monitoring the future

questionnaire responses from the nation's high school seniors

1981

Lloyd D. Johnston, Jerald G. Bachman, and
Patrick M. O'Malley

Survey Research Center • Institute for Social Research
The University of Michigan
Ann Arbor, Michigan

ISR Code Number 4525
ISSN 0190-9185
ISBN 0-87944-276-X
Library of Congress Catalog Card Number 79-640937

Published in 1982 by:
Institute for Social Research,
The University of Michigan, Ann Arbor, Michigan

Printed in the United States of America

Table of Contents

Preface

This volume is the latest in a series which presents descriptive statistical results from a national survey of young people entitled Monitoring the Future: A continuing Study of the Lifestyles and Values of Youth. Each year the study surveys a large sample of high school seniors, located in approximately 125 schools nationwide, and drawn to be representative of all seniors in the coterminous United States.

The first four volumes in this series, dealing with the high school classes of 1975, 1976, 1977, and 1978 were published simultaneously early in 1980. Additional volumes appear on an annual basis. The most important contribution of this series is likely to be the opportunity it provides for the exploration of trends, a process that obviously involves the use of several different volumes. With that in mind, we have kept the format highly consistent from one volume to another, and we have developed an index (described below) which should facilitate the process of matching data across years. It should be noted that the volume presenting 1975 data is different from the others in several respects.*

Although we designed the volumes to fit together as a series, we also saw distinct advantages in having each volume able to stand alone — to be usable without reference to any of the others. For that reason, the introductory material on research design and questionnaire content, the instructions for accessing the data tables, and the appendices on sampling errors are all included in each volume. Thus, the small price we pay for making each volume self-contained is that much of the text portion is repeated each year.

Purposes of this Series of Publications

Monitoring the Future, which is conducted by the University of Michigan's Institute for Social Research and receives its core funding from the National Institute on Drug Abuse, is an unusually comprehensive research project in several respects: surveys are conducted annually on an ongoing basis; the samples are large and nationally representative; and the subject matter is very broad, encompassing some 1,300 variables per year. Many people — scholars, policy makers, educators, and so on — will have an interest in the results.

The principal investigators are already writing for a number of these audiences and will continue to do so. Because of the limitations in our own time, interests, and expertise, however, there is an enormous amount of valuable information which may never be utilized if the initiative to digest and disseminate all of it must come from us alone. Further, since the project is in part a social indicator series, its value rests to a considerable degree on timely dissemination of the results. For these reasons, we wish to share the study's results with others in a number of fields on a rapid and regular basis. We have chosen to provide two major and complementary vehicles for doing this: (a) these annual reference volumes of descriptive results, and (b) machine-readable data archives for direct analysis by others.

We believe that many potential users who would not mount the effort required to conduct computer analyses of archived data will be able to get most of

---

*The 1975 volume does not include comparison data for black and white subgroups, nor does it include data for the subgroups who did and did not plan to complete four years of college. Also, somewhat fewer questionnaire items appear than in the other volumes. These restrictions are the result primarily of missing data problems that occurred only in the 1975 survey. In most respects, however, those seeking to compare different classes of high school seniors will find the 1975 data useful.

what they want from these volumes of descriptive results. The user of any one of these volumes can estimate — usually with considerable accuracy — a wide variety of characteristics of the high school class described in that volume. To take just one example, the user of the 1978 volume can ascertain that 50.2 percent of seniors in the high school class of 1978 reported using marijuana at least once during the preceding year. Further, by utilizing two or more of these volumes the reader can describe recent trends in any such characteristic. To continue with the same example, the volume describing the high school class of 1975 indicates that 40.0 percent of these seniors reported marijuana use during the preceding year; and when that is combined with the data from the 1978 volume the reader is able to discern a shift of 10.2 percent over the three years between the classes of 1975 and 1978. And if all of the first four volumes in the series are used, one can observe a steady increase in the proportion of high school seniors who report having used marijuana at least once during the twelve months preceding the survey:

40.0 percent of seniors in 1975
44.5 percent of seniors in 1976
47.6 percent of seniors in 1977
50.2 percent of seniors in 1978

A similar examination of trends can be carried out for over 1,300 different variables dealing with a wide variety of subject areas (listed in Table 2 of the Introduction). A simple indexing system (described below) has been developed which makes it quite straightforward for the reader wishing to do trend analyses to locate the results for a given question for any year of the study. The index in the present volume lists the location of all items included in the surveys from 1976 onward, as well as most items included in 1975.

Analyses such as those illustrated above need not be limited to the total sample. The data provided in these volumes also permit examination of a variety of subgroups (e.g., males, females, those from different regions, those with different levels of drug use experience).

We recognize that providing ready access to essentially undigested data carries certain risks, particularly the risk of mistaken interpretations based on inadequate controls, lack of awareness of sample limitations, etc. More than offsetting the risks, in our view, are the advantages of prompt and widespread dissemination of these nationally representative survey indicator data. Although we are unable to eliminate the risks, we hope to reduce them by providing the reader with an extensive list of caveats presented at the end of the Introduction section. We ask all who use the data to read these caveats carefully and take them seriously.

A Guide for the Reader

This volume is divided into three main parts: (1) the introductory section, (2) the section giving the descriptive results from the current year's survey, and (3) the cross-time item reference index.

Introductory Section. The introduction contains a description of the study — its purposes, major content areas, design, field procedures, response rates, and methods of publication and data dissemination. Since most of this material remains unchanged from year to year, anyone having read another of the volumes may wish to skim this section. We do, however, suggest reviewing the caveats, located at the end of the introductory section, which deal with interpreting and extrapolating from these data.

Descriptive Results Section. In this section all questions contained in this year's survey are presented along with percentagized frequency distributions of answers for the entire sample and for selected subgroups. The questions in this section are organized according to the number of the questionnaire form in which they were contained (forms one through five) and according to the order in which the questions occurred. There is one important exception, however. A major segment of questions common to all five forms of the questionnaire (dealing with drug use, background characteristics, and some other subjects) is presented only once, at the beginning of the Descriptive Results section, using the data from respondents on all five forms.

The first portion of the descriptive results section contains detailed definitions of all subgroups for whom data are presented. It also describes the statistical conventions used in generating the tables.

Cross-Time Index of Questionnaire Items. This index is intended to serve two purposes.

First it should be useful in locating items dealing with a subject area of interest. The subject area key at the beginning of the cross-time item index shows the alphabetical code assigned to various subject areas (e.g., "politics" or "work and leisure"). Having selected a subject area of interest, one can then scan the Subject Area column in the item index to locate all questions in any of the surveys (through 1981) which deal with that subject. To locate the results from any given question in the Descriptive Results section of this volume, simply look in column two of the item index for its page location.

The cross-time index can also be used to determine in which other years an item was used and where to locate it. If, in reviewing the Descriptive Results section, one locates an interesting item and would like to know in which of the other annual surveys of seniors it has appeared, it may be found in the cross-time index by its unique "item reference number." The index will indicate all years in which that same item appeared and show the questionnaire form, section, and item number for each year. This information thus can be used to decide which other volumes in this series might be of relevance; and the same item may be readily located by its reference number in the index of any other volume.

Sampling Appendices. Appendix A is provided for those wishing to determine the confidence limits around a percentage estimate, or to test the statistical significance of an observed difference between two groups, or to test the significance of a change from one year to another. It gives the necessary procedures and tables for such tests and provides the appropriate factors by which to correct for the fact that the study makes use of a multi-stage probability sample clustered in a limited number of schools (usually about 125). Appendix B provides further detail on sample design effects and the procedures which were used to derive the sampling error estimates.

Availability of Archived Data

As was mentioned earlier, this series of volumes will be complemented by an archiving of the raw data set for direct analysis by others not associated with the project. The present volumes should be a considerable help to those wishing to access the archived data since they provide a verbatim statement of items and answer categories, and also because they include basic univariate and bivariate frequency distributions for all items, as well as the missing data rates. The cross-time index of items contained in each of these volumes also provides an efficient way to identify the relevant variables in various content areas, as well as to determine when they were measured and their questionnaire locations. In fact, we hope that the availability of this series will not only facilitate the use of the archived data but actually stimulate interest in their use.

The individual level data which are summarized in this and previous volumes will be available from:

The Interuniversity Consortium for Political
and Social Research (ICPSR)
Institute for Social Research
P.O. Box 1248
Ann Arbor, Michigan 48106

The ICPSR archive makes individual-level data available to interested investigators for analysis. A few variables have been modified or deleted to ensure that the answers of an individual respondent cannot be located through pattern recognition (i.e., us-

ing various descriptor variables in combination to make a unique identification). The changed or deleted variables include month of birth, race, and the sampling weight, which adjusts for selection probability.

Other Publications from the Study

A number of different forms of publications based on Monitoring the Future data have been developed or are being planned. One series of reports, dealing with trends in drug use and drug-related attitudes and beliefs, is being published by the National Institute on Drug Abuse. The fist report in that series, *Drug Use Among American High School Students 1975-1977* (Johnston, Bachman, and O'Malley), was published in late 1977. Subsequent reports have been issued annually.

An Occasional Papers series has been launched by the project. It includes papers on design and methodological issues as well as special substantive analyses and early, and sometimes more detailed, drafts of articles planned for journal publication. The first occasional paper, "The Monitoring the Future Project Design and Procedures" (Bachman and Johnston, 1978), provides a detailed description of the study and its underlying rationale.

The present series of reference volumes is being published by the Institute for Social Research. A new volume will be added to this series each year.

Articles for academic journals, as well as for journals serving various professionals working with youths, are also being written. In addition, several integrative books based on the Monitoring the Future project are in the planning stages.

To request particular papers, reprints, or periodic notification of publications available from the study, write to Monitoring the Future, Room 2030. Institute for Social Research, The University of Michigan, Box 1248, Ann Arbor, Michigan 48108.

Acknowledgements

A great many people have contributed to the launching and development of this research effort. We are indebted to a number of officials of the National Institute on Drug Abuse and the Special Action Office for Drug Abuse Prevention for their encouragement and advice at the outset — in particular, Richard Bucher, Robert DuPont, William Pollin, and Louise Richards.

Our colleagues at the Institute for Social Research and elsewhere who shared their insights, and often their most cherished instrumentation, are too numer-

---

*Single copies of these reports may be ordered without cost from the National Clearinghouse for Drug Abuse Information, National Institute on Drug Abuse, 5600 Fishers Lane, Rockville, Maryland 20857. See References for a complete list of reports.

ous to mention; but their contributions are greatly appreciated. To the former director of the Survey Research Center's Sampling Section, Irene Hess, and to her colleagues we owe a particular debt for the creativity of the sampling design for the study. The contributions of the SRC Field Section also have been very valuable.

Major contributions to the production of this particular volume were made by staff members Dawn Bare and Deborah Poinier. We would also like to thank the staff of the Publishing Division of the Institute for Social Research for their work in arranging publication.

The present and former members of the project staff (listed below) have, of course, contributed greatly to the building of this large and complex research series.

Finally, we would like to acknowledge the tens of thousands of high school seniors, their teachers, and their principals, whose cooperation and generous contribution of time make the Montoring the Future project possible.

LLOYD D. JOHNSTON
JERALD G. BACHMAN
PATRICK M. O'MALLEY

Present and Former Members of the Project Staff

Donna Ando	Henry Freeman	Jim Neveaux
Margaret Bailey	Walter Gruhn	Dorothy Paulette
Dawn Bare	James Hersey	Susan Pauls
Ellen Berger	A. Regula Herzog	Sharon Pietila
Mary Lou Bewley	Jerome Hiniker	Joseph Pleck
Katherine Blatt	Pamela Kittel	Deborah Poinier
Mary Lea Bonucchi	Mark Krell	Judith Redmond
Marcy Breslow	Sally Lawson	Barbara Renaud
Susan Burek	Ludmilla Litus	Don Rubinstein
Mary Danneffel-Mashruwala	A. Kathryn Loker	Maria Sanchez
Mary Lou Davis	Regina Lumbard	Tina Smith
Mary Dempsy	Mary Lutz	Ann Taylor
William Diedrich	Oksana Malanchuk	Richard Taylor
Karen Donahue	Wayne McCulloch	Lynda Tolen
Leslie Eveland	Joan McGraw	Sandra Wronski
Halford Fairchild	John Miller	Thelma Wurzelbacher
Michael Fisher	Marion Morse	

Introduction

The Monitoring the Future project is designed to explore changes in many important values, behaviors, and lifestyle orientations of contemporary American youth. Two general types of tasks may be distinguished. The first is to provide a systematic and accurate *description* of the youth population of interest in a given year, and to quantify the direction and rate of the changes taking place among them over time. The second task, more analytic than descriptive, involves the *explanation* of the relationships and trends observed to exist.

The task of description may be subdivided into three parts: (1) the description of static conditions (which may be accomplished through a single cross-sectional study); (2) the description of cross-cohort or, in longer time-spans, generational changes (usually accomplished using repeated cross sections of the same age groups); and (3) the description of changes with aging (usually accomplished by means of longitudinal studies). The Monitoring the Future project has the capacity to provide each of these three types of description, since it incorporates all three types of research design into a single study. (This complex design, in which multiple cohorts are followed longitudinally, has been referred to as a cohort-sequential design.)

The content of this volume exemplifies the first of these types of description in that it contains cross-sectional data on a single high school class. When the data in this volume are used in combination with data from other such volumes in the series, the nature, direction, and rates of change from one cohort of seniors to another also may be described — the type of reporting which is often labeled as the social indicator approach. The third class of description — dealing with the maturational changes which occur during the years after high school — will not be dealt with in this series of volumes but will be reported in other publications from the study.*

The accurate characterization of American young people and the description of important changes occurring among them is but one class of objectives for the study. The second class of objectives involves the development of a greater understanding of what causes these young people to be as they are, and why the changes being documented are occurring. Explanation will be sought through both the analysis of change at the aggregate level and at the individual level. The results of these explorations will be disseminated via the various publications discussed in the Preface.

The merging of the social indicator approach and the analysis of relationships (particularly longitudinal relations) into a single cohort-sequential design is, in our view, synergistic: the effectiveness of the two approaches combined is greater than if the two were undertaken separately. Because the present series of volumes deals with senior year data only, our remarks here focus primarily on the project's social indicator contributions — the accurate description of high

---

* Panels of students from each graduating class are being randomly selected and followed longitudinally for up to ten years. Thus it soon will be possible tó characterize the changes which seem to take place consistently with aging during the early adult years. Not only will longitudinal development in the years after high school be studied, but once enough of these longitudinal panels have accumulated, it will also be possible to characterize cross-sectionally most American young people aged 18 to 28, (at least the major segment of the population who completed high school — roughly 80-85 percent), and to describe the changing characteristics of that age group each year.

1

school seniors and the documentation of trends over time. It is worth noting, however, that even the limited amount of bivariate data included in the present volumes will suggest promising directions for relational analyses, many of which can be carried out using the archived data tapes from the project.

The Need for Social Indicators

The fundamental argument for developing social indicators is that there are considerable scientific and practical benefits derived from having accurate information about current social realities and the way those realities have been changing. For the scientific community such indicators provide a rich set of information against which existing theory may be tested and from which new theory may be suggested. For the community at large, social indicators permit the "reality testing" of common perceptions and beliefs about the nation and its people. Past experience has demonstrated that widely held conceptions, which themselves may serve to create or exacerbate problems, can be most inaccurate. One example is the exaggerated popular conception of the size and nature of the "gap" between generations (see Adelson, 1970, 1979); another is the mistaken assumption that most young people condone the use of a variety of illegal drugs (Johnston, 1973; Johnston, Bachman, and O'Malley, 1977; 1979 a, b; 1981).

While deflating exaggerated perceptions, a continual monitoring of indicators on youth also can reveal the beginning of new problems and thus give rise to corrective efforts at a relatively early stage. For instance, most would view with concern the emergence of new types of drug use. Monitoring the Future has already documented and reported a sharp increase in regular marijuana use among high school seniors, and as a result more attention has been paid to the issue by policy makers, the media, and the general public. The discovery of such trends may trigger more intense efforts to discover the causes, consequences, and (when appropriate) preventatives of such behaviors.

Although social indicators seldom translate directly into specific policy decisions, the availability of descriptive information can substantially enhance the decision-making capabilities of policy makers. These data provide considerable insight into the size and nature of problems, the rate of change occurring nationally and in subgroups, and in some instances information about related factors and even the likely impacts of major social interventions (such as changed drug laws, or new incentives for recruitment into the military, to name but two). They also provide the possibility of feedback on the consequences of some social interventions as well as major historical events.

The particular topics included in our monitoring system are summarized later in this introduction and, of course, they are presented fully in the complete set of data tables. For present purposes, it is enough to indicate that the range of topics is very broad. This breadth is partly due to the wide interests of the principal investigators; but it also reflects our conviction that the concurrent examination of trends in a variety of areas is not only much more cost efficient but also more scientifically productive.

Research Design and Procedures*

The basic research design involves annual data collections from high school seniors during the spring of each year, beginning with the class of 1975. Each data collection takes place in approximately 125 public and private high schools selected to provide an accurate cross section of high school seniors throughout the coterminous United States. The design also provides for the longitudinal study of a subsample from each class of participating seniors; but since the focus of this series of volumes is exclusively on the data collected annually from seniors, the follow-up procedures will not be discussed here.

Reasons for Focusing on High School Seniors. There are several reasons for choosing the senior year of high school as an optimal point for monitoring the behaviors and attitudes of youth. One is that the completion of high school represents the end of an important developmental stage in this society, since it demarcates both the end of universal public education and, for many, the end of living in the parental home. Therefore, it is a logical point at which to take stock of the accumulated influences of these two environments on American youth.

Further, the completion of high school represents the jumping off point from which young people diverge into widely differing social environments, including college, business firms, military service, and homemaking. But these environmental transitions are not the only important changes which coincide with the end of high school. Most young men and women now reach the formal age of adulthood shortly before or after graduation; more significantly, they begin to assume adult roles, including financial self-support, marriage, and parenthood.

Finally, there are some important practical advantages to building a system of data collections around samples of high school seniors. The last year of high school constitutes the final point at which a reasonably good national sample of an age-specific cohort can be drawn and studied economically. The need for systematically repeated, large-scale samples from which to make reliable estimates of change requires

*A more extensive description of the research design and procedures may be found in Bachman and Johnston (1978).

that considerable stress be laid on efficiency and feasibility; the present design meets those requirements.

One limitation in the design is that it does not include in the target population those young men and women who drop out of high school before graduation (or before the last few months of the senior year, to be more precise). This excludes a relatively small proportion of each age cohort — between 15 and 20 percent (Dearman and Plisko, 1979) — though not an unimportant segment, since we know that certain behaviors such as illicit drug use (Johnston, 1973) and delinquency (Bachman, O'Malley, and Johnston, 1978) tend to be higher than average in this group. However, the addition of a representative sample of dropouts would increase the cost of the present research enormously, because of their dispersion and generally higher level of resistance to being located and interviewed.

For the purposes of estimating characteristics of the entire age group, the omission of high school dropouts does introduce certain biases; however, their small proportion sets outer limits on the bias (Johnston, O'Malley, and Eveland, 1975, Appendix B). For the purposes of estimating *changes* from one cohort of high school seniors to another, the omission of dropouts represents a problem only if different cohorts have considerably different proportions who drop out. We have no reason to expect dramatic changes in those rates for the foreseeable future, and recently published government statistics indicate a great deal of stability in dropout rates since 1970 (Dearman and Plisko, 1979, p. 185).

Some may use our high school data to draw conclusions about changes for the entire age group. While we do not encourage such extrapolation, we suspect that the conclusions reached often would be valid, since over 80 percent of the age group is in the surveyed segment of the population *and* we expect that change among those not in school are very likely to parallel the changes among those who are. Nevertheless, for purposes of characterizing the entire age group we would urge the user to check the results emanating from the present monitoring system against those emerging from other data collection systems using different methods, such as household interviews. (It is encouraging to note that when we have compared drug use data for this age group from the present study with those from interview studies, the findings have shown a high degree of similarity.)

Sampling Procedures. The procedure for securing a nationwide sample of high school seniors is a multistage one. Stage 1 is the selection of particular geographic areas, Stage 2 is the selection of one or more high schools in each area, and Stage 3 is the selection of seniors within each high school.

Stage 1: Geographic Areas. The geographic areas used in this study are the primary sampling units (PSUs) developed by the Sampling Section of the Survey Research Center for use in the Center's nationwide interview studies. These consist of 74 primary areas throughout the coterminous United States — including the 12 largest metropolitan areas, which contain about 30 percent of the nation's population. Of the 62 other primary areas, 10 are in the Northeast, 18 in the North Central area, 24 in the South, and 10 in the West. Because these same PSUs are used for personal interview studies by the Survey Research Center (SRC), local field representatives can be assigned to administer the data collections in practically all schools.

Stage 2: Schools. In the major metropolitan areas more than one high school is often included in the sampling design; in most other sampling areas a single high school is sampled. In all cases, the selections of high schools are made such that the probability of drawing a school is proportionate to the size of its senior class. The larger the senior class (according to recent records), the higher the selection probability assigned to the high school. When a sampled school is unwilling to participate, a replacement school as similar to it as possible is selected from the same geographic area.

Stage 3: Students. Within each selected school, up to about 400 seniors may be included in the data collection. In schools with fewer than 400 seniors, the usual procedure is to include all of them in the data collection. In larger schools, a subset of seniors is selected either by randomly sampling classrooms or by some other random method that is convenient for the school and judged to be unbiased. Sample weights are assigned to each respondent so as to take account of variations in the sizes of samples from one school to another, as well as the (smaller) variations in selection probabilities occurring at the earlier stages of sampling.

The three-stage sampling procedure described above yielded the number of participating schools and students indicated in Table 1.

One other important feature of the base-year sampling procedure should be noted here. All schools (except for half of the initial 1975 sample) are asked to participate in two data collections, thereby permitting replacement of half of the total sample of schools each year. One motivation for requesting that schools participate for two years is administrative efficiency; it is a costly and time-consuming procedure to secure the cooperation of schools, and a two-year period of participation cuts down that effort substantially. Another important advantage is that whenever an appreciable shift in scores from one graduating class to the next is observed, it is possible to check whether the shift might be attributable to some differences in the newly sampled schools. This is done simply by repeating the analysis using only the 60 or so schools which participated both years. Thus far, the half-sample approach

Table 1

Sample Sizes and Student Response Rates

	1975	1976	1977	1978	1979	1980	1981
Number of Public Schools	111	108	108	111	111	107	109
Number of Private Schools	14	15	16	20	20	20	19
Total Number of Schools	125	123	124	131	131	127	128
Actual Number of Participating Students	15792	16678	18438	18924	16662	16524	18267
Number of Weighted Cases (Total)*	15104	15299	15839	18924	16662	16524	18267
Student Response Rate**	78%	77%	79%	83%	82%	82%	81%

* Sample weights are assigned to each respondent to correct for unequal probabilities of selection which arise in the multi-stage sampling procedure.

** The student response rate is derived by dividing the attained sample by the target sample (both based on weighted numbers of cases). The target sample is based upon listings provided by schools. Since such listings may fail to take account of recent student attrition, the actual response rate may be slightly underestimated.

has worked quite well; and examination of drug prevalence data from the "matched half-samples" showed that the half samples of repeat schools yielded drug prevalence trends which were virtually identical to trends based on all schools.

School Recruiting Procedures. Early during the fall semester an initial contact is made with each sampled school. First a letter is sent to the principal describing the study and requesting permission to survey seniors. The letter is followed by a telephone call from a project staff member, who attempts to deal with any questions or problems and (when necessary) makes arrangements to contact and seek permission from other school district officials. Basically the same procedures are followed for schools asked to participate for the second year.

Once the school's agreement to participate is obtained, arrangements are made by phone for administering the questionnaires. A specific date for the survey is mutually agreed upon and a local SRC representative is assigned to carry out the administration.

Advance Contact with Teachers and Students. The local SRC representative is instructed to visit the school two weeks ahead of the actual date of administration. This visit serves as an occasion to meet the teachers whose classes will be affected and to provide them with a brochure describing the study, a brief set of guidelines about the questionnaire administration, and a supply of flyers to be distributed to the students a week to 10 days in advance of the questionnaire administration. The guidelines to the teachers include a suggested announcement to students at the time the flyers are distributed.

From the students' standpoint, the first information about the study usually consists of the teacher's announcement and the short descriptive flyer. In announcing the study, the teachers are asked to stress that the questionnaires used in the survey are not tests, and that there are no right or wrong answers. The flyer tells students that they will be invited to participate in the study, points out that their participation is strictly voluntary, and stresses confidentiality (including a reference to the fact that the Monitoring the Future project has a special government grant of confidentiality which allows their answers to be protected). The flyer also serves as an informative document which the students can show to their parents.

Questionnaire Administrations. The questionnaire administration in each school is carried out by the local SRC representatives and their assistants, following standardized procedures detailed in a project instruction manual. The questionnaires are administered in classrooms during normal class periods whenever possible, although circumstances in some schools require the use of larger group administrations. Teachers are not asked to do anything more than introduce the SRC staff members and (in most cases) remain in the classroom to help guarantee an orderly atmosphere for the survey. Teachers are urged to avoid walking around the room, so that students may feel free to write their answers without fear of being observed.

The actual process of completing the questionnaires is quite straightforward. Respondents are given sharpened pencils and asked to use them because the questionnaires are designed for automatic scanning. Most respondents can finish within a 45-minute class period; for those who cannot, an effort is made to provide a few minutes of additional time.

Procedures for Protecting Confidentiality. In any study that relies on voluntary reporting of drug use or other illegal acts, it is essential to develop procedures which guarantee the confidentiality of such reports. It is also desirable that these procedures be described adequately to respondents so that they are comfortable about providing honest answers.

We noted that the first information given to students about the survey consists of a descriptive flyer stressing confidentiality and voluntary participation. This theme is repeated at the start of the questionnaire administration. Each participating student is instructed to read the message on the cover of the questionnaire, which stresses the importance and value of the study, notes that answers will be kept strictly confidential, states that the study is completely voluntary, and tells the student "If there is any question you or your parents would find objectionable for any reason, just leave it blank." The instructions then point out that in a few months a summary of nationwide results will be mailed to all participants and also that a follow-up questionnaire will be sent to some students after a year. The cover message explains that these are the reasons for asking that name and address be written on a special form which will be removed from the questionnaire and handed in separately. The message also points out that the two different code numbers (one on the questionnaire and one on the tear-out form) cannot be matched except by a special computer tape at The University of Michigan. (The content of the inside and outside of the standard questionnaire cover, including the tear-out form, may be found in Appendix C.)

Content Areas and Questionnaire Design

Drug use and related attitudes are the topics which receive the most extensive coverage in the Monitoring the Future project; but the questionnaires also deal with a wide range of other subject areas, including attitudes about government, social institutions, race relations, changing roles for women, educational aspirations, occupational aims, and marital and family plans, as well as a variety of background and demographic factors.* (Table 2 provides an outline of the 19 general subject areas into which all items are categorized in the Question Index toward the end of this volume.) Given this breadth of content, the study is not presented to respondents as a "drug use study," nor do they tend to view it as such.

Because many questions are needed to cover all of these topic areas, much of the questionnaire content is divided into five different questionnaire forms which are distributed to participants in an ordered sequence that produces five virtually identical subsamples. About one-third of each questionnaire form consists of key or "core" variables which are common to all forms. All demographic variables and some measures of drug use are included in this "core" set of measures. This use of the full sample for drug and demographic measures provides a more accurate estimation on these dimensions and also makes it possible to link them statistically to all of the other measures which are included in a single form only.**

Representativeness and Validity

The samples for this study are intended to be representative of high school seniors throughout the 48 coterminous states. We have already discussed the fact that this definition of the sample excludes one important portion of the age cohort: those who have dropped out of high school before nearing the end of the senior year. But given the aim of representing high school seniors, it will now be useful to consider the extent to which the obtained samples of schools and students are likely to be representative of all seniors and the degree to which the data obtained are likely to be valid.

We can distinguish at least four ways in which survey data of this sort might fall short of being fully accurate. First, some sampled schools refuse to participate, which could introduce some bias. Second, the failure to obtain questionnaire data from 100 percent of the students sampled in participating schools would also introduce bias. Third, the answers provided by participating students are open to both conscious and unconscious distortions which could reduce validity. Finally, limitations in sample size and/or design could place limits on the accuracy of estimates. Each of these issues is treated extensively elsewhere (Johnston, Bachman, and O'Malley, 1979a, especially Appendices A and B), so in this section we will present only the highlights of each of those discussions.

School Participation. As noted in the description of the sampling design, schools are invited to participate

---

*An example of analyses relating background, demographic, and lifestyle factors to drug use is Bachman, Johnston, and O'Malley (1981); a much broader array of other subject areas included in the study is treated by Bachman and Johnston (1979).

**These core variables are the first ones on which data are presented in the Descriptive Results Section.

Table 2

Measurement Content Areas

A. **Drugs.** Drug use and related attitudes and beliefs, drug availability and exposure, surrounding conditions and social meaning of drug use. Views of significant others regarding drugs.

B. **Education.** Educational lifestyle, values, experiences, and environments. Media usage.

C. **Work and Leisure.** Vocational values, meaning of work and leisure, work and leisure activities, preferences regarding occupational characteristics and type of work setting.

D. **Sex Roles and Family.** Values, attitudes, and expectations about marriage, family structure, sex roles, and sex discrimination.

E. **Family Plans and Population Concerns.** Values, attitudes, and expectations about personal family plans. Views on sexual mores and concerns about overpopulation.

F. **Conservation, Materialism, Equity, etc.** Values, attitudes, and expectations related to conservation, pollution, materialism, equity, and the sharing of resources. Preferences regarding type of dwelling and urbanicity.

G. **Religion.** Religious affiliation, practices, and views.

H. **Politics.** Political affiliation, activities, and views.

I. **Social Change.** Values, attitudes, and expectations about social change.

J. **Social Problems.** Concern with various social problems facing the nation and the world.

K. **Major Social Institutions.** Confidence in and commitment to various major social institutions (business, unions, branches of government, press, organized religion, military, etc.).

L. **Military.** Views about the armed services and the use of military force. Personal plans for military service.

M. **Interpersonal Relationships.** Qualitative and quantitative characteristics of cross-age and peer relationships. Interpersonal conflict.

N. **Race Relations.** Attitudes toward and experiences with other racial groups.

O. **Concern for Others.** Radius of concern for others; voluntary and charitable activities.

P. **Happiness.** Happiness and life satisfaction, overall and in specific life domains.

Q. **Other Personality Variables.** Attitudes about self (including self-esteem), locus of control, loneliness, optimism, trust in others, somatic symptoms, importance placed on various life goals, counter-culture orientation.

R. **Background and School.** Demographic and family background characteristics, curriculum and grades in high school, victimization in school.

S. **Deviant Behavior and Victimization.** Delinquent behaviors, driving violations and accidents, violations and accidents under the influence of drugs, victimization experiences.

in the study for a two-year period. With very few exceptions, each school which has participated for one data collection has agreed to participate for a second. Thus far, from 66 percent to 80 percent of the schools initially invited to participate have agreed to do so each year; for each school refusal, a similar school (in terms of size, geographic area, urbanicity, etc.) was recruited as a replacement. The selection of replacement schools almost entirely removes problems of bias in region, urbanicity, and the like that might result from certain schools refusing to participate. Other potential biases are more subtle, however. For example, if it turned out that most schools with "drug problems" refused to participate, that could seriously bias the drug estimates derived from the sample. And if any other single factor were dominant in most refusals, that also might suggest a source of serious bias. In fact, however, the reasons for schools' refusals to participate are varied and largely a function of happenstance events of the particular year. Thus, we feel fairly confident that school refusals have not seriously biased the surveys.

Student Participation. Completed questionnaires are obtained from three-fourths to four-fifths of all students sampled. The single most important reason that students are missed is that they are absent from class at the time of data collection, and in most cases it is not workable to schedule a special follow-up data collection for them. Students with fairly high rates of absenteeism also report above-average rates of drug use; therefore, there is some degree of bias introduced by missing the absentees. That bias could be largely corrected through the use of special weighting; however, this course was not chosen because the bias in estimates (for drug use, where the potential effect was hypothesized to be largest) was determined to be quite small and because the necessary weighting procedures would have introduced undesirable complications (see Johnston et al., 1977).

In addition to absenteeism, student nonparticipation occurs because of schedule conflicts with school trips and other activities which tend to be more frequent than usual during the final months of the senior year. Of course, some students refuse to complete or turn in a questionnaire. However, the SRC representatives in the field estimate this proportion to be only about one percent.

Validity of Self-Report Data. Survey measures of delinquency and of drug use depend upon respondents reporting what are, in many cases, illegal acts. Thus, a critical question is whether such self-reports are likely to be valid. Like most studies dealing with

these areas, we have no direct, objective validation of the present measures; however, the considerable amount of inferential evidence which exists strongly suggests that the self-report questions produce largely valid data. A number of factors have given us reasonable confidence about the validity of the responses to what are presumably among the most sensitive questions in the study: a low nonresponse on the drug questions; a large proportion admitting to some illicit drug use; the consistency of findings across several years of the present study; strong evidence of construct validity (based on relationships observed between variables); a close match between our data and the findings from other studies using other methods; and the findings from several methodological studies which have used objective validation methods.*

As for others of the measures, a few have a long and venerable history — as scholars of the relevant literatures will recognize — though some of these measures have been modified to fit the present questionnaire format. Many (probably most) questions, however, have been developed specifically for this project through a careful process of question writing, pilot testing, pretesting, and question revision or elimination. Some already have been included in other publications from the study, but many have not; therefore, there currently exists little *empirical* evidence of their validity and reliability. On the other hand, the fact that virtually all results presented in this volume are based on individual items, rather than indexes or abstract concepts, should make it easy for the reader to judge the degree to which each item has "face validity" and also the degree to which there is some evidence of construct validity in the bivariate results.

Accuracy of the Sample. A sample survey never can provide the same level of accuracy as would be obtained if the entire target population were to participate in the survey — in the case of the present study, about three million seniors per year. But perfect accuracy of this sort would be extremely expensive and certainly not worthwhile considering the fact that a high level of accuracy can be provided by a carefully designed probability sample. The accuracy of the sample in this study is affected both by the size of the student sample and by the number of schools in which they are clustered. Appendix B presents a discussion of the ways in which this clustering and other aspects of the sampling design are taken into account in computing the precision or accuracy of the samples. For the purposes of this introduction, it is sufficient to note that virtually all estimates based on the total sample have confidence intervals of ±1.5 percentage points or smaller — sometimes considerably smaller.

* A more detailed discussion of the evidence for validity of the measures of illicit drug use may be found in Johnston et al. (1977; 1979a), Appendix A. An analysis of inconsistencies in students' reports of monthly versus yearly drug use is provided by Bachman and O'Malley (1981).

This means that, had we been able to invite all schools and all seniors in the 48 coterminous states to participate, the results from such a massive survey would be within an estimated 1.5 percentage points of our present sample findings at least 95 times out of 100. We consider this to be a quite high level of accuracy, and one that permits the detection of fairly small trends from one year to the next.

Consistency and the Measurement of Trends. One other point is worth noting in a discussion of the validity of our findings. The Monitoring the Future project is, by intention, a study designed to be sensitive to changes from one time to another. Accordingly, the measures and procedures have been standardized and applied consistently across each data collection. To the extent that any biases remain because of limits in school and/or student participation, and to the extent that there are distortions (lack of validity) in the responses of some students, it seems very likely that such problems will exist in much the same way from one year to the next. In other words, biases in the survey estimates should tend to be consistent from one year to another, which means that the measurement of *trends* should be affected very little by any such biases.

Caveats to Users of the Data

In attempting to understand and interpret the statistical results contained in this volume, the reader should keep in mind the several considerations discussed below.

Estimation of Sampling Errors. Appendix A provides figures which allow the reader to determine the 95 percent confidence interval around any observed percentage for both the total sample and the several subgroups for which statistics are given. Appendix A also provides tables and guidelines for testing the statistical significance of observed differences between subgroups (e.g., males vs. females) and the significance of year-to-year changes for the entire sample and for the various subgroups on any given variable. Estimates based on subgroups containing relatively few cases (e.g., those who have used heroin) will have substantially larger margins of error than those subgroups with large numbers of cases.

Subgroup Definitions. At the beginning of the Descriptive Results section there is a careful definition of each of the subgroups analyzed in this series of volumes. It is important for the reader to read these definitions so as not to be misled by the necessarily abbreviated descriptions given in the column headings of the data tables. For example, the column labeled "4-year college plans" includes data only for seniors who

expect to be graduated from a four-year college, which is only a subset of all who expect to receive some college training. To take another example, several column headings in the lifetime illicit drug use index use the term "pills"; however, these categories contain people who indicate that they used any of a number of drugs — including some which usually are not taken in pill form (e.g., cocaine and narcotics other than heroin).

Missing Data Notes. Each column of percentages for a given variable adds to 100 percent (with slight variations due to rounding), whether based on the entire sample or any one of the subgroups being described. Missing data were not included in computing these percentages, so it is up to the reader to determine whether an exceptional level of missing data exists on any given question. This can be done by comparing the weighted number of cases on which those percentages were based (given in italics under each percentage distribution) with the total number of weighted cases who took the questionnaire (given at the top of the same column). As would be expected, the missing data rate tends to rise modestly toward the end of each questionnaire. Occasionally there is an exceptional level of nonresponse for some other reason, the most common being that the respondent has been branched around a question or set of questions which are inappropriate for him or her. In thise case the percentages are based only on those for whom the question was appropriate *and* who answered. A footnote has been entered to help call attention to the fact that completing a particular question is contingent upon the answer on a prior question. Most such cases are contained in Form 1 of the questionnaire, which has several sets of detailed questions about drug use which are answered only by those respondents who have used a particular class of drug during the past year.

Characterizing Heroin Users. Because this project places a special emphasis on the study of drug use, one set of columns distinguishes respondents according to the extent to which they have been involved with illicit drugs. The five drug use categories are based on an index of seriousness of involvement. The index has Guttman-like properties — that is, anyone classified at a given level is also very likely to have exhibited any drug-using behaviors which are associated with the lower levels in the index.

The most extreme category in the index is defined in terms of the respondent's ever having used heroin during his or her lifetime. However, any interpretations made about heroin users from these data must be tempered with extreme caution, not only because the small number of cases makes estimation in a given year relatively unreliable, but also because heroin users are probably the most selectively represented of all of the subgroups presented here. Heroin users — especially continuing users — are among those most likely to drop out of high school (Johnston, 1973). Therefore, we feel that heroin users are particularly underrepresented in a sample of high school seniors. Furthermore, most of those included in the study report only very occasional heroin use. Frequent users — addicts, if you will — are not well represented in these data.

Given these problems with the representation of heroin users, the readers may wonder why it was decided to present them as a separate category of drug users. There are two reasons for doing so. First, because even occasional heroin use represents such an extreme point on the continuum of drug involvement, it seems preferable that the heroin users not be mixed in with the next highest category of use (the "more pills" category). It remains quite possible, of course, for anyone to *combine* any two or more categories in the drug use continuum (by computing means of percentages weighted by the number of cases in each category); therefore, those wishing to incorporate heroin users with the next category can do so whenever they wish. The second reason for keeping them separate is that we suspect the data based on high school seniors provide some indication of the characteristics which might be found among heavier heroin users who dropped out of school. Some variables in the study are strongly correlated with the drug use continuum, and the present heroin user category provides both an end point for that continuum and an indication of the direction (further out on the continuum) in which heavier heroin users are likely to lie.

In sum, the reporting of separate percentages for heroin users among high school seniors permits greater clarity in analyzing other levels of drug use and provides data which may be suggestive about the larger population of young heroin users. But the particular data are clearly limited and should be interpreted with these cautions in mind.

Interpreting Racial Differences. Data are given for the two largest racial/ethnic subgroups in the population — those who identify themselves as white or Caucasian and those who identify themselves as black or Afro-American. Data are not given for the other ethnic categories (American Indians, Asian Americans, Mexican Americans, Puerto Ricans, or other Latin Americans) since each of these groups comprises less than three percent of the sample in any given year, which means that their small Ns (in combination with their clustered groupings in a limited number of schools) would yield estimates which would be too unreliable. In fact, even blacks — who constitute approximately 12 percent of each year's sample — are represented by only 350 to 425 respondents per year on any single questionnaire form. Further, because our sample is a stratified clustered sample, it yields less accuracy than would be yielded by a pure random sample of equal size (see Appendix B for details). Therefore, because of the limited number of cases, the margin of sampling error around any statistic describing blacks is larger than for most other subgroups described in this volume.

There exists, however, a quick way to determine the replicability of any finding involving racial comparisons. Since most questions are repeated from year to year, one can readily establish the degree to which a finding is replicated by looking at the results for the same question in prior or subsequent years. Given the relatively small Ns for blacks, the reader is urged to seek such replication before putting much faith in the reliability of any particular racial comparison.

There are factors in addition to unreliability, however, which could be misleading in the interpretation of racial differences. Given the social importance which has been placed on various racial differences reported in the social science literature, we would like to caution the reader to consider the various factors which could account for differences. These factors fall into three categories: differential representation in the sample, differential response tendencies, and the confounding of race with a number of other background and demographic characteristics.

Differential Representation. Census data characterizing American young people in the approximate age range of those in our sample show that somewhat lower proportions of blacks than whites remain in school through the end of twelfth grade (Dearman and Plisko, 1979, p. 185). Therefore, a slightly different segment of the black population than of the white population resides in our target population of high school seniors. Further, our samples appear to underrepresent slightly those black males who, according to census figures, *are* in high school at the twelfth grade level. Identified black males comprise about 6 percent of our sample, whereas census data suggest that they should comprise around 7 percent (U.S. Bureau of the Census, 1978). Therefore, it appears that we are losing more black males from our target population than white males or females of either race. This may be due to generally poorer attendance rates on the part of some black males and/or an unwillingness on the part of some to participate in data collections of this sort.

In sum, a smaller segment of the black population than of the white population of high school age is represented by the data contained here. Insofar as any characteristic is associated with being a school dropout or absentee, it is likely to be somewhat disproportionately underrepresented among blacks in our sample.

Differential Response Tendencies. In examining our full range of variables, we have noted certain racial differences in response tendencies. First, the tendency to state agreement in response to agree-disagree questions is generally somewhat greater among blacks than among whites. For example, blacks tend to agree more with the positively worded items in our index of self-esteem, but they also tend to agree more with the negatively worded items. As it happens, that particular index has an equal number of positively and negatively worded items, so that any overall "agreement bias" should be self-cancelling when the index score is computed. Since all data in this volume are based on single items, however, group differences in agreement bias are likely to affect results on questions employing the agree-disagree format. Fortunately, most of our questions are not of that type.

We have also observed a somewhat greater than average tendency for black respondents to select extreme answer categories on attitudinal scales. For example, even if the same proportion of blacks as whites felt positively (or negatively) about some subject, fewer of the whites are likely to say they feel very positively (or very negatively). We do not have any ready explanations for these differences in response styles, but what seems important for our present purposes is that, in the process of interpreting racial differences, the reader should be aware that differences in responses to particular questions may be related to these more general tendencies.

A somewhat separate issue in response tendency is a respondent's willingness to answer particular questions. The missing data rate, which can be determined by dividing the number responding to a question by the number taking the questionnaire (given at the top of each page), may reflect willingness to answer particular questions. If a particular question or set of questions has a missing data rate higher than is true for the prior or subsequent questions, then presumably more respondents than usual were unwilling (or perhaps unable) to answer it. We have observed such an exaggerated missing data rate for black males on the set of questions dealing with the respondent's own use of illicit drugs. Clearly a respondent's willingness to be candid on such questions depends on his or her trust of the research process and of the researchers themselves. We interpret the exaggerated missing data rates for black males in these sections as possibly reflecting, at least in part, less trust. The reader is advised to check for exceptional levels of missing data when making comparisons on any variable in which candor is likely to be reduced by lower system trust. One bit of additional evidence related to trust in the research process is that higher proportions of blacks than whites indicated that if they had used marijuana or heroin they would not have been willing to report it in the survey.

Covariance with Other Factors. Some characteristics such as race are highly confounded (correlated) with other variables — variables which may in fact explain some observed racial differences. Put another way, at the aggregate level we might observe a consid-

erable racial difference on some characteristic, but once we control for some background characteristics such as socio-economic level or region of the country — that is, once we compare the black respondents with whites who come from similar backgrounds — there may be no racial difference at all.

Race happens to be correlated with important background and demographic variables much more than some of the other variables dealt with here (like the respondent's sex). When we compare males and females in this sample we know that observed differences between them are not likely to be explained by differences in their family background (such as the socioeconomic level of their families, the region of the country, or the size of the cities in which they grew up) because males and females on the average come from extremely similar backgrounds. A perusal of Section C of Questionnaire Forms 1 through 5, however, will illustrate that on the average the black subgroup in this sample is quite different from the white subgroup in a number of such respects. A higher proportion of blacks live in the South and a higher proportion grew up in families with the father and/or mother absent, and more had mothers who worked while they were growing up. A substantially higher proportion of blacks are Baptists, and blacks tend to attribute more importance to religion in their lives than do whites. Fewer are enrolled in a college-preparatory curriculum (though a higher proportion say they plan to attend some type of college). A slightly higher proportion of black respondents are married and have children, and on the average they are slightly older than the white sample. As was mentioned earlier, black males are more underrepresented in our sample than black females, with the result that each year roughly 58 percent of our black sample is female versus roughly 51 percent of the white sample.

We note these differences in demographic, background, and ascriptive characteristics because, in any attempt to understand *why* a racial difference exists, one would want to be able to examine the role of these covarying characteristics. It is not possible, given the amount of data contained in this volume, to "factor out" the contribution of most of these covarying characteristics when interpreting racial differences. Therefore, while the data here may provide a relatively accurate *description* of racial differences (keeping in mind our earlier cautions about representativeness and response style), they do not by themselves yield a great deal by way of explanation. However, since the full data sets now reside in two archives, described in the Preface, it is possible for the reader to conduct a more in depth exploration of observed differences — or nondifferences, for that matter. We particularly encourage readers interested in racial comparisons to make further explorations in the data in order to determine the possible role of the other variables discussed here. Users of the data are also encouraged to contact the principal investigators for information on the most recent analyses of racial differences, some of which are already underway.

Given the long list of caveats about interpreting racial differences, one might ask why we chose to publish the statistics for racial subgroups at all. After considerable deliberation among ourselves as well as with colleagues more knowledgeable in the field of race relations, we concluded that the expected benefits of making these data available (along with this cautionary discussion) outweigh the potential costs of having them misused. Unfortunately, because blacks constitute a relatively small proportion of the American population, they constitute too small a number in most surveys to be characterized separately. Because the sample sizes in the present survey are large in comparison to most, we have at least sufficient numbers of cases to consider publishing data on blacks separately. Further, given the iterative nature of the series, we are also able to provide checks for replication of findings on different samples each year. While there may be some risk that findings will be taken out of context or used carelessly in ways that might tend to increase racial misunderstandings, there is substantially greater risk that valuable information concerning the races (and relevant to their well-being) will be lost if it were not included here.

Descriptive Results

Introduction to the Table Format and Conventions

Univariate and selected bivariate percentage distributions are given in this section for all questions asked of this year's senior class. The definitions of column headings and the source of the standard contents for each table are given below under the numbers indicated in Figure 1.

Definitions of Column Headings

① **Questionnaire Form.** The form from which all data on the page were derived is given here. When the designation "Forms 1-5" is used, it indicates that responses from students completing all five questionnaires have been combined; accordingly, the numbers of respondents in each column are five times as large for questions contained in a single form only.

② **Total Sample.** Univariate percentage distributions based on the total sample of respondents are given in this column.

③ **Sex.** Percentage distributions are given separately for males (M) and females (F). Respondents with missing data on the question asking the respondent's sex (Question C03) are omitted from both groupings.

④ **Race.** Percentage distributions are given separately for those describing themselves as "White or Caucasian" (W) and "Black or Afro-American" (B) in answer to Question C04. Comparable columns for the other racial or ethnic groups (Mexican Americans, Asian Americans, American Indians, etc.) are not shown because of the low number of cases in each group. *Note:* See the caveats regarding the interpretation of racial differences in the introduction section of this volume.

⑤ **Region.** Percentage distributions are given separately for respondents living in each of four mutually exclusive regions of the country. The regional classifications are based on Census categories and are defined as follows:

Northeast (NE): Census classifications of New England and Middle Atlantic states; includes Maine, New Hampshire, Vermont, Massachusetts, Rhode Island, Connecticut, New York, New Jersey, and Pennsylvania.

North Central (NC): Census classifications of East North Central and West North Central states; includes Ohio, Indiana, Illinois, Michigan, Wisconsin, Minnesota, Iowa, Missouri, North Dakota, South Dakota, Nebraska, and Kansas.

South (S): Census classifications of South Atlantic, East South Central, and West South Central states; includes Delaware, Maryland, District of Columbia, Virginia, West Virginia, North Carolina, South Carolina, Georgia, Florida, Kentucky, Tennessee, Alabama, Mississippi, Arkansas, Louisiana, Oklahoma, and Texas.

West (W): Census classifications of Mountain and Pacific states; includes Montana, Idaho, Wyoming, Colorado, New Mexico, Arizona, Utah, Nevada, Washington, Oregon, and California.

⑥ **Four-Year College Plans.** Percentage distributions are given separately for (1) respondents who indicate that they "definitely will" or "probably will" graduate from a four-year college program and (2) those who say that they "definitely won't" or "probably won't" graduate from a four-year college program, based on responses to Question C21d. Respondents not answering question C21d are omitted from both columns. (A number of those who do not expect to complete a four-year college program *do* expect to get some post-secondary education, as may be seen in the tables for questions C21a and c.)

(7) **Illicit Drug Use: Lifetime.** Percentage distributions are given separately for five mutually exclusive subgroups differentiated by their degree of involvement with illicit drugs. Eligibility for each category is defined below.

None. This column contains data from those respondents who indicated that they had not used marijuana at any time and did not report use of any of the following illicit drugs in their lifetime: LSD, other psychedelics, cocaine, amphetamines, tranquilizers, methaqualone, barbiturates, heroin, or other narcotics.*

Marijuana Only. This column contains data from other respondents who indicated that they had used marijuana (or hashish) but had never used any of the other illicit drugs just listed.

Few Pills. This column contains data from those respondents who indicated having used one or more of the above listed drugs (other than marijuana) but who had not used any one class of them on three or more occasions *and* who had not used heroin at all.

More Pills. This column contains data from respondents who had used any of the above listed drugs (other than marijuana) on three or more occasions but who had never used heroin.

Any Heroin. This column contains data from those respondents who indicated having used heroin on one or more occasions in their lifetime.

(8) **Weighted Number of Cases.** This row contains the number of students who turned in questionnaires in each of the categories indicated by the column headings. The number of cases is stated in terms of the weighted number of respondents rather than the actual number, since all percentages in the tables have been calculated using weighted cases. The actual number of respondents generally is about 15 percent higher than the weighted number for data collected in 1975, 1976, and 1977. (A comparison of weighted and unweighted numbers is provided in Tables B-1 and B-2 in Appendix B.) For data collected in 1978 or later, the actual number of respondents is roughly equal to the weighted number. Weighting is used to improve the accuracy of estimates by correcting for unequal probabilities of selection which arise in the multi-stage sampling procedures.

(9) **Percentage of Weighted Total.** This row indicates the percentage of the total number of respondents who fall into the category indicated by each column heading. Unlike all other percentages on the page, which can be summed vertically, these percentages sum horizontally. To the extent that the subcategories in a column (e.g., Males and Females) fail to sum to 100 percent, cases have been eliminated because of missing data on the variable in question (e.g., Sex), or, in the case of Race, because several subcategories have been omitted intentionally.

Table Contents

(10) **Questions and Answers.** Each question along with its accompanying answer alternatives is presented verbatim. The alphanumeric prefix to the question indicates the section of the questionnaire in which it is located and its sequence within that section. So, for example, a prefix of B12c indicates that the item was question 12c in the B Section of the questionnaire.

(11) **Item Reference Number.** This is a unique identification number permanently assigned to each question. Any question may be located in the cross-time item index of this volume (or any other volume in this series) by using this reference number.

(12) **Percentage Distribution.** Each column of numbers beside a question gives the percentage of each group (defined by the column heading) who chose each answer alternative, rounded to the nearest tenth of a percent. These figures add vertically to 100 percent (with some rounding error). Nonrespondents to the question are excluded from the percentage calculations.

(13) **Number of Weighted Cases Answering (N Wtd.).** The number of students in the relevant group (defined by the column heading) who answered the question is given just below the percentage distribution. The number of nonrespondents may be determined by subtracting this weighted number answering from the weighted number taking the questionnaire, shown at the top of the same column. Nonresponse may be due to the subject not answering the question, even though it pertains to him or her, or to the subject skipping inappropriate questions as instructed on a prior item.

---

*Inhalants (including the amyl and butyl nitrites) are not included in this list of illicit drugs because the relevant questions are not contained in all questionnaire forms nor in all years of the study. Similarly, the use of PCP is counted only if it was reported under "other psychedelics" use, because specific questions about PCP are not included in all forms or years. This results in a few apparent inconsistencies in the tables relating the drug use index to specific questions about these drugs.

Figure 1
Guide to Table Format

	TOTAL	SEX		RACE		REGION				4YR COLLEGE PLANS		ILLICIT DRUG USE: LIFETIME				
QUESTIONNAIRE FORM 1-5 1980		M	F	White	Black	NE	NC	S	W	Yes	No	None	Mari-juana Only	Few Pills	More Pills	Any Her-oin
Weighted No. of Cases:	16524	7744	8078	12846	2098	3877	4873	5049	2726	8658	6578	5591	4357	2104	3760	180
% of Weighted Total:	100.0	46.9	48.9	77.7	12.7	23.5	29.5	30.6	16.5	52.4	39.8	33.8	26.4	12.7	22.8	1.1

These next questions ask for some background information about yourself.

C01: In what year were you born?

	TOTAL	M	F	White	Black	NE	NC	S	W	Yes	No	None	Mari-juana Only	Few Pills	More Pills	Any Her-oin
1. Before '60	.2	.3	.1	*	.7	.2	.2	.2	.1	.1	.2	.3	.1	.2	.1	1.1
2. 1960	2.0	2.4	1.5	1.4	4.2	2.0	2.0	2.5	.9	1.0	2.9	2.3	1.7	1.9	1.5	2.8
3. 1961	22.0	25.4	18.5	20.9	24.0	16.9	25.6	23.4	19.9	18.4	26.0	22.2	20.9	22.5	21.8	32.4
4. 1962	74.3	70.5	78.1	76.3	68.4	78.4	71.3	72.4	77.2	78.4	69.9	73.6	75.5	73.6	75.3	62.5
5. 1963	1.5	1.3	1.8	1.3	2.4	2.6	.9	1.3	1.7	2.0	.9	1.6	1.7	1.6	1.2	.6
6. 1964	.1	.1	*	*	.1	.1	.1	.1	.1	.1	*	.1	*	.1	*	-
7. 1965	*	*	*	*	*	*	*	*	*	*	*	*	*	*	*	-
8. After 1965	*	*	*	*	*	*	*	-	-	-	*	*	*	*	*	-
Item 10 N(Wtd)	16098	7740	8074	12842	2094	3662	4820	4931	2685	8617	6536	5527	4307	2076	3682	176

C02: In what month were you born?

	TOTAL	M	F	White	Black	NE	NC	S	W	Yes	No	None	Mari-juana Only	Few Pills	More Pills	Any Her-oin
01. January	8.2	8.3	8.2	8.0	9.3	8.5	8.1	8.3	8.0	8.0	8.4	8.3	8.6	8.6	7.7	2.3
02. February	7.7	7.6	7.7	7.8	8.0	8.2	7.1	8.0	7.4	7.9	7.4	7.8	8.1	6.7	7.5	8.6
03. March	8.5	8.4	8.7	8.5	8.6	8.9	8.1	8.8	7.8	8.4	8.6	8.4	7.7	8.9	9.3	7.4
04. April	7.3	7.3	7.3	7.4	6.2	7.6	7.5	6.3	8.3	7.3	7.4	7.0	7.2	7.1	7.9	8.0
05. May	8.0	8.1	8.0	7.9	8.2	8.2	7.9	7.9	8.1	8.4	7.4	7.9	8.0	8.6	7.9	9.1
06. June	7.9	8.3	7.6	7.8	7.9	8.0	8.1	7.4	8.0	7.6	8.0	8.2	7.4	7.5	8.1	6.9
07. July	9.3	9.4	9.1	9.2	9.8	9.1	9.0	9.4	10.0	9.4	9.5	9.6	9.0	9.3	9.4	7.4
08. August	9.4	9.0	9.7	9.4	10.3	9.1	9.3	10.1	8.9	9.7	9.3	9.1	9.2	10.4	9.2	14.9
09. September	9.2	9.3	9.3	9.1	8.7	9.2	9.2	9.5	8.2	8.7	9.4	9.3	9.5	9.1	8.0	12.6
10. October	8.5	7.9	8.7	8.7	7.0	8.3	8.8	8.1	8.7	8.6	8.5	8.7	9.0	7.1	8.3	6.9
11. November	7.7	7.5	7.5	7.6	6.8	7.0	7.2	7.9	9.0	7.7	7.4	7.1	7.9	7.9	8.2	8.0
12. December	8.5	9.1	8.1	8.5	9.2	7.9	9.6	8.3	7.6	8.2	8.8	8.6	8.3	8.6	8.5	8.0
Item 20 N(Wtd)	16070	7724	8069	12820	2094	3646	4818	4927	2679	8602	6529	5526	4305	2073	3664	175

C03: What is your sex?

	TOTAL	M	F	White	Black	NE	NC	S	W	Yes	No	None	Mari-juana Only	Few Pills	More Pills	Any Her-oin
1. Male	48.9	100.0	-	49.6	42.1	49.7	49.5	48.1	48.6	50.3	46.2	45.2	54.6	47.6	48.4	57.6
2. Female	51.1	-	100.0	50.4	57.9	50.3	50.5	51.9	51.4	49.7	53.8	54.8	45.4	52.4	51.6	42.4
Item 30 N(Wtd)	15822	7744	8078	12638	2050	3601	4757	4834	2630	8489	6418	5438	4231	2038	3628	170

C04: How do you describe yourself?

	TOTAL	M	F	White	Black	NE	NC	S	W	Yes	No	None	Mari-juana Only	Few Pills	More Pills	Any Her-oin
1. American Indian	1.1	1.3	.8	-	-	.7	1.0	1.2	1.2	.7	1.3	.6	.7	1.5	1.6	4.7
2. Black or Afro-American	13.1	11.2	14.8	-	100.0	6.9	9.3	26.7	3.4	12.9	11.5	15.7	15.7	10.6	5.6	11.2
3. Mexican American or Chicano	1.2	1.4	1.1	-	-	*	.5	.7	5.2	1.1	1.4	1.0	1.2	1.5	1.4	1.2
4. Puerto Rican or other Latin American	1.0	1.0	1.1	-	-	3.3	.3	.3	.5	1.1	.7	1.5	.9	1.3	.4	.6
5. Oriental or Asian American	1.0	1.1	1.0	-	-	.7	.6	.3	3.4	1.6	.4	1.5	.8	.8	.7	2.4
6. White or Caucasian	80.3	81.5	79.4	100.0	-	85.1	86.0	69.4	83.6	81.4	81.8	77.9	78.8	81.9	87.7	71.2
7. Other	2.3	2.6	1.9	-	-	3.2	2.3	1.3	2.8	1.3	3.0	1.8	2.0	2.4	2.6	9.4
Item 40 N(Wtd)	15995	7693	8025	12846	2098	3632	4798	4910	2656	8572	6503	5510	4281	2066	3650	170

C05: Where did you grow up mostly?

	TOTAL	M	F	White	Black	NE	NC	S	W	Yes	No	None	Mari-juana Only	Few Pills	More Pills	Any Her-oin
1. On a farm	7.9	8.7	7.2	8.5	4.9	2.4	13.4	8.3	4.7	4.9	12.4	10.2	7.0	6.4	6.4	10.4
2. In the country, not on a			11.5	11.1	14.7		9.3	12.2	15.7	6.0	8.4	16.1	13.4	10.7	10.3	9.5	21.4
3. In a small						41.0	26.3	27.7	31.7	29.8	33.0	31.5	30.1	32.6	31.7	29.0
							9.6	15.4	19.6	14.5	12.5	11.9	14.3	15.2		
								9.9	8.2	9.6	7.0	7.5	8.3			
									11.6	9.6	8.0	9.1				

QUESTIONNAIRE FORM 1-5 1981	TOTAL	SEX		RACE		REGION				4YR COLLEGE PLANS		ILLICIT DRUG USE: LIFETIME				
		M	F	White	Black	NE	NC	S	W	Yes	No	None	Mari- juana Only	Few Pills	More Pills	Any Her- oin
Weighted No. of Cases:	18267	8725	8865	13985	2265	4290	5484	5600	2893	9878	7008	6148	4179	2306	4925	189
% of Weighted Total:	100.0	47.8	48.5	76.6	12.4	23.5	30.0	30.7	15.8	54.1	38.4	33.7	22.9	12.6	27.0	1.0

These next questions ask for some background information about yourself.

C01: In what year were you born?

1. Before '60	.1	.1	.1	*	.4	.2	.1	.1	*	.1	.1	*	.1	-	.1	.5
2. 1960	.2	.3	.2	.1	.4	.2	.2	.3	.2	.2	.2	.3	.1	.4	.2	-
3. 1961	1.8	2.1	1.3	1.3	3.3	1.1	1.7	2.4	1.6	.9	2.7	1.9	1.6	2.1	1.3	2.7
4. 1962	23.0	26.6	19.0	21.6	25.5	15.7	26.7	24.9	22.8	19.4	27.1	22.9	22.6	24.3	21.7	31.0
5. 1963	73.5	69.9	77.6	75.9	67.4	80.8	70.3	70.9	74.0	77.6	68.9	73.3	74.3	71.9	75.3	64.7
6. 1964	1.4	.9	1.9	1.0	3.1	2.0	1.0	1.4	1.2	1.8	.9	1.6	1.2	1.2	1.4	1.6
7. 1965	*	*	*	*	.1	.1	.1	*	*	.1	*	*	.1	-	*	-
8. After 1965	*	*	-	*	-	*	*	*	-	*	-	-	*	*	*	-
Item 10 N(Wtd)	17880	8719	8864	13980	2262	4148	5417	5482	2832	9839	6958	6092	4138	2284	4828	184

C02: In what month were you born?

01. January	7.9	7.8	8.0	7.8	8.2	7.4	7.8	8.3	8.0	8.3	7.4	8.3	7.4	7.5	7.9	6.6
02. February	7.7	7.6	7.8	7.9	7.7	7.7	7.0	8.3	7.8	7.5	8.1	7.5	7.4	7.2	8.6	4.9
03. March	8.0	8.1	7.9	8.0	8.0	7.9	8.5	7.4	8.1	7.7	8.3	8.0	7.6	7.1	8.5	8.7
04. April	8.3	8.5	8.1	8.5	6.8	8.3	8.3	8.2	8.4	8.5	8.0	8.2	8.4	8.4	8.3	8.7
05. May	7.6	7.3	8.0	7.7	6.2	7.8	8.4	6.6	8.1	7.5	7.9	7.3	7.4	8.2	8.0	7.7
06. June	8.0	8.1	8.1	8.2	7.6	8.2	8.1	7.7	8.3	8.1	8.0	8.0	8.4	8.8	7.4	5.5
07. July	9.0	9.4	8.6	8.7	9.8	9.8	8.8	8.5	9.2	8.7	9.2	9.1	9.2	8.8	8.8	9.8
08. August	9.4	9.4	9.3	9.4	10.6	9.1	9.5	9.3	9.7	9.3	9.4	9.8	9.0	9.3	9.2	13.1
09. September	9.0	8.9	9.3	8.9	9.1	8.6	8.5	9.7	8.8	8.9	9.1	9.2	8.7	8.9	9.0	9.8
10. October	8.8	8.4	8.7	8.8	8.7	8.6	8.5	9.2	8.8	9.1	8.4	8.3	9.9	8.6	8.5	6.0
11. November	8.1	7.7	8.2	7.8	8.6	8.2	7.6	8.9	7.3	8.3	7.6	8.4	7.9	8.5	7.4	8.7
12. December	8.3	8.8	8.0	8.3	8.7	8.4	9.1	8.1	7.4	8.1	8.7	7.9	8.6	8.5	8.4	9.3
Item 20 N(Wtd)	17857	8709	8857	13967	2263	4137	5416	5476	2828	9832	6947	6087	4134	2282	4818	183

C03: What is your sex?

1. Male	49.6	100.0	-	50.0	46.3	51.5	48.6	50.2	47.7	49.8	48.2	47.5	54.5	47.7	48.0	58.5
2. Female	50.4	-	100.0	50.0	53.6	48.5	51.4	49.9	52.3	50.2	51.8	52.5	45.5	52.3	52.0	41.5
Item 30 N(Wtd)	17590	8725	8865	13781	2221	4083	5333	5380	2793	9716	6831	6006	4074	2248	4745	176

C04: How do you describe yourself?

1. American Indian	1.3	1.4	1.1	-	-	1.0	1.3	1.3	1.5	.5	2.0	.9	1.0	1.2	1.7	4.5
2. Black or Afro-American	12.8	11.9	13.5	-	100.0	6.2	7.1	27.4	4.8	12.9	10.7	15.8	18.2	9.0	4.1	11.7
3. Mexican American or Chicano	2.1	1.7	2.3	-	-	.2	.9	1.0	9.1	1.7	2.5	2.0	2.4	1.6	1.9	2.2
4. Puerto Rican or other Latin American	1.4	1.3	1.5	-	-	3.2	.6	1.1	.7	1.5	1.0	1.7	1.1	1.5	1.1	1.7
5. Oriental or Asian American	1.5	1.5	1.5	-	-	1.5	1.1	.5	4.0	2.1	.5	2.4	.9	.8	.9	1.7
6. White or Caucasian	78.7	79.5	78.2	100.0	-	85.1	86.2	67.7	76.5	79.4	80.4	75.0	74.4	83.3	87.8	73.7
7. Other	2.3	2.6	1.9	-	-	2.9	2.8	.9	3.3	1.8	2.8	2.2	1.9	2.6	2.5	4.5
Item 40 N(Wtd)	17762	8663	8809	13985	2265	4112	5397	5460	2792	9793	6910	6064	4107	2271	4798	179

C05: Where did you grow up mostly?

1. On a farm	8.1	9.1	7.0	9.1	4.1	2.0	10.6	12.0	4.7	5.3	12.4	10.2	6.8	9.1	5.7	14.3
2. In the country, not on a farm	13.9	13.6	14.1	13.4	18.5	11.0	11.9	20.2	9.9	10.6	18.6	15.7	13.6	13.2	11.7	15.5
3. In a small city or town (under 50,000 people)	29.9	30.0	30.0	32.3	19.6	38.4	31.2	23.0	28.3	30.1	30.3	29.1	30.9	29.7	30.8	20.2
4. In a medium-sized city (50,000 - 100,000)	13.1	12.4	13.7	12.9	11.7	9.4	12.0	13.1	20.4	13.5	12.4	13.0	12.6	12.9	13.7	10.7
5. In a suburb of a medium-sized city	7.8	7.9	7.9	8.7	4.5	10.7	6.2	7.6	7.2	8.9	6.1	6.6	7.4	8.7	9.6	7.7
6. In a large city (100,000 - 500,000)	9.4	8.3	10.4	7.0	19.3	6.2	11.5	7.7	13.3	9.9	8.4	9.1	10.0	9.4	9.1	12.5
7. In a suburb of a large city	6.8	7.3	6.4	7.7	3.0	7.8	7.7	6.1	5.0	8.3	4.8	6.1	6.8	6.1	8.2	5.4
8. In a very large city (over 500,000)	6.6	6.5	6.9	4.3	16.2	8.8	5.1	5.8	8.1	7.8	4.3	6.1	7.5	6.7	6.3	7.1
9. In a suburb of a very large city	4.3	5.0	3.7	4.7	3.2	5.6	3.9	4.5	3.1	5.6	2.6	4.1	4.4	4.2	4.7	6.5
Item 50 N(Wtd)	16669	8124	8219	13040	2106	3856	5139	5056	2618	9230	6479	5702	3883	2135	4457	168

* = less than .05 per cent.

QUESTIONNAIRE FORM 1-5 1981	TOTAL	SEX		RACE		REGION				4YR COLLEGE PLANS		ILLICIT DRUG USE: LIFETIME				
		M	F	White	Black	NE	NC	S	W	Yes	No	None	Marijuana Only	Few Pills	More Pills	Any Heroin
Weighted No. of Cases:	18267	8725	8865	13985	2265	4290	5484	5600	2893	9878	7008	6148	4179	2306	4925	189
% of Weighted Total:	100.0	47.8	48.5	76.6	12.4	23.5	30.0	30.7	15.8	54.1	38.4	33.7	22.9	12.6	27.0	1.0

C06: What is your present marital status?

	TOTAL	M	F	White	Black	NE	NC	S	W	Yes	No	None	Mari. Only	Few Pills	More Pills	Any Her.
1. Married	2.3	2.2	2.3	1.9	3.5	1.5	2.4	3.1	1.6	1.3	3.6	2.5	2.0	2.5	1.9	2.7
2. Engaged	6.7	3.9	9.3	6.7	5.8	4.7	7.2	7.6	6.7	3.1	11.9	5.5	5.7	7.8	8.2	12.6
3. Separated/divorced	.5	.6	.4	.3	1.6	.4	.6	.8	.3	.3	.8	.2	.6	.7	.7	3.3
4. Single	90.5	93.3	88.0	91.1	89.1	93.4	89.9	88.6	91.3	95.4	83.8	91.8	91.7	89.1	89.2	81.3
Item 60 N(Wtd)	17833	8651	8835	13931	2232	4128	5419	5464	2823	9832	6966	6065	4133	2275	4827	182

C07: Which of the following people live in the same household with you? (Mark ALL that apply.)

	TOTAL	M	F	White	Black	NE	NC	S	W	Yes	No	None	Mari. Only	Few Pills	More Pills	Any Her.
A. I live alone	.5	.6	.2	.3	.6	.3	.6	.4	.5	.3	.6	.4	.3	.3	.6	3.3
B. Father (or male guardian)	80.4	81.7	79.3	85.0	56.1	82.8	83.2	76.2	79.4	82.4	78.5	82.5	80.3	79.8	79.4	68.3
C. Mother (or female guardian)	92.1	91.6	92.8	93.5	86.3	93.9	92.7	90.5	91.2	94.1	90.0	93.3	92.6	92.7	90.8	78.9
D. Brother(s) and/or sister(s)	76.3	76.2	76.6	76.7	74.4	82.3	77.1	72.4	73.8	78.6	73.8	79.3	77.6	77.2	72.7	57.8
E. Grandparent(s)	5.4	5.2	5.5	4.5	9.3	6.0	4.4	6.7	4.0	5.5	5.4	5.6	5.7	5.8	4.7	1.1
F. My husband/wife	1.0	.5	1.4	1.0	1.2	.4	1.1	1.6	.5	.4	1.8	1.1	1.0	1.0	.8	3.9
G. My children	.9	.2	1.6	.5	4.0	.4	.7	1.8	.2	.6	1.4	.9	1.2	.3	.9	2.8
H. Other relative(s)	5.0	4.3	5.6	3.0	13.6	3.5	3.7	7.4	4.7	4.7	5.3	4.8	5.2	5.5	4.4	7.8
I. Non-relative(s)	2.9	2.6	3.3	3.0	2.4	3.0	2.9	2.3	4.2	2.6	3.3	1.6	3.0	3.2	4.2	8.3
Item 80-160 N(Wtd)	17816	8637	8833	13914	2237	4118	5414	5460	2824	9832	6964	6078	4126	2277	4802	180

The next three questions ask about your parents. If you were raised mostly by foster parents, step-parents, or others, answer for them. For example, if you have both a step-father and a natural father, answer for the one that was most important in raising you.

C08: What is the highest level of schooling your father completed?

	TOTAL	M	F	White	Black	NE	NC	S	W	Yes	No	None	Mari. Only	Few Pills	More Pills	Any Her.
1. Completed grade school or less	7.1	6.3	7.8	5.2	12.2	5.3	6.8	9.5	5.5	4.9	9.8	7.5	7.4	7.3	5.9	7.7
2. Some high school	15.2	15.2	15.2	13.8	21.9	13.1	15.0	18.4	12.3	10.4	21.8	14.4	15.4	15.4	15.2	22.4
3. Completed high school	30.6	31.3	30.0	31.4	30.3	29.4	35.9	29.3	24.9	26.1	37.0	31.8	29.3	32.7	29.3	26.8
4. Some college	13.6	13.2	14.1	14.7	9.7	13.0	13.8	11.5	18.3	15.7	10.9	13.5	13.7	12.7	14.5	12.0
5. Completed college	17.0	17.9	16.3	19.0	8.1	20.0	15.7	14.1	20.9	21.8	10.7	16.2	17.4	15.6	19.1	12.0
6. Graduate or professional school after college	12.0	12.3	11.7	13.4	4.6	16.5	9.0	10.4	14.5	17.8	4.1	11.7	12.1	12.2	12.7	14.2
7. Don't know, or does not apply	4.4	3.8	5.0	2.6	13.2	2.9	3.7	6.8	3.6	3.2	5.7	5.0	4.8	4.0	3.2	4.9
Item 310 N(Wtd)	17777	8613	8814	13890	2220	4095	5416	5444	2823	9825	6955	6055	4117	2260	4807	183

C09: What is the highest level of schooling your mother completed?

	TOTAL	M	F	White	Black	NE	NC	S	W	Yes	No	None	Mari. Only	Few Pills	More Pills	Any Her.
1. Completed grade school or less	4.0	3.3	4.5	2.4	5.8	4.0	3.5	4.2	4.3	3.0	5.0	4.7	3.3	4.9	2.7	5.5
2. Some high school	14.4	13.2	15.6	12.3	23.5	10.8	13.1	19.7	12.2	9.2	21.4	14.0	14.3	14.3	14.4	18.0
3. Completed high school	42.5	43.6	41.5	45.0	36.2	42.3	48.5	41.0	34.4	38.4	48.4	43.1	41.8	42.2	43.1	38.8
4. Some college	15.5	15.7	15.4	16.3	13.4	14.7	14.4	14.0	21.9	18.9	11.2	15.0	15.9	15.6	16.5	11.5
5. Completed college	14.6	15.3	13.9	15.4	11.2	17.1	13.6	12.4	17.0	19.8	7.8	14.4	15.8	14.0	14.6	10.9
6. Graduate or professional school after college	6.7	6.5	6.9	7.0	5.3	9.2	4.8	5.9	8.0	9.2	3.0	6.2	6.9	6.9	6.9	10.9
7. Don't know, or does not apply	2.3	2.3	2.2	1.6	4.4	2.0	2.1	2.7	2.2	1.6	3.2	2.7	2.1	2.0	1.8	4.4
Item 320 N(Wtd)	17791	8616	8827	13898	2228	4096	5420	5454	2821	9835	6967	6062	4119	2264	4815	183

C10: Did your mother have a paid job (half-time or more) during the time you were growing up?

	TOTAL	M	F	White	Black	NE	NC	S	W	Yes	No	None	Mari. Only	Few Pills	More Pills	Any Her.
1. No	31.7	32.6	30.6	34.3	15.0	35.8	33.1	27.8	30.6	32.1	31.2	34.4	31.2	31.4	29.2	33.3
2. Yes, some of the time when I was growing up	30.3	31.1	29.6	32.0	21.6	31.2	30.8	28.0	32.4	30.0	30.9	30.2	30.2	30.1	31.0	26.1
3. Yes, most of the time	16.9	16.9	16.7	16.0	21.7	16.9	16.2	18.0	16.0	16.4	17.5	15.4	16.2	17.4	18.6	20.6
4. Yes, all or nearly all of the time	21.1	19.3	23.1	17.7	41.7	16.2	19.9	26.2	21.0	21.5	20.4	20.0	22.4	21.1	21.2	20.6
Item 330 N(Wtd)	17726	8582	8800	13878	2204	4077	5410	5423	2816	9821	6942	6031	4111	2264	4800	180

QUESTIONNAIRE FORM 1-5 1981	TOTAL	SEX		RACE		REGION				4YR COLLEGE PLANS		ILLICIT DRUG USE: LIFETIME				
		M	F	White	Black	NE	NC	S	W	Yes	No	None	Mari-juana Only	Few Pills	More Pills	Any Her-oin
Weighted No. of Cases:	18267	8725	8865	13985	2265	4290	5484	5600	2893	9878	7008	6148	4179	2306	4925	189
% of Weighted Total:	100.0	47.8	48.5	76.6	12.4	23.5	30.0	30.7	15.8	54.1	38.4	33.7	22.9	12.6	27.0	1.0

C11: How would you describe your political preference?

1. Strongly Republican	8.2	10.6	5.9	9.2	3.2	7.4	8.0	8.6	9.1	9.1	7.1	8.8	7.7	8.7	7.8	11.1
2. Mildly Republican	15.2	16.3	14.4	17.6	4.1	13.9	16.5	14.1	17.0	17.0	13.1	16.3	14.3	17.2	14.2	13.3
3. Mildly Democrat	14.0	14.0	13.9	13.5	17.8	11.5	14.2	16.0	13.4	14.2	13.8	14.1	14.7	14.0	13.4	8.9
4. Strongly Democrat	10.3	10.0	10.5	6.5	35.0	7.2	7.6	17.2	6.8	10.5	9.7	11.4	12.0	8.9	7.9	7.2
5. American Independent Party	1.7	1.9	1.5	1.6	2.1	2.2	1.3	1.5	2.2	1.4	1.9	.9	1.5	2.1	2.5	2.2
6. No preference, independent	23.6	25.1	22.3	25.8	10.8	28.6	28.0	16.6	21.7	24.2	23.2	21.9	22.4	22.6	27.9	31.7
7. Other	1.4	2.0	.9	1.2	1.6	1.7	1.4	1.3	1.4	1.5	1.4	1.1	1.1	1.6	1.7	5.6
8. Don't know, haven't decided	25.4	20.2	30.6	24.7	25.5	27.5	23.0	24.8	28.5	22.3	29.8	25.4	26.3	25.0	24.7	20.0
Item 340 N(Wtd)	17647	8553	8751	13820	2188	4049	5399	5403	2797	9803	6913	6010	4095	2252	4768	180

C12: How would you describe your political beliefs?

1. Very conservative	3.4	4.3	2.3	3.0	6.0	2.6	3.1	4.4	3.0	3.3	3.2	4.6	3.1	2.5	2.4	4.9
2. Conservative	15.3	16.9	13.7	16.0	12.4	13.3	15.0	16.7	16.3	16.8	13.5	18.1	14.7	14.3	13.2	9.3
3. Moderate	32.7	33.0	32.5	34.6	26.7	31.6	34.8	33.2	29.2	33.8	31.4	33.5	31.8	36.1	31.8	24.2
4. Liberal	14.7	15.1	14.3	14.6	15.5	18.2	13.8	12.7	15.2	17.2	11.4	11.0	14.9	16.0	16.4	20.9
5. Very liberal	3.1	3.1	3.0	2.6	4.7	3.5	2.3	3.1	3.8	3.3	2.5	2.3	2.7	2.3	4.4	5.5
6. Radical	3.0	4.5	1.4	2.6	4.3	3.9	2.4	2.8	3.0	2.8	3.2	1.5	2.6	2.9	4.9	11.0
8. None of the above, or don't know	27.9	22.9	32.9	26.5	30.4	27.0	28.6	27.1	29.5	22.7	34.9	29.0	30.1	26.1	24.9	24.2
Item 350 N(Wtd)	17577	8512	8722	13785	2168	4024	5385	5375	2793	9780	6904	5995	4076	2238	4759	182

C13: The next three questions are about religion.

C13A: What is your religious preference?

01. Baptist	21.1	20.0	22.1	15.8	63.2	5.6	14.1	45.8	9.2	18.0	24.7	25.1	22.1	18.6	15.5	12.3
02. Churches of Christ	6.7	7.1	6.2	6.3	7.7	4.9	4.8	8.3	9.9	4.9	9.0	7.1	5.9	8.0	6.2	4.5
03. Disciples of Christ	.5	.5	.6	.5	.7	.2	.5	.8	.7	.6	.5	.6	.5	.5	.5	1.7
04. Episcopal	1.8	1.5	2.0	2.0	.9	2.8	.9	1.9	1.5	2.3	1.0	1.5	1.9	1.8	2.0	1.7
05. Lutheran	6.0	5.9	6.1	7.1	.8	4.7	11.9	1.6	5.1	5.8	6.6	5.8	6.2	5.9	6.3	3.4
06. Methodist	8.1	7.6	8.6	8.8	6.6	5.1	10.9	9.3	4.7	8.0	8.4	9.1	7.3	8.3	7.6	9.5
07. Presbyterian	3.6	3.2	4.0	4.3	.9	3.7	3.7	3.0	4.6	4.4	2.6	3.8	3.3	3.4	3.9	3.4
08. United Church of Christ	.9	.9	.9	1.0	.4	1.1	1.5	.4	.7	1.0	1.0	1.0	.8	1.0	1.0	1.7
09. Other Protestant	4.1	3.8	4.4	4.6	1.7	5.6	4.4	1.9	5.5	4.0	4.2	4.3	4.2	4.1	3.9	2.2
10. Unitarian	.2	.2	.2	.3	*	.3	.2	.1	.3	.3	.1	.2	.4	.2	.2	-
11. Roman Catholic	30.2	30.4	30.1	32.6	6.0	49.2	32.3	16.2	25.8	33.9	25.3	25.6	33.1	31.2	33.9	27.9
12. Eastern Orthodox	.6	.4	.8	.7	-	1.3	.6	.2	.4	.9	.2	.7	.5	.5	.6	-
13. Jewish	1.1	1.3	1.0	1.3	*	3.2	.5	.4	.8	1.7	.3	1.0	1.3	.9	1.3	1.1
14. Other religion	5.7	5.4	6.1	5.1	5.5	2.9	4.8	4.7	13.4	5.2	6.3	7.1	4.3	5.9	4.8	8.9
15. None	9.3	11.8	6.9	9.7	5.3	9.5	9.0	5.3	17.3	9.0	9.7	7.0	8.2	9.6	12.4	21.2
Item 360 N(Wtd)	17561	8492	8730	13758	2185	4014	5379	5401	2767	9764	6903	5984	4082	2240	4738	179

C13B: How often do you attend religious services?

1. Never	9.5	11.1	7.9	9.9	4.7	12.2	8.9	5.2	14.8	8.1	11.2	7.0	8.8	9.9	12.6	19.3
2. Rarely	33.5	35.6	31.3	33.4	31.2	35.9	34.0	28.9	37.8	30.1	37.7	24.7	34.2	34.8	43.5	34.8
3. Once or twice a month	17.0	17.5	16.7	15.7	24.5	16.3	16.9	18.5	15.4	17.8	16.2	15.8	18.5	16.7	17.2	18.2
4. About once a week or more	40.0	35.9	44.1	41.0	39.5	35.5	40.2	47.3	31.9	44.1	34.9	52.5	38.6	38.5	26.7	27.1
Item 370 N(Wtd)	17699	8559	8795	13863	2197	4054	5416	5427	2801	9832	6961	6036	4100	2256	4785	181

C13C: How important is religion in your life?

1. Not important	10.7	13.6	7.9	11.8	3.6	14.9	9.8	5.6	16.0	10.6	10.9	7.4	10.5	10.5	14.6	27.5
2. A little important	26.0	28.9	23.2	27.9	14.5	31.2	28.6	18.9	27.4	23.6	29.2	19.1	27.4	27.7	33.1	25.8
3. Pretty important	32.8	32.3	33.4	33.1	31.3	33.2	34.6	33.6	27.3	33.0	32.8	31.1	33.9	34.5	33.5	32.4
4. Very important	30.5	25.2	35.5	27.1	50.5	20.7	26.9	42.0	29.3	32.8	27.1	42.3	28.2	27.3	18.8	14.3
Item 380 N(Wtd)	17673	8542	8785	13841	2198	4040	5406	5427	2799	9823	6955	6025	4096	2258	4770	182

* = less than .05 per cent.

QUESTIONNAIRE FORM 1-5 1981	TOTAL	SEX		RACE		REGION				4YR COLLEGE PLANS		ILLICIT DRUG USE: LIFETIME				
		M	F	White	Black	NE	NC	S	W	Yes	No	None	Marijuana Only	Few Pills	More Pills	Any Heroin
Weighted No. of Cases:	18267	8725	8865	13985	2265	4290	5484	5600	2893	9878	7008	6148	4179	2306	4925	189
% of Weighted Total:	100.0	47.8	48.5	76.6	12.4	23.5	30.0	30.7	15.8	54.1	38.4	33.7	22.9	12.6	27.0	1.0

C14: When are you most likely to graduate from high school?

	TOTAL	M	F	White	Black	NE	NC	S	W	Yes	No	None	Marijuana Only	Few Pills	More Pills	Any Heroin
1. By this June	98.4	97.8	99.1	98.9	97.2	98.8	98.3	98.5	98.1	99.2	97.3	99.2	98.9	98.5	97.5	91.2
2. July to January	1.2	1.6	.8	.9	2.1	.8	1.4	1.3	1.5	.7	2.1	.6	.9	1.2	2.0	6.1
3. After next January	-	-	-	-	-	-	-	-	-	-	-	-	-	-	-	-
6. Don't expect to graduate	.3	.5	.2	.2	.8	.3	.4	.3	.4	.1	.6	.1	.3	.3	.5	2.8
Item 390 N(Wtd)	17679	8547	8770	13843	2177	4045	5419	5405	2809	9865	6987	6034	4095	2252	4777	181

C15: Which of the following best describes your present high school program?

	TOTAL	M	F	White	Black	NE	NC	S	W	Yes	No	None	Marijuana Only	Few Pills	More Pills	Any Heroin
1. Academic or college prep	47.0	46.8	47.6	50.3	35.2	64.9	42.6	41.5	40.1	68.3	18.7	51.5	49.5	46.2	41.7	31.1
2. General	31.0	30.0	31.7	29.8	34.6	20.1	33.2	33.1	38.1	22.8	41.8	28.0	31.2	31.8	33.9	31.7
3. Vocational, technical, or commercial	14.1	15.6	12.5	13.8	16.0	10.4	16.7	15.4	11.9	5.1	25.9	12.3	12.3	14.4	16.9	24.4
4. Other, or don't know	8.0	7.7	8.1	6.1	14.2	4.5	7.5	10.0	9.8	3.7	13.5	8.2	7.0	7.7	7.4	12.8
Item 400 N(Wtd)	17569	8492	8716	13761	2158	4012	5385	5377	2795	9821	6950	6003	4073	2240	4739	180

C16: Compared with others your age throughout the country, how do you rate yourself on school ability?

	TOTAL	M	F	White	Black	NE	NC	S	W	Yes	No	None	Marijuana Only	Few Pills	More Pills	Any Heroin
1. Far below average	.4	.4	.3	.2	.9	.3	.4	.4	.3	.2	.6	.4	.1	.5	.3	4.0
2. Below average	1.8	2.1	1.4	1.6	1.9	1.6	2.0	1.7	1.9	1.0	2.7	1.2	1.6	2.0	2.1	4.0
3. Slightly below average	4.9	6.0	3.7	4.4	6.1	4.3	5.2	5.0	5.0	2.8	7.6	3.5	4.6	6.1	6.0	8.5
4. Average	36.2	34.4	37.6	33.2	49.8	32.9	35.0	42.0	31.8	25.4	50.0	33.3	36.7	35.5	38.6	38.4
5. Slightly above average	23.9	23.2	24.7	25.0	20.1	24.6	24.8	21.8	25.2	25.4	22.4	23.3	24.7	25.1	23.9	20.3
6. Above average	27.3	27.0	28.1	29.7	17.5	29.6	27.5	24.4	29.5	36.8	14.8	31.1	26.8	26.5	24.9	17.5
7. Far above average	5.6	6.9	4.3	6.0	3.8	6.6	5.2	4.8	6.3	8.3	1.8	7.2	5.4	4.3	4.2	7.3
Item 410 N(Wtd)	17266	8391	8516	13602	2066	3916	5324	5271	2755	9706	6820	5890	4006	2192	4677	177

C17: How intelligent do you think you are compared with others your age?

	TOTAL	M	F	White	Black	NE	NC	S	W	Yes	No	None	Marijuana Only	Few Pills	More Pills	Any Heroin
1. Far below average	.3	.3	.3	.2	.8	.4	.4	.3	.3	.2	.5	.3	.2	.4	.3	2.8
2. Below average	1.2	1.3	1.1	1.0	1.5	1.1	1.2	1.2	1.4	.6	2.0	1.1	1.0	1.4	1.2	2.8
3. Slightly below average	3.9	3.6	4.0	3.8	2.6	3.3	4.5	3.7	3.8	1.9	6.4	2.8	4.7	4.6	4.1	4.0
4. Average	35.0	31.0	38.6	33.6	38.4	31.5	35.9	38.3	32.1	24.4	49.5	33.1	34.2	36.0	36.8	34.5
5. Slightly above average	24.0	24.3	23.9	24.8	22.2	23.9	24.8	23.4	23.9	25.0	22.9	23.9	24.5	24.5	24.0	18.1
6. Above average	28.8	30.6	27.3	30.2	25.2	32.0	27.4	26.5	31.1	38.4	15.8	31.0	28.8	26.8	27.6	29.9
7. Far above average	6.8	8.8	4.8	6.5	9.3	7.7	5.9	6.7	7.4	9.5	2.9	7.8	6.6	6.2	6.1	7.3
Item 420 N(Wtd)	17312	8341	8620	13623	2086	3952	5322	5278	2760	9733	6858	5914	4018	2196	4691	177

C18: During the LAST FOUR WEEKS, how many whole days of school have you missed...

C18A: Because of illness

	TOTAL	M	F	White	Black	NE	NC	S	W	Yes	No	None	Marijuana Only	Few Pills	More Pills	Any Heroin
1. None	57.4	63.2	52.0	58.9	52.6	55.9	59.8	57.0	55.6	61.0	53.3	64.0	57.9	54.8	50.7	49.1
2. 1 day	17.7	16.2	19.1	17.9	16.7	18.2	17.3	17.8	17.5	17.6	17.9	17.1	16.6	18.6	19.0	17.1
3. 2 days	10.9	9.4	12.3	10.6	11.7	10.5	10.6	11.0	11.6	9.8	12.2	9.0	10.8	11.5	12.9	12.6
4. 3 days	6.5	5.3	7.8	6.2	8.1	6.8	6.0	6.8	6.6	5.5	7.8	5.0	6.5	6.8	8.2	7.4
5. 4-5 days	4.8	3.9	5.6	4.2	6.7	5.4	3.6	5.0	6.0	3.8	5.9	3.5	5.1	4.9	6.0	6.3
6. 6-10 days	1.8	1.2	2.3	1.6	2.6	2.1	1.8	1.6	1.8	1.7	1.8	1.0	2.1	2.1	2.4	5.1
7. 11 or more	.9	.8	.9	.7	1.5	1.0	.9	.8	.8	.6	1.1	.5	1.0	1.1	.9	2.3
Item 430 N(Wtd)	17168	8295	8521	13487	2089	3887	5312	5257	2712	9652	6823	5884	3976	2177	4638	175

C18B: Because you skipped or "cut"

	TOTAL	M	F	White	Black	NE	NC	S	W	Yes	No	None	Marijuana Only	Few Pills	More Pills	Any Heroin
1. None	68.5	66.7	70.6	67.8	76.0	65.0	70.8	72.1	61.9	71.4	64.6	84.6	68.7	64.4	51.2	35.7
2. 1 day	13.6	13.7	13.4	14.1	10.0	14.7	13.9	11.7	15.2	13.3	14.3	8.8	15.0	16.2	17.3	17.0
3. 2 days	7.1	7.6	6.6	7.3	5.4	7.6	6.5	6.9	8.3	6.3	8.2	3.4	6.8	7.8	12.0	5.8
4. 3 days	4.4	4.8	4.0	4.5	3.5	5.2	3.5	4.4	5.4	4.1	4.8	1.3	4.3	5.2	7.7	14.0
5. 4-5 days	3.8	4.3	3.2	3.9	2.3	4.4	2.9	3.3	5.5	2.9	4.9	1.3	3.2	3.8	7.0	7.6
6. 6-10 days	1.6	1.6	1.6	1.5	1.3	1.9	1.5	1.0	2.4	1.2	2.0	.3	1.2	1.9	3.0	9.4
7. 11 or more	1.0	1.3	.6	.9	1.4	1.3	.8	.7	1.4	.7	1.3	.3	.8	.7	1.8	10.5
Item 440 N(Wtd)	16639	8052	8250	13137	1965	3772	5186	5055	2626	9392	6632	5676	3851	2126	4534	171

QUESTIONNAIRE FORM 1-5 1981	TOTAL	SEX		RACE		REGION				4YR COLLEGE PLANS		ILLICIT DRUG USE: LIFETIME				
		M	F	White	Black	NE	NC	S	W	Yes	No	None	Mari- juana Only	Few Pills	More Pills	Any Her- oin
Weighted No. of Cases:	18267	8725	8865	13985	2265	4290	5484	5600	2893	9878	7008	6148	4179	2306	4925	189
% of Weighted Total:	100.0	47.8	48.5	76.6	12.4	23.5	30.0	30.7	15.8	54.1	38.4	33.7	22.9	12.6	27.0	1.0

C18C: For other reasons

1. None	58.1	59.4	56.9	58.0	58.2	58.4	57.3	60.7	54.2	58.3	58.0	63.1	58.1	56.1	52.5	57.9
2. 1 day	19.7	19.6	19.6	20.2	17.5	19.6	20.8	18.5	19.8	20.5	18.5	18.9	19.2	21.8	20.6	14.6
3. 2 days	10.4	10.0	10.8	10.3	11.7	10.1	10.4	9.6	12.3	10.5	10.2	9.5	10.6	10.5	11.5	7.6
4. 3 days	5.7	5.3	6.1	5.7	6.0	5.2	5.6	5.8	6.6	5.2	6.4	4.2	5.9	5.7	7.4	7.6
5. 4-5 days	3.8	3.3	4.3	3.7	3.9	3.9	3.7	3.4	4.5	3.6	4.1	2.8	3.9	4.2	4.8	5.3
6. 6-10 days	1.5	1.4	1.5	1.4	1.7	1.7	1.3	1.2	1.8	1.3	1.7	1.0	1.6	.9	1.9	2.9
7. 11 or more	.8	1.0	.7	.8	1.1	1.1	.8	.7	.8	.7	1.1	.5	.7	.7	1.4	3.5
Item 450　N(Wtd)	16724	8083	8305	13180	1996	3771	5197	5097	2659	9458	6636	5795	3841	2124	4500	171

C19: During the last four weeks, how often have you gone to school, but skipped a class when you weren't supposed to?

1. Not at all	60.8	57.9	63.8	61.2	63.0	58.7	64.8	65.6	46.8	61.0	60.9	75.6	59.2	58.9	45.4	35.4
2. 1 or 2 times	23.0	23.7	22.1	22.3	24.6	22.9	21.3	21.4	29.4	22.9	22.8	17.5	24.7	25.2	27.1	19.9
3. 3-5 times	9.8	10.7	8.9	10.0	7.7	9.3	8.5	8.2	16.1	9.8	9.8	4.4	10.1	10.3	15.9	18.2
4. 6-10 times	3.8	4.4	3.3	4.1	2.0	5.0	3.3	2.9	5.0	3.9	3.7	1.2	3.9	3.3	7.3	8.3
5. 11-20 times	1.5	1.8	1.2	1.4	1.2	2.3	1.1	1.0	1.8	1.4	1.5	.6	1.2	1.5	2.6	8.3
6. More than 20 times	1.2	1.6	.7	1.0	1.5	1.8	1.0	1.0	1.0	1.0	1.3	.7	.9	.8	1.8	10.5
Item 460　N(Wtd)	17548	8476	8710	13767	2144	3982	5407	5368	2791	9854	6997	6004	4059	2236	4737	181

C20: Which of the following best describes your average grade so far in high school?

9. A (93-100)	8.8	7.9	9.8	10.0	3.1	7.8	9.4	9.5	7.6	12.7	3.7	13.8	7.5	6.3	5.1	7.2
8. A- (90-92)	11.1	8.8	13.6	12.3	6.0	11.3	10.8	11.1	11.8	14.6	6.3	14.9	10.2	10.7	7.9	6.1
7. B+ (87-89)	17.8	15.6	20.2	18.5	14.6	18.5	17.5	17.0	19.1	21.2	13.4	18.5	17.8	19.1	16.9	13.8
6. B (83-86)	20.5	18.8	22.2	21.3	16.5	21.3	19.4	19.8	22.9	20.9	20.5	19.6	21.0	22.4	20.9	12.7
5. B- (80-82)	14.8	16.2	13.4	14.3	17.6	16.1	14.5	14.3	14.5	13.3	16.6	12.7	15.3	15.4	17.0	14.4
4. C+ (77-79)	13.5	15.7	11.2	11.8	21.8	13.0	13.3	14.5	12.6	9.8	18.2	10.7	15.1	12.8	15.1	21.0
3. C (73-76)	8.7	10.7	6.6	8.0	12.1	8.1	10.0	8.4	7.6	5.4	13.1	6.5	8.9	8.4	11.0	9.4
2. C- (70-72)	3.5	4.6	2.3	2.8	6.5	2.8	3.8	4.0	2.9	1.7	5.9	2.6	3.1	3.4	4.5	9.9
1. D (69 or below)	1.2	1.8	.7	1.0	1.9	1.1	1.2	1.5	1.0	.4	2.2	.8	1.2	1.5	1.5	5.0
Item 470　N(Wtd)	17454	8421	8670	13694	2142	3964	5369	5361	2760	9827	6943	5976	4037	2221	4714	181

C21: How likely is it that you will do each of the following things after high school?

C21A: Attend a technical or vocational school

1. Definitely won't	42.5	38.8	46.4	44.5	34.6	60.1	40.1	38.0	31.3	55.4	26.3	45.5	44.2	42.2	38.2	42.0
2. Probably won't	29.3	29.8	28.8	29.9	26.0	21.6	31.4	29.4	35.9	30.0	28.8	28.6	28.1	31.0	30.5	26.6
3. Probably will	18.3	20.9	15.6	16.3	26.7	10.7	17.0	22.5	23.4	9.8	29.3	15.8	18.3	17.8	20.8	21.9
4. Definitely will	9.9	10.5	9.2	9.3	12.7	7.6	11.4	10.2	9.4	4.8	15.6	10.1	9.5	9.0	10.5	9.5
Item 480　N(Wtd)	16712	8032	8345	13192	1980	3735	5226	5124	2627	9471	6973	5771	3844	2127	4496	169

C21B: Serve in the armed forces

1. Definitely won't	58.9	41.9	75.5	60.6	49.6	63.4	60.3	54.4	58.8	61.6	56.1	60.1	57.1	59.1	59.9	53.2
2. Probably won't	26.7	34.7	19.0	27.7	21.3	24.1	26.6	28.3	27.5	27.9	25.3	26.7	26.3	28.1	26.8	27.6
3. Probably will	9.0	14.4	3.8	7.3	18.3	7.4	8.3	11.2	8.5	7.0	11.4	8.2	9.8	8.8	8.6	11.5
4. Definitely will	5.3	9.0	1.7	4.4	10.7	5.1	4.8	6.1	5.3	3.4	7.2	5.1	6.8	4.0	4.8	8.3
Item 490　N(Wtd)	16157	7743	8111	12867	1849	3646	5069	4922	2520	9261	6690	5578	3727	2068	4345	156

C21C: Graduate from a two-year college program

1. Definitely won't	36.2	37.3	35.2	37.3	32.4	47.3	34.4	36.7	23.2	40.9	31.0	38.1	38.7	33.4	32.7	40.8
2. Probably won't	29.8	32.4	27.3	30.8	27.3	24.6	33.1	31.2	27.9	31.1	29.0	29.6	29.4	30.2	30.5	30.2
3. Probably will	21.2	19.8	22.6	19.5	28.3	15.7	21.0	21.3	29.4	16.3	27.0	20.0	19.6	22.6	23.1	23.1
4. Definitely will	12.8	10.6	14.9	12.5	12.1	12.5	11.5	10.9	19.5	11.7	13.0	12.3	12.4	13.8	13.7	6.5
Item 500　N(Wtd)	16632	7930	8363	13141	1959	3710	5210	5082	2630	9383	6967	5730	3836	2110	4484	169

QUESTIONNAIRE FORM 1-5 1981	TOTAL	SEX		RACE		REGION				4YR COLLEGE PLANS		ILLICIT DRUG USE: LIFETIME				
		M	F	White	Black	NE	NC	S	W	Yes	No	None	Mari-juana Only	Few Pills	More Pills	Any Her-oin
Weighted No. of Cases:	18267	8725	8865	13985	2265	4290	5484	5600	2893	9878	7008	6148	4179	2306	4925	189
% of Weighted Total:	100.0	47.8	48.5	76.6	12.4	23.5	30.0	30.7	15.8	54.1	38.4	33.7	22.9	12.6	27.0	1.0
C21D: Graduate from college (four-year program)																
1. Definitely won't	23.2	22.5	23.6	23.5	20.2	19.9	25.9	26.0	17.1	-	55.9	20.2	20.6	23.4	27.9	27.7
2. Probably won't	18.3	18.0	18.5	18.2	16.8	12.9	20.3	17.9	23.1	-	44.1	16.1	17.1	20.1	21.3	20.2
3. Probably will	23.1	23.9	22.4	22.9	24.6	20.2	23.4	22.5	27.7	39.4	-	23.3	23.9	23.0	22.3	21.4
4. Definitely will	35.4	35.6	35.6	35.5	38.5	47.0	30.5	33.6	32.1	60.6	-	40.3	38.5	33.4	28.4	30.6
Item 510 N(Wtd)	16886	8131	8415	13334	2002	3815	5242	5169	2660	9878	7008	5820	3898	2159	4528	173
C21E: Attend graduate or professional school after college																
1. Definitely won't	31.6	30.7	32.2	32.0	29.5	27.0	35.4	34.5	25.0	10.7	60.1	27.8	29.8	32.0	36.5	41.4
2. Probably won't	33.5	33.7	33.3	34.7	29.1	29.0	36.3	32.6	36.1	35.5	31.1	34.5	33.9	34.8	32.5	23.1
3. Probably will	24.9	25.7	24.3	24.5	26.9	31.4	20.4	22.9	28.5	38.2	6.9	26.2	26.2	24.6	22.5	21.9
4. Definitely will	10.0	9.8	10.2	8.7	14.6	12.6	7.9	10.1	10.5	15.7	1.9	11.6	10.0	8.6	8.5	13.6
Item 520 N(Wtd)	16535	7929	8275	13063	1954	3693	5173	5072	2596	9420	6973	5714	3802	2116	4436	169
C22: Suppose you could do just what you'd like and nothing stood in your way. How many of the following things would you WANT to do? (Mark ALL that apply)																
A. Attend a technical or vocational school	26.8	30.0	23.7	26.1	29.4	17.8	28.7	30.0	29.9	13.4	45.7	25.1	26.1	25.7	29.8	31.2
B. Serve in the armed forces	13.4	19.2	7.8	11.6	23.8	12.0	12.7	16.0	11.8	11.0	16.7	12.8	16.0	12.8	12.0	11.8
C. Graduate from a two-year college program	26.4	21.3	31.2	25.7	26.4	20.6	27.8	23.7	36.9	17.5	38.4	24.8	25.0	28.9	28.6	19.4
D. Graduate from college (four year program)	60.9	61.0	61.3	61.6	62.8	65.3	58.9	58.5	63.4	89.5	22.7	64.9	64.1	60.2	55.2	48.2
E. Attend graduate or professional school after college	39.5	39.1	40.3	39.4	39.4	44.8	36.6	38.0	40.7	56.3	16.6	41.6	41.8	38.6	36.5	31.8
F. None of the above	9.0	8.7	9.0	9.4	4.5	9.3	9.7	8.8	7.3	2.7	17.9	8.1	7.7	8.7	10.7	17.6
Item 530-580 N(Wtd)	17224	8270	8597	13546	2095	3868	5326	5301	2730	9785	6881	5926	3998	2183	4623	170
C23: On the average over the school year, how many hours per week do you work in a paid or unpaid job?																
1. None	21.5	19.0	23.8	17.9	41.5	20.5	19.4	25.9	18.1	21.6	21.0	26.0	22.7	19.0	15.4	18.4
2. 5 or less hours	9.7	9.9	9.6	9.8	9.8	9.9	9.4	9.0	11.6	11.7	7.2	12.0	8.8	9.1	7.6	5.2
3. 6 to 10 hours	10.4	9.9	10.8	10.5	10.0	10.5	9.6	10.6	11.8	11.0	9.6	10.9	10.0	11.4	9.9	9.2
4. 11 to 15 hours	11.3	10.5	12.3	12.3	7.1	13.5	12.1	9.4	10.4	12.7	9.4	11.3	11.0	11.3	11.7	13.2
5. 16 to 20 hours	16.2	15.6	17.0	17.2	10.7	18.4	16.8	14.5	15.4	17.5	14.7	14.2	17.5	17.1	17.7	13.2
6. 21 to 25 hours	12.7	13.3	12.2	13.9	6.7	13.0	13.9	11.5	12.0	11.9	13.6	9.6	12.5	13.4	16.3	14.9
7. 26 to 30 hours	8.4	9.4	7.4	8.6	6.0	7.8	8.5	7.9	10.2	7.4	9.8	6.8	8.3	9.2	10.2	11.5
8. More than 30 hours	9.8	12.4	7.0	9.8	8.1	6.5	10.2	11.2	10.6	6.2	14.6	9.0	9.2	9.5	11.1	13.8
Item 590 N(Wtd)	17266	8329	8579	13602	2085	3867	5358	5297	2743	9783	6916	5929	4001	2190	4648	174
C24: During an average week, how much money do you get from...																
C24A: A job or other work																
1. None	24.7	22.2	27.4	22.0	39.7	22.6	23.8	28.0	23.4	26.1	23.3	30.3	25.0	22.2	18.8	18.8
2. $1-5	4.2	3.9	4.5	4.4	3.0	4.4	4.6	3.2	5.0	4.6	3.6	4.6	3.4	5.4	3.6	3.0
3. $6-10	4.5	4.1	4.9	4.5	4.0	4.7	4.8	4.1	4.5	4.5	4.6	5.2	3.7	4.4	4.1	9.1
4. $11-20	5.7	5.2	6.2	6.0	4.3	6.6	5.7	5.2	5.8	6.3	5.0	6.4	5.2	5.7	5.5	2.4
5. $21-35	10.3	9.6	11.0	10.7	9.5	11.5	10.1	10.6	8.6	10.8	9.8	10.6	11.9	9.9	9.7	10.3
6. $36-50	14.8	14.0	15.6	15.6	10.8	16.8	15.1	13.1	14.5	16.0	13.0	13.8	15.0	15.1	16.0	10.9
7. $51 +	35.7	41.0	30.4	36.8	28.5	33.5	36.0	35.8	38.2	31.8	40.6	29.2	36.5	37.1	42.2	46.1
Item 600 N(Wtd)	16494	7969	8194	13098	1909	3679	5167	5024	2623	9381	6631	5649	3817	2106	4473	165

QUESTIONNAIRE FORM 1-5 1981	TOTAL	SEX		RACE		REGION				4YR COLLEGE PLANS		ILLICIT DRUG USE: LIFETIME				
		M	F	White	Black	NE	NC	S	W	Yes	No	None	Mari-juana Only	Few Pills	More Pills	Any Her-oin
Weighted No. of Cases:	18267	8725	8865	13985	2265	4290	5484	5600	2893	9878	7008	6148	4179	2306	4925	189
% of Weighted Total:	100.0	47.8	48.5	76.6	12.4	23.5	30.0	30.7	15.8	54.1	38.4	33.7	22.9	12.6	27.0	1.0

C24B: Other sources (allowances, etc.)

1. None	39.4	39.1	39.7	41.4	26.4	42.3	41.2	36.1	38.3	37.8	41.9	40.7	39.1	39.0	38.6	32.9
2. $1-5	21.5	19.9	23.4	22.8	17.1	22.2	22.7	18.5	24.2	22.9	19.8	24.0	20.8	22.9	18.9	15.0
3. $6-10	17.5	17.1	17.9	17.1	18.7	17.4	17.2	18.1	17.3	18.5	16.1	16.9	18.6	16.6	18.3	10.2
4. $11-20	11.1	12.0	10.1	10.0	18.5	9.7	10.0	13.8	10.0	11.1	11.1	9.7	11.4	11.8	12.0	16.2
5. $21-35	4.9	5.5	4.3	4.3	8.2	4.1	4.4	6.5	3.9	4.9	4.7	4.0	5.0	5.6	5.5	2.4
6. $36-50	2.0	2.1	1.9	1.6	4.4	1.6	1.7	2.6	2.2	1.8	2.4	1.7	1.8	1.5	2.6	4.8
7. $51 +	3.5	4.2	2.6	2.8	6.8	2.7	2.9	4.3	4.1	3.0	4.0	2.9	3.2	2.6	4.0	18.0
Item 610 N(Wtd)	16065	7703	8045	12722	1899	3582	5033	4912	2538	9198	6422	5518	3723	2055	4339	167

C25: During a typical week, on how many evenings do you go out for fun and recreation?

1. Less than one	8.1	7.0	9.3	6.7	13.3	7.6	6.8	9.5	8.8	8.0	8.2	12.7	6.6	5.1	4.8	3.4
2. One	13.9	12.0	15.7	13.3	16.1	12.0	13.5	15.0	15.4	14.6	13.2	19.6	12.8	12.7	8.3	8.0
3. Two	30.5	30.3	30.8	30.7	30.1	30.6	30.2	30.8	30.3	32.8	27.7	33.0	35.2	32.9	22.9	10.9
4. Three	26.0	26.7	25.3	27.3	21.0	25.4	26.1	26.0	26.3	26.6	25.0	22.0	26.1	29.0	29.7	31.4
5. Four or five	15.2	16.3	14.0	16.2	11.4	16.0	17.2	13.4	13.7	13.7	17.2	9.6	13.9	15.2	23.3	24.0
6. Six or seven	6.3	7.6	4.9	5.9	8.2	8.3	6.1	5.3	5.6	4.3	8.9	3.0	5.4	5.2	11.0	21.7
Item 620 N(Wtd)	17230	8283	8590	13578	2073	3844	5359	5290	2738	9759	6908	5927	3989	2193	4627	175

C26: On the average, how often do you go out with a date (or your spouse, if you are married)?

1. Never	13.3	13.2	13.4	11.8	18.0	14.4	12.7	12.4	14.8	13.6	13.0	19.5	11.8	9.4	8.1	7.3
2. Once a month or less	19.1	20.6	17.6	19.4	16.9	18.0	19.7	17.6	22.1	21.5	15.7	22.3	18.9	17.7	16.1	15.3
3. 2 or 3 times a month	18.6	21.2	16.3	18.7	20.6	16.9	18.0	19.5	20.5	20.1	16.6	18.2	19.4	18.2	18.7	22.6
4. Once a week	16.3	17.1	15.5	15.9	19.3	16.2	15.9	17.9	13.9	16.3	16.3	16.0	16.7	19.1	15.0	13.0
5. 2 or 3 times a week	22.0	19.9	24.0	22.8	19.6	21.7	22.3	23.5	19.3	20.8	23.7	18.1	23.6	23.8	25.3	16.4
6. Over 3 times a week	10.7	7.9	13.4	11.5	5.6	12.8	11.4	9.1	9.5	7.6	14.8	5.9	9.5	11.7	16.8	24.9
Item 630 N(Wtd)	17042	8181	8511	13458	2024	3787	5308	5218	2727	9633	6808	5863	3959	2162	4573	177

C27: During an average week, how much do you usually drive a car, truck, or motorcycle?

1. Not at all	14.2	9.4	18.9	10.3	31.2	20.7	11.8	11.5	14.7	13.5	14.8	15.9	13.5	13.8	12.4	8.5
2. 1 to 10 miles	13.6	9.6	17.4	12.2	20.8	14.8	14.3	12.5	12.6	13.8	13.2	16.1	12.7	11.5	11.6	9.6
3. 11 to 50 miles	31.8	28.5	35.2	33.2	27.0	33.1	33.7	28.9	32.0	34.8	27.8	34.1	33.5	31.4	28.5	21.5
4. 51 to 100 miles	20.9	25.0	16.9	22.8	12.3	16.6	21.6	23.3	20.7	20.7	21.5	18.8	21.5	22.5	22.7	24.9
5. 100 to 200 miles	13.0	17.8	8.1	14.8	4.5	9.6	13.3	15.1	13.0	12.1	14.0	10.3	12.1	13.9	16.5	20.9
6. More than 200 miles	6.6	9.6	3.5	6.8	4.2	5.2	5.2	8.6	7.0	5.1	8.6	4.8	6.7	7.1	8.2	15.3
Item 640 N(Wtd)	17217	8287	8577	13582	2058	3839	5352	5276	2750	9736	6866	5931	3986	2187	4618	177

C28: Within the LAST 12 MONTHS, how many times, if any, have you received a ticket (OR been stopped and warned) for moving violations such as speeding, running a stop light, or improper passing?

0. None--GO TO Q.C30	73.3	63.7	82.7	71.4	83.2	80.2	70.8	73.8	67.7	73.5	73.0	82.3	73.0	68.8	65.0	50.9
1. Once	16.6	20.1	13.1	17.6	12.3	12.1	18.0	17.2	19.4	17.4	15.7	12.5	17.2	19.6	20.0	17.5
2. Twice	5.7	8.6	3.0	6.2	2.9	4.3	6.8	4.9	7.2	5.4	6.2	3.2	5.7	6.9	8.2	12.3
3. Three times	2.5	4.3	.8	2.8	.9	2.1	2.4	2.5	3.2	2.2	2.8	1.2	2.3	2.7	4.0	8.8
4. Four or more times	1.9	3.3	.4	2.0	.8	1.4	2.1	1.5	2.6	1.6	2.2	.8	1.8	2.1	2.9	11.1
Item 650 N(Wtd)	16810	8078	8396	13360	1940	3736	5258	5126	2690	9589	6642	5827	3887	2142	4495	171

C29: How many of these tickets or warnings occurred after you were...

QUESTIONNAIRE FORM 1-5 1981	TOTAL	SEX		RACE		REGION				4YR COLLEGE PLANS		ILLICIT DRUG USE: LIFETIME				
		M	F	White	Black	NE	NC	S	W	Yes	No	None	Marijuana Only	Few Pills	More Pills	Any Heroin
Weighted No. of Cases:	18267	8725	8865	13985	2265	4290	5484	5600	2893	9878	7008	6148	4179	2306	4925	189
% of Weighted Total:	100.0	47.8	48.5	76.6	12.4	23.5	30.0	30.7	15.8	54.1	38.4	33.7	22.9	12.6	27.0	1.0
C29A: Drinking alcoholic beverages?																
0. None	80.3	76.5	87.3	79.1	92.6	76.7	77.2	82.8	84.8	82.0	78.0	94.0	83.3	81.4	69.7	49.4
1. One	14.5	16.6	10.7	15.7	4.9	17.0	17.1	12.8	10.5	13.6	15.6	4.7	13.2	14.4	21.4	30.9
2. Two	3.9	5.1	1.4	4.0	1.5	4.8	4.7	2.8	3.2	3.2	5.0	1.1	3.1	3.9	6.1	11.1
3. Three	.5	.6	.3	.6	-	.5	.4	.7	.3	.5	.5	-	.2	.2	1.2	1.2
4. Four or more	.8	1.1	.2	.7	.6	.8	.6	.8	1.0	.8	.8	.2	.3	-	1.6	6.2
Item 660 N(Wtd) ★	4459	2907	1452	3794	326	734	1522	1340	863	2530	1779	1035	1057	665	1552	81
C29B: Smoking marijuana or hashish?																
0. None	91.3	89.7	94.7	91.0	94.6	88.0	90.6	93.4	92.3	92.7	89.5	100.0	98.2	96.5	80.5	52.4
1. One	6.1	6.9	4.3	6.3	3.5	7.9	7.2	4.7	4.6	5.3	7.2	-	1.2	2.8	14.0	26.8
2. Two	1.5	1.9	.7	1.5	1.3	2.8	1.3	.9	1.8	1.0	2.1	-	.3	.8	3.2	11.0
3. Three	.6	.8	.2	.6	-	.6	.5	.6	.6	.6	.5	-	.1	.2	1.4	2.4
4. Four or more	.5	.8	.1	.5	.6	.8	.4	.5	.8	.4	.7	-	.2	-	1.0	8.5
Item 670 N(Wtd) ★	4393	2851	1442	3747	317	722	1506	1312	852	2492	1755	1026	1026	652	1538	82
C29C: Using other illegal drugs?																
0. None	97.3	96.5	98.8	97.3	98.1	96.5	97.3	97.6	97.4	97.6	97.0	100.0	99.8	99.4	94.4	64.2
1. One	1.6	2.0	.8	1.7	.9	2.2	1.8	1.5	.9	1.4	1.9	-	-	.5	3.5	17.3
2. Two	.5	.7	.2	.5	.6	.6	.3	.3	1.1	.4	.5	-	-	.2	1.1	4.9
3. Three	.3	.4	.1	.3	-	.1	.4	.5	.2	.3	.3	-	-	-	.7	4.9
4. Four or more	.2	.3	.1	.2	.3	.6	.2	.1	.4	.2	.3	-	.1	-	.3	7.4
Item 680 N(Wtd) ★	4376	2838	1440	3732	318	718	1496	1313	849	2486	1746	1028	1025	651	1522	81
C30: We are interested in any accidents which occurred while you were driving a car, truck, or motorcycle. ("Accidents" means a collision involving property damage or personal injury--not bumps or scratches in parking lots.) During the LAST 12 MONTHS, how many accidents have you had while you were driving (whether or not you were responsible)?																
0. None--GO TO Q.C32	76.6	71.2	81.9	74.5	87.6	78.3	75.2	76.8	76.8	77.3	75.7	83.6	77.4	73.0	69.3	53.2
1. One	18.3	21.7	14.9	19.9	10.1	17.1	19.3	18.1	17.9	17.9	18.6	13.6	18.3	21.8	22.7	24.0
2. Two	3.9	5.3	2.4	4.3	1.5	3.5	4.1	3.8	3.9	3.8	4.0	2.3	3.4	3.9	5.8	11.1
3. Three	.8	1.1	.6	.9	.4	.8	.8	.9	.8	.7	1.0	.3	.6	1.0	1.5	6.4
4. Four or more	.5	.7	.2	.4	.5	.3	.6	.4	.5	.3	.6	.2	.2	.3	.8	5.3
Item 690 N(Wtd)	16630	8005	8289	13224	1903	3680	5220	5072	2658	9477	6589	5785	3829	2117	4444	171
C31: How many of these accidents occurred after you were...																
C31A: Drinking alcoholic beverages?																
0. None	84.4	81.4	89.1	83.9	92.9	80.5	84.0	87.4	84.5	84.8	83.7	96.2	89.3	87.3	73.7	48.7
1. One	13.1	15.6	9.5	13.8	4.1	16.9	13.5	10.3	12.9	13.3	13.0	3.8	9.4	10.3	22.1	32.9
2. Two	1.7	2.0	.9	1.7	1.2	1.6	1.6	1.9	1.5	1.5	2.0	.1	.9	2.0	2.6	11.8
3. Three	.5	.5	.5	.6	-	.4	.5	.3	1.0	.3	.7	-	-	.2	1.3	1.3
4. Four or more	.3	.5	-	.1	1.7	.6	.4	.1	.3	.1	.6	-	.2	.2	.4	5.3
Item 700 N(Wtd) ★	3862	2284	1490	3345	241	789	1288	1172	613	2139	1587	950	872	561	1355	76
C31B: Smoking marijuana or hashish?																
0. None	93.2	92.1	95.1	93.5	93.2	90.0	93.3	95.3	93.2	94.2	91.9	100.0	98.6	96.5	85.3	58.7
1. One	5.3	6.3	3.9	5.2	4.7	8.0	5.2	3.9	5.1	4.5	6.4	-	1.1	3.5	11.8	24.0
2. Two	1.0	1.1	.7	1.0	.8	1.5	1.0	.6	1.0	1.0	.9	-	-	-	2.3	10.7
3. Three	.2	.2	.2	.2	-	.1	.2	.1	.3	*	.5	-	-	-	.5	-
4. Four or more	.2	.3	-	.1	1.7	.5	.2	.2	.3	.2	.3	-	.2	-	.1	5.3
Item 710 N(Wtd) ★	3784	2228	1471	3278	236	779	1260	1140	605	2101	1548	940	850	550	1327	75

★ = excludes respondents for whom question was inappropriate.   * = less than .05 per cent.

QUESTIONNAIRE FORM 1-5 1981	TOTAL	SEX		RACE		REGION				4YR COLLEGE PLANS		ILLICIT DRUG USE: LIFETIME				
		M	F	White	Black	NE	NC	S	W	Yes	No	None	Mari- juana Only	Few Pills	More Pills	Any Her- oin
Weighted No. of Cases:	18267	8725	8865	13985	2265	4290	5484	5600	2893	9878	7008	6148	4179	2306	4925	189
% of Weighted Total:	100.0	47.8	48.5	76.6	12.4	23.5	30.0	30.7	15.8	54.1	38.4	33.7	22.9	12.6	27.0	1.0
C31C: Using other illegal drugs?																
0. None	97.9	97.5	98.6	98.0	98.3	96.5	98.0	98.9	97.3	98.2	97.5	100.0	99.8	99.8	95.7	72.2
1. One	1.5	1.7	1.1	1.4	.4	2.8	1.4	.6	1.7	1.4	1.7	-	.1	.2	3.4	15.3
2. Two	.3	.5	.1	.4	.9	.4	.4	.3	.3	.3	.5	-	-	-	.6	6.9
3. Three	.1	.1	.1	.1	-	.1	-	.1	.3	-	.2	-	-	-	.3	-
4. Four or more	.1	.2	-	.1	.4	.1	.2	.1	.3	.1	.2	-	.1	-	-	5.6
Item 720 N(Wtd) ★	*3741*	*2195*	*1463*	*3244*	*231*	*762*	*1253*	*1129*	*597*	*2083*	*1529*	*938*	*850*	*542*	*1297*	*72*
C32: If you have not entered military service, and do not expect to enter, GO TO PART D.																
What is, or will be, your branch of service?																
1. Army	21.1	20.0	24.8	17.3	34.5	17.4	20.2	26.2	15.1	19.8	23.2	22.5	21.1	19.7	18.8	31.8
2. Navy	15.7	16.7	11.7	17.6	9.9	16.5	18.5	12.4	17.6	14.3	16.3	13.4	17.7	17.3	16.7	2.3
3. Marine Corps	11.9	13.7	5.3	12.5	8.6	12.6	14.1	9.4	12.4	10.2	13.0	10.3	13.5	11.2	12.0	13.6
4. Air Force	33.9	31.9	41.1	34.6	32.3	32.6	32.8	34.3	36.8	38.8	30.3	34.3	34.0	34.2	34.7	22.7
5. Coast Guard	4.2	4.6	3.0	5.1	1.0	7.4	2.2	3.3	6.3	3.0	5.0	3.5	3.1	5.8	5.2	11.4
6. Uncertain	13.2	13.1	14.2	12.9	13.6	13.4	12.4	14.3	11.7	14.0	12.2	16.1	10.5	11.8	12.6	15.9
Item 730 N(Wtd) ★	*2758*	*2084*	*606*	*1859*	*595*	*516*	*813*	*1019*	*410*	*1181*	*1408*	*837*	*702*	*330*	*744*	*44*
C33: Do you expect to be an officer?																
1. No	15.6	14.8	18.2	14.4	16.4	14.7	18.6	12.7	17.8	7.7	21.0	14.9	12.2	15.5	18.3	14.3
2. Uncertain	43.3	43.1	44.2	45.4	36.1	38.3	47.9	40.7	46.6	33.1	52.0	39.4	43.0	44.8	47.2	57.1
3. Yes	41.1	42.1	37.5	40.2	47.4	47.0	33.5	46.5	35.3	59.3	26.9	45.7	44.8	39.7	34.5	31.0
Item 740 N(Wtd) ★	*2791*	*2110*	*611*	*1878*	*599*	*532*	*828*	*1014*	*416*	*1202*	*1421*	*845*	*714*	*335*	*760*	*42*
C34: Do you expect to have a career in the Armed Forces?																
1. No	30.7	31.2	28.9	33.2	23.4	34.8	32.9	26.0	32.4	32.9	27.5	29.6	29.5	32.0	32.4	27.5
2. Uncertain	46.9	48.4	41.7	49.3	40.7	43.1	50.5	45.5	48.1	46.6	49.0	43.5	46.4	46.5	52.8	45.0
3. Yes	22.4	20.4	29.4	17.5	35.8	22.0	16.6	28.4	19.6	20.5	23.5	26.9	24.1	21.5	14.8	27.5
Item 750 N(Wtd) ★	*2776*	*2098*	*609*	*1872*	*595*	*531*	*821*	*1010*	*414*	*1199*	*1408*	*841*	*711*	*331*	*757*	*40*

★=excludes respondents for whom question was inappropriate.

QUESTIONNAIRE FORM 1-5 1981	TOTAL	SEX		RACE		REGION				4YR COLLEGE PLANS		ILLICIT DRUG USE: LIFETIME				
		M	F	White	Black	NE	NC	S	W	Yes	No	None	Mari-juana Only	Few Pills	More Pills	Any Her-oin
Weighted No. of Cases:	18267	8725	8865	13985	2265	4290	5484	5600	2893	9878	7008	6148	4179	2306	4925	189
% of Weighted Total:	100.0	47.8	48.5	76.6	12.4	23.5	30.0	30.7	15.8	54.1	38.4	33.7	22.9	12.6	27.0	1.0

The following questions are about CIGARETTE SMOKING.

B01: Have you ever smoked cigarettes?

	TOTAL	M	F	White	Black	NE	NC	S	W	Yes	No	None	Mari-juana Only	Few Pills	More Pills	Any Her-oin
1. Never	29.0	31.4	26.7	27.7	33.9	29.2	26.1	29.0	33.9	33.4	23.0	56.3	17.0	19.7	10.4	11.4
2. Once or twice	30.9	32.6	29.4	30.3	38.0	28.5	29.9	32.5	33.0	33.4	28.2	30.1	40.3	34.5	22.9	16.8
3. Occasionally but not regularly	16.1	14.3	18.0	16.5	14.2	14.7	17.0	16.6	15.3	16.2	16.2	8.1	21.4	20.5	19.3	14.6
4. Regularly in the past	7.7	7.3	8.2	8.2	5.0	8.3	7.9	6.9	8.1	6.9	8.6	2.4	8.9	7.8	13.1	13.5
5. Regularly now	16.4	14.4	17.7	17.3	9.0	19.2	19.0	15.0	9.7	10.0	24.1	3.0	12.4	17.6	34.3	43.8
Item 760 N(Wtd)	17814	8546	8713	13797	2158	4180	5377	5440	2818	9729	6845	6024	4108	2252	4872	185

B02: How frequently have you smoked cigarettes during the past 30 days?

	TOTAL	M	F	White	Black	NE	NC	S	W	Yes	No	None	Mari-juana Only	Few Pills	More Pills	Any Her-oin
1. Not at all - incl. (1) in B01	70.6	73.5	68.4	69.9	77.7	68.5	67.7	71.1	78.2	77.7	61.9	91.3	72.0	66.9	47.2	38.9
2. Less than one cigarette per day	9.1	8.4	9.9	9.2	8.7	8.3	9.4	9.8	8.6	9.4	8.7	4.5	11.2	11.7	11.7	10.3
3. One to five cigarettes per day	6.7	5.3	8.0	6.3	8.0	6.7	6.9	7.1	5.9	5.3	8.6	2.0	7.2	7.5	11.5	10.8
4. About one-half pack per day	6.4	5.8	6.8	6.6	3.9	7.3	7.2	6.2	4.0	3.9	9.3	1.1	5.2	8.1	12.7	15.7
5. About one pack per day	5.6	5.6	5.5	6.3	1.2	7.3	6.9	4.5	2.7	2.9	9.0	.9	3.5	4.6	13.4	14.6
6. About one and one-half packs per day	1.2	1.1	1.3	1.4	.4	1.6	1.5	1.0	.4	.6	2.0	.2	.7	.9	2.9	5.9
7. Two packs or more per day	.3	.3	.2	.3	.1	.4	.4	.1	.1	.1	.5	*	.1	.3	.6	3.8
Item 780 N(Wtd)	17794	8537	8705	13778	2162	4168	5377	5431	2818	9722	6833	6030	4101	2250	4866	185

B03: Next we want to ask you about drinking alcoholic beverages, including beer, wine, and liquor.

Have you ever had any beer, wine, or liquor to drink?

	TOTAL	M	F	White	Black	NE	NC	S	W	Yes	No	None	Mari-juana Only	Few Pills	More Pills	Any Her-oin
1. No	7.1	6.5	7.7	5.4	13.7	3.5	5.5	10.3	9.6	7.2	6.7	18.0	1.0	2.6	.6	1.5
2. Yes	92.9	93.5	92.3	94.6	86.3	96.5	94.5	89.8	90.4	92.8	93.3	82.0	99.0	97.4	99.4	97.8
Item 790 N(Wtd)	13916	6724	6809	10896	1631	3277	4256	4180	2203	7669	5439	4748	3218	1785	3847	136

B04: On how many occasions have you had alcoholic beverages to drink...

B04A: ...in your lifetime?

	TOTAL	M	F	White	Black	NE	NC	S	W	Yes	No	None	Mari-juana Only	Few Pills	More Pills	Any Her-oin
1. 0 occasions - incl. (1) in B03	7.4	6.6	8.1	5.6	15.5	3.6	5.6	11.2	9.4	7.3	7.1	18.6	1.1	2.8	.6	1.7
2. 1-2	6.8	5.3	8.4	4.9	18.1	3.6	5.7	10.2	7.1	6.8	6.5	14.1	3.9	4.6	1.2	3.4
3. 3-5	7.7	6.3	9.1	6.6	13.9	5.6	7.0	9.7	8.4	8.0	7.5	14.8	6.3	5.4	1.5	1.7
4. 6-9	7.4	6.1	8.8	6.7	12.7	6.1	6.8	8.5	8.7	7.9	6.9	11.2	8.0	6.9	2.9	.6
5. 10-19	11.5	10.3	12.8	11.3	12.9	12.2	11.7	11.3	10.5	12.3	10.5	14.1	14.8	12.9	5.2	2.3
6. 20-39	13.5	11.8	15.2	14.3	9.6	15.3	13.3	12.6	12.8	14.1	12.8	11.7	17.2	18.2	10.8	5.2
7. 40 or more	45.7	53.5	37.6	50.5	17.2	53.6	49.8	36.6	43.1	43.7	48.7	15.5	48.6	49.2	77.8	85.6
Item 810 N(Wtd)	17131	8247	8381	13492	1939	4073	5220	5119	2719	9503	6496	5802	4012	2168	4733	174

B04B: ...during the last 12 months?

	TOTAL	M	F	White	Black	NE	NC	S	W	Yes	No	None	Mari-juana Only	Few Pills	More Pills	Any Her-oin
1. 0 occasions - incl. (1) in B03	13.0	11.1	14.9	9.9	29.3	6.2	10.9	19.3	15.5	12.6	13.0	29.9	5.1	6.1	2.0	4.0
2. 1-2	12.6	10.1	15.2	10.5	25.9	9.4	11.6	15.8	13.6	13.0	12.0	21.5	11.3	11.0	3.9	2.9
3. 3-5	11.8	10.4	13.2	11.1	15.6	10.7	12.1	12.3	11.7	12.3	11.3	15.9	14.0	11.7	5.2	3.5
4. 6-9	10.5	9.3	11.9	10.6	10.2	10.6	10.2	10.7	10.8	10.9	10.2	10.6	13.7	13.4	6.9	4.0
5. 10-19	15.6	15.8	15.6	17.3	7.5	17.9	16.6	13.0	15.2	16.3	15.2	10.7	19.7	20.2	16.5	8.7
6. 20-39	13.9	14.0	14.0	15.3	5.6	17.2	14.8	11.3	12.4	14.2	13.5	5.8	16.5	16.9	20.7	13.9
7. 40 or more	22.5	29.4	15.2	25.3	6.0	28.0	23.8	17.6	20.7	20.6	24.9	5.6	19.8	20.6	44.9	63.0
Item 820 N(Wtd)	17055	8207	8349	13451	1917	4057	5193	5089	2716	9450	6489	5760	3997	2151	4726	173

B04C: ...during the last 30 days?

	TOTAL	M	F	White	Black	NE	NC	S	W	Yes	No	None	Mari-juana Only	Few Pills	More Pills	Any Her-oin
1. 0 occasions - incl. (1) in B03	29.3	24.3	34.3	25.0	54.2	19.6	26.4	37.1	34.7	30.0	27.9	53.6	22.5	22.8	9.2	4.7
2. 1-2	21.9	20.2	23.8	21.4	25.0	20.4	22.5	22.9	21.3	23.1	20.8	25.9	25.0	24.9	13.6	12.4
3. 3-5	18.4	19.4	17.7	20.1	10.0	22.1	19.1	15.4	17.5	19.4	17.6	11.9	22.4	22.9	21.4	12.4
4. 6-9	13.6	15.2	11.9	15.0	5.0	16.7	14.1	10.3	14.0	13.7	13.4	4.5	15.9	15.3	22.0	15.3
5. 10-19	10.7	12.4	9.0	12.0	3.8	13.6	11.3	9.1	8.2	9.4	12.5	3.1	9.8	9.4	20.8	24.7
6. 20-39	3.4	4.5	2.2	3.8	1.0	4.1	4.0	2.9	2.5	2.8	4.2	.7	2.8	3.0	7.0	19.4
7. 40 or more	2.6	4.0	1.1	2.8	1.1	3.4	2.6	2.3	1.8	1.8	3.5	.4	1.6	1.6	6.1	11.2
Item 830 N(Wtd)	17051	8222	8327	13455	1906	4056	5197	5094	2705	9454	6482	5732	4012	2149	4743	170

* = less than .05 per cent.

QUESTIONNAIRE FORM 1-5 1981	TOTAL	SEX		RACE		REGION				4YR COLLEGE PLANS		ILLICIT DRUG USE: LIFETIME				
		M	F	White	Black	NE	NC	S	W	Yes	No	None	Mari- juana Only	Few Pills	More Pills	Any Her- oin
Weighted No. of Cases:	18267	8725	8865	13985	2265	4290	5484	5600	2893	9878	7008	6148	4179	2306	4925	189
% of Weighted Total:	100.0	47.8	48.5	76.6	12.4	23.5	30.0	30.7	15.8	54.1	38.4	33.7	22.9	12.6	27.0	1.0

B05: On the occasions that you drink alcoholic beverages, how often do you drink enough to feel pretty high?

	TOTAL	M	F	White	Black	NE	NC	S	W	Yes	No	None	Mari-juana Only	Few Pills	More Pills	Any Heroin
1. On none of the occasions	22.9	18.5	27.8	19.6	43.9	17.5	20.4	29.8	23.7	25.8	19.1	51.8	15.2	13.8	5.4	5.6
2. On few of the occasions	31.0	27.9	33.8	30.2	32.8	29.9	31.5	31.2	31.1	30.5	31.5	29.2	38.6	36.8	23.7	15.5
3. On about half of the occasions	18.0	19.3	16.6	19.3	10.6	20.4	18.0	15.8	18.1	17.9	18.0	9.3	20.7	20.7	23.2	19.7
4. On most of the occasions	18.8	22.0	15.6	20.9	7.4	21.4	19.5	15.4	19.7	18.3	19.7	7.1	18.4	19.6	30.5	25.4
5. On nearly all of the occasions	9.4	12.3	6.3	10.1	5.3	10.8	10.7	7.8	7.4	7.5	11.7	2.7	7.0	9.1	17.2	34.5
Item 840 N(Wtd) ★	13126	6409	6361	10440	1452	3208	4083	3827	2007	7192	5182	3920	3249	1771	3894	142

B06: Think back over the LAST TWO WEEKS. How many times have you had five or more drinks in a row? (A "drink" is a glass of wine, a bottle of beer, a shot glass of liquor, or a mixed drink.)

	TOTAL	M	F	White	Black	NE	NC	S	W	Yes	No	None	Mari-juana Only	Few Pills	More Pills	Any Heroin
1. None - incl. (1) in B03	58.6	48.4	69.2	54.7	82.8	50.7	55.1	65.3	64.4	62.6	53.3	84.0	56.4	56.4	31.8	13.5
2. Once	12.1	13.3	11.1	13.2	5.9	14.2	12.1	10.6	11.9	12.3	12.3	7.3	15.1	14.1	14.6	13.5
3. Twice	10.5	13.0	7.9	11.5	4.0	11.8	11.7	8.7	9.9	9.4	12.1	4.3	12.7	11.9	15.7	12.4
4. Three to five times	12.5	16.6	8.4	14.0	4.8	15.8	14.0	10.1	9.5	11.0	14.5	3.2	11.6	13.6	24.0	25.3
5. Six to nine times	4.0	5.4	2.4	4.3	1.6	5.1	4.4	3.2	2.9	3.1	4.9	.6	2.7	2.4	9.5	12.4
6. Ten or more times	2.2	3.4	.9	2.2	1.0	2.3	2.6	2.2	1.5	1.6	2.9	.6	1.4	1.6	4.4	22.9
Item 850 N(Wtd)	16975	8166	8322	13394	1914	4022	5180	5066	2707	9423	6441	5778	3967	2134	4685	170

The next major section of this questionnaire deals with various other drugs. There is a lot of talk these days about this subject, but very little accurate information. Therefore, we still have a lot to learn about the actual experiences and attitudes of people your age.

We hope that you can answer all questions; but if you find one which you feel you cannot answer honestly, we would prefer that you leave it blank.

Remember that your answers will be kept strictly confidential: they are never connected with your name or your class.

B07: On how many occasions (if any) have you used marijuana (grass, pot) or hashish (hash, hash oil)...

B07A: ...in your lifetime?

	TOTAL	M	F	White	Black	NE	NC	S	W	Yes	No	None	Mari-juana Only	Few Pills	More Pills	Any Heroin
1. 0 occasions	40.5	37.5	43.8	38.8	49.5	32.2	40.1	49.2	36.8	44.1	36.5	100.0	-	24.3	8.4	3.4
2. 1-2	10.5	10.4	10.7	9.9	14.4	9.6	10.6	11.6	9.7	10.9	10.2	-	32.8	13.3	3.8	3.4
3. 3-5	7.1	7.0	7.2	7.1	8.0	7.5	6.9	6.7	7.5	7.4	6.8	-	19.3	11.0	3.9	5.6
4. 6-9	5.3	5.1	5.5	5.5	5.1	5.4	5.5	5.1	5.2	5.2	5.4	-	12.3	9.2	4.4	2.2
5. 10-19	6.6	6.2	7.1	7.0	5.3	7.7	6.4	5.6	7.7	6.8	6.7	-	13.2	11.0	7.6	1.7
6. 20-39	6.3	5.9	6.7	6.7	4.3	7.7	6.3	4.7	7.1	6.4	6.2	-	10.1	9.5	9.6	3.9
7. 40 or more	23.7	27.9	18.8	25.0	13.5	29.8	24.3	17.1	26.0	19.3	28.2	-	12.5	21.7	62.3	79.8
Item 860 N(Wtd)	17540	8425	8620	13711	2081	4109	5335	5308	2787	9672	6724	6148	4149	2223	4812	178

B07B: ...during the last 12 months?

	TOTAL	M	F	White	Black	NE	NC	S	W	Yes	No	None	Mari-juana Only	Few Pills	More Pills	Any Heroin
1. 0 occasions	53.9	50.8	57.5	52.0	65.0	46.8	53.2	62.0	50.4	57.4	50.3	100.0	37.5	42.2	16.1	9.7
2. 1-2	10.2	9.5	11.0	10.4	10.4	10.8	10.0	10.0	10.3	10.8	9.5	-	25.4	15.9	7.8	8.0
3. 3-5	7.3	7.2	7.3	7.6	5.9	7.9	7.1	6.5	8.0	7.3	7.2	-	14.0	12.0	8.7	3.4
4. 6-9	4.9	5.0	4.9	5.2	4.2	5.4	5.2	3.9	6.0	4.8	5.3	-	8.3	8.3	7.0	2.3
5. 10-19	5.8	5.5	6.0	6.2	3.3	6.9	5.7	4.4	6.6	5.6	6.0	-	6.7	8.2	11.2	6.8
6. 20-39	5.0	5.0	5.0	5.1	4.0	6.0	4.9	4.2	5.3	4.3	5.8	-	4.3	5.8	11.3	12.5
7. 40 or more	12.9	17.0	8.3	13.5	7.2	16.2	14.0	9.0	13.3	9.9	15.9	-	3.8	7.6	37.9	58.0
Item 870 N(Wtd)	17455	8374	8589	13659	2068	4079	5323	5276	2776	9645	6677	6148	4109	2206	4786	176

★=excludes respondents for whom question was inappropriate.

QUESTIONNAIRE FORM 1-5 1981	TOTAL	SEX		RACE		REGION				4YR COLLEGE PLANS		ILLICIT DRUG USE: LIFETIME				
		M	F	White	Black	NE	NC	S	W	Yes	No	None	Mari-juana Only	Few Pills	More Pills	Any Her-oin
Weighted No. of Cases:	18267	8725	8865	13985	2265	4290	5484	5600	2893	9878	7008	6148	4179	2306	4925	189
% of Weighted Total:	100.0	47.8	48.5	76.6	12.4	23.5	30.0	30.7	15.8	54.1	38.4	33.7	22.9	12.6	27.0	1.0
B07C: ...during the last 30 days?																
1. 0 occasions	68.4	64.7	72.7	67.5	75.1	61.8	67.0	75.3	68.0	72.6	63.9	100.0	67.8	64.2	32.4	20.6
2. 1-2	10.1	10.1	10.2	10.5	9.4	11.9	10.2	8.3	11.0	10.3	10.1	-	18.3	17.7	12.8	8.0
3. 3-5	5.4	5.4	5.3	5.5	4.3	6.6	5.4	4.2	5.9	4.9	5.8	-	7.2	6.1	10.4	5.7
4. 6-9	3.9	4.4	3.3	4.0	2.4	4.8	3.9	3.1	3.9	3.2	4.8	-	3.1	4.9	8.8	11.4
5. 10-19	5.1	5.8	4.2	5.2	4.1	5.8	5.3	4.5	4.8	4.1	6.1	-	1.9	4.6	14.1	16.6
6. 20-39	3.6	4.6	2.5	3.7	2.7	4.4	4.2	2.5	3.2	2.6	4.8	-	1.0	1.7	10.9	13.1
7. 40 or more	3.4	5.0	1.7	3.5	2.0	4.7	4.0	2.0	3.1	2.3	4.6	-	.6	.9	10.7	24.6
Item 880 N(Wtd)	17453	8375	8589	13654	2069	4084	5321	5275	2772	9639	6681	6148	4102	2201	4793	175
B08: On how many occasions (if any) have you used LSD ("acid")...																
B08A: ...during your lifetime?																
1. 0 occasions	90.2	88.3	92.5	89.2	98.4	87.8	88.2	94.8	88.8	92.2	88.2	100.0	100.0	96.0	68.6	29.3
2. 1-2	4.3	4.7	3.6	4.7	.9	4.6	4.8	2.7	5.8	3.7	4.9	-	-	4.0	13.2	16.7
3. 3-5	2.1	2.4	1.7	2.3	.3	3.0	2.4	1.0	2.3	1.6	2.6	-	-	-	7.3	9.8
4. 6-9	1.3	1.6	.9	1.5	.1	1.7	1.5	.6	1.4	1.0	1.4	-	-	-	4.2	10.9
5. 10-19	1.1	1.4	.8	1.2	*	1.3	1.6	.5	1.1	.8	1.4	-	-	-	3.7	9.8
6. 20-39	.5	.7	.3	.6	.1	.8	.8	.1	.3	.3	.8	-	-	-	1.6	8.6
7. 40 or more	.5	.8	.2	.6	.1	.8	.7	.3	.3	.4	.7	-	-	-	1.5	14.4
Item 890 N(Wtd)	17771	8554	8720	13804	2181	4148	5387	5423	2812	9745	6855	6119	4165	2270	4863	174
B08B: ...during the last 12 months?																
1. 0 occasions	93.5	92.0	95.3	92.8	99.2	91.0	92.2	96.6	93.7	95.0	92.0	100.0	100.0	98.1	79.0	46.8
2. 1-2	3.6	4.2	2.7	4.0	.4	4.6	3.8	2.2	4.2	2.8	4.4	-	-	1.9	11.6	16.2
3. 3-5	1.4	1.6	1.2	1.6	.1	2.1	1.9	.5	1.4	1.1	1.8	-	-	-	4.8	12.1
4. 6-9	.7	1.0	.4	.8	*	.9	1.0	.4	.5	.6	.8	-	-	-	2.4	6.4
5. 10-19	.5	.7	.3	.5	.1	1.0	.7	.1	.2	.4	.7	-	-	-	1.6	8.1
6. 20-39	.2	.2	.1	.2	.1	.2	.3	.1	.1	.1	.2	-	-	-	.4	7.5
7. 40 or more	.1	.2	*	.1	*	.3	.1	.1	*	.1	.2	-	-	-	.3	2.3
Item 900 N(Wtd)	17760	8549	8715	13801	2177	4145	5389	5419	2808	9744	6849	6120	4167	2270	4848	173
B08C: ...during the last 30 days?																
1. 0 occasions	97.5	96.6	98.6	97.3	99.6	95.8	96.7	98.9	98.9	98.0	97.1	100.0	100.0	99.7	92.2	69.2
2. 1-2	1.9	2.5	1.2	2.1	.1	3.2	2.5	.8	.9	1.7	2.1	-	-	.3	6.3	16.9
3. 3-5	.3	.4	.2	.3	*	.4	.5	.1	.1	.1	.5	-	-	-	.9	5.2
4. 6-9	.1	.2	*	.1	*	.3	.2	*	.1	.1	.2	-	-	-	.4	4.1
5. 10-19	.1	.1	*	.1	.1	*	.1	*	*	*	.1	-	-	-	.1	3.5
6. 20-39	*	*	-	-	*	-	*	*	-	-	*	-	-	-	.1	1.2
7. 40 or more	.1	.1	*	.1	-	.1	*	*	-	*	.1	-	-	-	.2	.6
Item 910 N(Wtd)	17760	8551	8715	13802	2175	4144	5391	5418	2807	9742	6852	6120	4168	2270	4848	172
B09: On how many occasions (if any) have you used psychedelics other than LSD (like mescaline, peyote, psilocybin, PCP)...																
B09A: ...in your lifetime?																
1. 0 occasions	90.9	89.0	93.1	90.2	97.8	86.0	90.4	96.2	88.8	92.2	89.6	100.0	100.0	94.3	71.8	31.9
2. 1-2	4.6	5.5	3.6	4.9	1.4	6.5	4.7	2.3	5.6	4.1	5.1	-	-	5.7	13.4	15.9
3. 3-5	1.7	1.9	1.5	1.9	.4	2.5	2.0	.5	2.5	1.4	2.1	-	-	-	5.9	11.5
4. 6-9	.9	1.2	.6	1.0	.1	1.7	.9	.3	1.1	.8	1.0	-	-	-	3.2	4.9
5. 10-19	.9	1.0	.7	1.0	.1	1.6	.8	.2	1.3	.7	1.0	-	-	-	3.0	9.3
6. 20-39	.5	.7	.2	.4	*	1.0	.6	.1	.4	.3	.6	-	-	-	1.5	7.7
7. 40 or more	.5	.6	.3	.5	.1	.7	.7	.3	.4	.4	.6	-	-	-	1.2	18.1
Item 920 N(Wtd)	17698	8509	8697	13757	2171	4140	5374	5384	2800	9709	6831	6118	4121	2264	4833	182

* = less than .05 per cent.

QUESTIONNAIRE FORM 1-5 1981	TOTAL	SEX		RACE		REGION				4YR COLLEGE PLANS		ILLICIT DRUG USE: LIFETIME				
		M	F	White	Black	NE	NC	S	W	Yes	No	None	Mari-juana Only	Few Pills	More Pills	Any Her-oin
Weighted No. of Cases:	18267	8725	8865	13985	2265	4290	5484	5600	2893	9878	7008	6148	4179	2306	4925	189
% of Weighted Total:	100.0	47.8	48.5	76.6	12.4	23.5	30.0	30.7	15.8	54.1	38.4	33.7	22.9	12.6	27.0	1.0

B09B: ...during the last 12 months?

1. 0 occasions	94.4	93.1	96.0	94.0	98.8	91.0	94.3	98.0	93.1	95.0	94.0	100.0	100.0	97.9	82.6	47.5
2. 1-2	3.2	4.0	2.3	3.5	.7	4.8	3.5	1.5	3.4	3.0	3.4	-	-	2.2	9.9	20.1
3. 3-5	1.0	1.2	.8	1.1	.2	1.7	.9	.2	1.8	.9	1.1	-	-	-	3.5	3.9
4. 6-9	.6	.7	.4	.6	.1	1.0	.5	.1	.9	.5	.6	-	-	-	1.8	7.3
5. 10-19	.5	.7	.3	.5	*	1.1	.4	.1	.6	.4	.5	-	-	-	1.5	12.3
6. 20-39	.2	.3	.1	.2	*	.3	.3	.1	*	.2	.2	-	-	-	.5	5.6
7. 40 or more	.1	.1	.1	.1	-	.1	.1	*	.1	*	.1	-	-	-	.2	3.4
Item 930 N(Wtd)	17681	8497	8693	13747	2166	4136	5366	5383	2795	9698	6825	6119	4123	2262	4816	179

B09C: ...during the last 30 days?

1. 0 occasions	97.9	97.6	98.4	97.9	99.4	96.2	97.7	99.5	97.9	98.3	97.7	100.0	100.0	99.4	93.7	72.6
2. 1-2	1.4	1.5	1.1	1.5	.3	2.3	1.5	.3	1.8	1.2	1.5	-	-	.6	4.4	11.2
3. 3-5	.4	.5	.2	.3	.1	.9	.3	.1	.1	.3	.4	-	-	-	1.1	6.1
4. 6-9	.2	.3	.1	.2	.1	.4	.3	.1	.1	.1	.3	-	-	-	.6	7.8
5. 10-19	.1	.1	*	.1	*	.1	.1	*	-	*	.1	-	-	-	.2	.6
6. 20-39	*	-	*	*	-	*	*	-	*	*	*	-	-	-	.1	-
7. 40 or more	*	*	*	.1	-	*	.1	-	*	*	.1	-	-	-	.1	1.7
Item 940 N(Wtd)	17672	8493	8690	13741	2166	4130	5365	5384	2793	9694	6821	6119	4125	2261	4807	179

B10: On how many occasions (if any) have you use cocaine (sometimes called "coke")...

B10A: ...in your lifetime?

1. 0 occasions	83.5	81.3	86.2	82.7	92.3	78.3	86.0	90.0	73.6	85.6	81.9	100.0	100.0	81.0	51.7	14.3
2. 1-2	7.2	8.4	5.8	7.5	4.6	8.8	6.7	5.3	9.1	6.1	8.3	-	-	19.0	16.6	16.5
3. 3-5	3.1	3.5	2.6	3.3	1.2	4.0	2.9	1.6	5.1	2.6	3.4	-	-	-	10.9	11.5
4. 6-9	1.8	1.9	1.6	1.9	.7	2.3	1.3	1.2	3.4	1.7	1.8	-	-	-	6.3	10.4
5. 10-19	1.8	1.8	1.7	1.9	.6	2.6	1.4	.9	3.1	1.7	1.8	-	-	-	6.2	11.0
6. 20-39	1.1	1.1	1.0	1.1	.2	1.5	.6	.4	2.8	1.0	1.0	-	-	-	3.6	8.8
7. 40 or more	1.6	2.1	1.0	1.6	.4	2.4	1.1	.7	2.9	1.3	1.7	-	-	-	4.7	28.0
Item 950 N(Wtd)	17678	8509	8706	13783	2162	4119	5381	5381	2797	9717	6843	6096	4112	2268	4839	182

B10B: ...during the last 12 months?

1. 0 occasions	87.6	86.2	89.6	86.9	96.0	83.2	90.6	93.2	77.9	88.5	87.6	100.0	100.0	90.2	62.1	27.9
2. 1-2	5.8	6.8	4.6	6.2	2.1	7.4	5.0	3.8	8.7	5.3	6.0	-	-	9.8	15.9	16.4
3. 3-5	2.6	2.7	2.3	2.8	.8	3.1	2.0	1.3	5.2	2.3	2.6	-	-	-	8.7	15.8
4. 6-9	1.5	1.4	1.4	1.5	.5	2.7	.9	.7	2.4	1.6	1.1	-	-	-	5.1	10.4
5. 10-19	1.3	1.3	1.2	1.4	.3	1.6	.8	.6	3.1	1.2	1.3	-	-	-	4.4	7.7
6. 20-39	.6	.7	.5	.6	.2	1.0	.3	.3	1.4	.6	.7	-	-	-	2.1	8.7
7. 40 or more	.6	.8	.4	.7	.1	1.0	.5	.1	1.2	.5	.6	-	-	-	1.7	13.7
Item 960 N(Wtd)	17662	8502	8701	13777	2159	4115	5376	5377	2794	9711	6833	6097	4113	2262	4826	183

B10C: ...during the last 30 days?

1. 0 occasions	94.2	93.7	95.0	93.9	97.9	91.9	96.2	97.1	88.0	94.5	94.4	100.0	100.0	97.6	81.7	50.8
2. 1-2	3.5	3.6	3.2	3.6	1.5	4.6	2.4	1.9	6.7	3.3	3.3	-	-	2.4	10.7	21.9
3. 3-5	1.1	1.3	.8	1.2	.2	1.6	.5	.5	2.5	1.0	.9	-	-	-	3.7	6.6
4. 6-9	.7	.6	.7	.6	.2	1.0	.3	.3	1.4	.6	.6	-	-	-	2.1	8.2
5. 10-19	.4	.5	.3	.4	.2	.5	.3	.1	.9	.4	.4	-	-	-	1.1	8.7
6. 20-39	.1	.1	.1	.1	-	.1	.1	-	.3	*	.2	-	-	-	.3	1.1
7. 40 or more	.2	.2	*	.2	.1	.2	.1	.1	.2	.1	.2	-	-	-	.5	3.3
Item 970 N(Wtd)	17663	8504	8700	13777	2158	4115	5376	5375	2797	9710	6835	6097	4114	2261	4824	183

B11: Amphetamines are sometimes prescribed by doctors to help people lose weight or to give people more energy. They are sometimes called uppers, ups, speed, bennies, dexies, pep pills, and diet pills. On how many occasions (if any) have you taken amphetamines on your own--that is, without a doctor telling you to take them...

* = less than .05 per cent.

QUESTIONNAIRE FORM 1-5 1981	TOTAL	SEX		RACE		REGION				4YR COLLEGE PLANS		ILLICIT DRUG USE: LIFETIME				
		M	F	White	Black	NE	NC	S	W	Yes	No	None	Mari- juana Only	Few Pills	More Pills	Any Her- oin
Weighted No. of Cases:	18267	8725	8865	13985	2265	4290	5484	5600	2893	9878	7008	6148	4179	2306	4925	189
% of Weighted Total:	100.0	47.8	48.5	76.6	12.4	23.5	30.0	30.7	15.8	54.1	38.4	33.7	22.9	12.6	27.0	1.0
B11A: ...in your lifetime?																
1. 0 occasions	67.8	69.5	66.5	64.0	90.0	65.3	63.8	74.8	65.5	72.4	61.7	100.0	100.0	45.9	11.1	12.8
2. 1-2	8.5	7.9	9.2	9.3	4.5	8.2	8.8	7.7	10.1	8.2	9.2	-	-	54.1	5.6	6.1
3. 3-5	5.0	4.8	5.2	5.4	2.5	5.0	5.5	4.1	5.7	4.4	5.8	-	-	-	18.0	5.6
4. 6-9	3.6	3.5	3.6	4.1	.9	4.2	3.9	3.1	3.2	3.2	4.0	-	-	-	12.8	9.5
5. 10-19	4.7	4.7	4.6	5.3	1.1	5.2	5.0	3.9	5.1	4.1	5.6	-	-	-	16.9	9.5
6. 20-39	3.7	3.4	4.0	4.4	.4	4.4	4.2	2.6	4.0	3.1	4.5	-	-	-	13.3	8.4
7. 40 or more	6.6	6.2	6.9	7.5	.6	7.7	8.8	3.8	6.3	4.6	9.2	-	-	-	22.3	48.6
Item 980 N(Wtd)	17616	8521	8655	13736	2167	4116	5356	5359	2785	9696	6805	6061	4079	2259	4831	179
B11B: ...during the last 12 months?																
1. 0 occasions	74.0	75.2	73.1	70.4	94.4	71.2	69.9	80.4	73.4	77.7	69.1	100.0	100.0	71.2	21.4	16.4
2. 1-2	7.7	7.3	8.0	8.7	2.8	7.2	8.4	6.9	8.4	7.0	8.7	-	-	28.8	14.2	11.3
3. 3-5	4.8	5.0	4.5	5.4	1.3	5.7	5.3	3.8	4.6	4.1	5.5	-	-	-	17.0	13.0
4. 6-9	3.4	3.5	3.1	3.8	.4	4.0	3.6	2.6	3.7	2.9	3.9	-	-	-	12.1	7.9
5. 10-19	4.3	4.1	4.6	5.1	.6	5.4	4.7	3.1	4.4	3.7	5.2	-	-	-	15.4	11.9
6. 20-39	2.8	2.4	3.3	3.3	.2	3.3	3.8	1.5	3.0	2.3	3.5	-	-	-	10.0	11.3
7. 40 or more	3.0	2.4	3.5	3.4	.2	3.3	4.4	1.7	2.5	2.2	4.0	-	-	-	9.9	27.7
Item 990 N(Wtd)	17589	8501	8646	13717	2157	4112	5347	5352	2778	9683	6791	6065	4080	2239	4820	177
B11C: ...during the last 30 days?																
1. 0 occasions	84.2	85.3	83.3	82.2	96.8	81.6	81.1	88.5	85.7	87.0	80.6	100.0	100.0	91.0	48.9	33.5
2. 1-2	6.6	6.9	6.2	7.4	2.0	6.7	7.2	5.9	6.4	5.4	8.1	-	-	9.0	19.3	13.1
3. 3-5	3.6	3.4	3.8	4.1	.6	4.5	4.4	2.3	3.5	3.2	4.1	-	-	-	12.8	12.5
4. 6-9	2.3	2.1	2.5	2.7	.2	3.4	2.9	1.3	1.8	1.9	2.9	-	-	-	8.1	11.4
5. 10-19	2.1	1.6	2.5	2.3	.3	2.6	2.7	1.4	1.7	1.5	2.8	-	-	-	7.0	17.6
6. 20-39	.9	.4	1.3	1.0	.1	.8	1.3	.5	.9	.7	1.1	-	-	-	2.8	8.0
7. 40 or more	.3	.2	.4	.4	-	.4	.5	.1	.1	.2	.4	-	-	-	1.0	3.4
Item 1000 N(Wtd)	17583	8496	8648	13711	2160	4110	5349	5351	2773	9684	6789	6065	4080	2236	4818	176
B12: On how many occasions (if any) have you used quaaludes (quads, soapers, methaqualone) on your own--that is, without a doctor telling you to take them...																
B12A: ...in your lifetime?																
1. 0 occasions	89.4	87.7	91.5	88.4	97.7	87.9	89.9	89.4	90.7	91.9	86.6	100.0	100.0	93.1	67.1	29.8
2. 1-2	4.5	5.1	3.8	4.8	1.7	5.0	3.8	4.5	4.8	3.6	5.5	-	-	7.0	12.8	9.4
3. 3-5	2.1	2.5	1.7	2.4	.3	2.6	1.9	2.0	2.0	1.6	2.7	-	-	-	7.3	12.2
4. 6-9	1.3	1.4	1.1	1.5	.1	1.7	1.3	1.3	.9	.9	1.9	-	-	-	4.5	9.4
5. 10-19	1.0	1.2	.7	1.1	*	.8	1.2	1.0	.7	.8	1.2	-	-	-	3.2	11.0
6. 20-39	.7	.8	.6	.8	.1	.9	.7	.9	.3	.5	1.0	-	-	-	2.3	8.3
7. 40 or more	1.0	1.3	.6	1.0	*	1.1	1.1	.9	.6	.6	1.2	-	-	-	2.7	19.9
Item 1010 N(Wtd)	17669	8526	8715	13789	2175	4121	5370	5387	2791	9732	6832	6084	4103	2272	4817	181
B12B: ...during the last 12 months?																
1. 0 occasions	92.4	91.2	93.8	91.5	99.0	91.4	92.5	92.3	94.0	94.3	90.2	100.0	100.0	97.3	75.7	41.0
2. 1-2	3.8	4.4	3.3	4.3	.7	4.2	3.5	3.8	3.8	3.0	4.9	-	-	2.8	12.0	17.4
3. 3-5	1.5	1.8	1.2	1.7	.1	1.9	1.5	1.4	1.0	1.1	2.1	-	-	-	5.1	8.4
4. 6-9	.8	.9	.6	.9	-	.9	.8	.9	.5	.7	.9	-	-	-	2.7	8.4
5. 10-19	.8	1.0	.5	.9	*	.9	.8	.8	.4	.5	1.1	-	-	-	2.4	9.6
6. 20-39	.4	.4	.3	.4	.1	.4	.4	.5	.1	.3	.5	-	-	-	1.3	4.5
7. 40 or more	.3	.4	.2	.3	-	.2	.5	.3	.1	.2	.4	-	-	-	.7	9.6
Item 1020 N(Wtd)	17652	8517	8712	13780	2171	4114	5365	5384	2789	9725	6825	6084	4103	2269	4806	178
B12C: ...during the last 30 days?																
1. 0 occasions	96.9	96.3	97.6	96.6	99.5	96.6	96.8	96.5	98.4	97.9	95.8	100.0	100.0	99.2	90.3	63.8
2. 1-2	1.9	2.2	1.6	2.1	.2	2.4	1.8	2.3	1.0	1.3	2.7	-	-	.8	6.2	16.4
3. 3-5	.6	.8	.4	.7	.1	.5	.8	.6	.4	.5	.8	-	-	-	1.9	9.6
4. 6-9	.3	.3	.3	.3	*	.2	.4	.4	.1	.2	.4	-	-	-	1.0	4.5
5. 10-19	.2	.2	.1	.1	.1	.2	.1	.2	.1	.1	.2	-	-	-	.4	4.5
6. 20-39	.1	.1	*	.1	-	*	.1	.1	-	.1	.1	-	-	-	.2	.6
7. 40 or more	*	.1	-	*	-	.1	*	-	.1	*	*	-	-	-	.1	.6
Item 1030 N(Wtd)	17653	8518	8712	13781	2171	4116	5364	5383	2790	9726	6822	6087	4105	2267	4805	177

* = less than .05 per cent.

QUESTIONNAIRE FORM 1-5 1981	TOTAL	SEX		RACE		REGION				4YR COLLEGE PLANS		ILLICIT DRUG USE: LIFETIME				
		M	F	White	Black	NE	NC	S	W	Yes	No	None	Mari- juana Only	Few Pills	More Pills	Any Her- oin
Weighted No. of Cases:	18267	8725	8865	13985	2265	4290	5484	5600	2893	9878	7008	6148	4179	2306	4925	189
% of Weighted Total:	100.0	47.8	48.5	76.6	12.4	23.5	30.0	30.7	15.8	54.1	38.4	33.7	22.9	12.6	27.0	1.0

B13: Barbiturates are sometimes prescribed by doctors to help people relax or get to sleep. They are sometimes called downs, downers, goofballs, yellows, reds, blues, rainbows. On how many occasions (if any) have you taken barbiturates on your own-- that is, without a doctor telling you to take them...

B13A: ...in your lifetime?

	TOTAL	M	F	White	Black	NE	NC	S	W	Yes	No	None	Mari- juana Only	Few Pills	More Pills	Any Her- oin
1. 0 occasions	88.7	87.6	90.1	87.9	95.2	87.9	87.9	90.0	89.0	91.2	85.9	100.0	100.0	89.0	66.5	30.1
2. 1-2	5.0	5.3	4.7	5.3	2.9	4.9	5.5	4.4	5.3	4.3	5.9	-	-	11.0	12.6	13.7
3. 3-5	2.2	2.4	1.9	2.4	.8	2.5	2.2	2.2	2.0	1.7	2.8	-	-	7.8	8.7
4. 6-9	1.2	1.4	1.1	1.4	.6	1.6	1.4	.9	1.0	.9	1.7	-	-	-	4.4	5.5
5. 10-19	1.1	1.3	.9	1.2	.2	1.1	1.0	1.0	1.4	.8	1.3	-	-	-	3.5	13.1
6. 20-39	.8	.9	.7	.9	.1	1.0	1.0	.5	.7	.6	1.1	-	-	-	2.5	11.5
7. 40 or more	.9	1.2	.6	.9	.1	1.0	1.0	.9	.6	.6	1.2	-	-	-	2.7	16.4
Item 1040 N(Wtd)	17625	8496	8711	13758	2168	4103	5358	5376	2787	9716	6822	6070	4099	2265	4799	183

B13B: ...during the last 12 months?

	TOTAL	M	F	White	Black	NE	NC	S	W	Yes	No	None	Mari- juana Only	Few Pills	More Pills	Any Her- oin
1. 0 occasions	93.4	92.8	94.2	92.9	97.7	93.2	92.5	94.5	93.5	94.9	91.9	100.0	100.0	96.9	79.5	42.9
2. 1-2	3.2	3.3	3.0	3.4	1.4	3.3	3.6	2.4	3.7	2.6	3.7	-	-	3.1	9.6	16.5
3. 3-5	1.3	1.5	1.2	1.5	.4	1.2	1.7	1.1	1.3	1.1	1.7	-	-	-	4.7	6.0
4. 6-9	.9	1.0	.8	1.0	.2	1.0	1.0	.8	.8	.6	1.1	-	-	-	2.8	12.1
5. 10-19	.6	.8	.5	.6	.1	.8	.6	.6	.6	.4	.9	-	-	-	1.9	12.6
6. 20-39	.3	.4	.2	.3	.1	.4	.3	.3	.1	.2	.4	-	-	-	.9	4.9
7. 40 or more	.2	.2	.2	.2	-	.1	.2	.3	.1	.1	.3	-	-	-	.6	4.9
Item 1050 N(Wtd)	17615	8492	8705	13750	2167	4097	5360	5373	2785	9711	6817	6070	4099	2263	4790	182

B13C: ...during the last 30 days?

	TOTAL	M	F	White	Black	NE	NC	S	W	Yes	No	None	Mari- juana Only	Few Pills	More Pills	Any Her- oin
1. 0 occasions	97.4	97.1	97.6	97.2	98.8	97.3	97.2	97.3	97.8	98.0	96.8	100.0	100.0	99.3	91.9	66.1
2. 1-2	1.6	1.7	1.5	1.7	.7	1.8	1.7	1.5	1.4	1.2	1.9	-	-	.7	4.9	16.4
3. 3-5	.6	.6	.6	.6	.4	.6	.7	.6	.5	.4	.8	-	-	-	1.9	8.7
4. 6-9	.2	.2	.1	.2	*	.1	.2	.2	.2	.1	.3	-	-	-	.6	4.4
5. 10-19	.2	.2	.1	.2	.1	.2	.2	.2	.1	.1	.2	-	-	-	.5	2.2
6. 20-39	*	.1	*	*	-	*	*	.1	-	*	*	-	-	-	.1	1.1
7. 40 or more	*	.1	*	*	-	-	.1	*	*	*	*	-	-	-	.1	.5
Item 1060 N(Wtd)	17610	8490	8704	13745	2166	4099	5355	5373	2783	9712	6810	6070	4099	2260	4787	183

B14: Tranquilizers are sometimes prescribed by doctors to calm people down, quiet their nerves, or relax their muscles. Librium, Valium, and Miltown are all tranquilizers. On how many occasions (if any) have you taken tranquilizers on your own--that is, without a doctor telling you to take them...

B14A: ...in your lifetime?

	TOTAL	M	F	White	Black	NE	NC	S	W	Yes	No	None	Mari- juana Only	Few Pills	More Pills	Any Her- oin
1. 0 occasions	85.2	85.6	85.1	84.0	93.7	84.5	85.5	85.8	84.8	87.1	82.9	100.0	100.0	75.0	60.5	24.2
2. 1-2	7.3	6.5	7.8	7.8	3.5	7.4	6.7	7.3	8.1	6.6	7.9	-	-	25.0	14.2	17.0
3. 3-5	2.8	2.7	2.9	3.0	1.2	2.8	2.8	2.8	2.9	2.5	3.2	-	-	-	9.9	8.8
4. 6-9	1.6	1.6	1.5	1.7	.7	2.0	1.6	1.2	1.5	1.4	1.8	-	-	-	5.3	11.5
5. 10-19	1.4	1.6	1.3	1.6	.5	1.5	1.6	1.3	1.2	1.1	1.9	-	-	-	4.8	13.2
6. 20-39	.8	1.0	.7	.9	.1	.9	1.0	.8	.6	.6	1.2	-	-	-	2.7	9.9
7. 40 or more	.9	1.0	.7	1.0	.3	.9	.9	.9	.8	.7	1.1	-	-	-	2.6	15.9
Item 1070 N(Wtd)	17626	8513	8705	13776	2170	4099	5368	5378	2781	9714	6825	6064	4096	2264	4804	182

B14B: ...during the last 12 months?

	TOTAL	M	F	White	Black	NE	NC	S	W	Yes	No	None	Mari- juana Only	Few Pills	More Pills	Any Her- oin
1. 0 occasions	92.0	92.0	92.3	91.2	97.0	91.7	92.2	92.2	92.0	93.1	90.6	100.0	100.0	92.8	76.3	44.2
2. 1-2	4.4	4.2	4.5	4.8	1.7	4.6	3.8	4.5	5.1	4.1	4.9	-	-	7.2	12.2	14.9
3. 3-5	1.5	1.6	1.4	1.6	.7	1.7	1.6	1.3	1.5	1.2	1.9	-	-	-	5.2	9.9
4. 6-9	1.0	1.1	.9	1.1	.2	1.1	1.3	.8	.6	.8	1.1	-	-	-	3.2	11.6
5. 10-19	.6	.7	.5	.7	.2	.5	.7	.8	.5	.5	.8	-	-	-	1.9	10.5
6. 20-39	.3	.3	.3	.3	.1	.2	.4	.3	.3	.2	.4	-	-	-	.9	3.9
7. 40 or more	.1	.2	.1	.2	*	.1	.1	.2	.1	.1	.2	-	-	-	.4	3.9
Item 1080 N(Wtd)	17598	8495	8695	13758	2166	4094	5363	5363	2777	9701	6817	6065	4096	2252	4788	181

* = less than .05 per cent.

QUESTIONNAIRE FORM 1-5 1981	TOTAL	SEX		RACE		REGION				4YR COLLEGE PLANS		ILLICIT DRUG USE: LIFETIME				
		M	F	White	Black	NE	NC	S	W	Yes	No	None	Marijuana Only	Few Pills	More Pills	Any Heroin
Weighted No. of Cases:	18267	8725	8865	13985	2265	4290	5484	5600	2893	9878	7008	6148	4179	2306	4925	189
% of Weighted Total:	100.0	47.8	48.5	76.6	12.4	23.5	30.0	30.7	15.8	54.1	38.4	33.7	22.9	12.6	27.0	1.0
B14C: ...during the last 30 days?																
1. 0 occasions	97.3	97.3	97.4	97.2	98.8	97.3	97.0	97.4	97.7	97.8	96.7	100.0	100.0	98.5	92.2	65.6
2. 1-2	1.6	1.5	1.7	1.7	.6	2.0	1.6	1.4	1.5	1.4	1.9	-	-	1.5	4.8	12.2
3. 3-5	.6	.6	.5	.6	.3	.5	.8	.5	.5	.5	.7	-	-	-	1.7	12.2
4. 6-9	.3	.3	.2	.3	.2	.1	.3	.4	.1	.2	.4	-	-	-	.8	5.0
5. 10-19	.2	.2	.1	.2	.1	.1	.2	.2	.1	.1	.3	-	-	-	.4	5.0
6. 20-39	*	*	*	.1	-	*	.1	-	-	*	.1	-	-	-	.1	-
7. 40 or more	*	*	-	*	-	*	-	-	-	*	*	-	-	-	*	.6
Item 1090 N(Wtd)	17585	8487	8690	13744	2165	4091	5358	5360	2776	9693	6812	6065	4096	2247	4781	180
B15: On how many occasions (if any) have you used heroin (smack, horse, skag)...																
B15A: ...in your lifetime?																
1. 0 occasions	98.9	98.8	99.2	99.1	99.1	99.0	98.8	99.1	98.9	99.1	98.8	100.0	100.0	100.0	100.0	-
2. 1-2	.6	.6	.6	.6	.3	.7	.8	.4	.7	.6	.7	-	-	-	-	61.0
3. 3-5	.2	.3	.1	.2	.4	.1	.1	.3	.3	.1	.2	-	-	-	-	16.6
4. 6-9	.1	.1	.1	.1	*	.1	.1	.1	*	.1	.1	-	-	-	-	6.4
5. 10-19	*	.1	*	*	*	*	*	*	-	*	*	-	-	-	-	3.7
6. 20-39	*	.1	*	*	*	*	*	.1	*	*	.1	-	-	-	-	4.3
7. 40 or more	.1	.1	.1	.1	.1	.1	.1	*	.1	.1	.1	-	-	-	-	8.0
Item 1100 N(Wtd)	17639	8523	8730	13794	2178	4100	5376	5369	2794	9722	6845	6061	4100	2279	4801	187
B15B: ...during the last 12 months?																
1. 0 occasions	99.5	99.4	99.7	99.5	99.4	99.5	99.4	99.5	99.5	99.5	99.5	100.0	100.0	100.0	100.0	49.5
2. 1-2	.3	.4	.2	.3	.3	.3	.4	.3	.4	.3	.3	-	-	-	-	33.5
3. 3-5	*	.1	*	*	.1	.1	*	.1	-	*	*	-	-	-	-	4.4
4. 6-9	*	*	*	*	*	*	*	.1	-	*	*	-	-	-	-	3.3
5. 10-19	*	*	*	*	.1	*	*	*	-	*	.1	-	-	-	-	3.3
6. 20-39	*	.1	-	*	-	*	.1	*	*	*	*	-	-	-	-	1.1
7. 40 or more	.1	.1	*	.1	*	*	.1	*	*	.1	*	-	-	-	-	4.9
Item 1110 N(Wtd)	17635	8520	8729	13793	2175	4099	5375	5368	2793	9722	6843	6061	4100	2279	4801	182
B15C: ...during the last 30 days?																
1. 0 occasions	99.8	99.7	99.9	99.8	99.5	99.8	99.8	99.8	99.8	99.9	99.7	100.0	100.0	100.0	100.0	79.6
2. 1-2	.1	.2	.1	.1	.2	.1	.1	.1	.1	.1	.2	-	-	-	-	11.6
3. 3-5	*	*	*	*	*	.1	-	*	-	*	*	-	-	-	-	2.2
4. 6-9	*	*	*	*	*	*	*	*	-	-	*	-	-	-	-	.6
5. 10-19	*	*	*	*	*	*	*	*	.1	*	.1	-	-	-	-	2.8
6. 20-39	*	*	*	*	*	-	-	-	*	*	*	-	-	-	-	1.1
7. 40 or more	*	*	-	*	*	*	*	*	*	*	*	-	-	-	-	2.8
Item 1120 N(Wtd)	17635	8522	8728	13792	2177	4098	5375	5369	2793	9722	6842	6062	4100	2279	4801	181
B16: There are a number of narcotics other than heroin, such as methadone, opium, morphine, codeine, demerol, paregoric, talwin, and laudanum. These are sometimes prescribed by doctors. On how many occasions (if any) have you taken narcotics other than heroin on your own--that is, without a doctor telling you to take them...																
B16A: ...in your lifetime?																
1. 0 occasions	89.9	88.7	91.2	89.0	96.1	88.3	89.7	92.9	86.8	91.5	88.2	100.0	100.0	88.8	70.9	26.8
2. 1-2	4.7	5.3	4.0	5.1	2.4	5.6	4.7	3.3	6.5	4.2	5.2	-	-	11.2	11.3	20.7
3. 3-5	2.3	2.4	2.2	2.6	.5	2.2	2.6	1.7	3.1	2.0	2.6	-	-	-	8.0	11.7
4. 6-9	1.0	1.2	1.0	1.1	.3	1.4	1.1	.6	1.3	.7	1.4	-	-	-	3.5	7.8
5. 10-19	.9	1.1	.8	1.0	.4	1.3	.9	.8	.9	.7	1.3	-	-	-	3.0	12.3
6. 20-39	.4	.4	.4	.5	.1	.5	.3	.4	.5	.3	.6	-	-	-	1.4	5.6
7. 40 or more	.7	.9	.4	.7	.2	.8	.8	.3	1.0	.6	.8	-	-	-	1.9	15.6
Item 1130 N(Wtd)	17548	8518	8696	13762	2170	4080	5343	5343	2782	9690	6815	6038	4081	2264	4773	179

* = less than .05 per cent.

QUESTIONNAIRE FORM 1-5 1981	TOTAL	SEX		RACE		REGION				4YR COLLEGE PLANS		ILLICIT DRUG USE: LIFETIME				
		M	F	White	Black	NE	NC	S	W	Yes	No	None	Mari-juana Only	Few Pills	More Pills	Any Her-oin
Weighted No. of Cases:	18267	8725	8865	13985	2265	4290	5484	5600	2893	9878	7008	6148	4179	2306	4925	189
% of Weighted Total:	100.0	47.8	48.5	76.6	12.4	23.5	30.0	30.7	15.8	54.1	38.4	33.7	22.9	12.6	27.0	1.0

B16B: ...during the last 12 months?

1. 0 occasions	94.0	93.5	94.7	93.5	98.1	92.8	93.8	95.9	92.7	95.2	92.8	100.0	100.0	96.2	81.9	46.9
2. 1-2	3.2	3.5	2.8	3.5	1.0	3.6	3.4	2.2	3.9	2.6	3.7	-	-	3.8	9.2	18.6
3. 3-5	1.3	1.3	1.3	1.4	.3	1.5	1.3	.9	1.8	1.1	1.5	-	-	-	4.2	13.6
4. 6-9	.7	.8	.5	.7	.4	.8	.7	.4	.8	.4	1.0	-	-	-	2.2	5.6
5. 10-19	.4	.4	.4	.5	.1	.5	.5	.3	.4	.3	.6	-	-	-	1.3	8.5
6. 20-39	.2	.3	.2	.3	*	.5	.2	.1	.2	.3	.2	-	-	-	.8	3.4
7. 40 or more	.2	.2	.1	.2	*	.2	.1	.1	.2	.1	.2	-	-	-	.4	3.4
Item 1140 N(Wtd)	17529	8506	8690	13750	2168	4069	5343	5340	2777	9685	6805	6038	4082	2260	4759	177

B16C: ...during the last 30 days?

1. 0 occasions	97.9	97.6	98.2	97.8	99.3	97.3	97.8	98.5	97.9	98.6	97.0	100.0	100.0	98.9	93.8	72.7
2. 1-2	1.3	1.4	1.1	1.3	.5	1.4	1.3	1.0	1.3	.8	1.8	-	-	1.1	3.6	12.5
3. 3-5	.4	.5	.3	.5	.1	.6	.5	.2	.4	.3	.6	-	-	-	1.3	5.7
4. 6-9	.2	.3	.2	.2	*	.4	.3	.1	-	.2	.2	-	-	-	.7	2.3
5. 10-19	.1	.1	.1	.1	.1	.2	.1	.1	.1	.1	.2	-	-	-	.4	3.4
6. 20-39	.1	*	.1	.1	*	*	.1	.1	.1	*	.1	-	-	-	.1	1.7
7. 40 or more	*	*	-	*	-	-	-	-	.1	*	*	-	-	-	*	1.1
Item 1150 N(Wtd)	17520	8503	8687	13744	2169	4065	5343	5337	2775	9680	6803	6039	4082	2259	4751	176

B17: On how many occasions (if any) have you sniffed glue, or breathed the contents of aerosol spray cans, or inhaled any other gases or sprays in order to get high...

B17A: ...in your lifetime?

1. 0 occasions	87.7	84.7	90.6	87.2	92.3	84.9	88.3	89.7	86.9	89.0	85.9	97.4	91.7	85.7	74.3	51.4
2. 1-2	7.5	9.4	5.7	7.7	5.6	9.2	6.7	6.9	7.7	6.7	8.6	2.0	6.2	11.1	13.7	13.7
3. 3-5	2.2	2.7	1.7	2.3	1.0	2.5	2.2	1.8	2.5	1.8	2.5	.3	.9	2.3	5.3	6.8
4. 6-9	1.1	1.4	.9	1.3	.2	1.3	1.3	.8	1.4	1.1	1.3	.1	.6	.8	3.0	5.5
5. 10-19	.7	.9	.6	.8	.4	1.1	.7	.5	.5	.6	.9	-	.2	.2	1.9	9.6
6. 20-39	.3	.3	.2	.3	.1	.2	.4	.2	.1	.2	.3	.1	.1	.1	.6	2.7
7. 40 or more	.5	.6	.4	.5	.3	.8	.5	.3	.9	.5	.6	.1	.2	-	1.2	11.0
Item 1160 N(Wtd)	14230	6955	7011	11153	1784	3315	4336	4342	2236	7818	5630	4869	3294	1855	3911	146

B17B: ...during the last 12 months?

1. 0 occasions	95.9	94.9	96.8	95.6	97.6	94.8	96.1	96.8	95.3	96.0	95.7	99.4	98.1	95.4	90.8	69.7
2. 1-2	2.3	2.9	1.8	2.4	1.5	2.9	2.0	2.1	2.5	2.1	2.6	.5	1.3	4.0	4.6	9.7
3. 3-5	.8	1.1	.5	.9	.4	.9	.9	.5	.8	.8	.8	*	.3	.5	2.1	4.1
4. 6-9	.4	.4	.4	.5	.3	.6	.4	.3	.6	.5	.4	.1	.2	.1	1.0	4.8
5. 10-19	.3	.3	.2	.3	.1	.4	.3	.1	.3	.2	.3	*	.1	-	.6	6.2
6. 20-39	.1	.2	.1	.2	-	.4	.1	.1	.1	.2	.2	-	*	-	.4	2.8
7. 40 or more	.2	.2	.1	.2	.1	.1	.2	.1	.4	.2	.1	*	.1	-	.4	3.4
Item 1170 N(Wtd)	14218	6943	7010	11145	1782	3309	4337	4337	2235	7815	5626	4871	3287	1852	3909	145

B17C: ...during the last 30 days?

1. 0 occasions	98.5	98.1	98.9	98.4	98.9	98.1	98.5	98.8	98.3	98.5	98.4	99.7	99.5	98.9	96.5	81.3
2. 1-2	1.0	1.3	.7	1.0	.7	1.2	.9	.9	.8	1.0	1.0	.2	.4	.9	2.2	6.9
3. 3-5	.2	.3	.1	.2	.1	.3	.3	.1	.4	.2	.2	-	*	.1	.6	4.9
4. 6-9	.2	.2	.1	.2	.1	.2	.2	.1	.1	.1	.2	*	-	-	.3	5.6
5. 10-19	*	.1	*	*	.1	.1	*	*	*	.1	.1	-	*	-	.1	.7
6. 20-39	.1	.1	.1	.1	-	.2	-	-	.3	.1	.1	-	*	-	.3	-
7. 40 or more	*	*	.1	*	.1	-	*	*	.1	.1	*	*	*	-	*	.7
Item 1180 N(Wtd)	14218	6941	7012	11144	1781	3311	4334	4336	2236	7818	5623	4871	3287	1851	3911	144

* = less than .05 per cent.

QUESTIONNAIRE FORM 1 1981	TOTAL	SEX		RACE		REGION				4YR COLLEGE PLANS		ILLICIT DRUG USE: LIFETIME				
		M	F	White	Black	NE	NC	S	W	Yes	No	None	Marijuana Only	Few Pills	More Pills	Any Heroin
Weighted No. of Cases:	3644	1689	1795	2769	438	853	1075	1124	592	1969	1283	1213	853	430	958	37
% of Weighted Total:	100.0	46.3	49.3	76.0	12.0	23.4	29.5	30.8	16.3	54.0	35.2	33.3	23.4	11.8	26.3	1.0
A001: Taking all things together, how would you say things are these days--would you say you're very happy, pretty happy, or not too happy these days?																
3. Very happy	18.2	16.9	19.5	19.5	12.7	17.1	16.8	19.0	20.9	20.4	16.6	19.6	16.3	18.3	18.6	22.1
2. Pretty happy	66.6	66.6	66.8	68.7	57.4	66.8	69.1	64.6	65.5	66.3	66.8	66.9	68.3	66.8	65.9	47.0
1. Not too happy	15.2	16.5	13.7	11.8	29.9	16.1	14.1	16.5	13.7	13.4	16.5	13.4	15.4	14.9	15.6	31.0
Item 1190 N(Wtd)	3630	1680	1794	2764	435	849	1075	1117	589	1966	1280	1211	850	430	954	37
A002: How much do you agree or disagree with each of the following statements?																
A002A: The nation needs much more long-range planning and coordination to be prepared for the future																
1. Disagree	1.8	2.3	1.1	1.6	2.5	1.6	2.0	1.6	2.1	1.5	1.7	1.4	1.7	.4	2.4	8.3
2. Mostly disagree	3.2	2.7	3.6	3.0	3.9	2.4	3.6	3.6	3.1	2.6	3.7	2.8	3.5	3.6	3.0	2.0
3. Neither	7.2	7.6	7.0	7.7	3.8	7.3	8.8	4.7	9.2	6.0	8.8	6.4	6.4	9.7	8.0	8.4
4. Mostly agree	41.2	39.8	44.4	43.9	33.6	41.3	44.4	36.8	43.8	41.6	43.4	39.9	42.2	44.0	43.0	42.5
5. Agree	46.5	47.5	44.0	43.8	56.1	47.4	41.3	53.2	41.9	48.3	42.4	49.5	46.1	42.3	43.7	38.8
Item 1200 N(Wtd)	3604	1669	1784	2752	431	841	1068	1112	583	1960	1267	1206	847	427	950	37
A002B: I enjoy the fast pace and changes of today's world																
1. Disagree	14.7	14.7	14.3	11.6	29.3	11.7	13.9	19.8	10.8	12.4	16.8	16.7	13.3	12.7	12.3	10.7
2. Mostly disagree	19.7	19.1	20.8	20.5	19.0	16.8	19.3	21.7	21.1	18.0	23.2	18.8	19.9	26.4	18.6	18.6
3. Neither	20.3	22.0	18.7	22.2	10.4	22.5	20.4	17.2	22.5	20.6	19.8	21.7	18.2	21.1	20.9	9.3
4. Mostly agree	31.6	29.2	34.1	32.8	26.6	35.2	32.5	27.4	32.9	34.0	28.3	29.7	35.6	29.3	32.2	34.3
5. Agree	13.7	14.9	12.1	12.9	14.7	13.8	14.0	13.9	12.7	15.0	11.8	13.1	12.9	10.4	16.1	27.1
Item 1210 N(Wtd)	3600	1671	1782	2753	429	843	1065	1108	584	1956	1268	1205	846	427	948	35
A002C: Things change too quickly in today's world																
1. Disagree	11.3	12.5	9.9	11.0	12.1	12.5	11.8	9.6	11.8	12.0	10.1	9.0	13.2	9.5	12.3	23.7
2. Mostly disagree	20.4	21.7	19.6	22.4	10.2	21.4	21.7	16.7	23.8	22.7	18.4	19.3	21.2	21.1	22.2	12.7
3. Neither	17.9	18.4	17.9	19.9	8.1	19.3	18.9	14.8	19.9	19.8	14.8	18.6	15.9	19.9	20.2	5.1
4. Mostly agree	24.7	22.5	26.9	24.7	26.1	23.2	24.3	25.3	26.9	24.8	25.7	24.0	26.1	27.2	23.3	34.4
5. Agree	25.6	24.8	25.7	22.1	43.5	23.6	23.4	33.6	17.6	20.7	31.1	29.1	23.6	22.2	22.0	24.1
Item 1220 N(Wtd)	3601	1670	1782	2748	430	843	1065	1105	588	1955	1269	1205	848	424	949	35
A002D: I think the times ahead for me will be tougher and less fun than things are now																
1. Disagree	15.7	16.6	14.9	16.0	12.0	19.3	13.2	13.7	18.8	16.4	14.5	16.0	16.0	9.8	17.7	27.4
2. Mostly disagree	17.0	16.2	18.0	18.5	12.1	17.5	17.3	15.1	19.0	19.3	14.9	19.9	13.9	19.7	15.8	14.5
3. Neither	12.5	11.6	13.4	13.6	5.4	12.7	13.5	10.1	15.0	12.4	12.3	10.6	12.1	10.9	15.8	16.6
4. Mostly agree	24.3	24.2	24.6	25.3	22.8	23.2	26.1	24.5	22.2	25.1	24.3	24.7	26.7	28.1	21.1	15.0
5. Agree	30.5	31.4	29.1	26.6	47.6	27.2	29.9	36.5	25.0	26.8	34.0	28.8	31.4	31.5	29.6	26.5
Item 1230 N(Wtd)	3603	1673	1780	2752	433	839	1064	1114	585	1959	1267	1204	847	424	951	36
A003: Of all the time you spend with other people, about how much is spent with people over 30?																
1. Very little	20.9	24.3	17.3	17.7	36.5	21.2	21.8	21.9	16.6	19.1	22.0	19.2	24.7	17.8	19.7	16.2
2. Some	42.7	44.2	41.5	45.5	27.2	48.1	42.4	38.6	43.5	44.6	40.2	38.8	43.3	44.3	48.8	25.6
3. About half	29.4	25.1	33.6	30.1	28.0	24.8	29.5	31.4	32.1	30.1	29.5	33.7	27.5	31.6	24.5	47.5
4. Most	5.4	5.2	5.6	5.7	4.7	4.2	5.6	5.7	6.4	5.2	6.1	6.6	3.5	6.1	5.5	6.8
5. Nearly all	1.5	1.1	1.9	1.1	3.6	1.7	.6	2.4	1.3	1.0	2.2	1.8	1.0	.3	1.5	4.0
Item 1240 N(Wtd)	3631	1687	1792	2765	437	850	1072	1120	589	1966	1282	1211	851	430	958	36

QUESTIONNAIRE FORM 1 1981	TOTAL	SEX		RACE		REGION				4YR COLLEGE PLANS		ILLICIT DRUG USE: LIFETIME				
		M	F	White	Black	NE	NC	S	W	Yes	No	None	Mari- juana Only	Few Pills	More Pills	Any Her- oin
Weighted No. of Cases:	3644	1689	1795	2769	438	853	1075	1124	592	1969	1283	1213	853	430	958	37
% of Weighted Total:	100.0	46.3	49.3	76.0	12.0	23.4	29.5	30.8	16.3	54.0	35.2	33.3	23.4	11.8	26.3	1.0

A004: Would you like to spend more time, or less time, with people over 30 if you could?

1. Much less time	2.9	3.1	2.7	2.3	6.0	3.8	2.6	3.3	1.4	2.3	3.3	2.1	3.9	2.9	2.3	13.3
2. Somewhat less time	6.4	6.3	6.6	6.0	7.6	6.5	6.4	6.5	5.9	5.5	7.3	5.0	6.8	6.7	7.6	6.7
3. About the same as now	67.8	66.9	68.9	71.4	53.3	69.5	69.3	64.4	69.0	67.0	69.6	67.8	68.1	66.1	69.8	68.0
4. Somewhat more time	19.9	20.6	19.0	18.6	26.4	16.7	19.5	22.4	20.5	22.0	17.3	21.8	18.7	22.4	17.8	10.0
5. Much more time	3.0	3.2	2.8	1.7	6.7	3.4	2.3	3.4	3.2	3.1	2.6	3.3	2.6	1.9	2.5	2.0
Item 1250 N(Wtd)	3631	1685	1792	2764	437	848	1073	1120	589	1966	1282	1211	851	430	957	37

A005: Would you like to spend more time, or less time, working with or helping younger children?

1. Much less time	4.3	7.1	1.4	4.5	2.1	4.1	5.0	3.3	5.2	3.5	5.6	2.6	4.1	3.4	5.7	20.2
2. Somewhat less time	5.1	7.3	3.1	5.4	3.5	4.3	5.4	4.9	5.9	4.1	6.0	4.1	4.5	5.9	5.9	2.3
3. About the same as now	36.0	44.6	27.8	38.7	25.2	36.6	37.3	35.8	33.3	34.5	38.4	33.9	36.7	31.0	40.1	46.0
4. Somewhat more time	35.1	30.4	40.2	35.4	32.2	36.5	34.4	33.5	37.6	37.3	32.1	36.5	36.3	37.4	33.6	18.9
5. Much more time	19.5	10.7	27.4	16.0	36.9	18.5	18.0	22.4	18.1	20.6	17.8	22.9	18.3	22.3	14.6	12.6
Item 1260 N(Wtd)	3621	1683	1785	2755	437	841	1072	1120	588	1960	1280	1208	848	430	955	36

A006: The next questions ask how satisfied or dissatisfied you are with several aspects of your life. For each question, mark the circle that shows best how you feel. If you are neutral about something, or are just as satisfied as you are dissatisfied, mark the middle answer.

How satisfied are you with...

A006A: Your job? (If you have no job, leave blank)

7. Completely satisfied	20.8	21.2	20.4	19.6	25.6	20.0	18.7	25.0	19.0	19.7	22.2	24.0	17.4	18.4	21.4	13.0
6.	21.0	21.5	20.9	24.1	8.2	18.7	24.9	18.5	21.3	22.5	20.4	21.6	18.6	18.7	23.5	18.7
5.	14.3	15.6	13.2	15.1	9.0	14.5	13.3	12.2	19.1	16.8	11.2	14.8	15.1	15.0	13.0	21.9
4. Neutral	26.3	24.1	27.4	23.7	39.5	28.7	26.1	27.4	21.6	23.8	27.6	26.7	29.6	25.9	23.1	7.8
3.	6.7	6.1	7.4	7.4	2.1	8.4	7.2	5.0	6.5	7.6	6.0	5.4	6.8	12.1	5.8	18.7
2.	4.6	4.9	4.3	4.9	2.4	4.2	4.7	3.7	6.3	4.2	5.3	3.6	5.3	5.3	5.1	6.3
1. Completely dissatisfied	6.3	6.5	6.3	5.1	13.2	5.5	5.2	8.2	6.4	5.3	7.4	4.0	7.2	5.9	7.3	13.7
Item 1270 N(Wtd)	2400	1180	1121	1919	216	590	721	671	417	1294	857	732	565	300	691	23

A006B: The neighborhood where you live?

7. Completely satisfied	36.1	35.6	36.8	36.4	38.6	28.6	36.0	42.6	34.7	35.4	37.5	40.4	32.3	40.1	30.8	27.9
6.	18.7	20.0	17.6	20.9	8.8	20.5	22.2	12.9	20.9	21.4	15.3	18.8	20.1	19.0	18.8	10.7
5.	10.7	12.0	9.9	12.1	5.0	12.2	11.5	8.2	11.8	12.3	9.3	8.6	11.8	13.0	4.1	
4. Neutral	20.7	18.1	22.3	17.6	31.6	21.3	16.3	24.6	20.7	17.9	23.5	20.7	21.7	17.4	20.5	22.1
3.	5.2	5.3	5.1	5.4	3.4	5.3	5.4	4.3	6.3	5.0	5.4	4.0	5.5	5.9	5.9	10.0
2.	3.0	3.4	2.8	3.2	2.0	4.1	3.9	1.5	2.7	3.2	3.0	2.5	2.8	1.1	4.6	7.0
1. Completely dissatisfied	5.6	5.6	5.6	4.3	10.6	8.0	4.6	5.9	3.0	4.8	6.0	4.9	5.7	4.7	6.4	18.2
Item 1280 N(Wtd)	3622	1682	1791	2762	433	848	1072	1118	584	1962	1280	1210	851	429	955	35

A006C: Your personal safety in your neighborhood, on your job, and in your school--safety from being attacked and injured in some way?

7. Completely satisfied	39.4	46.4	33.2	40.5	34.3	41.7	39.8	39.4	35.5	40.6	38.3	39.3	35.7	40.5	42.0	24.1
6.	20.7	20.9	21.2	23.9	9.5	20.5	22.7	15.9	26.2	22.5	19.5	22.1	20.8	22.2	20.2	10.1
5.	9.7	8.5	10.8	10.2	6.5	8.4	10.7	9.1	10.6	10.4	9.0	9.3	10.5	9.4	10.2	6.6
4. Neutral	17.8	15.6	19.0	15.4	28.0	16.2	15.8	23.0	13.7	13.4	22.1	17.4	19.6	16.9	15.5	40.2
3.	4.9	3.4	6.4	5.0	3.2	5.0	4.8	4.1	6.7	5.5	4.5	4.1	5.0	5.1	5.8	11.1
2.	2.6	1.4	3.7	2.2	3.7	2.6	3.1	1.2	4.2	2.9	2.2	2.9	2.5	2.1	2.8	-
1. Completely dissatisfied	4.9	3.8	5.7	2.7	14.8	5.6	3.1	7.1	3.2	4.7	4.4	4.9	5.9	3.8	3.5	7.9
Item 1290 N(Wtd)	3624	1683	1790	2764	433	848	1071	1117	588	1961	1281	1210	850	429	956	35

QUESTIONNAIRE FORM 1 1981	TOTAL	SEX		RACE		REGION				4YR COLLEGE PLANS		ILLICIT DRUG USE: LIFETIME				
		M	F	White	Black	NE	NC	S	W	Yes	No	None	Mari- juana Only	Few Pills	More Pills	Any Her- oin
Weighted No. of Cases:	3644	1689	1795	2769	438	853	1075	1124	592	1969	1283	1213	853	430	958	37
% of Weighted Total:	100.0	46.3	49.3	76.0	12.0	23.4	29.5	30.8	16.3	54.0	35.2	33.3	23.4	11.8	26.3	1.0
A006D: The safety of things you own from being stolen or destroyed in your neighborhood, on your job, and in your school?																
7. Completely satisfied	18.2	19.4	16.9	16.7	24.8	16.5	18.8	20.5	15.3	17.7	19.3	18.9	16.7	14.9	18.9	18.2
6.	18.5	18.6	19.1	21.4	5.1	18.4	21.2	14.3	21.6	21.0	16.0	19.8	16.9	21.4	18.8	20.5
5.	13.6	15.4	12.2	15.1	7.4	13.3	16.2	11.0	14.2	15.4	11.6	13.2	12.4	14.3	14.9	11.4
4. Neutral	20.7	17.9	22.9	19.5	25.6	20.7	18.5	24.8	17.4	16.3	26.0	20.1	21.5	20.5	20.4	27.2
3.	10.3	9.6	11.2	11.6	6.1	10.1	11.2	8.2	12.9	11.9	9.0	9.9	11.9	10.9	10.2	9.7
2.	7.0	7.7	6.4	6.8	7.6	8.2	6.8	5.4	8.6	7.7	5.7	6.6	8.2	5.6	7.2	4.5
1. Completely dissatisfied	11.7	11.4	11.2	8.8	23.4	12.8	7.3	15.9	10.0	10.0	12.5	11.5	12.4	12.4	9.5	8.6
Item 1300 N(Wtd)	3614	1677	1785	2755	431	847	1068	1115	584	1956	1275	1208	848	426	956	35
A006E: Your educational experiences?																
7. Completely satisfied	21.9	21.2	21.8	19.7	32.7	24.1	19.0	26.4	15.4	21.9	22.3	27.2	21.0	20.3	16.2	11.1
6.	24.5	25.8	24.5	26.9	14.6	25.4	24.9	22.0	27.5	29.8	18.6	26.4	27.7	24.7	21.4	12.6
5.	15.8	17.0	14.7	17.4	9.8	16.4	18.9	10.8	19.1	16.7	15.1	15.8	13.4	16.7	17.7	28.3
4. Neutral	24.3	23.4	24.8	22.8	27.5	22.3	22.3	27.8	24.1	19.6	29.6	20.7	24.5	23.7	27.6	30.8
3.	6.2	5.4	6.9	6.5	3.6	4.9	8.1	5.4	6.2	5.4	6.8	4.5	5.9	6.8	8.5	6.5
2.	3.1	3.1	3.2	3.3	2.4	3.3	3.4	2.1	4.4	3.3	2.4	2.7	3.6	3.0	3.5	-
1. Completely dissatisfied	4.1	4.1	4.0	3.3	9.4	3.5	3.6	5.5	3.3	3.3	5.2	2.8	3.9	4.8	5.0	10.7
Item 1310 N(Wtd)	3616	1683	1781	2755	432	849	1067	1115	585	1957	1277	1205	848	427	958	35
A006F: Your friends and other people you spend time with?																
7. Completely satisfied	49.4	46.3	51.8	48.5	50.5	47.2	48.4	54.0	45.8	46.7	53.7	50.5	48.9	53.8	45.7	58.0
6.	25.3	26.0	25.4	28.3	13.5	25.4	26.8	21.6	29.5	28.1	22.7	25.8	26.5	23.4	26.2	12.9
5.	9.4	11.3	8.0	10.4	6.1	10.2	10.7	6.1	12.3	10.4	8.3	8.9	7.8	9.2	12.0	11.3
4. Neutral	11.1	11.2	10.9	8.6	23.9	11.4	9.6	13.8	8.0	9.6	12.3	11.9	10.3	8.0	10.7	16.5
3.	2.4	2.5	2.3	2.5	1.3	3.4	2.6	1.4	2.6	2.9	1.4	1.3	3.1	2.5	3.5	-
2.	.9	.9	.8	.7	1.8	.9	.6	1.4	.8	.8	.4	.5	1.3	1.1	1.0	-
1. Completely dissatisfied	1.4	1.8	1.0	1.1	2.8	1.4	1.3	1.6	1.1	1.4	1.2	1.0	2.1	2.1	.9	1.4
Item 1320 N(Wtd)	3624	1679	1792	2759	436	849	1070	1117	588	1960	1280	1208	852	428	957	35
A006G: The way you get along with your parents?																
7. Completely satisfied	37.5	36.0	38.4	34.3	53.7	36.0	33.8	43.6	34.9	36.6	38.4	44.8	36.9	33.2	30.0	25.3
6.	22.7	24.7	21.6	25.7	9.7	22.0	26.7	17.2	26.9	25.1	20.8	23.9	22.4	23.6	23.2	3.5
5.	10.8	11.0	10.9	12.4	4.3	11.1	12.3	9.2	10.6	11.9	10.2	9.3	11.3	12.1	12.5	7.0
4. Neutral	15.9	15.5	15.7	14.3	20.6	16.9	14.6	16.5	15.6	12.8	18.4	13.3	15.7	17.6	17.0	36.3
3.	5.2	5.3	5.1	5.7	2.4	5.1	5.1	4.9	6.6	5.7	4.5	4.5	4.7	6.9	6.0	10.0
2.	3.3	3.1	3.5	3.6	1.6	4.3	3.4	2.5	3.6	3.6	2.9	2.2	3.2	3.5	4.7	8.4
1. Completely dissatisfied	4.5	4.3	4.8	4.0	7.7	4.7	4.1	6.1	1.8	4.3	4.8	2.1	5.8	3.1	6.5	9.6
Item 1330 N(Wtd)	3617	1678	1786	2755	434	845	1067	1115	589	1961	1272	1208	851	424	955	35
A006H: Yourself?																
7. Completely satisfied	33.1	36.1	29.1	26.8	61.3	27.6	27.7	43.4	31.0	31.0	34.2	35.3	34.2	28.1	28.5	33.1
6.	28.6	29.2	28.8	32.3	14.7	33.6	29.0	22.7	31.9	32.4	25.1	31.8	27.1	28.8	28.2	19.1
5.	12.4	12.3	12.9	14.6	2.9	13.0	16.3	7.9	12.8	13.3	11.4	12.3	11.6	12.9	14.0	11.7
4. Neutral	18.0	14.5	20.8	18.3	14.6	17.9	17.8	19.0	16.2	15.1	21.6	15.1	18.4	18.8	20.5	25.6
3.	3.6	3.6	3.6	4.0	.6	3.4	4.4	2.3	4.6	3.4	3.7	1.9	3.5	5.4	4.7	4.2
2.	2.0	1.6	2.5	2.2	1.2	2.1	2.7	1.5	1.5	2.2	1.8	1.7	2.2	2.6	2.2	-
1. Completely dissatisfied	2.5	2.6	2.3	1.9	4.7	2.3	2.1	3.2	1.9	2.6	2.1	1.9	2.9	3.4	2.0	6.4
Item 1340 N(Wtd)	3609	1676	1784	2755	431	840	1069	1115	585	1957	1279	1208	847	427	949	36
A006I: Your standard of living--the things you have like housing, car, furniture, recreation, and the like?																
7. Completely satisfied	37.2	35.6	38.5	36.6	40.6	37.0	34.7	41.2	34.4	36.6	37.9	40.3	37.7	34.9	33.6	27.7
6.	26.9	27.7	26.9	29.8	15.3	29.6	25.9	24.2	29.9	31.1	22.3	30.7	23.6	28.9	25.9	22.6
5.	11.9	12.2	11.4	12.8	8.2	11.9	14.8	8.2	13.9	11.9	11.4	9.6	12.8	12.7	14.5	13.7
4. Neutral	13.9	13.7	13.8	11.7	22.3	11.9	14.7	16.6	10.4	10.9	17.4	11.8	14.4	15.4	14.7	4.3
3.	4.6	4.8	4.4	4.6	4.0	4.1	5.6	3.2	5.9	4.3	5.1	4.1	3.6	4.3	5.6	23.4
2.	2.0	2.2	1.8	1.9	2.8	2.1	2.0	1.7	2.4	2.1	1.9	.9	2.7	2.1	2.4	2.2
1. Completely dissatisfied	3.5	3.9	3.2	2.7	6.9	3.4	2.4	4.9	3.0	3.0	4.1	2.7	5.1	1.6	3.2	6.1
Item 1350 N(Wtd)	3630	1686	1791	2766	434	851	1072	1118	588	1966	1282	1212	850	430	957	37

QUESTIONNAIRE FORM 1 1981	TOTAL	SEX		RACE		REGION				4YR COLLEGE PLANS		ILLICIT DRUG USE: LIFETIME				
		M	F	White	Black	NE	NC	S	W	Yes	No	None	Mari-juana Only	Few Pills	More Pills	Any Her-oin
Weighted No. of Cases:	3644	1689	1795	2769	438	853	1075	1124	592	1969	1283	1213	853	430	958	37
% of Weighted Total:	100.0	46.3	49.3	76.0	12.0	23.4	29.5	30.8	16.3	54.0	35.2	33.3	23.4	11.8	26.3	1.0
A006J: The amount of time you have for doing things you want to do?																
7. Completely satisfied	16.7	16.2	16.1	14.9	23.4	16.4	14.5	19.0	16.7	15.4	17.9	16.8	17.0	15.9	14.9	22.6
6.	17.4	18.1	17.4	18.6	13.2	18.9	17.1	15.9	18.8	19.7	15.3	19.0	17.7	20.3	15.8	13.8
5.	15.5	16.2	15.4	17.4	9.6	14.9	18.6	11.2	18.6	17.8	13.3	15.8	16.6	14.0	15.0	21.7
4. Neutral	20.0	18.8	21.0	18.3	26.5	18.4	19.9	22.6	17.6	17.0	22.7	22.1	19.0	18.9	19.0	3.4
3.	11.7	12.3	11.6	13.4	4.2	11.2	13.3	9.3	14.1	12.7	11.0	12.2	10.1	9.8	13.6	3.9
2.	7.3	7.6	6.8	7.5	5.1	9.4	7.1	5.9	7.4	7.5	6.9	5.6	6.9	8.1	9.6	22.1
1. Completely dissatisfied	11.5	10.9	11.7	9.8	17.9	10.9	9.5	16.1	7.0	9.9	13.0	8.5	12.8	12.9	12.0	12.6
Item 1360 N(Wtd)	3630	1685	1791	2766	435	849	1070	1121	589	1965	1282	1211	852	429	958	36
A006K: The way you spend your leisure time--recreation, relaxation, and so on?																
7. Completely satisfied	31.3	32.4	29.6	29.4	38.1	30.0	27.7	36.5	30.0	29.4	33.8	31.4	31.1	29.2	30.9	33.8
6.	21.3	22.3	20.9	23.4	12.4	25.1	20.2	18.3	23.6	23.4	19.0	21.7	22.5	20.5	21.8	23.3
5.	15.3	16.1	14.9	17.6	7.0	15.5	18.8	11.4	16.2	16.6	14.2	15.8	15.3	15.7	15.8	4.5
4. Neutral	18.1	16.6	19.5	16.2	27.0	14.3	18.8	20.8	17.3	16.0	20.5	18.2	17.4	19.7	17.3	14.2
3.	7.3	6.5	8.0	7.8	3.8	8.1	8.9	5.3	7.3	8.0	6.4	6.2	5.7	8.2	9.3	13.5
2.	2.7	2.6	2.7	2.6	2.5	3.0	2.6	2.3	3.2	2.9	2.6	2.7	3.4	3.2	1.8	7.0
1. Completely dissatisfied	3.9	3.5	4.3	3.0	9.0	4.0	3.0	5.4	2.4	3.6	3.5	4.0	4.6	3.6	3.0	3.6
Item 1370 N(Wtd)	3630	1686	1791	2765	435	851	1073	1120	587	1965	1282	1211	852	429	958	37
A006L: Your life as a whole these days?																
7. Completely satisfied	20.8	20.0	21.5	19.1	29.7	21.2	17.0	23.5	21.8	21.3	19.6	23.6	20.8	18.0	16.9	13.8
6.	28.7	30.1	28.2	32.2	14.7	29.1	29.9	24.8	33.6	33.0	24.7	32.3	28.5	26.8	27.9	22.0
5.	17.8	18.3	17.3	19.5	10.0	17.2	20.6	16.2	16.8	19.2	16.5	16.0	16.8	18.9	21.2	29.3
4. Neutral	22.2	21.4	22.4	19.4	31.8	19.1	22.0	26.7	18.5	16.0	29.9	20.9	22.3	23.7	22.2	22.2
3.	4.7	4.9	4.4	4.7	5.1	6.0	5.2	3.4	4.6	4.7	4.0	2.9	4.9	6.7	5.4	4.7
2.	2.7	2.8	2.7	2.7	2.3	4.3	2.1	2.2	2.6	2.7	2.7	2.1	2.8	3.0	3.4	4.7
1. Completely dissatisfied	3.0	2.6	3.5	2.5	6.3	3.2	3.4	3.2	2.1	3.2	2.7	2.1	4.0	2.8	3.0	3.4
Item 1380 N(Wtd)	3622	1683	1786	2762	433	850	1069	1115	587	1963	1278	1207	850	430	956	37
A006M: The way our national government is operating?																
7. Completely satisfied	1.9	2.1	1.6	1.4	2.3	1.8	1.5	2.1	2.3	1.7	1.8	2.3	1.4	1.2	1.7	-
6.	4.4	5.5	3.3	5.0	1.4	4.2	5.2	4.0	4.3	5.5	2.9	5.1	4.4	5.0	3.2	7.2
5.	11.2	13.1	10.0	12.7	4.2	13.1	10.4	9.4	13.4	13.9	8.4	12.1	9.9	12.6	11.7	5.0
4. Neutral	33.6	28.3	39.3	34.5	27.7	36.1	33.5	33.4	30.6	32.4	36.0	34.7	32.7	35.2	33.8	21.4
3.	15.9	17.1	14.9	17.8	8.8	13.4	17.0	13.1	22.8	17.2	14.2	14.9	19.0	12.9	16.0	14.2
2.	12.0	13.6	10.9	12.5	10.0	11.7	14.0	11.2	10.5	12.0	12.1	12.4	10.1	11.9	13.5	16.6
1. Completely dissatisfied	21.0	20.3	20.0	16.0	45.6	19.7	18.5	26.9	16.1	17.2	24.6	18.5	22.4	21.2	20.0	35.7
Item 1390 N(Wtd)	3624	1683	1788	2762	435	850	1070	1117	588	1964	1279	1208	851	429	956	37
A006N: The amount of fun you are having?																
7. Completely satisfied	25.3	23.9	26.3	23.3	32.8	23.2	21.9	30.1	25.3	24.4	26.5	23.8	25.0	26.0	26.0	15.4
6.	25.3	26.2	24.6	28.2	14.3	28.6	24.9	22.1	27.1	28.9	20.7	27.3	24.5	22.4	27.4	25.9
5.	17.9	17.9	18.4	19.7	10.8	14.9	21.2	15.4	21.2	19.5	16.8	19.0	17.4	18.9	16.4	19.2
4. Neutral	19.2	20.1	18.3	17.5	26.5	18.4	19.6	21.5	15.6	14.9	24.3	20.3	20.2	17.7	17.1	11.6
3.	5.4	5.6	5.4	5.4	5.2	7.2	5.7	3.8	5.6	5.9	5.0	4.3	5.4	7.5	5.8	12.5
2.	2.9	3.0	2.8	3.0	2.2	3.7	3.8	1.6	2.3	3.0	2.7	2.1	3.1	3.3	3.8	-
1. Completely dissatisfied	4.0	3.4	4.3	2.9	8.2	4.0	2.9	5.6	2.9	3.4	3.9	3.3	4.5	4.3	3.5	15.4
Item 1400 N(Wtd)	3628	1686	1789	2763	437	850	1071	1118	588	1966	1279	1210	852	429	957	37
A007: How important is each of the following to you in your life?																
A007A: Being successful in my line of work																
1. Not important	1.0	1.5	.5	.9	1.6	1.0	.3	1.6	1.4	.8	1.4	.7	1.3	1.1	1.1	2.5
2. Somewhat important	9.8	9.6	9.7	9.9	8.3	11.2	9.5	8.5	11.1	6.8	12.8	8.3	9.5	10.7	11.7	7.8
3. Quite important	31.9	31.0	32.8	34.0	19.6	33.0	33.7	28.6	33.6	30.8	32.6	32.8	30.9	26.0	33.4	28.9
4. Extremely important	57.2	57.9	57.0	55.2	70.5	54.8	56.5	61.3	54.0	61.6	53.1	58.2	58.4	62.2	53.8	60.8
Item 1410 N(Wtd)	3579	1665	1761	2729	430	839	1059	1109	572	1946	1258	1194	843	424	937	37

QUESTIONNAIRE FORM 1 1981	TOTAL	SEX		RACE		REGION				4YR COLLEGE PLANS		ILLICIT DRUG USE: LIFETIME				
		M	F	White	Black	NE	NC	S	W	Yes	No	None	Marijuana Only	Few Pills	More Pills	Any Heroin
Weighted No. of Cases:	3644	1689	1795	2769	438	853	1075	1124	592	1969	1283	1213	853	430	958	37
% of Weighted Total:	100.0	46.3	49.3	76.0	12.0	23.4	29.5	30.8	16.3	54.0	35.2	33.3	23.4	11.8	26.3	1.0
A007B: Having a good marriage and family life																
1. Not important	4.2	5.4	2.7	3.8	5.5	3.2	3.5	3.9	7.2	3.5	4.6	3.3	3.4	3.4	5.0	31.9
2. Somewhat important	6.3	8.0	4.6	6.3	7.0	7.6	6.9	5.2	5.4	5.7	6.6	5.4	5.5	5.7	8.6	6.1
3. Quite important	13.2	15.3	11.0	12.5	14.4	14.6	12.6	11.6	15.5	14.0	12.2	12.0	13.6	14.7	13.2	12.5
4. Extremely important	76.3	71.2	81.8	77.4	73.2	74.5	77.0	79.3	71.9	76.8	76.6	79.3	77.5	76.2	73.1	49.5
Item 1420 N(Wtd)	3572	1657	1762	2722	427	835	1057	1102	578	1940	1260	1188	841	425	939	37
A007C: Having lots of money																
1. Not important	7.2	6.1	8.3	7.3	6.2	7.2	6.3	7.0	8.9	6.7	8.2	8.2	6.2	6.6	6.9	11.4
2. Somewhat important	41.0	34.0	48.4	44.5	26.3	38.6	42.3	41.6	41.1	42.5	40.3	45.5	39.0	44.8	36.5	38.5
3. Quite important	33.4	36.3	30.3	32.9	35.0	33.8	33.9	32.3	33.7	33.3	33.2	32.3	34.9	29.0	35.8	24.9
4. Extremely important	18.4	23.7	12.9	15.3	32.4	20.3	17.5	19.1	16.3	17.6	18.2	14.0	19.9	19.6	20.8	25.2
Item 1430 N(Wtd)	3582	1665	1764	2728	429	839	1056	1106	582	1946	1259	1193	844	424	941	37
A007D: Having plenty of time for recreation and hobbies																
1. Not important	2.5	2.9	2.3	2.0	5.0	1.8	2.3	3.4	2.3	2.3	3.3	3.6	2.1	1.2	1.8	-
2. Somewhat important	33.9	28.4	38.7	32.4	42.9	33.9	35.5	34.7	29.5	29.4	39.7	35.8	32.8	37.0	30.3	38.5
3. Quite important	40.6	39.9	42.0	42.0	33.8	38.6	40.5	41.0	43.1	43.9	36.7	40.2	41.6	41.3	40.9	33.6
4. Extremely important	22.9	28.8	17.0	23.6	18.3	25.7	21.6	20.9	25.1	24.4	20.2	20.4	23.5	20.4	26.9	27.9
Item 1440 N(Wtd)	3587	1672	1766	2733	434	838	1056	1111	581	1950	1263	1196	844	425	942	37
A007E: Having strong friendships																
1. Not important	1.4	1.5	1.2	.7	5.4	.9	.9	2.4	1.3	.9	1.6	1.1	2.2	.5	.9	-
2. Somewhat important	7.9	6.8	8.6	5.7	19.5	7.3	6.8	10.7	5.7	7.0	8.5	9.0	7.9	6.3	6.8	5.5
3. Quite important	28.7	31.3	25.7	28.0	31.4	25.8	31.4	28.0	29.5	25.8	32.0	27.5	29.1	30.1	28.9	42.2
4. Extremely important	61.9	60.4	64.5	65.6	43.7	66.0	61.0	59.0	63.4	66.4	57.8	62.5	60.8	63.1	63.4	52.3
Item 1450 N(Wtd)	3597	1670	1773	2737	434	842	1060	1112	583	1952	1265	1197	848	426	944	36
A007F: Being able to find steady work																
1. Not important	.9	1.2	.7	.9	.8	1.3	.4	1.4	.4	.5	1.4	.7	.6	.9	1.0	-
2. Somewhat important	5.3	5.2	5.7	5.6	3.3	6.0	4.7	4.3	7.3	5.9	4.5	5.4	5.4	4.4	5.5	6.7
3. Quite important	26.6	24.8	28.7	27.6	17.9	28.3	25.1	25.3	29.4	27.4	25.1	27.9	25.5	25.4	26.6	37.0
4. Extremely important	67.1	68.8	64.8	65.8	78.0	64.3	69.8	68.9	62.9	66.2	69.1	66.0	68.5	69.3	66.9	56.3
Item 1460 N(Wtd)	3590	1666	1771	2731	435	841	1058	1110	582	1951	1260	1197	844	422	945	37
A007G: Making a contribution to society																
1. Not important	6.9	7.7	5.8	6.6	7.0	6.8	7.9	5.1	8.5	4.7	9.6	5.9	9.2	4.3	6.3	13.2
2. Somewhat important	39.7	37.7	40.9	39.9	37.4	40.8	42.4	36.9	38.2	35.2	45.3	37.0	38.8	41.6	43.6	36.8
3. Quite important	35.5	35.6	36.1	35.4	34.9	35.3	34.6	36.6	35.4	37.4	32.7	36.5	34.9	36.9	34.9	17.8
4. Extremely important	18.0	19.0	17.2	18.1	20.8	17.1	15.2	21.3	17.9	22.7	12.4	20.6	17.1	17.1	15.2	32.2
Item 1470 N(Wtd)	3594	1670	1770	2738	433	840	1060	1112	582	1952	1265	1201	844	425	943	37
A007H: Being a leader in my community																
1. Not important	36.0	33.1	38.1	37.4	26.3	41.3	40.1	27.6	37.0	27.5	46.5	33.0	36.4	36.9	40.3	46.2
2. Somewhat important	38.8	39.6	38.2	39.3	37.2	39.2	35.8	40.1	40.9	41.6	34.4	37.2	39.9	36.5	40.7	34.8
3. Quite important	17.7	19.2	16.7	16.6	22.5	13.9	17.6	21.4	16.4	21.4	14.1	21.3	15.5	19.4	13.4	12.1
4. Extremely important	7.5	8.1	7.0	6.8	13.9	5.6	6.5	10.9	5.7	9.4	4.9	8.4	8.2	7.2	5.6	6.9
Item 1480 N(Wtd)	3579	1660	1766	2729	431	838	1055	1104	582	1943	1261	1196	838	422	942	37
A007I: Being able to give my children better opportunities than I've had																
1. Not important	2.8	3.2	2.1	2.9	1.6	3.0	2.7	2.3	3.5	2.6	2.8	1.6	3.2	1.8	3.3	9.9
2. Somewhat important	12.8	12.0	14.3	15.0	3.8	13.8	15.1	8.7	15.3	13.7	12.4	14.0	12.0	13.0	13.5	8.5
3. Quite important	30.5	30.8	30.6	34.6	11.4	34.1	31.3	26.5	31.7	30.4	31.2	28.1	31.9	32.5	31.1	36.3
4. Extremely important	53.9	54.0	53.1	47.4	83.3	49.1	51.0	62.5	49.5	53.2	53.5	56.3	52.8	52.7	52.0	45.3
Item 1490 N(Wtd)	3547	1649	1744	2695	431	831	1049	1101	566	1926	1247	1177	839	418	933	37

QUESTIONNAIRE FORM 1 1981	TOTAL	SEX		RACE		REGION				4YR COLLEGE PLANS		ILLICIT DRUG USE: LIFETIME				
		M	F	White	Black	NE	NC	S	W	Yes	No	None	Mari-juana Only	Few Pills	More Pills	Any Her-oin
Weighted No. of Cases:	3644	1689	1795	2769	438	853	1075	1124	592	1969	1283	1213	853	430	958	37
% of Weighted Total:	100.0	46.3	49.3	76.0	12.0	23.4	29.5	30.8	16.3	54.0	35.2	33.3	23.4	11.8	26.3	1.0
A007J: Living close to parents and relatives																
1. Not important	27.1	29.3	25.0	26.5	32.1	30.6	26.7	25.8	25.6	28.9	23.5	20.8	28.3	27.5	32.6	51.6
2. Somewhat important	41.3	39.7	42.7	42.6	34.0	39.2	41.5	41.1	43.9	40.5	43.9	42.2	41.2	41.4	41.8	37.7
3. Quite important	22.0	23.2	21.3	22.3	23.0	20.8	24.2	21.3	21.0	21.7	22.1	24.7	21.6	21.8	18.8	6.9
4. Extremely important	9.6	7.8	11.0	8.6	10.9	9.4	7.6	11.8	9.5	8.9	10.5	12.4	8.9	9.3	6.8	3.9
Item 1500 N(Wtd)	3589	1665	1770	2732	433	839	1059	1111	580	1949	1259	1195	846	426	941	37
A007K: Getting away from this area of the country																
1. Not important	55.1	54.7	56.3	58.2	42.3	48.6	52.4	60.7	58.7	56.6	55.6	61.1	56.5	55.0	48.4	35.5
2. Somewhat important	24.3	24.0	24.5	23.3	27.7	26.4	26.5	21.8	21.8	23.3	24.6	22.9	22.9	26.7	25.9	17.1
3. Quite important	10.7	10.5	10.5	9.3	16.5	13.1	10.6	8.7	11.1	10.4	10.9	9.0	10.3	10.2	12.2	21.7
4. Extremely important	10.0	10.8	8.7	9.3	13.5	11.9	10.6	8.8	8.4	9.8	8.8	7.0	10.3	8.0	13.4	25.8
Item 1510 N(Wtd)	3591	1668	1770	2735	436	840	1058	1113	580	1949	1263	1197	846	424	942	37
A007L: Working to correct social and economic inequalities																
1. Not important	19.5	24.4	15.2	22.1	7.2	19.2	23.6	15.9	19.5	18.3	22.1	18.8	20.4	18.1	20.1	25.8
2. Somewhat important	48.0	44.8	51.1	49.8	40.6	51.6	45.8	47.4	47.8	47.7	48.5	46.6	47.0	47.3	52.5	41.6
3. Quite important	23.0	21.8	23.9	20.9	31.1	20.1	21.9	25.4	24.8	23.1	22.0	23.2	22.6	27.1	19.7	30.6
4. Extremely important	9.5	9.0	9.9	7.3	21.0	9.1	8.8	11.3	7.9	10.9	7.4	11.4	10.0	7.5	7.7	2.0
Item 1520 N(Wtd)	3584	1668	1764	2731	432	837	1059	1109	579	1949	1262	1194	841	425	944	37
A007M: Discovering new ways to experience things																
1. Not important	8.0	9.4	7.0	8.4	7.6	6.8	8.7	8.3	7.9	7.3	9.6	10.5	8.2	6.5	5.0	4.7
2. Somewhat important	37.5	37.7	37.7	38.8	32.9	38.2	38.4	37.4	35.1	38.3	37.4	39.8	37.3	41.4	34.7	23.6
3. Quite important	37.1	36.1	37.5	37.1	37.3	36.1	36.8	37.7	37.7	36.4	36.9	34.5	38.3	36.1	38.7	49.6
4. Extremely important	17.4	16.9	17.7	15.7	22.2	18.8	16.1	16.6	19.4	18.1	16.1	15.2	16.2	16.1	21.6	22.1
Item 1530 N(Wtd)	3595	1668	1773	2737	436	839	1060	1115	582	1951	1267	1196	846	426	946	37
A007N: Finding purpose and meaning in my life																
1. Not important	2.7	4.2	1.2	3.0	1.2	2.4	3.3	2.0	3.5	2.1	3.7	2.6	2.3	2.7	2.9	8.6
2. Somewhat important	8.9	12.9	5.4	9.8	4.5	9.8	9.9	6.8	9.8	7.5	11.3	8.9	7.9	6.4	10.8	4.1
3. Quite important	26.4	30.9	21.9	28.4	16.5	27.4	28.1	23.5	27.3	25.1	29.1	26.4	27.0	32.8	23.5	28.1
4. Extremely important	62.0	51.9	71.5	58.9	77.7	60.4	58.7	67.8	59.4	65.2	55.9	62.1	62.8	58.1	62.8	59.1
Item 1540 N(Wtd)	3588	1666	1770	2731	434	838	1058	1111	582	1949	1260	1194	846	426	940	37
A008: Generally speaking, would you say that most people can be trusted or that you can't be too careful in dealing with people?																
3. Most people can be trusted	32.0	32.4	32.6	35.7	16.2	33.9	34.7	25.7	36.2	36.1	29.0	36.4	32.2	34.2	27.2	10.5
2. Don't know, undecided	27.8	27.5	27.6	28.4	20.5	28.6	29.7	24.8	28.8	26.7	28.1	26.8	28.9	28.7	27.8	29.8
1. Can't be too careful	40.2	40.1	39.7	36.0	63.3	37.6	35.6	49.5	35.0	37.2	42.9	36.8	38.9	37.1	45.0	59.7
Item 1550 N(Wtd)	3534	1637	1756	2700	421	830	1045	1086	573	1925	1242	1178	834	412	936	35
A009: Would you say that most of the time people try to be helpful or that they are mostly just looking out for themselves?																
3. Try to be helpful	33.2	31.0	36.0	34.3	31.0	32.8	34.3	30.1	37.9	34.8	32.7	37.8	32.5	37.4	25.8	13.7
2. Don't know, undecided	30.1	30.1	29.9	31.4	23.0	31.1	31.1	30.0	27.2	29.0	30.6	27.2	31.0	28.3	34.0	37.8
1. Just looking out for themselves	36.6	38.9	34.1	34.4	46.0	36.0	34.6	39.9	34.9	36.2	36.7	35.0	36.4	34.3	40.2	48.4
Item 1560 N(Wtd)	3591	1669	1772	2736	435	838	1058	1112	583	1951	1262	1195	844	425	946	37

QUESTIONNAIRE FORM 1 1981	TOTAL	SEX		RACE		REGION				4YR COLLEGE PLANS		ILLICIT DRUG USE: LIFETIME				
		M	F	White	Black	NE	NC	S	W	Yes	No	None	Marijuana Only	Few Pills	More Pills	Any Heroin
Weighted No. of Cases:	3644	1689	1795	2769	438	853	1075	1124	592	1969	1283	1213	853	430	958	37
% of Weighted Total:	100.0	46.3	49.3	76.0	12.0	23.4	29.5	30.8	16.3	54.0	35.2	33.3	23.4	11.8	26.3	1.0
A010: Do you think most people would try to take advantage of you if they got a chance or would they try to be fair?																
3. Would try to be fair	29.2	27.9	31.1	31.7	14.3	29.0	30.4	25.0	35.5	32.3	25.8	33.5	27.9	30.9	25.9	10.6
2. Don't know, undecided	34.3	34.6	34.3	37.1	19.3	36.3	34.0	31.7	36.8	34.0	34.5	33.6	33.7	36.1	35.7	40.4
1. Would try to take advantage of you	36.5	37.5	34.6	31.2	66.5	34.8	35.6	43.3	27.7	33.6	39.8	32.9	38.4	33.0	38.4	49.0
Item 1570 N(Wtd)	3588	1668	1770	2734	434	836	1058	1112	583	1947	1263	1196	843	425	942	37
A011: These next questions ask your opinions about a number of different topics. How much do you agree or disagree with each statement below?																
A011A: I feel that you can't be a good citizen unless you always obey the law																
1. Disagree	17.7	20.6	14.4	16.4	21.9	21.4	17.4	15.3	17.3	16.4	17.9	12.0	18.3	17.3	23.8	22.9
2. Mostly disagree	17.2	17.8	16.9	18.5	12.0	17.5	19.3	14.9	17.3	17.2	17.6	13.3	18.9	19.2	20.7	9.8
3. Neither	19.6	19.8	19.5	20.4	13.0	20.2	23.5	14.8	20.6	18.6	21.5	15.9	21.6	19.9	21.9	19.8
4. Mostly agree	33.6	30.4	37.1	34.9	29.3	31.5	31.7	35.9	35.9	37.1	29.2	40.1	32.5	34.3	27.1	45.2
5. Agree	12.0	11.4	12.1	9.8	23.9	9.4	8.1	19.1	8.9	10.7	13.9	18.7	8.6	9.2	6.5	2.3
Item 1580 N(Wtd)	3594	1672	1773	2740	435	841	1061	1112	580	1951	1266	1199	846	426	946	37
A011B: I feel a good citizen should go along with whatever the government does even if he disagrees with it																
1. Disagree	37.0	35.8	38.2	35.6	43.8	38.0	37.0	37.8	34.0	37.7	35.8	33.8	36.7	34.7	41.3	44.5
2. Mostly disagree	24.8	26.1	23.5	25.4	21.7	29.8	26.7	20.0	23.6	25.5	25.9	22.1	26.9	26.6	25.9	35.7
3. Neither	15.8	14.4	17.2	16.4	10.3	14.7	17.1	13.1	20.0	14.6	16.6	16.0	14.9	19.2	15.9	10.9
4. Mostly agree	16.5	16.3	16.7	17.5	13.4	12.6	15.6	19.5	18.1	16.9	15.3	20.9	16.9	14.8	11.9	2.6
5. Agree	5.9	7.4	4.5	5.1	10.9	5.0	3.6	9.6	4.3	5.2	6.4	7.2	4.7	4.7	5.0	6.3
Item 1590 N(Wtd)	3593	1672	1773	2737	435	840	1060	1113	580	1951	1265	1198	846	426	945	35
A011C: I feel a good citizen tries to change the government policies he disagrees with																
1. Disagree	6.4	6.2	6.4	4.9	12.8	5.7	5.7	8.4	5.0	5.2	7.8	6.4	7.2	5.5	5.5	5.9
2. Mostly disagree	9.1	9.1	8.7	8.8	8.5	10.7	8.4	8.0	10.1	8.7	9.9	9.8	8.4	8.8	8.4	15.4
3. Neither	24.8	22.3	27.4	25.0	22.0	24.3	27.7	23.4	22.9	22.4	27.5	23.6	26.2	24.6	26.0	18.1
4. Mostly agree	33.1	33.6	33.3	34.9	23.2	34.1	34.9	31.3	31.8	34.5	32.9	32.8	32.0	39.0	32.6	32.7
5. Agree	26.6	28.8	24.2	26.3	33.5	25.2	23.3	28.9	30.3	29.3	21.9	27.4	26.2	22.1	27.5	27.9
Item 1600 N(Wtd)	3578	1667	1764	2729	430	838	1051	1109	580	1945	1260	1194	843	423	942	35
A011D: The way people vote has a major impact on how things are run in this country																
1. Disagree	6.4	7.8	5.6	6.8	5.3	7.1	7.0	5.6	5.9	5.7	7.5	6.3	5.8	5.2	7.9	4.5
2. Mostly disagree	10.0	11.2	8.8	10.8	7.9	11.1	10.7	9.3	8.6	10.1	11.1	9.6	10.2	10.5	10.7	9.5
3. Neither	12.5	11.9	12.7	13.6	5.0	14.0	13.6	10.7	11.9	11.8	12.8	11.9	13.4	11.1	12.4	18.8
4. Mostly agree	32.4	31.4	33.5	33.1	28.6	33.8	34.0	28.6	34.8	33.0	31.8	32.0	30.8	36.7	31.6	43.5
5. Agree	38.6	37.7	39.4	35.6	52.8	34.0	34.7	45.7	38.7	39.3	36.8	40.2	39.9	36.4	37.3	23.8
Item 1610 N(Wtd)	3587	1668	1770	2735	432	839	1058	1111	579	1949	1262	1197	845	426	940	37
A011E: People who get together in citizen action groups to influence government policies can have a real effect																
1. Disagree	3.7	4.6	2.7	3.5	3.8	3.8	3.6	3.3	4.4	3.2	4.3	3.7	4.0	3.0	3.2	12.8
2. Mostly disagree	9.5	11.0	7.9	9.8	6.2	12.0	8.9	8.7	8.8	9.1	10.0	7.6	11.2	10.3	10.1	12.3
3. Neither	24.5	23.9	25.6	25.9	15.5	24.9	28.4	21.5	22.7	21.3	29.1	23.5	22.6	22.6	28.5	32.2
4. Mostly agree	38.3	37.0	39.1	39.5	32.7	36.4	38.9	37.5	41.7	40.0	36.9	38.6	39.0	41.5	37.7	31.2
5. Agree	23.9	23.4	24.8	21.3	41.7	22.9	20.2	29.0	22.4	26.4	19.8	26.7	23.2	22.6	20.5	11.5
Item 1620 N(Wtd)	3577	1666	1767	2733	429	836	1057	1107	576	1948	1259	1194	843	423	940	37

QUESTIONNAIRE FORM 1 1981	TOTAL	SEX		RACE		REGION				4YR COLLEGE PLANS		ILLICIT DRUG USE: LIFETIME				
		M	F	White	Black	NE	NC	S	W	Yes	No	None	Mari-juana Only	Few Pills	More Pills	Any Her-oin
Weighted No. of Cases:	3644	1689	1795	2769	438	853	1075	1124	592	1969	1283	1213	853	430	958	37
% of Weighted Total:	100.0	46.3	49.3	76.0	12.0	23.4	29.5	30.8	16.3	54.0	35.2	33.3	23.4	11.8	26.3	1.0

A011F: Despite its many faults, our system of doing things is still the best in the world

1. Disagree	5.1	4.3	5.6	3.7	11.3	5.2	4.9	6.3	3.2	4.5	6.0	4.4	4.6	4.9	5.7	12.8
2. Mostly disagree	6.6	6.7	6.2	5.4	12.1	5.6	6.5	7.9	5.9	5.4	8.0	5.1	7.5	7.0	7.0	18.7
3. Neither	20.0	17.5	22.4	19.8	20.1	19.7	24.1	16.4	20.0	15.7	25.8	18.0	20.7	22.2	20.6	18.7
4. Mostly agree	30.7	28.8	32.6	31.2	27.6	33.7	31.2	28.3	30.1	31.4	29.2	31.8	29.1	31.7	30.8	17.7
5. Agree	37.5	42.7	33.2	39.9	28.8	35.8	33.3	41.1	40.7	43.0	31.0	40.7	38.0	34.2	35.9	32.1
Item 1630 N(Wtd)	3580	1664	1769	2734	428	840	1057	1104	580	1947	1259	1195	841	424	943	37

A011G: America needs growth to survive, and that is going to require some increase in pollution

1. Disagree	34.1	33.9	34.7	35.5	29.6	34.4	32.9	35.1	34.1	36.3	31.0	33.9	35.1	30.0	35.9	33.3
2. Mostly disagree	22.7	23.3	22.0	23.9	16.6	24.4	25.2	19.7	21.4	23.8	22.1	23.3	24.0	24.3	21.9	20.4
3. Neither	20.6	18.3	23.0	20.7	15.9	21.3	20.1	20.3	21.0	19.1	23.0	19.3	19.2	21.9	23.5	18.7
4. Mostly agree	14.4	16.2	12.7	13.5	21.1	11.8	15.3	14.9	15.4	13.7	15.0	14.2	14.2	14.3	12.7	25.6
5. Agree	8.1	8.3	7.6	6.4	16.7	8.0	6.4	9.9	8.2	7.1	9.0	9.2	7.5	9.6	6.1	1.9
Item 1640 N(Wtd)	3577	1660	1767	2731	428	839	1056	1105	577	1944	1258	1190	843	425	941	37

A011H: If we just leave things to God, they will turn out for the best

1. Disagree	20.1	22.8	17.1	21.2	7.3	28.4	19.9	11.8	24.7	23.0	15.5	16.5	20.1	20.7	25.0	33.9
2. Mostly disagree	13.4	14.4	13.0	14.9	7.6	15.6	15.5	9.2	14.6	14.1	12.8	11.3	16.6	11.1	14.2	12.8
3. Neither	24.4	25.5	23.1	26.7	8.2	28.2	28.9	18.1	22.6	23.6	24.9	23.0	21.7	26.1	30.3	10.6
4. Mostly agree	18.2	16.9	19.6	17.5	22.7	14.3	18.0	21.9	17.1	17.2	20.0	17.2	19.5	21.8	15.2	20.2
5. Agree	23.9	20.4	27.3	19.8	54.2	13.6	17.7	39.0	21.0	22.1	26.8	32.1	22.2	20.2	15.4	22.6
Item 1650 N(Wtd)	3576	1666	1764	2731	428	836	1056	1107	577	1941	1260	1193	842	422	940	37

A011I: Going to school has been an enjoyable experience for me

1. Disagree	6.5	7.3	5.0	6.8	3.7	8.0	7.2	4.8	6.0	4.5	8.5	3.8	5.9	5.5	10.9	13.6
2. Mostly disagree	7.0	8.4	5.1	6.8	4.2	8.2	7.8	5.3	6.0	4.5	9.3	5.2	5.7	6.7	9.9	12.9
3. Neither	13.4	14.6	12.3	14.4	8.7	16.6	14.6	10.1	13.2	11.2	16.3	11.9	12.0	11.3	16.8	28.9
4. Mostly agree	40.2	40.6	40.9	42.0	35.2	40.6	40.1	39.4	41.4	42.0	38.2	39.2	43.3	40.4	40.0	21.3
5. Agree	32.9	29.1	36.7	29.7	48.2	26.6	30.3	40.5	32.5	37.8	27.5	40.0	33.1	36.1	22.4	23.3
Item 1660 N(Wtd)	3586	1667	1771	2736	431	841	1057	1110	578	1949	1262	1195	842	426	943	37

A011J: Doing well in school is important for getting a good job

1. Disagree	2.6	3.6	1.6	2.8	1.6	2.3	2.4	3.0	2.7	1.8	3.6	1.4	1.6	2.9	4.0	6.8
2. Mostly disagree	3.2	3.9	2.1	3.3	.3	3.5	4.2	2.3	2.9	2.0	4.5	2.1	2.8	2.9	5.2	11.6
3. Neither	6.7	8.4	5.1	7.1	3.7	6.9	7.5	5.3	7.7	5.4	8.0	5.3	6.8	6.2	8.9	7.3
4. Mostly agree	30.7	33.3	28.3	32.0	24.9	33.2	31.2	26.6	34.0	29.4	32.9	30.1	31.4	31.7	29.3	48.1
5. Agree	56.7	50.8	62.7	54.9	69.5	54.2	54.6	62.8	52.7	61.4	51.1	61.2	57.5	56.2	52.7	26.2
Item 1670 N(Wtd)	3587	1665	1773	2733	433	839	1059	1108	581	1948	1263	1196	844	426	941	37

The following questions are about CIGARETTE SMOKING.

B001: Have you ever smoked cigarettes?

1. Never--GO TO Q.B006	28.5	30.9	26.9	27.8	32.9	27.5	27.7	27.6	33.2	33.0	24.0	56.4	17.1	18.7	9.8	5.9
2. Once or twice	30.0	31.8	28.8	29.2	40.3	27.2	27.4	34.2	30.8	33.1	26.7	30.3	38.2	29.2	22.3	22.5
3. Occasionally but not regularly	17.1	15.3	19.2	17.8	13.2	17.3	15.7	18.2	17.7	17.8	17.1	8.2	24.8	23.1	18.6	10.5
4. Regularly in the past	7.5	7.4	7.6	7.9	5.4	8.2	8.3	6.1	7.9	6.4	8.6	2.2	8.5	8.9	12.8	16.4
5. Regularly now	16.8	14.6	17.5	17.3	8.2	19.9	20.9	13.9	10.5	9.7	23.7	3.0	11.4	20.1	36.5	44.7
Item 760 N(Wtd)	3545	1645	1756	2713	418	837	1043	1089	576	1937	1236	1169	840	419	941	37

QUESTIONNAIRE FORM 1 1981	TOTAL	SEX		RACE		REGION				4YR COLLEGE PLANS		ILLICIT DRUG USE: LIFETIME				
		M	F	White	Black	NE	NC	S	W	Yes	No	None	Mari- juana Only	Few Pills	More Pills	Any Her- oin
Weighted No. of Cases:	3644	1689	1795	2769	438	853	1075	1124	592	1969	1283	1213	853	430	958	37
% of Weighted Total:	100.0	46.3	49.3	76.0	12.0	23.4	29.5	30.8	16.3	54.0	35.2	33.3	23.4	11.8	26.3	1.0
B002: When did you first smoke cigarettes on a daily basis?																
0. Never smoked daily	49.1	52.7	48.2	51.1	47.1	44.9	46.9	50.7	57.2	59.8	40.9	72.5	57.0	46.2	31.9	19.6
1. Grade 6 or earlier	6.5	7.5	5.2	6.9	3.5	8.0	7.1	5.2	5.8	6.2	5.8	4.9	5.8	8.2	7.0	21.0
2. Grade 7 or 8	14.8	13.3	15.8	14.4	12.8	17.2	16.3	11.6	14.4	11.9	16.4	7.9	12.1	14.2	22.1	7.5
3. Grade 9 (Freshman)	9.0	9.0	7.8	8.3	8.2	9.8	9.6	8.8	6.6	5.5	12.5	5.5	8.1	9.3	10.8	15.8
4. Grade 10 (Sophomore)	9.8	7.8	11.3	9.6	11.0	10.7	9.8	10.5	6.8	7.4	11.9	2.5	8.8	8.9	14.3	23.5
5. Grade 11 (Junior)	6.7	5.7	7.4	6.1	8.8	6.7	7.1	6.6	5.8	5.2	7.7	3.1	4.3	9.0	9.6	8.8
6. Grade 12 (Senior)	4.2	3.9	4.3	3.5	8.5	2.8	3.2	6.6	3.4	4.0	4.9	3.7	4.0	4.4	4.3	3.8
Item 1680 N(Wtd) ★	2525	1131	1279	1950	280	607	754	782	382	1293	937	509	693	341	842	35
B003: How frequently have you smoked cigarettes during the past 30 days?																
1. Not at all	58.9	62.6	57.8	59.7	67.0	54.6	56.4	62.6	63.2	67.8	51.8	80.7	67.7	56.6	40.5	35.7
2. Less than one cigarette per day	11.8	11.8	11.8	11.8	10.1	11.7	9.5	12.7	14.3	13.4	10.3	8.8	12.7	11.7	13.0	9.4
3. One to five cigarettes per day	9.9	7.2	12.3	8.6	15.4	10.3	9.1	10.1	10.8	8.4	11.1	5.9	8.8	12.1	11.8	10.3
4. About one-half pack per day	9.2	7.2	9.7	9.4	3.2	10.2	10.8	8.0	7.2	5.1	12.6	2.2	5.4	11.0	15.9	14.4
5. About one pack per day	8.1	9.3	6.3	8.5	4.0	10.2	10.6	6.2	3.8	4.1	11.5	2.3	4.9	6.4	14.8	16.9
6. About one and one-half packs per day	1.5	1.4	1.5	1.4	.3	2.1	2.8	.4	.3	.8	2.0	.2	.4	1.6	3.0	6.3
7. Two packs or more per day	.5	.5	.6	.6	-	.9	.8	-	.4	.3	.7	-	-	.7	1.0	7.1
Item 780 N(Wtd) ★	2528	1131	1282	1952	280	603	755	788	382	1293	939	510	694	341	844	35
B004: Have you ever tried to stop smoking and found that you could not?																
1. Yes	15.2	13.5	16.0	15.4	10.1	18.9	18.9	11.7	9.0	10.5	18.8	8.4	9.0	17.3	24.1	10.5
2. No	84.8	86.5	84.0	84.6	89.9	81.1	81.1	88.3	91.0	89.5	81.2	91.6	91.0	82.7	75.9	89.5
Item 1690 N(Wtd) ★	2388	1055	1219	1852	253	567	723	737	360	1215	898	451	654	324	822	35
B005: Do you want to stop smoking now?																
1. Yes	15.6	13.7	16.4	14.7	14.2	18.1	17.6	13.2	12.6	11.2	19.1	8.0	10.7	20.6	22.0	25.6
2. No	18.2	17.4	18.0	18.6	10.4	20.4	20.7	15.5	15.6	12.7	22.5	7.2	12.6	18.7	28.2	31.4
8. Don't smoke now	66.2	68.9	65.6	66.7	75.5	61.5	61.6	71.3	71.8	76.1	58.5	84.8	76.6	60.7	49.8	43.0
Item 1700 N(Wtd) ★	2461	1095	1257	1911	266	589	734	760	377	1263	912	490	673	334	830	34
B006: Do you think you will be smoking cigarettes five years from now?																
1. I definitely will	.7	.7	.8	.8	.5	.8	1.0	.6	.6	.6	.9	.1	.4	.6	1.3	4.3
2. I probably will	13.1	11.3	13.7	12.3	12.5	14.7	15.4	11.7	9.5	7.9	18.1	4.1	11.3	15.3	24.7	17.1
3. I probably will not	27.2	24.4	29.4	26.6	26.3	29.2	25.8	29.2	23.0	25.9	28.0	17.9	29.1	31.1	34.3	43.3
4. I definitely will not	59.0	63.6	56.2	60.3	60.7	55.4	57.8	58.5	66.9	65.6	53.1	78.0	59.2	53.0	39.7	35.3
Item 1710 N(Wtd)	3557	1658	1749	2705	430	819	1053	1104	580	1929	1256	1183	834	424	938	37

The different questionnaire forms used in this study tend to emphasize somewhat different topics. The next major section in this form deals with alcohol and various other drugs. There is a lot of talk these days about these subjects, but very little accurate information. Therefore, we still have a lot to learn about the actual experiences and attitudes of people your age.

We hope that you can answer all questions; but if you find one which you feel you cannot answer honestly, we would prefer that you leave it blank.

★ = excludes respondents for whom question was inappropriate.

QUESTIONNAIRE FORM 1 1981	TOTAL	SEX		RACE		REGION				4YR COLLEGE PLANS		ILLICIT DRUG USE: LIFETIME				
		M	F	White	Black	NE	NC	S	W	Yes	No	None	Mari-juana Only	Few Pills	More Pills	Any Her-oin
Weighted No. of Cases:	3644	1689	1795	2769	438	853	1075	1124	592	1969	1283	1213	853	430	958	37
% of Weighted Total:	100.0	46.3	49.3	76.0	12.0	23.4	29.5	30.8	16.3	54.0	35.2	33.3	23.4	11.8	26.3	1.0

Remember that your answers will be strictly confidential. We never connect them with your name or your class.

The next questions are about ALCOHOLIC BEVERAGES, including beer, wine, and liquor.

B007: On how many occasions (if any) have you had alcohol to drink...

B007A: ...in your lifetime?

	TOTAL	M	F	White	Black	NE	NC	S	W	Yes	No	None	Mari-juana Only	Few Pills	More Pills	Any Her-oin
1. 0 occasions	8.0	6.7	9.4	6.1	20.0	3.7	5.5	13.9	8.0	7.8	8.4	19.6	1.5	3.2	.5	-
2. 1-2	7.9	7.1	9.0	6.1	18.9	4.7	7.2	11.0	8.4	7.9	8.3	15.3	5.7	4.8	1.7	2.5
3. 3-5	8.1	7.5	8.6	7.1	13.4	5.7	8.9	9.4	7.5	9.1	7.5	14.8	7.1	7.0	1.5	-
4. 6-9	8.4	7.2	9.8	7.3	16.3	6.0	8.0	9.7	10.5	8.6	8.7	11.9	8.9	6.9	4.4	-
5. 10-19	11.1	9.7	12.9	11.0	13.3	11.8	10.6	10.4	12.3	11.4	10.5	12.8	14.0	14.9	5.0	-
6. 20-39	13.6	11.5	15.7	14.8	7.7	17.8	13.2	10.7	13.6	14.1	12.6	11.3	18.4	16.4	11.7	5.4
7. 40 or more	42.9	50.4	34.6	47.5	10.4	50.3	46.6	35.0	39.8	41.2	43.8	14.2	44.4	46.8	75.3	92.1
Item 810 N(Wtd)	3402	1571	1695	2653	374	813	1019	1020	551	1882	1177	1157	813	403	902	34

B007B: ...during the last 12 months?

	TOTAL	M	F	White	Black	NE	NC	S	W	Yes	No	None	Mari-juana Only	Few Pills	More Pills	Any Her-oin
1. 0 occasions	14.8	12.6	17.1	11.6	34.8	7.4	13.1	22.2	15.2	14.6	16.1	33.4	6.7	5.8	2.4	2.4
2. 1-2	13.1	11.1	15.2	11.1	26.2	8.6	12.9	17.0	12.7	13.4	12.8	20.2	12.3	14.4	4.2	-
3. 3-5	12.2	10.9	13.6	11.6	15.0	10.7	12.8	11.8	14.1	13.3	11.0	15.8	15.7	10.9	5.6	6.1
4. 6-9	11.2	9.8	12.9	11.4	10.5	11.0	10.3	10.4	14.8	10.7	11.9	10.6	13.7	17.8	7.7	-
5. 10-19	14.8	14.9	15.2	16.9	5.3	19.6	14.7	11.2	14.8	15.6	13.9	8.7	19.0	16.7	18.0	13.4
6. 20-39	13.8	13.9	13.3	15.0	4.6	18.9	13.2	10.9	12.7	13.4	13.2	5.0	17.8	16.7	20.4	19.6
7. 40 or more	20.1	26.7	12.8	22.4	3.6	23.8	23.1	16.5	15.6	18.9	21.1	6.4	14.8	17.7	41.7	58.4
Item 820 N(Wtd)	3382	1556	1691	2645	369	811	1009	1013	549	1870	1169	1141	810	397	903	35

B007C: ...during the last 30 days?

	TOTAL	M	F	White	Black	NE	NC	S	W	Yes	No	None	Mari-juana Only	Few Pills	More Pills	Any Her-oin
1. 0 occasions	31.8	27.4	36.7	27.5	58.7	21.2	30.2	40.6	34.0	33.2	30.8	56.8	25.9	23.4	10.0	2.5
2. 1-2	21.8	19.9	24.1	21.1	26.6	19.9	20.1	23.8	24.0	23.3	20.1	23.6	25.3	28.0	13.4	15.0
3. 3-5	18.5	20.0	17.2	20.4	8.2	24.5	19.3	12.7	19.1	18.1	19.0	11.4	22.5	23.0	22.7	8.5
4. 6-9	13.2	14.7	11.8	15.0	2.6	15.9	13.9	10.5	12.8	13.0	13.3	4.5	15.2	12.3	23.0	18.9
5. 10-19	9.9	11.3	8.5	11.4	1.7	13.0	11.6	7.5	6.6	9.0	10.9	2.8	9.0	8.7	19.3	34.9
6. 20-39	3.0	3.6	1.6	2.9	1.5	3.9	3.1	2.9	1.8	1.9	3.7	.6	1.2	2.7	7.5	7.0
7. 40 or more	1.8	3.0	.2	1.7	.8	1.6	1.8	2.1	1.7	1.3	2.1	.1	.9	1.8	4.3	13.2
Item 830 N(Wtd)	3390	1562	1692	2646	372	810	1015	1014	551	1872	1176	1142	818	395	904	34

IF YOU HAVE NOT HAD ANY BEER, WINE, OR LIQUOR IN THE LAST TWELVE MONTHS, GO TO Q.B017.

B008: When you used alcohol during the last year, how often did you use it in each of the following situations?

B008A: When you were alone

	TOTAL	M	F	White	Black	NE	NC	S	W	Yes	No	None	Mari-juana Only	Few Pills	More Pills	Any Her-oin
1. Not at all	69.8	62.6	78.1	69.6	75.2	70.3	68.0	68.0	75.5	74.8	63.9	82.2	75.7	71.5	56.9	12.7
2. A few of the times	23.6	27.8	19.0	24.1	19.3	24.9	24.7	24.2	18.3	20.9	26.7	15.8	20.0	22.1	32.7	37.1
3. Some of the times	5.5	7.5	2.7	5.0	5.2	3.9	6.5	6.1	5.0	3.6	7.6	1.5	3.1	4.1	9.5	37.3
4. Most of the times	.9	1.5	.2	1.0	.2	1.0	.8	1.2	.6	.6	1.3	.3	.8	2.2	.7	7.8
5. Every time	.2	.5	-	.3	-	-	-	.5	.6	*	.5	.3	.3	-	.1	5.1
Item 1720 N(Wtd) ★	2919	1382	1416	2354	246	759	891	799	469	1605	1009	759	758	382	896	35

B008B: With just 1 or 2 other people

	TOTAL	M	F	White	Black	NE	NC	S	W	Yes	No	None	Mari-juana Only	Few Pills	More Pills	Any Her-oin
1. Not at all	12.0	9.1	15.4	10.6	20.3	13.1	12.3	11.1	11.5	15.5	8.1	26.6	9.4	9.5	3.7	-
2. A few of the times	32.0	28.1	36.5	31.5	36.7	31.9	30.8	31.8	34.7	33.5	29.6	35.8	39.6	32.8	22.4	11.8
3. Some of the times	26.0	27.0	23.9	26.4	17.8	31.1	26.7	21.1	24.8	23.4	28.8	12.6	22.0	26.3	40.5	39.4
4. Most of the times	24.0	29.2	18.8	25.8	13.2	20.4	25.1	28.4	20.5	21.4	27.7	15.4	24.0	27.1	29.5	37.5
5. Every time	5.9	6.6	5.4	5.6	12.0	3.5	5.1	7.5	8.6	6.2	5.8	9.5	5.0	4.4	3.9	11.3
Item 1730 N(Wtd) ★	2920	1387	1412	2357	246	757	894	800	469	1604	1010	758	757	383	898	36

* = less than .05 per cent.   ★ = excludes respondents for whom question was inappropriate.

QUESTIONNAIRE FORM 1 1981	TOTAL	SEX		RACE		REGION				4YR COLLEGE PLANS		ILLICIT DRUG USE: LIFETIME				
		M	F	White	Black	NE	NC	S	W	Yes	No	None	Mari- juana Only	Few Pills	More Pills	Any Her- oin
Weighted No. of Cases:	3644	1689	1795	2769	438	853	1075	1124	592	1969	1283	1213	853	430	958	37
% of Weighted Total:	100.0	46.3	49.3	76.0	12.0	23.4	29.5	30.8	16.3	54.0	35.2	33.3	23.4	11.8	26.3	1.0

B008C: At a party

1. Not at all	10.9	10.6	11.7	10.5	16.5	7.1	9.4	13.8	14.7	11.6	10.5	24.2	8.7	7.3	3.6	-
2. A few of the times	18.4	17.6	19.9	18.3	23.4	16.8	17.1	20.3	20.5	19.0	18.2	25.5	18.6	21.3	11.9	6.0
3. Some of the times	17.4	16.3	18.5	16.9	20.8	17.0	18.3	18.4	14.9	17.3	17.4	15.4	15.7	17.1	20.4	24.4
4. Most of the times	33.3	33.0	34.1	34.8	25.7	36.3	33.5	30.0	33.8	34.8	31.7	24.0	38.4	33.5	37.7	27.4
5. Every time	19.9	22.5	15.8	19.5	13.6	22.8	21.7	17.5	16.0	17.2	22.2	10.9	18.6	20.8	26.5	42.2
Item 1740 N(Wtd) ★	2909	1378	1409	2348	244	759	892	788	469	1602	1002	750	754	378	902	36

B008D: When your date or spouse was present

1. Not at all	31.3	35.7	27.7	28.4	53.0	27.8	30.3	33.0	35.7	35.0	27.6	50.6	34.1	26.0	14.5	15.7
2. A few of the times	27.2	27.7	27.2	28.4	24.8	26.8	25.4	29.0	28.1	27.9	28.0	25.4	29.9	27.3	26.2	27.9
3. Some of the times	20.0	19.6	19.3	20.1	14.1	23.6	19.9	17.7	18.5	18.8	18.2	11.7	17.9	22.7	28.3	17.6
4. Most of the times	16.2	13.3	18.6	17.5	4.9	17.3	18.2	15.0	12.6	13.3	19.4	7.5	14.2	16.8	25.1	27.2
5. Every time	5.3	3.7	7.2	5.6	3.3	4.5	6.2	5.3	5.0	5.0	6.7	4.7	3.9	7.2	5.9	11.6
Item 1750 N(Wtd) ★	2878	1360	1398	2320	245	738	884	788	468	1581	997	743	744	376	893	36

B008E: When people over age 30 were present

1. Not at all	28.5	28.4	29.4	26.6	51.1	22.2	28.1	37.0	24.8	28.9	29.0	35.1	32.5	29.6	18.4	13.4
2. A few of the times	40.3	41.7	38.6	41.8	32.6	43.6	38.7	37.6	42.7	40.6	38.9	35.5	40.6	42.7	43.9	28.4
3. Some of the times	18.5	18.7	17.6	18.5	9.2	22.4	18.1	15.2	18.5	17.6	18.5	10.7	16.5	17.9	26.9	27.0
4. Most of the times	8.5	8.1	8.9	8.7	4.5	8.0	10.2	6.2	9.9	8.2	9.3	9.5	8.0	7.7	8.5	15.9
5. Every time	4.2	3.1	5.6	4.3	2.6	3.8	4.8	3.9	4.2	4.7	4.2	9.1	2.3	2.2	2.3	15.3
Item 1760 N(Wtd) ★	2919	1383	1414	2355	245	758	894	797	470	1605	1010	759	754	384	899	35

B008F: During the daytime (before 4:00 p.m.)

1. Not at all	57.0	49.3	65.8	54.9	75.8	55.1	57.0	58.5	57.7	60.3	53.2	77.4	64.7	58.5	34.5	18.1
2. A few of the times	31.6	35.8	27.6	33.8	18.7	34.4	32.0	29.1	30.5	30.9	33.9	18.3	27.6	32.6	45.6	37.0
3. Some of the times	9.7	12.5	5.8	9.7	4.7	9.7	9.6	9.8	9.7	7.6	10.7	2.6	6.5	8.2	17.5	36.3
4. Most of the times	1.0	1.6	.4	1.0	.5	.4	1.0	1.6	1.2	.7	1.4	.5	1.1	.4	1.6	5.8
5. Every time	.7	.9	.4	.6	.2	.4	.4	1.1	.9	.6	.8	1.2	.1	.4	.7	2.8
Item 1770 N(Wtd) ★	2917	1383	1412	2354	244	760	892	795	470	1602	1010	758	755	383	899	36

B008G: At your home (or apartment or dorm)

1. Not at all	36.4	35.1	39.2	35.4	45.4	32.9	32.9	44.2	35.7	37.1	38.0	48.7	41.5	39.1	21.2	18.5
2. A few of the times	34.5	34.2	34.9	35.2	33.1	37.9	34.1	31.9	33.9	35.6	32.4	28.5	34.6	35.4	39.5	24.1
3. Some of the times	17.7	19.6	14.7	17.9	12.5	19.0	20.0	14.6	16.6	16.8	17.8	8.2	15.6	17.1	27.0	34.0
4. Most of the times	8.5	8.7	7.6	8.8	5.0	8.4	9.0	6.7	10.5	7.6	8.6	7.6	7.5	6.7	10.5	18.4
5. Every time	2.9	2.4	3.5	2.7	4.1	1.7	4.0	2.6	3.4	3.0	3.2	7.1	.7	1.7	1.8	5.0
Item 1780 N(Wtd) ★	2914	1383	1410	2350	247	759	889	796	470	1605	1005	757	752	382	901	36

B008H: At school

1. Not at all	86.2	81.6	91.5	86.7	88.1	87.8	88.2	84.5	82.7	89.2	83.7	96.7	88.2	85.0	77.9	43.0
2. A few of the times	10.1	12.8	7.2	10.0	6.9	9.2	8.7	11.1	12.7	8.0	11.7	2.1	9.1	11.1	17.0	18.7
3. Some of the times	2.8	3.9	1.3	2.5	4.3	2.3	2.3	3.1	3.9	2.3	3.1	.9	2.2	3.6	3.6	29.6
4. Most of the times	.7	1.3	*	.6	.7	.4	.8	1.1	.3	.4	1.1	-	.4	.3	1.4	6.4
5. Every time	.2	.4	-	.2	-	.3	-	.2	.5	*	.4	.3	.1	-	.2	2.2
Item 1790 N(Wtd) ★	2915	1382	1410	2350	245	760	892	794	468	1603	1010	758	753	384	896	36

B008I: In a car

1. Not at all	30.2	25.1	35.9	27.4	47.7	32.9	27.0	27.1	37.1	34.5	25.0	53.5	27.8	26.7	14.7	3.5
2. A few of the times	26.6	25.3	28.0	27.4	25.3	28.2	24.1	26.9	28.0	26.7	26.3	23.3	31.1	29.1	25.2	9.7
3. Some of the times	24.6	26.0	22.7	25.6	16.0	24.5	27.5	23.1	21.9	23.5	25.1	11.9	24.3	26.0	34.7	31.6
4. Most of the times	16.0	20.5	11.6	16.9	10.1	11.9	18.7	19.2	11.8	13.2	20.4	9.7	14.1	17.0	21.1	47.1
5. Every time	2.6	3.1	1.7	2.6	.8	2.5	2.6	3.6	1.2	2.0	3.2	1.5	2.7	1.2	4.1	8.2
Item 1810 N(Wtd) ★	2922	1387	1412	2355	247	760	895	796	470	1607	1010	758	754	384	901	36

★=excludes respondents for whom question was inappropriate.　　*=less than .05 per cent.

QUESTIONNAIRE FORM 1 1981	TOTAL	SEX		RACE		REGION				4YR COLLEGE PLANS		ILLICIT DRUG USE: LIFETIME				
		M	F	White	Black	NE	NC	S	W	Yes	No	None	Mari-juana Only	Few Pills	More Pills	Any Her-oin
Weighted No. of Cases:	3644	1689	1795	2769	438	853	1075	1124	592	1969	1283	1213	853	430	958	37
% of Weighted Total:	100.0	46.3	49.3	76.0	12.0	23.4	29.5	30.8	16.3	54.0	35.2	33.3	23.4	11.8	26.3	1.0

B009: What have been the most important reasons for your drinking alcoholic beverages? (Mark all that apply.)

	TOTAL	M	F	White	Black	NE	NC	S	W	Yes	No	None	Mari-juana Only	Few Pills	More Pills	Any Her-oin
A. To experiment--to see what it's like	38.8	35.6	42.1	36.6	56.8	36.4	39.5	41.8	36.3	42.5	35.4	48.7	42.7	37.9	28.4	27.5
B. To relax or relieve tension	39.3	38.9	38.4	41.5	17.8	44.6	41.5	36.3	31.5	38.6	39.6	26.0	35.8	40.0	51.7	68.0
C. To feel good or get high	53.6	56.7	50.0	55.3	41.3	60.2	54.1	49.0	49.9	52.1	54.6	23.2	56.1	55.6	74.3	90.7
D. To seek deeper insights and understanding	3.8	4.3	2.9	3.8	1.7	4.8	3.2	3.0	4.2	3.4	3.4	.9	3.3	4.2	5.6	11.8
E. To have a good time with my friends	72.5	74.6	70.2	73.8	60.5	78.1	74.0	67.2	69.6	72.6	71.7	56.8	79.9	71.7	79.5	70.8
F. To fit in with a group I like	11.2	13.3	9.3	11.5	10.1	9.6	12.7	12.4	8.9	12.4	10.9	11.2	13.0	9.8	10.4	15.1
G. To get away from my problems or troubles	17.7	15.9	19.0	18.2	8.9	19.8	19.1	17.1	12.5	16.0	20.4	9.6	14.7	16.4	25.4	44.4
H. Because of boredom, nothing else to do	20.5	21.9	18.7	21.1	19.5	21.1	20.3	23.2	15.2	20.3	19.0	12.2	20.4	18.8	26.7	44.1
I. Because of anger or frustration	14.3	13.3	15.0	14.7	8.6	14.3	14.9	14.9	11.9	12.4	15.7	7.4	10.7	16.1	21.4	25.2
J. To get through the day	1.6	1.8	1.2	1.5	2.3	2.3	1.7	1.0	1.0	1.1	2.1	.2	1.5	1.2	2.5	9.2
K. To increase the effects of some other drug(s)	7.4	8.5	5.1	7.1	4.4	9.7	7.1	5.5	7.5	6.1	6.6	-	1.6	2.1	18.9	47.2
L. To decrease (offset) the effects of some other drug(s)	.7	.9	.2	.4	.3	1.6	.5	.2	.3	.5	.5	-	.6	.9	1.0	1.4
M. To get to sleep	6.1	7.0	4.8	5.6	8.7	6.9	5.8	6.1	5.2	5.1	6.9	4.7	4.0	5.5	8.5	16.2
N. Because it tastes good	48.7	49.5	48.4	51.6	26.1	50.1	50.0	45.5	49.3	48.7	49.0	43.8	43.5	47.7	58.4	67.2
O. Because I am "hooked"--I feel I have to drink	.7	.8	.3	.5	.2	.6	.9	.6	.3	.4	.7	.4	.1	.6	1.3	2.2
Item 1820-1960 N(Wtd) ★	2843	1358	1365	2301	234	734	873	777	460	1549	991	706	744	380	897	36

B010: When you drink alcoholic beverages, how high do you usually get?

	TOTAL	M	F	White	Black	NE	NC	S	W	Yes	No	None	Mari-juana Only	Few Pills	More Pills	Any Her-oin
1. Not at all high	18.9	16.5	22.2	16.8	36.2	15.5	17.6	23.8	18.9	21.7	16.9	46.8	12.8	13.8	4.1	6.5
2. A little high	33.8	31.6	36.9	33.9	39.1	34.3	30.3	36.1	36.0	34.5	33.1	33.9	39.8	39.2	26.1	24.0
3. Moderately high	41.4	43.9	38.0	43.6	21.2	44.1	44.7	35.6	40.8	39.4	42.8	17.5	42.8	43.0	59.5	43.4
4. Very high	5.8	8.0	2.9	5.8	3.5	6.2	7.5	4.5	4.3	4.4	7.1	1.8	4.6	4.0	10.3	26.1
Item 1970 N(Wtd) ★	2912	1387	1401	2343	248	758	890	797	467	1601	1004	756	752	382	903	36

B011: When you drink alcoholic beverages, how long do you usually stay high?

	TOTAL	M	F	White	Black	NE	NC	S	W	Yes	No	None	Mari-juana Only	Few Pills	More Pills	Any Her-oin
1. Usually don't get high	20.9	18.2	24.0	18.4	39.6	16.2	18.9	26.7	22.2	23.6	18.4	48.8	14.7	16.5	5.5	6.5
2. One to two hours	40.3	38.0	44.1	42.0	34.7	41.0	39.6	39.7	41.4	40.6	40.0	35.2	47.2	48.4	36.3	23.0
3. Three to six hours	35.6	39.8	30.0	36.4	23.8	40.5	37.0	30.9	33.0	33.5	37.6	14.8	35.4	32.6	53.2	50.9
4. Seven to 24 hours	3.1	3.8	1.9	3.1	1.8	2.0	4.5	2.6	3.3	2.2	3.8	1.2	2.7	2.5	4.8	17.5
5. More than 24 hours	.1	.2	*	*	-	.3	-	-	.1	*	.2	-	-	-	.2	2.1
Item 1980 N(Wtd) ★	2892	1379	1391	2337	243	741	893	790	468	1585	1007	739	755	381	897	36

The following questions ask about how much you have to drink on the occasions when you drink alcoholic beverages. For these questions, a "drink" means any of the following: A 12-ounce can (or bottle) of beer, a 4-ounce glass of wine, a mixed drink or shot glass of liquor.

B012: Think back over the LAST TWO WEEKS. How many times have you had five or more drinks in a row?

	TOTAL	M	F	White	Black	NE	NC	S	W	Yes	No	None	Mari-juana Only	Few Pills	More Pills	Any Her-oin
1. None	58.3	47.8	70.6	56.3	85.4	52.7	54.6	64.3	64.3	63.2	53.7	81.3	64.0	61.5	34.9	10.2
2. Once	11.5	13.1	10.1	12.1	4.9	13.0	11.5	9.3	12.6	11.6	11.7	8.1	13.0	12.0	12.8	16.7
3. Twice	11.1	13.9	7.5	11.3	4.8	13.2	10.6	9.4	11.2	9.7	11.8	4.9	12.6	11.9	13.8	18.3
4. 3 to 5 times	14.3	18.5	9.6	15.7	2.9	15.7	17.9	12.2	8.7	12.1	17.3	4.2	8.3	12.3	28.1	27.1
5. 6 to 9 times	3.1	4.0	1.6	3.1	1.5	3.5	3.5	2.6	2.2	2.2	3.7	.9	1.5	1.2	6.9	3.8
6. 10 or more times	1.8	2.7	.5	1.5	.5	1.8	1.8	2.2	1.0	1.2	1.9	.6	.6	1.0	3.4	23.9
Item 850 N(Wtd) ★	2892	1377	1398	2338	242	746	883	791	473	1594	996	752	759	373	895	34

★ = excludes respondents for whom question was inappropriate.   * = less than .05 per cent.

QUESTIONNAIRE FORM 1 1981	TOTAL	SEX		RACE		REGION				4YR COLLEGE PLANS		ILLICIT DRUG USE: LIFETIME				
		M	F	White	Black	NE	NC	S	W	Yes	No	None	Marijuana Only	Few Pills	More Pills	Any Heroin
Weighted No. of Cases:	3644	1689	1795	2769	438	853	1075	1124	592	1969	1283	1213	853	430	958	37
% of Weighted Total:	100.0	46.3	49.3	76.0	12.0	23.4	29.5	30.8	16.3	54.0	35.2	33.3	23.4	11.8	26.3	1.0

B013: During the last two weeks, how many times have you had 3 or 4 drinks in a row (but no more than that)?

	TOTAL	M	F	White	Black	NE	NC	S	W	Yes	No	None	Marijuana Only	Few Pills	More Pills	Any Heroin
1. None	54.4	48.5	61.4	52.1	76.9	51.0	52.5	56.9	59.3	57.4	51.3	73.8	58.4	52.9	36.4	19.8
2. Once	19.7	20.2	19.0	21.1	9.7	20.8	19.9	18.2	20.2	20.3	20.0	16.7	19.8	23.5	20.9	13.9
3. Twice	13.6	15.0	11.8	14.1	8.6	15.6	15.0	11.4	11.6	12.6	14.7	6.2	12.5	12.7	20.5	35.7
4. 3 to 5 times	9.4	12.4	6.3	10.0	4.3	9.6	9.3	10.3	7.4	7.8	11.0	3.0	8.2	9.1	15.9	11.2
5. 6 to 9 times	1.8	2.4	1.2	2.0	-	1.9	2.1	2.1	.8	1.4	1.9	.3	.7	1.2	4.1	5.8
6. 10 or more times	1.1	1.5	.3	.7	.5	1.2	1.1	1.1	.7	.5	1.1	-	.4	.6	2.2	13.6
Item 1990 N(Wtd) ★	2885	1380	1395	2336	244	745	884	783	472	1593	994	753	755	371	895	33

B014: During the last two weeks, how many times have you had two drinks in a row (but no more than that)?

	TOTAL	M	F	White	Black	NE	NC	S	W	Yes	No	None	Marijuana Only	Few Pills	More Pills	Any Heroin
1. None	54.7	52.8	57.5	53.3	68.2	53.5	53.6	57.5	53.9	57.7	50.5	72.3	53.9	54.5	41.0	34.2
2. Once	21.9	21.7	22.3	22.3	16.2	21.6	23.5	18.4	25.3	20.8	24.3	16.3	25.3	22.5	24.1	26.4
3. Twice	11.1	11.3	10.5	11.6	8.4	10.9	11.7	11.7	9.5	10.8	11.7	6.6	11.5	13.4	13.4	11.9
4. 3 to 5 times	8.9	9.8	7.7	9.5	6.0	10.1	8.2	8.7	9.0	8.2	10.1	4.1	7.9	7.3	14.5	9.0
5. 6 to 9 times	1.8	2.1	1.1	1.7	1.1	2.5	2.0	1.3	1.1	1.6	1.4	.4	1.0	1.6	3.4	11.1
6. 10 to 19 times	1.2	1.6	.8	1.3	-	1.1	.9	1.8	.8	.6	1.6	.4	.4	.8	2.7	2.3
7. 20 or more times	.4	.6	.1	.3	-	.2	.2	.6	.3	.2	.3	-	-	-	.9	5.1
Item 2000 N(Wtd) ★	2861	1365	1384	2318	236	742	876	777	467	1573	989	745	744	374	884	35

B015: During the last two weeks, how many times have you had just one drink?

	TOTAL	M	F	White	Black	NE	NC	S	W	Yes	No	None	Marijuana Only	Few Pills	More Pills	Any Heroin
1. None	53.5	53.0	54.8	53.8	51.8	50.5	56.7	52.3	54.2	55.9	50.6	60.8	56.6	52.5	46.0	50.5
2. Once	27.1	26.4	27.6	27.1	30.7	28.9	23.7	28.7	27.9	27.0	27.3	26.3	25.1	28.9	28.6	27.2
3. Twice	9.9	9.3	10.2	9.5	10.7	10.1	10.3	9.5	9.4	8.8	10.7	8.0	10.7	11.3	9.8	6.5
4. 3 to 5 times	6.4	7.2	5.5	6.4	4.9	6.5	6.2	7.0	5.8	5.8	7.4	4.0	5.4	4.2	10.0	9.4
5. 6 to 9 times	1.8	1.9	1.5	1.8	1.6	2.8	1.7	1.5	.6	1.4	2.5	.7	1.3	2.2	2.9	-
6. 10 to 19 times	1.0	1.7	.5	1.2	-	.8	1.0	.6	1.9	.7	1.3	.1	.8	1.0	2.0	-
7. 20 or more times	.4	.6	-	.3	.3	.4	.4	.4	.2	.3	.3	.2	-	-	.7	6.3
Item 2010 N(Wtd) ★	2784	1330	1348	2271	216	722	859	747	455	1545	952	728	722	355	869	35

B016: Have you ever tried to stop using alcoholic beverages and found that you couldn't stop?

	TOTAL	M	F	White	Black	NE	NC	S	W	Yes	No	None	Marijuana Only	Few Pills	More Pills	Any Heroin
1. Yes	2.8	3.5	1.8	2.5	4.4	2.4	3.1	2.9	2.5	1.9	3.3	2.3	.9	4.4	3.5	7.1
2. No	97.2	96.5	98.2	97.5	95.6	97.6	96.9	97.1	97.5	98.1	96.7	97.7	99.1	95.6	96.5	92.9
Item 2020 N(Wtd) ★	2849	1366	1364	2314	232	734	877	776	463	1557	996	714	742	376	900	36

B017: Do you think you will be drinking alcoholic beverages five years from now?

	TOTAL	M	F	White	Black	NE	NC	S	W	Yes	No	None	Marijuana Only	Few Pills	More Pills	Any Heroin
1. I definitely will	15.8	18.5	13.1	18.3	2.1	25.2	16.4	9.7	13.1	17.3	14.1	7.6	17.7	12.0	26.2	43.9
2. I probably will	55.7	54.8	55.9	58.9	35.9	58.4	60.6	47.8	58.1	54.7	56.1	45.6	59.6	64.0	63.1	46.1
3. I probably will not	14.0	14.3	14.0	11.7	26.7	9.1	11.9	19.0	15.0	13.8	13.9	19.0	12.8	14.6	6.6	5.5
4. I definitely will not	14.5	12.4	17.0	11.1	35.2	7.4	11.1	23.5	13.8	14.2	15.8	27.8	9.9	9.4	4.1	4.5
Item 2030 N(Wtd)	3578	1667	1763	2733	431	830	1059	1105	585	1944	1260	1191	842	427	947	36

The next questions are about MARIJUANA and HASHISH.

Marijuana is sometimes called: grass, pot, dope.

Hashish is sometimes called: hash, hash oil.

★ = excludes respondents for whom question was inappropriate.

	TOTAL	SEX		RACE		REGION				4YR COLLEGE PLANS		ILLICIT DRUG USE: LIFETIME				
QUESTIONNAIRE FORM 1 **1981**		M	F	White	Black	NE	NC	S	W	Yes	No	None	Mari-juana Only	Few Pills	More Pills	Any Her-oin
Weighted No. of Cases:	3644	1689	1795	2769	438	853	1075	1124	592	1969	1283	1213	853	430	958	37
% of Weighted Total:	100.0	46.3	49.3	76.0	12.0	23.4	29.5	30.8	16.3	54.0	35.2	33.3	23.4	11.8	26.3	1.0
B018: On how many occasions (if any) have you used hashish...																
B018A: ...in your lifetime?																
1. 0 occasions	66.1	62.7	71.5	63.8	86.9	56.4	62.6	78.6	63.1	71.2	64.1	100.0	69.3	56.6	25.6	7.9
2. 1-2	12.0	12.1	12.0	12.9	7.0	13.3	11.8	10.8	12.6	11.3	12.7	-	19.7	22.2	15.7	4.9
3. 3-5	5.8	6.4	5.1	6.4	2.7	7.6	6.8	3.4	5.8	5.0	6.6	-	5.6	10.1	11.5	3.4
4. 6-9	3.5	3.5	3.2	3.6	1.2	4.0	3.7	2.7	4.0	3.1	4.1	-	1.9	5.0	8.9	9.9
5. 10-19	4.4	5.1	3.5	4.9	.8	6.1	4.9	2.0	5.5	3.8	4.0	-	1.5	2.9	13.5	9.3
6. 20-39	2.8	3.0	2.3	3.2	.1	3.8	3.7	.8	3.6	2.2	2.5	-	1.2	1.3	8.7	3.6
7. 40 or more	5.4	7.2	2.5	5.2	1.3	8.8	6.4	1.7	5.4	3.5	5.9	-	.8	1.9	16.2	60.8
Item 2040 N(Wtd)	3530	1640	1753	2718	410	828	1043	1077	582	1935	1241	1213	851	425	939	36
B018B: ...during the last 12 months?																
1. 0 occasions	76.0	73.0	80.9	74.2	92.0	68.4	72.0	85.6	76.1	80.8	73.1	100.0	83.8	74.8	40.2	15.3
2. 1-2	10.1	10.9	9.4	11.2	4.2	12.6	10.9	8.2	8.9	8.7	12.5	-	10.2	17.3	19.9	8.1
3. 3-5	4.9	5.1	4.2	5.2	2.1	5.8	5.9	2.7	5.8	4.0	5.1	-	3.2	4.2	12.9	17.0
4. 6-9	2.9	3.2	2.5	3.2	.4	4.6	3.7	1.1	2.7	2.4	3.0	-	1.6	1.9	8.2	15.2
5. 10-19	3.2	3.8	1.9	3.4	-	5.4	3.1	1.3	4.0	2.1	2.8	-	.9	1.1	10.4	10.7
6. 20-39	1.2	1.4	.7	1.2	.4	2.0	1.9	.3	.7	.7	1.5	-	.2	.2	3.8	11.3
7. 40 or more	1.6	2.7	.5	1.7	.9	1.2	2.6	.9	1.7	1.2	2.0	-	.2	.5	4.7	22.4
Item 2050 N(Wtd)	3507	1625	1750	2706	410	823	1040	1070	574	1927	1232	1213	844	422	931	36
B018C: ...during the last 30 days?																
1. 0 occasions	90.0	87.9	93.4	89.5	97.2	87.6	86.1	95.1	91.3	92.9	88.7	100.0	96.0	92.8	71.9	38.5
2. 1-2	5.4	6.0	4.4	5.7	1.4	7.3	6.8	3.1	4.4	4.1	6.1	-	3.4	6.7	13.5	16.0
3. 3-5	2.3	3.1	1.2	2.6	.1	2.8	3.8	.6	2.1	1.4	2.8	-	.2	.3	8.1	7.2
4. 6-9	1.0	1.4	.6	1.2	.2	1.0	1.5	.5	1.2	1.0	.9	-	.2	-	3.6	2.3
5. 10-19	.7	.7	.2	.5	.5	.8	1.0	.3	.4	.3	.6	-	.2	-	1.4	26.1
6. 20-39	.2	.3	.1	.2	.2	.1	.4	.1	.1	.2	.1	-	-	.2	.6	-
7. 40 or more	.4	.5	.2	.3	.4	.4	.3	.2	.6	.1	.7	-	-	-	1.0	9.9
Item 2060 N(Wtd)	3503	1624	1746	2699	412	820	1040	1069	574	1927	1227	1213	843	420	929	35
B019: On how many occasions (if any) have you used marijuana...																
B019A: ...in your lifetime?																
1. 0 occasions	39.7	37.5	43.6	39.0	47.2	33.3	38.6	46.7	38.4	44.8	36.7	100.0	.5	20.0	8.9	3.9
2. 1-2	10.0	9.9	10.8	9.0	16.0	9.3	8.5	11.8	10.9	10.4	10.2	-	29.4	15.0	3.4	-
3. 3-5	6.6	7.5	5.8	6.3	10.8	6.0	6.1	7.1	7.7	7.1	6.1	-	19.4	8.7	2.7	1.2
4. 6-9	5.3	4.8	5.6	5.5	4.1	5.8	5.8	4.8	4.6	5.3	4.7	-	13.4	8.6	3.1	2.3
5. 10-19	7.3	6.9	7.5	7.9	4.3	7.5	7.0	7.2	7.9	7.3	7.3	-	14.2	11.0	8.6	2.3
6. 20-39	6.4	6.4	6.7	7.0	3.5	7.0	7.9	4.6	6.3	5.6	8.3	-	10.5	10.9	9.2	-
7. 40 or more	24.5	27.2	20.0	25.3	14.1	31.1	26.2	17.8	24.3	19.4	26.7	-	12.6	25.8	64.0	90.4
Item 2070 N(Wtd)	3489	1613	1739	2696	394	825	1038	1056	570	1923	1218	1213	851	420	932	37
B019B: ...during the last 12 months?																
1. 0 occasions	53.4	50.9	57.9	51.8	66.6	47.7	51.2	60.7	52.5	58.6	51.0	100.0	34.9	41.4	17.8	7.6
2. 1-2	10.2	9.3	11.3	10.2	11.6	10.9	9.6	9.8	11.1	11.1	9.0	-	27.1	11.8	7.6	2.3
3. 3-5	6.5	7.2	5.8	7.1	3.5	7.2	6.5	6.1	6.4	5.7	7.4	-	13.0	11.9	7.1	-
4. 6-9	5.0	5.5	4.3	5.1	3.2	3.5	5.5	5.0	6.4	4.7	5.4	-	9.5	11.0	4.4	3.0
5. 10-19	5.8	5.6	6.3	6.7	3.3	6.6	6.9	4.8	4.9	5.6	6.4	-	6.9	8.0	11.4	6.8
6. 20-39	5.6	5.1	6.0	5.8	3.9	8.0	5.8	3.9	5.3	4.7	6.1	-	5.0	5.9	13.5	6.6
7. 40 or more	13.3	16.3	8.5	13.2	7.9	16.1	14.6	9.7	13.4	9.5	14.6	-	3.5	10.0	38.2	73.7
Item 2080 N(Wtd)	3455	1593	1726	2678	385	813	1029	1047	566	1908	1204	1213	835	416	924	35
B019C: ...during the last 30 days?																
1. 0 occasions	67.4	65.1	71.9	66.8	76.3	60.5	64.9	74.8	68.4	73.9	63.4	100.0	65.9	61.2	31.9	16.1
2. 1-2	10.9	11.1	10.7	11.2	9.9	13.4	10.3	9.0	12.0	10.4	11.7	-	21.1	18.7	12.5	11.9
3. 3-5	4.8	4.3	4.9	5.1	2.9	5.6	5.4	3.6	4.8	3.7	5.1	-	5.9	7.0	9.1	2.7
4. 6-9	4.3	4.7	3.8	4.4	2.1	5.0	4.6	4.2	3.2	3.8	5.1	-	3.8	6.1	9.2	2.2
5. 10-19	5.1	5.4	4.1	5.1	3.5	6.0	5.7	3.6	5.4	3.5	5.2	-	1.5	4.7	14.7	11.1
6. 20-39	3.6	4.0	2.8	3.5	3.3	4.9	4.2	2.2	2.9	2.5	4.7	-	1.1	1.3	11.1	12.9
7. 40 or more	3.9	5.4	1.8	3.9	2.1	4.6	4.9	2.6	3.3	2.3	4.8	-	.6	1.0	11.7	43.1
Item 2090 N(Wtd)	3450	1592	1722	2673	387	814	1027	1047	562	1904	1206	1213	832	415	922	35

QUESTIONNAIRE FORM 1 1981	TOTAL	SEX		RACE		REGION				4YR COLLEGE PLANS		ILLICIT DRUG USE: LIFETIME				
		M	F	White	Black	NE	NC	S	W	Yes	No	None	Mari-juana Only	Few Pills	More Pills	Any Her-oin
Weighted No. of Cases:	3644	1689	1795	2769	438	853	1075	1124	592	1969	1283	1213	853	430	958	37
% of Weighted Total:	100.0	46.3	49.3	76.0	12.0	23.4	29.5	30.8	16.3	54.0	35.2	33.3	23.4	11.8	26.3	1.0

IF YOU HAVE NOT USED MARIJUANA OR HASHISH IN THE LAST TWELVE MONTHS, GO TO Q.B028.

B020: When you used marijuana or hashish during the last year, how often did you use it in each of the following situations?

B020A: When you were alone

	TOTAL	M	F	White	Black	NE	NC	S	W	Yes	No	None	Mari-juana Only	Few Pills	More Pills	Any Her-oin
1. Not at all	63.0	56.0	73.3	65.1	56.9	61.7	59.9	66.4	66.0	69.4	59.9	-	84.8	71.9	47.9	7.5
2. A few of the times	23.2	25.8	19.6	22.4	24.3	24.8	24.7	21.5	20.6	18.2	27.2	-	12.3	18.5	31.7	32.6
3. Some of the times	10.5	14.0	5.7	9.9	14.7	11.0	10.8	9.2	11.2	10.4	9.7	-	1.6	8.3	16.5	27.6
4. Most of the times	2.3	3.3	1.2	2.3	2.9	1.4	3.3	2.4	1.7	1.6	2.4	-	1.3	1.3	3.2	6.3
5. Every time	.9	.9	.2	.3	1.2	1.2	1.3	.5	.6	.5	.8	-	-	-	.7	26.0
Item 2100 N(Wtd) ★	1615	785	734	1287	130	427	511	409	268	790	598	-	533	245	770	33

B020B: With just 1 or 2 other people

	TOTAL	M	F	White	Black	NE	NC	S	W	Yes	No	None	Mari-juana Only	Few Pills	More Pills	Any Her-oin
1. Not at all	5.9	5.3	7.2	6.0	7.1	4.4	4.2	10.3	4.7	5.9	6.9	-	10.8	7.2	2.0	-
2. A few of the times	32.0	30.2	34.7	31.3	38.3	31.7	34.1	29.6	32.2	33.7	32.3	-	44.1	41.9	21.3	9.5
3. Some of the times	19.6	19.8	18.0	18.9	19.4	24.2	18.3	15.1	21.7	17.4	19.7	-	13.0	22.0	23.1	26.4
4. Most of the times	33.3	35.3	31.6	34.8	25.5	33.7	32.7	34.5	32.2	33.5	33.5	-	22.1	24.7	44.1	34.6
5. Every time	9.1	9.5	8.6	8.9	9.7	6.0	10.6	10.5	9.2	9.4	7.6	-	10.0	4.2	9.4	29.5
Item 2110 N(Wtd) ★	1622	790	736	1289	135	429	511	412	270	797	597	-	535	244	772	34

B020C: At a party

	TOTAL	M	F	White	Black	NE	NC	S	W	Yes	No	None	Mari-juana Only	Few Pills	More Pills	Any Her-oin
1. Not at all	18.1	16.5	20.9	17.6	24.1	11.5	15.8	24.4	23.0	20.5	16.4	-	29.7	20.3	9.5	-
2. A few of the times	24.5	23.1	27.1	26.0	14.5	28.5	23.4	20.4	26.8	27.2	22.7	-	29.1	31.9	19.8	1.5
3. Some of the times	21.3	23.0	21.1	21.8	26.1	20.2	20.5	21.9	23.8	20.8	22.1	-	16.8	23.6	24.4	21.9
4. Most of the times	22.2	21.3	22.0	21.2	21.5	24.9	25.3	18.9	17.4	19.9	24.2	-	17.1	17.0	26.9	34.5
5. Every time	13.8	16.1	9.8	13.3	13.7	14.9	15.0	14.4	9.0	11.6	14.6	-	7.2	7.2	19.4	42.1
Item 2120 N(Wtd) ★	1610	785	730	1282	131	425	509	407	270	787	596	-	533	243	766	33

B020D: When your date or spouse was present

	TOTAL	M	F	White	Black	NE	NC	S	W	Yes	No	None	Mari-juana Only	Few Pills	More Pills	Any Her-oin
1. Not at all	42.3	49.3	36.2	41.3	51.5	42.6	39.9	43.2	45.3	49.4	36.5	-	60.1	51.1	27.6	20.9
2. A few of the times	22.6	22.2	23.9	24.3	19.9	23.4	19.7	21.8	28.1	22.5	23.0	-	22.2	23.4	23.9	6.4
3. Some of the times	16.5	14.8	16.7	15.8	15.4	19.9	18.4	13.4	12.4	14.6	17.2	-	7.6	10.3	23.2	38.8
4. Most of the times	12.9	9.8	16.1	13.0	10.2	9.2	15.4	15.0	10.9	9.2	16.9	-	6.1	11.3	18.2	18.8
5. Every time	5.6	4.0	7.1	5.7	3.0	4.9	6.6	6.7	3.3	4.3	6.4	-	4.0	3.8	7.1	15.2
Item 2130 N(Wtd) ★	1602	781	726	1272	132	419	506	410	267	788	590	-	528	243	763	34

B020E: When people over age 30 were present

	TOTAL	M	F	White	Black	NE	NC	S	W	Yes	No	None	Mari-juana Only	Few Pills	More Pills	Any Her-oin
1. Not at all	64.9	60.5	71.4	65.5	71.4	64.1	65.1	65.9	64.1	71.5	60.7	-	85.5	73.6	48.6	33.7
2. A few of the times	22.4	25.0	19.5	22.7	16.9	23.9	19.7	22.5	25.0	17.8	25.4	-	9.3	19.3	33.2	21.1
3. Some of the times	9.1	9.9	6.9	8.7	8.4	9.3	11.0	7.0	8.3	7.4	9.7	-	3.2	5.1	14.2	13.9
4. Most of the times	2.5	3.1	1.6	2.2	2.8	1.7	3.2	3.5	.9	2.0	3.4	-	1.1	2.0	3.0	20.1
5. Every time	1.1	1.5	.6	.9	.5	.9	.9	1.1	1.6	1.2	.8	-	.9	-	1.0	11.1
Item 2140 N(Wtd) ★	1618	789	732	1285	133	428	510	410	270	795	594	-	534	242	770	34

B020F: During the daytime (before 4:00 p.m.)

	TOTAL	M	F	White	Black	NE	NC	S	W	Yes	No	None	Mari-juana Only	Few Pills	More Pills	Any Her-oin
1. Not at all	36.0	33.0	40.5	35.7	48.8	31.1	37.0	40.4	35.5	43.2	31.1	-	58.1	43.7	18.8	2.3
2. A few of the times	26.6	26.0	29.3	27.5	21.2	25.0	26.6	28.4	26.3	24.5	30.4	-	27.5	34.6	24.5	9.9
3. Some of the times	23.7	25.9	19.7	23.7	18.7	29.8	21.4	21.5	21.8	22.6	21.8	-	10.1	17.9	34.9	30.1
4. Most of the times	10.6	11.9	8.3	10.4	7.6	11.5	10.6	7.6	13.6	7.3	13.6	-	3.1	2.5	17.6	29.0
5. Every time	3.1	3.3	2.2	2.7	3.8	2.7	4.4	2.1	2.9	2.4	3.1	-	1.1	1.3	4.1	28.7
Item 2150 N(Wtd) ★	1619	787	736	1285	135	429	508	413	269	795	595	-	532	244	772	34

★=excludes respondents for whom question was inappropriate.

QUESTIONNAIRE FORM 1 1981	TOTAL	SEX		RACE		REGION				4YR COLLEGE PLANS		ILLICIT DRUG USE: LIFETIME				
		M	F	White	Black	NE	NC	S	W	Yes	No	None	Mari-juana Only	Few Pills	More Pills	Any Her-oin
Weighted No. of Cases:	3644	1689	1795	2769	438	853	1075	1124	592	1969	1283	1213	853	430	958	37
% of Weighted Total:	100.0	46.3	49.3	76.0	12.0	23.4	29.5	30.8	16.3	54.0	35.2	33.3	23.4	11.8	26.3	1.0
B020G: At your home (or apartment or dorm)																
1. Not at all	51.3	48.4	57.1	52.2	54.5	47.3	50.8	59.5	45.9	54.9	50.3	-	73.5	60.1	34.3	5.2
2. A few of the times	21.6	20.7	22.5	22.1	18.1	23.8	19.4	21.4	22.6	19.8	24.0	-	16.4	21.5	26.0	18.5
3. Some of the times	14.9	16.9	11.2	14.3	16.2	15.9	15.0	12.7	16.6	13.8	14.5	-	6.6	11.4	21.2	28.5
4. Most of the times	9.5	10.7	8.2	9.3	8.2	10.2	11.2	4.8	12.4	9.5	8.0	-	3.3	6.2	14.3	22.5
5. Every time	2.7	3.3	1.1	2.1	3.0	2.8	3.7	1.7	2.4	2.0	3.1	-	.2	.8	4.1	25.4
Item 2160 N(Wtd) ★	1617	786	734	1284	133	427	509	411	269	793	595	-	531	245	769	34
B020H: At school																
1. Not at all	61.3	59.1	66.2	63.6	59.4	55.6	62.8	68.7	56.5	69.7	55.9	-	79.0	69.3	48.2	16.9
2. A few of the times	18.5	18.2	18.4	17.3	19.4	20.0	17.0	17.3	20.8	16.5	20.3	-	14.9	19.9	20.5	22.7
3. Some of the times	11.6	12.9	8.9	11.1	10.2	13.1	12.1	9.5	11.5	8.1	12.2	-	4.2	7.3	17.4	29.4
4. Most of the times	6.4	6.9	5.5	6.2	8.9	7.8	6.0	3.7	9.4	4.2	9.3	-	1.3	2.2	10.9	20.5
5. Every time	2.1	3.0	1.0	1.9	2.1	3.4	2.1	.9	1.8	1.5	2.4	-	.5	1.2	3.0	10.5
Item 2170 N(Wtd) ★	1617	789	732	1282	135	427	507	414	269	793	596	-	532	245	769	34
B020I: In a car																
1. Not at all	18.6	18.4	19.6	18.8	21.2	18.8	15.8	17.9	25.0	23.0	16.1	-	30.7	17.5	10.0	-
2. A few of the times	24.4	22.4	28.0	24.9	21.2	23.2	26.9	22.2	24.7	25.8	23.1	-	32.5	33.2	17.3	11.3
3. Some of the times	26.4	27.3	25.2	26.6	30.6	30.9	24.8	24.0	26.0	23.0	28.3	-	17.8	30.0	31.6	19.6
4. Most of the times	24.1	24.5	22.8	23.5	22.4	21.6	25.3	28.5	18.7	23.0	25.7	-	15.8	17.0	32.5	25.1
5. Every time	6.5	7.4	4.4	6.3	4.6	5.5	7.1	7.4	5.6	5.3	6.8	-	3.3	2.3	8.6	44.0
Item 2190 N(Wtd) ★	1616	788	734	1283	135	427	510	413	266	793	596	-	532	245	768	34
B021: How many of the times when you used marijuana or hashish during the last year did you use it along with alcohol--that is, so that their effects overlapped?																
1. Not at all	26.3	22.5	32.0	23.9	52.0	20.2	21.6	36.4	29.4	27.9	27.2	-	40.3	33.5	14.4	-
2. A few of the times	28.3	27.5	30.2	30.3	20.8	30.4	29.3	25.6	27.3	28.3	28.1	-	32.9	34.2	24.1	12.8
3. Some of the times	22.6	25.6	18.1	23.1	13.8	25.2	23.6	16.4	26.2	21.5	21.8	-	9.5	21.9	32.1	27.7
4. Most of the times	16.7	17.1	15.5	17.0	10.7	18.5	18.9	14.1	13.8	15.8	17.4	-	11.8	7.3	22.1	51.1
5. Every time	6.0	7.4	4.2	5.7	2.8	5.7	6.5	7.5	3.3	6.6	5.5	-	5.4	3.2	7.4	8.4
Item 2200 N(Wtd) ★	1604	785	726	1280	130	421	507	411	265	787	597	-	528	239	765	34
B022: What have been the most important reasons for your using marijuana or hashish? (Mark all that apply.)																
A. To experiment--to see what it's like	61.2	57.9	65.0	60.2	63.2	62.2	57.8	64.8	60.5	65.7	56.3	-	71.9	66.2	52.6	45.2
B. To relax or relieve tension	44.6	45.3	42.3	46.0	25.1	49.6	44.1	38.6	46.7	40.9	47.1	-	24.6	40.7	58.7	72.7
C. To feel good or get high	80.0	79.7	79.8	80.6	68.9	83.4	80.7	78.7	75.6	78.1	81.8	-	68.6	76.2	88.5	98.0
D. To seek deeper insights and understanding	14.1	14.6	12.0	14.0	6.5	16.7	12.2	12.4	16.2	14.5	13.2	-	6.7	13.0	18.5	44.8
E. To have a good time with my friends	66.8	65.9	68.5	68.4	61.1	71.0	68.7	61.6	64.5	65.7	69.1	-	60.5	63.4	72.2	72.6
F. To fit in with a group I like	14.3	15.9	13.0	14.0	11.0	13.8	15.3	16.0	10.6	15.7	14.4	-	17.6	14.5	12.0	15.8
G. To get away from my problems or troubles	17.7	16.1	18.5	17.6	10.9	16.9	20.3	16.2	16.4	15.1	21.5	-	11.0	13.9	22.9	32.1
H. Because of boredom, nothing else to do	26.2	26.6	25.6	25.7	29.9	32.5	24.3	24.5	22.7	24.0	27.1	-	18.6	18.6	33.6	45.1
I. Because of anger or frustration	15.0	12.0	17.3	14.1	11.6	14.2	16.0	16.3	12.4	12.0	18.0	-	8.7	12.3	20.0	14.3
J. To get through the day	7.1	7.7	5.5	7.3	4.4	7.4	7.5	6.3	7.1	5.6	8.7	-	2.0	2.7	10.3	41.0
K. To increase the effects of some other drug(s)	13.9	16.0	10.0	14.1	3.6	18.7	14.0	10.1	12.1	12.7	12.2	-	4.6	5.0	21.6	57.7
L. To decrease (offset) the effects of some other drug(s)	2.1	2.6	1.1	1.9	1.9	2.5	1.3	1.9	3.0	1.6	2.3	-	.4	.7	3.1	12.2
M. Because I am "hooked"--I have to have it	2.3	3.7	.7	2.3	1.8	2.8	2.6	1.3	2.6	1.5	2.9	-	.4	.4	3.3	20.9
Item 2210-2330 N(Wtd) ★	1607	783	729	1283	130	424	507	406	270	789	593	-	531	243	770	34

★=excludes respondents for whom question was inappropriate.

QUESTIONNAIRE FORM 1 1981	TOTAL	SEX		RACE		REGION				4YR COLLEGE PLANS		ILLICIT DRUG USE: LIFETIME				
		M	F	White	Black	NE	NC	S	W	Yes	No	None	Mari- juana Only	Few Pills	More Pills	Any Her- oin
Weighted No. of Cases:	3644	1689	1795	2769	438	853	1075	1124	592	1969	1283	1213	853	430	958	37
% of Weighted Total:	100.0	46.3	49.3	76.0	12.0	23.4	29.5	30.8	16.3	54.0	35.2	33.3	23.4	11.8	26.3	1.0
B023: When you use marijuana or hashish how high do you usually get?																
1. Not at all high	4.9	4.2	6.1	4.5	10.7	4.2	4.6	7.6	2.1	6.8	2.9	-	11.5	1.8	1.3	-
2. A little high	29.0	25.8	34.1	28.9	33.2	29.9	26.8	30.1	30.1	29.8	29.1	-	43.8	36.5	17.5	2.1
3. Moderately high	45.7	48.3	42.2	45.2	46.5	45.8	45.3	45.9	45.9	45.9	44.3	-	34.7	48.1	51.5	63.9
4. Very high	20.4	21.6	17.5	21.4	9.6	20.0	23.3	16.4	21.8	17.4	23.6	-	10.0	13.6	29.7	34.1
Item 2340 N(Wtd) ★	1607	783	729	1281	132	426	511	404	266	790	592	-	534	243	764	33
B024: When you use marijuana or hashish, how long do you usually stay high?																
1. Usually don't get high	7.6	6.7	9.0	7.1	15.7	5.8	6.6	12.1	5.9	9.7	5.6	-	17.7	1.9	2.1	-
2. One to two hours	52.5	50.1	56.9	54.1	43.1	56.3	50.0	52.0	51.7	50.6	53.5	-	54.8	65.4	48.5	22.1
3. Three to six hours	35.7	37.8	31.9	35.1	35.7	35.2	39.0	29.5	39.8	36.5	36.0	-	25.6	31.5	43.5	54.8
4. Seven to 24 hours	4.0	5.2	2.1	3.5	5.5	2.7	4.3	6.4	1.7	3.1	4.7	-	1.7	1.1	5.7	23.1
5. More than 24 hours	.2	.3	-	.2	-	-	.1	-	.9	.1	.3	-	.2	-	.2	-
Item 2350 N(Wtd) ★	1607	786	726	1280	131	427	509	404	267	788	592	-	529	242	767	34
B025: During the LAST MONTH, about how many marijuana cigarettes (joints, reefers), or the equivalent, did you smoke a day, on the average? (If you shared them with other people, count only the amount YOU smoked.)																
1. None	37.6	35.8	42.3	39.4	30.0	32.4	36.4	42.2	41.3	45.2	32.6	-	58.3	44.1	22.8	11.4
2. Less than 1 a day	36.5	34.8	38.8	37.6	25.9	41.8	33.5	32.7	39.8	38.7	35.2	-	34.0	41.9	38.1	20.4
3. 1 a day	8.0	8.6	7.3	7.5	13.8	7.4	8.7	8.4	6.7	5.4	9.9	-	3.6	5.3	11.6	7.1
4. 2 - 3 a day	11.2	13.2	7.8	10.2	18.8	11.3	13.6	10.7	6.8	7.0	15.0	-	3.0	7.3	16.7	25.6
5. 4 - 6 a day	3.9	4.0	3.1	3.4	6.8	4.5	3.8	4.0	2.7	2.6	4.3	-	.7	1.3	6.8	3.3
6. 7 - 10 a day	1.6	2.3	.1	1.1	1.9	2.2	1.7	1.5	.8	.5	1.8	-	-	-	2.3	19.0
7. 11 or more a day	1.2	1.5	.6	.8	2.9	.4	2.2	.5	1.8	.7	1.2	-	.4	.2	1.6	13.1
Item 2360 N(Wtd) ★	1537	752	694	1235	116	410	493	385	250	750	570	-	491	227	749	34
B026: Do you know how much marijuana you have used (in ounces) during the LAST MONTH?																
8. Don't know	16.6	12.1	21.8	16.0	24.7	13.9	17.8	18.2	15.9	12.8	21.7	-	19.0	15.7	15.2	7.7
1. None	34.6	33.6	38.0	35.7	34.2	29.1	35.1	39.5	34.9	41.3	30.9	-	52.1	42.5	21.7	11.4
2. Less than 1/2 ounce	23.8	23.7	23.3	24.3	17.5	28.2	19.3	20.7	30.2	26.4	19.3	-	21.3	28.8	24.7	6.3
3. About 1/2 ounce	8.7	11.4	5.8	8.1	9.7	11.1	9.2	6.7	6.9	8.2	9.2	-	4.0	6.5	12.4	12.1
4. About 1 ounce	6.7	7.5	5.9	7.0	5.6	7.1	7.0	6.2	5.9	4.3	9.7	-	2.0	2.6	10.7	17.4
5. About 2 ounces	6.1	7.1	3.3	5.3	6.9	6.3	7.3	5.6	4.4	4.8	5.2	-	1.0	3.7	9.9	17.0
6. 3 to 5 ounces	3.1	3.6	2.0	3.1	.7	3.7	3.6	2.8	1.7	2.0	3.5	-	.4	.2	4.7	24.8
7. 6 or more ounces	.5	.9	-	.5	.6	.6	.7	.3	.2	.2	.6	-	.2	-	.7	3.3
Item 2370 N(Wtd) ★	1529	746	691	1229	114	405	494	383	247	746	569	-	488	227	743	34
B027: Have you ever tried to stop using marijuana or hashish and found that you couldn't stop?																
1. Yes	5.7	6.7	4.4	4.8	9.3	4.7	5.0	6.8	7.0	4.1	7.4	-	2.1	2.6	8.5	8.7
2. No	94.3	93.3	95.6	95.2	90.7	95.3	95.0	93.2	93.0	95.9	92.6	-	97.9	97.4	91.5	91.3
Item 2380 N(Wtd) ★	1586	773	723	1269	127	415	505	405	261	777	591	-	521	242	759	34
B028: Do you think you will be using marijuana or hashish five years from now?																
1. I definitely will	3.3	4.2	1.7	2.9	3.7	3.7	4.4	2.0	3.1	2.4	3.8	.2	1.6	2.7	8.2	26.9
2. I probably will	16.4	17.4	14.2	16.8	11.6	19.3	17.8	13.1	15.7	13.7	18.3	.5	15.4	14.9	37.2	38.2
3. I probably will not	24.5	24.9	24.5	25.2	21.5	29.4	24.2	20.7	25.7	24.4	23.6	10.2	34.4	32.1	30.6	19.2
4. I definitely will not	55.8	53.5	59.6	55.0	63.1	47.6	53.6	64.3	55.5	59.6	54.2	89.0	48.6	50.2	24.0	15.6
Item 2390 N(Wtd)	3536	1651	1745	2703	426	819	1050	1093	574	1932	1240	1182	827	421	943	37

★=excludes respondents for whom question was inappropriate.

QUESTIONNAIRE FORM 1 1981	TOTAL	SEX		RACE		REGION				4YR COLLEGE PLANS		ILLICIT DRUG USE: LIFETIME				
		M	F	White	Black	NE	NC	S	W	Yes	No	None	Mari- juana Only	Few Pills	More Pills	Any Her- oin
Weighted No. of Cases:	3644	1689	1795	2769	438	853	1075	1124	592	1969	1283	1213	853	430	958	37
% of Weighted Total:	100.0	46.3	49.3	76.0	12.0	23.4	29.5	30.8	16.3	54.0	35.2	33.3	23.4	11.8	26.3	1.0

The next questions are about LSD, the psychedelic drug which is sometimes called "acid".

B029: On how many occasions (if any) have you taken LSD...

B029A: ...in your lifetime?

	TOTAL	M	F	White	Black	NE	NC	S	W	Yes	No	None	Mari-juana Only	Few Pills	More Pills	Any Heroin
1. 0 occasions	90.5	89.8	92.9	89.8	99.8	87.3	88.8	95.3	89.4	93.2	89.9	100.0	100.0	96.4	68.8	23.5
2. 1-2	4.2	4.2	3.7	4.7	.2	6.0	4.0	2.3	5.4	3.4	4.3	-	-	3.6	13.3	20.1
3. 3-5	1.7	2.1	1.1	1.9	-	2.4	2.1	.7	1.9	1.4	1.7	-	-	-	6.0	9.6
4. 6-9	1.1	1.3	.8	1.3	-	1.6	1.1	.7	1.4	.5	1.3	-	-	-	3.9	11.3
5. 10-19	1.2	1.1	.9	1.1	-	1.4	1.9	.4	1.0	1.0	.9	-	-	-	3.8	14.0
6. 20-39	.6	.5	.6	.6	-	.4	1.3	.1	.3	.2	1.0	-	-	-	2.0	2.6
7. 40 or more	.8	1.0	.1	.6	-	1.0	.8	.6	.6	.4	.9	-	-	-	2.2	19.0
Item 890 N(Wtd)	3489	1625	1736	2693	404	822	1033	1062	573	1931	1211	1197	846	420	937	31

B029B: ...during the last 12 months?

	TOTAL	M	F	White	Black	NE	NC	S	W	Yes	No	None	Mari-juana Only	Few Pills	More Pills	Any Heroin
1. 0 occasions	93.2	93.2	94.8	92.9	100.0	89.8	91.3	97.0	94.5	95.6	92.5	100.0	100.0	98.2	77.8	33.9
2. 1-2	3.6	3.4	2.9	3.8	-	5.7	4.2	1.7	3.0	2.5	3.7	-	-	1.8	11.8	22.0
3. 3-5	1.2	1.1	1.1	1.3	-	1.8	1.4	.4	1.3	.8	1.5	-	-	-	4.1	10.2
4. 6-9	.8	.8	.6	.9	-	.7	1.1	.5	.8	.7	.5	-	-	-	2.3	18.7
5. 10-19	.9	1.1	.7	.9	-	1.2	1.7	.3	.3	.4	1.5	-	-	-	3.2	10.7
6. 20-39	.2	.2	-	.1	-	.3	.2	.1	.1	*	.2	-	-	-	.6	2.9
7. 40 or more	.1	.2	-	.1	-	.4	-	-	-	.1	.1	-	-	-	.3	1.5
Item 900 N(Wtd)	3487	1625	1735	2692	404	824	1034	1061	568	1928	1212	1197	846	421	934	32

B029C: ...during the last 30 days?

	TOTAL	M	F	White	Black	NE	NC	S	W	Yes	No	None	Mari-juana Only	Few Pills	More Pills	Any Heroin
1. 0 occasions	97.2	96.8	98.3	97.3	100.0	94.7	96.6	98.8	99.2	98.0	97.3	100.0	100.0	99.7	90.8	68.9
2. 1-2	2.0	2.1	1.3	2.0	-	4.5	2.5	.4	.4	1.7	1.6	-	-	.3	6.9	15.9
3. 3-5	.5	.6	.3	.6	-	.4	.7	.6	.2	.2	.7	-	-	-	1.5	9.6
4. 6-9	.1	.3	-	.1	-	.2	.1	.1	.1	.1	.1	-	-	-	.4	2.6
5. 10-19	*	.1	-	.1	-	.1	.1	-	-	-	.1	-	-	-	.1	3.0
6. 20-39	*	-	-	-	-	-	-	.1	-	-	-	-	-	-	.1	-
7. 40 or more	.1	.2	-	*	-	.2	.1	-	-	.1	.1	-	-	-	.3	-
Item 910 N(Wtd)	3486	1625	1734	2692	404	822	1036	1060	568	1929	1211	1197	847	421	933	31

IF YOU HAVE NOT TAKEN LSD IN THE LAST TWELVE MONTHS, GO TO Q.B037.

B030: When you used LSD during the last year, how often did you use it in each of the following situations?

B030A: When you were alone

	TOTAL	M	F	White	Black	NE	NC	S	W	Yes	No	None	Mari-juana Only	Few Pills	More Pills	Any Heroin
1. Not at all	82.9	73.2	94.0	83.7	37.8	85.4	80.4	84.0	82.7	87.3	83.5	-	-	100.0	85.4	48.7
2. A few of the times	11.9	18.4	3.5	10.8	-	11.1	13.0	11.3	11.1	10.8	10.3	-	-	-	9.6	40.5
3. Some of the times	3.4	4.5	2.5	3.6	-	1.5	4.4	4.7	3.7	.4	4.5	-	-	-	3.6	3.7
4. Most of the times	1.8	3.8	-	1.9	62.2	2.0	2.2	-	2.5	1.5	1.7	-	-	-	1.4	7.1
5. Every time	-	-	-	-	-	-	-	-	-	-	-	-	-	-	-	-
Item 2400 N(Wtd) ★	241	116	91	196	1	80	93	36	32	88	93	-	-	8	206	22

B030B: With just 1 or 2 other people

	TOTAL	M	F	White	Black	NE	NC	S	W	Yes	No	None	Mari-juana Only	Few Pills	More Pills	Any Heroin
1. Not at all	15.8	20.1	10.3	15.7	-	16.7	11.1	21.8	21.1	14.8	15.2	-	-	41.5	14.6	8.1
2. A few of the times	43.9	35.7	56.1	44.5	37.8	43.4	44.3	49.5	37.8	38.2	56.0	-	-	50.9	44.7	37.5
3. Some of the times	11.4	12.1	8.2	11.0	-	13.3	9.8	12.6	9.8	10.0	10.2	-	-	-	12.1	10.2
4. Most of the times	16.6	21.9	9.0	15.5	62.2	9.7	27.0	8.8	12.1	17.7	11.4	-	-	-	15.5	35.2
5. Every time	12.3	10.2	16.4	13.4	-	16.9	7.8	7.3	19.2	19.3	7.5	-	-	7.6	13.0	9.0
Item 2410 N(Wtd) ★	240	113	93	194	1	80	92	34	33	87	93	-	-	8	207	22

* = less than .05 per cent.   ★ = excludes respondents for whom question was inappropriate.

QUESTIONNAIRE FORM 1 1981	TOTAL	SEX		RACE		REGION				4YR COLLEGE PLANS		ILLICIT DRUG USE: LIFETIME				
		M	F	White	Black	NE	NC	S	W	Yes	No	None	Marijuana Only	Few Pills	More Pills	Any Heroin
Weighted No. of Cases:	3644	1689	1795	2769	438	853	1075	1124	592	1969	1283	1213	853	430	958	37
% of Weighted Total:	100.0	46.3	49.3	76.0	12.0	23.4	29.5	30.8	16.3	54.0	35.2	33.3	23.4	11.8	26.3	1.0
B030C: At a party																
1. Not at all	29.5	24.7	39.1	31.8	-	30.4	20.8	29.9	50.8	32.3	27.2	-	-	39.2	28.8	24.7
2. A few of the times	27.7	25.6	29.1	26.7	100.0	32.0	28.0	20.2	24.3	30.4	25.0	-	-	60.8	28.5	12.2
3. Some of the times	18.8	20.1	15.1	18.3	-	10.3	26.3	28.2	9.0	13.1	24.1	-	-	-	20.0	15.7
4. Most of the times	13.7	19.0	7.3	13.0	-	21.6	11.9	5.2	8.6	10.2	14.8	-	-	-	13.9	18.3
5. Every time	10.3	10.7	9.5	10.2	-	5.7	13.0	16.5	7.3	14.0	9.0	-	-	-	8.8	29.1
Item 2420 N(Wtd) ★	238	112	92	193	1	80	90	35	32	87	91	-	-	6	208	21
B030D: When your date or spouse was present																
1. Not at all	58.3	65.9	43.0	56.7	-	63.7	58.8	42.2	60.4	60.0	54.7	-	-	77.6	58.9	41.0
2. A few of the times	21.0	18.6	26.9	23.1	-	18.2	23.2	26.1	16.3	20.9	23.6	-	-	22.4	21.3	20.3
3. Some of the times	7.4	6.0	9.6	6.9	100.0	1.7	8.0	12.6	14.2	5.6	8.4	-	-	-	6.3	19.5
4. Most of the times	6.7	6.2	9.7	6.9	-	8.5	5.6	11.4	-	6.0	8.7	-	-	-	7.5	2.3
5. Every time	6.7	3.3	10.8	6.4	-	8.0	4.4	7.6	9.0	7.5	4.5	-	-	-	6.0	17.0
Item 2430 N(Wtd) ★	239	113	92	194	1	80	92	34	32	87	93	-	-	8	206	22
B030E: When people over age 30 were present																
1. Not at all	67.5	63.8	76.9	71.1	37.8	74.6	63.7	61.1	67.0	72.1	64.2	-	-	100.0	67.1	55.6
2. A few of the times	16.4	17.9	13.5	14.1	-	14.9	21.8	7.2	14.6	13.8	19.2	-	-	-	17.2	15.9
3. Some of the times	13.1	13.1	9.2	11.5	-	9.0	12.2	27.1	10.9	8.5	15.3	-	-	-	13.4	16.6
4. Most of the times	2.1	3.6	-	2.3	62.2	1.5	2.2	3.3	2.2	4.2	.8	-	-	-	1.2	11.9
5. Every time	.9	1.6	.4	1.1	-	-	-	1.2	5.2	1.5	.5	-	-	-	1.0	-
Item 2440 N(Wtd) ★	238	112	92	193	1	80	91	34	32	88	91	-	-	6	206	22
B030F: During the daytime (before 4:00 p.m.)																
1. Not at all	51.9	47.4	60.7	54.9	-	60.3	47.1	60.1	36.1	56.2	47.7	-	-	92.0	51.0	37.4
2. A few of the times	24.8	26.6	19.7	22.8	-	24.2	28.2	19.3	23.0	20.4	29.2	-	-	-	27.8	7.9
3. Some of the times	13.6	15.4	9.3	12.8	-	10.2	17.9	10.5	12.7	13.2	12.1	-	-	-	14.1	15.8
4. Most of the times	5.9	6.9	6.3	4.9	100.0	3.3	4.8	6.9	14.5	3.4	8.6	-	-	-	4.3	25.2
5. Every time	3.8	3.7	4.1	4.6	-	2.0	1.9	3.3	13.8	6.8	2.5	-	-	8.0	2.8	13.8
Item 2450 N(Wtd) ★	238	113	91	193	1	79	92	35	32	86	93	-	-	8	207	19
B030G: At your home (or apartment or dorm)																
1. Not at all	53.5	52.9	53.8	54.6	-	50.4	54.5	65.5	45.1	51.2	56.5	-	-	100.0	52.2	43.9
2. A few of the times	23.8	20.5	29.5	24.6	-	31.5	25.5	5.0	19.6	27.0	20.9	-	-	-	26.1	13.9
3. Some of the times	13.0	17.2	5.4	10.1	62.2	14.1	11.8	17.4	8.7	7.5	17.8	-	-	-	14.4	5.6
4. Most of the times	6.1	8.6	4.0	6.4	-	2.5	7.6	7.5	9.8	8.2	3.0	-	-	-	4.7	23.3
5. Every time	3.7	.8	7.3	4.3	37.8	1.5	.5	4.6	16.9	6.1	1.8	-	-	-	2.6	13.3
Item 2460 N(Wtd) ★	239	113	92	194	1	80	92	34	32	87	93	-	-	8	207	22
B030H: At school																
1. Not at all	66.7	56.5	76.0	68.2	-	70.4	60.9	70.0	70.8	79.5	56.8	-	-	92.0	68.1	41.4
2. A few of the times	18.7	20.5	18.5	19.0	-	16.8	24.5	13.6	12.1	10.3	24.5	-	-	-	19.4	20.6
3. Some of the times	8.9	14.0	1.9	7.3	62.2	6.7	8.9	9.6	13.9	4.5	10.3	-	-	-	7.5	27.0
4. Most of the times	5.2	8.0	3.6	5.0	37.8	6.1	5.7	5.1	1.4	4.3	8.4	-	-	-	4.9	8.3
5. Every time	.5	1.1	-	.6	-	-	-	1.7	1.9	1.4	-	-	-	8.0	-	2.7
Item 2470 N(Wtd) ★	240	114	92	195	1	80	92	35	32	87	93	-	-	8	208	22
B030I: In a car																
1. Not at all	57.0	54.4	64.5	61.9	-	67.6	51.4	40.7	64.3	65.1	50.8	-	-	92.0	56.4	44.9
2. A few of the times	25.6	25.4	25.8	24.0	-	20.1	28.8	33.6	21.6	22.5	29.8	-	-	-	28.0	17.1
3. Some of the times	11.5	12.2	7.2	9.1	37.8	10.3	12.3	15.7	7.5	6.2	15.4	-	-	-	11.6	14.4
4. Most of the times	4.4	6.8	2.5	4.1	62.2	2.0	5.5	6.8	4.7	4.1	3.2	-	-	-	3.2	18.3
5. Every time	1.5	1.1	-	.9	-	-	2.1	3.3	1.9	2.0	.7	-	-	8.0	.9	5.3
Item 2490 N(Wtd) ★	240	114	92	195	1	80	92	35	32	88	93	-	-	8	207	22

★=excludes respondents for whom question was inappropriate.

QUESTIONNAIRE FORM 1 1981	TOTAL	M	F	White	Black	NE	NC	S	W	Yes	No	None	Mari- juana Only	Few Pills	More Pills	Any Her- oin
		SEX		RACE		REGION				4YR COLLEGE PLANS		ILLICIT DRUG USE: LIFETIME				
Weighted No. of Cases:	3644	1689	1795	2769	438	853	1075	1124	592	1969	1283	1213	853	430	958	37
% of Weighted Total:	100.0	46.3	49.3	76.0	12.0	23.4	29.5	30.8	16.3	54.0	35.2	33.3	23.4	11.8	26.3	1.0

B031: How many of the times when you used LSD during the last year did you use it along with each of the following drugs--that is, so that their effects overlapped?

B031A: With alcohol

	TOTAL	M	F	White	Black	NE	NC	S	W	Yes	No	None	Mari Only	Few Pills	More Pills	Heroin
1. Not at all	29.0	30.6	27.7	30.3	-	24.1	29.6	24.9	43.5	29.0	26.8	-	-	67.6	28.5	22.0
2. A few of the times	22.7	19.4	27.1	23.0	-	31.3	15.0	11.3	34.1	19.0	25.0	-	-	32.4	22.2	24.1
3. Some of the times	12.9	18.9	6.8	14.3	-	15.0	13.4	13.6	5.6	16.4	13.0	-	-	-	14.1	5.5
4. Most of the times	14.3	13.2	16.9	12.8	-	7.6	17.1	27.1	10.6	13.2	14.2	-	-	-	13.0	32.1
5. Every time	21.1	18.0	21.6	19.7	-	22.0	24.9	23.0	6.2	22.5	21.0	-	-	-	22.2	16.4
Item 2500 N(Wtd) ★	234	108	92	190	-	80	90	32	32	87	88	-	-	6	207	21

B031B: With marijuana

	TOTAL	M	F	White	Black	NE	NC	S	W	Yes	No	None	Mari Only	Few Pills	More Pills	Heroin
1. Not at all	23.5	16.3	32.7	24.0	-	25.5	18.0	9.8	47.5	33.8	13.6	-	-	88.6	23.6	3.3
2. A few of the times	21.4	21.1	16.6	19.7	-	25.8	18.8	17.8	21.6	13.0	21.2	-	-	11.4	20.6	31.6
3. Some of the times	11.1	15.6	7.7	11.6	-	12.8	7.2	24.5	4.3	6.7	15.0	-	-	-	12.6	-
4. Most of the times	20.6	20.6	21.1	20.9	-	16.3	26.5	23.7	11.9	22.0	23.2	-	-	-	19.9	33.6
5. Every time	23.4	26.4	21.8	23.7	100.0	19.7	29.5	24.1	14.7	24.6	27.0	-	-	-	23.3	31.5
Item 2510 N(Wtd) ★	235	109	92	190	1	80	91	32	32	87	88	-	-	6	207	22

B032: What have been the most important reasons for your taking LSD? (Mark all that apply.)

	TOTAL	M	F	White	Black	NE	NC	S	W	Yes	No	None	Mari Only	Few Pills	More Pills	Heroin
A. To experiment--to see what it's like	82.8	76.1	89.6	82.7	-	90.5	77.8	81.3	78.8	84.1	82.0	-	-	100.0	84.1	66.4
B. To relax or relieve tension	9.8	15.5	4.9	10.9	-	13.6	9.9	6.2	3.8	7.6	11.4	-	-	-	9.6	13.9
C. To feel good or get high	62.5	69.5	56.8	63.2	-	57.4	66.5	69.5	58.1	56.9	71.7	-	-	46.4	60.6	84.2
D. To seek deeper insights and understanding	32.8	40.3	21.4	33.3	-	31.5	30.4	29.8	44.6	34.6	30.1	-	-	12.2	30.3	60.6
E. To have a good time with my friends	51.4	56.1	46.2	49.8	-	53.9	49.7	49.4	51.7	51.0	51.1	-	-	52.6	51.7	
F. To fit in with a group I like	3.3	6.6	-	3.4	100.0	3.0	4.4	4.9	-	2.8	1.8	-	-	-	2.8	8.9
G. To get away from my problems or troubles	12.3	12.5	12.3	12.1	-	14.7	15.7	2.6	6.6	13.3	9.0	-	-	-	12.2	15.4
H. Because of boredom, nothing else to do	18.2	20.6	13.9	16.5	-	24.9	17.2	16.0	6.6	15.3	19.5	-	-	-	18.3	21.6
I. Because of anger or frustration	5.8	5.3	7.7	5.7	-	6.6	7.8	3.1	1.2	9.2	3.9	-	-	-	6.1	4.5
J. To get through the day	4.3	6.1	2.9	4.4	-	2.3	7.2	5.7	-	4.3	4.2	-	-	-	3.3	14.1
K. To increase the effects of some other drug(s)	11.2	18.0	4.6	12.0	-	8.6	14.5	10.8	9.0	11.0	12.2	-	-	-	10.3	21.8
L. To decrease (offset) the effects of some other drug(s)	1.2	2.2	.4	1.5	-	-	1.4	-	4.6	1.8	-	-	-	-	1.3	-
M. Because I am "hooked"--I have to have it	1.4	3.0	-	1.7	-	-	3.0	1.9	-	2.2	1.5	-	-	-	.6	8.5
Item 2520-2640 N(Wtd) ★	231	107	91	188	1	80	87	31	33	85	88	-	-	5	204	22

B033: When you take LSD how high do you usually get?

	TOTAL	M	F	White	Black	NE	NC	S	W	Yes	No	None	Mari Only	Few Pills	More Pills	Heroin
1. Not at all high	1.6	2.6	-	1.3	37.8	-	2.2	4.4	1.3	1.4	1.8	-	-	20.1	.3	-
2. A little high	9.6	9.2	10.6	9.7	62.2	11.9	8.5	8.4	8.3	11.0	9.2	-	-	29.0	10.7	3.3
3. Moderately high	23.3	20.5	27.7	22.5	-	19.8	28.3	16.2	24.6	23.9	22.6	-	-	29.0	24.9	8.1
4. Very high	65.5	67.7	61.8	66.5	-	68.3	61.0	70.9	65.8	63.8	66.3	-	-	50.9	64.1	88.6
Item 2650 N(Wtd) ★	236	110	93	192	1	78	92	32	34	88	89	-	-	8	205	22

B034: When you take LSD how long do you usually stay high?

	TOTAL	M	F	White	Black	NE	NC	S	W	Yes	No	None	Mari Only	Few Pills	More Pills	Heroin
1. Usually don't get high	1.6	1.6	1.5	1.4	37.8	1.8	1.4	1.9	1.3	3.1	-	-	-	-	1.6	-
2. One to two hours	5.4	.5	12.4	5.4	-	5.7	5.5	8.6	1.1	5.6	6.5	-	-	21.9	5.4	-
3. Three to six hours	35.5	39.3	27.8	33.5	62.2	33.6	37.9	39.9	29.9	35.3	25.1	-	-	35.9	37.5	17.7
4. Seven to 24 hours	54.6	56.3	53.8	56.4	-	54.7	52.4	49.5	65.3	49.1	67.6	-	-	42.2	53.1	74.2
5. More than 24 hours	2.9	2.4	4.5	3.3	-	4.3	2.8	-	2.4	6.9	.9	-	-	-	2.4	8.1
Item 2660 N(Wtd) ★	236	110	93	191	1	80	90	31	34	87	89	-	-	6	207	22

★=excludes respondents for whom question was inappropriate.

QUESTIONNAIRE FORM 1 1981	TOTAL	SEX		RACE		REGION				4YR COLLEGE PLANS		ILLICIT DRUG USE: LIFETIME				
		M	F	White	Black	NE	NC	S	W	Yes	No	None	Mari-juana Only	Few Pills	More Pills	Any Her-oin
Weighted No. of Cases:	3644	1689	1795	2769	438	853	1075	1124	592	1969	1283	1213	853	430	958	37
% of Weighted Total:	100.0	46.3	49.3	76.0	12.0	23.4	29.5	30.8	16.3	54.0	35.2	33.3	23.4	11.8	26.3	1.0
B035: Have you ever had a "bad trip" on LSD?																
1. No	75.7	75.6	72.3	75.6	37.8	80.8	72.3	64.1	83.5	79.2	68.9	-	-	75.7	76.9	63.3
2. Yes, once	20.2	21.4	23.5	21.2	-	19.2	23.2	27.8	7.0	15.4	30.3	-	-	24.3	19.7	24.4
3. Yes, more than once	4.1	3.0	4.2	3.3	62.2	-	4.5	8.1	9.5	5.4	.9	-	-	-	3.5	12.3
Item 2670 N(Wtd) ★	239	112	93	193	1	81	93	31	33	88	91	-	-	8	208	22
B036: Have you ever tried to stop using LSD and found that you couldn't stop?																
1. Yes	3.0	3.3	1.9	2.6	-	1.0	4.6	6.4	-	2.7	3.4	-	-	-	2.3	10.8
2. No	97.0	96.7	98.1	97.4	100.0	99.0	95.4	93.6	99.9	97.3	96.6	-	-	100.0	97.7	89.2
Item 2680 N(Wtd) ★	236	110	93	192	1	80	92	31	33	88	89	-	-	6	208	22
B037: Do you think you will be using LSD five years from now?																
1. I definitely will	1.0	1.1	.8	.9	1.8	.8	1.3	1.2	.5	.8	1.3	.4	.9	.8	1.6	7.2
2. I probably will	1.5	1.3	1.3	1.4	-	1.6	2.2	.8	1.6	1.2	1.7	-	-	1.5	4.8	9.3
3. I probably will not	9.4	10.7	7.5	9.7	5.1	12.6	9.1	7.4	9.2	8.2	9.7	2.5	5.7	8.0	21.5	43.5
4. I definitely will not	88.1	86.9	90.4	88.0	93.2	85.0	87.4	90.7	88.7	89.8	87.3	97.1	93.3	89.8	72.1	40.1
Item 2690 N(Wtd)	3382	1554	1701	2579	411	771	1006	1048	557	1843	1197	1169	779	405	881	34

The next questions are about PSYCHEDELICS OTHER THAN LSD.

This group would include the following drugs: mescaline, peyote, psilocybin, PCP.

B038: On how many occasions (if any) have you taken psychedelics other than LSD...

B038A: ...in your lifetime?

	TOTAL	M	F	White	Black	NE	NC	S	W	Yes	No	None	Mari-juana Only	Few Pills	More Pills	Any Her-oin
1. 0 occasions	89.3	88.6	91.7	88.7	98.2	83.8	88.8	95.1	87.4	91.4	89.1	100.0	100.0	92.4	66.2	22.1
2. 1-2	4.8	5.6	3.8	5.4	1.4	7.7	4.7	2.2	5.8	4.4	5.2	-	-	7.6	14.4	8.4
3. 3-5	2.0	1.9	1.9	2.1	.2	2.9	2.0	.6	3.6	1.6	2.4	-	-	7.3	10.5
4. 6-9	1.2	1.3	.7	1.3	-	1.9	.8	.6	1.7	.9	1.1	-	-	-	4.1	6.9
5. 10-19	1.1	.8	1.1	1.1	.2	2.4	1.0	.5	.5	.9	.7	-	-	-	3.6	15.2
6. 20-39	.6	.8	.2	.5	-	.9	1.1	.1	.2	.3	.6	-	-	-	2.1	4.5
7. 40 or more	1.0	1.0	.5	.9	-	.4	1.5	1.0	.7	.5	.9	-	-	-	2.3	32.5
Item 920 N(Wtd)	3410	1582	1704	2639	393	809	1015	1030	557	1895	1185	1196	805	414	903	37

B038B: ...during the last 12 months?

	TOTAL	M	F	White	Black	NE	NC	S	W	Yes	No	None	Mari-juana Only	Few Pills	More Pills	Any Her-oin
1. 0 occasions	93.0	92.4	94.8	92.6	99.5	89.8	92.4	96.6	92.0	94.7	92.4	100.0	100.0	97.2	77.3	28.1
2. 1-2	3.7	4.1	3.1	4.4	.2	5.5	3.7	1.8	4.7	2.9	4.6	-	-	2.8	11.9	23.9
3. 3-5	1.2	1.3	.9	1.2	.2	1.8	1.1	.5	1.6	1.0	1.0	-	-	-	4.4	-
4. 6-9	.7	.7	.5	.7	-	1.2	.7	.2	.6	.6	.6	-	-	-	2.3	7.2
5. 10-19	.9	.9	.2	.7	-	1.1	1.1	.6	.8	.5	.5	-	-	-	2.4	25.5
6. 20-39	.4	.4	.4	.4	-	.4	.8	.3	.1	.1	.7	-	-	-	1.3	9.3
7. 40 or more	.1	.2	.1	.1	-	.2	.2	.1	.1	.1	.1	-	-	-	.3	6.1
Item 930 N(Wtd)	3401	1576	1700	2631	390	807	1011	1029	554	1885	1186	1196	806	414	895	34

B038C: ...during the last 30 days?

	TOTAL	M	F	White	Black	NE	NC	S	W	Yes	No	None	Mari-juana Only	Few Pills	More Pills	Any Her-oin
1. 0 occasions	97.2	97.4	98.1	97.4	99.6	96.4	95.9	99.0	97.4	98.0	97.5	100.0	100.0	99.3	91.5	50.7
2. 1-2	1.8	1.6	1.4	1.8	.2	2.3	2.5	.5	2.2	1.6	1.5	-	-	.7	5.8	19.7
3. 3-5	.4	.4	.1	.3	-	.9	.2	.3	.1	.2	.2	-	-	-	1.2	7.2
4. 6-9	.4	.3	.3	.2	.2	.4	1.0	.1	.1	.1	.4	-	-	-	1.0	15.2
5. 10-19	.1	.2	*	.1	-	-	.2	.2	.1	-	.3	-	-	-	.4	2.7
6. 20-39	-	-	-	-	-	-	-	-	-	-	-	-	-	-	-	-
7. 40 or more	.1	.1	*	.1	-	-	.2	-	.1	.1	.1	-	-	-	.1	4.6
Item 940 N(Wtd)	3391	1569	1700	2626	391	800	1012	1029	551	1882	1181	1196	806	413	887	35

★ = excludes respondents for whom question was inappropriate.   * = less than .05 per cent.

QUESTIONNAIRE FORM 1 1981	TOTAL	SEX		RACE		REGION				4YR COLLEGE PLANS		ILLICIT DRUG USE: LIFETIME				
		M	F	White	Black	NE	NC	S	W	Yes	No	None	Mari-juana Only	Few Pills	More Pills	Any Her-oin
Weighted No. of Cases:	3644	1689	1795	2769	438	853	1075	1124	592	1969	1283	1213	853	430	958	37
% of Weighted Total:	100.0	46.3	49.3	76.0	12.0	23.4	29.5	30.8	16.3	54.0	35.2	33.3	23.4	11.8	26.3	1.0

IF YOU HAVE NOT TAKEN ANY PSYCHEDELICS OTHER THAN LSD IN THE LAST TWELVE MONTHS, GO TO Q.B042.

B039: When you take psychedelics other than LSD how high do you usually get?

1. Not at all high	2.3	2.1	3.2	2.7	-	5.0	-	2.6	1.3	.6	5.4	-	-	-	2.7	-
2. A little high	12.9	16.0	9.4	12.3	-	15.7	10.1	15.9	10.6	11.7	15.5	-	-	27.3	13.7	-
3. Moderately high	37.9	34.3	41.8	37.2	100.0	32.0	45.7	36.6	36.1	36.2	40.4	-	-	47.2	38.6	28.4
4. Very high	46.9	47.5	45.6	47.7	-	47.3	44.2	45.0	52.0	51.6	38.7	-	-	25.5	45.0	71.6
Item 2700 N(Wtd) ★	246	125	92	204	2	83	81	34	48	106	92	-	-	13	207	26

B040: When you take psychedelics other than LSD how long do you usually stay high?

1. Usually don't get high	2.8	3.2	3.2	3.0	-	5.7	.8	2.6	1.3	1.2	5.4	-	-	-	3.3	-
2. One to two hours	8.3	10.8	6.5	8.1	-	6.8	7.6	14.1	7.6	5.9	13.7	-	-	25.6	8.2	-
3. Three to six hours	47.1	49.2	45.3	49.0	33.9	52.9	33.9	49.9	57.5	50.6	42.2	-	-	60.6	49.9	18.9
4. Seven to 24 hours	38.7	33.3	42.4	36.6	66.1	31.3	52.4	31.6	33.6	36.7	37.7	-	-	6.3	36.2	74.3
5. More than 24 hours	3.1	3.6	2.6	3.2	-	3.2	5.3	1.8	-	5.8	.9	-	-	7.6	2.3	6.8
Item 2710 N(Wtd) ★	246	125	92	204	2	83	81	34	48	106	92	-	-	13	207	26

B041: What psychedelics other than LSD have you taken during the last year? (Mark all that apply.)

A. Mescaline	52.0	47.5	53.4	51.0	33.9	59.8	69.9	46.2	11.2	49.7	49.0	-	-	40.4	51.1	64.5
B. Peyote	13.0	15.5	8.6	12.7	-	13.5	11.4	6.5	19.3	18.0	1.8	-	3.0	10.9	33.8	
C. Psilocybin	22.5	22.8	20.4	23.2	-	12.1	18.2	3.1	61.7	27.9	18.4	-	-	16.1	19.7	47.1
D. PCP	31.7	30.6	28.2	29.5	-	39.1	28.1	47.7	13.9	19.3	38.2	-	-	29.7	29.9	47.0
E. Concentrated THC	30.1	30.4	20.7	27.1	-	30.8	34.9	40.1	13.7	26.0	29.6	-	-	11.1	28.8	49.4
F. Other	37.9	34.9	36.7	33.4	66.1	29.8	48.5	40.0	32.2	25.2	38.2	-	-	24.4	37.3	48.9
G. Don't know the names of some I have used	16.5	17.1	17.6	15.7	-	8.9	23.1	20.3	16.0	11.3	25.7	-	-	30.2	15.1	20.8
Item 2720-2780 N(Wtd) ★	240	121	92	200	2	81	80	32	46	107	88	-	-	13	201	26

The next questions are about AMPHETAMINES, which doctors sometimes prescribe to help people lose weight or to give people more energy. Drugstores are not supposed to sell them without a prescription.

Amphetamines are sometimes called: uppers, ups, speed, bennies, dexies, pep pills, diet pills. They include the following drugs: Benzedrine, Dexedrine, Methedrine, Ritalin, Preludin, Dexamyl, Methamphetamine.

B042: Have you ever taken amphetamines because a doctor told you to use them?

1. No	88.2	87.1	89.4	87.6	92.0	90.9	86.5	88.5	87.0	89.7	86.5	93.6	91.5	82.6	82.1	71.7
2. Yes, but I had already tried them on my own	3.6	3.8	3.1	3.7	1.8	2.7	4.6	2.5	5.1	2.3	4.9	.1	-	3.1	10.9	17.9
3. Yes, and it was the first time I took any	8.2	9.1	7.5	8.7	6.2	6.4	8.9	9.0	7.9	8.0	8.7	6.3	8.5	14.2	7.0	10.4
Item 2790 N(Wtd)	3431	1584	1723	2663	390	801	1031	1037	562	1892	1212	1171	792	421	937	37

B043: On how many occasions (if any) have you taken amphetamines on your own--that is, without a doctor telling you to take them...

★=excludes respondents for whom question was inappropriate.

QUESTIONNAIRE FORM 1 1981	TOTAL	SEX		RACE		REGION				4YR COLLEGE PLANS		ILLICIT DRUG USE: LIFETIME				
		M	F	White	Black	NE	NC	S	W	Yes	No	None	Mari-juana Only	Few Pills	More Pills	Any Her-oin
Weighted No. of Cases:	3644	1689	1795	2769	438	853	1075	1124	592	1969	1283	1213	853	430	958	37
% of Weighted Total:	100.0	46.3	49.3	76.0	12.0	23.4	29.5	30.8	16.3	54.0	35.2	33.3	23.4	11.8	26.3	1.0
B043A: ...in your lifetime?																
1. 0 occasions	69.9	71.0	70.7	67.4	91.4	66.0	67.5	76.1	68.3	75.9	64.7	100.0	100.0	53.1	13.8	7.9
2. 1-2	7.6	7.8	7.3	7.9	4.2	8.5	6.4	7.2	9.2	6.9	8.5	-	-	46.9	6.7	7.2
3. 3-5	4.7	4.9	4.4	4.9	2.1	4.2	5.6	3.9	5.1	3.6	5.7	-	-	-	17.1	1.7
4. 6-9	3.5	3.9	2.9	3.9	.8	4.4	3.3	3.2	2.8	3.1	3.5	-	-	-	12.3	11.9
5. 10-19	4.8	4.8	4.6	5.7	.4	5.0	4.5	3.9	6.7	4.1	5.1	-	-	-	17.3	8.5
6. 20-39	3.9	2.6	4.7	4.4	.3	5.1	4.0	2.9	3.6	2.9	4.6	-	-	-	14.1	5.0
7. 40 or more	5.7	5.0	5.3	5.8	.7	6.7	8.7	2.7	4.3	3.4	7.9	-	-	-	18.8	57.9
Item 980 N(Wtd)	3413	1584	1709	2653	386	800	1025	1032	556	1890	1205	1180	796	414	929	35
B043B: ...during the last 12 months?																
1. 0 occasions	75.3	76.7	75.7	73.0	94.5	71.3	72.4	80.9	76.2	80.9	70.8	100.0	100.0	73.7	24.1	8.1
2. 1-2	7.0	7.2	6.7	7.7	3.5	7.1	6.5	7.1	7.7	5.5	8.6	-	-	26.3	13.7	13.9
3. 3-5	4.5	5.3	3.4	4.8	1.2	6.1	5.4	3.1	3.5	3.7	4.7	-	-	-	16.5	6.0
4. 6-9	3.2	3.4	2.7	3.4	.2	3.5	3.2	2.6	3.9	2.7	3.1	-	-	-	11.5	10.4
5. 10-19	4.6	3.5	5.5	5.6	.3	5.5	4.8	4.0	4.3	3.6	5.8	-	-	-	16.8	7.1
6. 20-39	2.9	2.5	3.2	3.3	.3	3.9	4.0	1.2	2.4	2.4	3.5	-	-	-	10.3	10.2
7. 40 or more	2.4	1.3	2.6	2.2	-	2.5	3.7	1.1	2.0	1.2	3.5	-	-	-	7.1	44.2
Item 990 N(Wtd)	3406	1575	1710	2648	384	795	1025	1034	553	1883	1202	1181	796	412	924	34
B043C: ...during the last 30 days?																
1. 0 occasions	84.6	86.7	84.1	83.3	96.8	81.3	81.6	88.9	86.7	88.6	81.1	100.0	100.0	89.7	50.1	32.6
2. 1-2	6.5	6.3	6.2	6.9	2.7	7.0	6.4	6.2	6.4	5.2	7.6	-	-	10.3	19.0	7.9
3. 3-5	3.8	3.4	3.6	4.2	.2	5.4	4.2	2.4	3.2	3.0	4.2	-	-	-	13.2	18.6
4. 6-9	2.4	2.0	2.5	2.7	.3	3.5	3.2	1.1	1.6	1.6	3.0	-	-	-	8.5	10.2
5. 10-19	1.8	.9	2.4	1.7	-	1.6	3.1	1.0	1.2	1.0	2.7	-	-	-	6.0	18.0
6. 20-39	.7	.3	.8	.7	.1	.5	1.0	.5	.5	.5	.9	-	-	-	2.1	7.9
7. 40 or more	.3	.3	.3	.4	-	.6	.5	.1	.3	.1	.4	-	-	-	1.1	4.6
Item 1000 N(Wtd)	3401	1575	1707	2646	384	794	1024	1032	551	1883	1202	1181	796	410	920	34

IF YOU HAVE NOT TAKEN AMPHETAMINES IN THE LAST TWELVE MONTHS, GO TO Q.B052.

THE FOLLOWING QUESTIONS REFER ONLY TO TAKING AMPHETAMINES WITHOUT A DOCTOR'S ORDERS. IF YOU HAVE NOT DONE THIS IN THE LAST TWELVE MONTHS, GO TO Q.B052

B044: When you used amphetamines during the last year, how often did you use them in each of the following situations?

	TOTAL	M	F	White	Black	NE	NC	S	W	Yes	No	None	Mari-juana Only	Few Pills	More Pills	Any Her-oin
B044A: When you were alone																
1. Not at all	47.1	55.4	40.6	47.4	58.3	52.1	39.5	48.5	52.2	49.1	44.9	-	-	66.6	45.0	24.3
2. A few of the times	28.5	28.4	28.2	28.8	19.1	28.3	33.5	26.3	21.6	25.7	31.8	-	-	22.5	29.6	25.0
3. Some of the times	12.2	8.8	15.5	12.4	18.8	11.5	14.8	10.1	10.9	11.6	13.9	-	-	-	13.3	28.8
4. Most of the times	5.7	3.9	6.3	5.5	-	3.8	4.8	7.2	8.2	5.7	4.4	-	-	.5	5.7	21.9
5. Every time	6.6	3.4	9.3	5.9	3.8	4.4	7.4	7.8	7.1	7.9	5.0	-	-	10.3	6.4	-
Item 2800 N(Wtd) ★	814	359	396	691	21	221	270	193	129	350	339	-	-	97	683	29
B044B: With just 1 or 2 other people																
1. Not at all	20.4	20.1	22.2	20.1	32.3	20.8	16.6	25.7	20.4	26.2	16.4	-	-	49.6	16.6	5.4
2. A few of the times	39.4	38.2	40.3	40.3	36.1	46.2	33.7	38.8	41.1	38.1	40.0	-	-	37.1	40.7	25.7
3. Some of the times	23.0	22.1	22.3	22.7	15.8	18.6	30.0	19.0	21.3	19.2	25.9	-	-	.9	25.1	49.7
4. Most of the times	11.0	10.4	11.9	10.7	12.1	9.6	11.5	11.2	12.0	10.0	11.9	-	-	1.0	12.1	19.2
5. Every time	6.2	9.3	3.4	6.3	3.6	4.8	8.3	5.3	5.3	6.5	5.8	-	-	11.5	5.5	-
Item 2810 N(Wtd) ★	817	361	397	694	21	220	276	190	131	352	340	-	-	99	681	32

★=excludes respondents for whom question was inappropriate.

QUESTIONNAIRE FORM 1 1981	TOTAL	SEX		RACE		REGION				4YR COLLEGE PLANS		ILLICIT DRUG USE: LIFETIME				
		M	F	White	Black	NE	NC	S	W	Yes	No	None	Mari-juana Only	Few Pills	More Pills	Any Her-oin
Weighted No. of Cases:	3644	1689	1795	2769	438	853	1075	1124	592	1969	1283	1213	853	430	958	37
% of Weighted Total:	100.0	46.3	49.3	76.0	12.0	23.4	29.5	30.8	16.3	54.0	35.2	33.3	23.4	11.8	26.3	1.0

B044C: At a party

	TOTAL	M	F	White	Black	NE	NC	S	W	Yes	No	None	Mari-juana Only	Few Pills	More Pills	Any Her-oin
1. Not at all	42.6	39.0	48.7	43.0	60.9	43.9	33.1	50.9	48.5	51.8	38.9	–	–	81.8	38.5	6.2
2. A few of the times	21.3	23.2	20.8	22.4	29.1	21.1	20.7	20.8	23.6	19.8	22.3	–	–	8.1	24.0	5.4
3. Some of the times	18.9	19.5	16.3	18.1	3.4	19.6	27.0	10.0	13.9	15.4	20.1	–	–	1.6	20.3	44.5
4. Most of the times	11.4	11.5	10.2	10.9	3.9	12.0	11.5	10.7	11.3	8.2	12.5	–	–	1.6	12.7	15.7
5. Every time	5.7	6.8	4.0	5.6	2.7	3.5	7.6	7.6	2.6	4.8	6.3	–	–	6.9	4.5	28.2
Item 2820 N(Wtd) ★	812	357	399	690	21	220	272	190	129	350	336	–	–	97	679	32

B044D: When your date or spouse was present

	TOTAL	M	F	White	Black	NE	NC	S	W	Yes	No	None	Mari-juana Only	Few Pills	More Pills	Any Her-oin
1. Not at all	55.0	56.2	56.6	55.8	75.2	54.9	46.9	60.5	64.1	64.3	50.3	–	–	82.7	52.1	27.3
2. A few of the times	19.1	19.8	17.8	19.9	20.8	22.2	18.8	20.2	13.1	14.6	21.4	–	–	9.1	21.1	9.9
3. Some of the times	13.5	13.5	12.9	12.7	–	12.5	18.8	7.6	12.7	12.4	13.7	–	–	.4	14.4	36.2
4. Most of the times	7.9	4.7	9.5	7.0	4.0	6.8	9.5	7.0	7.9	5.9	8.1	–	–	1.5	8.5	16.1
5. Every time	4.4	5.7	3.3	4.6	–	3.6	6.0	4.7	2.1	2.8	6.5	–	–	6.3	3.9	10.6
Item 2830 N(Wtd) ★	801	350	396	681	21	215	269	189	128	349	334	–	–	96	672	31

B044E: When people over age 30 were present

	TOTAL	M	F	White	Black	NE	NC	S	W	Yes	No	None	Mari-juana Only	Few Pills	More Pills	Any Her-oin
1. Not at all	58.9	61.6	58.5	59.8	88.2	60.1	53.4	64.0	60.8	64.1	57.0	–	–	91.2	55.4	31.1
2. A few of the times	21.2	18.5	22.5	20.8	8.4	20.2	25.1	17.4	20.0	17.0	23.9	–	–	4.5	23.2	30.7
3. Some of the times	12.8	13.2	12.3	12.1	3.4	12.0	14.1	12.6	11.8	11.6	12.0	–	–	1.3	13.6	32.3
4. Most of the times	4.0	3.6	3.4	3.9	–	4.9	3.3	2.5	6.0	3.5	4.4	–	–	1.5	4.3	6.0
5. Every time	3.2	3.0	3.4	3.4	–	2.8	4.1	3.5	1.5	3.9	2.7	–	–	1.5	3.5	–
Item 2840 N(Wtd) ★	808	354	397	687	21	220	269	190	129	350	334	–	–	96	678	31

B044F: During the daytime (before 4:00 p.m.)

	TOTAL	M	F	White	Black	NE	NC	S	W	Yes	No	None	Mari-juana Only	Few Pills	More Pills	Any Her-oin
1. Not at all	22.9	30.2	18.8	23.3	43.2	23.3	18.4	29.1	22.6	27.4	21.2	–	–	41.4	20.6	8.3
2. A few of the times	26.1	25.9	25.2	25.4	38.4	29.2	25.4	22.2	28.3	24.8	26.0	–	–	26.1	25.9	34.8
3. Some of the times	18.2	19.1	16.5	18.4	10.3	17.0	22.5	16.1	14.7	15.2	19.4	–	–	9.8	19.5	18.2
4. Most of the times	18.9	11.6	24.3	17.9	–	15.8	23.3	17.6	16.7	17.1	20.4	–	–	3.6	20.9	22.1
5. Every time	13.9	13.1	15.2	15.1	8.1	14.8	10.5	15.0	17.7	15.4	13.1	–	–	19.0	13.1	16.7
Item 2850 N(Wtd) ★	809	355	398	688	21	221	270	189	129	349	336	–	–	95	681	31

B044G: At your home (or apartment or dorm)

	TOTAL	M	F	White	Black	NE	NC	S	W	Yes	No	None	Mari-juana Only	Few Pills	More Pills	Any Her-oin
1. Not at all	38.1	49.1	31.5	38.2	46.9	40.4	30.0	44.3	42.3	39.3	39.0	–	–	66.0	35.1	12.2
2. A few of the times	26.0	24.0	26.0	26.2	25.6	26.6	31.1	23.3	18.5	24.4	27.3	–	–	23.7	26.6	24.4
3. Some of the times	15.9	15.6	16.3	16.6	4.7	16.3	18.4	12.6	14.6	17.2	13.6	–	–	–	17.0	42.1
4. Most of the times	10.8	5.3	13.8	9.9	5.2	11.7	10.9	8.6	12.2	7.8	12.6	–	–	2.0	11.9	15.0
5. Every time	9.2	6.0	12.4	9.1	17.6	5.0	9.7	11.3	12.4	11.2	7.5	–	–	8.3	9.5	6.3
Item 2860 N(Wtd) ★	811	356	398	690	21	221	272	189	129	351	336	–	–	95	682	31

B044H: At school

	TOTAL	M	F	White	Black	NE	NC	S	W	Yes	No	None	Mari-juana Only	Few Pills	More Pills	Any Her-oin
1. Not at all	35.2	38.8	35.1	34.8	78.1	28.6	28.6	47.2	42.5	42.4	31.5	–	–	73.4	30.6	13.9
2. A few of the times	26.9	25.0	28.7	27.6	13.8	29.8	29.1	23.7	21.7	24.2	29.7	–	–	14.1	29.9	2.2
3. Some of the times	19.2	17.4	19.8	19.2	4.1	20.2	21.6	14.7	19.0	16.7	19.2	–	–	3.7	20.4	43.9
4. Most of the times	12.9	12.2	12.0	12.2	4.0	13.8	14.4	10.4	12.0	10.6	14.2	–	–	.7	14.0	25.2
5. Every time	5.8	6.6	4.4	6.2	–	7.5	6.2	4.0	4.8	6.0	5.4	–	–	8.2	5.1	14.8
Item 2880 N(Wtd) ★	809	354	397	687	21	220	271	188	130	350	335	–	–	94	680	31

B044I: In a car

	TOTAL	M	F	White	Black	NE	NC	S	W	Yes	No	None	Mari-juana Only	Few Pills	More Pills	Any Her-oin
1. Not at all	46.1	40.2	53.8	46.0	68.5	54.8	37.2	43.6	53.7	53.9	39.5	–	–	78.2	42.7	17.3
2. A few of the times	23.4	26.7	21.1	24.6	23.5	21.6	25.2	25.9	19.2	23.8	24.0	–	–	11.9	25.9	8.4
3. Some of the times	18.5	20.2	15.6	18.4	8.0	17.3	22.3	16.5	15.1	15.0	20.7	–	–	3.3	19.9	36.5
4. Most of the times	8.1	6.6	7.8	7.1	–	4.2	9.1	10.0	9.8	4.4	10.8	–	–	–	8.3	24.9
5. Every time	3.9	6.3	1.6	3.9	–	2.0	6.2	4.0	2.1	2.9	5.0	–	–	6.5	3.1	12.8
Item 2890 N(Wtd) ★	811	356	397	688	21	221	274	188	129	351	335	–	–	96	680	31

★=excludes respondents for whom question was inappropriate.

QUESTIONNAIRE FORM 1 1981	TOTAL	SEX		RACE		REGION				4YR COLLEGE PLANS		ILLICIT DRUG USE: LIFETIME				
		M	F	White	Black	NE	NC	S	W	Yes	No	None	Mari- juana Only	Few Pills	More Pills	Any Her- oin
Weighted No. of Cases:	3644	1689	1795	2769	438	853	1075	1124	592	1969	1283	1213	853	430	958	37
% of Weighted Total:	100.0	46.3	49.3	76.0	12.0	23.4	29.5	30.8	16.3	54.0	35.2	33.3	23.4	11.8	26.3	1.0

B045: How many of the times when you used amphetamines during the last year did you use them along with each of the following drugs--that is, so that their effects overlapped?

B045A: With alcohol

1. Not at all	39.4	35.4	45.1	39.9	55.8	36.5	35.2	46.1	43.5	43.0	39.4	-	-	82.1	34.1	13.1
2. A few of the times	26.6	28.3	25.3	27.4	32.4	31.2	25.4	23.7	25.6	25.6	26.5	-	-	9.5	29.8	14.5
3. Some of the times	15.3	13.4	15.8	15.0	-	18.6	17.4	10.8	11.7	12.3	16.0	-	-	1.5	16.7	29.4
4. Most of the times	11.5	13.7	9.2	11.4	-	7.1	13.5	11.5	14.7	11.3	11.6	-	-	.8	12.0	34.4
5. Every time	7.3	9.3	4.6	6.3	11.9	6.6	8.6	8.0	4.5	7.9	6.5	-	-	6.1	7.4	8.6
Item 2900 N(Wtd) ★	813	358	400	693	20	222	276	189	126	353	335	-	-	99	680	32

B045B: With marijuana

1. Not at all	42.7	36.3	52.2	43.8	60.6	43.9	36.9	45.8	48.6	51.0	42.4	-	-	87.2	37.6	10.2
2. A few of the times	20.5	25.0	16.2	20.6	19.9	20.4	19.6	21.1	21.9	19.2	18.9	-	-	4.8	23.1	15.2
3. Some of the times	15.5	14.1	14.4	14.4	7.5	16.2	17.9	11.9	14.4	12.5	15.6	-	-	4.1	17.3	13.0
4. Most of the times	15.3	16.4	13.3	15.1	4.8	12.6	19.1	15.7	11.4	12.8	16.5	-	-	.7	16.1	45.0
5. Every time	6.0	8.1	3.9	6.1	7.0	6.9	6.5	5.6	3.7	4.5	6.6	-	-	3.2	5.9	16.6
Item 2910 N(Wtd) ★	808	357	395	690	20	221	273	188	126	348	335	-	-	97	678	31

B045C: With LSD

1. Not at all	94.8	94.7	96.5	95.9	100.0	93.5	92.1	97.7	98.7	95.9	95.0	-	-	100.0	94.7	80.2
2. A few of the times	3.2	3.2	1.9	2.6	-	5.6	3.6	1.3	1.0	2.7	2.3	-	-	-	3.3	11.2
3. Some of the times	.8	.6	.7	.3	-	-	1.7	1.0	.3	.3	1.7	-	-	-	.7	6.0
4. Most of the times	.5	.7	.3	.6	-	.6	.9	-	-	.7	-	-	-	-	.6	-
5. Every time	.7	.7	.5	.7	-	.3	1.7	-	-	.3	1.0	-	-	-	.7	2.6
Item 2920 N(Wtd) ★	788	342	392	673	20	212	267	186	124	340	328	-	-	96	660	30

B045D: With psychedelics other than LSD

1. Not at all	93.8	93.2	96.4	95.1	96.3	94.9	90.7	95.8	95.9	96.3	92.7	-	-	98.5	95.0	53.8
2. A few of the times	3.2	3.7	1.6	2.6	-	3.9	4.4	2.1	1.2	1.3	4.6	-	-	1.5	2.6	22.8
3. Some of the times	2.0	1.8	1.5	1.5	-	.9	2.9	1.7	2.5	2.0	1.6	-	-	-	1.6	18.5
4. Most of the times	.2	.2	.3	.1	3.7	-	.3	.4	.3	-	.1	-	-	-	.2	2.4
5. Every time	.7	1.1	.2	.7	-	.3	1.7	-	-	.4	1.0	-	-	-	.7	2.5
Item 2930 N(Wtd) ★	794	348	393	679	20	213	270	186	125	343	329	-	-	97	663	31

B046: What have been the most important reasons for your taking amphetamines without a doctor's orders? (Mark all that apply.)

A. To experiment--to see what it's like	52.2	56.8	46.9	50.5	65.1	53.8	56.9	47.2	46.5	47.5	55.4	-	-	56.8	52.1	42.9
B. To relax or relieve tension	17.5	19.8	15.0	17.6	10.6	19.7	17.8	19.3	10.7	15.6	19.8	-	-	9.3	18.8	16.1
C. To feel good or get high	47.3	50.6	42.5	46.9	34.8	50.6	46.6	49.5	39.4	45.2	47.1	-	-	22.4	49.6	75.6
D. To seek deeper insights and understanding	4.2	5.4	1.6	3.7	6.2	3.5	6.4	3.6	1.6	2.5	4.5	-	-	1.3	4.5	6.6
E. To have a good time with my friends	29.9	34.3	26.0	29.2	41.6	28.0	30.5	31.5	29.5	26.9	32.0	-	-	14.5	32.1	29.5
F. To fit in with a group I like	4.1	5.4	2.2	4.1	3.4	5.4	3.7	5.2	1.0	4.2	3.7	-	-	5.1	3.8	6.6
G. To get away from my problems or troubles	9.2	10.6	8.6	9.5	14.9	8.0	13.1	7.6	5.0	6.8	12.5	-	-	4.2	10.3	1.4
H. Because of boredom, nothing else to do	12.6	14.6	10.9	12.2	12.6	12.6	14.7	10.1	11.6	10.1	13.9	-	-	3.3	13.9	12.8
I. Because of anger or frustration	7.6	8.9	7.0	7.5	15.5	6.6	9.6	8.6	3.4	6.9	10.1	-	-	6.4	7.9	4.5
J. To get through the day	24.0	23.4	24.0	25.4	13.3	21.5	26.7	25.8	19.7	21.0	27.2	-	-	5.1	26.4	31.7
K. To increase the effects of some other drug(s)	9.6	10.7	8.2	9.6	8.2	8.1	10.2	9.9	10.2	12.0	7.1	-	-	-	10.2	26.5
L. To decrease (offset) the effects of some other drug(s)	2.0	3.8	.2	1.9	-	2.1	3.5	.5	.9	2.8	1.0	-	-	-	2.2	3.9
M. To stay awake	59.5	57.3	60.9	61.0	7.5	59.4	62.9	55.7	57.6	54.4	63.2	-	-	35.3	62.7	65.0
N. To get more energy	61.8	59.1	64.9	62.8	39.7	65.2	62.3	56.1	63.3	59.6	62.3	-	-	36.1	65.7	59.2
O. To help me lose weight	39.4	9.6	66.0	39.5	36.8	36.8	40.7	34.8	47.7	36.9	43.9	-	-	37.6	39.5	42.3
P. Because I am "hooked"--I feel I have to have them	1.1	.8	1.4	1.1	-	.2	1.6	1.1	1.4	.6	1.5	-	-	-	.9	8.5
Item 2940-3090 N(Wtd) ★	813	357	401	694	21	222	278	186	128	355	333	-	-	98	683	31

★=excludes respondents for whom question was inappropriate.

QUESTIONNAIRE FORM 1 1981	TOTAL	SEX		RACE		REGION				4YR COLLEGE PLANS		ILLICIT DRUG USE: LIFETIME				
		M	F	White	Black	NE	NC	S	W	Yes	No	None	Mari-juana Only	Few Pills	More Pills	Any Heroin
Weighted No. of Cases:	3644	1689	1795	2769	438	853	1075	1124	592	1969	1283	1213	853	430	958	37
% of Weighted Total:	100.0	46.3	49.3	76.0	12.0	23.4	29.5	30.8	16.3	54.0	35.2	33.3	23.4	11.8	26.3	1.0
B047: When you take amphetamines, how high do you usually get?																
1. Not at all high	11.5	11.3	12.3	10.6	24.2	11.0	11.2	12.3	11.6	12.2	11.5	-	-	34.5	8.8	-
2. A little high	31.4	32.3	30.2	32.4	10.1	38.7	29.9	34.7	17.5	30.8	31.7	-	-	22.2	33.6	17.8
3. Moderately high	30.6	30.8	29.7	29.9	30.4	27.3	31.6	26.2	40.3	25.6	35.3	-	-	14.0	32.8	36.4
4. Very high	6.3	8.4	4.2	6.3	12.7	4.9	7.2	7.2	5.1	5.4	5.2	-	-	3.6	5.6	28.2
5. I don't take them to get high	20.2	17.1	23.6	20.9	22.7	18.1	20.0	19.6	25.5	26.0	16.4	-	-	25.8	19.3	17.6
Item 3100 N(Wtd) ★	788	349	384	672	20	213	277	177	121	343	321	-	-	95	658	32
B048: When you take amphetamines how long do you usually stay high?																
1. Usually don't get high	24.4	19.0	31.2	24.4	36.0	20.6	23.5	29.4	25.5	28.0	24.2	-	-	58.2	20.2	8.0
2. One to two hours	20.3	22.2	18.5	20.4	21.6	22.2	18.9	21.0	18.9	21.0	19.8	-	-	19.4	21.0	9.0
3. Three to six hours	38.2	41.5	32.4	37.7	22.6	38.7	38.2	35.5	41.0	36.7	37.2	-	-	17.1	40.8	48.6
4. Seven to 24 hours	16.3	16.7	16.7	16.5	19.7	18.0	18.6	12.3	14.1	13.8	17.7	-	-	2.1	17.8	28.1
5. More than 24 hours	.8	.6	1.2	1.0	-	.4	.7	1.7	.6	.4	1.1	-	-	3.1	.3	6.2
Item 3110 N(Wtd) ★	810	357	398	689	21	221	279	182	127	351	332	-	-	98	678	32
B049: What amphetamines have you taken during the last year without a doctor's orders? (Mark all that apply.)																
A. Benzedrine	15.1	16.6	11.7	14.3	8.3	12.8	17.9	13.6	15.4	13.4	16.0	-	-	5.2	15.0	48.7
B. Dexedrine	21.8	21.5	20.9	21.7	8.4	23.7	25.9	13.4	21.9	18.9	22.4	-	-	4.7	22.0	67.5
C. Methedrine	24.1	25.8	21.6	23.7	22.8	27.1	24.6	24.5	17.2	20.6	23.9	-	-	25.1	23.8	27.9
D. Ritalin	3.0	3.9	2.6	3.4	-	1.1	4.7	1.4	4.9	3.5	2.8	-	-	-	3.4	2.5
E. Preludin	7.1	7.1	4.8	6.3	4.2	2.7	11.8	7.2	4.8	4.7	9.2	-	-	-	7.4	22.9
F. Dexamyl	4.8	5.4	3.8	3.8	12.4	3.6	5.8	2.9	7.2	4.1	4.6	-	-	3.8	4.7	10.2
G. Methamphetamine	15.7	13.8	15.6	15.5	4.2	18.3	15.7	13.7	14.2	14.8	15.6	-	-	8.1	15.6	41.3
H. Other	32.4	33.3	30.3	31.3	38.8	29.8	35.7	33.2	28.8	30.2	35.0	-	-	26.5	33.1	36.3
I. Don't know the names of some amphetamines I have used	47.3	45.0	49.6	47.3	32.9	47.8	42.2	53.2	48.6	49.1	46.7	-	-	43.5	48.3	36.4
Item 3120-3200 N(Wtd) ★	786	343	392	671	20	213	267	180	126	347	318	-	-	94	661	32
B050: What methods have you used for taking amphetamines? (Mark all that apply.)																
A. By mouth	98.8	98.7	98.9	99.1	85.2	99.4	99.1	98.6	97.6	98.7	98.9	-	-	99.1	99.1	91.9
B. Injection	1.7	1.1	1.0	.8	3.5	-	2.8	2.2	1.6	.4	2.2	-	-	-	.6	30.0
C. Other	15.2	18.7	10.1	14.0	16.0	24.2	9.9	10.1	18.6	17.1	10.9	-	-	1.6	16.4	31.4
Item 3210-3230 N(Wtd) ★	811	357	402	693	21	220	280	184	128	355	334	-	-	98	681	32
B051: Have you ever tried to stop using amphetamines and found that you couldn't stop?																
1. Yes	2.8	2.2	2.7	2.3	10.9	1.7	4.1	3.1	1.8	1.4	4.1	-	-	6.2	2.1	8.2
2. No	97.2	97.8	97.3	97.7	89.1	98.3	95.9	96.9	98.2	98.6	95.9	-	-	93.8	97.9	91.8
Item 3240 N(Wtd) ★	806	351	399	686	21	217	276	185	127	350	334	-	-	94	676	32
B052: Do you think you will be using amphetamines without a doctor's orders five years from now?																
1. I definitely will	1.1	1.0	1.0	1.1	1.6	1.0	1.4	.9	.8	.8	1.7	.4	.8	.3	2.3	8.6
2. I probably will	8.5	7.5	8.7	9.0	3.9	10.5	10.4	5.4	8.2	7.2	10.0	.5	1.4	4.0	26.2	37.2
3. I probably will not	23.7	22.1	24.6	24.4	15.0	25.5	24.4	21.3	24.4	20.0	26.8	10.7	16.6	31.7	43.4	30.9
4. I definitely will not	66.7	69.4	65.6	65.5	79.5	63.0	63.7	72.4	66.6	72.0	61.5	88.4	81.2	64.0	28.1	23.3
Item 3250 N(Wtd)	3429	1587	1726	2636	413	785	1026	1054	564	1879	1226	1169	779	411	922	37

★=excludes respondents for whom question was inappropriate.

QUESTIONNAIRE FORM 1 1981	TOTAL	SEX		RACE		REGION				4YR COLLEGE PLANS		ILLICIT DRUG USE: LIFETIME				
		M	F	White	Black	NE	NC	S	W	Yes	No	None	Marijuana Only	Few Pills	More Pills	Any Heroin
Weighted No. of Cases:	3644	1689	1795	2769	438	853	1075	1124	592	1969	1283	1213	853	430	958	37
% of Weighted Total:	100.0	46.3	49.3	76.0	12.0	23.4	29.5	30.8	16.3	54.0	35.2	33.3	23.4	11.8	26.3	1.0

The next questions are about QUAALUDES (Methaqualone), which are sometimes prescribed by doctors. Drugstores are not supposed to sell them without a prescription.

Quaaludes are sometimes called: soapers, quads.

B053: On how many occasions (if any) have you taken quaaludes on your own--that is, without a doctor telling you to take them...

B053A: ...in your lifetime?

	TOTAL	M	F	White	Black	NE	NC	S	W	Yes	No	None	Marijuana Only	Few Pills	More Pills	Any Heroin
1. 0 occasions	88.7	86.5	91.9	87.8	97.9	87.6	89.3	88.1	90.0	92.2	86.7	100.0	100.0	89.3	64.9	31.4
2. 1-2	4.8	6.3	3.5	5.3	2.1	5.3	4.8	4.4	5.2	3.7	5.9	-	-	10.7	12.8	14.4
3. 3-5	2.3	3.2	1.3	2.6	-	2.8	2.1	2.0	2.5	1.6	2.7	-	-	-	8.3	8.3
4. 6-9	1.8	1.4	1.6	1.8	-	2.1	1.3	2.2	1.7	1.1	2.3	-	-	-	6.2	15.6
5. 10-19	.8	1.1	.6	1.0	-	.8	.9	1.2	.2	.6	.8	-	-	-	3.0	4.8
6. 20-39	.7	.7	.7	.8	-	.6	.5	1.1	.3	.5	.8	-	-	-	2.5	2.2
7. 40 or more	.9	.8	.5	.7	-	1.0	1.0	1.0	.1	.3	.8	-	-	-	2.3	23.2
Item 1010 N(Wtd)	3406	1578	1717	2647	395	800	1011	1041	554	1900	1197	1188	803	415	905	36

B053B: ...during the last 12 months?

	TOTAL	M	F	White	Black	NE	NC	S	W	Yes	No	None	Marijuana Only	Few Pills	More Pills	Any Heroin
1. 0 occasions	92.3	90.9	94.6	91.7	99.8	91.0	92.7	91.9	94.0	94.8	91.3	100.0	100.0	95.9	75.0	41.9
2. 1-2	4.0	5.5	2.4	4.4	.2	4.5	3.8	3.8	3.9	3.0	4.4	-	-	4.1	12.4	17.9
3. 3-5	1.5	1.4	1.2	1.6	-	2.1	1.3	1.1	1.4	.9	2.1	-	-	-	5.0	14.4
4. 6-9	.9	.9	.6	.9	-	1.2	.5	1.3	.4	.5	.9	-	-	-	3.3	3.2
5. 10-19	.5	.5	.5	.5	-	.5	.5	.8	.2	.2	.8	-	-	-	1.8	4.9
6. 20-39	.5	.5	.5	.5	-	.4	.6	.7	-	.4	.4	-	-	-	1.7	2.6
7. 40 or more	.4	.2	.2	.2	-	.2	.5	.4	.1	.2	.2	-	-	-	.8	15.1
Item 1020 N(Wtd)	3402	1575	1716	2645	393	797	1009	1041	554	1897	1196	1188	803	415	902	35

B053C: ...during the last 30 days?

	TOTAL	M	F	White	Black	NE	NC	S	W	Yes	No	None	Marijuana Only	Few Pills	More Pills	Any Heroin
1. 0 occasions	96.9	96.4	97.9	96.9	99.8	95.9	96.7	96.7	98.6	98.1	96.4	100.0	100.0	98.7	90.0	66.2
2. 1-2	2.3	2.7	1.3	2.3	-	3.5	2.0	2.3	1.1	1.4	2.8	-	-	1.3	7.2	21.8
3. 3-5	.2	.4	.1	.3	-	*	.5	.2	.1	.2	.1	-	-	-	.8	2.7
4. 6-9	.4	.3	.4	.3	.2	.3	.5	.5	-	.2	.4	-	-	-	1.2	4.9
5. 10-19	.1	.1	.2	.1	-	-	.3	.2	-	.1	.2	-	-	-	.5	2.2
6. 20-39	.1	.1	*	.1	-	.3	-	.1	-	*	.2	-	-	-	.3	-
7. 40 or more	*	.1	-	*	-	-	-	-	.1	-	-	-	-	-	-	2.3
Item 1030 N(Wtd)	3401	1577	1714	2644	395	798	1009	1041	553	1897	1196	1189	803	415	900	35

IF YOU HAVE NOT TAKEN QUAALUDES IN THE LAST TWELVE MONTHS, GO TO Q.B056.

THE FOLLOWING QUESTIONS REFER ONLY TO TAKING QUAALUDES WITHOUT A DOCTOR'S ORDERS. IF YOU HAVE NOT DONE THIS IN THE LAST TWELVE MONTHS, GO TO Q.B056.

B054: When you take quaaludes how high do you usually get?

	TOTAL	M	F	White	Black	NE	NC	S	W	Yes	No	None	Marijuana Only	Few Pills	More Pills	Any Heroin
1. Not at all high	1.7	2.0	1.9	1.7	-	-	3.7	.7	3.7	2.9	.8	-	-	9.9	1.0	-
2. A little high	16.3	17.4	15.7	16.5	-	21.7	9.7	17.5	16.0	14.5	19.8	-	-	27.3	16.2	10.4
3. Moderately high	39.2	42.0	37.9	39.4	100.0	33.7	39.7	44.3	38.0	37.1	44.6	-	-	41.0	39.4	42.0
4. Very high	39.9	36.2	44.4	40.9	-	41.6	43.2	37.0	35.9	44.3	34.8	-	-	19.1	42.5	34.0
5. I don't take them to get high	2.9	2.4	-	1.6	-	3.0	3.7	.5	6.5	1.2	-	-	-	2.8	1.0	13.5
Item 3260 N(Wtd) ★	258	140	91	213	2	72	74	80	32	97	100	-	-	16	219	20

* = less than .05 per cent.   ★ = excludes respondents for whom question was inappropriate.

QUESTIONNAIRE FORM 1 1981	TOTAL	SEX		RACE		REGION				4YR COLLEGE PLANS		ILLICIT DRUG USE: LIFETIME				
		M	F	White	Black	NE	NC	S	W	Yes	No	None	Mari-juana Only	Few Pills	More Pills	Any Her-oin
Weighted No. of Cases:	3644	1689	1795	2769	438	853	1075	1124	592	1969	1283	1213	853	430	958	37
% of Weighted Total:	100.0	46.3	49.3	76.0	12.0	23.4	29.5	30.8	16.3	54.0	35.2	33.3	23.4	11.8	26.3	1.0

B055: When you take quaaludes how long do you usually stay high?

1. Usually don't get high	3.3	3.7	3.5	3.2	-	2.2	6.2	1.3	3.8	4.9	1.9	-	-	12.6	2.5	-
2. One to two hours	21.4	20.2	26.4	22.3	53.4	22.8	9.8	29.1	26.1	21.3	27.3	-	-	38.6	20.4	19.6
3. Three to six hours	54.9	56.9	53.1	55.2	-	53.0	59.4	54.8	48.4	54.1	51.0	-	-	43.1	57.3	38.7
4. Seven to 24 hours	19.7	19.2	14.9	18.4	46.6	22.0	22.1	14.8	21.7	17.9	19.8	-	-	5.6	18.9	41.7
5. More than 24 hours	.7	-	2.0	.9	-	-	2.5	-	-	1.9	-	-	-	-	.8	-
Item 3270 N(Wtd) ★	255	138	92	212	2	70	74	80	31	98	100	-	-	16	220	19

The next questions are about BARBITURATES, which doctors sometimes prescribe to help people relax or get to sleep. Drugstores are not supposed to sell them without a prescription.

Barbiturates are sometimes called: downs, downers, goofballs, yellows, reds, blues, rainbows.

They include the following drugs: Phenobarbitol, Seconal, Tuinal, Nembutal, Luminal, Desbutal, Amytal.

B056: Have you ever taken barbiturates because a doctor told you to use them?

1. No	92.5	91.9	93.3	92.2	96.8	91.7	92.5	93.7	91.5	92.7	92.5	95.5	94.5	89.7	89.1	62.3
2. Yes, but I had already tried them on my own.	1.6	1.6	1.2	1.5	.2	2.3	1.3	1.1	2.3	1.0	2.0	.2	-	1.2	3.8	36.5
3. Yes, and it was the first time I took any	5.8	6.5	5.4	6.3	3.0	6.0	6.2	5.2	6.2	6.3	5.5	4.3	5.5	9.1	7.1	1.1
Item 3280 N(Wtd)	3347	1548	1695	2608	384	775	1005	1023	544	1862	1190	1165	789	404	886	34

B057: On how many occasions (if any) have you taken barbiturates on your own--that is, without a doctor telling you to take them...

B057A: ...in your lifetime?

1. 0 occasions	90.1	89.8	91.8	89.7	98.3	88.0	89.9	91.1	91.2	93.0	87.9	100.0	100.0	90.5	69.2	29.6
2. 1-2	4.4	4.5	4.0	4.6	1.1	5.0	4.9	3.3	4.8	3.7	5.3	-	-	9.5	12.1	8.3
3. 3-5	1.9	1.7	1.5	2.0	.3	2.5	1.4	2.2	1.6	1.1	2.5	-	-	-	6.9	11.1
4. 6-9	1.0	.9	.9	1.0	.4	1.1	.8	1.0	1.2	.6	1.3	-	-	-	3.5	6.5
5. 10-19	.9	1.1	.6	.9	-	1.3	1.3	.6	.1	.5	1.0	-	-	-	3.0	11.6
6. 20-39	.8	.9	.8	.9	-	.6	1.1	.8	.7	.5	1.1	-	-	-	2.8	8.5
7. 40 or more	.9	1.1	.5	.8	-	1.4	.6	1.0	.5	.6	.9	-	-	-	2.5	24.3
Item 1040 N(Wtd)	3353	1550	1699	2613	382	784	1004	1020	544	1878	1181	1176	798	407	878	35

B057B: ...during the last 12 months?

1. 0 occasions	94.4	94.0	95.5	94.3	99.2	93.4	94.2	95.4	94.2	96.3	93.2	100.0	100.0	97.6	82.2	34.6
2. 1-2	2.5	2.5	2.1	2.4	.7	3.0	2.4	1.5	3.9	1.9	3.0	-	-	2.4	7.4	28.1
3. 3-5	1.0	1.1	1.0	1.1	-	.8	1.2	1.0	1.2	.7	1.4	-	-	-	3.9	-
4. 6-9	.8	.6	.8	.8	-	1.0	1.4	.6	.1	.4	.8	-	-	-	2.6	16.2
5. 10-19	.7	1.1	.3	.8	.2	1.3	.4	.8	.4	.4	.9	-	-	-	2.4	11.3
6. 20-39	.2	.3	.1	.2	-	.1	.2	.3	-	.1	.3	-	-	-	.6	2.1
7. 40 or more	.3	.4	.2	.3	-	.3	.2	.5	.3	.2	.4	-	-	-	1.0	7.7
Item 1050 N(Wtd)	3347	1548	1696	2608	383	782	1002	1020	544	1876	1177	1176	798	406	872	36

B057C: ...during the last 30 days?

1. 0 occasions	97.3	97.0	97.8	97.2	99.6	96.8	96.9	97.5	98.3	98.3	96.5	100.0	100.0	99.3	91.4	62.3
2. 1-2	1.6	1.5	1.5	1.6	.2	2.1	2.2	.9	1.2	1.1	2.0	-	-	.7	5.2	16.2
3. 3-5	.6	.8	.4	.7	-	.5	.4	.9	.4	.2	.8	-	-	-	1.9	8.1
4. 6-9	.3	.3	.2	.3	.2	.2	.3	.5	.1	.2	.3	-	-	-	.8	10.2
5. 10-19	.2	.3	.1	.2	-	.4	.2	.1	-	.1	.4	-	-	-	.6	2.1
6. 20-39	*	*	-	*	-	*	-	-	-	-	-	-	-	-	-	1.0
7. 40 or more	.1	.1	-	.1	-	-	-	.2	-	.1	-	-	-	-	.2	-
Item 1060 N(Wtd)	3348	1548	1696	2609	383	781	1002	1021	544	1877	1177	1176	798	406	872	36

★=excludes respondents for whom question was inappropriate.   * =less than .05 per cent.

QUESTIONNAIRE FORM 1 1981	TOTAL	SEX		RACE		REGION				4YR COLLEGE PLANS		ILLICIT DRUG USE: LIFETIME				
		M	F	White	Black	NE	NC	S	W	Yes	No	None	Mari-juana Only	Few Pills	More Pills	Any Her-oin
Weighted No. of Cases:	3644	1689	1795	2769	438	853	1075	1124	592	1969	1283	1213	853	430	958	37
% of Weighted Total:	100.0	46.3	49.3	76.0	12.0	23.4	29.5	30.8	16.3	54.0	35.2	33.3	23.4	11.8	26.3	1.0

IF YOU HAVE NOT TAKEN BARBITURATES IN THE LAST TWELVE MONTHS, GO TO Q.B065.

THE FOLLOWING QUESTIONS REFER ONLY TO TAKING BARBITURATES WITHOUT A DOCTOR'S ORDERS. IF YOU HAVE NOT DONE THIS IN THE LAST TWELVE MONTHS, GO TO Q.B065

B058: When you used barbiturates during the last year, how often did you use them in each of the following situations?

B058A: When you were alone

	TOTAL	M	F	White	Black	NE	NC	S	W	Yes	No	None	Mari-juana Only	Few Pills	More Pills	Any Her-oin
1. Not at all	45.4	48.8	41.6	45.4	-	50.1	50.0	39.0	39.5	47.3	42.7	-	-	29.3	47.8	22.6
2. A few of the times	32.4	25.5	37.2	31.1	100.0	37.2	24.3	36.4	33.8	21.9	40.9	-	-	20.0	30.5	55.4
3. Some of the times	9.1	11.8	8.0	9.1	-	5.0	8.9	16.1	5.5	11.5	8.6	-	-	9.3	14.3
4. Most of the times	8.2	10.8	5.8	9.3	-	2.6	11.0	4.1	17.3	14.6	3.6	-	-	21.1	8.5	3.8
5. Every time	4.9	3.0	7.4	5.1	-	5.1	5.8	4.5	3.8	4.8	4.2	-	-	29.6	3.9	3.8
Item 3290 N(Wtd) ★	186	88	78	150	1	48	58	47	33	68	80	-	-	9	149	21

B058B: With just 1 or 2 other people

	TOTAL	M	F	White	Black	NE	NC	S	W	Yes	No	None	Mari-juana Only	Few Pills	More Pills	Any Her-oin
1. Not at all	19.4	20.3	19.0	17.6	56.8	20.5	20.5	14.5	22.5	26.6	16.4	-	-	87.1	14.0	11.8
2. A few of the times	35.1	31.4	36.7	34.9	-	40.4	30.7	37.6	31.9	27.3	39.4	-	-	12.9	38.4	30.3
3. Some of the times	19.4	22.2	14.5	19.9	-	26.8	19.8	18.6	8.8	16.7	19.2	-	-	-	20.2	21.8
4. Most of the times	16.9	18.3	19.3	17.7	43.2	4.4	25.5	21.0	14.1	19.4	18.1	-	-	-	17.0	28.1
5. Every time	9.2	7.8	10.6	9.8	-	7.9	3.5	8.3	22.7	10.0	7.0	-	-	-	10.4	8.0
Item 3300 N(Wtd) ★	187	88	78	150	2	48	59	47	33	68	80	-	-	9	149	22

B058C: At a party

	TOTAL	M	F	White	Black	NE	NC	S	W	Yes	No	None	Mari-juana Only	Few Pills	More Pills	Any Her-oin
1. Not at all	39.5	40.2	43.6	41.0	56.8	42.2	32.0	30.3	61.6	46.9	39.5	-	-	94.2	37.6	19.5
2. A few of the times	22.3	16.7	22.7	19.9	-	13.2	29.9	24.3	19.4	20.3	20.9	-	-	5.8	20.9	37.5
3. Some of the times	18.0	23.2	14.1	18.2	43.2	28.2	15.1	19.4	6.2	13.6	17.3	-	-	-	19.2	23.0
4. Most of the times	15.5	14.0	16.6	16.0	-	10.9	19.4	20.7	8.0	17.3	18.6	-	-	-	18.5	5.4
5. Every time	4.7	5.9	3.0	5.0	-	5.5	3.6	5.3	4.9	1.9	3.8	-	-	-	3.8	14.5
Item 3310 N(Wtd) ★	184	88	75	148	2	48	58	45	33	66	79	-	-	9	147	21

B058D: When your date or spouse was present

	TOTAL	M	F	White	Black	NE	NC	S	W	Yes	No	None	Mari-juana Only	Few Pills	More Pills	Any Her-oin
1. Not at all	56.9	62.1	53.6	56.5	56.8	50.5	59.1	54.2	66.5	66.5	56.4	-	-	78.9	54.0	59.5
2. A few of the times	20.6	15.4	21.8	18.7	-	17.5	21.3	21.0	23.3	24.7	16.9	-	-	21.1	22.5	10.1
3. Some of the times	11.2	12.1	12.5	13.6	-	17.5	12.9	6.5	5.2	7.0	14.2	-	-	-	12.4	10.5
4. Most of the times	4.2	3.6	4.5	3.4	43.2	4.4	3.2	8.3	-	1.7	3.3	-	-	-	3.7	10.2
5. Every time	7.1	6.8	7.6	7.9	-	10.1	3.5	10.0	5.0	-	9.2	-	-	-	7.4	9.7
Item 3320 N(Wtd) ★	183	88	76	148	2	48	59	45	31	66	79	-	-	9	147	22

B058E: When people over age 30 were present

	TOTAL	M	F	White	Black	NE	NC	S	W	Yes	No	None	Mari-juana Only	Few Pills	More Pills	Any Her-oin
1. Not at all	58.4	61.3	56.7	57.6	100.0	50.8	66.2	52.0	64.8	60.6	62.1	-	-	70.4	55.6	61.9
2. A few of the times	21.4	20.6	21.8	20.7	-	19.8	19.8	26.7	19.2	23.3	17.1	-	-	-	24.9	11.5
3. Some of the times	12.9	10.2	15.0	14.5	-	20.1	9.6	12.6	8.3	11.4	11.1	-	-	-	13.3	19.0
4. Most of the times	4.3	5.4	3.2	4.1	-	5.4	-	6.4	7.7	2.9	6.5	-	-	-	4.3	7.6
5. Every time	3.0	2.5	3.3	3.2	-	4.0	4.4	2.3	-	1.8	3.2	-	-	29.6	2.0	-
Item 3330 N(Wtd) ★	183	88	76	149	1	48	58	45	31	66	80	-	-	9	148	21

B058F: During the daytime (before 4:00 p.m.)

	TOTAL	M	F	White	Black	NE	NC	S	W	Yes	No	None	Mari-juana Only	Few Pills	More Pills	Any Her-oin
1. Not at all	51.6	51.2	53.0	52.4	56.8	44.1	53.7	52.3	57.9	54.4	55.9	-	-	78.9	49.3	46.2
2. A few of the times	21.5	13.9	32.0	22.3	-	27.3	23.0	14.8	19.4	22.1	19.1	-	-	-	22.3	27.7
3. Some of the times	15.1	19.8	8.2	15.0	-	15.7	16.1	16.2	10.6	9.6	17.6	-	-	-	16.7	13.8
4. Most of the times	9.1	11.4	6.3	8.1	43.2	8.9	7.1	12.4	8.3	12.1	5.7	-	-	21.1	8.3	12.3
5. Every time	2.8	3.6	.5	2.1	-	4.0	-	4.3	3.7	1.8	1.7	-	-	-	3.4	-
Item 3340 N(Wtd) ★	184	88	77	149	2	48	59	46	31	67	79	-	-	9	148	22

★=excludes respondents for whom question was inappropriate.

QUESTIONNAIRE FORM 1 1981	TOTAL	SEX		RACE		REGION				4YR COLLEGE PLANS		ILLICIT DRUG USE: LIFETIME				
		M	F	White	Black	NE	NC	S	W	Yes	No	None	Mari- juana Only	Few Pills	More Pills	Any Her- oin
Weighted No. of Cases:	3644	1689	1795	2769	438	853	1075	1124	592	1969	1283	1213	853	430	958	37
% of Weighted Total:	100.0	46.3	49.3	76.0	12.0	23.4	29.5	30.8	16.3	54.0	35.2	33.3	23.4	11.8	26.3	1.0
B058G: At your home (or apartment or dorm)																
1. Not at all	39.0	37.1	38.2	36.6	-	37.6	39.9	42.8	33.8	37.3	35.1	-	-	12.9	40.2	24.7
2. A few of the times	24.8	24.2	24.4	23.2	-	20.3	26.8	20.1	34.6	18.0	32.2	-	-	57.5	21.8	38.6
3. Some of the times	15.6	19.0	15.8	17.8	-	17.1	13.4	21.9	8.3	14.8	16.8	-	-	-	17.8	11.1
4. Most of the times	10.7	13.6	9.7	12.5	-	10.2	13.7	8.2	9.8	17.8	8.0	-	-	-	10.9	16.4
5. Every time	10.0	6.2	11.9	9.9	100.0	14.8	6.2	6.9	13.5	12.1	8.0	-	-	29.6	9.3	9.2
Item 3350 N(Wtd) ★	179	85	76	146	1	47	56	45	31	64	78	-	-	9	144	21
B058H: At school																
1. Not at all	55.1	51.4	57.8	55.1	56.8	41.6	63.0	53.5	62.9	62.1	55.0	-	-	62.4	54.2	46.3
2. A few of the times	20.9	19.0	24.4	20.8	-	33.5	11.0	20.9	20.4	15.1	18.2	-	-	37.6	21.7	14.4
3. Some of the times	16.0	22.6	9.1	15.8	43.2	14.4	21.6	17.7	5.8	10.8	21.6	-	-	-	18.4	10.1
4. Most of the times	4.6	4.2	6.2	4.6	-	7.7	4.4	3.1	2.2	7.3	4.5	-	-	-	3.1	17.4
5. Every time	3.4	2.7	2.6	3.7	-	2.8	-	4.8	8.7	4.7	.8	-	-	-	2.5	11.7
Item 3360 N(Wtd) ★	183	88	76	148	2	48	59	45	31	66	79	-	-	9	147	22
B058I: In a car																
1. Not at all	49.8	53.7	47.0	49.7	100.0	54.0	47.5	41.1	60.4	54.8	45.3	-	-	62.4	48.0	43.7
2. A few of the times	28.7	19.8	36.4	27.9	-	20.5	40.6	26.3	22.7	23.7	32.0	-	-	21.1	31.8	17.7
3. Some of the times	12.8	15.3	12.8	13.5	-	10.1	8.3	25.6	7.0	16.2	11.5	-	-	16.5	13.8	8.1
4. Most of the times	4.4	6.8	2.9	5.1	-	10.0	1.4	2.2	4.8	2.6	8.2	-	-	-	3.8	12.2
5. Every time	4.2	4.3	.9	3.8	-	5.4	2.3	4.8	5.0	2.8	3.1	-	-	-	2.6	18.3
Item 3380 N(Wtd) ★	180	86	76	147	1	47	57	45	31	65	78	-	-	9	145	21
B059: How many of the times when you used barbiturates during the last year did you use them along with each of the following drugs- -that is, so that their effects overlapped?																
B059A: With alcohol																
1. Not at all	35.7	37.2	42.5	39.0	56.8	27.7	28.6	35.5	61.7	41.9	40.4	-	-	83.5	33.0	18.4
2. A few of the times	23.9	17.4	22.9	19.2	-	29.9	31.3	12.4	17.5	14.7	21.7	-	-	16.5	23.2	38.5
3. Some of the times	17.1	15.6	16.5	18.3	43.2	14.8	15.4	33.8	-	15.9	15.2	-	-	-	19.6	11.3
4. Most of the times	13.9	18.8	11.1	13.8	-	14.4	18.8	10.4	8.9	17.7	15.4	-	-	-	14.1	21.4
5. Every time	9.4	11.0	7.1	9.8	-	13.2	5.9	7.8	12.0	9.7	7.4	-	-	-	10.1	10.4
Item 3390 N(Wtd) ★	184	88	76	149	2	48	59	45	31	66	80	-	-	9	148	22
B059B: With marijuana																
1. Not at all	31.7	30.6	39.0	34.3	100.0	35.4	19.4	25.6	57.8	41.3	30.8	-	-	83.5	28.5	14.1
2. A few of the times	17.5	13.7	19.5	14.6	-	23.2	11.3	26.7	7.3	6.8	16.8	-	-	16.5	19.3	10.0
3. Some of the times	21.4	22.3	17.9	21.6	-	16.9	25.8	26.8	12.1	20.6	19.2	-	-	-	23.6	20.4
4. Most of the times	16.3	19.1	11.1	15.7	-	12.8	27.4	9.2	10.8	16.4	21.9	-	-	-	16.4	26.5
5. Every time	13.2	14.4	12.5	13.8	-	11.6	16.1	11.8	11.9	14.9	11.2	-	-	-	12.2	29.0
Item 3400 N(Wtd) ★	182	87	76	148	1	47	58	45	31	65	79	-	-	9	147	21
B059C: With LSD																
1. Not at all	91.3	87.8	96.8	93.2	56.8	85.8	87.2	96.1	99.9	95.3	88.3	-	-	100.0	91.8	82.5
2. A few of the times	5.3	6.8	2.1	4.1	-	8.0	7.0	3.9	-	2.9	7.1	-	-	-	5.0	10.5
3. Some of the times	.8	.8	-	-	-	1.6	1.1	-	-	-	.9	-	-	-	1.0	-
4. Most of the times	2.6	4.6	1.0	2.7	43.2	4.5	4.6	-	-	1.8	3.7	-	-	-	2.2	6.9
5. Every time	-	-	-	-	-	-	-	-	-	-	-	-	-	-	-	-
Item 3410 N(Wtd) ★	179	85	76	147	2	45	58	45	31	65	77	-	-	7	145	22
B059D: With psychedelics other than LSD																
1. Not at all	88.5	88.7	94.4	92.9	56.8	86.5	87.1	86.2	97.4	91.3	92.4	-	-	83.5	92.5	61.0
2. A few of the times	7.0	5.9	3.6	3.6	-	7.3	6.0	11.2	2.6	4.1	3.1	-	-	-	5.7	20.8
3. Some of the times	2.7	2.5	1.0	1.3	43.2	4.7	2.6	2.5	-	1.8	2.9	-	-	16.5	.5	12.2
4. Most of the times	1.4	2.9	-	1.7	-	-	4.3	-	-	1.8	1.7	-	-	-	.8	6.0
5. Every time	.4	-	.9	.5	-	1.5	-	-	-	1.1	-	-	-	-	.5	-
Item 3420 N(Wtd) ★	179	85	76	146	2	46	57	45	31	65	77	-	-	9	143	22

★=excludes respondents for whom question was inappropriate.

QUESTIONNAIRE FORM 1 1981	TOTAL	SEX		RACE		REGION				4YR COLLEGE PLANS		ILLICIT DRUG USE: LIFETIME				
		M	F	White	Black	NE	NC	S	W	Yes	No	None	Mari-juana Only	Few Pills	More Pills	Any Her-oin
Weighted No. of Cases:	3644	1689	1795	2769	438	853	1075	1124	592	1969	1283	1213	853	430	958	37
% of Weighted Total:	100.0	46.3	49.3	76.0	12.0	23.4	29.5	30.8	16.3	54.0	35.2	33.3	23.4	11.8	26.3	1.0
B059E: With amphetamines																
1. Not at all	83.9	78.5	90.6	86.2	56.8	84.8	77.3	87.4	89.4	84.0	85.4	–	–	83.5	87.3	57.3
2. A few of the times	9.5	9.8	7.9	7.8	–	11.5	15.0	6.1	1.4	6.0	10.6	–	–	16.5	7.2	24.9
3. Some of the times	3.0	5.5	–	2.7	43.2	3.6	3.3	4.1	–	5.2	.8	–	–	–	2.9	6.2
4. Most of the times	2.4	4.1	1.1	1.8	–	–	4.3	2.4	2.5	1.6	3.2	–	–	–	2.4	3.7
5. Every time	1.2	2.0	.5	1.4	–	–	–	–	6.7	3.2	–	–	–	–	.3	8.0
Item 3430 N(Wtd) ★	181	86	77	148	2	47	57	46	31	66	77	–	–	9	145	22
B059F: With quaaludes																
1. Not at all	84.9	79.3 *	90.3	87.5	56.8	86.9	81.5	82.7	91.3	82.3	85.7	–	–	83.5	85.7	75.3
2. A few of the times	6.6	10.3	4.1	5.5	–	5.9	6.0	7.3	7.4	8.1	7.4	–	–	16.5	5.8	9.9
3. Some of the times	5.7	6.1	5.6	5.7	–	6.1	6.9	7.5	–	5.8	4.8	–	–	–	6.5	3.7
4. Most of the times	2.4	3.8	–	1.3	43.2	–	5.6	2.5	–	3.0	2.1	–	–	–	1.7	8.9
5. Every time	.5	.6	–	–	–	1.1	–	–	1.3	.7	–	–	–	–	.3	2.3
Item 3440 N(Wtd) ★	180	85	77	146	2	46	57	46	31	66	76	–	–	9	144	21
B060: What are the most important reasons for your taking barbiturates without a doctor's orders? (Mark all that apply.)																
A. To experiment--to see what it's like	48.3	47.0	45.8	44.0	–	52.7	45.3	49.6	45.3	49.2	44.5	–	–	50.4	49.5	37.0
B. To relax or relieve tension	59.0	55.2	61.6	57.7	56.8	62.4	55.2	74.4	40.7	56.7	52.6	–	–	20.0	60.5	66.1
C. To feel good or get high	58.4	68.6	44.5	60.7	–	65.3	50.7	73.3	42.3	52.9	57.6	–	–	26.9	59.6	64.3
D. To seek deeper insights and understanding	4.9	6.2	.6	4.7	–	5.6	4.4	4.5	5.4	6.5	3.3	–	–	–	4.0	13.8
E. To have a good time with my friends	31.2	34.9	29.0	33.8	43.2	34.8	26.8	36.3	27.0	26.9	30.8	–	–	–	34.3	22.6
F. To fit in with a group I like	1.9	1.8	2.5	2.4	–	.8	2.1	4.5	–	1.8	3.0	–	–	–	2.3	–
G. To get away from my problems or troubles	17.4	17.3	20.8	18.8	56.8	18.0	11.6	24.9	17.0	22.7	13.9	–	–	21.1	17.6	15.1
H. Because of boredom, nothing else to do	17.7	22.7	16.6	21.0	–	20.9	13.1	13.1	26.9	21.6	17.2	–	–	21.1	16.5	24.9
I. Because of anger or frustration	11.8	9.9	15.6	12.5	–	10.0	12.9	14.6	8.7	15.7	9.0	–	–	5.8	12.2	11.3
J. To get through the day	8.4	6.7	9.3	9.3	–	5.9	10.7	6.5	10.3	12.3	8.3	–	–	–	6.4	26.1
K. To increase the effects of some other drug(s)	14.8	18.9	8.6	15.7	–	17.3	17.2	17.2	3.8	19.8	9.4	–	–	–	15.8	13.8
L. To decrease (offset) the effects of some other drug(s)	4.7	8.9	1.3	5.2	–	2.0	7.6	2.3	6.6	9.0	3.3	–	–	–	3.8	13.1
M. To get to sleep	39.9	37.7	45.2	41.4	56.8	31.6	42.3	47.1	38.7	49.1	31.6	–	–	49.6	38.6	47.0
N. To relieve physical pain	36.2	37.7	34.1	38.3	56.8	33.0	30.0	40.3	46.4	42.1	31.8	–	–	21.1	35.2	50.8
O. Because I am "hooked"--I have to have them	1.1	2.3	–	1.3	–	–	2.3	1.4	–	.9	1.7	–	–	–	–	9.0
Item 3450-3580 N(Wtd) ★	178	83	76	142	2	47	57	42	32	65	76	–	–	9	149	21
B061: When you take barbiturates how high do you usually get?																
1. Not at all high	9.0	6.4	13.8	7.5	43.2	8.6	8.0	4.3	17.6	11.8	9.8	–	–	49.3	6.5	7.0
2. A little high	21.4	19.4	27.7	23.5	–	20.7	17.0	28.8	20.5	21.5	20.6	–	–	–	23.2	18.7
3. Moderately high	37.9	44.3	29.7	38.5	–	30.7	41.0	43.6	35.0	35.4	43.0	–	–	21.1	40.2	30.1
4. Very high	19.3	24.6	10.8	19.1	–	27.7	22.4	16.6	5.1	15.0	17.8	–	–	–	18.7	31.6
5. I don't take them to get high	12.4	5.3	18.0	11.4	56.8	12.3	11.7	6.6	21.8	16.3	8.7	–	–	29.6	11.4	12.6
Item 3590 N(Wtd) ★	176	83	76	143	2	45	57	42	31	63	77	–	–	9	145	22
B062: When you take barbiturates how long do you usually stay high?																
1. Usually don't get high	15.5	8.0	26.0	15.2	56.8	13.8	14.1	6.6	32.8	24.0	15.2	–	–	73.1	13.6	3.7
2. One to two hours	23.6	19.9	32.9	26.7	–	15.9	20.7	32.4	27.9	21.6	26.2	–	–	26.9	25.2	11.7
3. Three to six hours	45.6	54.1	29.6	43.4	–	51.3	43.4	52.8	31.7	44.8	42.9	–	–	–	44.3	73.4
4. Seven to 24 hours	14.9	17.9	10.6	14.3	43.2	19.0	20.7	8.2	7.6	9.6	14.8	–	–	–	16.4	11.2
5. More than 24 hours	.4	–	.9	.5	–	–	1.2	–	–	–	.9	–	–	–	.5	–
Item 3600 N(Wtd) ★	175	83	75	143	2	44	57	42	31	63	77	–	–	9	144	22

★ = excludes respondents for whom question was inappropriate.

QUESTIONNAIRE FORM 1 1981	TOTAL	SEX		RACE		REGION				4YR COLLEGE PLANS		ILLICIT DRUG USE: LIFETIME				
		M	F	White	Black	NE	NC	S	W	Yes	No	None	Marijuana Only	Few Pills	More Pills	Any Heroin
Weighted No. of Cases:	3644	1689	1795	2769	438	853	1075	1124	592	1969	1283	1213	853	430	958	37
% of Weighted Total:	100.0	46.3	49.3	76.0	12.0	23.4	29.5	30.8	16.3	54.0	35.2	33.3	23.4	11.8	26.3	1.0

B063: What barbiturates have you taken during the last year without a doctor's orders? (Mark all that apply.)

A. Phenobarbital	34.9	35.6	32.8	33.1	-	42.4	33.6	25.5	39.5	40.1	31.1	-	-	23.5	30.1	72.3
B. Seconal	23.8	27.2	22.2	25.3	-	15.2	26.1	26.8	27.7	20.0	23.1	-	-	20.0	24.6	20.6
C. Tuinal	16.9	20.3	16.3	18.1	-	18.2	22.2	8.7	16.1	21.3	13.9	-	-	-	16.8	24.7
D. Nembutal	13.0	12.3	9.1	9.9	-	9.6	21.6	5.4	12.5	11.0	13.6	-	-	-	10.0	38.9
E. Luminal	9.0	10.0	4.8	8.6	-	7.5	11.7	8.8	6.5	7.4	6.8	-	-	-	7.9	20.0
F. Desbutal	5.6	6.9	2.1	4.1	43.2	-	11.7	2.4	6.8	5.2	5.2	-	-	-	4.0	18.8
G. Amytal	9.3	12.7	6.0	11.0	-	6.7	9.0	8.1	14.9	15.0	3.1	-	-	7.1	8.6	14.9
H. Adrenocal	3.8	5.1	2.5	3.8	-	1.1	2.3	5.3	8.2	2.1	4.5	-	-	-	3.2	9.4
I. Other	42.2	50.8	27.7	39.1	-	44.6	42.4	46.0	33.7	37.0	37.5	-	-	21.1	44.7	35.7
J. Don't know the names of some that I have used	44.7	35.5	56.4	45.4	56.8	37.2	42.2	60.3	38.8	49.0	42.3	-	-	35.4	46.4	35.4
Item 3610-3700 N(Wtd) ★	175	83	75	143	2	44	57	42	31	63	77	-	-	9	144	22

B064: Have you ever tried to stop using barbiturates and found that you couldn't stop?

1. Yes	1.8	2.1	1.9	2.2	-	-	3.0	3.5	-	.9	3.4	-	-	-	1.4	2.7
2. No	98.2	97.9	98.1	97.8	100.0	100.0	97.0	96.5	99.9	99.1	96.6	-	-	100.0	98.6	97.3
Item 3710 N(Wtd) ★	175	83	75	143	2	44	57	42	31	63	77	-	-	9	144	22

B065: Do you think you will be using barbiturates without a doctor's prescription five years from now?

1. I definitely will	.7	.7	.6	.5	1.7	.6	1.1	.6	.3	.5	1.0	.4	.8	.5	.8	6.8
2. I probably will	2.6	2.9	2.1	2.7	.8	1.4	3.3	2.4	3.7	2.2	2.9	.2	.5	.9	7.8	27.8
3. I probably will not	18.7	17.8	18.7	19.4	12.1	23.2	19.2	16.3	16.2	15.7	21.1	8.2	11.8	20.6	38.4	44.5
4. I definitely will not	78.0	78.6	78.6	77.4	85.3	74.8	76.5	80.7	79.8	81.5	74.9	91.2	86.9	77.9	53.0	21.0
Item 3720 N(Wtd)	3349	1545	1701	2581	406	759	1000	1044	546	1849	1196	1163	791	398	853	36

The next questions are about TRANQUILIZERS, which doctors sometimes prescribe to calm people down, quiet their nerves, or relax their muscles.

They include the following drugs: Librium, Valium, Miltown, Equanil, Meprobamate, Serax, Atarax, Tranxene, Vistaril.

B066: Have you ever taken tranquilizers because a doctor told you to use them?

1. No	87.0	86.6	88.2	86.5	93.2	87.1	86.7	87.1	87.4	87.8	86.4	93.3	90.2	82.1	78.8	67.5
2. Yes, but I had already tried them on my own.	2.4	2.1	2.2	2.3	.8	3.2	2.1	1.8	2.6	1.7	2.7	.1	.2	2.5	6.5	23.7
3. Yes, and it was the first time I took any	10.6	11.3	9.6	11.2	6.0	9.7	11.2	11.1	10.0	10.5	10.9	6.6	9.5	15.4	14.7	8.8
Item 3730 N(Wtd)	3387	1572	1714	2646	389	790	1016	1038	543	1887	1205	1172	796	411	900	36

B067: On how many occasions (if any) have you taken tranquilizers on your own--that is, without a doctor telling you to take them...

B067A: ...in your lifetime?

1. 0 occasions	86.0	86.8	86.4	85.0	94.5	85.0	85.2	86.9	87.0	88.4	84.1	100.0	100.0	74.1	62.0	22.2
2. 1-2	6.7	5.7	7.1	7.4	2.6	7.2	6.1	6.9	6.7	5.7	7.7	-	-	25.9	12.9	15.3
3. 3-5	2.6	2.4	2.7	2.5	2.1	2.6	3.1	2.5	2.2	2.3	2.8	-	-	-	9.8	4.6
4. 6-9	1.5	1.1	1.8	1.7	.6	2.4	1.5	.9	1.3	1.4	1.6	-	-	-	5.3	7.9
5. 10-19	1.6	2.1	1.0	1.8	.3	1.0	2.5	1.5	1.0	1.1	2.3	-	-	-	5.4	14.9
6. 20-39	.7	.9	.4	.6	-	.4	1.0	.7	.5	.5	.5	-	-	-	2.3	8.7
7. 40 or more	.9	1.0	.6	1.1	-	1.3	.6	.6	1.2	.7	1.1	-	-	-	2.3	26.3
Item 1070 N(Wtd)	3376	1572	1706	2643	385	784	1015	1035	542	1889	1192	1177	798	410	894	36

★=excludes respondents for whom question was inappropriate.

QUESTIONNAIRE FORM 1 1981	TOTAL	SEX		RACE		REGION				4YR COLLEGE PLANS		ILLICIT DRUG USE: LIFETIME				
		M	F	White	Black	NE	NC	S	W	Yes	No	None	Mari- juana Only	Few Pills	More Pills	Any Her- oin
Weighted No. of Cases:	3644	1689	1795	2769	438	853	1075	1124	592	1969	1283	1213	853	430	958	37
% of Weighted Total:	100.0	46.3	49.3	76.0	12.0	23.4	29.5	30.8	16.3	54.0	35.2	33.3	23.4	11.8	26.3	1.0
B067B: ...during the last 12 months?																
1. 0 occasions	92.5	93.3	92.6	92.1	97.7	91.6	91.9	93.4	93.1	94.2	90.9	100.0	100.0	93.9	76.5	44.2
2. 1-2	3.7	2.7	4.4	4.0	1.3	3.9	3.5	3.8	3.7	3.0	4.6	-	-	6.1	11.2	5.4
3. 3-5	1.9	1.6	1.6	1.8	.8	2.6	2.1	1.2	1.9	1.3	2.6	-	-	-	6.6	14.8
4. 6-9	.8	1.0	.4	.8	.2	.7	1.3	.3	.6	.5	.7	-	-	-	2.4	13.1
5. 10-19	.7	.9	.5	.9	-	.8	.8	.8	.3	.8	.5	-	-	-	2.2	13.5
6. 20-39	.2	.3	.1	.2	-	.1	.2	.2	.1	.1	.4	-	-	-	.7	-
7. 40 or more	.2	.2	.2	.2	-	.3	.1	.2	.3	.2	.3	-	-	-	.5	8.9
Item 1080 N(Wtd)	3360	1561	1700	2629	385	781	1008	1030	541	1880	1185	1178	798	405	880	36
B067C: ...during the last 30 days?																
1. 0 occasions	97.3	97.2	97.6	97.2	98.8	97.4	96.5	97.9	97.3	97.7	96.6	100.0	100.0	99.3	91.5	60.3
2. 1-2	1.7	1.7	1.6	1.7	1.0	1.9	1.9	1.1	2.2	1.4	2.0	-	-	.7	5.5	13.9
3. 3-5	.6	.5	.4	.6	-	.4	.9	.6	.2	.6	.6	-	-	-	1.7	14.8
4. 6-9	.3	.4	.1	.3	.2	.1	.5	.3	-	.2	.4	-	-	-	.8	4.7
5. 10-19	.1	.1	.1	.1	-	.1	.1	.1	.3	.1	.2	-	-	-	.2	4.6
6. 20-39	*	.1	-	*	-	-	.1	-	-	-	.1	-	-	-	.1	-
7. 40 or more	*	*	-	*	-	.2	-	-	-	-	.1	-	-	-	.1	1.7
Item 1090 N(Wtd)	3359	1559	1701	2626	385	780	1009	1029	540	1878	1187	1178	799	403	881	36

IF YOU HAVE NOT TAKEN TRANQUILIZERS IN THE LAST TWELVE MONTHS, GO TO Q.B075.

THE FOLLOWING QUESTIONS REFER ONLY TO TAKING TRANQUILIZERS WITHOUT A DOCTOR'S ORDERS. IF YOU HAVE NOT DONE THIS IN THE LAST TWELVE MONTHS, GO TO Q.B075.

B068: When you used tranquilizers during the last year, how often did you use them in each of the following situations?

B068A: When you were alone

	TOTAL	M	F	White	Black	NE	NC	S	W	Yes	No	None	Mari- juana Only	Few Pills	More Pills	Any Her- oin
1. Not at all	46.4	48.3	48.2	45.3	81.3	41.2	36.2	56.2	58.3	46.3	46.7	-	-	66.9	44.5	20.2
2. A few of the times	26.2	25.3	25.1	26.4	-	29.3	30.0	25.0	15.6	24.3	29.6	-	-	16.6	27.9	30.6
3. Some of the times	11.2	14.0	6.0	11.0	-	7.8	18.7	9.2	4.3	8.3	9.4	-	-	-	11.4	26.3
4. Most of the times	8.1	6.2	9.9	8.8	14.6	11.1	8.3	5.7	7.3	10.1	6.9	-	-	-	7.9	22.9
5. Every time	8.2	6.3	10.8	8.5	4.1	10.6	6.9	3.9	14.5	11.0	7.4	-	-	16.5	8.4	-
Item 3740 N(Wtd) ★	238	104	115	197	11	59	77	65	37	100	101	-	-	21	191	19

B068B: With just 1 or 2 other people

	TOTAL	M	F	White	Black	NE	NC	S	W	Yes	No	None	Mari- juana Only	Few Pills	More Pills	Any Her- oin
1. Not at all	34.4	33.5	37.7	34.2	58.4	46.3	22.0	36.3	38.2	38.4	34.7	-	-	73.2	30.2	8.2
2. A few of the times	32.2	32.8	31.3	32.9	13.7	29.8	29.0	38.2	31.8	29.9	30.5	-	-	8.1	37.0	23.9
3. Some of the times	17.5	18.6	13.9	17.9	7.8	16.7	23.8	15.6	8.7	10.7	22.4	-	-	-	18.1	37.4
4. Most of the times	7.9	9.4	7.0	7.6	7.7	2.6	12.5	4.1	13.5	11.0	5.8	-	-	-	6.8	30.6
5. Every time	8.0	5.7	10.1	7.3	12.3	4.5	12.7	5.8	7.8	10.0	6.5	-	-	18.7	8.0	-
Item 3750 N(Wtd) ★	230	99	113	193	11	56	75	64	35	96	99	-	-	20	183	19

B068C: At a party

	TOTAL	M	F	White	Black	NE	NC	S	W	Yes	No	None	Mari- juana Only	Few Pills	More Pills	Any Her- oin
1. Not at all	56.8	56.0	63.1	57.3	86.1	63.1	46.2	59.6	64.3	65.8	52.3	-	-	91.1	54.9	19.7
2. A few of the times	17.3	12.3	18.8	16.9	7.4	14.2	18.3	17.1	20.3	15.6	16.9	-	-	8.9	17.6	31.0
3. Some of the times	13.3	16.4	7.9	13.4	-	10.6	18.1	10.0	13.1	5.9	16.4	-	-	-	14.8	17.8
4. Most of the times	5.9	8.4	4.0	6.3	6.5	6.5	7.4	5.9	2.3	6.9	5.1	-	-	-	6.9	5.8
5. Every time	6.7	6.9	6.2	6.2	-	5.5	10.1	7.5	-	5.7	9.3	-	-	-	5.8	25.7
Item 3760 N(Wtd) ★	230	99	114	193	11	55	76	64	36	97	99	-	-	20	183	19

* = less than .05 per cent.   ★ = excludes respondents for whom question was inappropriate.

QUESTIONNAIRE FORM 1 1981	TOTAL	SEX		RACE		REGION				4YR COLLEGE PLANS		ILLICIT DRUG USE: LIFETIME				
		M	F	White	Black	NE	NC	S	W	Yes	No	None	Mari- juana Only	Few Pills	More Pills	Any Her- oin
Weighted No. of Cases:	3644	1689	1795	2769	438	853	1075	1124	592	1969	1283	1213	853	430	958	37
% of Weighted Total:	100.0	46.3	49.3	76.0	12.0	23.4	29.5	30.8	16.3	54.0	35.2	33.3	23.4	11.8	26.3	1.0

B068D: When your date or spouse was present

1. Not at all	64.9	68.1	66.6	66.4	76.6	69.4	54.9	66.5	75.6	72.6	61.2	–	–	88.9	64.9	23.8
2. A few of the times	14.0	14.4	13.6	14.8	6.7	11.5	11.3	17.3	17.7	15.4	12.5	–	–	11.1	13.9	24.2
3. Some of the times	11.8	10.8	7.6	10.3	–	12.7	20.4	6.8	1.2	6.6	13.4	–	–	–	11.4	33.3
4. Most of the times	3.8	3.8	3.8	3.5	7.7	4.6	5.9	1.4	2.2	2.3	5.9	–	–	–	3.9	7.5
5. Every time	5.6	2.9	8.5	5.1	8.9	1.8	7.5	8.0	3.2	3.2	7.1	–	–	–	5.9	11.2
Item 3770 N(Wtd) ★	232	100	114	193	11	56	76	64	37	98	99	–	–	20	185	19

B068E: When people over age 30 were present

1. Not at all	56.3	58.9	53.0	55.1	59.3	59.4	57.1	50.4	60.2	55.6	58.0	–	–	36.1	56.1	60.6
2. A few of the times	21.4	19.4	23.0	22.1	13.8	21.2	17.4	29.8	15.1	24.3	19.1	–	–	13.6	23.8	16.3
3. Some of the times	10.3	10.8	9.1	11.3	–	11.3	12.5	8.0	8.2	6.1	12.7	–	–	8.9	10.4	15.4
4. Most of the times	4.4	5.9	3.7	3.9	6.5	7.0	7.5	.9	–	8.0	.8	–	–	–	4.7	7.8
5. Every time	7.7	5.0	11.2	7.6	20.4	1.1	5.6	10.9	16.4	5.9	9.5	–	–	41.4	5.0	–
Item 3780 N(Wtd) ★	231	100	114	193	11	56	75	64	36	98	99	–	–	20	184	19

B068F: During the daytime (before 4:00 p.m.)

1. Not at all	47.9	54.5	41.8	46.0	79.8	44.8	48.3	49.0	49.7	46.9	48.8	–	–	56.0	45.9	37.7
2. A few of the times	25.2	21.4	28.2	24.5	20.2	28.5	22.6	24.5	26.9	24.7	25.4	–	–	11.3	28.6	15.9
3. Some of the times	15.5	13.5	17.6	17.2	–	19.2	21.2	11.5	4.7	15.4	15.8	–	–	12.4	16.0	20.0
4. Most of the times	5.5	3.9	7.2	5.7	–	2.7	4.5	8.4	6.9	4.9	5.7	–	–	2.3	5.5	10.6
5. Every time	5.9	6.7	5.2	6.6	–	4.8	3.4	6.7	11.8	8.1	4.3	–	–	17.9	3.9	15.9
Item 3790 N(Wtd) ★	232	100	113	195	10	57	75	64	35	97	100	–	–	20	186	18

B068G: At your home (or apartment or dorm)

1. Not at all	28.2	33.0	23.4	27.3	31.0	25.5	25.7	30.3	33.9	18.2	34.3	–	–	3.0	28.5	25.4
2. A few of the times	25.8	25.9	27.1	26.2	28.9	28.5	26.0	28.9	15.6	29.8	22.1	–	–	31.8	27.7	10.4
3. Some of the times	17.1	20.0	12.0	16.8	–	17.9	24.9	9.3	13.5	14.1	21.5	–	–	21.3	15.4	35.8
4. Most of the times	10.3	8.3	13.8	11.8	–	10.1	11.9	11.4	5.5	12.8	8.3	–	–	5.3	10.5	18.1
5. Every time	18.5	12.8	23.7	17.9	40.1	18.0	11.5	20.1	31.6	25.0	13.8	–	–	38.6	17.9	10.3
Item 3800 N(Wtd) ★	231	99	113	193	11	55	76	64	36	96	99	–	–	20	185	19

B068H: At school

1. Not at all	68.9	60.0	77.4	68.6	86.3	66.5	69.0	71.3	68.0	72.7	68.1	–	–	100.0	66.5	47.3
2. A few of the times	13.7	13.8	11.8	13.0	7.0	14.0	11.9	13.4	17.8	9.9	14.4	–	–	–	15.8	13.4
3. Some of the times	13.3	19.0	9.4	15.3	–	12.6	17.3	12.4	7.2	14.2	13.2	–	–	–	14.1	24.4
4. Most of the times	3.2	5.0	1.4	1.9	6.7	3.6	1.8	2.9	5.8	1.5	3.7	–	–	–	2.4	14.9
5. Every time	1.0	2.2	–	1.2	–	3.2	–	–	1.2	1.7	.6	–	–	–	1.2	–
Item 3810 N(Wtd) ★	232	100	113	193	11	56	76	65	35	97	99	–	–	20	186	19

B068I: In a car

1. Not at all	66.4	63.1	70.1	64.5	100.0	73.6	57.8	60.7	83.2	74.0	59.3	–	–	100.0	64.1	37.9
2. A few of the times	15.8	14.9	15.4	16.5	–	19.6	14.5	17.2	10.0	11.7	17.7	–	–	–	17.7	20.6
3. Some of the times	12.4	14.5	9.9	13.2	–	4.8	22.3	12.3	3.4	11.4	15.5	–	–	–	13.7	17.5
4. Most of the times	4.4	5.0	4.6	4.5	–	2.0	2.6	9.2	3.4	3.0	5.7	–	–	–	3.9	16.8
5. Every time	1.1	2.5	–	1.3	–	–	2.8	.7	–	–	1.8	–	–	–	.7	7.2
Item 3830 N(Wtd) ★	230	99	114	193	10	56	74	64	36	97	99	–	–	20	184	18

B069: How many of the times when you used tranquilizers during the last year did you use them along with each of the following drugs- -that is, so that their effects overlapped?

★=excludes respondents for whom question was inappropriate.

QUESTIONNAIRE FORM 1 1981	TOTAL	SEX		RACE		REGION				4YR COLLEGE PLANS		ILLICIT DRUG USE: LIFETIME				
		M	F	White	Black	NE	NC	S	W	Yes	No	None	Marijuana Only	Few Pills	More Pills	Any Heroin
Weighted No. of Cases:	3644	1689	1795	2769	438	853	1075	1124	592	1969	1283	1213	853	430	958	37
% of Weighted Total:	100.0	46.3	49.3	76.0	12.0	23.4	29.5	30.8	16.3	54.0	35.2	33.3	23.4	11.8	26.3	1.0
B069A: With alcohol																
1. Not at all	57.3	55.0	61.1	56.4	83.3	61.0	46.0	67.1	57.6	61.0	54.1	-	-	88.8	53.2	44.8
2. A few of the times	20.8	24.7	18.5	23.6	8.3	15.8	23.0	17.7	29.5	21.5	21.1	-	-	11.2	23.9	8.8
3. Some of the times	8.1	7.1	6.1	7.0	-	7.3	13.5	4.0	5.3	4.7	6.8	-	-	-	8.6	15.2
4. Most of the times	7.6	6.2	10.0	7.8	8.4	7.8	10.0	6.5	4.3	8.3	9.3	-	-	-	8.3	13.1
5. Every time	6.2	7.0	4.3	5.2	-	8.1	7.5	4.7	3.3	4.5	8.7	-	-	-	6.0	18.2
Item 3840 N(Wtd) ★	234	100	115	195	10	56	76	65	37	97	102	-	-	20	187	18
B069B: With marijuana																
1. Not at all	52.3	47.8	58.7	50.7	77.7	65.1	34.1	55.8	64.9	61.0	45.9	-	-	100.0	49.1	11.5
2. A few of the times	13.8	16.6	12.3	15.3	7.7	8.4	14.5	18.9	11.0	11.9	14.2	-	-	-	16.9	4.1
3. Some of the times	12.2	15.2	10.2	14.3	6.7	13.8	12.9	9.3	13.7	4.9	18.2	-	-	-	13.6	17.2
4. Most of the times	12.2	11.5	8.8	10.9	7.8	5.0	25.7	4.6	8.0	14.6	9.3	-	-	-	11.0	42.4
5. Every time	9.5	8.9	10.1	8.9	-	7.7	12.7	11.4	2.3	7.6	12.4	-	-	-	9.5	24.8
Item 3850 N(Wtd) ★	231	99	113	193	11	56	76	64	35	96	99	-	-	20	184	19
B069C: With LSD																
1. Not at all	96.1	92.6	98.6	95.9	100.0	94.8	93.3	98.5	99.9	96.8	96.0	-	-	100.0	96.2	89.9
2. A few of the times	1.4	2.4	.7	1.6	-	1.4	3.2	-	-	3.2	-	-	-	-	1.7	-
3. Some of the times	1.7	4.0	-	2.0	-	3.8	2.4	-	-	-	2.1	-	-	-	2.1	-
4. Most of the times	.8	1.0	.7	.4	-	-	1.1	1.5	-	-	1.8	-	-	-	-	10.1
5. Every time	-	-	-	-	-	-	-	-	-	-	-	-	-	-	-	-
Item 3860 N(Wtd) ★	225	96	111	189	10	54	73	64	33	95	96	-	-	20	180	17
B069D: With psychedelics other than LSD																
1. Not at all	97.4	96.4	99.0	98.2	93.3	100.0	95.5	96.7	98.9	97.6	97.5	-	-	100.0	98.8	80.7
2. A few of the times	1.0	1.9	.3	.8	-	-	2.5	-	1.1	1.2	.7	-	-	-	1.2	-
3. Some of the times	.8	.7	-	.6	6.7	-	1.0	1.8	-	1.2	-	-	-	-	-	9.9
4. Most of the times	.8	1.0	.7	.4	-	-	1.0	1.5	-	-	1.8	-	-	-	-	9.3
5. Every time	-	-	-	-	-	-	-	-	-	-	-	-	-	-	-	-
Item 3870 N(Wtd) ★	228	98	113	192	11	55	74	64	35	96	97	-	-	20	181	19
B069E: With amphetamines																
1. Not at all	91.0	86.4	96.0	91.9	93.3	93.9	83.4	94.0	96.7	94.4	90.9	-	-	100.0	92.3	64.7
2. A few of the times	5.6	8.2	1.8	4.5	6.7	3.7	12.2	1.7	2.2	2.9	4.1	-	-	-	4.7	22.7
3. Some of the times	2.2	3.3	1.5	2.6	-	2.4	3.4	1.2	1.1	1.6	3.1	-	-	-	2.4	3.2
4. Most of the times	1.2	2.1	.7	1.0	-	-	1.1	3.2	-	1.1	1.8	-	-	-	.6	9.3
5. Every time	-	-	-	-	-	-	-	-	-	-	-	-	-	-	-	-
Item 3880 N(Wtd) ★	228	98	113	192	11	55	73	64	36	96	97	-	-	20	182	19
B069F: With quaaludes																
1. Not at all	91.8	87.4	95.2	91.2	93.3	97.4	88.3	87.8	97.7	87.1	95.7	-	-	100.0	92.4	73.3
2. A few of the times	5.1	9.8	2.0	5.8	-	1.7	6.4	8.1	2.3	7.9	3.5	-	-	-	6.0	4.4
3. Some of the times	.3	.7	-	.3	-	-	.9	-	-	-	-	-	-	-	.4	-
4. Most of the times	2.3	2.1	2.8	2.1	6.7	.9	4.4	2.3	-	3.9	.8	-	-	-	1.3	16.0
5. Every time	.5	-	-	.6	-	-	-	1.8	-	1.2	-	-	-	-	-	6.3
Item 3890 N(Wtd) ★	228	97	112	191	11	55	74	64	35	96	96	-	-	20	182	18
B069G: With barbiturates																
1. Not at all	93.2	89.9	96.5	93.2	93.3	96.7	90.6	91.2	96.6	94.2	91.9	-	-	100.0	94.1	74.0
2. A few of the times	3.7	4.3	2.8	3.7	6.7	.6	4.2	5.9	3.4	2.9	4.7	-	-	-	3.2	14.2
3. Some of the times	2.1	4.1	-	2.1	-	1.8	4.1	1.2	-	1.2	2.6	-	-	-	2.1	5.1
4. Most of the times	1.0	1.6	.7	1.0	-	.9	1.1	1.7	-	1.6	.8	-	-	-	.6	6.7
5. Every time	-	-	-	-	-	-	-	-	-	-	-	-	-	-	-	-
Item 3900 N(Wtd) ★	227	98	111	190	11	55	73	64	35	96	96	-	-	20	181	19

★ = excludes respondents for whom question was inappropriate.

QUESTIONNAIRE FORM 1 1981	TOTAL	SEX		RACE		REGION				4YR COLLEGE PLANS		ILLICIT DRUG USE: LIFETIME				
		M	F	White	Black	NE	NC	S	W	Yes	No	None	Mari-juana Only	Few Pills	More Pills	Any Her-oin
Weighted No. of Cases:	3644	1689	1795	2769	438	853	1075	1124	592	1969	1283	1213	853	430	958	37
% of Weighted Total:	100.0	46.3	49.3	76.0	12.0	23.4	29.5	30.8	16.3	54.0	35.2	33.3	23.4	11.8	26.3	1.0

B070: What have been the most important reasons for your taking tranquilizers without a doctor's orders? (Mark all that apply.)

	TOTAL	M	F	White	Black	NE	NC	S	W	Yes	No	None	Mari-juana Only	Few Pills	More Pills	Any Heroin
A. To experiment--to see what it's like	33.1	39.0	25.0	31.3	6.5	39.4	24.2	38.9	32.7	25.1	30.9	-	-	3.0	37.1	24.6
B. To relax or relieve tension	64.6	60.3	68.0	64.9	70.6	74.8	59.4	63.6	60.9	69.2	63.4	-	-	51.6	66.6	58.7
C. To feel good or get high	40.9	55.8	28.0	42.5	12.2	44.0	42.0	44.9	26.7	42.4	42.4	-	-	3.0	42.4	65.8
D. To seek deeper insights and understanding	4.0	6.4	.4	3.6	-	4.4	5.3	3.5	1.3	4.4	3.4	-	-	-	2.6	23.0
E. To have a good time with my friends	18.2	20.8	14.0	17.5	-	26.3	18.7	14.5	10.3	18.7	15.9	-	-	-	19.9	20.8
F. To fit in with a group I like	2.1	4.3	-	1.7	10.7	3.5	3.5	-	-	2.9	.4	-	-	-	2.1	4.1
G. To get away from my problems or troubles	15.1	10.5	20.5	15.9	12.3	18.9	15.2	16.9	5.9	17.7	15.2	-	-	15.1	16.2	4.5
H. Because of boredom, nothing else to do	14.0	19.5	10.7	15.2	-	14.5	16.1	11.5	12.7	12.0	14.1	-	-	-	14.0	29.4
I. Because of anger or frustration	13.1	10.6	16.6	13.8	22.8	15.3	16.0	11.6	5.7	17.2	10.2	-	-	4.0	15.2	2.4
J. To get through the day	6.1	6.5	6.2	6.4	10.7	5.5	10.9	-	6.8	4.9	7.9	-	-	-	5.4	20.2
K. To increase the effects of some other drug(s)	8.7	14.2	5.1	9.0	-	10.6	10.4	9.1	1.1	11.4	8.8	-	-	-	9.0	14.4
L. To decrease (offset) the effects of some other drug(s)	5.4	8.6	2.0	5.2	-	4.0	8.2	3.0	5.2	8.7	1.3	-	-	-	4.9	16.2
M. To get to sleep	45.4	41.6	49.4	46.1	12.3	52.6	41.4	33.7	61.7	51.2	41.2	-	-	40.0	46.0	45.3
N. To relieve physical pain	42.9	44.1	41.9	44.5	24.7	45.0	38.4	38.2	57.2	41.8	46.0	-	-	58.7	41.6	39.3
O. Because I am "hooked"--I have to have them	.6	1.5	-	.7	-	-	1.8	-	-	-	1.4	-	-	-	-	7.3
Item 3910-4040 N(Wtd) ★	217	89	111	185	7	55	74	55	34	93	94	-	-	19	180	18

B071: When you take tranquilizers how high do you usually get?

	TOTAL	M	F	White	Black	NE	NC	S	W	Yes	No	None	Mari-juana Only	Few Pills	More Pills	Any Heroin
1. Not at all high	17.0	13.6	21.5	15.5	54.6	15.0	6.4	29.6	22.4	23.1	15.9	-	-	40.5	14.6	6.3
2. A little high	28.7	30.9	25.7	30.9	-	30.8	30.4	25.7	26.2	25.1	28.4	-	-	21.8	31.3	13.9
3. Moderately high	22.9	26.2	23.0	25.3	9.0	24.0	21.6	26.3	17.4	19.8	25.2	-	-	-	26.1	22.4
4. Very high	12.4	18.6	4.6	11.0	7.9	12.6	16.2	9.5	8.0	11.2	13.5	-	-	-	11.1	42.1
5. I don't take them to get high	19.1	10.7	25.2	17.2	28.5	17.6	25.3	8.8	26.0	20.8	17.0	-	-	37.7	16.9	15.2
Item 4050 N(Wtd) ★	223	94	111	188	9	56	76	59	31	95	96	-	-	22	180	18

B072: When you take tranquilizers how long do you usually stay high?

	TOTAL	M	F	White	Black	NE	NC	S	W	Yes	No	None	Mari-juana Only	Few Pills	More Pills	Any Heroin
1. Usually don't get high	31.1	23.3	40.2	29.9	64.2	23.6	26.7	35.1	45.4	35.8	31.3	-	-	78.9	27.1	6.3
2. One to two hours	27.2	23.5	32.6	29.5	16.7	24.5	16.6	37.8	36.1	21.2	32.2	-	-	17.6	29.0	23.5
3. Three to six hours	32.1	41.7	19.9	31.5	-	39.0	42.7	23.3	14.1	34.3	28.4	-	-	-	34.9	46.5
4. Seven to 24 hours	9.5	11.4	7.2	9.1	19.1	13.0	14.0	3.8	4.5	8.6	8.1	-	-	3.5	8.9	23.7
5. More than 24 hours	-	-	-	-	-	-	-	-	-	-	-	-	-	-	-	-
Item 4060 N(Wtd) ★	221	94	109	186	8	54	73	58	35	93	98	-	-	22	179	18

B073: What tranquilizers have you taken during the last year without a doctor's orders? (Mark all that apply.)

	TOTAL	M	F	White	Black	NE	NC	S	W	Yes	No	None	Mari-juana Only	Few Pills	More Pills	Any Heroin
A. Librium	29.8	31.8	26.2	28.8	-	38.7	31.0	13.5	39.9	29.1	24.4	-	-	12.7	30.6	41.7
B. Valium	83.3	82.7	82.2	82.7	65.9	87.3	90.3	81.5	64.1	81.2	85.0	-	-	63.4	85.4	86.4
C. Miltown	2.9	2.7	3.5	2.5	-	2.3	.9	3.1	7.9	2.8	3.1	-	-	8.5	1.5	9.5
D. Equanil	2.9	1.3	2.8	2.3	-	6.7	3.5	-	-	2.8	1.7	-	-	-	3.0	4.9
E. Meprobamate	2.0	3.1	.4	1.5	-	-	2.5	3.8	1.2	2.5	1.7	-	-	-	1.3	11.3
F. Serax	2.5	4.4	1.4	3.0	-	3.8	1.6	2.6	2.4	1.6	1.3	-	-	-	2.7	4.2
G. Atarax	4.9	5.4	1.7	3.7	-	4.4	7.2	3.9	2.4	2.9	3.1	-	-	-	3.1	27.5
H. Tranxene	3.1	6.0	.8	3.1	-	1.6	3.6	1.3	7.7	2.7	3.7	-	-	-	3.4	4.2
I. Vistaril	5.2	5.6	3.2	3.4	10.7	-	11.8	2.6	3.6	2.6	4.0	-	-	-	2.2	39.7
J. Don't know the names of some tranquilizers I have used	24.8	22.5	25.5	23.7	23.4	18.4	23.4	31.3	27.2	23.0	23.4	-	-	32.1	23.2	31.0
Item 4070-4160 N(Wtd) ★	217	92	109	185	7	54	74	56	33	93	94	-	-	21	177	19

★= excludes respondents for whom question was inappropriate.

QUESTIONNAIRE FORM 1 1981	TOTAL	SEX		RACE		REGION				4YR COLLEGE PLANS		ILLICIT DRUG USE: LIFETIME				
		M	F	White	Black	NE	NC	S	W	Yes	No	None	Marijuana Only	Few Pills	More Pills	Any Heroin
Weighted No. of Cases:	3644	1689	1795	2769	438	853	1075	1124	592	1969	1283	1213	853	430	958	37
% of Weighted Total:	100.0	46.3	49.3	76.0	12.0	23.4	29.5	30.8	16.3	54.0	35.2	33.3	23.4	11.8	26.3	1.0

B074: Have you ever tried to stop using tranquilizers and found that you couldn't stop?

1. Yes	2.2	2.2	1.9	1.8	-	2.3	.9	5.2	-	-	4.4	-	-	-	2.7	-
2. No	97.8	97.8	98.1	98.2	100.0	97.7	99.1	94.8	99.9	100.0	95.6	-	-	100.0	97.3	100.0
Item 4170 N(Wtd) ★	224	93	113	189	8	55	76	58	35	96	97	-	-	21	182	19

B075: Do you think you will be using tranquilizers without a doctor's orders five years from now?

1. I definitely will	.6	.5	.6	.5	1.4	.8	.9	.5	-	.6	.6	.5	.5	.7	.6	3.2
2. I probably will	3.5	3.3	3.4	3.4	3.6	4.4	3.4	2.9	3.9	3.0	4.2	.7	1.3	2.3	9.5	17.0
3. I probably will not	27.4	25.1	29.2	28.6	15.6	29.5	28.3	23.3	30.5	24.2	29.6	14.6	20.9	33.0	48.4	50.9
4. I definitely will not	68.5	71.0	66.8	67.6	79.5	65.3	67.4	73.4	65.6	72.2	65.6	84.2	77.4	63.9	41.4	28.9
Item 4180 N(Wtd)	3349	1563	1700	2599	404	763	1008	1033	546	1855	1203	1156	785	403	863	35

The next questions are about COCAINE, which is sometimes called "coke".

B076: On how many occasions (if any) have you taken cocaine...

B076A: ...in your lifetime?

1. 0 occasions	82.7	81.0	86.3	82.3	91.1	78.4	84.7	89.4	73.1	84.9	83.6	100.0	100.0	77.2	49.8	6.0
2. 1-2	6.6	8.0	5.1	6.8	4.5	7.9	6.8	4.3	8.9	6.1	7.1	-	-	22.8	14.0	6.0
3. 3-5	3.3	3.4	2.9	3.6	1.2	4.4	3.3	1.7	4.7	2.6	2.9	-	-	-	11.9	9.9
4. 6-9	2.1	2.6	1.2	2.0	1.4	3.3	1.2	1.2	3.8	2.0	1.4	-	-	-	7.7	6.4
5. 10-19	1.9	1.8	1.8	2.0	.7	1.6	1.6	1.8	3.1	1.9	1.7	-	-	-	6.4	18.1
6. 20-39	1.1	.8	1.2	1.0	.4	1.0	.5	.8	2.6	.7	.9	-	-	-	3.7	5.6
7. 40 or more	2.3	2.4	1.6	2.2	.6	3.3	2.0	.9	3.8	1.8	2.4	-	-	-	6.5	48.0
Item 950 N(Wtd)	3413	1591	1726	2669	393	795	1026	1028	564	1912	1202	1180	801	421	915	37

B076B: ...during the last 12 months?

1. 0 occasions	87.0	86.0	89.7	86.8	93.7	82.6	89.8	92.3	78.6	88.1	89.4	100.0	100.0	88.9	60.1	16.5
2. 1-2	5.4	6.8	3.9	5.5	3.7	7.3	5.0	3.4	7.1	5.1	4.5	-	-	11.1	14.6	13.5
3. 3-5	2.9	2.7	2.4	3.0	.9	3.9	2.0	1.5	5.9	2.9	2.3	-	-	-	10.5	11.6
4. 6-9	1.4	1.6	1.0	1.4	.7	2.4	.8	1.1	2.0	1.4	.6	-	-	-	4.9	11.7
5. 10-19	1.4	1.0	1.9	1.6	.4	1.5	.6	1.2	3.1	1.1	1.7	-	-	-	5.0	6.4
6. 20-39	.8	.7	.5	.7	.1	.6	.6	.4	2.0	.6	.7	-	-	-	2.3	13.0
7. 40 or more	1.0	1.2	.5	.9	.4	1.7	1.2	.1	1.3	.9	.7	-	-	-	2.6	27.4
Item 960 N(Wtd)	3408	1588	1725	2666	392	795	1025	1027	562	1910	1199	1181	801	417	912	37

B076C: ...during the last 30 days?

1. 0 occasions	93.0	93.1	94.1	93.0	96.4	90.1	95.3	96.5	86.7	93.3	95.0	100.0	100.0	97.5	77.8	34.2
2. 1-2	4.0	3.8	3.9	4.1	2.3	5.9	2.8	2.1	7.3	4.1	2.7	-	-	2.5	12.8	24.7
3. 3-5	1.4	1.8	.8	1.5	.6	2.4	.3	.7	3.4	1.4	.8	-	-	-	4.9	7.7
4. 6-9	.8	.7	.8	.9	.2	.8	.8	.6	1.5	.6	.8	-	-	-	2.8	9.6
5. 10-19	.4	.3	.2	.3	-	.5	.6	.1	.6	.4	.3	-	-	-	.9	17.4
6. 20-39	.1	.1	.1	.1	-	-	.2	-	.2	.1	*	-	-	-	.3	-
7. 40 or more	.2	.2	*	.2	.4	.3	.1	.1	.4	.1	.3	-	-	-	.5	6.4
Item 970 N(Wtd)	3406	1587	1724	2666	391	795	1024	1027	560	1910	1199	1181	801	417	911	37

IF YOU HAVE NOT TAKEN COCAINE IN THE LAST TWELVE MONTHS, GO TO Q.B084.

B077: When you used cocaine during the Last year, how often did you use it in each of the following situations?

★ = excludes respondents for whom question was inappropriate.   * = less than .05 per cent.

QUESTIONNAIRE FORM 1 1981	TOTAL	SEX		RACE		REGION				4YR COLLEGE PLANS		ILLICIT DRUG USE: LIFETIME				
		M	F	White	Black	NE	NC	S	W	Yes	No	None	Marijuana Only	Few Pills	More Pills	Any Heroin
Weighted No. of Cases:	3644	1689	1795	2769	438	853	1075	1124	592	1969	1283	1213	853	430	958	37
% of Weighted Total:	100.0	46.3	49.3	76.0	12.0	23.4	29.5	30.8	16.3	54.0	35.2	33.3	23.4	11.8	26.3	1.0

B077A: When you were alone

	TOTAL	M	F	White	Black	NE	NC	S	W	Yes	No	None	Marijuana Only	Few Pills	More Pills	Any Heroin
1. Not at all	79.1	76.5	85.9	81.1	63.0	80.3	76.5	83.9	76.6	79.5	79.9	-	-	89.7	79.8	49.6
2. A few of the times	13.2	13.2	12.1	12.3	21.0	14.4	13.4	9.4	14.3	13.3	11.6	-	-	5.1	13.8	21.1
3. Some of the times	5.4	7.2	.9	4.7	7.1	3.0	8.5	3.6	6.7	5.6	6.1	-	-	-	4.9	20.7
4. Most of the times	1.2	1.4	1.1	1.1	5.9	-	1.6	.9	2.4	.3	2.3	-	-	-	.8	8.6
5. Every time	1.1	1.6	-	.8	2.9	2.3	-	2.2	-	1.2	-	-	-	5.2	.7	-
Item 4190 N(Wtd) ★	430	219	172	342	24	137	102	78	113	218	127	-	-	47	351	29

B077B: With just 1 or 2 other people

	TOTAL	M	F	White	Black	NE	NC	S	W	Yes	No	None	Marijuana Only	Few Pills	More Pills	Any Heroin
1. Not at all	10.7	11.4	10.6	10.7	14.0	10.1	12.3	10.7	10.0	11.5	10.4	-	-	19.6	8.5	10.0
2. A few of the times	34.4	38.6	33.0	35.6	44.7	35.2	32.9	33.3	35.7	31.0	40.2	-	-	52.0	34.7	6.8
3. Some of the times	14.4	15.3	8.7	12.3	9.3	13.8	18.7	11.6	13.5	9.5	16.7	-	-	-	14.5	39.7
4. Most of the times	20.9	16.0	25.2	21.6	8.4	22.8	14.7	21.2	24.0	25.5	15.4	-	-	-	23.5	27.8
5. Every time	19.5	18.6	22.6	19.7	23.6	18.2	21.5	23.2	16.9	22.5	17.3	-	-	28.4	18.8	15.7
Item 4200 N(Wtd) ★	444	225	178	355	25	140	103	81	120	228	131	-	-	50	360	31

B077C: At a party

	TOTAL	M	F	White	Black	NE	NC	S	W	Yes	No	None	Marijuana Only	Few Pills	More Pills	Any Heroin
1. Not at all	35.6	37.7	35.7	35.3	47.0	33.1	34.3	43.5	34.2	35.0	39.3	-	-	70.4	32.6	7.9
2. A few of the times	19.3	18.6	22.0	20.9	16.2	15.2	20.7	18.8	23.3	24.7	13.0	-	-	10.1	21.4	11.8
3. Some of the times	21.5	18.4	22.8	20.1	27.9	25.2	19.6	18.5	21.0	17.8	21.7	-	-	4.1	23.4	29.5
4. Most of the times	11.8	12.8	10.5	11.6	2.9	10.9	10.0	13.4	13.5	9.1	14.1	-	-	6.3	12.3	16.8
5. Every time	11.7	12.5	9.0	12.2	6.1	15.6	15.5	5.7	8.0	13.4	12.0	-	-	9.0	10.3	34.0
Item 4210 N(Wtd) ★	437	221	176	348	25	136	103	80	117	223	128	-	-	47	356	30

B077D: When your date or spouse was present

	TOTAL	M	F	White	Black	NE	NC	S	W	Yes	No	None	Marijuana Only	Few Pills	More Pills	Any Heroin
1. Not at all	45.5	59.0	32.0	44.6	61.9	43.0	42.8	61.4	39.7	50.3	40.3	-	-	71.8	43.1	25.7
2. A few of the times	19.4	19.3	20.7	20.3	21.1	22.4	18.9	13.7	20.5	17.0	23.1	-	-	20.0	19.7	17.8
3. Some of the times	12.8	12.4	10.2	12.1	10.3	15.1	13.2	8.7	12.4	12.9	10.4	-	-	-	14.0	18.6
4. Most of the times	9.5	6.3	13.6	9.7	3.2	11.2	7.3	5.4	12.2	10.9	6.3	-	-	-	11.0	7.2
5. Every time	12.9	3.0	23.5	13.2	3.4	8.3	17.8	10.8	15.2	9.0	19.9	-	-	8.2	12.1	30.7
Item 4220 N(Wtd) ★	435	219	177	347	25	135	103	80	117	224	127	-	-	45	356	29

B077E: When people over age 30 were present

	TOTAL	M	F	White	Black	NE	NC	S	W	Yes	No	None	Marijuana Only	Few Pills	More Pills	Any Heroin
1. Not at all	69.4	71.0	69.7	71.1	60.9	71.0	67.4	71.7	67.8	72.3	70.8	-	-	93.1	68.8	38.4
2. A few of the times	13.5	12.9	14.8	13.4	21.9	14.1	9.0	15.1	15.7	11.5	14.5	-	-	1.4	14.7	18.8
3. Some of the times	10.9	9.9	10.1	9.6	14.4	7.1	18.2	5.4	12.7	10.4	11.0	-	-	-	11.6	19.7
4. Most of the times	3.5	3.5	3.8	4.2	-	4.5	2.5	4.5	2.6	3.0	2.8	-	-	-	3.0	16.3
5. Every time	2.6	2.8	1.6	1.8	2.8	3.2	3.0	3.2	1.2	2.8	.9	-	-	5.5	1.9	6.8
Item 4230 N(Wtd) ★	435	219	177	346	25	136	101	80	117	223	126	-	-	44	357	30

B077F: During the daytime (before 4:00 p.m.)

	TOTAL	M	F	White	Black	NE	NC	S	W	Yes	No	None	Marijuana Only	Few Pills	More Pills	Any Heroin
1. Not at all	54.6	57.4	54.4	55.3	52.3	56.8	62.9	46.1	50.4	58.7	48.2	-	-	81.8	53.2	26.4
2. A few of the times	25.2	22.4	26.8	24.4	20.6	24.2	22.7	28.0	26.7	21.5	32.2	-	-	6.7	27.4	30.1
3. Some of the times	14.1	15.2	13.2	14.5	19.6	15.4	7.1	12.7	19.6	14.7	11.9	-	-	3.5	14.6	24.9
4. Most of the times	2.9	2.0	2.7	2.5	2.9	.8	6.6	3.2	1.9	1.0	5.4	-	-	-	2.4	12.6
5. Every time	3.2	2.9	2.9	3.3	4.5	2.7	.7	10.1	1.4	4.1	2.3	-	-	8.0	2.4	6.0
Item 4240 N(Wtd) ★	436	219	177	348	25	139	101	80	117	225	126	-	-	44	357	31

B077G: At your home (or apartment or dorm)

	TOTAL	M	F	White	Black	NE	NC	S	W	Yes	No	None	Marijuana Only	Few Pills	More Pills	Any Heroin
1. Not at all	54.8	55.6	58.7	55.7	68.7	56.3	47.0	66.7	51.7	54.1	54.4	-	-	79.8	52.9	35.0
2. A few of the times	19.7	20.2	18.2	20.2	11.8	17.2	24.4	17.0	20.7	20.1	22.2	-	-	13.9	20.1	27.1
3. Some of the times	11.4	11.1	9.6	11.0	6.9	9.8	12.5	6.4	15.7	12.4	10.2	-	-	-	12.7	13.5
4. Most of the times	7.7	6.3	8.8	6.8	2.9	9.1	6.2	6.2	8.5	8.2	7.1	-	-	-	8.1	15.1
5. Every time	6.4	6.8	4.6	6.3	9.7	7.7	10.0	3.6	3.5	5.1	6.1	-	-	6.4	6.2	9.4
Item 4250 N(Wtd) ★	436	219	177	347	25	138	100	80	118	226	126	-	-	44	357	31

★=excludes respondents for whom question was inappropriate.

QUESTIONNAIRE FORM 1 1981	TOTAL	SEX		RACE		REGION				4YR COLLEGE PLANS		ILLICIT DRUG USE: LIFETIME				
		M	F	White	Black	NE	NC	S	W	Yes	No	None	Mari- juana Only	Few Pills	More Pills	Any Her- oin
Weighted No. of Cases:	3644	1689	1795	2769	438	853	1075	1124	592	1969	1283	1213	853	430	958	37
% of Weighted Total:	100.0	46.3	49.3	76.0	12.0	23.4	29.5	30.8	16.3	54.0	35.2	33.3	23.4	11.8	26.3	1.0

B077H: At school

	TOTAL	M	F	White	Black	NE	NC	S	W	Yes	No	None	Mari- juana Only	Few Pills	More Pills	Any Her- oin
1. Not at all	80.5	80.7	82.7	82.0	68.2	78.9	86.0	78.4	78.9	82.1	78.1	-	-	100.0	81.1	41.7
2. A few of the times	10.6	9.3	12.6	10.3	18.9	12.0	4.2	13.5	12.3	9.2	12.0	-	-	-	11.7	13.9
3. Some of the times	6.9	7.9	3.3	6.3	9.6	6.8	8.0	3.9	8.1	6.3	8.8	-	-	-	5.9	29.6
4. Most of the times	1.1	1.0	1.5	.9	3.3	.4	1.7	2.1	.6	.8	1.0	-	-	-	.7	7.5
5. Every time	1.0	1.1	-	.5	-	1.9	-	2.2	-	1.6	-	-	-	-	.6	7.4
Item 4260　N(Wtd) ★	434	219	177	346	25	137	101	80	117	224	126	-	-	44	356	30

B077I: In a car

	TOTAL	M	F	White	Black	NE	NC	S	W	Yes	No	None	Mari- juana Only	Few Pills	More Pills	Any Her- oin
1. Not at all	56.8	59.2	56.3	59.5	54.8	59.7	59.6	60.6	48.5	59.3	56.7	-	-	74.8	56.0	32.7
2. A few of the times	18.5	18.7	20.5	18.0	21.5	15.1	17.7	18.1	23.5	18.5	18.1	-	-	23.8	18.8	9.7
3. Some of the times	14.6	13.1	12.3	12.8	14.0	17.1	12.8	10.2	16.4	14.1	15.4	-	-	-	14.9	36.8
4. Most of the times	5.4	4.2	6.7	5.0	9.7	4.6	5.2	3.7	7.8	3.3	5.1	-	-	-	5.8	9.9
5. Every time	4.6	4.9	4.1	4.7	-	3.5	4.7	7.5	3.8	4.8	4.7	-	-	1.4	4.5	10.8
Item 4280　N(Wtd) ★	436	222	177	349	25	136	104	80	117	224	129	-	-	47	356	30

B078: How many of the times when you used cocaine during the last year did you use it along with each of the following drugs-- that is, so that their effects overlapped?

B078A: With alcohol

	TOTAL	M	F	White	Black	NE	NC	S	W	Yes	No	None	Mari- juana Only	Few Pills	More Pills	Any Her- oin
1. Not at all	27.5	34.4	21.6	27.1	41.9	28.5	19.2	38.2	26.3	26.2	33.5	-	-	50.2	25.3	12.3
2. A few of the times	27.3	28.6	26.1	27.1	31.9	24.0	28.3	31.0	28.0	26.5	23.6	-	-	34.0	28.6	7.6
3. Some of the times	14.8	10.8	18.0	13.9	23.1	13.1	17.1	13.2	15.9	12.1	22.3	-	-	-	15.2	31.9
4. Most of the times	13.4	11.4	17.7	14.9	3.1	14.8	14.6	7.3	14.9	14.6	10.9	-	-	-	15.7	7.6
5. Every time	17.0	14.8	16.7	17.0	-	19.6	20.9	10.4	15.0	20.5	9.7	-	-	15.9	15.2	40.6
Item 4290　N(Wtd) ★	428	213	175	343	23	135	101	78	114	223	125	-	-	42	350	31

B078B: With marijuana

	TOTAL	M	F	White	Black	NE	NC	S	W	Yes	No	None	Mari- juana Only	Few Pills	More Pills	Any Her- oin
1. Not at all	28.1	25.9	33.7	30.2	12.0	24.1	14.6	34.9	40.1	35.6	22.4	-	-	63.1	24.6	7.6
2. A few of the times	28.0	30.3	25.7	26.6	56.4	33.2	28.4	25.5	23.4	25.8	27.1	-	-	24.3	29.6	18.7
3. Some of the times	15.3	18.5	10.4	15.7	19.6	16.3	13.2	16.6	15.1	9.3	24.0	-	-	2.3	17.0	16.2
4. Most of the times	11.0	8.4	13.7	10.3	3.7	8.8	13.0	10.7	12.1	11.0	8.8	-	-	-	12.3	13.9
5. Every time	17.6	16.9	16.3	17.2	8.4	17.6	30.8	12.3	9.3	18.3	17.6	-	-	10.3	16.5	43.6
Item 4300　N(Wtd) ★	431	219	174	346	23	134	104	78	115	219	130	-	-	44	354	30

B078C: With LSD

	TOTAL	M	F	White	Black	NE	NC	S	W	Yes	No	None	Mari- juana Only	Few Pills	More Pills	Any Her- oin
1. Not at all	94.7	94.3	96.3	95.6	96.9	95.0	91.4	95.0	97.4	96.4	92.7	-	-	100.0	94.8	86.4
2. A few of the times	3.1	2.5	2.7	2.3	-	2.5	5.7	2.6	1.9	3.4	2.3	-	-	-	3.2	6.9
3. Some of the times	.7	.9	.5	.8	-	-	-	2.4	.7	-	1.6	-	-	-	.8	-
4. Most of the times	1.0	1.6	.5	.9	3.1	2.0	1.5	-	-	.2	2.3	-	-	-	.6	6.7
5. Every time	.5	.7	-	.4	-	.5	1.4	-	-	-	1.2	-	-	-	.6	-
Item 4310　N(Wtd) ★	411	206	167	327	23	125	99	78	109	211	121	-	-	39	338	30

B078D: With psychedelics other than LSD

	TOTAL	M	F	White	Black	NE	NC	S	W	Yes	No	None	Mari- juana Only	Few Pills	More Pills	Any Her- oin
1. Not at all	95.3	94.4	97.0	95.4	100.0	97.8	94.2	96.0	92.9	96.4	93.5	-	-	100.0	96.5	74.6
2. A few of the times	2.9	2.5	2.3	2.7	-	1.8	3.6	1.5	4.5	2.6	3.8	-	-	-	2.2	15.1
3. Some of the times	1.0	1.8	.2	1.2	-	-	-	1.4	2.7	.8	.9	-	-	-	.7	6.0
4. Most of the times	.5	.7	.5	.2	-	.4	.8	1.1	-	.2	.6	-	-	-	.3	4.3
5. Every time	.3	.7	-	.4	-	-	1.4	-	-	-	1.2	-	-	-	.4	-
Item 4320　N(Wtd) ★	409	205	167	329	22	126	99	77	108	212	123	-	-	39	337	29

B078E: With amphetamines

	TOTAL	M	F	White	Black	NE	NC	S	W	Yes	No	None	Mari- juana Only	Few Pills	More Pills	Any Her- oin
1. Not at all	88.5	91.8	88.4	89.6	96.9	90.7	83.6	87.4	91.1	91.3	84.5	-	-	100.0	89.2	63.5
2. A few of the times	6.8	4.9	6.5	5.6	-	5.7	6.3	10.2	6.2	4.0	11.7	-	-	-	7.2	12.8
3. Some of the times	3.1	2.4	3.1	2.9	3.1	2.8	7.4	-	1.9	2.7	2.4	-	-	-	2.3	17.3
4. Most of the times	1.1	1.0	.8	1.4	-	.9	.8	2.4	.7	1.4	.6	-	-	-	.8	6.4
5. Every time	.5	-	1.2	.6	-	-	2.0	-	-	.5	.7	-	-	-	.6	-
Item 4330　N(Wtd) ★	412	204	170	328	23	129	99	76	109	212	121	-	-	39	340	30

★=excludes respondents for whom question was inappropriate.

MONITORING THE FUTURE

QUESTIONNAIRE FORM 1 1981	TOTAL	SEX		RACE		REGION				4YR COLLEGE PLANS		ILLICIT DRUG USE: LIFETIME				
		M	F	White	Black	NE	NC	S	W	Yes	No	None	Mari- juana Only	Few Pills	More Pills	Any Her- oin
Weighted No. of Cases:	3644	1689	1795	2769	438	853	1075	1124	592	1969	1283	1213	853	430	958	37
% of Weighted Total:	100.0	46.3	49.3	76.0	12.0	23.4	29.5	30.8	16.3	54.0	35.2	33.3	23.4	11.8	26.3	1.0
B078F: With quaaludes																
1. Not at all	91.2	90.1	93.2	90.7	96.9	87.7	91.7	86.2	98.2	91.6	92.9	-	-	100.0	91.7	73.1
2. A few of the times	4.5	5.3	3.6	5.3	-	4.8	2.5	11.2	1.4	4.8	4.3	-	-	-	4.8	8.4
3. Some of the times	3.1	3.1	2.2	3.1	-	5.2	3.9	2.6	.4	3.3	1.1	-	-	-	2.5	14.9
4. Most of the times	1.2	1.5	1.0	.9	3.1	2.3	1.9	-	-	.3	1.7	-	-	-	1.1	3.6
5. Every time	-	-	-	-	-	-	-	-	-	-	-	-	-	-	-	-
Item 4340 N(Wtd) ★	418	209	172	334	23	129	100	77	111	217	123	-	-	39	345	30
B078G: With barbiturates																
1. Not at all	97.0	97.7	97.8	98.1	96.9	97.6	93.5	96.7	99.7	98.4	98.9	-	-	100.0	98.1	79.7
2. A few of the times	1.7	1.9	1.2	1.7	3.1	1.9	2.6	2.2	.3	1.3	1.1	-	-	-	1.1	10.9
3. Some of the times	1.0	.4	.4	.2	-	.5	2.8	1.1	-	.3	-	-	-	-	.4	9.4
4. Most of the times	.3	-	.7	-	-	-	1.2	-	-	-	-	-	-	-	.3	-
5. Every time	-	-	-	-	-	-	-	-	-	-	-	-	-	-	-	-
Item 4350 N(Wtd) ★	416	208	171	331	23	128	99	78	111	215	123	-	-	39	344	29
B078H: With tranquilizers																
1. Not at all	96.3	96.3	98.1	97.0	93.2	97.0	93.8	93.6	99.7	97.6	94.9	-	-	100.0	97.1	82.1
2. A few of the times	1.7	2.4	.5	1.6	3.6	.6	2.7	4.5	-	1.5	3.1	-	-	-	1.5	6.3
3. Some of the times	.4	.4	.6	.3	3.1	.5	.7	-	.3	.3	-	-	-	-	.3	2.4
4. Most of the times	1.5	1.0	.9	1.1	-	1.6	2.8	1.9	-	.7	1.7	-	-	-	1.0	9.2
5. Every time	.1	-	-	-	-	.4	-	-	-	-	.4	-	-	-	.1	-
Item 4360 N(Wtd) ★	415	208	170	331	23	128	99	78	111	215	123	-	-	39	342	30
B079: What have been the most important reasons for your taking cocaine? (Mark all that apply.)																
A. To experiment--to see what it's like	73.0	72.8	76.4	73.0	69.7	82.6	68.1	70.9	67.2	77.0	68.6	-	-	84.6	73.2	51.8
B. To relax or relieve tension	23.1	22.9	21.7	21.3	25.9	27.0	25.8	24.8	15.0	19.4	24.5	-	-	5.3	24.7	33.5
C. To feel good or get high	73.8	73.7	71.9	74.7	58.6	79.8	73.4	66.2	72.1	70.8	76.1	-	-	26.3	78.6	95.5
D. To seek deeper insights and understanding	10.0	8.9	5.5	8.3	5.8	12.8	13.9	6.6	5.4	7.6	10.2	-	-	1.6	7.9	46.8
E. To have a good time with my friends	47.3	42.1	52.7	47.7	38.6	45.4	54.1	34.1	52.4	46.7	47.4	-	-	23.7	49.4	61.4
F. To fit in with a group I like	5.8	7.1	2.8	4.7	13.6	7.7	6.2	7.2	2.3	4.5	6.6	-	-	3.6	5.4	13.4
G. To get away from my problems or troubles	6.8	10.0	3.0	6.9	-	7.3	7.9	8.2	4.3	6.8	8.7	-	-	-	7.0	15.1
H. Because of boredom, nothing else to do	9.0	11.4	5.5	8.0	8.2	12.7	9.7	10.5	3.2	8.6	10.1	-	-	-	9.3	20.9
I. Because of anger or frustration	3.7	4.7	1.0	3.0	2.4	4.6	2.5	7.2	1.5	2.6	4.6	-	-	2.0	3.7	6.8
J. To get through the day	4.5	3.4	4.8	5.1	2.4	4.8	4.5	2.5	5.4	4.2	6.3	-	-	-	4.6	9.9
K. To increase the effects of some other drug(s)	11.4	11.0	9.8	10.7	8.2	14.3	10.8	8.7	10.4	10.6	9.9	-	-	-	12.5	17.3
L. To decrease (offset) the effects of some other drug(s)	2.5	3.5	1.4	2.1	1.6	3.8	1.2	-	3.7	2.6	2.1	-	-	-	2.8	3.5
M. To stay awake	17.8	16.7	19.1	18.0	13.4	13.9	17.4	16.7	23.4	16.7	21.8	-	-	10.2	18.0	26.8
N. To get more energy	24.3	20.3	29.3	25.0	15.7	18.4	23.3	15.9	37.9	24.0	24.9	-	-	7.0	24.9	45.7
O. Because I am "hooked"--I have to have it	1.7	1.2	1.1	1.4	-	2.5	1.3	1.0	1.7	2.1	1.0	-	-	-	1.4	8.7
Item 4370-4510 N(Wtd) ★	433	215	178	345	24	138	100	78	117	224	125	-	-	50	352	31
B080: When you take cocaine how high do you usually get?																
1. Not at all high	7.4	5.2	11.8	7.2	10.5	7.6	4.4	13.7	5.7	9.8	6.9	-	-	33.6	4.3	-
2. A little high	22.1	21.5	24.9	22.9	31.7	24.6	18.4	22.9	21.9	21.8	23.2	-	-	34.8	22.2	-
3. Moderately high	42.4	49.0	36.8	44.4	29.7	40.3	40.4	33.3	52.5	42.1	37.4	-	-	21.7	45.9	35.6
4. Very high	27.5	24.4	25.0	25.3	22.0	26.5	36.2	30.2	19.5	26.2	32.0	-	-	9.8	26.8	64.4
5. I don't take it to get high	.6	-	1.5	.2	6.1	1.1	.7	-	.4	.2	.5	-	-	-	.8	-
Item 4520 N(Wtd) ★	434	220	175	346	25	137	101	77	119	223	128	-	-	50	354	30

★ = excludes respondents for whom question was inappropriate.

QUESTIONNAIRE FORM 1 1981	TOTAL	SEX		RACE		REGION				4YR COLLEGE PLANS		ILLICIT DRUG USE: LIFETIME				
		M	F	White	Black	NE	NC	S	W	Yes	No	None	Marijuana Only	Few Pills	More Pills	Any Heroin
Weighted No. of Cases:	3644	1689	1795	2769	438	853	1075	1124	592	1969	1283	1213	853	430	958	37
% of Weighted Total:	100.0	46.3	49.3	76.0	12.0	23.4	29.5	30.8	16.3	54.0	35.2	33.3	23.4	11.8	26.3	1.0
B081: When you take cocaine how long do you usually stay high?																
1. Usually don't get high	8.2	4.8	14.0	7.4	17.3	8.6	5.8	10.0	8.4	9.7	6.8	-	-	36.8	5.0	-
2. One to two hours	45.9	48.2	46.1	49.3	32.2	46.1	40.1	44.9	51.3	51.8	39.3	-	-	35.3	49.7	18.9
3. Three to six hours	33.8	38.4	28.8	33.8	31.4	36.4	39.9	30.0	28.0	28.5	43.4	-	-	20.5	34.2	50.6
4. Seven to 24 hours	9.8	6.8	9.2	7.6	12.9	5.1	12.8	13.7	10.1	7.3	9.9	-	-	4.1	9.7	19.2
5. More than 24 hours	2.3	2.0	2.0	1.9	6.2	3.7	1.3	1.3	2.2	2.7	.6	-	-	3.3	1.4	11.3
Item 4530 N(Wtd) ★	432	218	175	344	25	136	102	76	119	221	127	-	-	48	354	30
B082: Have you ever tried to stop using cocaine and found that you couldn't stop?																
1. Yes	3.2	1.8	4.6	2.6	12.4	4.4	2.1	.9	4.4	3.0	3.0	-	-	3.3	3.0	6.6
2. No	96.8	98.2	95.4	97.4	87.6	95.6	97.9	99.1	95.6	97.0	97.0	-	-	96.7	97.0	93.4
Item 4540 N(Wtd) ★	430	218	175	343	25	134	102	76	119	220	127	-	-	47	353	29
B083: What methods have you used for taking cocaine? (Mark all that apply.)																
A. Sniffing or "snorting"	94.0	94.6	93.4	94.1	88.5	93.6	91.0	93.3	97.4	94.5	93.0	-	-	75.5	96.0	100.0
B. Smoking	22.6	23.4	18.5	20.9	20.5	15.8	33.7	18.6	23.5	15.4	28.6	-	-	11.6	22.2	44.9
C. Injection	2.8	1.9	1.0	1.7	-	2.3	5.2	1.4	2.1	1.5	3.3	-	-	-	.8	30.8
D. By mouth	41.8	37.1	47.4	42.3	31.6	45.4	39.0	37.7	42.6	39.7	41.1	-	-	29.8	43.3	43.4
E. Other	4.1	4.7	2.3	2.8	6.7	3.7	5.3	2.3	4.8	2.1	5.5	-	-	-	3.0	24.0
Item 4550-4590 N(Wtd) ★	433	220	175	345	25	137	101	76	119	222	128	-	-	49	353	30
B084: Do you think you will be using cocaine five years from now?																
1. I definitely will	2.3	2.3	1.6	2.3	1.2	2.7	2.2	.9	4.3	2.0	2.2	.5	.7	.3	5.9	35.8
2. I probably will	7.0	8.1	5.3	7.4	3.6	11.2	5.9	4.3	8.2	6.5	6.3	-	1.1	4.6	21.9	30.6
3. I probably will not	17.5	18.2	16.5	18.1	10.8	23.2	15.6	12.8	21.8	16.4	18.4	5.1	15.1	22.2	35.0	19.6
4. I definitely will not	73.3	71.4	76.6	72.3	84.4	63.0	76.4	82.0	65.7	75.1	73.1	94.4	83.2	72.8	37.2	14.0
Item 4600 N(Wtd)	3429	1605	1734	2666	410	784	1022	1052	571	1901	1219	1178	797	417	898	34

The next questions are about HEROIN.

Heroin is sometimes called: smack, horse, skag.

B085: On how many occasions (if any) have you taken heroin...

B085A: ...in your lifetime?

	TOTAL	M	F	White	Black	NE	NC	S	W	Yes	No	None	Marijuana Only	Few Pills	More Pills	Any Heroin
1. 0 occasions	98.9	99.0	99.3	99.0	99.6	98.9	98.4	99.6	98.7	99.1	98.7	100.0	100.0	100.0	100.0	-
2. 1-2	.7	.6	.4	.5	.4	1.0	1.1	.2	.7	.6	.7	-	-	-	-	65.7
3. 3-5	.1	.2	*	.2	-	-	-	.2	.5	.2	.1	-	-	-	-	12.2
4. 6-9	*	*	-	*	-	-	-	.1	-	*	-	-	-	-	-	1.6
5. 10-19	.1	.1	-	.1	-	-	.2	-	-	-	.2	-	-	-	-	6.1
6. 20-39	*	-	*	*	-	-	-	-	.1	*	-	-	-	-	-	2.2
7. 40 or more	.1	.1	.2	.2	-	.1	.3	-	.1	*	.3	-	-	-	-	12.3
Item 1100 N(Wtd)	3368	1572	1716	2644	390	781	1018	1016	553	1894	1194	1173	798	417	883	37

B085B: ...during the last 12 months?

	TOTAL	M	F	White	Black	NE	NC	S	W	Yes	No	None	Marijuana Only	Few Pills	More Pills	Any Heroin
1. 0 occasions	99.3	99.3	99.6	99.2	100.0	99.5	98.9	99.7	99.0	99.4	99.3	100.0	100.0	100.0	100.0	34.9
2. 1-2	.5	.5	.3	.5	-	.4	.6	.3	.9	.6	.3	-	-	-	-	48.6
3. 3-5	*	.1	-	*	-	-	.1	-	-	-	.1	-	-	-	-	3.6
4. 6-9	-	-	-	-	-	-	-	-	-	-	-	-	-	-	-	-
5. 10-19	*	.1	-	*	-	-	.1	-	-	-	.1	-	-	-	-	2.6
6. 20-39	-	-	-	-	-	-	-	-	-	-	-	-	-	-	-	-
7. 40 or more	.1	.1	.2	.1	-	.1	.3	-	.1	*	.2	-	-	-	-	10.3
Item 1110 N(Wtd)	3368	1572	1716	2643	390	781	1018	1015	553	1894	1194	1173	798	417	883	36

★ = excludes respondents for whom question was inappropriate.   * = less than .05 per cent.

QUESTIONNAIRE FORM 1 1981	TOTAL	SEX		RACE		REGION				4YR COLLEGE PLANS		ILLICIT DRUG USE: LIFETIME				
		M	F	White	Black	NE	NC	S	W	Yes	No	None	Marijuana Only	Few Pills	More Pills	Any Heroin
Weighted No. of Cases:	3644	1689	1795	2769	438	853	1075	1124	592	1969	1283	1213	853	430	958	37
% of Weighted Total:	100.0	46.3	49.3	76.0	12.0	23.4	29.5	30.8	16.3	54.0	35.2	33.3	23.4	11.8	26.3	1.0

B085C: ...during the last 30 days?

1. 0 occasions	99.8	99.6	99.9	99.8	99.8	99.9	99.5	99.9	99.8	100.0	99.7	100.0	100.0	100.0	100.0	81.6
2. 1-2	.1	.2	-	.1	-	-	.2	-	.1	-	.2	-	-	-	-	8.5
3. 3-5	-	-	-	-	-	-	-	-	-	-	-	-	-	-	-	-
4. 6-9	-	-	-	-	-	-	-	-	-	-	-	-	-	-	-	-
5. 10-19	*	.1	-	*	-	-	.1	-	-	-	.1	-	-	-	-	2.6
6. 20-39	*	*	.1	*	.2	-	.2	-	-	*	-	-	-	-	-	4.6
7. 40 or more	*	.1	-	*	-	.1	-	-	.1	-	.1	-	-	-	-	2.8
Item 1120 N(Wtd)	3368	1574	1716	2643	392	780	1019	1016	553	1894	1194	1174	798	417	883	36

IF YOU HAVE NOT TAKEN HEROIN IN THE LAST TWELVE MONTHS, GO TO Q.B093.

B086: When you used heroin during the last year, how often did you use it in each of the following situations?

B086A: When you were alone

1. Not at all	54.8	67.0	56.2	61.2	-	-	39.5	81.9	79.8	68.5	49.4	-	-	-	-	46.9
2. A few of the times	19.1	16.3	-	10.1	-	-	44.3	-	-	-	20.7	-	-	-	-	22.5
3. Some of the times	11.3	-	23.5	13.4	-	-	16.2	18.1	-	11.2	16.8	-	-	-	-	13.3
4. Most of the times	7.9	3.6	20.2	7.1	-	77.1	-	-	-	20.2	-	-	-	-	-	9.3
5. Every time	6.9	13.1	-	8.1	-	22.9	-	-	20.2	-	13.1	-	-	-	-	8.1
Item 4610 N(Wtd) ★	26	14	8	22	-	3	11	6	6	10	11	-	-	-	-	22

B086B: With just 1 or 2 other people

1. Not at all	33.6	38.1	-	23.6	-	-	36.1	55.6	20.4	12.8	32.5	-	-	-	-	21.9
2. A few of the times	24.4	26.1	21.6	26.7	-	18.4	20.2	44.4	13.6	16.1	36.5	-	-	-	-	28.7
3. Some of the times	7.0	-	23.5	8.2	-	-	16.2	-	-	-	16.8	-	-	-	-	8.2
4. Most of the times	9.5	-	32.3	11.3	-	58.7	8.3	-	-	24.5	-	-	-	-	-	11.2
5. Every time	25.5	35.9	22.6	30.2	-	22.9	19.3	-	66.0	46.6	14.2	-	-	-	-	30.0
Item 4620 N(Wtd) ★	26	14	8	22	-	3	11	6	6	10	11	-	-	-	-	22

B086C: At a party

1. Not at all	55.7	61.5	33.2	47.5	-	18.4	44.7	68.5	79.8	39.2	61.1	-	-	-	-	47.9
2. A few of the times	3.3	-	11.0	3.9	-	-	-	13.5	-	-	7.9	-	-	-	-	3.8
3. Some of the times	-	-	-	-	-	-	-	-	-	-	-	-	-	-	-	-
4. Most of the times	20.4	5.9	43.8	24.1	-	58.7	16.2	18.1	13.6	26.6	16.8	-	-	-	-	24.0
5. Every time	20.7	32.6	12.0	24.5	-	22.9	39.2	-	6.6	34.2	14.2	-	-	-	-	24.3
Item 4630 N(Wtd) ★	26	14	8	22	-	3	11	6	6	10	11	-	-	-	-	22

B086D: When your date or spouse was present

1. Not at all	58.9	67.0	33.6	53.3	-	18.4	60.1	81.9	50.1	56.2	56.9	-	-	-	-	51.9
2. A few of the times	20.2	14.1	43.8	21.2	100.0	58.7	32.2	-	-	15.4	28.9	-	-	-	-	23.6
3. Some of the times	7.7	6.4	-	9.4	-	-	7.8	18.1	-	11.2	8.6	-	-	-	-	9.0
4. Most of the times	1.4	2.7	-	1.8	-	-	-	-	6.6	-	-	-	-	-	-	1.7
5. Every time	11.8	9.8	22.6	14.3	-	22.9	-	-	43.3	17.2	5.6	-	-	-	-	13.8
Item 4640 N(Wtd) ★	27	14	8	22	1	3	12	6	6	10	11	-	-	-	-	23

B086E: When people over age 30 were present

1. Not at all	71.0	55.4	100.0	72.3	-	77.1	67.8	81.9	63.7	58.7	76.5	-	-	-	-	70.1
2. A few of the times	7.4	5.9	-	9.4	-	-	7.0	18.1	-	11.2	7.7	-	-	-	-	9.0
3. Some of the times	2.6	4.6	-	-	100.0	-	5.5	-	-	-	-	-	-	-	-	3.2
4. Most of the times	4.6	8.3	-	-	-	-	9.8	-	-	-	10.8	-	-	-	-	-
5. Every time	14.4	25.7	-	18.3	-	22.9	9.8	-	36.3	30.0	5.0	-	-	-	-	17.7
Item 4650 N(Wtd) ★	28	16	8	22	1	3	13	6	6	10	12	-	-	-	-	23

* = less than .05 per cent.   ★ = excludes respondents for whom question was inappropriate.

QUESTIONNAIRE FORM 1 1981	TOTAL	SEX		RACE		REGION				4YR COLLEGE PLANS		ILLICIT DRUG USE: LIFETIME				
		M	F	White	Black	NE	NC	S	W	Yes	No	None	Marijuana Only	Few Pills	More Pills	Any Heroin
Weighted No. of Cases:	3644	1689	1795	2769	438	853	1075	1124	592	1969	1283	1213	853	430	958	37
% of Weighted Total:	100.0	46.3	49.3	76.0	12.0	23.4	29.5	30.8	16.3	54.0	35.2	33.3	23.4	11.8	26.3	1.0
B086F: During the daytime (before 4:00 p.m.)																
1. Not at all	64.2	69.7	31.3	63.6	-	77.1	57.0	87.2	50.1	73.7	54.8	-	-	-	-	61.8
2. A few of the times	7.5	8.3	10.5	3.7	-	-	9.8	12.8	-	-	17.5	-	-	-	-	3.5
3. Some of the times	12.4	10.6	23.5	12.4	100.0	-	26.2	-	-	-	22.7	-	-	-	-	15.2
4. Most of the times	4.7	2.5	12.0	6.0	-	-	7.0	-	6.6	9.1	-	-	-	-	-	5.7
5. Every time	11.2	9.0	22.6	14.3	-	22.9	-	-	43.3	17.2	5.0	-	-	-	-	13.8
Item 4660 N(Wtd) ★	28	16	8	22	1	3	13	6	6	10	12	-	-	-	-	23
B086G: At your home (or apartment or dorm)																
1. Not at all	62.0	72.6	33.7	59.2	-	-	63.2	69.1	79.8	59.4	61.4	-	-	-	-	55.5
2. A few of the times	3.0	-	10.5	3.7	-	-	-	12.8	-	-	7.5	-	-	-	-	3.5
3. Some of the times	11.3	8.5	23.5	8.2	100.0	18.4	21.3	-	-	4.8	16.8	-	-	-	-	13.3
4. Most of the times	10.7	2.7	32.3	13.0	-	58.7	7.8	-	6.6	24.5	-	-	-	-	-	12.6
5. Every time	13.0	16.2	-	15.8	-	22.9	7.8	18.1	13.6	11.2	14.2	-	-	-	-	15.2
Item 4670 N(Wtd) ★	27	14	8	22	1	3	12	6	6	10	11	-	-	-	-	23
B086H: At school																
1. Not at all	81.5	84.6	64.4	83.0	-	58.7	71.0	99.9	93.4	86.0	77.5	-	-	-	-	78.3
2. A few of the times	-	-	-	-	-	-	-	-	-	-	-	-	-	-	-	-
3. Some of the times	9.5	5.1	23.5	8.2	100.0	-	21.3	-	-	-	16.8	-	-	-	-	11.1
4. Most of the times	5.3	3.4	12.0	4.2	-	18.4	7.8	-	-	14.0	-	-	-	-	-	6.2
5. Every time	3.7	6.9	-	4.5	-	22.9	-	-	6.6	-	5.6	-	-	-	-	4.3
Item 4680 N(Wtd) ★	27	14	8	22	1	3	12	6	6	10	11	-	-	-	-	23
B086I: In a car																
1. Not at all	75.5	79.6	53.4	73.3	-	58.7	64.0	86.5	93.4	86.0	57.6	-	-	-	-	71.2
2. A few of the times	11.8	9.5	23.1	14.0	-	-	19.9	13.5	-	9.1	20.0	-	-	-	-	13.9
3. Some of the times	7.0	-	23.5	8.2	-	-	16.2	-	-	-	16.8	-	-	-	-	8.2
4. Most of the times	1.9	3.6	-	-	-	18.4	-	-	-	4.8	-	-	-	-	-	2.2
5. Every time	3.8	7.3	-	4.5	-	22.9	-	-	6.6	-	5.6	-	-	-	-	4.5
Item 4700 N(Wtd) ★	26	14	8	22	-	3	11	6	6	10	11	-	-	-	-	22
B087: How many of the times when you used heroin during the last year did you use it along with each of the following drugs--that is, so that their effects overlapped?																
B087A: With alcohol																
1. Not at all	51.4	45.3	33.2	44.2	-	18.4	23.0	86.5	86.4	50.4	40.0	-	-	-	-	43.1
2. A few of the times	17.5	15.8	31.3	21.3	-	58.7	19.0	13.5	-	28.2	16.9	-	-	-	-	20.5
3. Some of the times	12.9	11.5	23.5	12.4	100.0	-	29.0	-	-	-	25.4	-	-	-	-	15.2
4. Most of the times	8.3	9.0	12.0	10.1	-	-	18.7	-	-	9.1	12.1	-	-	-	-	9.7
5. Every time	9.9	18.4	-	12.0	-	22.9	10.3	-	13.6	12.2	5.6	-	-	-	-	11.6
Item 4710 N(Wtd) ★	27	14	8	22	1	3	12	6	6	10	11	-	-	-	-	23
B087B: With marijuana																
1. Not at all	40.6	39.0	42.9	42.2	-	77.1	-	73.7	66.2	65.8	25.1	-	-	-	-	30.1
2. A few of the times	25.6	16.6	21.6	17.9	-	-	44.7	26.3	-	12.8	24.4	-	-	-	-	30.1
3. Some of the times	10.0	5.9	23.5	11.9	-	-	16.2	-	13.6	-	24.2	-	-	-	-	11.8
4. Most of the times	3.6	-	12.0	4.2	-	-	8.3	-	-	9.1	-	-	-	-	-	4.2
5. Every time	20.2	38.5	-	23.9	-	22.9	30.9	-	20.2	12.2	26.3	-	-	-	-	23.7
Item 4720 N(Wtd) ★	26	14	8	22	-	3	11	6	6	10	11	-	-	-	-	22

★ = excludes respondents for whom question was inappropriate.

QUESTIONNAIRE FORM 1 1981	TOTAL	SEX		RACE		REGION				4YR COLLEGE PLANS		ILLICIT DRUG USE: LIFETIME				
		M	F	White	Black	NE	NC	S	W	Yes	No	None	Marijuana Only	Few Pills	More Pills	Any Heroin
Weighted No. of Cases:	3644	1689	1795	2769	438	853	1075	1124	592	1969	1283	1213	853	430	958	37
% of Weighted Total:	100.0	46.3	49.3	76.0	12.0	23.4	29.5	30.8	16.3	54.0	35.2	33.3	23.4	11.8	26.3	1.0

B087C: With LSD

1. Not at all	94.2	88.9	100.0	96.3	-	100.0	93.9	99.9	86.4	100.0	100.0	-	-	-	-	93.1
2. A few of the times	-	-	-	-	-	-	-	-	-	-	-	-	-	-	-	-
3. Some of the times	2.8	5.3	-	-	100.0	-	6.1	-	-	-	-	-	-	-	-	3.3
4. Most of the times	-	-	-	-	-	-	-	-	-	-	-	-	-	-	-	-
5. Every time	3.1	5.8	-	3.7	-	-	-	-	13.6	-	-	-	-	-	-	3.6
Item 4730　N(Wtd) ★	26	14	8	21	1	2	12	6	6	10	10	-	-	-	-	22

B087D: With psychedelics other than LSD

1. Not at all	97.2	94.7	100.0	100.0	-	100.0	93.9	99.9	99.9	100.0	100.0	-	-	-	-	96.7
2. A few of the times	-	-	-	-	-	-	-	-	-	-	-	-	-	-	-	-
3. Some of the times	-	-	-	-	-	-	-	-	-	-	-	-	-	-	-	-
4. Most of the times	2.8	5.3	-	-	100.0	-	6.1	-	-	-	-	-	-	-	-	3.3
5. Every time	-	-	-	-	-	-	-	-	-	-	-	-	-	-	-	-
Item 4740　N(Wtd) ★	26	14	8	21	1	2	12	6	6	10	10	-	-	-	-	22

B087E: With amphetamines

1. Not at all	95.0	90.7	100.0	97.2	-	77.1	93.9	99.9	99.9	100.0	94.4	-	-	-	-	94.2
2. A few of the times	-	-	-	-	-	-	-	-	-	-	-	-	-	-	-	-
3. Some of the times	2.7	5.1	-	-	100.0	-	6.1	-	-	-	-	-	-	-	-	3.2
4. Most of the times	-	-	-	-	-	-	-	-	-	-	-	-	-	-	-	-
5. Every time	2.3	4.2	-	2.8	-	22.9	-	-	-	-	5.6	-	-	-	-	2.7
Item 4750　N(Wtd) ★	27	14	8	22	1	3	12	6	6	10	11	-	-	-	-	23

B087F: With quaaludes

1. Not at all	93.1	93.6	88.0	91.4	-	100.0	91.6	99.9	85.4	90.9	100.0	-	-	-	-	91.6
2. A few of the times	-	-	-	-	-	-	-	-	-	-	-	-	-	-	-	-
3. Some of the times	3.2	6.4	-	4.0	-	-	-	-	14.6	-	-	-	-	-	-	3.9
4. Most of the times	3.7	-	12.0	4.6	-	-	8.4	-	-	9.1	-	-	-	-	-	4.5
5. Every time	-	-	-	-	-	-	-	-	-	-	-	-	-	-	-	-
Item 4760　N(Wtd) ★	25	12	8	20	-	2	11	6	5	10	9	-	-	-	-	21

B087G: With barbiturates

1. Not at all	94.5	89.3	100.0	93.2	-	77.1	99.9	99.9	85.4	100.0	93.8	-	-	-	-	93.4
2. A few of the times	3.1	6.1	-	3.9	-	-	-	-	14.6	-	-	-	-	-	-	3.8
3. Some of the times	-	-	-	-	-	-	-	-	-	-	-	-	-	-	-	-
4. Most of the times	-	-	-	-	-	-	-	-	-	-	-	-	-	-	-	-
5. Every time	2.4	4.6	-	2.9	-	22.9	-	-	-	-	6.2	-	-	-	-	2.9
Item 4770　N(Wtd) ★	25	13	8	21	-	3	11	6	5	10	10	-	-	-	-	21

B087H: With tranquilizers

1. Not at all	91.9	84.6	100.0	93.2	-	77.1	93.8	99.9	85.4	100.0	93.8	-	-	-	-	90.2
2. A few of the times	3.0	5.8	-	3.9	-	-	-	-	14.6	-	-	-	-	-	-	3.6
3. Some of the times	2.8	5.3	-	-	100.0	-	6.2	-	-	-	-	-	-	-	-	3.3
4. Most of the times	-	-	-	-	-	-	-	-	-	-	-	-	-	-	-	-
5. Every time	2.3	4.4	-	2.9	-	22.9	-	-	-	-	6.2	-	-	-	-	2.8
Item 4780　N(Wtd) ★	26	14	8	21	1	3	12	6	5	10	10	-	-	-	-	22

B087I: With cocaine

1. Not at all	94.2	88.7	100.0	95.2	-	58.7	99.9	99.9	92.9	95.2	93.8	-	-	-	-	93.0
2. A few of the times	-	-	-	-	-	-	-	-	-	-	-	-	-	-	-	-
3. Some of the times	1.9	3.7	-	-	-	18.4	-	-	-	4.8	-	-	-	-	-	2.3
4. Most of the times	-	-	-	-	-	-	-	-	-	-	-	-	-	-	-	-
5. Every time	3.9	7.6	-	4.8	-	22.9	-	-	7.1	-	6.2	-	-	-	-	4.7
Item 4790　N(Wtd) ★	25	13	8	21	-	3	11	6	5	10	10	-	-	-	-	21

★＝excludes respondents for whom question was inappropriate.

QUESTIONNAIRE FORM 1 1981	TOTAL	SEX		RACE		REGION				4YR COLLEGE PLANS		ILLICIT DRUG USE: LIFETIME				
		M	F	White	Black	NE	NC	S	W	Yes	No	None	Marijuana Only	Few Pills	More Pills	Any Heroin
Weighted No. of Cases:	3644	1689	1795	2769	438	853	1075	1124	592	1969	1283	1213	853	430	958	37
% of Weighted Total:	100.0	46.3	49.3	76.0	12.0	23.4	29.5	30.8	16.3	54.0	35.2	33.3	23.4	11.8	26.3	1.0

B088: What have been the most important reasons for your taking heroin? (Mark all that apply.)

	TOTAL	M	F	White	Black	NE	NC	S	W	Yes	No	None	Marijuana Only	Few Pills	More Pills	Any Heroin
A. To experiment--to see what it's like	68.7	49.6	79.7	68.8	-	59.3	67.5	99.9	61.1	68.3	64.9	-	-	-	-	71.0
B. To relax or relieve tension	26.7	24.4	41.8	30.8	-	14.2	41.9	28.9	-	13.0	60.6	-	-	-	-	27.6
C. To feel good or get high	66.1	69.1	60.1	65.7	-	59.3	85.8	28.9	46.5	66.4	60.1	-	-	-	-	68.4
D. To seek deeper insights and understanding	35.2	26.8	30.0	26.9	-	14.2	44.2	28.9	31.9	31.7	26.2	-	-	-	-	36.4
E. To have a good time with my friends	26.6	29.6	21.3	33.3	-	-	36.4	40.7	14.6	21.7	38.5	-	-	-	-	27.5
F. To fit in with a group I like	12.9	10.9	21.3	16.1	-	-	25.5	-	-	11.3	22.4	-	-	-	-	13.3
G. To get away from my problems or troubles	10.2	5.4	21.3	12.8	-	17.6	15.2	-	-	-	30.0	-	-	-	-	10.6
H. Because of boredom, nothing else to do	13.6	4.3	32.2	14.5	-	14.2	22.9	-	-	13.0	22.4	-	-	-	-	14.1
I. Because of anger or frustration	7.7	-	21.3	9.6	-	-	15.2	-	-	-	22.4	-	-	-	-	7.9
J. To get through the day	19.6	18.0	30.7	16.5	100.0	23.1	32.2	-	-	7.3	38.5	-	-	-	-	16.8
K. To increase the effects of some other drug(s)	5.5	11.5	-	6.9	-	-	10.9	-	-	-	16.1	-	-	-	-	5.7
L. To decrease (offset) the effects of some other drug(s)	2.6	5.4	-	3.2	-	17.6	-	-	-	-	7.5	-	-	-	-	2.7
M. Because I am "hooked"--I have to have it	17.4	20.3	21.3	21.7	-	17.6	26.1	-	7.1	-	46.1	-	-	-	-	18.0
Item 4800-4920 N(Wtd) ★	24	11	8	19	1	3	12	3	5	11	8	-	-	-	-	23

B089: When you take heroin how high do you usually get?

	TOTAL	M	F	White	Black	NE	NC	S	W	Yes	No	None	Marijuana Only	Few Pills	More Pills	Any Heroin
1. Not at all high	8.2	14.8	-	-	-	-	15.2	-	-	-	13.9	-	-	-	-	-
2. A little high	-	-	-	-	-	-	-	-	-	-	-	-	-	-	-	-
3. Moderately high	27.2	17.1	45.1	31.9	100.0	-	18.0	73.5	31.9	28.4	37.0	-	-	-	-	31.0
4. Very high	64.6	68.1	54.9	68.1	-	100.0	66.8	26.5	68.1	71.6	49.1	-	-	-	-	69.0
5. I don't take it to get high	-	-	-	-	-	-	-	-	-	-	-	-	-	-	-	-
Item 4930 N(Wtd) ★	26	14	8	20	1	3	14	4	5	10	9	-	-	-	-	23

B090: When you take heroin how long do you usually stay high?

	TOTAL	M	F	White	Black	NE	NC	S	W	Yes	No	None	Marijuana Only	Few Pills	More Pills	Any Heroin
1. Usually don't get high	3.4	6.4	-	-	-	-	6.5	-	-	-	-	-	-	-	-	-
2. One to two hours	3.0	5.6	-	-	100.0	-	5.7	-	-	-	-	-	-	-	-	3.2
3. Three to six hours	27.3	30.0	21.6	33.9	-	-	17.2	73.5	31.9	40.6	32.5	-	-	-	-	29.5
4. Seven to 24 hours	46.7	32.9	58.2	41.7	-	18.4	60.3	-	61.1	31.2	59.9	-	-	-	-	50.5
5. More than 24 hours	19.7	25.2	20.2	24.4	-	81.6	10.2	26.5	7.1	28.2	7.5	-	-	-	-	16.9
Item 4940 N(Wtd) ★	25	13	8	20	1	3	13	4	5	10	8	-	-	-	-	23

B091: Have you ever tried to stop using heroin and found that you couldn't stop?

	TOTAL	M	F	White	Black	NE	NC	S	W	Yes	No	None	Marijuana Only	Few Pills	More Pills	Any Heroin
1. Yes	17.9	20.3	23.5	21.7	-	22.9	28.4	-	7.1	-	52.4	-	-	-	-	18.8
2. No	82.1	79.7	76.5	78.3	100.0	77.1	71.6	99.9	92.9	100.0	47.6	-	-	-	-	81.2
Item 4950 N(Wtd) ★	23	11	8	19	1	3	11	4	5	10	7	-	-	-	-	22

B092: What methods have you used for taking heroin? (Mark all that apply.)

	TOTAL	M	F	White	Black	NE	NC	S	W	Yes	No	None	Marijuana Only	Few Pills	More Pills	Any Heroin
A. Sniffing or "snorting"	31.6	46.7	23.5	37.9	-	-	41.9	-	46.5	30.0	45.9	-	-	-	-	33.0
B. Smoking	26.6	38.2	21.6	31.9	-	-	18.1	43.6	46.5	29.4	32.0	-	-	-	-	27.8
C. Injection	68.3	58.0	68.7	65.7	-	41.3	56.8	77.7	99.9	59.6	66.0	-	-	-	-	66.9
D. By mouth	22.3	23.0	32.3	23.0	100.0	58.7	24.8	-	14.6	37.4	-	-	-	-	-	23.2
E. Other	7.3	-	22.6	8.7	-	-	-	-	31.9	17.2	-	-	-	-	-	7.6
Item 4960-5000 N(Wtd) ★	24	12	8	20	1	3	12	4	5	10	8	-	-	-	-	23

★ = excludes respondents for whom question was inappropriate.

QUESTIONNAIRE FORM 1 1981	TOTAL	SEX		RACE		REGION				4YR COLLEGE PLANS		ILLICIT DRUG USE: LIFETIME				
		M	F	White	Black	NE	NC	S	W	Yes	No	None	Mari- juana Only	Few Pills	More Pills	Any Her- oin
Weighted No. of Cases:	3644	1689	1795	2769	438	853	1075	1124	592	1969	1283	1213	853	430	958	37
% of Weighted Total:	100.0	46.3	49.3	76.0	12.0	23.4	29.5	30.8	16.3	54.0	35.2	33.3	23.4	11.8	26.3	1.0

B093: Do you think you will be using heroin five years from now?

1. I definitely will	.6	.7	.5	.5	1.2	.7	1.0	.4	.1	.6	.7	.6	.8	.4	.4	5.0
2. I probably will	.4	.5	.2	.4	.6	.4	.4	.4	.4	.6	.2	-	-	-	1.0	13.4
3. I probably will not	7.3	7.8	6.8	7.2	6.8	7.4	7.5	6.9	7.8	6.6	8.3	3.6	7.6	8.5	11.5	20.3
4. I definitely will not	91.7	91.1	92.4	91.9	91.4	91.5	91.1	92.3	91.7	92.3	90.8	95.9	91.6	91.0	87.1	61.4
Item 5010 N(Wtd)	3345	1564	1706	2604	409	759	1003	1034	550	1856	1213	1170	789	405	839	34

The next questions are about NARCOTICS OTHER THAN HEROIN, which are sometimes prescribed by doctors. Drugstores are not supposed to sell them without a prescription.

These include: Methadone, Opium, Morphine, Codeine, Demerol, Paregoric, Talwin, Laudanum.

B094: Have you ever taken any narcotics other than heroin because a doctor told you to use them?

1. No	80.9	84.2	78.4	78.3	95.3	77.6	83.7	83.4	75.6	80.1	82.9	89.4	86.1	73.8	67.8	60.7
2. Yes, but I had already tried them on my own.	2.2	2.0	2.2	2.4	.9	2.9	2.1	1.8	2.4	1.4	2.9	.1	-	2.2	6.5	23.0
3. Yes, and it was the first time I took any	16.9	13.8	19.4	19.3	3.9	19.5	14.2	14.8	22.0	18.6	14.2	10.5	13.9	24.1	25.7	16.3
Item 5020 N(Wtd)	3339	1557	1707	2632	382	769	1004	1016	550	1876	1197	1164	785	413	873	34

B095: On how many occasions (if any) have you taken narcotics other than heroin on your own--that is, without a doctor telling you to take them...

B095A: ...in your lifetime?

1. 0 occasions	88.7	89.2	89.3	87.8	96.8	85.7	90.0	92.1	84.4	90.6	88.0	100.0	100.0	83.2	67.8	22.4
2. 1-2	5.3	5.1	4.8	5.8	2.2	8.1	4.1	3.5	7.3	4.8	5.3	-	-	16.8	11.9	17.0
3. 3-5	2.6	2.5	2.5	2.9	.5	2.5	2.9	2.0	3.2	2.2	2.8	-	-	-	9.5	9.4
4. 6-9	1.2	1.1	1.4	1.2	.2	1.1	1.1	.9	2.2	.5	1.6	-	-	-	4.3	8.9
5. 10-19	1.0	.9	1.0	1.0	.2	1.6	1.2	.6	.7	.9	1.1	-	-	-	3.5	10.1
6. 20-39	.5	.6	.4	.6	-	.4	.2	.8	.7	.4	.8	-	-	-	1.7	6.9
7. 40 or more	.6	.6	.5	.7	.1	.7	.6	.2	1.3	.6	.5	-	-	-	1.4	25.2
Item 1130 N(Wtd)	3319	1559	1691	2611	385	763	1001	1009	547	1868	1188	1163	788	410	867	33

B095B: ...during the last 12 months?

1. 0 occasions	93.5	93.8	93.8	92.8	98.5	91.0	94.0	95.4	92.4	95.1	92.6	100.0	100.0	94.6	80.0	34.6
2. 1-2	3.6	3.6	3.1	3.9	1.1	5.6	3.4	2.4	3.3	2.4	4.2	-	-	5.4	10.8	10.9
3. 3-5	1.4	1.1	1.7	1.6	.4	1.3	1.2	1.2	2.5	1.4	1.5	-	-	-	4.4	26.2
4. 6-9	.8	.7	.7	.7	-	1.2	.7	.4	.8	.3	.9	-	-	-	2.6	7.9
5. 10-19	.5	.6	.5	.6	-	.4	.5	.6	.6	.4	.7	-	-	-	1.5	12.0
6. 20-39	.1	.1	.2	.1	-	.2	.2	-	.2	.2	*	-	-	-	.4	2.8
7. 40 or more	.1	.1	.1	.2	-	.3	-	.1	.3	.2	.1	-	-	-	.3	5.6
Item 1140 N(Wtd)	3311	1555	1689	2606	385	759	999	1008	545	1865	1185	1163	788	408	861	33

B095C: ...during the last 30 days?

1. 0 occasions	98.0	97.8	98.3	97.9	99.4	98.0	97.7	98.7	97.5	98.6	97.3	100.0	100.0	98.3	94.5	65.9
2. 1-2	1.1	1.4	.9	1.3	.4	1.1	1.5	.7	1.3	.7	1.8	-	-	1.7	3.3	7.8
3. 3-5	.5	.5	.4	.4	.2	.6	.4	.4	.8	.4	.5	-	-	-	1.3	15.1
4. 6-9	.2	.1	.3	.2	-	.3	.2	.2	-	.2	.2	-	-	-	.7	2.2
5. 10-19	.1	.1	.1	.1	-	-	.2	-	.2	*	.2	-	-	-	.1	5.6
6. 20-39	*	-	-	*	-	-	-	.1	-	.1	-	-	-	-	-	3.4
7. 40 or more	*	*	-	*	-	-	-	-	.1	*	-	-	-	-	.1	-
Item 1150 N(Wtd)	3311	1557	1689	2607	385	757	1002	1007	545	1864	1187	1165	788	408	859	33

* = less than .05 per cent.

QUESTIONNAIRE FORM 1 1981	TOTAL	SEX		RACE		REGION				4YR COLLEGE PLANS		ILLICIT DRUG USE: LIFETIME				
		M	F	White	Black	NE	NC	S	W	Yes	No	None	Mari-juana Only	Few Pills	More Pills	Any Her-oin
Weighted No. of Cases:	3644	1689	1795	2769	438	853	1075	1124	592	1969	1283	1213	853	430	958	37
% of Weighted Total:	100.0	46.3	49.3	76.0	12.0	23.4	29.5	30.8	16.3	54.0	35.2	33.3	23.4	11.8	26.3	1.0

IF YOU HAVE NOT TAKEN NARCOTICS OTHER THAN HEROIN IN THE LAST TWELVE MONTHS, GO TO Q.B104.

THE FOLLOWING QUESTIONS REFER ONLY TO TAKING NARCOTICS OTHER THAN HEROIN WITHOUT A DOCTOR'S ORDERS. IF YOU HAVE NOT DONE THIS IN THE LAST TWELVE MONTHS, GO TO Q.B104.

B096: When you used narcotics other than heroin during the last year, how often did you use them in each of the following situations?

B096A: When you were alone

	TOTAL	M	F	White	Black	NE	NC	S	W	Yes	No	None	Mari.	Few	More	Any
1. Not at all	51.4	53.2	49.6	51.9	74.4	49.3	42.4	62.4	54.0	47.8	50.4	-	-	72.0	48.9	49.3
2. A few of the times	27.2	27.3	27.4	26.1	25.6	29.3	36.8	23.5	15.5	24.5	32.7	-	-	23.0	29.8	14.3
3. Some of the times	8.1	7.6	7.8	7.8	-	8.8	9.6	4.7	8.9	9.3	7.0	-	-	5.0	7.7	14.6
4. Most of the times	3.9	4.6	3.7	4.1	-	3.8	5.0	1.4	5.5	4.3	4.1	-	-	-	3.0	14.6
5. Every time	9.4	7.3	11.6	10.1	-	8.8	6.2	7.9	16.1	14.2	5.7	-	-	-	10.7	7.2
Item 5030 N(Wtd) ★	187	87	90	167	3	59	49	42	37	76	81	-	-	13	151	19

B096B: With just 1 or 2 other people

	TOTAL	M	F	White	Black	NE	NC	S	W	Yes	No	None	Mari.	Few	More	Any
1. Not at all	26.7	24.4	28.9	26.9	24.3	36.9	20.6	27.1	18.1	34.5	20.4	-	-	50.2	26.1	4.1
2. A few of the times	37.0	31.0	41.1	36.1	50.1	28.9	40.2	42.8	38.8	27.7	45.7	-	-	35.4	39.7	22.5
3. Some of the times	16.0	23.0	11.2	15.5	25.6	19.4	16.0	13.4	13.6	16.0	13.7	-	-	5.9	16.7	19.8
4. Most of the times	9.1	11.9	7.2	9.3	-	7.1	7.6	10.4	13.1	4.6	13.9	-	-	-	9.2	16.3
5. Every time	11.1	9.8	11.7	12.3	-	7.7	15.5	6.3	16.4	17.2	6.2	-	-	8.5	8.2	37.3
Item 5040 N(Wtd) ★	187	87	89	166	3	59	50	42	36	77	80	-	-	13	151	19

B096C: At a party

	TOTAL	M	F	White	Black	NE	NC	S	W	Yes	No	None	Mari.	Few	More	Any
1. Not at all	49.0	44.1	57.3	50.1	100.0	43.7	45.6	44.4	67.2	54.1	49.9	-	-	73.6	47.9	34.3
2. A few of the times	16.9	22.3	13.7	18.3	-	15.0	20.5	19.6	11.8	20.0	12.7	-	-	16.8	19.1	2.2
3. Some of the times	13.2	10.7	12.3	11.2	-	15.3	12.2	13.3	11.1	4.2	15.2	-	-	9.6	13.9	11.7
4. Most of the times	11.3	14.9	8.0	11.3	-	17.6	9.3	9.4	6.6	13.5	11.0	-	-	-	10.7	25.4
5. Every time	9.6	8.0	8.8	9.1	-	8.4	12.5	13.3	3.3	8.2	11.2	-	-	-	8.4	26.4
Item 5050 N(Wtd) ★	187	88	88	166	3	58	50	43	36	77	80	-	-	12	152	19

B096D: When your date or spouse was present

	TOTAL	M	F	White	Black	NE	NC	S	W	Yes	No	None	Mari.	Few	More	Any
1. Not at all	66.8	73.0	63.5	68.0	72.8	80.7	55.8	62.6	64.6	75.1	60.3	-	-	80.0	67.2	49.2
2. A few of the times	12.7	12.7	13.4	13.3	27.2	5.0	16.8	14.2	17.6	13.2	14.5	-	-	15.1	13.2	9.3
3. Some of the times	8.1	5.4	7.0	5.9	-	6.0	11.8	7.7	6.6	1.9	8.7	-	-	5.0	8.4	9.1
4. Most of the times	5.9	4.5	8.0	5.5	-	6.4	6.8	2.5	7.9	5.3	8.6	-	-	-	5.7	12.6
5. Every time	6.5	4.4	8.1	7.3	-	1.9	8.7	13.0	3.3	4.5	7.9	-	-	-	5.5	19.8
Item 5060 N(Wtd) ★	186	86	89	166	3	58	50	43	36	76	81	-	-	13	151	19

B096E: When people over age 30 were present

	TOTAL	M	F	White	Black	NE	NC	S	W	Yes	No	None	Mari.	Few	More	Any
1. Not at all	56.2	60.4	53.4	56.7	47.2	56.1	51.9	58.6	59.2	54.3	57.9	-	-	78.3	55.4	40.0
2. A few of the times	19.3	19.8	20.7	20.1	-	14.1	20.1	29.0	14.9	17.4	20.5	-	-	14.2	19.6	22.8
3. Some of the times	12.0	8.2	13.1	10.8	25.6	9.7	17.5	8.7	12.1	9.6	12.8	-	-	7.6	13.4	6.7
4. Most of the times	6.9	7.5	5.9	6.5	27.2	12.6	6.6	2.7	3.3	10.6	5.9	-	-	-	6.2	18.4
5. Every time	5.6	4.1	6.9	5.9	-	7.5	3.9	1.0	10.5	8.2	2.9	-	-	-	5.4	12.1
Item 5070 N(Wtd) ★	187	86	90	167	3	58	50	43	37	77	81	-	-	13	151	19

★=excludes respondents for whom question was inappropriate.

QUESTIONNAIRE FORM 1 1981	TOTAL	SEX		RACE		REGION				4YR COLLEGE PLANS		ILLICIT DRUG USE: LIFETIME				
		M	F	White	Black	NE	NC	S	W	Yes	No	None	Marijuana Only	Few Pills	More Pills	Any Heroin
Weighted No. of Cases:	3644	1689	1795	2769	438	853	1075	1124	592	1969	1283	1213	853	430	958	37
% of Weighted Total:	100.0	46.3	49.3	76.0	12.0	23.4	29.5	30.8	16.3	54.0	35.2	33.3	23.4	11.8	26.3	1.0

B096F: During the daytime (before 4:00 p.m.)

1. Not at all	37.8	43.6	33.4	39.6	50.1	41.2	39.1	28.7	41.1	40.2	35.9	-	-	72.4	33.2	39.4
2. A few of the times	29.2	34.3	26.2	29.9	49.9	20.6	37.2	30.2	30.9	24.4	33.2	-	-	15.1	31.0	29.9
3. Some of the times	21.6	15.0	25.3	19.0	-	25.3	14.9	29.7	15.7	21.8	21.7	-	-	5.0	23.3	23.8
4. Most of the times	6.6	4.7	9.2	7.0	-	6.3	5.0	9.7	5.7	6.4	8.2	-	-	7.6	6.6	6.9
5. Every time	4.8	2.5	5.9	4.5	-	6.7	3.9	1.8	6.5	7.2	.9	-	-	-	5.9	-
Item 5080 N(Wtd) ★	187	86	90	167	3	58	50	43	37	77	81	-	-	13	151	19

B096G: At your home (or apartment or dorm)

1. Not at all	36.2	41.3	29.8	36.6	22.9	37.2	34.6	38.5	34.3	34.5	35.8	-	-	68.2	32.8	31.1
2. A few of the times	19.7	23.4	18.5	21.0	-	15.8	20.3	21.2	23.0	19.7	19.0	-	-	19.3	20.4	17.2
3. Some of the times	17.4	18.3	14.5	15.1	25.6	20.5	22.0	15.5	8.7	13.8	20.2	-	-	-	18.8	21.7
4. Most of the times	12.0	6.0	19.2	11.6	27.2	13.0	11.3	12.4	10.8	10.3	15.3	-	-	12.5	12.9	6.3
5. Every time	14.7	10.9	18.0	15.6	24.3	13.5	11.8	12.3	23.2	21.6	9.7	-	-	-	15.2	23.7
Item 5090 N(Wtd) ★	188	87	90	167	3	58	50	43	37	77	81	-	-	13	152	19

B096H: At school

1. Not at all	65.4	65.8	63.9	67.4	75.7	58.5	71.7	61.4	72.4	61.9	67.2	-	-	80.0	63.7	63.4
2. A few of the times	16.5	15.4	19.6	16.2	24.3	20.9	9.8	19.2	15.3	18.8	13.8	-	-	9.2	19.2	2.5
3. Some of the times	12.8	11.4	13.8	11.9	-	13.7	16.2	13.6	5.7	12.1	14.9	-	-	10.8	12.5	18.0
4. Most of the times	3.2	5.1	1.9	3.0	-	4.7	2.3	1.4	4.4	4.1	3.2	-	-	-	3.2	6.1
5. Every time	2.1	2.4	.8	1.6	-	2.2	-	4.4	2.2	3.1	.9	-	-	-	1.3	10.0
Item 5100 N(Wtd) ★	187	86	90	167	3	58	50	43	37	77	81	-	-	13	151	19

B096I: In a car

1. Not at all	61.6	58.0	64.8	62.5	72.8	75.6	52.1	43.5	72.8	65.6	56.7	-	-	73.8	63.4	33.1
2. A few of the times	16.3	21.2	13.0	15.8	27.2	2.0	16.3	33.9	18.6	11.2	19.7	-	-	10.2	17.1	16.1
3. Some of the times	10.7	8.0	10.6	10.5	-	14.7	9.0	11.7	5.3	10.1	11.9	-	-	-	11.1	16.5
4. Most of the times	6.2	9.0	4.2	6.0	-	5.5	12.3	4.5	1.0	6.6	6.7	-	-	2.7	5.0	18.8
5. Every time	5.3	3.8	7.3	5.2	-	2.1	10.4	6.3	2.2	6.6	4.9	-	-	13.4	3.4	15.6
Item 5120 N(Wtd) ★	188	88	90	168	3	59	50	43	37	78	81	-	-	13	153	19

B097: How many of the times when you used narcotics other than heroin during the last year did you use them along with each of the following drugs--that is, so that their effects overlapped?

B097A: With alcohol

1. Not at all	50.8	48.9	52.9	50.3	100.0	56.4	40.9	47.3	59.9	55.5	52.3	-	-	86.9	49.4	28.7
2. A few of the times	23.6	27.7	21.8	24.2	-	16.7	25.4	29.2	25.0	21.4	21.6	-	-	4.5	26.7	16.2
3. Some of the times	6.8	6.3	7.9	7.5	-	2.9	8.9	8.8	7.4	3.5	8.1	-	-	-	8.4	-
4. Most of the times	9.5	6.5	10.0	7.9	-	8.5	13.8	9.0	5.5	9.6	9.8	-	-	5.9	7.9	25.2
5. Every time	9.4	10.6	7.4	10.1	-	15.5	11.0	5.7	2.2	10.0	8.2	-	-	2.7	7.5	29.9
Item 5130 N(Wtd) ★	185	87	90	167	3	55	50	43	37	76	82	-	-	13	149	19

B097B: With marijuana

1. Not at all	40.4	29.0	51.3	40.4	72.8	39.3	35.5	37.5	52.0	49.6	37.6	-	-	67.4	41.8	2.2
2. A few of the times	17.8	23.0	12.9	18.0	27.2	15.1	13.7	28.1	15.5	13.3	16.9	-	-	26.6	16.5	24.1
3. Some of the times	12.2	14.6	11.1	12.5	-	6.7	19.2	11.5	12.1	10.3	12.3	-	-	-	14.0	8.9
4. Most of the times	10.2	7.3	10.5	8.7	-	8.7	18.8	7.3	4.4	10.8	12.6	-	-	-	10.9	13.5
5. Every time	19.3	26.1	14.1	20.3	-	30.2	12.8	15.6	16.1	16.0	20.4	-	-	6.0	16.8	51.3
Item 5140 N(Wtd) ★	186	88	90	169	3	56	50	43	37	77	82	-	-	13	151	19

★ = excludes respondents for whom question was inappropriate.

QUESTIONNAIRE FORM 1 1981	TOTAL	SEX		RACE		REGION				4YR COLLEGE PLANS		ILLICIT DRUG USE: LIFETIME				
		M	F	White	Black	NE	NC	S	W	Yes	No	None	Mari- juana Only	Few Pills	More Pills	Any Her- oin
Weighted No. of Cases:	3644	1689	1795	2769	438	853	1075	1124	592	1969	1283	1213	853	430	958	37
% of Weighted Total:	100.0	46.3	49.3	76.0	12.0	23.4	29.5	30.8	16.3	54.0	35.2	33.3	23.4	11.8	26.3	1.0
B097C: With LSD																
1. Not at all	92.5	88.1	97.6	93.2	100.0	96.6	85.6	97.5	89.3	93.5	93.0	-	-	100.0	93.9	75.5
2. A few of the times	1.8	3.6	.4	1.6	-	-	3.8	2.5	1.1	1.6	2.2	-	-	-	2.3	-
3. Some of the times	3.1	4.1	.7	2.4	-	1.1	3.5	-	9.6	3.3	2.1	-	-	-	2.1	13.1
4. Most of the times	.5	1.1	-	.6	-	-	1.9	-	-	-	1.2	-	-	-	-	4.8
5. Every time	2.0	3.1	1.3	2.2	-	2.2	5.1	-	-	1.6	1.6	-	-	-	1.6	6.7
Item 5150 N(Wtd) ★	179	81	89	163	2	54	48	43	34	72	80	-	-	13	143	19
B097D: With psychedelics other than LSD																
1. Not at all	93.0	89.4	97.6	94.1	100.0	95.7	88.5	97.5	89.9	92.3	94.6	-	-	100.0	93.7	82.2
2. A few of the times	3.1	3.5	1.1	1.6	-	1.1	7.2	2.5	1.0	1.6	4.3	-	-	-	3.8	-
3. Some of the times	2.6	5.5	-	2.8	-	2.2	1.9	-	6.8	3.9	1.2	-	-	-	1.4	13.7
4. Most of the times	.4	1.0	-	.5	-	-	-	-	2.2	-	-	-	-	-	-	4.1
5. Every time	.9	.6	1.3	1.0	-	.9	2.4	-	-	2.2	-	-	-	-	1.1	-
Item 5160 N(Wtd) ★	182	84	90	165	3	54	49	43	37	75	80	-	-	13	146	19
B097E: With amphetamines																
1. Not at all	87.0	82.8	91.7	87.3	100.0	93.1	80.0	86.7	87.8	87.9	85.9	-	-	100.0	87.8	69.7
2. A few of the times	6.1	7.7	3.2	5.0	-	4.7	11.6	3.9	3.2	2.9	9.0	-	-	-	6.5	7.7
3. Some of the times	4.6	5.9	3.8	5.1	-	2.2	3.7	6.9	6.9	4.6	5.1	-	-	-	4.1	12.1
4. Most of the times	1.7	3.6	-	1.9	-	-	2.5	2.5	2.2	3.0	-	-	-	-	.7	10.4
5. Every time	.6	-	1.3	.7	-	-	2.3	-	-	1.5	-	-	-	-	.8	-
Item 5170 N(Wtd) ★	185	86	90	167	3	55	50	43	37	76	82	-	-	13	149	19
B097F: With quaaludes																
1. Not at all	91.0	90.0	92.6	90.6	100.0	88.4	94.7	89.6	91.9	86.9	96.0	-	-	94.0	92.9	73.5
2. A few of the times	4.2	4.6	4.1	4.2	-	6.8	5.3	3.2	-	5.0	1.8	-	-	-	4.3	7.0
3. Some of the times	2.9	3.5	2.6	3.2	-	3.3	-	3.1	5.9	4.7	2.2	-	-	-	2.4	9.2
4. Most of the times	1.8	1.9	.7	2.0	-	1.5	-	4.1	2.2	3.4	-	-	-	6.0	.4	10.3
5. Every time	-	-	-	-	-	-	-	-	-	-	-	-	-	-	-	-
Item 5180 N(Wtd) ★	180	83	90	164	3	54	47	43	36	75	78	-	-	13	145	19
B097G: With barbiturates																
1. Not at all	94.7	92.7	95.9	94.5	100.0	97.1	92.7	94.2	94.3	94.2	95.3	-	-	100.0	95.9	81.0
2. A few of the times	2.7	4.3	1.4	2.6	-	.7	3.8	1.4	5.7	2.4	1.9	-	-	-	1.8	11.1
3. Some of the times	1.1	1.6	.7	1.2	-	2.3	-	1.8	-	.8	1.7	-	-	-	.9	3.1
4. Most of the times	1.1	1.3	1.0	1.2	-	-	1.9	2.6	-	2.7	-	-	-	-	.7	4.8
5. Every time	.5	-	.9	.5	-	-	1.7	-	-	-	1.0	-	-	-	.6	-
Item 5190 N(Wtd) ★	181	83	89	163	3	54	49	42	36	75	80	-	-	12	146	19
B097H: With tranquilizers																
1. Not at all	94.4	93.0	96.4	94.1	100.0	96.2	92.9	92.4	95.5	92.8	95.8	-	-	100.0	95.1	84.4
2. A few of the times	2.1	3.6	1.0	2.0	-	.9	5.2	-	2.3	2.2	1.4	-	-	-	2.7	-
3. Some of the times	3.0	3.4	1.6	3.3	-	2.8	-	7.6	2.2	3.7	2.8	-	-	-	2.3	10.8
4. Most of the times	.5	-	1.1	.6	-	-	1.9	-	-	1.2	-	-	-	-	-	4.8
5. Every time	-	-	-	-	-	-	-	-	-	-	-	-	-	-	-	-
Item 5200 N(Wtd) ★	179	83	88	161	3	55	48	39	36	75	77	-	-	13	143	19
B097I: With cocaine																
1. Not at all	86.9	85.2	88.5	87.0	100.0	83.0	88.1	89.9	87.7	84.8	92.5	-	-	100.0	89.6	54.8
2. A few of the times	5.6	6.1	5.6	5.4	-	6.5	5.3	5.9	4.3	.8	5.1	-	-	-	5.5	11.1
3. Some of the times	4.3	7.1	2.0	4.0	-	6.7	2.4	-	8.0	8.4	1.3	-	-	-	3.7	12.3
4. Most of the times	2.7	.4	3.9	3.0	-	3.8	2.4	4.2	-	6.1	-	-	-	-	1.2	16.8
5. Every time	.5	1.1	-	.6	-	-	1.9	-	-	-	1.2	-	-	-	-	4.9
Item 5210 N(Wtd) ★	181	84	89	164	3	55	49	42	36	76	78	-	-	13	146	19

★=excludes respondents for whom question was inappropriate.

QUESTIONNAIRE FORM 1 1981	TOTAL	SEX		RACE		REGION				4YR COLLEGE PLANS		ILLICIT DRUG USE: LIFETIME				
		M	F	White	Black	NE	NC	S	W	Yes	No	None	Marijuana Only	Few Pills	More Pills	Any Heroin
Weighted No. of Cases:	3644	1689	1795	2769	438	853	1075	1124	592	1969	1283	1213	853	430	958	37
% of Weighted Total:	100.0	46.3	49.3	76.0	12.0	23.4	29.5	30.8	16.3	54.0	35.2	33.3	23.4	11.8	26.3	1.0

B097J: With heroin

	TOTAL	M	F	White	Black	NE	NC	S	W	Yes	No	None	Marij	Few Pills	More Pills	Any Heroin
1. Not at all	98.7	97.2	100.0	98.6	100.0	98.9	98.1	99.9	97.8	100.0	98.1	-	-	100.0	100.0	87.7
2. A few of the times	.4	1.0	-	.5	-	-	-	-	2.2	-	-	-	-	-	-	4.2
3. Some of the times	-	-	-	-	-	-	-	-	-	-	-	-	-	-	-	-
4. Most of the times	-	-	-	-	-	-	-	-	-	-	-	-	-	-	-	-
5. Every time	.8	1.8	-	.9	-	1.1	1.9	-	-	-	1.9	-	-	-	-	8.1
Item 5220 N(Wtd) ★	182	84	89	164	3	55	48	43	36	75	79	-	-	13	146	19

B098: What have been the most important reasons for your using narcotics other than heroin without a doctor's orders? (Mark all that apply.)

	TOTAL	M	F	White	Black	NE	NC	S	W	Yes	No	None	Marij	Few Pills	More Pills	Any Heroin
A. To experiment--to see what it's like	49.7	59.6	39.9	47.1	50.1	50.1	42.2	64.0	43.8	48.8	49.1	-	-	31.2	51.9	47.1
B. To relax or relieve tension	47.5	52.9	39.9	46.4	-	41.7	55.3	44.7	48.9	43.5	49.1	-	-	28.9	47.6	61.4
C. To feel good or get high	51.5	62.7	38.6	52.8	-	61.1	47.7	52.1	41.3	46.2	49.4	-	-	17.6	51.1	81.9
D. To seek deeper insights and understanding	8.4	12.2	3.8	8.2	-	5.9	18.5	4.6	3.2	8.1	9.1	-	-	-	6.7	28.8
E. To have a good time with my friends	25.5	31.2	19.9	24.5	-	32.1	30.6	21.0	13.5	19.5	27.1	-	-	9.8	25.7	36.4
F. To fit in with a group I like	3.5	6.4	1.0	3.9	-	2.8	6.8	3.6	-	3.8	4.4	-	-	-	2.9	10.9
G. To get away from my problems or troubles	14.9	18.0	11.6	14.3	-	13.8	23.6	11.4	8.9	13.3	17.8	-	-	17.4	14.8	13.8
H. Because of boredom, nothing else to do	15.4	21.2	9.6	14.9	-	19.7	14.8	18.3	6.8	7.8	19.3	-	-	18.3	14.7	18.6
I. Because of anger or frustration	7.8	9.2	5.3	6.5	-	9.2	10.7	7.3	2.3	6.9	8.1	-	-	-	8.6	7.4
J. To get through the day	5.6	6.3	3.7	4.7	-	2.1	10.8	5.8	4.2	4.0	7.7	-	-	-	5.4	12.0
K. To increase the effects of some other drug(s)	10.6	16.4	4.2	9.0	-	10.9	14.8	10.4	5.2	13.6	6.9	-	-	13.8	9.8	14.5
L. To decrease (offset) the effects of some other drug(s)	2.1	3.7	.7	1.6	-	3.2	2.4	-	2.0	3.9	-	-	-	-	2.5	-
M. To get to sleep	26.0	21.6	30.1	25.8	-	26.9	29.8	22.7	23.3	26.9	27.3	-	-	3.3	27.7	30.7
N. As a substitute for heroin	2.6	4.1	1.5	1.9	-	4.1	4.2	-	1.1	4.9	1.3	-	-	-	1.6	12.8
O. To relieve physical pain	52.9	43.2	59.0	51.4	49.9	55.7	43.7	44.3	69.6	54.2	51.4	-	-	41.8	55.0	45.6
P. To control coughing	20.2	16.1	24.1	20.0	25.6	24.0	30.2	9.0	13.4	25.1	16.6	-	-	17.9	20.1	23.5
Q. Because I am "hooked"--I have to have it	1.0	2.2	-	1.2	-	1.1	2.6	-	-	-	2.4	-	-	-	-	10.0
Item 5230-5370 N(Wtd) ★	185	87	89	164	3	58	49	40	38	79	79	-	-	15	151	19

B099: When you take narcotics other than heroin how high do you usually get?

	TOTAL	M	F	White	Black	NE	NC	S	W	Yes	No	None	Marij	Few Pills	More Pills	Any Heroin
1. Not at all high	11.6	8.8	14.2	11.9	25.6	14.1	10.1	8.2	13.3	13.2	13.0	-	-	24.0	11.3	4.4
2. A little high	30.0	29.4	32.3	31.5	-	28.8	26.6	29.3	37.0	26.5	31.6	-	-	29.6	31.0	22.5
3. Moderately high	29.4	31.2	24.5	28.0	27.2	33.2	30.1	34.1	17.9	24.3	29.2	-	-	-	32.6	26.6
4. Very high	14.5	22.0	7.8	14.8	-	11.7	17.4	16.0	13.4	15.3	13.9	-	-	16.3	10.3	46.5
5. I don't take them to get high	14.5	8.5	21.2	13.8	47.2	12.1	15.8	12.4	18.4	20.7	12.3	-	-	30.1	14.8	-
Item 5380 N(Wtd) ★	182	85	90	167	3	56	49	40	37	77	78	-	-	14	149	19

B100: When you take narcotics other than heroin how long do you usually stay high?

	TOTAL	M	F	White	Black	NE	NC	S	W	Yes	No	None	Marij	Few Pills	More Pills	Any Heroin
1. Usually don't get high	24.2	17.4	31.8	24.1	48.5	23.1	22.7	21.3	31.3	33.4	21.1	-	-	61.3	23.1	4.6
2. One to two hours	30.4	32.7	30.0	31.6	51.5	30.9	34.6	23.8	31.6	23.6	33.0	-	-	22.4	33.4	12.7
3. Three to six hours	33.2	33.1	30.3	32.5	-	32.4	24.6	52.3	24.5	27.1	34.5	-	-	10.7	34.0	43.7
4. Seven to 24 hours	9.8	12.8	7.0	10.0	-	11.4	11.7	2.7	12.6	11.6	10.3	-	-	5.6	7.5	31.9
5. More than 24 hours	2.3	4.0	.9	1.8	-	2.2	6.3	-	-	4.4	1.1	-	-	-	2.0	7.1
Item 5390 N(Wtd) ★	180	84	89	164	3	57	47	40	36	78	76	-	-	14	148	18

B101: What narcotics other than heroin have you taken during the last year without a doctor's orders? (Mark all that apply.)

	TOTAL	M	F	White	Black	NE	NC	S	W	Yes	No	None	Marij	Few Pills	More Pills	Any Heroin
A. Methadone	12.7	12.9	10.9	11.8	-	7.3	19.8	12.1	12.3	12.5	14.9	-	-	8.9	10.0	35.4
B. Opium	44.8	50.8	38.7	43.6	35.9	43.8	45.2	48.2	42.4	40.8	47.2	-	-	15.6	42.5	83.1
C. Morphine	20.3	25.7	13.1	18.5	-	21.7	15.2	21.9	23.0	20.8	19.6	-	-	-	15.6	70.3
D. Codeine	78.1	76.0	79.2	77.9	35.9	72.9	75.7	77.6	89.7	81.0	75.1	-	-	53.3	81.2	72.6
E. Demerol	25.1	21.4	26.1	24.8	-	26.6	14.6	37.6	23.5	29.5	16.4	-	-	-	25.8	36.9
F. Paregoric	2.7	4.9	.9	2.6	-	-	3.8	2.7	5.5	2.1	3.3	-	-	-	2.8	4.2
G. Talwin	1.1	2.0	.4	1.2	-	-	1.8	-	3.2	2.1	-	-	-	-	1.4	-
H. Laudanum	2.0	4.2	-	1.0	-	2.2	1.4	-	4.3	1.7	2.0	-	-	-	1.3	8.4
I. Other	11.3	8.5	13.7	9.0	64.1	8.8	11.6	12.7	13.7	10.6	13.8	-	-	5.3	10.6	21.4
J. Don't know the names of some I have used	11.8	14.7	10.0	10.6	33.9	11.3	5.7	17.4	14.7	10.3	13.3	-	-	25.5	10.7	9.8
Item 5400-5490 N(Wtd) ★	177	83	87	163	2	57	47	37	37	76	74	-	-	14	145	19

★=excludes respondents for whom question was inappropriate.

QUESTIONNAIRE FORM 1 1981	TOTAL	SEX		RACE		REGION				4YR COLLEGE PLANS		ILLICIT DRUG USE: LIFETIME				
		M	F	White	Black	NE	NC	S	W	Yes	No	None	Mari- juana Only	Few Pills	More Pills	Any Her- oin
Weighted No. of Cases:	3644	1689	1795	2769	438	853	1075	1124	592	1969	1283	1213	853	430	958	37
% of Weighted Total:	100.0	46.3	49.3	76.0	12.0	23.4	29.5	30.8	16.3	54.0	35.2	33.3	23.4	11.8	26.3	1.0
B102: Have you ever tried to stop using narcotics other than heroin and found that you couldn't stop?																
1. Yes	1.1	2.3	-	1.2	-	1.1	2.8	-	-	-	2.5	-	-	-	-	10.0
2. No	98.9	97.7	100.0	98.8	100.0	98.9	97.2	99.9	99.9	100.0	97.5	-	-	100.0	100.0	90.0
Item 5500 N(Wtd) ★	180	84	89	165	3	56	47	40	37	78	75	-	-	14	147	19
B103: What methods have you used for taking any of these narcotics other than heroin? (Mark all that apply.)																
A. Sniffing or "snorting"	17.6	20.7	12.2	15.9	-	16.3	18.6	24.2	11.2	11.5	22.5	-	-	5.1	15.5	43.6
B. Smoking	38.5	45.5	33.9	40.0	36.5	38.4	42.6	39.8	32.0	35.0	37.5	-	-	24.7	34.3	80.8
C. Injection	6.2	8.5	3.3	5.9	-	1.7	9.2	6.8	8.7	2.2	10.3	-	-	-	3.1	34.7
D. By mouth	82.3	78.6	85.7	81.6	100.0	76.7	79.4	88.0	88.6	85.1	78.9	-	-	76.4	84.2	72.6
E. Other	2.5	5.4	-	1.9	-	3.6	1.8	2.1	2.2	2.7	1.0	-	-	-	2.0	8.1
Item 5510-5550 N(Wtd) ★	180	83	89	165	2	56	47	40	37	77	76	-	-	14	147	19
B104: Do you think you will be using any narcotics other than heroin without a doctor's orders five years from now?																
1. I definitely will	.7	.9	.4	.7	1.3	.6	.8	.6	.7	.7	.8	.2	.9	.3	.8	14.2
2. I probably will	2.6	2.7	2.2	2.6	1.8	2.7	2.8	1.9	3.4	2.0	3.2	.4	-	1.7	8.0	16.1
3. I probably will not	15.6	14.9	16.2	16.9	9.0	17.9	15.1	14.0	16.6	13.7	17.8	6.4	11.0	20.1	30.3	45.6
4. I definitely will not	81.1	81.4	81.1	79.8	87.9	78.8	81.2	83.6	79.3	83.6	78.2	92.9	88.1	77.9	60.8	24.1
Item 5560 N(Wtd)	3414	1606	1741	2672	416	775	1023	1051	565	1913	1227	1186	794	419	872	34
B105: When (if ever) did you FIRST do each of the following things? Don't count anything you took because a doctor told you to.																
B105A: Smoke cigarettes on a daily basis																
8. Never	62.0	66.0	58.8	61.0	70.2	58.1	59.7	64.5	67.1	70.0	53.3	88.1	60.7	52.1	35.8	20.8
1. Grade 6 or below	5.9	7.0	4.8	6.5	1.8	6.2	6.4	5.2	6.0	5.6	5.7	2.6	6.3	7.6	8.6	21.4
2. Grade 7 or 8	11.0	9.3	12.7	11.8	6.3	12.8	13.0	8.1	10.1	8.6	13.9	3.0	11.7	14.4	19.3	5.6
3. Grade 9 (Freshman)	6.7	6.0	6.9	6.5	5.3	8.1	6.6	6.0	6.2	4.8	8.8	2.6	7.1	8.7	10.4	19.0
4. Grade 10 (Sophomore)	6.7	6.0	7.3	6.5	8.0	7.1	6.3	7.7	5.0	4.8	8.7	1.5	7.0	5.3	12.8	20.4
5. Grade 11 (Junior)	4.7	3.5	5.8	4.9	3.3	4.4	5.7	4.3	4.2	3.6	6.1	.8	4.5	7.5	8.8	7.4
6. Grade 12 (Senior)	2.9	2.1	3.7	2.8	5.0	3.2	2.3	4.2	1.4	2.7	3.4	1.4	2.7	4.5	4.3	5.4
Item 5570 N(Wtd)	3209	1499	1664	2578	342	739	980	955	535	1805	1168	1098	749	395	849	31
B105B: Try an alcoholic beverage-- more than just a few sips																
8. Never	8.0	6.6	9.3	6.1	20.4	3.8	4.9	14.4	8.2	8.1	8.1	21.7	1.0	1.9	.2	-
1. Grade 6 or below	8.6	10.9	6.4	8.6	5.6	9.6	9.9	8.1	10.1	8.5	8.7	5.2	8.5	8.4	12.1	23.2
2. Grade 7 or 8	24.8	27.5	22.0	26.2	14.8	28.1	22.9	22.2	28.1	23.0	26.8	13.3	22.7	30.5	37.8	29.4
3. Grade 9 (Freshman)	23.5	21.5	25.4	24.7	16.5	25.6	26.2	20.3	21.2	23.3	23.5	14.2	28.9	24.5	29.6	19.0
4. Grade 10 (Sophomore)	17.8	17.9	17.8	18.4	15.2	17.2	19.9	17.7	15.3	18.0	17.9	16.6	23.8	19.6	13.5	15.7
5. Grade 11 (Junior)	11.4	9.9	13.0	11.3	14.2	11.7	10.5	12.6	10.2	12.9	9.3	18.7	10.8	10.0	4.6	10.0
6. Grade 12 (Senior)	5.9	5.6	6.2	4.7	13.3	4.0	5.6	7.0	7.0	6.1	5.8	10.4	4.4	5.2	2.2	2.7
Item 5580 N(Wtd)	3078	1451	1584	2496	323	717	933	919	509	1731	1125	977	742	396	850	30
B105C: Try marijuana or hashish																
8. Never	41.2	38.4	43.9	39.3	51.2	34.1	39.7	49.4	38.6	45.1	37.3	100.0	-	20.5	8.9	-
1. Grade 6 or below	2.0	2.7	1.3	2.1	1.2	1.7	2.4	.8	4.2	2.1	1.8	-	2.0	2.1	4.4	14.8
2. Grade 7 or 8	14.7	16.7	12.8	15.8	6.8	21.2	14.8	8.8	16.2	13.2	16.2	-	13.8	16.3	33.9	43.2
3. Grade 9 (Freshman)	18.0	18.2	17.3	19.0	12.9	21.4	18.0	14.1	20.1	15.1	20.4	-	28.7	24.8	29.5	26.7
4. Grade 10 (Sophomore)	12.5	13.7	11.5	12.8	10.0	12.5	13.9	11.9	10.9	13.1	12.1	-	24.8	19.5	15.8	5.9
5. Grade 11 (Junior)	7.6	6.5	8.6	7.4	10.5	6.6	6.7	9.8	6.4	7.7	7.6	-	19.3	10.8	5.1	6.7
6. Grade 12 (Senior)	4.1	3.8	4.6	3.7	7.3	2.4	4.5	5.3	3.7	3.7	4.6	-	11.3	5.9	2.5	2.6
Item 5590 N(Wtd)	3218	1511	1664	2592	347	736	978	974	530	1834	1157	1122	732	397	854	31

★=excludes respondents for whom question was inappropriate.

QUESTIONNAIRE FORM 1 1981	TOTAL	SEX		RACE		REGION				4YR COLLEGE PLANS		ILLICIT DRUG USE: LIFETIME				
		M	F	White	Black	NE	NC	S	W	Yes	No	None	Mari-juana Only	Few Pills	More Pills	Any Her-oin
Weighted No. of Cases:	3644	1689	1795	2769	438	853	1075	1124	592	1969	1283	1213	853	430	958	37
% of Weighted Total:	100.0	46.3	49.3	76.0	12.0	23.4	29.5	30.8	16.3	54.0	35.2	33.3	23.4	11.8	26.3	1.0

B105D: Try LSD

	TOTAL	M	F	White	Black	NE	NC	S	W	Yes	No	None	Mari-juana Only	Few Pills	More Pills	Any Her-oin
8. Never	91.9	90.8	93.3	90.7	99.7	88.9	90.5	96.3	90.4	93.9	90.3	100.0	100.0	97.6	72.2	23.7
1. Grade 6 or below	.1	.2	-	.1	-	.2	.1	-	-	.1	.1	-	-	-	.3	-
2. Grade 7 or 8	.5	.4	.3	.4	-	.4	.8	.2	.6	.3	.6	-	-	.1	.9	22.8
3. Grade 9 (Freshman)	1.3	1.6	.9	1.4	.3	2.3	1.4	.5	1.3	.8	1.6	-	-	-	4.7	11.5
4. Grade 10 (Sophomore)	2.4	2.9	1.9	2.7	-	1.9	3.2	1.3	3.8	1.8	2.9	-	-	.3	8.3	27.2
5. Grade 11 (Junior)	2.4	2.8	1.9	2.9	-	3.9	2.2	1.3	2.4	1.8	2.7	-	-	1.2	8.4	8.1
6. Grade 12 (Senior)	1.5	1.4	1.6	1.8	-	2.5	1.7	.5	1.5	1.3	1.7	-	-	.8	5.2	6.7
Item 5600　N(Wtd)	3254	1531	1679	2580	381	729	983	1002	541	1845	1177	1136	767	399	828	30

B105E: Try any psychedelic other than LSD

	TOTAL	M	F	White	Black	NE	NC	S	W	Yes	No	None	Mari-juana Only	Few Pills	More Pills	Any Her-oin
8. Never	92.6	91.4	94.0	91.5	99.4	88.9	92.4	97.4	88.8	93.2	91.9	100.0	100.0	95.7	74.4	21.8
1. Grade 6 or below	.2	.4	-	.1	-	.4	.1	-	.3	.2	.2	-	-	.4	.4	5.8
2. Grade 7 or 8	.6	.7	.4	.5	-	.2	.9	.1	1.5	.6	.6	-	-	.6	1.6	15.6
3. Grade 9 (Freshman)	1.3	1.2	1.2	1.5	-	2.4	1.3	.6	1.3	1.0	1.6	-	-	1.3	4.2	15.0
4. Grade 10 (Sophomore)	1.9	2.2	1.5	2.1	-	2.7	2.1	.8	2.3	1.5	2.0	-	-	.1	6.8	24.0
5. Grade 11 (Junior)	2.1	2.9	1.4	2.5	.4	3.0	1.7	.7	4.2	1.9	2.4	-	-	.5	7.9	15.1
6. Grade 12 (Senior)	1.3	1.2	1.5	1.7	.2	2.3	1.5	.3	1.6	1.5	1.3	-	-	1.4	4.7	2.7
Item 5610　N(Wtd)	3189	1493	1653	2527	377	704	966	985	535	1810	1156	1135	772	391	765	30

B105F: Try amphetamines

	TOTAL	M	F	White	Black	NE	NC	S	W	Yes	No	None	Mari-juana Only	Few Pills	More Pills	Any Her-oin
8. Never	76.6	77.2	76.6	73.3	95.5	73.0	73.8	82.4	75.8	80.5	71.6	100.0	100.0	66.4	17.5	4.3
1. Grade 6 or below	.2	.3	.2	.2	.1	.5	.1	-	.6	.3	.1	-	-	.4	.2	14.8
2. Grade 7 or 8	.8	.7	.8	.9	.2	.8	1.3	.5	.5	.5	1.1	-	-	.8	3.1	1.5
3. Grade 9 (Freshman)	3.2	3.3	2.6	3.6	.4	3.5	3.4	2.7	3.2	2.3	4.2	-	-	4.1	11.2	17.1
4. Grade 10 (Sophomore)	6.1	6.4	5.8	7.0	.3	6.5	6.1	4.4	8.7	4.8	7.2	-	-	6.1	22.3	36.0
5. Grade 11 (Junior)	7.9	7.4	8.3	9.0	1.9	9.4	10.3	5.7	5.6	6.5	10.3	-	-	8.8	29.4	23.5
6. Grade 12 (Senior)	5.2	4.6	5.7	6.0	1.7	6.5	4.9	4.3	5.6	5.1	5.4	-	-	13.4	16.3	2.8
Item 5620　N(Wtd)	3038	1438	1560	2412	361	680	919	938	501	1749	1082	1133	771	318	696	29

B105G: Try quaaludes

	TOTAL	M	F	White	Black	NE	NC	S	W	Yes	No	None	Mari-juana Only	Few Pills	More Pills	Any Her-oin
8. Never	90.2	87.9	92.5	88.8	98.7	89.1	91.2	89.4	91.6	92.9	88.1	100.0	100.0	91.8	67.9	28.2
1. Grade 6 or below	*	-	.1	.1	-	-	.1	.1	-	*	-	-	-	-	.2	-
2. Grade 7 or 8	.2	.3	.1	.2	-	.1	.2	.2	.4	*	.3	-	-	.7	4.6	
3. Grade 9 (Freshman)	1.5	1.7	1.2	1.6	.7	1.7	1.1	1.9	1.4	1.1	2.0	-	-	.5	5.2	18.5
4. Grade 10 (Sophomore)	2.3	3.0	1.7	2.7	-	1.8	2.0	2.7	2.9	1.6	2.4	-	-	1.1	7.7	25.6
5. Grade 11 (Junior)	3.7	4.8	2.7	4.3	.4	4.5	3.6	3.9	2.2	3.0	4.6	-	-	3.2	12.3	20.4
6. Grade 12 (Senior)	2.0	2.3	1.7	2.3	.2	2.8	1.8	1.9	1.5	1.3	2.6	-	-	3.3	6.2	2.7
Item 5630　N(Wtd)	3245	1521	1681	2578	378	732	976	998	539	1842	1171	1135	772	394	820	29

B105H: Try barbiturates

	TOTAL	M	F	White	Black	NE	NC	S	W	Yes	No	None	Mari-juana Only	Few Pills	More Pills	Any Her-oin
8. Never	92.9	92.5	93.8	92.1	98.9	92.7	92.1	93.8	93.4	94.8	90.9	100.0	100.0	96.4	75.0	33.4
1. Grade 6 or below	-	-	-	-	-	-	-	-	-	-	-	-	-	-	-	-
2. Grade 7 or 8	.4	.4	.3	.4	-	.2	.4	.3	.6	.2	.2	-	-	.2	1.2	4.2
3. Grade 9 (Freshman)	1.5	1.5	1.3	1.7	.3	1.8	1.8	1.3	.9	.9	2.6	-	-	1.4	4.3	32.4
4. Grade 10 (Sophomore)	2.1	2.1	1.9	2.4	.5	1.3	2.4	2.4	1.9	1.6	2.2	-	-	.2	8.1	11.4
5. Grade 11 (Junior)	2.3	3.0	1.6	2.3	.4	3.1	2.2	1.9	2.1	1.8	2.8	-	-	1.1	8.3	15.9
6. Grade 12 (Senior)	.8	.5	1.1	1.0	-	.9	1.1	.4	1.1	.7	1.3	-	-	.7	3.0	2.8
Item 5640　N(Wtd)	3164	1486	1640	2510	376	703	963	974	524	1799	1148	1132	771	377	761	29

B105I: Try tranquilizers

	TOTAL	M	F	White	Black	NE	NC	S	W	Yes	No	None	Mari-juana Only	Few Pills	More Pills	Any Her-oin
8. Never	90.1	91.2	89.6	88.7	96.7	90.5	89.0	90.5	91.0	91.5	88.1	100.0	100.0	85.2	68.6	22.1
1. Grade 6 or below	.3	.3	.3	.4	-	*	.5	.3	.2	.3	.3	-	-	.6	.7	6.1
2. Grade 7 or 8	.8	1.0	.7	1.0	-	.9	.7	.8	.9	.8	.8	-	-	1.9	2.1	11.1
3. Grade 9 (Freshman)	2.1	2.2	1.9	2.6	-	1.7	2.4	2.3	1.9	1.6	3.0	-	-	3.4	6.8	14.7
4. Grade 10 (Sophomore)	2.6	1.9	3.3	3.0	.6	1.4	3.3	2.8	2.7	2.6	2.9	-	-	2.4	9.4	10.4
5. Grade 11 (Junior)	2.6	2.8	2.1	2.9	1.2	3.9	2.5	2.1	2.0	2.5	2.5	-	-	3.7	8.0	32.7
6. Grade 12 (Senior)	1.4	.7	2.0	1.4	1.5	1.5	1.5	1.2	1.3	.8	2.4	-	-	2.9	4.4	2.8
Item 5650　N(Wtd)	3110	1459	1613	2470	370	697	944	958	512	1779	1121	1134	771	342	740	29

* = less than .05 per cent.

QUESTIONNAIRE FORM 1 1981	TOTAL	SEX		RACE		REGION				4YR COLLEGE PLANS		ILLICIT DRUG USE: LIFETIME				
		M	F	White	Black	NE	NC	S	W	Yes	No	None	Mari- juana Only	Few Pills	More Pills	Any Her- oin
Weighted No. of Cases:	3644	1689	1795	2769	438	853	1075	1124	592	1969	1283	1213	853	430	958	37
% of Weighted Total:	100.0	46.3	49.3	76.0	12.0	23.4	29.5	30.8	16.3	54.0	35.2	33.3	23.4	11.8	26.3	1.0
B105J: Try cocaine																
8. Never	84.2	82.1	86.9	83.0	92.1	80.4	86.6	90.1	74.4	85.3	84.9	100.0	100.0	79.5	51.8	7.1
1. Grade 6 or below	.1	.1	.1	.1	-	.2	.1	-	.1	*	.2	-	-	-	.2	2.7
2. Grade 7 or 8	.4	.5	.3	.5	-	.5	.3	.1	.8	.2	.5	-	-	-	.6	24.5
3. Grade 9 (Freshman)	1.7	2.0	1.1	1.8	.6	2.0	1.4	1.2	2.9	1.5	1.9	-	-	1.3	5.5	14.0
4. Grade 10 (Sophomore)	3.8	4.5	3.2	4.3	1.8	4.4	3.9	2.6	5.2	3.3	3.4	-	-	3.4	12.6	22.1
5. Grade 11 (Junior)	5.7	6.2	5.1	6.1	2.6	6.4	4.5	3.2	11.6	5.4	5.8	-	-	8.7	17.5	17.1
6. Grade 12 (Senior)	4.0	4.7	3.3	4.1	2.9	6.1	3.3	2.7	5.0	4.3	3.3	-	-	7.1	11.8	12.4
Item 5660 N(Wtd)	3265	1541	1682	2599	378	738	982	1002	543	1854	1178	1134	772	396	841	29
B105K: Try heroin																
8. Never	99.0	98.9	99.3	99.1	99.6	99.0	98.8	99.5	98.8	99.1	98.8	100.0	100.0	100.0	100.0	-
1. Grade 6 or below	.1	.1	*	*	-	.2	-	-	.2	*	.1	-	-	-	-	4.0
2. Grade 7 or 8	.1	.1	.1	.1	-	.2	.1	-	.1	.1	.1	-	-	-	-	10.4
3. Grade 9 (Freshman)	.2	.1	.1	.1	-	*	.5	-	.1	.1	.4	-	-	-	-	19.6
4. Grade 10 (Sophomore)	.2	.2	.1	.2	.4	.3	.2	.2	-	.1	.2	-	-	-	-	15.5
5. Grade 11 (Junior)	.3	.3	.2	.3	-	.1	.4	.2	.5	.3	.3	-	-	-	-	29.5
6. Grade 12 (Senior)	.2	.2	.2	.2	-	.2	.1	.2	.3	.2	.1	-	-	-	-	21.0
Item 5670 N(Wtd)	3268	1536	1690	2597	377	740	987	997	543	1853	1183	1134	772	399	839	29
B105L: Try any narcotic other than heroin																
8. Never	92.2	92.2	92.4	90.9	98.3	89.4	92.9	95.1	89.3	93.8	90.8	100.0	100.0	91.9	74.9	15.2
1. Grade 6 or below	.3	.2	.4	.3	.1	.2	.5	-	.7	.2	.5	-	-	-	1.0	3.0
2. Grade 7 or 8	.7	.4	.9	.8	-	1.0	.3	.2	1.6	.6	.8	-	-	.5	2.0	12.9
3. Grade 9 (Freshman)	1.2	1.2	1.0	1.3	-	1.1	1.4	.9	1.5	.7	1.8	-	-	1.0	3.7	21.8
4. Grade 10 (Sophomore)	1.5	1.8	1.3	1.8	.6	2.0	1.3	1.2	1.6	1.2	1.1	-	-	1.1	5.2	12.1
5. Grade 11 (Junior)	2.7	2.9	2.6	3.3	.5	3.8	2.3	1.7	4.1	2.5	3.0	-	-	2.9	9.5	11.5
6. Grade 12 (Senior)	1.4	1.3	1.4	1.7	.4	2.4	1.3	.9	1.3	1.0	2.0	-	-	2.5	3.7	23.6
Item 5680 N(Wtd)	3140	1481	1622	2491	374	710	949	969	513	1780	1142	1128	770	363	757	27

The next questions are about your experiences in school.

D001: Some people like school very much. Others don't. How do you feel about going to school?

	TOTAL	M	F	White	Black	NE	NC	S	W	Yes	No	None	Mari- juana Only	Few Pills	More Pills	Any Her- oin
5. I like school very much	14.6	12.3	16.6	12.6	25.1	9.7	14.9	17.9	14.1	17.5	10.5	19.5	12.7	14.7	9.2	6.1
4. I like school quite a lot	32.9	32.8	33.4	33.1	31.8	32.9	32.5	32.3	34.8	38.8	24.6	38.1	35.7	32.6	23.7	14.4
3. I like school some	39.4	41.3	37.5	40.2	35.4	40.5	40.1	37.9	39.4	34.7	45.8	34.3	41.2	39.4	45.4	25.3
2. I don't like school very much	9.3	9.1	9.5	10.0	5.3	11.7	8.4	8.6	9.2	6.9	12.6	6.0	7.9	10.9	14.4	31.9
1. I don't like school at all	3.8	4.5	3.0	4.1	2.3	5.2	4.1	3.3	2.6	2.1	6.6	2.1	2.6	2.4	7.3	22.3
Item 7630 N(Wtd)	3278	1528	1699	2593	389	694	1009	1032	543	1914	1225	1161	784	402	786	31

D002: How often do you feel that the school work you are assigned is meaningful and important?

	TOTAL	M	F	White	Black	NE	NC	S	W	Yes	No	None	Mari- juana Only	Few Pills	More Pills	Any Her- oin
5. Almost always	12.9	11.9	14.0	10.3	26.2	11.2	12.2	16.1	10.2	14.7	10.0	17.4	10.9	14.7	7.5	2.2
4. Often	26.9	27.6	25.9	26.4	24.8	21.9	26.6	26.9	33.6	30.1	21.6	29.8	29.9	25.9	20.8	11.0
3. Sometimes	43.4	40.8	46.1	45.3	37.8	47.4	43.7	41.2	41.8	42.6	44.5	39.7	43.5	46.0	48.0	36.2
2. Seldom	14.6	16.2	12.8	15.7	8.9	16.8	14.7	13.7	13.4	11.3	20.1	11.8	14.7	11.8	19.4	38.0
1. Never	2.3	3.4	1.2	2.3	2.3	2.8	2.8	2.1	1.0	1.2	3.8	1.3	.9	1.6	4.3	12.7
Item 5700 N(Wtd)	3275	1525	1699	2591	388	692	1011	1028	544	1917	1221	1163	781	403	784	31

D003: How interesting are most of your courses to you?

	TOTAL	M	F	White	Black	NE	NC	S	W	Yes	No	None	Mari- juana Only	Few Pills	More Pills	Any Her- oin
5. Very exciting and stimulating	5.1	5.3	5.0	3.9	12.2	3.2	5.0	6.7	4.9	5.8	4.0	7.0	3.6	4.7	3.7	-
4. Quite interesting	32.0	30.7	33.1	30.2	36.4	32.0	31.5	31.5	33.7	35.7	26.5	37.4	30.4	33.4	25.8	20.9
3. Fairly interesting	43.3	42.6	43.8	45.4	35.5	42.5	42.4	43.8	45.0	42.5	44.7	40.9	47.7	40.4	43.9	32.1
2. Slightly dull	15.1	15.4	14.7	15.7	13.5	17.1	16.3	13.6	13.0	12.7	18.2	10.7	15.5	17.4	20.0	22.3
1. Very dull	4.6	5.9	3.3	5.0	2.5	5.2	4.8	4.4	3.4	3.3	6.5	4.0	2.7	4.0	6.6	24.7
Item 5710 N(Wtd)	3267	1523	1693	2583	387	690	1009	1028	540	1908	1221	1161	783	401	779	31

*=less than .05 per cent.

QUESTIONNAIRE FORM 1 1981	TOTAL	SEX		RACE		REGION				4YR COLLEGE PLANS		ILLICIT DRUG USE: LIFETIME				
		M	F	White	Black	NE	NC	S	W	Yes	No	None	Mari- juana Only	Few Pills	More Pills	Any Her- oin
Weighted No. of Cases:	3644	1689	1795	2769	438	853	1075	1124	592	1969	1283	1213	853	430	958	37
% of Weighted Total:	100.0	46.3	49.3	76.0	12.0	23.4	29.5	30.8	16.3	54.0	35.2	33.3	23.4	11.8	26.3	1.0

D004: How important do you think the things you are learning in school are going to be for your later life?

5. Very important	21.9	22.5	21.2	17.5	45.2	15.7	21.7	27.7	18.9	23.7	19.3	26.2	21.1	21.9	14.9	5.8
4. Quite important	29.9	28.8	31.0	30.3	27.2	27.2	30.5	31.3	29.3	32.4	25.8	33.4	31.0	28.4	25.6	14.1
3. Fairly important	30.9	30.4	31.3	33.7	17.4	34.1	30.8	26.3	35.9	29.8	32.6	27.7	30.5	31.5	37.0	33.8
2. Slightly important	15.0	15.7	14.5	16.2	8.5	20.0	14.6	12.2	14.6	12.8	18.6	10.7	15.8	16.5	19.1	29.5
1. Not at all important	2.4	2.7	2.0	2.3	1.7	3.0	2.4	2.6	1.3	1.3	3.8	2.1	1.6	1.8	3.4	16.9
Item 5720 N(Wtd)	3265	1518	1696	2583	387	687	1007	1029	543	1908	1220	1159	783	400	780	31

D005: How much competition for grades is there among students at your school?

1. None	6.0	6.9	5.1	5.5	7.3	4.3	5.2	6.1	9.4	3.3	9.7	4.4	5.1	8.6	6.3	4.9
2. A little	19.5	19.8	19.4	19.9	17.4	16.4	21.5	17.4	23.9	18.0	22.6	18.2	20.4	21.0	21.2	13.9
3. Some	34.9	33.8	35.9	36.0	30.6	34.5	35.0	34.9	35.1	31.8	39.3	35.6	32.7	32.8	37.9	34.2
4. Quite a bit	29.2	28.9	29.4	29.6	27.6	28.4	30.0	30.4	26.7	33.6	22.4	30.4	31.9	28.7	25.6	41.6
5. A great deal	10.4	10.5	10.2	9.0	17.1	16.4	8.3	11.3	4.9	13.2	6.0	11.4	9.9	9.0	9.0	5.4
Item 5730 N(Wtd)	3267	1523	1691	2586	384	693	1005	1032	538	1899	1212	1156	788	399	781	32

D006: How do you think most of the students in your classes would feel if you cheated on a test?

1. They would like it very much	2.0	2.8	1.4	1.6	4.2	3.0	1.5	2.5	1.1	1.8	2.3	1.9	1.6	1.9	1.9	6.5
2. They would like it	2.3	2.3	2.1	1.6	4.5	2.2	1.6	3.4	1.7	1.2	3.9	2.6	1.8	3.1	2.2	2.6
3. They would not care	77.2	77.0	77.3	78.9	74.0	76.4	78.0	77.6	75.9	75.8	79.3	73.0	80.6	75.2	81.3	72.5
4. They would dislike it	14.2	13.9	14.7	14.5	9.4	14.1	15.2	11.9	16.8	16.2	11.5	16.3	12.6	17.1	11.6	18.5
5. They would dislike it very much	4.2	4.0	4.6	3.5	7.9	4.4	3.7	4.6	4.5	5.1	3.1	6.2	3.4	2.7	3.0	-
Item 5740 N(Wtd)	3271	1520	1695	2591	383	688	1008	1033	542	1900	1212	1158	788	401	780	32

D007: How do you think most of the students in your classes would feel if you intentionally did things to make your teachers angry?

1. They would like it very much	3.4	5.3	1.6	2.7	6.2	4.5	3.1	4.0	1.4	3.3	3.4	2.5	3.3	4.1	3.8	8.2
2. They would like it	11.6	15.5	8.3	10.7	18.2	10.9	11.7	13.2	9.4	11.1	12.9	11.2	10.8	11.5	13.3	9.9
3. They would not care	42.7	43.1	41.9	42.0	43.9	43.8	44.5	42.0	39.1	39.0	48.2	41.0	43.8	38.7	46.3	47.1
4. They would dislike it	35.2	30.8	39.3	37.7	21.5	35.7	34.3	32.8	40.7	38.5	29.9	36.3	36.5	39.7	30.3	27.3
5. They would dislike it very much	7.1	5.3	8.9	6.9	10.2	5.1	6.4	8.0	9.5	8.0	5.6	9.0	5.6	6.1	6.2	7.4
Item 5750 N(Wtd)	3256	1516	1684	2582	380	682	1004	1030	539	1894	1204	1152	783	400	778	32

D008: How often do you find that your friends encourage you to do things which your teachers wouldn't like?

1. Never	35.7	24.5	45.8	33.5	43.3	37.2	31.6	34.5	43.4	35.7	34.2	40.0	34.4	39.0	29.4	13.6
2. Seldom	34.3	34.9	34.0	36.3	25.9	34.9	34.9	32.9	34.8	37.1	30.8	35.0	35.7	31.3	34.5	28.2
3. Sometimes	23.2	30.8	16.4	24.1	20.6	21.3	27.0	23.9	17.4	21.6	26.0	18.5	24.3	24.0	28.0	43.2
4. Often	5.5	7.9	3.3	5.2	8.2	4.8	4.9	7.5	3.9	4.6	7.4	5.5	5.0	4.6	6.0	6.4
5. Almost always	1.3	1.9	.5	1.0	2.1	1.8	1.5	1.2	.5	1.0	1.5	1.1	.7	1.0	2.1	8.6
Item 5760 N(Wtd)	3268	1518	1694	2587	381	689	1006	1033	540	1900	1208	1162	785	401	777	32

D009: Have you ever been in a work-study program--that is, a program where you work on a job as part of your schooling?

1. No, not ever	76.9	77.6	76.5	78.6	68.1	86.8	75.4	75.2	70.5	83.2	68.5	82.0	78.4	74.6	70.8	61.9
2. Yes, for a half year or less	8.5	8.2	8.8	7.7	11.4	5.3	8.4	6.9	15.5	7.0	10.5	7.2	8.4	10.7	9.0	4.7
3. Yes, for about a year	10.2	8.9	10.9	9.5	15.1	5.3	11.9	12.3	9.2	6.7	14.6	8.2	8.9	12.1	12.8	25.6
4. Yes, for about two years	3.3	3.9	2.8	3.2	3.0	1.7	3.5	4.1	3.6	1.9	5.5	2.0	3.4	1.7	5.6	2.3
5. Yes, for more than two years	1.1	1.4	.9	.9	2.4	1.0	.9	1.4	1.2	1.2	.9	.6	.9	.8	1.8	5.5
Item 5770 N(Wtd)	3260	1515	1690	2581	381	685	1005	1031	539	1897	1205	1161	783	399	774	32

QUESTIONNAIRE FORM 1 1981	TOTAL	SEX		RACE		REGION				4YR COLLEGE PLANS		ILLICIT DRUG USE: LIFETIME				
		M	F	White	Black	NE	NC	S	W	Yes	No	None	Marijuana Only	Few Pills	More Pills	Any Heroin
Weighted No. of Cases:	3644	1689	1795	2769	438	853	1075	1124	592	1969	1283	1213	853	430	958	37
% of Weighted Total:	100.0	46.3	49.3	76.0	12.0	23.4	29.5	30.8	16.3	54.0	35.2	33.3	23.4	11.8	26.3	1.0

These last questions are about you and the counselors in your school.

D010: How many times this school year have you seen a counselor individually?

	TOTAL	M	F	White	Black	NE	NC	S	W	Yes	No	None	Marijuana Only	Few Pills	More Pills	Any Heroin
1. No times	12.3	11.2	13.1	12.5	13.0	7.4	12.9	17.3	7.7	8.1	18.9	13.5	10.2	11.5	12.2	28.0
2. 1 time	12.0	12.0	12.4	12.2	12.7	11.6	11.1	14.0	10.7	9.8	15.1	12.5	11.4	10.7	12.6	5.3
3. 2 times	19.0	19.0	18.8	19.4	19.5	15.5	18.5	22.6	17.5	18.7	19.7	17.6	20.3	23.6	16.3	15.5
4. 3 or 4 times	29.1	29.8	28.5	29.6	26.2	31.0	28.4	25.5	33.1	30.9	26.5	28.2	28.9	30.4	30.6	25.7
5. 5 - 7 times	16.4	17.4	15.8	16.7	13.9	19.3	17.6	12.6	17.7	19.1	12.6	17.0	17.7	15.1	16.3	4.0
6. 8 - 10 times	5.3	5.2	5.3	4.7	6.1	6.3	6.3	3.4	5.9	6.2	4.0	5.2	5.6	3.7	5.5	21.5
7. 11 or more times	5.9	5.5	6.1	4.9	8.6	8.8	5.3	3.7	7.4	7.2	3.2	6.0	5.9	4.9	6.5	-
Item 5780 N(Wtd)	3257	1513	1687	2578	381	685	1005	1027	540	1897	1201	1160	783	395	775	32

D011: How many times this school year have you seen a counselor as a part of a group of other students?

	TOTAL	M	F	White	Black	NE	NC	S	W	Yes	No	None	Marijuana Only	Few Pills	More Pills	Any Heroin
1. No times	51.3	51.8	50.8	53.1	39.3	60.5	48.7	47.9	50.7	47.2	57.6	49.8	50.7	50.3	54.6	50.6
2. 1 time	15.7	14.6	16.7	16.0	14.0	14.2	18.1	13.7	16.8	15.7	16.0	14.8	16.6	17.3	16.0	20.8
3. 2 times	15.2	15.1	15.2	14.9	18.6	12.4	15.7	17.5	13.8	16.4	13.5	14.5	15.7	18.0	14.5	6.9
4. 3 or 4 times	11.9	12.4	11.5	11.2	17.7	8.3	10.5	14.9	13.3	14.0	8.3	13.5	11.3	10.3	9.9	19.4
5. 5 - 7 times	2.8	3.2	2.6	2.3	4.8	2.7	3.2	2.7	2.4	3.1	2.5	3.4	3.2	2.6	1.9	-
6. 8 - 10 times	1.6	1.6	1.7	1.3	2.6	.9	2.3	1.4	1.6	2.1	1.0	2.3	1.0	.9	1.6	2.3
7. 11 or more times	1.5	1.4	1.6	1.2	3.1	.9	1.5	1.9	1.4	1.5	1.3	1.6	1.4	.7	1.6	-
Item 5790 N(Wtd)	3254	1514	1686	2576	380	685	1005	1028	536	1892	1204	1159	784	392	776	32

D012: Would you have preferred to see a counselor more or less often than you have during the past year?

	TOTAL	M	F	White	Black	NE	NC	S	W	Yes	No	None	Marijuana Only	Few Pills	More Pills	Any Heroin
5. Much more often	9.3	9.9	8.6	7.1	20.1	8.4	8.2	10.3	10.6	10.5	7.1	8.7	11.0	9.1	8.5	15.0
4. A little more often	24.7	24.6	24.7	23.9	29.5	23.8	23.4	27.5	23.0	26.6	22.2	23.1	27.5	25.9	22.6	24.2
3. About as often	51.3	49.5	53.2	54.8	33.2	56.4	53.3	46.3	50.2	53.7	47.5	55.3	49.5	50.6	49.4	36.0
2. A little less often	6.2	5.3	6.9	5.8	7.7	5.6	5.8	6.6	6.7	4.4	8.9	6.0	4.7	6.4	7.8	4.3
1. Much less often	8.6	10.7	6.6	8.4	9.5	5.7	9.3	9.2	9.6	4.8	14.3	6.9	7.3	7.9	11.7	20.5
Item 5800 N(Wtd)	3208	1499	1657	2537	375	676	994	1006	531	1884	1174	1146	779	386	760	32

D013: How helpful have your sessions with a counselor been to you?

	TOTAL	M	F	White	Black	NE	NC	S	W	Yes	No	None	Marijuana Only	Few Pills	More Pills	Any Heroin
5. Extremely helpful	11.3	11.6	10.9	9.0	20.4	12.8	9.3	12.5	11.0	12.6	9.1	12.9	11.7	12.2	7.9	8.6
4. Quite helpful	25.3	25.2	25.4	24.3	29.0	24.4	22.2	27.5	27.8	27.8	21.3	27.7	26.6	24.4	21.2	18.9
3. Somewhat helpful	25.7	26.8	25.2	26.4	23.7	23.0	28.2	22.7	30.3	26.4	25.0	26.2	25.2	24.2	28.2	9.8
2. A little helpful	19.5	19.5	19.5	20.9	14.6	21.8	19.9	18.3	18.3	19.6	19.0	16.5	20.9	20.5	21.4	18.8
1. Not at all helpful	10.3	10.6	9.7	10.7	7.6	12.7	11.4	8.9	8.1	9.1	12.7	8.0	10.9	9.0	13.7	28.6
8. Did not see a counselor this year	7.8	6.2	9.3	8.7	4.8	5.4	9.0	10.0	4.5	4.6	13.0	8.8	4.7	9.7	7.7	15.4
Item 5810 N(Wtd)	3240	1505	1682	2567	377	680	1001	1022	536	1892	1193	1158	779	390	771	32

D014: Would you have preferred more or less of each of the following types of counseling in the last year?

D014A: Choosing what courses to take

	TOTAL	M	F	White	Black	NE	NC	S	W	Yes	No	None	Marijuana Only	Few Pills	More Pills	Any Heroin
5. Much more	21.6	20.8	21.7	17.8	38.4	20.9	19.3	24.6	20.9	20.8	22.3	20.7	21.0	23.0	21.0	27.2
4. A little more	25.9	26.2	25.8	26.8	21.9	25.2	24.6	26.6	28.1	27.3	24.4	24.7	27.6	29.6	24.3	30.5
3. About right	44.7	44.3	45.6	48.1	30.8	48.2	46.1	41.2	44.7	46.3	42.1	47.0	45.2	41.9	45.3	25.7
2. A little less	3.6	3.6	3.5	3.2	4.4	2.8	4.7	3.1	3.2	2.8	5.0	3.4	2.0	3.1	4.3	12.1
1. Much less	4.2	5.1	3.4	4.0	4.5	2.9	5.3	4.5	3.2	2.8	6.2	4.2	4.2	2.4	5.1	4.5
Item 5811 N(Wtd)	3178	1471	1658	2526	363	659	990	1000	529	1866	1166	1137	765	383	755	29

QUESTIONNAIRE FORM 1 1981	TOTAL	SEX		RACE		REGION				4YR COLLEGE PLANS		ILLICIT DRUG USE: LIFETIME				
		M	F	White	Black	NE	NC	S	W	Yes	No	None	Mari-juana Only	Few Pills	More Pills	Any Her-oin
Weighted No. of Cases:	3644	1689	1795	2769	438	853	1075	1124	592	1969	1283	1213	853	430	958	37
% of Weighted Total:	100.0	46.3	49.3	76.0	12.0	23.4	29.5	30.8	16.3	54.0	35.2	33.3	23.4	11.8	26.3	1.0
D014B: Discussing problems with course work																
5. Much more	14.2	13.3	14.5	10.9	30.0	13.3	14.7	16.8	9.8	14.4	14.3	13.1	13.7	12.7	15.9	22.8
4. A little more	24.3	23.9	25.0	23.0	29.5	23.4	22.1	25.1	28.0	24.1	24.6	21.7	26.7	26.1	25.2	28.8
3. About right	51.0	50.8	51.5	56.0	29.3	56.0	52.3	45.3	53.0	54.6	45.2	55.5	49.8	50.6	47.9	40.3
2. A little less	3.8	3.9	3.8	3.6	4.4	2.1	4.8	4.3	2.8	2.8	5.4	3.3	3.1	3.3	4.3	8.1
1. Much less	6.7	8.1	5.2	6.4	6.9	5.2	6.2	8.5	6.4	4.1	10.5	6.4	6.7	7.3	6.7	-
Item 5812 N(Wtd)	3129	1452	1627	2480	361	649	973	988	519	1835	1151	1119	754	382	738	28
D014C: Discussing any trouble you've gotten into																
5. Much more	9.5	10.3	8.4	6.5	22.0	9.8	10.0	10.1	7.0	9.1	9.5	7.8	9.4	8.7	11.1	40.7
4. A little more	10.3	12.4	8.5	9.5	12.5	11.0	7.8	12.0	11.0	9.8	11.1	9.8	11.4	10.3	9.8	12.2
3. About right	60.3	57.2	63.4	65.4	37.9	62.5	61.0	55.7	64.7	65.7	52.4	64.4	59.3	58.2	59.1	30.2
2. A little less	5.2	6.0	4.5	4.6	8.8	4.6	5.9	5.5	4.2	4.5	6.5	4.0	4.6	7.3	5.8	4.8
1. Much less	14.7	14.1	15.2	13.9	18.8	12.0	15.3	16.7	13.0	10.8	20.5	13.9	15.4	15.5	14.1	12.2
Item 5813 N(Wtd)	3052	1426	1580	2418	355	629	959	955	509	1790	1123	1086	736	373	725	30
D014D: Discussing military plans																
5. Much more	6.5	9.1	3.7	4.4	16.5	5.6	5.6	8.8	4.8	4.7	8.2	5.2	7.2	6.2	6.7	8.1
4. A little more	5.9	8.4	3.8	5.5	9.4	6.1	5.6	6.4	5.5	5.2	7.0	5.3	6.9	6.5	5.2	9.0
3. About right	48.6	47.1	50.2	53.2	25.7	51.0	50.9	44.1	49.6	55.0	39.5	53.8	48.3	46.5	46.3	42.5
2. A little less	5.5	6.8	4.3	5.1	8.6	3.9	4.4	6.8	7.3	4.9	6.9	6.1	4.7	5.3	5.5	3.0
1. Much less	33.5	28.7	37.9	31.7	39.8	33.2	33.4	33.9	32.9	30.2	38.5	29.7	32.9	35.6	36.3	37.4
Item 5814 N(Wtd)	2977	1409	1523	2361	344	603	942	933	499	1745	1095	1062	722	357	710	28
D014E: Discussing education or training plans																
5. Much more	25.0	22.4	27.0	20.7	48.2	22.3	23.4	28.0	25.7	27.5	21.0	25.6	26.0	25.9	21.2	24.0
4. A little more	32.2	31.7	33.1	34.8	21.0	32.9	32.6	31.3	32.4	34.9	28.1	31.3	32.5	34.1	33.8	30.4
3. About right	33.3	34.8	31.7	35.3	21.1	37.2	33.4	30.5	33.2	32.4	34.5	34.9	32.0	31.5	34.1	30.9
2. A little less	3.2	3.9	2.7	3.2	3.8	1.5	3.3	3.9	3.6	1.9	5.4	3.0	2.8	2.9	3.8	1.8
1. Much less	6.3	7.1	5.5	6.1	5.9	6.0	7.2	6.2	5.1	3.3	11.1	5.2	6.7	5.6	7.1	12.9
Item 5815 N(Wtd)	3119	1447	1623	2483	351	648	982	974	516	1835	1141	1111	759	375	741	28
D014F: Discussing career plans or job choice																
5. Much more	30.9	25.9	34.9	26.4	53.3	30.3	29.8	32.8	30.5	33.8	26.4	29.9	34.1	30.9	27.4	49.2
4. A little more	32.1	32.7	31.9	34.8	22.3	33.4	31.3	32.6	30.9	34.6	28.3	32.3	31.4	33.0	33.6	27.4
3. About right	29.9	33.3	27.2	32.4	16.1	31.8	30.9	26.2	32.7	28.3	32.6	31.9	28.2	29.8	30.2	21.7
2. A little less	1.7	1.9	1.5	1.5	2.2	.8	1.4	2.4	2.0	1.1	2.5	1.8	1.2	.9	2.1	1.8
1. Much less	5.3	6.2	4.5	4.9	6.1	3.6	6.7	5.9	3.9	2.2	10.2	4.1	5.1	5.3	6.7	-
Item 5816 N(Wtd)	3118	1444	1626	2477	354	646	976	977	519	1841	1134	1116	760	378	734	28
D014G: Discussing personal problems																
5. Much more	9.2	8.7	9.4	7.3	17.5	9.3	7.8	12.2	6.2	9.6	8.6	7.7	8.8	10.2	10.1	23.7
4. A little more	10.0	10.8	9.5	10.2	8.2	8.8	10.5	9.6	11.2	10.3	9.3	9.8	9.2	10.7	11.0	5.5
3. About right	54.7	53.6	56.1	58.9	34.5	56.3	54.6	50.2	61.3	58.9	48.4	59.3	55.0	55.1	49.5	40.4
2. A little less	4.9	6.1	3.5	4.8	6.4	6.0	5.8	4.0	3.6	4.7	5.4	3.6	5.3	3.6	6.9	9.4
1. Much less	21.2	20.9	21.4	18.8	33.4	19.6	21.2	24.0	17.7	16.5	28.2	19.6	21.7	20.4	22.5	21.1
Item 5817 N(Wtd)	3035	1423	1567	2410	345	630	948	954	503	1780	1117	1077	735	368	726	28

QUESTIONNAIRE FORM 2 1981	TOTAL	SEX		RACE		REGION				4YR COLLEGE PLANS		ILLICIT DRUG USE: LIFETIME				
		M	F	White	Black	NE	NC	S	W	Yes	No	None	Mari-juana Only	Few Pills	More Pills	Any Her-oin
Weighted No. of Cases:	3655	1762	1762	2761	467	869	1102	1117	567	1937	1462	1219	846	487	958	41
% of Weighted Total:	100.0	48.2	48.2	75.5	12.8	23.8	30.1	30.6	15.5	53.0	40.0	33.4	23.2	13.3	26.2	1.1

A01: Taking all things together, how would you say things are these days--would you say you're very happy, pretty happy, or not too happy these days?

	TOTAL	M	F	White	Black	NE	NC	S	W	Yes	No	None	Mari-juana Only	Few Pills	More Pills	Any Her-oin
3. Very happy	20.2	18.6	22.2	22.1	12.2	18.4	19.8	21.6	21.1	21.4	18.9	24.7	18.0	15.5	19.0	20.5
2. Pretty happy	66.0	67.9	64.5	67.0	60.8	67.0	66.3	64.3	67.2	66.1	67.4	61.7	69.0	70.9	68.1	53.8
1. Not too happy	13.8	13.5	13.3	10.8	27.0	14.5	13.9	14.1	11.7	12.4	13.8	13.6	13.0	13.6	12.9	23.1
Item 1190 N(Wtd)	3556	1702	1738	2692	459	843	1080	1092	540	1904	1410	1199	826	477	921	39

A02: The next questions ask about the kinds of things you might do. How often do you do each of the following?

A02A: Watch TV

	TOTAL	M	F	White	Black	NE	NC	S	W	Yes	No	None	Mari-juana Only	Few Pills	More Pills	Any Her-oin
5. Almost everyday	72.2	75.0	69.3	71.1	81.9	71.5	69.2	77.7	68.4	70.4	74.7	75.5	76.2	69.7	66.1	63.4
4. At least once a week	22.7	20.3	25.3	23.5	14.9	23.3	25.5	17.5	26.4	23.9	21.0	20.2	19.8	26.1	27.1	17.1
3. Once or twice a month	3.6	3.0	4.0	3.9	1.1	3.2	4.4	3.2	3.4	4.5	2.5	2.9	2.8	3.1	4.9	12.2
2. A few times a year	1.1	1.0	1.1	1.0	1.5	1.6	.8	.9	1.4	1.0	1.1	1.1	.9	1.0	1.2	4.9
1. Never	.4	.6	.2	.5	.2	.5	.1	.7	.5	.3	.6	.3	.2	-	.8	2.4
Item 5820 N(Wtd)	3630	1755	1749	2747	464	864	1100	1106	560	1926	1449	1211	844	479	955	41

A02B: Go to movies

	TOTAL	M	F	White	Black	NE	NC	S	W	Yes	No	None	Mari-juana Only	Few Pills	More Pills	Any Her-oin
5. Almost everyday	.3	.5	.2	.4	-	.5	-	.7	-	.2	.6	.6	.1	-	.3	2.5
4. At least once a week	8.7	9.4	8.0	7.8	10.2	7.9	9.5	8.2	9.3	7.9	9.8	8.9	9.4	9.5	6.4	12.5
3. Once or twice a month	54.6	52.7	57.1	57.0	46.8	51.5	57.0	55.4	53.0	57.3	52.9	51.9	55.1	60.2	56.8	52.5
2. A few times a year	34.7	35.9	33.2	33.6	39.2	38.4	32.2	33.5	36.3	32.9	35.4	36.3	34.4	29.6	35.1	30.0
1. Never	1.7	1.6	1.6	1.2	3.7	1.7	1.3	2.3	1.3	1.7	1.2	2.3	1.2	.4	1.4	2.5
Item 5830 N(Wtd)	3624	1751	1745	2739	462	864	1099	1102	559	1927	1444	1208	844	483	948	40

A02C: Attend art shows, musical performances, or theater plays

	TOTAL	M	F	White	Black	NE	NC	S	W	Yes	No	None	Mari-juana Only	Few Pills	More Pills	Any Her-oin
5. Almost everyday	.3	.5	.2	.3	.6	.3	.3	.4	.2	.1	.6	.3	.1	.6	.3	-
4. At least once a week	1.5	1.6	1.3	1.2	2.2	1.4	1.2	1.4	2.7	1.9	1.0	1.5	1.1	1.2	1.7	2.4
3. Once or twice a month	9.3	8.4	10.0	9.1	10.1	10.5	9.3	7.6	10.7	12.9	4.5	9.9	7.9	7.4	10.3	17.1
2. A few times a year	56.8	55.0	59.3	57.8	54.4	60.9	55.5	55.6	55.4	64.6	48.3	56.2	56.3	57.7	58.9	58.5
1. Never	32.1	34.4	29.3	31.6	32.7	26.9	33.8	35.0	31.1	20.6	45.6	32.2	34.5	32.8	28.8	22.0
Item 5840 N(Wtd)	3625	1748	1749	2740	465	861	1098	1102	563	1924	1448	1208	843	485	951	41

A02D: Ride around in a car (or motorcycle) just for fun

	TOTAL	M	F	White	Black	NE	NC	S	W	Yes	No	None	Mari-juana Only	Few Pills	More Pills	Any Her-oin
5. Almost everyday	31.6	36.1	26.8	30.9	31.0	30.2	32.1	33.9	28.4	24.8	40.5	20.6	34.4	34.2	40.4	53.7
4. At least once a week	33.8	34.7	33.4	35.2	33.0	32.1	35.5	35.1	30.7	33.3	34.5	33.4	34.4	37.1	33.5	29.3
3. Once or twice a month	15.8	13.9	17.6	16.8	12.7	16.0	15.7	14.0	19.1	17.8	13.8	19.6	13.0	16.6	13.6	7.3
2. A few times a year	10.9	9.1	12.8	10.5	12.2	11.1	10.9	9.8	12.9	14.3	6.6	14.4	11.7	6.8	7.7	9.8
1. Never	7.8	6.2	9.4	6.7	11.1	10.5	5.7	7.2	8.9	9.8	4.6	12.1	6.6	5.2	4.7	2.4
Item 5850 N(Wtd)	3634	1753	1752	2751	458	868	1096	1106	564	1929	1452	1216	838	483	954	41

A02E: Participate in community affairs or volunteer work

	TOTAL	M	F	White	Black	NE	NC	S	W	Yes	No	None	Mari-juana Only	Few Pills	More Pills	Any Her-oin
5. Almost everyday	2.6	3.2	2.0	2.2	4.8	1.9	2.5	3.2	2.5	2.2	2.8	2.8	1.9	1.5	3.3	5.1
4. At least once a week	8.0	6.9	9.3	7.9	8.6	9.1	5.4	9.4	8.5	10.2	5.4	11.2	7.6	4.8	5.9	10.3
3. Once or twice a month	13.1	12.3	13.9	12.5	16.8	11.2	13.2	15.3	11.5	15.9	10.1	14.8	13.7	16.3	9.3	10.3
2. A few times a year	45.9	44.9	47.1	48.2	38.7	47.2	47.9	44.1	43.3	48.1	43.8	44.9	47.3	44.7	47.4	43.6
1. Never	30.5	32.7	27.6	29.2	31.1	30.7	31.0	28.0	34.2	23.6	37.9	26.1	29.6	33.0	34.0	30.8
Item 5860 N(Wtd)	3627	1750	1751	2745	463	858	1094	1111	564	1924	1452	1209	845	479	956	39

QUESTIONNAIRE FORM 2 1981	TOTAL	SEX		RACE		REGION				4YR COLLEGE PLANS		ILLICIT DRUG USE: LIFETIME				
		M	F	White	Black	NE	NC	S	W	Yes	No	None	Marijuana Only	Few Pills	More Pills	Any Heroin
Weighted No. of Cases:	3655	1762	1762	2761	467	869	1102	1117	567	1937	1462	1219	846	487	958	41
% of Weighted Total:	100.0	48.2	48.2	75.5	12.8	23.8	30.1	30.6	15.5	53.0	40.0	33.4	23.2	13.3	26.2	1.1
A02F: Play a musical instrument or sing																
5. Almost everyday	30.7	27.1	34.4	30.4	31.7	29.4	32.2	31.0	29.1	36.3	24.3	33.8	26.2	32.2	30.5	43.9
4. At least once a week	10.9	9.3	12.8	11.0	11.9	11.0	10.0	12.1	10.5	12.2	9.8	12.3	10.2	10.1	10.8	12.2
3. Once or twice a month	5.1	3.7	6.4	4.7	6.5	3.4	4.6	6.6	5.7	5.7	4.2	5.5	4.2	3.5	5.5	17.1
2. A few times a year	10.9	11.8	9.8	10.9	12.1	10.4	9.7	11.5	12.7	11.2	9.8	9.4	12.7	9.9	11.5	12.2
1. Never	42.4	48.1	36.6	43.0	37.6	46.0	43.5	38.8	42.2	34.5	51.9	39.2	46.8	44.4	41.8	17.1
Item 5870 N(Wtd)	3621	1743	1751	2737	463	857	1093	1109	561	1920	1448	1208	840	484	946	41
A02G: Do creative writing																
5. Almost everyday	5.7	4.3	7.1	4.6	9.9	5.6	5.3	5.9	6.4	6.0	5.4	5.9	5.4	5.4	6.2	12.5
4. At least once a week	12.5	10.7	14.1	11.8	14.1	14.6	10.9	11.4	14.5	15.9	7.5	12.5	11.3	12.6	13.2	25.0
3. Once or twice a month	17.7	16.7	18.6	18.1	17.4	20.1	18.8	15.6	16.0	22.0	12.5	17.6	16.6	18.4	18.8	17.5
2. A few times a year	29.0	27.6	31.0	30.4	24.2	27.0	28.9	29.9	30.5	31.2	26.9	31.5	30.1	28.7	26.6	15.0
1. Never	35.0	40.7	29.3	35.1	34.7	32.7	36.2	37.1	32.4	25.0	47.7	32.7	36.7	34.9	35.3	30.0
Item 5880 N(Wtd)	3615	1741	1746	2746	455	854	1095	1102	564	1922	1444	1204	841	484	950	40
A02H: Actively participate in sports, athletics or exercising																
5. Almost everyday	47.6	56.4	38.7	46.7	53.2	49.9	46.7	45.8	49.4	54.1	38.7	50.3	51.0	47.3	41.4	39.0
4. At least once a week	25.1	22.7	27.9	26.3	17.9	26.7	24.6	24.5	25.0	24.4	26.3	21.0	25.3	28.6	29.8	19.5
3. Once or twice a month	11.6	8.7	14.8	12.2	9.7	10.5	13.1	11.6	10.5	10.3	13.8	11.6	9.9	9.7	14.5	19.5
2. A few times a year	9.7	7.2	12.0	9.1	12.1	7.3	9.9	11.3	10.3	7.5	12.6	10.3	8.6	7.6	9.8	2.4
1. Never	5.9	5.1	6.7	5.7	7.1	5.6	5.6	6.9	5.0	3.6	8.6	6.7	5.4	6.6	4.4	19.5
Item 5890 N(Wtd)	3635	1754	1751	2748	464	864	1100	1108	563	1927	1452	1216	841	486	953	41
A02I: Do art or craft work																
5. Almost everyday	13.7	12.8	14.6	13.5	10.7	12.3	15.8	11.8	15.3	11.2	16.9	15.2	11.6	12.7	13.8	7.3
4. At least once a week	11.3	10.9	11.6	11.5	9.2	11.0	9.5	11.2	15.5	11.7	11.1	11.3	10.6	12.2	11.4	12.2
3. Once or twice a month	19.4	17.8	21.3	20.0	17.2	17.7	19.7	18.0	23.8	20.7	18.2	17.6	20.0	20.7	21.3	17.1
2. A few times a year	31.0	31.1	31.3	32.1	25.5	34.2	32.1	27.9	29.5	33.7	27.1	30.2	31.4	32.4	32.3	29.3
1. Never	24.7	27.3	21.3	22.8	37.3	24.6	22.8	31.0	15.8	22.8	26.7	25.8	26.4	22.2	21.1	34.1
Item 5900 N(Wtd)	3616	1748	1740	2739	458	857	1095	1102	563	1925	1442	1207	838	482	947	41
A02J: Work around the house, yard, garden, car, etc.																
5. Almost everyday	40.2	32.3	48.1	37.8	52.4	35.6	40.1	43.8	40.2	34.7	47.2	44.1	38.0	41.1	36.2	39.0
4. At least once a week	38.7	45.8	32.2	41.5	28.7	41.6	37.7	37.3	38.8	41.5	35.7	36.1	41.8	39.3	39.6	39.0
3. Once or twice a month	14.8	15.7	13.8	15.4	11.4	14.8	16.1	13.5	14.7	17.5	11.5	13.5	15.4	14.5	17.0	7.3
2. A few times a year	5.1	5.1	4.9	4.8	4.7	6.0	5.1	4.4	5.3	5.4	4.4	4.7	4.1	5.0	6.0	9.8
1. Never	1.2	1.1	1.1	.6	3.0	2.0	.7	1.0	.9	.9	1.2	1.6	.5	.4	1.2	4.9
Item 5910 N(Wtd)	3640	1755	1756	2752	464	865	1097	1113	565	1933	1452	1218	844	484	952	41
A02K: Get together with friends, informally																
5. Almost everyday	49.2	54.1	44.1	48.8	51.2	54.3	46.8	47.1	50.3	47.7	51.2	40.8	49.9	49.9	58.2	58.5
4. At least once a week	38.7	37.3	40.5	40.3	32.7	36.0	42.2	37.9	38.1	40.7	36.5	42.1	39.8	39.0	34.5	26.8
3. Once or twice a month	8.7	6.2	11.2	8.5	9.5	6.9	8.6	10.4	8.3	8.7	8.3	12.0	7.9	8.0	5.9	4.9
2. A few times a year	2.5	1.6	3.4	1.9	4.5	2.2	1.7	3.5	2.8	2.2	2.8	3.7	1.8	2.7	1.3	9.8
1. Never	.9	.9	.7	.5	2.2	.6	.9	1.2	.5	.7	1.0	1.4	.6	.4	.2	-
Item 5920 N(Wtd)	3626	1750	1747	2742	465	858	1093	1110	565	1923	1452	1210	844	485	949	41
A02L: Go shopping or window-shopping																
5. Almost everyday	3.4	1.1	5.4	2.4	7.6	3.7	2.3	4.6	2.8	2.7	4.4	3.1	3.1	5.2	2.6	4.9
4. At least once a week	32.2	19.6	44.8	30.4	42.3	33.3	31.7	33.6	28.4	32.5	32.4	33.0	31.5	36.4	29.4	24.4
3. Once or twice a month	46.3	48.4	44.8	48.2	38.2	43.1	47.8	44.7	51.5	49.2	43.5	45.6	47.5	44.1	48.6	41.5
2. A few times a year	14.1	23.5	4.6	15.1	8.9	15.3	13.9	13.4	14.2	13.5	13.9	14.2	14.4	12.7	15.0	9.8
1. Never	4.0	7.3	.3	3.9	3.0	4.6	4.2	3.7	3.0	2.2	5.9	4.1	3.5	1.7	4.4	19.5
Item 5930 N(Wtd)	3619	1749	1742	2738	461	854	1090	1112	563	1918	1448	1209	840	481	949	41

QUESTIONNAIRE FORM 2 1981	TOTAL	SEX		RACE		REGION				4YR COLLEGE PLANS		ILLICIT DRUG USE: LIFETIME				
		M	F	White	Black	NE	NC	S	W	Yes	No	None	Marijuana Only	Few Pills	More Pills	Any Heroin
Weighted No. of Cases:	3655	1762	1762	2761	467	869	1102	1117	567	1937	1462	1219	846	487	958	41
% of Weighted Total:	100.0	48.2	48.2	75.5	12.8	23.8	30.1	30.6	15.5	53.0	40.0	33.4	23.2	13.3	26.2	1.1
A02M: Spend at least an hour of leisure time alone																
5. Almost everyday	43.5	41.9	45.0	42.3	51.6	45.9	41.6	43.3	44.5	45.2	41.2	39.8	46.7	43.6	46.0	43.9
4. At least once a week	35.4	36.8	34.4	36.8	29.0	36.8	36.1	33.4	35.8	36.6	34.3	38.0	31.8	37.2	34.9	29.3
3. Once or twice a month	11.9	11.6	12.4	12.9	8.0	9.0	14.0	13.1	10.1	11.7	12.7	12.9	12.9	9.1	11.8	9.8
2. A few times a year	5.0	5.3	4.6	5.0	5.6	4.7	4.6	6.2	3.9	3.5	6.7	5.0	3.9	6.8	4.3	9.8
1. Never	4.2	4.5	3.6	3.1	6.0	3.6	3.7	4.0	5.9	3.0	5.1	4.2	4.7	3.5	3.1	7.3
Item 5940 N(Wtd)	3636	1751	1755	2751	465	859	1100	1112	564	1932	1450	1213	843	484	953	41
A02N: Read books, magazines, or newspapers																
5. Almost everyday	58.7	57.6	60.3	58.9	63.8	62.4	59.5	56.8	55.0	66.1	49.6	60.7	62.0	56.3	54.6	68.3
4. At least once a week	26.1	25.1	26.9	25.9	22.7	23.9	25.8	27.6	27.3	23.6	29.1	25.8	23.9	28.7	26.9	12.2
3. Once or twice a month	10.4	10.6	9.6	10.3	9.9	9.4	10.0	9.9	13.5	7.8	13.7	9.4	8.9	10.3	13.4	-
2. A few times a year	3.5	4.8	2.4	3.6	2.8	3.1	2.9	4.4	3.5	2.1	5.3	2.5	4.4	3.7	3.5	14.6
1. Never	1.4	1.8	.9	1.4	.9	1.3	1.9	1.3	.7	.4	2.2	1.5	.8	1.0	1.6	4.9
Item 5950 N(Wtd)	3641	1756	1756	2751	467	866	1099	1110	565	1931	1455	1217	844	485	952	41
A02O: Go to taverns, bars or nightclubs																
5. Almost everyday	2.1	3.5	.7	2.2	1.9	2.3	2.7	1.7	1.6	1.9	2.3	.5	1.5	1.2	3.7	31.7
4. At least once a week	15.4	18.3	12.1	15.9	15.5	22.1	13.7	17.1	5.1	12.6	18.3	6.8	16.0	14.1	25.6	29.3
3. Once or twice a month	19.1	19.8	18.2	19.9	14.0	22.8	19.7	19.1	12.4	20.3	17.4	12.1	21.5	21.3	25.2	12.2
2. A few times a year	21.5	20.6	22.7	22.2	20.4	21.6	23.0	21.9	17.7	22.6	21.0	21.1	23.1	21.9	21.2	9.8
1. Never	41.8	37.8	46.4	39.9	48.2	31.2	40.9	40.1	63.1	42.6	41.0	59.5	37.9	41.6	24.3	19.5
Item 5960 N(Wtd)	3630	1750	1751	2744	465	860	1098	1108	564	1929	1447	1214	840	483	951	41
A02P: Go to parties or other social affairs																
5. Almost everyday	3.5	5.1	1.8	3.5	1.9	3.9	4.0	2.6	3.7	2.6	4.3	1.0	2.4	2.1	6.9	34.1
4. At least once a week	32.5	33.5	31.1	33.6	29.7	41.4	34.6	24.4	30.8	32.9	31.4	16.1	35.4	35.9	49.1	34.1
3. Once or twice a month	36.4	36.0	37.2	37.8	31.8	33.4	37.0	37.7	37.2	39.0	34.2	37.7	40.3	38.1	32.6	22.0
2. A few times a year	22.7	20.9	25.0	21.1	29.0	18.4	20.4	28.9	21.8	21.8	24.1	36.4	18.2	19.4	11.0	7.3
1. Never	4.9	4.6	5.0	4.0	7.5	2.9	3.9	6.5	6.7	3.6	6.0	8.8	3.7	4.7	.5	2.4
Item 5970 N(Wtd)	3637	1754	1755	2752	465	868	1092	1111	565	1931	1450	1213	844	485	954	41
A03: How much do you agree or disagree with each of the following statements?																
A03A: In the United States, we put too much emphasis on making profits and not enough on human well-being																
1. Disagree	4.8	7.1	2.5	4.9	3.9	4.7	3.7	6.5	3.9	4.3	5.4	5.2	4.2	5.0	4.5	7.3
2. Mostly disagree	9.9	11.8	7.9	11.0	4.6	8.1	9.2	9.9	14.1	10.9	8.0	10.1	10.7	8.7	9.6	12.2
3. Neither	13.6	16.1	10.8	13.7	10.8	15.7	14.0	11.3	13.7	13.5	13.2	13.2	15.3	12.2	12.4	14.6
4. Mostly agree	44.1	39.4	49.0	46.3	36.4	42.8	49.3	41.5	40.9	46.2	42.7	42.7	42.9	47.1	46.5	41.5
5. Agree	27.7	25.6	29.7	24.1	44.3	28.6	23.8	30.8	27.4	24.9	30.7	28.9	26.9	27.2	26.8	24.4
Item 5990 N(Wtd)	3615	1745	1744	2737	461	859	1087	1106	562	1912	1450	1200	843	482	950	41
A03B: People are too much concerned with material things these days																
1. Disagree	3.7	4.6	2.7	3.3	4.5	4.1	2.9	3.8	4.4	3.2	4.5	4.4	3.0	3.1	3.1	7.3
2. Mostly disagree	5.6	8.0	3.1	5.3	6.7	4.9	5.4	6.4	5.3	5.5	5.7	6.4	5.7	3.7	5.2	7.3
3. Neither	10.8	13.7	7.7	11.2	6.7	12.9	11.2	7.7	12.8	9.2	12.3	8.2	11.9	13.9	11.0	7.3
4. Mostly agree	39.0	38.1	40.2	41.6	30.1	39.2	40.5	37.6	38.9	41.8	36.8	37.2	40.5	39.8	40.2	29.3
5. Agree	41.0	35.6	46.3	38.5	51.9	39.0	40.0	44.7	38.5	40.3	40.8	43.8	38.9	39.5	40.4	48.8
Item 6000 N(Wtd)	3623	1745	1752	2742	462	860	1089	1110	563	1922	1448	1209	838	483	953	41

QUESTIONNAIRE FORM 2 1981	TOTAL	SEX		RACE		REGION				4YR COLLEGE PLANS		ILLICIT DRUG USE: LIFETIME				
		M	F	White	Black	NE	NC	S	W	Yes	No	None	Mari-juana Only	Few Pills	More Pills	Any Her-oin
Weighted No. of Cases:	3655	1762	1762	2761	467	869	1102	1117	567	1937	1462	1219	846	487	958	41
% of Weighted Total:	100.0	48.2	48.2	75.5	12.8	23.8	30.1	30.6	15.5	53.0	40.0	33.4	23.2	13.3	26.2	1.1
A03C: Since it helps the economy to grow, people should be encouraged to buy more																
1. Disagree	25.6	22.5	27.7	22.2	37.2	25.3	20.8	31.0	24.2	23.0	27.8	25.8	27.0	22.4	23.7	24.4
2. Mostly disagree	26.5	22.2	31.4	28.7	19.6	25.1	29.4	23.0	29.4	28.4	25.4	24.5	25.8	35.3	27.0	19.5
3. Neither	27.1	26.4	28.1	28.4	18.5	29.2	28.6	23.3	28.3	29.0	25.2	28.8	25.8	25.9	27.0	22.0
4. Mostly agree	14.3	19.4	9.5	14.8	15.9	13.4	14.7	15.8	11.9	13.9	14.5	14.3	14.5	12.7	15.8	9.8
5. Agree	6.6	9.5	3.3	5.8	8.7	7.1	6.4	6.9	6.1	5.7	7.1	6.6	6.9	3.9	6.5	24.4
Item 6010 N(Wtd)	3620	1744	1749	2743	460	860	1090	1108	561	1917	1451	1204	841	482	951	41
A03D: There is nothing wrong with advertising that gets people to buy things they don't really need																
1. Disagree	43.5	41.8	45.3	44.6	39.7	46.4	38.8	45.2	45.0	45.0	42.6	43.7	42.4	41.2	45.9	41.5
2. Mostly disagree	24.4	23.1	26.0	26.1	18.1	21.6	28.4	22.3	25.1	24.3	24.6	24.8	23.5	28.9	23.2	29.3
3. Neither	11.7	12.1	11.1	11.9	7.3	10.8	15.0	10.2	9.8	11.6	11.6	11.0	12.5	9.8	12.5	9.8
4. Mostly agree	10.1	11.4	9.3	9.7	12.9	11.6	9.5	9.2	10.8	10.3	10.0	9.7	10.6	10.6	9.9	9.8
5. Agree	10.2	11.7	8.4	7.7	22.0	9.6	8.1	13.1	9.4	8.9	11.1	10.9	11.0	9.4	8.4	12.2
Item 6020 N(Wtd)	3636	1757	1751	2749	464	864	1094	1112	565	1930	1454	1210	846	481	957	41
A03E: There will probably be more shortages in the future, so Americans will have to learn how to be happy with fewer "things"																
1. Disagree	6.6	7.6	5.2	5.7	9.3	8.0	5.7	6.4	7.1	6.4	6.0	7.7	5.6	5.6	5.8	17.1
2. Mostly disagree	8.0	8.8	7.3	8.0	5.2	9.6	8.1	6.6	8.5	8.5	7.7	7.8	8.6	7.2	8.8	2.4
3. Neither	8.2	7.9	8.5	8.8	6.3	6.4	9.8	7.5	9.8	7.8	9.1	8.5	7.6	8.1	8.5	12.2
4. Mostly agree	26.4	26.0	26.9	27.6	22.2	29.6	28.2	22.3	26.2	27.9	24.2	26.1	25.2	30.0	26.9	24.4
5. Agree	50.7	49.7	52.0	49.9	56.9	46.5	48.3	57.2	48.6	49.4	53.0	50.0	53.0	49.2	50.1	43.9
Item 6030 N(Wtd)	3637	1753	1756	2752	464	866	1096	1111	564	1928	1455	1212	844	484	956	41
A04: Below are several ways that people have used to protest about serious social issues. How much do you approve or disapprove of these actions?																
A04A: Signing petitions																
4. Strongly approve	23.5	24.7	22.5	25.3	16.6	26.7	24.1	20.3	23.7	29.4	16.6	24.0	22.1	20.9	26.3	26.8
3. Approve	45.8	43.7	47.9	48.3	33.4	46.3	47.2	42.4	49.1	47.6	44.8	44.2	46.1	50.5	45.7	53.7
2. Disapprove	3.3	4.6	2.1	3.1	4.4	2.2	3.7	4.8	1.6	2.2	4.4	3.7	2.6	3.7	3.0	4.9
1. Strongly disapprove	1.1	1.7	.5	.7	2.6	.7	1.5	1.1	.9	.7	1.3	1.3	.9	.6	.8	2.4
8. Don't know, or it depends	26.3	25.3	27.1	22.6	42.8	24.1	23.6	31.3	24.7	20.1	33.0	26.8	28.1	24.0	24.2	12.2
Item 6040 N(Wtd)	3624	1750	1752	2752	458	866	1090	1107	562	1927	1448	1202	846	483	958	41
A04B: Boycotting certain products or stores																
4. Strongly approve	19.2	22.3	15.8	19.9	15.4	26.0	17.9	16.2	16.8	23.9	13.4	17.8	20.5	16.0	20.3	39.0
3. Approve	37.7	40.2	36.1	40.0	31.7	40.3	37.9	35.0	38.9	40.8	35.1	37.4	37.9	36.3	41.2	24.4
2. Disapprove	11.3	9.8	12.5	10.9	11.7	8.7	11.5	12.9	11.8	8.6	13.9	12.5	10.4	13.7	8.9	14.6
1. Strongly disapprove	3.1	3.3	2.7	2.0	7.4	1.6	2.8	4.4	3.2	1.5	5.1	3.1	3.6	2.7	1.8	9.8
8. Don't know, or it depends	28.8	24.5	33.0	27.2	34.3	23.2	30.1	31.6	29.5	25.2	32.6	29.2	27.5	31.1	27.9	12.2
Item 6050 N(Wtd)	3617	1748	1748	2745	461	865	1090	1102	560	1922	1444	1199	844	482	957	41
A04C: Lawful demonstrations																
4. Strongly approve	19.1	22.1	16.3	19.2	19.6	25.4	16.7	17.2	18.0	24.5	12.5	17.5	19.0	16.7	22.9	24.4
3. Approve	45.6	45.7	46.4	47.8	36.7	43.2	47.5	43.8	49.5	47.4	44.8	46.4	46.5	46.9	44.6	36.6
2. Disapprove	8.7	9.3	8.1	8.6	10.1	7.7	9.0	10.0	6.8	7.5	10.0	10.3	8.2	10.0	6.7	2.4
1. Strongly disapprove	3.7	3.7	3.4	3.0	5.7	2.4	3.9	4.3	4.1	2.6	4.6	3.6	3.8	2.9	3.1	14.6
8. Don't know, or it depends	22.8	19.3	25.7	21.4	27.9	21.2	23.0	24.7	21.4	18.1	28.1	22.2	22.5	23.8	22.6	19.5
Item 6060 N(Wtd)	3604	1742	1744	2739	455	865	1086	1097	555	1917	1443	1200	841	480	953	41

QUESTIONNAIRE FORM 2 1981	TOTAL	SEX		RACE		REGION				4YR COLLEGE PLANS		ILLICIT DRUG USE: LIFETIME				
		M	F	White	Black	NE	NC	S	W	Yes	No	None	Mari-juana Only	Few Pills	More Pills	Any Her-oin
Weighted No. of Cases:	3655	1762	1762	2761	467	869	1102	1117	567	1937	1462	1219	846	487	958	41
% of Weighted Total:	100.0	48.2	48.2	75.5	12.8	23.8	30.1	30.6	15.5	53.0	40.0	33.4	23.2	13.3	26.2	1.1
A04D: Occupying buildings or factories																
4. Strongly approve	4.4	5.3	3.4	3.8	6.5	4.2	4.5	4.7	4.2	3.3	5.7	3.6	4.5	5.2	4.2	17.1
3. Approve	18.7	16.9	20.2	16.9	25.6	14.1	18.6	21.8	19.9	16.1	21.7	17.6	18.1	18.8	19.2	24.4
2. Disapprove	27.7	29.1	26.8	29.2	21.2	29.8	27.2	26.6	27.5	31.5	23.7	30.1	27.5	27.4	26.2	17.1
1. Strongly disapprove	11.6	14.4	8.9	12.9	7.8	14.5	10.6	11.1	10.1	14.3	7.8	14.4	11.4	11.3	9.2	12.2
8. Don't know, or it depends	37.6	34.3	40.7	37.2	39.2	37.5	39.1	35.8	38.2	34.8	41.1	34.3	38.4	37.2	41.2	31.7
Item 6070 N(Wtd)	3576	1736	1722	2723	449	857	1078	1090	552	1903	1429	1188	836	478	944	41
A04E: Wildcat strikes																
4. Strongly approve	2.7	4.1	1.5	2.6	3.8	3.6	2.5	2.5	2.5	2.5	3.1	1.8	2.9	1.9	3.5	14.6
3. Approve	13.8	17.0	10.1	13.5	14.0	14.0	12.8	14.8	13.6	14.0	13.7	12.5	14.5	13.6	14.5	14.6
2. Disapprove	29.1	29.9	28.6	30.6	21.3	30.4	31.9	28.5	23.0	30.0	27.9	31.1	26.8	29.6	28.9	22.0
1. Strongly disapprove	15.3	15.5	15.3	15.4	16.0	13.6	15.5	14.6	18.6	15.9	14.8	18.7	14.9	15.3	11.0	39.0
8. Don't know, or it depends	39.1	33.5	44.5	37.8	44.9	38.6	37.2	39.6	42.3	37.7	40.5	35.9	41.0	39.6	42.1	9.8
Item 6080 N(Wtd)	3565	1738	1708	2713	450	853	1074	1085	553	1898	1426	1188	835	470	942	41
A04F: Blocking traffic																
4. Strongly approve	1.9	2.8	1.0	1.6	2.8	2.2	1.0	2.4	2.2	1.5	2.4	1.5	1.4	2.7	2.0	9.8
3. Approve	3.2	3.7	2.5	2.5	4.8	3.0	3.0	3.4	3.4	2.4	4.1	3.3	2.5	2.1	3.6	9.8
2. Disapprove	41.6	38.7	44.2	41.4	42.2	41.9	39.2	45.4	38.5	40.8	42.0	40.8	39.3	47.2	41.6	29.3
1. Strongly disapprove	42.2	43.8	41.2	44.5	37.0	39.0	45.8	39.7	45.5	45.9	38.5	46.7	43.2	37.9	39.7	43.9
8. Don't know, or it depends	11.1	10.9	11.2	10.0	13.3	13.9	11.1	9.1	10.6	9.5	13.0	7.8	13.6	9.9	13.0	9.8
Item 6090 N(Wtd)	3610	1752	1737	2737	460	864	1083	1106	556	1919	1441	1200	843	483	952	41
A04G: Damaging things																
4. Strongly approve	2.2	2.5	1.7	1.6	4.1	2.4	2.0	2.5	1.3	1.4	3.2	1.7	1.8	2.3	2.7	7.3
3. Approve	2.1	2.9	1.2	1.5	4.4	1.7	2.2	2.7	1.4	1.8	2.1	2.4	1.2	1.4	2.2	12.2
2. Disapprove	19.2	20.8	17.6	17.0	25.7	20.6	15.2	22.4	18.8	14.8	23.3	17.2	16.5	21.1	22.0	24.4
1. Strongly disapprove	70.8	66.5	76.0	75.0	58.8	68.6	76.1	66.6	72.2	77.3	64.9	75.4	73.7	70.4	66.2	51.2
8. Don't know, or it depends	5.6	7.3	3.4	5.0	7.2	6.5	4.5	5.8	6.1	4.8	6.6	3.2	7.0	5.2	6.9	4.9
Item 6100 N(Wtd)	3618	1748	1751	2747	459	867	1089	1105	558	1920	1448	1203	844	483	955	41
A04H: Personal violence																
4. Strongly approve	2.7	2.8	2.2	2.1	3.3	3.6	2.7	2.4	2.0	1.6	3.8	2.4	1.7	3.5	3.1	9.8
3. Approve	2.9	4.0	1.5	2.0	6.3	2.1	2.7	4.1	2.3	1.8	3.8	2.5	1.5	3.1	3.8	4.9
2. Disapprove	16.8	19.6	13.6	15.1	20.4	17.4	15.6	17.3	17.3	14.2	19.3	13.8	16.1	18.3	19.2	17.1
1. Strongly disapprove	69.3	63.1	77.2	73.7	57.4	69.1	72.3	66.5	69.3	76.8	61.8	75.5	71.6	67.0	64.4	61.0
8. Don't know, or it depends	8.3	10.4	5.5	7.0	12.4	7.8	6.8	9.7	9.1	5.6	11.3	5.9	9.0	8.1	9.4	7.3
Item 6110 N(Wtd)	3624	1752	1752	2750	460	867	1091	1106	560	1925	1449	1208	846	482	956	41
A05: Do you think that you would prefer having a mate for most of your life, or would you prefer not having a mate?																
5. Definitely prefer to have a mate	60.4	57.2	64.8	63.4	50.0	59.5	62.0	59.9	59.7	61.4	60.7	64.1	61.4	58.1	58.3	57.5
4. Probably prefer to have a mate	27.5	29.3	25.5	27.2	28.9	30.0	27.4	25.4	27.6	28.3	26.3	25.2	26.1	31.8	29.4	27.5
3. Not sure	9.3	10.2	7.8	7.2	16.8	8.0	8.2	11.6	9.4	7.9	10.4	8.7	9.7	7.4	9.2	10.0
2. Probably prefer not to have a mate	2.1	2.4	1.6	1.8	3.2	1.6	1.9	2.5	2.1	1.7	2.1	1.4	2.4	1.8	2.3	7.5
1. Definitely prefer not to have a mate	.7	.9	.3	.5	1.1	.9	.5	.6	1.1	.7	.4	.7	.5	.6	.7	-
Item 6120 N(Wtd)	3637	1756	1758	2755	464	866	1098	1113	561	1930	1456	1216	844	487	953	40
A06: Which do you think you are most likely to choose in the long run?																
3. Getting married	77.6	75.3	80.9	81.6	64.0	76.3	81.3	75.7	76.1	80.9	74.8	79.9	78.6	81.2	75.0	60.5
2. I have no idea	17.3	20.1	13.7	14.7	24.8	19.0	15.0	17.1	19.0	15.1	19.3	15.5	15.9	14.9	20.3	18.4
1. Not getting married	4.4	4.5	4.0	2.9	10.7	4.6	3.2	5.7	4.0	3.7	4.5	4.0	4.3	3.7	4.0	15.8
8. Am already married	.8	.1	1.3	.8	.7	-	.7	1.5	.7	.3	1.4	.5	1.1	.4	.7	5.3
Item 6130 N(Wtd)	3565	1710	1732	2716	447	851	1075	1088	552	1910	1415	1187	829	483	935	38

QUESTIONNAIRE FORM 2 1981	TOTAL	SEX		RACE		REGION				4YR COLLEGE PLANS		ILLICIT DRUG USE: LIFETIME				
		M	F	White	Black	NE	NC	S	W	Yes	No	None	Marijuana Only	Few Pills	More Pills	Any Heroin
Weighted No. of Cases:	3655	1762	1762	2761	467	869	1102	1117	567	1937	1462	1219	846	487	958	41
% of Weighted Total:	100.0	48.2	48.2	75.5	12.8	23.8	30.1	30.6	15.5	53.0	40.0	33.4	23.2	13.3	26.2	1.1

A07: If you did get married (or are married)...

A07A: How likely do you think it is that you would stay married to the same person for life?

	TOTAL	M	F	White	Black	NE	NC	S	W	Yes	No	None	Marijuana Only	Few Pills	More Pills	Any Heroin
5. Very likely	62.2	56.7	68.3	64.6	49.2	57.3	64.2	62.9	64.2	63.0	61.7	70.2	60.7	64.4	53.8	55.0
4. Fairly likely	23.1	26.9	19.4	23.3	25.8	25.3	24.1	22.2	19.9	24.8	21.8	20.0	23.9	22.1	27.3	20.0
3. Uncertain	12.3	13.7	10.2	10.3	20.3	14.2	9.8	13.4	12.4	9.9	14.5	8.5	13.7	11.3	14.9	17.5
2. Fairly unlikely	1.5	1.4	1.6	1.3	1.8	2.0	1.2	.8	2.8	1.5	1.3	.6	1.0	1.3	2.9	-
1. Very unlikely	.8	1.3	.4	.5	2.9	1.3	.7	.8	.7	.8	.7	.7	.7	.9	.9	7.5
Item 6140 N(Wtd)	3446	1656	1673	2611	449	797	1045	1066	539	1833	1382	1163	805	452	897	40

A07B: How likely is it that you would want to have children?

	TOTAL	M	F	White	Black	NE	NC	S	W	Yes	No	None	Marijuana Only	Few Pills	More Pills	Any Heroin
5. Very likely	60.9	60.0	62.4	62.7	54.7	61.7	62.1	59.8	59.8	62.8	59.3	63.0	62.0	62.6	58.8	42.5
4. Fairly likely	20.2	23.9	16.7	19.4	23.0	19.9	21.0	20.2	18.8	19.7	21.0	20.4	19.1	17.8	21.0	17.5
3. Uncertain	12.0	11.4	12.2	11.6	12.4	11.7	11.2	12.3	13.0	10.8	13.1	11.0	10.8	13.2	13.1	20.0
2. Fairly unlikely	3.1	2.5	3.4	3.0	2.2	2.3	2.4	3.2	5.1	3.1	2.6	2.5	2.9	2.6	3.9	2.5
1. Very unlikely	2.6	1.8	3.4	2.7	3.1	3.7	2.5	2.0	2.7	2.9	2.0	1.8	3.9	2.9	2.1	7.5
8. Already have child(ren)	1.2	.4	2.0	.6	4.6	.7	.9	2.4	.4	.7	1.9	1.2	1.3	.9	1.1	10.0
Item 6150 N(Wtd)	3488	1679	1687	2640	453	814	1058	1069	547	1851	1398	1169	816	455	914	40

The questions in the next column ask you to imagine different kinds of married life that you might have. We want you to think about different ways you might share responsibilities for working, taking care of the home, and taking care of children. Please indicate how acceptable for you each of the different arrangements would be.

A08: Imagine you are married and have no children--how would you feel about each of the following working arrangements?

A08A: Husband works full-time, wife doesn't work

	TOTAL	M	F	White	Black	NE	NC	S	W	Yes	No	None	Marijuana Only	Few Pills	More Pills	Any Heroin
1. Not at all acceptable	25.9	13.5	37.4	23.8	38.8	29.7	27.5	23.1	22.2	28.1	21.5	24.3	25.9	21.7	28.3	35.0
2. Somewhat acceptable	34.3	32.2	36.7	34.5	35.1	34.2	32.9	35.4	34.9	33.3	36.5	32.9	34.4	38.1	34.1	37.5
3. Acceptable	31.7	42.6	21.1	32.9	22.2	28.3	32.3	32.4	34.2	31.1	32.7	33.7	32.2	32.1	29.5	22.5
4. Desirable	8.2	11.8	4.8	8.8	3.9	7.8	7.2	9.2	8.8	7.3	9.3	9.0	7.4	8.3	8.1	2.5
Item 6160 N(Wtd)	3617	1748	1747	2743	459	862	1093	1103	559	1920	1451	1212	841	483	948	40

A08B: Husband works full-time, wife works about half-time

	TOTAL	M	F	White	Black	NE	NC	S	W	Yes	No	None	Marijuana Only	Few Pills	More Pills	Any Heroin
1. Not at all acceptable	3.9	3.1	4.3	2.7	8.7	4.6	2.7	3.8	5.4	4.0	3.3	3.5	4.5	2.9	2.9	20.0
2. Somewhat acceptable	22.3	16.6	27.6	21.1	29.3	21.3	25.7	21.4	19.1	22.6	21.3	21.6	22.2	25.5	22.4	17.5
3. Acceptable	55.9	60.6	51.5	56.3	52.2	56.5	52.3	59.5	54.8	54.4	57.9	57.6	55.5	51.8	56.0	50.0
4. Desirable	17.9	19.6	16.7	19.9	9.8	17.5	19.3	15.3	20.7	19.0	17.5	17.4	17.9	19.9	18.6	10.0
Item 6170 N(Wtd)	3624	1750	1749	2745	460	863	1095	1106	560	1922	1451	1216	838	483	950	40

A08C: Both work full-time

	TOTAL	M	F	White	Black	NE	NC	S	W	Yes	No	None	Marijuana Only	Few Pills	More Pills	Any Heroin
1. Not at all acceptable	14.1	18.6	9.4	13.1	15.3	13.3	12.4	15.2	16.3	11.4	17.4	13.2	15.1	17.4	12.2	17.5
2. Somewhat acceptable	20.3	23.9	16.7	21.4	16.8	19.4	18.8	21.8	21.6	19.0	21.7	21.8	18.5	21.8	19.2	25.0
3. Acceptable	43.4	38.5	48.1	42.8	47.6	42.7	45.2	43.6	40.6	44.9	41.4	44.4	42.5	41.8	43.8	32.5
4. Desirable	22.2	19.1	25.9	22.8	20.3	24.7	23.6	19.2	21.3	24.7	19.5	20.8	23.8	18.7	24.9	25.0
Item 6180 N(Wtd)	3599	1742	1739	2735	458	851	1087	1102	559	1915	1440	1208	833	476	949	40

QUESTIONNAIRE FORM 2 1981	TOTAL	SEX		RACE		REGION				4YR COLLEGE PLANS		ILLICIT DRUG USE: LIFETIME				
		M	F	White	Black	NE	NC	S	W	Yes	No	None	Mari-juana Only	Few Pills	More Pills	Any Her-oin
Weighted No. of Cases:	3655	1762	1762	2761	467	869	1102	1117	567	1937	1462	1219	846	487	958	41
% of Weighted Total:	100.0	48.2	48.2	75.5	12.8	23.8	30.1	30.6	15.5	53.0	40.0	33.4	23.2	13.3	26.2	1.1
A08D: Both work about half-time																
1. Not at all acceptable	48.3	52.1	44.5	45.9	61.2	45.8	49.1	53.5	40.3	45.0	52.3	49.7	54.2	41.6	44.0	52.5
2. Somewhat acceptable	27.1	24.6	29.6	29.2	19.5	27.8	28.0	25.4	27.9	28.8	25.7	27.5	25.2	30.5	27.9	20.0
3. Acceptable	16.8	15.8	17.6	17.1	13.9	18.2	15.8	14.0	21.3	18.0	14.7	15.1	13.9	21.1	19.2	12.5
4. Desirable	7.9	7.5	8.2	7.7	5.4	8.2	7.1	7.0	10.6	8.2	7.3	7.7	6.9	6.7	8.9	15.0
Item 6190 N(Wtd)	3576	1732	1727	2725	446	850	1079	1089	559	1901	1432	1196	829	478	945	40
A08E: Husband works about half-time, wife works full-time																
1. Not at all acceptable	60.3	65.5	.54.7	58.2	68.5	56.0	57.5	67.5	58.4	56.0	65.6	58.7	64.9	59.3	58.2	52.5
2. Somewhat acceptable	24.4	20.1	29.1	26.7	16.3	26.3	27.5	19.0	26.0	28.0	20.2	25.6	21.7	26.8	25.2	27.5
3. Acceptable	11.8	9.7	14.2	12.5	9.0	14.4	12.1	9.4	12.3	13.6	9.6	12.0	10.1	11.6	13.4	12.5
4. Desirable	3.4	4.7	2.0	2.6	6.2	3.4	2.9	4.1	3.1	2.4	4.6	3.6	3.4	2.1	3.2	7.5
Item 6200 N(Wtd)	3596	1740	1734	2730	454	856	1090	1098	553	1911	1441	1206	835	482	941	40
A08F: Husband doesn't work, wife works full-time																
1. Not at all acceptable	81.7	82.3	80.9	81.5	84.0	80.4	82.0	83.1	80.4	80.1	83.6	79.7	84.5	82.8	82.4	70.0
2. Somewhat acceptable	10.6	8.4	13.3	11.7	7.3	11.2	11.7	8.7	11.3	13.0	8.3	12.1	9.1	10.6	10.3	15.0
3. Acceptable	4.1	4.1	4.1	4.3	2.9	5.6	3.5	3.3	4.7	4.5	3.5	4.3	3.5	3.9	4.3	5.0
4. Desirable	3.6	5.2	1.7	2.5	5.9	2.9	2.8	5.0	3.6	2.3	4.8	3.9	2.9	2.7	3.1	10.0
Item 6210 N(Wtd)	3604	1741	1741	2735	455	859	1090	1098	556	1914	1441	1205	834	482	949	40
A09: Imagine you are married and have one or more pre-school children. How would you feel about each of the following working arrangements?																
A09A: Husband works full-time, wife doesn't work																
1. Not at all acceptable	8.3	5.2	10.7	6.2	19.7	8.7	7.5	8.5	9.1	8.3	7.0	7.9	8.6	6.8	8.2	17.5
2. Somewhat acceptable	18.0	15.1	20.5	16.0	28.4	17.3	19.0	18.4	16.0	16.5	19.0	16.4	17.5	17.9	19.6	30.0
3. Acceptable	36.7	35.6	37.8	35.5	36.9	36.4	36.7	36.8	37.3	35.4	39.0	36.9	36.5	36.4	36.2	32.5
4. Desirable	37.0	44.2	31.0	42.2	14.8	37.7	36.8	36.2	37.8	39.9	34.8	38.8	37.5	38.9	36.0	20.0
Item 6220 N(Wtd)	3621	1746	1750	2746	458	861	1091	1107	561	1925	1447	1210	840	486	949	40
A09B: Husband works full-time, wife works about half-time																
1. Not at all acceptable	10.1	13.5	6.5	9.8	9.1	11.3	9.4	9.1	11.3	9.3	11.2	10.4	11.7	6.4	9.7	15.0
2. Somewhat acceptable	25.8	27.7	24.2	25.8	28.0	28.4	24.7	25.9	24.2	26.2	24.2	25.6	26.5	29.2	23.4	27.5
3. Acceptable	50.2	46.6	53.9	49.9	52.3	45.5	51.0	53.7	48.8	50.2	51.3	51.9	46.9	53.1	49.8	45.0
4. Desirable	13.9	12.2	15.4	14.5	10.4	14.8	14.9	11.2	15.7	14.4	13.4	12.0	14.9	11.5	17.1	12.5
Item 6230 N(Wtd)	3622	1748	1751	2745	461	864	1093	1107	559	1922	1452	1213	838	486	951	40
A09C: Both work full-time																
1. Not at all acceptable	61.5	65.1	58.6	65.8	42.3	68.1	61.4	54.4	65.6	64.4	58.6	60.7	60.6	62.2	64.2	52.5
2. Somewhat acceptable	20.1	17.7	22.6	19.9	21.5	17.9	21.2	21.7	18.0	19.3	21.2	21.2	20.7	19.4	19.1	17.5
3. Acceptable	13.2	12.0	13.6	10.2	26.1	9.2	12.3	17.9	12.1	11.2	15.2	12.9	12.7	15.1	12.1	17.5
4. Desirable	5.2	5.2	5.2	4.1	9.9	4.9	5.1	6.0	4.3	5.1	5.0	5.2	6.2	3.5	4.6	12.5
Item 6240 N(Wtd)	3606	1744	1740	2738	456	860	1092	1100	555	1918	1444	1205	837	484	948	40
A09D: Both work about half-time																
1. Not at all acceptable	48.3	52.8	44.2	46.7	55.7	46.6	47.6	52.4	44.4	42.9	55.1	48.2	51.7	45.6	46.8	52.5
2. Somewhat acceptable	30.4	29.0	32.0	32.6	24.6	30.1	34.0	28.1	28.3	32.8	28.3	30.6	29.4	33.6	30.4	27.5
3. Acceptable	15.5	12.5	18.3	15.7	12.9	17.9	13.5	14.4	18.1	17.9	12.1	16.5	13.3	15.9	15.6	15.0
4. Desirable	5.7	5.7	5.5	5.0	6.8	5.5	4.9	5.2	9.0	6.4	4.5	4.8	5.6	4.7	7.3	5.0
Item 6250 N(Wtd)	3603	1742	1740	2734	456	857	1088	1100	558	1917	1440	1204	836	485	945	40

QUESTIONNAIRE FORM 2 1981	TOTAL	SEX		RACE		REGION				4YR COLLEGE PLANS		ILLICIT DRUG USE: LIFETIME				
		M	F	White	Black	NE	NC	S	W	Yes	No	None	Mari-juana Only	Few Pills	More Pills	Any Her-oin
Weighted No. of Cases:	3655	1762	1762	2761	467	869	1102	1117	567	1937	1462	1219	846	487	958	41
% of Weighted Total:	100.0	48.2	48.2	75.5	12.8	23.8	30.1	30.6	15.5	53.0	40.0	33.4	23.2	13.3	26.2	1.1
A09E: Husband works about half-time, wife works full-time																
1. Not at all acceptable	68.1	70.5	65.4	68.0	66.1	66.4	64.5	73.2	68.1	63.7	74.0	65.5	70.8	70.1	68.3	67.5
2. Somewhat acceptable	19.2	17.4	21.2	19.9	19.5	19.7	22.6	15.8	18.6	23.0	14.5	20.9	16.7	20.8	18.9	22.5
3. Acceptable	9.5	8.5	10.9	9.9	8.1	11.4	9.9	7.1	10.6	11.0	7.5	10.4	9.1	6.9	10.7	2.5
4. Desirable	3.1	3.6	2.5	2.1	6.1	2.4	2.9	3.9	3.1	2.2	3.9	3.4	3.3	2.3	2.1	7.5
Item 6260 N(Wtd)	3603	1740	1741	2734	457	858	1091	1100	554	1914	1445	1207	836	481	947	40
A09F: Husband doesn't work, wife works full-time																
1. Not at all acceptable	78.5	78.9	77.9	77.7	83.0	75.5	77.4	81.8	79.0	74.7	83.0	76.1	79.4	82.2	79.2	80.0
2. Somewhat acceptable	10.0	8.8	11.8	10.9	7.9	10.9	11.7	7.8	9.7	13.0	7.1	10.9	9.9	9.3	9.9	12.5
3. Acceptable	7.5	7.4	7.7	8.4	3.3	10.3	7.4	5.6	7.4	9.0	5.5	8.7	7.2	6.0	7.6	-
4. Desirable	3.9	4.9	2.6	2.9	6.0	3.4	3.4	4.8	3.9	3.2	4.3	4.3	3.5	2.7	3.3	7.5
Item 6270 N(Wtd)	3606	1745	1740	2740	453	860	1090	1099	557	1916	1443	1208	835	482	949	40
A10: Imagine you are married and have one or more pre-school children. Imagine also that the husband is working full-time and the wife does not have a job outside the home. How would you feel about each of these arrangements for the day-to-day care of the child(ren)?																
A10A: Wife does all child care																
1. Not at all acceptable	32.1	28.6	35.8	32.3	30.7	36.6	31.3	29.0	32.8	35.6	28.3	33.8	29.9	30.2	34.0	27.5
2. Somewhat acceptable	29.1	29.1	29.3	29.9	27.7	26.3	29.5	30.2	31.0	27.3	31.2	26.9	26.8	36.0	30.6	30.0
3. Acceptable	28.6	28.6	28.3	27.8	33.6	26.4	29.4	30.6	26.7	27.7	29.6	29.5	32.8	25.8	24.3	35.0
4. Desirable	10.1	13.7	6.7	10.0	8.1	10.8	9.7	10.3	9.5	9.4	10.8	9.9	10.5	7.9	11.0	5.0
Item 6280 N(Wtd)	3617	1750	1742	2740	459	864	1091	1103	558	1920	1450	1210	839	484	947	40
A10B: Wife does most of it																
1. Not at all acceptable	10.7	11.0	9.8	9.3	16.4	11.4	9.5	10.5	12.2	9.7	10.7	10.4	12.6	8.6	9.0	17.5
2. Somewhat acceptable	29.2	28.9	29.4	28.1	31.4	28.4	30.0	28.3	30.6	26.9	31.6	29.1	26.9	32.1	30.2	20.0
3. Acceptable	42.8	40.4	45.6	43.5	41.3	42.6	41.9	45.7	38.8	44.2	42.2	42.3	43.4	43.0	42.7	57.5
4. Desirable	17.3	19.7	15.3	19.0	10.9	17.5	18.5	15.5	18.4	19.2	15.5	18.3	17.0	16.3	18.2	5.0
Item 6290 N(Wtd)	3614	1748	1743	2743	458	863	1086	1107	559	1921	1448	1207	839	486	949	40
A10C: Both do it equally																
1. Not at all acceptable	5.9	6.3	5.2	5.4	8.0	7.0	4.1	6.4	7.0	4.9	6.7	4.6	5.3	6.2	6.8	12.5
2. Somewhat acceptable	17.7	19.6	15.8	17.3	16.7	15.3	17.7	19.0	18.6	18.0	17.6	18.3	16.7	19.1	17.4	22.5
3. Acceptable	40.2	42.1	37.8	37.5	51.8	39.7	40.6	42.2	36.3	37.6	42.0	39.9	39.8	39.0	40.6	32.5
4. Desirable	36.2	32.0	41.3	39.8	23.4	38.1	37.7	32.3	38.1	39.5	33.8	37.2	38.2	35.7	35.2	32.5
Item 6300 N(Wtd)	3610	1742	1744	2734	461	862	1086	1103	559	1922	1440	1210	834	482	949	40
A10D: Husband does most of it																
1. Not at all acceptable	53.0	49.9	55.8	53.6	47.5	51.4	51.2	53.2	58.5	52.7	53.7	52.6	53.4	52.9	54.0	45.0
2. Somewhat acceptable	35.6	37.6	34.2	36.7	34.9	36.3	38.8	33.4	32.3	35.8	35.4	35.0	35.8	37.4	35.2	40.0
3. Acceptable	8.3	9.2	7.3	8.1	8.9	10.1	7.4	8.7	6.5	9.4	6.6	8.5	7.9	7.2	8.3	7.5
4. Desirable	3.1	3.4	2.7	1.6	8.9	2.2	2.4	4.7	2.7	2.0	4.2	3.8	2.9	2.5	2.4	7.5
Item 6310 N(Wtd)	3613	1747	1743	2738	459	863	1089	1104	557	1920	1447	1208	837	484	948	40
A10E: Husband does all of it																
1. Not at all acceptable	87.0	84.2	90.2	88.7	80.3	88.2	87.4	84.3	89.8	88.2	86.6	86.6	87.5	88.4	87.6	80.0
2. Somewhat acceptable	8.0	9.8	6.2	7.9	9.8	8.5	8.2	8.6	5.7	8.7	6.6	7.6	8.2	7.4	8.4	10.0
3. Acceptable	1.9	2.1	1.6	1.6	3.1	2.3	1.7	1.8	1.4	1.9	1.7	2.0	1.7	1.4	1.8	5.0
4. Desirable	3.1	3.8	2.1	1.8	6.8	1.0	2.7	5.3	2.9	1.2	5.1	3.9	2.5	2.5	2.2	7.5
Item 6320 N(Wtd)	3608	1745	1739	2737	457	862	1086	1100	560	1916	1444	1207	837	484	946	40

QUESTIONNAIRE FORM 2 1981	TOTAL	SEX		RACE		REGION				4YR COLLEGE PLANS		ILLICIT DRUG USE: LIFETIME				
		M	F	White	Black	NE	NC	S	W	Yes	No	None	Mari-juana Only	Few Pills	More Pills	Any Her-oin
Weighted No. of Cases:	3655	1762	1762	2761	467	869	1102	1117	567	1937	1462	1219	846	487	958	41
% of Weighted Total:	100.0	48.2	48.2	75.5	12.8	23.8	30.1	30.6	15.5	53.0	40.0	33.4	23.2	13.3	26.2	1.1

The next section of this questionnaire is about government and public affairs.

A11: Some people think about what's going on in government very often, and others are not that interested. How much of an interest do you take in government and current events?

	TOTAL	M	F	White	Black	NE	NC	S	W	Yes	No	None	Mari-juana Only	Few Pills	More Pills	Any Her-oin
1. No interest at all	3.3	4.1	2.5	3.1	3.4	3.6	3.4	2.9	3.6	1.6	5.6	3.5	2.8	2.9	3.4	12.5
2. Very little interest	14.0	9.5	18.3	13.4	13.3	13.8	12.8	14.3	15.8	10.5	17.8	13.1	12.8	14.6	14.9	17.5
3. Some interest	46.3	43.3	49.1	45.7	46.7	46.4	47.2	45.5	45.9	42.0	51.9	43.7	47.9	48.5	47.4	35.0
4. A lot of interest	25.7	28.7	22.8	27.0	25.6	23.4	26.9	27.0	24.2	30.9	19.8	26.1	25.8	25.9	25.1	27.5
5. A very great interest	10.7	14.5	7.3	10.8	11.0	12.8	9.7	10.3	10.3	15.1	4.9	13.7	10.5	8.2	9.2	10.0
Item 6330 N(Wtd)	3634	1755	1756	2752	465	865	1095	1112	562	1929	1456	1214	844	487	954	40

A12: Do you think some of the people running the government are crooked or dishonest?

	TOTAL	M	F	White	Black	NE	NC	S	W	Yes	No	None	Mari-juana Only	Few Pills	More Pills	Any Her-oin
1. Most of them are crooked or dishonest	11.0	10.3	11.1	8.7	21.5	11.5	8.2	14.7	8.2	9.4	12.6	11.7	9.7	10.3	10.9	22.5
2. Quite a few are	30.4	30.7	30.6	30.1	31.2	30.5	29.8	32.0	28.3	29.2	32.2	28.6	31.0	28.1	32.3	35.0
3. Some are	53.0	53.0	53.1	55.6	41.7	53.2	56.3	49.5	53.3	55.4	50.6	53.8	53.4	55.9	52.2	35.0
4. Hardly any are	5.2	5.7	4.7	5.4	4.1	4.4	5.6	3.2	9.3	6.0	4.2	5.2	5.9	5.3	4.3	7.5
5. None at all are crooked or dishonest	.5	.5	.4	.1	1.3	.3	.2	.6	.9	.1	.3	.7	-	.2	.2	2.5
Item 6340 N(Wtd)	3626	1752	1751	2746	465	866	1093	1109	559	1927	1450	1209	843	487	951	40

A13: Do you think the government wastes much of the money we pay in taxes?

	TOTAL	M	F	White	Black	NE	NC	S	W	Yes	No	None	Mari-juana Only	Few Pills	More Pills	Any Her-oin
1. Nearly all tax money is wasted	6.8	6.4	6.8	5.6	12.9	6.8	5.0	8.2	7.0	4.2	9.2	5.9	6.2	8.1	7.1	10.0
2. A lot of tax money is wasted	49.9	49.0	51.2	50.6	46.6	52.8	52.3	47.5	46.0	49.8	51.1	48.7	48.6	56.7	50.4	47.5
3. Some tax money is wasted	36.6	36.9	36.7	37.9	32.1	34.8	37.1	35.8	40.1	39.3	34.1	38.2	39.7	30.6	36.1	30.0
4. A little tax money wasted	6.0	7.2	4.6	5.8	5.4	5.6	5.1	7.0	6.6	6.3	4.5	6.4	5.0	4.3	6.2	12.5
5. No tax money is wasted	.6	.5	.7	.1	3.0	.1	.4	1.4	.4	.4	.9	.9	.6	.2	.2	2.5
Item 6350 N(Wtd)	3624	1754	1748	2745	464	864	1094	1106	559	1926	1451	1212	844	483	950	40

A14: How much of the time do you think you can trust the government in Washington to do what is right?

	TOTAL	M	F	White	Black	NE	NC	S	W	Yes	No	None	Mari-juana Only	Few Pills	More Pills	Any Her-oin
1. Almost always	8.1	9.4	7.0	8.7	3.7	7.9	7.2	8.2	9.6	9.7	5.9	8.6	8.7	7.4	7.9	2.5
2. Often	38.5	42.0	35.9	42.2	21.8	40.5	39.7	35.2	39.8	43.4	33.7	39.9	40.2	36.6	37.9	27.5
3. Sometimes	41.1	37.7	44.4	40.1	45.3	40.1	43.4	39.7	41.3	38.3	44.1	39.4	38.9	43.2	44.3	47.5
4. Seldom	10.4	9.2	10.9	7.9	23.1	9.5	8.0	14.5	8.4	7.1	14.0	10.3	10.5	11.6	8.3	17.5
5. Never	1.8	1.6	1.8	.9	6.3	2.0	1.7	2.4	.9	1.4	2.3	1.8	1.8	1.2	1.7	7.5
Item 6360 N(Wtd)	3622	1752	1749	2745	464	862	1092	1108	560	1925	1452	1212	841	484	951	40

A15: Do you feel that the people running the government are smart people who usually know what they are doing?

	TOTAL	M	F	White	Black	NE	NC	S	W	Yes	No	None	Mari-juana Only	Few Pills	More Pills	Any Her-oin
1. They almost always know what they are doing	12.8	15.2	10.4	12.9	10.2	11.2	11.8	13.6	15.8	13.4	11.4	14.5	14.5	7.8	12.0	10.0
2. They usually know what they are doing	53.2	54.1	53.0	56.2	39.4	54.0	54.6	50.9	53.9	56.8	49.6	49.7	55.3	54.2	56.2	47.5
3. They sometimes know what they are doing	28.3	25.6	31.0	26.7	37.2	27.0	30.5	28.3	26.0	25.4	32.1	31.0	25.2	29.1	27.6	25.0
4. They seldom know what they are doing	4.6	4.4	4.5	3.5	11.3	5.9	2.4	6.2	3.8	3.7	5.6	3.9	4.3	7.2	3.3	12.5
5. They never know what they are doing	1.0	.7	1.1	.7	1.9	2.0	.7	1.0	.4	.7	1.3	.8	.8	1.6	.8	5.0
Item 6370 N(Wtd)	3621	1753	1747	2747	462	863	1093	1107	558	1923	1453	1211	842	485	949	40

QUESTIONNAIRE FORM 2 1981	TOTAL	SEX		RACE		REGION				4YR COLLEGE PLANS		ILLICIT DRUG USE: LIFETIME				
		M	F	White	Black	NE	NC	S	W	Yes	No	None	Mari- juana Only	Few Pills	More Pills	Any Her- oin
Weighted No. of Cases:	3655	1762	1762	2761	467	869	1102	1117	567	1937	1462	1219	846	487	958	41
% of Weighted Total:	100.0	48.2	48.2	75.5	12.8	23.8	30.1	30.6	15.5	53.0	40.0	33.4	23.2	13.3	26.2	1.1

A16: Would you say the government is pretty much run for a few big interests looking out for themselves, or is it run for the benefit of all the people?

	TOTAL	M	F	White	Black	NE	NC	S	W	Yes	No	None	Mari- juana Only	Few Pills	More Pills	Any Her- oin
1. Nearly always run for a few big interests	7.8	9.0	6.4	6.6	11.5	7.3	6.6	9.4	8.1	6.1	9.9	7.8	8.3	7.5	7.2	7.5
2. Usually run for a few big interests	22.2	21.9	22.4	21.5	28.6	21.2	22.1	24.3	20.2	21.8	23.4	22.9	20.4	26.9	20.4	35.0
3. Run some for the big interests, some for the people	47.7	46.7	49.0	48.4	43.2	49.8	48.6	45.7	46.8	47.6	47.8	47.8	47.3	46.4	48.1	45.0
4. Usually run for the benefit of all the people	17.9	17.8	18.0	19.3	12.8	17.1	19.9	16.1	18.9	19.2	16.3	17.0	19.5	15.3	20.4	5.0
5. Nearly always run for the benefit of all the people	4.3	4.5	4.1	4.2	3.7	4.4	3.0	4.5	5.9	5.3	2.8	4.5	4.3	4.1	4.0	7.5
Item 6380　N(Wtd)	3611	1746	1747	2744	461	859	1092	1105	555	1920	1451	1208	839	483	951	40

A17: Have you ever done, or do you plan to do, the following things?

A17A: Vote in a public election

	TOTAL	M	F	White	Black	NE	NC	S	W	Yes	No	None	Mari- juana Only	Few Pills	More Pills	Any Her- oin
1. I probably won't do this	3.2	3.2	3.1	2.7	4.1	3.7	2.6	2.7	4.7	2.1	4.7	3.2	3.4	2.3	3.0	10.0
2. Don't know	6.5	6.2	6.6	4.8	9.5	6.9	4.7	7.0	8.6	2.9	9.8	6.2	5.8	9.3	5.7	-
3. I probably will do this	82.5	80.6	85.3	84.7	79.0	83.7	81.6	83.2	81.0	87.4	77.8	82.6	83.5	80.6	84.5	75.0
4. I have already done this	7.8	10.0	5.0	7.8	7.4	5.7	11.3	7.0	5.7	7.7	7.8	8.0	7.2	7.8	6.7	17.5
Item 6390　N(Wtd)	3627	1755	1755	2754	462	865	1096	1109	557	1928	1454	1218	844	485	952	40

A17B: Write to public officials

	TOTAL	M	F	White	Black	NE	NC	S	W	Yes	No	None	Mari- juana Only	Few Pills	More Pills	Any Her- oin
1. I probably won't do this	18.5	17.9	18.7	16.9	21.7	18.6	17.9	18.7	19.3	11.7	25.7	17.8	20.1	17.7	17.7	15.0
2. Don't know	46.5	45.7	47.3	47.0	46.2	46.1	47.4	47.7	43.0	42.9	50.9	47.3	43.0	50.3	45.7	50.0
3. I probably will do this	21.9	23.6	20.2	22.0	21.0	23.1	19.7	22.4	23.1	28.0	15.0	22.0	24.6	19.0	22.2	7.5
4. I have already done this	13.1	12.8	13.7	14.1	10.8	12.3	14.9	11.2	14.6	17.3	8.5	12.9	12.2	13.2	14.4	27.5
Item 6400　N(Wtd)	3618	1752	1750	2752	461	862	1094	1108	554	1926	1449	1214	841	485	951	40

A17C: Give money to a political candidate or cause

	TOTAL	M	F	White	Black	NE	NC	S	W	Yes	No	None	Mari- juana Only	Few Pills	More Pills	Any Her- oin
1. I probably won't do this	34.8	37.3	31.6	33.6	36.2	37.0	36.1	31.0	36.4	26.9	43.8	33.1	34.9	36.6	34.3	45.0
2. Don't know	39.4	38.1	40.8	40.1	37.9	39.2	39.1	41.0	36.9	41.9	36.3	39.9	38.3	39.8	40.1	30.0
3. I probably will do this	21.4	20.5	22.8	21.6	21.1	20.6	20.1	22.5	22.7	26.1	15.6	22.8	21.8	20.9	20.4	15.0
4. I have already done this	4.5	4.2	4.8	4.7	4.8	3.2	4.6	5.5	4.0	5.0	4.3	4.1	4.9	2.5	5.3	10.0
Item 6410　N(Wtd)	3619	1750	1754	2751	459	863	1094	1107	555	1925	1451	1216	843	483	951	40

A17D: Work in a political campaign

	TOTAL	M	F	White	Black	NE	NC	S	W	Yes	No	None	Mari- juana Only	Few Pills	More Pills	Any Her- oin
1. I probably won't do this	45.2	48.1	41.8	45.6	38.6	44.9	47.6	40.7	50.2	35.9	56.6	42.4	47.2	46.3	46.6	42.5
2. Don't know	37.3	36.4	38.8	37.1	40.8	38.3	34.6	40.5	34.5	39.7	34.0	38.8	37.2	34.5	36.9	30.0
3. I probably will do this	10.7	9.4	11.8	10.1	14.4	10.3	9.5	12.0	11.2	15.2	5.2	12.1	9.8	13.2	8.1	15.0
4. I have already done this	6.7	6.1	7.7	7.1	6.1	6.5	8.2	6.8	4.1	9.1	4.1	6.8	5.8	6.0	8.3	12.5
Item 6420　N(Wtd)	3616	1751	1749	2749	458	864	1091	1105	556	1928	1445	1213	841	484	950	40

A17E: Participate in a lawful demonstration

	TOTAL	M	F	White	Black	NE	NC	S	W	Yes	No	None	Mari- juana Only	Few Pills	More Pills	Any Her- oin
1. I probably won't do this	33.0	29.8	36.3	32.3	34.7	27.8	32.9	36.5	34.0	26.5	40.9	36.1	34.4	34.2	27.1	32.5
2. Don't know	46.8	47.5	46.1	47.6	46.3	44.1	49.4	46.8	45.9	49.2	44.3	47.5	46.6	45.5	47.7	45.0
3. I probably will do this	16.8	17.9	15.3	16.1	17.5	22.9	14.8	14.2	16.4	19.8	12.5	14.4	15.8	17.0	19.5	22.5
4. I have already done this	3.4	4.7	2.3	3.9	1.5	5.2	2.8	2.4	3.8	4.4	2.3	1.9	3.2	3.3	5.9	2.5
Item 6430　N(Wtd)	3615	1751	1748	2750	458	862	1093	1104	556	1925	1446	1215	841	483	950	40

A17F: Boycott certain products or stores

	TOTAL	M	F	White	Black	NE	NC	S	W	Yes	No	None	Mari- juana Only	Few Pills	More Pills	Any Her- oin
1. I probably won't do this	29.8	25.2	34.5	28.9	32.5	24.5	29.3	32.3	34.0	22.9	37.7	29.9	31.9	33.3	25.6	27.5
2. Don't know	44.3	46.0	42.5	44.0	48.4	37.7	48.6	47.0	40.3	45.4	43.2	45.8	43.0	45.8	43.7	22.5
3. I probably will do this	19.3	20.5	17.9	19.8	16.6	28.2	16.5	15.7	18.2	23.2	14.6	18.5	19.3	16.0	21.7	25.0
4. I have already done this	6.7	8.3	5.2	7.4	2.6	9.5	5.7	5.0	7.6	8.4	4.5	5.7	5.8	4.8	9.1	22.5
Item 6440　N(Wtd)	3611	1752	1743	2744	459	861	1090	1104	556	1926	1444	1213	844	480	949	40

QUESTIONNAIRE FORM 2 1981	TOTAL	SEX		RACE		REGION				4YR COLLEGE PLANS		ILLICIT DRUG USE: LIFETIME				
		M	F	White	Black	NE	NC	S	W	Yes	No	None	Marijuana Only	Few Pills	More Pills	Any Heroin
Weighted No. of Cases:	3655	1762	1762	2761	467	869	1102	1117	567	1937	1462	1219	846	487	958	41
% of Weighted Total:	100.0	48.2	48.2	75.5	12.8	23.8	30.1	30.6	15.5	53.0	40.0	33.4	23.2	13.3	26.2	1.1

A18: How much do you agree or disagree with each of the following statements?

A18A: The U.S. should begin a gradual program of disarming whether other countries do or not

	TOTAL	M	F	White	Black	NE	NC	S	W	Yes	No	None	Mari-juana Only	Few Pills	More Pills	Any Heroin
1. Disagree	47.3	61.8	32.5	51.5	29.6	45.6	47.1	48.9	46.6	50.1	44.6	48.2	47.1	43.6	48.2	52.5
2. Mostly disagree	17.8	15.1	21.0	18.4	16.5	18.2	20.0	14.7	18.9	19.3	17.5	16.9	17.7	21.5	17.8	12.5
3. Neither	19.1	12.3	25.8	17.3	28.1	19.2	18.7	19.1	19.6	16.3	21.9	18.2	20.1	20.0	18.4	20.0
4. Mostly agree	9.9	6.4	13.5	8.3	16.0	10.1	8.4	10.9	10.3	9.6	9.7	9.8	10.0	9.9	9.8	12.5
5. Agree	5.9	4.4	7.1	4.5	9.8	6.7	5.7	6.3	4.8	4.8	6.4	6.8	5.0	5.1	5.7	2.5
Item 6450 N(Wtd)	3564	1740	1714	2723	449	848	1085	1087	545	1900	1432	1198	834	475	937	40

A18B: There may be times when the U.S. should go to war to protect the rights of other countries

	TOTAL	M	F	White	Black	NE	NC	S	W	Yes	No	None	Mari-juana Only	Few Pills	More Pills	Any Heroin
1. Disagree	22.8	19.2	26.5	21.0	31.4	26.0	22.5	21.4	21.0	21.4	24.3	20.8	20.9	23.0	26.5	32.5
2. Mostly disagree	24.0	22.6	25.6	25.7	19.6	24.7	23.9	22.9	25.0	25.7	23.4	21.1	27.1	25.9	24.9	15.0
3. Neither	18.0	17.8	17.8	17.8	17.4	17.0	20.0	16.2	19.0	16.9	18.9	18.7	17.1	18.9	17.2	7.5
4. Mostly agree	22.4	24.0	20.4	23.8	17.4	20.6	24.4	23.0	19.9	23.9	20.5	24.1	20.6	22.0	22.3	30.0
5. Agree	12.9	16.2	9.7	11.8	14.2	11.7	9.2	16.4	15.0	12.0	12.9	15.3	14.4	10.2	9.1	17.5
Item 5690 N(Wtd)	3607	1749	1743	2745	459	860	1091	1105	552	1922	1446	1213	841	482	946	40

A18C: The U.S. should be willing to go to war to protect its own economic interests

	TOTAL	M	F	White	Black	NE	NC	S	W	Yes	No	None	Mari-juana Only	Few Pills	More Pills	Any Heroin
1. Disagree	9.0	8.1	10.2	8.1	11.4	11.3	9.0	7.0	9.5	8.7	9.5	10.4	7.9	7.5	9.1	7.5
2. Mostly disagree	13.4	12.2	15.1	14.2	10.5	14.5	14.2	10.4	16.2	13.8	13.3	12.3	13.4	16.2	13.8	17.5
3. Neither	17.7	15.1	19.9	18.0	16.6	15.7	19.6	15.5	21.3	18.7	16.9	18.1	17.9	17.7	17.7	12.5
4. Mostly agree	31.7	31.8	31.4	33.0	25.8	33.1	33.3	30.6	28.5	32.8	29.9	32.0	31.3	34.5	29.9	32.5
5. Agree	28.2	32.8	23.6	26.8	35.7	25.4	23.9	36.5	24.5	26.1	30.4	27.3	29.7	23.9	29.6	30.0
Item 6460 N(Wtd)	3593	1746	1732	2733	457	853	1088	1102	550	1919	1436	1207	838	481	944	40

A18D: The only good reason for the U.S. to go to war is to defend against an attack on our own country

	TOTAL	M	F	White	Black	NE	NC	S	W	Yes	No	None	Mari-juana Only	Few Pills	More Pills	Any Heroin
1. Disagree	7.8	9.8	5.5	6.8	9.8	8.6	5.8	9.6	6.9	7.6	7.3	8.9	7.1	7.5	5.4	10.0
2. Mostly disagree	10.4	13.2	7.7	11.4	5.7	11.5	10.4	11.1	7.5	13.0	7.2	12.2	9.8	9.7	8.8	22.5
3. Neither	9.0	8.3	9.7	9.4	6.8	9.3	8.9	8.3	10.4	9.3	8.9	7.8	7.6	13.5	10.2	7.5
4. Mostly agree	31.5	27.3	36.1	32.5	27.2	30.3	33.6	30.1	31.6	31.9	31.3	30.9	33.2	29.6	33.1	17.5
5. Agree	41.3	41.5	41.0	40.0	50.3	40.4	41.2	40.9	43.5	38.3	45.2	40.3	42.4	39.5	42.6	42.5
Item 6470 N(Wtd)	3594	1742	1739	2736	459	851	1091	1106	547	1913	1443	1209	834	483	944	40

A18E: The U.S. does not need to have greater military power than the Soviet Union

	TOTAL	M	F	White	Black	NE	NC	S	W	Yes	No	None	Mari-juana Only	Few Pills	More Pills	Any Heroin
1. Disagree	44.7	48.3	40.6	42.7	54.8	43.5	38.8	54.6	38.4	42.0	47.4	45.9	44.0	42.7	43.2	52.5
2. Mostly disagree	24.1	24.2	24.3	25.5	19.4	24.0	26.5	22.1	23.9	25.6	21.8	23.6	23.7	27.0	24.4	15.0
3. Neither	13.9	11.6	16.5	14.5	11.2	13.0	16.9	10.4	16.8	13.7	15.0	13.4	13.3	13.9	15.5	17.5
4. Mostly agree	10.1	9.1	11.1	10.7	5.9	11.5	10.6	6.8	13.5	11.2	8.9	10.6	10.4	10.8	9.3	7.5
5. Agree	7.2	6.8	7.5	6.7	8.6	8.1	7.4	6.1	7.7	7.6	6.8	6.4	8.6	5.4	7.7	7.5
Item 6480 N(Wtd)	3586	1743	1732	2736	454	851	1085	1100	549	1916	1436	1206	839	482	938	40

A18F: The U.S. ought to have much more military power than any other nation in the world

	TOTAL	M	F	White	Black	NE	NC	S	W	Yes	No	None	Mari-juana Only	Few Pills	More Pills	Any Heroin
1. Disagree	11.8	12.7	11.3	11.9	9.2	12.8	11.8	10.5	13.0	13.6	9.7	13.6	11.7	8.3	11.3	12.5
2. Mostly disagree	15.4	15.0	16.3	16.5	10.9	16.9	18.0	10.4	18.1	19.0	12.0	16.7	15.4	17.4	13.4	7.5
3. Neither	22.4	19.3	25.9	23.1	19.0	24.0	24.0	18.7	23.9	21.5	24.1	20.9	22.4	23.9	24.3	15.0
4. Mostly agree	21.7	20.3	22.8	22.1	19.4	22.2	22.3	21.8	19.5	21.9	21.4	20.3	21.8	21.8	24.4	20.0
5. Agree	28.7	32.8	23.8	26.4	41.3	24.1	23.8	38.7	25.4	24.1	32.8	28.5	28.8	28.8	26.5	45.0
Item 6490 N(Wtd)	3584	1745	1729	2728	458	851	1086	1099	548	1912	1437	1208	836	482	938	40

QUESTIONNAIRE FORM 2 1981	TOTAL	SEX		RACE		REGION				4YR COLLEGE PLANS		ILLICIT DRUG USE: LIFETIME				
		M	F	White	Black	NE	NC	S	W	Yes	No	None	Mari-juana Only	Few Pills	More Pills	Any Her-oin
Weighted No. of Cases:	3655	1762	1762	2761	467	869	1102	1117	567	1937	1462	1219	846	487	958	41
% of Weighted Total:	100.0	48.2	48.2	75.5	12.8	23.8	30.1	30.6	15.5	53.0	40.0	33.4	23.2	13.3	26.2	1.1

A18G: Our present foreign policy is based on our own narrow economic and power interests

	TOTAL	M	F	White	Black	NE	NC	S	W	Yes	No	None	Mari-juana Only	Few Pills	More Pills	Any Her-oin
1. Disagree	5.9	7.1	4.7	6.0	6.3	7.6	4.8	5.6	5.8	5.3	6.4	6.6	4.2	5.1	6.4	2.6
2. Mostly disagree	10.8	11.9	9.7	11.4	11.0	11.4	10.1	11.1	10.7	13.0	8.4	12.5	10.8	8.7	10.6	5.1
3. Neither	43.5	37.9	49.6	46.0	32.6	40.1	48.8	40.1	44.8	39.6	49.5	40.3	43.9	46.1	46.3	35.9
4. Mostly agree	26.2	27.9	24.5	25.9	27.9	24.8	26.0	28.2	25.0	27.8	23.6	25.8	25.6	32.0	24.8	30.8
5. Agree	13.6	15.3	11.6	10.6	22.2	16.2	10.1	15.0	13.5	14.3	12.0	14.9	15.5	7.9	12.0	25.6
Item 6500 N(Wtd)	3518	1724	1689	2683	445	833	1076	1076	533	1880	1413	1180	817	469	937	39

A18H: Servicemen should obey orders without question

	TOTAL	M	F	White	Black	NE	NC	S	W	Yes	No	None	Mari-juana Only	Few Pills	More Pills	Any Her-oin
1. Disagree	14.0	12.1	15.6	11.6	21.3	15.7	12.3	13.1	16.2	14.5	12.9	14.7	13.5	11.0	13.7	10.0
2. Mostly disagree	18.4	16.6	20.2	18.7	17.8	17.6	20.8	16.1	19.2	18.9	17.8	17.1	17.2	23.1	19.7	10.0
3. Neither	20.1	18.0	22.5	20.3	18.7	18.9	22.5	18.5	20.6	20.3	20.5	19.4	19.7	20.2	21.4	30.0
4. Mostly agree	30.5	32.9	28.4	33.0	22.6	30.7	30.6	31.5	28.1	31.6	29.6	31.8	30.8	29.9	30.1	25.0
5. Agree	17.0	20.4	13.3	16.4	19.3	16.9	13.7	20.8	15.7	14.7	19.3	16.9	18.9	15.8	15.3	25.0
Item 6510 N(Wtd)	3590	1746	1734	2736	455	856	1085	1101	548	1918	1435	1207	837	481	945	40

A19: This section deals with activities which may be against the rules or against the law. We hope you will answer all of these questions. However, if you find a question which you cannot answer honestly, we would prefer that you leave it blank. Remember, your answers will never be connected with your name. During the LAST 12 MONTHS, how often have you...

A19A: Argued or had a fight with either of your parents

	TOTAL	M	F	White	Black	NE	NC	S	W	Yes	No	None	Mari-juana Only	Few Pills	More Pills	Any Her-oin
1. Not at all	13.7	16.6	10.4	7.6	41.8	6.7	11.2	21.7	13.6	12.4	13.5	20.7	13.2	6.4	6.9	4.9
2. Once	10.0	10.3	9.2	8.9	13.6	9.1	9.0	11.9	9.2	9.3	9.9	12.1	11.1	9.9	5.9	7.3
3. Twice	11.8	13.0	10.7	12.4	9.3	12.7	12.1	10.1	12.9	12.3	11.7	14.1	12.0	11.5	9.5	12.2
4. 3 or 4 times	22.7	23.0	22.1	24.3	16.4	23.7	23.7	21.6	21.5	23.7	21.8	20.4	24.1	27.0	22.5	26.8
5. 5 or more times	41.8	37.1	47.5	46.8	18.8	47.8	43.9	34.8	42.7	42.5	43.1	32.6	39.7	45.1	55.0	46.3
Item 6520 N(Wtd)	3623	1751	1757	2748	464	864	1095	1106	557	1926	1452	1216	844	486	954	41

A19B: Hit an instructor or supervisor

	TOTAL	M	F	White	Black	NE	NC	S	W	Yes	No	None	Mari-juana Only	Few Pills	More Pills	Any Her-oin
1. Not at all	97.0	95.1	99.0	97.5	97.0	96.9	97.4	97.5	95.5	97.7	96.1	98.0	97.9	97.3	95.4	80.5
2. Once	2.0	3.3	.6	1.5	2.4	1.9	1.8	2.1	2.2	1.5	2.6	1.3	1.7	2.1	2.9	7.3
3. Twice	.6	.7	.3	.5	-	.7	.6	.3	.9	.6	.5	.2	.1	.2	1.2	7.3
4. 3 or 4 times	.2	.3	.1	.2	.2	.1	.1	.3	.5	-	.5	.1	.1	.4	.2	-
5. 5 or more times	.3	.6	-	.2	.4	.5	.2	-	.9	.3	.3	.3	.1	-	.3	7.3
Item 6530 N(Wtd)	3621	1753	1755	2751	463	860	1097	1107	556	1927	1452	1217	843	486	955	41

A19C: Gotten into a serious fight in school or at work

	TOTAL	M	F	White	Black	NE	NC	S	W	Yes	No	None	Mari-juana Only	Few Pills	More Pills	Any Her-oin
1. Not at all	84.6	79.1	90.1	84.8	86.2	81.8	84.2	86.7	85.3	87.1	81.9	91.3	84.9	83.5	77.3	68.3
2. Once	9.5	12.6	6.5	9.2	10.1	11.0	9.3	9.1	8.8	7.7	11.3	5.7	10.5	9.1	13.4	12.2
3. Twice	3.1	4.2	2.2	3.2	2.2	3.7	3.6	2.5	2.2	3.0	3.3	1.6	2.7	4.1	4.5	9.8
4. 3 or 4 times	1.8	2.6	1.0	1.8	.9	2.3	1.7	1.4	2.3	1.5	2.1	.6	1.7	1.9	3.0	9.8
5. 5 or more times	1.0	1.5	.3	1.0	.6	1.3	1.2	.3	1.4	.7	1.3	.6	.2	1.2	1.7	2.4
Item 6540 N(Wtd)	3628	1755	1759	2752	465	865	1098	1109	556	1930	1454	1219	845	486	954	41

A19D: Taken part in a fight where a group of your friends were against another group

	TOTAL	M	F	White	Black	NE	NC	S	W	Yes	No	None	Mari-juana Only	Few Pills	More Pills	Any Her-oin
1. Not at all	83.2	77.9	88.7	83.0	87.1	80.9	82.8	84.1	85.6	86.6	79.7	91.2	85.1	78.0	75.7	65.9
2. Once	9.5	11.6	7.3	9.6	7.1	9.5	10.3	9.7	7.7	7.3	12.0	5.5	9.1	13.6	12.7	4.9
3. Twice	3.6	4.8	2.5	3.6	3.0	4.3	3.6	3.0	3.8	3.0	4.1	1.6	2.5	5.3	5.9	9.8
4. 3 or 4 times	2.3	3.3	1.1	2.4	1.5	3.0	1.9	2.5	1.4	1.8	2.6	1.2	1.9	2.1	3.6	7.3
5. 5 or more times	1.4	2.3	.4	1.3	1.3	2.3	1.4	.7	1.4	1.3	1.4	.5	1.3	.8	2.3	14.6
Item 6550 N(Wtd)	3627	1753	1760	2753	464	865	1098	1108	556	1930	1454	1217	846	486	955	41

QUESTIONNAIRE FORM 2 1981	TOTAL	SEX		RACE		REGION				4YR COLLEGE PLANS		ILLICIT DRUG USE: LIFETIME				
		M	F	White	Black	NE	NC	S	W	Yes	No	None	Marijuana Only	Few Pills	More Pills	Any Heroin
Weighted No. of Cases:	3655	1762	1762	2761	467	869	1102	1117	567	1937	1462	1219	846	487	958	41
% of Weighted Total:	100.0	48.2	48.2	75.5	12.8	23.8	30.1	30.6	15.5	53.0	40.0	33.4	23.2	13.3	26.2	1.1
A19E: Hurt someone badly enough to need bandages or a doctor																
1. Not at all	90.4	83.6	97.4	90.7	90.3	88.6	90.8	91.6	90.3	92.8	87.9	94.3	91.3	91.1	85.2	73.2
2. Once	6.0	10.0	2.0	6.1	5.0	7.5	5.6	5.5	5.6	4.6	7.7	4.1	5.6	5.8	8.8	9.8
3. Twice	2.2	3.9	.5	2.0	3.0	2.0	2.6	1.9	2.2	1.5	2.8	.9	1.7	1.9	3.9	9.8
4. 3 or 4 times	.8	1.4	.1	.8	.6	1.3	.5	.9	.4	.6	.9	.2	1.2	.6	1.3	2.4
5. 5 or more times	.6	1.1	.1	.4	1.1	.7	.4	.2	1.6	.5	.7	.4	.2	.8	.8	2.4
Item 6560 N(Wtd)	3623	1753	1759	2751	463	863	1096	1107	556	1931	1452	1219	843	485	955	41
A19F: Used a knife or gun or some other thing (like a club) to get something from a person																
1. Not at all	97.5	96.2	99.1	98.1	95.9	97.6	97.7	97.5	97.3	98.3	96.9	98.8	98.6	98.6	95.8	82.9
2. Once	1.4	2.1	.7	1.2	2.2	1.6	1.3	1.3	1.8	1.1	1.5	.5	.9	1.2	2.6	12.2
3. Twice	.4	.6	-	.3	.6	.1	.5	.5	.2	.2	.6	.2	.1	-	.6	2.4
4. 3 or 4 times	.4	.7	.1	.4	.4	.2	.4	.5	.5	.3	.7	.4	.1	.2	.6	2.4
5. 5 or more times	.2	.4	.1	.1	.9	.5	.1	.3	.2	.2	.3	.1	.2	-	.4	4.9
Item 6570 N(Wtd)	3624	1754	1759	2753	463	864	1097	1108	556	1931	1452	1218	845	486	955	41
A19G: Taken something not belonging to you worth under $50																
1. Not at all	69.0	60.2	77.7	67.1	80.4	64.2	67.1	75.7	66.5	70.2	67.2	81.7	70.4	65.9	53.5	41.5
2. Once	14.6	17.0	11.7	15.1	9.5	14.9	15.9	13.0	15.1	13.4	16.0	11.5	13.1	16.4	19.1	9.8
3. Twice	6.0	7.3	4.8	6.5	4.1	7.4	6.5	4.2	6.4	5.7	6.4	2.6	6.9	7.3	8.7	12.2
4. 3 or 4 times	5.3	7.1	3.5	5.8	2.6	6.1	5.9	2.9	7.7	5.1	5.6	2.7	4.2	6.0	9.3	12.2
5. 5 or more times	5.2	8.3	2.2	5.5	3.4	7.4	4.6	4.4	4.4	5.6	4.8	1.6	5.5	4.4	9.4	24.4
Item 6580 N(Wtd)	3592	1738	1749	2725	464	854	1089	1101	549	1915	1442	1206	840	481	947	41
A19H: Taken something not belonging to you worth over $50																
1. Not at all	92.9	88.8	97.2	93.0	93.9	90.8	93.7	93.9	92.2	94.1	92.0	98.0	93.8	93.4	86.7	63.4
2. Once	3.9	6.0	1.7	3.9	3.0	4.6	3.9	3.6	3.4	3.1	4.6	1.2	3.4	3.7	7.1	17.1
3. Twice	1.5	2.5	.6	1.5	1.7	2.0	1.0	1.4	2.2	1.3	1.6	.4	.9	2.1	2.7	7.3
4. 3 or 4 times	.7	1.1	.3	.7	.4	1.0	.5	.6	.5	.6	.8	.2	.8	.6	1.3	-
5. 5 or more times	1.0	1.7	.2	1.0	.6	1.4	.8	.4	1.6	.9	1.0	.2	.8	.2	2.1	7.3
Item 6590 N(Wtd)	3611	1747	1755	2745	462	861	1092	1105	554	1926	1446	1211	843	486	954	41
A19I: Taken something from a store without paying for it																
1. Not at all	71.4	64.6	78.7	72.1	74.0	64.1	72.7	75.9	71.1	74.7	68.5	84.9	71.1	66.3	57.9	53.7
2. Once	12.8	14.7	10.5	12.1	12.9	14.7	11.9	12.5	12.2	11.2	14.4	9.1	13.8	16.7	14.3	9.8
3. Twice	6.1	7.0	5.1	6.0	5.0	7.8	6.0	4.5	6.5	5.3	6.6	2.2	5.6	7.3	10.3	14.6
4. 3 or 4 times	4.6	5.4	3.7	4.6	3.7	6.9	4.2	3.1	4.5	4.2	5.0	2.1	4.6	4.8	7.6	14.6
5. 5 or more times	5.1	8.3	2.1	5.2	4.4	6.5	5.1	3.8	5.6	4.6	5.6	1.7	4.9	5.0	9.9	9.8
Item 6600 N(Wtd)	3602	1745	1749	2744	458	859	1092	1100	551	1923	1442	1209	845	480	951	41
A19J: Taken a car that didn't belong to someone in your family without permission of the owner																
1. Not at all	96.1	94.5	97.8	96.3	95.9	95.5	96.6	96.9	94.4	96.6	95.5	97.5	98.0	95.9	93.4	87.8
2. Once	2.5	3.1	1.8	2.3	3.0	2.8	2.0	2.1	3.8	2.3	2.5	1.7	1.5	3.5	3.2	7.3
3. Twice	.7	1.3	.2	.7	.6	.9	.6	.6	.9	.6	.9	.5	.4	.4	1.6	2.4
4. 3 or 4 times	.3	.5	.2	.4	.2	.2	.3	.4	.4	.2	.5	.1	.1	-	.8	-
5. 5 or more times	.4	.7	-	.4	-	.6	.5	.1	.5	.3	.5	.1	.1	.2	.9	2.4
Item 6610 N(Wtd)	3621	1755	1757	2753	464	861	1095	1108	556	1930	1452	1219	845	486	954	41

QUESTIONNAIRE FORM 2 1981	TOTAL	SEX		RACE		REGION				4YR COLLEGE PLANS		ILLICIT DRUG USE: LIFETIME				
		M	F	White	Black	NE	NC	S	W	Yes	No	None	Mari- juana Only	Few Pills	More Pills	Any Her- oin
Weighted No. of Cases:	3655	1762	1762	2761	467	869	1102	1117	567	1937	1462	1219	846	487	958	41
% of Weighted Total:	100.0	48.2	48.2	75.5	12.8	23.8	30.1	30.6	15.5	53.0	40.0	33.4	23.2	13.3	26.2	1.1

A19K: Taken part of a car without permission of the owner

	TOTAL	M	F	White	Black	NE	NC	S	W	Yes	No	None	Mari- juana Only	Few Pills	More Pills	Any Her- oin
1. Not at all	94.7	90.3	99.0	94.2	97.2	92.8	95.1	95.0	96.0	95.5	94.0	97.3	94.9	94.2	92.0	75.6
2. Once	3.0	5.2	.8	3.4	1.5	4.1	2.9	3.0	1.8	2.6	3.2	2.2	3.3	2.7	3.6	12.2
3. Twice	1.2	2.2	.1	1.2	.9	1.2	1.5	1.2	.5	.8	1.2	.3	.8	1.6	2.1	2.4
4. 3 or 4 times	.7	1.3	.1	.8	.6	1.3	.5	.7	.4	.5	1.0	-	.5	1.2	1.5	2.4
5. 5 or more times	.4	.9	.1	.4	-	.8	.2	.1	1.1	.5	.5	.2	.4	.2	.8	7.3
Item 6620 N(Wtd)	3616	1753	1755	2749	463	859	1096	1106	555	1927	1450	1217	844	486	953	41

A19L: Gone into some house or building when you weren't supposed to be there

	TOTAL	M	F	White	Black	NE	NC	S	W	Yes	No	None	Mari- juana Only	Few Pills	More Pills	Any Her- oin
1. Not at all	77.1	69.7	84.6	76.1	84.0	73.7	76.1	80.2	78.6	78.4	76.0	84.5	79.8	77.5	66.8	39.0
2. Once	11.4	13.4	9.5	11.9	9.1	11.5	12.4	11.1	10.1	10.7	12.4	9.7	10.4	11.0	14.1	24.4
3. Twice	6.2	8.8	3.6	6.5	3.9	7.2	6.6	5.4	5.6	6.3	5.9	3.6	5.7	6.4	9.3	17.1
4. 3 or 4 times	2.7	4.2	1.2	2.8	2.2	3.6	2.5	2.1	3.2	2.6	3.0	1.4	3.0	2.5	4.3	2.4
5. 5 or more times	2.5	3.9	1.1	2.7	.9	4.0	2.5	1.3	2.7	1.9	2.8	.7	1.1	2.5	5.4	17.1
Item 6630 N(Wtd)	3614	1752	1754	2749	462	860	1095	1104	555	1925	1452	1215	843	484	955	41

A19M: Set fire to someone's property on purpose

	TOTAL	M	F	White	Black	NE	NC	S	W	Yes	No	None	Mari- juana Only	Few Pills	More Pills	Any Her- oin
1. Not at all	98.3	96.9	99.7	98.3	98.9	97.9	98.4	98.6	98.4	99.1	97.7	98.8	99.2	98.6	97.5	85.4
2. Once	1.2	2.1	.3	1.1	.6	1.4	1.3	.9	1.1	.7	1.6	.8	.8	1.2	1.6	4.9
3. Twice	.2	.5	-	.2	.2	.2	.1	.4	.2	.1	.3	.3	-	.2	.3	2.4
4. 3 or 4 times	.1	.3	-	.2	-	.2	.1	.1	-	-	.3	-	-	-	.3	2.4
5. 5 or more times	.2	.3	-	.2	.2	.2	.1	.1	.4	.2	.2	-	-	-	.4	4.9
Item 6640 N(Wtd)	3622	1755	1758	2753	464	861	1097	1108	556	1930	1453	1219	845	486	955	41

A19N: Damaged school property on purpose

	TOTAL	M	F	White	Black	NE	NC	S	W	Yes	No	None	Mari- juana Only	Few Pills	More Pills	Any Her- oin
1. Not at all	86.7	79.7	93.6	86.0	90.3	85.8	85.1	88.8	86.5	87.5	85.2	94.0	88.2	85.8	77.1	61.0
2. Once	7.3	10.8	3.7	7.3	5.4	8.2	7.2	6.4	7.9	6.7	8.2	3.9	6.2	8.5	12.4	4.9
3. Twice	3.5	5.2	1.9	4.0	2.4	3.3	4.8	2.9	2.5	3.4	3.7	1.4	3.8	4.1	5.5	14.6
4. 3 or 4 times	1.2	2.0	.5	1.2	1.3	1.4	1.1	1.0	1.6	1.5	.9	.1	1.1	1.2	2.4	9.8
5. 5 or more times	1.3	2.2	.4	1.4	.9	1.3	1.7	.8	1.4	.8	1.9	.5	.8	.6	2.6	12.2
Item 6650 N(Wtd)	3600	1738	1753	2737	463	851	1090	1103	556	1916	1445	1206	842	485	951	41

A19O: Damaged property at work on purpose

	TOTAL	M	F	White	Black	NE	NC	S	W	Yes	No	None	Mari- juana Only	Few Pills	More Pills	Any Her- oin
1. Not at all	93.5	89.1	97.9	92.8	96.1	92.5	92.6	94.3	95.3	93.7	93.2	95.8	93.4	93.6	90.5	87.8
2. Once	3.1	4.9	1.1	3.5	1.3	4.3	3.3	2.1	2.7	3.1	3.0	2.1	2.3	3.3	5.0	4.9
3. Twice	1.6	2.9	.5	1.8	1.5	1.4	1.8	2.0	.9	1.7	1.7	1.0	2.0	1.6	2.3	2.4
4. 3 or 4 times	1.1	1.9	.4	1.4	.7	.9	1.8	.9	.5	.9	1.5	.8	1.4	.8	1.6	-
5. 5 or more times	.6	1.1	.1	.5	.7	.9	.5	.6	.5	.6	.6	.3	.9	.4	.6	2.4
Item 6660 N(Wtd)	3610	1748	1755	2746	460	857	1094	1103	556	1926	1447	1217	844	486	948	41

A19P: Gotten into trouble with police because of something you did

	TOTAL	M	F	White	Black	NE	NC	S	W	Yes	No	None	Mari- juana Only	Few Pills	More Pills	Any Her- oin
1. Not at all	78.2	67.7	88.5	75.9	90.9	74.3	75.2	84.3	78.1	80.5	75.6	90.9	78.2	75.0	64.5	53.7
2. Once	12.9	17.2	8.5	14.4	6.3	16.0	14.5	9.7	11.3	12.2	13.8	5.9	14.8	16.1	18.4	14.6
3. Twice	5.2	8.9	1.7	5.6	2.2	5.0	6.7	3.7	5.8	4.7	5.8	1.6	4.9	6.2	9.2	17.1
4. 3 or 4 times	2.2	3.2	1.1	2.4	.2	3.0	1.6	1.4	3.6	1.7	2.8	.6	1.3	1.7	4.7	17.1
5. 5 or more times	1.5	3.0	.1	1.6	.4	1.6	2.1	1.0	1.1	.9	2.1	.9	.9	1.0	3.2	-
Item 6670 N(Wtd)	3619	1753	1758	2752	463	861	1095	1107	556	1929	1452	1219	844	484	955	41

A20: The next questions are about some things which may have happened TO YOU. During the LAST 12 MONTHS, how often...

QUESTIONNAIRE FORM 2 1981	TOTAL	SEX		RACE		REGION				4YR COLLEGE PLANS		ILLICIT DRUG USE: LIFETIME				
		M	F	White	Black	NE	NC	S	W	Yes	No	None	Mari- juana Only	Few Pills	More Pills	Any Her- oin
Weighted No. of Cases:	3655	1762	1762	2761	467	869	1102	1117	567	1937	1462	1219	846	487	958	41
% of Weighted Total:	100.0	48.2	48.2	75.5	12.8	23.8	30.1	30.6	15.5	53.0	40.0	33.4	23.2	13.3	26.2	1.1
A20A: Has something of yours (worth under $50) been stolen?																
1. Not at all	56.3	50.4	62.0	56.2	55.4	53.9	57.7	57.5	55.0	53.8	59.7	61.7	56.7	55.5	50.5	31.7
2. Once	24.9	26.8	23.3	25.1	26.0	23.9	24.1	26.3	24.8	25.8	24.1	22.0	26.7	25.4	26.3	29.3
3. Twice	11.5	13.3	9.5	11.3	11.3	13.5	11.2	8.8	14.1	13.0	9.3	10.5	9.9	12.2	13.6	22.0
4. 3 or 4 times	5.1	6.4	3.9	5.3	5.0	6.4	4.6	5.7	3.3	5.0	5.0	4.2	4.6	4.7	6.8	7.3
5. 5 or more times	2.2	3.0	1.3	2.2	2.4	2.2	2.4	1.6	2.9	2.3	1.9	1.6	2.1	2.3	2.8	9.8
Item 6680 N(Wtd)	3605	1743	1757	2744	462	857	1094	1102	553	1921	1450	1215	842	485	951	41
A20B: Has something of yours (worth over $50) been stolen?																
1. Not at all	83.3	80.3	87.1	85.1	76.6	84.1	83.3	83.8	81.2	83.9	83.6	86.3	84.2	83.3	80.3	53.7
2. Once	12.6	14.0	10.3	11.2	18.6	12.1	13.0	12.5	12.7	12.5	11.9	10.9	11.7	13.2	14.0	36.6
3. Twice	2.8	4.2	1.5	2.6	3.3	2.6	2.9	2.6	3.4	2.4	3.2	2.1	3.0	2.1	3.7	2.4
4. 3 or 4 times	1.0	1.1	.9	.9	1.1	1.1	.7	.8	2.0	.8	1.1	.4	1.0	1.2	1.6	7.3
5. 5 or more times	.3	.3	.2	.2	.4	.2	.1	.3	.7	.3	.3	.2	.2	.2	.4	2.4
Item 6690 N(Wtd)	3603	1744	1753	2744	458	857	1093	1100	552	1922	1451	1212	840	485	954	41
A20C: Has someone deliberately damaged your property (your car, clothing, etc.)?																
1. Not at all	65.8	57.9	73.5	65.4	68.7	69.7	61.7	67.9	63.9	67.4	64.0	70.6	69.8	60.6	59.7	37.5
2. Once	21.2	26.6	16.0	21.5	17.8	17.6	24.6	20.7	21.1	19.6	23.4	18.7	18.9	27.0	23.9	30.0
3. Twice	8.7	10.5	6.9	8.7	8.9	8.8	10.1	6.5	10.5	9.0	8.5	6.4	8.3	7.6	11.9	20.0
4. 3 or 4 times	2.8	3.0	2.7	2.8	2.8	2.3	2.5	3.7	2.4	2.6	2.9	3.1	1.9	2.7	3.2	-
5. 5 or more times	1.5	2.0	.9	1.5	2.0	1.6	1.2	1.3	2.2	1.4	1.2	1.4	1.0	2.1	1.3	10.0
Item 6700 N(Wtd)	3599	1743	1750	2745	460	856	1093	1098	551	1919	1451	1210	840	485	954	40
A20D: Has someone injured you with a weapon (like a knife, gun, or club)?																
1. Not at all	95.1	92.8	97.6	95.6	93.9	95.2	94.2	95.3	96.6	96.3	93.9	97.1	95.6	94.6	93.4	73.2
2. Once	3.7	5.5	1.8	3.5	3.9	3.3	4.7	3.5	2.7	2.9	4.5	2.1	3.8	4.1	4.9	17.1
3. Twice	.7	.9	.4	.5	2.0	.7	.5	.6	.7	.5	.9	.4	.2	1.2	1.2	2.4
4. 3 or 4 times	.3	.6	.1	.3	.2	.2	.4	.5	-	.3	.4	.2	.2	-	.4	4.9
5. 5 or more times	.2	.2	.2	.1	-	.5	.2	.1	.2	.1	.3	.1	.1	-	.2	4.9
Item 6710 N(Wtd)	3605	1746	1754	2748	457	858	1095	1099	553	1924	1451	1213	841	484	954	41
A20E: Has someone threatened you with a weapon, but not actually injured you?																
1. Not at all	82.1	74.8	89.9	83.8	75.6	81.9	82.8	80.2	85.0	85.8	78.4	87.7	83.0	82.1	76.0	58.5
2. Once	12.1	16.5	7.2	10.6	16.8	12.0	11.1	14.0	10.3	9.8	14.6	9.4	12.6	12.0	14.1	17.1
3. Twice	3.3	4.8	1.8	3.0	5.4	3.0	3.4	3.6	2.9	2.3	4.1	1.3	3.0	3.5	6.0	7.3
4. 3 or 4 times	1.4	2.1	.6	1.5	1.1	1.9	1.5	1.2	.9	1.2	1.4	.6	1.0	2.3	2.2	7.3
5. 5 or more times	1.1	1.8	.5	1.1	1.1	1.3	1.4	.9	.9	.8	1.4	1.0	.6	.4	1.8	9.8
Item 6720 N(Wtd)	3600	1743	1753	2743	459	857	1093	1098	552	1920	1450	1212	839	485	953	41
A20F: Has someone injured you on purpose without using a weapon?																
1. Not at all	85.7	84.4	87.1	85.8	87.4	83.8	84.6	88.1	86.6	87.5	83.9	90.6	88.7	85.2	78.4	65.9
2. Once	8.9	9.9	7.6	8.7	8.7	10.5	8.9	7.6	8.9	8.1	9.4	6.3	7.9	10.3	11.8	17.1
3. Twice	2.8	3.3	2.5	2.8	3.1	2.7	4.0	1.9	2.5	2.3	3.4	1.8	1.5	2.9	5.0	7.3
4. 3 or 4 times	1.5	1.4	1.5	1.5	.9	1.4	1.2	1.8	1.6	1.4	1.8	.7	1.3	1.0	2.6	9.8
5. 5 or more times	1.1	1.0	1.3	1.2	.2	1.7	1.3	.7	.5	.7	1.5	.7	.6	.6	2.3	2.4
Item 6730 N(Wtd)	3602	1745	1753	2744	459	858	1094	1097	552	1922	1450	1212	840	485	953	41
A20G: Has an unarmed person threatened you with injury, but not actually injured you?																
1. Not at all	72.4	64.8	79.7	71.0	75.8	70.0	71.1	73.7	75.9	74.5	69.3	80.1	75.0	68.6	62.3	53.7
2. Once	13.0	14.9	11.2	13.1	13.5	13.8	12.1	12.9	13.6	11.6	15.2	10.3	11.1	15.9	17.0	12.2
3. Twice	6.5	8.8	4.2	7.1	3.9	6.5	7.9	5.7	5.3	6.4	6.5	3.8	6.7	7.4	9.3	14.6
4. 3 or 4 times	4.0	5.3	2.7	4.3	3.1	4.8	4.5	3.8	1.8	3.8	4.4	3.2	3.2	3.7	5.5	4.9
5. 5 or more times	4.2	6.3	2.2	4.5	3.7	4.8	4.5	3.8	3.4	3.7	4.7	2.6	4.0	4.3	5.9	14.6
Item 6740 N(Wtd)	3603	1746	1755	2748	458	858	1095	1097	552	1923	1450	1212	841	484	954	41

QUESTIONNAIRE FORM 2 1981	TOTAL	SEX		RACE		REGION				4YR COLLEGE PLANS		ILLICIT DRUG USE: LIFETIME				
		M	F	White	Black	NE	NC	S	W	Yes	No	None	Mari-juana Only	Few Pills	More Pills	Any Her-oin
Weighted No. of Cases:	3655	1762	1762	2761	467	869	1102	1117	567	1937	1462	1219	846	487	958	41
% of Weighted Total:	100.0	48.2	48.2	75.5	12.8	23.8	30.1	30.6	15.5	53.0	40.0	33.4	23.2	13.3	26.2	1.1

A21: The following questions concern cigarettes, alcohol, and a number of other drugs. How difficult do you think it would be for you to get each of the following types of drugs, if you wanted some?

A21A: Marijuana (pot, grass)

	TOTAL	M	F	White	Black	NE	NC	S	W	Yes	No	None	Mari-juana Only	Few Pills	More Pills	Any Her-oin
1. Probably impossible	5.1	4.1	5.7	2.1	17.3	1.4	3.4	9.4	5.4	3.9	5.7	11.7	1.9	1.2	.9	7.3
2. Very difficult	2.0	1.7	2.4	1.1	5.0	.9	2.0	2.9	2.0	2.1	1.9	4.2	.7	1.7	.3	2.4
3. Fairly difficult	3.7	3.5	3.7	3.6	3.3	1.9	4.1	4.4	3.8	3.8	3.5	5.4	3.2	3.9	1.3	2.4
4. Fairly easy	25.0	23.8	26.4	26.2	20.1	20.0	26.0	29.2	22.1	25.9	24.9	33.3	26.0	22.5	15.7	2.4
5. Very easy	64.3	66.9	61.7	67.1	54.3	75.7	64.4	54.0	66.7	64.2	64.1	45.4	68.1	70.7	81.7	87.8
Item 6750 N(Wtd)	3578	1736	1740	2728	457	849	1086	1092	552	1913	1436	1198	841	484	953	41

A21B: LSD

	TOTAL	M	F	White	Black	NE	NC	S	W	Yes	No	None	Mari-juana Only	Few Pills	More Pills	Any Her-oin
1. Probably impossible	18.9	16.7	20.7	12.9	43.2	12.0	16.2	26.9	19.0	14.9	22.2	24.1	20.8	20.4	9.4	9.8
2. Very difficult	17.0	17.5	16.2	16.3	19.8	14.8	16.0	19.6	16.9	18.3	15.1	16.2	21.9	18.3	12.8	12.2
3. Fairly difficult	29.1	29.8	28.5	31.7	16.5	31.5	31.5	25.3	28.2	29.9	29.3	28.0	28.8	28.5	30.8	39.0
4. Fairly easy	26.2	25.5	27.4	30.4	11.6	30.3	27.3	22.2	25.8	29.2	23.4	24.5	23.5	27.5	31.0	22.0
5. Very easy	8.9	10.5	7.2	8.7	8.9	11.4	9.0	6.1	10.1	7.7	10.1	7.3	5.1	5.2	15.9	19.5
Item 6760 N(Wtd)	3527	1713	1717	2691	449	833	1071	1080	543	1879	1429	1176	831	480	942	41

A21C: Some other psychedelic(mescaline, peyote, psilocybin, PCP, etc.)

	TOTAL	M	F	White	Black	NE	NC	S	W	Yes	No	None	Mari-juana Only	Few Pills	More Pills	Any Her-oin
1. Probably impossible	22.4	19.1	25.1	16.6	49.1	13.0	19.1	33.1	22.2	18.0	26.8	27.8	25.7	21.6	12.5	7.3
2. Very difficult	19.8	19.4	20.0	19.8	19.6	18.5	20.3	19.9	20.7	20.8	18.4	20.9	22.4	19.3	16.2	19.5
3. Fairly difficult	25.0	26.3	24.0	27.9	11.5	24.3	26.8	23.1	26.4	27.2	23.2	24.6	25.1	25.8	25.8	22.0
4. Fairly easy	24.5	25.3	24.1	27.4	13.1	30.1	26.4	19.6	21.6	26.2	23.3	20.8	20.4	27.0	32.2	26.8
5. Very easy	8.3	9.9	6.8	8.4	6.5	14.0	7.4	4.3	9.1	7.7	8.3	6.0	6.3	6.3	13.1	26.8
Item 6770 N(Wtd)	3498	1704	1699	2677	444	828	1063	1067	541	1871	1415	1153	832	477	943	41

A21D: Amphetamines (uppers, pep pills, bennies, speed)

	TOTAL	M	F	White	Black	NE	NC	S	W	Yes	No	None	Mari-juana Only	Few Pills	More Pills	Any Her-oin
1. Probably impossible	10.9	8.5	12.6	6.0	31.3	6.4	7.6	16.6	13.4	8.5	12.6	18.6	11.8	6.8	2.2	4.9
2. Very difficult	6.7	6.9	6.6	5.4	14.0	4.0	5.6	10.3	5.5	7.6	5.2	8.6	9.0	6.2	2.0	9.8
3. Fairly difficult	13.0	14.5	11.7	13.3	12.0	12.6	13.5	12.3	13.7	14.4	11.8	17.3	15.5	13.9	5.1	4.9
4. Fairly easy	36.2	37.2	35.1	38.8	23.5	38.1	37.6	33.0	36.6	38.0	34.9	35.9	39.3	38.2	33.7	19.5
5. Very easy	33.3	33.0	34.1	36.4	19.3	39.0	35.7	27.9	30.8	31.5	35.5	19.6	24.5	35.1	56.9	61.0
Item 6780 N(Wtd)	3544	1723	1724	2708	451	834	1085	1080	546	1895	1432	1174	840	482	952	41

A21E: Barbiturates (downers, goofballs, reds, yellows, etc.)

	TOTAL	M	F	White	Black	NE	NC	S	W	Yes	No	None	Mari-juana Only	Few Pills	More Pills	Any Her-oin
1. Probably impossible	14.4	11.1	16.8	8.8	37.1	8.3	11.5	21.0	16.2	11.0	17.3	21.5	16.2	10.8	4.6	7.3
2. Very difficult	11.0	12.0	9.9	10.0	15.0	10.2	10.1	12.9	10.1	11.7	9.5	11.5	12.6	11.6	8.3	14.6
3. Fairly difficult	19.8	21.3	18.1	21.7	12.6	20.9	20.6	15.6	24.6	21.5	18.1	18.3	21.6	21.8	20.1	4.9
4. Fairly easy	33.1	34.4	32.2	35.9	21.2	36.3	34.5	30.0	31.4	35.6	31.4	32.8	33.0	33.5	34.5	24.4
5. Very easy	21.8	21.2	23.0	23.6	14.1	24.2	23.2	20.6	17.8	20.3	23.6	16.1	16.7	22.0	32.6	48.8
Item 6790 N(Wtd)	3531	1716	1718	2697	453	832	1076	1079	544	1887	1425	1170	834	481	949	41

A21F: Tranquilizers

	TOTAL	M	F	White	Black	NE	NC	S	W	Yes	No	None	Mari-juana Only	Few Pills	More Pills	Any Her-oin
1. Probably impossible	11.3	9.8	12.0	6.0	32.7	7.1	8.1	16.9	13.1	7.9	14.2	16.4	11.9	8.0	4.8	7.3
2. Very difficult	9.6	10.9	8.4	8.3	15.4	7.7	10.4	10.5	9.2	9.4	9.7	9.2	10.0	10.5	9.3	7.3
3. Fairly difficult	18.3	19.4	17.1	19.4	12.1	20.9	17.7	17.1	17.7	18.1	18.3	13.4	19.8	21.0	22.0	17.1
4. Fairly easy	32.4	33.5	31.6	35.8	18.6	33.1	35.7	29.5	30.6	34.8	30.9	33.3	33.9	30.4	31.8	22.0
5. Very easy	28.4	26.3	30.9	30.5	21.3	31.2	28.2	25.9	29.3	29.8	26.9	27.7	24.3	30.2	32.1	48.8
Item 6800 N(Wtd)	3526	1714	1716	2701	447	829	1078	1076	542	1888	1421	1175	837	477	943	41

QUESTIONNAIRE FORM 2 1981	TOTAL	SEX		RACE		REGION				4YR COLLEGE PLANS		ILLICIT DRUG USE: LIFETIME				
		M	F	White	Black	NE	NC	S	W	Yes	No	None	Marijuana Only	Few Pills	More Pills	Any Heroin
Weighted No. of Cases:	3655	1762	1762	2761	467	869	1102	1117	567	1937	1462	1219	846	487	958	41
% of Weighted Total:	100.0	48.2	48.2	75.5	12.8	23.8	30.1	30.6	15.5	53.0	40.0	33.4	23.2	13.3	26.2	1.1
A21G: Cocaine																
1. Probably impossible	15.7	13.4	17.3	10.8	36.0	7.7	15.0	23.9	12.7	11.5	19.8	24.0	17.0	12.3	5.2	7.3
2. Very difficult	14.2	15.1	13.3	14.1	15.2	9.8	16.4	17.5	10.1	14.6	13.9	17.1	14.6	15.2	9.7	7.3
3. Fairly difficult	22.6	22.5	22.9	24.8	14.1	23.6	26.6	20.6	16.8	25.2	19.9	24.6	25.7	19.2	20.0	9.8
4. Fairly easy	28.2	29.2	27.4	31.0	17.0	30.5	29.0	25.1	29.0	29.1	28.3	23.3	26.9	34.0	32.9	41.5
5. Very easy	19.4	19.6	19.1	19.2	17.9	28.3	12.8	12.9	31.4	19.6	18.1	11.0	15.8	19.4	32.4	34.1
Item 6810 N(Wtd)	3509	1703	1709	2682	447	827	1070	1070	542	1877	1416	1156	833	480	942	41
A21H: Heroin (smack, horse)																
1. Probably impossible	29.3	27.6	30.0	24.5	47.3	22.4	28.0	35.9	29.4	24.3	34.4	31.5	28.1	30.3	26.9	9.8
2. Very difficult	27.1	28.8	25.8	28.7	21.2	29.5	25.4	26.1	28.7	29.2	24.4	23.1	28.4	27.6	31.6	19.5
3. Fairly difficult	24.4	24.4	24.8	27.6	11.5	26.3	28.0	20.4	22.5	25.9	23.6	23.4	25.4	25.1	24.4	34.1
4. Fairly easy	13.5	13.1	14.2	14.3	10.8	13.0	13.8	13.1	14.5	15.3	11.8	16.3	12.8	12.5	11.5	19.5
5. Very easy	5.6	6.1	5.2	4.9	9.2	8.8	4.8	4.5	4.8	5.4	5.7	5.7	5.3	4.4	5.8	19.5
Item 6820 N(Wtd)	3487	1697	1695	2669	444	821	1069	1061	537	1868	1412	1149	830	479	934	41
A21I: Some other narcotic (methadone, opium, codeine, paregoric, etc.)																
1. Probably impossible	22.2	19.0	24.6	16.4	46.7	15.8	19.3	30.5	20.7	18.8	25.3	28.4	24.6	23.6	11.1	7.3
2. Very difficult	22.4	24.3	20.7	23.5	18.7	19.5	25.7	21.6	22.0	23.8	21.4	21.5	24.6	20.3	23.0	14.6
3. Fairly difficult	25.8	26.9	24.6	28.7	14.6	29.9	25.7	23.0	25.2	27.2	24.8	23.8	27.0	25.9	27.7	26.8
4. Fairly easy	20.0	19.4	21.0	21.9	11.7	22.1	20.4	17.3	21.3	21.3	18.5	18.3	17.2	22.2	23.8	19.5
5. Very easy	9.6	10.4	9.1	9.6	8.1	12.6	8.9	7.5	10.6	8.9	10.0	7.9	6.5	7.7	14.6	34.1
Item 6830 N(Wtd)	3495	1704	1696	2677	445	824	1064	1072	536	1872	1413	1151	830	478	940	41

This section asks for your views and feelings about a number of different things.

D01: How satisfied are you with your life as a whole these days?

	TOTAL	M	F	White	Black	NE	NC	S	W	Yes	No	None	Marijuana Only	Few Pills	More Pills	Any Heroin
1. Completely dissatisfied	2.7	2.8	2.4	2.2	5.6	2.6	2.7	3.4	1.7	2.1	3.7	3.0	2.6	2.2	2.1	7.3
2. Quite dissatisfied	9.8	9.5	10.4	10.1	9.0	10.1	8.0	10.6	11.6	9.6	9.7	9.1	10.4	12.1	9.1	2.4
3. Somewhat dissatisfied	10.9	11.1	10.6	10.4	12.2	11.5	12.3	9.8	9.8	10.4	11.7	9.6	9.9	11.2	13.3	9.8
4. Neither, or mixed feelings	12.5	12.1	12.7	11.8	13.9	13.2	11.9	12.1	13.3	10.8	14.5	8.7	12.2	13.4	16.8	14.6
5. Somewhat satisfied	23.7	25.7	22.0	24.0	23.7	24.1	22.3	23.8	25.9	24.2	23.0	22.9	22.9	26.2	24.0	29.3
6. Quite satisfied	33.4	32.3	34.8	35.4	26.8	34.0	35.9	33.0	28.5	36.3	29.9	36.9	35.6	30.0	29.9	29.3
7. Completely satisfied	6.9	6.5	7.1	6.2	8.8	4.6	7.0	7.3	9.2	6.6	7.5	9.7	6.3	4.7	4.9	2.4
Item 6840 N(Wtd)	3409	1651	1694	2663	410	759	1071	1046	533	1895	1403	1162	809	447	904	41

D02: These next questions ask you to guess how well you might do in several different situations. How good do you think you would be...

D02A: As a husband or wife?

	TOTAL	M	F	White	Black	NE	NC	S	W	Yes	No	None	Marijuana Only	Few Pills	More Pills	Any Heroin
1. Poor	.7	1.0	.4	.7	1.0	.7	.4	1.0	.8	.3	1.1	.6	.6	.9	.4	-
2. Not so good	1.8	1.7	1.8	1.7	2.2	2.2	2.1	1.4	1.3	1.8	1.6	1.1	2.2	1.8	1.9	5.0
3. Fairly good	10.1	10.9	9.1	9.8	11.8	9.7	11.0	10.4	7.9	8.1	13.0	10.0	8.2	11.0	11.9	10.0
4. Good	35.3	39.1	31.9	36.7	24.0	34.4	39.3	31.8	35.7	35.4	35.5	34.7	36.4	39.0	33.2	32.5
5. Very good	47.9	43.1	52.7	47.7	54.9	48.7	43.9	50.7	49.4	50.3	44.5	49.8	48.1	45.7	46.9	50.0
8. Don't know	4.2	4.2	4.2	3.6	6.1	4.2	3.4	4.6	5.1	4.2	4.3	3.8	4.5	1.6	5.5	2.5
Item 6850 N(Wtd)	3405	1644	1699	2664	408	759	1069	1047	530	1896	1399	1162	807	446	904	40

D02B: As a parent?

	TOTAL	M	F	White	Black	NE	NC	S	W	Yes	No	None	Marijuana Only	Few Pills	More Pills	Any Heroin
1. Poor	1.3	1.8	.8	1.4	1.2	1.7	.8	1.6	1.1	1.0	1.6	.8	1.6	1.8	1.2	2.5
2. Not so good	3.3	2.9	3.6	3.2	3.2	2.8	3.4	3.8	2.6	2.5	4.4	3.4	2.7	2.9	3.6	7.5
3. Fairly good	9.2	10.4	7.9	9.4	8.4	6.7	10.3	9.4	10.2	8.8	9.9	10.0	8.7	9.2	8.8	12.5
4. Good	34.4	37.7	31.2	36.4	19.7	35.8	37.2	30.8	33.6	34.2	34.7	32.3	35.0	36.9	35.6	37.5
5. Very good	46.3	41.5	51.3	44.0	63.1	47.6	42.7	49.4	45.5	48.4	43.5	49.6	46.3	43.7	44.1	35.0
8. Don't know	5.5	5.8	5.1	5.4	4.4	5.2	5.6	4.8	7.0	5.2	5.8	3.9	5.7	5.2	6.7	7.5
Item 6860 N(Wtd)	3393	1633	1697	2657	406	756	1065	1042	530	1892	1394	1161	805	444	898	40

QUESTIONNAIRE FORM 2 1981	TOTAL	SEX		RACE		REGION				4YR COLLEGE PLANS		ILLICIT DRUG USE: LIFETIME				
		M	F	White	Black	NE	NC	S	W	Yes	No	None	Mari-juana Only	Few Pills	More Pills	Any Her-oin
Weighted No. of Cases:	3655	1762	1762	2761	467	869	1102	1117	567	1937	1462	1219	846	487	958	41
% of Weighted Total:	100.0	48.2	48.2	75.5	12.8	23.8	30.1	30.6	15.5	53.0	40.0	33.4	23.2	13.3	26.2	1.1

D02C: As a worker on a job?

1. Poor	.5	.9	.1	.6	.2	.1	.8	.5	.4	.3	.8	.6	.6	.2	.2	2.4
2. Not so good	.4	.4	.5	.5	.5	.7	.6	.4	-	.3	.7	.3	.6	.2	.4	-
3. Fairly good	4.6	4.1	5.1	4.9	3.2	3.7	5.9	3.9	4.5	3.4	5.7	3.5	3.4	9.6	4.2	17.1
4. Good	30.2	30.0	30.3	31.7	21.7	26.4	33.2	30.2	29.8	28.2	33.0	30.4	28.3	32.3	31.0	22.0
5. Very good	63.5	63.8	63.4	61.9	72.9	68.2	58.9	64.1	64.7	67.2	58.3	64.9	66.2	56.7	63.3	56.1
8. Don't know	.8	.8	.7	.6	1.5	.8	.7	1.0	.6	.6	1.1	.4	1.0	.7	.7	2.4
Item 6870 N(Wtd)	3394	1636	1695	2657	406	758	1066	1041	530	1890	1397	1159	805	446	899	41

D03: Some people think a lot about the social problems of the nation and the world, and about how they might be solved. Others spend little time thinking about these issues. How much do you think about such things?

1. Never	4.1	5.6	2.6	3.6	3.5	4.3	4.2	4.3	3.0	2.2	6.2	4.9	2.8	4.3	3.0	15.0
2. Seldom	20.8	19.5	22.1	21.3	19.8	22.2	18.5	21.6	21.5	16.8	26.7	19.9	21.0	23.0	20.0	27.5
3. Sometimes	45.9	44.9	46.7	46.6	39.8	43.5	48.9	43.6	47.6	45.9	46.1	43.1	48.6	43.9	48.4	42.5
4. Quite often	22.9	23.2	22.5	22.2	30.3	22.5	22.0	24.6	21.7	26.2	18.2	24.0	23.0	23.4	22.0	10.0
5. A great deal	6.5	6.9	6.2	6.3	6.8	7.3	6.5	6.0	6.1	9.0	2.8	8.1	4.9	5.2	6.5	5.0
Item 6880 N(Wtd)	3375	1630	1682	2642	400	751	1065	1033	525	1884	1381	1154	797	444	896	40

D04: Now we'd like you to make some ratings of how honest and moral the people are who run the following organizations. To what extent are there problems of dishonesty and immorality in the leadership of...

D04A: Large corporations?

1. Not at all	3.8	5.1	2.5	2.8	6.1	3.6	4.6	3.6	3.1	2.3	5.9	4.1	3.2	3.5	3.3	7.3
2. Slight	14.5	16.6	12.5	14.5	16.1	14.9	13.2	15.7	14.6	13.7	15.6	14.6	17.4	14.3	11.5	29.3
3. Moderate	33.0	33.3	32.9	35.2	25.3	33.4	33.5	32.1	32.7	34.0	32.1	34.2	32.1	32.1	33.2	22.0
4. Considerable	26.2	25.9	26.3	27.2	24.2	26.4	26.0	27.2	24.4	31.2	20.2	27.4	25.1	27.0	26.6	17.1
5. Great	9.0	9.4	8.4	8.7	9.2	11.0	9.2	7.6	8.8	8.9	8.7	7.6	9.0	8.3	10.7	17.1
8. No opinion	13.5	9.6	17.3	11.6	19.1	10.9	13.6	13.8	16.4	9.8	17.5	12.0	13.1	14.8	14.5	7.3
Item 6890 N(Wtd)	3311	1600	1652	2597	392	727	1053	1018	513	1858	1349	1140	781	433	876	41

D04B: Major labor unions?

1. Not at all	4.1	4.9	3.4	3.2	7.4	3.6	3.3	5.8	3.1	2.4	6.4	4.6	4.4	1.9	4.2	4.9
2. Slight	16.3	16.9	15.4	16.4	19.1	16.2	15.4	17.6	15.6	16.6	16.0	15.8	17.2	17.9	15.1	22.0
3. Moderate	31.8	31.5	32.4	33.0	26.5	31.8	33.2	29.8	32.9	32.8	31.3	33.0	30.8	34.5	30.3	29.3
4. Considerable	20.9	23.1	18.7	22.1	16.1	21.5	20.5	21.7	19.1	23.1	17.6	21.8	19.9	18.9	22.7	9.8
5. Great	9.0	11.3	6.8	9.1	7.4	11.0	9.9	7.0	7.8	10.6	6.6	9.6	7.8	9.3	8.7	19.5
8. No opinion	17.9	12.4	23.4	16.0	23.7	16.0	17.6	17.9	21.4	14.3	22.1	15.3	19.9	17.5	19.2	12.2
Item 6900 N(Wtd)	3304	1599	1646	2594	392	724	1051	1016	513	1856	1344	1140	778	429	876	41

D04C: The nation's colleges and universities?

1. Not at all	8.2	8.7	7.8	7.7	8.7	8.2	8.2	8.7	7.0	6.9	10.1	7.8	8.6	8.4	7.8	17.5
2. Slight	34.5	34.5	34.7	37.1	24.4	37.3	34.1	34.0	32.2	40.2	27.3	34.4	36.7	33.6	33.7	32.5
3. Moderate	25.4	26.0	24.9	26.9	21.3	27.4	25.8	23.6	25.0	26.3	24.5	28.3	21.5	25.2	25.7	20.0
4. Considerable	13.3	14.0	12.4	11.8	20.6	12.8	12.5	14.4	13.4	13.5	13.0	12.6	14.6	15.9	11.6	15.0
5. Great	5.3	6.2	4.1	4.6	8.2	3.3	4.1	6.6	7.8	5.0	5.1	6.2	4.1	4.0	5.4	5.0
8. No opinion	13.4	10.7	16.0	12.0	16.7	11.0	15.3	12.6	14.6	8.2	20.1	10.8	14.4	12.6	15.9	10.0
Item 6910 N(Wtd)	3301	1593	1650	2591	389	729	1044	1014	515	1855	1341	1138	780	428	873	40

D04D: The nation's public schools?

1. Not at all	8.0	8.7	7.2	7.7	6.7	8.9	7.5	7.7	8.8	7.6	8.9	8.2	9.3	7.2	7.1	5.0
2. Slight	32.0	32.6	31.6	33.7	27.6	34.7	33.6	29.2	30.2	37.1	25.7	33.9	34.6	31.2	28.5	20.0
3. Moderate	26.4	25.9	27.3	27.6	22.5	28.3	25.3	26.4	25.9	26.6	26.1	26.9	25.2	24.2	28.4	27.5
4. Considerable	16.2	16.1	16.0	15.6	18.9	13.8	16.8	18.1	14.4	15.4	16.7	15.6	15.4	19.1	16.3	20.0
5. Great	7.4	8.2	6.7	6.5	12.7	5.9	6.4	9.0	8.8	7.0	8.2	7.8	4.9	6.7	8.6	20.0
8. No opinion	10.0	8.5	11.2	8.9	11.6	8.4	10.3	9.7	12.3	6.3	14.4	7.7	10.8	11.4	11.0	7.5
Item 6920 N(Wtd)	3292	1588	1646	2584	387	727	1039	1012	514	1854	1333	1135	775	430	870	40

QUESTIONNAIRE FORM 2 1981	TOTAL	SEX		RACE		REGION				4YR COLLEGE PLANS		ILLICIT DRUG USE: LIFETIME				
		M	F	White	Black	NE	NC	S	W	Yes	No	None	Mari- juana Only	Few Pills	More Pills	Any Her- oin
Weighted No. of Cases:	3655	1762	1762	2761	467	869	1102	1117	567	1937	1462	1219	846	487	958	41
% of Weighted Total:	100.0	48.2	48.2	75.5	12.8	23.8	30.1	30.6	15.5	53.0	40.0	33.4	23.2	13.3	26.2	1.1

D04E: Churches and religious organizations?

1. Not at all	20.5	20.3	20.6	21.3	14.2	23.5	20.4	20.2	17.0	20.3	21.0	21.5	21.6	20.9	17.4	22.0
2. Slight	34.4	35.7	33.6	37.6	21.2	35.1	37.7	30.9	33.8	39.1	28.6	37.4	34.4	34.1	32.1	24.4
3. Moderate	14.2	14.4	14.1	13.5	17.4	13.7	13.1	14.4	16.4	15.3	12.5	13.5	15.0	11.4	15.6	19.5
4. Considerable	9.8	10.0	9.3	9.1	13.7	9.7	9.4	9.9	10.2	8.6	11.2	9.4	7.2	10.2	12.4	9.8
5. Great	9.4	9.6	8.9	8.2	17.6	8.4	7.9	11.6	9.2	8.7	9.9	8.7	9.5	11.6	8.3	9.8
8. No opinion	11.8	10.1	13.5	10.4	15.8	9.7	11.5	13.0	13.3	7.9	16.8	9.4	12.3	12.3	14.1	12.2
Item 6930 N(Wtd)	3300	1589	1654	2594	386	729	1045	1014	512	1857	1337	1135	779	431	872	41

D04F: The national news media (TV, magazines, news services)?

1. Not at all	3.9	4.6	3.2	3.2	4.9	4.8	4.4	2.7	4.1	2.9	5.4	4.7	4.2	2.6	3.0	9.8
2. Slight	20.9	24.8	17.5	21.5	16.5	20.2	22.4	20.6	20.1	21.3	20.1	19.9	24.1	15.2	20.6	19.5
3. Moderate	28.1	29.4	27.1	29.5	26.9	30.6	24.4	29.3	29.9	30.7	24.6	30.3	27.3	26.5	27.0	22.0
4. Considerable	23.7	21.7	25.6	24.6	22.2	24.5	26.3	21.0	22.7	25.3	22.2	23.7	22.9	24.6	24.5	22.0
5. Great	13.5	12.5	14.2	12.8	14.0	11.8	13.8	14.4	13.3	13.9	13.4	13.4	11.4	17.6	13.0	14.6
8. No opinion	9.9	7.1	12.5	8.3	15.5	8.1	8.6	12.0	10.6	6.0	14.4	8.0	10.0	10.7	11.9	9.8
Item 6940 N(Wtd)	3297	1589	1650	2587	387	728	1043	1015	511	1853	1340	1137	780	431	866	41

D04G: The Presidency and the administration?

1. Not at all	5.1	6.0	4.1	4.0	9.3	3.4	4.5	6.3	6.5	4.8	5.9	5.6	6.8	4.4	3.4	5.3
2. Slight	24.7	29.2	20.7	26.2	15.5	26.7	26.1	22.6	23.2	27.4	21.7	27.0	24.3	23.1	23.8	18.4
3. Moderate	30.0	30.2	30.0	32.5	21.2	30.4	29.8	30.5	29.1	32.8	26.2	30.5	30.3	31.8	29.3	23.7
4. Considerable	18.2	16.7	19.9	17.8	21.8	19.0	18.6	17.8	16.9	18.5	17.5	17.3	17.0	16.8	21.0	23.7
5. Great	9.1	8.7	9.0	7.9	16.6	9.2	8.9	9.6	8.3	8.4	10.3	8.7	8.5	10.0	8.8	21.1
8. No opinion	12.8	9.2	16.4	11.5	15.3	11.3	12.1	13.2	15.9	8.2	18.4	10.8	13.2	13.8	13.9	10.5
Item 6950 N(Wtd)	3285	1577	1649	2580	386	727	1040	1011	508	1847	1335	1135	778	428	863	38

D04H: Congress--that is, the U.S. Senate and House of Representatives?

1. Not at all	3.8	4.4	3.2	2.8	5.7	3.7	3.3	4.2	4.5	2.4	5.7	2.7	5.3	4.2	3.4	5.3
2. Slight	20.7	23.7	18.1	21.4	16.9	20.6	21.8	18.7	22.4	22.2	19.1	20.6	20.7	21.6	20.9	18.4
3. Moderate	29.9	30.6	29.1	32.0	24.0	29.4	29.1	31.1	29.6	33.3	25.5	33.3	31.7	30.2	24.9	10.5
4. Considerable	21.4	21.8	21.4	21.7	20.6	23.9	21.7	21.1	17.8	22.5	19.8	20.8	18.1	19.5	25.6	31.6
5. Great	10.0	9.8	9.7	9.6	14.3	9.9	10.3	10.4	9.0	9.8	10.3	9.5	10.3	10.7	9.6	18.4
8. No opinion	14.2	9.7	18.4	12.5	18.2	12.7	13.9	14.5	16.7	9.8	19.6	13.1	13.9	13.9	15.5	13.2
Item 6960 N(Wtd)	3283	1580	1645	2576	384	725	1039	1009	510	1846	1335	1132	777	431	863	38

D04I: The U.S. Supreme Court?

1. Not at all	13.1	16.3	10.0	13.5	8.4	15.8	12.2	11.8	13.4	14.7	10.8	12.4	15.7	13.1	11.5	16.7
2. Slight	27.4	30.3	24.7	29.0	18.7	30.8	27.1	24.7	28.5	31.8	22.3	29.5	27.9	27.3	25.6	13.9
3. Moderate	22.1	21.5	23.0	23.2	20.8	18.5	23.5	22.5	23.5	22.0	22.4	23.4	20.4	20.7	22.9	13.9
4. Considerable	13.4	12.4	14.3	12.9	15.3	14.1	13.3	14.3	10.5	12.8	14.1	12.2	13.0	12.6	15.1	25.0
5. Great	6.6	6.9	6.1	6.0	12.4	6.2	6.6	7.7	5.1	6.4	6.8	6.4	5.7	8.6	6.7	8.3
8. No opinion	17.5	12.5	21.9	15.2	24.0	14.6	17.4	18.9	19.0	12.4	23.6	16.3	17.1	17.7	18.1	22.2
Item 6970 N(Wtd)	3253	1569	1627	2558	379	714	1035	999	506	1827	1324	1118	770	429	861	36

D04J: All the courts and the justice system in general?

1. Not at all	6.7	7.4	6.0	6.4	6.3	6.6	5.7	6.9	8.7	6.9	6.6	6.9	7.4	7.0	5.6	7.9
2. Slight	27.7	30.8	25.0	28.7	21.1	28.6	29.8	23.8	29.9	31.1	23.2	29.3	27.2	28.3	25.3	31.6
3. Moderate	28.0	28.0	28.0	29.9	21.8	26.6	27.9	29.2	27.8	29.2	26.9	30.1	28.0	25.0	28.0	13.2
4. Considerable	16.1	16.6	15.8	16.0	18.9	18.1	15.6	17.1	12.2	17.0	14.8	14.0	16.4	17.3	18.1	18.4
5. Great	6.1	5.5	6.3	5.8	10.3	7.8	5.4	6.4	4.9	5.9	6.5	5.9	5.1	6.8	6.8	10.5
8. No opinion	15.4	11.6	18.8	13.3	21.8	12.4	15.7	16.6	16.5	10.0	22.1	13.7	15.8	15.9	16.3	21.1
Item 6980 N(Wtd)	3261	1574	1630	2564	380	717	1033	1003	508	1833	1328	1128	768	428	858	38

QUESTIONNAIRE FORM 2 1981	TOTAL	SEX		RACE		REGION				4YR COLLEGE PLANS		ILLICIT DRUG USE: LIFETIME				
		M	F	White	Black	NE	NC	S	W	Yes	No	None	Mari-juana Only	Few Pills	More Pills	Any Her-oin
Weighted No. of Cases:	3655	1762	1762	2761	467	869	1102	1117	567	1937	1462	1219	846	487	958	41
% of Weighted Total:	100.0	48.2	48.2	75.5	12.8	23.8	30.1	30.6	15.5	53.0	40.0	33.4	23.2	13.3	26.2	1.1
D04K: The police and other law enforcement agencies?																
1. Not at all	4.8	4.6	4.9	4.0	7.0	4.0	4.5	5.6	4.5	3.8	6.0	5.2	4.8	4.9	3.7	7.9
2. Slight	23.6	24.8	22.6	24.6	16.7	24.0	25.5	20.0	26.4	24.5	23.0	25.4	25.6	22.5	20.0	15.8
3. Moderate	31.3	32.0	31.2	34.0	22.1	29.3	31.2	32.6	31.6	34.3	27.7	33.1	31.8	33.3	28.8	18.4
4. Considerable	20.1	20.3	19.9	19.9	22.7	23.5	19.2	20.2	17.2	21.4	18.2	18.4	18.3	21.8	23.0	31.6
5. Great	9.8	11.2	8.1	8.5	17.4	10.1	8.6	11.4	8.7	9.5	10.1	8.2	8.2	8.0	13.8	21.1
8. No opinion	10.4	7.2	13.3	9.0	14.1	9.0	10.9	10.2	11.4	6.5	14.9	9.5	11.4	9.6	10.8	5.3
Item 6990 N(Wtd)	3271	1576	1637	2571	384	720	1032	1012	507	1835	1333	1133	771	427	861	38
D04L: The U.S. military?																
1. Not at all	8.2	8.3	8.2	8.0	7.6	9.9	7.7	7.6	7.9	8.0	8.5	8.2	9.7	7.0	7.5	10.5
2. Slight	27.2	28.8	25.8	28.4	23.6	29.2	27.4	26.9	24.6	29.5	24.4	29.5	27.9	26.5	24.6	10.5
3. Moderate	25.9	28.3	23.7	28.0	19.4	24.4	26.5	26.2	25.8	28.1	23.6	26.7	26.6	26.1	25.0	15.8
4. Considerable	13.9	14.6	13.2	13.4	13.1	13.7	14.8	13.7	12.8	14.4	12.7	13.1	12.2	14.6	16.1	23.7
5. Great	6.9	8.3	5.3	5.8	12.3	6.8	6.0	6.4	9.6	6.8	6.8	5.9	6.1	7.0	7.5	26.3
8. No opinion	17.9	11.6	23.7	16.4	24.3	16.1	17.5	19.0	19.3	13.1	24.1	16.5	17.5	18.5	19.4	15.8
Item 7000 N(Wtd)	3264	1571	1635	2563	382	716	1033	1008	508	1830	1330	1131	771	426	859	38
D05: How much do you agree or disagree with each of the following statements?																
D05A: There is too much competition in this society																
1. Disagree	9.7	13.3	6.4	9.4	12.0	9.1	8.5	11.2	10.4	10.8	7.8	10.9	9.2	9.0	8.2	22.5
2. Mostly disagree	13.9	16.8	11.1	15.1	12.0	11.9	12.4	16.5	14.9	16.6	10.3	15.5	12.9	14.1	13.2	12.5
3. Neither	22.2	26.4	18.1	22.0	20.2	19.1	23.2	23.4	22.4	20.0	25.1	23.4	23.1	22.2	19.6	22.5
4. Mostly agree	33.2	27.8	38.5	34.1	29.3	36.7	35.1	29.6	31.1	33.3	33.4	29.6	34.1	33.6	37.6	20.0
5. Agree	21.0	15.8	25.9	19.4	26.3	23.3	20.8	19.3	21.1	19.3	23.5	20.7	20.9	20.8	21.4	22.5
Item 7010 N(Wtd)	3306	1586	1665	2592	392	724	1051	1013	517	1848	1353	1137	784	432	874	40
D05B: Too many young people are sloppy about their grooming and clothing, and just don't care how they look																
1. Disagree	14.3	15.0	13.8	13.5	17.6	16.2	13.7	13.9	13.5	14.3	14.8	11.3	13.6	13.0	18.7	30.0
2. Mostly disagree	29.6	30.6	28.9	31.6	18.6	31.0	31.6	25.9	30.9	32.3	25.5	28.7	30.2	29.0	30.1	37.5
3. Neither	20.3	22.7	18.0	21.1	14.8	19.9	22.2	17.6	22.4	20.2	20.9	19.8	21.4	20.4	20.7	5.0
4. Mostly agree	22.6	20.6	24.4	22.6	23.7	20.7	22.5	24.4	22.2	21.7	23.2	23.4	22.0	24.4	21.5	22.5
5. Agree	13.2	11.2	14.9	11.1	25.2	12.2	10.1	18.4	11.0	11.6	15.7	16.7	12.8	13.5	9.0	5.0
Item 7020 N(Wtd)	3312	1590	1666	2596	393	728	1049	1017	518	1851	1354	1141	786	431	876	40
D05C: There is too much hard rock music on the radio these days																
1. Disagree	42.9	49.1	37.1	45.5	30.9	53.4	43.5	38.1	36.5	42.7	43.6	27.9	45.6	41.4	60.1	67.5
2. Mostly disagree	20.9	19.7	22.3	22.0	13.3	21.8	21.9	19.8	19.5	23.4	17.2	22.4	20.8	22.1	18.4	15.0
3. Neither	18.4	16.5	20.0	17.5	25.3	15.1	20.2	18.5	18.9	17.8	18.7	24.2	17.5	17.2	13.2	2.5
4. Mostly agree	8.9	7.4	10.2	7.9	13.6	4.7	7.9	10.3	13.9	9.1	8.4	11.8	8.2	8.8	5.3	12.5
5. Agree	9.0	7.2	10.4	7.0	16.9	4.9	6.5	13.3	11.0	6.9	12.1	13.6	8.2	10.2	3.0	5.0
Item 7030 N(Wtd)	3309	1587	1665	2592	391	728	1047	1016	518	1851	1351	1139	785	430	874	40
D05D: People should do their own thing, even if other people think it's strange																
1. Disagree	3.0	3.6	2.2	2.0	6.2	3.3	1.7	4.1	2.7	2.4	3.6	4.1	3.0	1.4	1.8	4.9
2. Mostly disagree	6.5	7.0	6.0	6.8	5.4	4.7	6.5	7.4	7.4	6.9	6.1	8.8	4.9	5.3	5.2	7.3
3. Neither	12.4	12.1	12.5	12.3	10.1	9.6	13.7	12.8	13.2	11.4	13.5	13.5	13.2	14.6	9.3	14.6
4. Mostly agree	36.1	36.4	35.8	38.5	24.5	33.8	40.9	32.3	36.9	38.9	32.3	36.5	36.6	40.4	34.5	14.6
5. Agree	42.0	40.9	43.4	40.4	53.7	48.5	37.2	43.5	39.8	40.5	44.3	37.3	42.4	38.3	49.1	58.5
Item 7040 N(Wtd)	3287	1572	1658	2578	387	719	1043	1010	515	1835	1345	1130	779	431	867	41

QUESTIONNAIRE FORM 2 1981	TOTAL	SEX		RACE		REGION				4YR COLLEGE PLANS		ILLICIT DRUG USE: LIFETIME				
		M	F	White	Black	NE	NC	S	W	Yes	No	None	Mari-juana Only	Few Pills	More Pills	Any Her-oin
Weighted No. of Cases:	3655	1762	1762	2761	467	869	1102	1117	567	1937	1462	1219	846	487	958	41
% of Weighted Total:	100.0	48.2	48.2	75.5	12.8	23.8	30.1	30.6	15.5	53.0	40.0	33.4	23.2	13.3	26.2	1.1
D05E: I get a real kick out of doing things that are a little dangerous																
1. Disagree	23.8	15.1	32.1	20.6	42.3	18.6	21.8	30.3	22.0	21.1	26.9	32.1	23.1	18.4	16.8	9.8
2. Mostly disagree	22.8	19.2	26.6	23.4	21.1	22.0	23.1	22.2	24.7	26.1	18.9	26.0	20.6	24.2	20.7	12.2
3. Neither	25.5	27.4	23.7	26.3	17.3	30.0	27.5	21.8	22.6	26.7	24.0	22.5	24.4	30.5	27.7	34.1
4. Mostly agree	19.5	25.9	13.4	21.4	12.4	18.9	18.2	19.7	22.2	19.6	19.7	14.2	23.7	17.9	23.8	17.1
5. Agree	8.4	12.5	4.3	8.3	7.0	10.2	9.4	6.0	8.4	6.4	10.5	5.3	8.1	9.1	10.9	29.3
Item 7050 N(Wtd)	3275	1565	1653	2565	388	714	1042	1005	514	1832	1337	1126	775	430	863	41
D05F: I like to test myself every now and then by doing something a little risky																
1. Disagree	23.0	14.9	30.9	20.4	37.4	18.2	19.6	29.9	23.7	21.6	25.2	30.8	21.7	20.7	15.7	4.9
2. Mostly disagree	18.5	16.1	20.8	19.6	13.9	20.0	19.1	17.2	17.7	21.3	15.1	22.3	19.5	19.1	15.4	29.3
3. Neither	22.0	22.2	21.7	21.8	18.6	23.6	22.7	19.5	23.3	22.8	21.0	22.3	21.6	19.5	22.6	29.3
4. Mostly agree	24.1	29.9	18.5	26.1	17.0	23.6	26.7	21.5	24.7	24.9	23.0	17.9	25.7	29.8	28.4	22.0
5. Agree	12.4	16.8	8.0	12.0	13.4	14.5	12.1	12.0	10.9	9.4	15.8	10.1	11.4	11.2	15.0	39.0
Item 7060 N(Wtd)	3273	1561	1655	2565	388	715	1037	1005	515	1835	1332	1125	774	430	864	41
D06: How many of your friends would you estimate...																
D06A: Smoke cigarettes?																
1. None	11.5	12.6	10.2	10.9	9.4	9.2	9.9	9.6	21.6	13.0	9.4	19.0	10.0	9.2	3.9	9.8
2. A few	36.3	36.3	36.4	36.8	37.2	33.5	35.6	36.6	41.3	41.7	29.2	46.1	38.1	36.4	23.3	26.8
3. Some	29.7	32.2	27.4	31.0	26.6	31.9	29.4	31.8	23.2	30.9	28.2	24.0	31.5	34.8	32.8	34.1
4. Most	20.2	16.8	23.5	19.4	22.5	22.4	22.9	19.9	12.5	13.4	29.1	10.2	17.5	17.8	36.7	24.4
5. All	2.2	2.1	2.4	1.9	4.3	3.2	2.2	2.2	1.4	.9	4.1	.7	2.9	2.1	3.3	4.9
Item 7070 N(Wtd)	3307	1580	1671	2591	395	728	1044	1021	513	1846	1350	1127	782	437	877	41
D06B: Smoke marijuana (pot, grass) or hashish?																
1. None	17.0	16.1	18.0	17.1	14.9	10.5	18.2	20.0	17.8	17.3	17.0	34.5	9.8	11.2	3.6	4.9
2. A few	31.3	31.8	30.6	31.8	27.2	26.1	32.1	34.6	30.4	33.7	28.0	40.7	37.1	32.2	14.4	19.5
3. Some	24.1	23.4	24.8	24.7	23.6	26.4	22.4	22.9	22.8	24.9	22.8	18.4	28.4	29.5	25.1	24.4
4. Most	22.4	22.2	22.8	22.2	25.9	29.4	22.8	17.1	22.5	19.8	25.9	5.7	20.3	25.6	44.9	22.0
5. All	5.2	6.6	3.8	4.2	8.7	7.6	4.5	3.4	6.4	4.2	6.2	.7	4.2	1.6	12.1	29.3
Item 7080 N(Wtd)	3301	1580	1664	2588	390	724	1043	1017	516	1843	1349	1124	778	438	878	41
D06C: Take LSD?																
1. None	71.5	69.7	73.2	69.8	80.8	65.1	71.8	76.2	70.6	74.1	68.3	84.9	79.7	73.3	48.2	31.7
2. A few	20.1	20.1	20.0	21.6	14.4	23.0	19.0	18.4	21.4	19.6	20.8	12.4	17.0	22.3	30.7	36.6
3. Some	6.3	7.3	5.4	6.6	3.7	9.5	7.0	4.0	4.7	4.9	7.8	2.2	2.9	3.7	15.1	17.1
4. Most	1.6	2.1	1.2	1.6	.5	1.8	2.1	.6	2.1	1.1	2.2	.2	.1	.7	4.8	9.8
5. All	.5	.7	.4	.3	.8	.6	-	.8	1.4	.3	.9	.2	.3	-	1.1	4.9
Item 7090 N(Wtd)	3274	1566	1651	2574	381	723	1032	1006	513	1833	1336	1119	770	430	872	41
D06D: Take other psychedelics (mescaline, peyote, PCP, etc.)?																
1. None	73.7	71.1	76.3	72.2	81.3	60.7	74.8	80.5	76.5	75.9	71.0	88.0	80.4	74.9	50.9	24.4
2. A few	18.9	20.0	17.5	20.5	14.5	27.6	17.8	15.2	15.7	18.4	19.4	9.4	16.9	21.7	30.3	43.9
3. Some	5.4	6.1	4.8	5.4	3.4	8.5	5.4	3.5	4.9	4.2	7.0	2.4	1.9	3.2	13.2	17.1
4. Most	1.6	2.0	1.2	1.6	.8	2.5	1.5	.5	2.2	1.3	1.7	.1	.5	.2	4.6	9.8
5. All	.5	.8	.2	.3	.3	.7	.5	.2	.8	.3	.8	.1	.3	-	1.1	4.9
Item 7100 N(Wtd)	3276	1567	1655	2573	386	720	1038	1006	511	1828	1340	1115	774	434	871	41

QUESTIONNAIRE FORM 2 1981	TOTAL	SEX		RACE		REGION				4YR COLLEGE PLANS		ILLICIT DRUG USE: LIFETIME				
		M	F	White	Black	NE	NC	S	W	Yes	No	None	Marijuana Only	Few Pills	More Pills	Any Heroin
Weighted No. of Cases:	3655	1762	1762	2761	467	869	1102	1117	567	1937	1462	1219	846	487	958	41
% of Weighted Total:	100.0	48.2	48.2	75.5	12.8	23.8	30.1	30.6	15.5	53.0	40.0	33.4	23.2	13.3	26.2	1.1
D06E: Take amphetamines (uppers, pep pills, bennies, speed)?																
1. None	51.2	51.9	50.4	47.1	72.8	45.4	48.2	57.2	53.9	54.7	46.3	75.4	61.9	42.3	16.0	12.2
2. A few	29.7	28.3	31.2	32.5	17.9	31.9	30.7	28.3	27.1	30.9	29.0	20.4	29.7	43.9	34.3	41.5
3. Some	12.8	13.7	11.8	13.6	6.5	14.0	13.2	10.7	13.9	10.5	15.2	3.6	6.3	11.5	30.8	22.0
4. Most	5.1	4.7	5.7	5.7	2.1	6.9	6.8	2.8	3.7	3.3	7.2	.4	1.8	2.1	15.4	14.6
5. All	1.3	1.4	1.0	1.1	.8	1.8	1.1	1.0	1.6	.6	2.2	.2	.3	.5	3.3	12.2
Item 7110　N(Wtd)	3278	1564	1657	2571	386	724	1038	1006	510	1831	1338	1116	772	435	874	41
D06F: Take quaaludes (quads, methaqualone)?																
1. None	65.0	60.9	69.0	62.4	79.5	59.7	67.7	63.2	70.6	67.9	61.3	82.2	71.2	66.7	38.1	22.0
2. A few	23.0	25.9	20.2	25.0	14.8	26.9	21.0	23.0	21.6	23.7	22.3	13.9	24.4	25.4	32.2	29.3
3. Some	8.4	9.1	7.6	8.7	3.9	9.5	8.1	9.5	5.3	6.4	10.7	3.4	3.6	6.7	19.5	22.0
4. Most	2.8	3.1	2.6	3.0	.8	3.4	2.5	3.1	2.2	1.6	4.3	.2	.5	.7	8.6	17.1
5. All	.9	1.0	.7	.8	1.0	.6	.8	1.3	.6	.4	1.3	.3	.3	.7	1.6	7.3
Item 7120　N(Wtd)	3277	1566	1654	2572	385	725	1037	1005	510	1830	1338	1115	772	433	875	41
D06G: Take barbiturates (downers, goofballs, reds, yellows, etc.)?																
1. None	68.9	66.1	71.5	67.2	79.6	65.3	69.0	69.8	71.7	72.4	64.2	82.6	75.8	69.0	46.3	30.0
2. A few	23.1	25.5	20.8	25.0	14.9	25.4	23.6	22.2	20.7	22.2	24.4	13.9	21.2	24.1	35.6	42.5
3. Some	5.8	6.3	5.6	5.6	4.4	7.1	5.6	5.3	5.9	4.3	7.8	3.0	2.6	5.7	12.2	17.5
4. Most	1.6	1.5	1.7	1.7	.5	1.9	1.6	1.8	1.0	.8	2.8	.3	.1	.9	4.8	7.5
5. All	.6	.6	.4	.5	.8	.3	.2	.9	.8	.3	.8	.3	.3	.2	1.0	2.5
Item 7130　N(Wtd)	3270	1562	1651	2568	383	723	1035	1004	508	1825	1337	1113	769	435	872	40
D06H: Take tranquilizers?																
1. None	70.5	69.3	71.4	69.0	78.2	69.3	71.3	70.0	71.2	72.2	68.0	78.8	77.4	70.0	55.0	29.3
2. A few	22.8	22.6	23.2	24.7	16.6	22.4	22.9	23.2	22.2	22.7	23.4	17.3	19.1	25.3	31.6	43.9
3. Some	5.3	6.3	4.5	5.1	3.6	6.4	4.4	5.6	5.3	4.3	6.7	3.3	2.9	4.4	10.2	19.5
4. Most	1.0	1.1	.9	.9	1.0	1.5	1.1	.9	.4	.7	1.6	.4	.3	.5	2.5	4.9
5. All	.4	.6	.1	.3	.3	.4	.2	.3	1.0	.2	.4	.1	.3	-	.8	2.4
Item 7140　N(Wtd)	3273	1564	1652	2569	385	723	1035	1005	510	1827	1338	1114	771	434	873	41
D06I: Take cocaine?																
1. None	59.9	57.4	62.4	58.2	72.5	49.2	64.2	68.4	49.4	61.6	58.2	82.4	68.9	55.1	27.6	12.2
2. A few	23.5	24.7	22.7	25.2	17.3	28.6	22.4	21.0	23.9	23.6	23.6	13.6	25.0	28.6	32.4	26.8
3. Some	10.3	11.3	9.1	10.1	6.8	13.3	9.6	7.2	13.5	9.7	10.7	3.3	5.2	12.2	21.9	29.3
4. Most	4.7	4.6	4.6	4.9	2.6	6.5	3.2	2.5	9.2	4.0	5.2	.5	.6	2.8	13.7	24.4
5. All	1.6	2.0	1.1	1.5	1.0	2.4	.5	1.0	3.9	1.1	2.2	.3	.3	1.2	4.3	4.9
Item 7150　N(Wtd)	3270	1562	1651	2567	382	723	1036	1001	510	1827	1334	1107	772	434	876	41
D06J: Take heroin (smack, horse)?																
1. None	87.5	87.6	87.2	87.5	88.3	85.8	87.7	88.0	88.0	88.5	85.8	90.5	90.4	86.3	83.9	34.1
2. A few	10.1	9.2	11.1	10.4	8.1	11.3	10.5	9.0	9.6	9.7	10.9	7.0	8.0	11.3	13.9	39.0
3. Some	2.0	2.5	1.4	1.6	3.1	2.8	1.5	2.1	1.6	1.6	2.5	2.2	1.3	1.6	1.8	19.5
4. Most	.2	.2	.2	.2	-	-	.1	.6	-	.1	.4	.1	-	.7	.2	2.4
5. All	.3	.4	.1	.2	.5	-	.2	.3	.8	.2	.4	.2	.3	-	.1	2.4
Item 7160　N(Wtd)	3266	1561	1652	2562	383	720	1035	1003	509	1824	1334	1113	771	432	869	41
D06K: Take other narcotics (methadone, opium, codeine, paregoric, etc.)?																
1. None	76.9	74.5	79.3	76.0	83.8	73.0	77.0	80.4	75.1	79.3	74.3	87.2	83.3	77.4	59.7	29.3
2. A few	17.7	19.5	16.1	19.2	10.7	19.8	17.4	15.7	19.8	16.9	18.6	10.5	14.1	19.9	28.3	48.8
3. Some	3.9	4.3	3.5	3.4	3.1	5.8	4.2	2.8	2.7	2.9	5.0	1.8	2.0	2.3	8.7	12.2
4. Most	1.0	1.3	.8	1.1	1.0	1.3	1.0	.6	1.8	.5	1.7	.2	.5	.5	2.7	4.9
5. All	.4	.4	.2	.2	1.3	.1	.3	.5	.6	.3	.5	.3	.3	-	.5	4.9
Item 7170　N(Wtd)	3266	1561	1649	2563	383	718	1037	1001	510	1824	1333	1112	767	433	873	41

QUESTIONNAIRE FORM 2 1981	TOTAL	SEX		RACE		REGION				4YR COLLEGE PLANS		ILLICIT DRUG USE: LIFETIME				
		M	F	White	Black	NE	NC	S	W	Yes	No	None	Mari- juana Only	Few Pills	More Pills	Any Her- oin
Weighted No. of Cases:	3655	1762	1762	2761	467	869	1102	1117	567	1937	1462	1219	846	487	958	41
% of Weighted Total:	100.0	48.2	48.2	75.5	12.8	23.8	30.1	30.6	15.5	53.0	40.0	33.4	23.2	13.3	26.2	1.1
D06L: Use inhalants (sniffing glue, aerosols, laughing gas, etc.)?																
1. None	83.5	81.8	85.0	83.4	85.8	80.2	85.2	85.8	80.2	84.3	81.9	88.1	86.6	83.1	75.7	65.9
2. A few	12.9	13.9	12.2	13.3	9.7	15.1	11.2	11.5	16.2	12.6	13.5	9.5	11.1	14.8	18.1	17.1
3. Some	2.6	3.0	2.4	2.3	3.9	3.8	2.7	2.3	1.6	2.2	3.5	1.9	2.0	2.1	4.3	9.8
4. Most	.7	1.1	.4	.9	.3	1.0	.8	.3	1.2	.7	.8	.3	.1	.2	1.8	7.3
5. All	.2	.3	.1	.2	.5	.1	.2	.2	.8	.2	.4	.2	.3	-	.1	2.4
Item 7180 N(Wtd)	3255	1557	1643	2554	381	716	1031	997	511	1818	1329	1110	766	431	867	41
D06M: Drink alcoholic beverages (liquor, beer, wine)?																
1. None	5.3	5.1	5.2	3.6	11.9	2.6	3.6	7.2	8.2	3.8	7.0	8.9	5.0	3.2	1.3	2.4
2. A few	10.8	8.9	12.6	9.2	19.4	5.8	10.7	12.0	15.6	11.2	10.1	20.1	7.2	8.1	3.3	2.4
3. Some	16.3	15.5	17.2	15.2	23.6	10.8	15.2	22.3	14.3	16.6	15.9	25.8	14.2	15.2	7.1	7.3
4. Most	41.7	42.5	41.4	44.2	30.3	41.7	44.4	41.6	36.3	43.0	40.7	35.6	46.8	45.6	43.9	24.4
5. All	26.0	28.0	23.6	27.7	14.8	39.1	26.1	16.7	25.6	25.4	26.2	9.6	26.6	27.9	44.3	61.0
Item 7190 N(Wtd)	3285	1570	1659	2577	386	721	1043	1009	512	1834	1343	1119	775	434	874	41
D06N: Get drunk at least once a week?																
1. None	18.2	15.4	20.8	15.4	30.1	14.6	16.9	19.2	24.0	18.4	18.1	29.3	16.0	16.6	6.2	9.8
2. A few	25.2	23.4	26.6	24.9	26.5	20.1	25.6	27.7	26.4	26.3	23.9	33.5	23.2	23.9	17.6	9.8
3. Some	27.3	26.1	28.9	28.7	21.1	27.1	28.5	27.9	23.8	29.0	24.8	23.9	30.2	29.0	28.5	24.4
4. Most	19.9	23.3	16.8	21.5	14.7	23.3	20.6	17.8	17.6	18.0	22.3	10.6	21.6	21.1	30.2	19.5
5. All	9.5	11.8	6.9	9.6	7.5	14.9	8.4	7.4	8.0	8.2	10.9	2.7	8.8	9.2	17.4	34.1
Item 7200 N(Wtd)	3286	1572	1659	2577	389	720	1044	1011	512	1834	1344	1120	776	435	873	41
Lately there has been increased attention paid to two types of drugs: PCP and amyl or butyl nitrite.																
E01: How many of your friends would you estimate...																
E01A: Take PCP (angel dust, crystal, peace pill, killer weed, supergrass, crystal cyclone)?																
1. None	82.8	82.3	83.3	82.7	83.8	77.2	84.3	84.7	83.8	85.2	79.6	90.1	86.5	82.8	71.6	43.9
2. A few	13.1	12.9	13.3	13.8	11.2	16.3	12.6	11.7	12.1	11.6	15.2	7.8	11.1	14.7	20.8	17.1
3. Some	3.2	3.8	2.7	2.9	3.7	5.7	2.2	2.5	2.9	2.5	3.8	1.3	2.2	2.3	6.3	17.1
4. Most	.6	.8	.5	.5	.8	.7	.7	.6	.6	.6	.8	.4	.1	.2	.9	14.6
5. All	.2	.2	.2	.1	.8	-	.2	.4	.4	-	.6	.2	-	-	.3	4.9
Item 7201 N(Wtd)	3254	1558	1639	2557	383	705	1038	1001	511	1818	1326	1116	763	430	867	41
E01B: Take amyl or butyl nitrite (poppers, snappers, Locker Room, Vaporole, Rush, Kick, Bullet)?																
1. None	82.6	80.2	85.1	82.0	88.2	80.1	83.5	84.9	80.0	83.9	81.3	92.0	86.4	83.6	68.2	43.2
2. A few	13.2	14.7	11.9	14.0	9.4	15.1	12.2	12.0	15.1	12.9	13.3	6.6	11.8	13.3	23.3	18.9
3. Some	2.9	3.6	2.1	2.8	1.3	3.4	3.1	1.9	3.5	2.4	3.5	1.1	1.5	2.8	5.9	21.6
4. Most	.9	1.0	.8	1.0	.3	1.1	.7	.9	1.0	.6	1.4	.2	.4	.5	2.3	2.7
5. All	.3	.5	.1	.2	.8	.1	.5	.4	.4	.2	.6	.2	-	-	.3	10.8
Item 7202 N(Wtd)	3232	1543	1632	2543	374	700	1031	993	509	1805	1319	1109	757	428	862	37
E02: On how many occasions (if any) have you used PCP (angel dust, crystal, peace pill, killer weed, supergrass, crystal cyclone)?																

QUESTIONNAIRE FORM 2 1981	TOTAL	SEX		RACE		REGION				4YR COLLEGE PLANS		ILLICIT DRUG USE: LIFETIME				
		M	F	White	Black	NE	NC	S	W	Yes	No	None	Mari- juana Only	Few Pills	More Pills	Any Her- oin
Weighted No. of Cases:	3655	1762	1762	2761	467	869	1102	1117	567	1937	1462	1219	846	487	958	41
% of Weighted Total:	100.0	48.2	48.2	75.5	12.8	23.8	30.1	30.6	15.5	53.0	40.0	33.4	23.2	13.3	26.2	1.1
E02A: ...in your lifetime?																
1. 0 occasions	92.2	91.0	93.6	92.1	96.8	89.5	93.0	94.2	90.8	94.5	89.4	99.6	98.8	94.4	ˋ78.5	30.8
2. 1-2	4.5	4.5	4.5	4.8	1.6	6.6	3.9	2.8	6.5	3.2	6.1	-	.9	4.0	12.7	28.2
3. 3-5	1.1	1.8	.6	1.2	-	1.9	1.0	.9	1.2	.8	1.4	-	.3	.5	3.1	12.8
4. 6-9	.7	1.0	.4	.7	-	.9	.7	.8	.2	.5	.9	.3	-	-	1.9	7.7
5. 10-19	.5	.5	.6	.6	.3	.7	.6	.5	.2	.5	.5	-	-	.9	1.0	10.3
6. 20-39	.6	.8	.4	.4	1.1	-	.7	.7	1.0	.3	.9	-	-	.2	1.9	5.1
7. 40 or more	.4	.5	.1	.3	.3	.6	.3	.2	.4	.1	.8	.1	-	-	.8	5.1
Item 1181 N(Wtd)	3233	1546	1630	2547	374	693	1038	992	510	1809	1316	1115	762	426	859	39
E02B: ...during the last 12 months?																
1. 0 occasions	96.8	96.1	97.7	96.9	98.1	96.5	96.3	97.1	97.6	97.5	95.7	99.6	99.7	97.9	91.6	61.5
2. 1-2	1.7	2.0	1.3	1.7	.5	2.2	2.1	1.0	1.4	1.3	2.1	-	.3	.9	4.8	17.9
3. 3-5	.4	.3	.4	.5	-	.7	.2	.4	.2	.3	.5	-	-	.2	1.1	2.6
4. 6-9	.5	.6	.4	.4	.8	.1	.7	.7	.4	.4	.7	.3	-	-	1.6	-
5. 10-19	.5	.8	.2	.4	.3	.3	.7	.6	-	.4	.6	-	-	.9	.7	12.8
6. 20-39	.1	.1	-	*	.3	-	.1	.1	-	-	.2	-	-	-	-	5.1
7. 40 or more	.1	.1	.1	*	.3	-	.1	.1	.4	-	.3	.1	-	-	.2	-
Item 1182 N(Wtd)	3232	1545	1630	2544	374	693	1037	993	508	1810	1314	1115	762	426	856	39
E02C: ...during the last 30 days?																
1. 0 occasions	98.6	98.3	99.0	98.7	98.9	98.6	98.6	98.5	99.0	98.9	98.1	99.6	99.9	99.1	96.5	87.2
2. 1-2	.6	.7	.5	.5	.3	1.0	.4	.5	.6	.5	.7	-	.1	.2	1.9	2.6
3. 3-5	.2	.2	.2	.1	.8	.3	.3	.1	-	.2	.2	-	-	-	.5	5.1
4. 6-9	.5	.7	.4	.6	-	.3	.6	.9	-	.4	.8	.3	-	.7	1.2	5.1
5. 10-19	-	-	-	-	-	-	-	-	-	-	-	-	-	-	-	-
6. 20-39	*	.1	-	-	.3	-	.1	-	-	-	.1	-	-	-	-	2.6
7. 40 or more	.1	.1	-	*	-	-	.1	-	.4	-	.2	.1	-	-	.1	-
Item 1183 N(Wtd)	3231	1544	1630	2544	374	693	1037	992	508	1809	1314	1115	762	426	856	39
E03: On how many occasions (if any) have you used amyl or butyl nitrites (poppers, snappers, Locker Room, Vaporole, Rush, Kick, Bullet)?																
E03A: ...in your lifetime?																
1. 0 occasions	89.9	87.0	92.9	89.0	96.2	86.6	89.6	92.1	90.6	90.7	88.8	99.8	95.5	93.6	71.9	46.2
2. 1-2	5.6	6.9	4.2	6.0	3.0	7.5	5.7	4.0	5.9	5.4	5.7	.2	3.3	5.0	14.1	28.2
3. 3-5	2.3	2.9	1.8	2.6	-	3.3	2.4	1.8	1.6	2.0	2.6	-	.9	.7	7.1	7.7
4. 6-9	.5	.7	.3	.6	-	.4	.4	.5	.8	.4	.7	-	-	.5	1.6	-
5. 10-19	.7	1.0	.3	.7	.3	.4	1.3	.3	.4	.7	.8	-	.1	-	2.1	7.7
6. 20-39	.7	1.0	.4	.7	.5	1.4	.2	1.0	.2	.5	1.1	-	-	.5	2.3	2.6
7. 40 or more	.4	.6	.1	.4	-	.1	.5	.3	.6	.4	.4	.1	.1	-	.8	7.7
Item 1184 N(Wtd)	3222	1541	1624	2538	371	694	1035	984	509	1803	1311	1110	759	420	859	39
E03B: ...during the last 12 months?																
1. 0 occasions	96.3	94.9	97.7	96.0	98.6	96.0	96.7	96.1	96.1	96.6	95.6	100.0	98.8	98.3	89.2	74.4
2. 1-2	2.3	3.0	1.5	2.4	1.1	2.4	1.8	2.3	2.8	2.1	2.6	-	1.2	1.2	6.4	10.3
3. 3-5	.4	.6	.2	.5	-	.6	.2	.4	.6	.4	.4	-	-	.2	1.3	2.6
4. 6-9	.4	.6	.3	.5	.3	.1	.6	.5	.2	.4	.5	-	-	.2	1.3	2.6
5. 10-19	.3	.6	.1	.3	-	.3	.3	.3	-	.1	.5	-	-	-	.9	2.6
6. 20-39	.1	.1	.1	.2	-	.3	-	.1	.2	.1	.2	-	-	-	.5	-
7. 40 or more	.2	.3	-	.2	-	.1	.3	.2	.4	.3	.2	.1	.1	-	.2	7.7
Item 1185 N(Wtd)	3219	1542	1620	2536	370	695	1034	983	507	1805	1307	1110	759	420	855	39
E03C: ...during the last 30 days?																
1. 0 occasions	98.6	97.8	99.4	98.5	100.0	99.1	98.4	98.6	98.2	99.0	97.9	100.0	99.3	99.8	96.3	86.8
2. 1-2	.7	1.1	.4	.8	-	.6	.7	.5	1.4	.6	1.0	-	.5	.2	2.0	2.6
3. 3-5	.3	.6	.1	.3	-	.1	.6	.3	-	.2	.5	-	.1	-	.9	2.6
4. 6-9	.2	.2	.2	.2	-	.1	-	.6	-	.1	.4	-	-	-	.6	2.6
5. 10-19	.1	.2	-	.1	-	-	.3	-	-	.2	-	-	-	-	-	7.9
6. 20-39	-	-	-	-	-	-	-	-	-	-	-	-	-	-	-	-
7. 40 or more	.1	.1	-	*	-	-	.1	-	.4	-	.2	.1	-	-	.1	-
Item 1186 N(Wtd)	3219	1542	1620	2536	369	695	1034	983	507	1805	1307	1110	759	420	855	38

* = less than .05 per cent.

QUESTIONNAIRE FORM 2 1981	TOTAL	SEX		RACE		REGION				4YR COLLEGE PLANS		ILLICIT DRUG USE: LIFETIME				
		M	F	White	Black	NE	NC	S	W	Yes	No	None	Marijuana Only	Few Pills	More Pills	Any Heroin
Weighted No. of Cases:	3655	1762	1762	2761	467	869	1102	1117	567	1937	1462	1219	846	487	958	41
% of Weighted Total:	100.0	48.2	48.2	75.5	12.8	23.8	30.1	30.6	15.5	53.0	40.0	33.4	23.2	13.3	26.2	1.1

E04: When (if ever) did you FIRST do each of the following things?

E04A: Try PCP

	TOTAL	M	F	White	Black	NE	NC	S	W	Yes	No	None	Marijuana Only	Few Pills	More Pills	Any Heroin
8. Never	93.7	92.4	95.0	93.5	97.8	90.4	94.8	95.5	93.1	95.4	91.6	99.7	99.1	96.3	81.8	33.3
1. Grade 6 or below	.2	.3	-	.1	.5	.3	.2	.1	-	.1	.2	-	-	.2	.2	8.3
2. Grade 7 or 8	.8	.6	.9	.9	-	1.6	.6	.3	.8	.7	.9	-	-	.2	2.2	13.9
3. Grade 9(Freshman)	2.0	2.3	1.6	2.0	.5	2.9	1.6	1.9	1.8	1.7	2.4	-	.5	.2	5.4	36.1
4. Grade 10(Sophomore)	1.9	2.6	1.3	2.2	-	2.9	2.1	1.2	1.2	1.2	2.6	.3	.1	1.2	6.1	2.8
5. Grade 11(Junior)	1.2	1.4	1.0	1.1	.8	1.5	.6	.9	2.6	.8	1.7	-	.3	1.7	3.2	2.8
6. Grade 12(Senior)	.3	.3	.3	.3	-	.3	.3	.1	.6	.2	.4	.1	-	-	.9	2.8
Item 5686 N(Wtd)	3152	1503	1594	2493	364	679	1011	969	492	1777	1269	1111	754	410	808	36

E04B: $:try amyl or butyl nitrites

	TOTAL	M	F	White	Black	NE	NC	S	W	Yes	No	None	Marijuana Only	Few Pills	More Pills	Any Heroin
8. Never	91.8	89.2	94.4	91.2	96.9	89.8	91.7	93.6	91.3	91.8	91.8	99.5	97.0	95.1	76.1	47.1
1. Grade 6 or below	.1	.2	-	.1	-	.2	.1	.2	-	.1	.2	-	-	-	.3	2.9
2. Grade 7 or 8	.9	1.0	.8	1.1	-	1.4	.8	.5	1.2	.8	1.2	-	-	.5	3.2	2.9
3. Grade 9(Freshman)	2.3	3.1	1.4	2.6	1.1	3.0	2.4	1.7	1.8	2.3	2.1	-	.9	1.2	6.1	29.4
4. Grade 10(Sophomore)	2.5	3.5	1.6	2.5	.6	3.3	2.4	2.0	2.2	2.5	2.4	.4	1.1	1.5	6.9	11.8
5. Grade 11(Junior)	1.5	1.8	1.3	1.6	.6	.9	2.0	1.1	2.2	1.4	1.5	-	.1	1.5	4.8	2.9
6. Grade 12(Senior)	1.0	1.2	.6	1.0	.8	1.5	.5	.8	1.4	1.1	.8	.1	.8	.2	2.5	-
Item 5687 N(Wtd)	3101	1467	1581	2451	356	664	995	948	494	1763	1235	1099	740	407	788	34

E05: What is your best guess about whether your parents think you drink alcoholic beverages (beer, wine, liquor)?

	TOTAL	M	F	White	Black	NE	NC	S	W	Yes	No	None	Marijuana Only	Few Pills	More Pills	Any Heroin
1. They feel sure I don't drink	25.7	22.3	29.1	22.5	43.4	12.9	21.3	34.9	33.6	27.2	23.5	45.9	17.9	20.8	9.6	5.0
2. They think I probably don't drink	11.2	10.7	11.8	11.2	12.4	10.3	11.3	12.5	9.6	10.7	12.2	13.4	13.7	12.3	6.1	10.0
3. I don't know, or they differ in whether they think I drink	8.4	7.6	9.1	7.7	11.9	8.1	8.8	9.1	6.7	8.3	8.1	8.4	8.8	9.0	7.7	2.5
4. They think I probably drink	17.2	17.5	16.7	17.7	13.7	19.9	18.2	16.4	13.2	17.7	17.4	13.0	19.2	20.8	18.1	30.0
5. They feel sure (or know) that I drink	37.5	41.9	33.4	40.9	18.9	48.7	40.4	27.0	36.7	36.1	38.7	19.2	40.2	37.3	58.5	55.0
Item 7510 N(Wtd)	3215	1544	1616	2533	371	688	1027	992	509	1800	1308	1097	759	424	858	40

E06: What's your best guess about whether your parents think you smoke marijuana?

	TOTAL	M	F	White	Black	NE	NC	S	W	Yes	No	None	Marijuana Only	Few Pills	More Pills	Any Heroin
1. They feel sure I don't	66.4	62.2	70.8	67.3	64.0	59.2	65.9	72.1	66.0	70.3	62.4	93.7	66.2	64.8	34.7	22.5
2. They think I probably don't	12.3	12.2	12.4	11.6	16.9	13.8	12.7	11.1	12.1	12.1	12.2	4.1	18.4	15.8	16.0	10.0
3. I don't know, or they differ in whether they think I do	6.2	6.7	5.4	6.1	5.4	8.9	5.9	5.3	4.7	5.0	7.3	.8	5.6	7.7	11.7	12.5
4. They think I probably do	6.5	7.3	5.7	6.0	8.4	8.8	5.6	6.4	5.9	5.7	7.8	.6	6.4	6.5	14.1	12.5
5. They feel sure (or know) that I do	8.6	11.6	5.8	8.9	5.2	9.4	10.1	5.1	11.3	6.9	10.2	.6	3.5	5.3	23.6	42.5
Item 7520 N(Wtd)	3194	1529	1609	2517	367	682	1023	983	506	1791	1299	1096	749	418	852	40

E07: What's your best guess about whether your parents think you use any other drugs (uppers, downers, psychedelics, etc.) for non-medical reasons?

	TOTAL	M	F	White	Black	NE	NC	S	W	Yes	No	None	Marijuana Only	Few Pills	More Pills	Any Heroin
1. They feel sure I don't	85.2	82.5	88.2	85.2	88.5	83.4	84.9	87.2	84.7	88.3	81.2	97.2	93.2	89.9	62.8	35.9
2. They think I probably don't	8.1	9.2	6.8	8.3	6.3	11.2	7.2	7.1	7.6	7.4	9.0	2.1	4.7	5.1	20.5	7.7
3. I don't know, or they differ in whether they think I do	3.8	5.0	2.4	3.5	3.3	2.8	3.8	4.0	4.8	2.5	5.3	.3	.7	3.4	8.9	43.6
4. They think I probably do	1.9	2.3	1.5	2.0	1.4	1.5	3.0	1.0	2.0	1.1	3.1	.2	.4	1.2	5.4	7.7
5. They feel sure (or know) that I do	1.0	1.0	1.1	1.0	.8	1.2	1.3	.7	.8	.8	1.3	.2	.8	.5	2.4	5.1
Item 7530 N(Wtd)	3168	1514	1599	2493	366	676	1011	977	503	1782	1283	1091	740	414	845	39

E08: Within the past three months, how often have you...

QUESTIONNAIRE FORM 2 1981	TOTAL	SEX		RACE		REGION				4YR COLLEGE PLANS		ILLICIT DRUG USE: LIFETIME				
		M	F	White	Black	NE	NC	S	W	Yes	No	None	Mari- juana Only	Few Pills	More Pills	Any Her- oin
Weighted No. of Cases:	3655	1762	1762	2761	467	869	1102	1117	567	1937	1462	1219	846	487	958	41
% of Weighted Total:	100.0	48.2	48.2	75.5	12.8	23.8	30.1	30.6	15.5	53.0	40.0	33.4	23.2	13.3	26.2	1.1
E08A: Had arguments or quarrels with your parents or other older relatives?																
1. Not at all	18.4	22.2	14.5	13.5	42.6	10.7	16.8	24.6	19.7	16.4	20.9	23.6	17.9	13.8	12.9	7.9
2. Once or twice	48.1	50.4	46.0	49.8	42.0	46.6	49.6	47.5	48.5	49.1	46.6	51.4	50.1	49.5	42.3	47.4
3. Every month	13.5	12.2	14.9	15.3	4.9	16.1	13.5	10.9	15.2	13.5	13.5	10.3	13.6	13.1	18.1	13.2
4. Every week	14.8	12.0	17.6	16.2	6.5	20.7	14.4	11.8	14.0	16.0	13.7	10.8	13.4	17.4	20.3	26.3
5. Almost daily	5.1	3.3	6.9	5.3	4.3	5.9	5.8	5.2	2.4	5.1	5.4	4.0	5.0	6.2	6.3	5.3
Item 19530 N(Wtd)	3206	1534	1616	2526	371	682	1024	992	507	1797	1303	1108	755	420	843	38
E08B: Had arguments or quarrels with people in positions of authority?																
1. Not at all	58.0	49.4	66.3	55.3	69.1	49.6	57.6	63.3	60.3	56.4	60.6	67.0	59.4	56.7	45.5	39.5
2. Once or twice	32.8	37.0	28.8	35.0	26.1	34.6	34.2	30.5	31.8	34.2	30.8	27.7	32.9	34.5	39.6	34.2
3. Every month	5.7	8.2	3.4	5.9	4.0	9.5	5.4	4.0	4.5	5.7	5.7	3.3	4.8	6.2	8.9	13.2
4. Every week	2.7	4.2	1.4	3.3	.3	5.6	1.7	1.8	2.8	3.1	2.0	1.6	2.4	2.4	4.7	2.6
5. Almost daily	.8	1.2	.2	.6	.5	.7	1.2	.4	.6	.6	.9	.4	.4	.2	1.3	13.2
Item 19540 N(Wtd)	3199	1533	1610	2519	372	682	1021	989	506	1796	1298	1105	751	420	844	38
E08C: Been mad enough to feel like smashing something, but didn't?																
1. Not at all	25.7	23.3	28.1	23.8	31.4	20.0	25.3	27.3	31.2	24.8	27.0	32.7	23.7	20.0	20.5	23.7
2. Once or twice	47.0	44.8	49.2	47.6	46.5	44.5	46.5	49.8	45.5	48.8	44.7	46.8	48.5	50.1	44.8	44.7
3. Every month	12.8	15.0	10.6	14.2	6.8	15.0	13.6	10.9	11.9	13.4	11.9	9.3	12.5	15.5	16.8	7.9
4. Every week	11.0	13.1	8.9	11.3	8.9	14.9	11.3	8.9	8.9	10.1	12.0	8.1	12.3	11.0	13.2	21.1
5. Almost daily	3.5	3.8	3.2	3.1	6.5	5.5	3.3	2.9	2.4	2.8	4.3	3.2	3.2	3.1	4.5	2.6
Item 19550 N(Wtd)	3197	1530	1611	2517	370	685	1021	988	503	1795	1298	1104	751	419	843	38
E08D: Been mad enough so you actually did smash something?																
1. Not at all	74.2	64.4	83.7	73.1	82.2	69.5	76.7	74.9	74.2	77.3	70.0	83.7	77.4	69.9	62.1	50.0
2. Once or twice	19.7	26.2	13.4	21.0	12.6	22.4	18.3	19.6	19.1	17.4	22.5	13.0	17.9	23.7	28.6	21.1
3. Every month	3.3	5.1	1.6	3.5	2.5	4.3	2.8	3.0	3.6	2.5	4.6	1.5	2.5	3.3	5.9	21.1
4. Every week	2.0	3.2	.7	1.8	1.4	3.2	1.5	1.6	2.2	2.0	2.0	.9	1.7	2.4	3.1	5.3
5. Almost daily	.8	1.1	.6	.7	1.1	.6	.8	.8	1.0	.8	.9	.9	.4	.7	.6	5.3
Item 19560 N(Wtd)	3181	1522	1603	2509	366	679	1015	983	503	1787	1289	1099	749	418	837	38
E08E: Felt like getting into a fist fight with someone, but didn't?																
1. Not at all	50.6	34.7	65.8	50.1	53.7	47.9	50.0	51.6	53.3	52.8	48.1	60.5	47.4	48.3	41.4	39.5
2. Once or twice	36.1	45.5	27.1	36.5	34.1	34.9	37.2	37.0	33.7	35.0	37.0	31.7	37.7	37.1	41.0	26.3
3. Every month	6.7	10.3	3.1	7.1	3.5	7.6	6.4	5.4	8.5	6.6	7.1	2.9	7.9	6.9	10.2	18.4
4. Every week	4.4	6.7	2.1	4.4	4.4	6.6	4.2	3.9	2.8	3.6	5.4	3.1	5.1	5.7	4.8	2.6
5. Almost daily	2.3	2.7	1.9	1.9	4.4	2.9	2.1	2.2	1.8	2.0	2.4	1.9	2.0	1.9	2.6	10.5
Item 19570 N(Wtd)	3187	1526	1605	2514	367	680	1017	985	505	1793	1290	1100	749	418	841	38
E08F: Actually got into a fight and hit somebody?																
1. Not at all	87.6	81.0	94.1	87.5	88.0	86.0	87.5	88.9	87.1	90.6	83.7	93.4	91.1	85.6	79.2	63.2
2. Once or twice	10.3	15.8	5.1	10.2	9.8	11.8	10.2	9.1	10.7	8.4	12.6	5.5	7.6	11.8	17.6	23.7
3. Every month	1.2	1.6	.5	1.3	1.6	1.3	1.3	.9	1.8	.7	2.1	.5	.7	1.7	1.9	7.9
4. Every week	.5	.8	.1	.4	.3	.6	.5	.5	.4	.2	.8	.1	.5	.7	.5	5.3
5. Almost daily	.5	.8	.2	.4	.3	.4	.5	.7	-	.2	.9	.5	.1	.2	.6	2.6
Item 19580 N(Wtd)	3182	1523	1603	2509	367	680	1015	982	505	1792	1285	1097	749	416	841	38
E09: Some people like school very much. Others don't. How do you feel about going to school?																
5. I like school very much	14.7	14.8	14.7	12.8	24.7	12.1	11.4	19.8	14.7	17.7	10.5	18.7	16.8	12.0	8.6	13.2
4. I like school quite a lot	26.4	26.2	26.9	26.8	26.8	21.7	27.7	27.1	28.5	32.4	18.9	32.5	26.9	26.1	18.9	21.1
3. I like school some	41.2	41.3	41.2	41.5	38.4	45.3	42.5	38.2	39.0	37.1	46.5	39.6	40.1	41.7	44.4	36.8
2. I don't like school very much	11.7	11.0	12.1	12.4	6.8	12.3	12.5	10.0	12.5	9.1	15.2	6.2	11.5	14.1	17.7	10.5
1. I don't like school at all	6.0	6.9	5.0	6.5	3.0	8.4	5.9	4.9	5.2	3.9	8.9	3.1	4.5	6.0	10.4	21.1
Item 7630 N(Wtd)	3177	1515	1608	2510	365	677	1018	980	502	1777	1296	1096	748	417	837	38

QUESTIONNAIRE FORM 2 1981	TOTAL	SEX		RACE		REGION				4YR COLLEGE PLANS		ILLICIT DRUG USE: LIFETIME				
		M	F	White	Black	NE	NC	S	W	Yes	No	None	Marijuana Only	Few Pills	More Pills	Any Heroin
Weighted No. of Cases:	3655	1762	1762	2761	467	869	1102	1117	567	1937	1462	1219	846	487	958	41
% of Weighted Total:	100.0	48.2	48.2	75.5	12.8	23.8	30.1	30.6	15.5	53.0	40.0	33.4	23.2	13.3	26.2	1.1

E10: About how many hours do you spend in an average week on all your homework including both in school and out of school?

	TOTAL	M	F	White	Black	NE	NC	S	W	Yes	No	None	Marijuana Only	Few Pills	More Pills	Any Heroin
1. 0 hours	8.6	12.8	4.6	8.6	7.1	5.8	10.0	8.3	10.2	4.0	14.6	7.1	8.8	6.2	10.5	26.3
2. 1-4 hours	41.8	43.5	39.8	41.1	46.6	38.3	40.4	43.4	46.2	34.8	51.2	36.4	43.2	47.3	44.4	34.2
3. 5-9 hours	23.9	22.3	25.8	24.9	20.7	27.7	23.7	23.2	20.3	27.8	18.6	25.5	24.1	23.4	23.0	21.1
4. 10-14 hours	12.4	10.9	13.7	12.4	11.7	15.0	12.4	11.7	10.2	15.6	7.9	14.5	11.5	12.4	10.8	10.5
5. 15-19 hours	5.8	4.5	7.1	5.8	5.7	7.8	5.8	5.0	4.2	8.3	2.6	8.0	5.3	3.8	4.7	2.6
6. 20-24 hours	3.8	3.5	4.2	3.8	3.5	3.1	4.0	3.5	5.0	4.7	2.8	3.8	3.7	3.3	4.1	-
7. 25 or more hours	3.7	2.6	4.7	3.4	4.4	2.1	3.6	4.8	4.0	4.8	2.3	4.7	3.3	3.6	2.6	7.9
Item 7640 N(Wtd)	3174	1519	1602	2506	367	678	1017	977	502	1778	1292	1093	748	419	836	38

E11: In general, how much say or influence do you feel each of the following has on HOW YOUR SCHOOL IS RUN?

E11A: The principal

	TOTAL	M	F	White	Black	NE	NC	S	W	Yes	No	None	Marijuana Only	Few Pills	More Pills	Any Heroin
1. Little or no influence	11.1	12.6	9.4	9.1	16.2	9.5	11.7	11.3	11.6	7.9	15.9	10.1	12.5	11.5	10.0	23.7
2. Some influence	14.0	14.6	13.1	12.3	20.8	10.8	14.1	15.4	15.1	11.6	17.1	15.0	12.7	12.2	14.8	13.2
3. Moderate influence	12.8	13.2	12.3	13.6	9.9	13.3	12.6	10.2	17.5	11.7	14.1	12.9	10.2	12.0	14.2	28.9
4. Considerable influence	27.3	28.3	26.8	29.3	16.2	28.1	28.7	24.7	28.5	30.4	23.8	27.5	25.1	33.3	27.3	18.4
5. A great deal of influence	34.9	31.2	38.4	35.6	37.0	38.4	32.9	38.3	27.5	38.4	29.2	34.5	39.5	31.3	33.9	18.4
Item 7650 N(Wtd)	3159	1510	1592	2492	365	677	1012	979	491	1779	1274	1087	746	418	824	38

E11B: The teachers

	TOTAL	M	F	White	Black	NE	NC	S	W	Yes	No	None	Marijuana Only	Few Pills	More Pills	Any Heroin
1. Little or no influence	9.0	10.2	7.9	7.7	12.8	7.6	9.8	9.0	9.1	6.3	12.7	9.3	8.4	7.5	9.0	21.1
2. Some influence	22.1	23.0	21.1	21.1	29.2	21.8	20.2	24.4	22.1	20.0	25.2	21.1	19.2	26.9	22.7	36.8
3. Moderate influence	31.0	31.9	30.4	33.9	18.1	33.0	34.3	27.9	27.4	32.6	29.2	31.3	31.9	31.0	30.9	18.4
4. Considerable influence	28.4	26.4	30.5	29.1	22.0	28.1	27.8	27.8	31.0	31.7	23.6	29.8	28.4	28.1	27.8	10.5
5. A great deal of influence	9.5	8.6	10.1	8.2	17.5	9.4	8.1	10.7	10.3	9.5	9.3	8.3	12.0	6.7	9.7	10.5
Item 7660 N(Wtd)	3143	1498	1587	2479	359	670	1004	977	493	1770	1268	1083	739	416	825	38

E11C: The students

	TOTAL	M	F	White	Black	NE	NC	S	W	Yes	No	None	Marijuana Only	Few Pills	More Pills	Any Heroin
1. Little or no influence	30.5	31.3	29.9	31.8	26.5	31.8	34.5	29.5	22.4	28.6	33.1	27.8	29.1	31.3	34.3	39.5
2. Some influence	29.1	29.2	28.6	29.6	29.5	28.5	27.6	29.9	31.6	30.5	27.1	29.9	28.7	31.6	27.6	28.9
3. Moderate influence	19.4	18.4	20.4	19.3	15.0	21.6	16.8	18.9	22.6	20.7	17.5	20.3	20.2	16.6	19.3	13.2
4. Considerable influence	12.0	11.5	12.7	11.4	16.2	8.8	11.8	13.2	14.5	12.0	12.1	12.7	13.7	13.7	9.0	10.5
5. A great deal of influence	9.0	9.5	8.5	8.0	13.1	9.4	9.4	8.4	9.0	8.2	10.2	9.3	8.4	6.7	10.0	10.5
Item 7670 N(Wtd)	3133	1491	1587	2471	359	667	1002	972	491	1770	1260	1081	739	415	820	38

E11D: Parents of students

	TOTAL	M	F	White	Black	NE	NC	S	W	Yes	No	None	Marijuana Only	Few Pills	More Pills	Any Heroin
1. Little or no influence	23.6	24.6	22.5	23.1	23.4	26.2	23.0	23.9	20.5	21.5	27.2	22.4	22.0	25.2	24.7	39.5
2. Some influence	32.3	31.6	33.1	34.5	25.1	33.6	33.3	30.6	31.9	33.6	30.2	32.7	29.7	32.4	34.9	31.6
3. Moderate influence	21.3	21.2	21.7	21.6	17.3	20.1	23.1	19.7	22.4	23.4	19.1	21.3	20.3	24.5	21.5	10.5
4. Considerable influence	14.4	14.3	14.5	14.0	16.7	12.1	13.0	16.5	15.9	14.0	14.5	14.3	18.2	10.8	12.5	7.9
5. A great deal of influence	8.5	8.3	8.1	6.8	17.3	8.0	7.6	9.2	9.3	7.5	9.1	9.3	9.7	7.2	6.5	10.5
Item 7680 N(Wtd)	3135	1494	1585	2477	359	663	1005	975	492	1769	1263	1081	740	417	819	38

E12: Have you had any drug education courses or lectures in school?

	TOTAL	M	F	White	Black	NE	NC	S	W	Yes	No	None	Marijuana Only	Few Pills	More Pills	Any Heroin
1. No--GO TO Q.E16	23.5	28.0	19.4	22.6	27.5	23.3	24.9	25.4	17.3	21.6	26.1	25.9	26.0	18.6	21.1	18.2
2. No, and I wish I had-- GO TO Q.E16	4.2	2.9	5.4	4.3	4.0	3.9	5.1	4.3	2.5	5.0	3.2	2.9	4.9	5.4	4.5	6.1
3. Yes	72.4	69.2	75.3	73.1	68.2	72.8	70.0	70.4	80.2	73.4	70.7	71.2	69.1	76.0	74.4	75.8
Item 7690 N(Wtd)	2990	1402	1541	2398	324	644	963	902	481	1706	1186	1042	700	392	792	33

QUESTIONNAIRE FORM 2 1981	TOTAL	SEX		RACE		REGION				4YR COLLEGE PLANS		ILLICIT DRUG USE: LIFETIME				
		M	F	White	Black	NE	NC	S	W	Yes	No	None	Mari- juana Only	Few Pills	More Pills	Any Her- oin
Weighted No. of Cases:	3655	1762	1762	2761	467	869	1102	1117	567	1937	1462	1219	846	487	958	41
% of Weighted Total:	100.0	48.2	48.2	75.5	12.8	23.8	30.1	30.6	15.5	53.0	40.0	33.4	23.2	13.3	26.2	1.1

E13: Would you say that the information about drugs that you received in school classes or programs has...

	TOTAL	M	F	White	Black	NE	NC	S	W	Yes	No	None	Mari- juana Only	Few Pills	More Pills	Any Her- oin
1. Made you less interested in trying drugs	58.8	53.6	63.0	56.3	73.6	51.7	54.6	67.6	59.7	57.4	61.1	73.3	67.0	60.9	34.1	32.0
2. Not changed your interest in trying drugs	38.5	42.2	35.5	40.9	24.5	45.0	42.6	29.6	38.2	40.8	34.9	26.3	31.8	35.4	60.2	52.0
3. Made you more interested in trying drugs	2.7	4.2	1.6	2.8	1.8	3.2	2.8	2.8	1.8	1.8	3.9	.4	1.0	3.7	5.9	16.0
Item 7840 N(Wtd) ★	2163	977	1153	1756	220	462	672	642	387	1246	846	737	485	297	595	25

E14: How many of the following drug education experiences have you had in high school? (Mark all that apply.)

	TOTAL	M	F	White	Black	NE	NC	S	W	Yes	No	None	Mari- juana Only	Few Pills	More Pills	Any Her- oin
A. A special course about drugs	22.3	25.2	20.2	22.8	17.3	24.8	19.1	21.4	26.3	23.0	21.2	22.6	25.6	21.0	21.4	8.0
B. Films, lectures, or discussions in one of my regular courses	76.8	74.3	79.5	77.8	70.5	76.5	79.3	71.7	81.8	79.6	72.5	78.1	75.0	78.0	76.4	88.0
C. Films or lectures, outside of my regular courses	23.9	25.6	22.2	24.1	26.4	19.8	23.7	31.0	17.4	25.7	21.2	24.4	24.6	22.0	23.8	24.0
D. Special discussions ("rap" groups) about drugs	20.8	18.3	23.0	20.2	22.7	18.1	21.0	21.6	22.6	20.7	21.4	18.6	19.5	22.0	23.8	24.0
Item 7850-7880 N(Wtd) ★	2141	973	1134	1731	220	459	666	635	380	1235	835	735	476	291	589	25

E15: Overall, how valuable were the experiences to you?

	TOTAL	M	F	White	Black	NE	NC	S	W	Yes	No	None	Mari- juana Only	Few Pills	More Pills	Any Her- oin
1. Little or no value	15.4	18.2	13.3	16.2	11.7	18.3	15.6	13.9	14.0	15.7	14.6	16.4	12.0	13.0	18.0	24.0
2. Some value	43.7	45.0	42.1	46.3	24.8	44.2	47.4	41.0	41.6	45.5	42.3	36.5	41.8	44.0	53.6	52.0
3. Considerable value	25.0	22.6	27.4	24.0	31.1	24.6	23.0	25.0	29.2	25.0	24.9	25.1	29.0	29.7	19.8	16.0
4. Great value	15.9	14.2	17.2	13.5	32.0	13.1	14.0	20.3	15.2	13.7	18.2	22.0	17.4	13.3	8.6	8.0
Item 7890 N(Wtd) ★	2159	977	1148	1748	222	459	671	641	387	1245	842	737	483	293	595	25

E16: Some people have suggested that there be standard tests of high school skills in arithmetic, reading, and writing. What do you think about each of the following possible uses of such a test?

E16A: Any student age 16 or older who can pass such a test should be given a high school diploma and be allowed to leave high school early

	TOTAL	M	F	White	Black	NE	NC	S	W	Yes	No	None	Mari- juana Only	Few Pills	More Pills	Any Her- oin
1. Disagree	38.6	36.3	40.2	39.4	35.0	41.3	36.1	41.0	35.2	41.8	34.0	41.2	40.4	40.8	32.1	26.3
2. Mostly disagree	22.1	20.5	23.7	24.5	12.0	23.0	25.5	18.4	21.5	25.0	18.5	24.0	18.9	24.2	22.9	10.5
3. Neither	13.2	14.7	11.9	12.5	15.7	12.4	13.5	13.1	13.7	10.9	16.4	11.3	16.7	12.0	13.3	13.2
4. Mostly agree	14.1	14.6	13.9	13.5	15.4	11.8	15.5	13.5	15.7	12.9	16.1	12.2	13.4	13.0	17.2	23.7
5. Agree	12.0	13.9	10.2	10.1	21.9	11.5	9.4	14.1	14.1	9.5	15.2	11.2	10.5	10.3	14.4	26.3
Item 7900 N(Wtd)	3106	1477	1572	2453	351	652	1005	959	489	1755	1252	1070	731	409	812	38

E16B: Any student age 14 or older who can pass such a test should be given a high school diploma and be allowed to leave high school early

	TOTAL	M	F	White	Black	NE	NC	S	W	Yes	No	None	Mari- juana Only	Few Pills	More Pills	Any Her- oin
1. Disagree	63.5	60.5	66.4	66.2	52.6	68.0	62.8	62.3	61.1	68.3	57.1	67.0	61.8	67.3	60.4	39.5
2. Mostly disagree	19.3	19.1	19.7	19.1	22.3	17.0	20.4	19.5	19.6	17.6	22.0	18.1	21.3	18.0	20.1	10.5
3. Neither	9.6	10.7	8.3	8.8	10.3	8.9	10.2	9.0	10.4	8.1	11.6	8.2	9.3	9.3	11.1	21.1
4. Mostly agree	3.8	3.9	3.7	3.3	5.7	2.3	3.7	4.3	5.1	3.1	4.7	3.6	3.0	2.4	5.1	13.2
5. Agree	3.7	5.6	1.9	2.7	8.9	3.7	2.9	4.8	3.3	2.8	4.6	3.2	4.5	2.7	3.5	13.2
Item 7910 N(Wtd)	3102	1474	1572	2452	350	654	1006	953	489	1755	1249	1067	731	410	811	38

★=excludes respondents for whom question was inappropriate.

QUESTIONNAIRE FORM 2 1981	TOTAL	SEX		RACE		REGION				4YR COLLEGE PLANS		ILLICIT DRUG USE: LIFETIME				
		M	F	White	Black	NE	NC	S	W	Yes	No	None	Mari- juana Only	Few Pills	More Pills	Any Her- oin
Weighted No. of Cases:	3655	1762	1762	2761	467	869	1102	1117	567	1937	1462	1219	846	487	958	41
% of Weighted Total:	100.0	48.2	48.2	75.5	12.8	23.8	30.1	30.6	15.5	53.0	40.0	33.4	23.2	13.3	26.2	1.1

E16C: Before any student (no matter what age) is given a high school diploma, he or she should have to pass such a standard test

	TOTAL	M	F	White	Black	NE	NC	S	W	Yes	No	None	Mar.	Few	More	Heroin
1. Disagree	23.9	23.2	24.2	23.7	23.4	25.3	25.7	24.2	17.2	21.2	27.0	26.6	23.1	24.1	21.2	10.5
2. Mostly disagree	9.6	9.6	9.6	9.9	8.9	9.6	11.3	8.5	8.2	8.5	11.3	8.9	10.6	8.6	10.3	5.3
3. Neither	12.5	11.8	13.1	12.0	12.0	11.6	15.6	10.4	11.5	11.9	13.7	11.8	10.9	14.0	13.2	21.1
4. Mostly agree	21.2	22.1	20.5	22.3	18.6	21.8	20.9	20.0	23.6	23.7	18.1	19.6	21.2	22.9	22.5	39.5
5. Agree	32.8	33.2	32.6	32.1	37.1	31.8	26.3	37.0	39.4	34.7	30.0	33.2	34.3	30.7	33.0	23.7
Item 7920 N(Wtd)	3094	1469	1568	2444	350	648	1006	953	487	1748	1245	1063	728	407	813	38

E17: How often do you...

E17A: Eat breakfast?

	TOTAL	M	F	White	Black	NE	NC	S	W	Yes	No	None	Mar.	Few	More	Heroin
1. Never	7.7	6.6	8.6	7.6	7.5	7.5	8.2	7.6	7.0	6.3	9.7	5.5	6.9	8.9	10.5	10.5
2. Seldom	25.8	21.8	29.6	24.7	33.5	25.3	24.2	27.2	27.3	23.7	28.0	22.3	25.7	27.4	29.4	26.3
3. Sometimes	16.0	13.7	18.0	14.6	22.7	15.4	17.7	14.9	15.2	15.3	17.2	14.4	14.0	15.1	18.9	44.7
4. Most days	11.1	12.0	10.3	11.0	9.1	12.3	10.5	10.1	12.8	11.3	10.9	10.5	11.1	13.5	11.1	10.5
5. Nearly every day	12.2	12.8	11.9	12.9	11.4	11.5	12.3	13.0	11.4	13.8	10.6	11.8	13.9	13.2	11.7	2.6
6. Every day	27.2	33.2	21.6	29.1	15.8	28.0	27.1	27.2	26.3	29.7	23.6	35.6	28.4	22.1	18.5	7.9
Item 20740 N(Wtd)	3162	1508	1597	2494	361	669	1020	974	499	1784	1270	1086	742	416	831	38

E17B: Eat at least some green vegetables?

	TOTAL	M	F	White	Black	NE	NC	S	W	Yes	No	None	Mar.	Few	More	Heroin
1. Never	2.1	2.0	2.1	1.6	3.9	1.4	2.0	2.8	2.2	1.1	3.4	2.3	1.8	1.9	2.1	-
2. Seldom	7.5	6.3	8.7	6.3	15.4	7.7	7.1	8.3	6.4	5.7	10.1	5.7	8.0	7.8	8.6	10.5
3. Sometimes	18.4	17.8	18.6	17.3	25.1	14.7	20.2	19.8	16.7	15.0	22.8	18.1	14.9	18.9	21.4	26.3
4. Most days	23.0	21.1	24.6	23.0	23.2	20.5	24.0	24.8	21.1	23.6	21.8	19.9	24.2	26.5	23.5	23.7
5. Nearly every day	25.0	25.2	25.0	26.4	19.0	28.3	25.2	21.3	27.4	26.9	22.9	25.7	26.6	22.8	24.3	26.3
6. Every day	24.1	27.6	21.0	25.5	13.7	27.7	21.6	23.1	26.2	27.7	18.9	28.1	24.6	21.8	20.1	13.2
Item 20750 N(Wtd)	3138	1499	1582	2474	358	665	1010	965	497	1775	1256	1079	740	412	822	38

E17C: Eat at least some fruit?

	TOTAL	M	F	White	Black	NE	NC	S	W	Yes	No	None	Mar.	Few	More	Heroin
1. Never	1.3	1.2	1.4	1.1	1.1	.6	1.2	2.1	1.2	.4	2.6	1.2	1.0	1.7	1.3	2.6
2. Seldom	6.6	5.7	7.4	6.2	11.2	4.7	6.9	9.3	3.4	4.6	9.7	5.7	7.2	5.3	7.2	21.1
3. Sometimes	21.5	20.4	22.9	21.2	24.7	19.0	20.5	26.0	18.5	18.8	25.0	19.9	21.5	23.2	22.8	21.1
4. Most days	25.2	25.9	24.6	24.8	28.4	24.9	26.5	25.4	22.4	25.4	25.0	23.3	23.7	26.8	28.2	26.3
5. Nearly every day	23.0	23.1	22.6	23.6	19.9	23.7	24.1	19.1	27.0	24.5	21.1	23.7	25.6	23.4	20.2	13.2
6. Every day	22.4	23.8	21.2	23.1	14.9	27.1	20.9	18.1	27.2	26.2	16.7	26.2	21.2	19.3	20.2	18.4
Item 20760 N(Wtd)	3137	1493	1587	2475	356	663	1017	961	496	1772	1259	1078	735	414	825	38

E17D: Exercise vigorously (jogging, swimming, calisthenics, or any other active sports)?

	TOTAL	M	F	White	Black	NE	NC	S	W	Yes	No	None	Mar.	Few	More	Heroin
1. Never	2.8	2.6	3.0	2.0	7.5	1.2	3.0	4.0	2.0	1.4	4.7	3.0	3.2	1.7	1.9	7.9
2. Seldom	12.7	10.0	14.9	12.1	15.9	11.1	11.3	16.0	11.2	10.5	15.5	12.1	11.5	11.5	15.4	18.4
3. Sometimes	25.0	19.0	31.2	25.8	20.9	23.7	27.8	24.0	22.7	23.7	27.1	23.5	24.1	25.9	26.8	39.5
4. Most days	16.5	16.3	16.6	17.3	13.1	18.2	15.1	15.7	18.7	15.9	17.5	14.9	17.0	17.7	18.0	5.3
5. Nearly every day	18.3	19.8	17.0	18.6	16.5	18.3	18.4	18.1	18.9	20.0	15.8	19.0	18.5	19.4	17.4	15.8
6. Every day	24.7	32.5	17.4	24.2	26.3	27.5	24.3	22.1	26.3	28.5	19.4	27.6	26.5	23.3	20.5	18.4
Item 20770 N(Wtd)	3152	1503	1592	2488	358	666	1019	968	498	1782	1264	1080	742	417	829	38

E17E: Get at least seven hours of sleep?

	TOTAL	M	F	White	Black	NE	NC	S	W	Yes	No	None	Mar.	Few	More	Heroin
1. Never	2.0	2.5	1.5	1.8	2.5	3.6	1.5	1.9	1.4	1.5	2.9	1.2	2.0	1.7	2.7	8.3
2. Seldom	8.4	8.3	8.4	8.5	7.8	8.3	9.3	8.3	6.8	8.1	8.8	7.7	8.2	5.1	9.6	33.3
3. Sometimes	16.8	15.4	17.8	16.7	19.9	17.5	16.8	17.9	13.7	15.1	18.4	14.6	17.1	17.1	21.3	25.0
4. Most days	24.3	21.6	27.1	25.9	15.1	23.8	26.8	22.2	24.5	24.5	24.1	23.8	20.5	28.4	28.2	11.1
5. Nearly every day	26.7	27.9	25.6	27.2	25.2	25.5	25.5	28.3	27.9	29.1	24.1	27.0	31.3	26.0	23.5	8.3
6. Every day	21.8	24.2	19.7	19.9	29.1	21.4	20.0	21.7	26.1	21.7	21.9	25.7	23.5	21.9	14.8	13.9
Item 20780 N(Wtd)	3150	1503	1590	2490	357	664	1018	969	498	1780	1263	1080	742	415	830	36

QUESTIONNAIRE FORM 2 1981	TOTAL	SEX		RACE		REGION				4YR COLLEGE PLANS		ILLICIT DRUG USE: LIFETIME				
		M	F	White	Black	NE	NC	S	W	Yes	No	None	Mari- juana Only	Few Pills	More Pills	Any Her- oin
Weighted No. of Cases:	3655	1762	1762	2761	467	869	1102	1117	567	1937	1462	1219	846	487	958	41
% of Weighted Total:	100.0	48.2	48.2	75.5	12.8	23.8	30.1	30.6	15.5	53.0	40.0	33.4	23.2	13.3	26.2	1.1

E17F: Get less sleep than you think you should?

	TOTAL	M	F	White	Black	NE	NC	S	W	Yes	No	None	Mari- juana Only	Few Pills	More Pills	Any Her- oin
1. Never	8.6	9.0	8.2	6.7	18.6	8.7	7.9	10.0	7.7	6.6	11.6	10.1	9.1	8.5	5.4	5.3
2. Seldom	21.3	21.1	21.7	21.1	21.7	18.5	19.7	23.1	25.1	20.7	21.9	22.6	24.6	20.3	17.5	18.4
3. Sometimes	34.0	31.7	36.1	35.3	28.5	33.7	35.9	32.3	33.7	35.1	33.0	35.7	31.3	33.8	36.0	21.1
4. Most days	16.0	17.0	14.6	16.5	13.2	15.5	16.2	16.9	14.3	15.7	16.1	13.8	17.2	15.2	19.0	10.5
5. Nearly every day	10.1	11.0	9.6	10.9	6.2	11.6	10.5	9.1	9.5	11.5	8.3	8.8	9.5	14.5	9.9	23.7
6. Every day	9.9	10.1	9.9	9.5	11.8	11.9	9.9	8.7	9.7	10.4	9.1	9.0	8.5	7.7	12.1	21.1
Item 20790 N(Wtd)	3143	1496	1592	2487	355	665	1019	964	495	1777	1262	1079	739	414	827	38

QUESTIONNAIRE FORM 3 1981	TOTAL	SEX		RACE		REGION				4YR COLLEGE PLANS		ILLICIT DRUG USE: LIFETIME				
		M	F	White	Black	NE	NC	S	W	Yes	No	None	Mari-juana Only	Few Pills	More Pills	Any Her-oin
Weighted No. of Cases:	3658	1721	1795	2830	459	869	1100	1114	575	1980	1448	1228	894	433	990	41
% of Weighted Total:	100.0	47.0	49.1	77.4	12.5	23.8	30.1	30.5	15.7	54.1	39.6	33.6	24.4	11.8	27.1	1.1

A01: Taking all things together, how would you say things are these days-would you say you're very happy, pretty happy, or not too happy these days?

	TOTAL	M	F	White	Black	NE	NC	S	W	Yes	No	None	Mari-juana Only	Few Pills	More Pills	Any Her-oin
3. Very happy	18.3	17.5	19.4	18.9	15.7	17.7	17.5	18.3	20.8	20.1	15.8	21.2	18.8	15.2	16.2	10.0
2. Pretty happy	68.7	71.0	66.6	71.1	58.6	69.2	71.0	66.7	67.7	68.8	69.6	66.7	68.6	73.0	70.6	47.5
1. Not too happy	13.0	11.6	14.0	10.0	25.7	13.2	11.6	15.0	11.5	11.1	14.6	12.1	12.7	12.1	13.1	42.5
Item 1190 N(Wtd)	3631	1705	1787	2812	452	859	1092	1107	573	1972	1438	1218	889	429	984	40

A02: Some people think a lot about the social problems of the nation and the world, and about how they might be solved. Others spend little time thinking about these issues. How much do you think about such things?

	TOTAL	M	F	White	Black	NE	NC	S	W	Yes	No	None	Mari-juana Only	Few Pills	More Pills	Any Her-oin
1. Never	1.4	2.2	.7	1.3	.7	2.4	.9	1.4	1.2	1.2	1.9	1.5	.9	1.4	1.3	12.2
2. Seldom	12.3	12.7	12.0	12.9	10.3	13.9	11.8	12.2	11.3	9.9	15.5	8.9	13.5	12.4	15.4	17.1
3. Sometimes	51.5	49.3	53.9	53.9	41.4	51.4	55.8	46.4	53.1	50.1	54.4	54.4	52.8	49.0	49.4	31.7
4. Quite often	28.3	28.8	27.4	26.8	35.4	26.4	26.2	32.3	27.6	31.1	24.0	28.1	27.0	31.2	28.6	14.6
5. A great deal	6.5	7.0	6.0	5.1	12.5	5.9	5.3	7.7	6.8	7.7	4.2	7.0	6.0	6.1	5.2	22.0
Item 6880 N(Wtd)	3641	1709	1793	2817	457	864	1093	1111	573	1975	1439	1226	890	429	985	41

A03: The next questions ask your opinions about a number of different topics. How much do you agree or disagree with each statement below?

A03A: Men and women should be paid the same money if they do the same work

	TOTAL	M	F	White	Black	NE	NC	S	W	Yes	No	None	Mari-juana Only	Few Pills	More Pills	Any Her-oin
1. Disagree	1.7	2.7	.6	1.2	2.4	2.1	1.8	1.3	1.4	1.1	2.1	2.0	.8	.9	1.6	7.3
2. Mostly disagree	1.7	2.8	.7	1.6	1.7	1.2	1.8	2.3	1.0	1.4	2.0	2.0	1.2	1.4	1.5	2.4
3. Neither	1.5	2.7	.3	1.7	.9	1.4	2.2	.8	1.7	1.7	1.2	1.5	.6	.7	2.4	2.4
4. Mostly agree	14.5	19.6	8.7	14.5	12.2	12.5	15.1	14.7	16.0	13.5	15.2	13.2	16.1	15.7	14.2	9.8
5. Agree	80.6	72.2	89.7	81.1	82.8	82.9	79.1	80.9	79.8	82.4	79.5	81.2	81.3	81.0	80.3	78.0
Item 7930 N(Wtd)	3653	1719	1793	2826	459	867	1098	1114	574	1978	1447	1227	894	432	989	41

A03B: Women should be considered as seriously as men for jobs as executives or politicians

	TOTAL	M	F	White	Black	NE	NC	S	W	Yes	No	None	Mari-juana Only	Few Pills	More Pills	Any Her-oin
1. Disagree	4.1	6.4	1.4	3.4	5.7	4.5	3.7	5.1	1.7	3.1	5.1	4.8	3.2	1.9	3.5	19.5
2. Mostly disagree	3.9	6.2	1.6	3.8	3.1	2.5	4.6	4.4	3.7	3.4	4.4	3.7	3.4	4.0	4.5	4.9
3. Neither	4.4	6.5	2.1	4.5	2.8	4.0	3.9	4.7	4.9	3.7	5.1	5.1	3.5	2.1	5.2	4.9
4. Mostly agree	23.0	30.9	14.7	23.0	21.0	19.4	25.0	22.1	26.0	21.0	24.6	23.6	22.3	24.2	22.0	19.5
5. Agree	64.8	50.0	80.2	65.1	67.5	69.5	62.8	63.6	63.6	68.7	60.7	62.8	67.7	67.7	64.9	51.2
Item 7940 N(Wtd)	3649	1717	1793	2825	458	866	1098	1111	574	1977	1446	1227	894	430	988	41

A03C: A woman should have exactly the same job opportunities as a man

	TOTAL	M	F	White	Black	NE	NC	S	W	Yes	No	None	Mari-juana Only	Few Pills	More Pills	Any Her-oin
1. Disagree	7.7	11.5	4.1	7.0	10.6	7.1	5.6	11.1	6.3	5.2	10.3	8.3	6.7	6.3	6.9	20.0
2. Mostly disagree	6.4	9.0	3.7	6.5	4.9	6.8	6.0	7.2	5.1	5.0	7.9	5.6	4.8	7.7	7.5	10.0
3. Neither	5.6	7.3	3.7	5.8	3.7	5.0	6.8	4.6	5.8	5.3	5.4	6.7	5.0	5.4	5.1	2.5
4. Mostly agree	29.2	31.5	27.1	30.5	24.5	26.1	33.9	27.1	29.2	28.1	31.8	27.1	29.5	31.6	31.8	7.5
5. Agree	51.1	40.8	61.5	50.2	57.0	55.0	47.9	50.0	53.6	56.4	44.7	52.3	53.9	49.2	48.7	57.5
Item 7950 N(Wtd)	3618	1703	1776	2804	453	855	1092	1102	569	1958	1433	1215	881	427	984	40

A03D: A woman should have exactly the same educational opportunities as a man

	TOTAL	M	F	White	Black	NE	NC	S	W	Yes	No	None	Mari-juana Only	Few Pills	More Pills	Any Her-oin
1. Disagree	1.0	1.3	.4	.5	2.9	1.3	.7	1.3	.3	.5	1.2	1.5	.6	.2	.5	7.3
2. Mostly disagree	.9	1.2	.6	.8	.9	.8	.5	.9	1.4	.7	1.2	1.3	.7	.5	.7	2.4
3. Neither	1.4	1.8	1.1	1.5	.9	.5	2.1	1.5	1.2	.8	2.2	1.4	1.0	1.6	1.5	-
4. Mostly agree	10.3	12.6	7.3	8.6	15.6	8.5	12.0	11.3	7.9	8.2	12.6	11.0	10.1	10.0	9.2	7.3
5. Agree	86.5	83.1	90.5	88.6	79.6	89.0	84.7	84.9	89.4	89.9	82.8	84.8	87.6	87.6	88.0	80.5
Item 7960 N(Wtd)	3639	1713	1786	2814	456	861	1096	1109	573	1969	1442	1224	888	429	986	41

QUESTIONNAIRE FORM 3 1981	TOTAL	SEX		RACE		REGION				4YR COLLEGE PLANS		ILLICIT DRUG USE: LIFETIME				
		M	F	White	Black	NE	NC	S	W	Yes	No	None	Mari-juana Only	Few Pills	More Pills	Any Her-oin
Weighted No. of Cases:	3658	1721	1795	2830	459	869	1100	1114	575	1980	1448	1228	894	433	990	41
% of Weighted Total:	100.0	47.0	49.1	77.4	12.5	23.8	30.1	30.5	15.7	54.1	39.6	33.6	24.4	11.8	27.1	1.1
A03E: It is usually better for everyone involved if the man is the achiever outside the home and the woman takes care of the home and family																
1. Disagree	21.9	12.6	31.0	20.3	29.7	26.5	20.2	20.6	20.9	24.3	18.6	19.7	24.7	21.1	22.3	30.8
2. Mostly disagree	17.0	14.2	20.2	17.8	14.7	16.7	19.5	14.3	18.2	19.7	14.6	16.3	16.9	20.6	17.4	5.1
3. Neither	16.2	19.4	13.3	17.4	9.7	17.2	17.5	13.5	17.1	16.8	15.3	14.8	17.4	13.9	18.2	7.7
4. Mostly agree	25.6	28.8	22.6	26.0	22.9	22.7	27.0	26.9	24.8	23.8	28.2	26.6	23.2	27.6	25.8	17.9
5. Agree	19.3	25.0	12.9	18.4	22.9	16.9	15.8	24.7	19.0	15.4	23.2	22.6	17.8	16.7	16.2	33.3
Item 7970 N(Wtd)	3638	1713	1788	2822	455	862	1096	1108	573	1970	1444	1224	887	431	987	39
A03F: A preschool child is likely to suffer if the mother works																
1. Disagree	16.3	11.0	21.3	13.2	37.3	14.0	16.3	19.5	13.6	15.6	16.3	15.0	19.5	17.3	13.9	17.5
2. Mostly disagree	16.9	10.6	23.3	17.4	14.3	19.0	17.3	14.1	18.5	20.0	13.3	15.0	17.5	19.7	17.7	17.5
3. Neither	13.2	12.4	14.5	13.9	8.3	13.8	14.9	10.3	14.7	12.6	14.6	14.8	11.1	10.5	14.5	22.5
4. Mostly agree	25.5	27.7	22.7	26.1	19.0	28.1	24.6	24.2	26.2	26.5	24.0	24.7	28.1	24.1	25.2	10.0
5. Agree	28.0	38.3	18.1	29.3	21.2	25.1	27.0	31.9	27.1	25.2	31.9	30.4	23.8	28.1	28.6	30.0
Item 7980 N(Wtd)	3626	1706	1782	2816	448	860	1094	1098	573	1967	1436	1217	889	427	983	40
A03G: A working mother can establish just as warm and secure a relationship with her children as a mother who does not work																
1. Disagree	14.9	21.2	8.4	14.8	11.0	15.5	13.3	17.0	12.9	12.3	17.2	15.5	16.0	12.8	13.5	17.1
2. Mostly disagree	16.8	21.5	12.0	18.2	8.4	17.3	16.8	15.8	18.1	18.5	15.4	18.7	14.6	18.8	16.4	12.2
3. Neither	8.2	9.9	6.4	9.0	3.7	7.4	8.8	7.8	8.9	8.0	8.6	8.4	6.2	8.0	10.0	2.4
4. Mostly agree	27.6	25.3	30.3	28.7	21.8	28.4	30.7	25.0	25.6	27.7	27.7	26.8	27.0	26.7	29.9	26.8
5. Agree	32.5	22.2	42.9	29.2	55.2	31.4	30.4	34.4	34.3	33.5	31.1	30.5	36.3	33.2	30.2	39.0
Item 7990 N(Wtd)	3647	1715	1792	2824	455	866	1095	1112	574	1976	1444	1223	892	431	988	41
A04: The next questions are about pollution and the environment. How much do you agree or disagree with each statement below?																
A04A: Pollution of most types has increased in the U.S. in the last ten years																
1. Disagree	2.6	3.9	1.4	2.1	5.2	2.7	2.4	3.3	1.4	2.4	2.8	2.5	3.1	1.6	2.5	7.3
2. Mostly disagree	4.5	6.6	2.5	4.9	3.3	4.9	5.5	3.8	3.7	4.6	4.6	4.3	4.7	5.3	4.5	4.9
3. Neither	5.9	6.5	5.4	6.2	4.6	8.1	5.9	5.4	3.7	6.3	5.0	5.1	7.0	6.5	5.3	7.3
4. Mostly agree	26.1	25.4	26.9	26.9	21.6	25.3	30.3	23.5	24.6	25.8	26.6	25.0	24.5	26.0	29.8	17.1
5. Agree	60.9	57.5	63.9	59.8	65.3	59.0	56.1	64.0	66.7	60.8	61.1	63.1	60.7	60.8	58.1	63.4
Item 8000 N(Wtd)	3645	1716	1789	2821	458	864	1097	1111	573	1973	1446	1221	894	431	987	41
A04B: Government should take steps to deal with our environmental problems, even if it means that most of us pay higher prices or taxes																
1. Disagree	8.8	10.7	6.5	6.6	18.3	8.9	7.7	11.2	6.1	6.2	11.5	9.6	9.4	6.3	7.9	22.0
2. Mostly disagree	10.8	10.6	11.0	10.5	13.3	10.1	10.5	11.6	11.4	9.8	12.7	9.9	11.4	10.9	11.5	9.8
3. Neither	17.6	15.5	20.0	19.1	10.5	17.2	21.4	13.8	18.2	16.5	19.6	16.4	16.8	19.3	20.4	7.3
4. Mostly agree	37.0	36.6	38.2	38.9	30.3	36.9	36.6	36.2	39.7	39.7	34.0	40.3	35.5	36.0	35.2	31.7
5. Agree	25.7	26.5	24.4	24.8	27.3	26.9	23.8	27.1	24.8	27.7	22.3	23.7	27.0	27.7	25.1	29.3
Item 8010 N(Wtd)	3643	1715	1789	2819	458	862	1097	1113	572	1973	1446	1222	893	430	986	41
A04C: I would prefer to pay more money for things that will last a long time, rather than have them cost less and break sooner																
1. Disagree	.8	.9	.5	.4	2.0	.8	.7	.6	1.0	.6	.6	.9	.6	.7	.6	4.9
2. Mostly disagree	1.3	1.3	1.3	1.0	2.8	1.2	1.2	1.6	1.2	1.1	1.7	1.2	.6	1.6	1.9	-
3. Neither	3.5	3.2	4.0	3.6	2.2	2.9	4.3	3.1	4.0	3.0	4.3	3.4	2.5	5.1	3.7	9.8
4. Mostly agree	21.3	21.0	21.5	22.1	16.3	21.6	23.4	20.1	19.4	21.7	21.3	20.5	22.8	22.6	20.8	14.6
5. Agree	73.0	73.7	72.8	72.8	76.7	73.5	70.3	74.6	74.5	73.5	72.2	74.0	73.6	70.2	72.9	70.7
Item 8020 N(Wtd)	3641	1714	1787	2819	459	861	1096	1112	572	1973	1446	1223	893	429	985	41

QUESTIONNAIRE FORM 3 1981	TOTAL	SEX		RACE		REGION				4YR COLLEGE PLANS		ILLICIT DRUG USE: LIFETIME				
		M	F	White	Black	NE	NC	S	W	Yes	No	None	Mari-juana Only	Few Pills	More Pills	Any Her-oin
Weighted No. of Cases:	*3658*	*1721*	*1795*	*2830*	*459*	*869*	*1100*	*1114*	*575*	*1980*	*1448*	*1228*	*894*	*433*	*990*	*41*
% of Weighted Total:	*100.0*	*47.0*	*49.1*	*77.4*	*12.5*	*23.8*	*30.1*	*30.5*	*15.7*	*54.1*	*39.6*	*33.6*	*24.4*	*11.8*	*27.1*	*1.1*

A04D: I would probably be willing to use a bicycle or mass transit (if available) rather than a car to get to work

	TOTAL	M	F	White	Black	NE	NC	S	W	Yes	No	None	Mari-juana Only	Few Pills	More Pills	Any Her-oin
1. Disagree	19.8	21.2	18.0	17.5	32.6	17.4	16.7	25.7	18.0	16.6	22.8	19.2	19.1	21.7	19.7	19.5
2. Mostly disagree	16.0	18.0	14.0	16.1	12.7	18.4	16.0	15.5	13.4	16.3	15.7	15.1	15.2	17.2	17.5	24.4
3. Neither	10.9	11.6	10.3	11.7	7.4	10.1	13.0	9.8	10.2	10.5	12.0	11.0	10.4	8.9	12.4	4.9
4. Mostly agree	28.7	26.2	31.6	30.2	22.8	28.8	29.2	27.7	29.8	31.1	26.2	28.7	30.1	27.7	28.0	24.4
5. Agree	24.6	23.0	26.1	24.6	24.5	25.2	25.1	21.4	28.9	25.6	23.3	25.9	25.4	24.7	22.2	24.4
Item 8030 N(Wtd)	*3634*	*1712*	*1785*	*2814*	*457*	*860*	*1096*	*1110*	*568*	*1971*	*1440*	*1222*	*891*	*429*	*981*	*41*

A04E: I would be willing to eat less meat and more grains and vegetables, if it would help provide food for starving people

	TOTAL	M	F	White	Black	NE	NC	S	W	Yes	No	None	Mari-juana Only	Few Pills	More Pills	Any Her-oin
1. Disagree	9.6	15.6	3.4	9.8	8.4	11.1	9.3	8.3	10.5	8.4	10.5	7.7	9.1	9.6	11.2	24.4
2. Mostly disagree	8.6	13.0	4.5	9.2	5.9	8.9	9.2	7.8	8.7	9.0	8.0	8.5	9.0	10.7	7.7	7.3
3. Neither	13.1	16.2	9.7	14.3	5.9	13.2	15.1	11.0	13.1	13.7	12.5	12.2	12.7	12.4	14.7	19.5
4. Mostly agree	29.1	29.0	29.3	29.2	27.5	29.6	31.0	27.5	27.8	29.3	29.2	29.6	30.1	30.5	27.1	26.8
5. Agree	39.6	26.3	53.1	37.5	52.3	37.3	35.3	45.4	40.0	39.6	39.8	42.1	39.0	36.8	39.3	22.0
Item 8040 N(Wtd)	*3631*	*1710*	*1785*	*2813*	*455*	*855*	*1096*	*1107*	*572*	*1967*	*1444*	*1218*	*889*	*429*	*984*	*41*

A05: In the following list you will find some statements about leisure time and work. Please show whether you agree or disagree with each statement.

A05A: I like the kind of work you can forget about after the work day is over

	TOTAL	M	F	White	Black	NE	NC	S	W	Yes	No	None	Mari-juana Only	Few Pills	More Pills	Any Her-oin
1. Disagree	14.9	17.0	13.1	12.8	25.1	15.0	13.2	17.3	13.7	16.0	13.0	15.0	16.8	12.3	13.2	19.5
2. Mostly disagree	15.5	15.9	15.4	16.7	10.7	18.7	15.6	13.5	14.2	18.9	11.5	17.7	15.0	15.8	13.3	12.2
3. Neither	12.0	12.4	12.1	13.3	7.4	11.8	13.4	9.6	14.2	14.6	8.7	11.4	14.1	10.7	11.7	9.8
4. Mostly agree	24.7	22.8	26.1	25.4	21.2	23.7	26.7	23.5	24.4	22.9	27.1	24.2	22.1	25.1	27.9	17.1
5. Agree	32.9	31.9	33.3	31.8	35.6	30.8	30.9	36.2	33.7	27.5	39.6	31.6	31.8	36.2	33.8	41.5
Item 8050 N(Wtd)	*3640*	*1716*	*1786*	*2818*	*458*	*861*	*1096*	*1113*	*570*	*1974*	*1444*	*1223*	*892*	*431*	*984*	*41*

A05B: To me, work is nothing more than making a living

	TOTAL	M	F	White	Black	NE	NC	S	W	Yes	No	None	Mari-juana Only	Few Pills	More Pills	Any Her-oin
1. Disagree	43.6	40.5	47.3	44.0	43.8	42.0	42.1	44.8	46.5	47.2	39.1	46.4	44.6	42.9	40.0	22.0
2. Mostly disagree	27.5	27.6	27.8	29.6	15.3	30.5	31.8	21.1	26.9	28.7	26.8	25.5	28.5	28.1	29.8	19.5
3. Neither	7.9	8.0	7.7	8.4	4.4	10.8	7.3	5.7	8.6	8.0	7.5	7.6	7.2	8.8	8.2	12.2
4. Mostly agree	11.5	12.9	9.8	10.8	14.0	9.1	11.1	13.6	11.9	9.7	14.2	10.8	10.1	11.6	13.9	9.8
5. Agree	9.6	11.0	7.3	7.0	22.5	7.5	7.6	14.8	6.3	6.4	12.3	9.7	9.5	8.8	8.0	39.0
Item 8060 N(Wtd)	*3643*	*1715*	*1791*	*2822*	*457*	*861*	*1099*	*1111*	*572*	*1973*	*1446*	*1222*	*892*	*431*	*987*	*41*

A05C: I expect my work to be a very central part of my life

	TOTAL	M	F	White	Black	NE	NC	S	W	Yes	No	None	Mari-juana Only	Few Pills	More Pills	Any Her-oin
1. Disagree	4.3	3.7	4.7	3.9	4.6	4.1	3.6	4.2	5.8	3.9	4.7	3.9	4.0	4.9	4.4	12.2
2. Mostly disagree	9.1	7.4	10.5	9.8	5.9	10.2	9.9	7.6	8.9	8.6	9.6	9.9	6.6	7.4	11.1	17.1
3. Neither	12.2	11.5	13.3	13.8	4.6	13.3	14.1	8.8	13.8	12.4	12.6	11.2	14.0	10.0	13.8	2.4
4. Mostly agree	37.4	38.0	37.1	39.2	27.5	36.9	39.1	34.9	39.6	37.9	37.3	36.2	37.2	39.9	38.7	22.0
5. Agree	37.1	39.4	34.4	33.3	57.3	35.7	33.3	44.5	32.0	37.2	35.7	38.9	38.1	37.8	31.9	46.3
Item 8070 N(Wtd)	*3631*	*1709*	*1784*	*2813*	*454*	*857*	*1096*	*1108*	*571*	*1971*	*1439*	*1218*	*890*	*431*	*983*	*41*

A05D: I want to do my best in my job, even if this sometimes means working overtime

	TOTAL	M	F	White	Black	NE	NC	S	W	Yes	No	None	Mari-juana Only	Few Pills	More Pills	Any Her-oin
1. Disagree	1.4	1.3	1.2	1.0	2.4	1.7	1.4	1.6	.5	1.0	1.8	1.8	.7	1.9	1.2	2.5
2. Mostly disagree	2.1	2.1	2.1	2.2	1.5	2.4	1.7	2.3	1.9	1.7	2.2	1.7	2.7	.2	2.7	7.5
3. Neither	4.5	4.0	5.0	4.9	2.4	5.8	5.3	2.7	4.4	4.2	4.7	3.9	4.0	2.8	6.6	5.0
4. Mostly agree	31.5	32.7	30.0	32.7	23.9	34.5	33.2	27.1	32.3	32.5	30.8	31.1	32.1	30.9	32.7	25.0
5. Agree	60.5	59.9	61.6	59.3	70.0	55.8	58.4	66.3	60.8	60.6	60.5	61.6	60.5	64.3	56.9	62.5
Item 8080 N(Wtd)	*3640*	*1714*	*1788*	*2820*	*456*	*862*	*1095*	*1110*	*572*	*1972*	*1444*	*1220*	*893*	*431*	*985*	*40*

	TOTAL	SEX		RACE		REGION				4YR COLLEGE PLANS		ILLICIT DRUG USE: LIFETIME				
QUESTIONNAIRE FORM 3 1981		M	F	White	Black	NE	NC	S	W	Yes	No	None	Mari- juana Only	Few Pills	More Pills	Any Her- oin
Weighted No. of Cases:	3658	1721	1795	2830	459	869	1100	1114	575	1980	1448	1228	894	433	990	41
% of Weighted Total:	100.0	47.0	49.1	77.4	12.5	23.8	30.1	30.5	15.7	54.1	39.6	33.6	24.4	11.8	27.1	1.1

A05E: I would like to stay in the same job for most of my adult life

1. Disagree	13.4	12.7	13.9	11.9	19.6	12.7	12.4	15.8	11.6	11.1	14.9	11.4	13.4	12.1	15.9	31.7
2. Mostly disagree	12.1	10.4	13.7	11.8	12.7	14.5	11.3	10.1	13.7	11.6	12.2	11.2	10.7	13.5	13.9	7.3
3. Neither	16.2	15.9	16.6	17.9	8.2	20.2	16.5	11.9	17.9	17.9	14.3	16.6	17.1	16.0	15.6	7.3
4. Mostly agree	28.0	28.9	27.3	28.8	22.5	25.9	29.8	26.1	31.2	29.3	27.8	28.7	26.8	28.3	28.0	17.1
5. Agree	30.4	32.0	28.5	29.6	37.0	26.8	30.1	36.0	25.7	30.1	30.7	32.0	32.2	29.9	26.5	39.0
Item 8090 N(Wtd)	3626	1710	1780	2813	449	857	1091	1107	571	1962	1440	1211	889	431	985	41

A06: If you were to get enough money to live as comfortably as you'd like for the rest of your life, would you want to work?

1. I would want to work	79.4	77.9	80.5	78.5	83.1	78.1	79.6	81.0	78.1	79.0	79.8	82.3	83.3	78.5	73.3	59.0
2. I would not want to work	20.6	22.1	19.5	21.6	16.9	21.9	20.4	19.0	21.9	21.1	20.2	17.7	16.7	21.7	26.7	41.0
Item 8100 N(Wtd)	3556	1662	1764	2774	431	845	1081	1077	553	1932	1409	1194	869	424	965	39

The next questions are about living or working with people of different races. Please rate each of the statements below using the following terms:

Not at all acceptable: I'd avoid this if I possibly could.

Somewhat acceptable: I could live with this, but not be happy about it.

Acceptable: This would be O.K., or I'd be neutral about this.

Desirable: I'd really like this.

A07: How would you feel about...

A07A: Having close personal friends of another race?

1. Not at all acceptable	3.1	4.2	2.1	3.1	2.6	3.1	2.6	4.4	1.4	1.8	5.1	3.1	2.4	3.7	3.2	12.5
2. Somewhat acceptable	7.1	10.4	4.0	8.0	2.4	5.1	9.9	7.6	3.9	5.6	8.7	6.5	6.6	6.7	7.9	12.5
3. Acceptable	57.1	58.4	55.2	60.0	48.4	62.9	58.8	53.2	52.9	55.9	58.5	53.7	55.0	61.2	62.1	52.5
4. Desirable	32.7	26.9	38.7	28.9	46.4	28.9	28.7	34.8	41.8	36.7	27.7	36.7	36.0	28.4	26.7	25.0
Item 8110 N(Wtd)	3639	1713	1789	2823	455	862	1098	1109	569	1973	1442	1223	889	433	987	40

A07B: Having a job with a supervisor of a different race?

1. Not at all acceptable	2.8	4.3	1.3	2.9	1.5	3.4	2.6	3.2	1.4	2.1	3.7	2.0	2.3	3.0	3.4	17.5
2. Somewhat acceptable	10.4	13.2	8.0	11.2	8.1	9.0	12.6	11.6	6.0	9.6	11.6	10.5	8.1	10.5	12.2	22.5
3. Acceptable	70.0	69.5	70.2	70.8	68.8	73.4	69.9	68.3	68.1	71.5	67.9	68.6	72.4	69.3	70.9	45.0
4. Desirable	16.9	13.0	20.5	15.2	21.8	14.0	15.0	16.9	24.6	16.8	16.8	18.8	17.2	17.2	13.5	15.0
Item 8120 N(Wtd)	3636	1710	1789	2821	455	862	1098	1107	570	1973	1440	1223	888	430	987	40

A07C: Having a family of a different race (but same level of education and income) move next door to you?

1. Not at all acceptable	5.7	7.6	3.7	5.9	4.4	6.1	5.1	8.2	1.6	4.7	7.0	5.7	4.3	5.6	6.1	15.0
2. Somewhat acceptable	12.5	15.5	9.9	13.7	7.9	12.2	12.9	15.2	6.8	11.1	13.7	12.0	11.2	15.5	12.9	20.0
3. Acceptable	57.5	60.3	54.5	58.7	54.1	59.3	58.5	54.4	58.8	56.4	58.7	55.0	59.8	54.5	60.4	50.0
4. Desirable	24.3	16.6	31.9	21.7	33.8	22.4	23.5	22.2	32.8	27.8	20.7	27.3	24.5	24.4	20.7	15.0
Item 8130 N(Wtd)	3636	1713	1788	2822	453	862	1098	1106	570	1971	1443	1221	889	431	987	40

QUESTIONNAIRE FORM 3 1981	TOTAL	SEX		RACE		REGION				4YR COLLEGE PLANS		ILLICIT DRUG USE: LIFETIME				
		M	F	White	Black	NE	NC	S	W	Yes	No	None	Mari- juana Only	Few Pills	More Pills	Any Her- oin
Weighted No. of Cases:	3658	1721	1795	2830	459	869	1100	1114	575	1980	1448	1228	894	433	990	41
% of Weighted Total:	100.0	47.0	49.1	77.4	12.5	23.8	30.1	30.5	15.7	54.1	39.6	33.6	24.4	11.8	27.1	1.1
A07D: Having your (future) children's friends be all of your race?																
1. Not at all acceptable	17.7	15.6	19.8	16.1	25.5	17.6	16.1	18.2	19.8	18.3	16.8	19.1	18.3	14.5	17.5	12.5
2. Somewhat acceptable	19.4	20.3	18.9	19.6	17.8	20.6	18.8	18.0	21.4	21.3	17.5	17.9	21.5	19.3	19.7	15.0
3. Acceptable	43.4	43.3	43.6	44.3	39.7	44.3	45.8	41.1	41.8	43.8	42.2	43.9	43.3	45.0	42.3	37.5
4. Desirable	19.6	20.8	17.6	20.0	17.2	17.5	19.4	22.7	17.0	16.6	23.6	19.1	17.0	21.4	20.6	35.0
Item 8140 N(Wtd)	3594	1691	1769	2792	443	851	1088	1090	565	1962	1414	1209	876	429	974	40
A07E: Having some of your (future) children's friends be of other races?																
1. Not at all acceptable	3.9	5.5	2.2	4.0	3.1	3.2	3.7	5.4	2.3	2.4	5.6	3.4	4.0	3.7	4.2	10.0
2. Somewhat acceptable	9.3	12.2	6.8	9.9	7.5	7.6	11.0	10.8	5.7	7.8	11.0	8.1	8.9	8.4	11.1	12.5
3. Acceptable	52.0	55.3	48.4	54.2	43.1	56.4	54.0	48.8	48.1	50.7	53.0	49.7	51.2	53.0	55.9	55.0
4. Desirable	34.8	27.0	42.5	31.9	46.0	32.9	31.2	34.9	44.2	39.1	30.4	38.7	35.9	35.1	28.9	25.0
Item 8150 N(Wtd)	3622	1704	1782	2813	452	857	1096	1103	566	1966	1435	1219	883	430	984	40
A08: How would you feel about having a job where...																
A08A: ...all the employees are of your race?																
1. Not at all acceptable	5.8	5.1	6.1	3.4	14.0	4.9	3.8	7.3	8.3	5.6	5.9	7.0	6.6	5.4	3.7	2.5
2. Somewhat acceptable	14.1	13.4	15.1	11.9	25.6	14.5	12.9	14.6	14.9	14.3	13.8	15.0	16.3	12.5	11.8	17.5
3. Acceptable	53.4	52.9	54.1	55.3	47.4	57.4	52.4	50.7	54.7	56.7	48.3	52.3	54.2	52.0	54.7	42.5
4. Desirable	26.7	28.6	24.7	29.5	12.9	23.1	31.0	27.5	22.1	23.4	32.0	25.6	22.8	30.0	29.7	40.0
Item 8160 N(Wtd)	3615	1702	1779	2809	449	854	1097	1099	565	1967	1433	1218	885	423	985	40
A08B: ...some employees are of a different race?																
1. Not at all acceptable	1.0	1.5	.3	.7	1.3	1.5	.7	.8	.9	.7	1.1	.9	.7	.5	1.1	7.5
2. Somewhat acceptable	5.0	6.9	3.2	5.2	2.9	4.8	5.1	5.9	3.9	4.1	6.2	5.6	5.6	5.4	5.4	5.0
3. Acceptable	67.2	70.8	63.8	70.6	55.4	71.2	69.4	64.3	62.4	66.2	68.8	63.3	68.1	67.6	72.1	75.0
4. Desirable	26.8	20.9	32.7	23.6	40.6	22.5	24.7	29.0	33.0	29.1	23.8	30.3	27.7	26.8	21.4	15.0
Item 8170 N(Wtd)	3625	1706	1784	2815	453	855	1096	1105	569	1968	1438	1223	886	426	985	40
A08C: ...most employees are of a different race?																
1. Not at all acceptable	13.2	16.1	10.9	15.1	6.0	13.4	14.9	14.0	7.9	12.3	15.2	10.9	10.9	14.1	17.8	15.0
2. Somewhat acceptable	34.6	37.4	32.4	39.0	17.9	38.1	38.5	32.1	27.0	34.3	36.9	32.1	35.8	38.8	36.0	40.0
3. Acceptable	43.4	40.3	46.1	41.2	50.2	40.4	40.2	43.3	54.5	45.1	39.4	45.6	43.9	39.1	42.3	37.5
4. Desirable	8.7	6.2	10.7	4.7	25.7	8.2	6.4	10.6	10.4	8.3	8.5	11.3	9.4	8.0	4.1	10.0
Item 8180 N(Wtd)	3612	1700	1777	2806	448	852	1096	1097	567	1966	1431	1215	883	425	984	40
A09: How would you feel about living in an area where...																
A09A: ...all the neighbors are of your race?																
1. Not at all acceptable	3.7	2.8	3.9	1.8	11.1	3.5	2.3	4.5	5.3	3.5	3.7	4.6	4.1	3.1	1.9	2.5
2. Somewhat acceptable	9.2	9.0	9.6	7.3	17.6	10.0	7.5	10.0	9.7	8.9	9.4	8.9	10.1	10.1	9.0	2.5
3. Acceptable	50.3	50.0	51.0	50.3	51.2	54.8	49.9	43.3	57.7	54.3	44.3	50.6	52.3	46.9	49.9	45.0
4. Desirable	36.8	38.1	35.6	40.7	20.0	31.7	40.3	42.2	27.3	33.4	42.5	36.0	33.6	40.1	39.2	52.5
Item 8190 N(Wtd)	3613	1703	1776	2809	449	851	1096	1099	567	1967	1433	1218	883	426	982	40
A09B: ...some of the neighbors are of other races?																
1. Not at all acceptable	2.3	3.5	1.1	2.3	1.3	2.7	2.3	2.5	1.4	1.2	3.8	2.0	1.9	1.2	3.0	7.5
2. Somewhat acceptable	8.7	11.6	6.0	9.1	5.7	9.6	7.8	10.5	5.6	7.7	9.9	8.4	7.8	8.9	9.1	15.0
3. Acceptable	67.4	68.7	66.4	70.1	57.8	69.9	70.9	64.0	63.5	68.0	67.0	64.6	66.8	69.2	72.1	62.5
4. Desirable	21.6	16.3	26.6	18.5	34.9	17.8	19.1	22.9	29.5	23.2	19.3	24.9	23.5	20.5	16.0	15.0
Item 8200 N(Wtd)	3621	1707	1781	2813	453	853	1094	1107	567	1969	1438	1221	885	429	984	40

QUESTIONNAIRE FORM 3 1981	TOTAL	SEX		RACE		REGION				4YR COLLEGE PLANS		ILLICIT DRUG USE: LIFETIME				
		M	F	White	Black	NE	NC	S	W	Yes	No	None	Marijuana Only	Few Pills	More Pills	Any Heroin
Weighted No. of Cases:	3658	1721	1795	2830	459	869	1100	1114	575	1980	1448	1228	894	433	990	41
% of Weighted Total:	100.0	47.0	49.1	77.4	12.5	23.8	30.1	30.5	15.7	54.1	39.6	33.6	24.4	11.8	27.1	1.1

A09C: ...most of the neighbors are of other races?

1. Not at all acceptable	22.2	27.2	17.8	25.9	7.6	22.2	24.4	25.6	11.3	21.4	24.6	18.3	20.6	23.0	28.3	17.5
2. Somewhat acceptable	36.4	37.4	35.9	40.0	23.4	38.1	37.9	34.4	34.4	35.2	38.5	33.1	37.5	39.0	39.1	32.5
3. Acceptable	35.3	30.7	38.8	30.9	51.3	33.1	33.5	33.6	45.4	37.1	31.4	40.5	35.8	30.5	29.8	35.0
4. Desirable	6.2	4.6	7.6	3.2	17.9	6.6	4.2	6.4	8.9	6.3	5.5	8.1	6.0	7.5	2.7	15.0
Item 8210 N(Wtd)	3606	1700	1772	2807	448	850	1094	1098	564	1964	1430	1216	879	426	982	40

A10: How would you feel about having your (future) children go to schools where...

A10A: ...all the children are of your race?

1. Not at all acceptable	7.1	5.7	8.3	4.7	17.6	5.5	5.7	8.5	9.9	7.2	6.9	8.6	7.2	6.6	5.9	2.5
2. Somewhat acceptable	12.2	12.7	11.8	9.7	22.5	13.1	8.1	14.7	13.6	13.1	10.7	13.0	11.8	13.6	10.6	10.0
3. Acceptable	47.1	47.5	47.4	48.4	42.8	51.7	45.8	42.9	51.0	51.1	42.0	46.7	51.4	45.8	44.4	40.0
4. Desirable	33.6	34.1	32.6	37.2	17.4	29.6	40.3	34.0	25.4	28.5	40.4	31.8	29.6	34.0	39.1	50.0
Item 8220 N(Wtd)	3609	1702	1774	2806	449	847	1096	1098	567	1965	1431	1216	883	426	980	40

A10B: ...some of the children are of other races?

1. Not at all acceptable	1.4	2.2	.6	1.2	2.4	1.8	1.3	1.5	.9	.9	2.0	1.4	.7	1.2	1.7	10.0
2. Somewhat acceptable	5.9	7.6	3.7	5.6	5.3	6.5	6.2	5.7	4.7	4.7	7.0	5.5	4.9	6.8	6.1	10.0
3. Acceptable	64.0	67.3	61.1	66.3	56.5	67.1	65.6	62.6	59.1	63.7	64.6	61.5	65.0	64.3	67.3	67.5
4. Desirable	28.7	22.9	34.5	27.0	36.0	24.6	26.9	30.1	35.3	30.7	26.4	31.6	29.4	27.7	24.9	15.0
Item 8230 N(Wtd)	3616	1704	1778	2807	453	849	1093	1105	569	1966	1435	1217	883	429	981	40

A10C: ...most of the children are of other races?

1. Not at all acceptable	26.4	30.8	22.0	31.0	8.5	26.2	30.8	28.1	14.8	25.8	27.8	21.1	25.0	29.3	32.9	30.0
2. Somewhat acceptable	34.6	35.5	34.4	37.5	24.9	37.0	35.3	33.0	32.8	33.8	36.1	31.8	37.3	35.9	35.9	25.0
3. Acceptable	32.6	29.2	35.5	28.6	46.5	30.3	29.6	31.8	43.4	33.8	30.4	38.0	31.6	28.2	28.5	32.5
4. Desirable	6.4	4.4	8.0	2.9	20.0	6.4	4.3	7.1	8.8	6.6	5.7	9.0	6.1	6.6	2.7	12.5
Item 8240 N(Wtd)	3602	1696	1773	2804	445	848	1093	1094	567	1962	1431	1212	881	426	979	40

A11: What race are your close friends?

1. All my race	37.1	36.6	37.4	40.8	28.1	39.9	45.0	34.1	23.3	36.2	38.8	36.4	40.3	34.9	35.8	40.0
2. Almost all my race	31.5	32.2	31.1	35.3	18.8	32.4	33.7	28.8	31.3	32.1	31.9	28.6	29.4	34.7	36.0	20.0
3. Mostly my race	19.0	18.8	19.3	18.1	23.2	18.6	13.7	21.8	24.6	20.0	17.6	19.6	19.4	17.6	18.9	17.5
4. About half my race	7.4	7.5	7.6	4.5	18.6	4.2	4.7	10.4	11.7	6.6	7.5	8.8	7.1	8.4	5.8	5.0
5. Mostly other race(s)	2.3	2.7	1.9	.6	4.9	2.7	1.6	2.1	3.7	2.5	2.1	2.9	2.5	1.9	1.5	5.0
6. Almost all other race(s)	2.6	2.3	2.7	.7	6.4	2.1	1.5	2.8	5.3	2.5	2.2	3.8	1.4	2.3	1.7	10.0
Item 8250 N(Wtd)	3611	1700	1779	2808	452	853	1091	1105	562	1967	1429	1220	878	427	982	40

A12: What race are the people in your neighborhood?

1. All my race	52.0	50.7	53.4	57.5	38.5	52.3	57.0	55.3	34.8	49.8	55.7	50.0	52.4	56.0	52.7	47.5
2. Almost all my race	25.7	27.9	23.8	28.5	17.7	26.3	27.8	20.9	30.2	27.0	24.0	25.9	24.5	23.2	28.4	15.0
3. Mostly my race	10.0	10.1	9.8	9.5	13.5	10.2	7.3	10.8	13.4	10.2	9.3	9.5	11.1	8.9	9.9	12.5
4. About half my race	5.9	5.0	6.8	3.3	15.5	5.9	3.5	7.8	7.1	6.0	5.7	6.2	6.3	5.9	4.7	17.5
5. Mostly other race(s)	3.5	3.4	3.4	.7	8.6	2.8	2.5	3.4	6.4	3.7	2.9	4.4	3.5	3.5	1.9	2.5
6. Almost all other race(s)	2.9	2.9	2.7	.5	6.2	2.5	1.9	1.7	8.0	3.2	2.4	3.9	2.2	2.3	2.5	5.0
Item 8260 N(Wtd)	3609	1700	1780	2808	452	854	1091	1104	560	1967	1432	1220	879	427	979	40

A13: What race were the students in the elementary school where you spent the most time?

1. All my race	38.8	37.4	40.4	43.1	24.9	47.8	51.0	25.8	26.7	39.7	38.6	36.9	41.0	40.3	39.6	32.5
2. Almost all my race	28.7	29.9	27.6	32.1	15.2	27.7	31.7	25.3	31.3	29.2	28.7	28.9	26.3	29.2	30.5	30.0
3. Mostly my race	12.9	14.4	11.6	13.9	9.4	9.5	9.1	16.7	18.1	12.4	13.1	12.7	12.4	13.7	13.9	2.5
4. About half my race	11.6	11.3	11.6	8.5	28.0	7.3	3.9	23.0	10.5	9.4	13.7	10.7	12.3	11.1	11.0	27.5
5. Mostly other race(s)	4.3	3.8	4.9	1.5	11.9	4.2	2.1	5.5	6.4	5.0	3.2	5.5	4.9	2.6	2.9	5.0
6. Almost all other race(s)	3.7	3.3	3.9	.9	10.3	3.6	2.2	3.6	6.8	4.2	2.7	5.4	3.2	3.1	2.0	2.5
Item 8270 N(Wtd)	3600	1692	1778	2803	446	853	1090	1095	562	1965	1426	1219	878	424	977	40

QUESTIONNAIRE FORM 3 1981	TOTAL	SEX		RACE		REGION				4YR COLLEGE PLANS		ILLICIT DRUG USE: LIFETIME				
		M	F	White	Black	NE	NC	S	W	Yes	No	None	Marijuana Only	Few Pills	More Pills	Any Heroin
Weighted No. of Cases:	3658	1721	1795	2830	459	869	1100	1114	575	1980	1448	1228	894	433	990	41
% of Weighted Total:	100.0	47.0	49.1	77.4	12.5	23.8	30.1	30.5	15.7	54.1	39.6	33.6	24.4	11.8	27.1	1.1

A14: What race are the students in your present school (if you are in school)?

	TOTAL	M	F	White	Black	NE	NC	S	W	Yes	No	None	Marijuana Only	Few Pills	More Pills	Any Heroin
1. All my race	14.3	13.8	14.6	14.7	16.2	19.3	20.6	7.9	6.9	14.9	13.6	15.0	15.1	13.9	13.2	10.0
2. Almost all my race	35.6	38.4	33.2	41.4	13.6	43.7	42.5	24.5	31.6	37.2	34.2	31.5	35.6	36.2	41.3	35.0
3. Mostly my race	23.2	23.4	23.4	26.3	10.4	22.0	22.0	22.8	28.2	22.1	25.2	23.4	23.5	23.1	23.2	17.5
4. About half my race	17.0	15.3	18.4	14.3	30.4	6.9	8.2	32.9	18.4	15.8	18.6	17.1	16.2	17.2	16.3	25.0
5. Mostly other race(s)	5.7	5.8	5.5	1.9	17.6	4.3	3.1	8.0	8.5	5.9	4.5	8.0	5.5	4.9	3.2	10.0
6. Almost all other race(s)	4.2	3.3	4.9	1.2	12.0	4.0	3.7	3.7	6.4	4.1	3.9	5.0	4.1	4.5	2.9	2.5
Item 8280 N(Wtd)	3605	1697	1776	2801	450	854	1090	1096	564	1968	1426	1217	878	425	979	40

A15: What race are the people that you work with on your job (if you have a job)?

	TOTAL	M	F	White	Black	NE	NC	S	W	Yes	No	None	Marijuana Only	Few Pills	More Pills	Any Heroin
1. All my race	44.2	45.0	43.5	51.3	13.7	46.9	57.9	31.1	37.0	42.4	48.0	41.8	44.7	46.4	47.2	24.3
2. Almost all my race	23.0	22.5	23.6	26.1	9.3	25.7	20.9	23.0	23.1	24.7	21.1	22.4	21.1	23.6	24.6	27.0
3. Mostly my race	12.3	13.6	10.8	13.2	7.3	13.5	9.5	12.2	16.7	12.2	12.5	10.1	13.1	11.3	14.5	13.5
4. About half my race	9.7	8.5	11.0	6.9	25.7	6.0	6.0	17.7	7.5	9.5	9.4	12.5	9.0	9.7	7.5	-
5. Mostly other race(s)	6.1	5.6	6.4	1.5	25.9	4.4	3.0	9.8	8.1	6.4	4.5	7.5	7.0	5.1	3.7	13.5
6. Almost all other race(s)	4.7	4.6	4.6	1.0	17.8	3.5	2.6	6.3	7.5	4.9	4.3	5.6	5.1	4.0	2.5	21.6
Item 8290 N(Wtd)	3001	1486	1408	2379	343	682	960	891	467	1606	1220	961	743	373	837	37

A16: How often do you do things (like having a conversation, eating together, playing sports) with people of other races?

	TOTAL	M	F	White	Black	NE	NC	S	W	Yes	No	None	Marijuana Only	Few Pills	More Pills	Any Heroin
1. Not at all	11.4	10.8	12.3	12.7	6.9	11.4	17.5	7.8	6.7	9.0	14.7	10.5	11.8	12.9	11.6	20.5
2. A little	33.0	32.7	32.7	36.2	24.2	37.0	34.9	31.2	26.5	32.6	33.4	33.2	32.4	33.5	32.6	25.6
3. Some	37.4	37.1	37.9	37.9	34.0	37.1	33.4	40.0	40.4	37.9	37.0	35.8	37.1	35.4	40.9	35.9
4. A lot	18.2	19.3	17.2	13.2	34.9	14.5	14.3	21.0	26.4	20.5	14.9	20.5	18.7	18.3	14.9	17.9
Item 8300 N(Wtd)	3611	1699	1779	2809	447	851	1093	1102	565	1966	1432	1220	879	427	981	39

A17: Generally, how do you feel about the experiences you have had with people of other races?

	TOTAL	M	F	White	Black	NE	NC	S	W	Yes	No	None	Marijuana Only	Few Pills	More Pills	Any Heroin
5. Very good	25.5	20.5	30.1	22.9	33.4	24.7	24.9	23.4	32.1	27.7	21.7	30.4	24.7	23.6	20.6	22.5
4. Mostly good	41.0	39.3	43.2	41.2	43.0	39.7	42.6	40.2	41.4	42.1	40.3	40.4	42.0	43.3	40.3	40.0
3. Mixed	29.6	34.9	24.3	31.5	22.3	31.4	28.4	32.5	23.8	27.8	32.4	25.5	30.5	29.3	34.1	27.5
2. Mostly bad	2.7	3.7	1.8	3.1	1.1	2.5	2.7	3.0	2.5	1.8	3.7	2.5	2.2	2.6	3.4	5.0
1. Very bad	1.2	1.7	.6	1.4	.2	1.8	1.5	.9	.2	.5	2.0	1.1	.6	1.2	1.5	7.5
Item 8310 N(Wtd)	3593	1693	1767	2791	449	847	1085	1098	563	1958	1418	1219	871	423	975	40

A18: The next questions are about some of your own plans. Are you married or engaged?

	TOTAL	M	F	White	Black	NE	NC	S	W	Yes	No	None	Marijuana Only	Few Pills	More Pills	Any Heroin
1. Married--SKIP TO Q.A20	1.2	.1	2.2	1.2	1.1	.6	.9	2.2	.4	.3	2.5	1.6	.7	1.8	1.0	-
2. Engaged	8.2	4.3	11.8	8.1	9.6	5.3	9.2	10.0	7.6	3.8	14.6	7.6	5.7	10.3	10.4	11.8
3. Neither	90.6	95.6	86.0	90.8	89.3	94.0	89.8	87.7	92.0	95.9	82.9	90.8	93.5	88.0	88.6	88.2
Item 8320 N(Wtd)	3322	1541	1673	2657	355	806	1002	987	527	1855	1296	1108	802	399	929	34

A19: If it were just up to you, what would be the ideal time for you to get married?

	TOTAL	M	F	White	Black	NE	NC	S	W	Yes	No	None	Marijuana Only	Few Pills	More Pills	Any Heroin
1. Within the next year or so	7.7	3.4	11.8	8.1	6.8	4.9	9.3	9.9	4.6	1.9	16.4	8.5	5.7	6.8	8.7	14.3
2. Two or three years from now	19.3	12.8	25.8	18.8	19.2	11.8	22.1	21.3	21.5	11.9	29.2	19.4	18.2	19.1	20.2	22.9
3. Four or five years from now	34.8	35.9	34.2	36.0	30.3	34.0	35.6	34.4	35.0	38.7	29.6	37.4	37.1	35.2	30.5	17.1
4. Over five years from now	33.9	42.5	25.1	33.5	35.0	45.5	28.8	29.3	35.2	44.3	19.9	30.9	35.1	34.2	36.4	25.7
5. I don't want to marry	4.3	5.4	3.0	3.6	8.7	3.8	4.4	5.1	3.7	3.1	5.0	3.9	3.8	4.4	4.2	20.0
Item 8330 N(Wtd) ★	3403	1604	1679	2690	380	815	1033	1010	545	1892	1318	1128	844	409	931	35

★=excludes respondents for whom question was inappropriate.

QUESTIONNAIRE FORM 3 1981	TOTAL	SEX		RACE		REGION				4YR COLLEGE PLANS		ILLICIT DRUG USE: LIFETIME				
		M	F	White	Black	NE	NC	S	W	Yes	No	None	Mari-juana Only	Few Pills	More Pills	Any Her-oin
Weighted No. of Cases:	3658	1721	1795	2830	459	869	1100	1114	575	1980	1448	1228	894	433	990	41
% of Weighted Total:	100.0	47.0	49.1	77.4	12.5	23.8	30.1	30.5	15.7	54.1	39.6	33.6	24.4	11.8	27.1	1.1

A20: Have you thought at all about whether you'd like to have children or how many you'd like to have?

	TOTAL	M	F	White	Black	NE	NC	S	W	Yes	No	None	Mari-juana Only	Few Pills	More Pills	Any Her-oin
3. I've thought about it a lot	40.4	27.5	53.7	39.8	47.5	37.0	40.0	44.1	38.6	37.9	44.7	40.0	40.3	41.6	39.9	42.5
2. I've thought about it a little	50.6	58.1	43.1	51.6	43.2	54.0	51.0	45.8	54.3	55.2	44.4	50.4	51.5	49.4	51.2	45.0
1. I haven't thought about it at all	9.0	14.4	3.2	8.6	9.0	9.1	9.0	10.1	7.1	7.0	11.0	9.6	8.1	8.8	8.9	12.5
Item 8340 N(Wtd)	3511	1649	1736	2730	442	828	1059	1072	552	1910	1392	1167	860	421	961	40

A21: All things considered, if you could have exactly the number of children you want, what number would you choose to have?

	TOTAL	M	F	White	Black	NE	NC	S	W	Yes	No	None	Mari-juana Only	Few Pills	More Pills	Any Her-oin
1. None	3.5	3.6	3.4	3.3	4.0	2.6	2.9	4.1	5.0	3.1	3.7	3.7	2.5	3.8	3.8	10.0
2. One	4.9	4.4	5.6	4.3	9.1	3.1	4.3	6.2	6.4	4.0	6.0	4.8	3.4	7.3	5.5	7.5
3. Two	45.3	45.8	44.7	45.2	49.4	39.8	44.9	51.6	42.2	43.4	47.5	42.1	49.0	48.9	46.0	25.0
4. Three	21.6	22.4	20.6	22.2	16.9	23.9	22.7	18.7	21.6	22.4	20.7	23.5	19.7	20.3	20.9	27.5
5. Four	10.9	9.1	12.6	10.4	11.6	12.6	10.3	9.8	11.2	12.2	9.4	11.5	11.3	9.2	10.4	7.5
6. Five	2.6	2.1	3.1	2.7	2.0	3.3	2.6	1.6	3.7	2.8	2.4	2.8	2.6	2.6	2.5	5.0
7. Six or more	2.8	2.3	3.4	3.0	1.6	2.9	3.0	2.5	2.7	2.9	2.8	3.4	2.6	2.1	2.0	7.5
8. Don't know	8.4	10.3	6.6	8.8	5.6	11.8	9.1	5.6	7.1	9.2	7.4	8.2	9.0	5.7	9.1	10.0
Item 8350 N(Wtd)	3584	1685	1769	2785	449	850	1085	1088	561	1952	1416	1206	878	423	971	40

A22: If the "population explosion" were NOT a problem, would you choose to have a larger number of children?

	TOTAL	M	F	White	Black	NE	NC	S	W	Yes	No	None	Mari-juana Only	Few Pills	More Pills	Any Her-oin
4. Yes, I'm sure I would want more	6.9	5.7	8.1	6.7	5.7	7.9	5.7	6.8	8.0	6.3	7.8	6.5	5.4	5.1	8.7	10.0
3. I probably would want more	14.1	14.4	13.9	14.4	10.1	14.4	15.7	13.9	11.3	13.8	14.8	13.7	14.6	14.9	14.2	15.0
2. I probably would not want more	36.3	36.8	35.9	37.0	33.2	38.4	36.6	34.1	37.0	39.0	33.5	37.6	36.1	36.7	35.1	32.5
1. I'm sure I would not want more	28.1	27.4	28.7	27.1	36.9	23.2	28.1	31.3	28.8	26.7	29.2	25.6	29.4	30.2	28.8	30.0
8. Don't know, no idea	14.6	15.8	13.3	14.7	14.1	15.9	13.8	13.8	15.2	14.2	14.7	16.7	14.5	12.8	13.1	12.5
Item 8360 N(Wtd)	3629	1711	1786	2818	455	859	1098	1107	565	1969	1441	1220	889	430	985	40

A23: If it were just up to you, how soon after getting married would you want to have your first child?

	TOTAL	M	F	White	Black	NE	NC	S	W	Yes	No	None	Mari-juana Only	Few Pills	More Pills	Any Her-oin
1. I don't want to have children (or get married)	3.9	4.3	3.4	3.6	4.2	3.2	3.3	4.3	5.5	3.6	4.2	4.2	2.7	4.3	4.0	15.0
2. I wouldn't wait at all	4.3	6.1	2.3	3.8	5.1	5.4	4.0	4.0	3.8	3.4	5.5	5.2	3.9	3.8	3.6	10.0
3. I would wait one year	27.4	30.9	24.1	25.7	35.5	24.7	27.3	28.2	30.2	24.3	30.7	28.0	27.9	26.5	26.3	25.0
4. I would wait two years	30.8	28.4	33.2	31.8	25.7	31.6	32.6	28.8	29.5	33.3	27.9	29.7	32.6	33.3	30.0	22.5
5. I would wait three years	16.5	13.8	18.8	17.6	12.1	16.6	16.9	16.7	15.0	17.7	15.4	15.1	16.2	16.1	19.1	10.0
6. I would wait four or five years	6.8	4.4	9.3	7.5	4.7	5.4	7.3	7.6	6.6	6.6	7.4	7.1	6.2	7.3	6.9	5.0
7. I would wait more than five years	1.9	1.5	2.2	1.6	2.7	2.1	1.2	2.1	2.1	1.9	1.8	1.6	2.1	2.6	1.4	5.0
8. Don't know, or already have a child	8.4	10.4	6.6	8.2	10.3	10.9	7.5	8.1	7.3	9.1	7.3	9.1	8.5	6.1	8.8	7.5
Item 8370 N(Wtd)	3577	1680	1769	2781	448	850	1082	1085	560	1951	1413	1204	875	423	971	40

A24: Now we'd like you to make some ratings of how good or bad a job you feel each of the following organizations is doing for the country as a whole. For each one, mark the circle that best describes how you feel. How good or bad a job is being done for the country as a whole by...

A24A: Large corporations?

	TOTAL	M	F	White	Black	NE	NC	S	W	Yes	No	None	Mari-juana Only	Few Pills	More Pills	Any Her-oin
1. Very poor	3.7	5.1	2.1	3.8	1.3	4.6	3.1	3.4	4.0	4.0	3.3	3.6	3.0	2.3	4.1	22.5
2. Poor	12.0	15.0	9.2	12.2	11.0	13.4	12.1	11.2	11.2	12.5	11.9	11.6	12.4	13.0	12.6	5.0
3. Fair	35.6	35.8	35.2	36.0	36.6	33.1	36.9	34.1	39.9	35.3	36.1	34.8	35.4	38.4	36.3	37.5
4. Good	28.1	29.3	27.1	29.2	23.3	28.4	28.8	29.2	24.6	28.3	28.0	28.4	30.7	27.5	25.3	22.5
5. Very good	6.8	6.4	7.1	6.1	10.8	7.5	6.5	7.9	4.4	7.3	6.1	6.9	5.9	6.9	7.3	5.0
8. No opinion	13.7	8.4	19.2	12.8	16.7	13.0	12.6	14.4	15.8	12.6	14.6	14.8	12.8	11.8	14.3	7.5
Item 8380 N(Wtd)	3616	1708	1777	2809	454	852	1091	1103	569	1966	1434	1213	888	432	980	40

QUESTIONNAIRE FORM 3 1981	TOTAL	SEX		RACE		REGION				4YR COLLEGE PLANS		ILLICIT DRUG USE: LIFETIME				
		M	F	White	Black	NE	NC	S	W	Yes	No	None	Marijuana Only	Few Pills	More Pills	Any Heroin
Weighted No. of Cases:	3658	1721	1795	2830	459	869	1100	1114	575	1980	1448	1228	894	433	990	41
% of Weighted Total:	100.0	47.0	49.1	77.4	12.5	23.8	30.1	30.5	15.7	54.1	39.6	33.6	24.4	11.8	27.1	1.1
A24B: Major labor unions?																
1. Very poor	3.5	5.2	1.8	3.8	.7	3.3	3.9	3.5	2.8	3.2	4.0	3.0	3.7	4.2	3.4	10.0
2. Poor	10.6	13.5	8.0	11.1	8.4	10.7	13.5	9.4	7.0	11.3	9.6	10.6	12.7	11.1	8.7	15.0
3. Fair	34.1	35.2	33.0	34.8	34.1	32.2	33.7	34.8	36.6	33.8	34.4	35.6	31.2	33.3	35.2	47.5
4. Good	29.1	28.7	29.3	29.2	27.2	31.5	29.2	26.0	31.0	29.9	28.4	27.4	27.9	29.9	32.3	15.0
5. Very good	7.7	8.0	7.6	7.2	9.5	8.0	7.3	8.5	6.3	8.3	6.7	7.7	8.5	6.0	7.4	7.5
8. No opinion	15.1	9.5	20.3	13.9	20.1	14.4	12.1	17.8	16.2	13.6	16.9	15.8	16.0	15.0	13.2	7.5
Item 8390 N(Wtd)	3611	1708	1772	2807	452	852	1089	1102	568	1962	1434	1209	889	432	979	40
A24C: The nation's colleges and universities?																
1. Very poor	.9	1.1	.7	.6	.9	.6	1.0	.6	1.4	.7	1.2	1.2	.8	.5	.7	5.0
2. Poor	2.6	3.3	2.1	2.5	3.8	3.5	2.2	2.3	2.8	2.7	2.7	2.1	2.9	3.0	2.8	2.5
3. Fair	15.2	15.2	14.9	13.9	20.6	13.7	15.8	15.6	15.7	11.2	20.3	13.8	14.8	16.7	17.0	22.5
4. Good	46.2	44.9	47.4	47.8	40.7	47.5	47.8	45.3	42.7	47.6	44.8	47.5	47.2	46.5	44.4	22.5
5. Very good	30.5	31.2	30.0	31.3	26.8	29.0	29.4	31.5	33.0	35.0	24.2	29.8	31.2	28.7	30.7	42.5
8. No opinion	4.7	4.3	5.0	3.9	7.3	5.9	3.9	4.7	4.4	2.7	6.7	5.7	3.2	4.6	4.5	5.0
Item 8400 N(Wtd)	3612	1706	1775	2807	452	853	1089	1103	567	1966	1430	1212	888	432	978	40
A24D: The nation's public schools?																
1. Very poor	6.1	6.9	5.5	6.1	5.4	7.2	6.5	4.2	7.6	6.6	5.5	5.6	5.7	3.7	8.1	10.0
2. Poor	15.0	14.9	15.1	15.2	12.8	16.1	13.2	15.0	16.6	15.8	14.2	13.3	15.9	15.5	16.5	17.5
3. Fair	34.2	33.9	34.7	35.1	31.2	33.5	34.8	33.9	34.5	33.9	35.0	31.2	34.2	38.4	36.7	37.5
4. Good	31.0	32.0	29.9	31.7	30.9	30.7	33.8	30.2	27.6	31.7	30.5	35.0	30.8	30.3	27.0	15.0
5. Very good	10.2	9.1	10.9	9.2	13.9	8.1	8.8	12.6	11.1	9.7	10.0	11.2	10.8	9.5	7.9	12.5
8. No opinion	3.6	3.3	3.8	2.7	5.8	4.4	3.0	4.2	2.5	2.3	4.7	3.6	2.5	2.5	3.9	10.0
Item 8410 N(Wtd)	3599	1700	1770	2803	446	847	1090	1096	566	1954	1433	1204	887	432	976	40
A24E: Churches and religious organizations?																
1. Very poor	2.4	3.2	1.9	2.5	1.3	3.7	1.3	1.9	3.7	2.3	2.6	2.2	2.5	2.3	2.7	10.0
2. Poor	4.6	5.4	4.0	4.4	3.7	6.0	3.4	4.3	5.5	5.0	4.3	3.9	4.4	3.7	5.8	15.0
3. Fair	21.6	21.3	21.9	22.2	19.4	22.6	23.3	18.3	23.0	22.6	20.0	19.7	20.6	23.9	23.9	12.5
4. Good	38.0	37.5	38.5	38.9	35.9	38.0	37.9	40.1	34.6	39.0	37.6	40.3	38.8	37.8	35.6	22.5
5. Very good	21.6	20.9	22.0	20.4	28.4	15.6	21.4	26.2	21.7	21.2	22.0	23.7	22.1	20.9	19.2	12.5
8. No opinion	11.7	11.7	11.4	11.6	11.0	14.1	12.6	9.3	11.5	10.0	13.5	10.3	11.8	11.4	12.8	25.0
Item 8420 N(Wtd)	3601	1706	1766	2803	454	845	1088	1101	566	1957	1432	1207	884	431	980	40
A24F: The national news media (TV, magazines, news services)?																
1. Very poor	4.2	4.7	3.4	4.4	2.2	4.7	3.7	3.9	5.3	4.0	4.8	3.9	3.8	4.4	4.8	15.0
2. Poor	8.5	8.8	8.5	9.3	5.1	9.4	9.5	6.7	9.0	8.4	9.3	7.4	8.8	10.4	9.4	2.5
3. Fair	25.0	25.0	25.1	25.6	23.6	24.2	25.2	24.3	27.2	25.7	24.4	24.6	26.2	24.3	24.6	27.5
4. Good	36.2	37.4	35.7	37.2	30.2	33.7	38.1	35.6	37.5	37.2	35.4	36.2	34.9	37.0	37.1	35.0
5. Very good	21.4	20.1	22.0	19.3	31.8	23.3	19.2	23.4	18.7	21.5	20.4	22.1	22.2	19.4	20.8	15.0
8. No opinion	4.6	4.0	5.3	4.2	7.1	4.5	4.4	6.2	2.5	3.2	5.7	5.9	4.1	4.4	3.4	-
Item 8430 N(Wtd)	3606	1706	1771	2805	453	848	1091	1101	566	1963	1433	1212	887	432	977	40
A24G: The President and his administration?																
1. Very poor	7.0	6.9	6.9	4.5	18.1	6.4	5.8	9.2	5.8	6.1	7.8	6.2	9.0	3.7	6.3	25.0
2. Poor	9.4	8.0	10.3	7.2	22.3	7.4	9.9	11.2	7.4	8.0	10.8	9.5	9.7	7.4	9.2	20.0
3. Fair	28.7	27.8	29.6	29.4	27.0	29.8	28.1	29.4	27.0	28.0	29.9	27.2	29.5	27.8	31.5	15.0
4. Good	30.8	33.2	28.4	34.8	10.8	32.2	32.9	24.5	36.9	34.7	26.5	31.5	31.1	34.0	29.7	17.5
5. Very good	12.0	13.8	10.7	13.3	5.1	11.4	12.7	11.9	11.8	13.1	10.1	14.4	9.3	13.0	10.3	20.0
8. No opinion	12.2	10.4	14.2	10.8	16.8	12.8	10.6	13.9	11.0	10.1	14.9	11.2	11.2	14.1	12.9	5.0
Item 8440 N(Wtd)	3609	1708	1771	2807	452	849	1090	1103	566	1963	1432	1212	884	432	981	40

QUESTIONNAIRE FORM 3 1981	TOTAL	SEX		RACE		REGION				4YR COLLEGE PLANS		ILLICIT DRUG USE: LIFETIME				
		M	F	White	Black	NE	NC	S	W	Yes	No	None	Mari-juana Only	Few Pills	More Pills	Any Her-oin
Weighted No. of Cases:	3658	1721	1795	2830	459	869	1100	1114	575	1980	1448	1228	894	433	990	41
% of Weighted Total:	100.0	47.0	49.1	77.4	12.5	23.8	30.1	30.5	15.7	54.1	39.6	33.6	24.4	11.8	27.1	1.1

A24H: Congress--that is, the U.S. Senate and House of Representatives?

	TOTAL	M	F	White	Black	NE	NC	S	W	Yes	No	None	Mari-juana Only	Few Pills	More Pills	Any Her-oin
1. Very poor	5.0	6.6	3.3	4.3	7.5	4.0	5.5	5.9	3.7	4.2	5.6	4.5	5.5	2.3	5.6	15.0
2. Poor	11.5	12.4	10.8	10.7	18.0	11.6	9.7	13.8	10.2	11.4	11.6	11.1	11.8	11.8	11.7	17.5
3. Fair	36.7	37.1	36.3	38.0	32.5	36.4	37.1	35.3	39.0	37.0	36.6	36.6	36.3	37.0	37.6	30.0
4. Good	24.0	25.2	22.8	26.0	14.1	25.6	26.0	20.5	24.9	26.8	20.6	25.7	25.0	23.6	21.6	25.0
5. Very good	4.7	4.5	4.7	4.0	6.6	3.6	4.4	5.4	4.9	4.5	4.3	5.5	3.4	6.7	3.4	5.0
8. No opinion	18.1	14.2	22.0	17.1	21.5	18.6	17.2	19.1	17.3	16.0	21.4	16.6	17.9	18.5	20.2	10.0
Item 8450　N(Wtd)	3611	1708	1774	2807	455	850	1090	1103	567	1964	1434	1210	887	432	982	40

A24I: The U.S. Supreme Court?

	TOTAL	M	F	White	Black	NE	NC	S	W	Yes	No	None	Mari-juana Only	Few Pills	More Pills	Any Her-oin
1. Very poor	3.6	5.1	2.1	3.2	3.8	4.0	3.1	4.3	2.1	3.2	3.9	3.5	3.3	1.9	3.6	22.5
2. Poor	7.9	7.5	7.1	7.5	9.1	8.3	8.0	7.6	7.8	6.5	10.0	7.4	6.8	8.1	9.7	7.5
3. Fair	31.1	29.6	32.5	31.3	33.6	30.3	30.6	32.6	30.2	29.9	33.0	31.8	30.5	31.5	31.0	30.0
4. Good	29.4	33.2	26.0	30.9	24.1	30.4	32.1	26.5	28.6	32.9	24.1	29.9	31.4	28.5	28.2	10.0
5. Very good	7.8	7.7	8.0	6.9	11.5	7.0	7.4	7.8	9.7	8.2	7.0	8.4	7.7	7.9	6.9	10.0
8. No opinion	20.2	15.4	24.4	20.3	17.9	19.9	18.8	21.2	21.5	19.2	21.9	19.1	20.2	22.5	20.7	20.0
Item 8460　N(Wtd)	3599	1704	1768	2799	452	841	1091	1100	567	1955	1434	1209	882	432	976	40

A24J: All the courts and the justice system in general?

	TOTAL	M	F	White	Black	NE	NC	S	W	Yes	No	None	Mari-juana Only	Few Pills	More Pills	Any Her-oin
1. Very poor	7.3	10.3	4.3	7.1	7.0	8.1	7.0	7.5	6.0	7.0	7.5	6.9	7.2	4.4	7.7	35.0
2. Poor	16.6	17.9	15.5	17.3	13.0	21.0	13.9	15.1	18.3	19.2	13.0	16.1	16.3	15.5	18.7	5.0
3. Fair	35.8	34.3	37.5	36.1	37.8	33.3	37.3	36.1	35.8	35.7	36.7	34.1	37.0	38.7	35.6	35.0
4. Good	22.7	23.4	22.1	23.8	18.7	22.1	24.5	21.4	22.2	23.2	21.8	23.6	23.4	23.4	21.2	15.0
5. Very good	4.2	3.6	4.7	3.5	7.0	3.3	4.2	4.3	5.5	3.9	4.3	5.5	3.9	4.2	3.1	2.5
8. No opinion	13.5	10.4	15.9	12.1	16.3	12.0	13.0	15.7	12.4	11.1	16.6	13.7	12.1	13.9	13.6	7.5
Item 8470　N(Wtd)	3610	1706	1773	2807	455	849	1092	1105	564	1963	1433	1210	887	432	981	40

A24K: The police and other law enforcement agencies?

	TOTAL	M	F	White	Black	NE	NC	S	W	Yes	No	None	Mari-juana Only	Few Pills	More Pills	Any Her-oin
1. Very poor	6.9	8.1	5.7	5.9	12.1	7.1	5.9	8.7	5.1	6.0	8.4	4.9	6.9	6.7	8.6	30.0
2. Poor	16.1	16.3	16.2	15.5	18.8	16.7	16.1	17.2	13.1	15.9	16.2	13.6	16.0	18.5	18.7	17.5
3. Fair	37.7	37.7	37.5	38.2	37.1	38.3	37.9	36.9	37.7	39.0	36.0	40.0	37.3	32.2	39.1	25.0
4. Good	28.4	27.4	29.2	30.7	18.1	28.1	30.3	26.0	29.6	29.7	27.5	29.1	30.2	32.9	24.7	17.5
5. Very good	6.6	7.2	6.1	6.2	6.6	4.7	6.3	6.4	10.8	5.9	7.0	8.4	6.4	6.5	4.6	5.0
8. No opinion	4.3	3.2	5.2	3.5	7.3	4.9	3.6	4.7	3.7	3.5	4.8	4.1	3.4	3.2	4.5	5.0
Item 8480　N(Wtd)	3610	1706	1775	2809	453	851	1092	1102	565	1964	1435	1211	888	432	980	40

A24L: The U.S. military?

	TOTAL	M	F	White	Black	NE	NC	S	W	Yes	No	None	Mari-juana Only	Few Pills	More Pills	Any Her-oin
1. Very poor	4.9	7.3	2.6	5.5	2.2	6.3	4.9	3.8	4.9	6.2	3.4	4.3	4.5	4.4	5.7	15.0
2. Poor	10.5	13.7	7.7	11.1	7.3	12.1	9.8	9.7	11.3	12.8	7.7	9.6	10.1	13.9	10.9	15.0
3. Fair	29.3	29.1	30.8	30.3	26.5	29.0	30.1	28.0	30.5	30.3	28.9	31.3	29.5	26.4	28.5	27.5
4. Good	29.8	29.3	30.2	29.3	33.3	28.8	29.8	32.2	26.5	28.5	30.3	29.1	31.3	31.3	29.1	17.5
5. Very good	13.3	14.0	12.4	12.0	20.8	12.0	13.1	15.5	11.5	10.5	16.7	14.1	13.4	11.3	12.3	17.5
8. No opinion	12.2	7.7	16.3	11.9	9.9	11.8	12.1	10.8	15.5	11.7	13.0	11.6	11.2	12.7	13.5	5.0
Item 8490　N(Wtd)	3604	1703	1771	2800	453	844	1089	1104	567	1960	1430	1210	885	432	976	40

A25: All things considered, do you think the armed services presently have too much or too little influence on the way this country is run?

	TOTAL	M	F	White	Black	NE	NC	S	W	Yes	No	None	Mari-juana Only	Few Pills	More Pills	Any Her-oin
1. Far too little	6.6	7.9	5.4	6.5	7.5	5.6	5.8	8.8	5.4	5.9	7.6	6.2	5.0	7.3	8.0	15.0
2. Too little	28.7	28.2	29.1	29.8	24.6	32.0	29.0	27.8	24.7	30.5	27.1	27.9	28.9	31.7	28.3	32.5
3. About right	52.6	51.3	54.0	51.7	56.8	50.4	52.0	55.0	52.5	51.0	54.4	54.0	53.4	53.0	50.6	45.0
4. Too much	9.4	9.2	9.7	9.6	8.2	8.4	10.6	6.7	14.1	9.5	9.0	9.0	10.4	6.4	10.6	2.5
5. Far too much	2.7	3.4	1.7	2.4	2.9	3.6	2.6	1.7	3.2	3.1	1.8	3.0	2.4	1.4	2.6	7.5
Item 8500　N(Wtd)	3548	1685	1737	2750	451	835	1076	1082	554	1934	1407	1195	878	423	955	40

QUESTIONNAIRE FORM 3 1981	TOTAL	SEX		RACE		REGION				4YR COLLEGE PLANS		ILLICIT DRUG USE: LIFETIME				
		M	F	White	Black	NE	NC	S	W	Yes	No	None	Mari-juana Only	Few Pills	More Pills	Any Her-oin
Weighted No. of Cases:	3658	1721	1795	2830	459	869	1100	1114	575	1980	1448	1228	894	433	990	41
% of Weighted Total:	100.0	47.0	49.1	77.4	12.5	23.8	30.1	30.5	15.7	54.1	39.6	33.6	24.4	11.8	27.1	1.1
A26: Do you think the U.S. spends too much or too little on the armed services?																
1. Far too little	12.2	17.1	7.6	13.0	9.2	10.7	11.1	15.9	9.3	11.2	13.6	10.9	12.1	14.2	12.9	17.5
2. Too little	38.0	41.6	35.3	40.3	31.9	40.3	35.4	39.1	37.4	41.4	33.8	38.8	38.3	38.8	37.0	45.0
3. About right	32.1	26.0	37.4	30.7	35.7	30.9	34.2	31.9	30.7	29.0	35.9	30.8	31.0	31.2	34.9	25.0
4. Too much	14.0	11.6	16.3	12.7	19.4	14.1	15.8	10.3	17.6	13.9	14.1	15.5	14.6	13.5	11.7	2.5
5. Far too much	3.7	3.7	3.3	3.2	3.8	3.9	3.6	2.8	5.1	4.5	2.6	3.8	3.8	2.4	3.4	7.5
Item 8510 N(Wtd)	3550	1694	1731	2755	448	838	1076	1085	551	1932	1412	1197	871	423	962	40
A27: Next are some questions which ask about your experiences and attitudes concerning particular drugs. First we want your answers about some drugs that can be bought at a drugstore without a doctor's prescription--sometimes called over-the-counter or non-prescription drugs. DURING THE LAST 12 MONTHS, on how many occasions have you...																
A27A: ...used non-prescription drugs which are supposed to relieve pain (such as aspirin, Anacin, Bufferin, or Excedrin)?																
1. 0 occasions	9.1	11.4	5.9	6.2	18.2	9.8	8.9	8.0	11.0	6.8	11.3	11.8	9.2	7.5	5.5	10.0
2. 1-2	16.9	19.0	14.8	14.5	26.0	14.0	16.9	18.5	18.2	15.3	17.8	21.8	16.5	12.9	12.4	25.0
3. 3-5	18.1	20.4	16.0	17.1	22.9	16.0	15.7	21.2	20.0	18.7	17.0	21.6	19.3	14.7	14.7	12.5
4. 6-9	15.3	15.5	15.5	16.2	13.1	15.3	14.8	16.6	13.6	15.8	15.3	13.9	16.5	17.8	14.6	22.5
5. 10-19	17.5	15.3	19.7	19.3	12.0	20.8	20.0	14.4	13.8	19.7	15.0	16.0	16.9	21.0	18.5	2.5
6. 20-39	11.5	9.2	14.1	13.1	3.8	11.4	13.0	9.5	12.5	12.2	11.6	7.8	11.0	14.5	15.9	10.0
7. 40 or more	11.6	9.2	14.1	13.6	4.2	12.7	10.9	11.8	11.0	11.5	12.1	7.0	10.5	11.4	18.4	20.0
Item 8520 N(Wtd)	3610	1704	1779	2809	450	851	1096	1098	566	1965	1435	1222	889	428	982	40
A27B: ...used non-prescription drugs that are supposed to help people get to sleep (such as Sleep-Eze, Sominex, or Nytol)?																
1. 0 occasions	88.7	88.7	89.0	88.8	88.8	90.0	89.3	87.8	87.5	89.6	88.2	94.9	91.9	83.5	81.8	65.0
2. 1-2	6.0	6.2	5.7	5.9	5.3	4.9	5.9	6.3	7.4	5.9	6.1	3.2	4.2	11.8	8.6	5.0
3. 3-5	2.0	1.5	2.5	2.1	2.4	1.5	2.1	2.2	2.7	1.6	2.4	1.0	1.1	2.4	4.2	2.5
4. 6-9	1.2	1.2	1.3	1.4	.9	1.6	.6	1.5	1.2	1.1	1.4	-	1.6	.7	2.3	5.0
5. 10-19	1.1	1.4	.8	1.2	1.1	1.2	1.1	1.2	.9	1.1	1.1	.5	.7	.7	2.0	12.5
6. 20-39	.6	.6	.5	.5	1.1	.6	.5	.8	.4	.5	.6	.2	.4	.5	.8	7.5
7. 40 or more	.2	.2	.2	.2	.4	.1	.4	.4	-	.3	.2	.1	.1	.2	.3	2.5
Item 8530 N(Wtd)	3614	1706	1780	2808	454	853	1097	1098	566	1968	1433	1223	891	425	985	40
A27C: ...used non-prescription drugs that are supposed to help people stay awake (such as No-Doz, Wake, or Vivarin)?																
1. 0 occasions	84.9	83.5	86.3	83.5	93.0	86.5	84.8	85.2	82.1	85.6	84.3	95.9	92.7	80.3	67.0	62.5
2. 1-2	6.7	6.7	6.3	6.9	3.1	5.6	6.6	6.9	8.0	6.9	6.1	2.7	4.6	13.1	10.3	12.5
3. 3-5	3.1	3.8	2.5	3.7	.9	2.7	3.0	3.5	3.0	3.1	3.3	.9	1.2	4.0	7.3	2.5
4. 6-9	1.9	2.1	1.7	2.2	.7	2.1	1.8	1.2	3.2	1.6	2.1	.2	.6	1.4	5.5	5.0
5. 10-19	1.7	2.0	1.6	2.0	.7	1.4	2.1	1.5	1.9	1.5	2.2	.2	.7	.9	5.1	-
6. 20-39	.8	.8	.7	.7	1.5	.4	.5	1.1	1.1	.7	.8	.1	-	.2	2.1	12.5
7. 40 or more	.9	1.0	.7	.9	.2	1.2	1.2	.5	.5	.7	1.1	-	.1	-	2.7	7.5
Item 8540 N(Wtd)	3612	1706	1780	2807	454	852	1096	1100	565	1966	1435	1222	891	427	984	40
A27D: ...used non-prescription drugs that are supposed to calm people down--keep them from being nervous or in a bad mood (such as Cope, Compoz, Devarex, or Miles Nervine)?																
1. 0 occasions	94.0	94.3	93.9	94.6	93.1	95.1	95.8	91.8	93.4	96.0	91.8	97.6	97.9	91.1	88.5	72.5
2. 1-2	2.9	2.9	3.0	3.0	1.8	1.9	1.6	4.1	5.0	2.0	4.1	.8	.9	5.8	5.8	7.5
3. 3-5	1.2	1.0	1.5	1.1	1.8	1.2	.7	1.7	1.2	.9	1.5	1.0	.6	2.1	1.9	-
4. 6-9	.7	.6	.9	.7	1.1	.6	1.2	.6	.4	.7	.9	.1	.3	.5	1.9	-
5. 10-19	.4	.5	.3	.2	.7	.6	.2	.5	-	.2	.6	.4	.1	.5	.5	-
6. 20-39	.3	.4	.3	.2	1.3	.4	.2	.6	-	.2	.6	.1	.1	-	.6	10.0
7. 40 or more	.3	.4	.1	.2	.4	.5	.2	.5	-	.2	.4	-	.1	-	.7	7.5
Item 8550 N(Wtd)	3612	1708	1776	2809	452	852	1095	1100	564	1966	1433	1222	891	428	982	40

QUESTIONNAIRE FORM 3 1981	TOTAL	SEX		RACE		REGION				4YR COLLEGE PLANS		ILLICIT DRUG USE: LIFETIME				
		M	F	White	Black	NE	NC	S	W	Yes	No	None	Mari-juana Only	Few Pills	More Pills	Any Her-oin
Weighted No. of Cases:	3658	1721	1795	2830	459	869	1100	1114	575	1980	1448	1228	894	433	990	41
% of Weighted Total:	100.0	47.0	49.1	77.4	12.5	23.8	30.1	30.5	15.7	54.1	39.6	33.6	24.4	11.8	27.1	1.1

A28: Individuals differ in whether or not they disapprove of people doing certain things. Do YOU disapprove of people (who are 18 or older) doing each of the following?

A28A: Smoking one or more packs of cigarettes per day

1. Don't disapprove	30.1	29.5	30.5	31.3	24.1	32.0	33.7	29.2	22.0	23.8	39.0	17.9	26.0	30.4	48.2	47.5
2. Disapprove	37.1	36.4	37.6	37.4	36.9	39.3	34.9	38.5	35.2	38.8	34.8	40.4	40.7	40.7	28.6	32.5
3. Strongly disapprove	32.9	34.1	31.9	31.3	38.9	28.8	31.5	32.3	42.8	37.4	26.2	41.8	33.2	28.6	23.2	22.5
Item 8560 N(Wtd)	3610	1707	1776	2808	452	847	1095	1100	568	1963	1435	1219	891	427	983	40

A28B: Trying marijuana (pot, grass) once or twice

1. Don't disapprove	60.0	63.7	56.4	63.1	45.8	72.6	58.4	50.2	63.2	59.1	61.2	24.1	72.8	68.2	88.5	85.0
2. Disapprove	21.2	19.4	22.8	19.9	26.5	17.1	22.3	23.3	21.1	22.0	19.8	33.4	18.9	21.5	7.8	12.5
3. Strongly disapprove	18.8	16.9	20.8	17.0	27.7	10.4	19.3	26.4	15.8	18.8	19.0	42.5	8.2	10.1	3.7	5.0
Item 8570 N(Wtd)	3608	1707	1775	2810	452	847	1094	1101	565	1965	1432	1223	892	424	983	40

A28C: Smoking marijuana occasionally

1. Don't disapprove	47.4	51.6	43.4	50.2	34.7	59.5	46.4	37.3	50.8	44.9	50.6	13.4	52.8	52.5	81.2	82.1
2. Disapprove	25.1	22.7	27.1	24.1	29.8	23.5	25.1	26.9	23.9	26.3	23.1	31.0	29.3	31.4	11.3	12.8
3. Strongly disapprove	27.5	25.7	29.6	25.7	35.5	17.0	28.4	35.8	25.3	28.8	26.3	55.6	17.9	16.2	7.4	7.7
Item 8580 N(Wtd)	3602	1701	1775	2801	453	843	1094	1100	565	1957	1434	1222	885	427	981	39

A28D: Smoking marijuana regularly

1. Don't disapprove	22.6	27.6	17.4	23.2	17.7	26.3	21.5	19.5	25.2	18.5	28.3	5.2	17.0	20.6	48.1	77.5
2. Disapprove	29.3	29.1	29.3	29.1	32.7	33.3	28.6	26.2	30.7	29.4	28.1	19.6	37.0	34.0	32.1	10.0
3. Strongly disapprove	48.1	43.3	53.4	47.7	49.7	40.5	50.0	54.2	44.3	52.1	43.5	75.2	45.8	45.4	19.8	10.0
Item 8590 N(Wtd)	3599	1704	1770	2798	453	845	1090	1096	567	1959	1429	1221	888	427	977	40

A28E: Trying LSD once or twice

1. Don't disapprove	13.6	16.6	10.5	13.9	9.6	18.9	11.9	9.3	17.5	12.6	14.8	4.5	8.2	9.1	29.2	67.5
2. Disapprove	20.5	20.7	20.5	20.6	19.8	20.3	20.3	21.0	20.1	20.2	21.1	17.3	21.4	21.1	23.4	15.0
3. Strongly disapprove	65.9	62.7	69.1	65.4	70.7	60.7	67.8	69.6	62.4	67.2	64.1	78.2	70.4	69.8	47.4	17.5
Item 8600 N(Wtd)	3608	1709	1775	2810	450	847	1097	1098	567	1963	1435	1221	891	427	983	40

A28F: Taking LSD regularly

1. Don't disapprove	3.2	4.2	2.3	2.5	4.9	3.5	2.8	2.9	3.9	2.2	4.3	2.4	2.1	3.1	3.9	35.0
2. Disapprove	14.1	16.1	12.0	13.9	15.0	14.9	13.9	14.1	13.1	12.1	16.4	10.6	12.2	8.5	21.3	32.5
3. Strongly disapprove	82.7	79.7	85.7	83.6	80.3	81.5	83.3	82.9	83.0	85.6	79.4	87.0	85.7	88.2	74.8	32.5
Item 8610 N(Wtd)	3594	1700	1770	2801	446	847	1097	1085	565	1960	1425	1218	884	424	980	40

A28G: Trying heroin (smack, horse) once or twice

1. Don't disapprove	6.5	7.7	5.3	6.0	6.4	6.4	6.7	5.8	7.4	6.0	7.0	3.9	5.7	6.1	8.5	50.0
2. Disapprove	16.5	16.2	16.5	16.3	16.7	17.3	13.5	18.3	17.4	15.2	18.0	13.7	15.6	16.7	20.0	25.0
3. Strongly disapprove	77.1	76.0	78.2	77.8	76.7	76.3	79.9	75.9	75.2	78.8	75.0	82.3	78.8	77.2	71.6	25.0
Item 8620 N(Wtd)	3608	1705	1777	2805	454	844	1097	1099	568	1960	1436	1223	891	426	981	40

A28H: Taking heroin occasionally

1. Don't disapprove	2.9	3.6	2.3	2.3	4.9	3.0	2.5	2.9	3.2	2.2	3.5	2.4	1.8	3.0	3.3	27.5
2. Disapprove	12.6	13.4	11.6	11.8	15.7	13.0	11.7	14.0	10.9	10.9	14.3	11.0	11.9	10.5	14.3	37.5
3. Strongly disapprove	84.6	83.0	86.1	85.8	79.6	84.1	85.9	83.1	85.9	86.9	82.2	86.7	86.2	86.4	82.3	35.0
Item 8630 N(Wtd)	3606	1705	1777	2806	452	844	1096	1097	568	1962	1432	1222	890	427	980	40

QUESTIONNAIRE FORM 3 1981	TOTAL	SEX		RACE		REGION				4YR COLLEGE PLANS		ILLICIT DRUG USE: LIFETIME				
		M	F	White	Black	NE	NC	S	W	Yes	No	None	Marijuana Only	Few Pills	More Pills	Any Heroin
Weighted No. of Cases:	3658	1721	1795	2830	459	869	1100	1114	575	1980	1448	1228	894	433	990	41
% of Weighted Total:	100.0	47.0	49.1	77.4	12.5	23.8	30.1	30.5	15.7	54.1	39.6	33.6	24.4	11.8	27.1	1.1
A28I: Taking heroin regularly																
1. Don't disapprove	2.2	2.9	1.6	1.6	4.9	2.2	2.0	2.4	2.5	1.8	2.7	2.3	1.6	2.8	1.8	15.0
2. Disapprove	9.3	9.8	8.6	8.6	12.5	8.7	8.1	11.2	8.8	7.4	11.3	8.5	8.2	7.7	10.7	30.0
3. Strongly disapprove	88.5	87.2	89.8	89.8	82.6	88.9	90.0	86.4	88.7	90.8	86.1	89.2	90.2	89.4	87.5	52.5
Item 8640 N(Wtd)	3598	1701	1772	2801	449	846	1095	1092	566	1959	1430	1218	891	426	977	40
A28J: Trying a barbiturate (downer, goofball, red, yellow, etc.) once or twice																
1. Don't disapprove	17.6	19.2	·16.0	18.7	8.4	22.4	16.2	14.2	19.6	16.2	19.6	4.7	9.9	13.1	40.2	75.0
2. Disapprove	24.6	24.6	24.5	25.5	22.0	26.2	24.1	24.1	23.8	23.5	25.8	19.4	23.7	32.1	29.3	12.5
3. Strongly disapprove	57.8	56.3	59.5	55.8	69.6	51.2	59.6	61.7	56.6	60.3	54.7	76.0	66.6	55.0	30.6	12.5
Item 8650 N(Wtd)	3609	1706	1777	2808	454	847	1098	1098	567	1961	1436	1223	891	427	981	40
A28K: Taking barbiturates regularly																
1. Don't disapprove	5.8	7.6	4.0	5.3	7.1	6.6	4.9	6.2	5.6	4.1	8.0	2.7	2.6	5.4	10.7	47.5
2. Disapprove	23.7	24.6	22.8	23.5	24.6	25.8	22.7	24.1	22.0	21.2	26.4	15.4	20.3	21.3	37.3	42.5
3. Strongly disapprove	70.4	67.8	73.2	71.2	68.5	67.6	72.4	69.7	72.3	74.8	65.6	81.9	77.0	73.3	52.0	12.5
Item 8660 N(Wtd)	3607	1706	1776	2808	451	845	1096	1100	567	1965	1433	1221	891	427	981	40
A28L: Trying an amphetamine (upper, pep pill, bennie, speed) once or twice																
1. Don't disapprove	28.9	31.0	26.6	31.5	13.9	37.4	27.6	22.5	31.4	26.7	32.0	6.1	15.5	27.5	68.4	77.5
2. Disapprove	24.1	24.2	23.9	24.1	23.2	25.8	24.3	22.9	23.5	23.8	24.4	21.5	29.5	35.8	17.7	15.0
3. Strongly disapprove	47.0	44.8	49.5	44.4	62.6	36.7	48.2	54.6	45.3	49.5	43.7	72.4	55.0	36.7	14.0	10.0
Item 8670 N(Wtd)	3608	1708	1776	2808	452	844	1096	1101	567	1965	1434	1222	892	425	983	40
A28M: Taking amphetamines regularly																
1. Don't disapprove	8.3	9.5	7.1	8.3	6.4	9.6	7.9	7.4	8.7	6.4	10.7	2.3	2.6	5.0	20.3	60.0
2. Disapprove	24.1	26.1	21.7	24.5	20.2	27.6	23.4	22.5	23.5	21.1	27.7	13.7	18.1	25.5	41.4	30.0
3. Strongly disapprove	67.6	64.4	71.2	67.2	73.3	62.8	68.7	70.1	67.6	72.5	61.5	84.0	79.3	69.3	38.4	12.5
Item 8680 N(Wtd)	3592	1699	1768	2794	450	842	1094	1095	561	1961	1424	1218	890	424	974	40
A28N: Trying cocaine once or twice																
1. Don't disapprove	25.4	30.4	19.9	26.6	15.7	35.4	20.2	17.8	35.3	24.1	26.6	4.6	16.5	23.0	58.2	75.0
2. Disapprove	19.6	19.4	19.6	19.0	20.1	22.0	19.0	19.2	17.8	19.6	19.1	17.8	22.9	24.2	16.4	17.5
3. Strongly disapprove	55.0	50.2	60.5	54.4	64.2	42.7	60.7	63.1	46.9	56.3	54.2	77.5	60.6	53.1	25.4	7.5
Item 8690 N(Wtd)	3601	1705	1773	2802	452	845	1092	1097	567	1963	1431	1216	891	426	981	40
A28O: Taking cocaine regularly																
1. Don't disapprove	9.3	12.1	6.3	9.1	7.7	13.2	6.7	6.6	13.7	8.1	10.3	2.5	2.9	5.4	23.7	52.5
2. Disapprove	18.3	20.6	15.9	18.6	16.2	20.7	16.4	16.9	21.2	17.0	19.5	10.0	15.5	18.4	30.6	15.0
3. Strongly disapprove	72.3	67.4	77.8	72.2	76.1	66.1	76.9	76.4	65.1	74.9	70.1	87.6	81.6	76.1	45.7	30.0
Item 8700 N(Wtd)	3573	1687	1764	2784	444	840	1087	1086	561	1951	1417	1205	885	423	976	40
A28P: Trying one or two drinks of an alcoholic beverage (beer, wine, liquor)																
1. Don't disapprove	82.9	85.6	81.0	86.8	65.2	92.0	85.0	74.7	80.8	84.2	82.0	65.7	89.9	88.5	96.1	77.5
2. Disapprove	10.8	8.7	12.0	8.3	21.7	5.6	10.3	14.8	11.5	9.7	11.5	21.0	6.9	8.4	2.6	12.5
3. Strongly disapprove	6.4	5.6	7.0	4.8	13.1	2.4	4.6	10.4	7.8	6.1	6.5	13.3	3.3	2.8	1.4	12.5
Item 8710 N(Wtd)	3605	1705	1776	2805	451	842	1097	1099	567	1966	1430	1221	890	427	980	40

QUESTIONNAIRE FORM 3 1981	TOTAL	SEX		RACE		REGION				4YR COLLEGE PLANS		ILLICIT DRUG USE: LIFETIME				
		M	F	White	Black	NE	NC	S	W	Yes	No	None	Marijuana Only	Few Pills	More Pills	Any Heroin
Weighted No. of Cases:	3658	1721	1795	2830	459	869	1100	1114	575	1980	1448	1228	894	433	990	41
% of Weighted Total:	100.0	47.0	49.1	77.4	12.5	23.8	30.1	30.5	15.7	54.1	39.6	33.6	24.4	11.8	27.1	1.1
A28Q: Taking one or two drinks nearly every day																
1. Don't disapprove	30.9	38.8	23.7	33.8	17.7	37.0	32.4	27.4	26.2	28.7	34.6	18.4	31.3	31.6	44.2	67.5
2. Disapprove	42.2	40.5	43.6	41.8	42.1	42.4	42.4	41.6	42.3	42.9	41.2	42.7	44.2	45.7	39.5	20.0
3. Strongly disapprove	26.9	20.7	32.6	24.4	40.1	20.5	25.2	31.0	31.5	28.5	24.3	38.9	24.6	22.5	16.4	12.5
Item 8720 N(Wtd)	3595	1702	1769	2796	451	841	1094	1095	565	1961	1426	1220	886	427	975	40
A28R: Taking four or five drinks nearly every day																
1. Don't disapprove	8.2	11.8	4.5	8.3	6.0	9.4	8.2	8.4	6.0	5.9	11.1	4.5	6.7	5.9	13.7	37.5
2. Disapprove	29.3	35.1	24.1	31.3	21.5	29.1	30.6	28.7	28.5	27.1	32.1	22.3	31.0	33.5	34.2	45.0
3. Strongly disapprove	62.5	53.1	71.3	60.4	72.6	61.5	61.2	63.0	65.5	67.0	56.8	73.2	62.2	60.7	52.1	20.0
Item 8730 N(Wtd)	3599	1705	1769	2799	452	844	1091	1098	565	1965	1426	1217	889	427	979	40
A28S: Having five or more drinks once or twice each weekend																
1. Don't disapprove	44.5	52.6	36.2	49.9	18.8	54.2	48.2	36.9	37.7	41.8	48.7	20.9	45.7	45.7	71.0	75.0
2. Disapprove	26.4	24.7	28.3	25.3	31.6	27.1	25.7	26.6	26.5	27.1	25.0	31.2	28.9	31.4	16.7	17.5
3. Strongly disapprove	29.1	22.6	35.4	24.8	49.6	18.9	26.1	36.5	35.9	31.1	26.3	47.9	25.5	23.2	12.3	7.5
Item 8740 N(Wtd)	3602	1706	1772	2804	452	842	1096	1101	563	1962	1432	1221	887	427	980	40
A29: During the LAST 12 MONTHS, how often have you been around people who were taking each of the following to get high or for "kicks"?																
A29A: Marijuana (pot, grass) or hashish																
1. Not at all	19.8	15.9	23.2	18.0	26.7	13.1	21.2	24.2	18.6	21.1	17.7	45.7	7.1	10.8	4.0	5.0
2. Once or twice	20.4	19.9	21.3	19.7	23.8	15.8	21.8	22.6	20.4	20.7	20.6	27.1	23.2	23.4	8.3	10.0
3. Occasionally	26.7	28.4	24.9	27.5	22.9	30.1	24.7	26.3	26.0	27.0	25.9	18.2	40.5	33.5	21.8	12.5
4. Often	33.1	35.8	30.6	34.9	26.9	41.1	32.3	26.8	35.0	31.2	35.8	8.8	29.2	32.1	65.8	72.5
Item 20590 N(Wtd)	3608	1706	1780	2808	454	847	1098	1098	565	1964	1437	1223	891	427	985	40
A29B: LSD																
1. Not at all	82.6	79.8	85.5	80.0	95.7	75.2	82.7	88.5	82.5	83.2	81.8	93.4	90.5	86.4	63.3	13.2
2. Once or twice	9.8	11.0	8.3	11.5	3.4	12.6	10.0	7.4	9.7	10.7	8.8	5.5	6.8	8.1	17.6	36.8
3. Occasionally	5.5	6.6	4.6	6.3	.2	8.9	5.2	3.0	6.1	4.2	7.6	.6	1.8	4.3	14.6	26.3
4. Often	2.0	2.6	1.5	2.3	.7	3.3	2.0	1.2	1.6	1.9	1.8	.5	.9	1.2	4.5	23.7
Item 20600 N(Wtd)	3555	1686	1749	2781	439	840	1087	1074	554	1942	1413	1206	880	419	972	38
A29C: Other psychedelics (mescaline, peyote, PCP, etc.)																
1. Not at all	82.4	79.5	85.5	80.7	91.6	70.2	84.8	88.3	84.4	82.4	82.0	94.3	90.0	81.7	62.9	35.0
2. Once or twice	10.6	12.3	8.5	11.5	6.0	15.3	10.0	8.0	9.9	10.5	10.9	3.8	7.2	12.2	20.7	25.0
3. Occasionally	5.0	5.9	4.0	5.5	1.6	10.1	3.2	3.3	4.2	5.2	5.1	1.2	1.8	4.7	12.0	25.0
4. Often	2.0	2.2	1.9	2.3	.9	4.4	1.9	.5	1.4	2.0	2.0	.7	1.0	1.2	4.4	17.5
Item 20610 N(Wtd)	3595	1704	1770	2801	450	842	1095	1093	565	1960	1432	1216	890	426	981	40
A29D: Amphetamines (uppers, pep pills, bennies, speed)																
1. Not at all	50.5	47.9	53.0	45.2	76.4	42.1	47.9	57.9	53.6	53.1	46.2	77.7	61.1	38.3	14.2	15.0
2. Once or twice	21.7	22.0	21.0	23.1	15.1	23.5	23.1	19.0	21.3	22.4	21.3	16.4	25.0	33.8	20.3	10.0
3. Occasionally	15.8	18.3	13.6	17.9	4.7	19.7	16.6	12.4	14.7	14.3	17.7	4.0	9.1	20.2	33.9	17.5
4. Often	12.1	11.8	12.4	13.8	3.8	14.6	12.3	10.7	10.3	10.1	14.9	2.0	4.7	7.7	31.5	57.5
Item 20620 N(Wtd)	3599	1706	1771	2805	450	847	1097	1091	563	1961	1433	1213	892	426	986	40

QUESTIONNAIRE FORM 3 1981	TOTAL	SEX		RACE		REGION				4YR COLLEGE PLANS		ILLICIT DRUG USE: LIFETIME				
		M	F	White	Black	NE	NC	S	W	Yes	No	None	Mari- juana Only	Few Pills	More Pills	Any Her- oin
Weighted No. of Cases:	3658	1721	1795	2830	459	869	1100	1114	575	1980	1448	1228	894	433	990	41
% of Weighted Total:	100.0	47.0	49.1	77.4	12.5	23.8	30.1	30.5	15.7	54.1	39.6	33.6	24.4	11.8	27.1	1.1
A29E: Barbiturates (downers, goofballs, reds, yellows, etc.)																
1. Not at all	74.1	70.3	78.0	71.6	88.9	67.1	75.5	75.8	78.7	77.0	70.0	90.3	85.4	70.7	48.7	12.5
2. Once or twice	13.9	16.6	11.1	15.4	5.3	16.3	13.1	13.0	13.5	13.0	15.1	7.3	9.3	20.7	22.5	30.0
3. Occasionally	8.0	9.0	6.9	8.6	4.0	12.3	7.7	7.0	4.1	6.2	10.6	1.4	3.7	6.3	19.0	32.5
4. Often	4.0	4.1	4.1	4.3	1.6	4.3	3.7	4.1	3.5	3.7	4.2	1.0	1.6	2.3	9.7	25.0
Item 20630 N(Wtd)	3592	1701	1771	2799	450	843	1096	1089	564	1959	1428	1212	889	426	985	40
A29F: Tranquilizers (Librium, Valium, Miltown)																
1. Not at all	71.0	71.2	70.7	68.1	86.9	65.6	73.2	72.4	72.3	70.7	71.0	83.6	81.9	67.1	49.7	22.5
2. Once or twice	16.8	17.1	16.7	19.0	6.7	19.6	15.8	15.5	17.1	18.0	15.1	10.7	11.6	22.1	26.4	22.5
3. Occasionally	8.0	8.2	7.7	8.5	4.2	10.2	7.1	7.4	7.1	7.2	9.4	3.5	4.6	7.5	15.8	25.0
4. Often	4.2	3.6	5.0	4.4	2.0	4.6	3.8	4.6	3.6	4.0	4.5	2.1	1.8	3.5	8.1	32.5
Item 20640 N(Wtd)	3594	1702	1770	2799	451	846	1094	1090	563	1957	1431	1214	888	426	984	40
A29G: Cocaine ("coke")																
1. Not at all	63.7	60.0	67.4	61.3	76.5	49.9	70.9	73.7	50.5	63.4	64.9	86.9	68.5	60.7	33.8	7.5
2. Once or twice	19.5	21.6	17.7	20.5	15.9	24.9	17.1	16.7	21.7	20.1	18.4	9.0	22.4	27.3	26.4	32.5
3. Occasionally	10.2	11.7	8.6	11.3	4.6	14.8	7.6	6.5	15.4	9.7	10.3	2.6	7.1	10.1	22.1	20.0
4. Often	6.6	6.7	6.3	6.9	2.7	10.3	4.3	3.2	12.4	6.7	6.3	1.4	2.0	2.1	17.7	40.0
Item 20650 N(Wtd)	3598	1702	1774	2802	452	843	1097	1093	566	1961	1432	1218	892	425	982	40
A29H: Heroin (smack, horse)																
1. Not at all	93.4	93.1	93.8	93.4	95.7	92.5	94.5	92.5	94.3	93.8	92.8	96.3	95.9	90.5	91.9	35.0
2. Once or twice	5.0	4.9	5.0	5.1	3.1	6.0	4.2	5.7	3.2	4.8	5.6	2.7	3.3	8.1	6.5	40.0
3. Occasionally	1.1	1.5	.7	1.0	.4	.8	.7	1.3	1.6	.8	1.2	.5	.6	1.4	1.2	12.5
4. Often	.6	.5	.6	.5	.7	.6	.6	.5	.9	.7	.4	.5	.3	.2	.3	12.5
Item 20660 N(Wtd)	3575	1690	1765	2790	445	840	1088	1083	563	1948	1422	1209	888	419	978	40
A29I: Other narcotics (methadone, opium, codeine, paregoric, etc.)																
1. Not at all	82.5	80.6	84.6	81.2	92.1	78.3	83.2	86.6	79.8	83.0	82.4	93.8	90.8	82.7	63.9	25.0
2. Once or twice	11.9	13.0	10.6	13.0	4.7	14.5	11.5	10.0	12.2	12.0	11.2	4.8	7.1	12.2	23.9	35.0
3. Occasionally	3.9	4.5	3.2	4.2	1.8	4.7	3.8	2.7	5.0	3.1	5.0	.6	1.5	3.7	9.2	25.0
4. Often	1.7	1.9	1.6	1.6	1.3	2.5	1.5	.6	3.0	1.8	1.4	.7	.7	1.4	3.1	15.0
Item 20670 N(Wtd)	3591	1702	1769	2803	445	847	1092	1087	565	1959	1432	1211	887	427	985	40
A29J: Alcoholic beverages (beer, wine, liquor)																
1. Not at all	6.0	5.4	6.2	4.2	11.3	3.3	4.5	7.9	9.2	5.4	5.9	14.3	1.2	2.3	1.2	7.5
2. Once or twice	9.8	7.7	11.8	7.1	23.1	5.4	11.0	12.5	9.2	10.2	8.6	18.7	7.8	6.8	1.9	15.0
3. Occasionally	23.2	21.5	24.5	22.0	30.2	21.2	22.6	26.5	21.0	24.5	21.8	32.6	25.6	21.5	10.1	10.0
4. Often	61.0	65.5	57.5	66.7	35.3	70.0	62.0	53.2	60.8	60.0	63.6	34.5	65.4	69.3	86.8	70.0
Item 20680 N(Wtd)	3602	1704	1777	2807	451	846	1095	1095	566	1962	1435	1219	890	427	985	40

This section asks for your views and feelings about a number of different things.

D01: How satisfied are you with your life as a whole these days?	TOTAL	M	F	White	Black	NE	NC	S	W	Yes	No	None	Mari- juana Only	Few Pills	More Pills	Any Her- oin
1. Completely dissatisfied	2.0	2.1	2.0	1.2	6.0	1.3	1.4	2.9	2.8	1.7	2.3	2.3	1.2	2.6	1.8	2.4
2. Quite dissatisfied	9.8	9.4	9.9	10.4	6.7	11.1	9.7	8.8	9.7	10.8	8.3	9.7	9.3	10.2	10.0	17.1
3. Somewhat dissatisfied	11.5	11.2	11.8	10.6	15.4	10.8	10.6	13.3	10.6	10.8	12.4	8.7	12.2	9.8	14.5	14.6
4. Neither, or mixed feelings	13.4	13.7	13.4	13.1	12.3	13.5	13.0	13.2	14.7	11.9	15.6	12.8	14.6	13.6	12.7	19.5
5. Somewhat satisfied	24.9	27.0	22.8	25.4	24.3	25.5	25.9	25.0	22.0	24.1	25.9	21.9	27.3	25.0	27.3	12.2
6. Quite satisfied	33.2	32.0	34.4	34.8	26.9	34.3	33.8	30.7	35.8	36.1	30.0	36.9	32.7	33.3	30.1	22.0
7. Completely satisfied	5.2	4.6	5.7	4.5	8.4	3.7	5.5	6.2	4.6	4.7	5.5	7.6	2.7	5.5	3.7	12.2
Item 6840 N(Wtd)	3474	1645	1740	2750	416	793	1084	1052	545	1950	1408	1183	841	420	948	41

QUESTIONNAIRE FORM 3 1981	TOTAL	SEX		RACE		REGION				4YR COLLEGE PLANS		ILLICIT DRUG USE: LIFETIME				
		M	F	White	Black	NE	NC	S	W	Yes	No	None	Mari-juana Only	Few Pills	More Pills	Any Her-oin
Weighted No. of Cases:	3658	1721	1795	2830	459	869	1100	1114	575	1980	1448	1228	894	433	990	41
% of Weighted Total:	100.0	47.0	49.1	77.4	12.5	23.8	30.1	30.5	15.7	54.1	39.6	33.6	24.4	11.8	27.1	1.1

D02: These questions are about your health during the last MONTH.

D02A: Have you been bothered by shortness of breath when you were not exercising or working hard?

	TOTAL	M	F	White	Black	NE	NC	S	W	Yes	No	None	Mari-juana Only	Few Pills	More Pills	Any Her-oin
1. Never	75.8	79.3	72.6	75.8	75.1	74.9	75.0	75.9	78.6	77.1	74.1	83.0	77.6	77.3	65.9	51.2
2. Seldom	14.8	12.8	16.6	15.7	11.9	14.7	16.5	13.4	14.5	14.3	15.6	9.9	14.6	15.2	21.3	7.3
3. Sometimes	8.0	6.6	9.6	7.4	11.1	9.1	7.6	8.8	5.9	7.3	9.1	6.2	6.5	6.9	11.0	29.3
4. Often	1.3	1.3	1.3	1.2	1.9	1.3	.9	1.9	.9	1.2	1.2	.9	1.2	.9	1.8	12.2
Item 8850 N(Wtd)	3473	1643	1740	2753	413	790	1085	1055	543	1949	1410	1180	841	422	948	41

D02B: Have you been bothered by your heart beating hard?

	TOTAL	M	F	White	Black	NE	NC	S	W	Yes	No	None	Mari-juana Only	Few Pills	More Pills	Any Her-oin
1. Never	74.9	79.8	70.5	74.7	74.8	72.4	74.4	76.0	77.1	75.5	74.3	80.0	77.2	74.8	67.3	63.4
2. Seldom	16.6	13.7	19.0	17.3	13.8	19.0	17.6	14.7	15.0	16.9	16.2	14.1	14.8	16.4	20.9	17.1
3. Sometimes	7.1	5.1	9.2	6.7	8.7	7.8	7.1	6.7	7.0	6.2	8.2	5.4	6.4	7.9	9.6	9.8
4. Often	1.4	1.4	1.3	1.2	2.4	.9	.9	2.5	.9	1.4	1.3	.5	1.5	1.0	2.1	9.8
Item 8860 N(Wtd)	3464	1642	1733	2750	412	786	1082	1052	545	1943	1407	1176	839	420	948	41

D02C: Have you had spells of dizziness?

	TOTAL	M	F	White	Black	NE	NC	S	W	Yes	No	None	Mari-juana Only	Few Pills	More Pills	Any Her-oin
1. Never	60.5	69.3	51.7	59.3	68.2	61.7	58.4	61.0	61.9	62.7	56.8	66.5	65.0	58.1	50.1	43.9
2. Seldom	24.5	20.7	28.4	26.3	15.4	23.3	26.8	22.8	25.0	23.9	26.0	20.5	22.9	24.3	31.3	24.4
3. Sometimes	12.7	8.5	16.9	12.5	13.9	13.4	12.4	13.5	10.7	11.5	14.5	11.5	10.5	15.0	15.0	19.5
4. Often	2.3	1.5	3.0	2.0	2.5	1.5	2.5	2.7	2.6	1.9	2.8	1.5	1.6	2.9	3.5	12.2
Item 8870 N(Wtd)	3441	1630	1722	2739	403	781	1074	1046	540	1938	1391	1170	835	420	935	41

D02D: Have your hands trembled enough to bother you?

	TOTAL	M	F	White	Black	NE	NC	S	W	Yes	No	None	Mari-juana Only	Few Pills	More Pills	Any Her-oin
1. Never	79.8	84.6	74.8	79.6	81.1	79.9	78.4	79.6	82.7	81.5	77.1	85.7	83.3	75.5	71.6	65.9
2. Seldom	11.3	8.9	13.9	11.5	10.8	11.5	12.7	10.1	11.0	10.8	12.5	8.3	9.5	14.0	15.7	9.8
3. Sometimes	7.0	5.2	8.9	7.1	5.9	6.9	7.8	7.5	4.4	6.0	8.2	4.7	6.0	6.7	10.2	19.5
4. Often	1.9	1.4	2.4	1.8	2.2	1.8	1.1	2.8	1.8	1.7	2.1	1.3	1.1	3.6	2.5	4.9
Item 8880 N(Wtd)	3456	1638	1729	2745	408	786	1079	1048	543	1941	1403	1173	839	420	943	41

D02E: Have you been troubled by your hands sweating so that they felt damp and clammy?

	TOTAL	M	F	White	Black	NE	NC	S	W	Yes	No	None	Mari-juana Only	Few Pills	More Pills	Any Her-oin
1. Never	65.2	69.3	61.0	64.1	74.9	65.7	62.7	66.3	67.5	67.6	61.3	67.6	70.8	64.5	58.3	41.5
2. Seldom	21.9	19.1	24.8	23.3	14.0	23.9	23.0	19.7	20.7	20.8	24.0	20.9	19.4	23.8	24.6	26.8
3. Sometimes	8.8	7.2	10.5	9.0	6.4	7.4	10.2	9.1	7.3	8.4	9.4	8.3	7.2	7.9	10.9	14.6
4. Often	4.1	4.4	3.7	3.6	4.7	2.9	4.2	4.9	4.2	3.1	5.4	3.1	2.6	3.8	6.3	17.1
Item 8890 N(Wtd)	3458	1641	1728	2748	407	784	1082	1048	545	1941	1405	1174	839	420	945	41

D02F: Have there been times when you couldn't take care of things because you just couldn't get going?

	TOTAL	M	F	White	Black	NE	NC	S	W	Yes	No	None	Mari-juana Only	Few Pills	More Pills	Any Her-oin
1. Never	54.0	61.0	47.0	53.3	55.9	54.1	53.6	54.0	54.5	55.0	51.7	60.6	56.9	50.4	44.2	51.3
2. Seldom	27.0	24.5	29.4	28.1	20.6	26.3	26.9	27.2	28.1	27.6	26.8	24.2	25.4	32.5	30.3	15.4
3. Sometimes	15.7	12.3	19.2	15.8	19.1	16.5	16.4	15.3	13.9	14.7	17.4	12.8	14.9	14.5	20.5	23.1
4. Often	3.3	2.3	4.3	2.9	4.2	3.2	3.2	3.4	3.5	2.6	4.1	2.5	2.7	2.6	4.9	10.3
Item 8900 N(Wtd)	3459	1639	1731	2747	408	787	1081	1046	545	1943	1404	1174	838	421	946	39

D03: At any time during the LAST 12 MONTHS, have you felt in your own mind that you should REDUCE or STOP your use of...

QUESTIONNAIRE FORM 3 1981	TOTAL	SEX		RACE		REGION				4YR COLLEGE PLANS		ILLICIT DRUG USE: LIFETIME				
		M	F	White	Black	NE	NC	S	W	Yes	No	None	Marijuana Only	Few Pills	More Pills	Any Heroin
Weighted No. of Cases:	3658	1721	1795	2830	459	869	1100	1114	575	1980	1448	1228	894	433	990	41
% of Weighted Total:	100.0	47.0	49.1	77.4	12.5	23.8	30.1	30.5	15.7	54.1	39.6	33.6	24.4	11.8	27.1	1.1
D03A: Alcohol?																
1. Yes	33.8	37.7	29.5	33.9	30.7	27.4	37.0	35.5	33.5	33.0	35.0	20.0	38.0	41.5	41.3	28.6
2. No	52.9	52.0	54.1	55.1	38.0	67.9	52.0	44.3	48.3	53.1	53.6	45.3	57.3	52.6	57.0	62.9
8. Haven't used in last 12 months	13.3	10.3	16.4	11.0	31.7	4.8	10.9	20.1	18.1	13.9	11.5	34.7	4.8	6.2	1.7	8.6
Item 8910 N(Wtd)	3035	1468	1493	2500	300	707	953	901	474	1711	1219	922	756	386	903	35
D03B: Cigarettes?																
1. Yes	23.0	20.1	25.2	23.5	17.2	23.8	24.2	24.5	16.3	18.4	29.2	7.6	20.0	25.4	42.1	36.8
2. No	15.1	13.5	16.7	14.0	21.3	13.4	15.7	16.0	14.8	13.9	16.5	9.4	18.5	16.2	18.1	26.3
8. Haven't used in last 12 months	61.9	66.4	58.1	62.5	61.8	62.7	60.1	59.6	69.1	67.7	54.3	83.0	61.6	58.4	39.8	34.2
Item 8920 N(Wtd)	3369	1596	1685	2683	390	751	1060	1029	528	1892	1360	1130	813	413	938	38
D03C: Marijuana?																
1. Yes	23.4	28.5	18.0	24.2	18.1	25.8	22.4	21.2	26.3	21.8	25.4	-	30.8	31.3	42.0	28.9
2. No	23.4	23.8	23.1	23.5	22.7	29.8	22.1	20.1	22.8	22.2	25.0	-	32.3	23.6	41.8	63.2
8. Haven't used in last 12 months	53.3	47.7	58.9	52.3	59.5	44.4	55.5	58.7	50.9	55.9	49.5	100.0	36.9	44.8	16.3	7.9
Item 8930 N(Wtd)	3057	1466	1519	2484	321	698	965	911	483	1745	1211	1044	715	364	870	38
D03D: Psychedelics (LSD, etc.)?																
1. Yes	3.2	4.4	2.2	3.5	1.2	5.5	3.2	2.0	2.3	2.2	4.4	-	-	1.1	10.2	39.4
2. No	3.0	3.8	2.2	3.1	2.2	4.2	2.5	1.8	4.7	2.9	3.1	-	-	.5	9.9	27.3
8. Haven't used in last 12 months	93.8	91.8	95.7	93.4	96.9	90.3	94.2	96.1	93.0	94.8	92.3	100.0	100.0	98.4	79.9	33.3
Item 8940 N(Wtd)	3013	1421	1529	2455	323	690	944	909	471	1737	1176	1045	757	370	781	33
D03E: Amphetamines (uppers)?																
1. Yes	8.4	9.0	7.9	9.5	1.6	10.1	10.1	6.0	7.2	6.7	10.8	.3	-	6.2	32.7	30.6
2. No	10.7	10.2	11.3	11.8	4.4	11.2	10.4	10.0	12.1	10.0	12.0	.3	.1	7.6	40.7	63.9
8. Haven't used in last 12 months	80.9	80.8	80.8	78.6	94.1	78.8	79.6	84.0	80.4	83.2	77.2	99.4	99.9	86.6	26.6	5.6
Item 8950 N(Wtd)	2768	1320	1383	2230	320	626	874	839	429	1611	1061	1051	754	290	612	36
D03F: Tranquilizers?																
1. Yes	2.0	2.3	1.6	1.9	.9	2.3	1.5	2.6	1.9	1.2	3.1	.3	-	1.1	6.2	22.2
2. No	2.5	2.9	2.1	2.4	3.1	2.1	1.7	4.1	1.5	2.0	3.2	-	.1	2.0	6.5	59.3
8. Haven't used in last 12 months	95.5	94.8	96.4	95.7	96.0	95.6	96.8	93.2	96.6	96.7	93.8	99.7	100.0	96.6	87.1	14.8
Item 9005 N(Wtd)	2937	1378	1491	2378	324	660	935	874	469	1696	1142	1044	753	349	739	27
D03G: Barbiturates/Quaaludes (downers)?																
1. Yes	1.5	1.9	1.0	1.6	.3	2.8	1.9	.8	.4	1.0	2.2	.3	-	-	5.2	24.1
2. No	2.5	3.0	2.2	2.5	1.9	2.8	1.9	3.6	1.6	1.8	3.7	-	.1	.6	8.5	51.7
8. Haven't used in last 12 months	96.0	95.2	96.8	96.0	98.1	94.6	96.4	95.6	98.0	97.1	94.1	99.7	99.9	99.4	86.5	27.6
Item 8970 N(Wtd)	2869	1344	1458	2322	321	648	917	855	448	1682	1093	1049	757	352	657	29
D03H: Cocaine?																
1. Yes	2.4	2.9	1.8	2.4	1.9	2.6	2.0	2.4	2.7	2.1	2.5	-	-	1.4	6.4	40.0
2. No	9.5	11.0	7.8	10.0	3.1	14.2	5.9	4.6	19.3	8.7	10.1	-	-	4.4	31.1	40.0
8. Haven't used in last 12 months	88.2	86.1	90.5	87.6	95.3	83.2	92.0	93.0	78.1	89.2	87.4	100.0	100.0	94.2	62.5	22.9
Item 8980 N(Wtd)	3057	1433	1555	2490	322	691	964	920	483	1755	1202	1045	760	362	826	35
D03I: Heroin?																
1. Yes	.5	.6	.2	.2	.9	.4	.4	.6	.2	.2	.8	.3	-	-	-	40.0
2. No	.2	.3	.1	.1	1.2	-	.1	.5	-	.2	.2	-	-	-	.1	20.0
8. Haven't used in last 12 months	99.3	99.1	99.7	99.7	98.2	99.6	99.4	98.8	99.6	99.6	99.1	99.6	100.0	100.0	99.9	43.3
Item 8990 N(Wtd)	3085	1453	1559	2515	325	689	983	927	487	1767	1218	1048	757	374	851	30

QUESTIONNAIRE FORM 3 1981	TOTAL	SEX		RACE		REGION				4YR COLLEGE PLANS		ILLICIT DRUG USE: LIFETIME				
		M	F	White	Black	NE	NC	S	W	Yes	No	None	Mari- juana Only	Few Pills	More Pills	Any Her- oin
Weighted No. of Cases:	3658	1721	1795	2830	459	869	1100	1114	575	1980	1448	1228	894	433	990	41
% of Weighted Total:	100.0	47.0	49.1	77.4	12.5	23.8	30.1	30.5	15.7	54.1	39.6	33.6	24.4	11.8	27.1	1.1
D03J: Other narcotics?																
1. Yes	1.5	1.9	.9	1.2	1.6	2.4	1.0	1.2	1.3	.6	2.6	.3	.3	-	3.6	35.3
2. No	2.5	2.4	2.4	2.4	1.6	2.3	2.4	2.5	2.8	1.7	3.5	.3	-	.5	8.1	23.5
8. Haven't used in last 12 months	96.0	95.6	96.6	96.3	97.2	95.3	96.4	96.1	96.1	97.6	93.9	99.4	99.7	99.5	88.3	41.2
Item 9000 N(Wtd)	2980	1392	1515	2419	317	662	954	905	459	1719	1163	1051	758	364	749	34
D04: How likely is it that you will use marijuana in the next 12 months?																
1. Definitely will-GO TO Q.D05	15.2	20.3	10.8	16.3	9.7	20.7	14.0	11.9	16.2	14.7	16.1	1.8	9.6	13.6	39.2	63.6
2. Probably will-GO TO Q.D05	14.5	14.8	13.9	14.6	13.9	17.7	14.0	12.9	13.7	13.4	16.2	.8	22.7	18.1	24.4	15.2
3. Probably will not	19.4	19.1	20.1	20.2	17.2	22.9	19.2	18.4	17.0	21.1	16.8	9.6	31.6	28.2	17.7	15.2
4. Definitely will not	50.9	45.8	55.2	48.9	59.5	38.7	52.9	56.9	52.9	50.8	50.8	87.8	36.1	40.2	18.7	6.1
Item 9010 N(Wtd)	3065	1417	1573	2475	331	690	974	919	482	1759	1216	1118	737	376	770	33

Here are some reasons people give for not using marijuana, or for stopping use. If you have never used marijuana, or if you have stopped using it, please tell us which reasons are true for you. (Mark all that apply.)

	TOTAL	M	F	White	Black	NE	NC	S	W	Yes	No	None	Mari- juana Only	Few Pills	More Pills	Any Her- oin
A. Concerned about possible psychological damage	65.3	63.9	66.4	66.3	59.8	63.2	67.6	62.4	69.2	69.2	60.0	71.6	59.0	60.3	57.3	50.0
B. Concerned about possible physical damage	66.5	66.1	66.4	67.2	62.3	66.7	68.6	62.7	69.5	70.6	61.4	73.0	60.9	63.6	55.6	25.0
C. Concerned about getting arrested	40.8	43.5	38.7	40.6	42.6	35.3	42.2	42.3	41.7	40.9	41.0	42.4	42.6	38.9	34.8	12.5
D. Concerned about becoming addicted to marijuana	42.1	39.9	43.7	40.5	47.1	33.3	44.6	43.9	43.9	43.2	42.2	48.8	34.6	38.9	33.7	12.5
E. It's against my beliefs	53.6	49.0	57.2	55.0	47.5	42.2	57.1	56.0	55.5	56.6	50.4	66.6	42.2	43.7	36.6	25.0
F. Concerned about loss of energy or ambition	38.0	39.8	37.0	38.7	35.7	38.5	41.2	32.3	42.7	40.5	34.5	37.7	35.2	37.2	44.8	-
G. Concerned about possible loss of control of myself	47.8	42.0	52.0	47.5	45.1	40.7	52.7	45.8	49.8	51.8	43.7	55.0	38.1	48.6	36.9	-
H. It might lead to stronger drugs	50.0	49.2	50.8	49.4	52.5	42.5	51.8	51.7	51.4	50.1	50.7	55.8	43.9	51.4	39.4	-
I. Not enjoyable, I didn't like it	35.4	36.7	34.9	35.3	35.2	37.0	36.5	30.3	41.7	35.4	35.6	22.5	53.3	44.9	45.2	12.5
J. My parents would disapprove	58.6	54.9	61.6	59.8	53.7	50.9	62.9	58.9	58.3	60.9	56.1	61.9	56.4	61.9	48.4	12.5
K. My husband/wife (or boyfriend/ girlfriend) would disapprove	31.3	28.6	33.4	31.0	29.5	22.0	35.8	31.8	32.4	29.2	34.9	30.0	32.4	33.2	33.7	25.0
L. I don't like being with the people who use it	39.0	37.1	40.5	38.2	41.4	29.4	40.9	40.9	43.3	40.9	36.8	49.1	28.7	34.4	23.7	25.0
M. My friends don't use it	33.0	31.4	34.1	33.7	25.8	25.4	35.4	32.8	37.7	35.8	29.8	40.5	26.0	32.8	17.6	-
N. I might have a bad trip	20.3	17.5	22.5	18.4	28.3	15.6	21.4	20.3	23.7	20.3	21.0	21.8	19.3	19.8	16.1	-
O. Too expensive	25.2	29.3	22.2	26.0	21.3	21.0	29.4	23.7	24.9	24.4	27.2	24.0	26.0	27.5	27.6	-
P. Not available	5.8	6.0	5.2	5.0	7.0	5.2	5.6	4.7	9.0	6.3	5.1	6.1	5.7	5.7	3.9	-
Q. Don't feel like getting high	57.2	55.0	59.1	57.1	55.3	53.6	61.6	52.3	62.3	56.7	58.8	59.6	51.8	57.5	58.1	25.0
Item 9020-9180 N(Wtd) ★	2100	902	1148	1670	244	405	695	679	321	1219	808	1058	488	247	279	8

D05A: Has your use of alcohol ever caused any of the following problems for you?

Responses to this set of questions are not included because of complexities in the presentation and interpretation of the data.

Item 9190-9350

D05M: Has your use of marijuana ever caused any of the following problems for you? (Mark all that apply.)

★=excludes respondents for whom question was inappropriate.

QUESTIONNAIRE FORM 3 1981	TOTAL	SEX		RACE		REGION				4YR COLLEGE PLANS		ILLICIT DRUG USE: LIFETIME				
		M	F	White	Black	NE	NC	S	W	Yes	No	None	Mari-juana Only	Few Pills	More Pills	Any Her-oin
Weighted No. of Cases:	3658	1721	1795	2830	459	869	1100	1114	575	1980	1448	1228	894	433	990	41
% of Weighted Total:	100.0	47.0	49.1	77.4	12.5	23.8	30.1	30.5	15.7	54.1	39.6	33.6	24.4	11.8	27.1	1.1

Responses to this set of questions are not included because of complexities in the presentation and interpretation of the data.

Item 9360-9520

D05O: Has your use of other drugs ever caused any of the following problems for you? (Mark all that apply.)

Responses to this set of questions are not included because of complexities in the presentation and interpretation of the data.

Item 9530-9690

E01: Some people think about what's going on in government very often, and others are not that interested. How much of an interest do you take in government and current events?

	TOTAL	M	F	White	Black	NE	NC	S	W	Yes	No	None	Mari-juana Only	Few Pills	More Pills	Any Her-oin
5. A very great interest	8.7	12.6	5.1	7.9	13.3	7.8	7.3	11.2	8.1	11.1	5.4	10.6	8.0	6.7	7.5	16.2
4. A lot of interest	21.4	25.0	18.4	21.7	23.1	22.5	20.4	22.7	19.3	26.6	14.3	21.6	24.2	22.8	18.8	18.9
3. Some interest	48.2	45.7	50.3	49.1	41.5	47.2	51.8	44.6	49.2	48.0	48.1	51.6	44.7	50.3	46.2	35.1
2. Very little interest	17.5	12.4	22.1	17.7	15.2	17.8	17.2	16.9	18.9	12.1	25.5	13.9	19.3	16.4	21.5	10.8
1. No interest at all	4.2	4.3	4.2	3.6	6.6	4.7	3.2	4.7	4.4	2.2	6.7	2.4	3.8	3.6	5.8	18.9
Item 6330 N(Wtd)	3260	1528	1654	2609	376	707	1028	1007	518	1840	1303	1118	799	390	878	37

E02: Do you agree or disagree that most efforts to prevent (or clean up) pollution...

E02A: ...are just too expensive

	TOTAL	M	F	White	Black	NE	NC	S	W	Yes	No	None	Mari-juana Only	Few Pills	More Pills	Any Her-oin
1. Disagree	22.7	25.8	19.3	21.9	31.5	24.1	19.3	25.6	21.7	23.5	21.0	20.9	24.1	19.6	23.6	45.9
2. Mostly disagree	23.5	22.8	24.2	24.7	14.6	25.7	23.3	20.1	27.6	26.7	19.8	23.2	25.7	25.3	21.7	10.8
3. Neither	32.0	29.4	35.1	33.9	22.1	30.3	34.8	30.7	31.3	29.6	35.6	31.1	29.7	30.8	36.9	18.9
4. Mostly agree	15.6	14.8	16.3	15.7	17.3	14.9	17.2	15.6	13.5	15.4	15.9	16.9	15.6	19.1	12.8	8.1
5. Agree	6.2	7.1	5.1	3.9	14.0	4.9	5.4	7.9	5.9	4.8	7.6	7.7	4.9	5.5	5.0	16.2
Item 9700 N(Wtd)	3210	1510	1623	2570	371	696	1021	983	511	1819	1280	1098	794	383	860	37

E02B: ...cost more jobs than it's worth

	TOTAL	M	F	White	Black	NE	NC	S	W	Yes	No	None	Mari-juana Only	Few Pills	More Pills	Any Her-oin
1. Disagree	26.2	26.7	25.5	26.0	31.6	27.7	23.3	28.3	25.9	27.6	23.6	24.6	29.2	22.3	26.7	32.4
2. Mostly disagree	27.3	26.9	27.6	29.0	16.6	33.5	27.7	20.5	31.5	30.8	23.0	27.3	27.3	35.8	24.7	13.5
3. Neither	29.4	27.7	31.5	30.9	21.1	25.5	31.9	29.9	28.9	27.9	32.5	28.6	27.0	27.1	34.3	24.3
4. Mostly agree	11.6	12.3	11.0	10.5	19.7	8.4	12.3	14.4	8.9	9.7	13.7	11.5	12.9	11.9	10.1	16.2
5. Agree	5.5	6.4	4.2	3.6	10.8	4.9	4.8	6.8	5.0	4.0	7.1	8.0	3.7	2.9	4.2	13.5
Item 9710 N(Wtd)	3185	1504	1606	2560	361	687	1022	971	505	1809	1269	1092	785	377	859	37

E02C: ...are proposed by people who usually don't know what they are talking about

	TOTAL	M	F	White	Black	NE	NC	S	W	Yes	No	None	Mari-juana Only	Few Pills	More Pills	Any Her-oin
1. Disagree	19.4	21.8	17.2	19.2	24.6	20.2	19.4	18.1	20.6	21.7	16.2	18.6	23.6	14.7	18.1	22.2
2. Mostly disagree	24.2	23.9	24.4	25.4	15.0	26.5	25.9	21.5	22.8	27.3	20.0	24.6	21.9	27.4	24.3	25.0
3. Neither	32.3	27.0	37.3	33.1	28.8	30.1	34.6	31.2	32.9	29.6	36.7	32.5	30.5	33.4	33.8	19.4
4. Mostly agree	14.6	15.3	13.9	14.0	18.4	12.8	11.3	19.2	14.3	14.2	14.8	13.7	15.2	18.2	13.9	13.9
5. Agree	9.5	11.9	7.2	8.2	13.3	10.2	8.7	10.1	9.5	7.1	12.4	10.7	8.8	6.6	9.9	19.4
Item 9720 N(Wtd)	3165	1491	1601	2547	354	678	1014	969	505	1799	1262	1079	787	380	847	36

QUESTIONNAIRE FORM 3 1981	TOTAL	SEX		RACE		REGION				4YR COLLEGE PLANS		ILLICIT DRUG USE: LIFETIME				
		M	F	White	Black	NE	NC	S	W	Yes	No	None	Mari-juana Only	Few Pills	More Pills	Any Her-oin
Weighted No. of Cases:	3658	1721	1795	2830	459	869	1100	1114	575	1980	1448	1228	894	433	990	41
% of Weighted Total:	100.0	47.0	49.1	77.4	12.5	23.8	30.1	30.5	15.7	54.1	39.6	33.6	24.4	11.8	27.1	1.1
E02D: ...will not be enough anyhow																
1. Disagree	19.1	20.9	17.3	18.9	24.7	19.7	17.7	20.2	18.8	21.0	15.8	19.2	21.8	12.5	19.0	19.4
2. Mostly disagree	23.3	23.3	23.3	24.6	16.1	24.7	25.9	18.6	24.8	26.4	19.1	26.3	21.4	25.1	20.3	22.2
3. Neither	32.2	30.7	34.0	32.8	29.3	28.3	32.7	35.2	30.7	29.6	36.7	29.1	32.7	34.1	35.4	16.7
4. Mostly agree	17.8	16.5	19.2	18.1	15.5	17.8	17.2	18.2	18.2	16.9	18.9	16.0	16.5	23.2	18.8	25.0
5. Agree	7.7	8.8	6.3	5.7	14.1	9.5	6.4	7.8	7.4	6.1	9.3	9.4	7.6	4.8	6.5	16.7
Item 9730 N(Wtd)	3136	1483	1578	2528	348	675	1009	952	501	1793	1243	1070	781	375	842	36
E02E: ...are useless because this society won't last long enough for such efforts to do any good																
1. Disagree	37.8	42.0	34.4	40.6	28.2	40.8	38.6	35.0	37.9	43.8	28.8	38.9	41.8	32.2	35.8	27.8
2. Mostly disagree	21.3	18.8	23.6	22.1	14.4	22.7	22.3	18.2	23.4	22.5	19.8	22.4	19.4	26.9	19.7	19.4
3. Neither	26.3	23.6	28.9	26.2	28.8	24.2	27.2	28.1	23.8	22.2	32.7	23.0	27.5	24.8	30.5	5.6
4. Mostly agree	8.1	8.3	7.7	6.9	13.6	6.8	6.7	10.5	8.2	6.8	9.8	7.8	6.3	11.3	8.2	19.4
5. Agree	6.4	7.2	5.5	4.2	15.0	5.7	5.1	8.1	7.0	4.7	8.7	8.0	5.1	4.7	5.8	25.0
Item 9740 N(Wtd)	3150	1486	1592	2536	354	679	1007	962	501	1801	1250	1080	783	379	838	36
E03: There has been talk about shortages of energy, food, and raw materials in this country. Do you think that in the coming years we will have plenty to meet our needs, a sufficient amount, or will we have to consume less?																
1. Plenty to meet our needs	11.9	16.1	7.6	10.9	16.6	8.7	12.6	14.2	10.3	10.4	13.7	12.7	13.4	9.7	9.9	20.0
2. A sufficient amount	44.4	45.9	43.3	45.4	41.4	47.7	47.1	39.9	43.3	42.7	46.9	45.5	39.9	47.9	45.2	40.0
3. Will have to consume less	43.8	38.1	49.1	43.7	42.0	43.7	40.4	45.9	46.5	46.9	39.3	41.8	46.5	42.4	45.0	40.0
Item 9750 N(Wtd)	3121	1450	1597	2515	355	663	994	968	497	1784	1231	1073	766	380	832	35
E04: The questions in this section deal with population problems. How much do you agree or disagree with each statement?																
E04A: Our government should help other countries to control their population																
1. Disagree	24.5	28.4	21.4	23.7	29.2	23.4	24.4	24.7	26.0	22.3	28.0	25.0	22.9	23.4	25.0	40.0
2. Mostly disagree	20.0	17.9	21.8	22.0	14.2	21.0	19.7	20.5	18.1	21.4	18.1	21.6	20.9	16.3	19.8	11.4
3. Neither	23.0	20.7	25.0	23.4	17.7	22.9	25.6	19.6	24.6	23.1	22.9	22.6	22.5	24.1	23.7	8.6
4. Mostly agree	21.6	22.0	21.3	21.3	21.3	23.2	18.3	23.9	21.9	23.5	19.5	20.8	22.3	24.9	20.9	25.7
5. Agree	10.8	11.0	10.5	9.5	17.4	9.3	12.0	11.2	9.6	9.8	11.5	10.0	11.3	11.0	10.6	17.1
Item 9760 N(Wtd)	3182	1488	1617	2555	367	676	1008	990	508	1811	1259	1099	785	381	847	35
E04B: Governments should avoid making policy about population and let the individual decide																
1. Disagree	11.7	12.4	11.0	11.1	13.7	11.8	10.1	11.6	15.4	12.0	10.8	10.9	10.1	12.1	13.4	28.6
2. Mostly disagree	21.8	21.0	22.5	22.7	15.3	23.4	22.1	19.9	22.4	22.9	20.1	21.0	22.7	21.3	23.0	11.4
3. Neither	26.1	26.6	25.7	26.8	21.3	25.9	26.4	25.6	26.6	26.8	25.8	24.3	26.7	31.1	26.5	11.4
4. Mostly agree	24.3	22.4	26.4	23.9	29.8	24.6	26.2	24.5	19.8	23.7	25.1	25.9	23.2	23.9	23.3	25.7
5. Agree	16.1	17.6	14.5	15.5	19.7	14.2	15.3	18.4	15.8	14.5	18.2	18.0	17.2	11.6	14.0	22.9
Item 9770 N(Wtd)	3162	1483	1605	2542	366	671	1008	984	500	1804	1250	1092	783	380	838	35
E04C: I feel strongly enough about preventing overpopulation that I'd be willing to limit my family to two children																
1. Disagree	14.1	15.6	13.0	13.2	20.5	15.4	13.0	14.6	13.8	13.7	15.1	14.8	15.8	9.3	12.9	20.0
2. Mostly disagree	12.4	11.5	13.2	12.5	13.0	14.7	14.2	9.0	12.8	14.2	9.7	13.9	12.2	13.5	10.1	14.3
3. Neither	20.7	22.4	19.2	20.8	18.3	24.9	22.0	18.0	18.0	20.8	20.7	20.6	20.7	23.8	20.1	11.4
4. Mostly agree	23.6	22.0	24.8	23.8	21.9	23.3	23.3	25.4	20.8	23.5	23.6	23.4	23.9	22.2	24.0	22.9
5. Agree	29.1	28.4	29.8	29.7	26.3	21.9	27.7	33.1	34.3	27.8	30.9	27.3	27.5	31.2	32.8	28.6
Item 9780 N(Wtd)	3150	1475	1600	2537	361	662	1009	980	499	1792	1250	1085	779	378	839	35

QUESTIONNAIRE FORM 3 1981	TOTAL	SEX		RACE		REGION				4YR COLLEGE PLANS		ILLICIT DRUG USE: LIFETIME				
		M	F	White	Black	NE	NC	S	W	Yes	No	None	Marijuana Only	Few Pills	More Pills	Any Heroin
Weighted No. of Cases:	3658	1721	1795	2830	459	869	1100	1114	575	1980	1448	1228	894	433	990	41
% of Weighted Total:	100.0	47.0	49.1	77.4	12.5	23.8	30.1	30.5	15.7	54.1	39.6	33.6	24.4	11.8	27.1	1.1

E04D: To help prevent overpopulation, I might decide not to have any children of my own

	TOTAL	M	F	White	Black	NE	NC	S	W	Yes	No	None	Marijuana Only	Few Pills	More Pills	Any Heroin
1. Disagree	53.5	49.9	57.8	54.0	53.0	54.7	51.1	53.1	57.9	53.8	53.5	52.2	57.1	49.3	53.6	45.7
2. Mostly disagree	17.5	18.4	16.7	18.0	15.5	18.6	19.3	15.1	16.9	19.1	15.0	17.0	20.3	18.2	15.9	8.6
3. Neither	14.9	16.8	13.0	15.0	12.4	15.3	16.7	13.8	12.3	14.2	16.2	15.2	11.6	15.8	17.1	11.4
4. Mostly agree	7.1	8.0	5.7	6.5	11.0	5.6	5.1	10.7	5.6	6.7	7.4	7.8	5.4	8.2	6.7	22.9
5. Agree	7.0	7.0	6.8	6.4	8.3	5.6	7.7	7.2	7.3	6.2	8.0	7.7	5.7	8.4	6.7	8.6
Item 9790 N(Wtd)	3151	1474	1601	2535	362	666	1010	978	496	1797	1244	1090	778	379	836	35

E04E: High schools should offer instruction in birth control methods

	TOTAL	M	F	White	Black	NE	NC	S	W	Yes	No	None	Marijuana Only	Few Pills	More Pills	Any Heroin
1. Disagree	6.4	5.9	6.7	6.2	6.7	5.6	6.3	7.0	6.7	5.7	7.8	9.1	4.6	6.4	4.3	17.1
2. Mostly disagree	4.1	4.6	3.6	4.3	3.6	4.5	4.7	3.7	3.4	4.0	4.2	3.6	5.5	4.5	3.2	5.7
3. Neither	10.4	12.4	8.9	11.2	7.0	9.2	11.9	10.1	9.7	10.3	10.8	13.7	8.2	8.2	9.9	2.9
4. Mostly agree	26.5	29.6	23.9	26.9	23.7	26.6	25.7	28.0	25.2	26.9	26.0	26.9	26.1	28.7	25.5	34.3
5. Agree	52.4	47.7	57.0	51.4	58.9	54.0	51.4	51.1	55.2	53.1	51.1	46.6	55.6	51.9	57.2	40.0
Item 9800 N(Wtd)	3140	1472	1593	2530	358	661	1008	977	493	1792	1238	1083	779	376	832	35

E04F: I personally consider most methods of birth control to be immoral

	TOTAL	M	F	White	Black	NE	NC	S	W	Yes	No	None	Marijuana Only	Few Pills	More Pills	Any Heroin
1. Disagree	43.5	39.3	47.9	45.7	31.6	49.8	39.5	40.3	49.9	44.6	42.9	34.7	44.6	45.3	53.4	37.1
2. Mostly disagree	19.7	22.5	17.1	20.5	17.1	20.4	21.0	18.2	19.1	21.6	17.0	19.8	23.7	19.1	16.0	37.1
3. Neither	20.5	21.7	19.5	19.8	23.1	18.9	23.5	20.4	17.1	19.5	22.3	24.2	18.3	19.1	19.3	5.7
4. Mostly agree	8.2	9.3	7.0	7.7	11.1	5.9	7.3	11.2	7.1	7.5	9.0	9.7	7.5	10.2	5.8	14.3
5. Agree	8.0	7.2	8.5	6.2	16.8	4.7	8.8	9.9	6.7	6.9	8.7	11.5	6.1	6.5	5.5	5.7
Item 9810 N(Wtd)	3116	1459	1583	2514	351	656	1001	968	491	1783	1225	1075	776	371	824	35

E04G: The government should make birth control information and services available without cost to anyone who wants them

	TOTAL	M	F	White	Black	NE	NC	S	W	Yes	No	None	Marijuana Only	Few Pills	More Pills	Any Heroin
1. Disagree	7.2	7.9	6.8	7.6	4.2	8.4	6.8	6.6	7.7	7.5	6.9	10.7	5.4	6.4	4.8	8.8
2. Mostly disagree	7.2	7.7	6.3	7.5	6.8	6.5	8.4	7.1	5.9	7.7	6.3	7.9	6.2	7.2	7.2	5.9
3. Neither	14.0	17.5	10.8	14.5	9.3	14.3	15.6	13.7	10.8	14.1	14.5	14.6	14.6	13.4	13.0	5.9
4. Mostly agree	24.9	23.9	26.2	25.3	22.9	24.6	24.2	24.1	28.1	25.9	22.7	26.4	25.0	27.1	21.0	32.4
5. Agree	46.7	43.1	49.9	45.1	56.9	46.1	45.2	48.5	47.7	44.8	49.5	40.5	48.8	45.8	54.1	41.2
Item 9820 N(Wtd)	3115	1456	1586	2512	353	651	1003	969	491	1778	1228	1076	775	373	821	34

E05: What do you think would be the ideal population size for the United States?

	TOTAL	M	F	White	Black	NE	NC	S	W	Yes	No	None	Marijuana Only	Few Pills	More Pills	Any Heroin
1. Much smaller than it is now	10.1	10.7	9.3	9.5	10.6	10.2	9.6	9.3	12.8	8.4	12.5	10.0	9.0	9.3	11.7	17.6
2. Somewhat smaller than it is now	39.6	36.3	42.4	41.8	27.1	43.6	40.8	33.9	42.7	40.8	38.2	38.0	41.4	36.8	42.5	23.5
3. About the same as it is now	43.0	45.1	41.6	44.2	38.9	40.6	44.8	46.2	36.0	44.6	41.5	43.3	41.8	47.7	41.7	41.2
4. Somewhat larger than it is now	5.4	6.3	4.5	3.9	14.6	5.0	3.6	7.1	6.3	4.7	5.6	5.9	5.5	6.0	3.6	5.9
5. Much larger than it is now	1.9	1.7	2.2	.6	8.9	.6	1.1	3.4	2.0	1.5	2.1	2.9	2.1	.3	.6	8.8
Item 9830 N(Wtd)	3091	1453	1564	2489	350	640	999	958	494	1758	1221	1065	765	367	824	34

E06: What do you think would be the ideal population size for the entire world?

	TOTAL	M	F	White	Black	NE	NC	S	W	Yes	No	None	Marijuana Only	Few Pills	More Pills	Any Heroin
1. Much smaller than it is now	31.3	33.5	29.3	33.3	19.2	35.7	30.9	27.2	34.6	32.2	29.6	29.9	33.9	29.1	32.0	50.0
2. Somewhat smaller than it is now	41.5	39.2	43.7	43.7	28.4	43.6	44.8	38.1	38.9	43.6	39.5	41.6	39.9	43.1	43.8	20.6
3. About the same as it is now	21.0	22.0	19.9	20.0	27.5	16.9	20.0	25.3	19.6	19.2	23.6	20.5	19.7	22.5	21.6	14.7
4. Somewhat larger than it is now	3.9	3.6	4.2	2.3	13.8	3.0	3.2	4.9	4.5	3.4	4.2	4.6	4.3	4.1	1.5	11.8
5. Much larger than it is now	2.3	1.6	3.0	.7	10.9	1.0	1.0	4.5	2.4	1.5	3.1	3.2	2.2	1.1	1.2	2.9
Item 9850 N(Wtd)	3069	1453	1544	2475	349	628	991	959	491	1746	1211	1056	762	364	816	34

QUESTIONNAIRE FORM 3 1981	TOTAL	SEX		RACE		REGION				4YR COLLEGE PLANS		ILLICIT DRUG USE: LIFETIME				
		M	F	White	Black	NE	NC	S	W	Yes	No	None	Mari- juana Only	Few Pills	More Pills	Any Her- oin
Weighted No. of Cases:	3658	1721	1795	2830	459	869	1100	1114	575	1980	1448	1228	894	433	990	41
% of Weighted Total:	100.0	47.0	49.1	77.4	12.5	23.8	30.1	30.5	15.7	54.1	39.6	33.6	24.4	11.8	27.1	1.1

E07: Some people like school very much. Others don't. How do you feel about going to school?

5. I like school very much	15.0	13.5	16.4	12.9	26.6	8.7	13.3	19.1	18.5	17.6	10.9	22.2	13.4	13.8	6.8	23.5
4. I like school quite a lot	30.3	28.3	32.1	30.5	30.2	31.0	29.0	29.3	33.9	36.6	21.1	33.9	31.5	33.2	24.5	14.7
3. I like school some	39.4	41.8	37.4	40.1	36.8	41.7	42.2	37.7	34.3	35.9	44.5	34.4	41.1	39.9	44.4	26.5
2. I don't like school very much	10.6	11.4	9.7	11.5	5.8	13.0	10.9	9.7	8.7	7.3	15.4	6.9	10.0	9.8	15.9	23.5
1. I don't like school at all	4.7	4.9	4.6	4.9	.6	5.5	4.6	4.2	4.8	2.4	8.1	2.5	4.2	2.9	8.4	14.7
Item 7630 N(Wtd)	3141	1472	1595	2528	361	655	1007	983	496	1786	1241	1081	779	376	838	34

E08: Did you have a unit on sex education when you were in high school?

1. No, and I'm glad I didn't	7.4	8.7	6.2	7.1	8.0	4.3	7.3	10.3	5.7	7.0	8.2	9.7	4.7	6.0	7.4	9.4
2. No, and I wish I had	24.6	24.8	24.4	23.3	38.2	17.1	20.2	39.6	13.7	24.0	25.3	24.1	27.3	23.2	23.4	28.1
3. Yes, and it was very worthwhile	27.3	23.2	31.0	25.6	32.7	24.6	27.1	24.8	36.2	25.9	29.0	29.5	25.3	27.2	25.2	25.0
4. Yes, and it was somewhat worthwhile	32.0	34.0	30.1	34.6	17.2	41.7	37.3	17.7	36.0	34.5	28.3	29.7	33.8	35.7	32.5	25.0
5. Yes, but it was not worthwhile at all	8.8	9.3	8.3	9.5	3.9	12.3	7.9	7.4	8.4	8.7	9.2	6.9	8.8	8.2	11.5	15.6
Item 9860 N(Wtd)	3104	1458	1573	2493	361	650	996	970	489	1767	1226	1070	770	367	828	32

E09: Did you ever study about birth control methods in high school?

1. No, and I'm glad I didn't	10.7	13.3	8.3	10.5	8.9	6.5	11.3	12.6	11.3	9.6	12.4	13.9	6.9	10.8	9.9	12.5
2. No, and I wish I had	33.0	32.6	33.9	32.9	36.9	31.9	30.8	40.7	23.8	32.3	33.8	31.9	34.6	35.8	32.0	31.3
3. Yes, and it was very worthwhile	28.2	23.9	32.0	26.6	35.2	25.9	26.6	27.9	34.8	27.8	28.3	27.7	29.2	26.8	28.3	15.6
4. Yes, and it was somewhat worthwhile	22.9	24.1	21.6	24.5	15.9	29.1	25.1	14.7	26.4	25.1	19.9	22.1	24.4	21.4	23.4	25.0
5. Yes, but it was not worthwhile at all	5.2	6.1	4.3	5.4	3.4	6.4	6.1	4.1	3.9	5.1	5.6	4.4	4.7	5.1	6.4	12.5
Item 9870 N(Wtd)	3085	1441	1573	2481	358	642	995	961	488	1755	1221	1057	765	369	829	32

E10: Looking toward the future, how important would it be for you to have each of the following things?

E10A: At least one car

1. Not important	3.0	3.4	2.3	2.4	5.0	3.5	2.4	2.1	4.9	2.6	3.3	3.8	2.4	1.6	2.6	-
2. Somewhat important	17.3	15.2	19.6	16.4	21.4	17.1	17.1	15.9	20.7	18.4	16.0	20.6	16.7	17.8	13.2	27.3
3. Quite important	34.5	34.3	34.8	35.0	37.9	33.4	36.4	35.0	31.0	35.9	32.8	34.0	36.3	35.8	33.1	24.2
4. Extremely important	45.3	47.0	43.2	46.2	35.7	46.0	44.2	46.8	43.3	43.0	47.9	41.6	44.6	44.8	51.3	48.5
Item 13835 N(Wtd)	3168	1485	1602	2542	359	659	1011	985	513	1799	1257	1088	783	377	844	33

E10B: At least two cars

1. Not important	47.3	38.9	54.9	45.7	57.0	50.8	45.8	44.2	51.6	47.5	47.6	48.5	46.5	41.2	50.1	42.4
2. Somewhat important	31.7	35.0	29.0	32.9	25.4	28.9	33.4	32.5	30.1	32.8	30.1	31.0	33.5	34.6	30.0	24.2
3. Quite important	14.3	17.3	11.4	14.8	12.8	13.5	13.5	17.0	12.0	14.1	14.3	13.7	15.0	15.7	13.7	18.2
4. Extremely important	6.7	8.7	4.7	6.6	5.1	6.7	7.2	6.3	6.3	5.7	7.9	6.8	5.0	8.8	6.2	15.2
Item 13840 N(Wtd)	3146	1479	1591	2534	351	653	1013	972	508	1795	1252	1079	779	376	840	33

E10C: A large (full-sized) car

1. Not important	72.5	65.7	79.0	73.4	69.2	72.5	71.3	71.5	76.2	71.6	73.9	70.4	70.9	72.4	77.4	66.7
2. Somewhat important	15.8	18.4	13.4	16.0	14.5	16.0	16.7	15.3	15.1	16.5	15.0	16.0	17.6	16.9	13.6	23.3
3. Quite important	6.7	9.9	3.6	6.4	9.0	7.5	6.4	7.8	4.8	7.1	5.9	7.5	6.6	8.2	5.0	6.7
4. Extremely important	5.0	6.0	4.0	4.3	7.3	4.1	5.7	5.3	4.2	4.7	5.1	6.2	4.8	2.5	4.1	10.0
Item 13850 N(Wtd)	3100	1449	1575	2503	344	655	990	952	504	1773	1228	1063	774	366	828	30

QUESTIONNAIRE FORM 3 1981	TOTAL	SEX		RACE		REGION				4YR COLLEGE PLANS		ILLICIT DRUG USE: LIFETIME				
		M	F	White	Black	NE	NC	S	W	Yes	No	None	Mari-juana Only	Few Pills	More Pills	Any Her-oin
Weighted No. of Cases:	3658	1721	1795	2830	459	869	1100	1114	575	1980	1448	1228	894	433	990	41
% of Weighted Total:	100.0	47.0	49.1	77.4	12.5	23.8	30.1	30.5	15.7	54.1	39.6	33.6	24.4	11.8	27.1	1.1
E10D: A new car every two or three years																
1. Not important	70.3	62.5	78.0	70.8	69.9	70.1	67.2	71.4	75.1	69.1	72.7	73.2	67.8	68.5	70.3	66.7
2. Somewhat important	18.5	22.5	14.8	18.1	21.6	18.8	20.5	17.5	16.1	20.7	15.4	16.3	21.0	21.1	17.6	15.2
3. Quite important	6.9	9.3	4.6	7.1	5.1	6.9	7.9	7.1	4.6	6.8	6.8	6.3	7.7	6.7	7.2	9.1
4. Extremely important	4.2	5.9	2.6	4.0	3.4	4.4	4.4	4.0	4.2	3.4	5.2	4.2	3.5	3.5	5.0	9.1
Item 13860 N(Wtd)	3137	1468	1591	2523	352	655	1008	971	503	1786	1244	1077	776	375	835	33
E10E: Clothes in the latest style																
1. Not important	18.0	22.3	13.1	18.4	11.3	18.3	18.6	16.2	20.1	17.1	19.3	20.6	16.9	14.9	18.4	3.2
2. Somewhat important	39.1	39.0	40.0	40.5	31.0	39.2	39.4	37.4	41.7	41.6	37.0	40.6	37.1	39.5	38.0	48.4
3. Quite important	27.2	26.7	27.8	27.9	26.5	27.2	27.4	28.3	24.4	27.1	26.8	24.5	30.3	31.2	25.9	25.8
4. Extremely important	15.7	12.0	19.0	13.3	31.3	15.5	14.6	18.0	13.8	14.3	16.8	14.3	15.7	14.1	17.8	22.6
Item 13870 N(Wtd)	3144	1475	1591	2526	355	646	1012	978	508	1787	1248	1085	776	375	837	31
E10F: A house of my own (instead of an apartment or condominium)																
1. Not important	15.3	11.9	18.5	15.9	13.0	18.4	16.0	14.1	12.4	15.1	16.1	14.4	12.8	18.8	17.3	15.2
2. Somewhat important	24.0	20.5	27.2	24.9	16.1	23.6	27.8	20.5	23.6	25.1	23.1	22.6	24.8	22.8	26.6	12.1
3. Quite important	28.0	31.3	25.2	28.8	24.9	29.9	25.6	28.7	28.9	28.8	26.7	30.0	27.5	29.7	25.3	18.2
4. Extremely important	32.7	36.2	29.2	30.4	46.0	28.3	30.5	36.7	34.8	31.0	34.1	33.0	34.8	28.9	30.8	57.6
Item 13880 N(Wtd)	3153	1479	1597	2535	354	653	1015	977	508	1787	1257	1085	781	377	837	33
E10G: Lots of space around my house, a big yard																
1. Not important	12.5	10.6	14.6	11.1	17.2	11.7	12.6	12.9	12.6	11.9	13.4	12.3	8.6	17.1	14.2	12.1
2. Somewhat important	26.9	24.5	28.8	27.2	25.7	24.7	27.9	26.3	28.8	26.9	27.5	25.6	29.0	25.1	28.2	21.2
3. Quite important	31.8	34.0	30.1	33.4	26.8	33.9	31.5	32.3	28.8	32.4	30.2	31.4	32.9	31.7	31.1	30.3
4. Extremely important	28.8	30.9	26.6	28.3	30.2	29.8	28.0	28.5	29.8	28.8	28.9	30.7	29.2	26.1	26.5	39.4
Item 13890 N(Wtd)	3145	1477	1593	2530	354	652	1010	976	507	1786	1250	1085	775	375	838	33
E10H: A well-kept garden and lawn																
1. Not important	10.1	10.2	10.0	9.4	12.7	14.3	9.0	8.8	9.4	10.5	9.6	9.5	8.3	11.4	12.5	9.1
2. Somewhat important	30.0	29.3	30.4	30.6	23.2	32.3	31.1	28.1	28.5	30.2	30.2	27.6	30.2	31.7	32.3	27.3
3. Quite important	35.7	36.2	35.5	37.5	30.6	32.9	37.4	36.2	35.0	36.0	35.0	36.7	36.2	35.4	34.0	33.3
4. Extremely important	24.2	24.3	24.2	22.5	33.7	20.5	22.6	26.9	27.1	23.3	25.3	26.1	25.3	21.4	21.2	30.3
Item 13900 N(Wtd)	3140	1468	1594	2525	353	650	1009	972	509	1784	1247	1083	771	378	835	33
E10I: Major labor-saving appliances (washer, drier, dishwasher, etc.)																
1. Not important	10.1	9.4	10.9	9.5	11.9	11.7	10.1	9.2	9.4	9.7	11.2	11.3	8.4	9.0	10.2	21.2
2. Somewhat important	32.0	30.7	33.1	32.8	26.1	33.3	33.6	27.7	35.6	32.1	32.5	33.6	32.4	31.8	30.9	3.0
3. Quite important	34.1	38.2	30.5	35.0	33.1	31.6	35.9	35.4	31.3	34.8	32.3	32.3	36.4	35.8	33.9	36.4
4. Extremely important	23.8	21.8	25.4	22.6	29.2	23.1	20.4	27.6	23.8	23.4	24.1	22.9	22.7	23.3	25.2	39.4
Item 13910 N(Wtd)	3140	1470	1591	2526	353	648	1010	974	508	1781	1251	1082	771	377	836	33
E10J: A high-quality stereo																
1. Not important	18.1	11.4	24.7	17.3	24.8	14.8	20.3	18.4	17.5	16.9	20.4	25.6	16.0	15.6	11.8	3.0
2. Somewhat important	31.5	27.5	35.3	31.7	28.8	28.4	33.5	32.9	29.3	33.5	29.5	33.6	33.9	32.5	26.5	21.2
3. Quite important	26.6	31.0	22.7	27.1	25.4	28.4	25.3	25.9	28.1	26.2	26.2	25.3	27.6	28.0	27.8	12.1
4. Extremely important	23.8	30.2	17.3	24.0	21.0	28.7	20.9	22.8	25.0	23.4	23.9	15.5	22.5	23.8	34.1	60.6
Item 13920 N(Wtd)	3135	1469	1588	2526	347	649	1008	968	509	1785	1242	1080	769	378	834	33
E10K: A vacation house																
1. Not important	63.7	56.6	70.5	64.1	65.3	58.6	67.4	64.2	61.9	62.3	67.3	68.9	63.2	62.4	59.7	39.4
2. Somewhat important	20.7	25.7	16.2	21.3	18.2	26.0	18.1	19.5	21.3	22.9	17.1	17.8	22.7	21.6	22.3	18.2
3. Quite important	8.6	9.9	7.3	8.6	8.4	7.9	8.0	9.6	8.9	8.2	8.8	7.4	8.2	9.1	9.6	24.2
4. Extremely important	7.0	7.7	6.1	6.0	8.4	7.4	6.6	6.7	7.9	6.7	6.8	5.9	5.7	6.9	8.5	21.2
Item 13930 N(Wtd)	3120	1461	1582	2515	346	645	1005	963	507	1778	1238	1076	766	375	831	33

QUESTIONNAIRE FORM 3 1981	TOTAL	SEX		RACE		REGION				4YR COLLEGE PLANS		ILLICIT DRUG USE: LIFETIME				
		M	F	White	Black	NE	NC	S	W	Yes	No	None	Mari-juana Only	Few Pills	More Pills	Any Her-oin
Weighted No. of Cases:	3658	1721	1795	2830	459	869	1100	1114	575	1980	1448	1228	894	433	990	41
% of Weighted Total:	100.0	47.0	49.1	77.4	12.5	23.8	30.1	30.5	15.7	54.1	39.6	33.6	24.4	11.8	27.1	1.1

E10L: A motor-powered, recreational vehicle (powerboat, snowmobile)

1. Not important	57.0	41.5	71.9	55.1	72.3	57.3	55.6	60.3	53.4	59.9	53.3	63.6	59.3	53.3	49.5	27.3
2. Somewhat important	22.8	30.0	16.2	24.4	13.1	23.8	23.8	19.9	25.1	21.0	25.7	18.8	20.7	29.1	27.9	15.2
3. Quite important	10.8	15.1	6.7	11.1	7.4	12.1	11.3	10.0	9.6	10.9	10.1	9.8	12.9	8.3	10.2	24.2
4. Extremely important	9.4	13.5	5.2	9.4	6.9	6.8	9.3	9.8	11.8	8.3	10.8	8.0	7.2	9.1	12.5	36.4
Item 13940 N(Wtd)	3132	1465	1589	2523	350	646	1008	969	509	1781	1242	1081	769	375	833	33

E11: In the following list you will find some statements about leisure time. Please show whether you agree or disagree with each statement.†

E11A: I find that I don't know what to do with a lot of my leisure time

1. Disagree	41.3	41.6	40.9	41.5	45.7	41.9	38.6	43.6	41.8	44.3	37.5	41.9	42.7	37.4	40.8	48.5
2. Mostly disagree	28.1	27.1	29.2	29.8	17.6	33.0	27.3	26.5	26.5	29.7	25.4	28.0	28.9	27.0	28.6	18.2
3. Neither	13.1	14.6	11.6	13.2	9.7	10.8	15.0	11.6	14.7	10.7	16.6	13.6	9.9	16.0	14.1	9.1
4. Mostly agree	12.5	11.6	13.4	11.7	16.2	10.8	13.7	12.4	12.5	11.3	14.3	11.4	13.9	14.7	11.5	18.2
5. Agree	5.0	5.0	4.9	3.8	11.1	3.5	5.4	5.9	4.6	3.9	6.3	5.2	4.7	4.5	5.0	6.1
Item 9880 N(Wtd)	3117	1455	1584	2503	352	649	999	963	505	1776	1232	1074	771	374	824	33

E11B: Time seems to pass very quickly during my leisure hours

1. Disagree	5.9	5.2	6.5	4.9	11.8	5.3	4.5	7.1	7.2	4.9	7.2	6.0	6.0	5.7	5.1	9.7
2. Mostly disagree	7.0	7.2	6.8	7.1	8.3	7.7	6.5	7.1	7.2	6.8	7.7	6.0	7.9	7.0	7.5	6.5
3. Neither	9.7	11.0	8.5	9.7	7.5	11.1	8.4	7.6	14.1	9.5	9.9	8.8	9.9	10.0	10.5	9.7
4. Mostly agree	34.0	35.8	32.6	34.7	29.3	32.6	38.8	31.5	31.1	35.2	32.2	34.5	34.4	36.7	32.2	29.0
5. Agree	43.4	40.8	45.6	43.5	43.1	43.3	41.7	46.7	40.6	43.6	42.9	44.8	41.8	40.7	44.6	45.2
Item 9890 N(Wtd)	3108	1451	1579	2499	348	647	1002	957	502	1773	1228	1071	770	371	825	31

E11C: I feel that I waste a great deal of my free time because I don't end up doing things that are either productive or enjoyable

1. Disagree	25.0	24.8	25.0	24.3	31.9	26.6	23.0	25.4	25.9	25.9	24.3	26.4	24.0	24.0	23.6	34.4
2. Mostly disagree	25.0	25.1	25.0	26.6	16.5	28.6	27.8	20.8	23.2	26.9	22.8	25.0	28.4	19.4	24.9	18.8
3. Neither	19.5	21.3	17.7	20.5	13.6	16.6	21.4	19.5	19.2	18.2	21.2	18.0	18.0	24.0	21.1	6.3
4. Mostly agree	19.9	19.2	20.7	19.6	20.6	19.2	18.8	20.3	22.4	20.2	19.4	19.0	20.9	22.6	19.2	18.8
5. Agree	10.6	9.6	11.6	8.9	17.4	8.9	8.8	14.0	9.4	8.9	12.3	11.5	8.9	9.7	11.0	18.8
Item 9900 N(Wtd)	3095	1445	1573	2490	345	640	998	957	501	1766	1224	1070	767	371	818	32

E11D: I usually have enough time for the things I want to do

1. Disagree	14.5	13.2	15.5	13.8	17.9	14.2	13.8	15.2	14.5	15.0	13.6	15.4	15.8	15.4	11.6	15.6
2. Mostly disagree	22.5	20.8	24.1	24.0	16.1	22.7	22.3	20.9	26.0	24.8	19.6	22.8	22.0	21.8	23.8	3.1
3. Neither	10.8	11.9	9.6	10.8	9.2	12.7	9.7	10.3	11.1	10.3	11.4	11.2	10.4	10.8	10.5	15.6
4. Mostly agree	32.7	34.6	31.3	33.7	25.9	35.1	33.7	32.2	29.0	34.2	31.4	32.1	34.6	32.6	32.1	37.5
5. Agree	19.5	19.5	19.4	17.7	31.1	15.3	20.4	21.5	19.1	15.8	24.0	18.6	17.2	19.4	22.1	25.0
Item 9910 N(Wtd)	3098	1449	1572	2490	347	639	999	957	503	1764	1228	1070	768	371	820	32

E12: When (if ever) did you FIRST do each of the following things? Don't count anything you took because a doctor told you to.

E12A: Smoke cigarettes on a daily basis

8. Never	66.9	72.1	62.3	65.3	77.0	63.9	65.1	67.0	74.1	73.9	57.0	90.5	66.4	66.7	38.0	40.7
1. Grade 6 or below	4.6	4.2	5.0	4.8	4.9	4.4	5.0	4.6	4.4	4.1	5.2	1.6	6.4	4.6	6.9	6.7
2. Grade 7 or 8	9.5	7.0	11.8	10.0	4.5	10.1	11.4	8.1	7.8	6.8	13.3	2.5	9.0	8.3	18.7	33.3
3. Grade 9 (Freshman)	7.2	6.0	8.3	7.7	4.9	9.9	7.3	7.1	4.1	5.9	9.1	1.6	6.5	7.6	15.2	3.3
4. Grade 10 (Sophomore)	5.3	4.8	5.6	5.8	2.9	5.2	5.7	5.5	4.1	3.7	7.7	1.7	6.5	4.0	9.1	10.0
5. Grade 11 (Junior)	4.1	3.8	4.6	4.3	2.9	3.8	3.7	5.2	3.5	3.3	5.3	1.4	2.5	7.0	8.0	-
6. Grade 12 (Senior)	2.3	2.0	2.6	2.1	3.2	2.6	2.0	2.6	2.0	2.3	2.3	.7	2.8	1.8	4.2	-
Item 5570 N(Wtd)	2833	1324	1440	2291	309	574	923	877	459	1614	1125	994	675	327	771	30

QUESTIONNAIRE FORM 3 1981	TOTAL	SEX		RACE		REGION				4YR COLLEGE PLANS		ILLICIT DRUG USE: LIFETIME				
		M	F	White	Black	NE	NC	S	W	Yes	No	None	Mari- juana Only	Few Pills	More Pills	Any Her- oin
Weighted No. of Cases:	3658	1721	1795	2830	459	869	1100	1114	575	1980	1448	1228	894	433	990	41
% of Weighted Total:	100.0	47.0	49.1	77.4	12.5	23.8	30.1	30.5	15.7	54.1	39.6	33.6	24.4	11.8	27.1	1.1
E12B: Try an alcoholic beverage - more than just a few sips																
8. Never	9.0	7.7	9.7	7.0	20.2	2.8	7.8	12.8	12.6	9.5	8.1	24.3	.6	5.1	.7	3.7
1. Grade 6 or below	9.2	12.0	6.7	9.3	8.4	9.1	9.7	7.8	10.9	8.6	9.8	6.3	9.0	7.5	12.7	29.6
2. Grade 7 or 8	20.8	22.5	18.9	21.9	12.2	24.8	20.1	16.6	24.6	20.5	21.4	10.1	22.3	21.3	31.3	33.3
3. Grade 9 (Freshman)	24.2	24.3	24.3	25.1	18.6	26.3	26.1	21.1	23.0	23.7	25.4	15.9	28.5	24.6	30.2	11.1
4. Grade 10 (Sophomore)	19.3	18.9	20.1	20.2	14.4	21.0	19.5	20.2	15.2	20.0	18.3	18.3	24.6	20.4	15.8	11.1
5. Grade 11 (Junior)	12.1	10.3	13.7	11.6	15.6	11.8	12.0	14.0	9.6	12.1	12.2	16.0	11.1	16.5	7.4	3.7
6. Grade 12 (Senior)	5.3	4.2	6.6	4.8	10.3	4.1	4.8	7.5	4.1	5.6	4.9	9.2	4.1	5.1	1.8	11.1
Item 5580 N(Wtd)	2821	1344	1410	2335	263	604	934	823	460	1621	1111	889	723	334	812	27
E12C: Try marijuana or hashish																
8. Never	41.2	36.0	45.7	38.3	56.0	32.5	42.3	48.5	36.9	43.5	38.0	100.0	-	27.1	8.4	-
1. Grade 6 or below	2.4	3.7	1.0	2.3	2.8	2.0	2.0	2.1	4.1	2.2	2.4	-	2.4	1.7	4.8	20.7
2. Grade 7 or 8	13.0	14.9	11.2	13.7	7.9	18.0	11.5	9.6	16.0	11.6	15.5	-	14.6	10.8	28.6	41.4
3. Grade 9 (Freshman)	17.3	19.1	16.1	18.6	10.1	22.1	17.1	13.4	19.3	17.4	17.7	-	27.5	22.2	29.6	10.3
4. Grade 10 (Sophomore)	13.8	15.9	11.9	15.3	7.9	15.4	14.1	12.4	13.9	13.1	14.5	-	26.3	20.1	18.5	13.8
5. Grade 11 (Junior)	8.4	7.1	9.9	8.2	9.8	8.3	9.0	9.4	5.4	8.3	8.7	-	19.0	12.5	8.0	3.4
6. Grade 12 (Senior)	3.8	3.4	4.3	3.6	5.4	1.8	4.2	4.5	4.4	4.1	3.4	-	10.2	5.5	2.0	10.3
Item 5590 N(Wtd)	2946	1370	1502	2391	316	615	956	893	482	1693	1155	1039	699	343	805	29
E12D: Try LSD																
8. Never	92.2	89.5	94.7	91.3	98.8	90.1	91.6	95.5	89.8	94.4	88.9	100.0	100.0	96.3	73.8	24.1
1. Grade 6 or below	*	-	.1	*	-	-	.1	-	-	-	.1	-	-	-	.1	-
2. Grade 7 or 8	.4	.5	.4	.4	-	.2	.2	.1	1.6	.2	.7	-	-	.3	1.2	10.3
3. Grade 9 (Freshman)	1.5	2.7	.5	1.8	.3	2.3	1.8	.3	2.5	.9	2.3	-	-	.8	4.5	31.0
4. Grade 10 (Sophomore)	2.5	3.5	1.6	2.8	-	3.1	2.6	1.4	3.7	2.0	3.2	-	-	-	9.6	3.4
5. Grade 11 (Junior)	2.1	2.2	2.0	2.3	.9	3.1	1.9	1.6	2.0	1.5	3.0	-	-	1.1	6.7	24.1
6. Grade 12 (Senior)	1.2	1.6	.7	1.4	.3	1.1	1.8	1.0	.6	.9	1.8	-	-	1.1	4.0	10.3
Item 5600 N(Wtd)	2982	1395	1517	2400	336	616	960	917	489	1716	1170	1057	749	354	759	29
E12E: Try any psychedelic other than LSD																
8. Never	95.0	93.2	96.7	94.5	98.2	90.8	96.7	97.7	91.3	95.8	93.9	100.0	100.0	98.3	82.7	23.1
1. Grade 6 or below	*	.1	-	*	-	-	-	.1	-	-	.1	-	-	-	-	3.8
2. Grade 7 or 8	.3	.4	.1	.2	.6	.5	.1	.2	.4	.1	.6	-	-	-	.6	19.2
3. Grade 9 (Freshman)	.8	1.6	.1	1.0	.3	1.2	1.0	.3	1.0	.7	.8	-	-	.6	2.5	19.2
4. Grade 10 (Sophomore)	1.6	2.3	.9	1.8	-	3.2	1.2	.8	2.5	1.4	2.1	-	-	-	6.4	11.5
5. Grade 11 (Junior)	1.7	1.9	1.5	1.9	.9	3.4	.9	.6	3.1	1.5	1.9	-	-	-	6.4	19.2
6. Grade 12 (Senior)	.5	.4	.6	.7	-	.8	.2	.2	1.5	.5	.6	-	-	1.4	1.3	7.7
Item 5610 N(Wtd)	2941	1367	1506	2361	337	597	937	926	482	1702	1140	1059	757	357	706	26
E12F: Try amphetamines																
8. Never	78.7	78.4	78.7	75.4	96.6	75.3	78.0	83.8	74.5	80.5	75.0	99.9	99.7	68.4	15.8	-
1. Grade 6 or below	.3	.4	.2	.2	.6	.4	.2	.2	.2	.1	.6	-	-	-	.9	7.7
2. Grade 7 or 8	1.7	1.8	1.7	1.9	.3	.9	2.0	1.3	2.9	.8	3.1	-	-	.4	6.0	42.3
3. Grade 9 (Freshman)	2.9	3.1	2.6	3.2	.6	4.0	2.3	2.2	3.8	1.9	4.1	-	-	2.7	11.4	26.9
4. Grade 10 (Sophomore)	5.9	6.2	5.7	6.9	.3	7.0	5.9	4.2	7.6	5.4	7.0	-	-	3.6	26.6	7.7
5. Grade 11 (Junior)	5.9	6.0	5.8	6.7	.6	6.1	6.1	4.5	7.4	5.4	7.0	-	.1	9.8	23.6	7.7
6. Grade 12 (Senior)	4.7	4.1	5.4	5.7	.9	6.1	5.4	3.7	3.6	5.9	3.0	.1	.3	15.1	15.8	7.7
Item 5620 N(Wtd)	2646	1252	1327	2098	321	571	841	815	419	1565	989	1053	756	225	552	26
E12G: Try quaaludes																
8. Never	91.3	90.2	92.3	90.6	98.8	89.4	93.3	90.0	91.9	93.2	88.2	100.0	99.9	96.2	70.6	21.4
1. Grade 6 or below	.1	.3	-	.1	.6	-	.1	.2	.2	.1	.2	-	-	-	.1	10.7
2. Grade 7 or 8	.7	.9	.5	.6	-	.5	.6	.5	1.2	.4	1.0	-	-	.3	1.6	25.0
3. Grade 9 (Freshman)	1.1	1.4	.8	1.2	.3	1.8	.6	1.1	1.0	.8	1.5	-	-	.6	3.5	14.3
4. Grade 10 (Sophomore)	2.2	3.0	1.6	2.4	.3	3.5	1.7	2.5	1.2	1.6	3.1	-	-	.6	8.2	10.7
5. Grade 11 (Junior)	2.7	2.6	2.5	3.0	-	3.1	1.9	3.6	2.5	2.2	3.8	-	.1	1.5	9.6	7.1
6. Grade 12 (Senior)	1.9	1.6	2.1	2.2	-	1.6	1.9	2.1	1.9	1.7	2.3	-	-	1.2	6.4	10.7
Item 5630 N(Wtd)	2986	1379	1536	2404	332	620	964	920	483	1723	1164	1057	757	340	770	28

* = less than .05 per cent.

QUESTIONNAIRE FORM 3 1981	TOTAL	SEX		RACE		REGION				4YR COLLEGE PLANS		ILLICIT DRUG USE: LIFETIME				
		M	F	White	Black	NE	NC	S	W	Yes	No	None	Marijuana Only	Few Pills	More Pills	Any Heroin
Weighted No. of Cases:	3658	1721	1795	2830	459	869	1100	1114	575	1980	1448	1228	894	433	990	41
% of Weighted Total:	100.0	47.0	49.1	77.4	12.5	23.8	30.1	30.5	15.7	54.1	39.6	33.6	24.4	11.8	27.1	1.1
E12H: Try barbiturates																
8. Never	94.0	92.6	95.3	93.6	98.8	93.0	94.8	94.0	94.0	95.2	92.1	100.0	99.9	97.9	78.6	13.0
1. Grade 6 or below	.1	.2	-	.1	-	.3	.1	-	.2	.2	-	-	-	.6	.1	4.3
2. Grade 7 or 8	.7	.8	.5	.7	-	.7	.7	.2	1.7	.4	1.1	-	-	-	1.9	30.4
3. Grade 9 (Freshman)	1.5	1.6	1.4	1.7	.3	2.2	1.6	1.1	1.1	1.3	2.0	-	-	-	5.8	17.4
4. Grade 10 (Sophomore)	1.9	2.2	1.6	2.1	-	3.0	1.3	1.8	1.7	1.4	2.6	-	-	.3	7.6	8.7
5. Grade 11 (Junior)	1.3	1.7	.8	1.3	.6	1.0	.9	1.9	.9	.8	1.9	-	.1	.9	4.2	17.4
6. Grade 12 (Senior)	.5	.7	.4	.6	.6	-	.8	.7	.4	.7	.3	-	-	.3	1.8	8.7
Item 5640 N(Wtd)	2873	1343	1459	2295	332	602	918	888	465	1677	1100	1057	758	326	674	23
E12I: Try tranquilizers																
8. Never	92.8	92.5	93.1	92.0	98.8	91.7	94.6	92.3	91.8	94.2	90.6	100.0	99.9	95.0	74.3	21.7
1. Grade 6 or below	.1	.2	-	.1	-	-	.1	-	.4	.1	-	-	-	-	.2	4.3
2. Grade 7 or 8	.8	.8	.9	.8	.3	.5	1.0	.4	1.9	.5	1.2	-	-	.4	2.9	13.0
3. Grade 9 (Freshman)	1.8	1.9	1.7	2.1	.3	2.6	1.5	1.4	1.9	1.2	2.7	-	-	.4	6.0	43.5
4. Grade 10 (Sophomore)	2.0	1.8	2.2	2.3	.3	2.6	1.2	2.7	1.5	1.5	2.8	-	-	1.4	8.1	-
5. Grade 11 (Junior)	1.7	1.8	1.5	1.8	.3	1.6	1.2	2.4	1.7	1.6	1.9	-	.1	1.8	6.3	4.3
6. Grade 12 (Senior)	.8	.9	.6	.9	.3	1.1	.4	.9	.6	.7	.8	-	-	1.4	2.4	8.7
Item 5650 N(Wtd)	2800	1302	1436	2243	326	569	921	847	463	1614	1090	1053	757	280	654	23
E12J: Try cocaine																
8. Never	85.8	82.6	89.3	84.5	94.9	81.5	88.2	92.0	75.3	87.7	83.6	100.0	99.9	87.6	55.1	6.9
1. Grade 6 or below	.2	.3	.1	.1	.9	-	.2	.1	.2	.2	.1	-	-	.6	.1	6.9
2. Grade 7 or 8	.5	.6	.3	.5	-	.5	.6	.1	.6	.3	.7	-	-	.3	1.3	10.3
3. Grade 9 (Freshman)	1.2	1.6	.6	1.1	.6	1.6	.9	.3	2.4	.7	1.4	-	-	.3	4.2	3.4
4. Grade 10 (Sophomore)	3.4	4.5	2.2	3.7	-	4.8	3.1	2.1	5.1	2.4	5.0	-	-	1.7	11.4	24.1
5. Grade 11 (Junior)	5.3	6.6	4.3	6.0	1.8	6.6	4.3	3.1	9.9	5.0	5.8	-	-	3.7	17.7	27.6
6. Grade 12 (Senior)	3.6	3.8	3.3	4.1	1.5	4.8	2.6	2.4	6.5	3.7	3.6	-	.3	5.5	10.5	20.7
Item 5660 N(Wtd)	3019	1408	1537	2438	333	622	982	922	493	1736	1180	1055	760	347	792	29
E12K: Try heroin																
8. Never	99.2	98.8	99.6	99.3	99.1	99.0	99.6	98.9	99.2	99.5	98.8	100.0	100.0	100.0	99.9	-
1. Grade 6 or below	-	-	-	-	-	-	-	-	-	-	-	-	-	-	-	-
2. Grade 7 or 8	.1	.1	.1	.1	.3	-	.2	-	.4	.1	.3	-	-	-	-	16.7
3. Grade 9 (Freshman)	.1	.3	-	.2	-	.5	-	.1	-	-	.3	-	-	-	-	16.7
4. Grade 10 (Sophomore)	.1	.1	-	.1	-	.2	-	.1	-	.1	.1	-	-	-	.1	4.2
5. Grade 11 (Junior)	.2	.4	.1	.2	-	-	-	.5	.4	-	.5	-	-	-	-	29.2
6. Grade 12 (Senior)	.3	.3	.2	.2	.6	.3	.1	.4	.2	.3	.2	-	-	-	-	33.3
Item 5670 N(Wtd)	3041	1417	1550	2456	335	627	981	936	497	1746	1193	1055	760	360	807	24
E12L: Try any narcotic other than heroin																
8. Never	96.8	95.8	97.8	96.8	97.9	97.2	96.5	97.3	96.7	97.6	95.9	100.0	100.0	99.1	89.8	13.6
1. Grade 6 or below	.2	.3	.1	.2	.3	.3	.3	.1	-	.2	.3	-	-	-	.8	4.5
2. Grade 7 or 8	.2	.2	.2	.2	.3	-	.2	.1	.7	.1	.4	-	-	-	.8	4.5
3. Grade 9 (Freshman)	.5	.6	.4	.5	.6	.5	.5	.5	.4	.3	.7	-	-	-	1.5	18.2
4. Grade 10 (Sophomore)	.9	1.5	.4	1.0	-	.5	1.5	.5	1.3	.4	1.7	-	-	.9	3.2	13.6
5. Grade 11 (Junior)	.8	1.1	.6	1.0	.3	1.2	.7	.9	.7	.9	.7	-	-	-	2.9	22.7
6. Grade 12 (Senior)	.5	.5	.4	.4	.6	.2	.4	.8	.2	.4	.4	-	-	-	1.2	22.7
Item 5680 N(Wtd)	2849	1315	1462	2283	327	575	935	883	455	1653	1097	1056	753	327	655	22
E12M: Try inhalants																
8. Never	92.6	90.4	94.5	91.7	99.1	90.2	93.4	94.4	90.4	92.6	92.4	99.1	96.1	91.9	81.2	43.5
1. Grade 6 or below	1.0	1.7	.5	1.1	.3	1.2	1.1	.2	1.9	.9	.9	.3	.6	1.4	2.0	8.7
2. Grade 7 or 8	1.5	1.8	1.4	1.7	.3	1.3	1.4	1.6	1.9	1.3	2.0	.2	.7	2.6	3.7	8.7
3. Grade 9 (Freshman)	1.7	2.1	1.3	1.8	-	2.4	1.8	1.4	1.1	1.3	2.5	-	.7	1.4	4.5	26.1
4. Grade 10 (Sophomore)	1.2	1.6	1.0	1.5	-	2.0	1.1	.4	1.9	1.4	1.1	.1	.7	1.4	3.4	-
5. Grade 11 (Junior)	1.0	1.4	.7	1.2	.3	1.2	.4	1.1	1.5	1.3	.6	.1	.4	.9	2.8	4.3
6. Grade 12 (Senior)	1.0	1.1	.7	1.2	-	1.3	.7	.7	1.5	1.2	.7	.1	1.0	.6	2.4	4.3
Item 5685 N(Wtd)	2896	1328	1496	2341	321	593	936	899	468	1671	1128	1038	717	345	738	23

QUESTIONNAIRE FORM 4 1981	TOTAL	SEX		RACE		REGION				4YR COLLEGE PLANS		ILLICIT DRUG USE: LIFETIME				
		M	F	White	Black	NE	NC	S	W	Yes	No	None	Mari-juana Only	Few Pills	More Pills	Any Her-oin
Weighted No. of Cases:	3653	1751	1771	2804	441	846	1116	1117	574	1955	1393	1277	804	441	991	29
% of Weighted Total:	100.0	47.9	48.5	76.8	12.1	23.2	30.6	30.6	15.7	53.5	38.1	35.0	22.0	12.1	27.1	.8

A01: Taking all things together, how would you say things are these days-would you say you're very happy, pretty happy, or not too happy these days?

3. Very happy	18.2	14.7	21.4	19.4	11.6	18.9	16.8	18.2	19.9	21.0	15.0	20.7	16.7	17.4	16.0	6.9
2. Pretty happy	65.9	68.7	63.6	67.9	61.2	65.5	68.4	64.4	64.5	64.7	69.2	64.7	68.2	70.1	66.5	51.7
1. Not too happy	16.0	16.6	14.9	12.7	27.2	15.7	14.8	17.5	15.6	14.4	15.8	14.6	15.1	12.8	17.5	41.4
Item 1190 N(Wtd)	3640	1745	1770	2798	441	843	1109	1117	572	1952	1390	1277	802	438	990	29

A02: Looking ahead to the next five years, do you think that things in this country will get better or worse?

1. Get much better	3.1	4.4	1.9	2.9	3.4	3.3	3.6	2.6	3.2	3.5	2.3	4.4	2.2	2.5	2.3	6.9
2. Get somewhat better	32.6	38.0	27.1	34.5	23.1	34.1	34.6	30.4	31.0	36.4	27.6	34.4	35.2	31.9	29.6	37.9
3. Stay about the same	19.2	18.9	19.4	19.8	14.7	20.7	18.5	18.3	19.9	20.4	18.7	19.4	19.1	19.8	19.4	17.2
4. Get somewhat worse	37.5	32.0	43.7	36.7	44.2	35.7	35.8	39.6	39.1	33.8	42.3	35.8	37.5	40.1	38.9	27.6
5. Get much worse	7.6	6.7	7.9	6.1	14.5	6.2	7.5	9.1	6.9	5.9	9.1	6.1	5.9	5.9	9.8	10.3
Item 9940 N(Wtd)	3639	1743	1769	2799	441	842	1111	1117	568	1952	1388	1275	801	439	988	29

A03: Looking ahead to the next five years, do you think that things in the rest of the world will get better or worse?

1. Get much better	1.1	1.0	1.1	.7	1.6	1.3	1.3	.9	.9	1.1	.7	1.3	.9	1.1	.2	6.9
2. Get somewhat better	15.3	15.6	14.9	14.0	20.4	15.8	16.4	15.2	12.4	15.6	14.7	16.1	15.8	15.0	14.1	17.2
3. Stay about the same	27.3	28.3	26.4	28.9	20.6	29.1	28.2	25.2	27.4	28.9	26.3	27.7	28.8	28.7	25.8	24.1
4. Get somewhat worse	44.0	42.6	45.8	45.1	39.9	45.6	42.2	43.6	46.3	44.2	43.6	43.5	44.0	43.7	45.2	34.5
5. Get much worse	12.3	12.6	11.9	11.2	17.7	8.3	12.1	15.1	13.1	10.1	14.7	11.5	10.6	11.2	14.9	17.2
Item 9950 N(Wtd)	3642	1745	1770	2798	441	842	1111	1117	572	1953	1390	1276	802	439	989	29

A04: How do you think your own life will go in the next five years-- do you think it will get better or worse?

1. Get much better	38.1	35.6	40.6	36.3	44.8	39.5	36.5	39.0	37.1	39.6	35.8	38.5	37.5	36.9	39.1	31.0
2. Get somewhat better	48.2	51.0	45.4	49.9	43.6	47.3	47.8	48.3	50.0	47.9	49.3	47.3	49.6	48.7	48.5	34.5
3. Stay about the same	11.3	10.5	11.9	11.4	8.4	11.6	12.9	9.8	10.5	10.2	12.4	11.5	11.0	11.4	10.5	20.7
4. Get somewhat worse	2.2	2.3	2.0	2.1	3.2	1.2	2.5	2.6	2.1	1.8	2.4	2.5	1.6	3.0	1.5	10.3
5. Get much worse	.3	.5	.1	.2	.2	.2	.3	.4	.3	.4	.2	.4	.2	-	.3	3.4
Item 9960 N(Wtd)	3642	1746	1769	2801	440	842	1111	1116	572	1952	1390	1275	803	439	990	29

A05: Some people think a lot about the social problems of the nation and the world, and about how they might be solved. Others spend little time thinking about these issues. How much do you think about such things?

1. Never	1.6	2.1	1.1	1.6	1.6	1.2	1.7	2.0	1.6	1.0	2.5	1.2	2.0	1.8	1.6	6.9
2. Seldom	15.4	16.0	14.9	16.6	10.7	17.2	16.0	14.0	14.2	11.7	19.8	13.5	18.0	11.6	17.5	6.9
3. Sometimes	48.7	45.8	51.9	49.8	41.0	47.6	51.7	45.2	51.4	48.0	51.5	50.0	47.3	55.0	45.7	62.1
4. Quite often	27.9	28.7	27.2	27.2	33.9	27.1	25.7	30.9	27.7	31.9	21.7	28.8	26.3	25.6	30.1	13.8
5. A great deal	6.3	7.4	5.0	4.7	13.0	6.9	4.9	8.0	5.1	7.3	4.4	6.5	6.2	6.2	5.3	10.3
Item 6880 N(Wtd)	3639	1745	1768	2799	439	844	1110	1115	570	1950	1389	1276	801	438	989	29

A06: These questions are about pollution and the environment. Please mark the circle that shows how much you agree or disagree with each statement below.

A06A: In general, pollution has increased in the U.S. in the last ten years

1. Disagree	5.2	7.0	3.4	4.9	7.3	5.1	5.1	5.4	5.2	4.9	5.5	5.8	5.1	4.3	4.3	-
2. Mostly disagree	8.3	10.1	6.3	8.3	9.1	8.3	8.0	8.5	8.2	9.1	7.4	8.9	8.1	8.0	7.9	10.3
3. Neither	5.4	6.5	4.3	5.5	5.2	5.2	6.7	4.2	5.4	5.6	5.0	4.6	6.6	6.4	4.8	6.9
4. Mostly agree	31.1	29.4	33.1	32.2	26.3	30.7	33.9	30.0	28.6	32.9	28.3	31.7	30.7	30.3	31.4	37.9
5. Agree	50.0	47.0	52.9	49.1	51.9	50.7	46.3	51.9	52.7	47.5	53.8	49.0	49.5	50.8	51.7	44.8
Item 9970 N(Wtd)	3641	1746	1768	2797	441	844	1108	1116	573	1951	1390	1276	804	439	988	29

QUESTIONNAIRE FORM 4 1981	TOTAL	SEX		RACE		REGION				4YR COLLEGE PLANS		ILLICIT DRUG USE: LIFETIME				
		M	F	White	Black	NE	NC	S	W	Yes	No	None	Mari- juana Only	Few Pills	More Pills	Any Her- oin
Weighted No. of Cases:	3653	1751	1771	2804	441	846	1116	1117	574	1955	1393	1277	804	441	991	29
% of Weighted Total:	100.0	47.9	48.5	76.8	12.1	23.2	30.6	30.6	15.7	53.5	38.1	35.0	22.0	12.1	27.1	.8

A06B: The dangers of pollution are not really as great as government, the media, and environmental groups would like us to believe

1. Disagree	38.1	38.4	37.8	39.4	33.6	40.7	36.0	38.0	38.1	41.1	34.8	39.2	37.1	36.4	40.1	37.9
2. Mostly disagree	25.7	24.5	26.8	27.0	17.4	29.0	26.6	21.5	26.9	28.0	22.9	23.5	26.3	28.0	27.2	17.2
3. Neither	10.4	10.6	10.0	9.2	11.6	8.2	12.4	10.1	10.3	9.4	11.8	10.5	11.4	9.3	9.1	20.7
4. Mostly agree	15.8	15.6	16.5	15.5	21.7	13.1	15.9	18.0	15.4	13.8	18.3	17.0	15.1	17.5	14.3	3.4
5. Agree	10.0	11.0	9.0	8.8	15.8	8.7	9.0	12.5	8.9	7.8	12.3	9.8	10.1	8.7	9.3	20.7
Item 9980 N(Wtd)	3630	1740	1765	2792	438	838	1110	1111	572	1946	1385	1270	801	439	987	29

A06C: America needs growth to survive, and that is going to require some increase in pollution

1. Disagree	32.2	31.1	33.2	32.6	29.9	31.5	30.8	34.9	30.4	33.6	31.4	32.9	32.8	32.4	31.2	34.5
2. Mostly disagree	23.5	23.6	23.6	24.5	18.1	26.1	23.5	21.3	24.0	26.0	20.1	23.1	21.4	28.0	25.1	6.9
3. Neither	10.3	9.9	10.6	10.9	7.6	10.1	11.0	10.5	8.6	9.9	10.9	9.3	9.8	10.8	11.9	13.8
4. Mostly agree	19.8	20.6	19.1	20.4	18.8	20.0	21.4	17.1	21.6	20.2	19.5	21.0	20.2	17.5	17.7	37.9
5. Agree	14.2	14.8	13.4	11.6	25.5	12.3	13.2	16.2	15.3	10.3	18.1	13.7	15.8	11.3	14.1	6.9
Item 9990 N(Wtd)	3623	1742	1755	2792	432	839	1106	1108	570	1941	1383	1272	799	435	986	29

A06D: People will have to change their buying habits and way of life to correct our environmental problems

1. Disagree	10.1	12.1	8.1	9.1	15.6	11.4	8.1	12.6	7.5	8.6	11.7	11.0	10.4	9.4	8.5	10.3
2. Mostly disagree	11.1	11.8	10.8	11.3	10.8	12.9	10.6	10.4	11.0	11.0	11.4	10.3	11.6	13.8	10.4	17.2
3. Neither	11.3	11.8	10.6	11.9	8.0	10.2	12.6	11.1	10.7	10.3	12.9	10.8	9.7	10.8	12.8	13.8
4. Mostly agree	33.1	32.2	34.2	34.7	25.6	34.8	34.5	29.2	35.7	34.9	31.1	33.0	31.5	34.2	34.6	31.0
5. Agree	34.3	32.2	36.4	33.0	40.0	30.8	34.2	36.6	35.0	35.3	32.9	34.9	36.7	31.7	33.8	27.6
Item 10000 N(Wtd)	3624	1741	1756	2784	437	837	1104	1112	572	1940	1390	1271	801	436	982	29

A06E: Government should take action to solve our environmental problems even if it means that some of the products we now use would have to be changed or banned

1. Disagree	4.7	6.2	3.0	4.0	8.7	3.8	4.7	5.4	4.2	3.6	6.1	5.2	4.5	3.9	3.8	10.3
2. Mostly disagree	6.9	7.8	5.5	6.6	8.5	6.3	7.8	6.8	6.5	5.9	7.9	7.2	6.8	5.3	6.5	6.9
3. Neither	9.6	11.0	8.2	9.8	8.9	6.2	11.8	10.4	8.6	8.3	11.2	9.9	7.6	13.2	9.2	6.9
4. Mostly agree	34.9	32.5	37.6	35.4	32.5	34.5	34.8	32.2	40.6	36.1	33.5	34.5	37.6	31.5	35.3	27.6
5. Agree	43.9	42.6	45.5	44.2	41.6	49.0	40.9	45.1	40.2	46.0	41.3	43.2	43.6	46.3	45.3	48.3
Item 10010 N(Wtd)	3626	1741	1759	2787	437	840	1105	1111	569	1943	1386	1272	803	438	981	29

A06F: Government should place higher taxes on products which cause pollution in their manufacture or disposal, so that companies will be encouraged to find better ways to produce them

1. Disagree	15.2	15.4	14.5	13.8	24.4	12.8	15.0	16.7	15.7	13.6	17.5	16.1	17.8	10.3	13.0	17.2
2. Mostly disagree	13.0	13.8	12.2	13.3	11.8	12.1	14.8	11.9	11.7	12.7	14.2	12.7	12.4	16.1	12.2	27.6
3. Neither	13.6	12.6	15.0	14.2	11.8	13.4	15.7	12.0	12.9	12.5	15.6	11.4	14.4	14.7	15.0	13.8
4. Mostly agree	26.4	26.3	26.4	27.3	19.4	27.2	27.6	24.3	27.0	28.4	23.8	27.4	26.6	28.7	24.8	31.0
5. Agree	31.8	31.7	31.9	31.5	32.3	33.7	26.9	35.0	32.5	33.6	29.0	32.4	28.7	30.3	35.0	10.3
Item 10020 N(Wtd)	3627	1743	1761	2790	439	841	1106	1113	566	1946	1387	1274	804	436	980	29

A06G: I wish that government would ban throwaway bottles and beverage cans

1. Disagree	23.2	23.2	23.1	22.9	30.0	21.0	22.3	28.7	17.1	21.7	25.5	23.4	23.7	22.0	23.5	17.9
2. Mostly disagree	12.3	12.5	12.3	12.1	12.5	12.1	10.7	13.1	14.2	11.2	13.8	12.6	10.0	13.5	12.6	21.4
3. Neither	22.8	20.0	26.0	24.3	17.7	21.4	25.2	21.7	22.2	24.3	22.0	22.6	23.3	25.9	21.3	35.7
4. Mostly agree	17.1	16.3	17.5	16.8	14.3	19.4	16.5	14.7	19.5	17.8	15.5	17.6	16.5	16.9	16.3	7.1
5. Agree	24.7	28.0	21.1	24.0	25.5	26.2	25.4	21.9	27.2	25.1	23.2	23.8	26.7	22.0	26.3	17.9
Item 10030 N(Wtd)	3617	1734	1759	2778	440	837	1104	1112	563	1942	1379	1271	799	437	977	28

QUESTIONNAIRE FORM 4 1981	TOTAL	SEX		RACE		REGION				4YR COLLEGE PLANS		ILLICIT DRUG USE: LIFETIME				
		M	F	White	Black	NE	NC	S	W	Yes	No	None	Marijuana Only	Few Pills	More Pills	Any Heroin
Weighted No. of Cases:	3653	1751	1771	2804	441	846	1116	1117	574	1955	1393	1277	804	441	991	29
% of Weighted Total:	100.0	47.9	48.5	76.8	12.1	23.2	30.6	30.6	15.7	53.5	38.1	35.0	22.0	12.1	27.1	.8

A06H: T.V. commercials stimulate people to buy a lot of things they don't really need

	TOTAL	M	F	White	Black	NE	NC	S	W	Yes	No	None	Marijuana Only	Few Pills	More Pills	Any Heroin
1. Disagree	5.7	7.1	4.5	4.9	10.6	5.4	5.2	7.5	4.0	6.0	5.5	4.6	7.6	4.6	5.8	3.4
2. Mostly disagree	5.6	6.9	4.3	5.8	4.6	4.6	6.8	6.1	3.5	5.4	6.1	6.0	4.6	5.3	5.9	6.9
3. Neither	5.6	6.6	4.4	5.6	4.4	4.9	6.3	5.7	5.3	5.3	6.2	5.3	6.0	5.5	5.9	6.9
4. Mostly agree	25.5	26.6	24.2	26.8	18.6	26.9	26.4	22.0	28.5	25.3	24.7	24.3	28.3	25.3	24.7	34.5
5. Agree	57.6	52.8	62.5	57.0	61.7	58.2	55.3	58.8	58.5	57.9	57.6	60.0	53.5	59.1	57.6	48.3
Item 10040 N(Wtd)	3629	1743	1760	2790	436	840	1104	1114	571	1945	1387	1274	798	435	986	29

A06I: T.V. commercials do a lot of good by showing new products that we might not know about otherwise

	TOTAL	M	F	White	Black	NE	NC	S	W	Yes	No	None	Marijuana Only	Few Pills	More Pills	Any Heroin
1. Disagree	8.4	8.1	8.6	8.2	6.2	11.0	6.9	7.3	9.5	8.9	7.4	7.1	6.4	8.0	11.3	13.8
2. Mostly disagree	14.4	13.6	15.3	15.7	7.1	16.7	15.3	10.0	17.7	16.2	12.2	14.5	14.1	13.7	15.2	6.9
3. Neither	15.0	15.6	14.8	16.6	6.6	14.0	17.4	12.8	16.1	16.6	13.9	14.9	13.0	19.1	15.8	10.3
4. Mostly agree	34.0	33.8	33.6	35.1	29.2	36.3	33.3	32.0	35.7	34.1	34.2	32.1	37.0	34.9	33.4	34.5
5. Agree	28.2	28.8	27.7	24.3	51.3	21.9	27.2	37.9	20.8	24.3	32.4	31.3	29.4	24.6	24.4	34.5
Item 10050 N(Wtd)	3632	1747	1760	2792	439	845	1107	1110	571	1950	1385	1274	802	439	985	29

A06J: My family and I often buy things we don't really need; we could get along with much less

	TOTAL	M	F	White	Black	NE	NC	S	W	Yes	No	None	Marijuana Only	Few Pills	More Pills	Any Heroin
1. Disagree	12.8	13.1	12.3	10.9	23.1	12.7	11.2	14.7	12.5	12.5	13.2	13.4	12.0	10.8	12.8	24.1
2. Mostly disagree	14.0	15.8	12.3	14.2	13.0	15.5	14.2	11.3	16.8	13.7	14.3	15.7	14.2	13.3	12.4	17.2
3. Neither	11.8	12.6	11.0	11.9	9.4	11.2	13.4	10.2	12.7	11.9	12.1	12.3	11.2	11.7	11.7	6.9
4. Mostly agree	29.5	28.7	30.8	30.9	21.2	30.8	30.2	27.1	30.9	30.2	29.0	30.5	30.5	29.0	27.6	17.2
5. Agree	31.9	29.8	33.7	32.1	33.3	29.9	31.1	36.7	27.2	31.7	31.5	28.1	32.1	35.2	35.4	34.5
Item 10060 N(Wtd)	3622	1736	1761	2785	438	843	1102	1111	566	1943	1381	1272	797	435	985	29

A06K: By the year 2000, engineers and scientists will probably have invented devices that will solve our pollution problems

	TOTAL	M	F	White	Black	NE	NC	S	W	Yes	No	None	Marijuana Only	Few Pills	More Pills	Any Heroin
1. Disagree	13.0	15.2	10.4	12.7	15.0	14.9	12.2	13.5	10.9	11.6	14.0	12.3	14.1	9.5	14.4	10.3
2. Mostly disagree	19.2	20.0	18.9	20.8	10.5	19.3	19.1	17.4	22.6	20.1	18.5	18.0	18.7	20.9	20.8	17.2
3. Neither	21.7	20.0	23.7	22.9	18.2	19.5	21.9	22.1	24.3	22.2	21.8	20.7	22.6	24.5	21.6	24.1
4. Mostly agree	29.9	28.1	31.8	30.1	27.3	31.1	30.5	29.5	27.8	30.9	29.1	31.1	28.2	31.6	28.9	31.0
5. Agree	16.1	16.7	15.1	13.5	29.1	15.2	16.3	17.5	14.5	15.3	16.5	17.9	16.7	13.6	14.1	13.8
Item 10070 N(Wtd)	3638	1748	1763	2796	440	843	1111	1113	571	1950	1387	1275	804	440	985	29

A07: In your own actions--the things you buy and the things you do-- how much of an effort do you make to conserve energy and protect the environment?

	TOTAL	M	F	White	Black	NE	NC	S	W	Yes	No	None	Marijuana Only	Few Pills	More Pills	Any Heroin
1. None	4.1	4.4	3.5	3.7	5.9	4.8	3.2	5.1	2.8	3.8	4.6	2.3	4.5	5.7	5.0	3.6
2. A little	24.4	24.5	24.0	23.7	29.1	20.2	27.0	26.2	21.5	24.2	24.5	22.1	25.0	25.5	25.8	28.6
3. Some	54.8	53.4	56.7	56.9	45.8	58.1	53.8	53.0	55.4	55.4	54.4	57.6	55.6	52.4	52.8	39.3
4. Quite a bit	16.8	17.7	15.8	15.7	19.5	16.9	16.0	15.7	20.3	16.6	16.5	18.0	15.0	16.2	16.5	28.6
Item 10080 N(Wtd)	3501	1663	1719	2713	406	817	1076	1064	543	1889	1337	1244	773	420	947	28

The next questions are about work.

A08: Different people may look for different things in their work. Below is a list of some of these things. Please read each one, then indicate how important this thing is for you.

QUESTIONNAIRE FORM 4 1981	TOTAL	SEX		RACE		REGION				4YR COLLEGE PLANS		ILLICIT DRUG USE: LIFETIME				
		M	F	White	Black	NE	NC	S	W	Yes	No	None	Mari-juana Only	Few Pills	More Pills	Any Her-oin
Weighted No. of Cases:	3653	1751	1771	2804	441	846	1116	1117	574	1955	1393	1277	804	441	991	29
% of Weighted Total:	100.0	47.9	48.5	76.8	12.1	23.2	30.6	30.6	15.7	53.5	38.1	35.0	22.0	12.1	27.1	.8
A08A: A job where you can see the results of what you do																
1. Not important	1.2	1.8	.5	1.0	.9	1.4	1.0	1.4	.9	1.3	1.0	.9	1.0	.9	1.7	-
2. A little important	6.9	7.9	6.1	7.2	4.3	7.7	8.0	5.6	6.2	6.0	8.6	5.9	6.0	7.3	8.8	17.2
3. Pretty important	31.4	32.7	30.1	33.8	19.8	33.6	32.5	26.5	35.7	32.1	31.2	28.9	35.9	31.8	31.4	31.0
4. Very important	60.5	57.6	63.5	58.0	74.9	57.2	58.5	66.5	57.3	60.6	59.2	64.2	57.0	60.0	58.0	51.7
Item 10090 N(Wtd)	3634	1743	1763	2794	439	843	1108	1114	569	1944	1389	1272	800	440	986	29
A08B: A job that has high status and prestige																
1. Not important	8.3	8.4	8.2	8.8	4.3	8.7	8.3	7.3	9.9	8.4	8.7	10.7	7.9	5.9	6.7	10.3
2. A little important	26.6	26.1	27.0	29.0	13.9	27.9	27.4	22.7	31.0	27.6	26.5	27.0	26.3	26.9	26.8	24.1
3. Pretty important	37.0	36.9	37.3	37.8	34.2	37.7	40.0	35.0	33.9	38.4	35.4	34.8	36.3	40.9	39.7	37.9
4. Very important	28.0	28.5	27.5	24.3	47.7	25.7	24.2	35.0	25.2	25.6	29.3	27.5	29.4	26.5	26.9	27.6
Item 10100 N(Wtd)	3615	1733	1757	2783	438	840	1102	1110	564	1940	1380	1269	797	438	979	29
A08C: A job which is interesting to do																
1. Not important	.3	.5	.1	.1	1.4	.5	.4	.3	-	.1	.4	.2	.4	.5	.1	-
2. A little important	1.4	1.7	1.0	.9	4.0	1.2	.6	2.5	1.1	1.0	1.7	1.4	2.0	1.9	.3	-
3. Pretty important	10.1	12.5	7.5	9.6	12.4	9.4	10.6	10.5	9.7	8.3	11.1	9.1	9.0	8.1	11.9	34.5
4. Very important	88.2	85.3	91.4	89.4	82.5	89.0	88.4	86.7	89.2	90.5	86.8	89.1	88.8	89.6	87.7	65.5
Item 10110 N(Wtd)	3599	1720	1752	2775	428	839	1098	1094	567	1929	1370	1261	792	431	982	29
A08D: A job where the chances for advancement and promotion are good																
1. Not important	1.2	1.3	1.0	1.1	.9	1.1	.9	1.5	.9	.8	1.5	1.0	1.0	1.4	.7	6.9
2. A little important	6.9	6.1	7.7	7.3	3.7	6.9	7.2	5.6	8.8	7.9	5.7	9.5	5.6	6.3	4.4	6.9
3. Pretty important	25.6	26.0	25.6	27.0	18.5	25.3	26.3	21.9	32.2	27.6	23.0	27.6	23.8	28.1	23.7	31.0
4. Very important	66.3	66.6	65.8	64.7	76.9	66.6	65.6	71.0	58.0	63.8	69.8	62.0	69.5	63.9	71.2	55.2
Item 10120 N(Wtd)	3631	1743	1761	2795	438	842	1109	1111	569	1940	1391	1267	801	441	987	29
A08E: A job that gives you an opportunity to be directly helpful to others																
1. Not important	3.0	5.0	.7	3.1	1.8	4.2	3.0	2.3	2.3	2.5	3.2	1.8	2.4	4.1	4.1	10.3
2. A little important	14.7	21.4	8.5	16.6	8.0	15.1	15.5	13.6	14.9	13.2	17.0	12.1	15.9	11.6	18.5	17.2
3. Pretty important	34.4	38.0	31.1	35.2	28.1	35.0	35.4	30.6	39.1	35.1	34.3	33.8	33.9	35.4	35.1	37.9
4. Very important	47.9	35.6	59.7	45.1	61.9	45.7	46.3	53.5	43.9	49.2	45.5	52.3	47.8	48.9	42.3	34.5
Item 10130 N(Wtd)	3627	1739	1762	2792	438	842	1106	1112	565	1940	1388	1269	799	438	985	29
A08F: A job which provides you with a chance to earn a good deal of money																
1. Not important	1.5	1.2	1.8	1.5	.7	2.3	1.4	1.3	1.2	1.9	.9	1.9	1.5	1.4	1.0	3.4
2. A little important	8.5	7.3	9.9	9.4	2.5	9.6	8.3	7.6	8.9	11.1	5.4	11.8	7.5	7.9	6.0	6.9
3. Pretty important	34.0	32.0	36.3	36.5	20.8	33.9	35.7	27.9	42.6	36.5	32.2	35.4	34.6	38.1	31.5	20.7
4. Very important	56.0	59.4	52.0	52.5	76.3	54.3	54.5	63.2	47.2	50.5	61.4	50.9	56.6	52.6	61.5	65.5
Item 10140 N(Wtd)	3634	1742	1765	2796	438	844	1108	1112	570	1943	1390	1269	801	441	987	29
A08G: A job where you have the chance to be creative																
1. Not important	5.4	7.1	3.5	5.5	5.3	5.8	5.1	6.8	2.3	4.1	6.8	4.9	5.4	5.7	5.4	3.4
2. A little important	22.4	23.1	21.5	23.4	17.6	22.4	22.3	21.6	24.1	21.5	23.4	22.0	21.9	27.1	21.4	20.7
3. Pretty important	36.9	37.2	36.5	37.2	36.8	35.7	37.9	36.8	36.9	37.2	36.6	36.0	41.0	35.8	35.3	31.0
4. Very important	35.4	32.5	38.4	33.8	40.6	36.1	34.6	34.8	36.7	37.1	33.3	37.1	31.8	31.7	37.9	44.8
Item 10150 N(Wtd)	3630	1740	1764	2795	438	841	1107	1113	569	1945	1389	1271	800	439	987	29

QUESTIONNAIRE FORM 4 1981	TOTAL	SEX		RACE		REGION				4YR COLLEGE PLANS		ILLICIT DRUG USE: LIFETIME				
		M	F	White	Black	NE	NC	S	W	Yes	No	None	Mari-juana Only	Few Pills	More Pills	Any Her-oin
Weighted No. of Cases:	3653	1751	1771	2804	441	846	1116	1117	574	1955	1393	1277	804	441	991	29
% of Weighted Total:	100.0	47.9	48.5	76.8	12.1	23.2	30.6	30.6	15.7	53.5	38.1	35.0	22.0	12.1	27.1	.8

A08H: A job where the skills you learn will not go out of date

	TOTAL	M	F	White	Black	NE	NC	S	W	Yes	No	None	Mari-juana Only	Few Pills	More Pills	Any Her-oin
1. Not important	4.3	5.2	3.5	4.3	3.4	6.1	3.2	4.0	4.2	5.0	3.6	4.0	4.4	4.3	4.4	13.8
2. A little important	11.2	10.6	11.2	11.3	8.0	11.5	11.1	11.4	10.4	11.3	10.3	10.5	12.5	11.1	11.0	10.3
3. Pretty important	30.2	30.5	30.9	31.8	22.2	30.7	31.9	25.9	34.4	31.6	28.6	28.7	31.3	30.2	31.5	27.6
4. Very important	54.3	53.8	54.4	52.5	66.4	51.7	53.7	58.8	50.9	52.0	57.5	56.7	51.9	54.4	53.1	48.3
Item 10160 N(Wtd)	3631	1742	1762	2798	437	840	1108	1113	570	1943	1390	1271	800	441	986	29

A08I: A job that gives you a chance to make friends

	TOTAL	M	F	White	Black	NE	NC	S	W	Yes	No	None	Mari-juana Only	Few Pills	More Pills	Any Her-oin
1. Not important	2.4	2.9	1.9	1.7	6.6	3.6	1.2	3.1	1.8	2.2	2.3	2.7	2.8	1.4	1.3	6.9
2. A little important	9.8	10.8	8.9	9.1	13.0	10.7	9.6	8.7	10.8	8.4	10.7	9.3	10.4	7.5	9.8	10.3
3. Pretty important	34.5	38.1	31.1	35.8	30.5	34.8	35.4	32.4	36.2	34.0	36.3	33.2	37.1	38.7	33.6	27.6
4. Very important	53.4	48.1	59.0	53.5	49.9	51.0	53.8	55.7	51.4	55.4	50.6	54.8	49.8	52.6	55.3	51.7
Item 10170 N(Wtd)	3629	1741	1761	2793	439	843	1107	1113	566	1941	1389	1270	800	439	984	29

A08J: A job which uses your skills and abilities--lets you do the things you can do best

	TOTAL	M	F	White	Black	NE	NC	S	W	Yes	No	None	Mari-juana Only	Few Pills	More Pills	Any Her-oin
1. Not important	.7	1.2	.2	.6	.9	1.2	.5	.6	.5	.6	.9	.4	1.1	.2	.6	-
2. A little important	3.3	3.5	2.8	3.5	.9	2.7	3.6	2.8	4.7	2.5	4.2	2.0	3.6	3.9	4.0	10.3
3. Pretty important	23.4	25.1	21.5	24.0	19.1	23.8	24.1	21.8	24.2	22.6	24.5	19.8	25.5	25.9	24.2	27.6
4. Very important	72.7	70.2	75.5	72.0	78.8	72.3	71.9	74.8	70.7	74.4	70.5	77.7	69.7	69.8	71.2	62.1
Item 10180 N(Wtd)	3634	1744	1764	2796	439	842	1109	1113	570	1944	1390	1271	801	441	986	29

A08K: A job that is worthwhile to society

	TOTAL	M	F	White	Black	NE	NC	S	W	Yes	No	None	Mari-juana Only	Few Pills	More Pills	Any Her-oin
1. Not important	3.5	4.6	2.3	3.4	3.7	5.4	2.8	3.3	2.7	2.6	4.5	2.9	2.3	2.7	4.6	10.3
2. A little important	14.6	17.9	11.4	15.2	12.6	14.0	15.9	13.2	15.4	12.8	17.4	12.1	14.2	14.0	17.3	20.7
3. Pretty important	37.6	37.5	37.3	39.2	27.5	38.3	37.9	34.1	42.7	37.5	37.6	36.2	38.7	41.0	38.1	37.9
4. Very important	44.3	40.0	49.1	42.3	56.2	42.3	43.6	49.4	39.0	47.0	40.6	48.9	44.9	42.3	39.9	27.6
Item 10190 N(Wtd)	3601	1725	1750	2776	429	833	1104	1100	564	1930	1376	1263	791	437	977	29

A08L: A job where you have more than two weeks vacation

	TOTAL	M	F	White	Black	NE	NC	S	W	Yes	No	None	Mari-juana Only	Few Pills	More Pills	Any Her-oin
1. Not important	20.4	16.0	25.3	21.2	21.2	19.3	21.3	21.7	18.3	20.2	20.7	21.0	20.9	19.8	19.8	20.7
2. A little important	36.6	33.7	39.4	36.7	34.7	35.7	38.0	36.0	36.1	38.1	35.4	37.3	40.1	38.0	34.0	31.0
3. Pretty important	24.7	27.2	21.8	25.1	21.5	25.8	22.8	24.0	28.0	23.7	25.1	24.6	20.7	21.0	28.0	27.6
4. Very important	18.3	23.1	13.5	17.0	22.4	19.4	17.9	18.3	17.6	18.0	18.8	17.1	18.3	21.2	18.3	20.7
Item 10200 N(Wtd)	3627	1742	1761	2793	438	841	1105	1113	568	1942	1388	1271	799	439	985	29

A08M: A job where you get a chance to participate in decision making

	TOTAL	M	F	White	Black	NE	NC	S	W	Yes	No	None	Mari-juana Only	Few Pills	More Pills	Any Her-oin
1. Not important	4.0	4.0	4.0	3.9	3.4	4.1	4.7	3.2	3.7	2.6	5.8	3.9	4.0	2.5	4.2	13.8
2. A little important	21.8	21.7	22.0	22.7	16.1	21.8	22.5	20.0	23.9	20.1	23.9	21.4	22.5	23.3	21.4	20.7
3. Pretty important	42.8	43.8	42.0	43.7	41.3	42.2	42.6	43.1	43.3	43.9	43.0	44.6	43.4	45.5	39.1	27.6
4. Very important	31.4	30.5	32.0	29.6	39.0	32.0	30.0	33.5	29.2	33.3	27.3	30.1	30.2	28.6	35.3	37.9
Item 10210 N(Wtd)	3624	1740	1758	2793	436	844	1107	1108	566	1943	1385	1268	799	437	984	29

A08N: A job which leaves a lot of time for other things in your life

	TOTAL	M	F	White	Black	NE	NC	S	W	Yes	No	None	Mari-juana Only	Few Pills	More Pills	Any Her-oin
1. Not important	3.0	2.9	3.2	2.8	3.9	3.1	3.1	3.1	2.8	2.8	3.1	3.6	2.8	2.1	2.3	6.9
2. A little important	17.9	14.2	21.0	17.8	19.2	16.8	20.4	15.9	17.9	17.4	18.2	18.6	18.4	15.3	17.4	20.7
3. Pretty important	41.2	40.6	41.9	42.9	32.7	42.6	41.0	40.3	40.9	43.7	39.2	41.4	42.3	44.9	39.8	17.2
4. Very important	38.0	42.3	33.8	36.5	44.2	37.6	35.4	40.6	38.3	36.1	39.5	36.5	36.5	38.0	40.4	55.2
Item 10220 N(Wtd)	3624	1739	1760	2792	437	838	1106	1111	569	1938	1390	1266	799	439	986	29

	TOTAL	SEX		RACE		REGION				4YR COLLEGE PLANS		ILLICIT DRUG USE: LIFETIME				
QUESTIONNAIRE FORM 4 **1981**		M	F	White	Black	NE	NC	S	W	Yes	No	None	Mari-juana Only	Few Pills	More Pills	Any Her-oin
Weighted No. of Cases:	3653	1751	1771	2804	441	846	1116	1117	574	1955	1393	1277	804	441	991	29
% of Weighted Total:	100.0	47.9	48.5	76.8	12.1	23.2	30.6	30.6	15.7	53.5	38.1	35.0	22.0	12.1	27.1	.8
A08O: A job which allows you to establish roots in a community and not have to move from place to place																
1. Not important	9.8	8.6	11.0	9.5	10.0	13.2	9.4	8.4	8.1	11.6	7.3	8.8	8.3	7.9	11.9	31.0
2. A little important	19.4	18.9	20.2	19.4	18.5	21.2	20.7	16.7	19.7	20.6	18.5	17.6	19.4	17.9	22.1	34.5
3. Pretty important	32.8	32.6	33.1	32.8	33.6	32.8	34.3	30.4	34.8	33.9	31.8	31.2	36.1	37.2	31.3	27.6
4. Very important	38.0	39.8	35.8	38.3	38.1	32.8	35.6	44.5	37.6	33.9	42.4	42.4	36.3	36.7	34.7	6.9
Item 10230 N(Wtd)	3630	1745	1760	2794	438	844	1108	1109	569	1944	1388	1270	800	441	985	29
A08P: A job which leaves you mostly free of supervision by others																
1. Not important	9.4	9.0	9.9	9.3	11.0	9.9	9.8	9.9	6.9	8.7	10.1	10.4	11.1	8.8	7.1	13.8
2. A little important	26.2	23.0	29.7	27.0	21.6	27.5	25.5	26.0	25.8	27.3	24.6	28.5	26.5	28.3	22.1	17.2
3. Pretty important	39.4	39.4	38.9	39.9	37.2	38.2	39.7	38.4	42.4	40.2	39.2	39.0	39.3	36.1	42.1	34.5
4. Very important	25.0	28.5	21.6	23.7	30.1	24.5	24.8	25.8	24.8	23.8	26.1	22.1	23.2	26.8	28.6	34.5
Item 10240 N(Wtd)	3627	1739	1762	2795	435	840	1108	1110	569	1944	1387	1270	799	441	985	29
A08Q: A job that offers a reasonably predictable, secure future																
1. Not important	.9	1.1	.7	.9	.5	1.4	1.2	.5	.4	.9	1.1	.5	1.1	.5	1.2	3.4
2. A little important	6.1	6.6	5.7	6.1	6.2	7.1	4.9	6.2	6.5	5.9	6.1	6.0	5.5	6.6	6.3	13.8
3. Pretty important	28.3	29.7	27.4	30.0	19.0	29.2	29.1	25.1	31.8	30.1	27.3	26.9	31.7	26.0	28.7	24.1
4. Very important	64.7	62.7	66.2	63.0	74.4	62.3	64.8	68.1	61.3	63.1	65.5	66.5	61.7	67.0	63.8	62.1
Item 10250 N(Wtd)	3621	1739	1760	2791	437	840	1106	1109	566	1943	1384	1270	797	439	984	29
A08R: A job where you can learn new things, learn new skills																
1. Not important	1.2	1.3	1.0	1.2	.7	1.9	1.3	.9	.7	1.2	1.0	1.1	1.0	1.4	1.4	6.9
2. A little important	10.5	13.4	8.1	12.4	4.1	11.6	11.7	9.6	8.8	11.9	9.5	10.2	12.0	7.5	11.4	13.8
3. Pretty important	41.7	44.3	39.4	44.4	30.1	43.9	42.9	37.2	44.8	43.3	40.1	40.4	42.5	44.7	42.1	41.4
4. Very important	46.6	41.0	51.6	42.0	65.1	42.7	44.2	52.4	45.7	43.6	49.4	48.4	44.5	46.5	45.0	37.9
Item 10260 N(Wtd)	3624	1740	1761	2793	435	839	1106	1109	569	1943	1385	1269	797	441	984	29
A08S: A job where you do not have to pretend to be a type of person that you are not																
1. Not important	5.2	7.0	3.2	4.7	6.4	4.4	5.1	6.8	3.7	4.2	6.4	5.2	4.6	3.4	5.3	10.3
2. A little important	5.1	6.8	3.4	4.7	5.7	5.4	4.6	5.6	4.6	4.7	5.6	4.8	4.8	5.7	4.9	3.4
3. Pretty important	18.8	24.2	13.4	18.7	17.5	21.6	18.3	16.0	21.3	17.5	20.4	18.5	21.4	20.8	15.1	27.6
4. Very important	70.9	62.0	80.3	71.9	70.3	68.6	72.0	71.6	70.7	73.6	67.7	71.5	69.2	70.1	74.8	58.6
Item 10270 N(Wtd)	3614	1734	1759	2788	435	834	1104	1107	569	1939	1382	1268	796	438	981	29
A08T: A job that most people look up to and respect																
1. Not important	5.6	6.0	5.2	5.9	3.4	7.9	5.0	4.3	6.0	5.4	5.9	4.7	6.6	5.5	5.8	6.9
2. A little important	18.0	19.2	16.9	19.3	11.5	18.6	18.3	15.8	21.2	18.0	18.0	17.0	16.3	20.2	19.8	24.1
3. Pretty important	36.9	38.2	35.9	39.0	28.2	35.8	41.1	33.9	36.7	38.3	36.7	39.6	34.8	36.0	36.6	44.8
4. Very important	39.4	36.5	42.0	35.8	56.9	37.8	35.5	46.2	36.2	38.4	39.2	38.6	42.4	38.3	37.9	24.1
Item 10280 N(Wtd)	3613	1730	1762	2786	436	839	1103	1104	567	1944	1380	1268	797	436	982	29
A08U: A job that permits contact with a lot of people																
1. Not important	8.4	10.4	6.4	8.5	9.6	8.4	8.2	9.6	6.5	7.4	8.9	8.9	6.5	9.1	8.5	10.3
2. A little important	23.5	28.5	18.3	23.9	21.6	22.0	25.3	22.1	24.6	21.4	26.5	23.9	23.2	21.4	22.4	34.5
3. Pretty important	34.5	34.4	34.7	34.9	33.7	33.1	35.4	32.5	38.9	35.8	33.7	33.6	36.7	37.1	34.5	13.8
4. Very important	33.6	26.6	40.7	32.7	35.1	36.4	31.1	35.9	29.9	35.4	31.0	33.5	33.5	32.3	34.7	41.4
Item 10290 N(Wtd)	3616	1736	1758	2791	436	836	1106	1106	568	1942	1383	1269	796	439	984	29

QUESTIONNAIRE FORM 4 1981	TOTAL	SEX		RACE		REGION				4YR COLLEGE PLANS		ILLICIT DRUG USE: LIFETIME				
		M	F	White	Black	NE	NC	S	W	Yes	No	None	Mari-juana Only	Few Pills	More Pills	Any Her-oin
Weighted No. of Cases:	3653	1751	1771	2804	441	846	1116	1117	574	1955	1393	1277	804	441	991	29
% of Weighted Total:	100.0	47.9	48.5	76.8	12.1	23.2	30.6	30.6	15.7	53.5	38.1	35.0	22.0	12.1	27.1	.8

A08V: A job with an easy pace that lets you work slowly

1. Not important	29.0	27.8	30.2	30.3	24.1	31.9	28.1	28.2	28.3	31.7	26.1	31.6	27.6	26.7	27.4	34.5
2. A little important	39.6	39.8	39.3	40.2	36.7	39.5	40.8	37.4	41.9	41.2	37.5	37.9	38.2	40.1	42.7	24.1
3. Pretty important	22.2	23.4	21.5	21.4	25.2	21.1	21.9	24.3	20.6	20.2	24.7	21.6	23.1	26.2	21.0	31.0
4. Very important	9.1	9.0	9.0	8.1	14.0	7.5	9.2	10.1	9.2	6.9	11.6	8.7	11.1	7.1	8.8	10.3
Item 10300 N(Wtd)	3618	1736	1761	2791	436	837	1106	1106	568	1941	1386	1271	796	439	984	29

A08W: A job where most problems are quite difficult and challenging

1. Not important	16.0	14.9	16.5	15.6	17.0	15.0	15.0	20.3	11.3	12.6	20.1	13.7	16.6	18.4	16.7	24.1
2. A little important	36.1	34.9	38.3	38.5	28.3	34.7	39.8	33.2	36.7	33.3	40.1	35.1	38.0	36.4	36.5	27.6
3. Pretty important	34.7	36.1	32.9	33.7	38.2	37.3	33.0	31.9	39.2	38.4	29.9	37.6	31.9	32.5	34.3	31.0
4. Very important	13.2	14.0	12.3	12.3	16.6	12.9	12.1	14.6	12.7	15.6	9.9	13.6	13.5	12.7	12.5	17.2
Item 10310 N(Wtd)	3618	1736	1761	2793	435	836	1108	1107	566	1941	1385	1269	795	440	984	29

A09: What kind of work do you think you will be doing when you are 30 years old? Mark the one that comes closest to what you expect to be doing.

01. Laborer (car washer, sanitary worker, farm laborer)	.3	.7	-	.3	.3	.1	.6	.2	.2	.1	.6	-	-	.7	.6	-
02. Service worker (cook, waiter, barber, janitor, gas station attendant, practical nurse, beautician)	3.0	.6	5.3	3.3	1.0	3.6	3.0	2.8	2.6	1.1	5.8	2.1	2.9	3.1	4.0	3.7
03. Operative or semi-skilled worker (garage worker, taxicab, bus or truck driver, assembly line worker, welder)	2.9	5.0	.6	2.5	3.9	1.1	3.2	3.5	3.4	.5	6.1	2.3	2.2	1.9	3.8	11.1
04. Sales clerk in a retail store (shoe salesperson, department store clerk, drug store clerk)	1.2	.7	1.6	1.1	1.8	1.0	1.5	1.0	1.3	.6	2.1	1.4	1.2	1.7	.8	3.7
05. Clerical or office worker (bank teller, bookkeeper, secretary, typist, postal clerk or carrier, ticket agent)	10.6	1.2	19.8	10.3	13.8	9.8	11.1	11.4	9.2	5.9	17.2	11.6	10.9	9.4	10.0	7.4
06. Protective service (police officer, fireman, detective)	2.1	3.6	.8	2.3	1.6	2.4	1.8	2.1	2.8	1.8	2.8	2.3	2.5	2.7	1.4	3.7
07. Military service	3.2	5.1	1.2	2.6	6.8	2.3	2.5	5.0	2.4	2.1	4.5	2.8	4.6	4.4	1.7	-
08. Craftsman or skilled worker (carpenter, electrician, brick layer, mechanic, machinist, tool and die maker, telephone installer)	8.9	17.1	.5	8.6	9.4	6.8	10.4	8.5	10.0	3.2	15.7	7.6	8.2	8.7	10.7	11.1
09. Farm owner, farm manager	1.8	3.0	.7	2.2	.3	.4	2.7	2.5	.8	1.3	2.8	2.3	2.1	1.9	1.0	3.7
10. Owner of small business (restaurant owner, shop owner)	5.5	6.7	4.3	5.5	4.7	6.4	4.5	5.2	7.0	5.0	6.0	3.1	5.8	5.8	8.2	7.4
11. Sales representative (insurance agent, real estate broker, bond salesman)	1.4	1.4	1.4	1.7	.5	.6	1.6	1.9	1.1	1.1	1.8	1.1	1.2	1.9	1.8	3.7
12. Manager or administrator (office manager, sales manager, school administrator, government official)	6.7	7.4	6.1	7.0	7.0	10.1	5.3	6.5	5.1	8.6	4.9	5.6	8.2	8.0	6.6	7.4
13. Professional without doctoral degree (registered nurse, librarian, engineer, architect, social worker, technician, accountant, actor, artist, musician)	30.4	28.7	32.7	30.7	30.0	31.6	33.1	26.7	30.5	40.4	16.4	34.1	28.9	27.1	29.6	22.2
14. Professional with doctoral degree or equivalent (lawyer, physician, dentist, scientist, college professor)	13.1	13.8	12.5	13.0	12.0	15.8	10.6	13.3	13.5	20.7	2.1	15.4	13.4	12.3	10.8	11.1
15. Full-time homemaker or housewife	2.9	.1	5.7	3.1	1.6	2.3	2.5	3.0	4.3	1.9	4.7	3.3	2.9	2.2	2.7	3.7
16. Don't know-GO TO Q.A13	5.9	5.0	6.6	6.1	5.0	5.6	5.6	6.4	5.8	5.7	6.2	5.0	5.3	8.2	6.2	7.4
Item 10320 N(Wtd)	3397	1615	1679	2665	383	785	1055	1024	532	1871	1270	1190	760	413	931	27

MONITORING THE FUTURE

QUESTIONNAIRE FORM 4 1981	TOTAL	SEX		RACE		REGION				4YR COLLEGE PLANS		ILLICIT DRUG USE: LIFETIME				
		M	F	White	Black	NE	NC	S	W	Yes	No	None	Mari- juana Only	Few Pills	More Pills	Any Her- oin
Weighted No. of Cases:	3653	1751	1771	2804	441	846	1116	1117	574	1955	1393	1277	804	441	991	29
% of Weighted Total:	100.0	47.9	48.5	76.8	12.1	23.2	30.6	30.6	15.7	53.5	38.1	35.0	22.0	12.1	27.1	.8

A10: How likely do you think it is that you will actually get to do this kind of work?

1. Not very likely	1.9	2.1	1.4	1.4	3.7	2.1	1.8	1.9	1.9	1.2	2.4	1.4	1.6	1.8	1.9	–
2. Somewhat likely	6.9	6.8	6.8	6.8	7.9	6.4	7.2	7.3	6.5	5.7	8.3	6.8	7.3	7.8	6.1	12.0
3. Fairly likely	22.5	24.7	20.5	23.0	20.1	24.2	21.8	22.8	20.7	23.1	22.3	20.4	20.9	26.9	25.0	8.0
4. Very likely	44.8	45.4	44.7	44.6	44.5	45.9	46.4	42.0	45.2	47.7	40.6	44.4	48.1	42.0	44.8	36.0
5. Certain	16.4	13.5	19.4	16.0	20.6	15.2	14.5	18.5	17.8	17.9	14.6	18.8	15.2	15.4	15.4	16.0
6. I already do this kind of work	7.5	7.6	7.2	8.4	3.2	6.1	8.2	7.6	7.9	4.3	12.0	8.4	7.0	6.3	6.8	28.0
Item 10330 N(Wtd) ★	3318	1593	1616	2556	407	769	1025	1002	522	1797	1257	1182	738	383	900	25

A11: How certain are you that this kind of work is a good choice for you?

1. Not at all certain	2.9	3.2	2.6	2.6	3.4	3.9	2.4	3.0	2.5	2.5	3.2	2.3	3.5	3.9	2.3	4.0
2. Somewhat certain	8.5	8.4	8.2	8.4	9.6	7.6	9.1	8.8	7.6	8.1	9.7	7.6	6.9	11.1	8.7	4.0
3. Fairly certain	30.8	32.6	29.7	32.5	23.9	31.2	32.2	29.6	30.1	31.7	30.6	30.2	28.8	32.9	33.7	24.0
4. Very certain	41.1	39.6	42.3	40.9	43.1	40.2	41.0	40.9	43.2	41.5	40.6	40.8	46.4	38.1	39.6	36.0
5. Completely certain	16.6	16.2	17.1	15.6	19.7	17.2	15.2	17.8	16.4	16.2	15.9	19.1	14.4	14.0	15.7	32.0
Item 10340 N(Wtd) ★	3335	1599	1627	2572	406	773	1029	1007	525	1806	1262	1184	743	386	907	25

A12: How satisfying do you think this kind of work will be for you?

1. Not very satisfying	.9	1.0	.6	.5	2.5	1.2	1.0	.9	.4	.3	1.5	.4	.9	1.0	.8	8.0
2. Somewhat satisfying	6.9	7.0	6.5	6.5	7.9	7.8	7.3	6.6	5.2	4.9	9.4	6.5	6.5	6.0	7.8	4.0
3. Quite satisfying	24.0	26.6	21.2	24.2	22.7	20.7	26.2	24.8	23.1	20.7	28.2	20.3	23.1	29.8	26.4	16.0
4. Very satisfying	40.5	40.2	40.8	41.1	40.1	42.2	39.5	38.6	43.4	43.1	37.7	42.0	41.9	40.9	38.2	36.0
5. Extremely satisfying	27.8	25.2	30.8	27.8	26.8	28.2	26.0	29.2	27.9	30.9	23.2	30.6	27.6	22.5	26.9	36.0
Item 10350 N(Wtd) ★	3332	1600	1624	2570	406	773	1030	1006	523	1804	1261	1185	743	386	905	25

A13: To what extent do you think the things listed below will prevent you from getting the kind of work you would like to have?

A13A: Your religion

1. Not at all	89.8	89.2	91.1	92.2	81.2	92.1	92.0	86.7	88.6	91.6	88.2	89.1	92.4	88.9	91.2	89.7
2. Somewhat	4.4	4.4	4.3	4.3	4.4	4.0	3.7	4.8	5.9	4.3	4.9	4.5	4.0	4.5	4.3	–
3. A lot	1.7	2.0	1.3	1.0	4.9	1.4	.8	3.1	1.3	1.6	1.6	2.4	.9	.9	1.0	3.4
8. Don't know	4.0	4.4	3.4	2.5	9.4	2.7	3.4	5.4	4.2	2.4	5.3	4.1	2.6	5.4	3.4	10.3
Item 10360 N(Wtd)	3505	1674	1713	2722	405	810	1077	1073	545	1889	1346	1234	768	423	957	29

A13B: Your sex

1. Not at all	76.9	87.5	66.3	78.3	72.5	76.4	77.1	77.6	75.6	75.1	79.1	75.7	79.9	76.3	77.2	62.1
2. Somewhat	17.3	6.6	28.1	17.0	17.9	18.2	17.6	15.0	19.6	19.6	15.0	17.7	15.4	18.2	18.0	17.2
3. A lot	3.8	3.8	3.5	2.9	6.9	3.6	3.1	4.8	3.3	3.2	4.0	4.1	2.3	3.3	3.4	17.2
8. Don't know	2.1	2.1	2.2	1.8	2.7	1.7	2.2	2.6	1.7	2.1	1.9	2.4	2.2	1.9	1.3	3.4
Item 10370 N(Wtd)	3504	1677	1710	2721	408	811	1077	1073	542	1889	1347	1235	768	422	958	29

A13C: Your race

1. Not at all	82.4	81.7	83.6	91.5	37.2	84.2	86.2	75.6	85.3	83.1	84.3	79.8	81.8	81.7	89.6	62.1
2. Somewhat	11.3	10.9	11.3	5.8	38.2	11.0	9.5	14.7	8.6	11.1	9.6	12.1	12.3	14.0	6.7	17.2
3. A lot	4.0	4.8	3.2	1.8	16.7	2.8	3.3	5.9	3.3	4.1	3.6	5.0	3.4	2.9	2.8	13.8
8. Don't know	2.4	2.7	1.9	.8	8.0	2.1	1.1	3.8	2.8	1.8	2.5	2.9	2.6	1.7	.9	6.9
Item 10380 N(Wtd)	3508	1678	1711	2717	414	809	1076	1078	545	1891	1347	1235	773	420	957	29

A13D: Your family background

1. Not at all	87.2	86.9	87.7	90.4	75.4	86.5	88.3	85.8	88.4	88.5	86.6	87.0	89.1	85.5	88.7	65.5
2. Somewhat	7.2	6.7	7.7	6.3	9.1	8.5	7.6	5.9	6.8	7.4	6.9	7.3	6.4	7.6	6.5	24.1
3. A lot	2.7	3.5	1.9	1.5	7.6	2.5	2.0	3.7	2.0	2.2	3.2	3.0	1.8	2.1	2.4	10.3
8. Don't know	3.0	3.0	2.7	1.8	7.9	2.5	2.0	4.5	2.8	2.0	3.3	2.6	2.7	4.7	2.4	–
Item 10390 N(Wtd)	3506	1676	1711	2720	407	810	1079	1073	544	1890	1346	1234	768	422	958	29

★=excludes respondents for whom question was inappropriate.

QUESTIONNAIRE FORM 4 1981	TOTAL	SEX		RACE		REGION				4YR COLLEGE PLANS		ILLICIT DRUG USE: LIFETIME				
		M	F	White	Black	NE	NC	S	W	Yes	No	None	Marijuana Only	Few Pills	More Pills	Any Heroin
Weighted No. of Cases:	3653	1751	1771	2804	441	846	1116	1117	574	1955	1393	1277	804	441	991	29
% of Weighted Total:	100.0	47.9	48.5	76.8	12.1	23.2	30.6	30.6	15.7	53.5	38.1	35.0	22.0	12.1	27.1	.8

A13E: Your political views

	TOTAL	M	F	White	Black	NE	NC	S	W	Yes	No	None	Marijuana Only	Few Pills	More Pills	Any Heroin
1. Not at all	82.9	81.7	84.7	86.3	67.7	84.8	83.8	79.8	84.6	85.0	81.3	82.5	83.3	82.0	85.4	69.0
2. Somewhat	8.8	10.2	7.3	7.5	15.4	8.3	8.4	9.9	8.5	8.9	8.8	8.7	9.2	8.5	8.1	17.2
3. A lot	2.0	2.3	1.7	1.5	4.5	1.4	2.7	2.2	1.3	1.8	2.2	2.1	1.4	2.4	1.5	6.9
8. Don't know	6.2	5.7	6.4	4.7	12.4	5.6	5.2	8.1	5.7	4.3	7.7	6.8	6.0	6.9	4.9	10.3
Item 10400　N(Wtd)	3497	1671	1710	2720	402	809	1077	1067	544	1886	1343	1229	768	423	958	29

A13F: Your education

	TOTAL	M	F	White	Black	NE	NC	S	W	Yes	No	None	Marijuana Only	Few Pills	More Pills	Any Heroin
1. Not at all	49.0	49.1	49.2	49.2	48.2	51.7	44.6	51.0	49.8	54.6	41.5	53.0	48.1	45.7	46.7	44.8
2. Somewhat	24.0	23.4	24.3	25.3	17.3	24.3	25.6	21.2	25.9	20.1	29.9	20.5	24.9	24.4	27.4	34.5
3. A lot	23.4	23.5	23.1	22.2	29.7	21.1	26.4	23.9	19.7	22.7	23.8	22.3	24.1	26.1	22.0	17.2
8. Don't know	3.6	3.9	3.4	3.3	4.6	3.0	3.3	3.9	4.8	2.6	4.7	4.1	2.7	3.8	4.0	3.4
Item 10410　N(Wtd)	3507	1677	1713	2720	411	810	1080	1073	544	1890	1346	1233	771	422	959	29

A13G: Lack of vocational training

	TOTAL	M	F	White	Black	NE	NC	S	W	Yes	No	None	Marijuana Only	Few Pills	More Pills	Any Heroin
1. Not at all	52.8	53.6	51.9	54.9	44.0	55.7	49.0	54.3	53.1	57.8	46.7	54.0	53.5	51.8	52.3	44.8
2. Somewhat	24.4	24.1	24.7	23.7	28.1	22.0	28.3	22.3	24.1	21.6	28.6	21.3	24.7	29.5	24.8	24.1
3. A lot	14.0	13.7	14.3	12.8	19.3	11.6	14.8	14.9	14.4	11.9	16.4	14.1	13.6	10.9	15.1	24.1
8. Don't know	8.8	8.5	9.0	8.7	8.6	10.8	8.0	8.4	8.2	8.8	8.2	10.6	8.1	7.6	7.9	6.9
Item 10420　N(Wtd)	3497	1673	1706	2716	405	809	1068	1072	548	1878	1350	1230	764	421	961	29

A13H: Lack of ability

	TOTAL	M	F	White	Black	NE	NC	S	W	Yes	No	None	Marijuana Only	Few Pills	More Pills	Any Heroin
1. Not at all	58.7	60.6	56.9	59.2	57.9	60.5	54.6	59.7	61.9	60.9	55.6	58.1	57.4	57.1	61.6	41.4
2. Somewhat	15.1	14.8	15.4	15.1	15.0	15.1	16.6	14.0	14.0	13.4	17.2	14.4	17.1	15.7	14.2	24.1
3. A lot	22.2	20.6	23.9	22.2	22.4	20.2	25.2	21.8	20.0	21.7	23.2	23.1	21.9	23.6	20.7	24.1
8. Don't know	4.0	4.0	3.9	3.6	4.9	4.0	3.6	4.5	4.1	4.0	3.9	4.3	3.6	3.6	3.5	6.9
Item 10430　N(Wtd)	3494	1667	1709	2716	406	806	1077	1071	541	1884	1344	1232	768	420	956	29

A13I: Not knowing the right people

	TOTAL	M	F	White	Black	NE	NC	S	W	Yes	No	None	Marijuana Only	Few Pills	More Pills	Any Heroin
1. Not at all	44.7	42.0	47.3	45.9	41.6	38.5	43.4	48.4	48.9	42.5	48.1	47.5	45.3	39.9	42.8	34.5
2. Somewhat	37.8	37.8	37.8	37.8	36.9	41.5	39.9	33.6	36.3	41.0	33.5	35.8	36.7	41.6	39.2	48.3
3. A lot	10.5	12.0	8.8	9.9	12.0	11.9	11.1	9.1	9.9	10.4	10.9	9.8	10.5	9.0	12.3	13.8
8. Don't know	7.1	8.1	6.0	6.4	9.5	8.1	5.8	8.9	4.8	6.1	7.5	7.0	7.5	9.5	5.6	3.4
Item 10440　N(Wtd)	3507	1679	1711	2719	409	813	1076	1073	546	1891	1343	1236	771	421	958	29

A13J: Not wanting to work hard

	TOTAL	M	F	White	Black	NE	NC	S	W	Yes	No	None	Marijuana Only	Few Pills	More Pills	Any Heroin
1. Not at all	61.1	61.5	60.8	62.0	57.2	62.1	59.1	62.1	62.1	61.5	61.3	60.5	61.3	60.0	62.8	55.2
2. Somewhat	9.2	10.3	8.2	8.6	11.4	8.3	10.1	8.3	10.9	9.0	9.0	8.0	9.5	9.5	10.1	20.7
3. A lot	26.6	24.5	28.7	27.2	26.0	26.4	28.0	26.2	25.2	27.0	26.6	27.9	26.7	28.8	24.5	20.7
8. Don't know	3.0	3.8	2.2	2.2	5.7	3.2	2.9	3.6	1.8	2.5	3.1	3.6	2.5	1.7	2.7	3.4
Item 10450　N(Wtd)	3491	1668	1706	2713	404	807	1075	1066	543	1885	1340	1232	765	420	955	29

A13K: Not wanting to conform

	TOTAL	M	F	White	Black	NE	NC	S	W	Yes	No	None	Marijuana Only	Few Pills	More Pills	Any Heroin
1. Not at all	51.6	49.5	53.1	51.8	49.6	51.2	49.7	52.5	54.1	51.0	52.8	52.2	50.3	48.4	52.8	48.3
2. Somewhat	22.1	25.1	19.6	22.8	20.0	24.2	23.5	19.5	21.6	25.6	17.3	22.2	24.7	20.4	20.9	37.9
3. A lot	15.5	15.1	16.2	15.7	16.5	14.5	16.7	15.6	14.6	14.4	17.2	16.2	13.8	20.4	14.3	6.9
8. Don't know	10.8	10.3	11.1	9.7	14.0	9.9	10.2	12.5	9.9	9.0	12.6	9.3	11.3	10.8	12.1	6.9
Item 10460　N(Wtd)	3470	1654	1699	2698	401	805	1072	1057	536	1884	1323	1225	761	417	953	29

A14: If you were to get enough money to live as comfortably as you'd like for the rest of your life, would you want to work?

	TOTAL	M	F	White	Black	NE	NC	S	W	Yes	No	None	Marijuana Only	Few Pills	More Pills	Any Heroin
1. I would want to work	81.4	80.5	81.9	80.6	83.8	81.4	81.2	80.7	82.8	83.0	79.1	84.8	80.9	84.5	76.1	65.5
2. I would not want to work	18.6	19.5	18.1	19.4	16.2	18.6	18.8	19.3	17.0	17.0	20.9	15.2	19.1	15.5	23.9	34.5
Item 8100　N(Wtd)	3614	1734	1759	2791	433	837	1107	1106	565	1939	1385	1267	796	438	986	29

QUESTIONNAIRE FORM 4 1981	TOTAL	SEX		RACE		REGION				4YR COLLEGE PLANS		ILLICIT DRUG USE: LIFETIME				
		M	F	White	Black	NE	NC	S	W	Yes	No	None	Marijuana Only	Few Pills	More Pills	Any Heroin
Weighted No. of Cases:	3653	1751	1771	2804	441	846	1116	1117	574	1955	1393	1277	804	441	991	29
% of Weighted Total:	100.0	47.9	48.5	76.8	12.1	23.2	30.6	30.6	15.7	53.5	38.1	35.0	22.0	12.1	27.1	.8

A15: How much do you agree or disagree with each statement below?

A15A: One sees so few good or happy marriages that one questions it as a way of life

1. Disagree	30.0	29.9	31.0	32.5	21.2	30.3	29.7	29.7	30.9	32.6	28.2	36.7	29.1	24.3	25.8	10.7
2. Mostly disagree	20.6	20.9	20.3	22.8	11.1	23.4	22.7	16.7	19.4	22.9	17.7	20.1	21.3	22.4	20.5	17.9
3. Neither	18.0	20.1	15.9	18.3	15.2	17.8	19.1	16.5	18.9	16.8	19.9	14.6	17.7	22.7	20.7	21.4
4. Mostly agree	18.6	17.1	19.8	17.2	23.6	17.0	18.1	19.1	21.0	17.1	20.0	16.3	17.9	20.1	21.2	25.0
5. Agree	12.9	12.0	13.0	9.2	28.9	11.5	10.5	18.1	9.7	10.6	14.2	12.2	14.1	10.5	12.0	25.0
Item 10470 N(Wtd)	3604	1734	1752	2787	433	836	1106	1096	566	1936	1383	1266	795	437	983	28

A15B: It is usually a good idea for a couple to live together before getting married in order to find out whether they really get along

1. Disagree	31.0	24.4	37.9	31.3	32.3	23.2	28.4	40.2	29.8	31.9	30.0	46.7	23.8	28.5	18.4	10.3
2. Mostly disagree	14.0	14.5	13.5	14.5	11.9	11.9	16.5	14.8	10.9	15.3	12.8	14.6	17.0	12.1	12.3	6.9
3. Neither	16.2	17.8	14.8	17.1	12.4	16.6	17.4	14.9	16.2	18.3	13.8	15.0	19.8	15.7	15.3	20.7
4. Mostly agree	19.9	21.3	18.4	20.3	16.3	24.2	20.2	15.0	22.5	18.7	21.7	12.6	21.2	24.6	27.2	10.3
5. Agree	18.8	22.0	15.3	16.8	26.8	24.1	17.7	15.1	20.6	15.7	21.7	11.1	18.2	19.1	27.0	55.2
Item 10480 N(Wtd)	3619	1740	1762	2795	436	838	1106	1107	568	1943	1389	1271	798	439	987	29

A15C: Having a close intimate relationship with only one partner is too restrictive for the average person

1. Disagree	39.9	33.8	46.7	42.0	32.3	39.4	40.8	39.5	39.4	41.2	39.7	48.1	38.6	35.1	34.5	24.1
2. Mostly disagree	22.8	23.7	22.3	24.1	17.7	23.1	22.9	20.5	26.9	23.6	21.7	19.3	22.7	28.0	25.8	20.7
3. Neither	13.6	15.9	11.2	13.7	11.9	13.3	13.8	13.7	13.6	13.9	13.3	12.6	14.1	14.6	13.6	13.8
4. Mostly agree	14.3	16.1	11.9	13.0	19.0	15.1	14.1	14.1	14.0	13.4	14.5	11.8	13.6	15.3	16.4	24.1
5. Agree	9.4	10.4	7.9	7.2	19.0	9.2	8.3	12.2	6.2	7.9	10.7	8.1	11.0	6.8	9.8	20.7
Item 10490 N(Wtd)	3613	1737	1760	2791	436	837	1105	1105	566	1941	1387	1269	797	439	986	29

A15D: Having a job takes away from a woman's relationship with her husband

1. Disagree	47.1	38.1	56.3	45.7	58.9	48.7	44.8	49.5	44.8	46.9	48.2	47.4	47.6	46.5	47.3	25.0
2. Mostly disagree	27.9	30.4	26.0	29.7	17.2	28.0	31.0	24.1	28.8	30.1	25.6	25.7	29.6	34.2	26.7	39.3
3. Neither	12.3	15.9	8.5	12.6	9.9	11.8	12.5	11.5	14.6	11.6	12.8	12.3	11.2	10.3	14.1	10.7
4. Mostly agree	8.7	10.0	7.1	8.6	8.7	7.9	8.9	9.3	8.2	8.1	9.1	10.1	8.4	7.3	7.6	14.3
5. Agree	4.0	5.5	2.1	3.4	5.7	3.7	2.9	5.5	3.7	3.2	4.4	4.6	3.4	1.8	4.3	10.7
Item 10500 N(Wtd)	3612	1732	1763	2791	436	838	1107	1104	563	1941	1388	1269	798	439	983	28

A15E: Having a job gives a wife more of a chance to develop herself as a person

1. Disagree	4.6	6.0	3.2	4.2	5.5	3.9	4.2	5.8	3.7	3.1	6.0	5.7	3.4	.9	5.0	10.7
2. Mostly disagree	3.9	5.0	3.0	3.9	3.2	4.3	2.4	4.5	5.1	4.2	3.5	5.3	2.3	4.1	3.2	10.7
3. Neither	7.9	11.6	4.2	8.4	2.5	6.3	8.6	7.1	10.1	7.1	9.0	8.3	7.8	6.8	8.2	-
4. Mostly agree	30.5	37.2	24.0	32.5	20.8	29.9	34.3	28.1	28.5	31.2	29.5	27.2	32.9	34.9	30.8	32.1
5. Agree	53.1	40.3	65.5	50.9	67.8	55.6	50.5	54.4	52.5	54.4	52.0	53.5	53.7	53.2	52.8	46.4
Item 10510 N(Wtd)	3613	1736	1761	2793	438	837	1106	1105	564	1939	1389	1270	799	438	985	28

A15F: Being a father and raising children is one of the most fulfilling experiences a man can have

1. Disagree	4.9	5.9	3.9	4.5	5.7	5.1	5.4	4.5	4.3	4.5	5.3	4.2	4.3	4.6	6.1	13.8
2. Mostly disagree	5.2	6.3	4.0	5.1	5.5	4.2	6.8	3.5	6.8	4.7	6.1	4.8	5.1	4.1	6.2	3.4
3. Neither	19.0	15.9	22.4	21.4	10.3	20.9	20.9	15.9	18.6	19.6	19.0	17.2	19.3	19.5	21.7	24.1
4. Mostly agree	32.5	31.6	33.4	33.5	27.8	32.9	33.3	29.9	35.6	33.3	30.7	31.7	31.9	32.8	33.7	24.1
5. Agree	38.4	40.3	36.3	35.5	50.7	37.0	33.6	46.4	34.5	38.0	38.9	42.1	39.3	39.2	32.3	34.5
Item 10520 N(Wtd)	3586	1739	1731	2762	436	828	1101	1098	559	1931	1371	1267	792	436	968	29

QUESTIONNAIRE FORM 4 1981	TOTAL	SEX		RACE		REGION				4YR COLLEGE PLANS		ILLICIT DRUG USE: LIFETIME				
		M	F	White	Black	NE	NC	S	W	Yes	No	None	Marijuana Only	Few Pills	More Pills	Any Heroin
Weighted No. of Cases:	3653	1751	1771	2804	441	846	1116	1117	574	1955	1393	1277	804	441	991	29
% of Weighted Total:	100.0	47.9	48.5	76.8	12.1	23.2	30.6	30.6	15.7	53.5	38.1	35.0	22.0	12.1	27.1	.8

A15G: Most mothers should spend more time with their children than they do now

1. Disagree	5.1	5.1	5.3	5.4	4.4	7.5	5.8	2.8	4.8	5.7	4.4	3.9	5.1	6.9	5.6	14.3
2. Mostly disagree	10.3	10.8	9.9	11.7	4.4	13.1	12.3	6.6	9.6	11.3	9.7	7.9	10.4	12.9	13.0	7.1
3. Neither	23.2	27.1	19.6	24.8	14.2	28.1	25.2	15.2	27.3	25.6	20.4	19.8	23.8	27.4	25.4	35.7
4. Mostly agree	30.9	30.4	31.1	31.3	29.8	29.8	29.7	32.8	31.2	30.6	30.6	29.2	33.5	29.2	32.3	21.4
5. Agree	30.6	26.8	34.1	26.7	47.2	21.4	27.0	42.7	27.1	26.8	34.9	39.2	27.2	24.1	23.7	25.0
Item 10530 N(Wtd)	3612	1739	1754	2787	436	835	1106	1106	564	1935	1388	1272	797	435	982	28

A15H: If a wife works, her husband should take a greater part in housework and child-care

1. Disagree	7.1	8.4	5.8	6.7	6.9	5.9	6.4	8.9	6.7	5.8	8.9	7.2	6.0	5.9	7.7	13.8
2. Mostly disagree	6.4	6.9	5.7	6.1	6.7	6.8	7.1	5.3	6.7	5.5	7.3	6.7	5.8	7.8	6.0	-
3. Neither	12.2	13.4	11.0	12.6	9.9	13.5	12.3	10.6	13.2	11.3	13.5	10.9	14.2	14.4	11.1	13.8
4. Mostly agree	36.2	37.7	34.7	37.2	31.0	35.7	38.2	35.2	34.7	37.5	34.2	35.4	36.5	36.1	38.5	27.6
5. Agree	38.1	33.6	42.8	37.4	45.6	38.1	36.0	40.1	38.6	39.8	36.0	39.8	37.7	35.8	36.8	44.8
Item 10540 N(Wtd)	3615	1739	1759	2792	436	837	1104	1107	567	1939	1390	1270	798	438	985	29

A16: How much TV do you estimate you watch on an average weekday?

1. None	3.2	2.5	3.9	3.2	1.6	3.6	3.3	2.3	4.1	3.4	2.8	3.1	3.8	2.5	3.5	-
2. Half-hour or less	11.5	10.5	13.1	12.7	5.0	12.3	11.7	16.4	19.3	13.7	9.4	11.2	10.1	11.3	13.2	17.2
3. About one hour	20.1	20.6	19.5	22.3	8.4	22.6	22.6	16.4	19.3	21.9	17.9	18.6	18.1	19.5	25.0	17.2
4. About two hours	22.6	23.7	21.2	24.0	14.2	26.0	22.0	19.2	25.4	24.4	20.1	21.1	22.6	25.2	23.0	24.1
5. About three hours	17.6	19.5	16.0	17.7	19.4	17.4	16.7	18.7	17.5	16.0	19.9	17.6	18.9	17.0	16.5	24.1
6. About four hours	11.5	11.1	11.7	10.5	15.5	9.5	12.4	13.7	8.1	10.3	12.7	12.4	10.8	10.2	11.2	6.9
7. Five hours or more	13.5	12.1	14.6	9.6	36.1	8.6	11.4	20.8	10.8	10.5	17.2	16.1	15.8	14.5	7.6	10.3
Item 10550 N(Wtd)	3616	1740	1760	2793	438	838	1106	1107	566	1938	1390	1270	800	441	985	29

A17: In the past year, how many books have you read just because you wanted to--that is, without their being assigned?

1. None	16.1	23.0	9.3	16.4	14.2	15.8	16.1	16.8	15.2	12.0	21.5	13.8	17.9	19.1	15.6	27.6
2. One	12.4	13.5	11.6	12.8	10.8	11.8	12.4	12.6	12.6	11.2	13.6	11.2	13.6	14.7	12.6	3.4
3. Two to five	40.4	38.4	41.7	39.5	45.5	42.9	40.8	39.1	38.2	40.3	40.3	40.6	40.8	39.6	39.5	24.1
4. Six to ten	11.9	11.0	12.7	11.4	14.2	12.5	10.8	13.2	10.9	14.3	9.0	13.2	10.6	9.2	12.2	20.7
5. Ten or more	19.2	14.1	24.7	19.9	15.3	17.1	19.7	18.3	23.1	22.1	15.5	21.1	17.1	17.1	20.1	20.7
Item 10560 N(Wtd)	3624	1742	1766	2795	437	837	1110	1106	571	1948	1388	1277	801	434	991	29

A18: Some people think about what's going on in government very often, and others are not that interested. How much of an interest do you take in government and current events?

1. No interest at all	3.3	3.6	2.8	3.0	3.7	4.2	2.7	3.3	3.2	1.8	5.3	2.6	3.0	2.8	4.1	13.8
2. Very little interest	16.2	11.2	21.0	15.5	18.0	17.3	16.8	15.7	14.3	11.9	21.6	15.5	17.2	15.0	15.9	10.3
3. Some interest	46.3	42.0	50.9	46.9	43.6	44.4	49.4	43.7	48.2	45.4	48.0	45.7	47.3	51.7	45.1	44.8
4. A lot of interest	24.1	28.6	19.5	24.6	23.7	22.4	23.4	25.2	25.7	27.9	19.2	24.4	23.0	20.3	26.4	17.2
5. A very great interest	10.1	14.6	5.8	10.0	11.2	11.7	7.7	12.1	8.8	13.0	5.8	11.8	9.4	10.2	8.3	10.3
Item 6330 N(Wtd)	3619	1739	1766	2791	438	836	1109	1107	568	1948	1387	1275	801	433	991	29

A19: Some people think that there ought to be changes in the amount of influence and power that certain organizations have in our society. Do you think the following organizations should have more influence, less influence, or about the same amount of influence as they have now?

QUESTIONNAIRE FORM 4 1981	TOTAL	SEX		RACE		REGION				4YR COLLEGE PLANS		ILLICIT DRUG USE: LIFETIME				
		M	F	White	Black	NE	NC	S	W	Yes	No	None	Mari- juana Only	Few Pills	More Pills	Any Her- oin
Weighted No. of Cases:	3653	1751	1771	2804	441	846	1116	1117	574	1955	1393	1277	804	441	991	29
% of Weighted Total:	100.0	47.9	48.5	76.8	12.1	23.2	30.6	30.6	15.7	53.5	38.1	35.0	22.0	12.1	27.1	.8

A19A: Large corporations?

1. Much less	8.3	10.2	6.6	8.9	4.1	10.1	8.2	8.0	6.5	9.9	6.3	8.7	6.3	8.3	9.8	6.9
2. Less	35.8	37.9	34.2	40.5	17.7	38.2	39.5	29.5	37.0	40.3	31.6	34.8	35.0	40.2	37.7	34.5
3. Same as now	29.6	28.5	30.3	29.5	32.0	31.2	28.4	28.4	31.9	29.8	30.0	29.2	33.0	25.9	29.3	27.6
4. More	10.1	10.0	10.1	7.8	20.3	7.6	9.9	13.2	8.5	7.4	12.9	10.6	10.9	8.3	8.1	13.8
5. Much more	3.4	3.5	3.2	2.1	8.1	2.3	2.4	5.3	3.5	2.5	4.0	3.7	3.1	3.7	2.5	10.3
8. No opinion	12.7	9.9	15.7	11.3	17.7	10.6	11.6	15.6	12.4	10.3	15.2	12.9	11.7	13.9	12.6	6.9
Item 10570 N(Wtd)	3596	1733	1750	2778	434	828	1105	1098	565	1935	1380	1270	795	433	981	29

A19B: Major labor unions?

1. Much less	8.8	12.0	5.5	10.5	1.6	8.7	10.4	8.1	7.3	10.6	6.8	9.3	7.5	9.9	8.7	10.3
2. Less	21.8	25.7	18.1	24.8	10.0	23.8	22.6	19.8	21.2	26.0	17.0	25.3	22.3	19.6	18.9	24.1
3. Same as now	29.8	28.2	31.7	30.8	25.5	29.3	31.5	26.1	34.0	30.5	30.1	28.8	30.1	28.4	31.8	27.6
4. More	20.3	18.6	21.9	17.7	32.6	19.8	18.4	24.1	17.3	18.3	22.6	17.1	21.8	21.5	22.3	20.7
5. Much more	6.7	6.4	6.8	4.8	12.0	6.3	5.3	8.6	6.4	4.3	9.0	6.6	6.1	5.8	6.7	13.8
8. No opinion	12.5	9.2	16.1	11.3	18.3	12.1	11.7	13.2	13.6	10.4	14.5	12.9	12.3	14.5	11.6	3.4
Item 10580 N(Wtd)	3586	1730	1744	2775	432	828	1098	1096	565	1928	1377	1269	790	433	978	29

A19C: Churches and religious organizations?

1. Much less	5.9	7.3	4.4	6.5	2.5	7.5	6.0	3.1	9.0	6.8	4.8	4.0	5.3	5.3	9.1	6.9
2. Less	8.6	10.6	6.8	9.4	3.7	9.1	9.8	5.2	12.6	8.5	8.6	7.4	8.3	9.2	10.3	17.2
3. Same as now	33.1	34.8	31.0	35.1	22.4	40.9	34.7	25.5	31.2	35.4	30.1	30.0	35.9	31.2	36.6	31.0
4. More	25.1	23.1	27.5	25.6	24.4	22.3	27.5	27.3	20.4	25.5	23.8	26.5	24.5	26.6	23.5	31.0
5. Much more	19.0	16.6	21.5	16.2	37.3	13.0	13.9	29.6	17.5	17.2	21.2	24.7	18.1	17.6	12.4	6.9
8. No opinion	8.2	7.6	8.7	7.3	9.9	7.3	7.1	9.4	9.2	6.6	10.1	7.3	7.9	10.2	8.1	10.3
Item 10590 N(Wtd)	3596	1733	1752	2776	434	826	1106	1099	565	1934	1381	1271	796	433	980	29

A19D: The national news media (TV, magazines, news services)?

1. Much less	8.6	9.2	7.9	9.1	6.5	10.8	7.6	7.9	8.8	9.3	7.9	9.6	6.8	7.6	9.6	-
2. Less	27.0	26.7	27.6	29.7	13.5	28.8	30.0	23.9	24.4	30.5	23.4	26.1	27.2	32.3	27.3	24.1
3. Same as now	39.0	39.7	38.5	39.9	36.0	38.7	39.5	38.0	40.7	39.7	39.0	38.8	41.6	36.0	38.8	48.3
4. More	13.3	13.3	13.2	11.6	20.9	12.0	11.1	15.6	15.0	11.8	14.9	13.5	12.6	10.4	13.5	13.8
5. Much more	5.7	5.5	5.6	4.1	12.8	5.1	5.3	7.0	4.6	4.4	6.3	6.5	5.9	3.5	4.7	10.3
8. No opinion	6.4	5.5	7.3	5.6	10.2	4.6	6.4	7.7	6.5	4.4	8.6	5.5	5.8	10.2	6.0	3.4
Item 10600 N(Wtd)	3592	1732	1750	2777	430	827	1107	1093	565	1934	1379	1269	793	433	981	29

A19E: The Presidency and the administration?

1. Much less	4.0	4.3	3.6	3.4	7.5	3.6	4.6	4.3	3.0	2.9	5.2	3.8	4.5	2.3	4.6	3.4
2. Less	10.3	10.3	10.3	9.7	15.4	10.7	10.5	9.4	10.4	9.4	11.5	7.4	10.9	11.3	13.2	3.4
3. Same as now	35.7	34.0	36.9	36.9	31.0	39.0	37.2	33.3	32.4	38.6	32.1	36.3	38.9	33.0	34.1	31.0
4. More	25.5	28.0	23.0	26.9	18.6	24.8	26.1	24.2	27.8	28.7	22.8	28.6	22.6	28.2	22.7	20.7
5. Much more	15.5	16.1	15.2	15.1	14.2	14.5	12.9	17.8	17.3	13.5	17.6	15.0	13.5	15.2	17.2	31.0
8. No opinion	9.1	7.3	10.9	8.0	13.1	7.2	8.6	11.1	9.2	7.0	10.7	9.0	9.4	9.9	8.3	10.3
Item 10610 N(Wtd)	3590	1731	1746	2776	429	828	1103	1094	565	1932	1379	1268	795	433	979	29

A19F: The Congress--that is, the U.S. Senate and House of Representatives?

1. Much less	3.6	4.2	2.9	3.3	4.4	2.8	3.6	4.3	3.4	2.5	4.6	2.9	3.9	3.0	4.4	6.9
2. Less	11.7	14.0	9.5	12.6	8.2	10.8	12.1	11.9	11.9	11.0	13.0	9.9	11.9	13.8	12.7	6.9
3. Same as now	39.8	38.6	40.8	40.7	36.4	41.9	40.8	37.8	38.2	42.4	37.3	41.2	42.3	32.6	39.9	44.8
4. More	23.4	23.3	23.2	23.7	22.2	22.7	24.8	22.8	22.9	25.5	21.5	23.8	20.4	28.6	22.7	24.1
5. Much more	11.0	11.5	10.5	10.2	13.8	11.9	8.6	12.0	12.4	9.9	11.3	11.7	10.6	10.3	10.6	13.8
8. No opinion	10.5	8.4	12.9	9.6	15.0	10.0	10.0	11.2	11.0	8.6	12.2	10.4	10.6	11.9	9.6	6.9
Item 10620 N(Wtd)	3577	1726	1741	2772	428	824	1097	1094	563	1927	1374	1269	789	427	978	29

QUESTIONNAIRE FORM 4 1981	TOTAL	SEX		RACE		REGION				4YR COLLEGE PLANS		ILLICIT DRUG USE: LIFETIME				
		M	F	White	Black	NE	NC	S	W	Yes	No	None	Mari-juana Only	Few Pills	More Pills	Any Her-oin
Weighted No. of Cases:	3653	1751	1771	2804	441	846	1116	1117	574	1955	1393	1277	804	441	991	29
% of Weighted Total:	100.0	47.9	48.5	76.8	12.1	23.2	30.6	30.6	15.7	53.5	38.1	35.0	22.0	12.1	27.1	.8

A19G: The U.S. Supreme Court?

	TOTAL	M	F	White	Black	NE	NC	S	W	Yes	No	None	Mari-juana Only	Few Pills	More Pills	Any Her-oin
1. Much less	2.2	2.5	1.7	2.3	1.4	2.4	3.2	1.5	1.4	1.6	3.1	2.2	1.4	1.4	2.8	6.9
2. Less	6.2	6.4	6.0	6.3	5.1	6.7	5.7	6.3	6.2	6.0	6.8	5.4	6.5	7.2	6.4	10.3
3. Same as now	41.2	41.6	40.5	42.1	37.1	41.1	43.5	38.8	41.6	42.7	39.9	41.4	43.6	36.9	41.8	44.8
4. More	26.2	26.8	26.0	26.9	24.5	25.5	25.3	27.0	27.4	28.9	23.5	27.0	26.0	25.1	26.6	13.8
5. Much more	13.0	13.6	12.2	11.8	17.9	13.5	11.3	14.2	13.1	11.8	13.2	13.4	12.5	13.9	12.2	20.7
8. No opinion	11.2	8.9	13.6	10.6	14.2	10.7	11.1	12.2	10.3	9.1	13.4	10.6	10.0	15.5	10.2	6.9
Item 10630 N(Wtd)	3581	1726	1744	2769	429	823	1101	1092	565	1927	1376	1268	787	431	978	29

A19H: All the courts and the justice system in general?

	TOTAL	M	F	White	Black	NE	NC	S	W	Yes	No	None	Mari-juana Only	Few Pills	More Pills	Any Her-oin
1. Much less	2.0	2.5	1.4	1.9	1.9	1.7	2.7	1.8	1.4	1.5	2.8	1.5	2.2	2.1	2.1	6.9
2. Less	6.3	6.4	6.2	6.5	5.8	6.3	6.5	5.7	7.1	6.0	7.3	4.7	5.8	4.9	9.0	3.4
3. Same as now	38.4	39.4	36.9	38.9	34.9	37.8	42.5	35.1	37.8	40.1	36.9	36.5	42.5	33.8	40.2	48.3
4. More	29.4	30.6	28.5	30.9	24.7	30.0	28.8	29.4	29.1	31.7	27.0	31.3	26.1	38.0	26.9	17.2
5. Much more	13.5	13.3	13.8	12.2	18.4	14.1	10.3	16.3	13.5	11.8	14.0	15.4	13.2	9.7	12.3	17.2
8. No opinion	10.4	7.9	13.1	9.6	14.7	10.0	9.1	11.6	11.3	8.9	12.0	10.6	10.1	11.6	9.6	6.9
Item 10640 N(Wtd)	3584	1728	1745	2770	430	823	1106	1091	564	1928	1377	1268	789	432	979	29

A19I: The police and other law enforcement agencies?

	TOTAL	M	F	White	Black	NE	NC	S	W	Yes	No	None	Mari-juana Only	Few Pills	More Pills	Any Her-oin
1. Much less	2.8	3.8	1.7	2.7	3.2	2.8	2.7	3.1	2.5	2.6	3.1	.9	2.0	2.3	5.5	6.9
2. Less	7.8	9.0	5.7	7.6	7.2	8.1	8.0	7.0	8.7	6.6	9.7	4.8	7.3	6.5	12.1	20.7
3. Same as now	25.6	28.2	23.0	26.5	25.1	27.8	26.6	22.5	26.7	27.1	24.1	21.7	30.0	25.0	28.4	27.6
4. More	33.1	31.5	35.5	34.5	26.5	32.0	36.6	30.8	32.6	35.9	29.8	37.4	34.0	35.9	27.0	20.7
5. Much more	24.5	21.6	27.8	23.4	27.8	23.7	21.0	28.5	24.4	23.2	25.8	29.6	21.5	23.1	20.4	20.7
8. No opinion	6.2	5.8	6.4	5.3	10.2	5.6	5.2	8.1	5.1	4.6	7.6	5.6	5.0	7.2	6.5	6.9
Item 10650 N(Wtd)	3588	1730	1747	2775	431	826	1105	1093	565	1933	1378	1268	794	432	981	29

A19J: The U.S. military?

	TOTAL	M	F	White	Black	NE	NC	S	W	Yes	No	None	Mari-juana Only	Few Pills	More Pills	Any Her-oin
1. Much less	4.4	4.6	4.2	4.3	4.9	3.9	4.5	3.5	7.1	4.4	4.6	4.0	2.8	5.8	5.9	-
2. Less	7.6	8.1	7.2	7.8	7.2	7.8	7.4	5.8	10.8	8.2	6.8	6.5	8.2	6.2	8.7	10.3
3. Same as now	32.1	29.2	34.7	33.2	26.0	34.2	35.7	27.3	31.1	33.6	30.6	32.5	34.8	31.2	31.1	24.1
4. More	24.8	26.2	23.6	25.3	22.3	26.5	23.6	25.7	23.1	26.2	23.3	25.3	24.2	21.2	26.5	24.1
5. Much more	20.5	24.9	15.9	19.8	25.5	17.7	18.3	26.6	16.7	18.3	22.3	20.3	20.4	20.8	19.4	27.6
8. No opinion	10.6	7.1	14.3	9.6	14.4	9.8	10.4	11.1	11.4	9.3	12.3	11.3	9.6	14.5	8.4	10.3
Item 10660 N(Wtd)	3588	1732	1745	2773	431	824	1105	1095	563	1930	1378	1269	793	433	978	29

The next questions ask your views about drugs.

A20: Do you think that people (who are 18 or older) should be prohibited by law from doing each of the following?

A20A: Smoking marijuana (pot, grass) in private

	TOTAL	M	F	White	Black	NE	NC	S	W	Yes	No	None	Mari-juana Only	Few Pills	More Pills	Any Her-oin
1. No	49.6	51.6	47.9	50.1	47.1	58.9	48.0	42.5	52.8	48.6	51.4	29.0	50.9	55.1	73.1	69.0
2. Not sure	15.0	13.4	16.3	14.6	16.6	13.5	16.1	15.3	14.4	15.8	13.5	16.9	18.9	15.7	9.1	10.3
3. Yes	35.4	34.9	35.8	35.2	36.3	27.7	35.8	42.1	32.6	35.6	35.1	54.1	30.4	29.2	17.8	20.7
Item 10780 N(Wtd)	3611	1735	1765	2790	435	835	1108	1101	568	1944	1386	1276	800	432	989	29

A20B: Smoking marijuana in public places

	TOTAL	M	F	White	Black	NE	NC	S	W	Yes	No	None	Mari-juana Only	Few Pills	More Pills	Any Her-oin
1. No	19.6	22.9	15.9	17.6	29.5	20.2	19.0	20.1	19.2	15.4	24.2	13.9	16.1	19.4	28.3	48.3
2. Not sure	13.0	14.0	11.9	13.0	10.1	13.8	13.8	10.8	14.6	11.5	14.2	3.9	13.4	15.7	22.8	27.6
3. Yes	67.4	63.1	72.1	69.4	60.4	66.1	67.2	69.1	66.2	73.1	61.5	82.1	70.5	64.8	49.0	24.1
Item 10790 N(Wtd)	3606	1732	1763	2786	434	835	1103	1100	568	1943	1382	1276	800	432	984	29

QUESTIONNAIRE FORM 4 1981	TOTAL	SEX		RACE		REGION				4YR COLLEGE PLANS		ILLICIT DRUG USE: LIFETIME				
		M	F	White	Black	NE	NC	S	W	Yes	No	None	Mari-juana Only	Few Pills	More Pills	Any Her-oin
Weighted No. of Cases: % of Weighted Total:	3653 100.0	1751 47.9	1771 48.5	2804 76.8	441 12.1	846 23.2	1116 30.6	1117 30.6	574 15.7	1955 53.5	1393 38.1	1277 35.0	804 22.0	441 12.1	991 27.1	29 .8
A20C: Taking LSD in private																
1. No	25.8	29.3	22.3	23.4	35.7	28.6	24.2	24.6	27.0	22.6	29.6	20.4	23.2	22.4	34.5	58.6
2. Not sure	11.6	10.8	12.4	11.1	10.9	10.6	13.2	9.5	14.1	11.1	12.0	10.3	10.1	12.8	14.0	20.7
3. Yes	62.6	60.0	65.3	65.5	53.4	60.6	62.5	65.9	58.9	66.3	58.3	69.3	66.8	64.6	51.5	20.7
Item 10800 N(Wtd)	3596	1725	1760	2780	431	831	1102	1096	567	1940	1379	1272	794	429	987	29
A20D: Taking LSD in public places																
1. No	14.4	17.1	11.0	11.5	27.2	13.0	12.1	17.9	14.3	10.3	19.3	13.2	14.5	14.4	14.1	24.1
2. Not sure	4.9	5.7	4.1	4.5	6.9	4.8	6.5	3.6	4.1	4.5	5.2	2.1	3.6	4.9	9.2	24.1
3. Yes	80.7	77.1	84.9	84.0	65.9	82.1	81.2	78.4	81.7	85.2	75.6	84.7	81.9	80.7	76.7	51.7
Item 10810 N(Wtd)	3597	1723	1763	2780	434	832	1103	1096	567	1941	1379	1268	799	431	986	29
A20E: Taking amphetamines (uppers) or barbiturates (downers) in private																
1. No	32.2	35.2	29.4	30.6	37.4	36.4	30.6	29.5	34.6	29.7	35.9	21.6	26.8	28.5	51.0	72.4
2. Not sure	15.8	15.3	15.9	15.6	14.8	15.9	16.8	14.4	16.4	14.9	16.2	14.4	16.4	19.4	15.1	6.9
3. Yes	52.0	49.5	54.7	53.7	48.0	47.7	52.6	56.1	49.0	55.4	48.0	64.0	56.8	52.1	34.0	17.2
Item 10820 N(Wtd)	3608	1735	1763	2790	433	835	1108	1098	567	1943	1386	1275	799	432	989	29
A20F: Taking amphetamines or barbiturates in public places																
1. No	16.8	19.6	13.6	14.2	27.5	15.6	15.3	19.0	17.1	12.7	21.8	13.2	14.5	16.5	21.7	34.5
2. Not sure	9.0	10.1	8.1	9.1	8.1	9.4	10.3	7.7	8.6	7.9	10.1	4.4	6.0	11.1	16.3	24.1
3. Yes	74.2	70.3	78.4	76.7	64.7	75.0	74.4	73.2	74.3	79.5	68.0	82.4	79.5	72.4	62.0	41.4
Item 10830 N(Wtd)	3605	1731	1763	2786	433	832	1106	1099	567	1942	1384	1274	800	431	987	29
A20G: Taking heroin (smack, horse) in private																
1. No	22.0	23.8	20.0	19.2	34.6	23.1	20.0	23.0	21.9	18.9	25.5	19.6	23.5	19.5	23.2	48.3
2. Not sure	9.3	8.8	9.4	8.0	12.1	7.9	9.8	9.2	10.2	8.1	10.1	8.4	8.5	10.5	10.1	13.8
3. Yes	68.8	67.4	70.6	72.8	53.4	68.9	70.2	67.7	67.9	73.0	64.4	72.1	68.0	70.0	66.7	37.9
Item 10840 N(Wtd)	3599	1727	1761	2783	431	835	1103	1094	567	1939	1380	1267	800	430	989	29
A20H: Taking heroin in public places																
1. No	13.7	15.9	10.7	10.7	26.2	11.6	11.9	17.3	13.0	9.7	18.1	13.4	13.8	14.7	11.5	27.6
2. Not sure	3.9	4.7	3.1	3.3	6.9	3.7	4.7	3.6	3.0	3.0	5.0	2.3	3.4	3.7	6.4	13.8
3. Yes	82.4	79.4	86.2	86.0	66.9	84.5	83.4	79.0	83.8	87.3	77.0	84.4	82.9	81.6	82.1	58.6
Item 10850 N(Wtd)	3603	1728	1764	2788	432	833	1104	1099	568	1941	1384	1273	800	430	988	29
A20I: Getting drunk in private																
1. No	66.9	69.3	65.4	69.7	54.3	75.5	68.9	59.5	65.1	68.6	65.8	52.8	71.0	70.1	81.8	72.4
2. Not sure	13.5	10.9	15.3	13.1	14.8	10.3	12.7	16.5	13.9	14.0	12.4	20.4	12.3	12.1	6.0	6.9
3. Yes	19.6	19.7	19.4	17.3	31.2	14.2	18.5	23.9	21.2	17.4	21.7	26.8	16.6	17.9	12.2	17.2
Item 10860 N(Wtd)	3604	1732	1762	2788	433	831	1105	1100	567	1940	1385	1275	800	431	988	29
A20J: Getting drunk in public places																
1. No	29.3	32.4	26.3	28.8	30.6	29.8	33.5	25.8	27.2	25.0	35.2	19.6	27.4	31.7	41.3	44.8
2. Not sure	21.6	21.6	21.5	23.6	12.2	21.4	25.5	18.7	19.6	22.0	21.0	18.0	25.6	23.8	22.7	13.8
3. Yes	49.1	46.0	52.2	47.6	57.2	48.8	41.0	55.4	53.1	53.1	43.8	62.4	46.9	44.4	36.0	41.4
Item 10870 N(Wtd)	3604	1733	1759	2787	435	832	1106	1099	567	1940	1382	1275	797	432	987	29

QUESTIONNAIRE FORM 4 1981	TOTAL	SEX		RACE		REGION				4YR COLLEGE PLANS		ILLICIT DRUG USE: LIFETIME				
		M	F	White	Black	NE	NC	S	W	Yes	No	None	Mari-juana Only	Few Pills	More Pills	Any Her-oin
Weighted No. of Cases:	3653	1751	1771	2804	441	846	1116	1117	574	1955	1393	1277	804	441	991	29
% of Weighted Total:	100.0	47.9	48.5	76.8	12.1	23.2	30.6	30.6	15.7	53.5	38.1	35.0	22.0	12.1	27.1	.8
A20K: Smoking tobacco in certain specified public places																
1. No	41.5	40.2	43.1	42.6	38.9	45.0	41.3	41.4	37.2	38.8	45.7	32.2	41.5	47.7	51.1	53.6
2. Not sure	15.5	15.2	15.8	14.3	19.1	11.7	17.2	16.5	15.7	13.7	17.2	18.5	16.8	13.0	11.1	14.3
3. Yes	43.0	44.6	41.0	43.0	41.8	43.3	41.4	42.1	47.1	47.5	37.1	49.3	41.8	39.4	37.7	28.6
Item 10760 N(Wtd)	3608	1732	1765	2789	435	832	1108	1102	567	1944	1384	1275	800	432	990	28
A21: In particular, there has been a great deal of public debate about whether marijuana use should be legal. Which of the following policies would you favor?																
1. Using marijuana should be entirely legal	23.2	27.6	18.7	23.5	20.5	25.3	25.9	17.0	26.5	19.9	27.2	6.6	19.4	21.6	46.9	55.2
2. It should be a minor violation --like a parking ticket-- but not a crime	29.3	26.7	32.1	28.7	32.5	36.0	26.0	25.3	33.8	29.7	28.3	19.2	37.2	36.0	33.7	27.6
3. It should be a crime	32.1	31.2	32.9	32.9	28.8	23.1	32.7	40.7	27.3	34.5	29.5	56.3	23.8	25.1	11.7	6.9
4. Don't know	15.4	14.7	16.4	14.8	18.2	15.5	15.2	17.1	12.6	15.9	14.9	17.9	19.4	17.4	7.7	13.8
Item 10880 N(Wtd)	3593	1726	1758	2782	434	830	1103	1095	565	1933	1381	1272	793	431	988	29
A22: If it were legal for people to USE marijuana, should it also be legal to SELL marijuana?																
1. No	27.7	27.7	28.1	27.3	28.1	23.2	26.7	31.8	28.3	28.3	27.6	42.0	24.7	22.0	13.8	17.2
2. Yes, but only to adults	48.6	50.1	47.1	49.7	46.5	51.4	48.1	45.8	51.2	49.4	48.3	34.4	53.9	51.4	62.4	41.4
3. Yes, to anyone	10.5	10.6	10.3	9.7	14.1	10.6	11.2	10.6	8.7	9.5	11.6	9.9	7.9	10.6	12.9	34.5
4. Don't know	13.3	11.8	14.6	13.4	11.3	14.9	14.0	11.9	12.0	12.9	12.6	13.6	13.7	15.7	10.9	6.9
Item 10890 N(Wtd)	3599	1727	1764	2783	434	832	1105	1097	565	1937	1382	1275	798	432	988	29
A23: If marijuana were legal to use and legally available, which of the following would you be most likely to do?																
1. Not use it, even if it were legal and available	55.2	51.3	59.1	54.6	60.5	47.1	54.1	62.3	55.3	59.5	50.4	88.3	52.4	44.6	21.0	10.3
2. Try it	6.0	5.8	6.2	5.8	6.4	6.7	7.3	5.2	3.9	6.7	5.1	6.0	7.5	7.6	4.0	3.4
3. Use it about as often as I do now	24.8	26.7	23.0	26.5	17.7	31.8	25.0	18.2	26.9	21.5	29.1	.8	24.4	31.2	53.3	41.4
4. Use it more often than I do now	4.6	5.7	3.3	4.9	3.7	5.5	4.7	3.9	4.8	3.9	5.2	.2	4.0	3.9	10.5	27.6
5. Use it less than I do now	2.5	3.2	1.8	2.2	2.3	2.3	2.9	1.8	3.4	2.0	2.8	.2	2.5	3.5	5.0	6.9
6. Don't know	6.9	7.2	6.6	6.1	9.4	6.6	6.0	8.7	5.8	6.4	7.2	4.4	9.1	9.0	6.3	6.9
Item 10900 N(Wtd)	3598	1727	1764	2782	435	830	1106	1096	566	1940	1380	1274	799	433	987	29

This section asks for your views and feelings about a number of different things.

	TOTAL	M	F	White	Black	NE	NC	S	W	Yes	No	None	Mari-juana Only	Few Pills	More Pills	Any Her-oin
D01: How satisfied are you with your life as a whole these days?																
1. Completely dissatisfied	2.3	2.5	2.1	2.0	4.1	3.0	1.8	1.9	3.0	1.9	3.0	2.3	1.4	3.4	1.5	24.0
2. Quite dissatisfied	10.0	9.2	10.7	9.9	8.0	10.2	9.7	10.1	10.2	10.5	9.4	11.1	8.6	8.8	10.4	4.0
3. Somewhat dissatisfied	12.5	12.6	12.4	11.7	15.7	12.8	12.7	12.1	12.2	11.8	13.1	9.1	14.6	13.7	14.5	-
4. Neither, or mixed feelings	13.3	13.3	13.3	12.9	16.5	11.5	14.3	13.7	13.4	11.9	15.5	9.7	14.0	12.7	17.1	16.0
5. Somewhat satisfied	23.1	25.4	20.8	23.2	20.6	23.3	22.3	24.1	22.8	23.7	21.7	22.4	23.1	24.9	23.3	36.0
6. Quite satisfied	32.3	31.1	33.5	33.7	27.2	31.7	35.2	30.2	31.4	33.3	31.1	36.9	30.9	31.0	29.2	12.0
7. Completely satisfied	6.6	5.9	7.2	6.6	8.0	7.4	4.2	8.0	7.1	6.8	6.4	8.5	7.4	5.6	3.8	4.0
Item 6840 N(Wtd)	3418	1648	1699	2712	389	756	1086	1036	539	1917	1354	1221	767	410	939	25
D02: FOR THOSE WHO HAVE A JOB: All things considered, how satisfied are you with your present job?																
1. Completely dissatisfied	4.5	4.4	4.6	3.9	6.9	5.8	3.4	4.7	4.4	3.1	6.8	4.3	4.3	2.1	5.7	-
2. Quite dissatisfied	11.0	12.2	9.7	10.9	9.8	10.7	10.9	10.7	12.1	10.3	12.3	8.8	11.8	9.1	14.1	-
3. Somewhat dissatisfied	14.1	13.6	14.6	13.6	18.5	14.5	14.0	13.5	14.8	14.4	13.9	12.6	12.4	18.2	14.2	35.7
4. Neither, or mixed feelings	14.7	15.1	14.7	14.3	17.3	14.8	13.1	16.2	15.1	14.9	14.7	14.9	13.0	14.0	16.0	14.3
5. Somewhat satisfied	25.0	26.0	23.7	26.1	20.2	22.6	29.2	23.1	23.6	25.5	23.2	25.5	24.3	24.9	25.7	28.6
6. Quite satisfied	23.7	21.9	25.8	23.7	22.0	25.0	22.7	24.3	23.3	24.9	21.7	24.4	27.0	26.0	20.4	14.3
7. Completely satisfied	6.8	6.9	6.9	7.4	4.6	6.8	6.5	7.4	6.8	6.8	7.1	9.6	7.1	5.6	4.1	7.1
Item 10910 N(Wtd) ★	2308	1160	1097	1938	173	532	758	653	365	1285	920	783	507	285	682	14

★=excludes respondents for whom question was inappropriate.

QUESTIONNAIRE FORM 4 1981	TOTAL	SEX		RACE		REGION				4YR COLLEGE PLANS		ILLICIT DRUG USE: LIFETIME				
		M	F	White	Black	NE	NC	S	W	Yes	No	None	Marijuana Only	Few Pills	More Pills	Any Heroin
Weighted No. of Cases:	3653	1751	1771	2804	441	846	1116	1117	574	1955	1393	1277	804	441	991	29
% of Weighted Total:	100.0	47.9	48.5	76.8	12.1	23.2	30.6	30.6	15.7	53.5	38.1	35.0	22.0	12.1	27.1	.8
D03: People have different opinions about world problems. How much do you agree or disagree with each of the following statements?																
D03A: I feel that I can do very little to change the way the world is today																
1. Disagree	10.2	11.0	9.5	9.0	15.9	11.0	8.2	11.6	10.2	10.2	10.0	11.8	9.9	8.0	8.8	17.4
2. Mostly disagree	18.5	16.8	20.1	19.2	16.7	18.2	18.6	18.8	18.2	22.2	13.5	20.4	16.7	17.3	19.4	13.0
3. Neither	21.5	20.9	21.8	22.0	16.9	22.2	20.0	21.1	24.1	20.8	23.2	21.4	23.1	23.3	18.3	34.8
4. Mostly agree	32.9	33.5	32.7	34.2	25.7	30.2	37.6	30.6	31.8	33.4	31.4	30.8	34.1	36.6	34.5	8.7
5. Agree	16.9	17.7	15.9	15.6	25.1	18.3	15.7	17.7	15.6	13.4	21.9	15.8	16.2	15.0	19.0	30.4
Item 10920 N(Wtd)	3351	1610	1668	2667	378	726	1071	1022	532	1889	1313	1203	754	399	917	23
D03B: It does little good to clean up air and water pollution because this society will not last long enough for it to matter																
1. Disagree	43.3	42.7	44.2	45.8	32.2	49.2	40.9	40.6	45.3	48.4	36.0	43.6	43.8	42.4	44.0	30.4
2. Mostly disagree	27.1	27.0	27.1	28.9	18.1	25.3	29.4	24.6	29.6	28.0	26.0	28.5	29.6	24.3	25.2	17.4
3. Neither	14.4	14.6	14.6	13.4	18.4	12.6	16.3	14.5	13.0	11.4	18.7	12.9	11.9	19.3	16.1	34.8
4. Mostly agree	8.8	9.2	7.6	7.4	16.2	7.1	8.3	11.3	7.5	7.4	10.3	8.2	8.6	8.5	9.4	-
5. Agree	6.4	6.4	6.4	4.4	15.4	5.8	5.1	8.9	4.5	4.8	8.9	6.8	6.0	5.5	5.2	21.7
Item 10930 N(Wtd)	3343	1604	1668	2660	376	723	1071	1020	530	1890	1307	1202	754	399	915	23
D03C: When things get tough enough, we'll put our minds to it and find a technological solution																
1. Disagree	5.9	5.4	6.2	5.4	6.7	6.1	6.6	5.2	4.9	4.4	7.5	5.4	5.1	6.8	6.3	4.3
2. Mostly disagree	9.6	9.0	10.2	10.0	7.0	10.8	10.5	7.3	11.0	10.0	9.0	8.9	8.8	8.8	11.6	17.4
3. Neither	19.7	17.4	22.4	19.1	19.6	16.5	19.0	20.8	23.6	17.2	23.7	18.7	18.9	21.4	20.7	39.1
4. Mostly agree	40.4	41.2	39.8	42.3	31.7	41.5	43.2	37.4	38.8	43.8	35.6	40.0	43.4	41.1	38.8	26.1
5. Agree	24.4	27.1	21.5	23.2	34.7	25.1	20.7	29.2	21.9	24.7	24.2	27.0	23.7	22.2	22.7	17.4
Item 10940 N(Wtd)	3328	1598	1658	2649	372	721	1069	1012	526	1887	1296	1195	746	397	915	23
D03D: When I think about all the terrible things that have been happening, it is hard for me to hold out much hope for the world																
1. Disagree	17.6	19.0	16.3	18.1	16.9	21.6	17.0	16.8	15.0	19.5	15.3	19.9	16.4	17.1	15.9	13.0
2. Mostly disagree	25.8	27.1	24.9	28.1	13.1	26.1	27.7	23.4	26.6	30.4	20.4	27.5	25.7	25.7	24.4	17.4
3. Neither	23.2	23.7	22.7	23.5	22.0	20.9	24.3	22.5	25.4	20.3	27.3	20.9	23.9	25.9	23.6	43.5
4. Mostly agree	23.4	21.5	25.1	22.1	29.5	22.3	22.1	24.8	25.2	22.6	24.0	22.5	22.9	21.9	26.6	4.3
5. Agree	10.0	8.7	10.9	8.1	18.5	9.2	8.9	12.7	7.8	7.3	13.1	9.2	11.1	9.3	9.7	21.7
Item 10950 N(Wtd)	3322	1597	1655	2643	373	719	1062	1014	527	1880	1296	1196	746	397	911	23
D03E: I often wonder if there is any real purpose to my life in light of the world situation																
1. Disagree	27.3	26.5	28.4	28.7	21.0	29.9	25.8	25.1	31.0	31.9	21.1	32.7	24.5	25.7	24.1	13.0
2. Mostly disagree	20.6	20.4	21.1	22.0	14.2	23.1	21.9	18.3	18.9	22.8	17.1	22.5	20.7	20.2	19.0	21.7
3. Neither	25.4	25.1	25.3	26.0	20.7	25.5	25.8	25.0	25.3	21.3	31.8	21.4	26.1	29.0	28.0	34.8
4. Mostly agree	18.8	19.7	17.8	17.1	26.6	15.0	19.2	21.0	18.9	18.0	19.7	15.7	20.8	19.1	20.8	4.3
5. Agree	7.9	8.3	7.5	6.1	17.5	6.5	7.3	10.7	5.9	6.1	10.3	7.7	7.9	6.3	8.2	26.1
Item 10960 N(Wtd)	3312	1595	1648	2636	372	713	1065	1009	525	1875	1294	1193	744	397	905	23
D03F: My guess is that this country will be caught up in a major world upheaval in the next 10 years																
1. Disagree	9.2	10.3	8.1	9.2	11.5	9.8	9.1	10.4	5.9	9.3	8.9	11.4	8.6	7.1	7.7	4.3
2. Mostly disagree	14.6	16.0	13.3	16.0	9.8	18.8	14.2	11.8	15.3	15.3	14.1	13.2	17.7	11.6	16.0	13.0
3. Neither	30.6	27.5	33.9	30.3	27.6	32.5	31.4	27.4	32.3	30.6	30.7	31.6	29.2	34.3	28.7	43.5
4. Mostly agree	29.8	29.3	29.7	29.9	27.3	25.7	32.1	30.2	29.6	30.5	28.9	28.5	27.8	30.5	32.7	21.7
5. Agree	15.9	16.9	15.1	14.6	23.5	13.3	13.1	20.0	17.0	14.4	17.4	15.2	16.7	16.4	14.7	17.4
Item 10970 N(Wtd)	3305	1595	1641	2634	366	713	1064	1005	523	1875	1288	1188	742	397	905	23

QUESTIONNAIRE FORM 4 1981	TOTAL	SEX		RACE		REGION				4YR COLLEGE PLANS		ILLICIT DRUG USE: LIFETIME				
		M	F	White	Black	NE	NC	S	W	Yes	No	None	Mari- juana Only	Few Pills	More Pills	Any Her- oin
Weighted No. of Cases:	3653	1751	1771	2804	441	846	1116	1117	574	1955	1393	1277	804	441	991	29
% of Weighted Total:	100.0	47.9	48.5	76.8	12.1	23.2	30.6	30.6	15.7	53.5	38.1	35.0	22.0	12.1	27.1	.8

D03G: Nuclear or biological annihilation will probably be the fate of all mankind, within my lifetime

1. Disagree	15.7	18.5	13.2	17.0	9.5	17.9	14.9	15.6	14.6	18.7	11.0	18.7	15.2	14.9	13.3	-
2. Mostly disagree	17.6	19.6	15.4	19.6	9.3	22.2	18.4	14.3	15.8	20.5	14.0	18.3	19.3	13.4	17.6	21.7
3. Neither	35.1	29.5	40.5	35.0	34.1	33.5	36.8	33.7	36.2	33.3	37.7	34.8	35.7	39.1	33.6	34.8
4. Mostly agree	19.1	18.1	20.0	17.8	26.2	15.1	18.3	22.1	20.0	16.5	22.6	18.3	15.5	22.5	21.3	13.0
5. Agree	12.6	14.3	10.8	10.7	21.0	11.2	11.5	14.2	13.3	11.0	14.8	9.9	14.4	9.8	14.1	26.1
Item 10980 N(Wtd)	3291	1589	1633	2623	367	708	1059	1004	520	1869	1281	1180	737	396	905	23

D03H: The human race has come through tough times before, and will do so again

1. Disagree	3.9	4.7	3.1	3.1	5.7	3.1	4.0	4.0	4.0	2.9	5.1	2.7	2.8	5.3	5.1	17.4
2. Mostly disagree	7.0	7.1	6.9	6.4	10.5	5.7	6.5	8.0	8.0	6.8	7.2	6.4	7.3	5.6	7.3	8.7
3. Neither	19.5	18.6	20.7	18.9	18.9	17.7	19.0	19.1	23.6	18.0	21.8	18.6	19.2	24.0	18.5	21.7
4. Mostly agree	37.7	36.8	38.8	39.7	30.0	38.3	40.4	34.9	37.0	38.7	36.2	38.4	38.1	36.4	38.0	26.1
5. Agree	31.9	32.8	30.6	32.0	34.9	35.2	30.0	34.0	27.2	33.5	29.7	33.8	32.6	28.8	31.0	30.4
Item 10990 N(Wtd)	3295	1590	1635	2625	370	705	1062	1006	522	1870	1281	1182	740	396	906	23

The next questions are about alcohol use-- this time asking separately about beer, wine, and hard liquor.

D04: On how many occasions (if any) have you had beer to drink...

D04A: ...in your lifetime?

1. 0 occasions	11.2	8.5	14.1	9.1	23.2	6.7	8.2	16.5	13.8	12.0	10.2	26.4	3.1	5.9	1.0	9.1
2. 1-2	9.8	7.2	12.4	8.4	19.5	7.1	8.5	12.9	10.2	10.1	9.2	18.5	6.8	6.2	2.4	9.1
3. 3-5	7.6	5.3	9.7	6.9	12.4	6.4	7.7	7.6	8.8	7.7	7.3	11.7	7.7	7.5	2.7	-
4. 6-9	7.7	6.5	8.5	7.1	10.2	7.3	7.3	9.1	6.3	7.6	7.9	9.6	10.2	5.7	3.9	-
5. 10-19	10.3	9.4	10.9	10.5	10.5	12.7	9.8	9.8	8.6	11.6	8.8	11.2	13.1	14.0	5.6	4.5
6. 20-39	10.9	10.6	11.3	11.3	8.0	12.4	11.2	8.5	12.6	11.4	10.5	7.2	16.4	13.2	10.4	-
7. 40 or more	42.6	52.5	32.9	46.7	15.8	47.6	47.1	35.6	39.9	39.5	46.1	15.3	42.6	47.5	74.0	77.3
Item 11000 N(Wtd)	3199	1541	1592	2593	323	702	1036	951	509	1818	1244	1117	732	387	903	22

D04B: ...during the last 12 months?

1. 0 occasions	22.0	16.0	28.2	18.6	43.7	16.4	18.1	27.9	26.9	23.1	20.3	44.3	11.7	12.6	6.8	9.1
2. 1-2	11.2	9.2	13.3	10.2	16.8	8.9	10.4	14.1	10.7	10.5	12.4	16.0	12.0	12.0	4.9	9.1
3. 3-5	10.3	8.9	11.2	9.8	14.6	11.3	11.2	9.9	8.1	11.1	9.4	12.1	14.3	10.5	5.2	4.5
4. 6-9	8.8	7.3	10.3	9.2	7.3	8.5	9.8	8.7	7.9	9.7	7.8	7.9	11.8	11.3	6.8	4.5
5. 10-19	13.3	15.2	11.5	14.6	4.7	15.8	14.5	9.4	14.7	13.6	13.3	8.5	19.7	16.2	12.9	4.5
6. 20-39	11.7	12.4	11.0	12.8	6.3	11.0	12.5	11.6	11.1	10.6	12.4	4.3	12.9	16.2	17.5	18.2
7. 40 or more	22.7	31.0	14.3	24.8	6.6	28.3	23.7	18.6	20.8	21.4	24.3	6.8	18.7	21.5	45.9	54.5
Item 11010 N(Wtd)	3168	1528	1577	2573	316	697	1023	943	505	1803	1231	1104	727	382	897	22

D04C: ...during the last 30 days?

1. 0 occasions	37.3	28.6	46.1	33.2	62.1	32.9	32.6	42.5	43.2	39.0	35.0	63.5	28.6	30.3	15.1	13.6
2. 1-2	17.4	16.9	17.4	17.0	18.6	16.0	18.3	17.4	17.0	18.3	16.4	18.0	21.6	19.1	12.7	18.2
3. 3-5	15.4	16.2	14.7	17.1	6.0	15.2	17.6	13.5	14.5	16.2	14.9	8.6	21.6	20.4	16.8	4.5
4. 6-9	12.8	15.4	10.0	14.0	4.7	12.4	14.7	11.3	12.1	12.4	12.9	5.6	15.0	14.6	19.3	13.6
5. 10-19	11.2	13.9	8.4	12.1	6.0	14.2	9.7	10.8	10.9	9.7	12.7	2.9	10.0	9.4	22.4	31.8
6. 20-39	3.6	5.1	2.2	4.1	.6	5.9	4.0	2.6	1.6	2.7	4.8	.6	2.1	3.9	8.1	9.1
7. 40 or more	2.4	3.9	1.1	2.4	1.6	3.4	3.0	1.9	.8	1.8	3.4	.6	1.1	2.3	5.4	18.2
Item 11020 N(Wtd)	3168	1528	1576	2572	317	699	1026	938	505	1801	1231	1100	727	383	900	22

D05: Think back over the LAST TWO WEEKS. How many times have you had five or more 12-ounce cans of beer (or the equivalent) in a row?

1. None	62.0	50.6	73.4	58.9	82.3	57.9	56.4	66.1	71.5	65.8	57.2	84.8	58.6	61.7	37.6	27.3
2. Once	10.3	12.1	8.5	11.2	5.4	9.6	11.1	11.2	8.2	10.5	10.6	6.7	14.0	11.7	11.3	4.5
3. Twice	9.7	11.2	8.1	10.5	5.4	9.6	11.9	8.5	7.4	8.5	11.0	3.7	13.0	7.4	15.6	4.5
4. Three to five times	11.4	16.1	6.6	12.5	3.5	12.9	13.5	9.2	9.0	10.5	11.8	3.4	10.3	14.1	20.6	31.8
5. Six to nine times	4.4	6.6	2.4	4.9	1.6	7.0	4.9	3.0	2.6	3.2	6.3	.8	2.5	4.0	10.5	4.5
6. Ten or more times	2.1	3.3	.8	2.0	1.9	2.9	2.2	2.0	1.2	1.4	3.3	.5	1.7	1.1	4.4	27.3
Item 11030 N(Wtd)	3130	1497	1570	2542	317	689	1013	927	502	1795	1200	1095	715	376	884	22

QUESTIONNAIRE FORM 4 1981	TOTAL	SEX		RACE		REGION				4YR COLLEGE PLANS		ILLICIT DRUG USE: LIFETIME				
		M	F	White	Black	NE	NC	S	W	Yes	No	None	Marijuana Only	Few Pills	More Pills	Any Heroin
Weighted No. of Cases:	3653	1751	1771	2804	441	846	1116	1117	574	1955	1393	1277	804	441	991	29
% of Weighted Total:	100.0	47.9	48.5	76.8	12.1	23.2	30.6	30.6	15.7	53.5	38.1	35.0	22.0	12.1	27.1	.8

D06: On how many occasions (if any) have you had wine to drink...

D06A: ...in your lifetime?

1. 0 occasions	13.6	13.6	13.2	10.8	26.2	8.5	9.8	20.0	16.5	12.5	15.0	28.0	5.4	7.3	3.3	23.8
2. 1-2	16.7	15.9	17.3	16.4	20.8	13.2	14.7	22.2	15.5	16.2	17.9	24.8	14.8	16.5	8.1	-
3. 3-5	16.7	18.0	15.5	16.5	18.0	13.7	17.4	18.3	16.3	16.0	17.7	16.7	19.5	18.1	14.2	-
4. 6-9	13.9	14.1	13.8	14.8	13.2	12.9	15.4	13.4	13.5	13.7	14.4	11.2	19.2	15.0	13.3	9.5
5. 10-19	15.6	16.3	15.2	16.4	11.0	18.4	17.1	13.2	13.5	16.6	13.8	10.3	16.6	18.1	21.3	4.8
6. 20-39	12.1	10.2	13.9	13.0	6.6	16.8	14.0	6.4	12.3	13.6	10.2	5.9	14.9	13.9	16.7	23.8
7. 40 or more	11.4	11.7	11.2	12.1	4.1	16.6	11.7	6.7	12.5	11.4	11.1	3.1	9.7	10.8	22.9	38.1
Item 11040 N(Wtd)	3173	1524	1582	2576	317	692	1030	947	503	1810	1230	1121	718	381	896	21

D06B: ...during the last 12 months?

1. 0 occasions	31.3	32.3	30.1	27.6	50.8	21.9	25.9	42.0	35.3	29.0	35.1	48.1	24.2	25.7	17.7	23.8
2. 1-2	24.8	25.5	24.0	25.1	26.2	19.1	27.7	26.3	24.2	25.3	24.0	26.3	27.7	26.5	20.3	9.5
3. 3-5	15.8	16.9	15.1	16.5	12.6	17.5	17.9	14.1	12.4	15.7	16.2	12.9	19.6	17.2	15.9	14.3
4. 6-9	12.3	11.9	12.7	13.7	5.0	16.9	13.8	7.9	11.0	13.3	10.4	8.0	14.0	13.8	15.8	14.3
5. 10-19	9.4	8.2	10.6	10.2	2.8	13.1	9.0	6.6	10.4	9.9	8.6	3.3	9.0	11.7	16.9	4.8
6. 20-39	3.3	2.2	4.5	3.7	.9	6.6	2.8	1.5	3.2	3.7	2.8	.6	4.1	3.2	5.9	4.8
7. 40 or more	3.0	3.0	3.1	3.2	1.6	4.8	2.9	1.6	3.6	3.2	2.9	.6	1.4	2.1	7.4	28.6
Item 11050 N(Wtd)	3152	1512	1573	2557	317	685	1030	937	499	1801	1220	1105	723	377	892	21

D06C: ...during the last 30 days?

1. 0 occasions	63.4	64.7	61.8	60.3	77.7	48.4	61.5	73.7	68.3	60.9	67.1	79.0	59.4	57.7	49.4	50.0
2. 1-2	21.5	23.0	20.4	23.6	14.3	27.9	24.2	16.3	17.0	23.5	18.8	16.1	23.6	24.1	26.3	4.5
3. 3-5	9.3	7.3	11.1	9.9	4.5	13.9	9.4	6.3	8.2	9.4	8.5	3.2	10.9	12.2	14.3	4.5
4. 6-9	3.5	3.1	3.8	3.8	1.3	6.1	2.8	2.3	3.4	3.9	3.0	1.2	3.8	4.2	5.6	9.1
5. 10-19	1.7	.9	2.5	1.8	1.3	3.1	1.4	1.0	1.6	1.5	1.9	.4	1.8	1.3	3.3	9.1
6. 20-39	.3	.2	.4	.3	-	-	.2	-	1.4	.3	.2	.1	.1	.3	.8	-
7. 40 or more	.4	.7	.1	.3	1.0	.4	.6	.4	-	.4	.4	.2	.4	-	.4	18.2
Item 11060 N(Wtd)	3145	1506	1572	2555	314	684	1022	938	501	1797	1217	1104	717	378	891	22

D07: Think back over the LAST TWO WEEKS. How many times have you had five or more 4-ounce glasses of wine in a row (or the equivalent, which is about three-fourths of a bottle)?

1. None	87.1	87.8	86.5	86.5	90.8	82.2	86.1	90.1	90.2	87.4	86.8	95.3	88.0	81.3	79.0	60.0
2. Once	6.7	6.2	7.2	7.1	4.4	8.8	6.4	5.5	6.4	6.8	6.5	3.1	6.3	8.8	11.0	-
3. Twice	3.6	3.8	3.4	3.7	2.9	5.8	4.0	2.4	2.2	3.4	3.8	1.3	2.8	6.9	5.6	5.0
4. Three to five times	1.7	1.1	2.3	1.9	.6	1.9	2.5	1.3	.8	1.8	1.5	.3	1.8	2.9	2.8	15.0
5. Six to nine times	.5	.5	.5	.5	.3	1.0	.6	.2	.2	.4	.7	.1	.6	-	1.3	-
6. Ten or more times	.4	.7	.2	.3	1.0	.3	.4	.5	.2	.2	.8	-	.7	-	.5	20.0
Item 11070 N(Wtd)	3118	1489	1567	2532	315	684	1008	927	499	1796	1190	1101	716	375	870	20

These next questions are about hard liquor. (Hard liquor includes whiskey, Scotch, bourbon, gin, vodka, rum, etc., or mixed drinks made with liquor.)

D08: On how many occasions (if any) have you had liquor to drink...

D08A: ...in your lifetime?

1. 0 occasions	17.5	16.1	18.9	13.7	39.3	12.1	14.9	23.8	18.5	18.1	16.8	38.4	8.5	6.3	2.5	14.3
2. 1-2	11.6	11.2	12.0	10.7	20.4	10.1	11.0	13.0	12.2	12.7	9.7	18.1	12.1	12.3	2.9	4.8
3. 3-5	14.3	14.8	13.6	14.8	13.3	15.0	13.9	14.8	13.3	15.3	13.0	17.2	17.2	13.4	8.9	-
4. 6-9	12.5	11.8	12.9	13.1	8.4	12.7	13.0	11.8	12.4	12.8	12.0	8.5	18.2	17.6	10.9	-
5. 10-19	12.8	12.5	13.2	13.7	5.0	13.9	15.0	11.3	9.4	13.0	12.6	7.7	16.6	16.8	14.7	-
6. 20-39	12.8	12.5	13.0	13.8	6.8	13.9	13.3	10.9	14.3	12.2	13.9	5.2	14.3	20.2	18.7	9.5
7. 40 or more	18.5	21.1	16.2	20.1	6.5	22.5	18.8	14.5	20.1	16.0	22.1	4.9	12.9	13.1	41.5	71.4
Item 11080 N(Wtd)	3169	1530	1572	2568	323	693	1031	947	498	1808	1226	1116	719	381	895	21

QUESTIONNAIRE FORM 4 1981	TOTAL	SEX		RACE		REGION				4YR COLLEGE PLANS		ILLICIT DRUG USE: LIFETIME				
		M	F	White	Black	NE	NC	S	W	Yes	No	None	Marijuana Only	Few Pills	More Pills	Any Heroin
Weighted No. of Cases:	3653	1751	1771	2804	441	846	1116	1117	574	1955	1393	1277	804	441	991	29
% of Weighted Total:	100.0	47.9	48.5	76.8	12.1	23.2	30.6	30.6	15.7	53.5	38.1	35.0	22.0	12.1	27.1	.8

D08B: ...during the last 12 months?

	TOTAL	M	F	White	Black	NE	NC	S	W	Yes	No	None	Marijuana Only	Few Pills	More Pills	Any Heroin
1. 0 occasions	29.4	28.2	30.6	24.9	59.1	21.6	26.1	36.6	33.1	29.7	28.6	53.5	22.2	17.8	9.1	19.0
2. 1-2	19.6	19.5	19.5	20.3	17.3	21.6	20.9	18.6	16.3	21.7	16.5	22.3	23.6	21.5	12.9	4.8
3. 3-5	14.1	14.4	13.7	14.6	11.0	13.6	14.7	14.6	12.9	13.5	15.6	10.6	17.3	22.3	12.9	-
4. 6-9	11.6	12.1	11.1	12.6	5.7	11.4	11.7	12.8	9.8	12.6	10.2	6.6	14.6	13.8	14.8	9.5
5. 10-19	12.3	12.2	12.6	13.3	4.1	15.7	13.2	8.6	12.7	11.2	13.6	4.3	13.6	11.4	21.5	23.8
6. 20-39	7.2	6.6	7.9	8.1	1.3	8.2	7.2	5.1	9.8	6.5	8.7	1.5	5.5	8.5	15.3	9.5
7. 40 or more	5.8	7.0	4.5	6.3	1.6	8.3	6.1	3.8	5.4	4.8	6.8	1.1	3.2	4.3	13.6	38.1
Item 11090 N(Wtd)	3148	1523	1558	2555	318	686	1025	939	498	1795	1223	1109	712	376	894	21

D08C: ...during the last 30 days?

	TOTAL	M	F	White	Black	NE	NC	S	W	Yes	No	None	Marijuana Only	Few Pills	More Pills	Any Heroin
1. 0 occasions	55.4	54.7	55.6	52.4	77.9	50.6	52.8	61.2	56.7	57.0	53.0	78.8	52.8	48.8	31.5	22.7
2. 1-2	22.1	23.3	21.2	23.2	14.8	22.4	23.2	21.0	21.5	22.5	21.9	13.8	25.6	27.3	27.6	9.1
3. 3-5	11.5	11.9	11.2	12.8	2.5	12.2	12.4	10.0	11.7	11.5	11.6	4.3	12.8	13.3	18.7	27.3
4. 6-9	5.3	4.7	6.1	5.7	2.2	6.5	5.6	4.3	5.4	4.5	6.2	1.5	5.5	4.8	10.2	18.2
5. 10-19	4.1	3.7	4.5	4.4	1.3	6.4	4.2	2.9	3.0	3.3	5.5	1.1	2.2	5.3	8.8	4.5
6. 20-39	.9	.6	1.0	.8	.3	1.5	1.0	.1	1.2	.8	.8	.1	.7	.8	1.9	-
7. 40 or more	.7	1.0	.4	.6	.9	.6	.9	.6	.6	.4	1.0	.3	.4	-	1.3	18.2
Item 11100 N(Wtd)	3147	1517	1564	2555	317	688	1024	938	497	1798	1220	1106	712	377	895	22

D09: Think back over the LAST TWO WEEKS. How many times have you had five or more mixed drinks or shot-glasses of hard liquor in a row?

	TOTAL	M	F	White	Black	NE	NC	S	W	Yes	No	None	Marijuana Only	Few Pills	More Pills	Any Heroin
1. None	78.7	77.0	80.3	77.5	90.9	75.1	77.1	82.0	80.8	82.0	73.7	92.6	82.0	74.8	61.4	28.6
2. Once	8.1	9.0	7.4	8.8	2.2	9.7	8.6	6.0	8.8	7.8	8.6	2.9	9.2	13.7	11.4	-
3. Twice	6.5	6.7	6.2	7.0	2.8	7.2	6.9	6.4	4.8	5.0	8.7	2.8	3.7	6.4	12.6	33.3
4. Three to five times	4.4	4.9	3.9	4.5	2.5	5.8	3.9	4.1	4.0	3.6	5.7	1.3	3.7	4.0	9.1	14.3
5. Six to nine times	1.2	1.2	1.2	1.2	.9	1.0	2.0	.8	.8	.7	2.1	.5	.7	.3	2.9	9.5
6. Ten or more times	1.1	1.2	.9	1.0	.9	1.3	1.4	.8	.8	.8	1.4	.1	.9	.8	2.4	9.5
Item 11110 N(Wtd)	3063	1470	1537	2487	318	670	996	917	480	1774	1162	1090	683	373	858	21

These next questions ask for your opinions about the military services in the United States.

E01: To what extent do you think the following opportunities are available to people who work in the military services?

E01A: A chance to get ahead

	TOTAL	M	F	White	Black	NE	NC	S	W	Yes	No	None	Marijuana Only	Few Pills	More Pills	Any Heroin
1. To a very little extent	8.3	10.7	5.8	8.1	6.4	9.6	9.0	7.1	7.8	7.6	9.1	8.0	8.0	8.2	8.5	13.0
2. To a little extent	12.5	15.5	9.6	13.1	10.2	11.1	13.6	10.6	15.6	12.4	12.8	13.1	10.8	13.9	12.6	4.3
3. To some extent	45.5	42.9	48.0	47.3	35.6	47.1	48.6	42.3	43.1	48.0	42.7	43.5	46.9	47.9	47.0	52.2
4. To a great extent	22.5	20.6	24.9	21.7	27.6	21.7	19.6	25.5	24.0	21.7	23.8	23.7	22.5	21.1	21.4	17.4
5. To a very great extent	11.1	10.3	11.8	9.7	20.2	10.4	9.2	14.4	9.4	10.3	11.5	11.6	11.8	8.8	10.4	17.4
Item 11120 N(Wtd)	3193	1546	1580	2542	362	665	1038	990	501	1824	1239	1171	712	388	849	23

E01B: A chance to get more education

	TOTAL	M	F	White	Black	NE	NC	S	W	Yes	No	None	Marijuana Only	Few Pills	More Pills	Any Heroin
1. To a very little extent	4.1	5.1	3.3	3.5	7.2	4.5	3.4	4.6	4.4	3.8	4.3	4.2	4.6	3.9	3.3	4.3
2. To a little extent	8.1	10.3	5.9	8.9	3.0	9.2	10.5	5.0	7.8	8.5	7.4	8.0	5.6	9.0	10.0	4.3
3. To some extent	32.3	33.2	31.1	32.6	28.1	32.0	33.3	30.9	33.3	34.9	29.6	33.7	31.3	31.8	31.6	26.1
4. To a great extent	36.4	35.0	38.2	38.1	28.9	38.3	36.1	35.1	37.1	35.3	38.5	35.8	37.0	38.0	36.8	43.5
5. To a very great extent	19.1	16.5	21.6	16.9	32.8	16.1	16.6	24.4	17.4	17.5	20.3	18.3	21.3	17.3	18.2	17.4
Item 11130 N(Wtd)	3190	1543	1578	2537	363	666	1035	989	499	1821	1235	1170	713	387	847	23

E01C: A chance to advance to a more responsible position

	TOTAL	M	F	White	Black	NE	NC	S	W	Yes	No	None	Marijuana Only	Few Pills	More Pills	Any Heroin
1. To a very little extent	4.8	6.4	3.3	4.5	5.8	5.7	4.7	4.6	4.2	4.0	5.9	4.9	4.4	2.8	5.6	-
2. To a little extent	8.0	9.0	7.1	8.7	4.7	7.6	9.9	6.0	8.6	7.6	8.7	8.3	5.9	9.3	9.0	4.3
3. To some extent	32.8	35.2	29.9	34.2	25.4	35.5	34.1	29.5	32.8	33.8	31.4	32.0	34.8	31.3	33.3	26.1
4. To a great extent	36.6	33.8	39.7	36.4	37.3	34.9	35.4	38.0	38.6	37.8	35.3	37.4	36.0	39.6	34.3	52.2
5. To a very great extent	17.8	15.5	20.0	16.2	27.1	16.2	15.8	21.9	15.6	16.8	18.7	17.4	18.8	16.6	17.9	17.4
Item 11140 N(Wtd)	3177	1537	1573	2527	362	662	1029	985	500	1814	1231	1170	706	386	842	23

QUESTIONNAIRE FORM 4 1981	TOTAL	SEX		RACE		REGION				4YR COLLEGE PLANS		ILLICIT DRUG USE: LIFETIME				
		M	F	White	Black	NE	NC	S	W	Yes	No	None	Mari- juana Only	Few Pills	More Pills	Any Her- oin
Weighted No. of Cases:	3653	1751	1771	2804	441	846	1116	1117	574	1955	1393	1277	804	441	991	29
% of Weighted Total:	100.0	47.9	48.5	76.8	12.1	23.2	30.6	30.6	15.7	53.5	38.1	35.0	22.0	12.1	27.1	.8

E01D: A chance to have a personally more fulfilling job

1. To a very little extent	8.2	9.6	7.1	8.5	6.2	9.7	7.4	8.1	8.5	8.3	8.1	7.9	7.9	8.3	8.6	4.3
2. To a little extent	12.7	14.0	11.2	13.7	7.0	12.0	14.7	9.8	14.9	13.1	12.0	13.6	8.9	16.1	13.2	13.0
3. To some extent	37.2	37.9	36.4	38.7	27.5	37.7	39.0	34.8	37.5	38.9	35.2	37.5	38.2	33.2	38.2	26.1
4. To a great extent	28.5	27.0	30.1	28.2	31.4	29.5	27.9	29.3	26.6	27.4	30.2	26.4	29.5	31.2	29.5	34.8
5. To a very great extent	13.4	11.6	15.3	10.9	27.7	11.2	11.1	18.0	12.3	12.3	14.6	14.7	15.5	11.2	10.5	21.7
Item 11150 N(Wtd)	3168	1532	1568	2524	357	661	1031	980	496	1811	1229	1165	705	385	840	23

E01E: A chance to get their ideas heard

1. To a very little extent	18.4	22.5	14.4	19.6	10.1	21.6	16.5	16.1	22.5	20.7	15.3	17.6	17.7	18.1	20.0	8.7
2. To a little extent	21.8	23.7	19.7	23.2	13.2	24.1	24.6	17.4	21.7	24.1	18.6	21.8	20.7	21.8	23.4	26.1
3. To some extent	36.3	33.6	39.1	36.9	33.2	34.5	37.7	36.0	36.3	35.5	37.7	36.7	35.7	36.7	36.5	30.4
4. To a great extent	15.6	13.2	18.1	14.0	25.4	12.4	14.5	19.9	13.3	12.8	19.5	16.0	15.7	16.5	14.4	17.4
5. To a very great extent	7.9	7.0	8.8	6.3	18.3	7.3	6.6	10.6	6.4	6.9	9.0	8.0	10.1	7.1	5.6	17.4
Item 11160 N(Wtd)	3149	1522	1562	2510	355	647	1031	974	498	1794	1226	1158	705	381	832	23

E02: To what extent is it likely that a person in the military can get things changed and set right if he is being treated unjustly by a superior?

1. To a very little extent	24.3	25.8	22.7	25.6	16.7	29.5	25.2	19.7	24.4	25.9	22.6	23.8	21.5	27.1	27.2	21.7
2. To a little extent	27.6	28.1	26.8	28.6	20.4	30.6	27.8	24.1	29.9	29.9	24.5	27.4	28.3	25.7	27.9	30.4
3. To some extent	34.0	31.2	36.9	33.8	34.0	30.2	33.7	36.7	34.1	33.0	35.1	33.3	35.7	31.1	34.6	30.4
4. To a great extent	11.0	10.8	11.2	9.4	21.8	7.1	10.1	15.1	9.8	8.6	13.9	11.5	11.1	13.4	8.5	21.7
5. To a very great extent	3.2	4.0	2.3	2.6	7.4	2.5	3.2	4.4	1.6	2.6	3.9	4.0	3.4	2.7	1.8	-
Item 11170 N(Wtd)	3119	1512	1539	2482	353	648	1015	965	492	1771	1219	1144	703	373	827	23

E03: To what extent do you think there is any discrimination against women who are in the armed services?

1. To a very little extent	14.4	15.1	13.9	13.9	15.7	11.2	14.4	17.0	13.6	12.3	17.7	16.4	13.6	13.2	12.7	17.4
2. To a little extent	25.3	25.0	25.5	25.9	25.5	23.8	26.3	24.9	25.8	25.7	24.8	26.8	22.6	26.4	25.0	26.1
3. To some extent	37.7	37.8	37.5	38.3	33.9	38.6	38.4	35.4	39.6	38.0	37.1	35.5	41.0	38.3	37.9	30.4
4. To a great extent	16.2	15.7	16.6	15.8	16.8	19.1	14.0	17.4	14.8	17.7	14.3	15.8	16.9	15.1	16.7	17.4
5. To a very great extent	6.4	6.3	6.5	6.0	7.8	7.2	7.0	5.5	5.9	6.3	6.2	5.4	5.8	7.3	7.7	8.7
Item 11180 N(Wtd)	3131	1513	1551	2493	357	650	1016	972	492	1788	1214	1151	705	371	833	23

E04: To what extent do you think there is any discrimination against black people who are in the armed services?

1. To a very little extent	32.6	33.7	31.7	34.2	23.6	27.6	30.9	37.2	33.5	29.7	37.0	34.7	31.6	32.9	31.4	17.4
2. To a little extent	27.1	28.6	25.9	26.7	25.6	29.3	24.6	25.8	31.7	28.7	24.8	25.5	28.5	26.1	28.3	34.8
3. To some extent	29.0	26.4	31.3	29.5	27.8	32.4	32.8	24.5	25.4	30.6	26.4	28.4	29.5	29.6	29.0	21.7
4. To a great extent	7.7	6.8	8.5	6.8	13.6	7.1	8.3	8.1	6.5	7.4	8.1	8.0	6.8	7.8	7.7	17.4
5. To a very great extent	3.6	4.5	2.5	2.7	9.7	3.5	3.4	4.3	2.6	3.6	3.7	3.4	3.6	3.5	3.6	4.3
Item 11190 N(Wtd)	3119	1518	1535	2488	352	648	1016	964	492	1779	1211	1141	702	371	834	23

E05: Do you personally feel that you would receive more just and fair treatment as a civilian or as a member of the military service?

1. Much more fair in the military service	6.9	5.5	4.4	17.8	5.8	4.9	9.6	2.9	4.8	8.3	7.1	5.7	7.3	4.2	18.2	
2. More fair in the military service	10.0	11.3	9.0	10.0	10.6	10.2	9.1	11.0	9.7	9.6	10.8	8.4	11.3	10.8	10.5	9.1
3. About the same	44.1	40.0	48.4	45.1	41.3	42.1	46.0	44.6	41.6	42.3	46.9	45.1	45.6	41.4	43.7	36.4
4. More fair as a civilian	15.4	18.4	12.1	16.3	6.6	14.5	18.0	12.0	17.9	16.3	14.0	14.4	14.8	16.2	16.4	9.1
5. Much more fair as a civilian	12.0	15.7	8.5	13.2	6.6	15.4	11.5	10.2	12.1	15.1	7.5	11.4	11.0	13.5	13.7	4.5
6. Question not appropriate for me	12.2	7.8	16.6	10.9	16.9	11.9	10.5	12.6	15.6	12.0	12.4	13.5	11.7	10.5	11.6	22.7
Item 11200 N(Wtd)	3127	1519	1540	2502	349	655	1020	967	486	1786	1212	1144	702	370	842	22

QUESTIONNAIRE FORM 4 1981	TOTAL	SEX		RACE		REGION				4YR COLLEGE PLANS		ILLICIT DRUG USE: LIFETIME				
		M	F	White	Black	NE	NC	S	W	Yes	No	None	Mari-juana Only	Few Pills	More Pills	Any Her-oin
Weighted No. of Cases:	*3653*	*1751*	*1771*	*2804*	*441*	*846*	*1116*	*1117*	*574*	*1955*	*1393*	*1277*	*804*	*441*	*991*	*29*
% of Weighted Total:	*100.0*	*47.9*	*48.5*	*76.8*	*12.1*	*23.2*	*30.6*	*30.6*	*15.7*	*53.5*	*38.1*	*35.0*	*22.0*	*12.1*	*27.1*	*.8*

E06: If YOU felt that it was necessary for the U.S. to fight in some future war, how likely is it that you would volunteer for military service in that war?

	TOTAL	M	F	White	Black	NE	NC	S	W	Yes	No	None	Mari-juana Only	Few Pills	More Pills	Any Her-oin
1. I'm sure that I would volunteer	12.3	19.3	5.1	12.6	7.7	12.4	13.9	12.1	9.5	11.2	14.4	11.9	12.9	12.9	11.6	27.3
2. I would very likely volunteer	7.8	11.0	5.0	8.2	7.4	8.1	5.4	9.7	8.9	7.9	7.9	8.1	7.6	6.9	7.4	4.5
3. I would probably volunteer	18.2	22.6	13.6	18.5	13.6	17.7	18.5	18.3	17.6	19.7	16.6	15.7	22.4	19.0	17.3	27.3
4. I would probably NOT volunteer	18.0	15.8	20.3	18.9	14.5	18.8	16.3	18.4	19.7	17.3	18.7	17.6	16.5	21.7	18.7	9.1
5. I would very likely NOT volunteer	8.3	5.7	10.8	8.4	8.5	7.4	8.3	8.9	8.3	9.5	6.5	8.7	7.2	10.7	8.0	-
6. I would definitely NOT volunteer	15.2	9.8	20.4	13.4	27.3	13.8	16.2	15.5	13.9	14.8	14.8	16.6	16.1	12.1	14.0	4.5
7. In my opinion, there is no such thing as a "necessary" war	20.2	15.6	24.7	19.9	21.3	21.7	21.4	17.1	22.0	19.6	21.3	21.3	17.0	16.8	23.0	22.7
Item 11220 N(Wtd)	*3112*	*1496*	*1549*	*2486*	*352*	*645*	*1018*	*967*	*482*	*1779*	*1205*	*1150*	*695*	*364*	*836*	*22*

E07: How closely do your ideas agree with your PARENTS' ideas about ...

Our ideas are...

E07A: What you should do with your life.

	TOTAL	M	F	White	Black	NE	NC	S	W	Yes	No	None	Mari-juana Only	Few Pills	More Pills	Any Her-oin
1. Very similar	27.9	25.6	30.4	28.2	30.7	29.9	26.8	28.6	26.4	31.7	22.2	35.8	27.5	21.9	21.6	30.4
2. Mostly similar	44.6	43.6	45.2	47.4	30.7	46.6	46.6	40.6	45.9	48.0	40.4	41.4	47.5	50.4	45.0	30.4
3. Mostly different	10.8	11.2	10.3	10.1	10.9	10.7	10.2	11.3	11.2	8.0	14.9	7.9	10.6	12.1	13.8	17.4
4. Very different	7.9	6.8	9.1	6.3	16.7	6.3	7.0	10.1	7.7	5.5	11.3	5.8	7.3	7.7	10.4	17.4
8. Don't know	8.7	12.7	4.9	8.0	11.2	6.5	9.3	9.5	8.9	6.9	11.2	9.2	7.1	7.9	9.1	8.7
Item 11230 N(Wtd)	*3190*	*1522*	*1598*	*2553*	*348*	*665*	*1036*	*981*	*508*	*1823*	*1230*	*1158*	*708*	*379*	*871*	*23*

E07B: What you do in your leisure time

	TOTAL	M	F	White	Black	NE	NC	S	W	Yes	No	None	Mari-juana Only	Few Pills	More Pills	Any Her-oin
1. Very similar	9.0	7.7	10.2	8.9	11.0	7.9	9.2	10.0	7.9	9.2	9.1	12.2	8.4	9.3	5.3	4.3
2. Mostly similar	35.8	31.9	40.2	37.6	27.5	40.0	35.3	33.2	36.4	39.7	30.4	42.6	37.6	33.3	27.0	26.1
3. Mostly different	27.5	30.7	24.5	28.6	18.2	26.9	28.7	24.7	30.8	27.0	28.5	24.1	26.0	32.8	31.0	39.1
4. Very different	21.3	22.1	19.9	19.6	31.2	20.1	21.5	23.9	17.6	19.4	23.1	14.5	21.1	18.5	31.6	30.4
8. Don't know	6.4	7.6	5.2	5.2	11.8	5.1	5.3	8.2	7.1	4.7	8.9	6.6	7.0	6.1	5.2	4.3
Item 11240 N(Wtd)	*3179*	*1519*	*1590*	*2548*	*346*	*662*	*1036*	*976*	*506*	*1821*	*1226*	*1155*	*705*	*378*	*868*	*23*

E07C: How you dress--what clothes you wear

	TOTAL	M	F	White	Black	NE	NC	S	W	Yes	No	None	Mari-juana Only	Few Pills	More Pills	Any Her-oin
1. Very similar	26.3	21.5	31.0	27.4	21.4	25.0	25.0	27.2	28.9	28.1	23.9	28.5	26.9	28.2	23.1	4.5
2. Mostly similar	43.9	43.6	44.2	46.1	33.4	47.8	46.9	39.4	41.6	47.1	39.5	45.0	43.5	43.6	43.2	31.8
3. Mostly different	14.7	17.8	11.9	14.0	16.7	14.7	14.4	14.8	15.2	14.5	14.8	12.1	14.9	14.9	17.6	31.8
4. Very different	10.6	10.6	10.3	8.9	19.9	9.2	10.6	12.6	8.1	7.1	15.5	10.0	10.3	9.0	11.7	27.3
8. Don't know	4.5	6.5	2.6	3.6	8.5	3.2	3.1	6.0	5.9	3.2	6.3	4.4	4.4	4.5	4.4	-
Item 11250 N(Wtd)	*3163*	*1504*	*1590*	*2539*	*341*	*661*	*1033*	*965*	*505*	*1815*	*1216*	*1153*	*699*	*376*	*865*	*22*

E07D: How you spend your money

	TOTAL	M	F	White	Black	NE	NC	S	W	Yes	No	None	Mari-juana Only	Few Pills	More Pills	Any Her-oin
1. Very similar	12.8	10.2	15.4	12.5	15.1	12.6	11.8	14.6	11.5	13.8	11.3	16.5	11.3	16.3	7.5	9.1
2. Mostly similar	34.4	33.1	36.0	36.1	24.9	32.9	35.8	32.6	36.6	38.2	29.0	40.5	33.2	32.4	28.5	18.2
3. Mostly different	25.8	26.6	24.8	26.7	22.2	26.9	26.2	23.4	27.9	26.0	25.8	21.3	29.9	27.8	28.0	18.2
4. Very different	22.9	24.5	21.2	21.0	31.7	24.0	23.4	24.7	16.8	18.4	28.9	17.4	21.1	20.6	32.1	59.1
8. Don't know	4.2	5.7	2.7	3.7	6.2	3.5	2.7	4.6	7.3	3.5	5.0	4.5	4.4	3.2	3.8	-
Item 11260 N(Wtd)	*3158*	*1509*	*1579*	*2536*	*338*	*657*	*1031*	*964*	*506*	*1806*	*1220*	*1151*	*698*	*374*	*863*	*22*

E07E: What things are O.K. to do when you are on a date

	TOTAL	M	F	White	Black	NE	NC	S	W	Yes	No	None	Mari-juana Only	Few Pills	More Pills	Any Her-oin
1. Very similar	17.1	14.4	20.1	16.3	22.4	12.6	15.5	20.8	19.2	18.4	15.4	23.9	15.1	13.6	11.8	18.2
2. Mostly similar	31.4	30.5	32.3	32.9	27.4	30.9	33.0	30.3	31.1	34.2	28.1	34.2	34.1	31.9	25.3	13.6
3. Mostly different	19.0	19.4	18.6	19.8	13.7	20.4	19.9	18.1	17.0	19.3	18.5	14.8	21.0	20.7	21.8	27.3
4. Very different	18.5	18.2	18.6	17.7	22.4	18.8	19.7	17.5	17.6	14.6	23.9	13.3	15.5	19.4	27.5	27.3
8. Don't know	14.0	17.6	10.5	13.3	14.0	17.3	11.9	13.4	15.2	13.7	14.2	13.8	14.1	14.6	13.6	13.6
Item 11270 N(Wtd)	*3161*	*1511*	*1581*	*2534*	*343*	*658*	*1027*	*972*	*505*	*1809*	*1219*	*1151*	*701*	*376*	*862*	*22*

QUESTIONNAIRE FORM 4 1981	TOTAL	SEX		RACE		REGION				4YR COLLEGE PLANS		ILLICIT DRUG USE: LIFETIME				
		M	F	White	Black	NE	NC	S	W	Yes	No	None	Marijuana Only	Few Pills	More Pills	Any Heroin
Weighted No. of Cases:	3653	1751	1771	2804	441	846	1116	1117	574	1955	1393	1277	804	441	991	29
% of Weighted Total:	100.0	47.9	48.5	76.8	12.1	23.2	30.6	30.6	15.7	53.5	38.1	35.0	22.0	12.1	27.1	.8

E07F: Whether it is O.K. to drink

1. Very similar	23.9	21.5	26.2	22.3	34.9	19.1	20.7	29.5	25.9	25.2	22.0	37.4	17.6	16.5	15.5	9.1
2. Mostly similar	31.8	32.8	31.0	33.6	22.4	34.5	35.1	26.6	31.7	33.6	29.3	27.7	36.1	35.9	31.8	45.5
3. Mostly different	17.9	19.1	16.8	19.0	12.2	20.2	18.0	16.5	17.0	18.7	17.1	13.0	20.7	20.2	20.9	4.5
4. Very different	20.9	20.0	21.5	20.6	21.5	20.8	21.6	21.6	17.8	17.9	24.8	14.4	20.5	21.8	28.9	36.4
8. Don't know	5.6	6.8	4.5	4.5	9.0	5.5	4.6	5.7	7.5	4.5	6.8	7.5	5.1	5.9	2.8	4.5
Item 11280 N(Wtd)	3169	1511	1589	2540	344	658	1031	975	505	1810	1225	1154	704	376	864	22

E07G: Whether it is O.K. to use marijuana

1. Very similar	42.8	40.2	45.4	43.5	43.8	36.0	41.8	50.7	38.7	46.4	38.2	70.1	33.5	36.6	18.4	9.5
2. Mostly similar	12.6	12.3	12.9	12.8	11.0	14.9	12.4	10.7	13.9	14.5	9.9	10.9	18.1	12.3	10.1	23.8
3. Mostly different	8.7	8.3	9.1	9.2	4.5	9.0	10.0	5.9	10.9	7.9	9.6	2.4	11.2	10.2	14.2	4.3
4. Very different	28.0	30.2	26.0	27.9	26.5	34.5	29.1	23.6	25.8	24.8	32.2	7.8	27.4	33.4	52.9	57.1
8. Don't know	7.9	9.1	6.7	6.6	14.3	5.6	6.8	9.1	10.9	6.4	10.0	8.7	9.9	7.5	4.4	9.5
Item 11290 N(Wtd)	3152	1499	1584	2531	336	656	1025	966	504	1803	1217	1153	696	374	860	21

E07H: Whether it is O.K. to use other drugs

1. Very similar	53.8	50.1	57.3	55.5	50.4	49.5	53.4	58.4	51.9	58.9	47.6	74.4	58.5	52.1	26.2	4.5
2. Mostly similar	11.8	11.6	12.0	11.6	11.4	12.0	12.5	10.7	12.0	13.2	9.7	9.7	14.0	13.0	11.5	13.6
3. Mostly different	4.3	4.9	3.7	4.5	4.4	4.9	4.3	4.3	3.8	3.7	5.5	1.6	5.0	5.9	6.3	4.5
4. Very different	22.6	24.6	20.8	22.2	20.2	28.5	23.5	17.8	22.4	18.2	28.0	6.3	14.6	21.5	50.4	68.2
8. Don't know	7.5	8.8	6.2	6.2	13.2	5.2	6.5	8.8	10.2	5.9	9.2	7.9	7.9	7.4	5.5	9.1
Item 11300 N(Wtd)	3157	1502	1586	2535	341	657	1027	971	501	1805	1222	1152	699	376	861	22

E07I: What values are important in life

1. Very similar	35.6	32.1	39.0	35.3	42.2	32.7	33.2	40.1	35.9	41.1	28.7	45.9	36.2	30.1	24.8	14.3
2. Mostly similar	41.3	43.1	40.0	43.5	26.5	43.5	44.4	36.8	40.6	41.1	41.7	38.5	42.8	47.9	42.4	33.3
3. Mostly different	11.6	13.2	9.9	11.7	10.6	10.7	12.1	11.5	12.2	9.6	14.2	7.5	10.0	11.2	18.0	19.0
4. Very different	6.6	6.2	6.9	5.6	11.5	9.0	5.8	6.4	5.4	4.9	8.6	3.6	5.9	7.4	10.0	28.6
8. Don't know	4.8	5.4	4.2	3.8	8.6	4.1	4.3	5.1	6.4	3.4	6.7	4.5	4.9	3.2	4.8	9.5
Item 11310 N(Wtd)	3153	1503	1581	2529	339	655	1026	970	502	1800	1222	1152	698	376	859	21

E07J: The value of education

1. Very similar	54.6	53.3	55.9	53.8	59.2	55.8	53.8	55.4	52.9	65.5	38.7	63.4	55.4	50.1	45.3	38.1
2. Mostly similar	30.4	29.6	30.9	32.4	21.6	29.1	31.1	29.6	32.3	26.4	36.4	26.2	32.5	34.4	33.3	23.8
3. Mostly different	7.1	8.2	6.1	7.3	5.3	6.4	7.6	6.5	8.1	3.7	12.2	3.8	6.3	7.7	11.6	14.3
4. Very different	5.2	5.0	5.3	4.5	8.3	6.4	5.3	5.3	3.4	2.8	8.4	3.8	3.6	5.3	7.6	19.0
8. Don't know	2.8	3.9	1.7	2.0	5.6	2.3	2.2	3.3	3.4	1.5	4.3	2.8	2.3	2.7	2.3	4.8
Item 11320 N(Wtd)	3153	1506	1579	2529	338	652	1027	969	505	1807	1214	1150	699	375	859	21

E07K: What are appropriate roles for women

1. Very similar	30.0	23.9	35.9	30.2	31.2	30.5	28.2	32.1	28.9	32.9	26.1	34.3	30.4	27.4	25.9	28.6
2. Mostly similar	40.5	41.0	39.7	43.1	24.8	42.3	42.0	38.1	39.6	40.7	40.1	39.3	41.8	43.4	40.7	19.0
3. Mostly different	10.7	12.7	9.1	10.3	12.8	9.5	11.6	10.4	11.0	10.2	12.0	9.2	10.3	10.6	13.1	9.5
4. Very different	6.3	5.3	7.3	5.4	11.4	6.6	6.0	7.0	5.4	5.3	7.5	4.9	4.9	4.5	9.1	28.6
8. Don't know	12.5	17.1	7.9	10.9	19.2	10.9	12.1	12.5	15.1	11.0	14.3	12.2	12.5	13.8	11.1	9.5
Item 11330 N(Wtd)	3146	1498	1579	2521	343	650	1023	971	502	1798	1213	1148	698	376	854	21

E07L: Conservation and pollution issues

1. Very similar	22.8	22.0	23.2	23.0	24.0	23.6	18.6	25.6	24.8	23.9	21.4	27.2	21.7	20.7	19.5	14.3
2. Mostly similar	35.4	39.1	32.1	37.1	26.4	33.5	38.1	34.9	32.9	36.8	33.5	34.7	36.9	39.2	33.6	19.0
3. Mostly different	8.3	8.8	7.8	8.4	7.0	7.8	9.3	7.1	9.8	8.3	8.7	6.8	7.6	8.3	10.9	14.3
4. Very different	4.3	4.5	4.3	3.7	6.5	3.6	4.2	4.9	4.2	2.9	5.9	3.3	4.0	5.1	5.3	14.3
8. Don't know	29.2	25.7	32.6	27.8	35.8	31.5	29.9	27.5	28.3	28.1	30.5	28.0	30.0	26.6	30.8	38.1
Item 11340 N(Wtd)	3141	1498	1575	2521	341	645	1024	972	501	1797	1213	1148	697	372	853	21

QUESTIONNAIRE FORM 4 1981	TOTAL	SEX		RACE		REGION				4YR COLLEGE PLANS		ILLICIT DRUG USE: LIFETIME				
		M	F	White	Black	NE	NC	S	W	Yes	No	None	Mari-juana Only	Few Pills	More Pills	Any Her-oin
Weighted No. of Cases:	3653	1751	1771	2804	441	846	1116	1117	574	1955	1393	1277	804	441	991	29
% of Weighted Total:	100.0	47.9	48.5	76.8	12.1	23.2	30.6	30.6	15.7	53.5	38.1	35.0	22.0	12.1	27.1	.8
E07M: Racial issues																
1. Very similar	29.9	29.6	29.9	27.9	44.7	28.5	25.7	35.8	28.6	32.5	26.7	35.0	29.4	24.6	26.3	9.5
2. Mostly similar	34.0	34.4	33.6	36.3	24.4	32.8	36.9	31.2	35.4	34.4	33.6	33.3	35.7	36.9	33.1	38.1
3. Mostly different	10.4	11.2	9.7	10.8	5.9	12.3	11.1	8.3	11.0	10.8	10.1	8.0	10.9	13.4	12.3	4.8
4. Very different	7.1	6.3	7.8	7.0	7.1	9.1	6.6	7.1	5.4	6.5	7.6	5.2	5.6	7.8	9.6	19.0
8. Don't know	18.6	18.5	18.9	18.0	17.6	17.3	19.7	17.8	19.8	15.7	22.0	18.6	18.5	17.1	18.8	28.6
Item 11350　N(Wtd)	3140	1501	1570	2521	340	649	1022	969	500	1789	1216	1144	698	374	853	21
E07N: Religion																
1. Very similar	40.5	37.0	43.8	38.9	54.0	34.8	37.9	49.0	37.0	41.5	39.8	51.1	39.0	38.3	29.7	9.5
2. Mostly similar	33.9	34.6	33.2	36.1	23.5	34.4	36.2	30.4	35.2	34.9	32.0	29.5	37.7	34.6	36.6	28.6
3. Mostly different	10.1	10.9	9.4	10.7	7.0	13.0	11.2	7.1	10.1	10.3	9.7	6.8	9.4	12.9	14.2	4.8
4. Very different	6.9	7.7	6.0	6.4	7.6	7.9	6.2	6.9	7.4	6.3	7.7	4.4	5.7	7.8	10.0	33.3
8. Don't know	8.6	9.9	7.5	8.0	7.6	10.1	8.6	6.6	10.3	7.0	10.8	8.3	8.3	6.4	9.4	23.8
Item 11360　N(Wtd)	3145	1502	1574	2521	341	646	1024	973	503	1796	1218	1149	700	373	852	21
E07O: Politics																
1. Very similar	19.1	20.4	17.8	18.0	31.3	16.1	17.2	24.9	15.4	18.6	19.9	24.2	19.0	14.4	14.4	9.5
2. Mostly similar	35.1	36.9	33.5	37.6	22.2	36.3	35.8	32.7	36.7	38.1	30.6	33.2	36.9	37.4	35.5	23.8
3. Mostly different	9.9	11.3	8.5	10.0	5.6	10.2	10.4	7.3	13.4	10.7	9.1	8.0	7.1	12.3	13.3	14.3
4. Very different	6.5	6.5	6.3	5.9	8.8	8.1	6.9	6.0	4.8	6.4	6.8	5.2	5.4	7.5	8.0	23.8
8. Don't know	29.4	25.0	33.9	28.6	31.9	29.0	29.8	29.1	29.5	26.3	33.6	29.3	31.5	28.3	28.9	23.8
Item 11370　N(Wtd)	3141	1502	1570	2521	342	644	1023	973	501	1792	1214	1147	701	374	849	21
E08: How do you think your CLOSE FRIENDS feel (or would feel) about YOU doing each of the following things?																
E08A: Smoking one or more packs of cigarettes per day																
1. Not disapprove	26.2	25.8	26.1	26.2	25.4	27.9	29.1	26.1	17.9	19.4	35.6	16.5	22.4	26.2	41.1	57.1
2. Disapprove	36.1	37.2	35.2	36.8	33.4	37.1	34.1	38.1	34.8	37.4	33.6	33.9	41.2	40.5	33.2	23.8
3. Strongly disapprove	37.8	36.9	38.8	37.0	41.1	35.1	36.9	35.8	47.3	43.2	30.7	49.6	36.4	33.2	25.7	19.0
Item 11470　N(Wtd)	3119	1486	1566	2502	338	639	1020	968	491	1777	1210	1136	697	370	846	21
E08B: Trying marijuana (pot, grass) once or twice																
1. Not disapprove	53.6	55.5	51.6	55.3	43.5	66.8	55.0	41.0	58.2	51.3	56.4	23.3	63.6	64.2	81.2	90.5
2. Disapprove	21.5	22.2	21.0	21.0	25.0	18.1	21.4	24.7	20.0	23.5	18.3	28.3	21.9	22.8	11.2	4.8
3. Strongly disapprove	24.9	22.3	27.4	23.7	31.5	15.1	23.6	34.2	21.6	25.2	25.2	48.4	14.5	12.7	7.6	4.8
Item 11480　N(Wtd)	3115	1487	1561	2500	336	641	1020	964	491	1776	1205	1135	698	369	847	21
E08C: Smoking marijuana occasionally																
1. Not disapprove	44.1	46.2	41.9	45.0	38.6	57.7	44.4	32.4	48.3	39.2	50.1	15.9	46.0	51.2	76.7	85.0
2. Disapprove	24.1	24.0	24.3	24.0	25.1	20.5	24.0	27.2	23.2	27.2	20.4	26.9	32.3	27.8	11.9	5.0
3. Strongly disapprove	31.8	29.7	33.8	31.0	36.5	21.7	31.6	40.4	28.3	33.7	29.5	57.2	21.8	20.8	11.3	10.0
Item 11490　N(Wtd)	3114	1485	1561	2500	334	640	1018	965	491	1774	1205	1133	696	371	847	20
E08D: Smoking marijuana regularly																
1. Not disapprove	25.0	28.3	21.5	24.1	27.2	31.5	26.1	19.1	26.0	18.4	34.1	9.7	19.9	22.2	49.6	81.0
2. Disapprove	29.0	30.4	27.8	29.3	28.1	30.4	26.6	28.9	32.2	30.1	27.0	21.3	35.2	39.0	29.9	9.5
3. Strongly disapprove	46.0	41.3	50.7	46.5	44.6	38.0	47.3	51.9	41.8	51.5	39.0	69.1	44.9	38.5	20.6	9.5
Item 11500　N(Wtd)	3106	1479	1559	2495	334	639	1017	963	488	1768	1204	1129	697	369	843	21

QUESTIONNAIRE FORM 4 1981	TOTAL	SEX		RACE		REGION				4YR COLLEGE PLANS		ILLICIT DRUG USE: LIFETIME				
		M	F	White	Black	NE	NC	S	W	Yes	No	None	Mari-juana Only	Few Pills	More Pills	Any Her-oin
Weighted No. of Cases:	3653	1751	1771	2804	441	846	1116	1117	574	1955	1393	1277	804	441	991	29
% of Weighted Total:	100.0	47.9	48.5	76.8	12.1	23.2	30.6	30.6	15.7	53.5	38.1	35.0	22.0	12.1	27.1	.8
E08E: Trying LSD once or twice																
1. Not disapprove	13.5	16.0	10.7	13.6	10.4	17.1	14.3	8.8	16.3	10.4	17.8	7.6	5.4	7.0	29.8	71.4
2. Disapprove	21.7	23.5	19.4	21.1	22.0	21.8	21.1	21.8	22.4	20.6	23.9	18.3	22.2	28.0	22.5	9.5
3. Strongly disapprove	64.8	60.4	69.8	65.3	67.6	60.9	64.5	69.5	61.2	69.0	58.4	74.1	72.3	65.0	47.8	19.0
Item 11510 N(Wtd)	3115	1483	1564	2501	336	642	1018	965	490	1775	1206	1133	698	371	846	21
E08F: Trying an amphetamine (upper, pep pill, bennie, speed) once or twice																
1. Not disapprove	25.6	28.2	22.8	27.1	12.4	32.1	26.9	17.3	30.6	22.2	30.2	10.8	12.3	23.7	56.9	57.1
2. Disapprove	23.3	23.5	22.9	23.2	23.7	23.2	23.7	23.9	21.2	23.9	22.9	19.8	26.5	31.5	21.1	19.0
3. Strongly disapprove	51.1	48.3	54.3	49.8	63.6	44.5	49.4	58.8	48.2	53.9	46.9	69.5	61.2	44.7	22.0	23.8
Item 11520 N(Wtd)	3116	1483	1565	2500	338	642	1017	967	490	1774	1207	1133	698	371	847	21
E08G: Taking one or two drinks nearly every day																
1. Not disapprove	30.5	39.5	21.5	30.9	27.6	34.1	30.8	30.8	25.0	25.1	38.2	22.3	29.4	32.1	41.7	54.5
2. Disapprove	39.3	38.8	39.7	40.6	32.0	38.7	40.0	38.5	39.9	40.5	37.2	37.0	40.9	43.4	39.3	31.8
3. Strongly disapprove	30.2	21.8	38.8	28.5	40.5	27.2	29.2	30.7	35.1	34.4	24.5	40.7	29.8	24.5	19.2	13.6
Item 11530 N(Wtd)	3120	1492	1560	2505	341	636	1020	968	496	1775	1203	1134	697	371	845	22
E08H: Taking four or five drinks nearly every day																
1. Not disapprove	13.6	19.5	7.6	13.1	15.9	15.1	14.8	12.8	10.5	9.3	19.8	10.8	11.8	11.1	18.6	54.5
2. Disapprove	30.3	34.1	26.3	30.6	27.6	31.0	29.9	31.2	28.4	28.1	32.8	25.2	29.7	33.2	35.3	22.7
3. Strongly disapprove	56.2	46.5	66.1	56.4	56.5	53.9	55.3	56.1	61.1	62.6	47.4	64.0	58.3	55.9	46.0	22.7
Item 11540 N(Wtd)	3112	1484	1560	2498	340	636	1017	963	496	1771	1200	1130	696	370	843	22
E08I: Having five or more drinks once or twice each weekend																
1. Not disapprove	49.7	57.5	41.8	53.8	24.3	57.7	53.9	42.9	43.9	47.3	53.3	31.2	50.4	57.6	70.1	90.9
2. Disapprove	22.2	19.9	24.3	22.0	23.7	21.2	20.9	23.5	23.9	22.8	21.2	23.5	25.5	25.7	16.7	-
3. Strongly disapprove	28.1	22.6	33.9	24.2	52.1	21.3	25.2	33.6	32.2	29.9	25.5	45.3	24.1	16.8	13.2	9.1
Item 11550 N(Wtd)	3105	1484	1553	2494	338	633	1016	961	494	1767	1198	1130	693	370	839	22
E09: The next questions ask about different places to live and how desirable they might be to you. Please rate each kind of place below using the following terms: Not at all acceptable: You would not live in a place like this if you could possibly avoid it. Somewhat acceptable: You would live in a place like this, but not be very happy about it. Acceptable: A place like this would be O.K. Desirable: This is the kind of place where you would really like to live.																
E09A: A rural area																
1. Not at all acceptable	14.0	12.7	15.1	11.3	29.7	12.5	11.4	17.3	14.9	12.8	15.9	11.9	16.5	11.6	15.3	18.2
2. Somewhat acceptable	27.6	27.3	27.9	26.5	34.2	27.8	26.0	28.1	29.6	27.8	27.2	25.6	30.1	29.4	27.5	31.8
3. Acceptable	39.0	38.6	39.1	40.6	29.1	38.7	41.9	35.8	39.7	40.6	36.6	39.8	39.2	42.7	35.9	40.9
4. Desirable	19.4	21.5	17.8	21.6	7.3	21.0	.20.7	18.7	16.0	18.7	20.2	22.7	14.3	16.4	21.1	9.1
Item 17860 N(Wtd)	3025	1449	1508	2434	330	615	993	947	469	1736	1157	1112	665	354	824	22

QUESTIONNAIRE FORM 4 1981	TOTAL	SEX		RACE		REGION				4YR COLLEGE PLANS		ILLICIT DRUG USE: LIFETIME				
		M	F	White	Black	NE	NC	S	W	Yes	No	None	Marijuana Only	Few Pills	More Pills	Any Heroin
Weighted No. of Cases:	3653	1751	1771	2804	441	846	1116	1117	574	1955	1393	1277	804	441	991	29
% of Weighted Total:	100.0	47.9	48.5	76.8	12.1	23.2	30.6	30.6	15.7	53.5	38.1	35.0	22.0	12.1	27.1	.8
E09B: A small town																
1. Not at all acceptable	11.8	11.5	12.1	8.8	29.3	9.7	12.1	13.3	10.9	12.0	11.4	9.7	8.5	11.1	17.1	18.2
2. Somewhat acceptable	23.4	22.2	24.8	22.7	27.2	19.6	24.0	25.4	23.3	24.0	22.2	22.4	23.3	23.1	25.0	22.7
3. Acceptable	42.9	43.0	42.2	44.5	31.6	40.8	43.1	42.7	45.5	43.0	42.4	43.9	48.9	44.7	36.0	45.5
4. Desirable	21.9	23.3	20.9	24.0	11.6	29.8	20.7	18.7	20.3	20.9	23.9	24.1	19.1	21.1	21.8	13.6
Item 17870 N(Wtd)	3042	1453	1523	2445	335	618	998	949	477	1747	1162	1119	669	360	825	22
E09C: A small city																
1. Not at all acceptable	8.5	9.5	7.4	7.3	15.1	9.7	7.8	9.2	6.7	7.0	10.4	8.0	7.8	7.0	9.1	36.4
2. Somewhat acceptable	25.1	24.9	25.5	25.3	27.4	27.8	26.0	25.6	19.1	24.6	26.5	26.2	22.9	27.0	25.5	18.2
3. Acceptable	49.7	49.6	49.9	50.2	45.2	50.3	47.9	48.4	55.1	51.2	47.1	49.4	51.6	45.4	50.4	45.5
4. Desirable	16.7	16.1	17.3	17.2	12.3	12.1	18.2	16.9	19.1	17.2	16.1	16.5	17.7	20.3	15.2	4.5
Item 17880 N(Wtd)	3036	1448	1520	2441	332	618	998	943	477	1745	1156	1119	667	359	821	22
E09D: A suburb																
1. Not at all acceptable	18.0	17.6	17.9	17.3	22.2	14.9	14.9	23.1	17.8	12.1	26.4	20.2	18.1	13.2	16.5	13.6
2. Somewhat acceptable	26.7	27.3	26.4	26.2	27.5	25.3	28.4	25.1	28.5	25.7	27.7	25.7	24.5	35.8	25.4	50.0
3. Acceptable	36.1	35.6	36.5	36.8	32.0	37.9	37.0	32.9	38.3	38.5	32.8	35.8	37.0	32.4	37.8	22.7
4. Desirable	19.2	19.5	19.1	19.9	18.0	21.9	19.6	18.9	15.6	23.7	13.3	18.3	20.2	18.6	20.3	13.6
Item 17890 N(Wtd)	3024	1439	1517	2428	334	617	992	942	473	1745	1146	1116	664	355	818	22
E09E: A large city																
1. Not at all acceptable	42.0	46.5	37.6	46.8	14.2	47.2	42.2	40.1	38.4	36.3	50.0	43.2	42.9	44.2	39.3	47.6
2. Somewhat acceptable	21.5	22.5	20.9	21.6	20.2	20.5	21.1	20.8	24.9	22.6	20.6	22.2	21.4	22.3	20.1	23.8
3. Acceptable	23.8	21.2	26.1	21.2	40.4	19.8	25.6	24.7	23.5	27.7	18.4	23.9	23.7	20.0	24.5	14.3
4. Desirable	12.7	9.8	15.5	10.4	25.2	12.5	11.0	14.5	13.0	13.4	11.1	10.5	12.0	13.5	16.0	14.3
Item 17900 N(Wtd)	3035	1446	1522	2434	337	615	997	946	477	1742	1158	1120	667	355	826	21
Type of Housing: How would you rate...																
E09F: A single family home																
1. Not at all acceptable	5.5	6.6	3.9	3.8	15.7	3.4	5.1	6.4	7.1	4.8	6.2	5.6	5.3	2.2	6.1	13.6
2. Somewhat acceptable	11.5	11.9	10.9	10.0	18.1	5.8	11.8	13.4	14.0	9.1	14.8	10.8	11.3	12.8	11.7	9.1
3. Acceptable	25.7	25.7	25.5	24.6	30.7	26.0	26.1	24.2	27.4	22.1	30.1	22.6	28.4	25.3	26.5	54.5
4. Desirable	57.4	55.7	59.7	61.7	35.2	64.6	57.0	56.1	51.5	63.9	48.9	61.1	55.1	59.6	55.7	22.7
Item 17910 N(Wtd)	3032	1452	1514	2446	332	616	999	939	478	1739	1159	1113	666	359	822	22
E09G: A two-family house																
1. Not at all acceptable	36.9	35.2	38.6	38.1	30.8	31.5	35.5	43.9	33.0	37.0	37.0	37.6	37.0	35.7	36.1	36.4
2. Somewhat acceptable	28.4	31.4	25.8	28.8	26.1	28.1	30.6	24.7	31.7	29.3	27.7	27.6	26.6	33.1	29.4	22.7
3. Acceptable	28.5	27.0	29.7	27.7	31.1	35.4	28.6	23.8	28.3	28.4	27.9	27.8	29.9	27.0	28.6	36.4
4. Desirable	6.2	6.4	5.9	5.3	11.6	4.9	5.3	7.7	7.2	5.3	7.4	7.0	6.5	4.2	5.9	4.5
Item 17920 N(Wtd)	3000	1435	1499	2434	318	615	991	924	470	1720	1149	1101	659	356	817	22
E09H: A condominium																
1. Not at all acceptable	22.1	26.7	17.7	22.7	16.6	24.4	22.5	24.1	14.6	17.6	28.2	24.7	20.3	21.3	20.3	31.8
2. Somewhat acceptable	22.6	23.2	22.3	23.4	18.1	25.4	22.6	20.7	22.8	23.5	21.9	25.2	24.4	22.1	18.3	13.6
3. Acceptable	34.0	32.1	35.7	33.7	34.7	30.8	35.3	31.4	40.1	38.3	27.1	32.5	33.4	30.5	37.5	31.8
4. Desirable	21.3	18.0	24.3	20.2	30.6	19.2	19.5	23.8	22.6	20.5	22.9	17.6	21.8	26.1	23.9	27.3
Item 17930 N(Wtd)	3001	1433	1501	2427	320	610	990	927	474	1721	1153	1096	655	357	821	22
E09I: A one- or two-story apartment building																
1. Not at all acceptable	24.8	31.8	18.1	24.5	28.5	28.0	24.4	25.6	20.0	23.7	26.0	26.8	27.4	18.0	21.8	40.9
2. Somewhat acceptable	32.3	32.7	32.2	33.6	26.1	32.9	34.0	30.5	31.4	32.9	31.9	32.2	30.7	38.5	31.3	27.3
3. Acceptable	34.6	29.0	39.7	34.5	33.1	33.6	33.9	33.9	39.2	36.9	31.6	33.7	33.3	35.7	37.5	22.7
4. Desirable	8.2	6.5	9.9	7.4	12.3	5.4	7.8	10.0	9.3	6.5	10.5	7.2	8.4	7.9	9.3	9.1
Item 17940 N(Wtd)	3013	1438	1508	2431	326	614	992	932	474	1723	1158	1106	657	356	824	22

QUESTIONNAIRE FORM 4 1981	TOTAL	SEX		RACE		REGION				4YR COLLEGE PLANS		ILLICIT DRUG USE: LIFETIME				
		M	F	White	Black	NE	NC	S	W	Yes	No	None	Mari- juana Only	Few Pills	More Pills	Any Her- oin
Weighted No. of Cases:	3653	1751	1771	2804	441	846	1116	1117	574	1955	1393	1277	804	441	991	29
% of Weighted Total:	100.0	47.9	48.5	76.8	12.1	23.2	30.6	30.6	15.7	53.5	38.1	35.0	22.0	12.1	27.1	.8

E09J: A tall(high-rise) apartment building

1. Not at all acceptable	42.6	46.2	39.2	44.1	35.2	45.2	41.5	41.3	43.9	40.6	45.2	44.6	43.1	42.9	38.9	36.4
2. Somewhat acceptable	25.7	23.8	27.8	26.1	21.7	24.2	27.8	24.1	26.6	26.7	24.1	26.7	26.1	29.0	23.2	27.3
3. Acceptable	22.9	21.7	23.9	22.3	27.2	23.2	21.8	24.6	21.9	26.0	19.2	21.2	22.7	20.2	26.9	22.7
4. Desirable	8.8	8.3	9.2	7.6	15.9	7.4	8.9	10.0	7.6	6.7	11.4	7.6	8.2	8.0	11.1	13.6
Item 17950 N(Wtd)	3002	1430	1506	2422	327	611	986	932	474	1725	1145	1106	656	352	818	22

The following questions ask you to imagine different kinds of married life that you might have. We want you to think about different ways you might share responsibilities for working, taking care of the home and children. Please indicate how acceptable for you each of the different arrangements would be.

E10: Imagine both you and your spouse are working full-time.

How would you feel about each of these arrangements for doing things like cooking, cleaning, and laundry?

E10A: Wife does all cooking, cleaning, laundry

1. Not at all acceptable	46.2	36.8	55.9	46.8	43.9	51.9	45.9	42.8	46.5	51.1	39.4	45.3	49.0	42.3	48.1	27.3
2. Somewhat acceptable	29.1	31.7	26.4	29.3	28.2	27.1	30.7	28.7	29.2	27.2	31.5	28.0	26.6	35.6	30.1	22.7
3. Acceptable	16.3	18.8	13.4	15.6	19.1	14.2	14.9	18.1	17.9	14.6	19.1	16.7	19.1	14.0	13.5	31.8
4. Desirable	8.4	12.7	4.3	8.2	8.8	6.8	8.5	10.5	6.7	7.1	10.1	9.9	5.3	7.8	8.3	22.7
Item 11560 N(Wtd)	3013	1436	1511	2417	330	605	991	937	480	1728	1151	1096	665	357	823	22

E10B: Wife does most of it

1. Not at all acceptable	26.4	24.3	28.6	25.2	33.3	31.6	24.6	24.7	27.0	27.7	24.3	26.3	26.6	24.4	26.7	13.6
2. Somewhat acceptable	38.6	36.3	41.2	39.3	33.9	36.4	39.0	36.8	43.5	38.6	38.8	36.1	41.5	40.3	39.1	45.5
3. Acceptable	25.2	26.8	23.2	25.6	23.3	23.3	27.1	26.1	22.2	24.6	26.7	25.0	24.8	26.6	25.5	22.7
4. Desirable	9.8	12.6	7.0	9.8	9.7	8.7	9.2	12.4	7.5	9.1	10.2	12.5	7.1	8.4	8.7	18.2
Item 11570 N(Wtd)	3006	1433	1508	2412	330	601	990	937	478	1725	1146	1093	661	357	823	22

E10C: Both do it equally

1. Not at all acceptable	5.4	6.8	3.9	5.1	7.3	5.5	6.0	5.4	3.8	4.6	6.4	5.0	4.7	6.2	4.8	18.2
2. Somewhat acceptable	17.8	23.5	12.2	17.5	19.0	15.9	19.4	18.7	15.2	16.6	19.9	17.8	16.1	20.4	17.1	36.4
3. Acceptable	31.1	35.8	26.4	30.4	34.9	32.2	30.0	32.4	29.2	30.2	31.8	29.7	34.2	29.7	30.9	18.2
4. Desirable	45.8	33.9	57.6	47.0	38.8	46.6	44.6	43.4	51.8	48.6	41.9	47.4	45.0	43.7	47.2	27.3
Item 11580 N(Wtd)	3005	1439	1502	2418	327	599	990	937	479	1726	1147	1098	660	357	818	22

E10D: Husband does most of it

1. Not at all acceptable	56.3	57.1	55.8	57.0	54.1	58.2	57.6	56.3	51.4	56.8	55.5	55.5	56.4	55.8	57.4	47.6
2. Somewhat acceptable	33.5	33.7	32.9	33.8	30.6	32.1	32.4	32.7	38.6	34.2	32.8	33.6	34.3	34.9	32.1	33.3
3. Acceptable	8.3	7.3	9.4	7.8	10.7	8.5	7.7	8.7	8.6	7.5	9.3	9.3	7.7	7.6	7.8	19.0
4. Desirable	1.9	1.9	1.9	1.4	4.6	1.0	2.1	2.3	1.7	1.4	2.5	1.7	1.5	1.4	2.7	-
Item 11590 N(Wtd)	2989	1426	1497	2400	327	598	984	929	479	1722	1135	1087	659	355	819	21

E10E: Husband does all of it

1. Not at all acceptable	85.2	85.5	85.2	86.8	75.1	86.2	84.7	84.9	85.4	88.0	81.1	85.1	84.7	89.0	84.8	68.2
2. Somewhat acceptable	9.7	9.5	9.4	9.4	11.6	9.2	11.2	8.8	9.0	8.6	11.6	9.2	11.1	9.0	9.1	22.7
3. Acceptable	3.1	3.1	3.2	2.2	8.5	2.9	2.2	4.0	3.5	2.3	4.1	3.6	2.6	.8	3.4	9.1
4. Desirable	2.1	2.0	2.2	1.7	4.9	1.8	1.8	2.4	2.3	1.1	3.2	2.1	1.7	1.1	2.6	4.5
Item 11600 N(Wtd)	3001	1431	1503	2409	329	596	989	936	480	1722	1146	1094	659	355	820	22

QUESTIONNAIRE FORM 4 1981	TOTAL	SEX		RACE		REGION				4YR COLLEGE PLANS		ILLICIT DRUG USE: LIFETIME				
		M	F	White	Black	NE	NC	S	W	Yes	No	None	Mari-juana Only	Few Pills	More Pills	Any Her-oin
Weighted No. of Cases:	3653	1751	1771	2804	441	846	1116	1117	574	1955	1393	1277	804	441	991	29
% of Weighted Total:	100.0	47.9	48.5	76.8	12.1	23.2	30.6	30.6	15.7	53.5	38.1	35.0	22.0	12.1	27.1	.8

E11: Imagine you are married and have one or more pre-school children and both you and your spouse have to work full-time.

How would you feel about each of these arrangements for the day-to-day care of the child(ren) after working hours and on weekends?

E11A: Wife does all of it

	TOTAL	M	F	White	Black	NE	NC	S	W	Yes	No	None	Mari-juana Only	Few Pills	More Pills	Any Her-oin
1. Not at all acceptable	64.4	57.6	71.4	65.4	61.6	67.7	62.4	64.4	64.5	67.9	58.5	64.5	66.4	65.0	64.6	36.4
2. Somewhat acceptable	21.4	25.2	17.3	21.7	18.6	19.2	24.6	19.1	22.0	19.8	24.3	18.4	22.1	24.5	22.5	36.4
3. Acceptable	9.7	10.6	8.7	8.9	14.6	8.3	9.2	11.4	8.9	8.9	10.9	12.8	7.4	7.4	8.2	13.6
4. Desirable	4.5	6.6	2.6	4.1	5.5	4.6	3.8	5.3	4.7	3.3	6.2	4.3	4.3	3.1	4.7	13.6
Item 11610 N(Wtd)	2979	1429	1487	2390	328	589	986	932	473	1715	1137	1092	651	351	814	22

E11B: Wife does most of it

	TOTAL	M	F	White	Black	NE	NC	S	W	Yes	No	None	Mari-juana Only	Few Pills	More Pills	Any Her-oin
1. Not at all acceptable	31.5	29.4	33.6	31.4	32.8	38.5	29.6	28.2	32.9	32.2	29.4	31.8	34.2	32.2	29.0	22.7
2. Somewhat acceptable	42.9	43.2	42.7	43.1	38.6	37.0	46.0	43.3	42.9	42.9	44.1	41.3	42.0	45.7	45.5	54.5
3. Acceptable	20.4	20.4	20.1	20.7	21.9	19.1	19.6	22.7	19.1	19.9	21.4	22.0	17.9	19.9	20.5	13.6
4. Desirable	5.3	7.1	3.6	4.9	6.7	5.5	4.8	5.8	5.1	5.0	5.0	4.9	5.8	4.8	4.9	13.6
Item 11620 N(Wtd)	2975	1427	1484	2386	329	587	986	931	471	1715	1130	1089	653	351	811	22

E11C: Both do it equally

	TOTAL	M	F	White	Black	NE	NC	S	W	Yes	No	None	Mari-juana Only	Few Pills	More Pills	Any Her-oin
1. Not at all acceptable	3.2	4.8	1.7	2.9	3.4	3.1	3.6	3.2	2.5	2.5	3.7	2.4	2.4	4.3	3.7	18.2
2. Somewhat acceptable	13.5	17.3	9.5	12.7	16.3	12.5	13.7	13.9	13.6	10.9	17.7	13.0	12.4	15.1	13.2	45.5
3. Acceptable	28.8	34.2	23.7	27.5	36.2	27.1	27.8	31.0	28.2	26.3	32.5	29.1	32.0	23.3	28.3	-
4. Desirable	54.5	43.8	65.1	56.9	43.9	57.3	54.8	51.7	55.4	60.3	46.1	55.5	53.2	57.4	54.7	40.9
Item 11630 N(Wtd)	2975	1426	1484	2389	326	586	990	928	471	1712	1133	1086	654	352	813	22

E11D: Husband does most of it

	TOTAL	M	F	White	Black	NE	NC	S	W	Yes	No	None	Mari-juana Only	Few Pills	More Pills	Any Her-oin
1. Not at all acceptable	51.2	49.5	52.7	51.5	51.2	56.7	50.2	51.9	44.9	50.0	52.8	50.1	52.6	53.7	50.4	54.5
2. Somewhat acceptable	37.6	38.7	36.4	38.1	31.1	32.9	38.0	35.1	47.2	39.8	35.3	38.4	38.3	36.3	37.1	27.3
3. Acceptable	9.3	9.5	9.3	9.1	11.9	8.5	10.0	10.2	6.8	8.8	9.7	9.4	7.2	9.4	10.6	13.6
4. Desirable	1.9	2.2	1.6	1.3	5.5	1.9	1.6	2.6	.8	1.6	2.3	2.1	1.8	.6	1.8	-
Item 11640 N(Wtd)	2971	1425	1482	2383	328	586	986	928	472	1713	1129	1086	652	350	813	22

E11E: Husband does all of it

	TOTAL	M	F	White	Black	NE	NC	S	W	Yes	No	None	Mari-juana Only	Few Pills	More Pills	Any Her-oin
1. Not at all acceptable	83.5	82.4	84.4	85.7	70.7	87.0	82.0	82.3	84.5	85.8	79.2	82.8	84.5	83.5	84.6	86.4
2. Somewhat acceptable	10.9	11.4	10.3	10.0	13.7	8.9	12.6	9.8	11.9	10.2	12.6	10.6	11.7	12.0	9.7	13.6
3. Acceptable	3.8	4.0	3.7	3.0	10.1	2.2	4.1	5.1	2.8	2.6	5.6	4.5	2.1	4.3	3.8	4.5
4. Desirable	1.8	2.2	1.6	1.3	5.2	1.7	1.3	2.9	.8	1.4	2.7	2.1	1.7	-	1.8	-
Item 11650 N(Wtd)	2973	1424	1485	2385	328	586	986	930	471	1714	1131	1089	652	351	811	22

QUESTIONNAIRE FORM 5 1981	TOTAL	SEX		RACE		REGION				4YR COLLEGE PLANS		ILLICIT DRUG USE: LIFETIME				
		M	F	White	Black	NE	NC	S	W	Yes	No	None	Mari- juana Only	Few Pills	More Pills	Any Her- oin
Weighted No. of Cases:	3656	1803	1741	2820	459	853	1091	1127	586	2036	1422	1210	782	515	1027	40
% of Weighted Total:	100.0	49.3	47.6	77.1	12.6	23.3	29.8	30.8	16.0	55.7	38.9	33.1	21.4	14.1	28.1	1.1
A01: Taking all things together, how would you say things are these days--would you say you're very happy, pretty happy, or not too happy these days?																
3. Very happy	16.9	16.0	17.6	18.6	9.2	17.7	14.7	16.6	20.3	19.3	13.8	20.9	15.0	15.6	15.1	12.5
2. Pretty happy	66.5	67.3	66.6	68.2	61.1	66.0	68.6	65.2	65.7	65.8	69.1	64.4	67.5	67.6	67.7	77.5
1. Not too happy	16.6	16.8	15.8	13.2	29.7	16.4	16.6	18.3	13.9	14.9	17.2	14.7	17.5	16.8	17.2	10.0
Item 1190 N(Wtd)	3642	1797	1736	2813	458	849	1090	1123	581	2026	1422	1209	781	512	1023	40
A02: Some people think a lot about the social problems of the nation and the world, and about how they might be solved. Others spend little time thinking about these issues. How much do you think about such things?																
1. Never	1.5	2.1	1.0	1.3	1.3	1.5	1.5	1.3	1.9	.9	2.4	1.2	1.4	2.3	1.7	2.5
2. Seldom	11.5	11.2	11.7	11.6	12.2	11.4	11.4	12.0	10.6	9.2	14.8	11.8	10.5	12.1	11.5	17.5
3. Sometimes	50.7	48.5	52.7	52.8	37.9	52.4	53.0	46.8	51.4	48.9	54.6	50.5	50.4	51.2	50.8	50.0
4. Quite often	29.4	30.1	29.0	28.0	38.1	28.3	28.3	31.3	29.6	32.2	24.6	29.9	30.0	29.0	28.5	22.5
5. A great deal	6.9	8.1	5.6	6.4	10.2	6.4	5.8	8.6	6.7	8.7	3.7	6.6	7.7	5.4	7.4	10.0
Item 6880 N(Wtd)	3647	1798	1741	2817	459	849	1088	1125	584	2034	1420	1206	781	514	1027	40
A03: Of all the problems facing the nation today, how often do you worry about each of the following?																
A03A: Chance of nuclear war																
1. Never	10.0	8.4	11.7	8.7	17.5	8.8	9.1	12.2	8.9	8.0	12.1	10.2	8.6	10.0	9.2	17.9
2. Seldom	25.7	24.2	27.3	26.1	23.9	23.5	26.5	26.4	25.9	25.2	27.7	24.5	27.7	26.8	25.4	33.3
3. Sometimes	40.7	40.2	41.4	41.9	33.5	44.4	43.0	34.7	42.8	41.7	38.6	40.8	41.8	40.5	41.0	25.6
4. Often	23.6	27.2	19.7	23.3	25.2	23.3	21.4	26.6	22.3	25.1	21.6	24.5	21.8	22.5	24.5	23.1
Item 11660 N(Wtd)	3638	1795	1735	2813	457	850	1087	1120	582	2034	1413	1210	777	511	1025	39
A03B: Population growth																
1. Never	19.2	21.6	16.6	19.6	18.0	23.2	20.7	17.6	13.5	19.5	19.4	17.1	21.5	18.4	19.9	25.6
2. Seldom	41.0	40.2	42.0	43.0	32.5	42.9	46.0	35.9	38.8	40.7	42.1	40.9	39.3	43.6	41.0	41.0
3. Sometimes	29.9	28.8	31.1	29.5	32.0	26.9	26.9	33.8	32.5	30.5	29.2	32.4	28.0	28.6	29.7	25.6
4. Often	9.9	9.3	10.4	8.0	17.5	7.0	6.5	12.8	15.2	9.3	9.2	9.5	11.2	9.2	9.3	7.7
Item 11670 N(Wtd)	3628	1790	1732	2808	456	848	1085	1117	578	2032	1409	1206	776	511	1022	39
A03C: Crime and violence																
1. Never	1.8	2.7	.7	1.5	3.3	1.8	1.4	2.1	1.7	.8	2.8	1.6	1.4	1.2	2.2	7.7
2. Seldom	10.4	15.7	4.5	11.1	5.7	10.0	11.8	8.6	11.7	9.1	12.4	7.8	10.9	12.4	11.4	15.4
3. Sometimes	34.6	41.7	27.7	38.2	17.5	37.8	36.4	30.1	35.7	36.4	33.2	32.3	32.8	35.3	38.7	41.0
4. Often	53.2	40.0	67.0	49.1	73.5	50.4	50.5	59.2	50.9	53.7	51.6	58.2	54.9	51.1	47.7	33.3
Item 11680 N(Wtd)	3632	1788	1738	2812	456	849	1086	1118	580	2033	1411	1209	778	507	1023	39
A03D: Pollution																
1. Never	6.8	8.1	5.8	6.1	11.5	7.7	7.0	7.5	4.3	6.2	7.7	5.9	6.0	7.9	8.1	2.5
2. Seldom	31.2	31.1	32.0	31.0	36.2	27.6	34.9	32.9	26.2	31.0	32.3	30.4	33.4	33.0	29.5	45.0
3. Sometimes	39.3	36.6	40.7	40.2	34.4	38.2	37.1	40.5	42.9	40.3	37.7	39.1	40.8	40.1	37.8	30.0
4. Often	22.7	24.1	21.4	22.7	17.7	26.6	21.0	19.1	26.6	22.6	22.2	24.6	19.9	19.3	24.5	20.0
Item 11690 N(Wtd)	3614	1779	1729	2798	453	849	1079	1111	576	2032	1399	1203	770	509	1020	40
A03E: Energy shortages																
1. Never	4.3	4.5	4.2	3.8	8.2	4.2	2.9	5.0	5.5	3.6	5.3	4.0	3.6	4.3	5.2	2.6
2. Seldom	20.6	18.5	23.0	19.6	25.1	19.9	20.1	19.7	24.6	19.9	21.6	18.6	22.8	19.4	22.3	12.8
3. Sometimes	38.9	37.4	40.1	39.7	33.3	40.4	39.6	36.1	40.6	38.7	39.1	39.2	38.1	36.6	39.8	46.2
4. Often	36.2	39.5	32.6	36.9	33.3	35.4	37.2	39.2	29.5	37.8	33.9	38.2	35.4	39.7	32.8	38.5
Item 11700 N(Wtd)	3621	1786	1732	2808	450	848	1085	1111	577	2029	1406	1201	776	511	1020	39

QUESTIONNAIRE FORM 5 1981	TOTAL	SEX		RACE		REGION				4YR COLLEGE PLANS		ILLICIT DRUG USE: LIFETIME				
		M	F	White	Black	NE	NC	S	W	Yes	No	None	Marijuana Only	Few Pills	More Pills	Any Heroin
Weighted No. of Cases:	3656	1803	1741	2820	459	853	1091	1127	586	2036	1422	1210	782	515	1027	40
% of Weighted Total:	100.0	49.3	47.6	77.1	12.6	23.3	29.8	30.8	16.0	55.7	38.9	33.1	21.4	14.1	28.1	1.1
A03F: Race relations																
1. Never	17.7	20.4	14.7	19.2	8.4	19.8	17.8	16.5	16.9	13.1	23.6	16.4	17.1	15.4	20.5	20.5
2. Seldom	35.2	38.7	32.0	39.3	17.0	33.9	39.2	30.9	38.1	34.8	36.7	36.2	33.8	37.5	35.0	28.2
3. Sometimes	28.0	25.5	30.9	27.8	28.4	30.2	27.6	27.2	27.3	30.2	25.0	27.8	27.9	30.0	27.1	35.9
4. Often	19.0	15.4	22.4	13.7	46.5	16.1	15.3	25.4	17.7	21.8	14.6	19.5	21.2	17.2	17.3	12.8
Item 11710 N(Wtd)	3606	1774	1726	2791	454	847	1071	1113	575	2026	1394	1192	773	507	1019	39
A03G: Hunger and poverty																
1. Never	8.4	12.9	3.8	9.0	6.1	9.9	8.2	7.6	8.1	6.6	11.2	7.2	7.8	8.7	10.2	10.3
2. Seldom	34.4	42.4	26.7	38.0	21.0	33.4	36.8	30.0	39.5	37.1	30.8	32.2	35.8	34.8	36.6	30.8
3. Sometimes	36.6	31.6	41.5	36.9	33.3	38.6	39.1	34.8	32.4	36.6	37.2	36.2	38.4	37.2	35.5	30.8
4. Often	20.6	13.1	28.0	16.1	39.4	18.2	15.8	27.5	19.9	19.8	20.8	24.5	18.2	19.4	17.7	28.2
Item 11720 N(Wtd)	3618	1784	1728	2796	457	848	1079	1114	577	2025	1404	1205	771	506	1021	39
A03H: Using open land for housing or industry																
1. Never	31.9	29.4	34.6	31.5	37.1	34.9	33.1	32.6	23.7	34.0	29.1	30.5	32.8	34.4	32.1	25.6
2. Seldom	32.9	32.4	33.8	33.0	32.3	30.2	36.2	33.3	30.3	33.2	32.6	33.8	34.7	31.2	31.7	33.3
3. Sometimes	21.8	23.0	20.2	21.7	21.3	19.5	19.6	21.7	29.4	21.0	23.5	23.3	20.9	20.6	21.1	20.5
4. Often	13.4	15.2	11.4	13.7	9.5	15.4	11.3	12.3	16.6	11.9	14.8	12.5	11.7	13.9	15.2	17.9
Item 11730 N(Wtd)	3630	1788	1735	2809	455	848	1084	1119	578	2033	1410	1208	775	509	1023	39
A03I: Urban decay																
1. Never	39.1	36.7	42.0	39.3	43.9	34.8	41.4	42.0	35.1	35.4	45.5	37.8	39.2	41.6	40.2	25.0
2. Seldom	39.4	40.3	38.1	40.7	29.0	39.7	38.4	39.6	40.2	42.1	35.3	41.7	39.4	37.6	37.0	47.5
3. Sometimes	17.0	17.2	16.9	16.4	19.6	17.9	17.1	14.9	19.4	17.5	15.9	16.5	16.8	15.9	18.0	25.0
4. Often	4.6	5.8	3.1	3.7	7.3	7.6	3.1	3.5	5.2	5.1	3.4	4.1	4.7	5.2	4.8	2.5
Item 11740 N(Wtd)	3595	1778	1716	2793	449	843	1074	1106	572	2022	1392	1197	770	503	1012	40
A03J: Economic problems																
1. Never	5.0	5.3	4.8	4.6	5.7	5.4	5.5	4.5	4.5	3.2	7.5	4.5	5.5	5.1	4.9	5.1
2. Seldom	21.4	21.7	21.2	21.4	21.7	21.0	20.2	22.3	22.8	19.1	25.0	20.2	22.1	22.0	21.7	30.8
3. Sometimes	41.5	39.7	43.0	42.4	36.4	42.4	41.4	39.5	44.6	42.0	40.8	41.4	40.8	41.2	42.4	38.5
4. Often	31.9	33.3	31.1	31.6	36.2	31.1	32.9	33.6	28.0	35.7	26.8	33.8	31.6	31.8	31.0	25.6
Item 11750 N(Wtd)	3632	1792	1734	2813	456	846	1085	1122	579	2032	1412	1207	779	510	1022	39
A03K: Drug abuse																
1. Never	9.2	13.6	4.3	8.7	9.5	10.7	8.8	8.5	8.6	7.7	11.1	8.9	8.0	8.2	10.6	10.3
2. Seldom	22.3	28.1	16.6	23.6	16.5	22.4	21.8	21.0	26.1	22.8	21.5	20.9	24.3	22.5	21.9	25.6
3. Sometimes	35.5	33.8	37.4	36.7	32.5	37.2	37.6	33.0	33.9	36.4	34.1	34.4	36.8	34.3	37.0	33.3
4. Often	33.0	24.5	41.7	31.0	41.3	29.8	31.8	37.5	31.4	33.0	33.2	35.9	30.9	34.9	30.5	30.8
Item 11760 N(Wtd)	3632	1789	1737	2811	455	849	1085	1119	579	2034	1412	1208	777	510	1023	39
A04: How well do you think your experiences and training (at home, school, work, etc.) have prepared you to be a good...																
A04A: Husband or wife																
1. Poorly	2.2	2.9	1.5	2.1	2.9	2.9	2.4	1.5	2.3	2.4	1.9	1.6	2.1	2.8	2.6	10.0
2. Not so well	4.9	5.7	3.9	4.7	5.8	4.6	4.9	4.5	6.0	4.7	5.5	4.3	4.3	6.4	4.5	7.5
3. Fairly well	22.7	26.6	18.4	23.1	21.1	22.2	22.6	22.5	24.0	22.5	23.2	20.9	22.2	22.0	25.7	20.0
4. Well	40.7	43.5	38.7	41.9	32.6	42.8	42.7	39.1	37.4	40.7	41.2	40.7	42.9	39.9	41.0	25.0
5. Very well	29.4	21.4	37.6	28.2	37.8	27.5	27.4	32.4	30.2	29.7	28.2	32.4	28.6	28.9	26.1	37.5
Item 11770 N(Wtd)	3566	1765	1697	2772	445	828	1072	1099	567	1999	1388	1185	767	501	1002	40

QUESTIONNAIRE FORM 5 1981	TOTAL	SEX		RACE		REGION				4YR COLLEGE PLANS		ILLICIT DRUG USE: LIFETIME				
		M	F	White	Black	NE	NC	S	W	Yes	No	None	Mari- juana Only	Few Pills	More Pills	Any Her- oin
Weighted No. of Cases:	3656	1803	1741	2820	459	853	1091	1127	586	2036	1422	1210	782	515	1027	40
% of Weighted Total:	100.0	49.3	47.6	77.1	12.6	23.3	29.8	30.8	16.0	55.7	38.9	33.1	21.4	14.1	28.1	1.1

A04B: Parent

	TOTAL	M	F	White	Black	NE	NC	S	W	Yes	No	None	Mari- juana Only	Few Pills	More Pills	Any Her- oin
1. Poorly	2.6	3.6	1.6	2.3	3.8	2.9	2.7	2.0	3.3	2.4	2.5	2.0	3.0	3.6	2.4	7.5
2. Not so well	7.1	8.7	5.4	7.4	6.2	5.9	8.3	6.8	7.3	6.9	7.7	4.8	6.9	8.3	9.2	7.5
3. Fairly well	22.9	26.7	18.7	24.3	15.4	24.0	23.3	20.4	25.2	21.6	24.4	22.9	21.5	20.0	25.6	15.0
4. Well	36.4	36.1	37.0	37.6	27.8	36.0	38.6	36.2	33.6	36.1	37.9	36.1	36.1	38.9	36.5	35.0
5. Very well	31.0	24.8	37.2	28.4	46.5	31.3	27.1	34.7	30.6	32.9	27.5	34.2	32.4	29.2	26.3	35.0
Item 11780 N(Wtd)	3595	1782	1708	2788	449	833	1078	1109	575	2014	1394	1194	771	506	1009	40

A04C: Worker on a job

	TOTAL	M	F	White	Black	NE	NC	S	W	Yes	No	None	Mari- juana Only	Few Pills	More Pills	Any Her- oin
1. Poorly	.9	1.2	.6	.8	1.1	.7	1.3	.4	1.4	.7	1.2	.9	.1	1.2	1.5	2.5
2. Not so well	2.3	2.1	2.4	2.2	2.0	3.1	2.1	1.5	3.1	2.4	1.8	1.9	2.7	1.6	2.6	-
3. Fairly well	13.5	12.2	14.7	13.9	9.1	13.7	13.9	13.1	13.0	14.3	12.4	13.1	13.4	11.9	14.3	20.0
4. Well	39.1	40.3	38.0	40.0	33.3	38.3	44.0	36.1	36.6	37.7	41.9	37.6	39.3	40.5	40.8	30.0
5. Very well	44.2	44.3	44.3	43.0	54.7	44.1	38.7	48.8	46.1	44.9	42.6	46.3	44.6	45.0	41.0	45.0
Item 11790 N(Wtd)	3626	1788	1730	2812	453	845	1083	1118	579	2028	1409	1202	776	511	1023	40

A05: Apart from the particular kind of work you want to do, how would you rate each of the following settings as a place to work?

A05A: Working in a large corporation

	TOTAL	M	F	White	Black	NE	NC	S	W	Yes	No	None	Mari- juana Only	Few Pills	More Pills	Any Her- oin
1. Not at all acceptable	6.3	6.5	6.0	6.6	3.9	6.3	5.7	5.4	9.3	5.5	7.4	6.7	4.0	6.1	6.7	17.5
2. Somewhat acceptable	24.6	22.2	27.2	25.8	17.7	22.8	26.1	24.2	25.5	23.0	27.0	23.3	24.7	25.6	26.0	20.0
3. Acceptable	47.2	49.6	44.5	48.1	45.7	44.1	47.7	48.8	47.4	47.2	48.3	47.7	46.1	49.6	46.7	47.5
4. Desirable	21.9	21.8	22.3	19.5	32.6	26.9	20.6	21.5	17.8	24.2	17.2	22.4	25.2	18.7	20.4	15.0
Item 11800 N(Wtd)	3635	1795	1734	2815	457	848	1085	1122	580	2032	1416	1208	781	508	1023	40

A05B: Working in a small business

	TOTAL	M	F	White	Black	NE	NC	S	W	Yes	No	None	Mari- juana Only	Few Pills	More Pills	Any Her- oin
1. Not at all acceptable	4.5	4.6	4.2	3.6	6.3	5.1	4.3	4.7	3.5	4.0	4.3	4.3	4.6	3.7	4.3	15.0
2. Somewhat acceptable	23.6	24.5	22.8	20.6	32.8	21.0	24.4	24.9	23.6	22.5	25.0	25.2	23.5	20.0	22.5	25.0
3. Acceptable	52.7	50.9	54.7	54.4	49.2	54.8	52.6	50.6	54.1	54.2	51.1	50.6	55.5	55.5	53.0	35.0
4. Desirable	19.2	19.9	18.4	21.5	11.6	19.1	18.7	19.9	18.9	19.3	19.6	19.9	16.4	20.6	20.2	22.5
Item 11810 N(Wtd)	3629	1790	1734	2810	457	848	1085	1118	577	2031	1411	1208	780	510	1020	40

A05C: Working in a government agency

	TOTAL	M	F	White	Black	NE	NC	S	W	Yes	No	None	Mari- juana Only	Few Pills	More Pills	Any Her- oin
1. Not at all acceptable	20.5	21.0	19.4	21.4	14.9	18.2	21.1	20.6	22.4	16.9	25.5	20.4	18.9	19.4	22.3	12.5
2. Somewhat acceptable	32.6	32.7	33.4	35.5	21.7	33.7	35.4	27.5	36.0	33.0	33.7	32.5	32.8	33.4	32.8	40.0
3. Acceptable	31.1	30.8	31.9	30.3	36.2	30.1	30.6	33.5	29.3	33.5	27.5	32.3	31.4	30.8	30.3	22.5
4. Desirable	15.7	15.5	15.5	12.8	27.2	18.0	12.8	18.4	12.4	16.6	13.3	14.8	17.0	16.3	14.6	22.5
Item 11820 N(Wtd)	3633	1793	1733	2812	456	845	1084	1122	581	2029	1417	1206	777	509	1024	40

A05D: Working in the military service

	TOTAL	M	F	White	Black	NE	NC	S	W	Yes	No	None	Mari- juana Only	Few Pills	More Pills	Any Her- oin
1. Not at all acceptable	47.3	41.8	53.7	49.2	39.8	48.1	48.6	41.7	54.9	50.6	43.1	47.6	43.8	49.7	49.5	35.0
2. Somewhat acceptable	28.7	27.7	29.8	29.2	28.6	28.8	27.5	30.7	26.9	28.6	28.9	28.8	30.4	29.6	27.5	22.5
3. Acceptable	16.0	19.6	11.8	15.4	15.2	15.5	16.8	17.1	12.8	14.5	18.1	16.3	15.6	13.0	16.6	20.0
4. Desirable	8.0	10.9	4.7	6.2	16.5	7.6	7.2	10.6	5.4	6.3	9.8	7.3	10.0	7.7	6.3	20.0
Item 11830 N(Wtd)	3626	1789	1734	2813	455	844	1085	1118	579	2029	1413	1205	780	507	1025	40

A05E: Working in a school or university

	TOTAL	M	F	White	Black	NE	NC	S	W	Yes	No	None	Mari- juana Only	Few Pills	More Pills	Any Her- oin
1. Not at all acceptable	24.4	30.4	17.9	25.5	18.1	25.9	23.8	24.6	22.5	17.0	34.3	21.6	23.0	26.0	28.6	22.5
2. Somewhat acceptable	34.0	35.9	31.9	33.9	31.6	34.5	33.0	34.7	33.9	34.4	32.9	33.8	33.7	34.6	34.2	27.5
3. Acceptable	28.5	24.7	32.6	27.9	31.6	27.1	29.8	27.3	30.4	31.4	25.4	28.9	30.1	27.0	26.9	35.0
4. Desirable	13.1	9.0	17.5	12.8	18.8	12.4	13.3	13.5	13.3	17.2	7.4	15.8	13.1	12.6	10.4	12.5
Item 11840 N(Wtd)	3628	1787	1734	2812	453	849	1086	1115	579	2030	1413	1204	777	508	1024	40

QUESTIONNAIRE FORM 5 1981	TOTAL	SEX		RACE		REGION				4YR COLLEGE PLANS		ILLICIT DRUG USE: LIFETIME				
		M	F	White	Black	NE	NC	S	W	Yes	No	None	Mari-juana Only	Few Pills	More Pills	Any Her-oin
Weighted No. of Cases:	*3656*	*1803*	*1741*	*2820*	*459*	*853*	*1091*	*1127*	*586*	*2036*	*1422*	*1210*	*782*	*515*	*1027*	*40*
% of Weighted Total:	*100.0*	*49.3*	*47.6*	*77.1*	*12.6*	*23.3*	*29.8*	*30.8*	*16.0*	*55.7*	*38.9*	*33.1*	*21.4*	*14.1*	*28.1*	*1.1*

A05F: Working in a police department or police agency

1. Not at all acceptable	31.8	32.6	31.2	31.1	37.1	33.5	30.9	31.9	30.9	31.9	31.2	29.7	31.8	26.7	36.9	32.5
2. Somewhat acceptable	34.6	34.4	35.1	36.5	30.8	33.3	35.9	34.4	34.5	36.6	33.2	34.0	35.7	40.5	31.7	42.5
3. Acceptable	24.0	23.4	24.7	24.1	18.7	24.1	23.8	23.6	25.3	23.3	24.5	26.5	23.2	23.7	22.5	7.5
4. Desirable	9.5	9.6	9.1	8.4	13.4	9.1	9.3	10.0	9.3	8.2	11.1	9.9	9.2	9.1	8.8	15.0
Item 11850 N(Wtd)	*3631*	*1794*	*1731*	*2816*	*455*	*847*	*1085*	*1119*	*580*	*2031*	*1414*	*1206*	*779*	*506*	*1024*	*40*

A05G: Working in a social service organization

1. Not at all acceptable	21.9	32.9	10.3	23.2	12.6	22.3	22.5	20.6	22.9	19.7	24.6	20.4	25.2	21.9	22.0	15.0
2. Somewhat acceptable	33.7	38.8	28.6	33.3	38.1	32.6	31.8	37.1	32.4	32.5	35.4	33.9	34.2	32.9	33.3	32.5
3. Acceptable	29.6	22.5	36.9	28.7	32.6	30.4	30.2	29.0	28.4	31.6	27.2	32.2	26.7	29.8	28.8	30.0
4. Desirable	14.8	5.8	24.2	14.9	16.7	14.7	15.5	13.3	16.3	16.2	12.7	13.6	13.8	15.4	15.8	22.5
Item 11860 N(Wtd)	*3618*	*1783*	*1730*	*2806*	*454*	*846*	*1082*	*1112*	*577*	*2028*	*1405*	*1202*	*774*	*507*	*1023*	*40*

A05H: Working with a small group of partners

1. Not at all acceptable	10.2	10.3	9.8	8.6	17.1	9.6	10.6	11.5	8.1	7.8	12.6	10.1	8.6	10.4	10.0	23.1
2. Somewhat acceptable	27.7	26.1	29.3	25.4	35.0	27.3	26.1	30.4	26.1	25.4	30.3	28.4	29.7	28.0	26.2	17.9
3. Acceptable	43.0	44.4	41.8	45.4	34.1	42.9	45.5	41.4	41.8	44.8	42.2	43.9	45.4	43.1	41.0	28.2
4. Desirable	19.0	19.2	19.1	20.7	13.8	20.2	17.7	16.8	24.0	22.0	15.0	17.6	16.4	18.5	22.8	30.8
Item 11870 N(Wtd)	*3631*	*1794*	*1730*	*2811*	*457*	*847*	*1083*	*1122*	*579*	*2030*	*1413*	*1205*	*779*	*508*	*1023*	*39*

A05I: Working on your own (self-employed)

1. Not at all acceptable	8.1	5.1	11.2	7.9	9.8	8.8	9.0	7.7	6.2	8.4	7.6	8.9	8.2	10.4	5.5	10.0
2. Somewhat acceptable	15.9	12.6	19.5	15.2	15.7	16.7	14.4	14.9	19.3	16.3	15.0	17.6	18.5	15.1	13.2	2.5
3. Acceptable	29.8	30.3	29.7	30.1	28.6	31.7	32.0	27.2	27.5	30.7	28.4	29.0	34.4	28.5	27.5	35.0
4. Desirable	46.2	52.1	39.6	46.8	45.6	42.7	44.6	50.1	47.0	44.6	49.0	44.6	39.0	46.0	53.9	52.5
Item 11880 N(Wtd)	*3632*	*1791*	*1735*	*2815*	*458*	*848*	*1086*	*1120*	*579*	*2032*	*1415*	*1207*	*780*	*509*	*1023*	*40*

A06: If you were to get enough money to live as comfortably as you'd like for the rest of your life, would you want to work?

1. I would want to work	82.4	81.0	83.7	82.0	83.5	81.0	82.3	83.6	82.4	83.3	80.7	85.5	82.3	83.1	78.1	84.6
2. I would not want to work	17.6	19.0	16.3	18.0	16.3	19.0	17.7	16.4	17.6	16.7	19.3	14.5	17.7	17.1	22.0	15.4
Item 8100 N(Wtd)	*3606*	*1775*	*1727*	*2797*	*442*	*841*	*1080*	*1107*	*578*	*2019*	*1398*	*1196*	*770*	*510*	*1017*	*39*

A07: The next questions are about race relations. How much have you gotten to know people of other races...

A07A: In school?

1. Not at all	8.8	10.0	7.5	9.6	7.7	13.6	11.4	3.8	6.7	8.7	8.9	9.2	7.7	8.4	9.3	12.5
2. A little	24.1	24.7	24.1	27.0	14.0	28.6	29.1	17.3	21.5	25.6	22.6	22.6	24.3	26.3	24.7	35.0
3. Some	30.0	30.5	29.4	32.0	19.7	28.2	30.6	29.6	32.5	28.2	32.9	31.4	28.3	27.1	31.2	22.5
4. A lot	34.6	32.1	37.0	28.8	56.7	26.1	25.2	48.3	38.3	34.9	33.4	34.6	36.3	36.7	32.4	27.5
8. Does not apply to me	2.4	2.8	2.0	2.7	2.0	3.7	3.8	1.0	1.0	2.6	2.3	2.2	3.3	1.4	2.3	5.0
Item 11890 N(Wtd)	*3633*	*1793*	*1733*	*2808*	*457*	*844*	*1084*	*1123*	*582*	*2030*	*1412*	*1203*	*782*	*510*	*1023*	*40*

A07B: In your neighborhood?

1. Not at all	35.4	35.6	35.6	39.8	18.6	35.2	42.4	30.3	32.5	37.2	34.5	34.2	35.0	34.2	38.5	30.0
2. A little	22.0	22.6	21.3	21.8	20.4	24.3	18.9	22.1	24.0	21.5	21.9	21.5	20.1	24.4	23.2	22.5
3. Some	18.0	17.3	18.8	16.0	23.5	18.8	15.4	18.2	21.4	17.1	19.0	18.2	19.8	16.9	16.7	22.5
4. A lot	12.3	12.0	12.3	8.3	30.5	10.0	8.6	16.7	14.2	12.2	11.7	12.1	13.5	12.8	10.2	12.5
8. Does not apply to me	12.3	12.5	12.1	14.0	6.8	11.7	14.6	12.7	7.9	12.1	12.7	14.1	11.7	11.8	11.2	10.0
Item 11900 N(Wtd)	*3625*	*1790*	*1730*	*2806*	*456*	*844*	*1082*	*1120*	*579*	*2031*	*1407*	*1201*	*778*	*509*	*1025*	*40*

QUESTIONNAIRE FORM 5 1981	TOTAL	SEX		RACE		REGION				4YR COLLEGE PLANS		ILLICIT DRUG USE: LIFETIME				
		M	F	White	Black	NE	NC	S	W	Yes	No	None	Mari-juana Only	Few Pills	More Pills	Any Her-oin
Weighted No. of Cases:	3656	1803	1741	2820	459	853	1091	1127	586	2036	1422	1210	782	515	1027	40
% of Weighted Total:	100.0	49.3	47.6	77.1	12.6	23.3	29.8	30.8	16.0	55.7	38.9	33.1	21.4	14.1	28.1	1.1

A07C: In church?

1. Not at all	39.6	41.9	37.5	42.6	28.5	45.1	45.3	34.4	30.7	39.3	39.9	33.3	39.8	42.9	45.4	42.5
2. A little	20.2	19.0	21.6	20.4	18.3	20.3	19.4	19.7	22.2	21.7	19.1	24.0	19.9	16.6	18.6	12.5
3. Some	12.6	11.9	13.3	10.8	20.3	9.8	10.7	16.0	13.9	11.1	13.8	15.0	12.6	12.1	9.8	7.5
4. A lot	7.6	7.4	7.7	4.5	21.4	3.6	4.6	12.2	10.4	7.7	7.2	9.7	7.2	7.3	4.8	7.5
8. Does not apply to me	20.0	19.9	19.8	21.7	11.7	21.3	20.1	17.7	22.6	20.2	20.0	17.9	20.6	21.3	21.4	30.0
Item 11910 N(Wtd)	3617	1787	1726	2804	453	841	1085	1115	576	2029	1405	1198	778	506	1022	40

A07D: On sports teams?

1. Not at all	19.9	16.7	23.3	21.7	13.2	25.0	23.1	14.1	17.5	18.5	21.8	19.3	17.5	21.2	21.6	27.5
2. A little	16.4	16.6	16.7	17.2	10.4	17.3	18.8	13.3	16.6	16.7	16.5	15.9	17.5	14.3	17.2	20.0
3. Some	20.0	23.0	16.6	19.9	18.7	19.9	17.7	21.6	21.0	19.8	19.8	20.6	21.4	19.1	18.5	17.5
4. A lot	25.3	30.4	19.8	21.1	47.1	19.0	20.5	33.6	27.6	27.5	21.4	24.4	29.1	27.5	22.5	17.5
8. Does not apply to me	18.4	13.3	23.7	20.2	10.6	18.7	19.9	17.3	17.2	17.5	20.4	19.8	14.4	17.9	20.2	15.0
Item 11920 N(Wtd)	3620	1788	1728	2803	454	840	1084	1120	577	2026	1409	1199	777	509	1023	40

A07E: In clubs?

1. Not at all	27.5	29.4	25.4	29.8	18.3	33.8	33.7	19.0	23.1	25.8	30.2	26.2	25.4	25.9	31.3	32.5
2. A little	19.8	20.6	18.9	21.3	14.1	21.0	18.9	19.9	19.2	20.8	18.3	20.0	20.0	19.3	19.1	20.0
3. Some	19.4	17.7	21.1	18.2	23.6	16.4	15.0	25.8	19.8	21.3	17.1	19.2	22.3	18.5	17.7	20.0
4. A lot	14.3	12.4	16.2	10.9	30.8	9.3	10.5	19.8	17.9	15.8	11.3	15.4	14.2	17.7	11.4	10.0
8. Does not apply to me	19.1	19.8	18.3	19.9	13.2	19.6	21.9	15.6	20.3	16.4	23.1	19.2	17.8	18.7	20.5	15.0
Item 11930 N(Wtd)	3620	1784	1731	2803	454	843	1082	1118	577	2028	1405	1198	779	509	1021	40

A07F: On a job?

1. Not at all	15.4	17.1	14.2	17.4	6.4	16.5	20.5	10.6	14.0	15.1	16.7	16.2	15.6	14.8	14.9	20.0
2. A little	16.7	17.6	15.8	18.3	9.0	18.8	19.1	12.2	18.0	17.3	16.2	16.7	16.5	17.3	17.3	7.5
3. Some	23.3	23.7	22.9	22.8	24.9	24.1	21.3	24.1	24.8	22.7	24.3	22.2	22.4	21.3	25.8	22.5
4. A lot	32.4	31.2	33.7	28.6	51.1	27.4	25.4	42.7	33.1	33.0	30.4	29.8	32.8	36.2	32.8	42.5
8. Does not apply to me	12.1	10.4	13.5	12.8	8.8	13.2	13.8	10.6	10.1	11.9	12.3	15.0	13.0	10.4	9.4	7.5
Item 11940 N(Wtd)	3624	1788	1731	2804	454	844	1085	1118	577	2030	1409	1201	778	508	1025	40

A08: Thinking about the country as a whole, would you say relations between white people and black people have been getting better, getting worse, or staying pretty much the same?

1. Better	18.5	19.5	16.8	18.8	18.1	15.9	16.5	19.8	23.8	18.2	18.8	19.4	16.6	19.6	18.7	17.5
2. A little better	43.1	43.1	43.5	43.1	46.1	42.8	42.9	43.0	44.1	45.1	41.0	43.9	45.0	38.3	43.4	47.5
3. Same	23.7	23.5	24.2	23.8	21.0	27.1	25.2	21.4	20.3	23.3	23.8	22.5	24.0	26.5	23.5	15.0
4. A little worse	10.8	9.9	11.7	10.7	10.9	10.5	11.8	11.3	8.3	9.8	12.3	11.2	10.4	10.7	10.3	15.0
5. Worse	3.9	4.0	3.7	3.7	3.9	3.7	3.5	4.7	3.3	3.6	4.2	3.1	3.9	4.7	4.1	7.5
Item 11950 N(Wtd)	3641	1794	1739	2814	458	848	1089	1124	580	2031	1418	1207	778	514	1026	40

The next questions are about driving.

A09: Do you have a driver's license?

1. Yes	87.3	92.5	82.0	90.4	73.5	78.1	91.8	89.6	87.7	87.5	87.8	86.8	87.6	85.1	89.2	92.5
2. No, but I soon will-- GO TO Q.A13	9.9	5.9	14.1	7.6	19.6	17.1	5.5	8.1	11.2	9.7	9.6	10.2	9.4	11.3	9.0	5.0
3. No--GO TO Q.A13	2.8	1.6	3.9	2.0	6.9	4.8	2.6	2.2	1.1	2.8	2.6	3.0	3.2	3.6	1.8	-
Item 11960 N(Wtd)	3511	1742	1675	2777	404	808	1067	1083	553	1983	1363	1165	747	497	1003	40

A10: Do you own a car?

1. Yes	49.9	58.5	39.4	51.4	37.1	36.7	49.6	56.3	54.9	44.1	58.2	46.0	48.8	51.0	54.6	64.9
2. No, but I expect to own one in another year or two	30.6	26.1	36.0	28.5	44.5	34.0	31.3	30.0	26.1	28.8	32.8	27.7	32.6	31.7	31.7	27.0
3. No	19.5	15.4	24.6	20.1	18.4	29.1	19.2	13.7	18.9	27.0	9.0	26.3	18.7	17.4	13.6	8.1
Item 11970 N(Wtd) ★	3065	1612	1372	2507	299	632	979	968	486	1734	1195	1011	654	420	896	37

★=excludes respondents for whom question was inappropriate.

QUESTIONNAIRE FORM 5 1981	TOTAL	SEX		RACE		REGION				4YR COLLEGE PLANS		ILLICIT DRUG USE: LIFETIME				
		M	F	White	Black	NE	NC	S	W	Yes	No	None	Mari- juana Only	Few Pills	More Pills	Any Her- oin
Weighted No. of Cases:	3656	1803	1741	2820	459	853	1091	1127	586	2036	1422	1210	782	515	1027	40
% of Weighted Total:	100.0	49.3	47.6	77.1	12.6	23.3	29.8	30.8	16.0	55.7	38.9	33.1	21.4	14.1	28.1	1.1

A11: Are you able to use someone else's car when you want to?

	TOTAL	M	F	White	Black	NE	NC	S	W	Yes	No	None	Mari- juana Only	Few Pills	More Pills	Any Her- oin
1. Yes, whenever I wish	31.4	31.1	31.4	32.6	24.4	27.6	34.0	31.9	29.7	31.2	32.0	31.4	30.4	33.1	31.2	24.3
2. Yes, most of the time	44.9	43.5	46.7	45.3	46.2	46.0	43.9	44.4	46.8	46.5	43.4	47.6	44.6	41.4	43.6	56.8
3. Sometimes	16.5	17.7	15.3	15.5	19.4	17.8	14.8	17.4	16.1	15.5	17.6	14.3	18.0	19.3	16.6	10.8
4. Rarely	4.5	5.2	3.8	4.2	7.0	5.7	4.2	4.5	4.1	4.3	4.4	4.6	3.7	4.5	5.3	-
5. Never	2.7	2.5	2.8	2.5	2.7	2.9	3.0	1.9	3.3	2.4	2.6	2.1	2.9	1.7	3.4	10.8
Item 11980 N(Wtd) ★	3055	1608	1366	2498	299	630	979	962	485	1727	1193	1005	654	420	893	37

A12: Do you make an effort to cut down on driving, in order to save gasoline?

	TOTAL	M	F	White	Black	NE	NC	S	W	Yes	No	None	Mari- juana Only	Few Pills	More Pills	Any Her- oin
1. Not at all	8.6	10.2	6.7	8.7	9.4	12.3	7.2	7.7	8.2	8.5	8.1	5.1	8.3	8.1	12.5	10.8
2. Not very much	27.4	27.8	27.5	27.9	23.4	28.6	27.1	27.6	26.3	27.2	27.8	25.0	31.0	24.9	28.8	35.1
3. Yes, to some extent	48.9	47.0	50.7	48.9	49.8	44.0	49.5	51.2	49.4	48.0	51.0	51.9	48.2	53.1	44.6	29.7
4. Yes, quite a bit	12.7	13.3	12.1	12.4	13.7	11.9	13.7	11.6	14.2	13.9	10.8	15.8	10.6	11.8	11.5	16.2
8. Don't know	2.3	1.9	3.0	2.1	3.7	3.3	2.6	1.8	1.9	2.2	2.3	2.2	2.0	1.9	2.6	8.1
Item 11990 N(Wtd) ★	3064	1612	1371	2507	299	632	979	966	486	1736	1194	1010	654	422	895	37

A13: Do you make an effort to cut down on the amount of electricity you use in order to save energy?

	TOTAL	M	F	White	Black	NE	NC	S	W	Yes	No	None	Mari- juana Only	Few Pills	More Pills	Any Her- oin
1. Not at all	4.5	5.7	3.3	4.7	5.0	5.5	3.9	5.2	2.9	4.6	4.5	3.1	5.1	2.7	6.1	15.0
2. Not very much	22.0	23.3	21.2	22.6	18.6	20.4	21.5	22.5	24.4	22.4	22.0	21.3	23.1	20.4	22.7	25.0
3. Yes, to some extent	52.0	51.1	52.6	52.8	49.0	53.9	54.3	50.3	48.1	50.8	53.2	52.4	50.9	53.5	51.5	47.5
4. Yes, quite a bit	19.9	18.1	21.6	18.9	24.1	18.8	19.2	19.4	23.7	21.2	17.9	21.2	19.9	22.0	17.9	15.0
8. Don't know	1.6	1.8	1.3	1.2	3.1	1.3	1.1	2.6	.9	.8	2.3	1.9	.8	1.4	1.8	-
Item 12000 N(Wtd)	3644	1800	1739	2817	457	850	1088	1125	582	2033	1419	1207	782	514	1027	40

A14: In the house or apartment where you live, is an effort made to reduce heat during the winter, in order to save energy?

	TOTAL	M	F	White	Black	NE	NC	S	W	Yes	No	None	Mari- juana Only	Few Pills	More Pills	Any Her- oin
1. Not at all	3.7	3.7	3.3	2.4	10.3	3.1	1.4	6.1	4.1	3.4	3.7	3.5	3.2	4.1	3.7	7.5
2. Not very much	11.7	12.2	10.9	9.8	20.6	6.4	12.5	13.4	15.3	10.7	12.9	11.4	11.8	11.1	11.1	22.5
3. Yes, to some extent	39.8	41.7	38.0	39.9	38.9	37.3	41.5	40.2	39.5	40.2	39.2	38.0	42.6	38.8	40.9	35.0
4. Yes, quite a bit	42.8	40.6	45.8	46.5	27.6	50.7	43.0	38.5	39.2	44.1	42.1	44.6	40.8	43.9	43.2	30.0
8. Don't know	2.0	1.8	2.2	1.4	2.6	2.7	1.7	2.0	1.7	1.6	2.2	2.6	1.7	2.3	1.1	5.0
Item 12010 N(Wtd)	3643	1798	1739	2817	457	850	1089	1123	582	2032	1419	1206	782	513	1027	40

A15: How do you feel about each of the following?

A15A: How much do you enjoy shopping for things like clothes, records, sporting goods, and books?

	TOTAL	M	F	White	Black	NE	NC	S	W	Yes	No	None	Mari- juana Only	Few Pills	More Pills	Any Her- oin
1. Not at all	2.1	3.7	.4	2.2	.7	2.4	1.9	2.2	1.7	1.7	2.7	1.8	1.8	1.9	2.8	2.5
2. Not very much	10.4	17.1	3.7	11.2	3.9	12.0	11.2	8.5	10.7	9.6	10.9	10.8	9.7	9.1	11.0	17.5
3. Pretty much	32.5	44.4	20.0	34.2	23.6	34.8	32.1	32.1	30.8	33.2	31.5	33.6	32.4	31.3	31.8	37.5
4. Very much	54.9	34.9	76.0	52.4	71.8	50.9	54.7	57.3	56.9	55.5	55.0	53.8	56.3	57.6	54.3	42.5
Item 12020 N(Wtd)	3642	1798	1739	2817	457	850	1087	1123	582	2033	1419	1207	782	514	1027	40

A15B: How much do you care about having the latest fashion in your clothes, records, leisure activities, and so on?

	TOTAL	M	F	White	Black	NE	NC	S	W	Yes	No	None	Mari- juana Only	Few Pills	More Pills	Any Her- oin
1. Not at all	5.9	7.9	3.7	6.2	2.2	9.9	3.9	4.4	6.9	6.0	5.4	6.3	4.9	5.1	6.2	12.5
2. Not very much	26.9	32.0	21.8	29.2	15.3	26.7	29.7	22.9	29.8	26.6	27.6	29.9	23.4	29.8	24.9	35.0
3. Pretty much	39.2	39.0	39.3	40.7	30.6	37.4	40.8	38.6	40.0	40.2	38.2	38.9	39.8	36.8	40.3	40.0
4. Very much	27.9	21.1	35.2	23.9	52.1	25.9	25.6	34.0	23.4	27.2	28.8	24.8	31.8	28.3	28.7	12.5
Item 12030 N(Wtd)	3639	1799	1737	2814	457	850	1087	1122	580	2032	1418	1207	782	513	1025	40

★ = excludes respondents for whom question was inappropriate.

QUESTIONNAIRE FORM 5 1981	TOTAL	SEX		RACE		REGION				4YR COLLEGE PLANS		ILLICIT DRUG USE: LIFETIME				
		M	F	White	Black	NE	NC	S	W	Yes	No	None	Mari-juana Only	Few Pills	More Pills	Any Her-oin
Weighted No. of Cases:	3656	1803	1741	2820	459	853	1091	1127	586	2036	1422	1210	782	515	1027	40
% of Weighted Total:	100.0	49.3	47.6	77.1	12.6	23.3	29.8	30.8	16.0	55.7	38.9	33.1	21.4	14.1	28.1	1.1

A15C: How much do you care about whether your family has most of the things your friends and neighbors have?

1. Not at all	27.1	25.9	28.4	25.9	31.4	32.6	26.3	23.5	27.4	25.9	27.7	26.8	25.1	27.4	27.8	37.5
2. Not very much	47.5	49.5	45.3	48.5	41.1	45.4	48.2	47.7	49.0	48.2	47.2	48.8	46.7	47.1	47.8	42.5
3. Pretty much	19.0	18.6	19.5	20.3	15.4	17.4	19.4	20.1	18.8	19.7	18.9	18.7	21.8	18.7	17.8	10.0
4. Very much	6.4	6.0	6.7	5.3	12.3	4.6	6.1	8.7	5.0	6.3	6.2	5.7	6.5	6.6	6.5	10.0
Item 12040 N(Wtd)	3634	1796	1736	2813	455	850	1082	1122	580	2032	1415	1203	781	514	1025	40

A16: When you are older, do you expect to own more possessions than your parents do now, or about the same, or less?

I expect to own...

1. Much less than my parents	2.0	2.1	1.9	1.9	1.3	2.4	2.0	1.7	1.7	1.5	2.5	2.1	1.7	1.2	2.5	2.5
2. Somewhat less than my parents	8.6	8.0	9.3	9.3	4.4	9.6	9.3	6.6	9.4	7.9	9.5	7.7	7.6	9.2	9.8	5.0
3. About as much as my parents	37.2	33.6	40.7	40.0	25.1	36.7	38.0	37.1	36.9	34.3	41.9	41.6	33.2	33.7	36.6	45.0
4. Somewhat more than my parents	36.3	36.4	36.1	35.6	37.4	35.0	36.8	37.4	35.0	37.7	34.8	34.6	40.8	35.9	35.4	27.5
5. Much more than my parents	15.9	19.9	12.2	13.2	31.9	16.4	13.8	17.1	16.8	18.7	11.4	14.1	16.7	19.9	15.8	20.0
Item 12050 N(Wtd)	3624	1791	1729	2800	455	843	1084	1120	577	2018	1415	1198	777	513	1023	40

A17: Compared with your parents, what is the smallest amount that you could be content or satisfied to own?

The least I could be content to own is...

1. Much less than my parents	10.3	10.7	9.7	11.3	6.2	11.5	9.5	9.3	11.7	10.9	9.1	10.2	10.0	7.8	11.5	23.1
2. Somewhat less than my parents	31.6	29.6	34.0	35.6	14.6	31.5	36.6	25.2	35.0	32.6	31.2	32.7	31.0	28.0	34.6	12.8
3. About as much as my parents	40.9	40.4	41.3	39.4	46.4	38.8	38.8	46.6	36.4	38.8	43.8	41.8	40.1	44.8	37.0	43.6
4. Somewhat more than my parents	12.8	13.7	11.9	10.4	23.6	12.7	11.6	13.9	13.1	13.2	12.3	10.9	14.0	15.5	12.5	10.3
5. Much more than my parents	4.4	5.5	3.2	3.3	9.5	5.4	3.4	5.0	3.7	4.5	3.6	4.4	4.8	3.9	4.2	10.3
Item 12060 N(Wtd)	3595	1772	1720	2779	453	832	1079	1113	571	2007	1401	1194	770	511	1013	39

A18: These next questions ask your opinions about a number of different topics. How much do you agree or disagree with each statement below?

A18A: We ought to worry about our own country and let the rest of the world take care of itself

1. Disagree	21.5	22.8	20.4	19.5	28.2	22.1	20.4	21.5	22.7	22.7	19.2	24.4	21.5	20.5	18.7	17.5
2. Mostly disagree	24.8	22.3	28.0	27.0	17.5	27.0	23.7	24.2	25.0	28.9	19.8	25.0	25.4	26.6	23.8	35.0
3. Neither	14.2	13.2	14.8	13.9	9.6	15.6	13.1	11.9	18.5	14.1	14.3	11.7	14.9	13.9	17.0	10.0
4. Mostly agree	26.0	24.8	27.2	27.4	24.7	24.9	29.9	25.2	21.8	24.0	28.5	26.3	25.3	25.8	26.2	27.5
5. Agree	13.5	17.0	9.7	12.2	19.9	10.6	12.9	17.1	12.0	10.4	18.1	12.6	13.0	13.5	14.3	10.0
Item 12070 N(Wtd)	3634	1797	1734	2811	457	848	1087	1122	577	2030	1416	1206	778	512	1026	40

A18B: It would be better if we all felt more like citizens of the world than of any particular country

1. Disagree	10.6	12.9	7.9	11.1	7.5	11.3	8.4	12.2	10.3	10.4	10.5	9.0	10.7	14.1	10.5	15.0
2. Mostly disagree	13.0	13.9	11.8	14.8	6.4	13.2	14.7	12.8	9.9	13.0	13.1	13.7	13.1	14.6	11.8	7.5
3. Neither	18.1	19.3	17.0	18.6	14.5	16.5	20.4	15.8	20.3	18.0	18.6	16.6	16.0	20.3	20.5	17.5
4. Mostly agree	28.5	25.5	31.4	28.3	27.7	28.8	29.6	27.0	28.9	28.3	29.0	28.4	29.8	25.8	28.1	30.0
5. Agree	30.0	28.3	31.8	27.2	44.2	30.2	27.0	32.3	30.8	30.4	28.8	32.3	30.4	25.4	29.1	30.0
Item 12080 N(Wtd)	3620	1793	1727	2802	455	844	1085	1116	575	2025	1412	1202	779	512	1019	40

QUESTIONNAIRE FORM 5 1981	TOTAL	SEX		RACE		REGION				4YR COLLEGE PLANS		ILLICIT DRUG USE: LIFETIME				
		M	F	White	Black	NE	NC	S	W	Yes	No	None	Mari-juana Only	Few Pills	More Pills	Any Her-oin
Weighted No. of Cases:	3656	1803	1741	2820	459	853	1091	1127	586	2036	1422	1210	782	515	1027	40
% of Weighted Total:	100.0	49.3	47.6	77.1	12.6	23.3	29.8	30.8	16.0	55.7	38.9	33.1	21.4	14.1	28.1	1.1
A18C: I find it hard to be sympathetic toward starving people in foreign lands, when there is so much trouble in our own country																
1. Disagree	35.2	23.4	47.4	34.0	42.5	36.0	32.0	38.0	34.5	35.8	33.3	37.6	34.7	32.3	33.2	47.5
2. Mostly disagree	24.2	23.4	25.2	25.5	16.6	25.8	25.6	21.3	24.5	26.5	21.5	23.5	25.4	25.3	24.7	10.0
3. Neither	13.5	16.4	10.0	13.7	10.8	13.7	14.7	11.4	14.8	13.5	13.4	11.1	13.3	14.2	16.1	20.0
4. Mostly agree	16.2	21.2	10.9	16.7	15.3	14.9	16.9	16.9	15.3	14.9	18.0	16.0	15.6	14.8	17.0	15.0
5. Agree	11.0	15.5	6.5	10.2	14.6	9.5	10.8	12.4	10.8	9.2	13.8	11.9	11.1	13.4	8.8	7.5
Item 12090 N(Wtd)	3624	1790	1733	2809	452	845	1086	1117	576	2029	1414	1202	777	514	1023	40
A18D: Maybe some minority groups do get unfair treatment, but that's no business of mine																
1. Disagree	41.8	33.1	51.2	39.0	55.9	43.6	38.2	41.8	45.8	46.7	35.5	47.5	41.6	39.6	37.3	30.0
2. Mostly disagree	28.8	30.6	27.4	31.0	18.7	29.3	32.4	26.5	25.8	29.8	27.3	24.9	29.5	35.5	29.8	37.5
3. Neither	17.7	21.4	13.5	19.3	10.2	16.4	19.1	17.0	18.4	14.9	21.8	15.7	18.8	14.3	20.8	22.5
4. Mostly agree	7.0	8.7	5.1	6.4	8.5	7.3	6.5	8.1	5.9	5.7	8.8	6.8	5.3	7.4	8.2	5.0
5. Agree	4.7	6.2	2.8	4.2	6.7	3.6	3.8	6.6	4.2	2.8	6.6	5.3	4.8	3.1	3.9	5.0
Item 12100 N(Wtd)	3619	1789	1730	2809	449	841	1085	1117	577	2023	1416	1199	776	512	1023	40
A18E: I get very upset when I see other people treated unfairly																
1. Disagree	2.9	3.2	2.4	3.0	3.1	3.6	2.3	3.1	2.8	2.7	3.2	2.3	3.1	3.9	2.9	5.0
2. Mostly disagree	4.9	7.1	2.5	5.0	4.2	4.5	5.4	4.3	5.2	4.7	4.6	3.8	6.9	4.1	5.0	7.5
3. Neither	8.1	12.6	3.6	9.0	5.0	7.6	10.0	6.4	8.5	6.4	10.7	6.8	7.3	7.4	10.8	10.0
4. Mostly agree	31.3	35.5	26.3	32.4	27.4	29.6	32.9	31.4	30.2	31.5	31.3	29.1	31.0	33.3	32.6	30.0
5. Agree	52.9	41.6	65.2	50.7	60.3	54.8	49.5	54.6	53.4	54.8	50.2	57.9	51.7	51.5	48.7	47.5
Item 12110 N(Wtd)	3625	1789	1734	2805	456	845	1083	1120	577	2026	1414	1200	780	513	1023	40
A18F: I would agree to a good plan to make a better life for the poor, even if it cost me money																
1. Disagree	8.0	12.0	4.1	8.7	4.6	7.5	8.0	7.8	9.2	6.7	10.1	6.7	8.0	8.4	9.5	7.5
2. Mostly disagree	10.3	12.8	7.7	11.4	5.3	9.5	10.7	10.5	9.9	10.1	10.5	8.3	11.7	10.2	12.0	5.0
3. Neither	22.8	24.4	20.9	25.1	14.3	23.3	25.7	20.0	21.8	21.3	25.5	19.2	23.2	23.5	27.0	17.5
4. Mostly agree	36.2	33.6	39.2	36.7	32.8	38.9	38.1	33.5	33.8	38.9	31.9	39.4	36.2	35.6	33.6	27.5
5. Agree	22.8	17.2	28.1	18.1	43.2	20.7	17.4	28.2	25.4	22.9	22.0	26.5	21.1	22.5	18.0	42.5
Item 12120 N(Wtd)	3618	1788	1728	2799	454	844	1084	1116	574	2024	1412	1201	777	511	1019	40
A18G: It's not really my problem if others are in trouble and need help																
1. Disagree	40.6	32.0	49.3	38.2	49.7	42.3	36.6	42.7	41.5	42.6	37.2	45.5	40.1	36.5	37.3	35.0
2. Mostly disagree	35.4	37.5	33.5	37.7	26.0	37.4	39.4	31.9	31.8	37.3	33.6	31.5	38.8	38.9	36.5	45.0
3. Neither	13.2	15.9	10.3	13.8	10.6	11.4	14.9	12.2	14.4	11.7	15.1	10.9	12.3	14.8	16.5	7.5
4. Mostly agree	7.8	10.3	5.2	7.7	7.3	7.0	6.7	8.3	9.7	6.4	9.7	8.8	5.5	7.6	7.2	5.0
5. Agree	3.1	4.3	1.8	2.6	6.4	2.0	2.4	4.9	2.6	2.0	4.3	3.3	3.2	2.3	2.6	10.0
Item 12130 N(Wtd)	3620	1791	1729	2802	453	840	1085	1118	576	2022	1413	1205	775	512	1019	40
A18H: Americans could change their eating habits to provide more food for the hungry people in other parts of the world, and at the same time be healthier themselves																
1. Disagree	9.8	14.8	4.5	9.8	10.1	8.5	10.0	10.7	9.5	9.7	10.2	9.0	12.3	9.0	9.1	10.0
2. Mostly disagree	9.8	11.9	7.4	10.4	8.4	8.9	11.0	9.6	9.2	9.2	10.7	8.7	9.7	11.3	10.5	20.0
3. Neither	16.3	19.4	13.3	16.8	14.3	16.5	17.9	14.6	16.2	17.0	15.2	16.5	16.4	16.2	16.5	10.0
4. Mostly agree	29.3	29.1	29.9	30.1	26.0	29.8	29.8	28.9	28.2	28.6	30.5	29.2	29.4	27.9	29.7	25.0
5. Agree	34.8	24.8	44.8	33.0	41.2	36.2	31.2	36.1	36.8	35.6	33.4	36.4	32.2	35.4	34.4	32.5
Item 12140 N(Wtd)	3624	1792	1733	2806	454	843	1087	1116	579	2028	1414	1205	780	512	1021	40

QUESTIONNAIRE FORM 5 1981	TOTAL	SEX		RACE		REGION				4YR COLLEGE PLANS		ILLICIT DRUG USE: LIFETIME				
		M	F	White	Black	NE	NC	S	W	Yes	No	None	Mari- juana Only	Few Pills	More Pills	Any Her- oin
Weighted No. of Cases:	3656	1803	1741	2820	459	853	1091	1127	586	2036	1422	1210	782	515	1027	40
% of Weighted Total:	100.0	49.3	47.6	77.1	12.6	23.3	29.8	30.8	16.0	55.7	38.9	33.1	21.4	14.1	28.1	1.1

A18I: My family and I often buy things we really don't need; we could get along with much less

1. Disagree	14.2	17.0	11.4	12.4	23.2	16.0	13.5	14.0	13.0	12.9	15.7	14.8	14.8	13.5	12.9	12.5
2. Mostly disagree	16.0	17.5	14.5	16.8	12.4	16.8	14.8	14.7	19.6	15.4	17.1	16.4	17.0	17.6	14.5	15.0
3. Neither	15.6	17.7	13.4	15.9	10.0	17.2	16.7	12.1	17.9	15.5	15.5	14.9	15.5	16.1	16.1	10.0
4. Mostly agree	30.1	28.9	31.6	31.1	25.7	29.3	33.0	29.2	27.3	31.7	28.1	30.4	28.4	30.8	30.5	42.5
5. Agree	24.1	19.0	29.2	23.7	28.3	20.5	22.0	29.9	22.2	24.6	23.5	23.6	24.4	22.0	25.8	17.5
Item 10060 N(Wtd)	3617	1787	1730	2805	452	843	1085	1114	576	2024	1411	1202	776	510	1022	40

A18J: Most people will have fuller and happier lives if they choose legal marriage rather than staying single, or just living with someone

1. Disagree	21.6	20.0	23.2	21.0	24.8	28.5	20.5	15.9	24.3	21.3	22.2	12.3	21.3	25.4	29.7	40.0
2. Mostly disagree	13.3	13.5	13.7	13.3	14.1	14.6	13.1	11.8	14.9	13.3	13.1	8.0	13.8	15.3	18.4	20.0
3. Neither	24.9	25.5	24.0	25.0	22.4	26.5	25.7	23.3	23.9	25.6	23.9	25.0	28.4	20.9	24.6	20.0
4. Mostly agree	15.9	17.3	14.0	16.7	12.7	15.3	16.8	16.2	14.2	15.3	16.3	18.3	13.9	17.2	13.7	7.5
5. Agree	24.3	23.7	25.1	24.0	25.7	14.9	23.9	32.8	22.7	24.4	24.5	36.4	22.6	21.3	13.7	12.5
Item 12150 N(Wtd)	3620	1788	1731	2805	455	841	1087	1115	577	2024	1412	1203	778	511	1022	40

A18K: Parents should encourage just as much independence in their daughters as in their sons

1. Disagree	5.8	8.6	2.5	4.8	8.2	7.3	4.7	6.0	5.0	6.1	4.7	6.2	5.8	4.9	5.2	15.0
2. Mostly disagree	7.6	11.6	3.8	7.5	6.9	8.9	8.0	6.6	6.9	9.0	4.9	7.3	8.9	8.4	6.9	2.5
3. Neither	8.5	13.5	3.5	8.4	7.1	8.5	8.2	8.4	9.2	7.3	10.2	7.3	9.5	9.0	8.8	5.0
4. Mostly agree	24.0	29.2	18.7	24.5	18.9	23.3	25.4	24.4	21.8	22.2	26.8	24.0	24.7	25.0	22.6	20.0
5. Agree	54.1	37.1	71.5	54.8	59.1	52.0	53.7	54.5	57.1	55.4	53.4	55.3	51.1	53.1	56.5	55.0
Item 12160 N(Wtd)	3614	1782	1732	2801	450	838	1085	1113	578	2026	1407	1197	777	512	1020	40

A18L: Being a mother and raising children is one of the most fulfilling experiences a woman can have

1. Disagree	7.2	5.0	9.6	7.1	8.0	6.8	7.3	6.3	9.0	7.7	6.5	5.5	5.3	8.9	9.5	17.9
2. Mostly disagree	6.6	6.3	7.1	7.1	4.7	7.1	6.3	5.3	8.8	6.9	6.4	5.6	6.6	5.3	8.2	10.3
3. Neither	27.1	39.2	15.3	29.3	16.0	31.6	30.1	21.1	26.6	29.6	23.9	24.9	27.6	26.7	30.6	12.8
4. Mostly agree	26.6	23.9	28.7	26.9	22.2	26.9	28.5	25.1	25.0	25.5	27.2	26.1	30.4	29.3	22.2	30.8
5. Agree	32.6	25.7	39.3	29.6	48.9	27.4	27.8	42.1	30.7	30.2	35.8	37.9	30.0	29.7	29.5	28.2
Item 12170 N(Wtd)	3551	1727	1729	2747	450	828	1066	1090	567	1994	1378	1174	767	505	1000	39

A18M: Most fathers should spend more time with their children than they do now

1. Disagree	1.6	2.0	1.2	1.5	1.8	2.7	.8	1.4	1.6	1.3	2.0	1.2	2.3	1.8	1.4	5.0
2. Mostly disagree	2.8	2.7	2.9	3.0	1.8	3.4	3.6	1.2	3.6	3.0	2.3	3.5	1.8	2.3	2.8	5.0
3. Neither	13.4	14.4	12.6	14.7	6.9	16.9	13.7	9.9	14.8	13.7	12.6	10.6	14.2	13.3	16.2	17.5
4. Mostly agree	34.4	36.2	32.6	35.9	27.7	34.6	38.3	30.9	33.2	35.5	32.7	32.8	35.5	35.1	35.7	20.0
5. Agree	47.8	44.7	50.7	44.9	62.2	42.4	43.5	56.7	47.0	46.5	50.4	52.0	46.2	47.8	43.9	55.0
Item 12180 N(Wtd)	3618	1787	1732	2804	452	841	1086	1115	576	2026	1409	1203	777	513	1017	40

A18N: The husband should make all the important decisions in the family

1. Disagree	40.5	25.7	56.4	41.3	41.4	44.0	40.7	37.1	41.6	44.9	35.6	38.9	39.3	40.5	44.7	30.0
2. Mostly disagree	20.3	21.2	19.6	21.5	16.1	20.3	23.5	18.2	18.5	20.2	20.1	19.2	22.0	20.4	20.4	20.0
3. Neither	16.6	23.1	10.0	16.5	14.5	15.7	16.7	15.5	19.8	16.5	17.2	16.2	15.1	16.9	18.1	25.0
4. Mostly agree	14.2	17.9	9.8	13.6	16.5	11.9	13.0	19.0	10.6	11.5	17.6	16.5	12.9	15.4	11.0	10.0
5. Agree	8.4	12.1	4.3	7.1	11.5	8.1	6.2	10.2	9.4	6.9	9.5	9.2	10.7	6.8	5.9	15.0
Item 12190 N(Wtd)	3621	1787	1734	2808	454	841	1087	1116	577	2028	1410	1207	776	514	1019	40

QUESTIONNAIRE FORM 5 1981	TOTAL	SEX		RACE		REGION				4YR COLLEGE PLANS		ILLICIT DRUG USE: LIFETIME				
		M	F	White	Black	NE	NC	S	W	Yes	No	None	Mari-juana Only	Few Pills	More Pills	Any Her-oin
Weighted No. of Cases:	3656	1803	1741	2820	459	853	1091	1127	586	2036	1422	1210	782	515	1027	40
% of Weighted Total:	100.0	49.3	47.6	77.1	12.6	23.3	29.8	30.8	16.0	55.7	38.9	33.1	21.4	14.1	28.1	1.1

A19: Some people think about what's going on in government very often, and others are not that interested. How much of an interest do you take in government and current events?

1. No interest at all	2.7	2.9	2.6	2.4	3.5	3.0	2.5	3.0	2.3	1.6	4.1	2.5	2.4	2.7	3.1	2.5
2. Very little interest	14.2	11.1	17.2	13.9	16.1	15.8	13.6	13.6	14.2	10.8	18.9	14.0	15.3	14.3	12.9	10.0
3. Some interest	47.1	43.1	50.9	46.6	50.2	45.3	50.6	45.5	46.4	44.3	52.0	46.1	45.1	49.8	48.4	45.0
4. A lot of interest	25.9	29.1	22.9	26.6	23.1	25.4	24.5	27.0	27.4	29.5	20.3	27.4	25.8	23.8	26.0	25.0
5. A very great interest	10.0	13.7	6.5	10.6	7.0	10.8	8.8	11.0	9.5	13.8	4.7	9.9	11.2	9.4	9.6	17.5
Item 6330 N(Wtd)	3619	1785	1736	2805	454	844	1086	1113	576	2025	1413	1203	778	512	1020	40

A20: If you have at least an average income in the future, how likely is it that you will contribute money to the following organizations? If you have already contributed, mark the last circle only. Are you likely to contribute to...

A20A: The United Fund or other community charities?

1. Definitely not	3.8	5.4	1.9	3.8	2.7	4.1	3.0	4.0	4.6	2.8	5.1	2.3	4.1	4.9	4.3	5.0
2. Probably not	15.4	18.5	11.9	16.9	9.5	15.0	16.0	13.8	17.9	15.9	14.6	14.1	14.1	17.1	17.6	12.5
3. Don't know	43.1	43.5	42.9	43.6	38.5	41.3	42.0	42.8	48.8	40.3	47.6	41.8	43.7	41.7	45.4	30.0
4. Probably will	26.9	23.9	29.9	25.4	35.2	28.1	27.1	28.1	22.6	29.9	22.7	30.6	27.4	27.5	21.9	35.0
5. Definitely will	3.2	2.8	3.7	2.4	7.1	3.7	2.8	4.0	1.9	3.3	3.0	4.0	3.2	2.8	2.5	2.5
6. Already have	7.5	5.8	9.6	7.9	7.3	7.9	9.1	7.4	4.2	7.8	6.9	7.2	7.3	6.1	8.4	15.0
Item 12200 N(Wtd)	3592	1775	1721	2789	452	836	1078	1108	570	2014	1403	1190	778	509	1012	40

A20B: International relief organizations (CARE, UNICEF, etc.)?

1. Definitely not	4.0	6.3	1.5	4.4	1.5	3.9	4.2	3.5	4.7	3.4	5.2	2.6	4.5	5.1	4.6	7.5
2. Probably not	12.2	16.1	8.2	13.5	7.3	10.6	12.0	12.6	14.4	12.0	12.4	12.1	11.1	10.5	14.4	2.5
3. Don't know	29.7	33.0	26.0	29.9	26.7	25.3	30.5	32.1	29.8	26.5	33.9	30.2	29.2	29.2	29.8	22.5
4. Probably will	35.1	30.7	39.6	34.2	41.2	33.8	36.3	34.6	35.4	37.2	32.5	36.9	36.1	37.9	31.7	20.0
5. Definitely will	7.8	6.2	9.4	6.2	14.8	10.6	5.0	8.8	7.0	8.0	7.2	7.4	8.4	7.6	7.0	22.5
6. Already have	11.3	7.7	15.2	11.8	8.6	15.7	12.1	8.4	8.9	12.9	8.7	10.7	10.7	9.5	12.5	27.5
Item 12210 N(Wtd)	3603	1779	1727	2795	454	837	1083	1112	571	2020	1408	1195	778	514	1015	40

A20C: Minority group organizations (NAACP, SCLS, etc.)?

1. Definitely not	11.6	16.9	6.2	13.7	1.3	11.4	11.0	12.4	11.6	11.3	12.2	10.8	11.0	13.1	12.6	10.0
2. Probably not	25.6	26.5	24.9	30.7	4.7	23.8	30.4	22.6	25.1	26.7	24.7	24.0	25.0	24.6	29.1	25.0
3. Don't know	40.0	36.6	43.5	41.9	23.5	44.4	39.5	36.1	42.2	36.8	44.6	40.0	38.1	39.2	42.4	42.5
4. Probably will	15.4	13.7	17.1	11.6	33.9	15.6	14.4	16.8	14.4	17.0	13.3	17.0	17.4	16.4	11.4	17.5
5. Definitely will	5.4	4.5	6.1	1.4	26.2	3.7	3.2	8.8	5.6	6.2	3.6	6.0	6.1	5.5	3.4	5.0
6. Already have	1.9	1.8	2.1	.6	10.4	1.1	1.6	3.4	1.1	2.0	1.8	2.3	2.6	1.2	1.2	2.5
Item 12220 N(Wtd)	3579	1767	1716	2780	451	833	1074	1103	569	2010	1395	1189	775	505	1008	40

A20D: Church or religious organizations?

1. Definitely not	5.2	6.8	3.6	5.8	1.6	7.4	3.8	2.9	9.1	5.6	5.3	4.2	4.3	5.5	6.9	15.4
2. Probably not	8.3	7.8	9.0	9.2	2.7	9.7	8.4	4.9	13.2	8.4	8.0	5.2	7.4	10.8	12.1	5.1
3. Don't know	13.5	14.9	12.0	12.8	12.0	14.1	14.7	11.0	14.7	10.7	17.4	10.9	14.3	13.1	15.3	20.5
4. Probably will	24.1	25.6	22.3	24.0	27.3	23.5	24.4	24.4	24.0	21.8	27.2	23.0	24.4	25.2	24.6	28.2
5. Definitely will	16.2	15.8	16.5	14.6	27.5	13.7	14.9	21.9	11.4	17.8	13.9	19.3	17.8	14.9	12.5	7.7
6. Already have	32.6	29.2	36.6	33.7	29.0	31.7	33.9	34.8	27.4	35.7	28.4	37.4	32.0	30.5	28.8	25.6
Item 12230 N(Wtd)	3595	1776	1723	2790	451	839	1080	1106	570	2013	1406	1195	775	511	1012	39

QUESTIONNAIRE FORM 5 1981	TOTAL	SEX		RACE		REGION				4YR COLLEGE PLANS		ILLICIT DRUG USE: LIFETIME				
		M	F	White	Black	NE	NC	S	W	Yes	No	None	Marijuana Only	Few Pills	More Pills	Any Heroin
Weighted No. of Cases:	3656	1803	1741	2820	459	853	1091	1127	586	2036	1422	1210	782	515	1027	40
% of Weighted Total:	100.0	49.3	47.6	77.1	12.6	23.3	29.8	30.8	16.0	55.7	38.9	33.1	21.4	14.1	28.1	1.1

A20E: Political parties or organizations?

1. Definitely not	16.7	18.0	15.2	15.8	21.4	18.2	15.6	15.7	17.8	15.0	19.0	16.4	17.3	13.9	18.0	17.9
2. Probably not	25.6	23.0	28.3	26.8	18.5	26.2	28.0	23.0	24.9	25.8	25.8	23.6	24.7	29.0	27.1	20.5
3. Don't know	33.9	33.6	34.5	32.8	37.9	31.8	34.9	34.9	33.0	31.5	37.8	35.3	36.4	32.3	31.0	28.2
4. Probably will	16.7	17.7	15.3	17.2	15.8	17.3	15.9	17.3	16.0	18.8	12.6	17.5	14.9	17.0	17.0	17.9
5. Definitely will	3.8	3.9	3.3	3.7	3.4	2.9	2.5	5.2	4.8	4.4	2.9	3.7	3.9	3.7	3.7	5.1
6. Already have	3.4	3.7	3.2	3.7	3.2	3.5	3.0	3.8	3.5	4.3	2.0	3.6	2.8	4.1	3.2	7.7
Item 12240 N(Wtd)	3579	1766	1720	2785	443	833	1080	1100	567	2012	1394	1185	773	511	1011	39

A20F: Citizen lobbies (Common Cause, Public Citizen, etc.)?

1. Definitely not	10.2	12.1	8.0	10.3	9.0	10.9	10.6	9.7	9.0	9.2	11.8	9.1	10.8	11.4	10.0	15.0
2. Probably not	24.3	25.2	24.0	26.6	16.9	25.1	26.4	21.2	25.5	25.9	22.2	24.4	23.7	24.0	26.4	17.5
3. Don't know	45.4	43.2	47.8	45.4	42.2	44.8	45.6	45.2	46.4	44.4	47.6	45.3	46.8	46.6	44.3	40.0
4. Probably will	16.0	15.5	16.0	14.4	23.6	15.0	14.2	18.8	15.8	16.0	15.2	17.4	14.8	14.5	15.5	17.5
5. Definitely will	3.0	2.9	3.1	2.2	7.4	2.8	2.5	3.8	2.7	3.2	2.7	2.8	3.2	2.6	2.9	5.0
6. Already have	1.0	1.0	1.0	1.1	.9	1.6	.7	1.3	.7	1.2	.6	1.0	.8	1.2	1.0	5.0
Item 12250 N(Wtd)	3573	1762	1715	2785	445	829	1074	1104	565	2007	1393	1181	772	509	1012	40

A20G: Charities to help fight diseases (cancer, heart disease, etc.)?

1. Definitely not	1.1	1.6	.5	1.0	.9	1.8	.8	.6	1.4	.9	1.4	.9	1.0	2.1	.8	2.6
2. Probably not	2.6	4.5	.7	2.7	2.0	2.5	2.7	2.7	2.5	2.3	2.9	2.8	2.3	2.0	2.7	-
3. Don't know	11.9	15.2	8.4	11.5	12.0	11.7	10.8	10.8	16.2	10.7	13.4	12.2	12.9	9.4	11.8	7.7
4. Probably will	37.3	40.2	34.7	38.4	33.6	34.8	38.1	36.5	40.8	37.5	37.2	38.4	36.7	36.5	38.0	28.2
5. Definitely will	27.9	24.8	30.7	25.5	38.2	26.8	27.4	30.7	25.4	28.4	27.2	27.1	28.5	29.1	26.9	28.2
6. Already have	19.2	13.6	24.9	20.8	13.6	22.4	20.2	18.7	13.6	20.3	18.0	18.5	18.4	20.7	19.9	33.3
Item 12260 N(Wtd)	3589	1774	1718	2789	450	838	1078	1104	568	2013	1403	1189	776	512	1012	39

A20H: Organizations concerned with population problems (Planned Parenthood, ZPG, etc.)?

1. Definitely not	7.9	11.0	4.8	8.7	4.2	9.8	7.1	8.0	6.3	7.6	8.3	8.2	8.2	7.3	7.8	5.1
2. Probably not	19.8	22.7	16.6	21.7	12.2	19.5	22.5	17.9	18.7	21.9	17.3	20.3	18.9	19.4	20.5	10.3
3. Don't know	40.7	41.9	39.7	40.7	41.5	39.6	41.3	41.7	39.4	39.8	42.5	43.1	42.6	41.1	36.5	38.5
4. Probably will	22.4	18.2	26.8	21.3	27.5	21.9	21.8	22.7	23.8	23.2	21.1	20.6	22.4	23.4	23.8	28.2
5. Definitely will	7.6	5.0	10.1	5.9	12.0	7.8	5.6	8.3	9.8	6.2	8.9	6.6	6.2	7.5	9.4	10.3
6. Already have	1.6	1.2	2.1	1.5	2.7	1.4	1.8	1.4	2.1	1.2	1.9	1.1	1.7	1.4	2.1	7.7
Item 12270 N(Wtd)	3595	1776	1723	2791	451	835	1080	1109	571	2017	1405	1192	777	509	1016	39

A20I: Organizations concerned with environmental problems (Sierra Club, Friends of Earth, etc.)?

1. Definitely not	6.9	8.4	5.5	6.7	7.5	7.4	6.9	7.3	5.4	6.2	8.1	6.7	5.8	7.6	7.4	5.1
2. Probably not	17.9	16.8	19.1	18.8	16.8	14.7	22.0	16.8	17.1	18.5	17.4	17.5	19.7	16.4	18.1	10.3
3. Don't know	39.6	34.8	44.4	38.1	45.7	38.8	41.0	41.8	33.6	37.4	42.7	42.1	42.9	37.8	34.7	38.5
4. Probably will	23.2	25.1	20.8	23.4	21.2	22.7	21.0	24.2	26.0	24.1	21.8	23.3	21.1	23.7	24.8	25.6
5. Definitely will	9.3	11.2	7.6	9.5	6.4	12.2	7.2	7.5	12.7	10.4	7.7	7.9	7.6	10.8	11.4	17.9
6. Already have	3.1	3.6	2.7	3.5	2.2	4.2	1.9	2.5	5.1	3.5	2.3	2.5	3.0	3.9	3.6	5.1
Item 12280 N(Wtd)	3598	1778	1724	2790	453	837	1078	1109	574	2016	1409	1194	777	511	1014	39

Now we have a different kind of question.

A21: How satisfied are you with your life as a whole these days?

1. Completely dissatisfied	1.5	1.5	1.5	1.3	1.8	2.5	1.1	1.1	1.6	1.7	1.1	1.4	1.4	1.4	1.7	2.6
2. Quite dissatisfied	6.2	6.4	6.0	6.4	5.5	7.2	6.6	5.4	5.4	6.1	6.4	6.0	6.3	5.3	6.8	7.9
3. Somewhat dissatisfied	10.9	11.4	10.2	10.5	10.8	11.4	12.5	8.8	11.4	10.1	11.5	8.7	11.9	9.4	13.4	7.9
4. Neither, or mixed feelings	13.7	12.8	14.7	12.8	18.3	13.5	12.6	15.3	12.9	13.8	13.4	11.8	13.2	12.2	16.6	23.7
5. Somewhat satisfied	27.7	29.3	26.2	27.7	26.9	26.5	26.3	31.3	25.0	26.0	29.9	27.9	26.6	29.9	27.2	28.9
6. Quite satisfied	34.0	33.2	35.0	35.9	28.7	33.7	34.6	31.9	37.6	36.2	32.0	37.1	34.5	35.8	30.0	23.7
7. Completely satisfied	6.0	5.3	6.5	5.4	7.9	5.5	6.3	6.2	6.1	6.2	5.6	7.2	6.0	5.5	4.4	10.5
Item 6840 N(Wtd)	3611	1786	1728	2799	453	839	1085	1114	572	2022	1408	1207	779	508	1016	38

QUESTIONNAIRE FORM 5 1981	TOTAL	SEX		RACE		REGION				4YR COLLEGE PLANS		ILLICIT DRUG USE: LIFETIME				
		M	F	White	Black	NE	NC	S	W	Yes	No	None	Mari-juana Only	Few Pills	More Pills	Any Her-oin
Weighted No. of Cases:	3656	1803	1741	2820	459	853	1091	1127	586	2036	1422	1210	782	515	1027	40
% of Weighted Total:	100.0	49.3	47.6	77.1	12.6	23.3	29.8	30.8	16.0	55.7	38.9	33.1	21.4	14.1	28.1	1.1

A22: These questions are about whether you think women are discriminated against in each of the following areas. To what extent are women discriminated against...

A22A: In getting a college education?

	TOTAL	M	F	White	Black	NE	NC	S	W	Yes	No	None	Mari-juana Only	Few Pills	More Pills	Any Her-oin
1. Not at all	42.8	47.6	38.0	42.8	44.6	43.6	42.1	44.4	40.0	42.2	43.1	42.0	47.2	40.6	42.8	27.5
2. Very little	33.1	29.0	37.7	36.4	18.1	34.6	34.2	31.0	32.7	35.8	30.9	31.7	32.8	34.1	35.0	40.0
3. Some	12.2	10.0	14.9	12.4	13.5	12.2	12.6	10.4	14.8	12.8	11.8	13.4	9.4	13.8	12.3	15.0
4. A good deal	2.8	2.7	2.7	1.8	5.5	2.1	2.7	3.0	3.8	2.3	3.2	3.2	2.7	3.0	1.9	-
5. A great deal	1.7	1.9	1.4	.8	6.0	.7	1.6	2.8	1.2	.9	2.6	2.2	1.4	2.0	.8	-
8. Don't know	7.3	8.8	5.3	5.9	12.1	6.5	6.7	8.4	7.5	5.9	8.5	7.4	6.7	6.5	7.3	15.0
Item 12290 N(Wtd)	3613	1789	1725	2799	453	841	1085	1112	575	2020	1411	1207	780	508	1016	40

A22B: In gaining positions of leadership over men and women?

	TOTAL	M	F	White	Black	NE	NC	S	W	Yes	No	None	Mari-juana Only	Few Pills	More Pills	Any Her-oin
1. Not at all	5.1	7.5	2.3	4.8	6.6	4.5	4.3	6.4	4.5	4.2	6.0	4.3	6.5	6.5	4.1	7.5
2. Very little	12.5	15.2	9.9	13.2	10.4	11.4	11.3	14.2	13.2	11.8	13.3	14.4	12.3	12.2	11.1	10.0
3. Some	34.8	37.1	32.6	36.3	25.2	34.5	35.4	32.9	37.8	35.8	34.4	34.9	33.8	34.1	36.0	25.0
4. A good deal	28.3	25.4	31.7	29.6	24.1	30.6	31.7	25.5	23.9	30.1	26.3	26.1	29.2	31.1	29.0	30.0
5. A great deal	14.1	8.5	20.0	12.0	25.9	13.8	13.2	14.1	16.7	14.2	13.8	15.1	13.4	11.2	14.8	15.0
8. Don't know	5.2	6.4	3.5	4.1	7.7	5.1	4.2	6.9	3.8	4.0	6.2	5.1	4.9	4.9	5.1	12.5
Item 12300 N(Wtd)	3608	1786	1724	2800	452	841	1083	1110	574	2021	1406	1205	782	508	1015	40

A22C: In obtaining executive positions in business?

	TOTAL	M	F	White	Black	NE	NC	S	W	Yes	No	None	Mari-juana Only	Few Pills	More Pills	Any Her-oin
1. Not at all	6.2	8.6	3.8	5.8	7.4	5.5	5.1	8.2	5.4	4.4	8.3	5.7	7.3	7.3	5.1	7.5
2. Very little	13.8	15.6	11.6	14.2	13.0	11.4	14.2	15.4	13.4	13.4	14.3	15.2	12.5	13.9	13.7	5.0
3. Some	32.4	33.2	31.6	34.0	24.8	32.3	34.0	31.3	31.6	32.4	32.0	32.2	32.0	31.5	33.7	42.5
4. A good deal	27.3	26.0	28.9	27.9	23.7	29.6	28.1	24.3	27.9	28.3	26.8	26.8	27.2	27.1	28.2	20.0
5. A great deal	13.9	9.1	18.9	12.8	21.7	14.7	12.9	13.0	16.6	15.4	11.9	13.6	14.4	13.9	13.7	12.5
8. Don't know	6.4	7.5	5.3	5.3	9.6	6.4	5.7	7.8	5.1	6.2	6.6	6.4	6.6	6.3	5.5	10.0
Item 12310 N(Wtd)	3598	1777	1721	2793	447	839	1080	1107	573	2013	1403	1203	776	505	1014	40

A22D: In obtaining top jobs in the professions?

	TOTAL	M	F	White	Black	NE	NC	S	W	Yes	No	None	Mari-juana Only	Few Pills	More Pills	Any Her-oin
1. Not at all	8.8	11.1	6.5	8.3	11.2	8.6	7.6	10.8	7.7	7.6	9.6	8.1	10.9	10.6	7.0	12.8
2. Very little	16.9	18.7	15.3	17.5	14.7	15.5	17.6	17.0	17.6	17.3	16.6	18.1	13.9	16.9	19.0	2.6
3. Some	30.1	30.9	29.2	31.4	23.0	29.9	30.4	30.0	29.8	29.8	30.6	27.9	30.4	31.5	32.1	20.5
4. A good deal	24.8	23.3	26.4	25.6	22.8	28.2	26.1	21.8	23.0	25.7	23.3	25.1	25.3	24.4	24.1	30.8
5. A great deal	13.1	8.4	17.7	11.6	21.2	11.2	13.1	13.8	14.7	13.2	13.6	14.2	13.7	11.0	11.6	12.8
8. Don't know	6.3	7.6	4.9	5.6	7.1	6.6	5.3	6.7	7.2	6.4	6.3	6.5	5.8	5.3	6.3	20.5
Item 12320 N(Wtd)	3605	1784	1724	2797	448	839	1086	1106	573	2019	1405	1203	779	508	1014	39

A22E: In getting skilled labor jobs?

	TOTAL	M	F	White	Black	NE	NC	S	W	Yes	No	None	Mari-juana Only	Few Pills	More Pills	Any Her-oin
1. Not at all	9.8	12.1	7.6	9.6	9.4	10.1	9.6	9.8	9.9	8.9	10.4	8.5	10.4	11.3	10.3	12.5
2. Very little	18.3	19.6	17.3	19.2	15.4	17.4	18.2	18.4	19.9	18.8	18.4	20.0	18.0	16.1	18.0	5.0
3. Some	33.1	33.1	33.1	33.8	30.5	34.4	34.0	32.3	31.2	34.1	32.2	34.4	35.0	31.7	32.2	30.0
4. A good deal	21.1	19.6	22.5	21.6	18.3	21.0	21.8	20.3	21.5	20.8	21.4	20.9	18.4	24.2	21.7	25.0
5. A great deal	8.7	7.1	10.4	7.5	16.5	7.8	7.8	10.1	9.4	7.6	10.0	7.6	9.1	6.9	9.8	12.5
8. Don't know	8.9	8.6	9.1	8.2	10.2	9.3	8.7	9.1	8.2	9.9	7.7	8.7	9.0	9.7	7.9	15.0
Item 12330 N(Wtd)	3590	1777	1718	2782	449	835	1078	1104	573	2009	1402	1197	778	504	1011	40

A22F: In getting elected to political office?

	TOTAL	M	F	White	Black	NE	NC	S	W	Yes	No	None	Mari-juana Only	Few Pills	More Pills	Any Her-oin
1. Not at all	5.1	7.9	2.2	4.9	6.0	4.3	3.7	6.9	5.7	4.5	5.8	4.6	6.4	5.9	4.1	7.5
2. Very little	12.6	15.8	9.1	12.8	10.6	10.7	12.6	12.8	14.8	11.7	13.5	12.7	12.6	13.8	11.5	15.0
3. Some	24.9	27.4	22.3	26.2	15.9	26.2	24.8	24.4	24.2	25.5	24.5	26.7	23.1	24.4	24.3	20.0
4. A good deal	23.3	21.8	24.8	24.2	22.1	23.0	25.6	22.3	21.2	24.6	22.2	22.2	26.8	24.8	21.7	15.0
5. A great deal	28.0	20.3	36.2	26.4	37.4	29.6	27.8	27.1	27.7	27.8	27.8	27.8	25.5	26.0	32.0	27.5
8. Don't know	6.1	6.8	5.3	5.5	8.0	6.2	5.5	6.4	6.6	5.8	6.3	6.1	5.5	5.1	6.3	15.0
Item 12340 N(Wtd)	3608	1783	1727	2795	452	840	1084	1109	575	2018	1408	1205	780	508	1013	40

QUESTIONNAIRE FORM 5 1981	TOTAL	SEX		RACE		REGION				4YR COLLEGE PLANS		ILLICIT DRUG USE: LIFETIME				
		M	F	White	Black	NE	NC	S	W	Yes	No	None	Marijuana Only	Few Pills	More Pills	Any Heroin
Weighted No. of Cases:	3656	1803	1741	2820	459	853	1091	1127	586	2036	1422	1210	782	515	1027	40
% of Weighted Total:	100.0	49.3	47.6	77.1	12.6	23.3	29.8	30.8	16.0	55.7	38.9	33.1	21.4	14.1	28.1	1.1
A22G: In getting equal pay for equal work?																
1. Not at all	14.3	19.8	8.3	14.1	14.9	13.3	12.7	16.4	14.4	12.8	16.0	14.3	14.5	15.0	14.2	7.5
2. Very little	17.7	20.8	14.7	18.8	14.0	16.3	17.8	18.1	18.6	19.4	15.3	17.8	16.8	17.5	18.8	22.5
3. Some	27.4	27.0	27.5	28.0	24.0	29.6	28.0	25.8	26.3	28.8	26.1	25.8	28.3	29.1	27.8	25.0
4. A good deal	17.1	13.8	20.6	18.0	11.8	16.9	20.2	14.1	17.4	17.5	15.9	16.6	15.9	18.3	18.2	7.5
5. A great deal	17.9	12.0	24.3	16.1	28.9	17.3	16.5	19.6	18.6	16.0	21.0	19.7	18.3	15.0	16.1	32.5
8. Don't know	5.6	6.6	4.5	4.9	6.4	6.5	4.7	6.1	4.7	5.4	5.7	5.7	6.2	5.1	5.0	5.0
Item 12350 N(Wtd)	3607	1784	1725	2796	450	840	1082	1110	575	2019	1408	1208	780	508	1012	40
A23: The next questions ask for your opinions on the effects of using certain drugs and other substances. First, how much do you think people risk harming themselves (physically or in other ways), if they...																
A23A: Smoke one or more packs of cigarettes per day																
1. No risk	1.2	1.4	.8	.4	2.7	1.0	.9	1.0	2.4	.5	1.7	.7	1.5	1.4	.8	5.0
2. Slight risk	5.9	6.0	5.8	5.8	6.0	5.2	6.8	6.9	3.3	3.9	5.4	7.1	7.0	20.0
3. Moderate risk	28.3	29.2	27.6	29.6	23.7	27.7	30.2	28.6	25.1	25.5	33.1	23.8	31.1	24.5	33.3	27.5
4. Great risk	63.3	61.7	65.0	63.3	64.3	64.7	61.0	62.0	67.8	68.0	56.8	69.7	61.1	65.8	58.1	27.5
5. Can't say, drug unfamiliar	1.4	1.7	.8	.9	3.3	1.5	1.2	1.4	1.2	1.0	1.4	1.8	.9	1.2	.7	10.0
Item 12360 N(Wtd)	3604	1784	1723	2796	451	839	1081	1110	574	2018	1409	1204	781	506	1014	40
A23B: Try marijuana (pot, grass) once or twice																
1. No risk	42.6	44.8	40.5	46.0	29.9	49.4	43.0	33.9	48.8	43.0	42.7	17.0	52.1	45.9	64.0	72.5
2. Slight risk	30.5	28.4	32.5	31.0	27.7	30.7	32.1	31.2	25.8	32.0	28.2	33.3	32.0	32.3	25.4	15.0
3. Moderate risk	11.4	10.9	11.8	10.6	14.4	9.8	11.4	12.5	11.5	10.7	12.2	17.9	8.8	9.1	6.5	5.0
4. Great risk	13.0	13.0	13.0	10.8	21.7	8.2	11.4	19.1	11.3	12.1	14.2	27.1	5.6	9.9	3.7	5.0
5. Can't say, drug unfamiliar	2.6	2.8	2.2	1.6	6.2	1.9	2.2	3.4	2.4	2.2	2.7	4.7	1.3	2.8	.5	2.5
Item 12370 N(Wtd)	3603	1786	1720	2795	451	840	1082	1107	574	2019	1406	1203	781	505	1014	40
A23C: Smoke marijuana occasionally																
1. No risk	13.7	15.2	12.0	14.0	11.3	16.8	13.8	10.5	15.0	11.4	16.7	3.3	13.0	12.9	26.0	32.5
2. Slight risk	31.8	32.8	31.0	33.9	23.0	34.4	31.9	27.5	36.4	33.1	29.8	15.3	37.9	38.2	43.5	42.5
3. Moderate risk	33.0	29.7	36.2	34.3	27.5	35.1	33.5	32.8	29.5	35.6	30.5	39.7	36.4	32.1	24.1	22.5
4. Great risk	19.1	19.8	18.5	16.1	31.5	12.0	18.6	25.2	18.0	17.6	20.7	37.4	11.4	13.3	5.9	2.5
5. Can't say, drug unfamiliar	2.5	2.4	2.3	1.6	6.8	1.9	2.1	3.9	1.2	2.3	2.4	4.3	1.2	3.4	.5	2.5
Item 12380 N(Wtd)	3589	1775	1718	2793	444	835	1077	1105	572	2014	1402	1199	778	502	1011	40
A23D: Smoke marijuana regularly																
1. No risk	3.4	4.9	1.6	2.5	6.2	3.2	3.4	3.5	3.5	1.9	5.1	1.4	3.5	2.8	5.5	10.0
2. Slight risk	11.7	13.2	9.8	12.5	7.8	13.7	12.3	8.5	14.3	10.5	13.1	2.0	10.3	11.2	23.3	35.0
3. Moderate risk	25.0	26.1	24.0	26.6	18.7	25.5	25.5	22.9	27.3	24.8	25.6	11.5	29.5	28.9	35.8	27.5
4. Great risk	57.6	53.5	62.5	57.0	61.8	55.6	56.9	61.8	54.0	60.5	54.4	80.9	55.9	53.6	35.1	25.0
5. Can't say, drug unfamiliar	2.3	2.3	2.0	1.5	5.6	1.9	2.0	3.3	1.0	2.3	1.9	4.2	.8	3.4	.4	2.5
Item 12390 N(Wtd)	3592	1773	1722	2788	450	833	1076	1111	572	2017	1401	1202	776	502	1012	40
A23E: Try LSD once or twice																
1. No risk	4.5	6.3	2.4	4.2	3.6	5.3	3.9	3.8	5.8	3.5	5.6	2.0	3.3	3.6	7.8	22.5
2. Slight risk	16.6	16.7	16.4	17.8	11.0	18.5	18.2	12.9	17.7	16.3	16.9	9.3	16.2	18.5	24.2	37.5
3. Moderate risk	24.0	22.0	26.5	25.5	17.4	24.0	26.4	22.1	22.7	25.7	22.2	26.6	23.6	22.3	23.0	15.0
4. Great risk	45.5	45.5	45.6	44.7	50.3	42.2	42.4	50.4	46.7	46.2	45.0	52.7	46.3	44.7	38.3	17.5
5. Can't say, drug unfamiliar	9.5	9.6	9.1	7.8	17.9	9.8	9.1	10.8	7.2	8.3	10.2	9.5	10.6	10.9	6.8	7.5
Item 12400 N(Wtd)	3595	1775	1722	2795	447	836	1079	1108	572	2017	1407	1200	777	503	1016	40

QUESTIONNAIRE FORM 5 1981	TOTAL	SEX		RACE		REGION				4YR COLLEGE PLANS		ILLICIT DRUG USE: LIFETIME				
		M	F	White	Black	NE	NC	S	W	Yes	No	None	Marijuana Only	Few Pills	More Pills	Any Heroin
Weighted No. of Cases:	3656	1803	1741	2820	459	853	1091	1127	586	2036	1422	1210	782	515	1027	40
% of Weighted Total:	100.0	49.3	47.6	77.1	12.6	23.3	29.8	30.8	16.0	55.7	38.9	33.1	21.4	14.1	28.1	1.1

A23F: Take LSD regularly

	TOTAL	M	F	White	Black	NE	NC	S	W	Yes	No	None	Mari-juana Only	Few Pills	More Pills	Any Heroin
1. No risk	1.8	2.4	.8	.9	3.4	1.6	1.0	2.1	2.6	.5	3.1	1.0	1.9	1.8	1.7	7.5
2. Slight risk	1.1	1.5	.5	1.2	.2	1.2	1.2	.6	1.2	.7	1.5	.4	.6	.4	2.3	-
3. Moderate risk	4.4	4.7	4.2	4.5	3.6	4.7	4.6	4.2	4.0	3.6	5.5	2.1	4.0	3.4	7.4	22.5
4. Great risk	83.5	81.8	85.8	85.9	75.6	82.7	84.5	82.8	84.8	87.1	79.9	87.6	82.9	84.5	81.6	62.5
5. Can't say, drug unfamiliar	9.3	9.6	8.7	7.5	17.0	9.9	8.6	10.4	7.3	8.0	10.0	9.0	10.4	10.1	7.1	7.5
Item 12410 N(Wtd)	3597	1779	1721	2797	447	837	1078	1109	572	2019	1406	1200	780	503	1014	40

A23G: Try heroin (smack, horse) once or twice

	TOTAL	M	F	White	Black	NE	NC	S	W	Yes	No	None	Mari-juana Only	Few Pills	More Pills	Any Heroin
1. No risk	2.8	3.3	2.0	2.0	3.8	2.9	2.2	3.1	3.0	1.9	3.8	1.7	3.1	2.4	3.1	12.5
2. Slight risk	10.0	9.1	10.7	10.2	7.8	10.2	10.8	8.4	11.2	10.2	10.0	9.2	9.5	9.3	10.9	42.5
3. Moderate risk	23.8	23.7	23.9	25.5	17.6	25.0	26.4	21.7	20.8	24.6	22.4	24.0	24.6	25.2	23.1	12.5
4. Great risk	52.9	53.5	52.9	53.5	52.9	49.9	51.0	55.3	56.3	54.7	51.1	55.2	51.2	51.7	53.7	25.0
5. Can't say, drug unfamiliar	10.6	10.4	10.6	8.8	18.0	12.1	9.4	11.4	8.6	8.5	12.6	10.0	11.4	11.3	9.2	7.5
Item 12420 N(Wtd)	3599	1778	1723	2795	450	837	1080	1110	572	2017	1408	1202	779	503	1015	40

A23H: Take heroin occasionally

	TOTAL	M	F	White	Black	NE	NC	S	W	Yes	No	None	Mari-juana Only	Few Pills	More Pills	Any Heroin
1. No risk	1.6	2.2	.6	.9	2.9	1.4	1.1	1.8	2.3	.6	2.7	.8	2.2	1.8	1.3	10.0
2. Slight risk	1.4	1.3	1.4	1.2	1.8	1.6	1.9	1.2	1.0	1.3	1.4	1.2	1.5	1.6	1.3	2.5
3. Moderate risk	14.8	13.7	15.9	15.2	11.8	15.5	16.3	14.0	12.5	13.8	16.3	15.0	14.7	14.1	14.7	27.5
4. Great risk	72.2	72.8	72.1	74.5	66.3	70.0	71.8	72.1	76.3	76.1	67.8	73.3	70.9	71.6	73.9	55.0
5. Can't say, drug unfamiliar	10.0	9.9	10.0	8.3	17.3	11.6	9.0	11.0	7.8	8.2	11.8	9.6	10.8	10.9	8.7	7.5
Item 12430 N(Wtd)	3600	1780	1722	2795	451	838	1079	1109	574	2018	1408	1203	781	504	1012	40

A23I: Take heroin regularly

	TOTAL	M	F	White	Black	NE	NC	S	W	Yes	No	None	Mari-juana Only	Few Pills	More Pills	Any Heroin
1. No risk	1.5	2.1	.5	.6	2.9	1.3	1.1	1.6	2.1	.5	2.6	.8	1.8	1.8	1.0	7.5
2. Slight risk	.3	.3	.3	.3	.5	.6	.1	.3	.4	.2	.4	.3	.4	-	.1	2.5
3. Moderate risk	1.1	1.0	1.2	.9	2.0	1.6	.7	1.5	.7	.9	1.3	1.3	1.0	1.0	1.0	2.5
4. Great risk	87.5	86.8	88.7	90.3	77.5	85.4	89.7	86.0	89.5	90.4	84.5	88.9	86.0	86.9	89.1	82.5
5. Can't say, drug unfamiliar	9.6	9.6	9.4	7.9	17.1	11.1	8.5	10.6	7.5	7.9	11.2	8.8	10.7	10.2	8.7	7.5
Item 12440 N(Wtd)	3579	1770	1711	2782	444	831	1073	1106	570	2009	1396	1195	774	498	1011	40

A23J: Try barbiturates (downers, goofballs, reds, yellows, etc.) once or twice

	TOTAL	M	F	White	Black	NE	NC	S	W	Yes	No	None	Mari-juana Only	Few Pills	More Pills	Any Heroin
1. No risk	8.7	10.1	7.1	8.9	5.2	10.2	8.4	6.7	10.7	7.1	10.7	2.8	6.5	7.0	16.9	37.5
2. Slight risk	22.7	21.2	24.2	24.5	14.1	26.0	23.3	19.4	23.1	23.2	22.4	16.0	19.1	26.3	31.9	35.0
3. Moderate risk	30.2	29.9	30.3	31.9	23.3	30.4	31.1	29.1	30.2	32.7	27.3	29.1	32.7	29.9	30.9	10.0
4. Great risk	28.4	28.9	28.0	26.8	35.7	23.7	28.1	32.2	28.1	27.6	29.3	40.2	29.4	26.7	14.6	10.0
5. Can't say, drug unfamiliar	10.1	9.9	10.3	7.8	21.7	9.8	9.1	12.6	7.9	9.5	10.3	11.9	12.1	10.4	5.9	7.5
Item 12450 N(Wtd)	3592	1774	1722	2795	446	836	1078	1107	572	2017	1405	1200	779	502	1014	40

A23K: Take barbiturates regularly

	TOTAL	M	F	White	Black	NE	NC	S	W	Yes	No	None	Mari-juana Only	Few Pills	More Pills	Any Heroin
1. No risk	1.7	2.5	.6	1.0	2.9	1.9	1.1	2.2	1.6	.6	3.1	.8	2.2	1.8	1.9	7.5
2. Slight risk	3.6	3.7	3.6	3.8	2.3	4.0	4.2	2.6	4.0	2.5	5.1	1.0	1.9	1.4	8.9	10.0
3. Moderate risk	15.2	16.5	13.4	16.2	10.6	14.0	15.3	15.5	16.1	15.4	15.6	8.3	12.0	17.9	24.6	30.0
4. Great risk	69.9	67.8	72.8	71.9	62.9	70.2	70.6	67.8	71.9	72.5	66.5	79.0	72.9	68.6	58.9	45.0
5. Can't say, drug unfamiliar	9.6	9.4	9.7	7.1	21.3	9.8	8.8	11.8	6.3	9.0	9.8	10.9	11.0	10.5	5.8	7.5
Item 12460 N(Wtd)	3579	1766	1718	2790	442	833	1074	1102	570	2009	1401	1197	775	503	1008	40

A23L: Try amphetamines (uppers, pep pills, bennies, speed) once or twice

	TOTAL	M	F	White	Black	NE	NC	S	W	Yes	No	None	Mari-juana Only	Few Pills	More Pills	Any Heroin
1. No risk	13.4	15.7	11.1	14.3	6.7	17.0	13.6	9.1	16.2	11.7	15.7	3.4	8.8	11.3	28.7	47.5
2. Slight risk	24.7	24.4	24.9	26.9	12.3	27.6	26.8	19.5	26.7	24.4	25.9	16.2	20.5	29.2	36.8	27.5
3. Moderate risk	28.5	27.5	29.6	29.6	26.6	29.3	28.9	28.7	26.3	30.7	25.8	31.0	32.0	30.2	23.0	5.0
4. Great risk	26.4	25.7	27.3	24.5	37.3	20.4	24.6	33.2	25.8	26.6	26.1	39.7	28.9	23.1	10.3	15.0
5. Can't say, drug unfamiliar	7.0	6.6	7.1	4.6	17.6	5.7	6.1	9.6	5.1	6.7	6.6	9.6	9.7	6.2	1.3	7.5
Item 12470 N(Wtd)	3595	1776	1724	2795	448	837	1077	1107	574	2019	1404	1199	781	503	1014	40

QUESTIONNAIRE FORM 5 1981	TOTAL	SEX		RACE		REGION				4YR COLLEGE PLANS		ILLICIT DRUG USE: LIFETIME				
		M	F	White	Black	NE	NC	S	W	Yes	No	None	Mari- juana Only	Few Pills	More Pills	Any Her- oin
Weighted No. of Cases:	3656	1803	1741	2820	459	853	1091	1127	586	2036	1422	1210	782	515	1027	40
% of Weighted Total:	100.0	49.3	47.6	77.1	12.6	23.3	29.8	30.8	16.0	55.7	38.9	33.1	21.4	14.1	28.1	1.1
A23M: Take amphetamines regularly																
1. No risk	2.3	3.3	1.2	1.5	3.8	2.9	1.8	2.5	2.3	1.1	3.7	.9	2.4	1.8	3.6	15.0
2. Slight risk	6.2	7.7	4.8	6.8	2.0	7.7	7.2	4.3	5.9	5.2	7.5	1.0	2.8	4.8	15.8	12.5
3. Moderate risk	17.0	18.6	15.2	18.5	10.5	17.6	17.6	14.7	19.2	16.2	18.5	9.2	13.4	16.9	28.8	30.0
4. Great risk	66.1	62.6	70.2	67.5	64.0	63.7	66.1	67.8	66.1	70.1	61.3	78.7	70.2	69.0	48.6	35.0
5. Can't say, drug unfamiliar	8.4	7.9	8.6	5.7	19.7	8.1	7.2	10.7	6.3	7.3	8.9	10.1	11.2	7.8	3.3	7.5
Item 12480　N(Wtd)	3588	1777	1717	2793	447	830	1079	1107	572	2014	1408	1203	778	503	1009	40
A23N: Try cocaine once or twice																
1. No risk	14.3	16.4	12.0	15.3	6.7	18.8	11.9	10.1	20.8	13.1	15.9	2.5	9.3	13.6	31.6	50.0
2. Slight risk	21.1	20.7	20.8	22.0	16.7	29.3	20.7	13.8	23.7	21.9	19.6	11.8	21.4	25.5	29.9	17.5
3. Moderate risk	25.8	25.3	26.7	25.9	24.5	24.3	28.1	25.5	24.3	27.4	23.5	29.7	27.8	25.9	20.5	15.0
4. Great risk	32.1	30.9	33.9	31.6	38.5	22.1	32.8	41.1	27.9	32.3	32.9	48.0	32.5	29.1	15.2	10.0
5. Can't say, drug unfamiliar	6.7	6.7	6.5	5.3	14.0	5.4	6.5	9.5	3.3	5.3	8.1	8.0	9.1	6.0	3.0	7.5
Item 12490　N(Wtd)	3592	1779	1718	2792	449	832	1077	1110	573	2013	1406	1197	781	501	1014	40
A23O: Take cocaine regularly																
1. No risk	3.5	4.8	2.0	2.6	4.0	4.7	2.1	3.0	4.9	2.1	5.0	.9	2.4	1.4	7.2	20.0
2. Slight risk	5.0	5.1	4.7	5.4	2.7	6.5	3.8	3.2	8.4	4.7	5.2	.8	2.4	4.0	12.1	17.5
3. Moderate risk	13.7	15.8	11.1	14.4	9.4	18.2	12.9	8.9	17.7	14.4	12.4	3.9	11.8	16.0	25.6	25.0
4. Great risk	71.2	67.5	75.9	72.4	70.2	64.9	74.7	75.5	65.7	73.7	69.4	87.1	74.7	72.1	51.6	32.5
5. Can't say, drug unfamiliar	6.6	6.7	6.3	5.2	13.9	5.9	6.3	9.3	3.1	5.1	8.0	7.3	8.6	6.4	3.4	7.5
Item 12500　N(Wtd)	3577	1768	1713	2782	447	831	1074	1100	572	2008	1398	1193	778	499	1009	40
A23P: Try one or two drinks of an alcoholic beverage (beer, wine, liquor)																
1. No risk	55.4	58.1	52.8	59.4	36.5	67.5	56.5	45.7	54.4	57.2	53.4	37.6	59.0	62.6	71.3	70.0
2. Slight risk	30.9	29.3	32.7	30.2	36.3	24.7	32.4	33.8	31.8	30.6	31.3	39.0	31.3	27.6	22.2	20.0
3. Moderate risk	8.3	7.3	9.2	7.0	14.3	4.5	7.4	12.0	8.2	7.3	9.5	12.7	6.7	6.8	4.9	7.5
4. Great risk	4.6	4.5	4.6	3.1	9.2	2.4	3.3	7.2	5.1	4.1	5.2	9.3	2.2	2.8	1.5	2.5
5. Can't say, drug unfamiliar	.8	.8	.7	.3	3.8	.8	.5	1.2	.5	.8	.6	1.5	.8	.4	-	
Item 12510　N(Wtd)	3597	1779	1723	2797	446	837	1081	1107	572	2017	1407	1201	780	503	1015	40
A23Q: Take one or two drinks nearly every day																
1. No risk	10.5	13.6	6.9	9.8	9.8	12.1	10.5	9.7	9.6	8.3	12.7	6.9	10.9	10.6	14.0	12.5
2. Slight risk	28.1	29.5	26.6	29.6	22.2	31.1	31.3	26.2	21.2	27.1	30.0	22.5	30.2	31.5	30.9	37.5
3. Moderate risk	38.8	38.4	39.7	39.9	36.4	37.6	39.0	39.2	39.5	40.7	36.9	39.1	41.5	34.9	39.6	32.5
4. Great risk	21.6	17.7	25.9	20.3	27.3	18.3	18.7	23.3	28.6	23.1	19.5	29.8	16.5	22.7	15.4	15.0
5. Can't say, drug unfamiliar	.9	1.0	.9	.3	4.2	.8	.6	1.5	.9	.8	.9	1.7	.9	.4	.2	-
Item 12520　N(Wtd)	3596	1778	1721	2793	451	835	1081	1111	570	2017	1407	1201	781	502	1013	40
A23R: Take four or five drinks nearly every day																
1. No risk	2.9	4.3	1.2	1.9	4.5	3.4	2.4	3.3	2.6	1.3	4.6	1.3	3.6	2.6	3.6	10.0
2. Slight risk	7.8	10.0	5.5	8.5	4.3	7.9	8.6	7.0	8.0	6.4	9.9	5.7	8.3	7.6	10.3	2.5
3. Moderate risk	23.7	25.4	21.9	24.6	18.4	22.8	28.1	23.3	17.4	23.0	25.0	20.0	25.0	27.9	24.1	40.0
4. Great risk	64.5	59.0	70.6	64.5	68.2	65.1	60.1	64.8	70.9	68.4	59.4	71.2	62.1	61.1	61.5	47.5
5. Can't say, drug unfamiliar	1.1	1.3	.9	.4	4.5	.8	.6	1.7	1.2	.9	1.1	1.8	.9	.8	.3	-
Item 12530　N(Wtd)	3595	1778	1723	2798	446	834	1081	1107	574	2018	1406	1202	779	501	1015	40
A23S: Have five or more drinks once or twice each weekend																
1. No risk	11.0	14.9	7.0	11.1	7.8	15.5	11.9	8.2	8.0	8.1	14.5	5.2	10.8	12.0	16.9	20.0
2. Slight risk	20.1	23.8	15.9	22.2	10.7	22.4	22.1	17.1	18.6	18.9	21.9	12.1	20.7	21.9	27.2	40.0
3. Moderate risk	31.4	29.1	33.9	33.6	22.3	30.9	33.8	30.2	30.3	33.1	29.7	30.3	33.0	31.9	32.8	20.0
4. Great risk	36.3	30.8	42.2	32.7	54.1	30.2	31.2	42.8	42.0	38.8	32.8	50.6	34.3	32.9	23.0	17.5
5. Can't say, drug unfamiliar	1.2	1.4	1.0	.4	5.3	.8	.9	1.8	1.2	1.1	1.1	1.9	1.2	1.4	.2	-
Item 12540　N(Wtd)	3600	1780	1724	2799	449	834	1081	1111	574	2019	1409	1203	781	502	1015	40

QUESTIONNAIRE FORM 5 1981	TOTAL	SEX		RACE		REGION				4YR COLLEGE PLANS		ILLICIT DRUG USE: LIFETIME				
		M	F	White	Black	NE	NC	S	W	Yes	No	None	Mari-juana Only	Few Pills	More Pills	Any Her-oin
Weighted No. of Cases:	3656	1803	1741	2820	459	853	1091	1127	586	2036	1422	1210	782	515	1027	40
% of Weighted Total:	100.0	49.3	47.6	77.1	12.6	23.3	29.8	30.8	16.0	55.7	38.9	33.1	21.4	14.1	28.1	1.1

This section asks for your views and feelings about a number of different things.

D01: Do you agree or disagree with each of the following?

D01A: I take a positive attitude toward myself

	TOTAL	M	F	White	Black	NE	NC	S	W	Yes	No	None	Mari Only	Few Pills	More Pills	Heroin
1. Disagree	1.9	1.9	1.6	1.4	2.8	2.9	1.2	1.9	1.6	1.5	2.5	1.8	1.6	1.4	2.2	2.8
2. Mostly disagree	4.7	3.1	6.4	4.9	3.6	5.6	5.0	3.9	4.5	4.6	4.8	4.0	4.5	4.3	6.2	2.8
3. Neither	7.7	7.3	7.8	7.6	4.0	9.4	7.6	6.1	8.3	7.2	8.1	7.0	5.5	8.8	9.0	11.1
4. Mostly agree	48.3	45.3	51.2	51.4	30.3	49.1	51.7	44.0	49.3	46.5	51.8	47.1	49.1	51.3	48.6	30.6
5. Agree	37.4	42.3	33.0	34.6	59.2	32.8	34.6	44.0	36.2	40.1	32.8	40.1	39.3	34.4	34.0	50.0
Item 12550 N(Wtd)	3454	1699	1683	2735	422	752	1068	1079	556	1996	1375	1162	741	491	973	36

D01B: Good luck is more important than hard work for success

	TOTAL	M	F	White	Black	NE	NC	S	W	Yes	No	None	Mari Only	Few Pills	More Pills	Heroin
1. Disagree	37.7	34.3	41.4	37.5	40.7	37.5	35.9	40.1	36.7	38.3	36.2	42.9	37.1	35.2	34.5	25.0
2. Mostly disagree	36.6	36.8	36.5	39.8	21.5	35.3	39.6	34.4	37.1	39.0	34.1	33.5	35.9	39.5	39.9	33.3
3. Neither	14.8	16.9	12.7	14.7	14.1	17.5	15.0	12.5	15.3	14.0	15.8	13.4	14.6	13.9	16.6	13.9
4. Mostly agree	7.8	8.4	6.8	5.9	14.1	7.2	6.4	9.1	8.5	6.4	9.5	6.5	8.9	9.2	6.8	19.4
5. Agree	3.1	3.5	2.6	2.1	9.3	2.4	3.2	3.9	2.5	2.2	4.4	3.7	3.4	2.0	2.2	8.3
Item 12560 N(Wtd)	3448	1695	1678	2729	418	747	1069	1076	556	1988	1376	1161	738	489	974	36

D01C: I feel I am a person of worth, on an equal plane with others

	TOTAL	M	F	White	Black	NE	NC	S	W	Yes	No	None	Mari Only	Few Pills	More Pills	Heroin
1. Disagree	1.6	1.5	1.5	1.0	4.1	1.3	1.0	2.3	1.8	1.4	2.0	1.9	.9	1.4	1.5	2.8
2. Mostly disagree	3.4	3.8	2.9	3.5	3.4	3.7	3.4	2.8	3.8	2.6	4.5	2.7	3.9	3.5	3.5	5.6
3. Neither	8.3	9.2	7.1	8.3	6.5	10.3	7.0	8.5	7.8	6.7	10.8	8.4	6.6	6.6	10.3	5.6
4. Mostly agree	41.9	38.0	45.6	43.9	29.3	40.4	48.5	37.9	39.3	40.6	44.2	39.4	42.5	45.2	43.2	44.4
5. Agree	44.8	47.4	42.8	43.3	56.7	44.3	40.1	48.5	47.5	48.8	38.5	47.5	46.0	43.1	41.5	38.9
Item 12570 N(Wtd)	3440	1693	1672	2723	416	748	1067	1073	552	1983	1372	1159	737	487	971	36

D01D: I am able to do things as well as most other people

	TOTAL	M	F	White	Black	NE	NC	S	W	Yes	No	None	Mari Only	Few Pills	More Pills	Heroin
1. Disagree	1.0	1.2	.7	.9	1.4	.8	1.1	1.3	.4	.9	1.0	1.3	.4	.8	1.2	2.8
2. Mostly disagree	2.4	2.1	2.6	2.3	2.9	3.1	1.9	2.4	2.2	1.6	3.4	2.5	2.0	3.1	2.1	2.8
3. Neither	4.9	5.0	4.8	4.5	5.0	6.9	5.0	3.7	4.4	4.3	5.4	4.9	6.0	3.5	4.3	11.1
4. Mostly agree	44.6	40.2	48.9	46.3	33.7	42.3	50.2	40.5	44.6	41.8	48.7	41.4	44.3	45.3	48.5	27.8
5. Agree	47.2	51.5	43.1	45.9	57.2	46.9	41.9	52.2	48.6	51.3	41.5	50.0	47.1	47.3	43.8	58.3
Item 12580 N(Wtd)	3440	1693	1672	2725	416	744	1070	1075	551	1982	1372	1159	736	486	973	36

D01E: Every time I try to get ahead, something or somebody stops me

	TOTAL	M	F	White	Black	NE	NC	S	W	Yes	No	None	Mari Only	Few Pills	More Pills	Heroin
1. Disagree	19.5	17.9	21.2	18.7	25.5	19.7	19.2	19.3	20.7	21.3	16.7	22.7	19.2	17.4	17.4	13.9
2. Mostly disagree	34.1	32.7	35.8	37.0	21.2	34.6	35.1	31.5	36.7	37.7	29.7	32.7	37.2	37.8	32.4	33.3
3. Neither	23.2	24.6	21.8	23.1	21.4	23.0	25.1	21.7	22.7	21.6	25.6	22.3	22.3	23.3	25.2	16.7
4. Mostly agree	16.9	18.0	15.7	16.1	20.9	17.3	14.6	19.3	16.2	15.0	19.4	16.1	16.0	14.5	18.6	33.3
5. Agree	6.3	6.9	5.4	5.1	11.3	5.4	6.0	8.3	4.0	4.3	8.7	6.3	5.2	7.2	6.4	2.8
Item 12590 N(Wtd)	3436	1690	1671	2722	416	745	1070	1070	551	1982	1369	1159	736	484	971	36

D01F: Planning only makes a person unhappy since plans hardly ever work out anyway

	TOTAL	M	F	White	Black	NE	NC	S	W	Yes	No	None	Mari Only	Few Pills	More Pills	Heroin
1. Disagree	31.6	30.2	32.9	31.8	34.2	29.6	29.8	33.4	34.1	35.7	24.9	34.9	29.7	30.0	30.5	16.7
2. Mostly disagree	32.7	31.4	33.9	35.0	20.9	32.5	36.2	28.9	33.4	33.8	31.7	33.7	37.2	30.4	30.1	36.1
3. Neither	16.3	18.2	14.5	16.2	13.8	18.5	15.6	14.6	17.9	15.5	17.5	11.9	16.5	18.0	20.2	22.2
4. Mostly agree	13.2	14.5	12.0	12.5	18.2	12.7	12.6	15.5	11.0	10.7	17.0	13.6	10.5	14.0	14.0	11.1
5. Agree	6.2	5.6	6.7	4.5	12.9	6.7	5.8	7.6	3.6	4.3	8.9	6.0	6.0	7.6	5.3	13.9
Item 12600 N(Wtd)	3426	1680	1672	2720	412	742	1065	1066	554	1976	1368	1156	733	484	971	36

QUESTIONNAIRE FORM 5 1981	TOTAL	SEX		RACE		REGION				4YR COLLEGE PLANS		ILLICIT DRUG USE: LIFETIME				
		M	F	White	Black	NE	NC	S	W	Yes	No	None	Marijuana Only	Few Pills	More Pills	Any Heroin
Weighted No. of Cases:	3656	1803	1741	2820	459	853	1091	1127	586	2036	1422	1210	782	515	1027	40
% of Weighted Total:	100.0	49.3	47.6	77.1	12.6	23.3	29.8	30.8	16.0	55.7	38.9	33.1	21.4	14.1	28.1	1.1
D01G: People who accept their condition in life are happier than those who try to change things																
1. Disagree	19.9	20.1	20.1	20.3	22.9	22.8	19.4	18.2	20.5	23.7	14.3	19.1	19.1	22.9	20.9	5.6
2. Mostly disagree	24.2	24.6	23.9	25.9	16.2	24.2	26.1	21.0	26.6	27.1	20.4	25.1	24.2	25.2	23.1	25.0
3. Neither	19.2	20.1	18.3	19.7	15.0	21.5	19.7	17.6	18.1	19.0	19.4	17.5	19.4	16.9	21.9	25.0
4. Mostly agree	21.6	21.0	21.9	20.6	24.9	17.6	21.6	23.9	22.3	17.8	26.9	23.0	21.9	21.3	19.1	16.7
5. Agree	15.0	14.1	15.8	13.4	21.0	13.8	13.2	19.2	12.5	12.3	19.0	15.2	15.3	13.4	14.9	27.8
Item 12610 N(Wtd)	3429	1684	1671	2718	414	740	1067	1070	552	1977	1370	1161	732	484	968	36
D01H: On the whole, I'm satisfied with myself																
1. Disagree	3.0	2.9	3.0	2.8	4.6	5.0	2.1	2.9	2.4	2.7	3.2	2.0	4.0	2.3	3.9	2.9
2. Mostly disagree	6.3	6.7	6.1	5.7	9.0	5.7	6.9	6.6	6.0	6.2	6.6	5.6	6.1	5.6	7.5	8.6
3. Neither	9.1	9.9	8.0	9.4	5.9	9.3	9.9	8.0	9.4	8.9	9.6	8.0	8.5	10.0	10.4	8.6
4. Mostly agree	41.0	37.6	44.4	42.7	32.9	42.6	43.0	38.1	40.5	39.7	42.5	41.8	40.5	42.3	40.4	28.6
5. Agree	40.6	43.0	38.4	39.4	47.6	37.6	38.3	44.5	41.8	42.5	38.0	42.6	40.8	40.0	37.8	54.3
Item 12620 N(Wtd)	3421	1678	1668	2715	410	740	1064	1064	553	1972	1366	1159	726	480	970	35
D01I: People like me don't have much of a chance to be successful in life																
1. Disagree	58.1	56.0	60.3	57.4	67.1	58.2	53.3	60.4	62.6	64.3	48.9	60.8	59.9	59.3	53.2	58.3
2. Mostly disagree	27.3	27.3	27.5	29.6	14.5	26.7	31.9	24.7	24.1	25.7	29.9	25.6	27.2	29.0	29.4	16.7
3. Neither	7.5	8.8	6.0	7.2	6.5	7.9	7.8	6.7	7.6	5.2	10.5	5.4	6.6	6.5	10.3	16.7
4. Mostly agree	5.0	5.0	4.7	4.4	6.5	4.9	5.3	4.9	4.9	3.5	7.2	5.5	4.7	3.8	4.9	8.3
5. Agree	2.2	2.9	1.5	1.5	5.3	2.4	1.9	3.2	.7	1.3	3.4	2.8	1.8	1.5	2.2	-
Item 12630 N(Wtd)	3420	1676	1670	2712	414	735	1066	1067	551	1970	1367	1156	729	479	970	36
D01J: When I make plans, I am almost certain that I can make them work																
1. Disagree	2.2	2.4	2.0	1.8	5.3	3.0	2.1	2.5	.9	2.0	2.4	1.6	2.5	2.5	2.4	8.3
2. Mostly disagree	6.1	5.4	6.9	6.5	4.6	7.3	7.2	5.7	3.3	5.4	7.2	6.8	4.7	6.2	6.4	13.9
3. Neither	15.3	15.2	15.2	16.2	9.4	16.7	14.4	14.8	16.1	14.5	16.6	12.4	15.7	16.1	18.4	13.9
4. Mostly agree	47.0	45.6	48.7	48.3	40.1	44.6	50.5	43.6	50.1	47.1	47.3	48.4	47.1	50.5	44.4	30.6
5. Agree	29.3	31.3	27.2	27.2	40.6	28.5	25.7	33.2	29.7	30.9	26.5	30.9	30.0	24.8	28.4	33.3
Item 12640 N(Wtd)	3422	1675	1673	2714	414	738	1067	1065	553	1977	1362	1157	731	483	968	36
D01K: A lot of times I feel lonely																
1. Disagree	16.5	17.4	15.3	15.9	19.5	18.1	14.9	16.4	17.5	16.0	17.1	16.0	16.3	14.7	17.4	27.8
2. Mostly disagree	30.2	29.0	31.9	32.0	21.7	30.9	32.4	27.5	30.7	31.4	28.6	30.1	30.5	34.4	29.4	13.9
3. Neither	18.0	20.4	15.4	18.6	12.3	18.6	19.6	14.2	21.5	18.0	18.0	17.7	18.2	16.6	19.4	11.1
4. Mostly agree	22.8	22.1	23.7	23.0	24.4	20.9	23.3	24.2	21.5	22.6	23.1	23.7	23.4	21.0	21.4	36.1
5. Agree	12.4	11.0	13.6	10.5	22.2	11.3	9.6	17.8	8.8	11.9	13.0	12.5	11.7	13.3	12.3	13.9
Item 12650 N(Wtd)	3390	1658	1659	2689	406	724	1058	1060	548	1959	1349	1144	718	482	958	36
D01L: I feel I do not have much to be proud of																
1. Disagree	45.8	46.7	44.8	45.1	54.6	42.9	44.0	47.5	49.5	49.5	40.3	47.9	45.8	40.7	45.5	57.1
2. Mostly disagree	33.0	31.3	34.7	35.3	20.2	34.1	35.5	30.9	30.8	32.8	33.3	31.8	33.5	38.6	32.5	17.1
3. Neither	8.9	9.8	8.2	8.6	8.1	10.7	8.8	7.6	9.1	7.8	10.7	8.1	9.6	9.3	9.1	8.6
4. Mostly agree	8.4	7.9	8.9	7.6	9.9	6.9	8.7	9.3	8.0	6.6	10.8	7.9	7.8	9.1	8.5	8.6
5. Agree	4.0	4.4	3.4	3.3	7.2	5.4	3.0	4.5	2.6	3.3	4.9	4.4	3.3	2.3	4.5	8.6
Item 12660 N(Wtd)	3387	1654	1658	2688	405	722	1057	1061	548	1958	1346	1142	719	482	958	35
D01M: There is always someone I can turn to if I need help																
1. Disagree	3.8	4.3	3.3	3.2	5.2	4.5	3.0	4.3	3.7	4.0	3.6	4.6	2.6	2.5	4.3	2.8
2. Mostly disagree	4.8	5.5	4.1	5.0	2.5	6.3	5.9	3.2	3.7	4.8	4.6	3.1	4.9	5.0	6.4	11.1
3. Neither	6.1	7.9	4.4	6.0	5.9	8.2	6.1	4.7	5.9	5.9	6.0	5.8	7.1	4.8	6.2	5.6
4. Mostly agree	30.3	32.3	28.0	30.9	23.3	34.1	33.2	24.2	31.3	30.4	30.2	27.1	29.8	32.8	33.2	33.3
5. Agree	55.1	50.0	60.2	54.8	62.6	47.1	51.8	63.5	55.3	54.9	55.5	59.6	55.6	54.7	49.9	44.4
Item 12670 N(Wtd)	3376	1651	1651	2679	404	719	1056	1055	546	1955	1339	1141	717	479	953	36

QUESTIONNAIRE FORM 5 1981	TOTAL	SEX		RACE		REGION				4YR COLLEGE PLANS		ILLICIT DRUG USE: LIFETIME				
		M	F	White	Black	NE	NC	S	W	Yes	No	None	Mari-juana Only	Few Pills	More Pills	Any Her-oin
Weighted No. of Cases:	3656	1803	1741	2820	459	853	1091	1127	586	2036	1422	1210	782	515	1027	40
% of Weighted Total:	100.0	49.3	47.6	77.1	12.6	23.3	29.8	30.8	16.0	55.7	38.9	33.1	21.4	14.1	28.1	1.1
D01N: Sometimes I think that I am no good at all																
1. Disagree	33.5	36.2	31.0	30.6	52.0	31.6	30.2	37.8	34.0	34.7	31.8	36.7	35.7	29.8	29.4	36.1
2. Mostly disagree	25.5	26.2	24.9	27.3	16.9	24.5	27.2	22.9	28.9	26.0	25.0	24.2	25.2	30.4	25.4	27.8
3. Neither	16.2	17.1	15.2	17.1	10.2	15.8	18.3	15.5	14.3	15.3	17.4	15.5	16.2	16.5	17.5	13.9
4. Mostly agree	15.2	12.4	18.1	16.0	9.2	15.7	16.3	13.6	15.4	15.3	15.3	13.6	15.5	15.6	16.4	13.9
5. Agree	9.5	8.2	10.8	9.0	11.2	12.5	7.9	10.3	7.4	8.7	10.5	10.0	7.4	7.6	11.4	5.6
Item 12680 N(Wtd)	3370	1643	1652	2678	402	713	1053	1059	544	1945	1344	1138	718	473	954	36
D01O: I often feel left out of things																
1. Disagree	21.0	21.6	20.2	19.5	28.9	23.4	18.3	21.4	22.2	21.5	20.5	19.3	23.4	18.1	21.6	33.3
2. Mostly disagree	28.3	30.0	26.8	29.9	19.4	29.2	28.5	27.9	27.8	29.0	27.4	28.6	29.0	31.1	27.0	19.4
3. Neither	18.6	19.3	18.2	19.2	15.4	18.3	21.1	16.1	18.8	18.2	18.6	17.0	18.3	23.5	19.1	5.6
4. Mostly agree	21.5	19.7	23.4	22.0	20.6	19.2	23.2	20.5	23.2	22.2	20.8	24.1	20.3	18.5	20.5	27.8
5. Agree	10.6	9.4	11.5	9.4	15.7	9.9	8.9	14.1	8.1	9.2	12.6	11.0	9.0	8.8	11.9	13.9
Item 12690 N(Wtd)	3368	1646	1648	2676	402	715	1053	1057	544	1948	1341	1138	714	476	953	36
D01P: I believe a person is master of his/her own fate																
1. Disagree	4.4	4.5	4.1	4.3	4.2	4.9	5.4	3.6	3.5	4.0	4.9	6.3	3.1	4.0	3.2	2.8
2. Mostly disagree	4.7	4.7	4.8	4.9	3.0	5.4	4.8	4.6	4.1	4.5	5.2	4.7	3.4	7.4	4.7	-
3. Neither	17.1	13.8	20.4	17.6	12.9	19.2	15.4	17.3	17.0	16.5	17.9	15.4	16.6	14.0	20.7	22.2
4. Mostly agree	36.0	34.9	37.4	37.7	25.3	36.0	41.0	30.2	37.5	36.9	35.5	34.8	37.3	37.2	36.3	25.0
5. Agree	37.8	42.1	33.3	35.4	54.8	34.5	33.4	44.2	38.2	38.1	36.6	38.7	39.5	37.4	35.1	50.0
Item 12700 N(Wtd)	3362	1649	1639	2669	403	719	1046	1055	542	1947	1337	1138	716	470	952	36
D01Q: There is usually someone I can talk to, if I need to																
1. Disagree	2.4	2.4	2.2	2.1	3.0	3.5	1.2	2.4	3.1	2.5	2.2	2.6	2.2	1.7	2.4	2.8
2. Mostly disagree	4.4	5.6	3.2	4.3	3.0	7.0	4.4	2.8	3.8	4.8	3.6	3.3	3.4	3.6	6.5	8.3
3. Neither	4.2	5.8	2.7	4.2	3.8	4.6	4.4	3.9	4.4	4.2	4.2	4.8	4.2	4.0	3.8	2.8
4. Mostly agree	29.0	31.2	27.1	29.6	22.6	31.1	33.5	22.6	29.9	29.1	29.0	26.2	28.9	30.5	31.6	30.6
5. Agree	60.0	55.0	64.8	59.8	67.7	53.7	56.5	68.4	58.8	59.5	61.1	63.0	61.3	60.4	55.7	55.6
Item 12710 N(Wtd)	3368	1647	1648	2679	399	717	1052	1053	546	1943	1344	1138	716	475	954	36
D01R: I feel that I can't do anything right																
1. Disagree	44.6	45.5	43.7	44.7	48.6	44.2	44.3	43.5	47.7	48.8	38.4	47.4	46.1	40.0	41.5	64.5
2. Mostly disagree	30.7	29.8	31.9	32.4	21.5	31.5	32.9	28.7	29.7	31.3	30.1	28.6	31.0	36.9	31.2	9.7
3. Neither	12.6	10.8	14.4	12.2	10.6	11.7	12.3	13.3	13.2	10.9	15.1	12.0	11.1	13.0	14.4	6.5
4. Mostly agree	8.5	9.5	7.3	7.9	10.1	9.2	8.2	9.2	6.7	6.1	11.8	8.7	8.5	6.7	8.7	19.4
5. Agree	3.6	4.3	2.7	2.7	9.1	3.5	2.4	5.2	3.0	2.8	4.4	3.3	3.2	3.6	4.1	-
Item 12720 N(Wtd)	3345	1635	1637	2667	395	718	1042	1045	539	1936	1329	1132	709	477	951	31
D01S: I often wish I had more good friends																
1. Disagree	15.9	14.0	17.7	15.6	17.0	19.2	15.5	14.3	15.4	15.9	15.7	15.3	19.1	13.7	14.8	11.4
2. Mostly disagree	15.0	14.3	15.7	15.6	13.0	15.7	13.7	14.6	17.6	15.4	14.4	12.9	15.3	22.2	14.1	17.1
3. Neither	17.6	18.5	16.6	17.8	15.0	16.4	19.6	15.6	18.9	17.6	17.6	16.7	16.5	18.4	18.7	20.0
4. Mostly agree	28.2	30.2	26.6	28.7	23.3	29.0	30.6	25.6	27.8	29.1	27.5	28.3	28.5	28.3	27.9	34.3
5. Agree	23.3	23.0	23.4	22.2	31.3	19.7	20.6	29.9	20.2	21.9	24.8	26.8	20.6	17.3	24.3	17.1
Item 12730 N(Wtd)	3348	1633	1642	2661	399	715	1043	1050	539	1934	1333	1132	708	474	950	35
D01T: Planning ahead makes things turn out better																
1. Disagree	3.2	2.7	3.5	2.4	7.1	3.2	2.7	4.4	1.9	2.1	4.7	3.0	3.2	2.7	3.6	2.8
2. Mostly disagree	6.8	5.9	7.7	6.0	10.1	8.4	6.5	7.1	4.5	5.7	8.5	5.8	6.8	8.8	6.9	8.3
3. Neither	18.1	17.4	19.0	18.7	12.3	22.6	18.0	16.0	16.7	18.0	18.8	13.9	16.2	23.2	22.0	25.0
4. Mostly agree	41.2	40.5	42.0	43.4	32.7	41.6	43.8	38.0	42.4	41.8	40.4	42.7	41.9	39.6	39.5	41.7
5. Agree	30.7	33.5	27.7	29.6	37.8	24.2	29.1	34.6	34.8	32.5	27.6	34.8	31.9	25.7	28.0	22.2
Item 12740 N(Wtd)	3351	1638	1640	2669	397	712	1049	1051	538	1937	1335	1132	709	475	951	36

QUESTIONNAIRE FORM 5 1981	TOTAL	SEX		RACE		REGION				4YR COLLEGE PLANS		ILLICIT DRUG USE: LIFETIME				
		M	F	White	Black	NE	NC	S	W	Yes	No	None	Mari-juana Only	Few Pills	More Pills	Any Her-oin
Weighted No. of Cases:	3656	1803	1741	2820	459	853	1091	1127	586	2036	1422	1210	782	515	1027	40
% of Weighted Total:	100.0	49.3	47.6	77.1	12.6	23.3	29.8	30.8	16.0	55.7	38.9	33.1	21.4	14.1	28.1	1.1

D01U: I feel that my life is not very useful

1. Disagree	52.7	52.4	53.0	51.4	61.5	50.0	50.5	56.5	52.8	54.9	49.1	56.0	53.6	50.4	48.8	60.6
2. Mostly disagree	27.7	27.8	27.7	29.5	19.0	28.7	30.4	23.3	29.2	27.9	27.5	25.7	28.7	30.5	29.0	21.2
3. Neither	11.1	11.2	11.1	11.7	6.5	11.3	12.1	10.9	9.4	9.5	13.7	10.4	9.1	11.4	13.2	12.1
4. Mostly agree	5.6	5.5	5.3	5.0	6.5	6.8	4.9	5.3	6.2	4.8	6.7	4.6	5.7	5.5	6.1	6.1
5. Agree	3.0	3.1	2.9	2.3	6.5	3.2	2.1	4.0	2.4	2.9	2.9	3.4	2.9	1.9	2.9	-
Item 12750 N(Wtd)	3326	1623	1628	2659	384	710	1045	1037	534	1921	1327	1130	700	472	945	33

D01V: I usually have a few friends around that I can get together with

1. Disagree	4.8	4.7	4.8	3.9	9.7	5.5	3.3	5.6	5.0	4.2	5.6	5.3	4.1	3.6	5.1	5.6
2. Mostly disagree	5.9	5.4	6.3	6.0	3.8	7.3	4.2	6.0	7.2	6.0	5.8	6.1	6.1	5.5	5.6	11.1
3. Neither	7.1	7.7	6.7	6.7	6.9	5.8	8.5	6.1	8.2	7.2	7.0	8.1	7.9	4.4	7.0	-
4. Mostly agree	36.2	37.8	34.8	37.1	30.8	32.7	41.2	34.9	33.5	35.3	37.5	36.9	35.3	34.7	37.2	22.2
5. Agree	46.0	44.3	47.4	46.3	49.1	48.6	42.7	47.4	46.1	47.3	44.2	43.7	46.5	51.8	45.2	61.1
Item 12760 N(Wtd)	3345	1633	1638	2665	393	712	1045	1051	538	1936	1331	1133	705	475	947	36

D01W: I am eager to leave home and live on my own--independent from my parents

1. Disagree	9.4	9.1	9.4	8.3	11.7	8.3	8.9	10.4	9.9	7.9	11.3	11.4	10.0	8.2	7.2	8.6
2. Mostly disagree	11.9	12.4	11.6	12.4	9.2	11.7	12.8	10.9	12.3	12.1	12.0	15.9	11.1	11.4	8.7	2.9
3. Neither	20.5	23.3	17.8	20.9	16.6	22.1	20.9	17.9	22.9	21.6	19.1	23.3	22.2	18.9	17.1	14.3
4. Mostly agree	28.9	28.2	29.5	29.1	30.9	30.2	29.6	29.1	25.3	29.8	27.7	28.1	29.2	30.9	28.2	28.6
5. Agree	29.3	27.0	31.7	29.2	31.6	27.7	27.9	31.6	29.7	28.7	29.9	21.4	27.5	30.5	38.7	45.7
Item 13950 N(Wtd)	3339	1633	1633	2665	392	711	1048	1043	538	1932	1328	1132	702	475	950	35

D01X: I feel hesitant about taking a full- time job and becoming part of the "adult world"

1. Disagree	35.2	34.4	36.5	34.6	41.8	32.0	35.3	36.4	37.4	31.8	39.6	32.5	32.5	35.6	40.4	57.1
2. Mostly disagree	21.7	21.7	22.0	22.4	18.9	23.1	22.6	20.6	20.3	23.4	19.5	20.8	24.8	23.8	20.2	11.4
3. Neither	14.1	17.4	10.7	14.6	9.2	15.0	14.2	13.6	13.4	15.1	12.7	15.2	14.0	12.4	13.4	11.4
4. Mostly agree	19.0	17.7	20.2	19.8	16.6	19.9	19.8	17.2	19.9	20.7	16.9	21.5	19.5	17.9	16.3	14.3
5. Agree	10.0	8.7	10.6	8.7	13.8	9.9	8.1	12.2	9.1	9.0	11.3	10.0	9.1	10.3	9.8	5.7
Item 13960 N(Wtd)	3345	1635	1636	2666	392	709	1049	1048	538	1933	1333	1136	702	475	949	35

D02: These next questions ask how you feel about your present financial situation and your future financial security.

D02A: I feel that I have enough money to get along pretty well

1. Never	12.8	10.8	14.7	11.0	22.4	12.7	12.0	14.7	10.6	11.0	15.5	12.7	13.8	11.8	12.4	18.9
2. Seldom	19.4	18.8	20.2	18.6	23.0	20.1	21.1	17.7	18.5	18.8	20.5	17.7	19.2	21.7	21.0	5.4
3. Sometimes	36.1	35.1	36.7	36.3	34.3	33.4	37.8	36.4	35.8	34.8	38.0	36.9	37.0	35.4	34.1	56.8
4. Often	23.3	25.7	21.3	25.5	11.9	26.0	21.8	22.2	24.9	24.9	20.9	24.3	22.4	24.2	23.0	10.8
5. Always	8.4	9.6	7.0	8.5	8.4	7.8	7.2	9.0	10.4	10.5	5.1	8.4	7.7	6.9	9.4	8.1
Item 12990 N(Wtd)	3297	1609	1616	2636	379	695	1039	1033	530	1904	1317	1114	689	466	941	37

D02B: I get very concerned about how I am going to be able to pay my next bills

1. Never	26.5	25.6	27.5	25.7	33.2	28.2	26.0	25.8	26.9	30.1	21.7	29.3	26.4	25.4	24.1	24.3
2. Seldom	24.5	24.1	25.0	26.3	17.4	23.9	23.9	24.4	26.9	25.1	23.8	24.7	26.4	24.5	24.0	10.8
3. Sometimes	28.1	28.8	27.4	28.4	24.3	28.2	29.7	28.3	25.0	26.1	31.2	25.7	28.0	30.8	28.9	40.5
4. Often	14.2	15.1	12.9	13.7	15.8	13.9	14.1	14.2	15.0	12.9	16.0	13.6	13.0	14.0	15.4	21.6
5. Always	6.6	6.3	7.1	5.9	9.4	6.0	6.4	7.4	6.3	5.8	7.3	6.6	6.0	5.6	7.4	2.7
Item 13000 N(Wtd)	3265	1600	1594	2611	374	689	1027	1025	525	1889	1300	1099	685	465	933	37

QUESTIONNAIRE FORM 5 1981	TOTAL	SEX		RACE		REGION				4YR COLLEGE PLANS		ILLICIT DRUG USE: LIFETIME				
		M	F	White	Black	NE	NC	S	W	Yes	No	None	Mari-juana Only	Few Pills	More Pills	Any Her-oin
Weighted No. of Cases:	3656	1803	1741	2820	459	853	1091	1127	586	2036	1422	1210	782	515	1027	40
% of Weighted Total:	100.0	49.3	47.6	77.1	12.6	23.3	29.8	30.8	16.0	55.7	38.9	33.1	21.4	14.1	28.1	1.1

D02C: I worry whether I will have any job at all in a few months

	TOTAL	M	F	White	Black	NE	NC	S	W	Yes	No	None	Mari-juana Only	Few Pills	More Pills	Any Her-oin
1. Never	35.9	35.7	36.5	37.1	29.6	36.2	33.2	35.3	41.7	39.4	30.4	36.0	34.1	39.0	35.8	35.1
2. Seldom	22.8	23.8	21.7	23.9	15.3	24.3	23.1	21.2	23.5	23.9	21.6	21.9	24.0	23.5	22.6	18.9
3. Sometimes	19.9	20.5	19.1	19.6	22.2	19.8	19.8	21.5	17.0	18.4	22.3	19.6	20.4	19.2	19.7	27.0
4. Often	13.9	13.0	14.9	13.1	18.5	12.3	16.7	13.3	11.9	12.2	16.6	14.1	13.4	12.3	15.0	16.2
5. Always	7.5	7.0	7.9	6.2	14.0	7.2	7.2	8.7	5.9	6.2	9.2	8.3	8.2	6.0	6.8	-
Item 13010 N(Wtd)	3250	1590	1588	2595	378	676	1028	1023	523	1882	1294	1096	680	464	924	37

D02D: I feel sure that I could go out and get a new job (with decent pay) whenever I want one

	TOTAL	M	F	White	Black	NE	NC	S	W	Yes	No	None	Mari-juana Only	Few Pills	More Pills	Any Her-oin
1. Never	10.2	9.9	10.4	8.6	19.3	10.3	10.6	10.6	8.5	9.1	12.0	10.5	10.6	12.1	8.3	10.8
2. Seldom	24.6	21.9	27.2	24.4	22.5	23.1	29.1	21.9	22.5	21.8	28.5	22.1	26.0	28.7	24.6	24.3
3. Sometimes	33.8	30.3	37.2	34.5	30.7	35.4	33.6	33.1	33.3	33.9	33.6	35.7	34.9	29.7	33.3	29.7
4. Often	20.3	23.0	17.9	21.6	13.4	22.0	18.4	19.3	23.7	22.7	16.7	21.3	17.9	19.6	21.6	13.5
5. Always	11.2	15.0	7.2	10.9	13.9	9.3	8.3	15.0	12.3	12.5	9.1	10.6	10.7	9.9	12.0	18.9
Item 13020 N(Wtd)	3250	1600	1579	2598	374	681	1031	1018	520	1877	1296	1096	680	464	924	37

FOR THOSE WHO HAVE A JOB:

D02E: I feel sure I that can keep working steadily with my present employer as long as I want to

	TOTAL	M	F	White	Black	NE	NC	S	W	Yes	No	None	Mari-juana Only	Few Pills	More Pills	Any Her-oin
1. Never	5.2	4.9	5.5	4.1	12.5	5.4	5.4	6.0	3.2	4.3	6.3	4.1	4.4	4.0	6.6	11.5
2. Seldom	5.0	4.0	6.1	4.6	7.5	4.3	6.3	4.5	4.5	4.1	6.1	3.9	6.0	4.0	5.8	7.7
3. Sometimes	13.7	12.9	14.9	12.6	18.0	13.6	14.5	12.3	14.6	11.9	16.0	13.7	14.1	16.9	11.5	15.4
4. Often	27.3	27.7	26.8	28.5	22.5	28.9	29.5	23.8	27.4	27.4	27.6	29.6	23.0	28.0	28.1	23.1
5. Always	48.9	50.4	46.7	50.2	39.0	47.7	44.3	53.5	50.5	52.3	44.0	48.5	52.8	47.4	48.1	42.3
Item 13030 N(Wtd) ★	2194	1112	1027	1813	200	463	688	667	376	1244	896	685	434	325	686	26

D02F: I worry about getting fired or laid-off from my job

	TOTAL	M	F	White	Black	NE	NC	S	W	Yes	No	None	Mari-juana Only	Few Pills	More Pills	Any Her-oin
1. Never	56.5	54.2	59.1	57.6	51.3	57.0	55.4	58.1	54.9	59.4	52.6	59.2	54.9	55.4	56.2	38.5
2. Seldom	25.8	26.6	25.2	25.9	26.2	26.5	26.5	24.4	26.1	26.2	25.2	23.9	26.5	27.1	26.7	38.5
3. Sometimes	11.3	12.6	9.7	11.3	9.4	11.6	12.0	10.3	11.5	9.1	14.1	9.3	11.6	12.3	12.3	19.2
4. Often	4.0	3.8	4.2	3.5	7.3	3.0	4.4	3.9	4.5	3.4	4.8	4.3	4.7	4.3	2.9	3.8
5. Always	2.5	2.9	2.0	1.8	5.8	2.2	1.8	3.3	2.7	1.9	3.3	3.4	2.3	.9	1.9	-
Item 13040 N(Wtd) ★	2182	1106	1020	1810	191	465	682	661	375	1240	889	681	430	325	682	26

D03: Please think about all the money you earned during the past year, including last summer.

About how much of your past year's earnings have gone into:

D03A: Savings for your future education

	TOTAL	M	F	White	Black	NE	NC	S	W	Yes	No	None	Mari-juana Only	Few Pills	More Pills	Any Her-oin
1. None	46.9	46.7	46.2	46.1	48.6	43.4	45.2	50.1	48.4	38.2	60.1	39.5	46.8	56.1	50.1	68.6
2. A little	23.3	23.9	23.1	24.1	20.7	22.4	22.5	23.0	26.8	26.1	19.0	23.1	26.0	18.9	24.2	20.0
3. Some	12.4	12.1	12.8	12.4	14.7	12.0	14.4	11.8	10.1	13.3	10.9	14.6	11.4	8.8	12.6	2.9
4. About half	6.4	6.6	6.5	6.6	6.6	8.4	6.5	5.9	5.0	7.8	4.4	7.3	6.1	6.5	5.9	2.9
5. Most	6.4	6.1	6.7	6.7	2.5	8.7	7.7	4.7	3.8	8.4	3.5	9.1	5.5	5.4	4.4	2.9
6. Almost all	3.7	3.6	3.8	3.6	3.8	4.7	3.3	2.8	5.0	5.4	1.0	5.4	3.3	3.4	2.2	-
7. All	.9	1.1	.8	.5	3.1	.5	.3	1.7	1.0	.7	1.0	1.0	.9	.9	.6	-
Item 20830 N(Wtd)	3083	1504	1512	2512	319	643	987	949	504	1802	1212	1028	639	444	892	35

★ = excludes respondents for whom question was inappropriate.

QUESTIONNAIRE FORM 5 1981	TOTAL	SEX		RACE		REGION				4YR COLLEGE PLANS		ILLICIT DRUG USE: LIFETIME				
		M	F	White	Black	NE	NC	S	W	Yes	No	None	Mari-juana Only	Few Pills	More Pills	Any Her-oin
Weighted No. of Cases:	3656	1803	1741	2820	459	853	1091	1127	586	2036	1422	1210	782	515	1027	40
% of Weighted Total:	100.0	49.3	47.6	77.1	12.6	23.3	29.8	30.8	16.0	55.7	38.9	33.1	21.4	14.1	28.1	1.1

D03B: Savings or payments for a car or car expenses

	TOTAL	M	F	White	Black	NE	NC	S	W	Yes	No	None	Mari-juana Only	Few Pills	More Pills	Any Her-oin
1. None	45.7	35.5	55.5	43.7	61.1	50.0	43.3	47.0	42.2	50.4	38.7	49.1	46.5	45.3	41.8	40.0
2. A little	16.7	17.5	15.8	17.3	11.1	18.2	17.3	14.8	16.9	17.3	15.6	17.1	14.5	18.0	16.9	20.0
3. Some	14.7	17.1	12.8	15.7	8.6	13.1	17.0	14.0	13.7	14.0	16.2	13.1	16.6	11.6	16.8	14.3
4. About half	11.1	14.9	7.5	11.3	9.6	9.8	11.1	11.9	11.2	8.9	14.6	9.9	10.9	10.0	13.1	17.1
5. Most	6.6	8.2	4.9	7.2	3.5	5.0	6.0	7.0	9.0	5.5	7.9	5.7	6.5	7.7	7.1	5.7
6. Almost all	3.6	4.3	2.7	3.4	4.1	3.0	3.5	3.1	5.6	2.6	4.9	3.6	3.6	4.8	2.7	-
7. All	1.7	2.5	1.0	1.4	1.6	.8	1.8	2.2	1.4	1.2	2.2	1.6	1.6	2.3	1.6	-
Item 20840 N(Wtd)	3068	1500	1502	2502	314	642	984	940	502	1791	1208	1019	643	439	887	35

D03C: Other savings for long-range purposes

	TOTAL	M	F	White	Black	NE	NC	S	W	Yes	No	None	Mari-juana Only	Few Pills	More Pills	Any Her-oin
1. None	45.8	46.1	44.9	44.9	53.7	44.6	47.7	47.5	40.8	47.5	43.6	45.3	49.7	45.4	43.6	64.7
2. A little	24.9	26.7	23.5	26.4	16.2	27.8	24.1	22.5	27.6	26.0	23.6	24.8	23.3	22.9	28.0	20.6
3. Some	13.4	13.0	14.1	13.3	14.9	11.0	14.2	14.4	13.3	12.2	15.2	11.5	13.8	14.7	13.8	8.8
4. About half	7.0	6.5	7.3	6.8	5.7	7.6	6.4	7.0	7.4	6.0	8.3	7.8	5.7	8.8	6.3	2.9
5. Most	4.3	3.8	4.9	4.1	5.1	5.0	3.7	4.0	5.0	4.4	4.0	4.6	3.6	3.2	4.9	2.9
6. Almost all	3.2	2.8	3.7	3.3	1.9	2.5	3.0	2.9	5.2	3.0	3.6	4.1	3.5	3.2	2.1	-
7. All	1.4	1.1	1.7	1.3	2.2	1.6	1.2	1.9	.8	1.0	1.7	1.8	.6	1.4	1.4	-
Item 20850 N(Wtd)	3054	1489	1498	2490	315	634	980	942	497	1787	1201	1015	636	441	886	34

D03D: Spending on your own needs and activities -- things such as clothing, stereo, TV, records, other possessions, movies, eating out, other recreation, hobbies, gifts for others, and other personal expenses

	TOTAL	M	F	White	Black	NE	NC	S	W	Yes	No	None	Mari-juana Only	Few Pills	More Pills	Any Her-oin
1. None	4.8	5.7	3.9	3.8	10.7	3.0	5.3	6.2	3.2	4.3	5.4	6.0	5.9	2.5	3.4	8.6
2. A little	19.8	21.7	17.2	19.9	15.0	18.2	19.0	21.7	19.6	19.6	20.0	22.0	20.8	19.5	16.9	14.3
3. Some	19.1	20.5	17.8	19.7	16.6	19.6	19.5	17.6	20.4	19.0	19.5	21.2	17.8	19.0	17.9	8.6
4. About half	17.1	18.6	16.1	17.9	11.9	17.4	18.2	16.2	16.2	17.9	16.4	16.0	15.5	18.1	19.4	14.3
5. Most	16.8	16.2	17.9	17.8	11.6	17.3	15.8	15.2	21.6	16.4	17.4	15.3	16.7	16.6	18.7	25.7
6. Almost all	14.0	11.1	16.7	13.3	20.1	13.8	14.5	13.4	13.8	14.3	13.2	12.5	15.8	15.0	14.0	14.3
7. All	8.4	6.2	10.4	7.7	14.1	10.7	7.6	9.6	4.8	8.6	8.1	7.1	7.4	9.1	9.7	14.3
Item 20860 N(Wtd)	3063	1496	1500	2497	319	637	983	945	499	1792	1206	1021	639	441	886	35

D03E: Helping to pay family living expenses (groceries, housing, etc.)

	TOTAL	M	F	White	Black	NE	NC	S	W	Yes	No	None	Mari-juana Only	Few Pills	More Pills	Any Her-oin
1. None	55.4	54.3	56.2	59.8	31.9	55.8	59.4	52.6	52.3	59.1	50.3	57.1	55.6	51.4	56.3	48.6
2. A little	26.6	29.8	23.8	26.9	25.9	28.9	25.0	26.6	26.7	26.1	27.2	24.7	26.6	29.8	28.3	17.1
3. Some	9.7	9.1	10.1	7.8	21.1	9.8	8.9	10.2	10.0	8.4	11.3	9.7	10.7	8.9	8.2	17.1
4. About half	3.6	3.1	4.3	2.4	8.2	3.3	2.5	4.7	4.4	2.7	5.0	3.6	3.6	3.4	3.5	8.6
5. Most	2.0	1.3	2.5	1.5	5.4	1.1	1.8	2.5	2.4	1.7	2.2	2.2	1.6	3.2	1.1	8.6
6. Almost all	1.7	1.2	1.9	.9	4.7	.6	1.5	1.7	3.4	1.3	2.3	1.6	1.3	1.8	1.6	2.9
7. All	1.1	1.2	1.1	.7	3.2	.6	1.1	1.6	1.0	.7	1.7	1.3	.8	1.1	.9	-
Item 20870 N(Wtd)	3055	1490	1499	2490	317	633	977	943	501	1787	1202	1014	638	440	887	35

E01: Do YOU think that people who smoke marijuana several times a week tend to be...

E01A: More creative than average

	TOTAL	M	F	White	Black	NE	NC	S	W	Yes	No	None	Mari-juana Only	Few Pills	More Pills	Any Her-oin
1. No	61.2	62.2	59.7	63.4	48.3	60.5	61.1	59.1	66.2	65.3	55.2	68.2	62.8	64.1	51.4	44.4
2. Yes	14.7	15.6	14.0	14.3	15.5	14.7	15.7	14.0	13.7	12.2	18.1	6.4	12.2	14.1	26.0	30.6
3. Not sure, no opinion	24.1	22.2	26.3	22.3	36.2	24.8	23.1	26.8	20.1	22.6	26.7	25.4	25.1	21.9	22.5	25.0
Item 13060 N(Wtd)	3212	1561	1577	2581	362	661	1023	1011	518	1875	1268	1096	678	448	911	36

E01B: Less sensible than average

	TOTAL	M	F	White	Black	NE	NC	S	W	Yes	No	None	Mari-juana Only	Few Pills	More Pills	Any Her-oin
1. No	27.9	30.2	25.6	28.7	23.8	27.2	27.7	27.7	29.8	25.1	31.4	13.9	26.9	31.2	43.4	63.9
2. Yes	55.2	53.5	56.8	56.3	51.2	53.1	57.5	53.3	57.0	59.4	49.6	67.2	55.5	53.1	42.8	27.8
3. Not sure, no opinion	16.9	16.3	17.7	15.0	24.9	19.7	14.8	19.0	13.2	15.5	18.9	18.9	17.7	15.7	13.8	8.3
Item 13070 N(Wtd)	3206	1555	1577	2578	361	661	1021	1009	516	1869	1267	1096	677	446	907	36

QUESTIONNAIRE FORM 5 1981	TOTAL	SEX		RACE		REGION				4YR COLLEGE PLANS		ILLICIT DRUG USE: LIFETIME				
		M	F	White	Black	NE	NC	S	W	Yes	No	None	Mari- juana Only	Few Pills	More Pills	Any Her- oin
Weighted No. of Cases:	3656	1803	1741	2820	459	853	1091	1127	586	2036	1422	1210	782	515	1027	40
% of Weighted Total:	100.0	49.3	47.6	77.1	12.6	23.3	29.8	30.8	16.0	55.7	38.9	33.1	21.4	14.1	28.1	1.1
E01C: More interesting people than average																
1. No	66.0	64.8	67.1	68.7	52.4	63.5	66.3	65.8	69.2	69.9	60.6	75.4	67.2	67.5	55.0	50.0
2. Yes	15.2	17.7	13.0	14.4	21.4	15.9	16.2	14.3	14.3	13.0	18.3	5.0	14.9	16.4	26.4	30.6
3. Not sure, no opinion	18.7	17.6	19.9	16.9	26.2	20.8	17.5	20.0	16.3	17.0	21.2	19.5	17.9	16.1	18.7	19.4
Item 13080 N(Wtd)	3198	1552	1572	2575	359	660	1019	1003	516	1866	1262	1091	676	446	906	36
E01D: Less hard-working than average																
1. No	28.1	28.5	27.6	28.9	26.3	28.0	30.6	26.8	25.9	24.2	33.8	15.3	28.6	32.1	40.9	44.1
2. Yes	56.2	57.2	55.4	57.0	52.2	54.1	55.3	57.4	58.6	60.4	50.4	66.0	56.1	52.8	47.2	38.2
3. Not sure, no opinion	15.6	14.3	16.9	14.2	21.5	17.9	14.0	15.7	15.7	15.4	15.8	18.7	15.4	15.3	11.8	14.7
Item 13090 N(Wtd)	3194	1551	1570	2572	358	658	1013	1006	517	1865	1260	1090	675	445	908	34
E01E: More independent than average																
1. No	52.5	50.2	54.5	53.5	51.0	48.2	52.3	54.5	54.1	53.0	51.6	55.0	53.3	53.1	49.2	42.9
2. Yes	26.9	30.5	23.4	27.6	21.8	28.3	29.4	23.5	26.7	27.8	25.5	20.3	27.4	28.3	33.8	34.3
3. Not sure, no opinion	20.6	19.3	22.1	18.9	27.5	23.4	18.3	21.9	19.3	19.2	22.9	24.7	19.3	18.4	16.9	22.9
Item 13100 N(Wtd)	3185	1549	1562	2566	357	653	1016	1003	514	1859	1257	1090	675	441	904	35
E01F: More emotionally unstable than average																
1. No	26.8	29.7	23.6	27.6	24.2	26.5	28.8	24.7	27.2	24.1	30.3	13.4	26.9	26.1	41.9	72.2
2. Yes	56.1	52.7	59.6	56.7	52.2	56.4	56.2	56.9	53.8	60.1	50.2	68.0	56.4	55.3	43.7	13.9
3. Not sure, no opinion	17.2	17.7	16.8	15.7	23.3	17.1	15.2	18.4	19.0	15.8	19.6	18.5	16.7	18.4	14.4	13.9
Item 13110 N(Wtd)	3185	1544	1568	2566	360	656	1015	1000	515	1863	1252	1090	672	445	903	36
E01G: More concerned about other people than average																
1. No	70.3	70.6	70.0	72.5	62.2	65.2	72.1	70.9	72.1	73.7	65.7	75.1	72.4	72.9	63.7	52.8
2. Yes	10.2	11.7	8.9	9.9	11.2	11.9	10.0	10.3	8.6	7.7	13.5	4.0	9.8	8.4	18.3	27.8
3. Not sure, no opinion	19.4	17.6	21.1	17.6	26.9	22.8	17.8	18.8	19.3	18.6	20.8	21.1	17.8	18.8	18.1	19.4
Item 13120 N(Wtd)	3181	1542	1566	2563	357	653	1016	1000	512	1862	1251	1087	675	442	903	36
E01H: More weak-willed than average																
1. No	28.7	29.9	27.1	29.1	26.4	30.8	30.7	25.9	27.6	25.1	33.5	15.0	28.4	30.9	43.8	55.6
2. Yes	51.7	51.6	51.8	52.4	50.0	48.2	52.4	53.9	50.3	56.2	45.4	63.5	52.2	49.2	40.1	30.6
3. Not sure, no opinion	19.6	18.5	21.1	18.5	23.6	21.0	17.0	20.3	22.1	18.7	21.0	21.6	19.5	20.1	16.1	13.9
Item 13130 N(Wtd)	3175	1536	1566	2561	356	653	1014	997	511	1859	1248	1085	673	443	898	36
E01I: More criminal than average																
1. No	29.7	30.1	29.5	31.0	23.9	30.0	32.4	26.7	29.4	26.7	33.1	16.0	26.8	32.4	46.7	48.6
2. Yes	49.8	52.1	47.0	50.4	50.6	48.9	49.9	51.4	47.5	53.5	45.0	61.5	52.3	49.3	35.0	40.0
3. Not sure, no opinion	20.5	17.7	23.6	18.7	25.3	21.1	17.6	21.8	22.9	19.8	21.9	22.4	20.7	18.2	18.4	11.4
Item 13140 N(Wtd)	3179	1541	1565	2560	360	653	1014	1003	510	1862	1250	1087	675	444	898	35

Next we want to ask you how you think most of the people you know would answer the same questions.

E02: Do you think that MOST OF THE PEOPLE YOU KNOW feel that individuals who smoke marijuana several times a week tend to be...

QUESTIONNAIRE FORM 5 1981	TOTAL	SEX		RACE		REGION				4YR COLLEGE PLANS		ILLICIT DRUG USE: LIFETIME				
		M	F	White	Black	NE	NC	S	W	Yes	No	None	Marijuana Only	Few Pills	More Pills	Any Heroin
Weighted No. of Cases:	3656	1803	1741	2820	459	853	1091	1127	586	2036	1422	1210	782	515	1027	40
% of Weighted Total:	100.0	49.3	47.6	77.1	12.6	23.3	29.8	30.8	16.0	55.7	38.9	33.1	21.4	14.1	28.1	1.1

E02A: More creative than average

1. No	56.9	57.0	56.6	59.0	46.3	56.1	59.7	55.2	55.9	59.9	52.6	60.1	57.9	60.8	52.3	38.2
2. Yes	20.6	21.6	19.6	20.2	24.6	21.5	19.8	20.2	21.3	19.5	21.9	13.9	18.7	20.6	28.9	38.2
3. Not sure, no opinion	22.5	21.4	23.7	20.8	29.1	22.4	20.4	24.6	22.7	20.6	25.7	26.0	23.2	18.6	18.8	23.5
Item 13190 N(Wtd)	3131	1520	1538	2525	350	642	1003	989	497	1832	1235	1066	667	436	888	34

E02B: Less sensible than average

1. No	30.9	31.2	30.2	31.6	28.0	32.1	29.7	28.9	35.9	28.7	32.9	21.7	29.9	33.4	41.0	41.2
2. Yes	50.2	49.8	50.9	51.4	47.3	49.1	52.8	49.9	46.8	53.8	46.0	56.5	50.5	50.9	43.9	38.2
3. Not sure, no opinion	18.8	19.0	18.9	17.0	24.8	18.7	17.5	21.1	17.3	17.5	21.1	21.8	19.4	15.9	15.0	20.6
Item 13200 N(Wtd)	3120	1515	1533	2519	347	641	1000	985	496	1825	1232	1064	665	434	886	34

E02C: More interesting people than average

1. No	58.7	57.9	59.6	60.8	48.3	56.7	59.6	59.4	57.9	61.3	54.9	62.7	60.9	59.1	54.2	32.4
2. Yes	20.5	21.1	19.8	20.3	23.9	22.6	20.0	18.6	22.8	19.6	21.6	13.6	18.1	23.1	29.2	38.2
3. Not sure, no opinion	20.8	21.1	20.5	18.9	27.9	20.7	20.3	21.9	19.4	19.0	23.6	23.8	21.1	18.0	16.6	32.4
Item 13210 N(Wtd)	3115	1512	1530	2514	348	637	1001	981	496	1827	1225	1062	663	433	885	34

E02D: Less hard-working than average

1. No	30.0	30.2	29.4	30.6	30.1	30.1	29.7	28.5	33.5	28.2	32.2	21.0	29.3	34.3	39.1	41.2
2. Yes	51.3	51.2	51.7	52.2	46.4	50.5	52.5	52.3	48.2	55.0	46.1	57.8	51.5	49.9	45.1	44.1
3. Not sure, no opinion	18.7	18.6	19.0	17.2	23.5	19.3	17.9	19.3	18.5	16.8	21.8	21.2	19.2	15.6	15.7	17.6
Item 13220 N(Wtd)	3115	1513	1529	2515	345	641	997	981	496	1826	1226	1061	662	435	886	34

E02E: More independent than average

1. No	48.4	46.0	50.6	49.4	46.8	44.7	49.5	50.5	46.8	50.2	46.0	49.3	51.0	50.6	45.5	29.4
2. Yes	29.3	31.6	26.9	29.9	25.4	32.3	29.9	25.9	30.8	29.4	28.9	24.8	26.8	30.7	35.8	44.1
3. Not sure, no opinion	22.3	22.3	22.5	20.7	27.7	23.0	20.5	23.6	22.4	20.4	25.3	25.9	22.0	18.7	18.5	26.5
Item 13230 N(Wtd)	3113	1514	1526	2515	346	638	999	980	496	1826	1227	1061	663	433	885	34

E02F: More emotionally unstable than average

1. No	28.9	29.8	27.9	30.0	23.7	29.4	29.3	25.9	33.3	27.6	30.6	20.0	29.3	32.7	36.8	52.9
2. Yes	51.5	50.0	53.1	52.3	49.7	51.0	52.3	53.5	46.5	54.3	47.3	59.4	49.2	48.2	46.8	29.4
3. Not sure, no opinion	19.6	20.1	19.1	17.7	26.6	19.4	18.4	20.6	20.1	18.1	22.2	20.5	21.5	19.1	16.4	17.6
Item 13240 N(Wtd)	3110	1511	1526	2514	346	639	999	979	492	1824	1223	1061	662	434	885	34

E02G: More concerned about other people than average

1. No	66.0	65.5	66.5	68.5	57.6	63.5	67.2	67.0	64.8	68.8	61.6	68.2	69.4	68.0	61.8	44.1
2. Yes	11.7	12.5	10.8	11.1	14.4	12.8	12.0	10.9	11.3	10.4	13.5	7.7	9.3	12.2	17.4	23.5
3. Not sure, no opinion	22.3	22.1	22.7	20.4	28.0	23.8	20.8	22.0	23.8	20.9	24.9	24.0	21.2	19.8	20.8	32.4
Item 13250 N(Wtd)	3114	1510	1532	2517	347	639	999	980	495	1826	1226	1061	664	434	885	34

E02H: More weak-willed than average

1. No	30.7	32.3	28.8	31.4	27.5	32.2	31.4	27.5	33.3	28.7	33.1	22.1	29.8	31.6	41.3	47.1
2. Yes	48.4	47.3	49.5	49.1	46.5	46.2	48.9	50.6	45.5	51.9	43.5	55.3	48.3	49.1	40.9	29.4
3. Not sure, no opinion	21.0	20.4	21.7	19.5	26.0	21.4	19.7	21.9	21.2	19.5	23.4	22.6	22.0	19.4	17.8	26.5
Item 13260 N(Wtd)	3109	1508	1528	2513	346	639	997	978	495	1824	1222	1062	665	434	880	34

E02I: More criminal than average

1. No	30.1	28.5	31.3	31.2	23.1	31.6	32.6	24.6	33.9	28.8	31.6	20.7	27.9	34.1	41.3	33.3
2. Yes	49.3	51.0	47.7	50.2	47.6	47.7	48.1	53.3	46.0	51.8	45.8	57.5	48.8	48.6	41.3	39.4
3. Not sure, no opinion	20.6	20.5	20.9	18.6	29.1	20.8	19.3	22.1	20.2	19.5	22.5	21.9	23.2	17.1	17.4	27.3
Item 13270 N(Wtd)	3113	1510	1530	2516	347	640	997	980	496	1825	1224	1060	664	434	886	33

QUESTIONNAIRE FORM 5 1981	TOTAL	SEX		RACE		REGION				4YR COLLEGE PLANS		ILLICIT DRUG USE: LIFETIME				
		M	F	White	Black	NE	NC	S	W	Yes	No	None	Mari-juana Only	Few Pills	More Pills	Any Her-oin
Weighted No. of Cases:	3656	1803	1741	2820	459	853	1091	1127	586	2036	1422	1210	782	515	1027	40
% of Weighted Total:	100.0	49.3	47.6	77.1	12.6	23.3	29.8	30.8	16.0	55.7	38.9	33.1	21.4	14.1	28.1	1.1

The next few questions ask how YOU view cigarette smoking.

E03: In my opinion, when a guy my age is smoking a cigarette, it makes him look...

E03A: Cool, calm, in-control

	TOTAL	M	F	White	Black	NE	NC	S	W	Yes	No	None	Mari-juana Only	Few Pills	More Pills	Any Her-oin
1. Disagree	62.7	64.1	61.1	64.1	56.2	61.0	58.0	63.2	73.0	65.7	58.1	73.8	60.0	58.2	54.4	44.1
2. Mostly disagree	12.3	12.2	12.4	12.3	13.6	11.5	14.4	10.8	12.0	12.3	12.2	10.9	12.7	17.5	11.7	2.9
3. Neither	18.8	17.4	20.2	18.6	18.0	21.9	19.8	18.8	12.6	17.2	21.2	10.3	21.9	18.6	25.6	41.2
4. Mostly agree	4.1	3.8	4.5	3.8	5.8	4.2	5.1	4.5	1.4	3.2	5.6	2.6	4.2	3.7	5.7	8.8
5. Agree	2.1	2.5	1.8	1.2	6.4	1.4	2.7	2.9	.8	1.6	3.0	2.4	1.2	2.1	2.5	-
Item 20880 N(Wtd)	3117	1513	1531	2513	345	643	994	980	500	1836	1217	1069	662	435	875	34

E03B: Insecure

	TOTAL	M	F	White	Black	NE	NC	S	W	Yes	No	None	Mari-juana Only	Few Pills	More Pills	Any Her-oin
1. Disagree	16.7	15.2	17.9	16.0	23.3	16.7	16.8	18.6	13.0	13.9	20.7	11.5	14.4	17.4	24.0	20.6
2. Mostly disagree	10.0	9.4	10.5	9.9	13.4	10.2	11.1	8.5	10.6	9.6	10.8	6.8	10.5	11.1	13.1	11.8
3. Neither	31.3	30.0	32.5	32.0	27.1	34.7	31.2	31.7	26.3	30.0	33.4	24.4	34.5	33.1	35.3	50.0
4. Mostly agree	20.2	21.1	19.8	20.9	14.0	17.3	21.9	20.3	20.2	22.9	16.1	24.3	20.7	21.8	14.9	8.8
5. Agree	21.8	24.2	19.2	21.3	22.4	21.1	19.0	20.9	29.9	23.5	19.1	33.1	19.9	16.9	12.8	5.9
Item 20890 N(Wtd)	3104	1505	1527	2503	343	636	989	978	501	1831	1209	1062	658	432	878	34

E03C: Rugged, tough, independent

	TOTAL	M	F	White	Black	NE	NC	S	W	Yes	No	None	Mari-juana Only	Few Pills	More Pills	Any Her-oin
1. Disagree	56.3	57.7	55.0	58.0	50.6	56.2	52.0	57.9	61.5	57.7	53.8	63.7	55.1	53.2	50.2	50.0
2. Mostly disagree	13.9	14.4	13.5	14.4	11.0	12.7	16.1	12.4	13.8	14.1	13.8	12.3	15.1	14.6	15.0	5.9
3. Neither	21.2	19.5	22.5	20.9	20.8	24.3	22.6	19.7	17.6	19.8	23.4	14.9	20.2	24.1	27.4	35.3
4. Mostly agree	5.8	5.5	6.2	5.1	10.4	5.2	7.6	5.9	3.2	5.8	6.1	4.8	7.1	6.3	5.6	5.9
5. Agree	2.8	2.9	2.8	1.7	6.9	1.7	1.8	4.0	3.8	2.7	3.1	4.2	2.3	1.9	1.7	-
Item 20900 N(Wtd)	3104	1505	1527	2503	346	639	990	977	499	1828	1213	1066	662	432	873	34

E03D: Conforming

	TOTAL	M	F	White	Black	NE	NC	S	W	Yes	No	None	Mari-juana Only	Few Pills	More Pills	Any Her-oin
1. Disagree	30.2	27.7	32.0	28.6	40.2	25.7	29.6	33.4	31.2	26.0	36.6	31.1	30.2	28.0	29.8	32.4
2. Mostly disagree	9.7	10.5	9.0	10.0	7.9	9.7	10.2	8.2	11.5	9.8	9.5	8.4	9.4	11.5	10.7	11.8
3. Neither	34.6	34.9	34.2	34.3	35.9	34.3	36.1	35.2	31.0	32.1	38.4	29.2	38.5	34.6	37.5	52.9
4. Mostly agree	13.2	13.7	13.2	13.8	11.1	15.0	12.8	12.9	12.1	16.6	8.3	14.2	12.6	14.6	12.1	-
5. Agree	12.2	13.2	11.6	13.3	5.0	15.2	11.3	10.3	14.2	15.5	7.1	17.0	9.3	11.3	9.8	2.9
Item 20910 N(Wtd)	3075	1489	1514	2481	343	638	981	962	494	1824	1189	1053	659	425	866	34

E03E: Mature, sophisticated

	TOTAL	M	F	White	Black	NE	NC	S	W	Yes	No	None	Mari-juana Only	Few Pills	More Pills	Any Her-oin
1. Disagree	61.2	61.0	61.5	62.3	57.9	58.3	57.2	63.2	68.8	63.5	57.6	72.0	59.8	56.7	52.7	29.4
2. Mostly disagree	13.3	13.7	12.9	13.7	10.8	14.2	14.6	10.8	14.4	13.9	12.5	11.5	14.4	17.2	13.3	5.9
3. Neither	20.1	19.3	20.7	20.2	19.9	23.6	21.5	19.7	13.8	17.8	23.6	11.4	19.7	20.9	28.7	58.8
4. Mostly agree	3.9	3.9	4.1	3.0	8.5	2.5	4.9	5.0	2.0	3.6	4.8	3.3	4.7	3.7	4.4	2.9
5. Agree	1.4	2.1	.8	.7	2.9	1.3	1.6	1.4	1.0	1.3	1.5	1.7	1.2	1.4	1.0	2.9
Item 20920 N(Wtd)	3095	1501	1522	2500	342	635	990	969	500	1823	1210	1059	660	430	871	34

E03F: Like he's TRYING to appear mature and sophisticated

	TOTAL	M	F	White	Black	NE	NC	S	W	Yes	No	None	Mari-juana Only	Few Pills	More Pills	Any Her-oin
1. Disagree	14.8	13.9	15.3	13.6	22.9	14.2	14.5	16.8	12.2	11.1	19.8	10.2	12.5	16.7	20.4	23.5
2. Mostly disagree	5.6	5.3	5.9	5.8	5.3	5.8	7.9	4.1	3.6	4.9	6.9	4.6	5.0	6.0	7.1	5.9
3. Neither	18.1	18.9	17.3	18.4	17.0	20.0	18.3	19.1	13.6	16.6	20.2	9.9	21.0	18.3	24.7	29.4
4. Mostly agree	20.5	19.7	21.3	21.4	15.8	22.2	22.2	17.6	21.0	23.0	17.2	19.8	22.7	20.4	19.7	29.4
5. Agree	40.9	42.2	40.1	40.7	39.0	37.9	37.2	42.3	49.5	44.5	35.9	55.5	38.8	38.5	27.9	5.9
Item 20930 N(Wtd)	3101	1501	1528	2506	341	641	990	972	499	1829	1212	1066	657	431	876	34

QUESTIONNAIRE FORM 5 1981	TOTAL	SEX		RACE		REGION				4YR COLLEGE PLANS		ILLICIT DRUG USE: LIFETIME				
		M	F	White	Black	NE	NC	S	W	Yes	No	None	Mari- juana Only	Few Pills	More Pills	Any Her- oin
Weighted No. of Cases:	3656	1803	1741	2820	459	853	1091	1127	586	2036	1422	1210	782	515	1027	40
% of Weighted Total:	100.0	49.3	47.6	77.1	12.6	23.3	29.8	30.8	16.0	55.7	38.9	33.1	21.4	14.1	28.1	1.1

E04: In my opinion, when a girl my age is smoking a cigarette, it makes her look...

E04A: Cool, calm, in-control

1. Disagree	68.3	69.6	66.7	69.5	64.8	65.9	64.3	70.3	75.2	71.1	63.7	78.0	66.3	66.0	60.5	44.1
2. Mostly disagree	11.3	11.5	11.1	11.1	10.9	10.3	14.4	8.8	11.3	11.0	12.0	9.7	11.9	14.7	11.1	11.8
3. Neither	14.9	13.3	16.5	14.7	15.5	17.9	15.4	15.3	9.5	13.8	16.5	7.8	15.2	14.9	22.2	35.3
4. Mostly agree	3.6	3.3	4.0	3.4	4.1	4.1	4.2	3.2	2.6	2.9	4.8	2.6	4.6	2.6	4.4	8.8
5. Agree	1.9	2.3	1.6	1.3	4.7	1.9	1.7	2.4	1.4	1.2	3.0	2.0	1.8	1.9	1.7	-
Item 20940 N(Wtd)	3063	1456	1538	2470	341	633	980	956	495	1811	1191	1045	653	430	859	34

E04B: Insecure

1. Disagree	18.9	18.1	18.8	17.8	28.5	18.2	19.8	21.4	12.9	14.8	24.6	12.3	16.8	21.2	26.7	23.5
2. Mostly disagree	7.9	7.8	8.2	7.8	9.8	7.9	6.6	7.8	10.7	7.8	8.3	5.2	10.0	8.1	9.4	5.9
3. Neither	25.8	24.4	27.0	26.0	23.4	30.7	25.5	25.1	21.6	24.8	27.3	20.0	27.3	27.7	30.1	32.4
4. Mostly agree	16.9	15.8	18.3	17.7	10.4	15.2	20.3	14.8	16.2	19.1	13.9	19.4	16.0	18.4	14.5	8.8
5. Agree	30.5	33.8	27.8	30.6	27.9	27.6	27.8	31.1	38.6	33.6	25.8	42.9	29.8	24.9	19.3	26.5
Item 20950 N(Wtd)	3053	1452	1532	2465	337	631	974	953	495	1808	1183	1039	648	430	864	34

E04C: Independent and liberated

1. Disagree	56.2	55.2	56.9	56.9	56.8	51.7	53.9	59.8	60.0	58.4	52.8	65.9	53.7	50.0	50.9	35.3
2. Mostly disagree	13.2	14.2	12.4	13.5	12.6	12.6	15.0	11.3	14.4	13.7	12.7	11.6	14.2	17.1	13.0	8.8
3. Neither	19.4	18.8	19.9	19.2	18.0	22.9	20.0	18.6	15.4	17.6	21.7	12.3	19.9	20.3	25.3	47.1
4. Mostly agree	7.5	7.3	8.0	7.6	6.3	9.7	8.7	5.5	6.1	6.3	9.5	5.4	8.5	9.1	8.4	8.8
5. Agree	3.7	4.5	2.9	2.8	6.3	3.3	2.5	4.9	4.1	3.9	3.2	4.7	3.7	3.7	2.6	-
Item 20960 N(Wtd)	3050	1447	1534	2466	333	629	982	947	492	1807	1182	1041	648	428	861	34

E04D: Conforming

1. Disagree	34.3	33.2	34.5	32.4	45.0	29.3	34.2	37.9	34.2	29.9	41.1	34.0	34.7	32.6	34.5	44.1
2. Mostly disagree	8.6	8.9	8.2	8.6	9.1	7.5	9.9	7.3	10.0	7.8	10.1	7.7	9.0	7.6	9.7	23.5
3. Neither	30.5	29.3	31.7	30.4	30.7	30.9	31.0	31.0	27.7	28.9	33.0	25.8	33.3	30.2	33.8	29.4
4. Mostly agree	12.5	13.3	12.4	13.5	8.8	14.0	12.3	12.3	11.7	15.6	7.8	13.9	11.6	15.7	10.6	2.9
5. Agree	14.0	15.2	13.2	15.0	6.4	18.3	12.5	11.6	16.2	17.8	8.2	18.5	11.6	14.0	11.3	2.9
Item 20970 N(Wtd)	3020	1433	1518	2444	329	628	970	934	488	1797	1164	1026	648	420	856	34

E04E: Mature, sophisticated

1. Disagree	63.9	64.7	63.2	65.4	58.1	60.6	61.1	65.5	70.8	66.2	60.6	73.7	61.3	60.7	56.9	41.2
2. Mostly disagree	12.8	12.3	13.1	12.7	13.6	11.5	15.1	10.8	13.6	12.9	12.8	10.9	13.6	16.8	12.5	11.8
3. Neither	16.4	15.7	17.0	16.7	15.1	20.4	17.1	16.2	10.5	14.6	18.8	10.3	16.0	14.3	23.9	41.2
4. Mostly agree	4.6	4.4	4.8	3.8	7.8	5.3	5.0	4.3	3.7	4.3	5.3	2.8	6.9	5.6	4.4	5.9
5. Agree	2.3	2.9	1.8	1.4	5.4	2.4	1.5	3.4	1.6	2.1	2.5	2.2	2.0	2.6	2.3	-
Item 20980 N(Wtd)	3045	1446	1530	2465	332	627	978	947	493	1804	1180	1036	648	428	861	34

E04F: Like she's TRYING to appear mature and sophisticated

1. Disagree	15.8	15.7	15.6	15.0	22.8	15.9	15.7	18.2	11.3	12.7	19.7	11.4	14.8	15.5	20.8	38.2
2. Mostly disagree	4.6	4.5	4.6	4.8	3.6	6.2	4.9	3.8	3.6	3.8	6.0	2.7	5.2	4.7	6.1	2.9
3. Neither	14.9	14.6	15.2	14.9	15.3	16.5	15.4	15.6	10.7	13.4	17.3	9.5	14.3	15.3	20.9	32.4
4. Mostly agree	19.8	19.3	20.5	20.4	15.9	20.8	22.7	16.6	19.0	20.5	19.1	19.4	20.6	22.4	18.9	20.6
5. Agree	44.8	45.9	44.1	44.8	42.6	40.5	41.3	45.8	55.4	49.6	38.0	57.0	45.0	42.1	33.3	8.8
Item 20990 N(Wtd)	3052	1453	1529	2470	333	629	981	946	496	1806	1185	1043	649	425	862	34

E05: Do you agree or disagree..

E05A: Smokers know how to enjoy life more than nonsmokers

1. Disagree	76.1	75.4	77.3	77.3	72.3	78.3	72.9	75.4	80.7	79.7	70.3	83.3	77.7	73.5	69.2	50.0
2. Mostly disagree	8.4	7.4	9.1	8.1	10.4	7.5	10.4	7.1	8.0	7.7	9.5	7.6	8.9	9.8	8.2	14.7
3. Neither	12.7	13.9	11.2	12.3	12.1	11.8	14.7	13.2	8.9	10.4	16.3	7.0	11.5	13.0	19.2	29.4
4. Mostly agree	1.3	1.3	1.2	1.2	1.7	1.6	.6	1.8	1.2	1.2	1.4	.6	.9	2.3	1.7	-
5. Agree	1.5	1.9	1.2	1.0	3.7	.9	1.4	2.4	1.2	1.0	2.5	1.6	.9	1.4	1.8	5.9
Item 21000 N(Wtd)	3112	1502	1539	2504	347	636	999	974	503	1832	1216	1063	660	430	882	34

QUESTIONNAIRE FORM 5 1981	TOTAL	SEX		RACE		REGION				4YR COLLEGE PLANS		ILLICIT DRUG USE: LIFETIME				
		M	F	White	Black	NE	NC	S	W	Yes	No	None	Marijuana Only	Few Pills	More Pills	Any Heroin
Weighted No. of Cases:	3656	1803	1741	2820	459	853	1091	1127	586	2036	1422	1210	782	515	1027	40
% of Weighted Total:	100.0	49.3	47.6	77.1	12.6	23.3	29.8	30.8	16.0	55.7	38.9	33.1	21.4	14.1	28.1	1.1
E05B: I prefer to date people who don't smoke																
1. Disagree	10.5	9.0	11.7	9.7	16.7	9.6	12.1	11.5	6.2	7.7	14.2	5.3	11.1	11.8	15.5	17.6
2. Mostly disagree	3.9	3.5	4.4	3.4	6.9	4.1	4.1	4.2	2.8	2.7	5.4	2.3	4.4	3.7	5.2	2.9
3. Neither	19.1	16.0	21.9	19.5	15.3	20.3	20.6	18.7	15.4	16.2	23.8	10.2	19.3	20.8	27.5	47.1
4. Mostly agree	9.9	9.3	10.8	10.0	9.2	11.0	11.5	8.1	8.6	10.3	9.7	9.7	9.7	10.2	10.1	8.8
5. Agree	56.6	62.3	51.3	57.5	51.9	55.0	51.6	57.4	67.0	63.0	46.9	72.5	55.4	53.5	41.6	20.6
Item 21010 N(Wtd)	3104	1500	1533	2497	347	634	996	975	500	1828	1212	1056	659	432	879	34
E05C: The harmful effects of cigarettes have been exaggerated																
1. Disagree	46.2	47.8	45.1	47.7	39.5	48.5	42.3	45.3	53.2	49.3	41.3	54.6	42.4	44.8	40.5	35.3
2. Mostly disagree	21.6	19.1	23.7	22.6	16.1	22.7	24.3	17.5	22.5	22.7	20.5	19.9	22.6	22.4	22.6	29.4
3. Neither	16.7	17.5	15.8	16.6	15.5	14.8	18.6	17.2	14.1	14.6	20.0	11.7	18.2	16.4	21.2	14.7
4. Mostly agree	8.7	8.3	9.2	8.3	9.6	9.0	8.5	9.8	6.4	7.8	9.9	5.7	9.3	11.1	10.4	14.7
5. Agree	6.8	7.4	6.1	4.9	19.3	4.7	6.2	10.2	4.0	5.6	8.3	8.0	7.3	5.1	5.2	8.8
Item 21020 N(Wtd)	3095	1495	1530	2498	342	633	994	970	498	1827	1207	1056	655	433	879	34
E05D: I think that becoming a smoker reflects poor judgment																
1. Disagree	12.5	11.1	13.7	11.4	19.2	12.7	12.2	14.2	9.6	9.6	16.4	8.3	13.2	12.5	16.5	8.8
2. Mostly disagree	8.4	7.8	9.0	7.9	12.2	7.0	10.8	7.0	7.8	8.0	8.5	4.6	9.2	11.1	11.1	8.8
3. Neither	22.2	20.4	23.6	22.4	16.9	25.6	24.7	19.2	18.4	21.7	23.4	16.8	21.8	24.4	27.8	29.4
4. Mostly agree	17.7	17.9	17.9	18.9	11.1	18.6	18.4	15.9	18.4	19.3	15.1	17.6	19.8	17.4	16.1	29.4
5. Agree	39.3	42.7	36.0	39.4	40.2	36.0	33.9	43.5	45.8	41.3	36.5	52.8	35.9	34.3	28.6	20.6
Item 21030 N(Wtd)	3088	1489	1529	2490	343	628	988	972	500	1817	1209	1054	652	431	877	34
E05E: I personally don't mind being around people who are smoking																
1. Disagree	33.7	36.1	31.5	33.4	36.6	33.7	29.0	34.8	41.0	38.2	27.0	44.6	34.3	27.4	23.9	8.8
2. Mostly disagree	14.6	15.4	14.2	15.1	10.4	18.1	14.6	11.5	16.3	16.3	12.2	17.9	15.9	13.7	10.6	17.6
3. Neither	13.5	15.2	11.8	13.5	11.5	13.7	14.7	12.4	12.9	12.9	14.4	11.2	13.9	15.1	15.6	8.8
4. Mostly agree	19.1	17.9	19.8	19.8	15.9	16.3	21.7	19.4	16.3	17.4	21.7	15.0	18.2	22.8	22.1	29.4
5. Agree	19.1	15.5	22.8	18.2	25.4	18.3	20.0	21.9	13.3	15.1	24.6	11.3	17.7	20.9	27.9	32.4
Item 21040 N(Wtd)	3096	1494	1532	2493	347	630	990	974	502	1823	1209	1058	654	430	879	34
E05F: Smoking is a dirty habit																
1. Disagree	11.2	12.1	10.4	9.6	20.7	10.3	11.4	12.4	10.0	9.9	13.1	8.9	10.7	11.0	14.3	14.7
2. Mostly disagree	6.9	7.2	6.7	6.6	8.4	7.6	8.1	6.6	4.2	6.3	7.8	4.3	8.0	7.7	8.8	2.9
3. Neither	16.4	16.4	16.3	15.8	15.9	14.9	20.3	14.1	14.9	15.6	17.6	12.3	18.0	18.9	18.8	20.6
4. Mostly agree	17.7	16.4	19.1	19.1	11.2	22.4	16.6	16.5	16.3	18.7	16.6	16.3	18.8	18.9	17.6	32.4
5. Agree	47.8	48.0	47.6	48.9	43.2	44.7	43.7	50.4	54.8	49.5	44.9	58.3	44.5	43.8	40.6	29.4
Item 21050 N(Wtd)	3094	1492	1532	2491	347	629	990	973	502	1819	1211	1058	654	429	877	34

The next questions are about military service.

QUESTIONNAIRE FORM 5																
E06: Do you favor or oppose a military draft at the present time?																
1. Strongly oppose	29.1	30.8	28.0	28.2	35.7	29.1	29.9	28.5	28.7	27.5	31.9	25.6	29.6	28.7	33.1	28.6
2. Mostly oppose	23.1	22.0	24.4	24.3	20.5	22.3	26.4	19.3	25.1	24.7	21.5	23.6	23.7	22.1	23.3	14.3
3. No opinion, or mixed	30.5	24.6	36.1	29.3	32.9	29.7	28.7	32.5	31.3	30.3	30.2	32.5	30.2	31.0	27.9	28.6
4. Mostly favor	12.1	15.0	8.8	12.8	8.4	12.6	11.5	13.1	10.6	12.1	11.9	13.0	11.1	13.2	11.0	20.0
5. Strongly favor	5.2	7.6	2.7	5.5	2.6	6.3	3.6	6.7	4.4	5.5	4.4	5.3	5.6	4.8	4.7	8.6
Item 21060 N(Wtd)	3107	1506	1531	2500	347	636	997	972	502	1828	1214	1055	659	439	881	35

QUESTIONNAIRE FORM 5 1981	TOTAL	SEX		RACE		REGION				4YR COLLEGE PLANS		ILLICIT DRUG USE: LIFETIME				
		M	F	White	Black	NE	NC	S	W	Yes	No	None	Mari-juana Only	Few Pills	More Pills	Any Her-oin
Weighted No. of Cases:	3656	1803	1741	2820	459	853	1091	1127	586	2036	1422	1210	782	515	1027	40
% of Weighted Total:	100.0	49.3	47.6	77.1	12.6	23.3	29.8	30.8	16.0	55.7	38.9	33.1	21.4	14.1	28.1	1.1

E07: Do you think any military draft in the U.S. should include women as well as men?

1. No	29.9	18.9	40.6	28.4	42.4	25.1	27.7	36.3	27.9	28.4	32.5	33.7	26.1	34.4	25.8	22.9
2. Uncertain	30.6	25.0	36.4	30.9	29.1	31.2	29.4	30.0	33.5	30.0	31.4	30.0	30.2	31.2	31.7	25.7
3. Yes	39.5	56.2	23.0	40.7	28.5	43.8	42.8	33.7	38.6	41.6	36.2	36.3	43.5	34.2	42.5	51.4
Item 21070　N(Wtd)	3104	1503	1530	2495	347	634	992	976	502	1821	1216	1057	658	439	877	35

One idea for getting more high school graduates to serve in the military is to offer them a paid college education after three years of service in the armed forces. During the three years of military duty their pay would be fairly low, but afterward the government would pay their tuition plus $300 a month living expenses for up to four academic years.

E08: Do you think it would be a good idea for the U.S. to have such a program of paid college in return for military service?

1. Definitely not	3.8	3.8	3.8	3.3	6.6	4.3	4.0	4.0	2.8	3.8	4.1	3.3	4.0	3.7	4.1	8.6
2. Probably not	5.7	6.8	4.8	5.6	6.6	5.3	7.3	4.8	5.2	5.4	6.1	6.0	5.5	3.9	6.2	2.9
3. No opinion or uncertain	17.4	13.8	20.9	16.9	17.6	13.6	18.4	19.3	16.5	13.3	23.7	16.4	21.4	16.5	15.8	20.0
4. Yes, probably	34.7	33.8	35.8	37.0	21.0	33.5	34.4	33.8	38.4	34.4	35.7	33.3	31.4	41.4	35.8	42.9
5. Yes, definitely	38.3	41.7	34.8	37.1	47.8	43.6	35.9	38.2	37.0	43.1	30.4	41.1	37.7	34.6	38.1	28.6
Item 21080　N(Wtd)	3086	1495	1520	2480	347	626	987	971	503	1813	1209	1054	653	437	869	35

E09: If paid college in return for military sevice were available NOW, how likely is it that you would sign up for such a plan?

1. Definitely would not	30.1	25.4	35.2	31.7	23.3	28.9	31.4	28.7	31.9	29.7	31.2	32.5	25.5	26.5	32.6	25.7
2. Probably would not	38.6	36.9	40.4	40.6	28.3	41.8	39.0	35.8	39.0	40.7	35.9	36.6	40.0	42.4	38.9	34.3
3. Probably would	24.8	28.9	20.3	22.4	34.2	23.1	22.4	28.3	24.8	22.7	27.3	24.5	27.0	24.8	23.3	25.7
4. Definitely would	6.5	8.8	4.1	5.3	13.9	6.5	7.2	7.1	4.2	6.8	5.6	6.4	7.5	6.6	5.4	17.1
Item 21090　N(Wtd)	3043	1474	1499	2448	339	620	979	950	495	1790	1191	1044	640	427	859	35

E10: The next question is about cola drinks like Coca-Cola, Pepsi-Cola, Diet-Pepsi,Tab, Dr. Pepper, and other cola drinks. (Do not include decaffeinated colas.) About how many 12-ounce cans or bottles (or the equivalent) of cola do you drink per day, on the average?

1. None	10.8	10.8	10.8	9.5	15.0	12.8	8.0	8.0	19.1	11.2	9.9	11.8	11.0	11.1	9.1	14.3
2. Less than one a day	27.7	27.8	28.0	28.4	24.3	34.5	30.2	20.1	28.6	30.9	22.6	29.4	26.9	26.7	26.5	25.7
3. About one	21.9	22.5	21.4	22.2	21.6	22.4	22.2	22.9	19.1	23.2	20.0	25.0	23.0	18.3	20.4	8.6
4. About two	21.6	20.2	22.6	22.4	17.4	17.1	22.6	24.8	18.5	19.8	24.7	19.6	19.7	24.8	24.4	14.3
5. About three	10.1	9.3	10.5	9.9	13.5	6.7	10.7	13.2	7.3	7.5	13.8	8.3	10.9	10.4	10.4	20.0
6. About four	4.3	4.8	3.8	4.2	4.8	3.1	3.6	6.3	3.5	4.4	4.5	3.4	5.2	6.3	3.9	5.7
7. About five to six	2.0	2.0	1.9	2.0	2.4	1.3	1.7	2.2	2.7	1.8	2.2	1.1	2.2	1.6	2.8	5.7
8. Seven or more	1.6	2.4	.9	1.3	1.2	2.0	.9	2.4	1.5	1.1	2.4	1.5	1.3	.7	2.4	5.7
Item 21100　N(Wtd)	3010	1467	1475	2425	333	608	972	948	482	1782	1164	1026	635	431	844	35

E11: About how many cups of coffee do you drink per day on the average? Do not include decaffeinated coffees, such as Sanka or Brim. (NOTE: If you use a mug that would hold two regular coffee cups, for instance, count that as two cups.)

1. None	69.2	65.8	72.3	69.4	72.8	65.9	70.5	72.6	64.5	70.9	67.1	76.3	71.6	68.0	59.9	57.1
2. Less than one a day	14.4	16.5	12.5	14.1	13.3	15.2	13.7	13.5	16.6	13.0	16.4	12.9	14.1	13.8	17.1	11.4
3. About one	7.1	6.6	7.7	6.9	6.0	9.9	5.7	6.5	7.3	7.1	6.6	5.5	6.0	6.5	9.8	8.6
4. About two	5.1	6.3	4.0	5.4	4.2	5.2	6.0	3.6	6.3	4.9	5.5	3.2	4.7	7.5	6.4	11.4
5. About three	1.8	1.8	1.7	1.8	2.1	1.1	2.0	1.5	2.8	1.3	2.5	1.1	1.7	1.6	2.5	8.6
6. About four	1.2	1.6	.9	1.3	.9	1.3	1.0	1.4	1.0	1.4	.9	.4	.5	1.4	2.5	-
7. About five to six	.5	.5	.5	.4	-	.3	.5	.2	1.2	.6	.5	.2	.6	.9	.6	2.9
8. Seven or more	.7	1.0	.4	.7	.6	1.1	.5	.7	.4	.7	.5	.5	.9	.2	.9	2.9
Item 21110　N(Wtd)	3040	1471	1499	2456	331	618	981	948	493	1796	1180	1038	638	428	863	35

QUESTIONNAIRE FORM 5 1981	TOTAL	SEX		RACE		REGION				4YR COLLEGE PLANS		ILLICIT DRUG USE: LIFETIME				
		M	F	White	Black	NE	NC	S	W	Yes	No	None	Mari- juana Only	Few Pills	More Pills	Any Her- oin
Weighted No. of Cases:	3656	1803	1741	2820	459	853	1091	1127	586	2036	1422	1210	782	515	1027	40
% of Weighted Total:	100.0	49.3	47.6	77.1	12.6	23.3	29.8	30.8	16.0	55.7	38.9	33.1	21.4	14.1	28.1	1.1

E12: About how many cups of tea (or glasses of iced tea) do you drink per day on the average?

1. None	41.5	46.1	37.6	40.2	46.4	34.7	47.7	33.9	52.6	41.3	42.1	45.2	42.3	43.3	36.0	31.4
2. Less than one a day	21.3	21.5	21.3	21.8	18.8	27.3	23.3	15.2	21.7	22.9	19.1	19.7	22.9	21.3	22.6	8.6
3. About one	13.5	11.0	15.9	13.7	10.7	15.3	11.1	15.4	12.6	13.9	12.8	12.1	12.8	14.6	15.1	17.1
4. About two	10.5	7.6	13.3	10.9	9.8	9.5	8.6	15.5	5.9	9.7	11.5	9.9	10.8	8.6	11.4	28.6
5. About three	6.2	6.0	6.1	6.4	6.8	5.6	4.0	10.0	4.3	5.8	7.1	6.5	4.8	6.3	6.7	8.6
6. About four	3.4	3.9	2.6	3.4	3.9	3.1	2.6	5.0	2.0	3.3	3.5	3.0	3.0	3.0	4.5	-
7. About five to six	2.0	1.8	2.3	1.9	2.4	2.3	1.6	2.6	1.4	1.7	2.4	2.3	1.9	2.3	1.5	5.7
8. Seven or more	1.5	2.2	.7	1.6	1.2	2.3	1.1	2.2	-	1.5	1.4	1.3	1.6	.5	2.2	-
Item 21120 N(Wtd)	3060	1474	1514	2467	336	622	984	959	494	1803	1191	1049	641	432	863	35

E13: The next questions are about some things which may have happened TO YOU while you were at school (inside or outside or in a schoolbus).

During the LAST 12 MONTHS, how often ...

E13A: Has something of yours (worth under $50) been stolen?

1. Not at all	64.1	60.8	67.2	63.7	64.2	59.4	64.3	68.7	60.9	62.4	66.9	71.2	65.1	59.6	57.1	45.7
2. Once	24.5	26.3	22.8	24.9	21.6	25.3	24.2	22.7	27.8	25.4	23.2	19.3	22.4	29.9	29.6	42.9
3. Twice	7.7	8.5	7.1	7.5	10.9	10.6	7.5	5.9	7.5	7.7	7.7	6.2	9.4	7.7	8.3	5.7
4. 3 or 4 times	2.6	3.2	1.9	2.7	2.4	3.2	2.6	2.0	2.8	3.1	1.8	2.7	2.2	1.6	3.3	-
5. 5 or more times	1.1	1.2	.9	1.1	.9	1.3	1.3	.6	1.2	1.4	.6	.5	1.1	1.2	1.6	5.7
Item 9871 N(Wtd)	3060	1477	1514	2462	338	620	986	958	496	1802	1195	1046	639	428	868	35

E13B: Has something of yours (worth over $50) been stolen?

1. Not at all	87.4	83.8	90.9	88.1	84.4	87.1	90.6	87.3	81.5	87.7	87.3	91.2	87.3	86.5	84.4	71.4
2. Once	10.2	12.6	7.7	9.7	12.1	10.1	7.3	10.9	14.5	10.2	10.1	8.0	10.9	10.3	11.8	20.0
3. Twice	1.7	2.6	.9	1.5	3.2	2.1	1.5	1.2	2.8	1.6	1.7	.6	1.7	2.1	2.6	5.7
4. 3 or 4 times	.5	.7	.3	.5	.3	.5	.5	.2	.8	.3	.7	.1	.2	.9	.9	-
5. 5 or more times	.2	.1	.3	.2	-	-	.1	.4	.4	.2	.3	.1	-	.5	.2	2.9
Item 9872 N(Wtd)	3057	1473	1515	2462	339	621	986	954	496	1802	1190	1044	640	429	868	35

E13C: Has someone deliberately damaged your property (your car, clothing, etc.)?

1. Not at all	69.5	59.6	79.1	69.6	70.3	69.0	71.9	71.4	61.2	70.2	68.7	72.3	69.9	70.6	64.8	71.4
2. Once	20.7	27.1	14.4	20.9	19.2	21.4	18.6	19.9	25.7	19.6	22.1	18.8	21.1	21.5	22.8	17.1
3. Twice	6.5	8.9	4.0	6.2	7.5	6.0	5.8	5.7	10.1	6.4	6.8	6.1	6.9	4.7	7.3	8.6
4. 3 or 4 times	2.4	3.4	1.5	2.4	1.8	2.6	2.4	2.3	2.2	2.8	1.5	1.7	1.3	2.3	3.9	-
5. 5 or more times	1.0	.9	1.0	.9	1.5	1.3	1.2	.6	.8	1.1	.8	1.0	.6	.9	1.3	2.9
Item 9873 N(Wtd)	3041	1467	1506	2455	333	616	982	948	495	1796	1184	1043	634	428	861	35

E13D: Has someone injured you with a weapon (like a knife, gun, or club)?

1. Not at all	93.4	90.5	96.6	94.9	86.6	92.2	93.1	93.9	94.3	94.3	92.4	96.3	95.2	93.4	89.2	82.4
2. Once	4.7	7.1	2.0	3.5	11.0	4.7	5.2	4.5	4.1	4.1	5.1	2.8	3.6	4.4	7.6	11.8
3. Twice	1.2	1.4	1.0	1.0	1.8	2.6	1.0	.4	1.4	1.1	1.4	.7	.9	1.4	1.7	2.9
4. 3 or 4 times	.5	.7	.1	.4	.6	.2	.6	.7	.2	.4	.6	.3	.2	.2	.9	-
5. 5 or more times	.3	.3	.3	.3	-	.5	.1	.4	.2	.2	.4	-	-	.5	.6	5.9
Item 9874 N(Wtd)	3044	1468	1508	2455	337	619	983	950	492	1796	1185	1045	640	427	858	34

E13E: Has someone threatened you with a weapon, but not actually injured you?

1. Not at all	85.2	79.7	90.6	86.6	76.4	83.6	86.0	85.1	85.8	86.1	84.1	90.8	85.1	84.7	79.4	71.4
2. Once	9.5	12.9	6.1	8.5	15.8	10.1	8.6	11.2	7.7	8.8	10.3	6.7	11.1	7.5	11.9	20.0
3. Twice	3.0	3.9	2.0	2.7	3.9	3.1	3.6	1.5	4.5	3.1	3.0	1.2	2.2	4.7	4.9	-
4. 3 or 4 times	1.2	2.2	.3	1.2	2.1	2.1	.9	1.1	1.0	1.1	1.4	.7	.9	1.4	1.9	-
5. 5 or more times	1.2	1.3	.9	1.0	2.1	1.1	1.0	1.3	.8	1.0	1.2	.6	.6	1.6	1.9	5.7
Item 9875 N(Wtd)	3041	1468	1505	2452	335	616	982	950	493	1797	1183	1043	638	426	860	35

QUESTIONNAIRE FORM 5 1981	TOTAL	SEX		RACE		REGION				4YR COLLEGE PLANS		ILLICIT DRUG USE: LIFETIME				
		M	F	White	Black	NE	NC	S	W	Yes	No	None	Mari- juana Only	Few Pills	More Pills	Any Her- oin
Weighted No. of Cases:	3656	1803	1741	2820	459	853	1091	1127	586	2036	1422	1210	782	515	1027	40
% of Weighted Total:	100.0	49.3	47.6	77.1	12.6	23.3	29.8	30.8	16.0	55.7	38.9	33.1	21.4	14.1	28.1	1.1
E13F: Has someone injured you on purpose without using a weapon?																
1. Not at all	85.4	81.6	89.3	86.2	81.0	82.7	85.5	87.5	84.6	86.2	83.9	90.1	86.7	86.4	78.3	85.7
2. Once	8.9	11.5	6.1	8.1	13.4	10.0	9.2	7.9	8.5	9.0	8.7	6.7	8.6	8.2	12.0	5.7
3. Twice	3.1	4.2	2.1	3.1	2.4	3.8	3.4	1.9	4.3	2.7	3.9	1.3	2.4	2.1	6.1	8.6
4. 3 or 4 times	1.4	1.2	1.5	1.4	1.5	1.8	1.2	1.3	1.0	1.2	1.6	1.4	1.1	1.6	1.2	-
5. 5 or more times	1.3	1.6	1.0	1.2	1.8	1.8	.7	1.5	1.8	.9	1.9	.4	1.3	1.6	2.5	2.9
Item 9876 N(Wtd)	3036	1465	1502	2449	336	611	982	951	492	1796	1178	1044	638	427	853	35
E13G: Has an unarmed person threatened you with injury, but not actually injured you?																
1. Not at all	76.3	67.7	84.8	76.4	75.1	76.2	75.4	77.8	75.3	76.3	76.4	85.0	75.4	71.7	69.0	65.7
2. Once	12.0	16.1	7.9	11.6	14.5	11.0	12.1	11.9	13.2	12.2	11.7	8.2	13.6	15.2	13.6	17.1
3. Twice	5.0	6.5	3.4	5.0	5.9	5.8	5.3	3.8	5.7	5.3	4.5	2.4	5.0	5.9	7.4	8.6
4. 3 or 4 times	3.1	4.6	1.7	3.3	2.7	3.9	3.6	2.6	2.2	3.1	3.0	1.4	3.3	4.2	4.6	-
5. 5 or more times	3.6	5.0	2.2	3.8	2.1	3.2	3.6	3.9	3.4	3.2	4.3	3.0	2.8	3.0	5.3	5.7
Item 9877 N(Wtd)	3045	1469	1507	2454	338	618	985	950	493	1798	1184	1043	639	427	861	35
E14: If you had ever used marijuana or hashish, do you think that you would have said so in this questionnaire?																
1. No	5.2	6.7	3.4	3.8	11.0	2.6	5.2	7.9	3.5	3.7	7.6	8.5	3.1	3.3	2.7	-
2. Not sure	5.1	5.9	4.5	4.9	6.0	5.0	5.3	4.9	5.1	4.2	6.4	8.5	3.1	3.5	3.4	5.7
3. Yes	61.4	60.3	62.7	61.5	59.1	60.7	61.9	63.0	58.0	63.9	57.6	80.5	55.8	61.3	45.2	25.7
4. I did say so	28.3	27.1	29.4	29.7	23.9	31.7	27.5	24.2	33.5	28.1	28.5	2.5	37.9	32.2	48.8	65.7
Item 20800 N(Wtd)	3033	1463	1501	2448	335	618	979	946	490	1791	1178	1036	638	429	859	35
E15: If you had ever used amphetamines (without a doctor's orders), do you think that you would have said so in this questionnaire?																
1. No	7.2	9.6	4.2	5.2	14.1	5.2	7.1	8.8	6.6	5.5	9.6	8.0	8.3	6.6	4.1	2.9
2. Not sure	6.6	7.3	5.9	6.1	9.9	8.0	5.8	6.1	7.0	6.0	7.3	9.7	5.4	4.2	4.4	8.6
3. Yes	69.4	66.6	72.4	70.3	66.5	69.4	68.9	72.0	65.1	72.5	65.4	79.5	80.0	76.3	48.7	37.1
4. I did say so	16.9	16.4	17.4	18.5	9.3	17.0	18.2	13.0	21.6	16.0	17.8	2.8	6.5	12.9	42.8	54.3
Item 20810 N(Wtd)	3020	1456	1496	2437	334	612	978	944	487	1788	1172	1032	635	427	856	35
E16: If you had ever used heroin, do you think that you would have said so in this questionnaire?																
1. No	9.1	12.8	5.1	7.4	15.9	8.3	8.3	10.5	9.1	7.8	11.1	9.2	9.3	8.2	8.1	-
2. Not sure	8.6	9.0	8.4	8.5	9.6	11.4	8.0	8.4	6.8	8.4	8.7	10.3	7.1	6.1	8.8	8.6
3. Yes	74.4	69.7	79.1	76.0	68.2	72.4	73.7	75.6	75.5	76.9	70.9	77.6	77.1	81.3	68.3	28.6
4. I did say so	7.9	8.6	7.4	8.1	6.3	8.0	9.9	5.5	8.8	7.0	9.4	2.9	6.6	4.2	14.9	62.9
Item 20820 N(Wtd)	3022	1457	1496	2439	333	615	978	943	486	1785	1175	1032	637	428	855	35

Cross-Time Index of Questionnaire Items, 1975-1981

Introduction to the Indexing Conventions

This cross-time index of question locations is organized in numerical sequence according to item reference number, which is the unique numerical identifier assigned to each question in the study.

The Content Index may be used in two major ways:

1. **Locating a Question Across Years.** Having located a question of interest in the Descriptive Results section, the reader may determine in what other years that same question has appeared simply by looking it up here under its unique item reference number. The Index will show all years in which that item has appeared and also show its location each year (by questionnaire form, section, and item number). All items will retain their unique reference numbers in future years as well, and thus may be located in exactly the same way in subsequent volumes in this series.

EXAMPLE: A reader interested in a particular item about enjoying the fast pace of today's life would find that it has been assigned item Reference Number 1210. The index entry for item 1210 shows that this item has appeared in Section A of questionnaire Form 1 in all annual surveys in the series. Its question number was 4B in 1975 and 2B thereafter. By looking up the same item reference number in the index of any other volume of interest, the reader can ascertain the page location in that volume for the descriptive results on the same question.

2. **Locating Questions by Subject Area.** Given an interest in some particular subject area, one can quickly scan the Index to locate all questions dealing with that area. Table 3 shows the 19 general subject areas into which all items are classified, along with the alphabetical code assigned each area. (Category A, Drugs, is further subdivided into numerically identified subcategories.)

EXAMPLE: A reader interested in items dealing with religion should first locate the relevant code in Table 3: Code G, "Religion." The second step is to scan all pages of the item index looking for entries in Column G under the heading Subject Area, noting for every item showing a G, its item reference number and page location in this volume. The reader may or may not find the abbreviated description of the item (given in the third column of the index and further described below) helpful in deciding whether to look up a particular item in the Descriptive Results section. Some of these descriptions are rather clear as to their meaning, but others are less so.

Definitions of the Column Headings

The definitions of column headings, and the conventions used for the entries in each column, are given below under the numbers indicated in the following key.

① **Item Reference Number.** A unique identification number is assigned to each question for the duration of this research and reporting series. It appears below that question in the Descriptive Results section, as well as in this index and the indices of all other volumes in the series.

② **Page Location.** The second column of the Question Index gives the page number of the present volume on which a verbatim statement of the question may be found along with this year's descriptive results.

③ **Item Description (Abbreviated).** This is a brief mnemonic description — up to 16 characters in length

— which attempts to characterize the content of the question. Originally developed for question identification on OSIRIS computer files, it may in many cases allow one to determine the relevance of the question to one's own interest and thus reduce the number of irrelevant questions which must be looked up in the Descriptive Results section.

④ **Questionnaire Location by Year.** An entry is provided for every year in which an item appeared in one of the study's questionnaire forms. The six (or fewer) characters comprising the entry indicate the form in which the question appeared, the section of that form, and the question number. Take as an example the questionnaire location 1A004A. This location code indicates that the question appeared in Form 1, Section A, and was labeled as Question 4a.

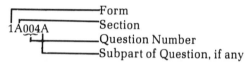

Occasionally an entry will be enclosed in parentheses. This indicates that there was a change (usually minor) in the wording of the question and/or the answer alternatives in subsequent years.

A form number (ranging from 1 to 5) is usually shown in the first character location. However, two substitute characters will replace the form number at times:

+ A plus sign indicates that the item appeared in all five forms that year and that it appeared in the same location on all forms.
* An asterisk indicates that the item appeared in four forms (Forms 2 through 5) and in the same location on all forms.

⑤ **Subject Area.** Table 3 shows the subject content areas which have been distinguished here and gives the alphabetical code assigned to each of them. Every question item in the index has been classified into one or more of the subject areas, and the alphabetical codes for those subject areas are printed in the appropriate column(s) next to each item under the general heading "Subject Area." A separate column has been assigned to each subject area code to facilitate rapid scanning. (Note that area A, dealing with drugs, has been given numerically identified subcategories because there were so many questions dealing with this general subject area.)

Figure 2

Guide to Cross-Time Index

Item Reference Number	Page Loc. in this Volume	ITEM DESCRIPTION (ABBREVIATED)	QUESTIONNAIRE LOCATION BY YEAR (FORM, SECTION, AND QUESTION NUMBER)						SUBJECT AREA	
			1975	1976	1977	1978	1979	1980/1	A	B C D E F G H I J K L M N O P Q R S
10	16	R'S BIRTH YEAR		+C001	+C001	+C001	+C001	+C001		R
20	16	R'S BIRTH MONTH		+C002	+C002	+C002	+C002	+C002		R
30	16	R'S SEX		+C003	+C003	+C003	+C003	+C003		R
40	16	R'S RACE		+C004	+C004	+C004	+C004	+C004		R
50	16	R SPD >TIM R-URB		+C005	+C005	+C005	+C005	+C005		R
60	17	R NOT MARRIED		+C006	+C006	+C006	+C006	+C006	D	R
80	17	R'S HSHLD ALONE		+C007A	+C007A	+C007A	+C007A	+C007A	M	R
90	17	R'S HSHLD FATHER		+C007B	+C007B	+C007B	+C007B	+C007B	M	R
100	17	R'S HSHLD MOTHER		+C007C	+C007C	+C007C	+C007C	+C007C	M	R
110	17	R'S HSHLD BR/SR		+C007D	+C007D	+C007D	+C007D	+C007D	M	R
120	17	R'S HSHLD GRPRNT		+C007E	+C007E	+C007E	+C007E	+C007E	M	R
130	17	R'S HSHLD SPOUSE		+C007F	+C007F	+C007F	+C007F	+C007F	M	R
140	17	R'S HSHLD CHLDRN		+C007G	+C007G	+C007G	+C007G	+C007G	M	R
150	17	R'S HSHLD RELTVS		+C007H	+C007H	+C007H	+C007H	+C007H	M	R
160	17	R'S HSHLD NONRLT		+C007I	+C007I	+C007I	+C007I	+C007I	M	R
310	17	FATHR EDUC LEVEL		+C008	+C008	+C008	+C008	+C008	B	R
320	17	MOTHR EDUC LEVEL		+C009	+C009	+C009	+C009	+C009	B	R
330	17	MOTH PD JB R YNG		+C010	+C010	+C010	+C010	+C010	C	R
340	18	R'S POLTL PRFNC		+C011	+C011	+C011	+C011	+C011	H	R
350	18	R'POL BLF RADCL		+C012	+C012	+C012	+C012	+C012	H	R
360	18	R'S RELGS PRFNC		+C013A	+C013A	+C013A	+C013A	+C013A	G	R
370	18	R'ATTND REL SVC		+C013B	+C013B	+C013B	+C013B	+C013B	G	R
380	18	RLGN IMP R'S LF		+C013C	+C013C	+C013C	+C013C	+C013C	G	R
390	19	WHEN R XPCT GRAD		+C014	+C014	+C014	+C014	+C014	B	R
400	19	R'S HS PROGRAM		+C015	+C015	+C015	+C015	+C015	B	R
410	19	RT SF SCH AB>AVG		+C016	+C016	+C016	+C016	+C016		R
420	19	RT SF INTELL>AVG		+C017	+C017	+C017	+C017	+C017		R
430	19	#DA/4W SC MS ILL		+C018A	+C018A	+C018A	+C018A	+C018A	B	
440	19	#DA/4W SC MS CUT		+C018B	+C018B	+C018B	+C018B	+C018B	B	
450	20	#DA/4W SC MS OTH		+C018C	+C018C	+C018C	+C018C	+C018C	B	
460	20	#DA/4W SKP CLASS		+C019	+C019	+C019				
470	20	R HS GRADE/D=1		+C020	+C020					R
480	20	R WL DO VOC/TEC		+C021A						R
490	20	R WL DO ARMD FC		+C021						
500	20	R WL DO 2YR CLG								
510	21	R WL DO 4YR CLG								
520	21	R WL DO GRD/PRF								
530	21	R WNTDO VOC/TEC								
540	21	R WNTDO								

Table 3

Subject Area Key
(Referenced by letter in the Question Index)

A **Drugs.** Drug use and related attitudes and beliefs, drug availability and exposure, surrounding conditions and social meaning of drug use. Views of significant others regarding drugs.

    A01   Use of Drugs
            A01A— . . . in lifetime
            A01B — . . . in the last 12 months
            A01C — . . . in the last 30 days
            A01D — Quantity used
            A01E — How high? (How often?)
            A01F — How long high?
            A01G — Incidence of first use
            A01H — Use with other drugs
            A01I — Try to stop?
            A01J — . . . on doctor's orders?
            A01K — Bad trip?
            A01L — Kinds of drugs

    A02   Exposure to Drug Use
            A02A — Friends' use of drugs
            A02B — Exposure to users

    A03   Availability of Drugs

    A04   Expected Future Use

    A05   Conditions of Use
            A05A — Alone
            A05B — With others
            A05C — Settings
            A05D — Mode of drug administration

    A06   Reasons for Use, Abstention, and Stopping

    A07   Problems with Drugs

    A08   Sources of Help regarding Drugs

    A09   Parental Awareness of Use

    A10   Drug Education

    A11   Own Attitudes regarding Drugs and Drug Users
            A11A — For adults
            A11C — For own children
            A11D — Perception of drug users

    A12   Others' Attitudes regarding Drugs and Drug Users
            A12A — Parents
            A12B — Friends
            A12C — Students in school
            A12D — Perception of Drug Users

Table 3 (continued)

A13   Legal Issues regarding Drugs
    A13A — Preferred legality for adults
    A13C — Own response to legalization
    A13D — Knowledge of marijuana laws

A14   Risk of Drug Harm
    A14A — To self
    A14B — To others

B. Education. Educational lifestyle, values, experiences, and environments. Media usage.

C. Work and Leisure. Vocational values, meaning of work and leisure, work and leisure activities, preferences regarding occupational characteristics and type of work setting.

D. Sex Roles and Family. Values, attitudes, and expectations about marriage, family structure, sex roles, and sex discrimination.

E. Family Plans and Population Concerns. Values, attitudes, and expectations about personal family plans. Views on sexual mores and concerns about overpopulation.

F. Conservation, Materialism, Equity, Etc. Values, attitudes, and expectations related to conservation, pollution, materialism, equity, and the sharing of resources. Preferences regarding type of dwelling and urbanicity.

G. Religion. Religious affiliation, practices, and views.

H. Politics. Political affiliation, activities, and views.

I. Social Change. Values, attitudes, and expectations about social change.

J. Social Problems. Concern with various social problems facing the nation and the world.

K. Major Social Institutions. Confidence in and commitment to various major social institutions (business, unions, branches of government, press, organized religion, military, etc.).

L. Military. Views about the armed services and the use of military force. Personal plans for military service.

M. Interpersonal Relationships. Qualitative and quantitative characteristics of cross-age and peer relationships. Interpersonal conflict.

N. Race Relations. Attitudes toward and experiences with other racial groups.

O. Concern for Others. Radius of concern for others, voluntary and charitable activities.

P. Happiness. Happiness and life satisfaction, overall and in specific life domains.

Q. Other Personality Variables. Attitudes about self (including self-esteem), locus of control, loneliness, optimism, trust in others, somatic symptoms, importance placed on various life goals, counter-culture orientation.

R. Background and School. Demographic and family background characteristics, curriculum and grades in high school, victimization in school.

S. Deviant Behavior and Victimization. Delinquent behaviors, driving violations and accidents, violations and accidents under the influence of drugs, victimization experiences.

Item Reference Number	Page Loc. in this Volume	ITEM DESCRIPTION (ABBREVIATED)	1975	1976	1977	1978	1979	1980/1	A	B	C	D	E	F	G	H	I	J	K	L	M	N	O	P	Q	R	S
						QUESTIONNAIRE LOCATION BY YEAR (FORM, SECTION, AND QUESTION NUMBER)										SUBJECT AREA											
10	16	R'S BIRTH YEAR		+C001	+C001	+C001	+C001	+C001																		R	
20	16	R'S BIRTH MONTH		+C002	+C002	+C002	+C002	+C002																		R	
30	16	R'S SEX		+C003	+C003	+C003	+C003	+C003																		R	
40	16	R'S RACE		+C004	+C004	+C004	+C004	+C004																		R	
50	16	R SPD >TIM R-URB		+C005	+C005	+C005	+C005	+C005																		R	
60	17	R NOT MARRIED		+C006	+C006	+C006	+C006	+C006				D														R	
80	17	R'S HSHLD ALONE		+C007A	+C007A	+C007A	+C007A	+C007A													M					R	
90	17	R'S HSHLD FATHER		+C007B	+C007B	+C007B	+C007B	+C007B													M					R	
100	17	R'S HSHLD MOTHER		+C007C	+C007C	+C007C	+C007C	+C007C													M					R	
110	17	R'S HSHLD BR/SR		+C007D	+C007D	+C007D	+C007D	+C007D													M					R	
120	17	R'S HSHLD GRPRNT		+C007E	+C007E	+C007E	+C007E	+C007E													M					R	
130	17	R'S HSHLD SPOUSE		+C007F	+C007F	+C007F	+C007F	+C007F													M					R	
140	17	R'S HSHLD CHLDRN		+C007G	+C007G	+C007G	+C007G	+C007G													M					R	
150	17	R'S HSHLD RELTVS		+C007H	+C007H	+C007H	+C007H	+C007H													M					R	
160	17	R'S HSHLD NONRLT		+C007I	+C007I	+C007I	+C007I	+C007I													M					R	
310	17	FATHR EDUC LEVEL		+C008	+C008	+C008	+C008	+C008		B																R	
320	17	MOTHR EDUC LEVEL		+C009	+C009	+C009	+C009	+C009		B																R	
330	17	MOTH PD JB R YNG		+C010	+C010	+C010	+C010	+C010			C															R	
340	18	R'S POLTL PRFNC		+C011	+C011	+C011	+C011	+C011								H										R	
350	18	R'POL BLF RADCL		+C012	+C012	+C012	+C012	+C012								H										R	
360	18	R'S RELGS PRFNC		+C013A	+C013A	+C013A	+C013A	+C013A							G											R	
370	18	R'ATTND REL SVC		+C013B	+C013B	+C013B	+C013B	+C013B							G											R	
380	18	RLGN IMP R'S LF		+C013C	+C013C	+C013C	+C013C	+C013C							G											R	
390	19	WHEN R XPCT GRAD		+C014	+C014	+C014	+C014	+C014		B																R	
400	19	R'S HS PROGRAM		+C015	+C015	+C015	+C015	+C015		B																R	
410	19	RT SF SCH AB>AVG		+C016	+C016	+C016	+C016	+C016																		R	
420	19	RT SF INTELL>AVG		+C017	+C017	+C017	+C017	+C017																		R	
430	19	#DA/4W SC MS ILL		+C018A	+C018A	+C018A	+C018A	+C018A		B																	
440	19	#DA/4W SC MS CUT		+C018B	+C018B	+C018B	+C018B	+C018B		B																	
450	20	#DA/4W SC MS OTH		+C018C	+C018C	+C018C	+C018C	+C018C		B																	
460	20	#DA/4W SKP CLASS		+C019	+C019	+C019	+C019	+C019		B																	
470	20	R HS GRADE/D=1		+C020	+C020	+C020	+C020	+C020																		R	
480	20	R WL DO VOC/TEC		+C021A	+C021A	+C021A	+C021A	+C021A		B	C															R	
490	20	R WL DO ARMD FC		+C021B	+C021B	+C021B	+C021B	+C021B		B										L						R	
500	20	R WL DO 2YR CLG		+C021C	+C021C	+C021C	+C021C	+C021C		B																R	
510	21	R WL DO 4YR CLG		+C021D	+C021D	+C021D	+C021D	+C021D		B																R	
520	21	R WL DO GRD/PRF		+C021E	+C021E	+C021E	+C021E	+C021E		B																R	
530	21	R WNTDO VOC/TEC		+C022A	+C022A	+C022A	+C022A	+C022A		B	C															R	
540	21	R WNTDO ARMD FC		+C022B	+C022B	+C022B	+C022B	+C022B		B										L						R	
550	21	R WNTDO 2YR CLG		+C022C	+C022C	+C022C	+C022C	+C022C		B																R	
560	21	R WNTDO 4YR CLG		+C022D	+C022D	+C022D	+C022D	+C022D		B																R	
570	21	R WNTDO GRD/PRF		+C022E	+C022E	+C022E	+C022E	+C022E		B																R	
580	21	R WNTDO NONE		+C022F	+C022F	+C022F	+C022F	+C022F		B																R	
590	21	HRS/W WRK SCHYR		+C023	+C023	+C023	+C023	+C023			C														Q		
600	21	R$/AVG WEEK JOB		+C024A	+C024A	+C024A	+C024A	+C024A																		R	
610	22	R$/AVG WEEK OTH		+C024B	+C024B	+C024B	+C024B	+C024B																		R	
620	22	#X/AV WK GO OUT		+C025	+C025	+C025	+C025	+C025			C										M						
630	22	#X DATE 3+/WK		+C026	+C026	+C026	+C026	+C026			C										M						
640	22	DRIVE>200 MI/WK		+C027	+C027	+C027	+C027	+C027						F													
650	22	#X/12MO R TCKTD		+C028	+C028	+C028	+C028	+C028	A07A																		S
660	23	#TCKTS AFT DRNK		+C029A	+C029A	+C029A	+C029A	+C029A	A07A																		S
670	23	#TCKTS AFT MARJ		+C029B	+C029B	+C029B	+C029B	+C029B	A07A																		S
680	23	#TCKTS AFT OTDG		+C029C	+C029C	+C029C	+C029C	+C029C	A07A																		S
690	23	#ACCIDNTS/12 MO		+C030	+C030	+C030	+C030	+C030	A07A																		S
700	23	#ACDTS AFT DRNK		+C031A	+C031A	+C031A	+C031A	+C031A	A07A																		S
710	23	#ACDTS AFT MARJ		+C031B	+C031B	+C031B	+C031B	+C031B	A07A																		S
720	24	#ACDTS AFT OTDG		+C031C	+C031C	+C031C	+C031C	+C031C	A07A																		S
730	24	R'S BRANCH SERV		+C032	+C032	+C032	+C032	+C032												L						R	
740	24	R XPCTS B OFFCR		+C033	+C033	+C033	+C033	+C033												L						R	
750	24	R XPCTS MLTR CR		+C034	+C034	+C034	+C034	+C034												L						R	
760		EVR SMK CIG,REGL	1A018 *B01	+B001	+B001	+B001	+B001	+B001	A01A A01A																		
780	41	#CIGS SMKD/30DAY	1A020 *B02	1B003 *B02	1B003 *B02	1B003 *B02	1B003 *B02	1B003 *B02	A01C A01C																		
790		EVER DRINK	1A026 *B03	*B03	*B03	*B03	*B03	*B03	A01A A01A																		

Item Reference Number	Page Loc. in this Volume	ITEM DESCRIPTION (ABBREVIATED)	1975	1976	1977	1978	1979	1980/1	A	B C D E F G H I J K L M N O P Q R S
810	42	#X DRNK/LIFETIME	1A028A	1B007A	1B007A	1B007A	1B007A	1B007A	A01A	
			*B04A	*B04A	*B04A	*B04A	*B04A	*B04A	A01A	
820	42	#X DRNK/LAST 12MO	1A028B	1B007B	1B007B	1B007B	1B007B	1B007B	A01B	
			*B04B	*B04B	*B04B	*B04B	*B04B	*B04B	A01B	
830	42	#X DRNK/LAST 30DA	1A028C	1B007C	1B007C	1B007C	1B007C	1B007C	A01C	
			*B04C	*B04C	*B04C	*B04C	*B04C	*B04C	A01C	
840		#X DRK ENF FL HI	*B05	*B05	*B05	*B05	*B05	*B05	A01E	
850	44	5+DRK ROW/LST 2W	1A035	1B012	1B012	1B012	1B012	1B012	A01D	
			*B06	*B06	*B06	*B06	*B06	*B06	A01D	
860	46	#XMJ+HS/LIFETIME	1A044A	1B019X	1B019X	1B019X	1B019X	1B019	A01A	
			*B07A	*B07A	*B07A	*B07A	*B07A	*B07A	A01A	
870	46	#XMJ+HS/LAST 12MO	1A044B	1B019Y	1B019Y	1B019Y	1B019Y	1B019	A01B	
			*B07B	*B07B	*B07B	*B07B	*B07B	*B07B	A01B	
880	46	#XMJ+HS/LAST 30DA	1A044C	1B019Z	1B019Z	1B019Z	1B019Z	1B019	A01C	
			*B07C	*B07C	*B07C	*B07C	*B07C	*B07C	A01C	
890	50	#X LSD/LIFETIME	1A057A	1B029A	1B029A	1B029A	1B029A	1B029A	A01A	
			*B08A	*B08A	*B08A	*B08A	*B08A	*B08A	A01A	
900	50	#X LSD/LAST 12MO	1A057B	1B029B	1B029B	1B029B	1B029B	1B029B	A01B	
			*B08B	*B08B	*B08B	*B08B	*B08B	*B08B	A01B	
910	50	#X LSD/LAST 30DA	1A057C	1B029C	1B029C	1B029C	1B029C	1B029C	A01C	
			*B08C	*B08C	*B08C	*B08C	*B08C	*B08C	A01C	
920	53	#X PSYD/LIFETIME	1A071A	1B038A	1B038A	1B038A	1B038A	1B038A	A01A	
			*B09A	*B09A	*B09A	*B09A	*B09A	*B09A	A01A	
930	53	#X PSYD/LAST 12MO	1A071B	1B038B	1B038B	1B038B	1B038B	1B038B	A01B	
			*B09B	*B09B	*B09B	*B09B	*B09B	*B09B	A01B	
940	53	#X PSYD/LAST 30DA	1A071C	1B038C	1B038C	1B038C	1B038C	1B038C	A01C	
			*B09C	*B09C	*B09C	*B09C	*B09C	*B09C	A01C	
950	69	#X COKE/LIFETIME	1A144A	1B076A	1B076A	1B076A	1B076A	1B076A	A01A	
			*B10A	*B10A	*B10A	*B10A	*B10A	*B10A	A01A	
960	69	#X COKE/LAST 12MO	1A144B	1B076B	1B076B	1B076B	1B076B	1B076B	A01B	
			*B10B	*B10B	*B10B	*B10B	*B10B	*B10B	A01B	
970	69	#X COKE/LAST 30DA	1A144C	1B076C	1B076C	1B076C	1B076C	1B076C	A01C	
			*B10C	*B10C	*B10C	*B10C	*B10C	*B10C	A01C	
980	55	#X AMPH/LIFETIME	1A087A	1B043A	1B043A	1B043A	1B043A	1B043A	A01A	
			*B11A	*B11A	*B11A	*B11A	*B11A	*B11A	A01A	
990	55	#X AMPH/LAST 12MO	1A087B	1B043B	1B043B	1B043B	1B043B	1B043B	A01B	
			*B11B	*B11B	*B11B	*B11B	*B11B	*B11B	A01B	
1000	55	#X AMPH/LAST 30DA	1A087C	1B043C	1B043C	1B043C	1B043C	1B043C	A01C	
			*B11C	*B11C	*B11C	*B11C	*B11C	*B11C	A01C	
1010	59	#X QUAD/LIFETIME	1A102A	1B053A	1B053A	1B053A	1B053A	1B053A	A01A	
			*B12A	*B12A	*B12A	*B12A	*B12A	*B12A	A01A	
1020	59	#X QUAD/LAST 12MO	1A102B	1B053B	1B053B	1B053B	1B053B	1B053B	A01B	
			*B12B	*B12B	*B12B	*B12B	*B12B	*B12B	A01B	
1030	59	#X QUAD/LAST 30DA	1A102C	1B053C	1B053C	1B053C	1B053C	1B053C	A01C	
			*B12C	*B12C	*B12C	*B12C	*B12C	*B12C	A01C	
1040	60	#X BRBT/LIFETIME	1A116A	1B057A	1B057A	1B057A	1B057A	1B057A	A01A	
			*B13A	*B13A	*B13A	*B13A	*B13A	*B13A	A01A	
1050	60	#X BRBT/LAST 12MO	1A116B	1B057B	1B057B	1B057B	1B057B	1B057B	A01B	
			*B13B	*B13B	*B13B	*B13B	*B13B	*B13B	A01B	
1060	60	#X BRBT/LAST 30DA	1A116C	1B057C	1B057C	1B057C	1B057C	1B057C	A01C	
			*B13C	*B13C	*B13C	*B13C	*B13C	*B13C	A01C	
1070	65	#X TRQL/LIFETIME	1A131A	1B067A	1B067A	1B067A	1B067A	1B067A	A01A	
			*B14A	*B14A	*B14A	*B14A	*B14A	*B14A	A01A	
1080	65	#X TRQL/LAST 12MO	1A131B	1B067B	1B067B	1B067B	1B067B	1B067B	A01B	
			*B14B	*B14B	*B14B	*B14B	*B14B	*B14B	A01B	
1090	65	#X TRQL/LAST 30DA	1A131C	1B067C	1B067C	1B067C	1B067C	1B067C	A01C	
			*B14C	*B14C	*B14C	*B14C	*B14C	*B14C	A01C	
1100	73	#X "H"/LIFETIME	1A158A	1B085A	1B085A	1B085A	1B085A	1B085A	A01A	
			*B15A	*B15A	*B15A	*B15A	*B15A	*B15A	A01A	
1110	73	#X "H"/LAST 12MO	1A158B	1B085B	1B085B	1B085B	1B085B	1B085B	A01B	
			*B15B	*B15B	*B15B	*B15B	*B15B	*B15B	A01B	
1120	74	#X "H"/LAST 30DA	1A158C	1B085C	1B085C	1B085C	1B085C	1B085C	A01C	
			*B15C	*B15C	*B15C	*B15C	*B15C	*B15C	A01C	
1130	78	#X NARC/LIFETIME	1A173A	1B095A	1B095A	1B095A	1B095A	1B095A	A01A	
			*B16A	*B16A	*B16A	*B16A	*B16A	*B16A	A01A	
1140	78	#X NARC/LAST 12MO	1A173B	1B095B	1B095B	1B095B	1B095B	1B095B	A01B	

Item Reference Number	Page Loc. in this Volume	ITEM DESCRIPTION (ABBREVIATED)	1975	1976	1977	1978	1979	1980/1	A	B	C	D	E	F	G	H	I	J	K	L	M	N	O	P	Q	R	S
1150	78	#X NARC/LAST30DA	*B16B 1A173C *B16C	*B16B 1B095C *B16C	*B16B 1B095C *B16C	*B16B 1B095C *B16C	*B16B 1B095C *B16C	*B16B 1B095C *B16C	A01B A01C A01C																		
1160		#X INHL/LIFETIME		*B17A	*B17A	*B17A	*B17A	*B17A	A01A																		
1170		#X INHL/LAST12MO		*B17B	*B17B	*B17B	*B17B	*B17B	A01B																		
1180		#X INHL/LAST30DA		*B17C	*B17C	*B17C	*B17C	*B17C	A01C																		
1181	112	#X PCP/LIFETIME					2E02A	2E02A	A01A																		
1182	112	#X PCP/LAST12MO					2E02B	2E02B	A01B																		
1183	112	#X PCP/LAST30DA					2E02C	2E02C	A01C																		
1184	112	#X PPRS/LIFETIME					2E03A	2E03A	A01A																		
1185	112	#X PPRS/LAST12MO					2E03B	2E03B	A01B																		
1186	112	#X PPRS/LAST30DA					2E03C	2E03C	A01C																		
1190		VRY HPY THS DAYS		+A001	+A001	+A001	+A001	+A001																P	Q	R	
1200	33	US NEEDS PLANNG	1A004A	1A002A	1A002A	1A002A	1A002A	1A002A									I										
1210	33	ENJOY FAST PACE	1A004B	1A002B	1A002B	1A002B	1A002B	1A002B									I								Q		
1220	33	THG CHG 2 QUICK	1A004D	1A002C	1A002C	1A002C	1A002C	1A002C									I								Q		
1230	33	X AHEAD TOUGHER	1A004G	1A002D	1A002D	1A002D	1A002D	1A002D									I								Q		
1240	33	TM SPT ADLT MST	1A006	1A003	1A003	1A003	1A003	1A003													M						
1250	34	LK MR TM ADLT	1A007	1A004	1A004	1A004	1A004	1A004													M						
1260	34	LK MR TM YG CHD	1A008	1A005	1A005	1A005	1A005	1A005													M						
1270	34	SAT PRESENT JOB	1A009A	1A006A	1A006A	1A006A	1A006A	1A006A			C													P			
1280	34	SAT NEIGHBORHOD	1A009B	1A006B	1A006B	1A006B	1A006B	1A006B																P			
1290	34	SAT PRSNL SAFTY	1A009C	1A006C	1A006C	1A006C	1A006C	1A006C																P			
1300	35	SAT OWN PROP SF	1A009D	1A006D	1A006D	1A006D	1A006D	1A006D																P			
1310	35	SAT EDUC EXPRNCS	1A009E	1A006E	1A006E	1A006E	1A006E	1A006E		B														P			
1320	35	SAT OWN FRIENDS	1A009F	1A006F	1A006F	1A006F	1A006F	1A006F													M			P			
1330	35	SAT GT ALNG PRNT	1A009G	1A006G	1A006G	1A006G	1A006G	1A006G													M			P			
1340	35	SAT YOURSELF	1A009H	1A006H	1A006H	1A006H	1A006H	1A006H																P	Q		
1350	35	SAT STD OF LVG	1A009I	1A006I	1A006I	1A006I	1A006I	1A006I						F										P			
1360	36	SAT TIME FR THGS	1A009J	1A006J	1A006J	1A006J	1A006J	1A006J																P			
1370	36	SAT SPD LEISR	1A009K	1A006K	1A006K	1A006K	1A006K	1A006K			C													P			
1380	36	SAT LIFE AS WHLE	1A009L	1A006L	1A006L	1A006L	1A006L	1A006L																P			
1390	36	SAT GOVT OPRTNG		1A006M	1A006M	1A006M	1A006M	1A006M								H			K								
1400	36	SAT AMT OF FUN		1A006N	1A006N	1A006N	1A006N	1A006N																P	Q	R	
1410	36	IMP B SUCCSS WK		1A007A	1A007A	1A007A	1A007A	1A007A			C														Q		
1420	37	IMP GD MRRG&FAM		1A007B	1A007B	1A007B	1A007B	1A007B				D													Q		
1430	37	IMP LOTS OF $		1A007C	1A007C	1A007C	1A007C	1A007C						F											Q		
1440	37	IMP TM RCRN&HBY		1A007D	1A007D	1A007D	1A007D	1A007D			C														Q		
1450	37	IMP STRG FRDSHP		1A007E	1A007E	1A007E	1A007E	1A007E													M				Q		
1460	37	IMP STEADY WORK		1A007F	1A007F	1A007F	1A007F	1A007F			C														Q		
1470	37	IMP CNTRBTN SOC		1A007G	1A007G	1A007G	1A007G	1A007G															O		Q		
1480	37	IMP LDR COMUNTY		1A007H	1A007H	1A007H	1A007H	1A007H													M				Q		
1490	37	IMP CHLD BTR OPP		1A007I	1A007I	1A007I	1A007I	1A007I																	Q		
1500	38	IMP LIV CLS PRNT		1A007J	1A007J	1A007J	1A007J	1A007J													M				Q		
1510	38	IMP GT AWY AREA		1A007K	1A007K	1A007K	1A007K	1A007K																	Q		
1520	38	IMP CRRCT INEQL		1A007L	1A007L	1A007L	1A007L	1A007L															O		Q		
1530	38	IMP NEW XPRNCE		1A007M	1A007M	1A007M	1A007M	1A007M																	Q		
1540	38	IMP FND PRPS LF		1A007N	1A007N	1A007N	1A007N	1A007N																	Q		
1550	38	PPL CAN B TRSTD	1A010	1A008	1A008	1A008	1A008	1A008																	Q		
1560	38	PPL TRY B HLPFL	1A011	1A009	1A009	1A009	1A009	1A009																	Q		
1570	39	PPL TRY BE FAIR	1A012	1A010	1A010	1A010	1A010	1A010																	Q		
1580	39	-OBY LW=-GD CTZN		1A011A	1A011A	1A011A	1A011A	1A011A								H											
1590	39	GD CTZN ALG GOVT		1A011B	1A011B	1A011B	1A011B	1A011B								H											
1600	39	GD CTZN CHG GOVT	1A013B	1A011C	1A011C	1A011C	1A011C	1A011C								H											
1610	39	VOTE->MAJ IMPCT		1A011D	1A011D	1A011D	1A011D	1A011D								H	I										
1620	39	CTZN GRP HV EFCT		1A011E	1A011E	1A011E	1A011E	1A011E								H	I										
1630	40	OUR SYST ST BS	1A013C	1A011F	1A011F	1A011F	1A011F	1A011F								H											
1640	40	US NEEDS GROWTH	1A013E	1A011G	1A011G	1A011G	1A011G	1A011G						F													
1650	40	LV THNGS TO GOD	1A004C	1A011H	1A011H	1A011H	1A011H	1A011H									I										
1660	40	GO SCH ENJY XPR	1A013I	1A011I	1A011I	1A011I	1A011I	1A011I		B																	
1670	40	DO WL SC IMP/JB	1A013H	1A011J	1A011J	1A011J	1A011J	1A011J		B	C																
1680	41	SMK CIG DLY/12G	1A019	1B002	(1B002)	1B002	1B002	1B002	A01G																		
1690	41	*TRY STP SMK&FL	1A021	1B004	1B004	1B004	1B004	1B004	A01I																		
1700	41	*WNT STP SMK NW	1A022	1B005	1B005	1B005	1B005	1B005	A01I																		
1710	41	NO SMK IN 5 YR	1A023	1B006	1B006	1B006	1B006	1B006	A04A																		
1720	42	#X/YR ALC ALONE		1B008A	1B008A	1B008A	1B008A	1B008A	A05A																		

Item Reference Number	Page Loc. in this Volume	ITEM DESCRIPTION (ABBREVIATED)	1975	1976	1977	1978	1979	1980/1	A	B C D E F G H I J K L M N O P Q R S
1730	42	#X/YR ALC-2 PPL		1B008B	1B008B	1B008B	1B008B	1B008B	A05B	
1740	43	#X/YR ALC@PARTY		1B008C	1B008C	1B008C	1B008C	1B008C	A05C	
1750	43	#X/YR ALC-DT/SP		1B008D	1B008D	1B008D	1B008D	1B008D	A05B	
1760	43	#X/YR ALC-ADLTS		1B008E	1B008E	1B008E	1B008E	1B008E	A05B	
1770	43	#X/YR ALC-DATIM		1B008F	1B008F	1B008F	1B008F	1B008F	A05C	
1780	43	#X/YR ALC@HOME		1B008G	1B008G	1B008G	1B008G	1B008G	A05C	
1790	43	#X/YR ALC@SCHL		1B008H	1B008H	1B008H	1B008H	1B008H	A05C	
1810	43	#X/YR ALCIN CAR		1B008I	1B008I	1B008I	1B008I	1B008I	A05C	
1820	44	ALC EXPERIMENT		1B009A	1B009A	1B009A	1B009A	1B009A	A06A	
1830	44	ALC RELAX	1A032A	1B009B	1B009B	1B009B	1B009B	1B009B	A06A	
1840	44	ALC GET HIGH	1A032B	1B009C	1B009C	1B009C	1B009C	1B009C	A06A	
1850	44	ALC SEEK INSGHT	1A032C	1B009D	1B009D	1B009D	1B009D	1B009D	A06A	
1860	44	ALC GD TM FRNDS	1A032D	1B009E	1B009E	1B009E	1B009E	1B009E	A06A	
1870	44	ALC FIT IN GRP	1A032E	1B009F	1B009F	1B009F	1B009F	1B009F	A06A	
1880	44	ALC GET AWY PRB	1A032F	1B009G	1B009G	1B009G	1B009G	1B009G	A06A	
1890	44	ALC BOREDOM	1A032G	1B009H	1B009H	1B009H	1B009H	1B009H	A06A	
1900	44	ALC ANGR&FRSTRN	1A032H	1B009I	1B009I	1B009I	1B009I	1B009I	A06A	
1910	44	ALC GT THRU DAY	1A032J	1B009J	1B009J	1B009J	1B009J	1B009J	A06A	
1920	44	ALC INCRS EF DR	1A032K	1B009K	1B009K	1B009K	1B009K	1B009K	A06A	
1930	44	ALC DECRS EF DR	1A032L	1B009L	1B009L	1B009L	1B009L	1B009L	A06A	
1940	44	ALC GET SLEEP		1B009M	1B009M	1B009M	1B009M	1B009M	A06A	
1950	44	ALC TASTES GOOD	1A032N	1B009N	1B009N	1B009N	1B009N	1B009N	A06A	
1960	44	ALC I AM HOOKED	1A032M	1B009O	1B009O	1B009O	1B009O	1B009O	A06A	
1970	44	#X DRK ENF FL 4	1A033	1B010	1B010	1B010	1B010	1B010	A01E	
1980	44	DRK AL,HI24+HR	1A034	1B011	1B011	1B011	1B011	1B011	A01F	
1990	45	#X/2W,3-4 DR RW	1A036	1B013	1B013	1B013	1B013	1B013	A01D	
2000	45	#X/2WK,2 DRK RW	1A037	1B014	1B014	1B014	1B014	1B014	A01D	
2010	45	#X/2WK,JST 1DRK	1A038	1B015	1B015	1B015	1B015	1B015	A01D	
2020	45	*TRY STP ALC&FL	1A039	1B016	1B016	1B016	1B016	1B016	A04A	
2030	45	NO ALC IN 5 YR	1A040	1B017	1B017	1B017	1B017	1B017	A04A	
2040	46	#X HASH/LIFETIM		1B018A	1B018A	1B018A	1B018A	1B018A	A01A	
2050	46	#X HASH/LAST12M		1B018B	1B018B	1B018B	1B018B	1B018B	A01B	
2060	46	#X HASH/LAST30D		1B018C	1B018C	1B018C	1B018C	1B018C	A01C	
2070	46	#X MARJ/LIFETIME		1B019A	1B019A	1B019A	1B019A	1B019A	A01A	
2080	46	#X MARJ/LAST12MO		1B019B	1B019B	1B019B	1B019B	1B019B	A01B	
2090	46	#X MARJ/LAST30DA		1B019C	1B019C	1B019C	1B019C	1B019C	A01C	
2100	47	#X/YR MJ ALONE	1A045	1B020A	1B020A	1B020A	1B020A	1B020A	A05A	
2110	47	#X/YR MJ-2 PPL		1B020B	1B020B	1B020B	1B020B	1B020B	A05B	
2120	47	#X/YR MJ@PARTY		1B020C	1B020C	1B020C	1B020C	1B020C	A05C	
2130	47	#X/YR MJ-DT/SP		1B020D	1B020D	1B020D	1B020D	1B020D	A05B	
2140	47	#X/YR MJ-ADLTS		1B020E	1B020E	1B020E	1B020E	1B020E	A05B	
2150	47	#X/YR MJ-DATIME		1B020F	1B020F	1B020F	1B020F	1B020F	A05C	
2160	48	#X/YR MJ@HOME		1B020G	1B020G	1B020G	1B020G	1B020G	A05C	
2170	48	#X/YR MJ@SCHL		1B020H	1B020H	1B020H	1B020H	1B020H	A05C	
2190	48	#X/YR MJIN CAR		1B020I	1B020I	1B020I	1B020I	1B020I	A05C	
2200	48	#X OVL MJ + ALC		1B021	1B021	1B021	1B021	1B021	A06A	
2210	48	MJ EXPERIMENT	1A049A	1B022A	1B022A	1B022A	1B022A	1B022A	A06A	
2220	48	MJ RELAX	1A049B	1B022B	1B022B	1B022B	1B022B	1B022B	A06A	
2230	48	MJ GET HIGH	1A049C	1B022C	1B022C	1B022C	1B022C	1B022C	A06A	
2240	48	MJ SEEK INSIGHT	1A049D	1B022D	1B022D	1B022D	1B022D	1B022D	A06A	
2250	48	MJ GD TM FRNDS	1A049E	1B022E	1B022E	1B022E	1B022E	1B022E	A06A	
2260	48	MJ FIT IN GRP	1A049F	1B022F	1B022F	1B022F	1B022F	1B022F	A06A	
2270	48	MJ GET AWY PRB	1A049G	1B022G	1B022G	1B022G	1B022G	1B022G	A06A	
2280	48	MJ BOREDOM	1A049H	1B022H	1B022H	1B022H	1B022H	1B022H	A06A	
2290	48	MJ ANGR&FRUSTRN	1A049I	1B022I	1B022I	1B022I	1B022I	1B022I	A06A	
2300	48	MJ GET THRU DAY	1A049K	1B022J	1B022J	1B022J	1B022J	1B022J	A06A	
2310	48	MJ INCRS EF DRG	1A049L	1B022K	1B022K	1B022K	1B022K	1B022K	A06A	
2320	48	MJ DECRS EF DRG	1A049M	1B022L	1B022L	1B022L	1B022L	1B022L	A06A	
2330	48	MJ I AM HOOKED		1B022M	1B022M	1B022M	1B022M	1B022M	A06A	
2340	49	MJ/HSH,VRY HIGH	1A050	1B023	1B023	1B023	1B023	1B023	A01E	
2350	49	MJ/HSH,HI 24+HR	1A051	1B024	1B024	1B024	1B024	1B024	A01F	
2360	49	JOINT/DA LST MO		1B025	1B025	1B025	1B025	1B025	A01D	
2370	49	OZS.MJ LST MO/6		1B026	1B026	1B026	1B026	1B026	A01D	
2380	49	*TRY STP MJ &FL	1A052	1B027	1B027	1B027	1B027	1B027	A01I	
2390	49	NO MJ/HSH IN5YR	1A053	1B028	1B028	1B028	1B028	1B028	A04A	
2400	50	#X/YR LSD ALONE		1B030A	1B030A	1B030A	1B030A	1B030A	A05A	

Item Reference Number	Page Loc. in this Volume	ITEM DESCRIPTION (ABBREVIATED)	QUESTIONNAIRE LOCATION BY YEAR (FORM, SECTION, AND QUESTION NUMBER)						SUBJECT AREA	
			1975	1976	1977	1978	1979	1980/1	A	B C D E F G H I J K L M N O P Q R S
2410	50	#X/YR LSD-2 PPL		1B030B	1B030B	1B030B	1B030B	1B030B	A05B	
2420	51	#X/YR LSD@PARTY		1B030C	1B030C	1B030C	1B030C	1B030C	A05C	
2430	51	#X/YR LSD-DT/SP		1B030D	1B030D	1B030D	1B030D	1B030D	A05B	
2440	51	#X/YR LSD-ADLTS		1B030E	1B030E	1B030E	1B030E	1B030E	A05B	
2450	51	#X/YR LSD-DATIM		1B030F	1B030F	1B030F	1B030F	1B030F	A05C	
2460	51	#X/YR LSD@HOME		1B030G	1B030G	1B030G	1B030G	1B030G	A05C	
2470	51	#X/YR LSD@SCHL		1B030H	1B030H	1B030H	1B030H	1B030H	A05C	
2490	51	#X/YR LSDIN CAR		1B030I	1B030I	1B030I	1B030I	1B030I	A05C	
2500	52	#X OVL LSD+ ALC		1B031A	1B031A	1B031A	1B031A	1B031A	A01H	
2510	52	#X OVL LSD+ MJ		1B031B	1B031B	1B031B	1B031B	1B031B	A01H	
2520	52	LSD EXPERIMENT	1A062A	1B032A	1B032A	1B032A	1B032A	1B032A	A06A	
2530	52	LSD RELAX	1A062B	1B032B	1B032B	1B032B	1B032B	1B032B	A06A	
2540	52	LSD GET HIGH	1A062C	1B032C	1B032C	1B032C	1B032C	1B032C	A06A	
2550	52	LSD SEEK INSGHT	1A062D	1B032D	1B032D	1B032D	1B032D	1B032D	A06A	
2560	52	LSD GD TM FRNDS	1A062E	1B032E	1B032E	1B032E	1B032E	1B032E	A06A	
2570	52	LSD FIT IN GRP	1A062F	1B032F	1B032F	1B032F	1B032F	1B032F	A06A	
2580	52	LSD GT AWY PRB	1A062G	1B032G	1B032G	1B032G	1B032G	1B032G	A06A	
2590	52	LSD BOREDOM	1A062H	1B032H	1B032H	1B032H	1B032H	1B032H	A06A	
2600	52	LSD ANGR&FRSTRN	1A062I	1B032I	1B032I	1B032I	1B032I	1B032I	A06A	
2610	52	LSD GT THRU DAY	1A062K	1B032J	1B032J	1B032J	1B032J	1B032J	A06A	
2620	52	LSD INCRS EF DR	1A062L	1B032K	1B032K	1B032K	1B032K	1B032K	A06A	
2630	52	LSD DCRS EF DRG	1A062M	1B032L	1B032L	1B032L	1B032L	1B032L	A06A	
2640	52	LSD I AM HOOKED		1B032M	1B032M	1B032M	1B032M	1B032M	A06A	
2650	52	LSD,GET VERY HI	1A063	1B033	1B033	1B033	1B033	1B033	A01E	
2660	52	LSD,HIGH 24+ HR	1A064	1B034	1B034	1B034	1B034	1B034	A01F	
2670	53	1+ BAD TRIP LSD	1A065	1B035	1B035	1B035	1B035	1B035	A01K	
2680	53	*TRY STP LSD&FL	1A066	1B036	1B036	1B036	1B036	1B036	A01I	
2690	53	NO LSD IN 5 YRS	1A067	1B037	1B037	1B037	1B037	1B037	A04A	
2700	54	PSYD,GT VERY HI	1A077	1B039	1B039	1B039	1B039	1B039	A01E	
2710	54	PSYD,HI 24+ HRS	1A078	1B040	1B040	1B040	1B040	1B040	A01F	
2720	54	TKN YR,MESCALIN	1A079A	1B041A	1B041A	1B041A	1B041A	1B041A	A01L	
2730	54	TKN YR,PEYOTE	1A079B	1B041B	1B041B	1B041B	1B041B	1B041B	A01L	
2740	54	TKN YR,PSILOCYB	1A079C	1B041C	1B041C	1B041C	1B041C	1B041C	A01L	
2750	54	TKN YR,PCP		1B041D	1B041D	1B041D	1B041D	1B041D	A01L	
2760	54	TKN YR,CNCT THC	1A079D	1B041E	1B041E	1B041E	1B041E	1B041E	A01L	
2770	54	TKN YR,OTH PSYD	1A079E	1B041F	1B041F	1B041F	1B041F	1B041F	A01L	
2780	54	TKN YR,DK NAME	1A079F	1B041G	1B041G	1B041G	1B041G	1B041G	A01L	
2790	54	DR TOLD TK AMPH	1A085	1B042	1B042	1B042	1B042	1B042	A01J	
2800	55	#X/YR AMPH ALNE		1B044A	1B044A	1B044A	1B044A	1B044A	A05A	
2810	55	#X/YR AMPH-2PPL		1B044B	1B044B	1B044B	1B044B	1B044B	A05B	
2820	56	#X/YR AMPH@PRTY		1B044C	1B044C	1B044C	1B044C	1B044C	A05C	
2830	56	#X/YR AMPH-DT/S		1B044D	1B044D	1B044D	1B044D	1B044D	A05B	
2840	56	#X/YR AMPH-ADLT		1B044E	1B044E	1B044E	1B044E	1B044E	A05B	
2850	56	#X/YR AMPH-DATM		1B044F	1B044F	1B044F	1B044F	1B044F	A05C	
2860	56	#X/YR AMPH@HOME		1B044G	1B044G	1B044G	1B044G	1B044G	A05C	
2880	56	#X/YR AMPH@SCHL		1B044H	1B044H	1B044H	1B044H	1B044H	A05C	
2890	56	#X/YR AMPH@CAR		1B044I	1B044I	1B044I	1B044I	1B044I	A05C	
2900	57	#X OVL AMPH+ALC		1B045A	1B045A	1B045A	1B045A	1B045A	A01H	
2910	57	#X OVL AMPH+MJ		1B045B	1B045B	1B045B	1B045B	1B045B	A01H	
2920	57	#X OVL AMPH+LSD		1B045C	1B045C	1B045C	1B045C	1B045C	A01H	
2930	57	#X OVL AMPH+PSY		1B045D	1B045D	1B045D	1B045D	1B045D	A01H	
2940	57	AMPH EXPERIMENT	1A092A	1B046A	1B046A	1B046A	1B046A	1B046A	A06A	
2950	57	AMPH RELAX	1A092B	1B046B	1B046B	1B046B	1B046B	1B046B	A06A	
2960	57	AMPH GET HIGH	1A092C	1B046C	1B046C	1B046C	1B046C	1B046C	A06A	
2970	57	AMPH SK INSIGHT	1A092D	1B046D	1B046D	1B046D	1B046D	1B046D	A06A	
2980	57	AMPH GD TM FRND	1A092E	1B046E	1B046E	1B046E	1B046E	1B046E	A06A	
2990	57	AMPH FIT IN GRP	1A092F	1B046F	1B046F	1B046F	1B046F	1B046F	A06A	
3000	57	AMPH GT AWY PRB	1A092G	1B046G	1B046G	1B046G	1B046G	1B046G	A06A	
3010	57	AMPH BOREDOM	1A092H	1B046H	1B046H	1B046H	1B046H	1B046H	A06A	
3020	57	AMPH ANGR&FRSTN	1A092I	1B046I	1B046I	1B046I	1B046I	1B046I	A06A	
3030	57	AMPH GT THRU DA	1A092K	1B046J	1B046J	1B046J	1B046J	1B046J	A06A	
3040	57	AMPH INCR EF DR	1A092L	1B046K	1B046K	1B046K	1B046K	1B046K	A06A	
3050	57	AMPH DCRS EF DR	1A092M	1B046L	1B046L	1B046L	1B046L	1B046L	A06A	
3060	57	AMPH STAY AWAKE	1A092N	1B046M	1B046M	1B046M	1B046M	1B046M	A06A	
3070	57	AMPH GET>ENERGY	1A092O	1B046N	1B046N	1B046N	1B046N	1B046N	A06A	
3080	57	AMPH LOSE WGHT	1A092P	1B046O	1B046O	1B046O	1B046O	1B046O	A06A	

Item Reference Number	Page Loc. in this Volume	ITEM DESCRIPTION (ABBREVIATED)	QUESTIONNAIRE LOCATION BY YEAR (FORM, SECTION, AND QUESTION NUMBER)						SUBJECT AREA	
			1975	1976	1977	1978	1979	1980/1	A	B C D E F G H I J K L M N O P Q R S
3090	57	AMPH I AM HOOKD	1A092Q	1B046P	1B046P	1B046P	1B046P	1B046P	A06A	
3100	58	AMPH, GT VERY HI	1A093	1B047	1B047	1B047	1B047	1B047	A01E	
3110	58	AMPH, HI 24 + HRS	1A094	1B048	1B048	1B048	1B048	1B048	A01F	
3120	58	TKN YR, BENZDRIN	1A095A	1B049A	1B049A	1B049A	1B049A	1B049A	A01L	
3130	58	TKN YR, DEXEDRIN	1A095B	1B049B	1B049B	1B049B	1B049B	1B049B	A01L	
3140	58	TKN YR, METHDRIN	1A095C	1B049C	1B049C	1B049C	1B049C	1B049C	A01L	
3150	58	TKN YR, RITALIN	1A095D	1B049D	1B049D	1B049D	1B049D	1B049D	A01L	
3160	58	TKN YR, PRELUDIN	1A095E	1B049E	1B049E	1B049E	1B049E	1B049E	A01L	
3170	58	TKN YR, DEXAMYL	1A095F	1B049F	1B049F	1B049F	1B049F	1B049F	A01L	
3180	58	TKN YR, METHAMPH	1A095G	1B049G	1B049G	1B049G	1B049G	1B049G	A01L	
3190	58	TKN YR, OTH AMPH	1A095H	1B049H	1B049H	1B049H	1B049H	1B049H	A01L	
3200	58	TKN YR, DNT KN N	1A095I	1B049I	1B049I	1B049I	1B049I	1B049I	A01L	
3210	58	MTHD AMPH-MOUTH		1B050A	1B050A	1B050A	1B050A	1B050A	A05D	
3220	58	MTHD AMPH-INJCT		1B050B	1B050B	1B050B	1B050B	1B050B	A05D	
3230	58	MTHD AMPH-OTHER		1B050C	1B050C	1B050C	1B050C	1B050C	A05D	
3240	58	*TRY STP AMP&FL	1A096	1B051	1B051	1B051	1B051	1B051	A01I	
3250	58	NO AMPH IN 5YR	1A097	1B052	1B052	1B052	1B052	1B052	A04A	
3260	59	QUAD GT VERY HI	1A108	1B054	1B054	1B054	1B054	1B054	A01E	
3270	60	QUAD, HI 24 + HRS	1A109	1B055	1B055	1B055	1B055	1B055	A01F	
3280	60	DR TOLD TK BARB	1A114	1B056	1B056	1B056	1B056	1B056	A01J	
3290	61	#X/YR BRBT ALNE		1B058A	1B058A	1B058A	1B058A	1B058A	A05A	
3300	61	#X/YR BRBT-2PPL		1B058B	1B058B	1B058B	1B058B	1B058B	A05B	
3310	61	#X/YR BRBT@PRTY		1B058C	1B058C	1B058C	1B058C	1B058C	A05C	
3320	61	#X/YR BRBT-DT/S		1B058D	1B058D	1B058D	1B058D	1B058D	A05B	
3330	61	#X/YR BRBT-ADLT		1B058E	1B058E	1B058E	1B058E	1B058E	A05B	
3340	61	#X/YR BRBT-DATM		1B058F	1B058F	1B058F	1B058F	1B058F	A05C	
3350	62	#X/YR BRBT@HOME		1B058G	1B058G	1B058G	1B058G	1B058G	A05C	
3360	62	#X/YR BRBT@SCHL		1B058H	1B058H	1B058H	1B058H	1B058H	A05C	
3380	62	#X/YR BRBT@CAR		1B058I	1B058I	1B058I	1B058I	1B058I	A05C	
3390	62	#X OVL BARB+ALC		1B059A	1B059A	1B059A	1B059A	1B059A	A01H	
3400	62	#X OVL BARB+MJ		1B059B	1B059B	1B059B	1B059B	1B059B	A01H	
3410	62	#X OVL BARB+LSD		1B059C	1B059C	1B059C	1B059C	1B059C	A01H	
3420	63	#X OVL BARB+PSY		1B059D	1B059D	1B059D	1B059D	1B059D	A01H	
3430	63	#X OVL BARB+AMP		1B059E	1B059E	1B059E	1B059E	1B059E	A01H	
3440	63	#X OVL BARB+QUA		1B059F	1B059F	1B059F	1B059F	1B059F	A01H	
3450	63	BARB EXPERIMENT	1A121A	1B060A	1B060A	1B060A	1B060A	1B060A	A06A	
3460	63	BARB RELAX	1A121B	1B060B	1B060B	1B060B	1B060B	1B060B	A06A	
3470	63	BARB GET HIGH	1A121C	1B060C	1B060C	1B060C	1B060C	1B060C	A06A	
3480	63	BARB SK INSIGHT	1A121D	1B060D	1B060D	1B060D	1B060D	1B060D	A06A	
3490	63	BARB GD TM FRND	1A121E	1B060E	1B060E	1B060E	1B060E	1B060E	A06A	
3500	63	BARB FIT IN GRP	1A121F	1B060F	1B060F	1B060F	1B060F	1B060F	A06A	
3510	63	BARB GT AWY PRB	1A121G	1B060G	1B060G	1B060G	1B060G	1B060G	A06A	
3520	63	BARB BOREDOM	1A121H	1B060H	1B060H	1B060H	1B060H	1B060H	A06A	
3530	63	BARB ANGR&FRSTN	1A121I	1B060I	1B060I	1B060I	1B060I	1B060I	A06A	
3540	63	BARB GT THRU DA	1A121K	1B060J	1B060J	1B060J	1B060J	1B060J	A06A	
3550	63	BARB INCR EF DR	1A121L	1B060K	1B060K	1B060K	1B060K	1B060K	A06A	
3560	63	BARB DCRS EF DR	1A121M	1B060L	1B060L	1B060L	1B060L	1B060L	A06A	
3570	63	BARB GET SLEEP	1A121N	1B060M	1B060M	1B060M	1B060M	1B060M	A06A	
3575	63	BARB RLV PHYS PN				1B060N	1B060N	1B060N	A06A	
3580	63	BARB I AM HOOKD	1A121O	1B060N	1B060N	1B060O	1B060O	1B060O	A06A	
3590	63	BARB, GT VERY HI	1A122	1B061	1B061	1B061	1B061	1B061	A01E	
3600	64	BARB, HI 24 + HRS	1A123	1B062	1B062	1B062	1B062	1B062	A01F	
3610	64	TKN YR, PHNOBARB	1A124A	1B063A	1B063A	1B063A	1B063A	1B063A	A01L	
3620	64	TKN YR, SECONAL	1A124B	1B063B	1B063B	1B063B	1B063B	1B063B	A01L	
3630	64	TKN YR, TUINAL	1A124C	1B063C	1B063C	1B063C	1B063C	1B063C	A01L	
3640	64	TKN YR, NEMBUTAL	1A124D	1B063D	1B063D	1B063D	1B063D	1B063D	A01L	
3650	64	TKN YR, LUMINAL	1A124E	1B063E	1B063E	1B063E	1B063E	1B063E	A01L	
3660	64	TKN YR, DESBUTAL	1A124F	1B063F	1B063F	1B063F	1B063F	1B063F	A01L	
3670	64	TKN YR, AMYTAL	1A124G	1B063G	1B063G	1B063G	1B063G	1B063G	A01L	
3680	64	TKN YR, ADRNOCAL	1A124H	1B063H	1B063H	1B063H	1B063H	1B063H	A01L	
3690	64	TKN YR, OTH BRBT	1A124I	1B063I	1B063I	1B063I	1B063I	1B063I	A01L	
3700	64	TKN YR, DNT KNOW	1A124J	1B063J	1B063J	1B063J	1B063J	1B063J	A01L	
3710	64	TRY STP BARB&FL	1A125	1B064	1B064	1B064	1B064	1B064	A01I	
3720	64	NO BARB IN 5YR	1A126	1B065	1B065	1B065	1B065	1B065	A04A	
3730	64	DR TOLD TK TRNQ	1A129	1B066	1B066	1B066	1B066	1B066	A01J	
3740	65	#X/YR TRQL ALNE		1B068A	1B068A	1B068A	1B068A	1B068A	A05A	

Item Reference Number	Page Loc. in this Volume	ITEM DESCRIPTION (ABBREVIATED)	QUESTIONNAIRE LOCATION BY YEAR (FORM, SECTION, AND QUESTION NUMBER)						SUBJECT AREA	
			1975	1976	1977	1978	1979	1980/1	A	B C D E F G H I J K L M N O P Q R S
3750	65	#X/YR TRQL-2PPL		1B068B	1B068B	1B068B	1B068B	1B068B	A05B	
3760	66	#X/YR TRQL@PRTY		1B068C	1B068C	1B068C	1B068C	1B068C	A05C	
3770	66	#X/YR TRQL-DT/S		1B068D	1B068D	1B068D	1B068D	1B068D	A05B	
3780	66	#X/YR TRQL-ADLT		1B068E	1B068E	1B068E	1B068E	1B068E	A05B	
3790	66	#X/YR TRQL-DATM		1B068F	1B068F	1B068F	1B068F	1B068F	A05C	
3800	66	#X/YR TRQL@HOME		1B068G	1B068G	1B068G	1B068G	1B068G	A05C	
3810	66	#X/YR TRQL@SCHL		1B068H	1B068H	1B068H	1B068H	1B068H	A05C	
3830	66	#X/YR TRQL@CAR		1B068I	1B068I	1B068I	1B068I	1B068I	A05C	
3840	67	#X OVL TRQL+ALC		1B069A	1B069A	1B069A	1B069A	1B069A	A01H	
3850	67	#X OVL TRQL+MJ		1B069B	1B069B	1B069B	1B069B	1B069B	A01H	
3860	67	#X OVL TRQL+LSD		1B069C	1B069C	1B069C	1B069C	1B069C	A01H	
3870	67	#X OVL TRQL+PSY		1B069D	1B069D	1B069D	1B069D	1B069D	A01H	
3880	67	#X OVL TRQL+AMP		1B069E	1B069E	1B069E	1B069E	1B069E	A01H	
3890	67	#X OVL TRQL+QUA		1B069F	1B069F	1B069F	1B069F	1B069F	A01H	
3900	67	#X OVL TRQL+BRB		1B069G	1B069G	1B069G	1B069G	1B069G	A01H	
3910	68	TRNQ EXPERIMENT	1A136A	1B070A	1B070A	1B070A	1B070A	1B070A	A06A	
3920	68	TRNQ RELAX	1A136B	1B070B	1B070B	1B070B	1B070B	1B070B	A06A	
3930	68	TRNQ GET HIGH	1A136C	1B070C	1B070C	1B070C	1B070C	1B070C	A06A	
3940	68	TRNQ SK INSIGHT	1A136D	1B070D	1B070D	1B070D	1B070D	1B070D	A06A	
3950	68	TRNQ GD TM FRND	1A136E	1B070E	1B070E	1B070E	1B070E	1B070E	A06A	
3960	68	TRNQ FIT IN GRP	1A136F	1B070F	1B070F	1B070F	1B070F	1B070F	A06A	
3970	68	TRNQ GT AWY PRB	1A136G	1B070G	1B070G	1B070G	1B070G	1B070G	A06A	
3980	68	TRNQ BOREDOM	1A136H	1B070H	1B070H	1B070H	1B070H	1B070H	A06A	
3990	68	TRNQ ANGR&FRSTN	1A136I	1B070I	1B070I	1B070I	1B070I	1B070I	A06A	
4000	68	TRNQ GT THRU DA	1A136K	1B070J	1B070J	1B070J	1B070J	1B070J	A06A	
4010	68	TRNQ INCR EF DR	1A136L	1B070K	1B070K	1B070K	1B070K	1B070K	A06A	
4020	68	TRNQ DCRS EF DR	1A136M	1B070L	1B070L	1B070L	1B070L	1B070L	A06A	
4030	68	TRNQ GET SLEEP	1A136N	1B070M	1B070M	1B070M	1B070M	1B070M	A06A	
4035	68	TRNQ RLV PHYS PN				1B070N	1B070N	1B070N	A06A	
4040	68	TRNQ I AM HOOKD	1A136O	1B070N	1B070N	1B070O	1B070O	1B070O	A06A	
4050	68	TRNQ,GT VERY HI	1A137	1B071	1B071	1B071	1B071	1B071	A01E	
4060	68	TRNQ,HI 24+ HRS	1A138	1B072	1B072	1B072	1B072	1B072	A01F	
4070	68	TKN YR,LIBRIUM		1B073A	1B073A	1B073A	1B073A	1B073A	A01L	
4080	68	TKN YR,VALIUM		1B073B	1B073B	1B073B	1B073B	1B073B	A01L	
4090	68	TKN YR,MILTOWN		1B073C	1B073C	1B073C	1B073C	1B073C	A01L	
4100	68	TKN YR,EQUANIL		1B073D	1B073D	1B073D	1B073D	1B073D	A01L	
4110	68	TKN YR,MEPRBMTE		1B073E	1B073E	1B073E	1B073E	1B073E	A01L	
4120	68	TKN YR,SERAX		1B073F	1B073F	1B073F	1B073F	1B073F	A01L	
4130	68	TKN YR,ATARAX		1B073G	1B073G	1B073G	1B073G	1B073G	A01L	
4140	68	TKN YR,TRANXENE		1B073H	1B073H	1B073H	1B073H	1B073H	A01L	
4150	68	TKN YR,VISTARIL		1B073I	1B073I	1B073I	1B073I	1B073I	A01L	
4160	68	TKN YR,DNT KNW		1B073J	1B073J	1B073J	1B073J	1B073J	A01L	
4170	69	*TRY STP TRQ&FL	1A139	1B074	1B074	1B074	1B074	1B074	A01I	
4180	69	NO TRNQ IN 5YR	1A140	1B075	1B075	1B075	1B075	1B075	A04A	
4190	70	#X/YR COKE ALNE		1B077A	1B077A	1B077A	1B077A	1B077A	A05A	
4200	70	#X/YR COKE-2PPL		1B077B	1B077B	1B077B	1B077B	1B077B	A05B	
4210	70	#X/YR COKE@PRTY		1B077C	1B077C	1B077C	1B077C	1B077C	A05C	
4220	70	#X/YR COKE-DT/S		1B077D	1B077D	1B077D	1B077D	1B077D	A05B	
4230	70	#X/YR COKE-ADLT		1B077E	1B077E	1B077E	1B077E	1B077E	A05B	
4240	70	#X/YR COKE-DATM		1B077F	1B077F	1B077F	1B077F	1B077F	A05C	
4250	70	#X/YR COKE@HOME		1B077G	1B077G	1B077G	1B077G	1B077G	A05C	
4260	71	#X/YR COKE@SCHL		1B077H	1B077H	1B077H	1B077H	1B077H	A05C	
4280	71	#X/YR COKE@CAR		1B077I	1B077I	1B077I	1B077I	1B077I	A05C	
4290	71	#X OVL COKE+ALC		1B078A	1B078A	1B078A	1B078A	1B078A	A01H	
4300	71	#X OVL COKE+MJ		1B078B	1B078B	1B078B	1B078B	1B078B	A01H	
4310	71	#X OVL COKE+LSD		1B078C	1B078C	1B078C	1B078C	1B078C	A01H	
4320	71	#X OVL COKE+PSY		1B078D	1B078D	1B078D	1B078D	1B078D	A01H	
4330	71	#X OVL COKE+AMP		1B078E	1B078E	1B078E	1B078E	1B078E	A01H	
4340	72	#X OVL COKE+QUA		1B078F	1B078F	1B078F	1B078F	1B078F	A01H	
4350	72	#X OVL COKE+BRB		1B078G	1B078G	1B078G	1B078G	1B078G	A01H	
4360	72	#X OVL COKE+TRN		1B078H	1B078H	1B078H	1B078H	1B078H	A01H	
4370	72	COKE EXPERIMENT	1A149A	1B079A	1B079A	1B079A	1B079A	1B079A	A06A	
4380	72	COKE RELAX	1A149B	1B079B	1B079B	1B079B	1B079B	1B079B	A06A	
4390	72	COKE GET HIGH	1A149C	1B079C	1B079C	1B079C	1B079C	1B079C	A06A	
4400	72	COKE SK INSIGHT	1A149D	1B079D	1B079D	1B079D	1B079D	1B079D	A06A	
4410	72	COKE GD TM FRND	1A149E	1B079E	1B079E	1B079E	1B079E	1B079E	A06A	

Item Reference Number	Page Loc. in this Volume	ITEM DESCRIPTION (ABBREVIATED)	QUESTIONNAIRE LOCATION BY YEAR (FORM, SECTION, AND QUESTION NUMBER)						SUBJECT AREA	
			1975	1976	1977	1978	1979	1980/1	A	B C D E F G H I J K L M N O P Q R S
4420	72	COKE FIT IN GRP	1A149F	1B079F	1B079F	1B079F	1B079F	1B079F	A06A	
4430	72	COKE GT AWY PRB	1A149G	1B079G	1B079G	1B079G	1B079G	1B079G	A06A	
4440	72	COKE BOREDOM	1A149H	1B079H	1B079H	1B079H	1B079H	1B079H	A06A	
4450	72	COKE ANGR&FRSTN	1A149I	1B079I	1B079I	1B079I	1B079I	1B079I	A06A	
4460	72	COKE GT THRU DA	1A149K	1B079J	1B079J	1B079J	1B079J	1B079J	A06A	
4470	72	COKE INCR EF DR	1A149L	1B079K	1B079K	1B079K	1B079K	1B079K	A06A	
4480	72	COKE DCRS EF DR	1A149M	1B079L	1B079L	1B079L	1B079L	1B079L	A06A	
4490	72	COKE STAY AWAKE		1B079M	1B079M	1B079M	1B079M	1B079M	A06A	
4500	72	COKE GET>ENERGY	1A149N	1B079N	1B079N	1B079N	1B079N	1B079N	A06A	
4510	72	COKE I AM HOOKD	1A149O	1B079O	1B079O	1B079O	1B079O	1B079O	A06A	
4520	72	COK,GET VERY HI	1A150	1B080	1B080	1B080	1B080	1B080	A01E	
4530	73	COK,HIGH 24+ HR	1A151	1B081	1B081	1B081	1B081	1B081	A01F	
4540	73	*TRY STP COK&FL	1A152	1B082	1B082	1B082	1B082	1B082	A01I	
4550	73	MTHD COKE SNORT	1A153A	1B083A	1B083A	1B083A	1B083A	1B083A	A05D	
4560	73	MTHD COKE-SMOKE	1A153B	1B083B	1B083B	1B083B	1B083B	1B083B	A05D	
4570	73	MTHD COKE-INJCT	1A153C	1B083C	1B083C	1B083C	1B083C	1B083C	A05D	
4580	73	MTHD COKE-MOUTH	1A153D	1B083D	1B083D	1B083D	1B083D	1B083D	A05D	
4590	73	MTHD COKE-OTHER	1A153E	1B083E	1B083E	1B083E	1B083E	1B083E	A05D	
4600	73	NO COKE IN 5YR	1A154	1B084	1B084	1B084	1B084	1B084	A04A	
4610	74	#X/YR HER ALONE		1B086A	1B086A	1B086A	1B086A	1B086A	A05A	
4620	74	#X/YR HER-2 PPL		1B086B	1B086B	1B086B	1B086B	1B086B	A05B	
4630	74	#X/YR HER@PARTY		1B086C	1B086C	1B086C	1B086C	1B086C	A05C	
4640	74	#X/YR HER-DA/SP		1B086D	1B086D	1B086D	1B086D	1B086D	A05B	
4650	74	#X/YR HER-ADULT		1B086E	1B086E	1B086E	1B086E	1B086E	A05B	
4660	75	#X/YR HER-DATIM		1B086F	1B086F	1B086F	1B086F	1B086F	A05C	
4670	75	#X/YR HER@HOME		1B086G	1B086G	1B086G	1B086G	1B086G	A05C	
4680	75	#X/YR HER@SCHL		1B086H	1B086H	1B086H	1B086H	1B086H	A05C	
4700	75	#X/YR HER@CAR		1B086I	1B086I	1B086I	1B086I	1B086I	A05C	
4710	75	#X OVL HER +ALC		1B087A	1B087A	1B087A	1B087A	1B087A	A01H	
4720	75	#X OVL HER +MJ		1B087B	1B087B	1B087B	1B087B	1B087B	A01H	
4730	76	#X OVL HER +LSD		1B087C	1B087C	1B087C	1B087C	1B087C	A01H	
4740	76	#X OVL HER +PSY		1B087D	1B087D	1B087D	1B087D	1B087D	A01H	
4750	76	#X OVL HER +AMP		1B087E	1B087E	1B087E	1B087E	1B087E	A01H	
4760	76	#X OVL HER +QUA		1B087F	1B087F	1B087F	1B087F	1B087F	A01H	
4770	76	#X OVL HER +BRB		1B087G	1B087G	1B087G	1B087G	1B087G	A01H	
4780	76	#X OVL HER +TRN		1B087H	1B087H	1B087H	1B087H	1B087H	A01H	
4790	76	#X OVL HER +COK		1B087I	1B087I	1B087I	1B087I	1B087I	A01H	
4800	77	HERIN EXPERMENT	1A163A	1B088A	1B088A	1B088A	1B088A	1B088A	A06A	
4810	77	HERIN RELAX	1A163B	1B088B	1B088B	1B088B	1B088B	1B088B	A06A	
4820	77	HERIN GET HIGH	1A163C	1B088C	1B088C	1B088C	1B088C	1B088C	A06A	
4830	77	HERIN SK INSIGT	1A163D	1B088D	1B088D	1B088D	1B088D	1B088D	A06A	
4840	77	HERIN GD TM FRN	1A163E	1B088E	1B088E	1B088E	1B088E	1B088E	A06A	
4850	77	HERIN FT IN GRP	1A163F	1B088F	1B088F	1B088F	1B088F	1B088F	A06A	
4860	77	HERIN GT AWY PB	1A163G	1B088G	1B088G	1B088G	1B088G	1B088G	A06A	
4870	77	HERIN BOREDOM	1A163H	1B088H	1B088H	1B088H	1B088H	1B088H	A06A	
4880	77	HERIN ANGR&FRST	1A163I	1B088I	1B088I	1B088I	1B088I	1B088I	A06A	
4890	77	HERIN GT THR DA	1A163K	1B088J	1B088J	1B088J	1B088J	1B088J	A06A	
4900	77	HERIN INC EF DG	1A163L	1B088K	1B088K	1B088K	1B088K	1B088K	A06A	
4910	77	HERIN DEC EF DG	1A163M	1B088L	1B088L	1B088L	1B088L	1B088L	A06A	
4920	77	HERIN I AM HOOK	1A163N	1B088M	1B088M	1B088M	1B088M	1B088M	A06A	
4930	77	HER,GT VERY HI	1A164	1B089	1B089	1B089	1B089	1B089	A01E	
4940	77	HER,HI 24+ HRS	1A165	1B090	1B090	1B090	1B090	1B090	A01F	
4950	77	TRY STP HER& FL	1A166	1B091	1B091	1B091	1B091	1B091	A01I	
4960	77	METHD HRN SNORT	1A167A	1B092A	1B092A	1B092A	1B092A	1B092A	A05D	
4970	77	METHD HRN-SMOKE	1A167B	1B092B	1B092B	1B092B	1B092B	1B092B	A05D	
4980	77	METHD HRN-INJCT	1A167C	1B092C	1B092C	1B092C	1B092C	1B092C	A05D	
4990	77	METHD HRN-MOUTH	1A167D	1B092D	1B092D	1B092D	1B092D	1B092D	A05D	
5000	77	METHD HRN-OTHER	1A167E	1B092E	1B092E	1B092E	1B092E	1B092E	A05D	
5010	78	NO HER IN 5 YR	1A168	1B093	1B093	1B093	1B093	1B093	A04A	
5020	78	DR TOLD TK NARC	1A171	1B094	1B094	1B094	1B094	1B094	A01J	
5030	79	#X/YR NARC ALNE		1B096A	1B096A	1B096A	1B096A	1B096A	A05A	
5040	79	#X/YR NARC-2PPL		1B096B	1B096B	1B096B	1B096B	1B096B	A05B	
5050	79	#X/YR NARC@PRTY		1B096C	1B096C	1B096C	1B096C	1B096C	A05C	
5060	79	#X/YR NARC-DT/S		1B096D	1B096D	1B096D	1B096D	1B096D	A05B	
5070	79	#X/YR NARC-ADLT		1B096E	1B096E	1B096E	1B096E	1B096E	A05B	
5080	80	#X/YR NARC-DATM		1B096F	1B096F	1B096F	1B096F	1B096F	A05C	

Item Reference Number	Page Loc. in this Volume	ITEM DESCRIPTION (ABBREVIATED)	QUESTIONNAIRE LOCATION BY YEAR (FORM, SECTION, AND QUESTION NUMBER)						SUBJECT AREA	
			1975	1976	1977	1978	1979	1980/1	A	B C D E F G H I J K L M N O P Q R S
5090	80	#X/YR NARC@HOME		1B096G	1B096G	1B096G	1B096G	1B096G	A05C	
5100	80	#X/YR NARC@SCHL		1B096H	1B096H	1B096H	1B096H	1B096H	A05C	
5120	80	#X/YR NARC @CAR		1B096I	1B096I	1B096I	1B096I	1B096I	A05C	
5130	80	#X OVL NARC+ALC		1B097A	1B097A	1B097A	1B097A	1B097A	A01H	
5140	80	#X OVL NARC+MJ		1B097B	1B097B	1B097B	1B097B	1B097B	A01H	
5150	81	#X OVL NARC+LSD		1B097C	1B097C	1B097C	1B097C	1B097C	A01H	
5160	81	#X OVL NARC+PSY		1B097D	1B097D	1B097D	1B097D	1B097D	A01H	
5170	81	#X OVL NARC+AMP		1B097E	1B097E	1B097E	1B097E	1B097E	A01H	
5180	81	#X OVL NARC+QUA		1B097F	1B097F	1B097F	1B097F	1B097F	A01H	
5190	81	#X OVL NARC+BRB		1B097G	1B097G	1B097G	1B097G	1B097G	A01H	
5200	81	#X OVL NARC+TRN		1B097H	1B097H	1B097H	1B097H	1B097H	A01H	
5210	81	#X OVL NARC+COK		1B097I	1B097I	1B097I	1B097I	1B097I	A01H	
5220	82	#X OVL NARC+HER		1B097J	1B097J	1B097J	1B097J	1B097J	A01H	
5230	82	NARC EXPERIMENT	1A178A	1B098A	1B098A	1B098A	1B098A	1B098A	A06A	
5240	82	NARC RELAX	1A178B	1B098B	1B098B	1B098B	1B098B	1B098B	A06A	
5250	82	NARC GET HIGH	1A178C	1B098C	1B098C	1B098C	1B098C	1B098C	A06A	
5260	82	NARC SK INSIGTS	1A178D	1B098D	1B098D	1B098D	1B098D	1B098D	A06A	
5270	82	NARC GD TM FRND	1A178E	1B098E	1B098E	1B098E	1B098E	1B098E	A06A	
5280	82	NARC FIT IN GRP	1A178F	1B098F	1B098F	1B098F	1B098F	1B098F	A06A	
5290	82	NARC GT AWY PBM	1A178G	1B098G	1B098G	1B098G	1B098G	1B098G	A06A	
5300	82	NARC BOREDOM	1A178H	1B098H	1B098H	1B098H	1B098H	1B098H	A06A	
5310	82	NARC ANGR&FRSTN	1A178I	1B098I	1B098I	1B098I	1B098I	1B098I	A06A	
5320	82	NARC GT THRU DA	1A178K	1B098J	1B098J	1B098J	1B098J	1B098J	A06A	
5330	82	NARC INC EF DG	1A178L	1B098K	1B098K	1B098K	1B098K	1B098K	A06A	
5340	82	NARC DEC EF DG	1A178M	1B098L	1B098L	1B098L	1B098L	1B098L	A06A	
5350	82	NARC GET SLEEP		1B098M	1B098M	1B098M	1B098M	1B098M	A06A	
5360	82	NARC SBST HERIN	1A178O	1B098N	1B098N	1B098N	1B098N	1B098N	A06A	
5363	82	NARC RLV PHYS PN				1B098O	1B098O	1B098O	A06A	
5366	82	NARC RLV COUGHNG				1B098P	1B098P	1B098P	A06A	
5370	82	NARC I AM HOOKD	1A178N	1B098O	1B098O	1B098Q	1B098Q	1B098Q	A06A	
5380	82	NARC,GT VERY HI	1A179	1B099	1B099	1B099	1B099	1B099	A01E	
5390	82	NARC,HI 24+ HRS	1A180	1B100	1B100	1B100	1B100	1B100	A01F	
5400	82	NARC TKN MTHDNE	1A181A	1B101A	1B101A	1B101A	1B101A	1B101A	A01L	
5410	82	NARC TKN OPIUM	1A181B	1B101B	1B101B	1B101B	1B101B	1B101B	A01L	
5420	82	NARC TKN MRPHNE	1A181C	1B101C	1B101C	1B101C	1B101C	1B101C	A01L	
5430	82	NARC TKN CODEIN	1A181D	1B101D	1B101D	1B101D	1B101D	1B101D	A01L	
5440	82	NARC TKN DEMROL	1A181E	1B101E	1B101E	1B101E	1B101E	1B101E	A01L	
5450	82	NARC TKN PARGRC	1A181F	1B101F	1B101F	1B101F	1B101F	1B101F	A01L	
5460	82	NARC TKN TALWIN	1A181G	1B101G	1B101G	1B101G	1B101G	1B101G	A01L	
5470	82	NARC TKN LDANUM	1A181H	1B101H	1B101H	1B101H	1B101H	1B101H	A01L	
5480	82	NARC TKN OTHER	1A181I	1B101I	1B101I	1B101I	1B101I	1B101I	A01L	
5490	82	NARC TKN DNT KN	1A181J	1B101J	1B101J	1B101J	1B101J	1B101J	A01L	
5500	83	TRY STP NARC&FL	1A182	1B102	1B102	1B102	1B102	1B102	A01I	
5510	83	METH NARC SNORT	1A183A	1B103A	1B103A	1B103A	1B103A	1B103A	A05D	
5520	83	METH NARC SMOKE	1A183B	1B103B	1B103B	1B103B	1B103B	1B103B	A05D	
5530	83	METH NARC INJCT	1A183C	1B103C	1B103C	1B103C	1B103C	1B103C	A05D	
5540	83	METH NARC MOUTH	1A183D	1B103D	1B103D	1B103D	1B103D	1B103D	A05D	
5550	83	METH NARC OTHER	1A183E	1B103E	1B103E	1B103E	1B103E	1B103E	A05D	
5560	83	NO NARC 5YR	1A184	1B104	1B104	1B104	1B104	1B104	A04A	
5570	83	GR 1ST SMOK DLY	1A019	1B105A	1B105A	1B105A	1B105A	1B105A	A01G	
	142				3E12A	3E12A	3E12A	3E12A	A01G	
5580	83	GR 1ST TRY ALC	1A027	1B105B	1B105B	1B105B	1B105B	1B105B	A01G	
	143				3E12B	3E12B	3E12B	3E12B	A01G	
5590	83	GR 1ST TRY MJ	1A043	1B105C	1B105C	1B105C	1B105C	1B105C	A01G	
	143				3E12C	3E12C	3E12C	3E12C	A01G	
5600	84	GR 1ST TRY LSD	1A056	1B105D	1B105D	1B105D	1B105D	1B105D	A01G	
	143				3E12D	3E12D	3E12D	3E12D	A01G	
5610	84	GR 1ST TRY PSY	1A070	1B105E	1B105E	1B105E	1B105E	1B105E	A01G	
	143				3E12E	3E12E	3E12E	3E12E	A01G	
5620	84	GR 1ST TRY AMP	1A086	1B105F	1B105F	1B105F	1B105F	1B105F	A01G	
	143				3E12F	3E12F	3E12F	3E12F	A01G	
5630	84	GR 1ST TRY QUA	1A101	1B105G	1B105G	1B105G	1B105G	1B105G	A01G	
	143				3E12G	3E12G	3E12G	3E12G	A01G	
5640	84	GR 1ST TRY BRB	1A115	1B105H	1B105H	1B105H	1B105H	1B105H	A01G	
	144				3E12H	3E12H	3E12H	3E12H	A01G	
5650	84	GR 1ST TRY TRN	1A130	1B105I	1B105I	1B105I	1B105I	1B105I	A01G	

Item Reference Number	Page Loc. in this Volume	ITEM DESCRIPTION (ABBREVIATED)	1975	1976	1977	1978	1979	1980/1	A	B C D E F G H I J K L M N O P Q R S
	144				3E12I	3E12I	3E12I	3E12I	A01G	
5660	85	GR 1ST TRY COK	1A143	1B105J	1B105J	1B105J	1B105J	1B105J	A01G	
	144				3E12J	3E12J	3E12J	3E12J	A01G	
5670	85	GR 1ST TRY HER	1A157	1B105K	1B105K	1B105K	1B105K	1B105K	A01G	
	144				3E12K	3E12K	3E12K	3E12K	A01G	
5680	85	GR 1ST TRY NRC	1A172	1B105L	1B105L	1B105L	1B105L	1B105L	A01G	
	144				3E12L	3E12L	3E12L	3E12L	A01G	
5685	144	GR 1ST TRY INHAL				3E12M	3E12M		A01G	
5686	113	GR 1ST TRY PCP						2E04A	A01G	
5687	113	GR 1ST TRY PPRS						2E04B	A01G	
5690	99	US GO WAR FR OTH	2A38B	2A18B	2A18B	2A18B	2A18B	2A18B		H L
5700	85	*SC WRK NVR MNG		1D002	1D002	1D002	1D002	1D002		B
5710	85	*MST COUR V DUL		1D003	1D003	1D003	1D003	1D003		B
5720	86	*LRN SCH NT IMPT		1D004	1D004	1D004	1D004	1D004		B
5730	86	LOT CMPTN GRADE		1D005	1D005	1D005	1D005	1D005		B
5740	86	STDTS DSLK CHTG		1D006	1D006	1D006	1D006	1D006		B
5750	86	ST -LK PROV TCH		1D007	1D007	1D007	1D007	1D007		B
5760	86	FRD NCG/TCH -LK		1D008	1D008	1D008	1D008	1D008		B
5770	86	R IN WK-STDY PG		1D009	1D009	1D009	1D009	1D009		B C
5780	87	#X/YR COUNS IND		1D010	1D010	1D010	1D010	1D010		B M
5790	87	#X/YR COUNS GRP		1D011	1D011	1D011	1D011	1D011		B M
5800	87	R LK C COUNS MR		1D012	1D012	1D012	1D012	1D012		B M
5810	87	CSLNG VRY HLPFL		(1D013)	1D013	1D013	1D013	1D013		B M
5811	87	CNSL COURSES					1D014A	1D014A		B M
5812	88	CNSL CL PROB					1D014B	1D014B		B M
5813	88	CNSL TRBL R IN					1D014C	1D014C		B M
5814	88	CNSL MILTRY PLN					1D014D	1D014D		B M
5815	88	CNSL EDUC PLANS					1D014E	1D014E		B M
5816	88	CNSL CAREER PLN					1D014F	1D014F		B M
5817		CNSL PRNL PROB					1D014G	1D014G		B M
5820	89	DALY WATCH TV		2A02A	2A02A	2A02A	2A02A	2A02A		B C
5830	89	DALY GO TO MOVIE		2A02B	2A02B	2A02B	2A02B	2A02B		B C
5840	89	DALY ART,MSC,PLA		2A02C	2A02C	2A02C	2A02C	2A02C		B C
5850		DALY RIDE FORFUN			2A02D	2A02D	202D2	202D		C
5860	89	DALY CMNTY AFFRS		2A02E	2A02E	2A02E	2A02E	2A02E		C O
5870	90	DALY PLA MSC,SNG		2A02F	2A02F	2A02F	2A02F	2A02F		C
5880	90	DALY CREAT WRTNG		2A02G	2A02G	2A02G	2A02G	2A02G		C
5890	90	DALY ACTV SPORTS		2A02H	2A02H	2A02H	2A02H	2A02H		C
5900	90	DALY ART/CRAFTS		2A02I	2A02I	2A02I	2A02I	2A02I		C
5910	90	DALY WRK HSE,CAR		2A02J	2A02J	2A02J	2A02J	2A02J		C
5920	90	DALY VIST W/FRDS		2A02K	2A02K	2A02K	2A02K	2A02K		C M
5930	90	DALY GO SHOPPING		2A02L	2A02L	2A02L	2A02L	2A02L		C F
5940	91	DALY ALONE LEISR		(2A02M)	2A02M	2A02M	2A02M	2A02M		C
5950	91	DALY READ BK,MAG		2A02N	2A02N	2A02N	2A02N	2A02N		B C
5960	91	DALY GO TO BARS		2A02O	2A02O	2A02O	2A02O	2A02O		C
5970	91	DALY GO TO PARTY		2A02P	2A02P	2A02P	2A02P	2A02P		C
5980		DALY GO CHURCH		2A02D						C G
5990	91	US 2 MUCH PROFIT	2A23J	2A03A	2A03A	2A03A	2A03A	2A03A		F O
6000	91	2MUCH CNCRN MTRL	2A23K	2A03B	2A03B	2A03B	2A03B	2A03B		F
6010	92	ENCOURG PPL BUY>	2A23L	2A03C	2A03C	2A03C	2A03C	2A03C		F
6020	92	-WRNG ADVERTISNG	2A23M	2A03D	2A03D	2A03D	2A03D	2A03D		F
6030	92	MOR SHORTGS FUTR	2A23N	2A03E	2A03E	2A03E	2A03E	2A03E		F
6040	92	APRV PETITIONS	2A21A	2A04A	2A04A	2A04A	2A04A	2A04A		H I
6050	92	APRV BOYCOTT	2A21B	2A04B	2A04B	2A04B	2A04B	2A04B		H I
6060	92	APRV LWFL DMSTN	2A21C	2A04C	2A04C	2A04C	2A04C	2A04C		H I
6070	93	APRV OCCUPY BLDG	2A21D	2A04D	2A04D	2A04D	2A04D	2A04D		H I
6080	93	APRV WLDCAT STRK	2A21E	2A04E	2A04E	2A04E	2A04E	2A04E		H I
6090	93	APRV BLK TRAFFIC	2A21F	2A04F	2A04F	2A04F	2A04F	2A04F		H I
6100	93	APRV DAMAG THING	2A21G	2A04G	2A04G	2A04G	2A04G	2A04G		H I
6110	93	APRV PSNL VIOLNC	2A21H	2A04H	2A04H	2A04H	2A04H	2A04H		H I
6120	93	DFNTLY PRFR MATE	2A10	2A05	2A05	2A05	2A05	2A05		D
6130	93	THINK WILL MARRY	2A11	2A06	2A06	2A06	2A06	2A06		D
6140	94	LIKLY STAY MARRD	2A12A	2A07A	2A07A	2A07A	2A07A	2A07A		D
6150	94	LIKLY HAVE KIDS	2A12B	2A07B	2A07B	2A07B	2A07B	2A07B		D E
6160	94	-CHL,HB WK1.,W=0	2A15A	2A08A	2A08A	2A08A	2A08A	2A08A		C D
6170	94	-CHL,HB WK1.,W.5	2A15B	2A08B	2A08B	2A08B	2A08B	2A08B		C D

Item Reference Number	Page Loc. in this Volume	Item Description (Abbreviated)	1975	1976	1977	1978	1979	1980/1	A	B	C	D	E	F	G	H	I	J	K	L	M	N	O	P	Q	R	S
6180	94	-CHL,HB&WF WK 1.	2A15C	2A08C	2A08C	2A08C	2A08C	2A08C			C	D															
6190	95	-CHL,HB&WF WK .5	2A15D	2A08D	2A08D	2A08D	2A08D	2A08D			C	D															
6200	95	-CHL,W WK 1.,H.5	2A15E	2A08E	2A08E	2A08E	2A08E	2A08E			C	D															
6210	95	-CHL,W WK 1.,H=0	2A15F	2A08F	2A08F	2A08F	2A08F	2A08F			C	D															
6220	95	PSCH,HB WK1.,W=0	2A16A	2A09A	2A09A	2A09A	2A09A	2A09A			C	D															
6230	95	PSCH,HB WK1.,W.5	2A16B	2A09B	2A09B	2A09B	2A09B	2A09B			C	D															
6240	95	PSCH,HB&WF WK 1.	2A16C	2A09C	2A09C	2A09C	2A09C	2A09C			C	D															
6250	95	PSCH,HB&WF WK .5	2A16D	2A09D	2A09D	2A09D	2A09D	2A09D			C	D															
6260	96	PSCH,WF WK1.,H.5	2A16E	2A09E	2A09E	2A09E	2A09E	2A09E			C	D															
6270	96	PSCH,WF WK1.,H=0	2A16F	2A09F	2A09F	2A09F	2A09F	2A09F			C	D															
6280	96	H WK,W -WK,W CCR	2A17A	2A10A	2A10A	2A10A	2A10A	2A10A				D															
6290	96	H WK,W -WK,W>CCR	2A17B	2A10B	2A10B	2A10B	2A10B	2A10B				D															
6300	96	H WK,W -WK,=CHCR	2A17C	2A10C	2A10C	2A10C	2A10C	2A10C				D															
6310	96	H WK,W -WK,H>CCR	2A17D	2A10D	2A10D	2A10D	2A10D	2A10D				D															
6320	96	H WK,W -WK,H CCR	2A17E	2A10E	2A10E	2A10E	2A10E	2A10E				D															
6330	97	INTEREST IN GOVT	2A31	2A11	2A11	2A11	2A11	2A11									H									Q		
	137		4A29	3E01	3E01	3E01	3E01	3E01									H									Q		
	155		5A40	4A18	4A18	4A18	4A18	4A18									H									Q		
	181			5A19	5A19	5A19	5A19	5A19									H									Q		
6340	97	GOVT PPL -DSHNST	2A32	2A12	2A12	2A12	2A12	2A12									H			K								
6350	97	GOVT DSNT WASTE$	2A33	2A13	2A13	2A13	2A13	2A13									H			K								
6360	97	NEVER TRUST GOVT	2A34	2A14	2A14	2A14	2A14	2A14									H			K								
6370	97	GVT PPL DK DOING	2A35	2A15	2A15	2A15	2A15	2A15									H			K								
6380	98	GOVT RUN FOR PPL	2A36	2A16	2A16	2A16	2A16	2A16									H			K								
6390	98	DO OR PLN VOTE	2A37A	2A17A	2A17A	2A17A	2A17A	2A17A									H	I										
6400	98	DO OR PLN WRITE	2A37B	2A17B	2A17B	2A17B	2A17B	2A17B									H	I										
6410	98	DO OR PLN GIVE $	2A37C	2A17C	2A17C	2A17C	2A17C	2A17C									H	I										
6420	98	DO OR PLN WK CPG	2A37D	2A17D	2A17D	2A17D	2A17D	2A17D									H	I										
6430	98	DO OR PLN DEMNST	2A37E	2A17E	2A17E	2A17E	2A17E	2A17E									H	I										
6440	98	DO OR PLN BOYCOT	2A37F	2A17F	2A17F	2A17F	2A17F	2A17F									H	I										
6450	99	US SHD DISARM	2A38A	2A18A	2A18A	2A18A	2A18A	2A18A									H				L							
6460	99	US WAR PRTCT ECN	2A38C	2A18C	2A18C	2A18C	2A18C	2A18C									H				L							
6470	99	US ONLY WAR DFNS	2A38D	2A18D	2A18D	2A18D	2A18D	2A18D									H				L							
6480	99	-US MIL PWR>USSR	2A38E	2A18E	2A18E	2A18E	2A18E	2A18E									H				L							
6490	99	US NEED>PWR OTHS	2A38F	2A18F	2A18F	2A18F	2A18F	2A18F									H				L							
6500	100	US FRN PLCY NRRW	2A38G	2A18G	2A18G	2A18G	2A18G	2A18G									H				L							
6510	100	SRVCMEN SHD OBEY	2A38H	2A18H	2A18H	2A18H	2A18H	2A18H													L							
6520	100	FRQ FIGHT PARNTS	2A39A	2A19A	2A19A	2A19A	2A19A	2A19A														M						S
6530	100	FRQ HIT SUPRVISR	2A39B	2A19B	2A19B	2A19B	2A19B	2A19B														M						S
6540	100	FRQ FGT WRK/SCHL	2A39C	2A19C	2A19C	2A19C	2A19C	2A19C		B	C																	S
6550	100	FRQ GANG FIGHT	2A39D	2A19D	2A19D	2A19D	2A19D	2A19D																			S
6560	101	FRQ HURT SM1 BAD	2A39E	2A19E	2A19E	2A19E	2A19E	2A19E																			S
6570	101	FRQ THREAT WEAPN	2A39F	2A19F	2A19F	2A19F	2A19F	2A19F																			S
6580	101	FRQ STEAL <$50	2A39G	2A19G	2A19G	2A19G	2A19G	2A19G																			S
6590	101	FRQ STEAL >$50	2A39H	2A19H	2A19H	2A19H	2A19H	2A19H																			S
6600	101	FRQ SHOPLIFT	2A39I	2A19I	2A19I	2A19I	2A19I	2A19I																			S
6610	101	FRQ CAR THEFT	2A39J	2A19J	2A19J	2A19J	2A19J	2A19J																			S
6620	102	FRQ STEAL CAR PT	2A39K	2A19K	2A19K	2A19K	2A19K	2A19K																			S
6630	102	FRQ TRESPAS BLDG	2A39L	2A19L	2A19L	2A19L	2A19L	2A19L																			S
6640	102	FRQ ARSON	2A39M	2A19M	2A19M	2A19M	2A19M	2A19M																			S
6650	102	FRQ DMG SCH PPTY	2A39N	2A19N	2A19N	2A19N	2A19N	2A19N		B																	S
6660	102	FRQ DMG WK PRPTY	2A39O	2A19O	2A19O	2A19O	2A19O	2A19O			C																S
6670	102	FRQ TRUBL POLICE	2A39P	2A19P	2A19P	2A19P	2A19P	2A19P																			S
6680	103	SM1 ROB YRS <$50		2A20A	2A20A	2A20A	2A20A	2A20A																			R	S
6690	103	SM1 ROB YRS >$50		2A20B	2A20B	2A20B	2A20B	2A20B																			R	S
6700	103	SM1 DMG YR PRPTY		2A20C	2A20C	2A20C	2A20C	2A20C																			R	S
6710	103	SM1 INJR U W/WPN		2A20D	2A20D	2A20D	2A20D	2A20D																			R	S
6720	103	SM1 THRTN U W/WP		2A20E	2A20E	2A20E	2A20E	2A20E																			R	S
6730	103	SM1 INJR YU -WPN		2A20F	2A20F	2A20F	2A20F	2A20F																			R	S
6740	103	SM1 THRT U W/INJ		2A20G	2A20G	2A20G	2A20G	2A20G																			R	S
6750	104	EASY GT MARIJUAN	2A40A	2A21A	2A21A	2A21A	2A21A	2A21A	A03A																			
6760	104	EASY GT LSD	2A40B	2A21B	2A21B	2A21B	2A21B	2A21B	A03A																			
6770	104	EASY GT PSYDELIC	2A40C	2A21C	2A21C	2A21C	2A21C	2A21C	A03A																			
6780	104	EASY GT AMPHTMNS	2A40D	2A21D	2A21D	2A21D	2A21D	2A21D	A03A																			
6790	104	EASY GT BBTUATES	2A40F	2A21E	2A21E	2A21E	2A21E	2A21E	A03A																			
6800	104	EASY GT TRANQLIZ	2A40G	2A21F	2A21F	2A21F	2A21F	2A21F	A03A																			

Item Reference Number	Page Loc. in this Volume	ITEM DESCRIPTION (ABBREVIATED)	1975	1976	1977	1978	1979	1980/1	A	B	C	D	E	F	G	H	I	J	K	L	M	N	O	P	Q	R	S
6810	105	EASY GT COCAINE	2A40H	2A21G	2A21G	2A21G	2A21G	2A21G	A03A																		
6820	105	EASY GT HEROIN	2A40I	2A21H	2A21H	2A21H	2A21H	2A21H	A03A																		
6830	105	EASY GT NARCOTIC	2A40J	2A21I	2A21I	2A21I	2A21I	2A21I	A03A																		
6840	105	CMP SATFD W/LIFE		2D01	2D01	2D01	2D01	2D01																	P	Q	R	
	133			3D01	3D01	3D01	3D01	3D01																P	Q	R	
	159			4D01	4D01	4D01	4D01	4D01																P	Q	R	
	182			5A21	5A21	5A21	5A21	5A21																P	Q	R	
6850	105	HOW GD AS SPOUSE	2A19A	2D02A	2D02A	2D02A	2D02A	2D02A				D													Q		
6860	105	HOW GD AS PARENT	2A19B	2D02B	2D02B	2D02B	2D02B	2D02B				D													Q		
6870	106	HOW GD AS WORKER	2A19C	2D02C	2D02C	2D02C	2D02C	2D02C			C														Q		
6880	106	THK ABT SOC ISSU	*A06	2D03	2D03	2D03	2D03	2D03										J							Q		
	119			3A02	3A02	3A02	3A02	3A02										J							Q		
	145			4A05	4A05	4A05	4A05	4A05										J							Q		
	172			5A02	5A02	5A02	5A02	5A02										J							Q		
6890	106	DHNSTY LARG CORP	2A20A	2D04A	2D04A	2D04A	2D04A	2D04A											K								
6900	106	DHNSTY LBR UNION	2A20B	2D04B	2D04B	2D04B	2D04B	2D04B											K								
6910	106	DHNSTY COLL&UNIV	2A20C	2D04C	2D04C	2D04C	2D04C	2D04C		B									K								
6920	106	DHNSTY PBLC SCHL	2A20D	2D04D	2D04D	2D04D	2D04D	2D04D		B									K								
6930	107	DHNSTY CHURCHES	2A20E	2D04E	2D04E	2D04E	2D04E	2D04E							G				K								
6940	107	DHNSTY NEWS MDIA	2A20F	2D04F	2D04F	2D04F	2D04F	2D04F		B									K								
6950	107	DHNSTY PRES&ADMN	2A20G	2D04G	2D04G	2D04G	2D04G	2D04G								H			K								
6960	107	DHNSTY CONGRESS	2A20H	2D04H	2D04H	2D04H	2D04H	2D04H								H			K								
6970	107	DHNSTY SUPRM CRT	2A20I	2D04I	2D04I	2D04I	2D04I	2D04I								H			K								
6980	107	DHNSTY JUSTC SYS	2A20J	2D04J	2D04J	2D04J	2D04J	2D04J								H			K								
6990	108	DHNSTY POLICE	2A20K	2D04K	2D04K	2D04K	2D04K	2D04K											K								
7000	108	DHNSTY MILITARY	2A20L	2D04L	2D04L	2D04L	2D04L	2D04L											K	L							
7010	108	2MCH COMPTN SCTY	2A23C	2D05A	2D05A	2D05A	2D05A	2D05A																	Q		
7020	108	2MANY YNG SLOPPY	2A23H	2D05B	2D05B	2D05B	2D05B	2D05B																	Q		
7030	108	2MUCH HARD ROCK	2A23I	2D05C	2D05C	2D05C	2D05C	2D05C																	Q		
7040	108	SHD DO OWN THING	2A23A	2D05D	2D05D	2D05D	2D05D	2D05D																	Q		
7050	109	KICK DO DANGR TH		2D05E	2D05E	2D05E	2D05E	2D05E																	Q		
7060	109	LIKE RISK SOME X		2D05F	2D05F	2D05F	2D05F	2D05F																	Q		
7070	109	ALL FRD SMK CIGS	2A41A	2D06A	2D06A	2D06A	2D06A	2D06A	A02A																		
7080	109	ALL FRD SMK MARJ	2A41B	2D06B	2D06B	2D06B	2D06B	2D06B	A02A																		
7090	109	ALL FRD TAKE LSD	2A41C	2D06C	2D06C	2D06C	2D06C	2D06C	A02A																		
7100	109	ALL FRD TK PSYDL	2A41D	2D06D	2D06D	2D06D	2D06D	2D06D	A02A																		
7110	110	ALL FRD TK AMPH	2A41E	2D06E	2D06E	2D06E	2D06E	2D06E	A02A																		
7120	110	ALL FRD TK QUALD	2A41F	2D06F	2D06F	2D06F	2D06F	2D06F	A02A																		
7130	110	ALL FRD TK BARBT	2A41G	2D06G	2D06G	2D06G	2D06G	2D06G	A02A																		
7140	110	ALL FRD TK TRNQL	2A41H	2D06H	2D06H	2D06H	2D06H	2D06H	A02A																		
7150	110	ALL FRD TK COKE	2A41I	2D06I	2D06I	2D06I	2D06I	2D06I	A02A																		
7160	110	ALL FRD TK HERON	2A41J	2D06J	2D06J	2D06J	2D06J	2D06J	A02A																		
7170	110	ALL FRD TK NARC	2A41K	2D06K	2D06K	2D06K	2D06K	2D06K	A02A																		
7180	111	ALL FRD TK INHL	2A41L	2D06L	2D06L	2D06L	2D06L	2D06L	A02A																		
7190	111	ALL FRD DRK ALCL	2A41M	2D06M	2D06M	2D06M	2D06M	2D06M	A02A																		
7200	111	ALL FRD GT DRUNK	2A41N	2D06N	2D06N	2D06N	2D06N	2D06N	A02A																		
7201	111	# FRNDS TAKE PCP					2E01A	2E01A	A02A																		
7202	111	# FRNDS TK PPRS					2E01B	2E01B	A02A																		
7210		FBD CHLD CIG RGL			2E01A				A11C																		
7220		FBD CHLD MJ OCCS			2E01B				A11C																		
7230		FBD CHLD MJ RGLY			2E01C				A11C																		
7240		FBD CHLD LSD OCC			2E01D				A11C																		
7250		FBD CHLD AMPH OC			2E01E				A11C																		
7260		FBD CHLD BARB OC			2E01F				A11C																		
7270		FBD CHLD COKE OC			2E01G				A11C																		
7280		FBD CHLD HRN OCC			2E01H				A11C																		
7290		FBD CHLD DRNK OC			2E01I				A11C																		
7300		FBD CHLD DRNK RG			2E01J				A11C																		
7310		FBD CHLD DRUNKOC			2E01K				A11C																		
7320		RSK/OT CIG1+PK/D		2E01A					A14B																		
7330		RSK/OT MJ 1-2 X		2E01B					A14B																		
7340		RSK/OT MJ OCSNLY		2E01C					A14B																		
7350		RSK/OT MJ REGLY		2E01D					A14B																		
7360		RSK/OT LSD 1-2 X		2E01E					A14B																		
7370		RSK/OT LSD REGLY		2E01F					A14B																		
7380		RSK/OT 'H' 1-2 X		2E01G					A14B																		

Item Reference Number	Page Loc. in this Volume	ITEM DESCRIPTION (ABBREVIATED)	1975	1976	1977	1978	1979	1980/1	A	B	C	D	E	F	G	H	I	J	K	L	M	N	O	P	Q	R	S
7390		RSK/OT 'H' OCSNL		2E01H					A14B																		
7400		RSK/OT 'H' REGLY		2E01I					A14B																		
7410		RSK7OT BARB 1-2X		2E01J					A14B																		
7420		RSK/OT BARB REGY		2E01K					A14B																		
7430		RSK/OT AMPH 1-2X		2E01L					A14B																		
7440		RSK/OT AMPH REG		2E01M					A14B																		
7450		RSK/OT COKE 1-2X		2E01N					A14B																		
7460		RSK/OT COKE REG		2E01O					A14B																		
7470		RSK/OT 1-2 DRINK		2E01P					A14B																		
7480		RSK/OT 1-2 DR/DA		2E01Q					A14B																		
7490		RSK/OT 4-5 DR/DA		2E01R					A14B																		
7500		RSK/OT 5+DR/WKND		2E01S					A14B																		
7510	113	PRNT THK U DRINK			2E02	2E01	2E04	2E05	A09A																		
7520	113	PRNT THK U SM MJ			2E03	2E02	2E05	2E06	A09A																		
7530	113	PRNT THK USE DRG			2E04	2E03	2E06	2E07	A09A																		
7540		TRN FA/MO DRG HP			2E05A		2E07A		A08A																		
7550		TRN SR/BR DRG HP			2E05B		2E07B		A08A																		
7560		TRN RLTVS DRG HP			2E05C		2E07C		A08A																		
7570		TRN FRND DRG HP			2E05D		2E07D		A08A																		
7580		TRN DOCTR DRG HP			2E05E		2E07E		A08A																		
7590		TRN CLINC DRG HP			2E05F		2E07F		A08A																		
7600		TRN CNSLR DRG HP			2E05G		2E07G		A08A																		
7610		TRN TCHR DRG HP			2E05H		2E07H		A08A																		
7620		TRN MNSTR DRG HP			2E05I		2E07I		A08A																		
7630	85	R LIKES SCHOOL		1D001	1D001	1D001	1D001	1D001		B															Q		
	114			2E02	2E06	2E06	2E08	2E09		B															Q		
	140			3E08	3E07	3E07	3E07	3E07		B															Q		
				4E10	5E05	5E05	5E03	5E05*		B															Q		
				5E04						B															Q		
7640	115	HRS/WK SPND HMWK		2E03	2E07	2E07	2E09	2E10		B																	
7650	115	PRCL INFL SCL RN		2E04A	2E08A	2E08A	2E10A	2E11A		B																	
7660	115	TCHR INFL SCL RN		2E04B	2E08B	2E08B	2E10B	2E11B		B																	
7670	115	STDS INFL SCL RN		2E04C	2E08C	2E08C	2E10C	2E11C		B																	
7680	115	PRTS INFL SCL RN		2E04D	2E08D	2E08D	2E10D	2E11D		B																	
7690	115	HAD DRUG EDUCATN		2E05	2E09	2E09	2E11	2E12	A10A																		
7700		NOW OWN HAIR DRY		2E09A										F												R	
7710		NOW OWN WT/S SKI		2E09B										F												R	
7720		NOW OWN CAMERA		2E09C										F												R	
7730		NOW OWN WATCH		2E09D										F												R	
7740		NOW OWN HKG BKPK		2E09E										F												R	
7750		NOW OWN CK RADIO		2E09F										F												R	
7760		NOW OWN EL SHAVR		2E09G										F												R	
7770		NOW OWN TENIS RQ		2E09H										F												R	
7780		NOW OWN TV SET		2E09I										F												R	
7790		NOW OWN BICYCLE		2E09J										F												R	
7800		NOW OWN CAR		2E09K										F												R	
7810		NOW OWN TAPE REC		2E09L										F												R	
7820		NOW OWN ELT CALC		2E09M										F												R	
7830		NOW OWN BT/SNMBL		2E09N										F												R	
7840	116	DG ED,>DG INTRST		2E06	2E10	2E10	2E12	2E13	A10A																		
7850	116	DG ED,SPC COURSE		2E07A	2E11A	2E11A	2E13A	2E14A	A10A																		
7860	116	DG ED,IN REG CRS		2E07B	2E11B	2E11B	2E13B	2E14B	A10A																		
7870	116	DG ED,NT REG CRS		2E07C	2E11C	2E11C	2E13C	2E14C	A10A																		
7880	116	DG ED,SPC DISCUS		2E07D	2E11D	2E11D	2E13D	2E14D	A10A																		
7890	116	DG ED,GRT VALUE		2E08	2E12	2E12	2E14	2E15	A10A																		
7900	116	16YR+,TEST->DIPL			2E13A	(2E13A)	5E07A	2E16A		B																	
7910	116	14YR+,TEST->DIPL			2E13B	(2E13B)	5E07B	2E16B		B																	
7920	117	ALL STD H.S.TEST			2E13C	(2E13C)	5E07C	2E16C		B																	
7930	119	MEN&WOMN/=$,=WRK	3A17A	3A03A	3A03A	3A03A	3A03A	3A03A			C	D															
7940	119	CNSDR WMN/HI JOB	3A17B	3A03B	3A03B	3A03B	3A03B	3A03B				D				H										
7950	119	WMN SHD =JOB OPP	3A17C	3A03C	3A03C	3A03C	3A03C	3A03C			C	D															
7960	119	WMN SHD =ED OPP	3A17D	3A03D	3A03D	3A03D	3A03D	3A03D		B		D															
7970	120	MN=ACHV/WMN=HOME	3A17H	3A03E	3A03E	3A03E	3A03E	3A03E				D															
7980	120	CHL SUFF W WK MO	3A17I	3A03F	3A03F	3A03F	3A03F	3A03F				D															
7990	120	WK MO AS WRM REL	3A17J	3A03G	3A03G	3A03G	3A03G	3A03G			C	D															
8000	120	POLLUT INCREASED	3A31A	3A04A	3A04A	3A04A	3A04A	3A04A						F													

* 1980 only.

Item Reference Number	Page Loc. in this Volume	ITEM DESCRIPTION (ABBREVIATED)	1975	1976	1977	1978	1979	1980/1	A	B	C	D	E	F	G	H	I	J	K	L	M	N	O	P	Q	R	S
8010	120	GOVT DEAL ENV PR	3A31D	3A04B	3A04B	3A04B	3A04B	3A04B						F		H											
8020	120	MR$ FR LASTG THG	3A31E	3A04C	3A04C	3A04C	3A04C	3A04C						F													
8030	121	USE BYC/MAS TRAN	3A31F	3A04D	3A04D	3A04D	3A04D	3A04D						F													
8040	121	EAT DIF->FD STRV	3A31G	3A04E	3A04E	3A04E	3A04E	3A04E						F									O				
8050	121	LIK WRK CAN FRGT	3A08D	3A05A	3A05A	3A05A	3A05A	3A05A			C																
8060	121	WRK=ONLY MK LVNG	3A08E	3A05B	3A05B	3A05B	3A05B	3A05B			C																
8070	121	WRK CNTRL PRT LF	3A08G	3A05C	3A05C	3A05C	3A05C	3A05C			C																
8080	121	OVTM 2DO BST JOB	3A08H	3A05D	3A05D	3A05D	3A05D	3A05D			C																
8090	122	SAME JOB MST LIF	3A08I	3A05E	3A05E	3A05E	3A05E	3A05E			C																
8100	122	ENUF$,NT WNT WRK	3A10	3A06	3A06	3A06	3A06	3A06			C																
	153		4A09A	4A14	4A14	4A14	4A14	4A14			C																
	175		5A11	5A06	5A06	5A06	5A06	5A06			C																
8110	122	DES FRND OTH RC	3A19A	3A07A	3A07A	3A07A	3A07A	3A07A														N					
8120	122	DES SUPVR DIF RC	3A19B	3A07B	3A07B	3A07B	3A07B	3A07B			C											N					
8130	122	DES FAM NX DF RC	3A19C	3A07C	3A07C	3A07C	3A07C	3A07C														N					
8140	123	DES CHL FD SM RC	3A19D	3A07D	3A07D	3A07D	3A07D	3A07D														N					
8150	123	DES CHL FD OT RC	3A19E	3A07E	3A07E	3A07E	3A07E	3A07E														N					
8160	123	DES AL WKS SM RC	3A19F	3A08A	3A08A	3A08A	3A08A	3A08A			C											N					
8170	123	DES SO WKS DF RC	3A19G	3A08B	3A08B	3A08B	3A08B	3A08B			C											N					
8180	123	DES MS WKS DF RC	3A19H	3A08C	3A08C	3A08C	3A08C	3A08C			C											N					
8190	123	DES AL NGB SM RC	3A19I	3A09A	3A09A	3A09A	3A09A	3A09A														N					
8200	123	DES SO NGB OT RC	3A19J	3A09B	3A09B	3A09B	3A09B	3A09B														N					
8210	124	DES MS NGB OT RC	3A19K	3A09C	3A09C	3A09C	3A09C	3A09C														N					
8220	124	DES AL CHL SM RC	3A19L	3A10A	3A10A	3A10A	3A10A	3A10A		B												N					
8230	124	DES SM CHL OT RC	3A19M	3A10B	3A10B	3A10B	3A10B	3A10B		B												N					
8240	124	DES MS CHL OT RC	3A19N	3A10C	3A10C	3A10C	3A10C	3A10C		B												N					
8250	124	FRNDS AL OT RC	3A22	3A11	3A11	3A11	3A11	3A11														N				R	
8260	124	NGBHD AL OT RC	3A23	3A12	3A12	3A12	3A12	3A12														N				R	
8270	124	ELEMSCH AL OT RC	3A21	3A13	3A13	3A13	3A13	3A13														N				R	
8280	125	HISCH AL OT RC	3A20	3A14	3A14	3A14	3A14	3A14														N				R	
8290	125	WRKRS AL OT RC		3A15	3A15	3A15	3A15	3A15														N					
8300	125	DO LOT THG OT RC	3A24	3A16	3A16	3A16	3A16	3A16														N					
8310	125	VRY GD EXP OT RC	3A25	3A17	3A17	3A17	3A17	3A17														N					
8320	125	MARRD OR ENGAGED	3A41	3A18	3A18	3A18	3A18	3A18					E													R	
8330	125	WHN WANT GT MARR	3A42	3A19	3A19	3A19	3A19	3A19					E														
8340	126	THGT LOT HAV CHL	3A43	3A20	3A20	3A20	3A20	3A20					E														
8350	126	# CHLDN WANT(6+)	3A44	3A21	3A21	3A21	3A21	3A21					E														
8360	126	IF -POP, MR CHLD	3A45	3A22	3A22	3A22	3A22	3A22					E														
8370	126	WHN 1ST CHL(5+Y)	3A46	3A23	3A23	3A23	3A23	3A23					E								M						
8380	126	GD JB LARG CORPS	3A27A	3A24A	3A24A	3A24A	3A24A	3A24A											K								
8390	127	GD JB LBR UNIONS	3A27B	3A24B	3A24B	3A24B	3A24B	3A24B											K								
8400	127	GD JB COLLG&UNIV	3A27C	3A24C	3A24C	3A24C	3A24C	3A24C		B									K								
8410	127	GD JB PBLC SCHOL	3A27D	3A24D	3A24D	3A24D	3A24D	3A24D		B									K								
8420	127	GD JB CHURCHES	3A27E	3A24E	3A24E	3A24E	3A24E	3A24E							G				K								
8430	127	GD JB NEWS MEDIA	3A27F	3A24F	3A24F	3A24F	3A24F	3A24F		B									K								
8440	127	GD JB PRES&ADMIN	3A27G	3A24G	3A24G	3A24G	3A24G	3A24G								H			K								
8450	128	GD JB CONGRESS	3A27H	3A24H	3A24H	3A24H	3A24H	3A24H								H			K								
8460	128	GD JB SUPRM CRT	3A27I	3A24I	3A24I	3A24I	3A24I	3A24I								H			K								
8470	128	GD JB JUSTC SYST	3A27J	3A24J	3A24J	3A24J	3A24J	3A24J								H			K								
8480	128	GD JB POLICE	3A27K	3A24K	3A24K	3A24K	3A24K	3A24K											K								
8490	128	GD JB MILITARY	3A27L	3A24L	3A24L	3A24L	3A24L	3A24L											K	L							
8500	128	MIL TOO MCH INFL	3A28	3A25	3A25	3A25	3A25	3A25												L							
8510	129	US TOO MCH$ MILT	3A29	3A26	3A26	3A26	3A26	3A26												L							
8520	129	12MO,#OCC PAINRF	3A48A	3A27A	3A27A	3A27A	3A27A	3A27A	A01B																		
8530	129	12MO,#OCC SLP PL	3A48B	3A27B	3A27B	3A27B	3A27B	3A27B	A01B																		
8540	129	12MO,#OCC AWK PL	3A48C	3A27C	3A27C	3A27C	3A27C	3A27C	A01B																		
8550	129	12MO,#OCC CALM P	3A48D	3A27D	3A27D	3A27D	3A27D	3A27D	A01B																		
8560	130	DAP SMK 1PCK CIG	(3A53A)	3A28A	3A28A	3A28A	3A28A	3A28A	A11A																		
8570	130	DAP TRY MRJ 1-2T	(3A53B)	3A28B	3A28B	3A28B	3A28B	3A28B	A11A																		
8580	130	DAP SMK MRJ OCCS	(3A53C)	3A28C	3A28C	3A28C	3A28C	3A28C	A11A																		
8590	130	DAP SMK MRJ REGL	(3A53D)	3A28D	3A28D	3A28D	3A28D	3A28D	A11A																		
8600	130	DAP TRY LSD 1-2T	(3A53E)	3A28E	3A28E	3A28E	3A28E	3A28E	A11A																		
8610	130	DAP TKG LSD REGL	(3A53F)	3A28F	3A28F	3A28F	3A28F	3A28F	A11A																		
8620	130	DAP TRY HRN 1-2T	(3A53G)	3A28G	3A28G	3A28G	3A28G	3A28G	A11A																		
8630	130	DAP TKG HRN OCCS	(3A53H)	3A28H	3A28H	3A28H	3A28H	3A28H	A11A																		
8640	131	DAP TKG HRN REGL	(3A53I)	3A28I	3A28I	3A28I	3A28I	3A28I	A11A																		

Item Reference Number	Page Loc. in this Volume	ITEM DESCRIPTION (ABBREVIATED)	QUESTIONNAIRE LOCATION BY YEAR (FORM, SECTION, AND QUESTION NUMBER)						SUBJECT AREA	
			1975	1976	1977	1978	1979	1980/1	A	B C D E F G H I J K L M N O P Q R S
8650	131	DAP TRY BRB 1-2T	(3A53J)	3A28J	3A28J	3A28J	3A28J	3A28J	A11A	
8660	131	DAP TKG BRB REGL	(3A53K)	3A28K	3A28K	3A28K	3A28K	3A28K	A11A	
8670	131	DAP TRY AMP 1-2T	(3A53L)	3A28L	3A28L	3A28L	3A28L	3A28L	A11A	
8680	131	DAP TKG AMP REGL	(3A53M)	3A28M	3A28M	3A28M	3A28M	3A28M	A11A	
8690	131	DAP TRY COC 1-2T	(3A53N)	3A28N	3A28N	3A28N	3A28N	3A28N	A11A	
8700	131	DAP TKG COC REGL	(3A53O)	3A28O	3A28O	3A28O	3A28O	3A28O	A11A	
8710	13†	DAP TRY DRK ALCL	(3A53P)	3A28P	3A28P	3A28P	3A28P	3A28P	A11A	
8720	132	DAP 1-2 DRK/DAY	(3A53Q)	3A28Q	3A28Q	3A28Q	3A28Q	3A28Q	A11A	
8730	132	DAP 4-5 DRK/DAY	(3A53R)	3A28R	3A28R	3A28R	3A28R	3A28R	A11A	
8740	132	DAP 5+ DRK WKNDS	(3A53S)	3A28S	3A28S	3A28S	3A28S	3A28S	A11A	
8750		OFT W PL TK MARJ	3A55A	5E07A	5E08A	5E08A			A02B	
8760		OFT W PL TK LSD	3A55B	5E07B	5E08B	5E08B			A02B	
8770		OFT W PL TK PSYC	3A55C	5E07C	5E08C	5E08C			A02B	
8780		OFT W PL TK QUAL		5E07D	5E08D	5E08D			A02B	
8790		OFT W PL TK BARB	3A55E	5E07E	5E08E	5E08E			A02B	
8800		OFT W PL TK TRQL	3A55F	5E07F	5E08F	5E08F			A02B	
8810		OFT W PL TK COKE	3A55G	5E07G	5E08G	5E08G			A02B	
8820		OFT W PL TK HRN	3A55H	5E07H	5E08H	5E08H			A02B	
8830		OFT W PL TK NARC	3A55I	5E07I	5E08I	5E08I			A02B	
8835		OFT W PL TK INHL		5E07J	5E08J	5E08J			A02B	
8840		OFT W PL TK ALCL	3A55K	5E07K	5E08K	5E08K			A02B	
8850	134	OFTN SHRTNS BRTH		(3D02A)	3D02A	3D02A	3D02A	3D02A		Q
8860	134	OFTN HEART BEATG		(3D02B)	3D02B	3D02B	3D02B	3D02B		Q
8870	134	OFTN SPLLS DZZNS		(3D02C)	3D02C	3D02C	3D02C	3D02C		Q
8880	134	OFTN HNDS TRMBLE		(3D02D)	3D02D	3D02D	3D02D	3D02D		Q
8890	134	OFTN HNDS SWEATG		(3D02E)	3D02E	3D02E	3D02E	3D02E		Q
8900	134	OFTN CDNT GT GNG		(3D02F)	3D02F	3D02F	3D02F	3D02F		Q
8910	135	12MO REDUCE ALCL		3D03A	3D03A	3D03A	3D03A	3D03A	A01I	
8920	135	12MO REDUCE CIG		3D03B	3D03B	3D03B	3D03B	3D03B	A01I	
8930	135	12MO REDUCE MARJ		3D03C	3D03C	3D03C	3D03C	3D03C	A01I	
8940	135	12MO REDUCE PSYC		3D03D	3D03D	3D03D	3D03D	3D03D	A01I	
8950	135	12MO REDUCE AMPH		3D03E	3D03E	3D03E	3D03E	3D03E	A01I	
8960		12MO REDUCE QUAL		3D03F	3D03F	3D03F			A01I	
8970	135	12MO REDUCE BARB		3D03G	3D03G	(3D03G)	3D03G	3D03G	A01I	
8980	135	12MO REDUCE COKE		3D03H	3D03H	3D03H	3D03H	3D03H	A01I	
8990	135	12MO REDUCE HRN		3D03I	3D03I	3D03I	3D03I	3D03I	A01I	
9000	136	12MO REDUCE NARC		3D03J	3D03J	3D03J	3D03J	3D03J	A01I	
9005	135	12MO REDUCE TRQL					3D03F	3D03F	A01I	
9010	136	NXT 12MOS USE MJ			3D04	3D04	3D04	3D04	A01B	
9020	136	CNCRN PSYCH DAMG		3D04A	3D04A	3D04A	3D04A	3D04A	A06A	
9030	136	CNCRN PHYSCL DMG		3D04B	3D04B	3D04B	3D04B	3D04B	A06A	
9040	136	CNCRN GT ARRESTD		3D04C	3D04C	3D04C	3D04C	3D04C	A06A	
9050	136	CNCRN BECOM ADCT		3D04D	3D04D	3D04D	3D04D	3D04D	A06A	
9060	136	AGST MY BELIEFS		3D04E	3D04E	3D04E	3D04E	3D04E	A06A	
9070	136	CNCRN LEGY&AMBTN		3D04F	3D04F	3D04F	3D04F	3D04F	A06A	
9080	136	CNCRN LOSS CNTRL		3D04G	3D04G	3D04G	3D04G	3D04G	A06A	
9090	136	MJ ->STRNGR DRGS		3D04H	3D04H	3D04H	3D04H	3D04H	A06A	
9100	136	MJ NOT ENJOYABLE		3D04I	3D04I	3D04I	3D04I	3D04I	A06A	
9110	136	PRNTS DISAPPROVE		3D04J	3D04J	3D04J	3D04J	3D04J	A06A	
9120	136	HS/WF DISAPPROVE		3D04K	3D04K	3D04K	3D04K	3D04K	A06A	
9130	136	DONT LIKE USERS		3D04L	3D04L	3D04L	3D04L	3D04L	A06A	
9140	136	FRNDS DNT USE IT		3D04M	3D04M	3D04M	3D04M	3D04M	A06A	
9150	136	PSSBLY BAD TRIP		3D04N	3D04N	3D04N	3D04N	3D04N	A06A	
9160	136	TOO EXPENSIVE			3D04O	3D04O	3D04O	3D04O	A06A	
9170	136	NOT AVAILABLE			3D04P	3D04P	3D04P	3D04P	A06A	
9180	136	NOT WNT GET HIGH			3D04Q	3D04Q	3D04Q	3D04Q	A06A	
9190	136	AL CS BEHV REGRT		3D05A	3D05A	3D05A	3D05A	3D05A	A07A	
9200	136	AL HURT REL PRNT		3D05A	3D05A	3D05A	3D05A	3D05A	A07A	
9210	136	AL HURT REL SPSE		3D05A	3D05A	3D05A	3D05A	3D05A	A07A	
9220	136	AL HURT REL FRND		3D05A	3D05A	3D05A	3D05A	3D05A	A07A	
9230	136	AL HURT REL TCHR		3D05A	3D05A	3D05A	3D05A	3D05A	A07A	
9240	136	AL INV PL BD INF		3D05A	3D05A	3D05A	3D05A	3D05A	A07A	
9250	136	AL HURT PERF JOB		3D05A	3D05A	3D05A	3D05A	3D05A	A07A	
9260	136	AL CAUS<INTERSTD		3D05A	3D05A	3D05A	3D05A	3D05A	A07A	
9270	136	AL CS<STABL EMTN		3D05A	3D05A	3D05A	3D05A	3D05A	A07A	
9280	136	AL CS HAV<ENERGY		3D05A	3D05A	3D05A	3D05A	3D05A	A07A	

Item Reference Number	Page Loc. in this Volume	ITEM DESCRIPTION (ABBREVIATED)	1975	1976	1977	1978	1979	1980/1	A	Subject Area (B C D E F G H I J K L M N O P Q R S)
9290	136	AL INTF THNK CLR		3D05A	3D05A	3D05A	3D05A	3D05A	A07A	
9300	136	AL BD PSYCH EFCT		3D05A	3D05A	3D05A	3D05A	3D05A	A07A	
9310	136	AL CS HEALTH BAD		3D05A	3D05A	3D05A	3D05A	3D05A	A07A	
9320	136	AL CS DRIV UNSAF		3D05A	3D05A	3D05A	3D05A	3D05A	A07A	
9330	136	AL GT TRBL W POL		3D05A	3D05A	3D05A	3D05A	3D05A	A07A	
9340	136	AL CS NO PROBLEM			3D05A	3D05A	3D05A	3D05A	A07A	
9350	136	AL NEVER USED DG			3D05A	3D05A	3D05A	3D05A	A07A	
9360	136	MJ CS BEHV REGRT		3D05M	3D05M	3D05M	3D05M	3D05M	A07A	
9370	136	MJ HURT REL PRNT		3D05M	3D05M	3D05M	3D05M	3D05M	A07A	
9380	136	MJ HURT REL SPSE		3D05M	3D05M	3D05M	3D05M	3D05M	A07A	
9390	136	MJ HURT REL FRND		3D05M	3D05M	3D05M	3D05M	3D05M	A07A	
9400	136	MJ HURT REL TCHR		3D05M	3D05M	3D05M	3D05M	3D05M	A07A	
9410	136	MJ INV PL BD INF		3D05M	3D05M	3D05M	3D05M	3D05M	A07A	
9420	136	MJ HURT PERF JOB		3D05M	3D05M	3D05M	3D05M	3D05M	A07A	
9430	136	MJ CAUS<INTERSTD		3D05M	3D05M	3D05M	3D05M	3D05M	A07A	
9440	136	MJ CS<STABL EMTN		3D05M	3D05M	3D05M	3D05M	3D05M	A07A	
9450	136	MJ CS HAV<ENERGY		3D05M	3D05M	3D05M	3D05M	3D05M	A07A	
9460	136	MJ INTF THNK CLR		3D05M	3D05M	3D05M	3D05M	3D05M	A07A	
9470	136	MJ BD PSYCH EFCT		3D05M	3D05M	3D05M	3D05M	3D05M	A07A	
9480	136	MJ CS HEALTH BAD		3D05M	3D05M	3D05M	3D05M	3D05M	A07A	
9490	136	MJ CS DRIV UNSAF		3D05M	3D05M	3D05M	3D05M	3D05M	A07A	
9500	136	MJ GT TRBL W POL		3D05M	3D05M	3D05M	3D05M	3D05M	A07A	
9510	136	MJ CS NO PROBLEM			3D05M	3D05M	3D05M	3D05M	A07A	
9520	136	MJ NEVER USED DG			3D05M	3D05M	3D05M	3D05M	A07A	
9530	137	OT CS BEHV REGRT		3D05O	3D05O	3D05O	3D05O	3D05O	A07A	
9540	137	OT HURT REL PRNT		3D05O	3D05O	3D05O	3D05O	3D05O	A07A	
9550	137	OT HURT REL SPSE		3D05O	3D05O	3D05O	3D05O	3D05O	A07A	
9560	137	OT HURT REL FRND		3D05O	3D05O	3D05O	3D05O	3D05O	A07A	
9570	137	OT HURT REL TCHR		3D05O	3D05O	3D05O	3D05O	3D05O	A07A	
9580	137	OT INV PL BD INF		3D05O	3D05O	3D05O	3D05O	3D05O	A07A	
9590	137	OT HURT PERF JOB		3D05O	3D05O	3D05O	3D05O	3D05O	A07A	
9600	137	OT CAUS<INTERSTD		3D05O	3D05O	3D05O	3D05O	3D05O	A07A	
9610	137	OT CS<STABL EMTN		3D05O	3D05O	3D05O	3D05O	3D05O	A07A	
9620	137	OT CS HAV<ENERGY		3D05O	3D05O	3D05O	3D05O	3D05O	A07A	
9630	137	OT INTF THNK CLR		3D05O	3D05O	3D05O	3D05O	3D05O	A07A	
9640	137	OT BD PSYCH EFCT		3D05O	3D05O	3D05O	3D05O	3D05O	A07A	
9650	137	OT CS HEALTH BAD		3D05O	3D05O	3D05O	3D05O	3D05O	A07A	
9660	137	OT CS DRIV UNSAF		3D05O	3D05O	3D05O	3D05O	3D05O	A07A	
9670	137	OT GT TRBL W POL		3D05O	3D05O	3D05O	3D05O	3D05O	A07A	
9680	137	OT CS NO PROBLEM			3D05O	3D05O	3D05O	3D05O	A07A	
9690	137	OT NEVER USED DG			3D05O	3D05O	3D05O	3D05O	A07A	
9700	137	PRVNT POL TOO >$		3E02A	3E02A	3E02A	3E02A	3E02A		F
9710	137	PRVNT POL CST JB		3E02B	3E02B	3E02B	3E02B	3E02B		F
9720	137	PRVNT POL PPL DK		3E02C	3E02C	3E02C	3E02C	3E02C		F
9730	138	PRVNT POL -ENUF		3E02D	3E02D	3E02D	3E02D	3E02D		F
9740	138	PRVNT POL USELSS		3E02E	3E02E	3E02E	3E02E	3E02E		F
9750	138	FUTR,HAV2 CNSUM<		3E03	3E03	3E03	3E03	3E03		F
9760	138	GOV HP PRB POPL	3A32N	3E04A	3E04A	3E04A	3E04A	3E04A		E H
9770	138	GOV NO POP PLCY	3A32A	3E04B	3E04B	3E04B	3E04B	3E04B		E H
9780	138	STR OVPOP,LMT FM	3A32B	3E04C	3E04C	3E04C	3E04C	3E04C		E
9790	139	PRV OVPOP,NO CHL	3A32C	3E04D	3E04D	3E04D	3E04D	3E04D		E
9800	139	HISCH INS BRTH C	3A32E	3E04E	3E04E	3E04E	3E04E	3E04E		B E
9810	139	BRTH CNT IMMORAL	3A32I	3E04F	3E04F	3E04F	3E04F	3E04F		E
9820	139	GOV BRTHC NO CST	3A32M	3E04G	3E04G	3E04G	3E04G	3E04G		E H
9830	139	US POP SZ LRGER	3A34	3E06	3E05	3E05	3E05	3E05		E
9840		GVNG FOOD O CNTY	3A33	3E05						E O
9850	139	WRLD POP SZ LRGR	3A35	3E07	3E08	3E08	3E08	3E08		E
9860	140	HAD SEX ED IN HS		3E09	3E09	3E09	3E09	3E09		D E
9870	140	STUDY BC IN HS		3E10	3E09	3E09	3E09	3E09		D E
9871	199	SM1 SCL ROB <$50		4E11A	3E10A	3E10A	5E06A	5E08A†		R S
9872	199	SM1 SCL ROB >$50		4E11B	3E10B	3E10B	5E06B	5E08B†		R S
9873	199	SM1 SCL DMG PRTY		4E11C	3E10C	3E10C	5E06C	5E08C†		R S
9874	199	SM1 SCL IN U W/W		4E11D	3E10D	3E10D	5E06D	5E08D†		R S
9875	199	SM1 SCL TH U W/W		4E11E	3E10E	3E10E	5E06E	5E08E†		R S
9876	200	SM1 SCL IN U -WP		4E11F	3E10F	3E10F	5E06F	5E08F†		R S
9877	200	SM1 SCL TH U W/I		4E11G	3E10G	3E10G	5E06G	5E08G†		R S

† 5E13A-G in 1981.

Item Reference Number	Page Loc. in this Volume	ITEM DESCRIPTION (ABBREVIATED)	QUESTIONNAIRE LOCATION BY YEAR (FORM, SECTION, AND QUESTION NUMBER) 1975	1976	1977	1978	1979	1980/1	SUBJECT AREA (A B C D E F G H I J K L M N O P Q R S)
9880	142	DK DO W LEISR TM			3E11A		3E11A	3E11A	C
9890	142	TM QUIK/LEIS HRS			3E11B		3E11B	3E11B	C
9900	142	WASTE LEIS TIME			3E11C		3E11C	3E11C	C
9910	142	ENUF TIME FR THG			3E11D		3E11D	3E11D	C
9920		R WL VOTE IN '76		3E11					H
9940	145	FUTR CNTRY WORSE	4A01	4A02	4A02	4A02	4A02	4A02	I
9950	145	FUTR WORLD WORSE	4A02	4A03	4A03	4A03	4A03	4A03	I
9960	145	FUTR R LIFE WRSE	4A03	4A04	4A04	4A04	4A04	4A04	I
9970	145	PLLTN INCR IN US	4A22A	4A06A	4A06A	4A06A	4A06A	4A06A	F
9980	146	PLLTN NT SO DANG	4A22B	4A06B	4A06B	4A06B	4A06B	4A06B	F
9990	146	PLLTN NEC 4 GRTH	4A22C	4A06C	4A06C	4A06C	4A06C	4A06C	F
10000	146	INDVL RESP 4 ENV	4A22D	4A06D	4A06D	4A06D	4A06D	4A06D	F
10010	146	GOVT RESP 4 ENV	4A22E	4A06E	4A06E	4A06E	4A06E	4A06E	F H
10020	146	GOVT TAX PLLTRS	4A22F	4A06F	4A06F	4A06F	4A06F	4A06F	F H
10030	146	GOVT BAN DSPSBLE	4A22G	4A06G	4A06G	4A06G	4A06G	4A06G	F H
10040	147	TV COMM CRT NDS	4A22H	4A06H	4A06H	4A06H	4A06H	4A06H	B F
10050	147	TV COMMRCLS GOOD	4A22I	4A06I	4A06I	4A06I	4A06I	4A06I	B F
10060	147	FAM BUYS THG -ND	4A22L	4A06J	4A06J	4A06J	4A06J	4A06J	F
	180			5A18I	5A18I	5A18I	5A18I		F
10070	147	POL SLVD BY 2000	4A22M	4A06K	4A06K	4A06K	4A06K	4A06K	F
10080	147	R EFRT 2 HLP ENV	4A23	4A07	4A07	4A07	4A07	4A07	F
10090	148	JOB IMPC SE RSLT	4A08A	4A08A	4A08A	4A08A	4A08A	4A08A	C
10100	148	JOB IMPC STATUS	4A08B	4A08B	4A08B	4A08B	4A08B	4A08B	C
10110	148	JOB IMPC INTRSTG	4A08C	4A08C	4A08C	4A08C	4A08C	4A08C	C
10120	148	JOB IMPC ADVNCMT	4A08D	4A08D	4A08D	4A08D	4A08D	4A08D	C
10130	148	JOB IMPC HLP OTH	4A08E	4A08E	4A08E	4A08E	4A08E	4A08E	C ... O
10140	148	JOB IMPC EARN $	4A08F	4A08F	4A08F	4A08F	4A08F	4A08F	C F
10150	148	JOB IMPC CREATVY	4A08G	4A08G	4A08G	4A08G	4A08G	4A08G	C
10160	149	JOB IMPC UTILITY	4A08H	4A08H	4A08H	4A08H	4A08H	4A08H	C
10170	149	JOB IMPC MK FRND	4A08I	4A08I	4A08I	4A08I	4A08I	4A08I	C M
10180	149	JOB IMPC USE SKL	4A08J	4A08J	4A08J	4A08J	4A08J	4A08J	C
10190	149	JOB IMPC WRTHWLE	4A08K	4A08K	4A08K	4A08K	4A08K	4A08K	C ... O
10200	149	JOB IMPC VACATN	4A08L	4A08L	4A08L	4A08L	4A08L	4A08L	C
10210	149	JOB IMPC MK DCSN	4A08M	4A08M	4A08M	4A08M	4A08M	4A08M	C
10220	149	JOB IMPC FRE TIM		4A08N	4A08N	4A08N	4A08N	4A08N	C
10230	150	JOB IMPC NO MVNG	4A08O	4A08O	4A08O	4A08O	4A08O	4A08O	C
10240	150	JOB IMPC NO SPRV	4A08P	4A08P	4A08P	4A08P	4A08P	4A08P	C
10250	150	JOB IMPC SECURTY	4A08Q	4A08Q	4A08Q	4A08Q	4A08Q	4A08Q	C
10260	150	JOB IMPC LRNING	4A08R	4A08R	4A08R	4A08R	4A08R	4A08R	B C
10270	150	JOB IMPC BE SELF	4A08S	4A08S	4A08S	4A08S	4A08S	4A08S	C
10280	150	JOB IMPC RESPECT	4A08T	4A08T	4A08T	4A08T	4A08T	4A08T	C
10290	150	JOB IMPC CNTC PL	4A08U	4A08U	4A08U	4A08U	4A08U	4A08U	C M
10300	151	JOB IMPC EZ PACE		4A08V	4A08V	4A08V	4A08V	4A08V	C
10310	151	JOB IMPC HRD PRB		4A08W	4A08W	4A08W	4A08W	4A08W	C
10320	151	KIND OF WORK @30	4A09	4A09	4A09	4A09	4A09	4A09	C
10330	152	R SURE GT THS WK		4A10	4A10	4A10	4A10	4A10	C
10340	152	R SURE WK GD CHC		4A11	4A11	4A11	4A11	4A11	C
10350	152	R THNK WK BE SAT		4A12	4A12	4A12	4A12	4A12	C ... P
10360	152	JOB OBSTC RELGN		4A13A	4A13A	4A13A	4A13A	4A13A	C G
10370	152	JOB OBSTC SEX		4A13B	4A13B	4A13B	4A13B	4A13B	C D
10380	152	JOB OBSTC RACE		4A13C	4A13C	4A13C	4A13C	4A13C	C ... N
10390	152	JOB OBSTC BKGRND		4A13D	4A13D	4A13D	4A13D	4A13D	C ... R
10400	153	JOB OBSTC POL VW		4A13E	4A13E	4A13E	4A13E	4A13E	C H
10410	153	JOB OBSTC EDUCTN		4A13F	4A13F	4A13F	4A13F	4A13F	B C
10420	153	JOB OBSTC -VOC T		4A13G	4A13G	4A13G	4A13G	4A13G	C
10430	153	JOB OBSTC -ABLTY		4A13H	4A13H	4A13H	4A13H	4A13H	C ... R
10440	153	JOB OBSTC - PULL		4A13I	4A13I	4A13I	4A13I	4A13I	C ... R
10450	153	JOB OBSTC -WK HD		4A13J	4A13J	4A13J	4A13J	4A13J	C ... Q
10460	153	JOB OBSTC -CONFM		4A13K	4A13K	4A13K	4A13K	4A13K	C ... Q
10470	154	FEW GD MAR, ? IT	4A11A	4A15A	4A15A	4A15A	4A15A	4A15A	D
10480	154	GD LIV TG BF MRG	4A11B	4A15B	4A15B	4A15B	4A15B	4A15B	D E
10490	154	1 PRTNR = RSTRCTVE	4A11C	4A15C	4A15C	4A15C	4A15C	4A15C	D E
10500	154	JB INTFR REL HBD	4A11E	4A15D	4A15D	4A15D	4A15D	4A15D	C D
10510	154	JB DVLP WF PERSN	4A11G	4A15E	4A15E	4A15E	4A15E	4A15E	C D
10520	154	RS CHLD + FR MAN	4A11H	4A15F	4A15F	4A15F	4A15F	4A15F	D
10530	155	MO SH B W CHL>TM	4A11I	4A15G	4A15G	4A15G	4A15G	4A15G	D

Item Reference Number	Page Loc. in this Volume	ITEM DESCRIPTION (ABBREVIATED)	QUESTIONNAIRE LOCATION BY YEAR (FORM, SECTION, AND QUESTION NUMBER)						SUBJECT AREA																		
			1975	1976	1977	1978	1979	1980/1	A	B	C	D	E	F	G	H	I	J	K	L	M	N	O	P	Q	R	S
10540	155	WF WK,HBD SHD>HW	4A11K	4A15H	4A15H	4A15H	4A15H	4A15H			C	D															
10550	155	#HRS TV/DAY/5+		4A16	4A16	4A16	4A16	4A16		B																	
10560	155	#BKS LAST YR/10+		4A17	4A17	4A17	4A17	4A17		B																	
10570	156	>INFLC LARG CORP	4A14A	4A19A	4A19A	4A19A	4A19A	4A19A											K								
10580	156	>INFLC LBR UNION	4A14B	4A19B	4A19B	4A19B	4A19B	4A19B											K								
10590	156	>INFLC CHURCHES	4A14C	4A19C	4A19C	4A19C	4A19C	4A19C							G				K								
10600	156	>INFLC NEWS MDIA	4A14D	4A19D	4A19D	4A19D	4A19D	4A19D		B									K								
10610	156	>INFLC PRES&ADMN	4A14E	4A19E	4A19E	4A19E	4A19E	4A19E								H			K								
10620	156	>INFLC CONGRESS	4A14F	4A19F	4A19F	4A19F	4A19F	4A19F								H			K								
10630	157	>INFLC SUPRM CRT	4A14G	4A19G	4A19G	4A19G	4A19G	4A19G								H			K								
10640	157	>INFLC JUSTC SYS	4A14H	4A19H	4A19H	4A19H	4A19H	4A19H								H			K								
10650	157	>INFLC POLICE	4A14I	4A19I	4A19I	4A19I	4A19I	4A19I											K								
10660	157	>INFLC MILITARY	4A14J	4A19J	4A19J	4A19J	4A19J	4A19J											K	L							
10760	159	LAW 4 SMK TOBPUB			4A20K	4A20K	4A20K	4A20K	A13A																		
10770		ILGL AD SMK CIG		4A20A					A13A																		
10780	157	ILGL AD MRJ PRIV		4A20B	4A20A	4A20A	4A20A	4A20A	A13A																		
10790	157	ILGL AD MRJ PUBL		4A20C	4A20B	4A20B	4A20B	4A20B	A13A																		
10800	158	ILGL AD LSD PRIV		4A20D	4A20C	4A20C	4A20C	4A20C	A13A																		
10810	158	ILGL AD LSD PUBL		4A20E	4A20D	4A20D	4A20D	4A20D	A13A																		
10820	158	ILGL AD AMP PRIV		4A20F	4A20E	4A20E	4A20E	4A20E	A13A																		
10830	158	ILGL AD AMP PUBL		4A20G	4A20F	4A20F	4A20F	4A20F	A13A																		
10840	158	ILGL AD HRN PRIV		4A20H	4A20G	4A20G	4A20G	4A20G	A13A																		
10850	158	ILGL AD HRN PUBL		4A20I	4A20H	4A20H	4A20H	4A20H	A13A																		
10860	158	ILGL AD DRNK PRV		4A20J	4A20I	4A20I	4A20I	4A20I	A13A																		
10870	158	ILGL AD DRNK PBL		4A20K	4A20J	4A20J	4A20J	4A20J	A13A																		
10880	159	CRIME 2 USE MARJ	4A32	4A21	4A21	4A21	4A21	4A21	A13C																		
10890	159	LEGAL 2 SELL MRJ	4A33	4A22	4A22	4A22	4A22	4A22	A13C																		
10900	159	USE<MJ IF LEGAL	4A34	4A23	4A23	4A23	4A23	4A23	A13C																		
10910	159	CMP SATFD W/JOB		4D02	4D02	4D02	4D02	4D02			C													P			
10920	160	I CNT CHNG WORLD	4A28A	4D03A	4D03A	4D03A	4D03A	4D03A									I	J							Q		
10930	160	SOCTY WONT LAST	4A28B	4D03B	4D03B	4D03B	4D03B	4D03B						F				J									
10940	160	THG TUF,TCHN SLV	4A28C	4D03C	4D03C	4D03C	4D03C	4D03C									I	J							Q		
10950	160	NO HOPE 4 WORLD	4A28D	4D03D	4D03D	4D03D	4D03D	4D03D										J							Q		
10960	160	WNDR PURPS 2 LIF	4A28E	4D03E	4D03E	4D03E	4D03E	4D03E										J							Q		
10970	160	WRLD UPHVL 10 YR	4A28F	4D03F	4D03F	4D03F	4D03F	4D03F										J							Q		
10980	161	ANNIHLTN IN LFTM	4A28G	4D03G	4D03G	4D03G	4D03G	4D03G										J							Q		
10990	161	HMN RCE RSILIENT	4A28H	4D03H	4D03H	4D03H	4D03H	4D03H										J							Q		
11000	161	#X BEER/LIFETIME		4D04A	4D04A	4D04A	4D04A	4D04A	A01A																		
11010	161	#X BEER/LAST12MO		4D04B	4D04B	4D04B	4D04B	4D04B	A01B																		
11020	161	#X BEER/LAST30DA		4D04C	4D04C	4D04C	4D04C	4D04C	A01C																		
11030	161	5+BR/LST2WK,10+X		4D05	4D05	4D05	4D05	4D05	A01D																		
11040	162	#X WINE/LIFETIME		4D06A	4D06A	4D06A	4D06A	4D06A	A01A																		
11050	162	#X WINE/LAST12MO		4D06B	4D06B	4D06B	4D06B	4D06B	A01B																		
11060	162	#X WINE/LAST30DA		4D06C	4D06C	4D06C	4D06C	4D06C	A01C																		
11070	162	#X 20OZ+WN/2WK		4D07	4D07	4D07	4D07	4D07	A01D																		
11080	162	#X LIQR/LIFETIME		4D08A	4D08A	4D08A	4D08A	4D08A	A01A																		
11090	163	#X LIQR/LAST12MO		4D08B	4D08B	4D08B	4D08B	4D08B	A01B																		
11100	163	#X LIQR/LAST30DA		4D08C	4D08C	4D08C	4D08C	4D08C	A01C																		
11110	163	#X 5+LIQ/LST 2WK		4D09	4D09	4D09	4D09	4D09	A01D																		
11120	163	MLTRY GET AHEAD		4E01A	4E01A	4E01A	4E01A	4E01A												L							
11130	163	MLTRY MORE ED		4E01B	4E01B	4E01B	4E01B	4E01B		B										L							
11140	163	MLTRY ADVNC RESP		4E01C	4E01C	4E01C	4E01C	4E01C												L							
11150	164	MLTRY >FLFLLG JB		4E01D	4E01D	4E01D	4E01D	4E01D			C									L							
11160	164	MLTRY IDEAS HERD		4E01E	4E01E	4E01E	4E01E	4E01E												L							
11170	164	EXTNT MLTRY JSTC		4E02	4E02	4E02	4E02	4E02												L							
11180	164	MLTRY DSCRM WOMN		4E03	4E03	4E03	4E03	4E03				D								L							
11190	164	MLTRY DSCRM BLKS		4E04	4E04	4E04	4E04	4E04												L		N					
11200	164	>FAIR MLTRY CVLN		4E05	4E05	4E05	4E05	4E05												L							
11210		-MLTRY COUP U.S.		4E06	4E06												H				L							
11220	165	NT VOL 4 NEC WAR		4E07	4E07	4E06	4E06	4E06												L							
11230	165	P'IDEA OF DO LIF	4A27A	4E08A	4E08A	4E07A	4E07A	4E07A													M						
11240	165	P'IDEA OF LSR TM	4A27B	4E08B	4E08B	4E07B	4E07B	4E07B			C										M						
11250	165	P'IDEA OF CLTHES	4A27C	4E08C	4E08C	4E07C	4E07C	4E07C													M						
11260	165	P'IDEA OF SPND $	4A27D	4E08D	4E08D	4E07D	4E07D	4E07D													M						
11270	165	P'IDEA OF DATE	4A27E	4E08E	4E08E	4E07E	4E07E	4E07E													M						
11280	166	P'IDEA OF OK DRK	4A27F	4E08F	4E08F	4E07F	4E07F	4E07F													M						

Item Reference Number	Page Loc. in this Volume	ITEM DESCRIPTION (ABBREVIATED)	QUESTIONNAIRE LOCATION BY YEAR (FORM, SECTION, AND QUESTION NUMBER)						SUBJECT AREA																		
			1975	1976	1977	1978	1979	1980/1	A	B	C	D	E	F	G	H	I	J	K	L	M	N	O	P	Q	R	S
11290	166	P'IDEA OF OK MRJ	4A27G	4E08G	4E08G	4E07G	4E07G	4E07G													M						
11300	166	P'IDEA OF OK DRG	4A27H	4E08H	4E08H	4E07H	4E07H	4E07H													M						
11310	166	P'IDEA OF VALUES	4A27I	4E08I	4E08I	4E07I	4E07I	4E07I													M						
11320	166	P'IDEA OF EDUC	4A27J	4E08J	4E08J	4E07J	4E07J	4E07J		B											M						
11330	166	P'IDEA OF SX RLS	4A27K	4E08K	4E08K	4E07K	4E07K	4E07K				D									M						
11340	166	P'IDEA OF ECLOGY	4A27L	4E08L	4E08L	4E07L	4E07L	4E07L						F							M						
11350	167	P'IDEA OF RCL IS	4A27M	4E08M	4E08M	4E07M	4E07M	4E07M													M	N					
11360	167	P'IDEA OF RLGION	4A27N	4E08N	4E08N	4E07N	4E07N	4E07N							G						M						
11370	167	P'IDEA OF PLTICS	4A27O	4E08O	4E08O	4E07O	4E07O	4E07O								H					M						
11380		PRNT DAP CIGS	4A35A	4E09A	4E09A	4E08A	4E08A		A12A																		
11390		PRNT DAP TRY MRJ	4A35B	4E09B	4E09B	4E08B	4E08B		A12A																		
11400		PRNT DAP MJ OCC	4A35C	4E09C	4E09C	4E08C	4E08C		A12A																		
11410		PRNT DAP MJ REG	4A35D	4E09D	4E09D	4E08D	4E08D		A12A																		
11420		PRNT DAP TRY LSD	4A35E	4E09E	4E09E	4E08E	4E08E		A12A																		
11430		PRNT DAP TRY AMP	4A35F	4E09F	4E09F	4E08F	4E08F		A12A																		
11440		PRNT DAP 1-2DR/D	4A35G	4E09G	4E09G	4E08G	4E08G		A12A																		
11450		PRNT DAP 4-5DR/D	4A35H	4E09H	4E09H	4E08H	4E08H		A12A																		
11460		PRNT DAP 5+DR/WE	4A35I	4E09I	4E09I	4E08I	4E08I		A12A																		
11470	167	FRD DAP CIGS			4E10A		4E09A	4E08A	A12B																		
11480	167	FRD DAP TRY MARJ			4E10B		4E09B	4E08B	A12B																		
11490	167	FRD DAP MJ OCC			4E10C		4E09C	4E08C	A12B																		
11500	167	FRD DAP MJ REG			4E10D		4E09D	4E08D	A12B																		
11510	168	FRD DAP TRY LSD			4E10E		4E09E	4E08E	A12B																		
11520	168	FRD DAP TRY AMP			4E10F		4E09F	4E08F	A12B																		
11530	168	FRD DAP 1-2DR/DA			4E10G		4E09G	4E08G	A12B																		
11540	168	FRD DAP 4-5DR/DA			4E10H		4E09H	4E08H	A12B																		
11550	168	FRD DAP 5+DR/WKD			4E10I		4E09I	4E08I	A12B																		
11560	170	H&W WK,WF AL HWK			4E11A	4E10A	4E10A	4E10A				D															
11570	170	H&W WK,WF MS HWK			4E11B	4E10B	4E10B	4E10B				D															
11580	170	H&W WK,DO = HWRK			4E11C	4E10C	4E10C	4E10C				D															
11590	170	H&W WK,HB MS HWK			4E11D	4E10D	4E10D	4E10D				D															
11600	170	H&W WK,HB AL HWK			4E11E	4E10E	4E10E	4E10E				D															
11610	171	H&W WK+CH,W CHCR			4E12A	4E11A	4E11A	4E11A				D															
11620	171	H&W WK+CH,W>CHCR			4E12B	4E11B	4E11B	4E11B				D															
11630	171	H&W WK+CH,=CHCAR			4E12C	4E11C	4E11C	4E11C				D															
11640	171	H&W WK+CH,H>CHCR			4E12D	4E11D	4E11D	4E11D				D															
11650	171	H&W WK+CH,H CHCR			4E12E	4E11E	4E11E	4E11E				D															
11660	172	WR/NT NUCLER WAR	5A04A	5A03A	5A03A	5A03A	5A03A	5A03A										J								
11670	172	WR/NT POP GROWTH	5A04B	5A03B	5A03B	5A03B	5A03B	5A03B					E					J								
11680	172	WR/NT CRIME&VLNC	5A04C	5A03C	5A03C	5A03C	5A03C	5A03C										J								
11690	172	WR/NT POLLUTION	5A04D	5A03D	5A03D	5A03D	5A03D	5A03D						F				J								
11700	172	WR/NT ENRGY SHRT	5A04E	5A03E	5A03E	5A03E	5A03E	5A03E						F				J								
11710	173	WR/NT RACE RELTN	5A04F	5A03F	5A03F	5A03F	5A03F	5A03F										J				N					
11720	173	WR/NT HNGR&PVRTY	5A04G	5A03G	5A03G	5A03G	5A03G	5A03G						F				J								
11730	173	WR/NT USE OPN LD	5A04H	5A03H	5A03H	5A03H	5A03H	5A03H						F				J								
11740	173	WR/NT URBN DECAY	5A04I	5A03I	5A03I	5A03I	5A03I	5A03I										J								
11750	173	WR/NT ECON PRBLM	5A04J	5A03J	5A03J	5A03J	5A03J	5A03J										J								
11760	173	WR/NT DRUG ABUSE	5A04K	5A03K	5A03K	5A03K	5A03K	5A03K										J								
11770	173	XPRC MK R GD SPS		5A04A	5A04A	5A04A	5A04A	5A04A				D															
11780	174	XPRC MK R GD PRT		5A04B	5A04B	5A04B	5A04B	5A04B				D															
11790	174	XPRC MK R GD WKR		5A04C	5A04C	5A04C	5A04C	5A04C			C																
11800	174	PLC WRK LG CORPN	5A09A	5A05A	5A05A	5A05A	5A05A	5A05A			C																
11810	174	PLC WRK SM BSNSS	5A09B	5A05B	5A05B	5A05B	5A05B	5A05B			C																
11820	174	PLC WRK GVT AGCY	5A09C	5A05C	5A05C	5A05C	5A05C	5A05C			C					H											
11830	174	PLC WRK MLTY SVC	5A09D	5A05D	5A05D	5A05D	5A05D	5A05D			C									L							
11840	174	PLC WRK SCH/UNIV	5A09E	5A05E	5A05E	5A05E	5A05E	5A05E		B	C																
11850	175	PLC WRK PLC DEPT	5A09F	5A05F	5A05F	5A05F	5A05F	5A05F			C																
11860	175	PLC WRK SOC SVCS	5A09G	5A05G	5A05G	5A05G	5A05G	5A05G			C													O				
11870	175	PLC WRK SML GRP	5A09H	5A05H	5A05H	5A05H	5A05H	5A05H			C																
11880	175	PLC WRK SLF EMPL	5A09I	5A05I	5A05I	5A05I	5A05I	5A05I			C																
11890	175	RCL CNTCT SCHOOL		5A07A	5A07A	5A07A	5A07A	5A07A		B													N					
11900	175	RCL CNTCT NGHBHD		5A07B	5A07B	5A07B	5A07B	5A07B															N					
11910	176	RCL CNTCT CHURCH		5A07C	5A07C	5A07C	5A07C	5A07C							G								N					
11920	176	RCL CNTCT SPORTS		5A07D	5A07D	5A07D	5A07D	5A07D															N					
11930	176	RCL CNTCT CLUBS		5A07E	5A07E	5A07E	5A07E	5A07E															N					
11940	176	RCL CNTCT JOB		5A07F	5A07F	5A07F	5A07F	5A07F			C											N						

Item Reference Number	Page Loc. in this Volume	ITEM DESCRIPTION (ABBREVIATED)	QUESTIONNAIRE LOCATION BY YEAR (FORM, SECTION, AND QUESTION NUMBER)						SUBJECT AREA	
			1975	1976	1977	1978	1979	1980/1	A	B C D E F G H I J K L M N O P Q R S
11950	176	B/W RLTNS WRSE	5A15	5A08	5A08	5A08	5A08	5A08		N
11960	176	DNT HV DRVR LCNS	5A22	5A09	5A09	5A09	5A09	5A09		F
11970	176	DONT OWN CAR	5A23	5A10	5A10	5A10	5A10	5A10		F
11980	177	NEVR USE OTHS CR	5A24	5A11	5A11	5A11	5A11	5A11		F
11990	177	R CUT DRIVING	5A32	5A12	5A12	5A12	5A12	5A12		F
12000	177	R CUT ELECTRICTY	5A33	5A13	5A13	5A13	5A13	5A13		F
12010	177	RDCE HEAT R'S HM	5A34	5A14	5A14	5A14	5A14	5A14		F
12020	177	ENJOY SHOPPING	5A35A	5A15A	5A15A	5A15A	5A15A	5A15A		F
12030	177	CARE LATST FASHN	5A35B	5A15B	5A15B	5A15B	5A15B	5A15B		F
12040	178	CR FAM HV NBR HV	5A35C	5A15C	5A15C	5A15C	5A15C	5A15C		F
12050	178	XPCT 2 OWN>PRNTS	5A36	5A16	5A16	5A16	5A16	5A16		F
12060	178	LST CNT OWN>PRNT	5A37	5A17	5A17	5A17	5A17	5A17		F
12070	178	WRRY ABT OW CTRY	5A19A	5A18A	5A18A	5A18A	5A18A	5A18A		O
12080	178	BTTR IF CTZ WRLD	5A19C	5A18B	5A18B	5A18B	5A18B	5A18B		O
12090	179	-SYMP TWD STARVG	5A19E	5A18C	5A18C	5A18C	5A18C	5A18C		F O
12100	179	MNRTY NT MY BSNS	5A19F	5A18D	5A18D	5A18D	5A18D	5A18D		N O
12110	179	UPST PL TR -FAIR	5A19G	5A18E	5A18E	5A18E	5A18E	5A18E		O
12120	179	HELP POOR W MY $	5A19I	5A18F	5A18F	5A18F	5A18F	5A18F		O
12130	179	-MY PRB OT ND HP	5A19K	5A18G	5A18G	5A18G	5A18G	5A18G		O
12140	179	RB CHNG ETG HABT		5A18H	5A18H	5A18H	5A18H	5A18H		F O
12150	180	FULLR LVS IF MRY	5A12A	5A18J	5A18J	5A18J	5A18J	5A18J		D
12160	180	ENCRG=INDP DT/SN	5A12B	5A18K	5A18K	5A18K	5A18K	5A18K		D
12170	180	BNG MOTH V FULFL	5A12D	5A18L	5A18L	5A18L	5A18L	5A18L		D
12180	180	FTHR>TIME W CHLD	5A12G	5A18M	5A18M	5A18M	5A18M	5A18M		D
12190	180	HSB MAK IMP DCSN	5A12H	5A18N	5A18N	5A18N	5A18N	5A18N		D
12200	181	CTB TO UNTD FUND	5A20A	5A20A	5A20A	5A20A	5A20A	5A20A		O
12210	181	CTB TO INTL RELF	5A20B	5A20B	5A20B	5A20B	5A20B	5A20B		O
12220	181	CTB TO MNRTY GRP	5A20C	5A20C	5A20C	5A20C	5A20C	5A20C		N O
12230	181	CTB TO RELGS ORG	5A20D	5A20D	5A20D	5A20D	5A20D	5A20D		G O
12240	182	CTB TO PLTCL PTY	5A20E	5A20E	5A20E	5A20E	5A20E	5A20E		H O
12250	182	CTB TO CTZN LBBY	5A20F	5A20F	5A20F	5A20F	5A20F	5A20F		H I O
12260	182	CTB TO VS DISEAS	5A20G	5A20G	5A20G	5A20G	5A20G	5A20G		O
12270	182	CTB TO POP PRBMS	5A20H	5A20H	5A20H	5A20H	5A20H	5A20H		E O
12280	182	CTB TO ENVIR PBM	5A20I	5A20I	5A20I	5A20I	5A20I	5A20I		F O
12290	183	DSCM WN COLLG ED	5A21A	5A22A	5A22A	5A22A	5A22A	5A22A		B D
12300	183	DSCM WN LDRSHP	5A21B	5A22B	5A22B	5A22B	5A22B	5A22B		D
12310	183	DSCM WN EXEC/BSN	5A21C	5A22C	5A22C	5A22C	5A22C	5A22C		C D
12320	183	DSCM WN TOP/PRFN	5A21D	5A22D	5A22D	5A22D	5A22D	5A22D		C D
12330	183	DSCM WN SKL LABR	5A21E	5A22E	5A22E	5A22E	5A22E	5A22E		C D
12340	183	DSCM WN PLTCL OF	5A21F	5A22F	5A22F	5A22F	5A22F	5A22F		D H
12350	184	DSCM WN =PAY =WK	5A21G	5A22G	5A22G	5A22G	5A22G	5A22G		C D
12360	184	RSK OF CIG1+PK/D	5A41A	5A23A	5A23A	5A23A	5A23A	5A23A	A14A	
12370	184	RSK OF MJ 1-2 X	5A41B	5A23B	5A23B	5A23B	5A23B	5A23B	A14A	
12380	184	RSK OF MJ OCSNLY	5A41C	5A23C	5A23C	5A23C	5A23C	5A23C	A14A	
12390	184	RSK OF MJ REGLY	5A41D	5A23D	5A23D	5A23D	5A23D	5A23D	A14A	
12400	184	RSK OF LSD 1-2 X	5A41E	5A23E	5A23E	5A23E	5A23E	5A23E	A14A	
12410	185	RSK OF LSD REGLY	5A41F	5A23F	5A23F	5A23F	5A23F	5A23F	A14A	
12420	185	RSK OF 'H' 1-2 X	5A41G	5A23G	5A23G	5A23G	5A23G	5A23G	A14A	
12430	185	RSK OF 'H' OCSNL	5A41H	5A23H	5A23H	5A23H	5A23H	5A23H	A14A	
12440	185	RSK OF 'H' REGLY	5A41I	5A23I	5A23I	5A23I	5A23I	5A23I	A14A	
12450	185	RSK OF BARB 1-2X	5A41J	5A23J	5A23J	5A23J	5A23J	5A23J	A14A	
12460	185	RSK OF BARB REGY	5A41K	5A23K	5A23K	5A23K	5A23K	5A23K	A14A	
12470	185	RSK OF AMPH 1-2X	5A41L	5A23L	5A23L	5A23L	5A23L	5A23L	A14A	
12480	186	RSK OF AMPH REG	5A41M	5A23M	5A23M	5A23M	5A23M	5A23M	A14A	
12490	186	RSK OF COKE 1-2X	5A41N	5A23N	5A23N	5A23N	5A23N	5A23N	A14A	
12500	186	RSK OF COKE REG	5A41O	5A23O	5A23O	5A23O	5A23O	5A23O	A14A	
12510	186	RSK OF 1-2 DRINK	5A41P	5A23P	5A23P	5A23P	5A23P	5A23P	A14A	
12520	186	RSK OF 1-2 DR/DA	5A41Q	5A23Q	5A23Q	5A23Q	5A23Q	5A23Q	A14A	
12530	186	RSK OF 4-5 DR/DA	5A41R	5A23R	5A23R	5A23R	5A23R	5A23R	A14A	
12540	186	RSK OF 5+DR/WKND	5A41S	5A23S	5A23S	5A23S	5A23S	5A23S	A14A	
12550	187	POS ATT TWD SELF	5A39A	5D01A	5D01A	5D01A	5D01A	5D01A		Q
12560	187	LUCK>IMP HRD WRK	5A39B	5D01B	5D01B	5D01B	5D01B	5D01B		Q
12570	187	AM PRSN OF WORTH	5A39C	5D01C	5D01C	5D01C	5D01C	5D01C		Q
12580	187	DO WELL AS OTHRS	5A39D	5D01D	5D01D	5D01D	5D01D	5D01D		Q
12590	187	TRY GT AHD,STOPD	5A39E	5D01E	5D01E	5D01E	5D01E	5D01E		Q
12600	187	PLNNG MKS UNHPPY	5A39F	5D01F	5D01F	5D01F	5D01F	5D01F		Q

Item Reference Number	Page Loc. in this Volume	Item Description (Abbreviated)	1975	1976	1977	1978	1979	1980/1	A	B	C	D	E	F	G	H	I	J	K	L	M	N	O	P	Q	R	S
12610	188	ACPT LIFE->HAPPR	5A39G	5D01G	5D01G	5D01G	5D01G	5D01G																	Q		
12620	188	SATISFD W MYSELF	5A39H	5D01H	5D01H	5D01H	5D01H	5D01H																P	Q		
12630	188	PPL LK ME -CHANC	5A39I	5D01I	5D01I	5D01I	5D01I	5D01I																	Q		
12640	188	MY PLANS DO WORK			5D01J	5D01J	5D01J	5D01J																	Q		
12650	188	OFTN FEEL LONELY			5D01K	5D01K	5D01K	5D01K													M				Q		
12660	188	-MUCH TO B PROUD			5D01L	5D01L	5D01L	5D01L																	Q		
12670	188	ALWYS SM1 HELP R			5D01M	5D01M	5D01M	5D01M													M				Q		
12680	189	I AM NO GOOD			5D01N	5D01N	5D01N	5D01N																	Q		
12690	189	OFTN FL LEFT OUT			5D01O	5D01O	5D01O	5D01O													M				Q		
12700	189	PPL MASTER FATE			5D01P	5D01P	5D01P	5D01P																	Q		
12710	189	USLY SM1 TALK TO			5D01Q	5D01Q	5D01Q	5D01Q													M				Q		
12720	189	I DO WRONG THING			5D01R	5D01R	5D01R	5D01R																	Q		
12730	189	OFT WSH MOR FRND			5D01S	5D01S	5D01S	5D01S													M				Q		
12740	189	PLANS->BTR RSLTS			5D01T	5D01T	5D01T	5D01T																	Q		
12750	190	MY LIFE NT USEFL			5D01U	5D01U	5D01U	5D01U																	Q		
12760	190	USLY FRDS BE WTH			5D01V	5D01V	5D01V	5D01V													M				Q		
		LV TGTH=BD MRLTY		5D05	5D02	5D02	5D02	5D02*				D															
		FAM-MAR=BD MRLTY		5D06	5D03	5D03	5D03	5D03*				D															
12780		PSN TKG MJ/AMBTS		5D02A					A12D																		
12790		PSN TKG MJ/-SOCL		5D02B					A12D																		
12800		PSN TKG MJ/CNFMG		5D02C					A12D																		
12810		PSN TKG MJ/CRMNL		5D02D					A12D																		
12820		PSN TKG MJ/-STBL		5D02E					A12D																		
12830		PSN TKG MJ/INTRS		5D02F					A12D																		
12840		PSN TKG MJ/RBLS		5D02G					A12D																		
12850		PSN TKG MJ/SNSBL		5D02H					A12D																		
12860		PSN TKG MJ/SX PR		5D02I					A12D																		
12870		PSN TKG MJ/WKWLD		5D02J					A12D																		
12890		PSN TKG DG/AMBTS		5D03A					A12D																		
12900		PSN TKG DG/-SOCL		5D03B					A12D																		
12910		PSN TKG DG/CNFMG		5D03C					A12D																		
12920		PSN TKG DG/CRMNL		5D03D					A12D																		
12930		PSN TKG DG/-STBL		5D03E					A12D																		
12940		PSN TKG DG/INTRS		5D03F					A12D																		
12950		PSN TKG DG/RBLS		5D03G					A12D																		
12960		PSN TKG DG/SNSBL		5D03H					A12D																		
12970		PSN TKG DG/SX PR		5D03I					A12D																		
12980		PSN TKG DG/WKWLD		5D03J					A12D																		
12990	190	I HAVE ENOUGH $			5D04A	5D04A	5D04A	5D04A†			C																	
13000	190	I LACK $ FR BILL			5D04B	5D04B	5D04B	5D04B†			C																	
13010	191	I WRY @-FINDG JOB			5D04C	5D04C	5D04C	5D04C†			C																	
13020	191	I CAN FIND JOB			5D04D	5D04D	5D04D	5D04D†			C																	
13030	191	I CAN KEEP MYJOB			5D04E	5D04E	5D04E	5D04E†			C																	
13040	191	I WRY @LOSS MYJOB			5D04F	5D04F	5D04F	5D04F†			C																	
13050		R'S STATE LAW/MJ		5D04	5D05	5D05	5D05	5D05*	A13D																		
13060	192	I/MJ USR,>CREATV			5E01A	5E01A	5E01A	5E01A	A11D																		
13070	192	I/MJ USR,<SENSBL			5E01B	5E01B	5E01B	5E01B	A11D																		
13080	192	I/MJ USR,>INTRST			5E01C	5E01C	5E01C	5E01C	A11D																		
13090	192	I/MJ USR,<HRDWKG			5E01D	5E01D	5E01D	5E01D	A11D																		
13100	192	I/MJ USR,>INDPND			5E01E	5E01E	5E01E	5E01E	A11D																		
13110	193	I/MJ USR,>UNSTBL			5E01F	5E01F	5E01F	5E01F	A11D																		
13120	193	I/MJ USR,>CNCRND			5E01G	5E01G	5E01G	5E01G	A11D																		
13130	193	I/MJ USR,>WKWLD			5E01H	5E01H	5E01H	5E01H	A11D																		
13140	193	I/MJ USR,>CRMNL			5E01I	5E01I	5E01I	5E01I	A11D																		
13150		FAM+REL GD/CHILD		5E01A								D										M						
13160		FAM+REL GD/PARNT		5E01B								D										M						
13170		FAM+REL GD/GRPNT		5E01C								D										M						
13180		FAM+REL,R LIK/PT		5E01D								D										M						
13190	193	PPL/MJUSR>CREATV			5E02A	5E02A		5E02A	A12D																		
13200	193	PPL/MJUSR<SENSBL			5E02B	5E02B		5E02B	A12D																		
13210	193	PPL/MJUSR>INTRST			5E02C	5E02C		5E02C	A12D																		
13220	194	PPL/MJUSR<HRDWKG			5E02D	5E02D		5E02D	A12D																		
13230	194	PPL/MJUSR>INDPND			5E02E	5E02E		5E02E	A12D																		
13240	194	PPL/MJUSR>UNSTBL			5E02F	5E02F		5E02F	A12D																		
13250	194	PPL/MJUSR>CNCRND			5E02G	5E02G		5E02G	A12D																		
13260	194	PPL/MJUSR>WKWLD			5E02H	5E02H		5E02H	A12D																		

* 1980 only.   † 5D02A-F in 1981.

Item Reference Number	Page Loc. in this Volume	ITEM DESCRIPTION (ABBREVIATED)	1975	1976	1977	1978	1979	1980/1	A	B	C	D	E	F	G	H	I	J	K	L	M	N	O	P	Q	R	S
13270	194	PPL/MJUSR>CRMNL			5E02I	5E02I		5E02I	A12D																		
13280		FAM+CPL GD/CHILD		5E02A								D															
13290		FAM+CPL GD/PARNT		5E02B								D															
13300		FAM+CPL GD/GRPNT		5E02C								D															
13310		FAM+CPL,LIK/PRNT		5E02D								D															
13320		FAM+CPL,LIK/-CHD		5E02E								D															
13330		I/DG USR,>CREATV			5E03A	5E03A		5E03A*	A11D																		
13340		I/DG USR,<SENSBL			5E03B	5E03B		5E03B*	A11D																		
13350		I/DG USR,>INTRST			5E03C	5E03C		5E03C*	A11D																		
13360		I/DG USR,<HRDWKG			5E03D	5E03D		5E03D*	A11D																		
13370		I/DG USR,>INDPND			5E03E	5E03E		5E03E*	A11D																		
13380		I/DG USR,>UNSTBL			5E03F	5E03F		5E03F*	A11D																		
13390		I/DG USR,>CNCRND			5E03G	5E03G		5E03G*	A11D																		
13400		I/DG USR,>WKWLD			5E03H	5E03H		5E03H*	A11D																		
13410		I/DG USR,>CRMNL			5E03I	5E03I		5E03I*	A11D																		
13420		CPL+OTH+CHD MAR		5E03A								D															
13430		CPL+OTH+CHD DVC		5E03B								D															
13440		CPL+OTH+MAR CPL		5E03C								D															
13450		CPL+OTH+DIV PRT		5E03D								D															
13460		CPL+OTH+UNMARRD		5E03E								D															
13470		CPL+OTH,LK,MR PT		5E03F								D															
13480		CPL+OTH,LK,DVC P		5E03G								D															
13490		PPL/DGUSR>CREATV			5E04A	5E04A		5E04A*	A12D																		
13500		PPL/DGUSR<SENSBL			5E04B	5E04B		5E04B*	A12D																		
13510		PPL/DGUSR>INTRST			5E04C	5E04C		5E04C*	A12D																		
13520		PPL/DGUSR<HRDWKG			5E04D	5E04D		5E04D*	A12D																		
13530		PPL/DGUSR>INDPND			5E04E	5E04E		5E04E*	A12D																		
13540		PPL/DGUSR>UNSTBL			5E04F	5E04F		5E04F*	A12D																		
13550		PPL/DGUSR>CNCRND			5E04G	5E04G		5E04G*	A12D																		
13560		PPL/DGUSR>WKWLD			5E04H	5E04H		5E04H*	A12D																		
13570		PPL/DGUSR>CRMNL			5E04I	5E04I		5E04I*	A12D																		
13580		STS SCH RT FAMLY		5E05A	5E06A	5E06A	5E04A	5E06A*		B																	R	
13590		STS SCH LDS STU		5E05B	5E06B	5E06B	5E04B	5E06B*		B												M						
13600		STS SCH NIC CAR		5E05C	5E06C	5E06C	5E04C	5E06C*		B				F													
13610		STS SCH HI GRDE		5E05D	5E06D	5E06D	5E04D	5E06D*		B																		
13620		STS SCH GD ATHLT		5E05E	5E06E	5E06E	5E04E	5E06E*		B																		
13630		STS SCH INTLCTL		5E05F	5E06F	5E06F	5E04F	5E06F*		B																		
13640		STS SCH PLN CLG		5E05G	5E06G	5E06G	5E04G	5E06G*		B																		
13650		DRG USE+,MAJ STD		5E06A	5E07A	5E07A	5E05A	5E07A*	A12C																		
13660		DRG USE+,MY FRND		5E06B	5E07B	5E07B	5E05B	5E07B*	A12B																		
13670		DRG USE+,MY FLGS			5E07C	5E07C	5E05C	5E07C*	A11D																		
13700		BY SOON HAIR DRY		2E10A										F													
13710		BY SOON WT/S SKI		2E10B										F													
13720		BY SOON CAMERA		2E10C										F													
13730		BY SOON WATCH		2E10D										F													
13740		BY SOON HKG BKPK		2E10E										F													
13750		BY SOON CK RADIO		2E10F										F													
13760		BY SOON EL SHAVR		2E10G										F													
13770		BY SOON TENIS RQ		2E10H										F													
13780		BY SOON TV SET		2E10I										F													
13790		BY SOON BICYCLE		2E10J										F													
13800		BY SOON CAR		2E10K										F													
13810		BY SOON TAPE REC		2E10L										F													
13820		BY SOON ELT CALC		2E10M										F													
13830		BY SOON BT/SNMBL		2E10N										F													
13835	140	IMP HAV 1 CAR		3E12A		3E11A	3E10A	3E10A						F													
13840	140	IMP HAV 2 CARS		3E12B		3E11B	3E10B	3E10B						F													
13850	140	IMP HAV LARG CAR		3E12C		3E11C	3E10C	3E10C						F													
13860	141	IMP HAV NW CR OF		3E12D		3E11D	3E10D	3E10D						F													
13870	141	IMP HAV NW CLTHS		3E12E		3E11E	3E10E	3E10E						F													
13880	141	IMP HAV OWN HSE		3E12F		3E11F	3E10F	3E10F						F													
13890	141	IMP HAV BIG YARD		3E12G		3E11G	3E10G	3E10G						F													
13900	141	IMP HAV NEAT LWN		3E12H		3E11H	3E10H	3E10H						F													
13910	141	IMP HAV APPLINCS		3E12I		3E11I	3E10I	3E10I						F													
13920	141	IMP HAV G STEREO		3E12J		3E11J	3E10J	3E10J						F													
13930	141	IMP HAV VAC HSE		3E12K		3E11K	3E10K	3E10K						F													

* 1980 only.

Item Reference Number	Page Loc. in this Volume	ITEM DESCRIPTION (ABBREVIATED)	QUESTIONNAIRE LOCATION BY YEAR (FORM, SECTION, AND QUESTION NUMBER)						SUBJECT AREA	
			1975	1976	1977	1978	1979	1980/1	A	B C D E F G H I J K L M N O P Q R S
13940	142	IMP HAV REC VEH		3E12L		3E11L	3E10L	3E10L		F
13950	190	EAGR TO LEAV HOM						5D01W		I Q
13960	190	HEST PRT ADLT WL						5D01X		I Q
16320		EFCTV WRIT OFCLS				2E04A				H I .
16330		EFCTV WRK PL CPN				2E04B				H I
16340		EFCTV VOTING				2E04C				H I
16350		EFCTV PETITIONS				2E04D				H I
16360		EFCTV BOYCOTT				2E04E				H I
16370		EFCTV LWFL DMSTN				2E04F				H I
16380		EFCTV OCPY BLDGS				2E04G				H I
16390		EFCTV WLDCT STRK				2E04H				H I
16400		EFCTV BLK TRAFIC				2E04I				H I
16410		EFCTV DAMAG THNG				2E04J				H I
16420		EFCTV PSNL VLNC				2E04K				H I
16430		SAT EVB CAR POOL				2E05A				F O
16440		SAT EAT<BEEF>GRN				2E05B				F O
16450		SAT TAX FR ECLGY				2E05C				F
17570		PPL SHD CONFORM					5E02A			Q
17580		PPL SHD LV HRMNY					5E02B			Q
17590		PPL SHD B FRANK					5E02C			Q
17600		PPL SHD THK FREE					5E02D			Q
17610		PPL SHD B INDPNT					5E02E			Q
17860	168	DESRD LVG RURAL				4E09A		4E09A		F
17870	169	DESRD LVG SM TWN				4E09B		4E09B		F
17880	169	DESRD LVG SM CTY				4E09C		4E09C		F
17890	169	DESRD LVG SUBURB				4E09D		4E09D		F
17900	169	DESRD LVG LG CTY				4E09E		4E09E		F
17910	169	DSRD HSG 1 FAMLY				4E09F		4E09F		F
17920	169	DSRD HSG 2 FAMLY				4E09G		4E09G		F
17930	169	DSRD HSG CNDMINM				4E09H		4E09H		F
17940	169	DSRD HSG APT BLD				4E09I		4E09I		F
17950	170	DSRD HSG HI RISE				4E09J		4E09J		F
19470		EAT<FD,>OWN CITY					5E08A			F O
19480		EAT<FD,>NRBY STT					5E08B			F O
19490		EAT<FD,>DIF REGN					5E08C			F O
19500		EAT<FD,>ASIAN CN					5E08D			F O
19530	114	3MO/DLY ARG PRNT						2E08A		M Q
19540	114	3MO/DLY ARG AUTH						2E08B		Q
19550	114	3MO/DLY MAD						2E08C		Q
19560	114	3MO/DLY MAD,SMSH						2E08D		Q
19570	114	3MO/DLY WANT FGT						2E08E		Q
19580	114	3MO/DLY DID FGHT						2E08F		Q
20590	132	12MO NR OTH MARJ		3A29A	3A29A	3A29A	3A29A	3A29A	A02B	
20600	132	12MO NR OTH LSD		3A29B	3A29B	3A29B	3A29B	3A29B	A02B	
20610	132	12MO NR OTH PSYC		3A29C	3A29C	3A29C	3A29C	3A29C	A02B	
20620	132	12MO NR OTH AMPH		3A29D	3A29D	3A29D	3A29D	3A29D	A02B	
20630	133	12MO NR OTH BARB		3A29E	3A29E	3A29E	3A29E	3A29E	A02B	
20640	133	12MO NR OTH TRQL		3A29F	3A29F	3A29F	3A29F	3A29F	A02B	
20650	133	12MO NR OTH COKE		3A29G	3A29G	3A29G	3A29G	3A29G	A02B	
20660	133	12MO NR OTH HRN		3A29H	3A29H	3A29H	3A29H	3A29H	A02B	
20670	133	12MO NR OTH NARC		3A29I	3A29I	3A29I	3A29I	3A29I	A02B	
20680	133	12MO NR OTH ALCL		3A29J	3A29J	3A29J	3A29J	3A29J	A02B	
20690		ATTN TO NUTRITON					2E15A			Q
20700		MIN CHOLESTEROL					2E15B			Q
20710		AVOID ADDITIVES					2E15C			Q
20720		TRY GET EXERCISE					2E15D			Q
20730		CNTRL OWN HEALTH					2E16			Q
20740	117	OFTN EAT BRKFST					2E17A	2E17A		Q
20750	117	OFTN EAT GN VEG					2E17B	2E17B		Q
20760	117	OFTN EAT FRUIT					2E17C	2E17C		Q
20770	117	OFTN EXERCISE					2E17D	2E17D		Q
20780	117	OFTN 7HRS SLEEP					2E17E	2E17E		Q
20790	118	OFTN SLEEP <SHLD					2E17F	2E17F		Q
20800	200	WLD ADMT USE MJ					5E09	5E09†	A15	
20810	200	WLD ADMT USE AMP					5E10	5E10†	A15	
20820	200	WLD ADMT USE HER					5E11	5E11†	A15	

† 5E14-5E16 in 1981

Item Reference Number	Page Loc. in this Volume	ITEM DESCRIPTION (ABBREVIATED)	QUESTIONNAIRE LOCATION BY YEAR (FORM, SECTION, AND QUESTION NUMBER)						SUBJECT AREA	
			1975	1976	1977	1978	1979	1980/1	A	B C D E F G H I J K L M N O P Q R S
20830	191	% $ SAVE FUTR EDUC						5D03A*		C
20840	192	% $ SAVE/SPEND CAR						5D03B*		C
20850	192	% $ SAVE OTHER						5D03C*		C
20860	192	% $ SPEND ON SELF						5D03D*		C
20870	192	% $ SPEND HELP FAM						5D03E*		C
20880	195	GUY SMK COOL						5E03A*	A11d	
20890	195	GUY SMK INSECURE						5E03B*	A11d	
20900	195	GUY SMK INDPNDNT						5E03C*	A11d	
20910	195	GUY SMK CONFORMG						5E03D*	A11d	
20920	195	GUY SMK MATURE						5E03E*	A11d	
20930	195	GUY SMK TRY MATUR						5E03F*	A11d	
20940	196	GIRL SMK COOL						5E04A*	A11d	
20950	196	GRL SMK INSECURE						5E04B*	A11d	
20960	196	GRL SMK INDPNDNT						5E04C*	A11d '	
20970	196	GRL SMK CONFORMG						5E04D*	A11d	
20980	196	GRL SMK MATURE						5E04E*	A11d	
20990	196	GRL SM TRY MATUR						5E04F*	A11d	
21000	196	SMKRS ENJOY LIFE						5E05A*	A11d	
21010	197	PRFR DATE N-SMKR						5E05B*	A11d	
21020	197	HARMFUL CIG EXAG						5E05C*	A11d	
21030	197	SMKR POOR JDGMNT						5E05D*	A11d	
21040	197	DONT MIND SMOKNG						5E05E*	A11d	
21050	197	SMKG DIRTY HABIT						5E05F*	A11d	
21060	197	FAVOR MLTY DRAFT						5E06*		L
21070	198	DRAFT INCL WOMEN						5E07*		L
21080	198	MLTRY PAY CLG GD						5E08*		L
21090	198	R WD DO MLTY/CLG						5E09*		L
21100	198	# CANS COLA/DAY						5E10*	A01d	
21110	198	# CUPS COFF/DAY						5E11*	A01d	
21120	199	# CUPS TEA/DAY						5E12*	A01d	

* 1981 only

Appendix A
Sampling Error Estimates and Tables

All of the percentages reported in this volume are really *estimates* of the response percentages that would have been obtained if, instead of using a sample survey, we had asked all high schools throughout the United States to participate, and in all schools that agreed to participate we had invited the whole senior class to fill out the questionnaires. The question naturally arises: How accurate are the present percentage estimates based on a limited number of schools and seniors? For any particular percentage resulting from a sample survey we cannot know exactly how much error has resulted from sampling, but we can make reasonably good estimates of "confidence intervals" — ranges within which the "true" population value is very likely to fall. The word "true" in this context is defined quite narrowly; it refers only to the value that would be found if we had set out to survey the total population — all high school seniors in the United States. Thus this concept of "true" population value does *not* take account of biases that might occur due to refusals, distortion of responses, faulty question wording, and other factors. Each of these sources of possible error is discussed in the "Representativeness and Validity" section of the Introduction to this volume. The reader is urged to review this material and take it into account along with the sampling error estimates included in this appendix.

The estimation of confidence intervals in surveys involving complex samples can be a highly complicated combination of statistical science plus informed judgment. It is an area in which there is no single "right answer" or "best approach." We suspect that many of those using this volume will not be especially interested in *how* we have chosen to solve the problems involved in estimating confidence intervals, so long as we provide guidelines that can be applied in a fairly simple and straightforward manner. This appendix is designed to accomplish that. Appendix B provides a more extensive discussion of how we obtained the confidence intervals shown here, and it also provides guidelines for computing specific confidence intervals for a wider range of possible applications than can be covered in the tables provided in this appendix.

A very rough example of a confidence interval can be stated in these terms: For percentages based on the total sample (all five questionnaire forms), the "true" values are rarely more than 1.5 percent higher or lower than the percentage estimates reported in this volume. How rarely? The chances are much lower than 1 in 20. Indeed, many of the percentages reported for the total sample are accurate to within one percent.

Of course, most of the data reported here are based on items included only in one or another of the five questionnaire forms. Since such percentages are based on only one-fifth of the total sample, they are somewhat less accurate. The loss in accuracy is less than might be imagined, however, for reasons spelled out in Appendix B. For present purposes, it is enough to say that percentages based on 3,000 or more seniors responding to one questionnaire form are rarely (less than 1 in 20) farther than 2.4 percent away from the "true" value.

We have thus far provided two very rough illustrations of confidence intervals — a range of ± 1.5 percent for percentages based on the total sample, and a range of ± 2.4 percent for percentages based on the number of seniors responding to one questionnaire form. While these two intervals provide some notion of the overall range of accuracy of the sample, they fall short of our needs in a number of respects. We need to be able to assign confidence intervals for subgroups such as males, females, those who plan to complete college, and so forth, all of which involve smaller numbers of cases and thus some reduction in accuracy. We also need to take account of the fact that, other things equal, confidence intervals grow smaller when one moves from the middle of the scale (percentages near 50 percent) to the extremes (e.g., 4 percent or 96 percent). Further, we need to provide guidelines for evaluating the *difference* between two percentages; for example, we may wish to know whether the difference between male and female percentages in response to a particular question is large enough so that it is not likely to be merely the result of sampling error. Another type of difference of considerable interest is that between percentages from two different years; for example, we may wish to know whether an increase in the percentage of daily marijuana users from one year to the next is large enough to be considered a statistically significant change.

Each of the requirements mentioned above is taken into account in the tables of confidence intervals which follow.

Confidence Intervals for Single Percentages

Table A-1 provides confidence intervals for single percentages that are reasonably good approximations for most *variables* and for most *subgroups* (as well as for the total sample). The table entries slightly underestimate the confidence intervals for regional subgroups and for blacks. These underestimates can be corrected reasonably well by multiplying the entries in Table A-1 by a factor of 1.1 for data based on a single form and by a factor of 1.33 for data based on all five forms. A more serious problem is that the table entries substantially underestimate the confidence intervals for certain variables which tend to be somewhat homogeneous within schools, as well as other factors likely to show clustering according to geographical area or socioeconomic level. A discussion of some of these variables is provided at the end of this appendix.

Table A-1 accommodates various numbers of cases (presented as different columns in the table), and various percentages (presented as different rows in the table). The table entries, when added to and subtracted from the observed percentage, establish the 95 percent confidence interval (calculated as 1.96 sampling errors). Thus, for example, to determine the accuracy of a result of 67.4 percent based on a sample of 1,632 cases, one should first look for the closest values in the table (in this case, about 70 percent and a number of cases approximately equal to 1,500); next determine the values to be added to and subtracted from the observed percentage (in this case the values

would be + 2.8 percent and − 2.9 percent); and then compute the confidence interval around the observed percentage of 67.4 percent (in this case an interval ranging from 64.5 percent to 70.2 percent). This procedure yields an interval such that, for most variables, the chances are 95 in 100 that if all high school seniors in the country had been asked to participate in the survey the resulting percentage would fall within the interval.

Confidence Intervals for Differences between Two Percentages

Table A-2 provides confidence intervals for differences between certain percentages. Specifically, the table can be used for *comparisons* between males and females, between those who do and do not plan to complete four years of college, and between those falling into different categories of the five-level index of drug usage. The above comparisons are appropriate for data from any single year (e.g., male seniors in 1976 compared with female seniors in 1976, or the "marijuana only" seniors in 1977 compared with the "no illicit drugs" seniors in 1977). Table A-2 is also useful in assessing *one-year* trends for any of the above subgroups as well as for the total sample. For example, one may be interested in a confidence interval (or significance level) for the difference between the percentage of female seniors in 1977 who used marijuana and the percentage of female seniors in 1978 who did so. The values in Table A-2 are appropriate for confidence intervals across adjacent years (e.g., 1976 compared with 1977), provided the same subgroup (e.g., females) is being considered both years. The confidence intervals for comparisons across non-adjacent years (e.g., 1976 compared with 1978), are slightly larger.

With appropriate corrections, the entries in Table A-2 can be used for trends covering more than one year and for trends or comparisons involving regional subgroups and blacks. Each of these applications requires some upward adjustment of the table entries; guidelines for such adjustments are provided in the notes accompanying Table A-2.

For information on the derivation of Table A-2 and for guidelines to be used in computing confidence intervals not covered in that table, the reader is referred to Appendix B.

In order to find the appropriate confidence interval in Table A-2, one must first locate that portion of the table which deals with percentage values closest to the two percentages being compared (for example, if one wished to compare a value of 28.1 percent with one of 35.4 percent, the "p = 30 percent or 70 percent" portion of the table would be closest). The next step is to locate the specific table entry which corresponds most closely to the numbers of cases involved in the two percentages being compared (e.g., if those numbers were 1,478 and 1,563 for 28.1 percent and 35.4 percent, the correct table entry would be 3.9 percent). That table entry, when added to and subtracted from the difference between the two percentages, yields the 95 percent confidence interval for the difference. (In the above illustration that would be 7.3 percent ± 3.9 percent or an interval from 3.4 percent to 11.2 percent.) The chances are only 1 in 20 that the "true" difference between two percentages lies outside of this interval.

Another use of Table A-2 is to test whether a difference between two percentages is "statistically significant." If the table entry is smaller than the difference between the two percentages (as is true in the above illustration), then the difference is statistically significant at the 95 percent level (sometimes indicated as $p < .05$).

Some Cautions

The tables provided here are based on averages of large numbers of sampling errors computed across a wide range of the variables which appear in this volume, as well as across all of the subgroups for which data are reported here. We are confident that the values in the tables are reasonably accurate for most purposes, but we must repeat the caution that the tables slightly underestimate confidence intervals for the following groups and comparisons:

> Blacks
> Regions (Northeast, North Central,
>   South, West)
> Comparisons among regions
> Comparisons across non-adjacent years
>   (e.g., 1976 vs. 1978)

A more important problem is that the tables substantially underestimate the confidence intervals for certain variables that, for various reasons, show greater than average homogeneity within schools. After an extensive, but by no means exhaustive, sampling of the kinds of variables which might show such clustering by school, we can provide the following examples of the kinds of variables for which Tables A-1 and A-2 substantially underestimate the confidence intervals.

Variables Related to Educational Background and Aspirations. The questionnaire items dealing with father's education, mother's education, high school curriculum (college preparatory versus all other), and plans for completing four years of college, all show an appreciable amount of clustering by school. Accordingly, for such variables the confidence intervals provided in the tables should be doubled.

Other items dealing with plans for technical/vocational schooling, a two-year college program, or graduate/professional study, also require adjustment. The confidence intervals in the tables should be multiplied by a factor of 1.5 in order to be applicable to these variables.

It seems clear that the common factor underlying these particular variables is the tendency for family socioeconomic level to be somewhat homogeneous within school districts — some schools serve wealthier populations than others. That makes the form of sampling we use somewhat less efficient for measuring those variables (like those listed above) which are closely associated with family socioeconomic level. Therefore, we urge the reader to treat with caution any variables which are likely to be strongly linked to socioeconomic factors. In the absence of more specific computations of sampling errors, a good rule of thumb for dealing with such variables would be to double the confidence intervals provided in Tables A-1 and A-2.

Variables Related to Geographic Location. Another category of variables which are somewhat homogeneous within schools and school districts consists of those things which reflect differences in region and/or urbanicity. An obvious example is a background question asking where the respondent grew up; the response category "on a farm" shows a very high degree of clustering within schools. One would have to more than double the confidence intervals in the tables to deal with such a measure. Similarly high clustering was found for some responses about religious preference; for example, those whose preference is Baptist are located primarily in the South (and probably heavily in rural areas), whereas those whose preference is Jewish are located primarily in the Northeast (especially in larger cities). The confidence intervals in Tables A-1 and A-2 should be multiplied by a factor as large as 3 in order to be applicable to such variables.

Other variables which show some greater than average homogeneity within schools include such ideologically related dimensions as frequency of attending religious services, importance of religion, and political preference. Still other variables showing high homogeneity, probably because of their association with urbanicity, include driving (percentage who usually do not drive at all), working (percentage with no job), and household composition (percentage with father not living in the home). For each of the variables mentioned in this paragraph, the confidence intervals shown in Tables A-1 and A-2 should be multiplied by a factor of about 1.5.

Variables Involving Use of Alcohol and Marijuana. Extensive work has been done to compute sampling errors and confidence intervals for the drug use measures included in this volume (see Johnston, Bachman, and O'Malley, 1977, 1979, especially Appendix B). Most drug use variables show sampling errors which lie within the range of those provided in Tables A-1 and A-2. Usage levels for alcohol and marijuana, however, show some degree of homogeneity within schools, thus requiring that the table levels be adjusted. For items dealing with alcohol use, the entries in Table A-1 should be multiplied by a factor of 1.6; for items dealing with marijuana use, the correction factor is 1.35.

As noted earlier, this appendix has presented guidelines for using the tables of confidence intervals provided herein. Those readers interested in learning more about the rationale underlying such tables, the procedures used to derive the particular tables presented here, and guidelines for further computations of confidence intervals may consult Appendix B of this volume.

Notes to Table A-1

Caution: The entries in this table systematically underestimate confidence intervals for regional subgroups and for blacks. In order to correct these underestimates, the table entries should be multiplied by a factor of 1.10 for data from a single form and by a factor of 1.33 for data based on five forms. Further cautions and corrections are required for some specific variables which relate to educational background and aspirations, geographic location, and the use of alcohol and marijuana (see discussion in the final sections of Appendix A).

The values in this table, when added to and subtracted from an observed percentage, establish the 95 percent confidence interval around that percentage, incorporating a design effect. Table values were calculated using the following formula (adapted from Hays, 1973, p. 379):

$$\text{lower limit} = p - \frac{2N'p + (1.96)^2 - 1.96\sqrt{4N'p\,(1-p) + (1.96)^2}}{2[N' + (1.96)^2]}$$

$$\text{upper limit} = \frac{2N'p + (1.96)^2 + 1.96\sqrt{4N'p\,(1-p) + (1.96)^2}}{2[N' + (1.96)^2]} - p$$

where p = the percentage, and N' is the "effective N," $N' = N/(1.3 + .00015N)$. (See Appendix B for a discussion of the concept of "effective N.")

Table A-1

Confidence Intervals (95% Level) around Percentage Values

Number of Cases

	100	200	300	400	500	700	1000	1500	2000	2500	3000	3500	4000	5000	7000	10000	15000	20000
99%+	0.9	0.8	0.7	0.7	0.6	0.6	0.5	0.5	0.4	0.4	0.4	0.4	0.3	0.3	0.3	0.3	0.3	0.2
−	5.6	3.2	2.4	1.9	1.7	1.3	1.1	0.8	0.7	0.6	0.6	0.6	0.5	0.5	0.4	0.4	0.3	0.3
97%+	2.1	1.8	1.6	1.4	1.3	1.2	1.0	0.9	0.8	0.8	0.7	0.7	0.6	0.6	0.6	0.5	0.5	0.5
−	6.6	4.1	3.2	2.6	2.3	1.9	1.6	1.3	1.1	1.0	0.9	0.9	0.8	0.8	0.7	0.6	0.6	0.5
95%+	3.1	2.5	2.2	2.0	1.8	1.6	1.4	1.2	1.1	1.0	0.9	0.9	0.9	0.8	0.7	0.7	0.6	0.6
−	7.4	4.7	3.7	3.1	2.7	2.3	1.9	1.5	1.4	1.2	1.1	1.1	1.0	0.9	0.8	0.8	0.7	0.7
90%+	4.9	3.8	3.3	2.9	2.7	2.3	2.0	1.7	1.5	1.4	1.3	1.3	1.2	1.1	1.0	0.9	0.9	0.8
−	8.8	5.8	4.6	4.0	3.5	2.9	2.5	2.0	1.8	1.6	1.5	1.4	1.4	1.3	1.1	1.0	0.9	0.9
85%+	6.6	4.8	4.1	3.6	3.3	2.9	2.5	2.1	1.9	1.7	1.6	1.5	1.5	1.4	1.2	1.1	1.0	1.0
−	9.7	6.6	5.3	4.5	4.0	3.4	2.9	2.4	2.1	1.9	1.8	1.7	1.6	1.5	1.3	1.2	1.1	1.1
80%+	7.4	5.6	4.7	4.2	3.8	3.3	2.8	2.4	2.1	2.0	1.8	1.7	1.7	1.5	1.4	1.3	1.2	1.1
−	10.3	7.1	5.7	4.9	4.4	3.7	3.1	2.6	2.3	2.1	2.0	1.8	1.8	1.6	1.5	1.3	1.2	1.2
70%+	9.1	6.8	5.6	5.0	4.5	3.9	3.3	2.8	2.5	2.3	2.1	2.0	1.9	1.8	1.6	1.5	1.4	1.3
−	11.1	7.7	6.3	5.5	4.9	4.2	3.5	2.9	2.6	2.4	2.2	2.1	2.0	1.8	1.7	1.5	1.4	1.3
50%+	11.0	7.9	6.5	5.7	5.1	4.4	3.7	3.1	2.8	2.5	2.4	2.2	2.1	2.0	1.8	1.6	1.5	1.4
−	11.0	7.9	6.5	5.7	5.1	4.4	3.7	3.1	2.8	2.5	2.4	2.2	2.1	2.0	1.8	1.6	1.5	1.4
30%+	11.1	7.7	6.3	5.5	4.9	4.2	3.5	2.9	2.6	2.4	2.2	2.1	2.0	1.8	1.7	1.5	1.4	1.3
−	9.1	6.8	5.6	5.0	4.5	3.9	3.3	2.8	2.5	2.3	2.1	2.0	1.9	1.8	1.6	1.5	1.4	1.3
20%+	10.3	7.1	5.7	4.9	4.4	3.7	3.1	2.6	2.3	2.1	2.0	1.8	1.8	1.6	1.5	1.3	1.2	1.2
−	7.4	5.6	4.7	4.2	3.8	3.3	2.8	2.4	2.1	2.0	1.6	1.7	1.7	1.5	1.4	1.3	1.2	1.1
15%+	9.7	6.6	5.3	4.5	4.0	3.4	2.9	2.4	2.1	1.9	1.8	1.7	1.6	1.5	1.3	1.2	1.1	1.1
−	6.3	4.8	4.1	3.6	3.3	2.9	2.5	2.1	1.9	1.7	1.6	1.5	1.5	1.4	1.2	1.1	1.0	1.0
10%+	8.8	5.8	4.6	4.0	3.5	2.9	2.5	2.0	1.8	1.6	1.5	1.4	1.4	1.3	1.1	1.0	0.9	0.9
−	4.9	3.8	3.3	2.9	2.7	2.3	2.0	1.7	1.5	1.4	1.3	1.3	1.2	1.1	1.0	0.9	0.9	0.8
5%+	7.4	4.7	3.7	3.1	2.7	2.3	1.9	1.5	1.4	1.2	1.1	1.1	1.0	0.9	0.8	0.8	0.7	0.7
−	3.1	2.5	2.2	2.0	1.8	1.6	1.4	1.2	1.1	1.0	0.9	0.9	0.9	0.8	0.7	0.7	0.6	0.6
3%+	6.6	4.1	3.2	2.6	2.3	1.9	1.6	1.3	1.1	1.0	0.9	0.9	0.8	0.8	0.7	0.6	0.6	0.5
−	2.1	1.8	1.6	1.4	1.3	1.2	1.0	0.9	0.8	0.8	0.7	0.7	0.6	0.6	0.6	0.5	0.5	0.5
1%+	5.6	3.2	2.4	1.9	1.7	1.3	1.1	0.8	0.7	0.6	0.6	0.6	0.5	0.5	0.4	0.4	0.3	0.3
−	0.9	0.8	0.7	0.7	0.6	0.6	0.5	0.5	0.4	0.4	0,4	0.4	0.3	0.3	0.3	0.3	0.3	0.2

Notes to Table A-2

The entries in this table (which appear on the next two pages) are appropriate for *comparisons* between (a) males and females, (b) those who do and do not plan four years of college, and (c) those falling into different categories of the five-level index of drug usage. The table entries are also appropriate for *one-year trends* for the total sample and any of the subgroups except region. Most other trends and subgroup comparisons require that the table entries be multiplied by an adjustment factor, given below.

Outline of Steps to Follow (see text of appendix for illustrations)

1. Locate the portion of the table with "p" values closest to the two percentages being compared.

2. Locate the specific entry closest to the weighted Ns for the two percentages.

3. Multiply that entry by any necessary adjustment factor (see below).

4. That table value (or adjusted table value), when added to and subtracted from the difference between the two percentages, yields the 95 percent confidence interval for the difference.

5. Also, if the table value (or adjusted table value) is smaller than the difference between the two percentages, then the difference may be described as "statistically significant at the 95 percent level."

	Adjustment Factor (to be multiplied by table entry)
Adjustment Factors	
For comparisons between blacks and whites	
based on single form data	*
based on five form data	1.25
For comparisons between any two regions	
based on single form data	1.15
based on five form data	1.50
For one-year trends involving any region	
based on single form data	*
based on five form data	1.25
For trends over two or more years involving any region	
based on single form data	*
based on five form data	1.35
For trends over two or more years involving all other groups	
based on single form data	*
based on five form data	1.15

*indicates that no adjustment is necessary for category shown

NOTE: The table entries were calculated using the following formula: $1.96\sqrt{p(1-p)\dfrac{1}{N'_1}+\dfrac{1}{N'_2}}$

where $N'_1 = N_1/DEFF$, and $N'_2 = N_2/DEFF$, $DEFF = 1.3 + .000075\left[\dfrac{N_1 N_2}{N_1 + N_2}\right]$

Table A-2

**Confidence Intervals (95% Confidence Level)
for Differences Between Two Percentages**

p = 1% or 99%

	N_1 = 100	200	300	400	500	700	1000	1500	2000	3000	4000	5000	7000	10000	15000	20000
N_2 = 100	3.2															
200	2.7	2.2														
300	2.6	2.0	1.8													
400	2.5	1.9	1.7	1.6												
500	2.4	1.9	1.6	1.5	1.4											
700	2.4	1.8	1.6	1.4	1.3	1.2										
1000	2.3	1.7	1.5	1.3	1.2	1.1	1.0									
1500	2.3	1.7	1.4	1.3	1.2	1.0	0.9	0.8								
2000	2.3	1.7	1.4	1.2	1.1	1.0	0.9	0.8	0.7							
3000	2.3	1.6	1.4	1.2	1.1	1.0	0.8	0.7	0.7	0.6						
4000	2.3	1.6	1.4	1.2	1.1	0.9	0.8	0.7	0.7	0.6	0.6					
5000	2.3	1.6	1.3	1.2	1.1	0.9	0.8	0.7	0.6	0.6	0.5	0.5				
7000	2.3	1.6	1.3	1.2	1.1	0.9	0.8	0.7	0.6	0.5	0.5	0.5	0.4			
10000	2.2	1.6	1.3	1.2	1.0	0.9	0.8	0.7	0.6	0.5	0.5	0.5	0.4	0.4		
15000	2.2	1.6	1.3	1.2	1.0	0.9	0.8	0.6	0.6	0.5	0.5	0.4	0.4	0.4	0.4	
20000	2.2	1.6	1.3	1.1	1.0	0.9	0.8	0.6	0.6	0.5	0.5	0.4	0.4	0.4	0.3	0.3

p = 3% or 97%

	N_1 = 100	200	300	400	500	700	1000	1500	2000	3000	4000	5000	7000	10000	15000	20000
N_2 = 100	5.4															
200	4.7	3.8														
300	4.4	3.5	3.1													
400	4.3	3.3	2.9	2.7												
500	4.2	3.2	2.8	2.6	2.4											
700	4.1	3.1	2.7	2.4	2.3	2.1										
1000	4.0	3.0	2.5	2.3	2.1	1.9	1.8									
1500	4.0	2.9	2.4	2.2	2.0	1.8	1.6	1.5								
2000	3.9	2.9	2.4	2.1	1.9	1.7	1.5	1.4	1.3							
3000	3.9	2.8	2.3	2.1	1.9	1.7	1.5	1.3	1.2	1.1						
4000	3.9	2.8	2.3	2.0	1.9	1.6	1.4	1.2	1.1	1.0	0.9					
5000	3.9	2.8	2.3	2.0	1.8	1.6	1.4	1.2	1.1	1.0	0.9	0.9				
7000	3.9	2.8	2.3	2.0	1.8	1.6	1.4	1.2	1.0	0.9	0.9	0.8	0.8			
10000	3.9	2.8	2.3	2.0	1.8	1.5	1.3	1.1	1.0	0.9	0.8	0.8	0.7	0.7		
15000	3.8	2.7	2.3	2.0	1.8	1.5	1.3	1.1	1.0	0.9	0.8	0.7	0.7	0.6	0.6	
20000	3.8	2.7	2.3	2.0	1.8	1.5	1.3	1.1	1.0	0.9	0.8	0.7	0.7	0.6	0.6	0.6

MONITORING THE FUTURE

Table A-2 (continued)

	$N_1 = 100$	200	300	400	500	700	1000	1500	2000	3000	4000	5000	7000	10000	15000	20000
$N_2 = 100$	6.9															
200	6.0	4.9														
300	5.6	4.5	4.0													
400	5.5	4.3	3.8	3.5												
500	5.4	4.1	3.6	3.3	3.1											
700	5.2	3.9	3.4	3.1	2.9	2.7			$p = 5\%$ or 95%							
1000	5.1	3.8	3.2	2.9	2.7	2.5	2.2									
1500	5.1	3.7	3.1	2.8	2.6	2.3	2.1	1.9								
2000	5.0	3.6	3.1	2.7	2.5	2.2	2.0	1.7	1.6							
3000	5.0	3.6	3.0	2.6	2.4	2.1	1.9	1.6	1.5	1.4						
4000	5.0	3.6	3.0	2.6	2.4	2.1	1.8	1.6	1.4	1.3	1.2					
5000	4.9	3.6	2.9	2.6	2.3	2.0	1.8	1.5	1.4	1.2	1.2	1.1				
7000	4.9	3.5	2.9	2.6	2.3	2.0	1.7	1.5	1.3	1.2	1.1	1.0	1.0			
10000	4.9	3.5	2.9	2.5	2.3	2.0	1.7	1.4	1.3	1.1	1.1	1.0	0.9	0.9		
15000	4.9	3.5	2.9	2.5	2.3	2.0	1.7	1.4	1.3	1.1	1.0	1.0	0.9	0.8	0.8	
20000	4.9	3.5	2.9	2.5	2.3	1.9	1.7	1.4	1.3	1.1	1.0	0.9	0.9	0.8	0.7	0.7

	$N_1 = 100$	200	300	400	500	700	1000	1500	2000	3000	4000	5000	7000	10000	15000	20000
$N_1 = 100$	9.5															
200	8.2	6.7														
300	7.8	6.2	5.5													
400	7.5	5.9	5.2	4.8												
500	7.4	5.7	4.9	4.6	4.3											
700	7.2	5.4	4.7	4.3	4.0	3.7			$p = 10\%$ or 90%							
1000	7.1	5.2	4.5	4.0	3.7	3.4	3.1									
1500	7.0	5.1	4.3	3.8	3.5	3.2	2.8	2.6								
2000	6.9	5.0	4.2	3.7	3.4	3.0	2.7	2.4	2.2							
3000	6.9	4.9	4.1	3.6	3.3	2.9	2.6	2.2	2.1	1.9						
4000	6.8	4.9	4.1	3.6	3.3	2.8	2.5	2.2	2.0	1.8	1.7					
5000	6.8	4.9	4.0	3.6	3.2	2.8	2.4	2.1	1.9	1.7	1.6	1.5				
7000	6.8	4.9	4.0	3.5	3.2	2.8	2.4	2.0	1.8	1.6	1.5	1.4	1.3			
10000	6.8	4.8	4.0	3.5	3.2	2.7	2.3	2.0	1.8	1.6	1.4	1.4	1.3	1.2		
15000	6.8	4.8	4.0	3.5	3.1	2.7	2.3	2.0	1.8	1.5	1.4	1.3	1.2	1.1	1.1	
20000	6.8	4.8	4.0	3.5	3.1	2.7	2.3	1.9	1.7	1.5	1.4	1.3	1.2	1.1	1.0	1.0

Table A-2 (continued)

p = 15% or 85%

	N₁ = 100	200	300	400	500	700	1000	1500	2000	3000	4000	5000	7000	10000	15000	20000
N₂ = 100	11.3															
200	9.8	8.0														
300	9.3	7.3	6.6													
400	9.0	7.0	6.2	5.7												
500	8.8	6.7	5.9	5.4	5.1											
700	8.6	6.5	5.6	5.1	4.8	4.4										
1000	8.4	6.2	5.3	4.8	4.5	4.0	3.7									
1500	8.3	6.1	5.1	4.6	4.2	3.8	3.4	3.0								
2000	8.2	6.0	5.0	4.5	4.1	3.6	3.2	2.9	2.7							
3000	8.2	5.9	4.9	4.3	3.9	3.5	3.0	2.7	2.5	2.2						
4000	8.1	5.8	4.9	4.3	3.9	3.4	2.9	2.6	2.3	2.1	2.0					
5000	8.1	5.8	4.8	4.2	3.8	3.3	2.9	2.5	2.3	2.0	1.9	1.8				
7000	8.1	5.8	4.8	4.2	3.8	3.3	2.8	2.4	2.2	1.9	1.8	1.7	1.6			
10000	8.1	5.8	4.8	4.2	3.8	3.2	2.8	2.4	2.1	1.9	1.7	1.6	1.5	1.4		
15000	8.1	5.7	4.7	4.1	3.7	3.2	2.7	2.3	2.1	1.8	1.7	1.6	1.4	1.3	1.3	
20000	8.0	5.7	4.7	4.1	3.7	3.2	2.7	2.3	2.1	1.8	1.6	1.5	1.4	1.3	1.2	1.2

p = 20% or 80%

	N₁ = 100	200	300	400	500	700	1000	1500	2000	3000	4000	5000	7000	10000	15000	20000
N₂ = 100	12.7															
200	11.0	9.0														
300	10.4	8.2	7.4													
400	10.0	7.8	6.9	6.4												
500	9.8	7.5	6.6	6.1	5.7											
700	9.6	7.2	6.2	5.7	5.3	4.9										
1000	9.4	7.0	6.0	5.4	5.0	4.5	4.1									
1500	9.3	6.8	5.7	5.1	4.7	4.2	3.8	3.4								
2000	9.2	6.7	5.6	5.0	4.6		3.6	3.2	3.0							
3000	9.1	6.6	5.5	4.9	4.4	3.9	3.4	3.0	2.8	2.5						
4000	9.1	6.5	5.4	4.8	4.3	3.8	3.3	2.9	2.6	2.4	2.2					
5000	9.1	6.5	5.4	4.7	4.3	3.7	3.2	2.8	2.6	2.3	2.1	2.0				
7000	9.1	6.5	5.4	4.7	4.2	3.7	3.2	2.7	2.5	2.2	2.0	1.9	1.8			
10000	9.0	6.5	5.3	4.7	4.2	3.6	3.1	2.7	2.4	2.1	1.9	1.8	1.7	1.6		
15000	9.0	6.4	5.3	4.6	4.2	3.6	3.1	2.6	2.3	2.0	1.9	1.7	1.6	1.5	1.4	
20000	9.0	6.4	5.3	4.6	4.2	3.6	3.1	2.6	2.3	2.0	1.8	1.7	1.6	1.5	1.4	1.3

Table A-2 (continued)

	$N_1 = 100$	200	300	400	500	700	1000	1500	2000	3000	4000	5000	7000	10000	15000	20000
$N_2 = 100$	14.5															
200	12.6	10.3														
300	11.9	9.4	8.4													
400	11.5	8.9	7.9	7.3												
500	11.3	8.6	7.6	7.0	6.6											
700	11.0	8.3	7.2	6.5	6.1	5.6										
1000	10.8	8.0	6.8	6.2	5.7	5.2	4.7									
1500	10.6	7.8	6.6	5.9	5.4	4.8	4.3	3.9								
2000	10.6	7.7	6.4	5.7	5.2	4.6	4.1	3.7	3.4							
3000	10.5	7.6	6.3	5.6	5.1	4.4	3.9	3.4	3.2	2.9						
4000	10.4	7.5	6.2	5.5	5.0	4.3	3.8	3.3	3.0	2.7	2.5					
5000	10.4	7.5	6.2	5.4	4.9	4.3	3.7	3.2	2.9	2.6	2.4	2.3				
7000	10.4	7.4	6.1	5.4	4.9	4.2	3.6	3.1	2.5	2.3	2.2	2.1				
10000	10.4	7.4	6.1	5.3	4.8	4.2	3.6	3.0	2.7	2.4	2.2	2.1	1.9	1.8		
15000	10.3	7.4	6.1	5.3	4.8	4.1	3.5	3.0	2.7	2.3	2.1	2.0	1.8	1.7	1.6	
20000	10.3	7.4	6.1	5.3	4.8	4.1	3.5	3.0	2.6	2.3	2.1	2.0	1.8	1.7	1.6	1.5

$p = 30\%$ or 70%

	$N_1 = 100$	200	300	400	500	700	1000	1500	2000	3000	4000	5000	7000	10000	15000	20000
$N_2 = 100$	15.8															
200	13.7	11.2														
300	13.0	10.3	9.2													
400	12.6	9.8	8.6	8.0												
500	12.3	9.4	8.2	7.6	7.2											
700	12.0	9.0	7.8	7.1	6.7	6.1										
1000	11.8	8.7	7.5	6.7	6.2	5.6	5.1									
1500	11.6	8.5	7.2	6.4	5.9	5.3	4.7	4.3								
2000	11.5	8.4	7.0	6.2	5.7	5.1	4.5	4.0	3.7							
3000	11.4	8.2	6.9	6.1	5.5	4.8	4.3	3.7	3.4	3.1						
4000	11.4	8.2	6.8	6.0	5.4	4.7	4.1	3.6	3.3	3.0	2.8					
5000	11.3	8.1	6.7	5.9	5.4	4.7	4.1	3.5	3.2	2.8	2.7	2.5				
7000	11.3	8.1	6.7	5.9	5.3	4.6	4.0	3.4	3.1	2.7	2.5	2.4	2.2			
10000	11.3	8.1	6.7	5.8	5.3	4.5	3.9	3.3	3.0	2.6	2.4	2.3	2.1	2.0		
15000	11.3	8.0	6.6	5.8	5.2	4.5	3.8	3.3	2.9	2.5	2.3	2.2	2.0	1.9	1.8	
20000	11.3	8.0	6.6	5.8	5.2	4.5	3.8	3.2	2.9	2.5	2.3	2.1	2.0	1.8	1.7	1.6

$p = 35\%$ or 65%

Appendix B
Procedures Used to Derive Design Effects and Sampling Errors

Appendix A provided a very brief and relatively nontechnical explanation of sampling error estimates, accompanied by two tables of confidence intervals which can be used to ascertain the accuracy of most percentages reported in this volume. The present appendix is intended to provide some background concerning the strategy and rationale involved in computing these confidence intervals. It also offers guidance for those wishing to make sampling computations beyond those contained in Appendix A.

This appendix, like the first, is intended to be readable and usable by the nonstatistician. For that reason, we take the time to outline (albeit briefly) a number of relatively elementary factors involved in estimating confidence intervals.

Factors Influencing the Size of Confidence Intervals

The most straightforward types of samples, from a statistical standpoint at least, are simple random samples. In such samples the confidence limits for a proportion are influenced by the size of the sample or subgroups being considered and also by the size of the proportion. For example, the 95 percent confidence interval for a proportion p based on a simple random sample of N cases is approximated by:
$p \pm 1.96 \sqrt{p(1-p)/N}$. In a complex probability sample such as the present one, there are a number of other factors which influence the size of confidence limits. This section lists all of the factors which have been taken into account in calculating confidence intervals for use with the data in this volume, beginning with the most simple factors and then proceeding to the more complex.

Number of Cases (N). Other things equal, the larger a sample (or subgroup within a sample), the smaller or more precise will be the confidence interval for a percentage based on that sample. One of the factors determining the size of the confidence interval is $1/\sqrt{N}$. Thus, for example, if all other things were equal, a sample of 400 would have confidence intervals half as large (or twice as precise) as a sample of 100, because $1/\sqrt{400}$ is half as large as $1/\sqrt{100}$.

Size of Percentage. Other things equal, percentage values around 50 percent have larger confidence intervals than higher or lower percentage values. This is because another of the factors determining the size of the confidence interval is $\sqrt{p(1-p)}$ where p is a proportion ranging from 0 to 1.0 (or, to put it in percentage terms, the factor is $\sqrt{x\%(100-x\%)}$). Thus, for example, a proportion of either .1 or .9 (a percentage of either 10 percent or 90 percent) will have a confidence interval only three-fifths as large as the confidence interval around a proportion of .5 (or 50 percent), because $\sqrt{.1(1-.1)}$ is three-fifths as large as $\sqrt{.5(1-.5)}$.

Design Effects in Complex Samples. Under conditions of simple random sampling, a confidence interval can be determined solely on the basis of the number of cases and the percentage value involved. More complex samples such as the one used in the present study make use of stratification and clustering and often differential weighting of respondent scores, and these all influence sampling error. While stratification tends to heighten the precision of a sample, the effects of clustering and weighting reduce precision (compared with a simple random sample of the same size). Therefore, it is not appropriate to apply the

241

standard, simple random sampling formulas to such complex samples in order to obtain estimates of sampling errors, because they would almost always underestimate the actual sampling errors.

Methods exist for correcting for this underestimation, however. Kish (1965, p. 258) defines a correction term called the design effect (DEFF), where:

$$\text{DEFF} = \frac{\text{actual sampling variance}}{\begin{array}{l}\text{expected sampling variance} \\ \text{from a simple random sample} \\ \text{with same number of elements}\end{array}}$$

Thus, if the actual sampling variance in a complex sample is four times as large as the expected sampling variance from a simple random sample with the same number of cases, the DEFF is 4.0. Since confidence intervals are proportionate to the square root of variance, the confidence intervals for such a sample would be twice as large (because the square root of 4 is 2) as the confidence interval for a simple random sample with the same number of cases. A fairly simple and straightforward way of applying the concept of design effect may be to note that an increase in design effect has the same impact on precision as a reduction in the number of cases in a simple random sample. For example, a sample of 16,000 cases with a design effect of 4.0 would have the same degree of precision (the same size confidence intervals around various percentages) as a simple random sample of 4,000.

In principle, every different statistic resulting from a complex sample can have its own design effect, and different statistics in the same sample may have quite different design effects. However, it is not feasible to compute every design effect, nor would it be feasible to report every one. Thus, in practice, design effects are averaged across a number of statistics and these average values are used to estimate the design effects for other statistics based on the same sample. Sometimes a single design effect is applied to all statistics of a given type (e.g., percentages) for a given sample. In the present study, however, a rather extensive exploration of design effects revealed a number of systematic differences. These systematic differences have to do with the particular measures being examined, the subgroups involved, and the question of whether a trend over time is being considered. The most consistent difference involves the number of cases in the group or subgroup for which the design effect is computed.

The Relationship between Subgroup Size and Design Effects. Kish et al. (1976) have observed that design effects tend to be smaller for subgroups than for total samples; moreover, the smaller the subgroup the smaller the design effect is likely to be. The ex-

planation for this widespread phenomenon is that the average number of cases in each sampling cluster is an important factor in determining the size of the design effect, and as subgroup size decreases so does this average number of cases per cluster. This point is illustrated by several subgroups treated in the present volume — males, females, those planning four years of college, and those not planning four years of college. All (or virtually all) of the schools in the sample have both male and female students, as well as some students who plan four years of college and others who do not. Thus, each of these four subgroups is spread more or less evenly across the full number of clusters (schools). Since each of these subgroups includes roughly half of the total sample, the average number of cases per cluster is about half as large as for the total sample, and this leads to a smaller design effect than is found for the total sample. Other subgroups involving different patterns of drug use are also distributed more or less evenly across all clusters and thus are subject to the same phenomenon of smaller design effects because of the smaller number of cases per cluster.

One very important exception to the pattern of smaller design effects for subgroups involves the four geographic region subgroups presented in this volume. These subgroups do not cut across all clusters; instead, regions have been described as "segregated" subgroups, in contrast to the "cross-class" subgroups discussed above. For such segregated subgroups the average number of cases per cluster is about the same as is found in the total sample, and thus the design effects are not lower than those for the total sample (Kish et al., 1976). Another subgroup which is in some respects similar to regional subgroups is the category of blacks. Black respondents are not found equally across high schools throughout the United States. There are, of course, regional differences in proportions of blacks, and these contribute substantially to this lack of equal distribution. In addition, there are patterns of segregation in housing which continue to be reflected in the unequal distribution of blacks in high schools. The net effect of these several factors is that the black subgroup in our sample is "partially segregated" in a sampling sense as well as in the more usual usage of that word. For that reason, the design effects for blacks are somewhat larger than for other subgroups of approximately similar size.

Because the subgroups consisting of blacks and the four regional groups all have larger design effects than other subgroups of the same size, it is necessary to adjust the confidence intervals for these subgroups as indicated in Appendix A. (At a later point in the present appendix we will say more about these adjustment factors.)

One other kind of "subgroup" must be noted in this discussion of the relationship between subgroup size and design effects. One-fifth of the total sample filled out each of the five separate questionnaire forms, and thus the respondents to each of these forms may be viewed as a "cross-class" subgroup of the total sample. The average cluster size for a single form is exactly 20 percent of the average cluster size for the total sample. That means, of course, that the single form samples (which are the basis for the large majority of the data presented in this volume) are distinctly more "efficient" than the sample based on all five forms. Accordingly, single form data have much smaller design effects (as displayed later in this appendix).

Design Effects for Comparisons between Subgroups. We noted above that a number of subgroups treated in this volume can be described as "cross-class" subgroups, meaning that members of the subgroup are distributed more or less evenly across sampling clusters. For these kinds of subgroups, it turns out that *comparisons* are relatively efficient, from a sampling standpoint. The technical explanation for this phenomenon is that there is a higher degree of covariance between such subgroup pairs than would be the case in a comparison of independent subgroups. Now let us offer a fairly nontechnical illustration to indicate why this is so. Suppose that a researcher interested in use of marijuana during the senior year of high school obtained data from five high schools concerning female seniors' marijuana use and data from five other high schools concerning male seniors' marijuana use. Suppose that the percentage values for marijuana use during senior year were as follows:

Female seniors (five schools): 60%, 20%, 65%, 30%, 50%

Male seniors (five other schools): 40%, 80%, 25%, 70%, 60%

Even though there is a difference of ten percentage points between males and females (if the five schools in each case are averaged), there is still so much variability among schools that one would not conclude with very much confidence that females in general are less likely than males to use marijuana during the senior year of high school. Suppose, on the other hand, that the researcher had obtained data from a total of only five schools and had obtained data concerning both male and female seniors in each school as follows:

	Females	Males
School A	60%	70%
School B	20%	25%
School C	65%	80%
School D	30%	40%
School E	50%	60%

The same group of percentages, this time based on five pairings of males and females rather than independent observations, are much more strongly suggestive of systematic differences between the sexes.

A process analogous to that illustrated above is involved when "cross-class" subgroups are compared, and the increased accuracy or sampling efficiency is reflected in relatively small sampling errors and design effects.

Design Effects for Trends. Thus far this discussion of factors influencing design effects and confidence intervals has focused only on groups and subgroups within a single year. But one of the central purposes of the Monitoring the Future project is to monitor trends over time; indeed, the study procedures have been standardized across years insofar as possible in order to provide the opportunity for sensitive measurement of change. One of the factors designed to produce an added degree of consistency from one year to the next is the use of each school for two data collections, which means that for any two successive years half of the sample of schools is the same. This, plus the fact that the other half of the school sample in a given year is from the same primary sampling units as the half sample it replaced, means that there is a good deal of consistency in the sampling and clustering of the sample from one year to the next. As a result, when cross-year comparisons are made (say, between 1976 and 1977), the design effects are appreciably smaller (i.e., the efficiency is greater) than if completely independent samples of schools had been drawn each year. In other words, the 1976 and 1977 samples are not independent; on the contrary, there is a considerable degree of covariance between them. A similar level of covariance occurs between any pair of adjacent-year samples (e.g., 1977 and 1978), because about half of the schools in both samples were the same. This covariance, or partial "matching," reduces the design effect for differences observed between adjacent years, compared to what they would have been with totally independent samples.

It follows from the discussion above that a trend over an interval greater than one year (e.g., a comparison between 1976 and 1978 which involves totally non-overlapping school samples) is likely to have a design effect which is larger than that for a comparison between adjacent-year samples.

Variables with Unusually Large Design Effects. Kish et al. (1976) stress the importance of computing sampling errors for many kinds of variables, and they point out that they have found "very wide ranges in values of sampling errors (standard errors and design effects) between diverse variables within the same survey" (p. 21). Our own experience has been that, among most variables, the variation in sampling errors and design effects seems more random than consistent, and thus we are reasonably comfortable with the use of averaging procedures (described below) in order to derive a set of general purpose tables. There are some important exceptions to the above generalization, however. Variables which are likely to be grouped according to geographical area (region and/or urbanicity), as well as variables that may differ systematically from one school to another, show much higher than usual amounts of homogeneity within sample clusters. It follows necessarily that such variables also have much higher than usual design effects. The variables in the Monitoring the Future study which seem most likely to show such high design effects tend to be grouped into the questionnaire segment dealing with background factors and educational aspirations (Section C of all questionnaire forms). These variables were excluded from the process of computing overall design effects and the confidence intervals provided in Tables A-1 and A-2. Appendix A provides a further discussion of some of these variables and offers some suggestions for adjusting the confidence interval tables to deal with them.

Procedures Used in Deriving Design Effects and Tables of Confidence Intervals

Having taken some pains to review the several factors which can influence design effects and confidence intervals, it is now a fairly simple matter for us to summarize the steps followed to compute the tables of confidence intervals shown in Appendix A. We were heavily influenced in this effort by the work of Kish and his colleagues (Kish, 1965; Kish et al., 1976) in two ways. First, we followed their recommendation that sampling errors be computed and averaged across a goodly number of variables and subgroups. Second, we paid particular attention to their observation that design effects tend to be smaller for subgroups than for total samples (a point discussed earlier in this appendix).

Confidence Intervals for Single Percentages. Our procedure was to compute sampling errors and design effects for most of the variables which are common to all five forms (those in the C sections of all questionnaires, and those in the B sections of Forms 2 through 5), and for every twentieth variable in the A, D, and E sections of Forms 2 through 5. (Form 1 was omitted because most of this form is comprised of drug-related items, and such items involve high proportions of missing data because respondents are instructed to skip over many questions which are not applicable to them). Design effects were computed for each of the subgroups reported in this volume, as well as for the total sample. Design effects for each subgroup and for the total were averaged across variables for the C sec-

tion material (all five forms), the B section material (drug use measures, all five forms), and the sampling of variables from the A, D, and E sections (single form data). As noted earlier, the variables which showed unusually high levels of homogeneity within sample clusters were excluded from the C section variables when they were averaged. The 1977 data were used for this analysis. Later replication using 1976 data provided nearly identical values.

The averaging process consisted of taking a mean of the *square roots* of the design effects. Kish and his colleagues (1976) refer to the design effect as DEFF, and to the square root of the design effect as DEFT; thus, $\sqrt{DEFF} = DEFT$. We will find it useful to use this terminology in what follows. The rationale for computing means of DEFT rather than DEFF is that the former value is directly proportional to the size of confidence intervals. A further reason for doing so is that the values of DEFT approximate a normal distribution much more closely than the values of DEFF, which are skewed upward. (A comparison of mean DEFTs and median DEFTs showed them to be quite similar, something which certainly is not true of mean and median DEFFs).

Bearing in mind that design effects tend to be smaller for subgroups than for total samples, and bearing in mind also that confidence intervals are directly proportionate to DEFT and to $\sqrt{N}$, we plotted the mean DEFT values for the total sample and for all subgroups, in each case relating DEFT to $\sqrt{N}$. The results are shown in Figure B-1. Note that distinctions are made between "cross-class" and "segregated" subgroups, and between mean DEFTs based on five forms and those based on single forms (the $\sqrt{N}$ values for the latter are, of course, much smaller).*

Setting aside the "segregated" subgroups (regions and blacks) for the moment, it is clear that the rest of the mean DEFTs in Figure B-1 show a very clear and consistent pattern: the higher the value $\sqrt{N}$ the higher the mean DEFT. It turns out that these mean DEFT values are very closely approximated by the function $DEFT = \sqrt{1.3 + .00015N}$, as shown by the solid line in the figure. (The function can also be stated as $DEFF = 1.3 + .00015N$.) The particular parameters in that function were derived empirically, but the basic function (i.e., $DEFT = \sqrt{a + bN}$) was adapted directly from the work of Kish et al. (1976).

Given the above function that fitted the mean DEFT values for the total sample and the "cross-class" subgroups, we returned to the problem of assigning DEFT values for the "segregated" subgroups. The simplest solution was to select two adjustment factors which could be multiplied by the confidence interval values in Table A-1. These adjustment factors are shown by the dashed lines in Figure B-1; they cor-

---

* The five form data consisted of C section material, excluding those variables related to region, urbanicity, and/or socioeconomic level.

Figure B-1
Design Effects for Single Percentages

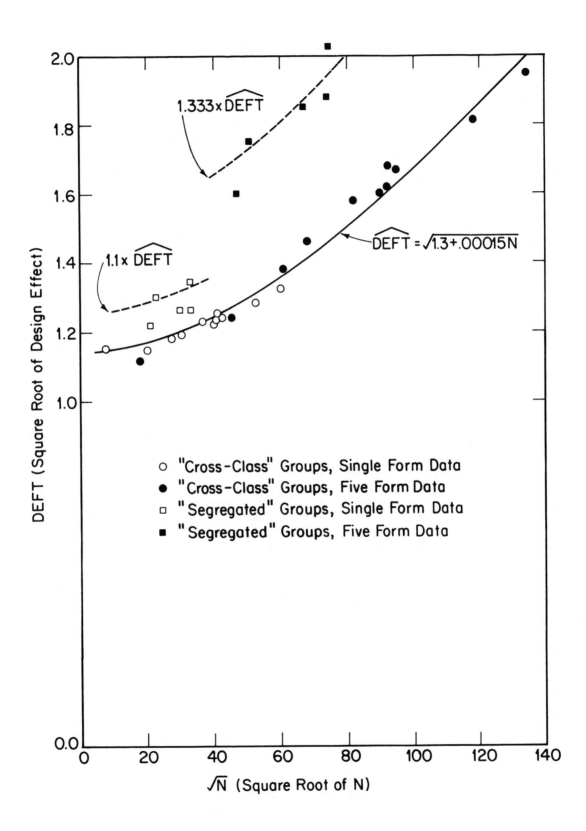

respond to multiplying the "standard" DEFT (solid line) by a factor of 1.1 for single form data and by a factor of 1.33 for five form data. These adjustments, which were selected on empirical grounds, yield design effects for the "segregated" subgroups which are approximately equal to the design effects for the total sample (treating single form and five form data separately, of course). This is reassuring, since Kish et al. (1976) have reported that "segregated" subgroups can in general be expected to show design effects approximately equivalent to the design effects for the total sample.

After the data in Figure B-1 were plotted and the form of the main function (indicated by the solid line) was determined, DEFT values for drug use measures (material in Section B of all forms) were checked. It was found that the DEFTs for only two drug categories, alcohol and marijuana, exceeded the values indicated by the function; accordingly, adjustment factors were developed for these two drugs (1.6 and 1.35, respectively).

Confidence Intervals for Differences between Two Percentages. Our procedure here was directly parallel to that followed in determining confidence intervals for single percentages. DEFT values for the differences between 1977 and 1976 percentages were computed using virtually the same set of items as used earlier. Also computed were mean DEFT values for comparisons in the same year between subgroups such as males and females, those who did and did not plan to complete four years of college, blacks and whites, pairings of regions, and pairings of drug use groups. It was found that, for any given level of N, the mean DEFT values for subgroup comparisons were quite similar to the mean DEFT values for one-year trends; accordingly, all of these mean DEFTs were included in Figure B-2, which plots mean DEFTs for differences between percentages. In this figure, as in Figure B-1, the strong relationship was evident between mean DEFTs and the numbers of cases in the two groups being compared. This relationship can be very closely approximated by the function DEFT = $\sqrt{1.3 + .000075N}$ (which can also be stated DEFF = 1.3 + .000075N), where N = $2N_1N_2/N_1 + N_2$.

It was expected on grounds of sampling theory that as we found earlier, the function which fit most differences between percentages would not fit differences involving regions and differences involving blacks. In fact, the data indicated that some adjustment is necessary for black-white comparisons using data from all five forms, and also for comparisons as well as trends involving any region. We have not tried to show those adjustments in Figure B-2, but the several values involved are shown in the guidelines to Table A-2.

It was also expected on the grounds of sampling theory that trends across an interval of two or more years would show somewhat higher values of DEFT than one-year trends. It turned out that this was true only for data from all five forms; data based on one form only did not show significantly higher values. The adjustment factors for trends involving five forms over two or more years are shown in Table A-2.

Use of Weighted Numbers of Cases in Entering Confidence Interval Tables. We should mention in passing that the recommendations for using the tables in Appendix A indicate that *weighted* N values should be used. The computer program which generated our design effect statistics makes use of weights in calculating percentages and actual sampling variances. But in computing the DEFF ratio, defined as the actual sampling variance divided by the expected sampling variance from a simple random sample with the same number of elements, the program makes use of the *unweighted* numbers of cases to determine "the same number of elements." Since the mean weights used in the 1975, 1976, and 1977 data tables are slightly lower than 1.0, this means that when entering the tables in Appendix A with weighted data from those years, one is being very slightly "conservative" (slightly reduced risk of a Type 1 error, slightly increased risk of a Type 2 error). It is important to realize that if one took the trouble to make corrections for this "conservatism," the correction would rarely be as great as multiplying the Table A-1 and Table A-2 entries by a factor of .95; and in the large majority of cases the correction would involve multiplying by a factor of about .98. We find such discrepancies to be trivially small, particularly when compared with what Kish et al. (1976, p. 12) describe as the "heroic simplifications" required in some of the steps leading to general purpose tables of design effects and confidence intervals.

Before the 1978 data tables were produced we had come to realize the advantages in having weighted values which averaged 1.0; accordingly, beginning with the 1978 data, the weighted N values in the tables do approximate the actual numbers of cases quite closely. But it was impractical to redo the 1975 through 1977 data tables to incorporate this refinement. Another alternative would have been to employ slightly different versions of Tables A-1 and A-2, containing slightly different confidence intervals for each of those three years; however, we felt that such an approach could introduce confusion when cross-year comparisons were made. Thus, we opted for the solution which seems to us to be most simple and manageable, even though it involves the slight degree of "conservatism" noted above. For readers who find this solution undesirable, we have included Tables B-1 and B-2, which present weighted and unweighted Ns for the various subgroups for each year. Table B-1 contains Ns for all five forms (except for 1975 which shows Ns for Forms 2 through 5), and Table B-2 con-

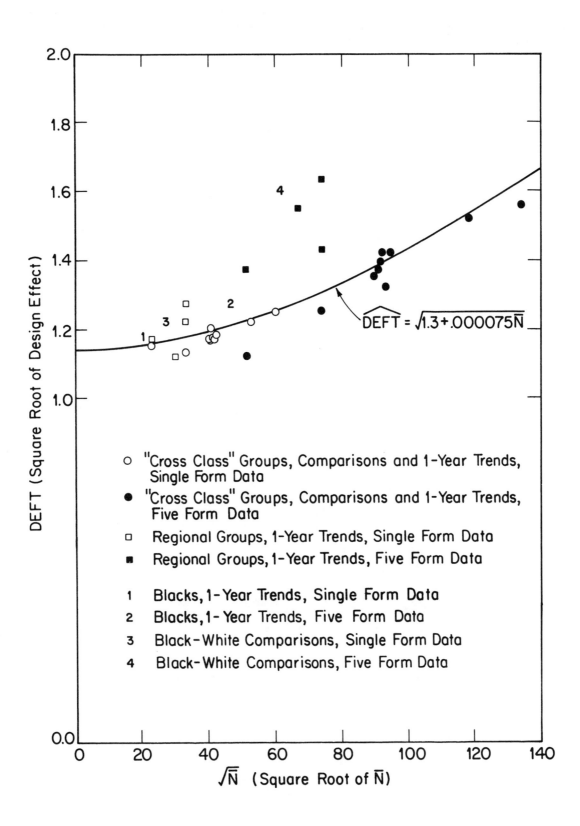

Figure B-2
Design Effects for Differences Between Percentages

$$\widehat{DEFT} = \sqrt{1.3 + .000075\overline{N}}$$

DEFT (Square Root of Design Effect)

$\sqrt{\overline{N}}$ (Square Root of $\overline{N}$)

○ "Cross Class" Groups, Comparisons and 1-Year Trends, Single Form Data

● "Cross Class" Groups, Comparisons and 1-Year Trends, Five Form Data

□ Regional Groups, 1-Year Trends, Single Form Data

■ Regional Groups, 1-Year Trends, Five Form Data

1 Blacks, 1-Year Trends, Single Form Data
2 Blacks, 1-Year Trends, Five Form Data
3 Black-White Comparisons, Single Form Data
4 Black-White Comparisons, Five Form Data

tains approximate Ns for a single form. Thus, readers who wish to avoid the slight "conservatism" (and also to be more precise for subgroups in 1978 and later whose average weight is not exactly 1.0) may determine the unweighted Ns. Some correction for missing data should be made in this case; this can be accom- plished by calculating the percentage of missing data (using the weighted Ns from the data table and the weighted N from Table B-1 or B-2) and adjusting the unweighted N accordingly. These adjusted un- weighted Ns can then be used in Appendix A.

Table B-1

Sample Sizes (Unweighted and Weighted) in Subgroups by Year

Number of Cases

	Class of 1975[a]		Class of 1976		Class of 1977		Class of 1978		Class of 1979		Class of 1980		Class of 1981	
	Unwtd.	Wtd.	Unwtd.	Wtd.	Unwtd.	Wtd.	Unwtd.	Wtd.	Unwtd.	Wtd.	Unwtd.	Wtd.	Unwtd.	Wtd.
Total Sample	12627	12108	16678	15138	18436	15830	18924	18916	16662	16662	16524	16524	18267	18267
Sex:														
Male	5799	5571	7999	7241	8449	7358	8603	8779	7889	7778	7935	7744	8775	8725
Female	6371	6100	7924	7257	9188	7850	9416	9266	8139	8232	7874	8078	8752	8865
Race:														
White	b	b	12933	11796	13818	12240	14663	14847	13432	13299	12894	12846	13625	13985
Black	b	b	1806	1716	2500	1938	2205	2096	1617	1742	1939	2098	2495	2265
Region:														
Northeast	3014	2695	4034	3570	4760	3959	4841	4607	3926	4016	4281	3877	4269	4290
North Central	3951	3832	5098	4687	5697	4758	5576	5411	5385	4874	4340	4873	5069	5484
South	3366	3857	4177	4597	4908	4820	5566	6292	4713	5055	4667	5049	5513	5600
West	2296	1724	3369	2284	3071	2294	2941	2605	2638	2717	3236	2726	3416	2893
College Plans:														
Complete 4 yrs	b	b	7963	6994	8933	7407	9264	8844	8571	8203	5995	6578	6486	7008
None or under 4 yrs	b	b	7179	6877	7764	7048	7857	8413	6715	7063	9191	8658	10256	9878
Illicit Drug Use:														
None	4329	4400	6532	6091	6672	5878	6400	6595	5426	5654	5322	5591	5954	6148
Marijuana Only	2044	1894	3950	3457	4955	4050	5354	5214	4756	4610	4480	4357	4313	4179
Few Pills	1163	1113	1942	1736	2173	1813	2329	2304	2171	2168	2150	2104	2297	2306
More Pills	2157	1989	3427	2987	3857	3266	3906	3885	3622	3543	3873	3760	4972	4925
Any Heroin	231	216	319	268	321	280	289	302	193	186	186	180	183	189

[a] The number of cases shown for 1975 is based on Forms 2 through 5 only, because the data from Form 1 are intentionally not included in tabulations based on drug and demographic items which appeared in all forms.

[b] Missing data problems were severe for race and college plans in 1975; accordingly, these data have been excluded from all tables in the 1975 report.

Table B-2

Sample Sizes (Unweighted and Weighted) in Subgroups by Year for Questions on a Single Form

Number of Cases

	Class of 1975		Class of 1976		Class of 1977		Class of 1978		Class of 1979		Class of 1980		Class of 1981	
	Unwtd.	Wtd.	Unwtd.	Wtd.	Unwtd.	Wtd.	Unwtd.	Wtd.	Unwtd.	Wtd.	Unwtd.	Wtd.	Unwtd.	Wtd.
Total Sample	3157	3027	3336	3028	3687	3166	3785	3783	3332	3332	3305	3305	3653	3653
Sex:														
Male	1450	1393	1600	1488	1690	1472	1721	1756	1578	1556	1587	1549	1755	1745
Female	1371	1525	1585	1451	1838	1570	1883	1853	1628	1646	1575	1616	1750	1773
Race:														
White	a	a	2587	2359	2764	2448	2933	2969	2686	2660	2579	2569	2725	2797
Black	a	a	361	343	500	388	441	419	323	348	388	420	499	453
Region:														
Northeast	754	674	807	714	952	792	968	921	785	803	856	775	854	858
North Central	988	958	1020	937	1139	952	1115	1082	1077	975	868	975	1014	1097
South	842	964	835	919	982	964	1113	1258	943	1011	933	1010	1103	1120
West	574	431	674	457	614	459	588	521	528	543	647	545	683	579
College Plans:														
Complete 4 yrs	a	a	1593	1399	1787	1481	1853	1769	1714	1641	1199	1316	1297	1402
None or under 4 yrs	a	a	1436	1375	1553	1410	1571	1683	1343	1413	1838	1732	2051	1976
Illicit Drug Use:														
None	1082	1100	1306	1218	1334	1176	1280	1319	1085	1131	1064	1118	1191	1230
Marijuana Only	511	474	790	691	991	810	1071	1043	951	922	896	871	863	836
Few Pills	291	278	388	347	435	363	466	461	434	434	430	421	459	461
More Pills	539	497	685	597	771	653	781	777	724	709	775	752	994	985
Any Heroin	58	54	64	54	64	56	58	60	39	37	37	36	37	38

aMissing data problems were severe for race and college plans in 1975; accordingly, these data have been exicluded from all tables in the 1975 report.

Further Applications of these Design Effects and Sampling Errors

One of the reasons for providing the above review of the factors influencing design effects and confidence intervals, and the procedures used in computing our confidence interval tables, is to provide sufficient background and data to permit the interested reader to go beyond the material provided in Appendix A. In this section we consider two specific extensions, the calculation of levels of "statistical significance" higher than 95 percent and the computation of means and their confidence intervals.

Calculating Confidence Intervals for Higher Levels of Statistical Significance. The entries contained in Tables A-1 and A-2 provide the 95 percent confidence level (also referred to as the .05 level of significance). These entries were computed by multiplying the standard error (square root of sample variance) by a factor of 1.96. The 99 percent confidence interval (.01 level of significance) uses a factor of 2.58 standard errors, and the 99.9 percent confidence interval (.001 level of significance) uses a factor of 3.29 standard errors. To convert the entries in Tables A-1 and A-2 to these higher levels, it is necessary only to multiply the entries by the appropriate constant shown below (keeping in mind that any other adjustments required in the tables must also be applied):

Confidence Interval	Significance Level	Multiply entries in Tables A-1 and A-2 by the following:
99%	.01	2.58/1.96 = 1.32
99.9%	.001	3.29/1.96 = 1.68

Computing Means and Their Confidence Intervals. Many of the questionnaire items included in this volume have ordinal response scales (e.g., agree, agree mostly, neither, disagree mostly, disagree), and it is often the case that a survey analyst will be willing to treat such scales as if they involved equal intervals. In such cases, means and standard deviations are more "efficient" in their use of information than are dichotomies which yield a single percentage or a pair of percentages (e.g., those who respond "agree" or "agree mostly," versus all others). It is a relatively straightforward matter to compute means and standard deviations for the total sample or any of the subgroups treated in this volume. The problem, then, is to be able to specify confidence intervals for the means, or for the differences between pairs of means. In the case of simple random samples, one needs only the means, standard deviations (or variances), and numbers of cases in order to compute confidence intervals. But in complex samples such as the present one,

it is also necessary to take account of design effects. If an estimate of design effect is available, one of the simplest procedures to follow is to divide the actual numbers of cases by the design effect (thereby "depreciating" the actual number to its equivalent value in simple random sample terms) and then employ the standard statistical procedures which have been developed for application to simple random samples. Thus, for example, if the design effect (DEFF) for a sample of 18,000 were 4.0, then one could divide the 18,000 by 4.0 and the result, 4,500, could be entered as the value of "N" in statistical tables and formulas designed for use with simple random samples. To take another example, if one were comparing means based on two subgroups, each involving about 9,000 cases, and if DEFF (for both subgroups) was 2.0, then one could compute the significance of the difference between the two means as if the N for each group were 4,500 (i.e., 9,000 divided by 2.0).

In short, the strategy involves dividing the actual number of cases by the appropriate DEFF in order to get a "simple random sampling equivalent N" or, more simply, an "effective N" for use in statistical procedures designed for random samples.

Design Effects for Use in Computing "Effective Ns." In order to employ the strategy outlined above, one must have estimates of design effects which are judged to be appropriate for one's purposes. In the case of means based on the percentages reported in this volume, we are confident (based on personal communications with Kish) that it is appropriate to use the same DEFF values as were used in developing Tables A-1 and A-2. For other, more complex statistics, we cannot make the same assertion, although it is generally the case that design effects for such statistics are not larger than those for means and percentages (Kish and Frankel, 1970; Frankel, 1971).

In Table B-3 we provide guidelines for computing DEFF values for single percentages (or means) and for differences between two percentages (or means). For reasons discussed elsewhere in this appendix, we must provide for different (and somewhat higher) DEFFs for "segregated" subgroups (regional subgroups and sometimes also blacks), and for trends over two or more years (in contrast to one-year trends). And in all instances, of course, the DEFF values are very much influenced by the average size of sampling clusters, which is always dependent on the number of cases (N). Accordingly, all of the design effect formulas in Table B-3 require computations which take account of N. (It should also be noted that the formulas in Table B-3 correspond exactly to the values of design effects and adjustment factors used in Tables A-1 and A-2 in Appendix A.

A Concluding Note. In their very useful paper dealing with sampling errors for fertility surveys, Kish

Table B-3
Guidelines for Computing Design Effects (DEFFs) for Percentages
and Means Derived from Monitoring the Future Samples

DEFINITIONS

$$\text{DEFF (design effect} = \frac{\text{(estimated sampling variance}}{\text{expected sampling variance from simple}}$$
random sample with same number of elements

N = number of respondents on whom a single percentage or mean is based

$\overline{N}$ = $2N_1N_2/(N_1 + N_2)$, for use in comparisons of two percentages or means, based on two groups of sizes N_1 and N_2.

DESIGN EFFECT FORMULAS

1. For single percentages or means involving . . .
   a. regional subgroups or blacks
      DEFF for single form data ....(1.3 + .00015N) (1.21)
      DEFF for five form data ....(1.3 + .00015N) (1.78)

   b. all other subgroups or total sample
      DEFF for single form or five form data ....1.3 + .00015N

2. For comparisons between . . .
   a. any two regions
      DEFF for single form data ....(1.3 + .000075$\overline{N}$) (1.32)
      DEFF for five form data ....(1.3 + .000075$\overline{N}$) (2.25)

   b. blacks and whites
      DEFF for single form data...1.3 + .000075$\overline{N}$
      DEFF for five form data ....(1.3 + .000075$\overline{N}$) (1.56)

   c. genders, college plans groups, or any two "drug use" subgroups
      DEFF for single form or five form data ....1.3 + .000075$\overline{N}$

3. For one-year trends involving . . .
   a. any region
      DEFF for single form data..1.3 + .000075$\overline{N}$
      DEFF for five form data ....(1.3 + .000075$\overline{N}$) (1.56)
   b. all other subgroups or total sample
      DEFF for single form or five form data ....1.3 + .000075$\overline{N}$

4. For trends over two or more years involving . . .
   a. any region
      DEFF for single form data..1.3 + .000075$\overline{N}$
      DEFF for five form data ....(1.3 + .000075$\overline{N}$) (1.82)
   b. all other subgroups or total sample
      DEFF for single form data..1.3 + .000075$\overline{N}$
      DEFF for five form data ....(1.3 + .000075$\overline{N}$) (1.32)

et al. (1976) commented that some of the methods they used "... emerged after several false starts." They went on to say that the volume and diversity of the data they were dealing with "... presented new challenges and opportunities." And they added, "Our methods are subject to further developments and modifications, and we invite participation and suggestions" (p. 10). Our own attempts to apply the methods of Kish and his colleagues to the data reported in this volume have been challenged by the diversity of the data, have involved several false starts, and we hope are subject to further developments and modifications. We invite readers to offer their suggestions, and we also encourage readers to inquire about further work that we and/or others may carry out during the coming months and years.

Appendix C
Questionnaire Covers, Instructions, and Sample Page

monitoring the future
a continuing study of the lifestyles and values of youth

This questionnaire is part of a nationwide study of high school seniors, conducted each year by the University of Michigan's Institute for Social Research. The questions ask your opinions about a number of things — the way things are now and the way you think they ought to be in the future. In a sense, many of your answers on this questionnaire will count as "votes" on a wide range of important issues.

If this study is to be helpful, it is important that you answer each question as thoughtfully and frankly as possible. All your answers will be kept strictly confidential, and will never be seen by anyone who knows you.

This study is completely voluntary. If there is any question that you or your parents would find objectionable for any reason, just leave it blank.

In a few months, we would like to mail each of you a summary of the nationwide results from this study. Also, in about a year we would like to mail another questionnaire to some of you, asking about how your plans have worked out and what's happening in your lives.

In order to include you in these mailings, we ask for your name and address on a special form at the end of this questionnaire. This form is to be torn out and handed in separately. Once the address form and the questionnaire have been separated, there is no way they can be matched again, except by using a special computer tape at the University of Michigan. The only purpose for that tape is to match a follow-up questionnaire with this one.

Other seniors have said that these questionnaires are very interesting and that they enjoy filling them out. We hope you will too. Be sure to read the instructions on the other side of this cover page before you begin to answer. Thank you very much for being an important part of this project.

INSTITUTE FOR SOCIAL RESEARCH
THE UNIVERSITY OF MICHIGAN
ANN ARBOR, MICHIGAN

INSTRUCTIONS

1. This is not a test, so there are no right or wrong answers; we would
    like you to work fairly quickly, so that you can finish.

2. All of the questions should be answered by marking one of the answer spaces.
    If you don't always find an answer that fits exactly, use the one that comes
    closest. If any question does not apply to you, or you are not sure of what it
    means, just leave it blank.

3. Your answers will be read automatically by a machine called an optical mark
    reader. Please follow these instructions carefully:

    • Use only the black lead pencil you have been given.

    • Make heavy black marks inside the circles.

    • Erase cleanly any answer you wish to change.

    • Make no other markings or comments on the
      answer pages, since they interfere with the
      automatic reading. (If you want to add a
      comment about any question, please use the
      space provided below.)

    These kinds of markings
    will work: ● ◖ ◑

    These kinds of markings
    will NOT work: ⊙ ✦ ○

(THIS SPACE FOR WRITTEN COMMENTS)

WHY YOUR NAME AND ADDRESS?

As we told you earlier, we'd like to send you a summary of the nationwide results of the present study, and in about a year we want to mail a shorter questionnaire to some of you. In order to include you in these follow-ups, we would like to have an address where information will be sure to reach you during the coming year.

HOW IS CONFIDENTIALITY PROTECTED?

- The information on this page will be used ONLY for mailing, and will always be kept separate from your answers. A special Grant of Confidentiality from the U.S. government protects all information gathered in this research project.

- The questionnaire and address pages will be collected separately, sealed immediately in separate envelopes, and sent to two different cities for processing.

- Once a questionnaire and address page have been separated, there is no way they can be matched, except by using a special computer tape at the University of Michigan. That tape contains the two DIFFERENT numbers that appear on the back of this address page and on the back of the questionnaire. These numbers will be used ONLY to match a follow-up questionnaire with this one.

Before filling out this address page, please separate it from the rest of the questionnaire by FOLDING ALONG THE PERFORATED LINE AND TEARING CAREFULLY.

Please **PRINT** your name and the address where you can most likely be reached during the coming year.

Mr.
Miss _
Ms.   FIRST NAME   INITIAL   LAST NAME
Mrs.

STREET _

CITY _

STATE _ _ _ _ _ _ _ _ _ _ _ _ _ _ _ _ _ _ _ ZIP _ _ _ _ _ _ _ _ _

TELEPHONE NO.   (   ) — _ _ _ _ _ _ _ _ _ _ _ _ _ _ _ _
                      AREA

In case we should have trouble getting mail to you, if you move, please **PRINT** the name and address of one other person (with a different address than your own) who will know where to reach you in the future. (Examples of such a person: aunt or uncle, older sister or brother, or close friend.)

Mr.
Miss _
Ms.   FIRST NAME   INITIAL   LAST NAME
Mrs.

STREET _

CITY _

STATE _ _ _ _ _ _ _ _ _ _ _ _ _ _ _ _ _ _ _ ZIP _ _ _ _ _ _ _ _ _

TELEPHONE NO.   (   ) — _ _ _ _ _ _ _ _ _ _ _ _ _ _ _ _
                      AREA

THANK YOU AGAIN FOR YOUR HELP

258   **MONITORING THE FUTURE**

PART A

* **BEFORE BEGINNING BE SURE YOU HAVE READ THE INSTRUCTIONS ON THE COVER.**

1. Taking all things together, how would you say things are these days–would you say you're very happy, pretty happy, or not too happy these days?

   ○ Very happy
   ○ Pretty happy
   ○ Not too happy

2. Some people think a lot about the social problems of the nation and the world, and about how they might be solved. Others spend little time thinking about these issues. How much do you think about such things?

   ① Never
   ② Seldom
   ③ Sometimes
   ④ Quite often
   ⑤ A great deal

3. **Of all the problems facing the nation today, how often do you worry about each of the following?** (Mark one circle for each line.)

   Never / Seldom / Sometimes / Often

   a. Chance of nuclear war .... ①②③④
   b. Population growth .... ①②③④
   c. Crime and violence .... ①②③④
   d. Pollution .... ①②③④
   e. Energy shortages .... ①②③④
   f. Race relations .... ①②③④
   g. Hunger and poverty .... ①②③④
   h. Using open land for housing or industry .... ①②③④
   i. Urban decay .... ①②③④
   j. Economic problems .... ①②③④
   k. Drug abuse .... ①②③④

4. How well do you think your experiences and training (at home, school, work, etc.) have prepared you to be a good. . .

   Poorly / Not So Well / Fairly Well / Well / Very Well

   a. ...husband or wife? .... ①②③④⑤
   b. ...parent? .... ①②③④⑤
   c. ...worker on a job? .... ①②③④⑤

5. **Apart from the particular kind of work you want to do, how would you rate each of the following settings as a place to work?** (Mark one circle for each line.)

   Not At All Acceptable / Somewhat Acceptable / Acceptable / Desirable

   a. Working in a large corporation .... ①②③④
   b. Working in a small business .... ①②③④
   c. Working in a government agency .... ①②③④
   d. Working in the military service .... ①②③④
   e. Working in a school or university .... ①②③④
   f. Working in a police department or police agency .... ①②③④
   g. Working in a social service organization .. ①②③④
   h. Working with a small group of partners ... ①②③④
   i. Working on your own (self-employed) ..... ①②③④

6. **If you were to get enough money to live as comfortably as you'd like for the rest of your life, would you want to work?**

   ① I would want to work
   ② I would not want to work

—1—   (Base Year & Follow-up: Form 5—Part A)

References

Adelson, J. "What Generation Gap?" *New York Times Magazine*, January 18, 1870, pp. 1–11.

Adelson J. "Adolescence and the Generation Gap." *Psychology Today*, February 1979, pp. 33–37.

Bachman, J.G., and Johnston, L.D. "The Monitoring the Future Project Design and Procedures," (Occasional Paper #1). Institute for Social Research, The University of Michigan, Ann Arbor, 1978.

Bachman, J.G., and Johnston, L.D. "The Freshmen, 1979." *Psychology Today*, September 1979, pp. 79–87.

Bachman, J.G.; Johnston, L.D.; and O'Malley, P.M. "Smoking, Drinking, and Drug Use Among American High School Students: Correlates and Trends, 1975-1979." *American Journal of Public Health* 71 (1981): 59–69.

Bachman, J.G., and O'Malley, P.M. "When Four Months Equal a Year: Inconsistencies in Students' Reports of Drug Use." *Public Opinion Quarterly* 45 (1981): 536–548.

Bachman, J.G.; O'Malley, P.M.; and Johnston, J. Youth in Transition, Volume VI: *Adolescence to Adulthood — A Study of Change and Stability in the Lives of Young Men*. Ann Arbor: Institute for Social Research, The University of Michigan, 1978.

Dearman, N.B., and Plisko, V.W. *The Condition of Education*. National Center for Education Statistics. Washington, D.C.: U.S. Government Printing Office, 1979.

Frankel, M.R. *Inference from Survey Samples: An Empirical Investigation*. Ann Arbor: Institute for Social Research, The University of Michgian, 1971.

Hays, W.L. *Statistics for the Social Sciences* (2nd ed.). New York: Holt, Rinehart, & Winston, 1973.

Johnston, L.D. *Drugs and American Youth*. Ann Arbor: Institute for Social Research, The University of Michigan, 1973.

Johnston, L.D.; Bachman, J.G.; and O'Malley, P.M. *Drug Use Among American High School Students, 1975-1977* (National Institute on Drug Abuse). Washington, D.C.: U.S. Government Printing Office, 1977.

Johnston, L.D.; Bachman, J.G.; and O'Malley, P.M. *Drugs and the Class of 1978: Behaviors, Attitudes, and Recent National Trends* (National Institute on Drug Abuse). Washington, D.C.: U.S. Government Printing Office, 1979 (a).

Johnston, L.D.; Bachman, J.G.; and O'Malley, P.M. *1979 Highlights: Drugs and the Nation's High School Students, Five Year National Trends* (National Institute on Drug Abuse). Washington, D.C.: U.S. Government Printing Office, 1979(b).

Johnston, L.D.; Bachman, J.G.; and O'Malley, P.M. *Highlights from Student Drug Use in America: 1975-1980* (National Institute on Drug Abuse). Washington, D.C.: U.S. Government Printing Office, 1981.

Johnston, L.D.; O'Malley, P.M.; and Eveland, L.K. "Some Preliminary Results from Drugs and American Youth II: A Longitudinal Resurvey." (Interim report to the National Institute on Drug Abuse.) Institute for Social Research, The University of Michigan, Ann Arbor, 1975. Mimeograph.

Kish, L. *Survey Sampling*. New York: John Wiley & Sons, 1965.

Kish, L., and Frankel, M.R. "Balanced Repeated Replication for Standard Errors." *Journal of the American Statistical Association* 65 (1970): 1071–1094.

Kish, L.; Groves, R.M.; and Krotki, K.P. *Sampling Errors for Fertility Surveys* (Occasional Papers Series No. 17). Voorburg, The Netherlands: International Statistical Institute, 1976.

U.S. Bureau of the Census, *Current Population Reports*. Series P-20, No. 319, School enrollment — social and economic characteristics of students, October 1976. Washington, D.C.: U.S. Government Printing Office, 1978.